Jan Schwochow

THE WORLD EXPLAINED

in 264 Infographics

PRESTEL
Munich · London · New York

Contents

Preface

Visual Journalism

Fig. 1 My first journalism job in 1990 at the weekly magazine *Stern*; here I am copying layout pages for the editorial staff — in black and white.

Fig. 2 An oil rig in airbrushed acrylics, by Reinald Blanck, for *Stern*, about 1980.

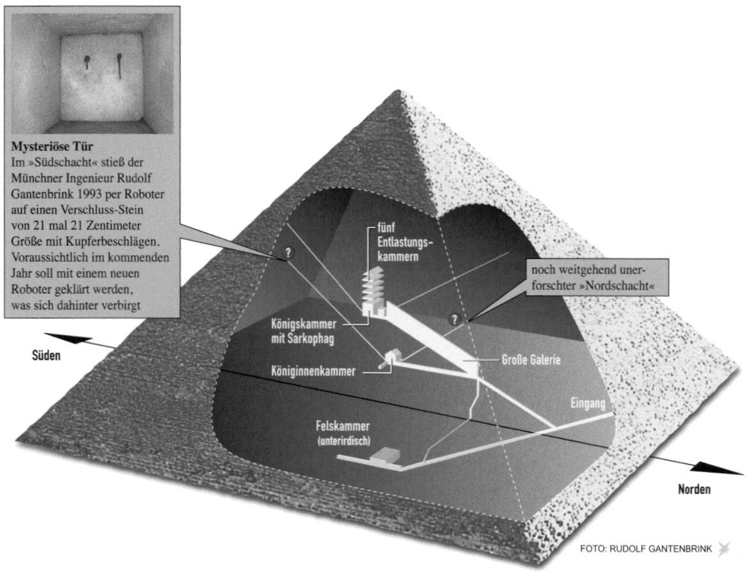
Mysteriöse Tür
Im »Südschacht« stieß der Münchner Ingenieur Rudolf Gantenbrink 1993 per Roboter auf einen Verschluss-Stein von 21 mal 21 Zentimeter Größe mit Kupferbeschlägen. Voraussichtlich im kommenden Jahr soll mit einem neuen Roboter geklärt werden, was sich dahinter verbirgt
fünf Entlastungs-kammern
noch weitgehend uner-forschter »Nordschacht«
Königskammer mit Sarkophag
Süden
Königinnenkammer
Große Galerie
Eingang
Felskammer (unterirdisch)
Norden
FOTO: RUDOLF GANTENBRINK

Fig. 3 The Great Pyramid of Giza. One of my first computer graphics, created on a Macintosh Quadra 950, appeared in *Stern* in 1993 and 1999.

You are holding a special book in your hands. It is a compendium of the best work that I have produced with my team since opening our doors in 2007, mostly for ourselves but also for and with our customers. Alltogether, more than one hundred people have contributed their diverse skills to this book which covers hundreds of topics. It really feels as if almost the entire world is contained and explained within these pages. Some graphics, which were previously published elsewhere, have been updated to reflect recent developments. Many have been produced especially for this book. This is therefore not only a showcase of my company's diverse work in the field of infographics, but also an elaborately produced book that may even help you to gain a better understanding of the world.

What is an infographic?

The word »infographic« is not particularly old. Its first reported use was in English in the 1960s. In the late 1970s, the UK computer manufacturer Ferranti established a subsidiary, Ferranti Infographics Ltd., to create modern illustrations of product functions for publications and catalogs. The first media-related use of the term that we are familiar with today only dates back, however, to 1979.

Infographics became extremely popular in the early 1980s, as advances in modern printing practices finally made it possible to print in four colors. Some newspapers were redesigned accordingly. In 1982, the American daily USA Today burst onto the scene with a new, full-page, color weather infographic every morning. The title page and every section header contained a daily »snapshot« — an illustrated statistic. Infographics became an important instrument for journalists, making complex information more accessible and easily digestible. The arrival in editorial rooms of personal computers, especially Apple's Macintosh, provided further impetus. When I began working at Hamburg's *Stern* magazine in the early 1990s, no one had a computer there or knew the word »infographic«. We were still doing everything by hand, in the most literal sense.

The first German »infographics« appeared in 1993 in a new weekly magazine, Focus, which placed a strong emphasis on the use of maps, pie charts, and bar graphs right from the start. Many can still remember the magazine's ads featuring a photo of Editor-in-Chief Helmut Markwort, for whom »Facts, Facts, Facts« were indispensable.

If you dig deeper into the archives, however, you will discover that informational graphics have always existed. Numerous wonderfully elaborate infographics are to be found in many old books, newspapers, and magazines, such as those that you might encounter in Fortune, an economics magazine which was launched in 1930. The magazine's artists were not only responsible for infographics; they also drew advertisements and provided impressive artwork for the covers. The Austrian graphic designer Herbert Bayer, a student and junior master at the Bauhaus, was one such illustrator.

These artists drew maps, diagrams, organizational charts, tables, and illustrations — seemingly everything we now produce with computers. Complex data visualizations existed even in the 19th century. There were many painters, statisticians, scientists, researchers, and engineers who, in principle, were also information graphic artists. Leonardo da Vinci, Albrecht Dürer, Isaac Newton, Charles Darwin, Alexander von Humboldt could all draw or illustrate their works graphically on paper. In 1925, the sociologist Otto Neurath and the graphic artist Gerd Arntz began working together. Their »Vienna Method of Pictorial Statistics« (known since 1934 as Isotype, the acronym for International System of Typographic Picture Education) perfected the combination of statistics and appealing graphic design containing diagrams and pictograms. Science and graphics formed a perfect union. The goal of pictorial statistics was to make education accessible to underprivileged members of society who could neither read nor write. Informational graphics were an optimal solution.

We will introduce the individual chapters of this book with a few examples that provide a historical context for the different types of infographic illustrations. There are now a number of excellent books that approach the topic of infographics on both a theoretical and a scientific level. I do not favor any one philosophical approach to data and information. Instead, I have always been fascinated by the topic in question and the relevant history I need to consider. This curiosity has defined the methods I use in my work. Such an approach is not unlike that of archaeologists or detectives: They gather puzzle pieces over a long period of time that gradually form a complete picture, thereby delivering greater insights.

My first infographics

I had the good fortune to be hired by the *Stern* magazine in 1990. I started working there as an assistant during my studies (Fig. 1) and entered the world of journalism at the age of 22 — a world I have never left. After spending time in the graphics lab, followed by the *Stern* title page department, I eventually ended up in the team of draftspersons. My mentors were my colleagues Monica Polasz, Reinald Blanck, and his nephew Harald Blanck, all of whom were employed there as illustrators. Our job was to put everything into graphic form that could not be explained using either photos or text. This mainly covered maps, diagrams, and schematics, but also larger-sized illustrations, which, at the time, were still drawn or airbrushed by hand (Fig. 2). *Stern* had a long tradition of employing well-known artists and caricaturists, among them Neugebauer, Wolf, Markus, Papan, Loriot, Tetsche, Haderer and Til Mette. When I began my career on the banks of the Alster in the so-called »monkey cliffs« (a nickname reflecting the building's architecture — others called it the »shark tank«) that neighbored the US Embassy, I could still feel the spirit of Henri Nannen who had founded *Stern* in 1948. At Nannen's side in those days was the press illustrator Günter Radtke, who, from *Stern's* earliest days, set the tone for cover layouts, illustrations and graphics, thereby laying a cornerstone of visual journalism upon which many others have built.

I was part of their third generation of illustrators and infographic artists. I spent nearly six years at *Stern's* publisher, Gruner + Jahr, learning my craft. When computers arrived in 1993, we began creating graphics on our Macs; we too had finally arrived in the digital age and began calling ourselves infographic artists (Fig. 3).

Upon a wave of digitalization ushered in by the growth of the internet in the late 1990s, infographics grew in popularity. The small monitor sizes of the time meant that many people were averse to long texts. Photos, videos, and infographics therefore increased in importance. The introduction of the iPhone and other smartphones in 2007 provided another leap forward. Fledgling social media platforms boomed.

As infographic artists, we also had to reconsider how best to share information in graphic form, as smartphones provided much smaller displays, but could nevertheless deliver a virtually unending stream of content if organized in a series of images to be clicked through in order. At the start of the new millennium, interactive infographics suddenly gained in popularity. And today we are researching voice assistants, augmented reality (AR), virtual reality (VR), and artificial intelligence (AI) to see how we can share knowledge with the help of such technologies.

Infographics appear in all areas of our lives. They provide direction (navigation) and orientation (building maps); they help us spot trends within election results (seat allocation) and even weather patterns (weather maps). Many of these visualizations are like second nature to us, because we have seen, understood, and used them so often. The human brain can process such images extremely well, enabling us to make decisions more quickly. To a certain extent therefore, these images simplify life itself.

Telling stories

Graphic artists are trained to develop ideas and create graphics with the help of various pieces of software. In principle, anyone who can use a computer can learn how to do this. And once you have gathered a few years of experience with such tools, you are in a better position to use them in the future. But what is it that defines my uniqueness as a graphic artist?

To start with, I do not consider myself to be *just* a graphic artist. In fact, I am primarily a storyteller — a visual author, not unlike a film director. I tell a story — visually — with as little text as possible. As infographic artists, we do not, however, create fiction — our primary objective is to present real and complex issues in a more understandable form. We are ultimately providing a service to society because we make knowledge possible and accessible to everyone.

The world is growing ever more complex. Untold amounts of data are being collected and made publicly available. We are immersed in a jungle of numbers and information. And, unfortunately, not all of them are correct. There are also piles of garbage data, fake news, and conspiracy theories. Part of the service that we provide to our readers is therefore to search for only true, valid data and create informative and entertaining graphics based on that data.

Using data and information, we build a visual knowledge base from which readers can form their own opinion. It might also occur to you that we could abuse readers' trust in our graphics by knowingly manipulating data or simply leaving out important facts. Unfortunately, this is an increasingly common practice, especially among those who seek to communicate a very specific message. It may well apply to politically motivated individuals or groups, but also to corporations or businesses hoping to improve their public image. Indeed, the trust many readers now place in infographics lends itself to their growing popularity among those who aim to deceive. It is also possible to create a misleading infographic by presenting truthful information in an entirely false context. Just look at the discussions about climate change over the past few years. The media is full of self-styled experts, and it is increasingly common to see politicians holding up infographics containing some sort of chart to the cameras to back up their political position. Unfortunately, the evidence is often much more complex than can be summarized in any single graphic and requires much more time to sort through — which is traditionally the domain of science.

Many people have difficulty understanding that certain questions have no definitive answer. Was there really a Big Bang? What came before it? What exists beyond our universe? There are many things that will remain unexplained forever. We can only try to research these issues as much as possible, use the data to form an increasing number of connections and draw some conclusions: about our universe, our Earth, our history, our environment, and ourselves, taking into account the smallest living cells and every pulsing molecule.

We will never understand everything in its entirety. The weather alone is too complex, eluding accurate prediction. Therefore, we discuss future weather patterns in terms of probability. When we see tomorrow's weather report with its rain cloud positioned above our city, do we know whether our street will get any rain? We must apply the same skepticism about daily weather forecasts to any graphic representation of future political developments, for the simple reason that we cannot make any definite predictions about such things. Infographics do not have to go into every last detail of an issue, but rather illustrate the basic operational modes and tendencies of real processes. They can then serve as the basis for an objective exchange on a given issue, allowing us to make specific decisions for the future together.

No info, no graphics

Creating infographics is a complex task. By introducing individual workflow steps, I will explain how graphics are created. Before I can begin to create one, I first need to collect information from a wide variety of sources: from tables, texts, maps, illustrations, photos, videos, and objects. As a rule, I try to gather as much information on each specific topic as possible in order to form the most complete and objective view. In the digital age, it has become easier than ever to gather information and evidence quickly, but it can also be worthwhile visiting a library or a relevant location if such a visit is feasible and might yield some benefits.

To put it more simply, facts have to be the priority. We have to ensure that our sources of information are trustworthy, complete, faultless, current, and accurately prepared. It is even better if we have multiple, independent sources and can compare their data ourselves. It is also important to question the data: How was it gathered? Where is the original source? Who gathered or financed it?

One of my most important rules is to never trust anyone else's infographic! Unfortunately, it has become common practice to take existing infographics and copy or recreate them in part or in whole, without thinking anything about it. The worst situation of all is when a supposedly correct graphic is copied so many times that people start to believe that it must be true if they have seen it everywhere.

When I was working on an infographic for the 50th anniversary of the erection of the Berlin Wall in 2011, I soon discovered that many sources, including some very old ones, were contradictory and, in some cases, completely wrong. Old maps marking the length of the Berlin Wall were especially inaccurate, often showing the wrong course entirely. One erroneous map had been copied so many times that it eventually became the »truth« (Fig. 4). I therefore headed to Berlin's geoinformation office and retrieved copies of detailed aerial photographs from 1988 and 1989, from which I could ascertain the final position of the Berlin Wall. My map remains the most accurate on this topic to-date, and I have allowed the Berlin Wall Foundation to make use of it. In the ensuing years, my passion for the visual interpretation of the Berlin Wall grew further. Part of that work is also published in this book (see the HISTORY chapter).

My journalistic work often resembles that of a crime detective. During my long career, I have witnessed a few special cases — for example, in October 2002, when 40–50 terrorists took over Moscow's Dubrovka Theater (home to the Russian musical, »Nord-Ost«), holding over 800 people hostage, to demand the withdrawal of Russian troops from Chechnya. Russian special forces stormed the building after releasing an aerosol anesthetic through the building's ventilation system. The terrorists were killed, but so were 130 hostages: 5 at the hands of their hostage takers, 125 from a lack of medical treatment following the gas attack. At the time, I was working for *Max* magazine, a semimonthly giving publications such as *Stern*, *Focus*, and *Spiegel* a run for their money. It was my job to describe the chain of events in and around the theater in one graphic. For us infographic artists, topical events like this can be difficult to illustrate, particularly when they take place far from home. From such a distance, we often know too little to create a truthful graphic. Under such conditions, it is better simply to wait, because both the necessary technology and the quality of the reporting demand far more time than is available in such a pressurized situation. If you have a couple of days or weeks of breathing space, a far clearer picture eventually forms and it is possible to slowly pick your way through the subject. In the case of the Dubrovka Theater, I had four entire weeks in which to complete my usual daily responsibilities as well as tell this story graphically (Fig. 5). At the time, it was unbelievably difficult to find information about the theater building itself, specifically the internal layout of rooms (this was, of course, in the time before Google Maps). So I compiled satellite images with the help of our photo editors. Using many photographs and videos from various news agencies, I pieced the puzzle together bit by bit, eventually forming a sketch of the entire building complex. I had to be cautious with Russian sources, because the Russian government's information policy appeared to be quite restrictive. Getting a copy of the building's architectural plans was unthinkable. But what did the inside of the theater even look like? In an attempt to find more specific information on that aspect, I explored certain Russian webpages and online fora, eventually meeting a young actor who had worked in the theater. I sent him a copy of my sketch by email, which he then corrected, improved, and labeled, returning it to me a few days later. This sketch was an important missing piece in the puzzle. Together with a further item of information from a colleague at *Stern*, it enabled me to complete the graphic to the very best of my ability (and in gratitude I also sent the actor a heavy metal music DVD he was desperate to get his hands on).

Fig. 4. Tourists at Potsdamer Platz photograph a map showing the incorrect route of the Berlin Wall. The map was published by the city of Berlin. This is one example of how incorrect information becomes its own truth and spreads across the globe. View the correct path of the Berlin Wall in the HISTORY chapter.

The art of absence

As infographic artists, we very often work on boring tables. Sometimes they are composed of countless lines of data, which it is our job to screen, format, or convert. Things get more complicated when we need to combine two different sources of data, each bound by different formats, measures, or notations. We have to look at the data very closely, because if a mistake happens at this point, any subsequent work is in vain. It gets especially interesting if our aim is to visualize such data. What format should I choose? A bar chart? Or maybe a map with data points would be better? What if I simply change the background color of the relevant table cells?

There are hundreds, if not thousands of possibilities for visualizing data. Which method is the right one? The only way to find out is to start experimenting and trying out different options. A common mistake is to prefer a certain visualization format over another for aesthetic reasons. While it may look nice, the wrong format may indeed provide the reader with no insights at all.

The first question I always ask myself is: What is the story I am trying to recount? What does the data tell us? Can I obtain an answer from the data, or can it be used to answer a specific question? Does the data give me an entirely new perspective, leading me to another story altogether? For this reason, it is very important to remain relatively open at this stage of the task. At the beginning, everything is still possible; during the brainstorming phase, there are no limitations. Once you have made as many infographics as I have, you will be able to recognize more quickly which path is the right one. Experience is a definite asset in this field. It is indeed much harder to decide which things to leave out. What time frame shall I include in this diagram? What is essential and what is superfluous for my readers or users? What could be confusing? And what aspects are even relevant for us and our readers?

There is one graphic in this book that clearly illustrates why data cannot always be easily evaluated and why it is worth digging deeper into every statistic. When I was working with the data for the »50th Anniversary of the German Soccer League« story (see the SPORTS chapter), I received an Excel spreadsheet with the results of every game over the last fifty years. The table was straightforward to read. »1:1 is the most common score in the German Soccer League«, has been published by every press outlet, repeating and copying it throughout their reporting and graphics. There was just one problem, as one of my employees pointed out to me. It was actually 2:1 that was the most common score if you looked at the data carefully, because 1:1 scores did not differentiate between home or away games, whereas 2:1 (home) or 1:2 (away) did. As a result, the actual number of 1:1 draws was half the number it appeared to be. This meant that the correct interpretation was that 2:1 was the most common or probable result — an answer that bookies can also confirm. I have placed this data in a matrix so that you can understand it better.

Who even cares?

As graphic artists, and editors, we must naturally consider who will be receiving our output. What level of knowledge does the reader or user already have? How good is their general education and how old are they? Are we speaking to the broader public — as in this book — or to the specialized workers of a given corporation? Can we assume previous knowledge? These questions must be answered in advance, because our customers want us to present complex content to them in a way that can be easily understood.

In my opinion, one rule always applies. People need an easy entrée into every topic; they should never feel overwhelmed — especially as we find ourselves in a world that increasingly floods all of us with images and information. We must reach out to our readers and users, leading them by the hand through our graphics. What should they see first? How do I pique their curiosity? How do I make it more inviting to engage with this topic or specific elements of it?

As a graphic artist, we do not only use our color palette to make a graphic more attractive. We mainly use it to make things easier for our readers, for example, in a graphic's legend. Or we use a signal color to amplify certain elements of the graphic. Typography is used systematically, using bold for certain texts and italics for others, such as the names of rivers on maps. There are endless possibilities to apply the tools that graphic artists have at their disposal in a sensible manner. The culture we grew up in also attributes specific meanings to a broad range of items. In the West, for example, the color green is associated with something positive. We play on and take advantage of such cultural assumptions and conventions.

Given the variety of both graphics and content in this book, you will quickly see that some graphics require a lot of time to absorb fully. Other graphics can be »read« more quickly and are quite entertaining. My experience has shown that you cannot please everyone in this job, but that is also what makes it so fascinating. After all, every person is unique.

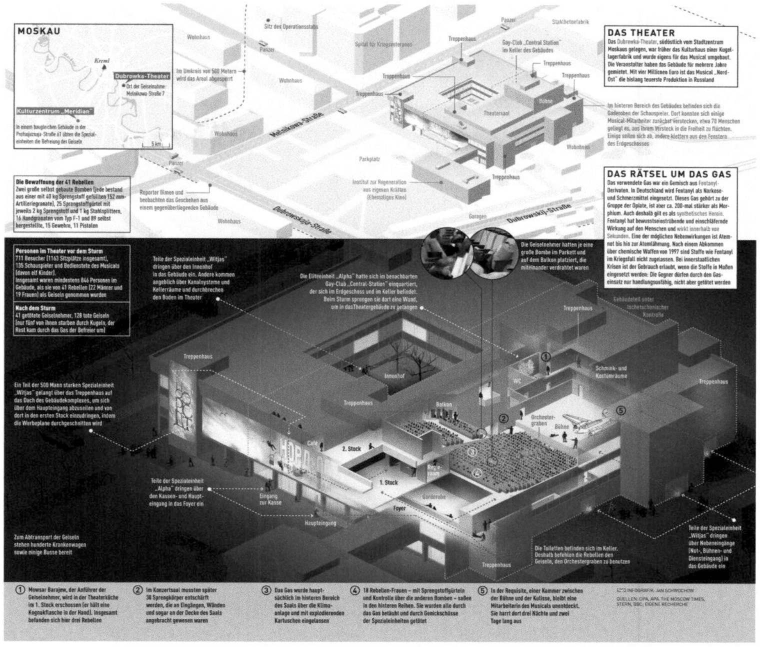

Fig. 5. Graphic of the October 2002 hostage situation in Moscow's Dubrovka Theater, published in *Max* magazine, Vol. 1, 2003.

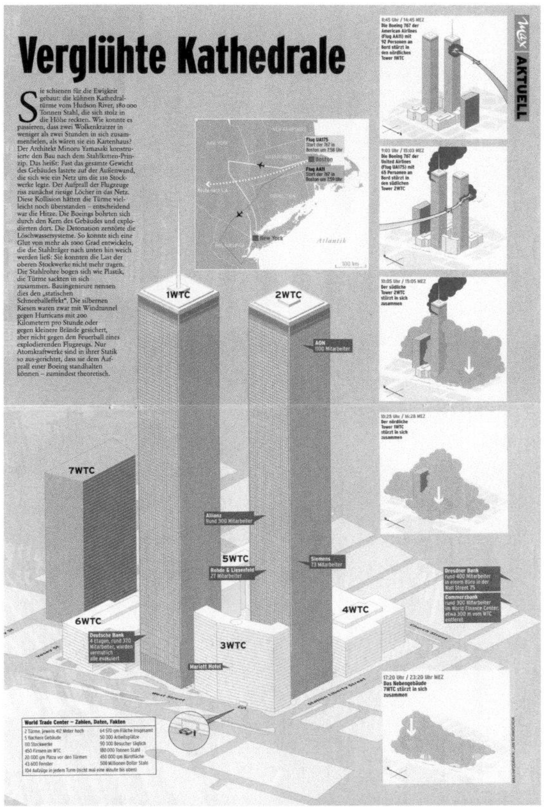

Fig. 6. Graphic of the September 11 terror attacks on the World Trade Center, published in *Max* magazine's special issue, September 14, 2001.

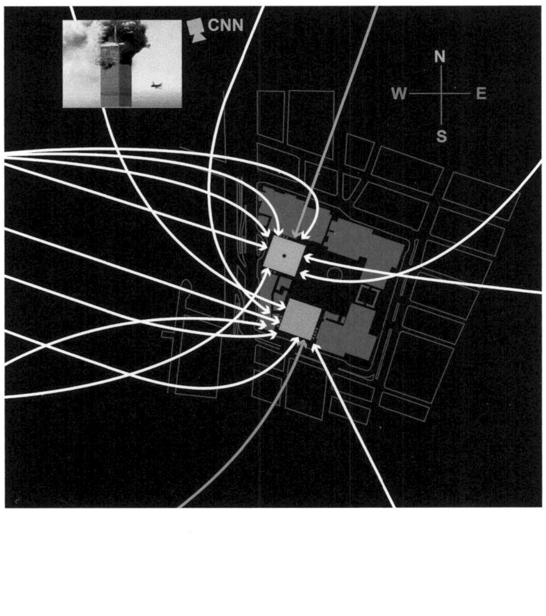

Fig. 7. In the weeks following 9/11, I analyzed countless media infographics and plotted all illustrated flight paths in a single graphic. I came to the conclusion that numerous colleagues had incorrectly interpreted television images of the crashes. The correct flight routes are shown in orange and blue.

Fig. 8. One of my finest infographics to-date – everything you need to know about the Orca whale. Text, pictures, illustrations and infographics combine to serve one single goal: the graphic should be a source of both pleasure and detailed information. It appeared in the Sunday newspaper *Welt am Sonntag* (2.1.2005).

What is the story?

Most people would call even a simple chart an infographic. I do not agree. Diagrams, maps, pictures, and fonts are all tools that storytellers employ like directors. A good film does not make itself, even if it employs talented actors, an accomplished cinematographer, and an attractive backdrop. We need a good story, a leitmotif, that transports and entertains our readers. We need an arc of suspense, as well as clarity on what comprises the main story and what remains subtext, perhaps hinted at between the lines. These are all questions we must ask ourselves. For this reason, the first step is to make one or more sketches, working from rough outlines to finer and finer points, before we begin realizing our vision. Only when the story is clear, and we have all the necessary information and data, can we begin with implementation. If, in the process of developing our graphic, we notice that something is missing, we must do further research. In this case, part of the process then goes back to the drawing board.

In the last few years, data visualization programs have entered the market. Newly developed software makes it possible for us to evaluate millions of data points simultaneously and illustrate them graphically. Such visualizations bring with them an entirely new aesthetic. In this book you will also find illustrations of some quite complex data sets. To me, it is still important to guide the reader through such data; it is not necessary to label every single data point, rather only those that are truly relevant for the topic at hand.

Choosing Your Visualization Method

Imagine you recently returned from vacation. You run into a friend on the street, but only have a couple of minutes to tell him about the sensational trip that is still so fresh in your memory. What are the most important things to share in the short time available? It is a completely different story than if you had invited your friend over for dinner and a slide show on your 4K monitor the next evening. In that case, you would have the space and time to go into much greater detail — you would likely take a chronological approach to help you recall the best, most interesting, and most important moments from your trip, with ample room for every story worth telling.

This example is quite revealing – as graphic artists, we face this problem every time we are asked to reduce our graphic to an image for a social media post. Or is it a large A2 poster we need to design, or perhaps a double page spread as in this book? Or maybe a seemingly infinite website? How much time do we want to invest in creating this graphic? The limits of time and available space are therefore incredibly important factors. We have invested much — arguably too much — time in this book. But we think it was worth it. You will discover a wide variety of graphic styles, from simple computer vector graphics to 3D graphics and wonderful, hand-drawn illustrations. Once the story and its development are set, style is the next major hurdle. Aesthetic or economic reasons often guide our style choices and the time we allocate to execution. That is what makes this book a real grab bag, as I have always encouraged my employees to find their own style and develop it further.

The devil is in the detail

Whoever works on such complex topics must protect themselves against errors. We have, of course, completed these graphics to the best of our knowledge, but nevertheless cannot exclude that, despite all efforts to the contrary, some errors may still have sneaked in. We believe that quality trumps speed and that it is our responsibility to ensure that the book you hold in your hands gives you the feeling of being thoroughly and truthfully informed.

During my career, I have made a few errors that taught me some important lessons. One terrible slip came the first night after the September 11 attacks in 2001. *Max* produced a special edition with 139 pages. That volume included three large graphics designed by me, produced in just a few hours with the bare minimum of information. One of these graphics showed the World Trade Center towers with two airplanes headed towards them, but unfortunately I had drawn one of their flight paths coming from the wrong direction (Fig. 6). That mistake annoyed me greatly at the time, and regrettably we never published a correction or apology for the error. In my haste, I had misinterpreted the television images of the attack. There had not been enough time, and, when in doubt, it is better to be less ambitious. In the days following publication, I studied what other colleagues around the world produced at the same time and was shocked. My analysis of the other infographics showed the airplanes flying into the towers from virtually every direction (Fig. 7). Ten years later, my team and I picked up this topic once again (see the HISTORY chapter) and could use the gift of time to reconstruct the events of that day with much greater precision.

When a graphic sees the light of day

The best moment for me is when an infographic is first published. During my time at *Stern*, I was able to experience this feeling every week, providing accurate information to millions of German readers. *Stern* was fortunate to have a so-called 'documentation department' – an editorial department that re-examined every graphic with a fine-tooth comb before publication. The final edit ensured error-free copy. This impressed me at the time and continues to do so to this day. I am shocked to witness that this essential final editorial step has now been removed from almost every modern newsroom. Speed has usurped accuracy – something which has become increasingly problematic. These days, all that matters is being the fastest, accumulating the most clicks, or expanding readership, even if it comes at the cost of truthful reporting.

Careful and precise ways of working are a standard I will never abandon. I am concerned at the degree to which younger colleagues pay little thought to the information they come across and the limited awareness they have of their own responsibility. »Someone else will take care of that«, they seem to think. Today we publish and share all kinds of information on the internet and across social networks at the speed of a double-click and rarely stop to ask ourselves whether or not these actions are good or correct. In the end, it doesn't matter one iota if information is spread by analog or digital means. What matters most to me is that any graphic I publish gives me the feeling that I have delivered the best, most error-free work possible. We can and will continue to update our graphics, as we will surely do for the next edition of this book. In the modern age, anything that has already been released into the world can hardly be controlled or even stopped. I therefore attach a huge amount of importance to my work and am passionate about achieving the best results, irrespective of the fact that my employees and I earn our livings this way.

Understanding the world

These lines were crafted in my home office while the coronavirus was paralyzing the world. My team and I could continue working on our book from home, but these events have granted us a new perspective on our work. This book inadvertently describes our old world and its sacred principles — things which have seemingly disappeared during a lockdown of unforeseen length.

You have the opportunity to curl up on your sofa with this book and study the ways of our old world. You do not have to read it all at once. You can pick it up again and again, giving yourself space to reflect. Perhaps certain graphics will take on an entirely new meaning to you in the shadow of a global pandemic?

No one could have predicted that our everyday lives could be completely disrupted so abruptly. Every single one of us — the entire world over — is affected by this global crisis in their own way. But if we are honest, it was only a matter of time until something like this happened. Until now, we have been stuck in a kind of rat race — and now external forces have applied the brakes to the wheel in our cage to such an extent that we have been forcibly ejected from it, flying head over heels to a screeching stop. Things that humanity has done to life on our planet have now come back to haunt us.

The coronavirus is a kind of mirror. The virus is oblivious, knows no borders, cannot differentiate between rich and poor. We must understand this lesson: As far as the virus is concerned, we are all the same. This crisis may be just the chance we need to leave our children and all future generations a different and possibly better world than the one that came before.

We will have to consider what it truly means to »be human« on this planet. Even during the coronavirus crisis, we have witnessed in spectacular fashion how our human values far exceed economic ones. We are facing the essential question: What is the value of one human life?

We know that our old way of life really only benefited a handful of people. Perhaps this crisis will help remove the negative elements in our society. We can only hope that many people will finally learn to stop listening to populist beliefs and instead take their guidance from experts and scientists. Even in Germany we will address the question of whether, for example, a universal basic income during crisis periods wouldn't be an appropriate solution. Do we need a better health care system — perhaps a pan-European or even a global system? Should the responsibility for certain areas no longer remain with individual countries? Does everything need to be privatized? Just how social or how liberal should our future state – and our life together – be?

It won't all be as negative as it perhaps appears at the moment. I want this book to spread hope as well. Our natural world, our whole Earth is so beautiful and unique. We should do everything in our power to preserve that gift. Perhaps this book may contribute to that end. In the pages that follow, you will find many intellectual approaches to various topics that have occupied us before and during this crisis, as well as things we will certainly address in the coming years: social systems, the EU on the verge of Brexit, medicine and health care systems, natural disasters, globalization and climate change, natural resources and their exploitation, wars, colonization, religion, corporations, value-added and supply chains, inventions and discoveries, and much more.

Otherwise, simply see where the pages take you and allow yourself to be entertained. And if you come to the conclusion that none of this is important and there is nothing to be learned here, please turn to the final page (P. 552) before showing yourself out. It is a powerful reminder of just how small and inconsequential all of humanity is in the context of our entire universe. In some seven billion years, our sun will become a red giant, thereby making Earth uninhabitable. If we have not already done so, we will have reached the end of our story by then.

Jan Schwochow, May 2020

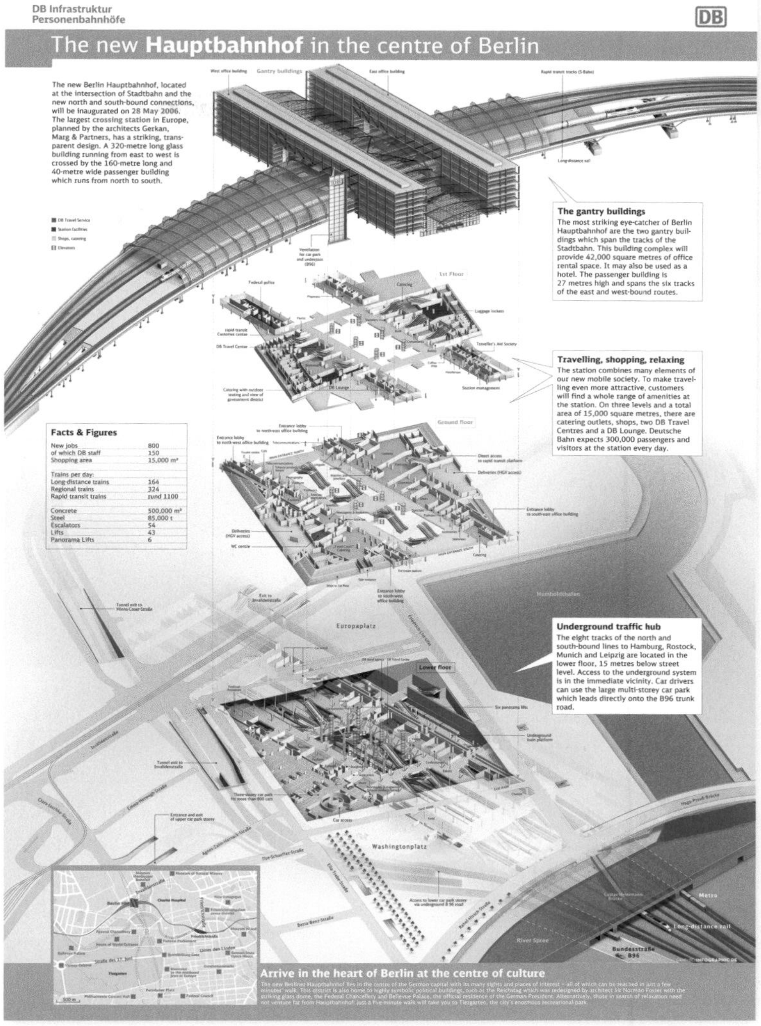
DB Infrastruktur
Personenbahnhöfe
DB
The new Hauptbahnhof in the centre of Berlin
The new Berlin Hauptbahnhof, located at the intersection of Stadtbahn and the new north and south-bound connections, will be inaugurated on 28 May 2006. The largest crossing station in Europe, planned by the architects Gerkan, Marg & Partners, has a striking, transparent design. A 320-metre long glass building running from east to west is crossed by the 160-metre long and 40-metre wide passenger building which runs from north to south.
Gantry buildings
The gantry buildings
The most striking eye-catcher of Berlin Hauptbahnhof are the two gantry buildings which span the tracks of the Stadtbahn. This building complex will provide 42,000 square metres of office rental space. It may also be used as a hotel. The passenger building is 27 metres high and spans the six tracks of the east and west-bound routes.
1st Floor
Travelling, shopping, relaxing
The station combines many elements of our new mobile society. To make travelling even more attractive, customers will find a whole range of amenities at the station. On three levels and a total area of 15,000 square metres, there are catering outlets, shops, two DB Travel Centres and a DB Lounge. Deutsche Bahn expects 300,000 passengers and visitors at the station every day.
Facts & Figures
New jobs 800
of which DB staff 150
Shopping area 15,000 m²
Trains per day:
Long-distance trains 164
Regional trains 324
Rapid transit trains rund 1100
Concrete 500,000 m³
Steel 85,000 t
Escalators 54
Lifts 43
Panorama Lifts 6
Ground floor
Europaplatz
Humboldthafen
Underground traffic hub
The eight tracks of the north and south-bound lines to Hamburg, Rostock, Munich and Leipzig are located in the lower floor, 15 metres below street level. Access to the underground system is in the immediate vicinity. Car drivers can use the large multi-storey car park which leads directly onto the B96 trunk road.
Lower floor
Washingtonplatz
Arrive in the heart of Berlin at the centre of culture

Fig. 9 Infographics can also be useful for companies. I designed this poster for Deutsche Bahn to present the newly built central station in Berlin. The graphic was published in May 2006 and was printed in many German newspapers and magazines.

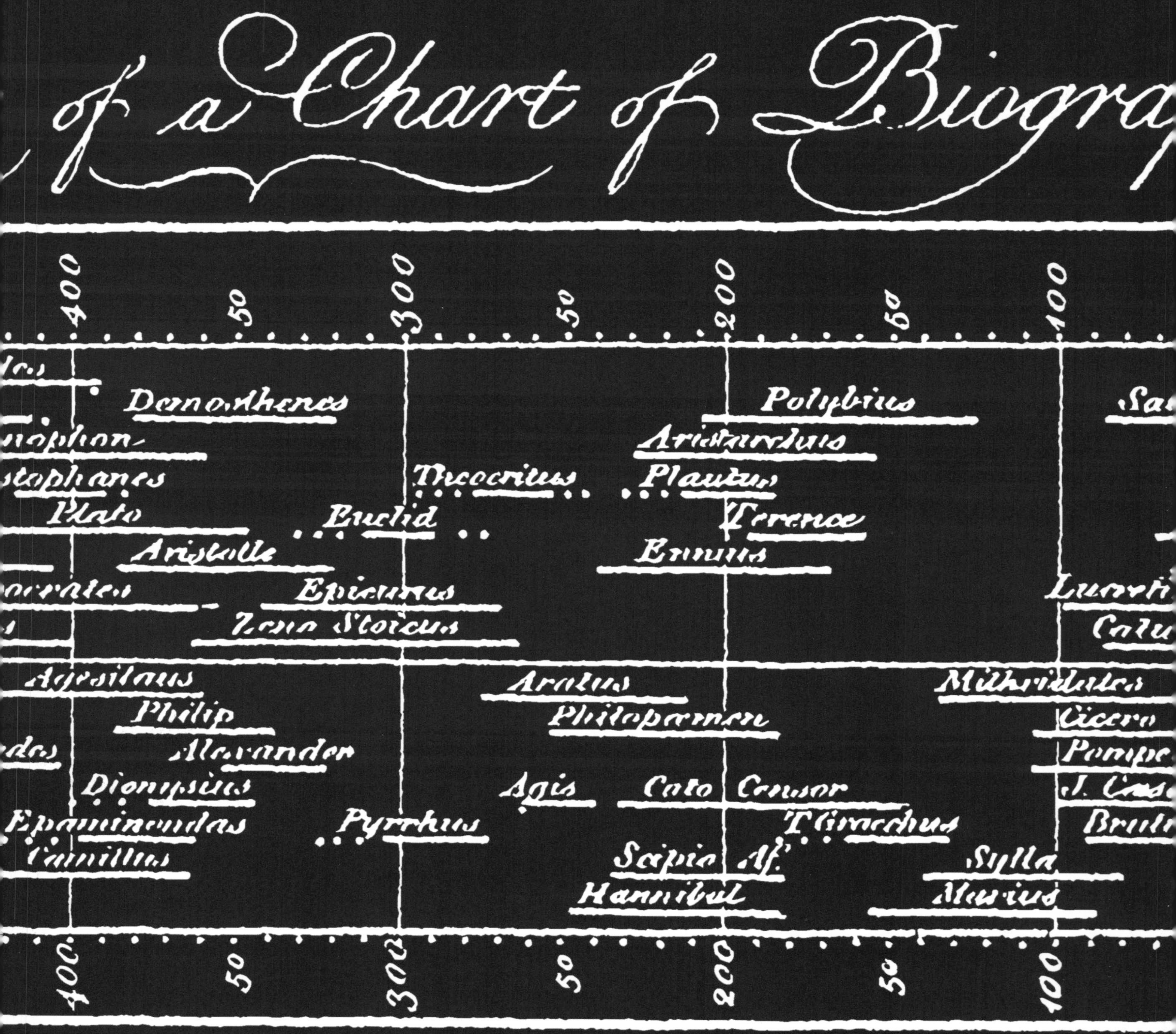
of a Chart of Biogra
400
50
300
50
200
50
100
Demosthenes
Polybius
Aristarchus
Plato
Theocritus
Plautus
Euclid
Terence
Aristotle
Ennius
Epicurus
Zeno Stoicus
Agesilaus
Aratus
Mithridates
Philip
Philopoemen
Cicero
Alexander
Dionysius
Agis
Cato Censor
Epaminondas
Pyrrhus
T. Gracchus
Camillus
Scipio Af.
Sylla
Hannibal
Marius

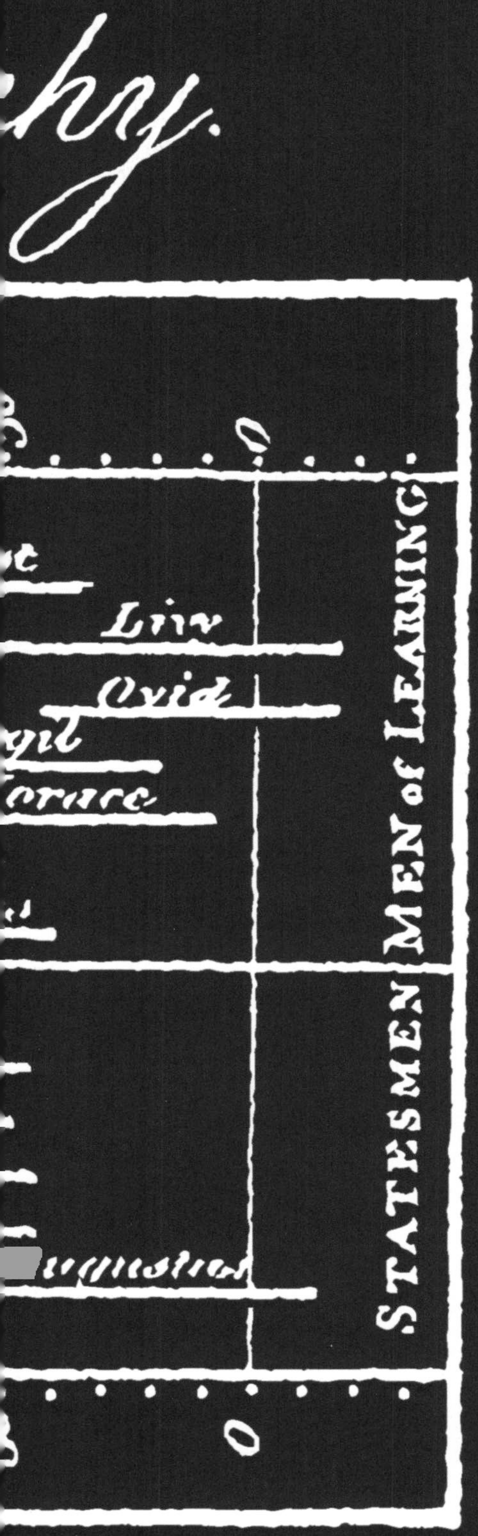

HISTORY

Time plays a central role in historical infographics. While historical facts and figures are most often conveyed in text form, illustrations regularly complement such written content. Their purpose is generally to visualize conditions at a given time or to relate information to a specific date. In this case, we have opted for a timeline which provides a linear presentation of temporal processes such as a person's lifespan or various segments of a trip linearly, thereby simplifying the reader's understanding and ability to reconstruct past events.

For example, **Joseph Priestley's »Specimen of a Chart of Biography«** from 1765 uses proportional graphic elements (in this case, horizontal lines) to visualize the lives and deaths of important historical figures relative to one another. Priestley was the first to use the timeline format in a consistent manner, thereby defining the most basic elements of such illustrations, including uniform measurements and labels.

Infographics with timelines are easy to follow and offer a wide scope for design. As a result, they remain popular to the present day when visualizing historical events, biographies, as well as workflows and operating processes.

BY ORDER OF THE EMPEROR

1433: For nearly three decades Admiral Zheng He travelled the seas on the orders of the Chinese emperor Zhu Di with a huge fleet of ships. China is on its way to world domination. But with the death of Zheng He this era ends – and with it the era of the treasure ships. For centuries afterwards, China isolates itself from the outside world. Only since China has regained its position as a world power has the story of Zheng He and his treasure ships drawn new attention.

»Baochuan« Treasure ship

With nine masts and sails made from red silk and bamboo—the largest sail weighed five tons and had a height of about 20 meters.

FLAGSHIP TO THE EMPIRE

Admiral Zheng He's flagship Baochuan dwarfed the other ocean-faring ships, including the fleet Christopher Columbus commanded to the New World, though there is some scholarly debate about the actual size and seaworthiness of the Admiral's massive ships. Each ship was crewed by a cross section of the Ming Dynasty population, but most on board were convicted criminals. Each team was led by specialists including captains, helmsmen, anchormen, astrologers, geomancers, scholars and craftsmen. When Zheng He died in 1433, the era of the Treasure Ships ended and China returned to isolation—until today.

Huge anchors weighing several tons
Crew's quarters
Gunpowder magazine
Sick bay
Workshops
24 bronze cannons
»Qilin« the Chinese unicorn: Admiral Zheng He brought a giraffe from Africa as a gift for the Emperor—a strange creature nobody had ever seen before.

1355 | 1360 | 1365 | 1370 | 1375

- Zheng He and his time
- Zheng He's voyages

China was under mongol rule from 1271 until 1368. The land then came under the rule of Hongwu, who became the first Emperor of the Ming Dynasty. This was the beginning of an economic and military ascent.

- **1360**: Hongwu's fourth son—the future Emperor Zhu Din—is born in the capital Nanjing.
- **1368**: Hongwu founds the Ming Dynasty and declares himself Emperor of China.
- **1371**: Zheng He, born in Southwest China, is the son of a Muslim rebel from Yunnan Province. His name at birth is Ma He.

Signal flags
Wheelhouse
The Admiral's launch
The Admiral's cabin served Zheng He as a residence during his travels.
Officers' Quarters: here lived astrologers, pharmacologists, clergymen, pharmacists, secretaries, interpreters, Imperial ambassadors and officers.
Guest accommodation
Festival room-saloon
Ship's hold
The deck house served as the quarters for the Admiral's elite troops.

Treasure ship »Baochuan« (1405–1433)		»Santa Maria« (1480–1492)
Admiral Zheng He	Captain	Christoph Columbus
130 m/426 ft	Length	23 m/75 ft
48 m/157 ft	Width	7 m/23 ft
300–500	Crew	40

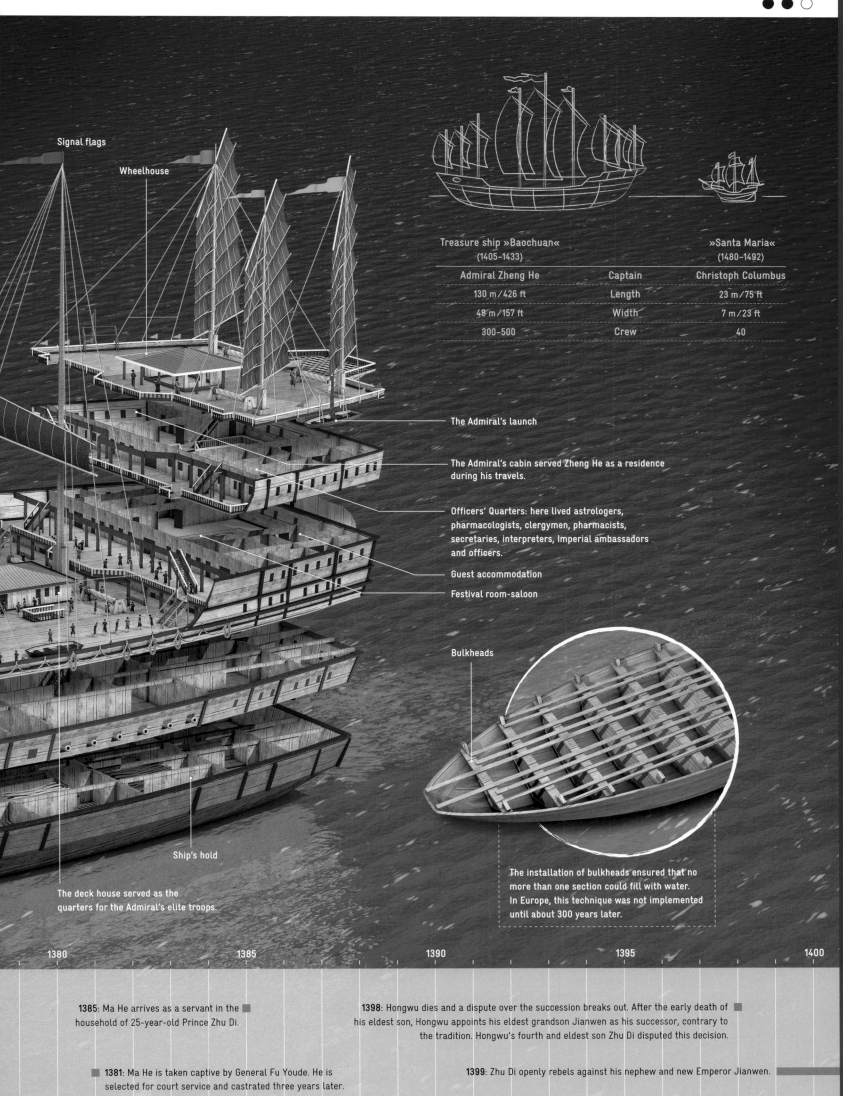

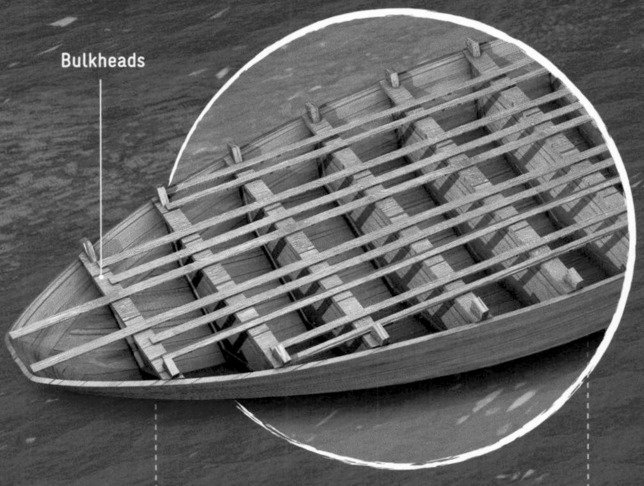
Bulkheads

The installation of bulkheads ensured that no more than one section could fill with water. In Europe, this technique was not implemented until about 300 years later.

1380 1385 1390 1395 1400

1385: Ma He arrives as a servant in the household of 25-year-old Prince Zhu Di.

1381: Ma He is taken captive by General Fu Youde. He is selected for court service and castrated three years later.

1398: Hongwu dies and a dispute over the succession breaks out. After the early death of his eldest son, Hongwu appoints his eldest grandson Jianwen as his successor, contrary to the tradition. Hongwu's fourth and eldest son Zhu Di disputed this decision.

1399: Zhu Di openly rebels against his nephew and new Emperor Jianwen.

THE TREASURE VOYAGES

In the early Ming Dynasty (1368-1644), China was on its way to world domination with a fleet of ships that ruled the seas under the command of Admiral Zheng He. For 30 years, he commanded the Baochuan or Treasure Ships on trade missions, collected tribute payments, pursued pirates and spread the glory of the Chinese empire. At the height of the Ming Voyages, the admiral commanded 300 ships and 30,000 crew. In all, Zheng He made seven voyages from China to India and from the Persian Gulf to East Africa. Today, he is celebrated in Chinese communities abroad as a god.

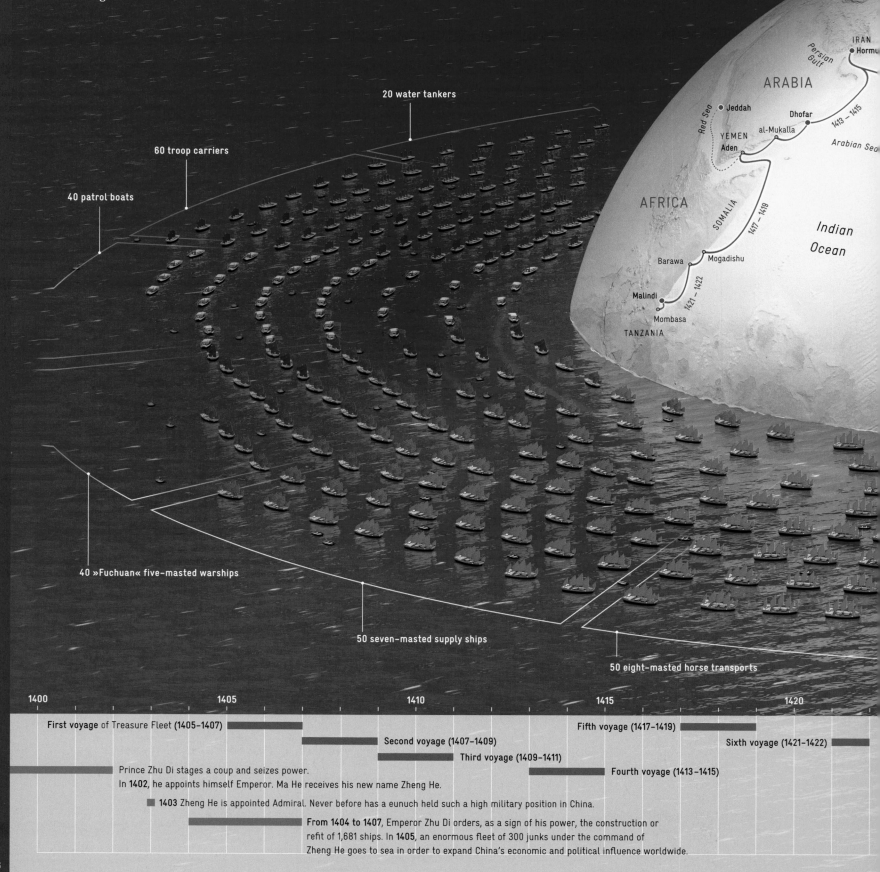

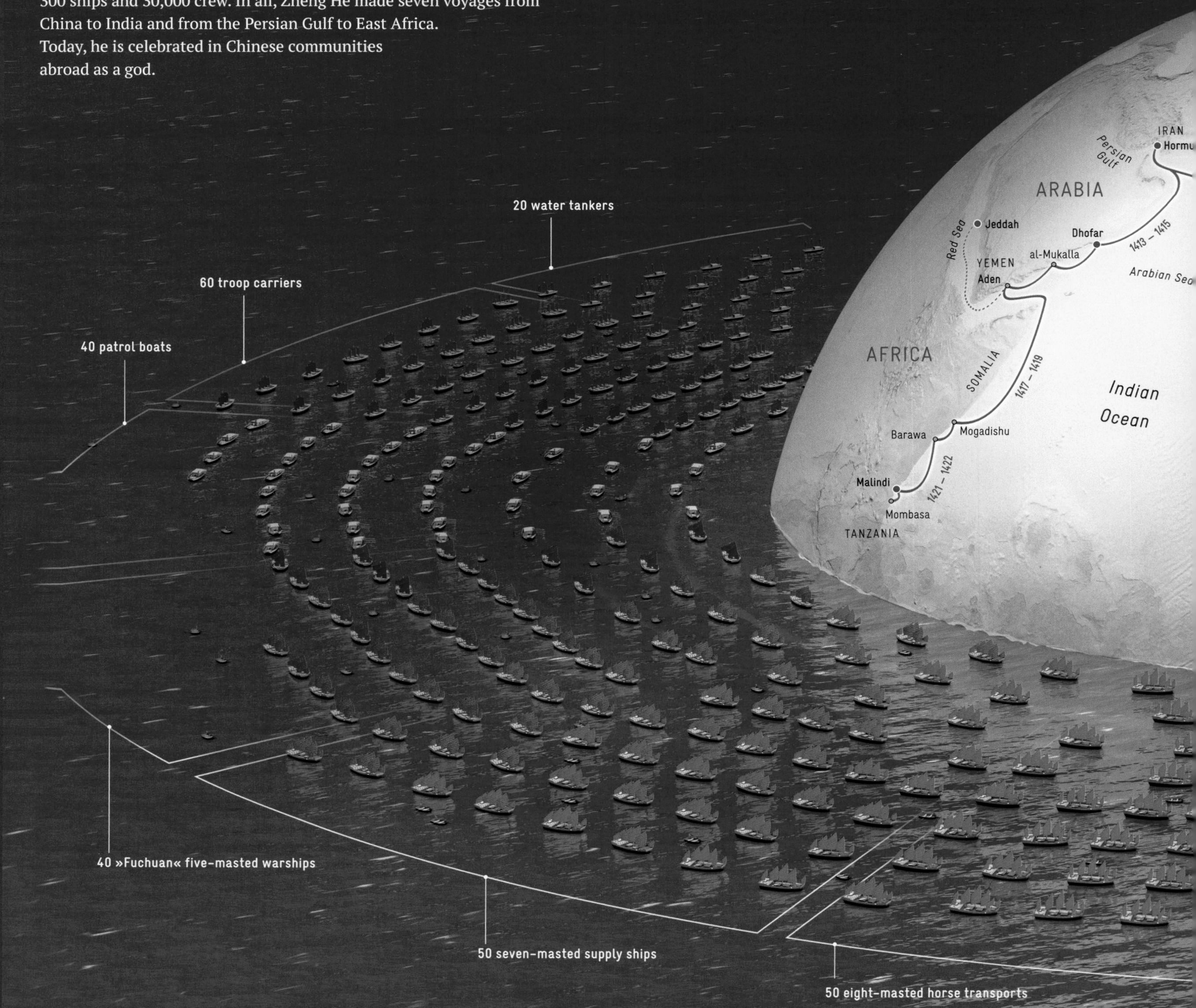
IRAN
Hormu
Persian Gulf
ARABIA
Red Sea
Jeddah
Dhofar
1413 – 1415
YEMEN
al-Mukalla
Aden
Arabian Sea
AFRICA
SOMALIA
1417 – 1419
Indian Ocean
Barawa
Mogadishu
Malindi
1421 – 1422
Mombasa
TANZANIA
20 water tankers
60 troop carriers
40 patrol boats
40 »Fuchuan« five-masted warships
50 seven-masted supply ships
50 eight-masted horse transports

1400 · 1405 · 1410 · 1415 · 1420

- **First voyage** of Treasure Fleet **(1405–1407)**
- **Second voyage (1407–1409)**
- **Third voyage (1409–1411)**
- **Fourth voyage (1413–1415)**
- **Fifth voyage (1417–1419)**
- **Sixth voyage (1421–1422)**

Prince Zhu Di stages a coup and seizes power.
In **1402**, he appoints himself Emperor. Ma He receives his new name Zheng He.

1403 Zheng He is appointed Admiral. Never before has a eunuch held such a high military position in China.

From 1404 to 1407, Emperor Zhu Di orders, as a sign of his power, the construction or refit of 1,681 ships. In **1405**, an enormous fleet of 300 junks under the command of Zheng He goes to sea in order to expand China's economic and political influence worldwide.

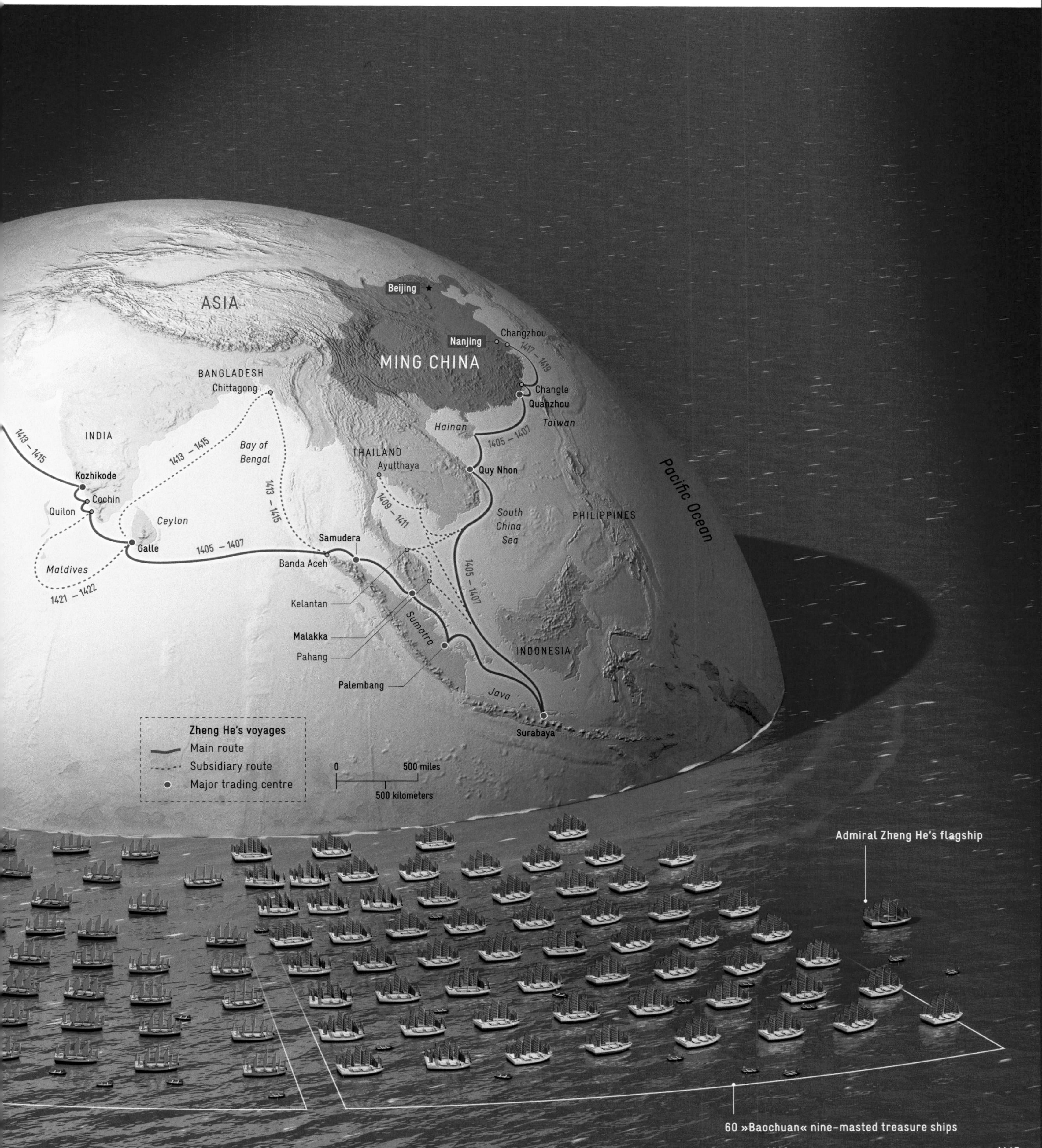

ASIA
Beijing
Nanjing
Changzhou
1417 – 1419
MING CHINA
BANGLADESH
Chittagong
Changle
Quanzhou
Taiwan
Hainan
1405 – 1407
INDIA
1413 – 1415
1413 – 1415
Bay of Bengal
THAILAND
Ayutthaya
Quy Nhon
Pacific Ocean
Kozhikode
Cochin
Quilon
1413 – 1415
1409 – 1411
South China Sea
PHILIPPINES
Ceylon
Galle
1405 – 1407
Samudera
Banda Aceh
Maldives
1421 – 1422
1405 – 1407
Kelantan
Sumatra
Malakka
Pahang
INDONESIA
Palembang
Java
Surabaya
Zheng He's voyages
Main route
Subsidiary route
Major trading centre
0
500 miles
500 kilometers
Admiral Zheng He's flagship
60 »Baochuan« nine-masted treasure ships

1425 | 1430 | 1435 | 1440 | 1445

Seventh and final voyage of the Treasure Fleet **(1431–1433)**

■ **1424** Zhu Di dies. Zheng He loses the support of the court. For financial reasons the new Emperor Zhu Gaozhi halts all Treasure Fleet voyages.

■ Zheng He dies probably in **1433** on the return from his final journey. This ends the era of the Treasure Fleets. Most ships are docked and left to rot.

■ Admiral Zheng He is relieved of his command and is appointed military commander of Nanjing.

■ Without the voyages of the Treasure Ships tribute payments drop off sharply. The successor to Zhu Gaozhi—the emperor Zhu Zhanji—orders Zheng He to sail once more.

FROZEN IN TIME

Ötzi the Iceman is now one of the most famous mummies in the world. The state in which he was found makes him so unique: a man, complete with clothing and equipment, frozen for over 5,000 years in the glacial ice of the Alps. The Dutch brothers Adrie and Alfons Kennis have reconstructed a scientific model of Ötzi based on his anatomy. This model and the mummy can be seen in the South Tyrol Museum of Archaeology in Bolzano.

Cap
Made from bearskin stitched together, and attached with two leather straps.
Coat
Made of dark and light goat hide.
Bow
The 1.82 meter longbow made from one piece of yew was found leaning against a rock.
Pants
Made from domestic goat hide and at the lower end of one flap made of deer skin, all stitched together with animal sinews.
Underwear
Narrow strips of goat hide.
Shoes
An inner shoe, made from grass netting and lined with hay for insulation, was covered with an outer shoe made of deerskin. Leather straps of bearskin hold the shoe together.

IMPORTANT FACTS

Age:	45–46 years
	(today: ca. 5,300 years)
Height:	1.60 m (today: 1.54 m)
Weight:	50 kg (today: 13 kg)
Shoe size:	38 (EU) / 5 (UK) / 6 (US)
Eye color:	brown
Hair:	medium length dark brown to black curly hair

Distinctive features:
A three millimeter wide gap between the two upper incisors; lack of all four wisdom teeth and the twelfth pair of ribs

ITALIAN OR AUSTRIAN?

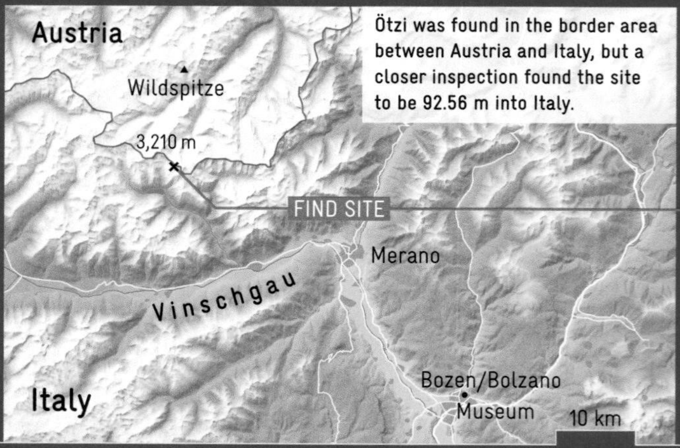
Austria
Wildspitze
3,210 m
FIND SITE
Merano
Vinschgau
Italy
Bozen/Bolzano
Museum
10 km
Ötzi was found in the border area between Austria and Italy, but a closer inspection found the site to be 92.56 m into Italy.

Axe

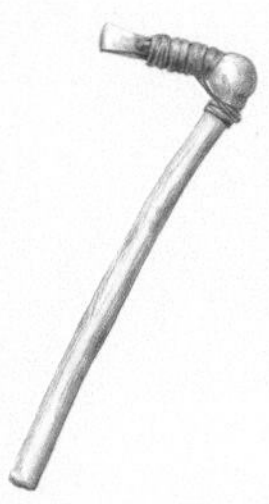

Shaft of yew; copper blade attached with birch tar and leather straps.

Dagger with raffia sheath

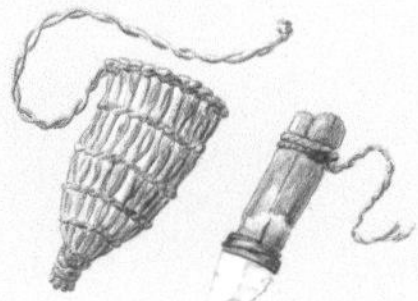

A dagger, about 13 cm long with a flint blade and ash wood handle: The dagger was kept in a sheath, which was likely attached to the belt.

Belt and pouch

4-5 cm wide belt of calf leather, originally 2 meters long, and twice tied around the hip.

Quiver with contents

A chamois hide quiver with arrows and rough arrow shafts, four antler points, a bent antler tip, a cord and two animal sinews.

Backpack

A two-meter long, U-shaped stick of hazel and two narrow wooden boards of larch wood.

Birch bark baskets

Two light containers made from birch bark with a diameter of 15 cm - 18 cm and a height of ca. 20 cm.

Simple first-aid kit

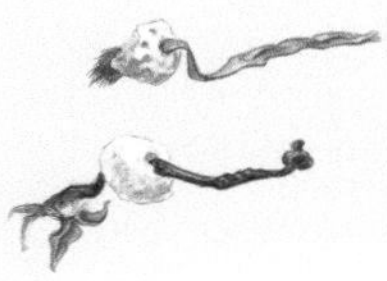

Two strips of hide, each threaded with a ball of fungus that were thought to have many medical purposes.

Bird belt

The disc of white dolomite marble has a hole and is tied to a hide strip. It is attached to a cord of twisted leather.

Net

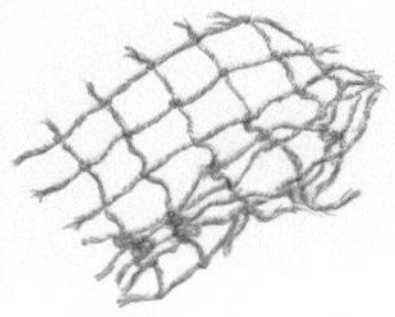

Coarse meshed net of raffia, was probably used to catch birds or hare.

Retoucher

A 12 cm long, pencil-like tool, made from a piece of lime wood—it was used for working flint, the tip is the fire-hardened point of a stag's antler.

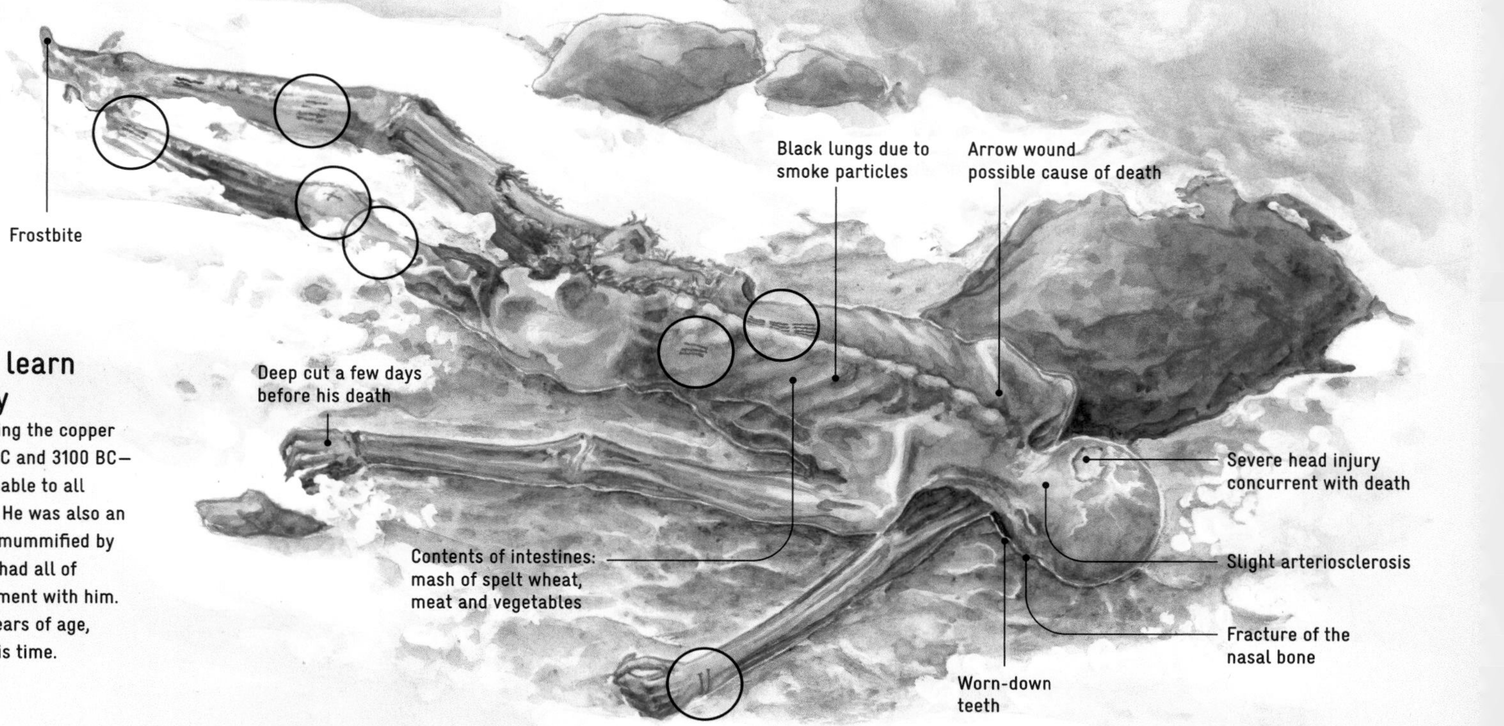

Frostbite
Black lungs due to smoke particles
Arrow wound possible cause of death
Deep cut a few days before his death
Severe head injury concurrent with death
Contents of intestines: mash of spelt wheat, meat and vegetables
Slight arteriosclerosis
Fracture of the nasal bone
Worn-down teeth

What we can learn from his body

The iceman lived during the copper age—between 3350 BC and 3100 BC—making him very valuable to all sorts of researchers. He was also an accidental mummy—mummified by the elements—so he had all of his organs and equipment with him. At an estimated 45 years of age, he was very old for his time.

HOW HE WAS FOUND

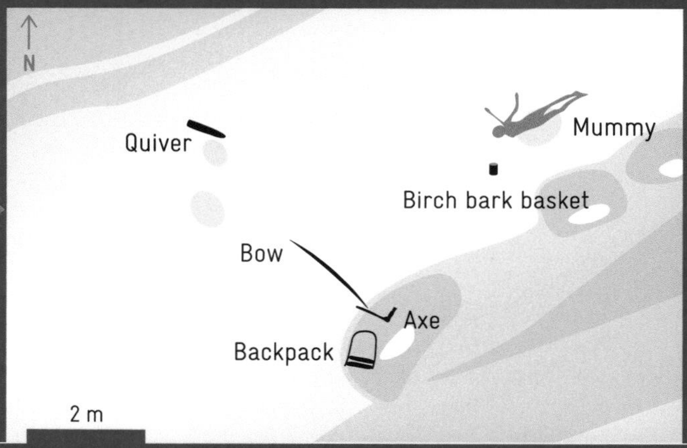

N
Quiver
Mummy
Birch bark basket
Bow
Axe
Backpack
2 m

TATTOOS AS ANCIENT MEDICINE?

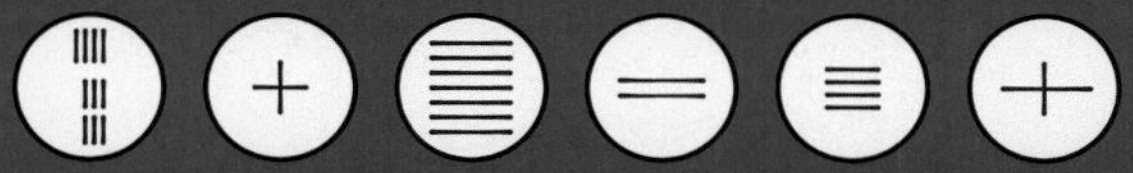

Ötzi was found to have several lines tattooed all over his body. Researchers theorize these were done as medical treatments on areas where he suffered strain.
Unlike modern tattoos done with needles, Ötzi's tattoos were likely made with fine incisions into the skin that were then rubbed with charcoal.

A NEW PALACE

The Neues Museum on Berlin's Museum Island is the home to thousands of years of human history. But its prize exhibit is the bust of Nefertiti dating from 1345 BC. The 19th century building suffered heavy damage during the Second World War and underwent a major renovation led by architect David Chipperfield. Today, tourists wander through the halls, in awe of both the building and the treasures it holds.

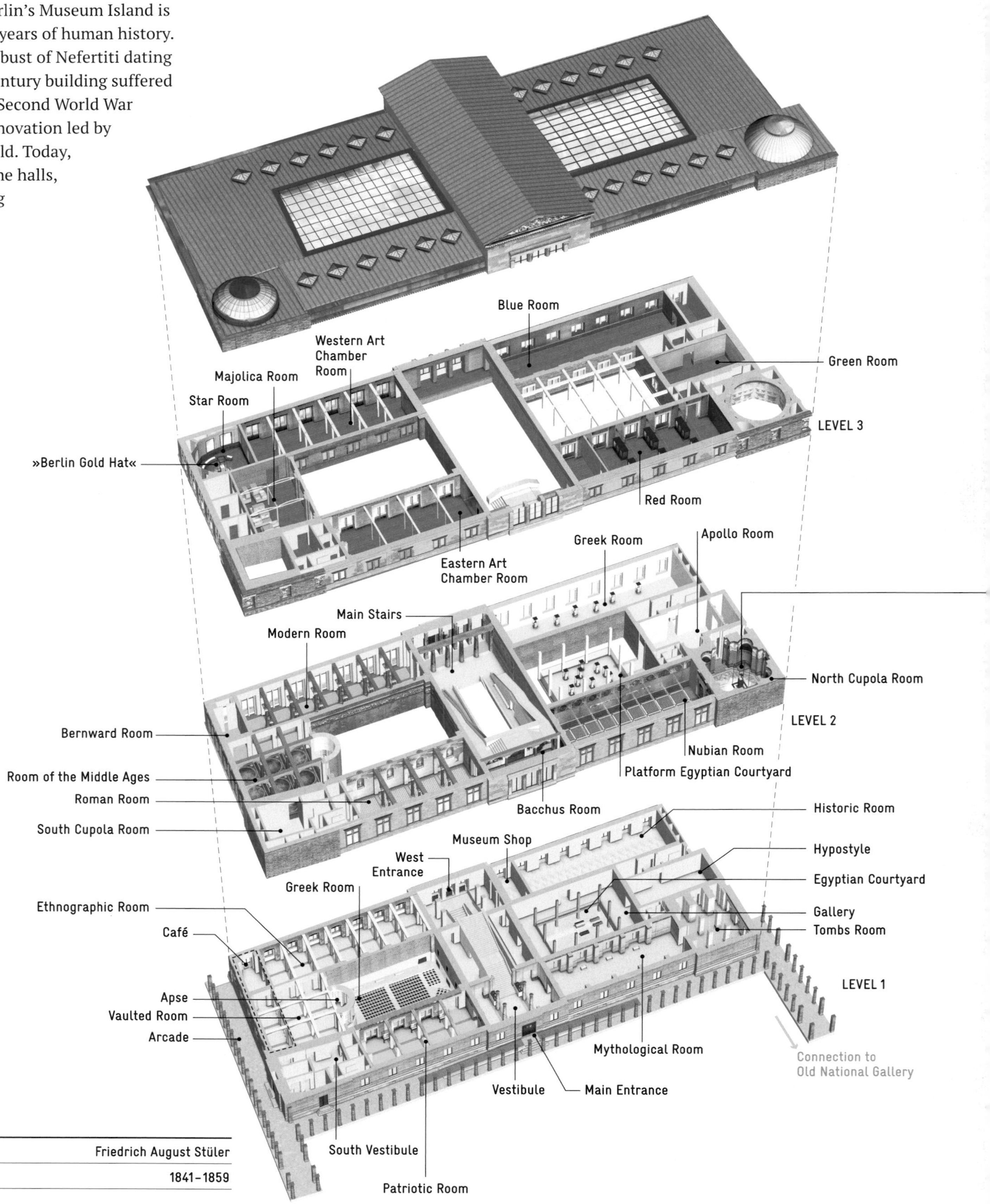

FACTS

Design	Friedrich August Stüler
Construction time	1841–1859

THE REBUILDING

Architects	David Chipperfield Architects, Julian Harrap
Contracting body	Stiftung Preußischer Kulturbesitz
Construction time	11-2003 until 3-2009
Construction costs	€212 m.
Gross floor area	20,500 m^2
Reopening	10-16-2009

A 19th century building constructed to the plans of Friedrich August Stüler. The building suffered heavy damage during the Second World War. Under the direction of the leading British architect, David Chipperfield, the remains were restored and modern elements added. The museum offers the visitor objects of antiquity from the treasures of the Egyptian Museum and Papyrus Collection and the Museum of Prehistory and Early History.

Nefertiti

NEFERTITI'S BURIAL CHAMBER?

In 1922, the Englishman Howard Carter discovered Pharaoh Tutankhamun's tomb. Further investigations of the 3,300-year-old complex are now suggesting that there are more chambers. In August 2015, the archaeologist Nicholas Reeves published »The Burial of Nefertiti?« with the thesis that there could be two more chambers in tomb KV62 and that the tomb is originally that of Tutankhamun's predecessor, Neferneferuaton (Nefertiti). Until 2018, further investigations were made and Reeves' thesis has been judged differently since its publication. At the Tutankhamun conference in May 2018, the results of further radar analyses, which were carried out by three independent teams at the beginning of the year, were announced. As no doors or cavities could be detected, further hidden burial chambers can be excluded with a high degree of certainty.

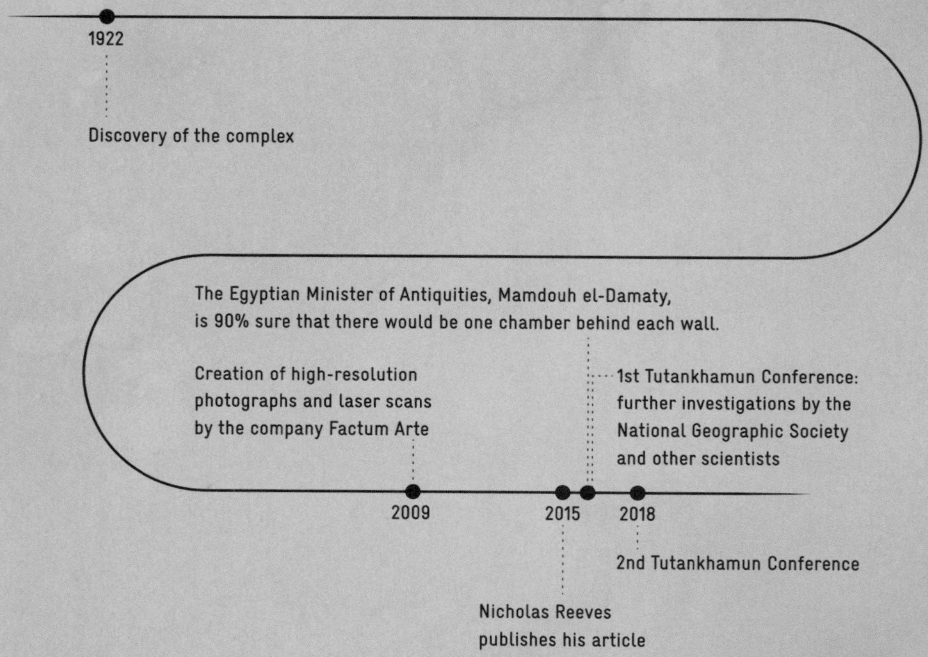
1922
Discovery of the complex
The Egyptian Minister of Antiquities, Mamdouh el-Damaty, is 90% sure that there would be one chamber behind each wall.
Creation of high-resolution photographs and laser scans by the company Factum Arte
1st Tutankhamun Conference: further investigations by the National Geographic Society and other scientists
2009
2015
2018
2nd Tutankhamun Conference
Nicholas Reeves publishes his article

The Valley of the Kings
NILE
KARNAK
LUXOR
Egypt

The Valley of the Kings is on the west bank of the Nile where primarily the tombs of the emperors of Egypt's New Kingdom are located. Akhenaten is believed to have been buried in Amarna first and later reburied here. However, the last burial chamber of Nefertiti (which means »the beautiful one has come«) is one of Egyptology's biggest mysteries.

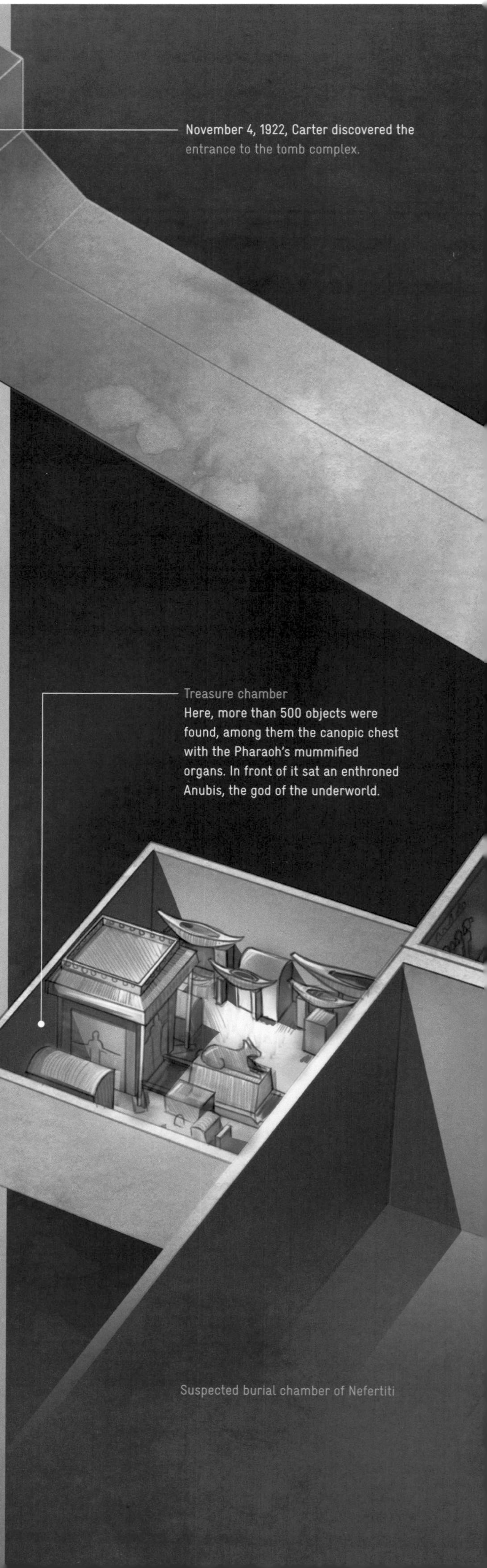
November 4, 1922, Carter discovered the entrance to the tomb complex.
Treasure chamber
Here, more than 500 objects were found, among them the canopic chest with the Pharaoh's mummified organs. In front of it sat an enthroned Anubis, the god of the underworld.
Suspected burial chamber of Nefertiti

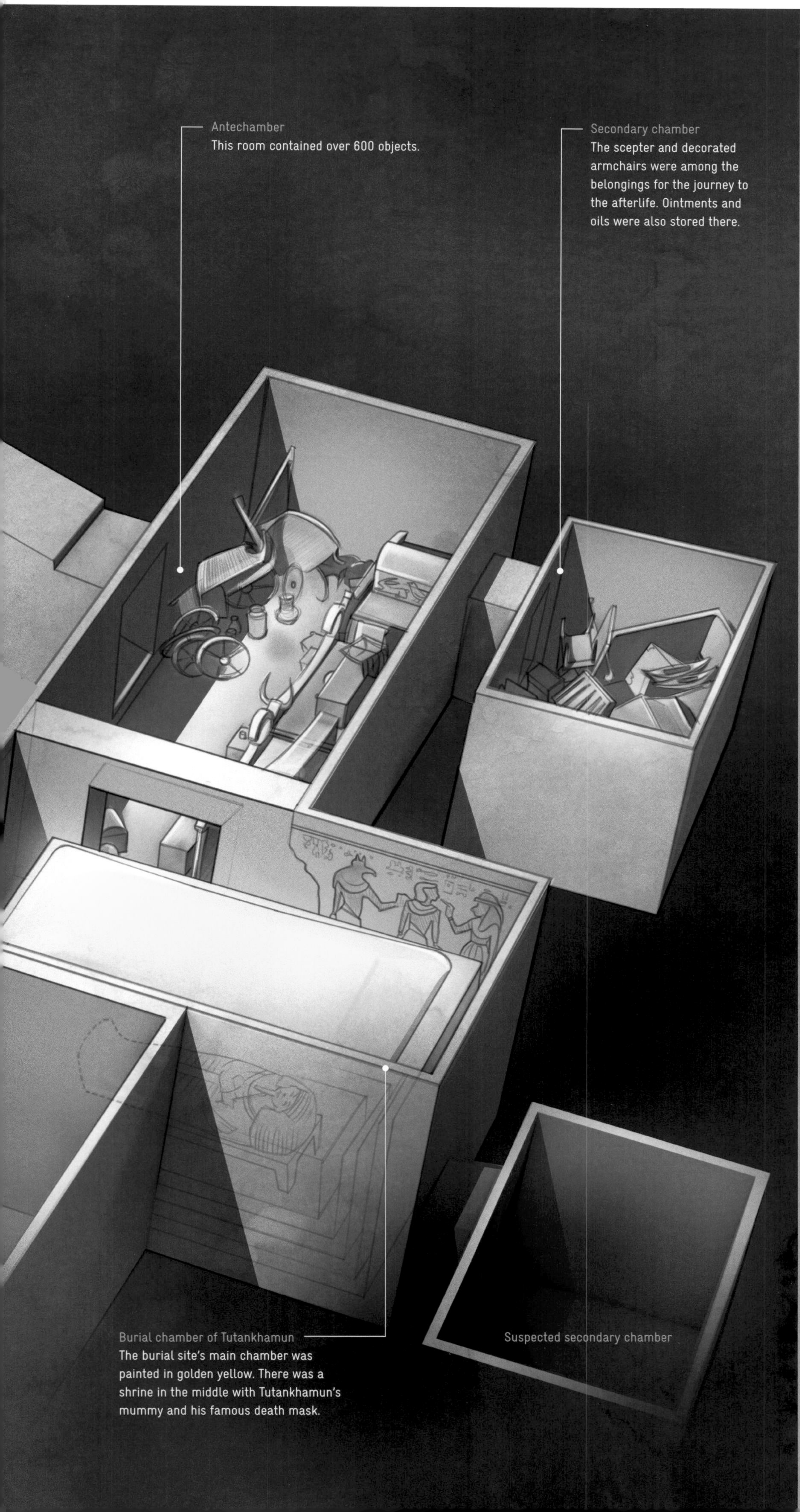

Antechamber
This room contained over 600 objects.
Secondary chamber
The scepter and decorated armchairs were among the belongings for the journey to the afterlife. Ointments and oils were also stored there.
Burial chamber of Tutankhamun
The burial site's main chamber was painted in golden yellow. There was a shrine in the middle with Tutankhamun's mummy and his famous death mask.
Suspected secondary chamber

THE THEORY OF THE TWO TOMBS IN THE KV62 COMPLEX

construction of the burial chamber

rooms discovered during excavation in 1923

Queen Nefertiti
The burial chamber for the wife of the »Heretic Pharaoh« Akhenaten was carved into the rocks.

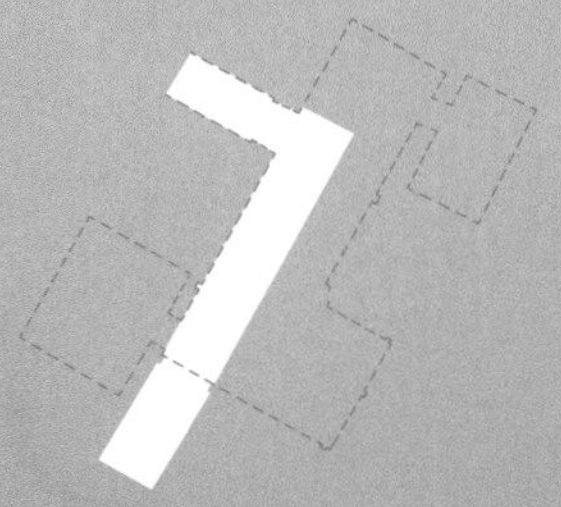

Nefertiti as co-regent
Akhenaten made Nefertiti his co-regent shortly before he died. The burial site was enlarged in honor of her.

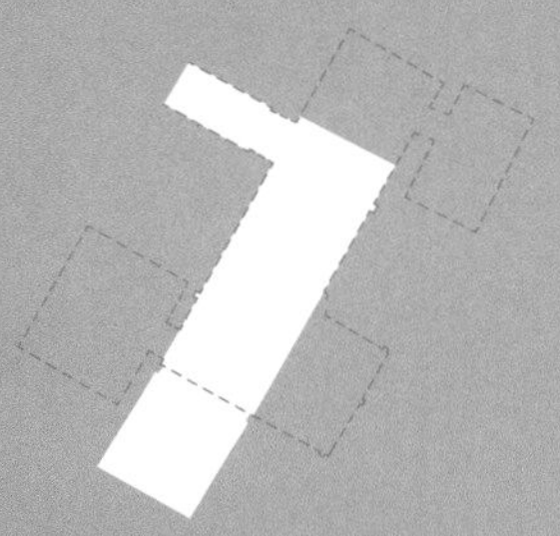

Nefertiti as Pharaoh
After the Pharaoh's death, Nefertiti reigned over Egypt on her own. Another secondary chamber was built behind the western wall. After her death, she was buried behind the northern wall.

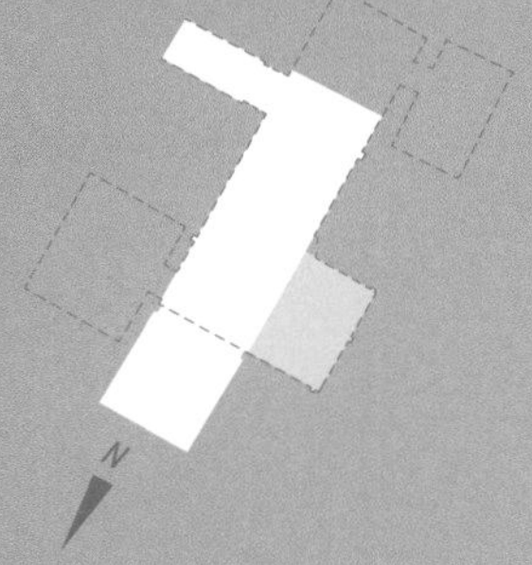

Tutankhamun's tomb
The tomb was expanded by three rooms after Tutankhamun's death. The boy king was buried in the antechamber to Nefertiti's burial chamber.

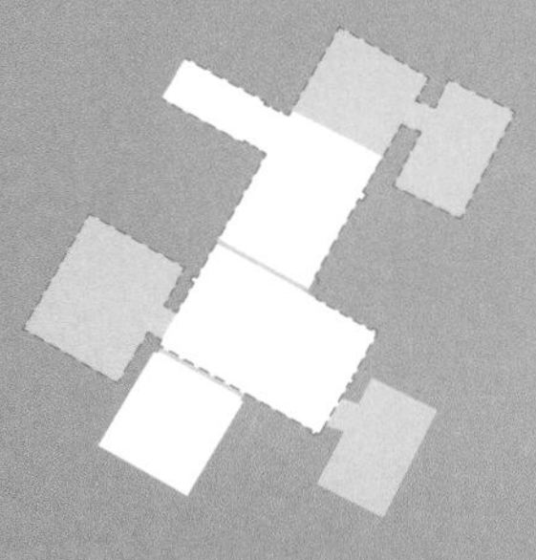

THE WORLD UPSIDE DOWN

Our globe with its view on Europe and Northern Africa shows the political situation around 1914. Back then, colonialism ruled the world. About 100 years later, the situation has hardly changed due to the tribes and peoples still living in their former areas. Moreover, the British, French and Italians are still very important trade partners of Egypt, Libya, Tunisia and Algeria.

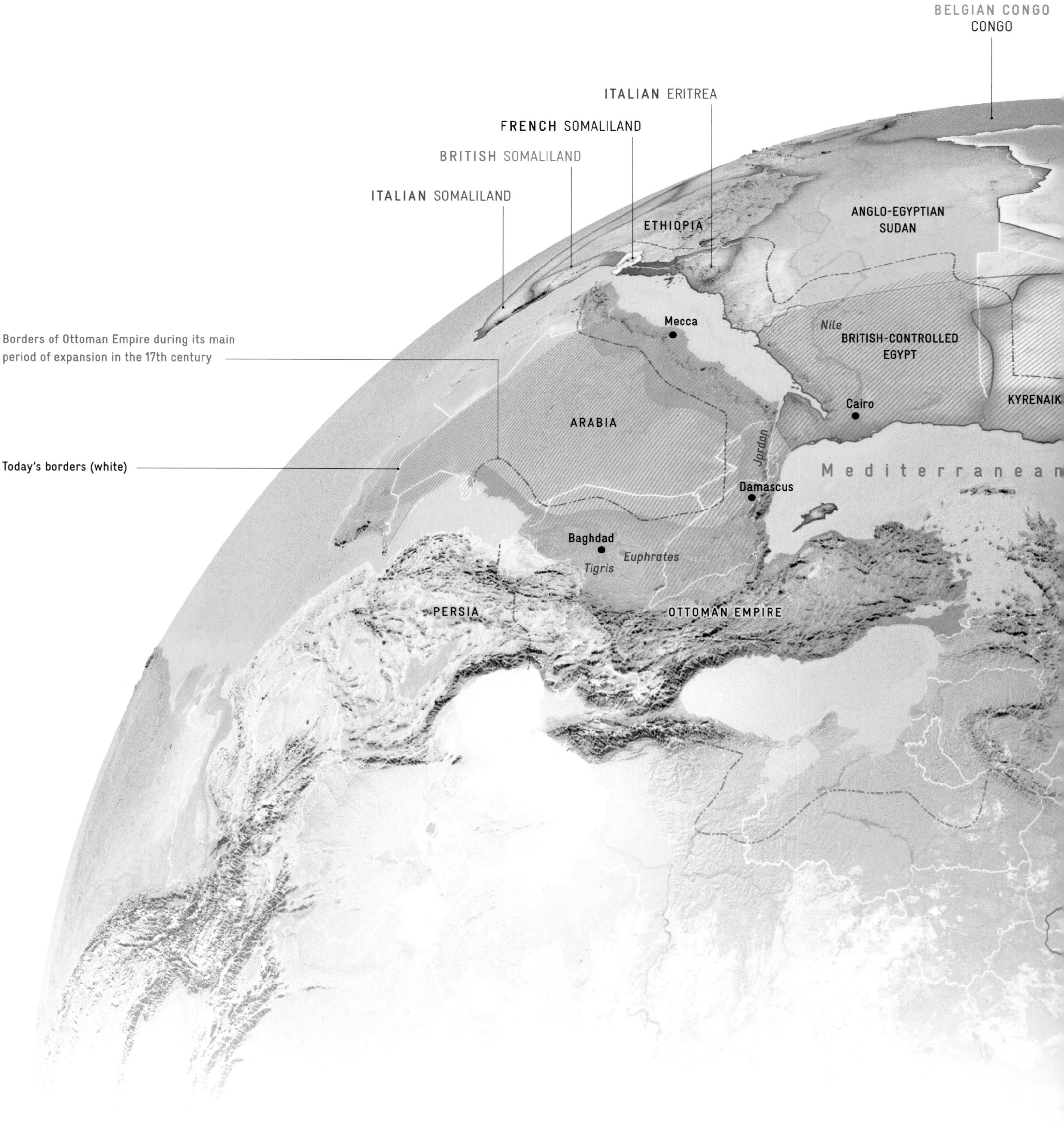

BELGIAN CONGO
CONGO
ITALIAN ERITREA
FRENCH SOMALILAND
BRITISH SOMALILAND
ITALIAN SOMALILAND
ETHIOPIA
ANGLO-EGYPTIAN SUDAN
Mecca
Nile
BRITISH-CONTROLLED EGYPT
Borders of Ottoman Empire during its main period of expansion in the 17th century
Cairo
KYRENAIK
ARABIA
Jordan
Today's borders (white)
Mediterranean
Damascus
Baghdad
Euphrates
Tigris
PERSIA
OTTOMAN EMPIRE

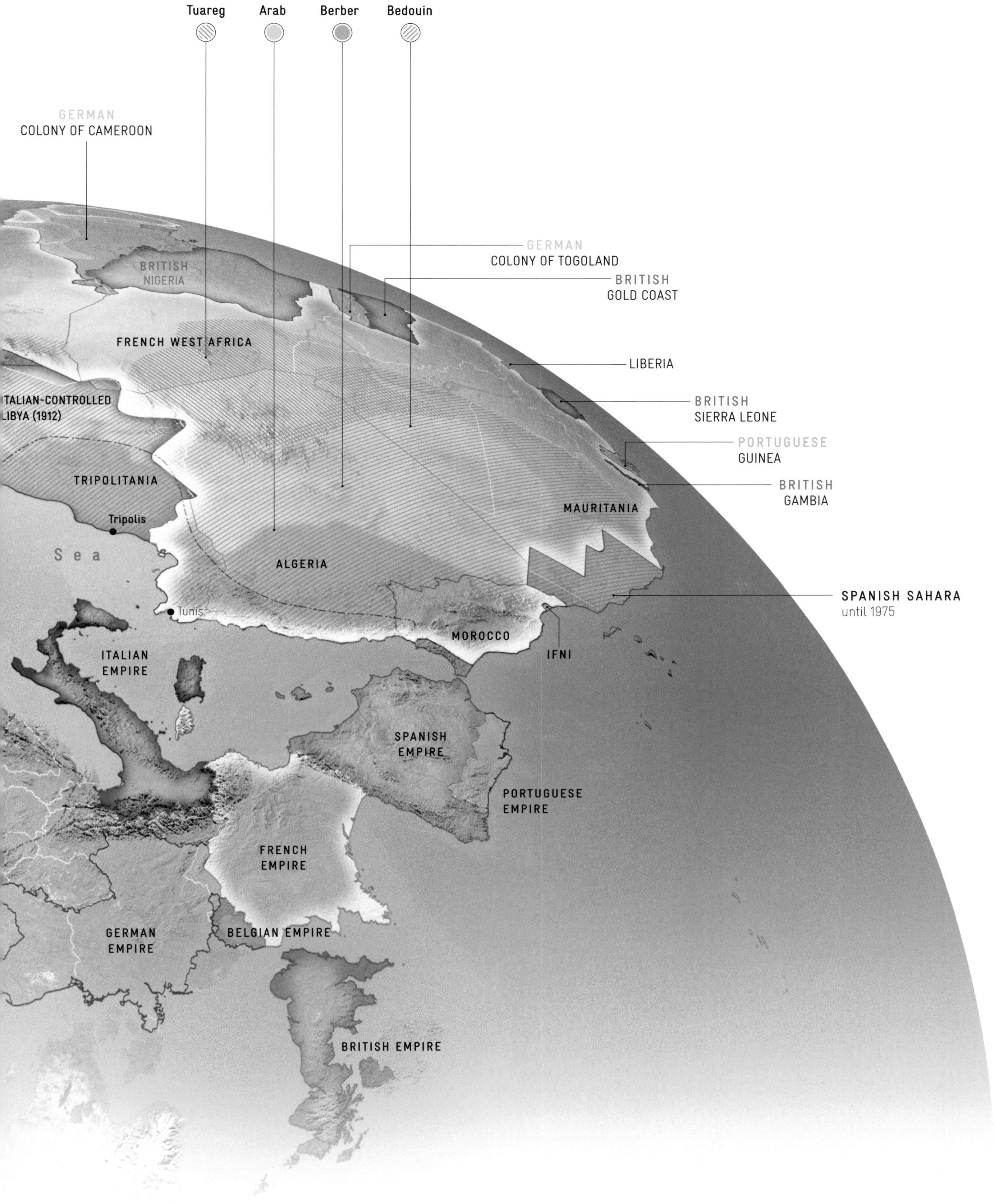

Tuareg
Arab
Berber
Bedouin
GERMAN
COLONY OF CAMEROON
BRITISH
NIGERIA
GERMAN
COLONY OF TOGOLAND
BRITISH
GOLD COAST
FRENCH WEST AFRICA
LIBERIA
TALIAN-CONTROLLED
IBYA (1912)
BRITISH
SIERRA LEONE
PORTUGUESE
GUINEA
TRIPOLITANIA
BRITISH
GAMBIA
MAURITANIA
Tripolis
Sea
ALGERIA
SPANISH SAHARA
until 1975
Tunis
MOROCCO
IFNI
ITALIAN
EMPIRE
SPANISH
EMPIRE
PORTUGUESE
EMPIRE
FRENCH
EMPIRE
GERMAN
EMPIRE
BELGIAN EMPIRE
BRITISH EMPIRE

THE FATE OF THE »TITANIC«

The glory of the »Titanic« echoes to this day. From the plans drawn in 1907 to the keel being laid in Belfast in 1909 and the launch in 1911, she was the world's largest passenger ship until her fateful maiden voyage in 1912. »God himself couldn't sink this ship«, a crew member told an embarking passenger. Perhaps not God, but an iceberg did, taking around 1,500 souls with her. The »Titanic« was a symbol of her era, the pre-eminence of power over nature. And what a beautiful ship she was.

TITANIC

THE »TITANIC« SINKS

April 15, 1912 • 41° 43.5' N, 49° 56.8' W • 2:20 a.m.

Shortly before the sinking, smoke was seen coming out of the rear funnel, which was not a true fume outlet, but a ventilation shaft. The water pressure inside the ship forced smoke out from the engine rooms, away from the ship.

How the tragedy unfolded

More than a century ago, an iceberg, faulty engineering calculations and neglected safety issues led to an unprecedented catastrophe. Within two hours, the Atlantic Ocean swallowed a proud ship and, with it, humanity's faith in the greatness of technological progress. The first ship to respond to the SOS signal, the Carpathia, found only a few lifeboats and many bodies. Only approximately 720 of the ship's 2,222 passengers and crew survived.

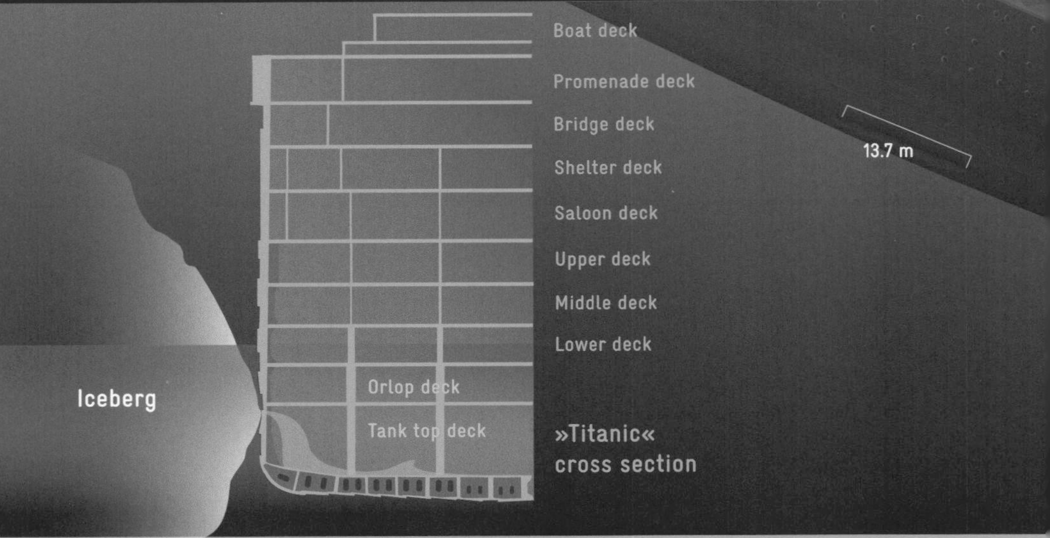
Boat deck
Promenade deck
Bridge deck
Shelter deck
Saloon deck
Upper deck
Middle deck
Lower deck
Orlop deck
Tank top deck
13.7 m
Iceberg
»Titanic« cross section

How did the »Titanic« sink?

11:40 p.m.
The starboard bow of the »Titanic«, under full steam, collides with an iceberg of about 1.5 million tonnes.

12:40 a.m.
Within an hour, up to 25,000 tonnes of water flood the hull. Five forward compartments are flooded and the tilt of the ship is about five degrees.

1:40 a.m.
During the second hour after the collision, only about 6,000 tonnes of water flood the ship. Slowly but surely, the non-waterproof parts of the ship, like portholes, ventilation shafts and hatchways sink below the water line. This hastens the sinking.

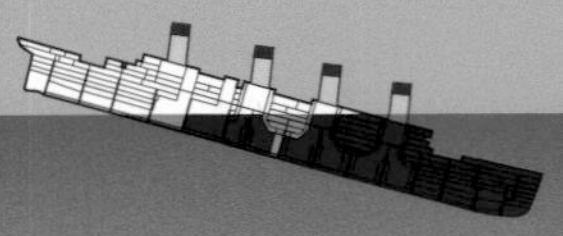

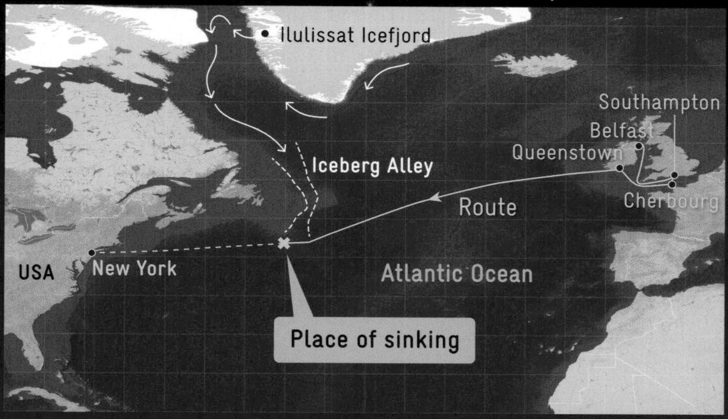

The »Titanic« sank about 340 nautical miles from the coast of Newfoundland, Canada. That year saw an unusual number of icebergs traveling far south.

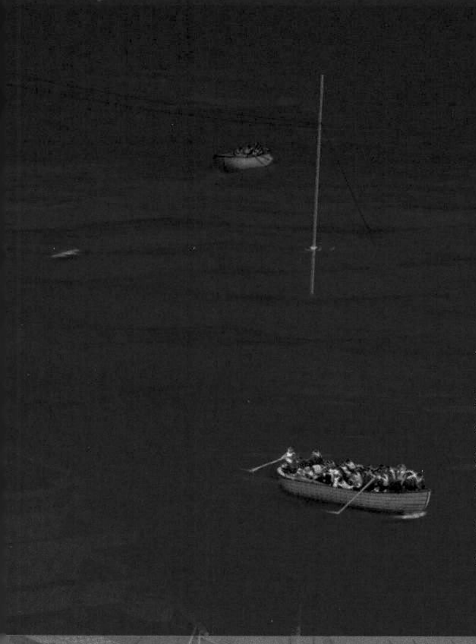

LIFEBOATS

The 20 lifeboats provided space for nearly 1,200 people, but there were about 2,200 passengers on board. The ship was actually allowed to carry 2,400 passengers.
But even so, only 60% of the given capacity was used. The crew was not well trained and the rules were not enforced for such eventualities.

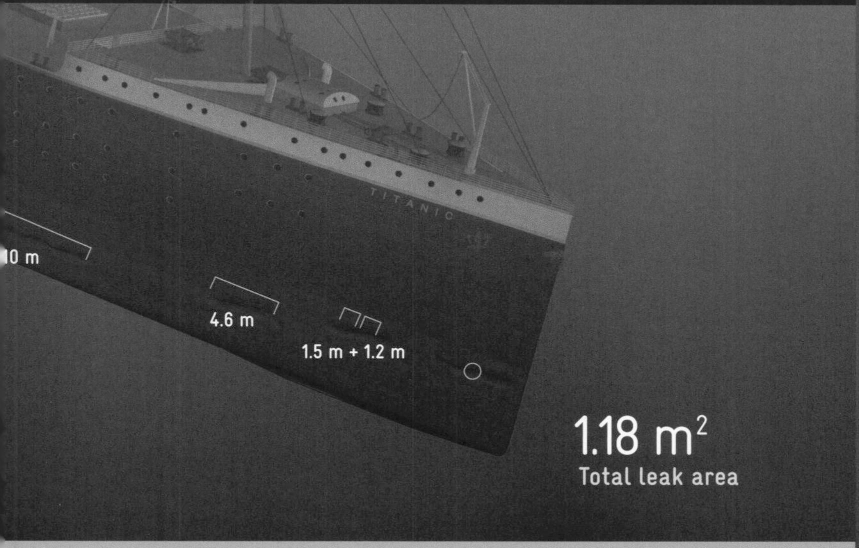

10 m
4.6 m
1.5 m + 1.2 m
1.18 m²
Total leak area

2:20 a.m.
The stern rises out of the water to an angle of between 15° and 20° and breaks apart due to the stress that the vessel was subject to. There are two ways this might have happened—we've illustrated both possibilities.

stern
≈ 600 m
bow

THE WRECK

The »Titanic« sank to a depth of 3,803 meters. For 73 years no light reached the wreck until it was located in 1985. The bow lay in relatively good condition about 600 meters from the heavily damaged stern, with much debris in between. It is estimated that about 5,500 artefacts have been recovered to date. By the way: A private dive cruise to the wreck is available for about €30,000.

»RMS TITANIC«

TECHNICAL DATA

Length	269.04 m
Width	28.19 m
Draft	10.54 m
Displacement	53,147 t
Speed	21 kn (39 km/h)
Horse power	51,000 HP
Coal	5,344 t
Approved passengers	2,400
Crew	897
First Class	750
Second Class	550
Third Class	1,100

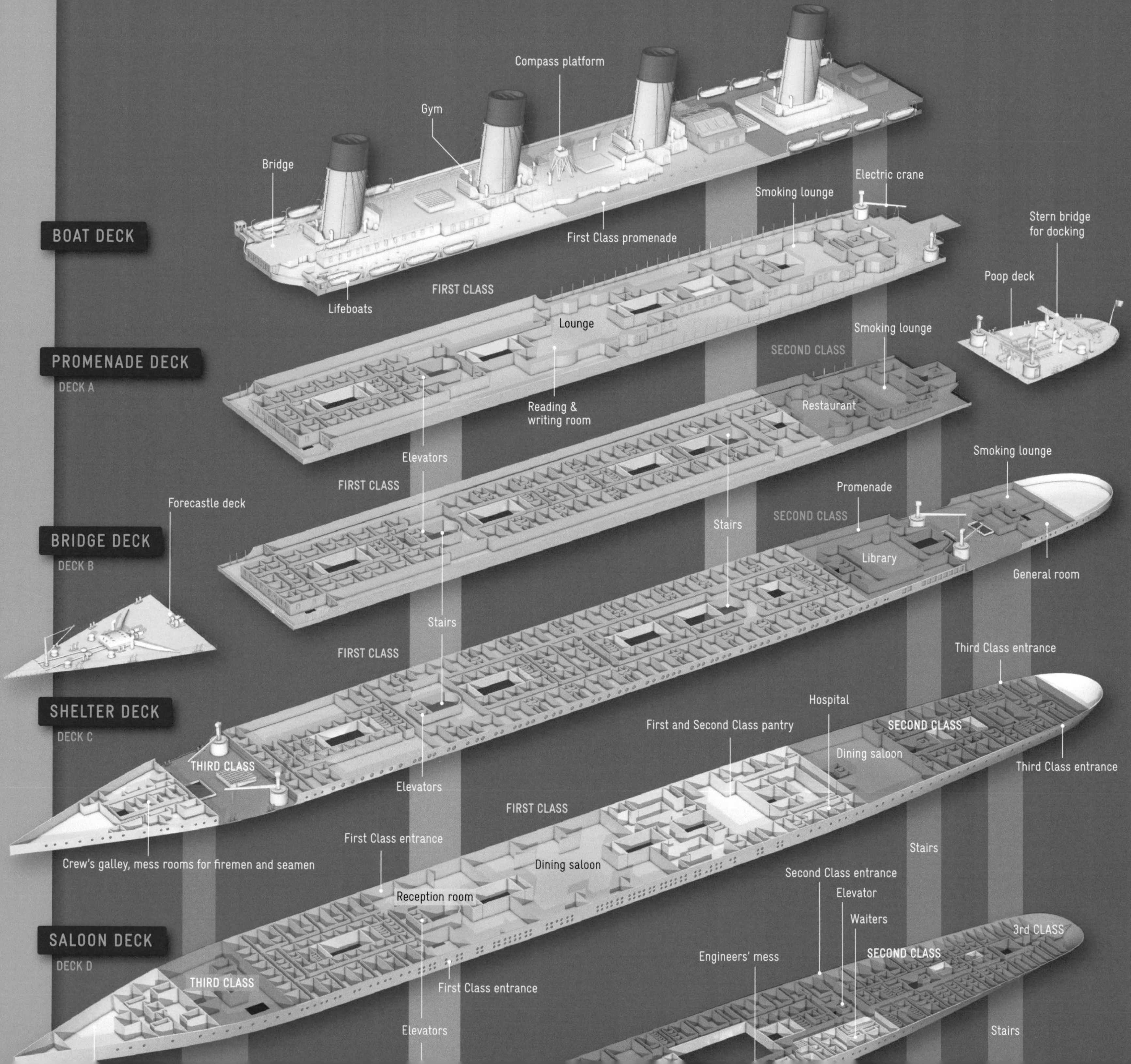

BOAT DECK
Bridge
Gym
Compass platform
Lifeboats
First Class promenade
Smoking lounge
Electric crane
FIRST CLASS
PROMENADE DECK
DECK A
Lounge
Reading & writing room
Elevators
SECOND CLASS
Smoking lounge
Restaurant
Stern bridge for docking
Poop deck
BRIDGE DECK
DECK B
Forecastle deck
FIRST CLASS
Stairs
SECOND CLASS
Promenade
Library
Smoking lounge
General room
SHELTER DECK
DECK C
THIRD CLASS
FIRST CLASS
Stairs
Elevators
Crew's galley, mess rooms for firemen and seamen
First and Second Class pantry
Hospital
SECOND CLASS
Dining saloon
Third Class entrance
Third Class entrance
SALOON DECK
DECK D
THIRD CLASS
First Class entrance
Reception room
Dining saloon
FIRST CLASS
First Class entrance
Elevators
Engineers' mess
Second Class entrance
Elevator
Waiters
SECOND CLASS
3rd CLASS
Stairs
Stairs

THREE-CLASS SOCIETY

Dividing passengers into three classes was common practice at the time. The »Titanic« provided accommodation for 1,100 3rd class and 550 2nd class passengers. 1st class had access to the largest areas of the ship—including the famous stairway. The 750 members of the »Titanic's« upper crust also had access to salons, cafés, a Turkish bath, dining room and restaurant facilities.
Even third class had relatively comfortable quarters compared to other ships.
Passengers were provided with six, four or two bed cabins instead of the more common dormitories.

CONSTRUCTION

The keel of the »Titanic« was laid in 1909 in Belfast as the second of the Olympic-class vessels by shipmakers Harland & Wolff. On May 31, 1911, around 10,000 people gathered to see the »Titanic« travel the slipway into the water—though there was no ceremony around the launch in accordance with White Star Line policy. To gain »Royal Mail Ship« status, the »Titanic« had a post office on board. It cost £1.1 million (approx. €120 million today).

THE ENGINE

The »Titanic« was designed for a cruising speed of 21 knots (approx. 39 km/h). The engines provided more than 50,000 horse power and burned through 630 tonnes of coal a day. There were 159 furnaces that could heat 29 boilers, which provided steam to drive the three propeller shafts. There were also four generators on board providing electrical power to the ship.

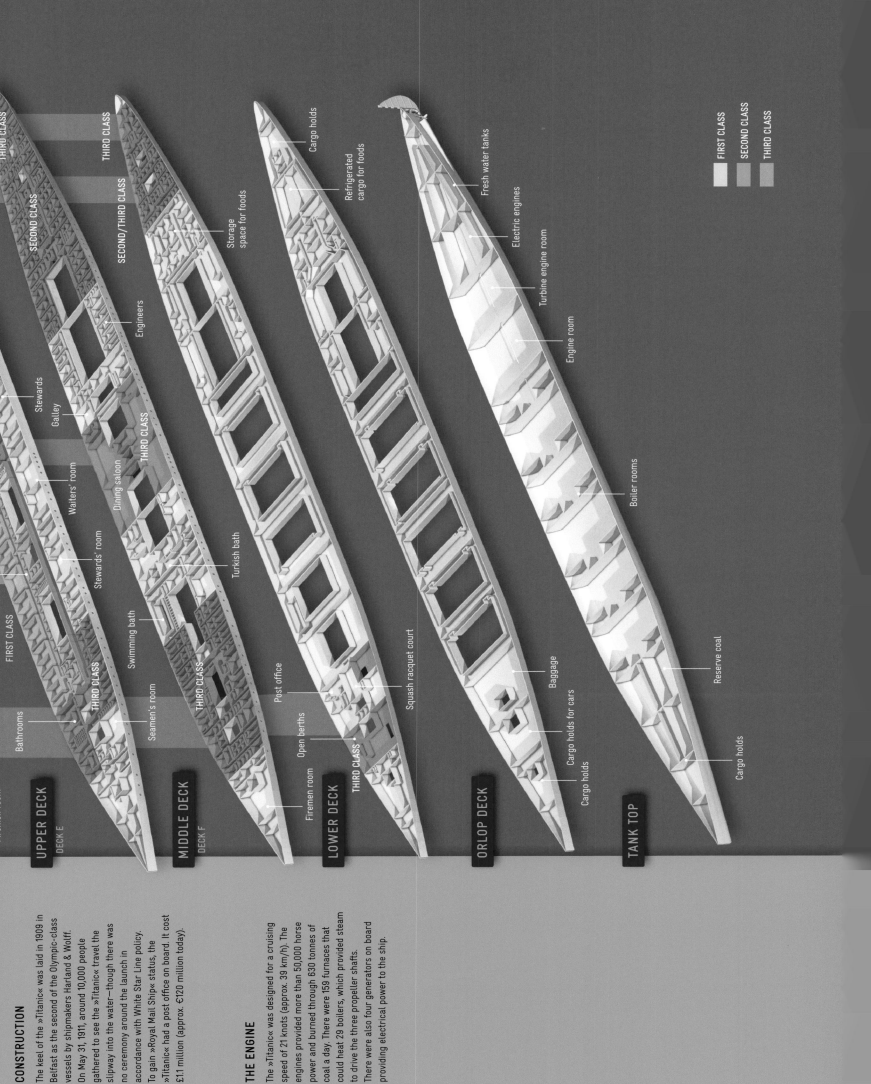

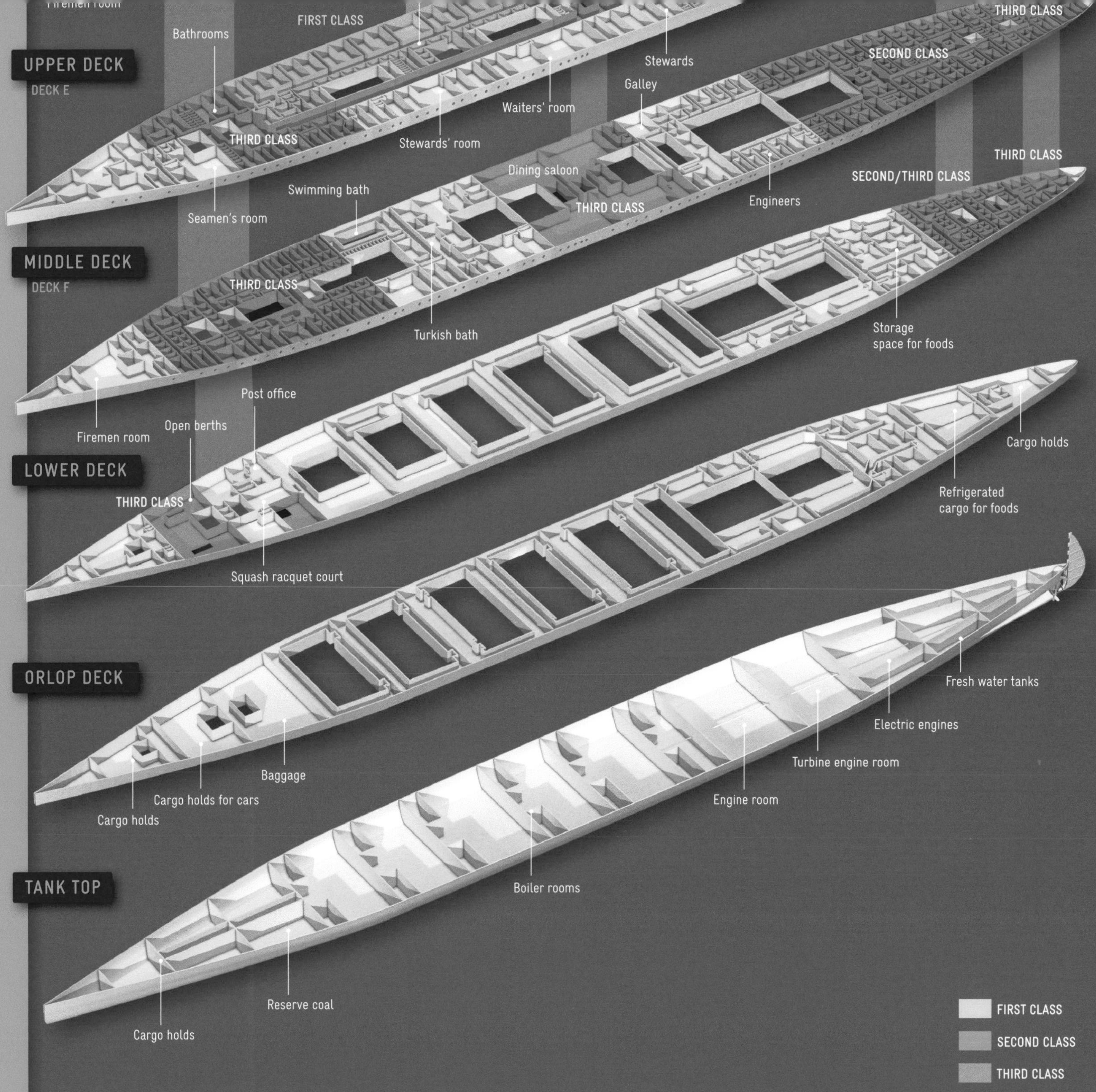

Firemen room
FIRST CLASS
THIRD CLASS
Bathrooms
UPPER DECK
DECK E
Stewards
SECOND CLASS
Galley
Waiters' room
THIRD CLASS
Stewards' room
Dining saloon
THIRD CLASS
SECOND/THIRD CLASS
Swimming bath
THIRD CLASS
Engineers
Seamen's room
MIDDLE DECK
DECK F
THIRD CLASS
Turkish bath
Storage space for foods
Post office
Firemen room
Open berths
LOWER DECK
THIRD CLASS
Cargo holds
Refrigerated cargo for foods
Squash racquet court
ORLOP DECK
Fresh water tanks
Electric engines
Turbine engine room
Baggage
Engine room
Cargo holds for cars
Cargo holds
TANK TOP
Boiler rooms
Reserve coal
Cargo holds
FIRST CLASS
SECOND CLASS
THIRD CLASS

WOMEN AND CHILDREN FIRST

Passengers from 28 nations were on board the »Titanic«, nearly half of them British and American. Women and children had the best chance to survive, particularly if they were travelling in a higher class. Men of all ages, and in all classes, had little chance to escape death in the cold North Atlantic.

Victims and survivors by age

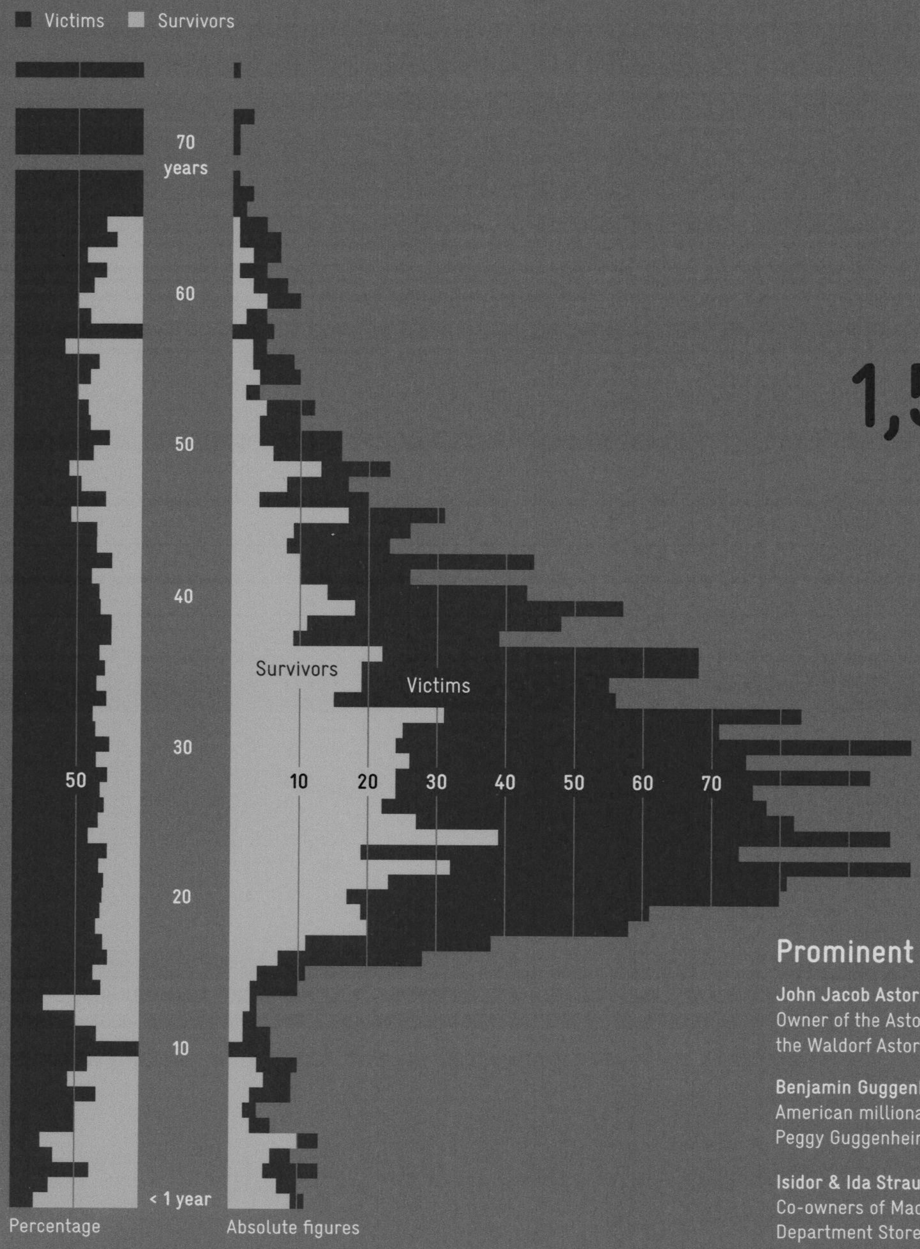

Victims
Survivors
70 years
60
50
40
30
20
10
< 1 year
50
Survivors
Victims
10
20
30
40
50
60
70
Percentage
Absolute figures

Victims and survivors by sex and class

1,514
Victims
710
Survivors
First Class 325
Second Class 285
Passengers Third Class 706
Crew 908
123 (38 %)
167 (59 %)
528 (75 %)
696 (77 %)
202 (62 %)
118 (41 %)
178 (25 %)
212 (23 %)

Prominent victims

John Jacob Astor IV.
Owner of the Astoria Hotel (later the Waldorf Astoria) in New York

Benjamin Guggenheim
American millionaire and Peggy Guggenheim's father

Isidor & Ida Straus
Co-owners of Macy's Department Store

Charles Hays
President of Canadian Railroad

John Borland Thayer
US cricket player

William Thomas Stead
English journalist

Thomas Andrews
Chief constructor of the Titanic

Archibald Butt
US military aide

Jacques Futrelle
US writer

The last survivors

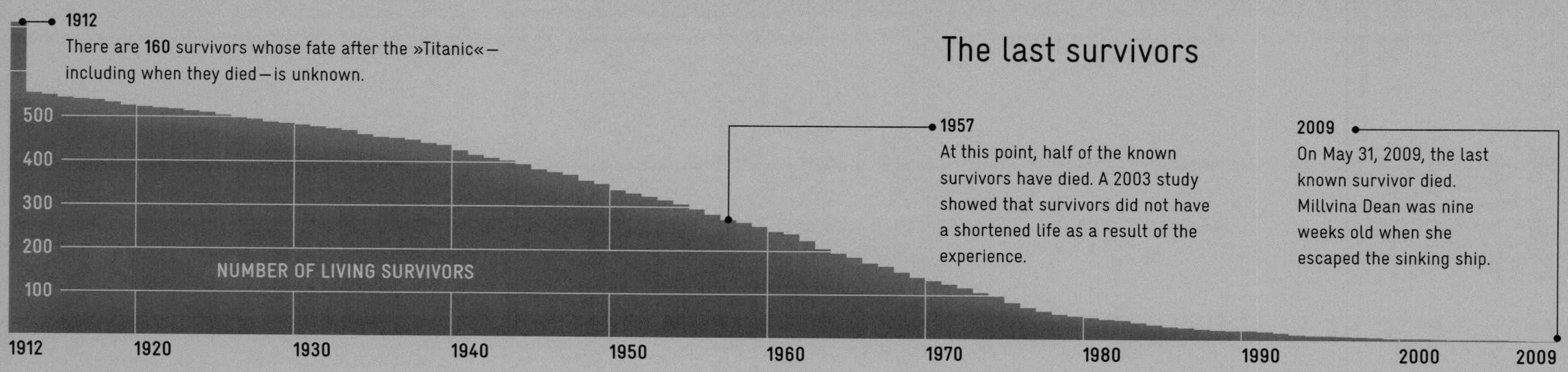

1912
There are 160 survivors whose fate after the »Titanic«—including when they died—is unknown.
1957
At this point, half of the known survivors have died. A 2003 study showed that survivors did not have a shortened life as a result of the experience.
2009
On May 31, 2009, the last known survivor died. Millvina Dean was nine weeks old when she escaped the sinking ship.
NUMBER OF LIVING SURVIVORS
500
400
300
200
100
1912
1920
1930
1940
1950
1960
1970
1980
1990
2000
2009

Steam- and motorships: Balance sheet of victims from an epoch

Significant catastrophes involving steam- or motor-driven ships per decade. Each alternating color band shows single events and the area size shows the number of victims. Figures are rounded and designed to provide an overview of each time period.

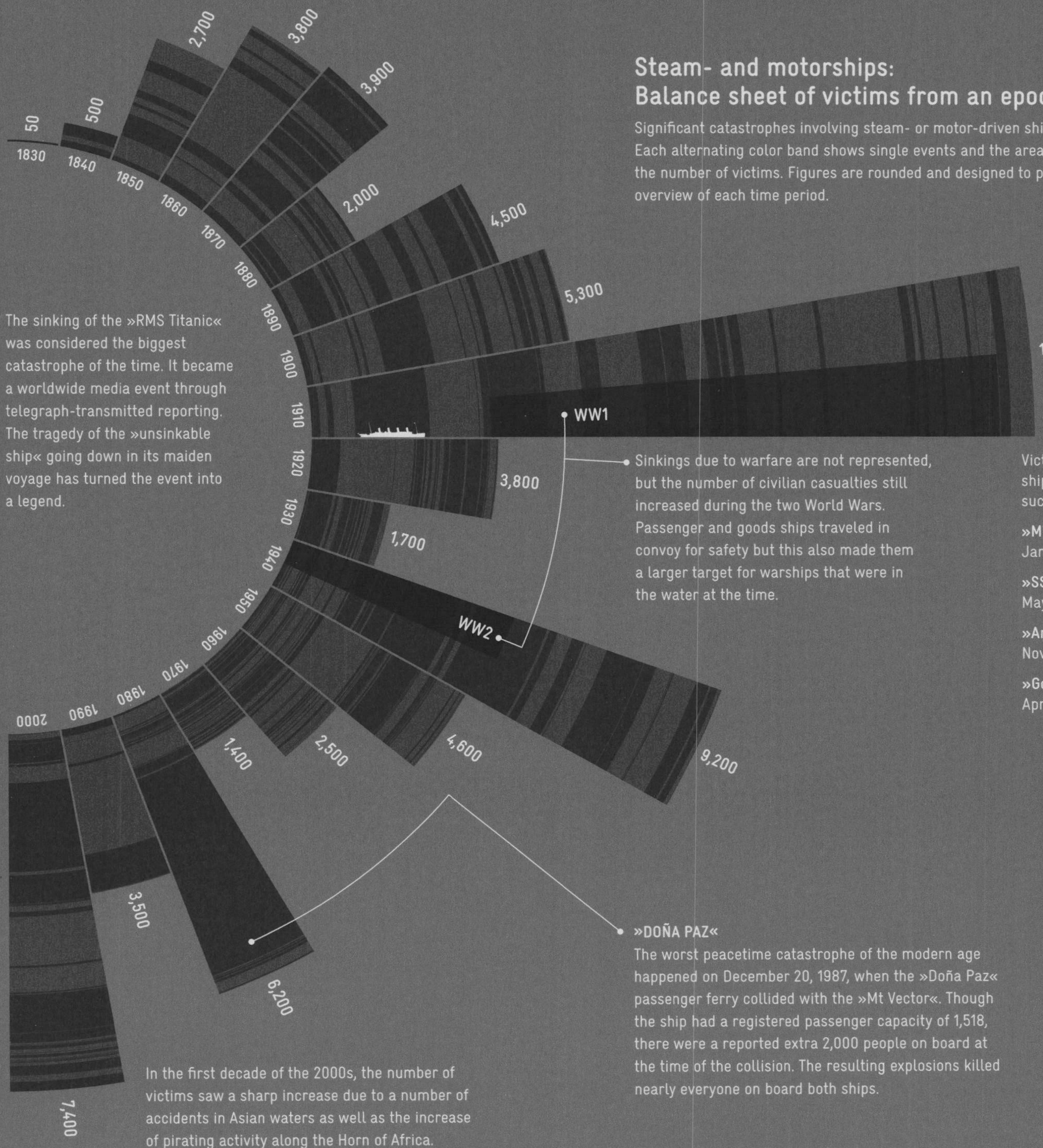

The sinking of the »RMS Titanic« was considered the biggest catastrophe of the time. It became a worldwide media event through telegraph-transmitted reporting. The tragedy of the »unsinkable ship« going down in its maiden voyage has turned the event into a legend.

Sinkings due to warfare are not represented, but the number of civilian casualties still increased during the two World Wars. Passenger and goods ships traveled in convoy for safety but this also made them a larger target for warships that were in the water at the time.

Victims of acts of war against passenger ships are not represented in this graphic, such as:

»MV Wilhelm Gustloff«
January 30, 1945: up to 9,300 victims

»SS Cap Arcona« and »SS Thielbeck«
May 3, 1945: 7,000 to 8,000 victims

»Armenia«
November 7, 1941: up to 7,000 victims

»Goya«
April 16, 1945: up to 7,000 victims

»DOÑA PAZ«
The worst peacetime catastrophe of the modern age happened on December 20, 1987, when the »Doña Paz« passenger ferry collided with the »Mt Vector«. Though the ship had a registered passenger capacity of 1,518, there were a reported extra 2,000 people on board at the time of the collision. The resulting explosions killed nearly everyone on board both ships.

In the first decade of the 2000s, the number of victims saw a sharp increase due to a number of accidents in Asian waters as well as the increase of pirating activity along the Horn of Africa.

Changing the safety protocols

The »International Convention for the Safety of Life at Sea« was formed following the »RMS Titanic« tragedy. This maritime treaty became part of the UN's »International Maritime Organization« (logo, left). This set international standards for lifeboat numbers, safety regulations related to ship design and 24-hour radio service staffing.

After the iceberg sunk the »RMS Titanic«, Canada and the United States formed the »International Ice Patrol« (IIP). Coast guard crews conduct flyovers of their area of responsibility to provide iceberg reports. There are now 17 member countries.

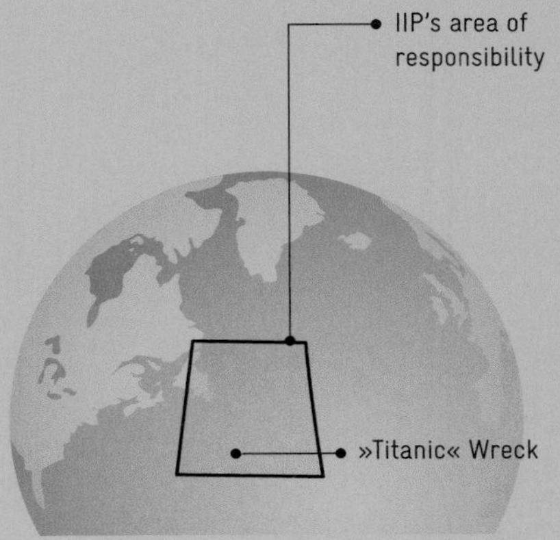
IIP's area of responsibility
»Titanic« Wreck

BY SEA OR BY AIR

When the »RMS Titanic« sank, ships were the only way to traverse the world's oceans. Aviation was in its infancy. The LZ 127 »Graf Zeppelin« offered the first commercial trans-Atlantic aircraft service in 1928. It carried 24 passengers and was crewed by a further 36 people.

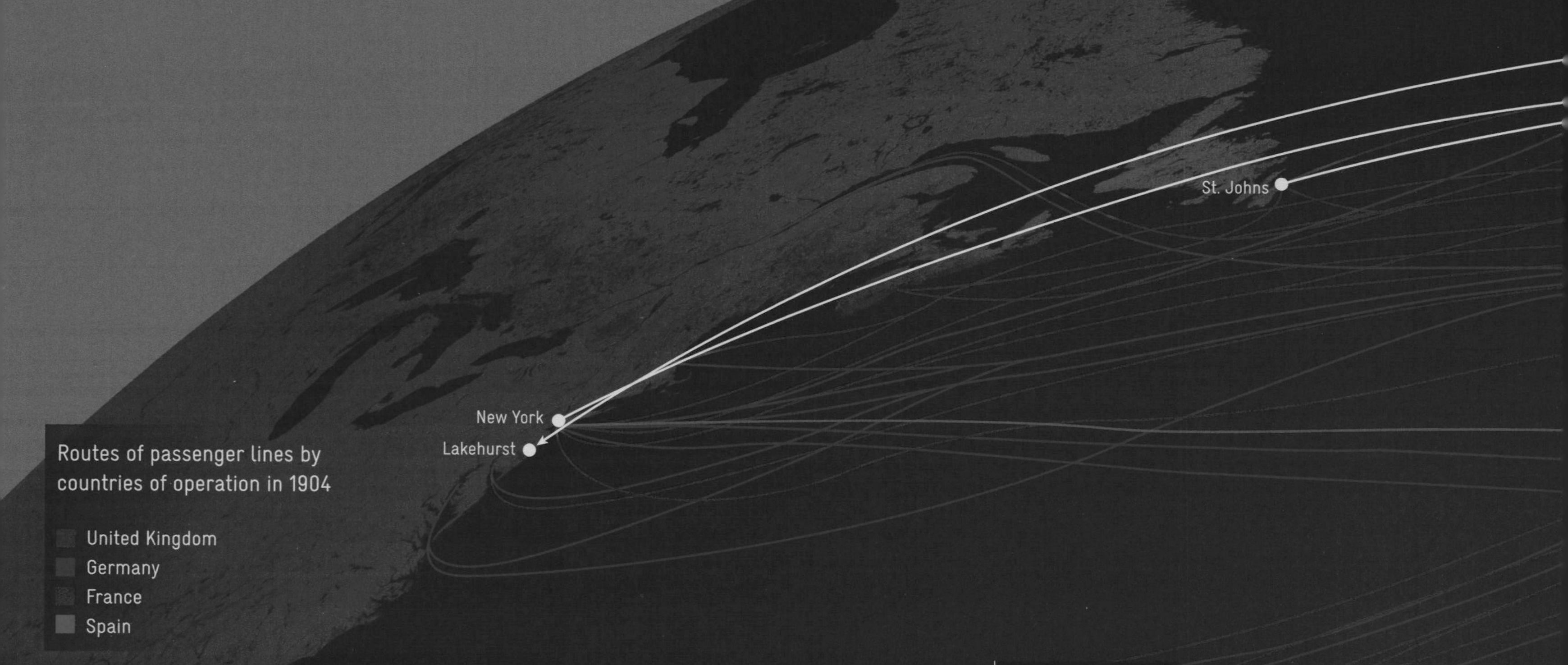
St. Johns
New York
Lakehurst
Routes of passenger lines by countries of operation in 1904
United Kingdom
Germany
France
Spain

Moving People

Crises in Europe led to waves of western emigration. Getting people to the US was big business for passenger carriers, like Hapag, whose ship numbers grew with the demand.

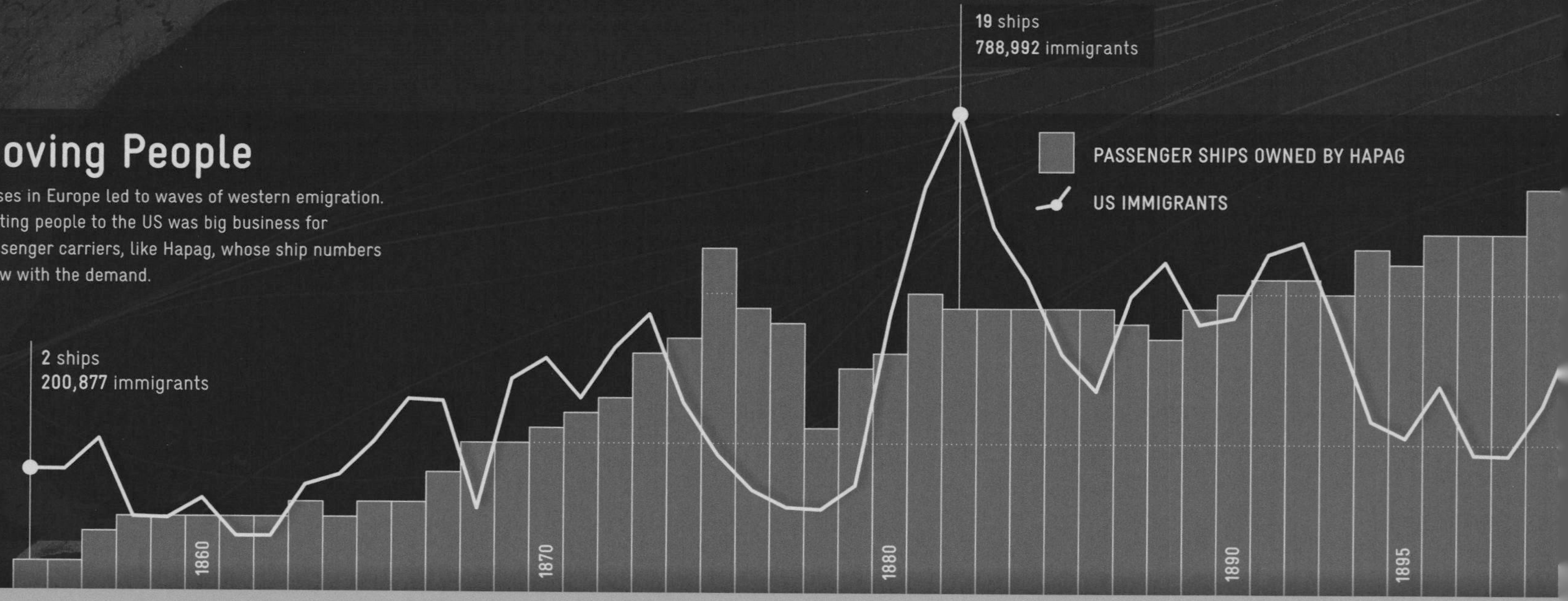
19 ships
788,992 immigrants
PASSENGER SHIPS OWNED BY HAPAG
US IMMIGRANTS
2 ships
200,877 immigrants
1860
1870
1880
1890
1895

Making the trans-Atlantic crossing

Ship	»Pauline« 1838	»Britannia« 1840	»RMS Titanic« 1912	»Allure of the Seas« 2010
Type	Brig	Paddle steamer	Ocean Liner	Cruise ship
Length	31.5 m	65 m	269 m	360 m
max. Passengers	about 83	115	2,435	6,296
Approx. duration of Atlantic crossing	36 days	14 days	5 days	5 days

»Pauline«
Typical vessel of the pre-steam era

»Britannia«
Steam engine with sails

»RMS Titanic« World's biggest passenger ship in 1912

Pioneers of the air

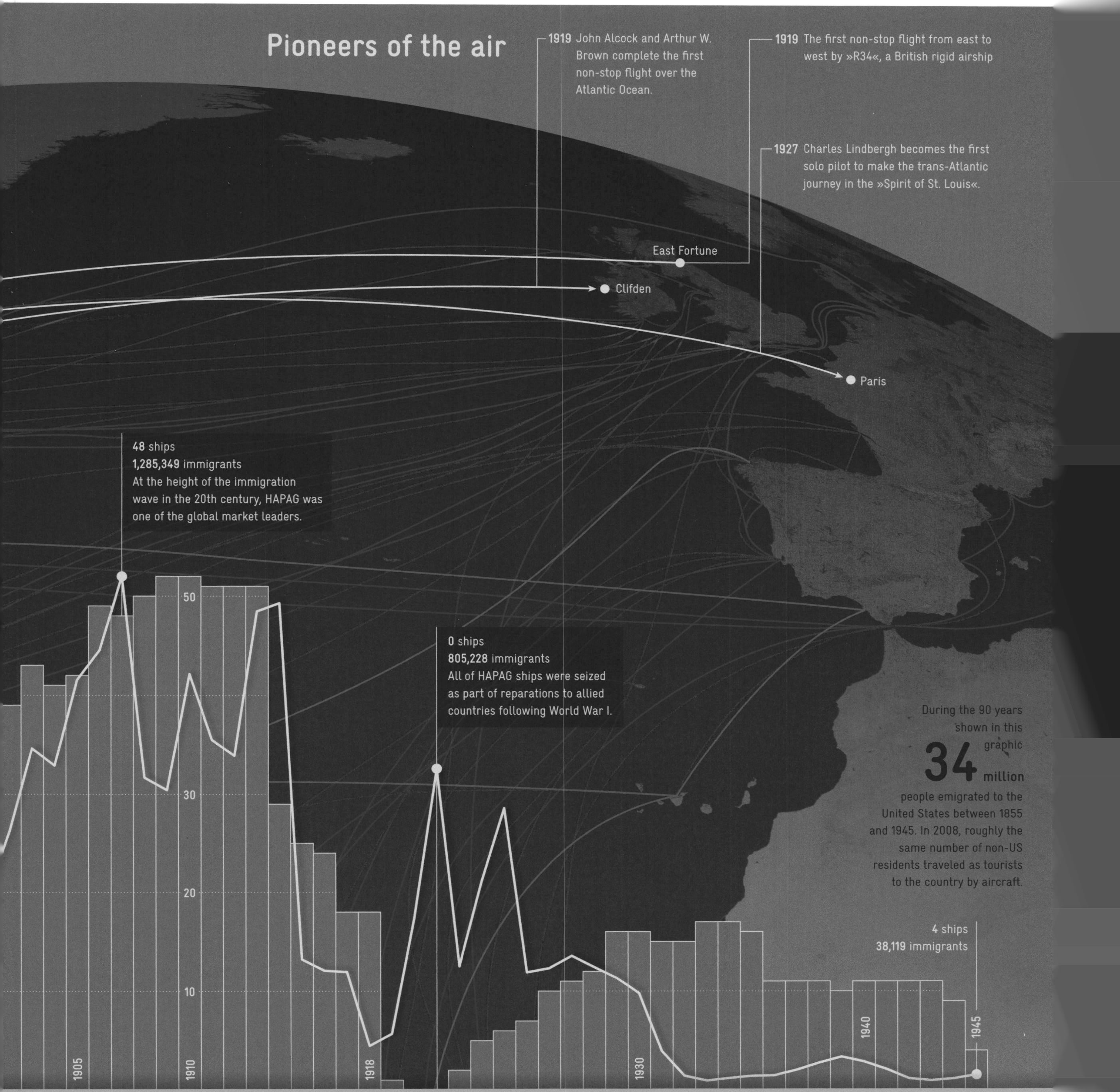
1919 John Alcock and Arthur W. Brown complete the first non-stop flight over the Atlantic Ocean.
1919 The first non-stop flight from east to west by »R34«, a British rigid airship
1927 Charles Lindbergh becomes the first solo pilot to make the trans-Atlantic journey in the »Spirit of St. Louis«.
East Fortune
Clifden
Paris
48 ships
1,285,349 immigrants
At the height of the immigration wave in the 20th century, HAPAG was one of the global market leaders.
0 ships
805,228 immigrants
All of HAPAG ships were seized as part of reparations to allied countries following World War I.
During the 90 years shown in this graphic
34 million
people emigrated to the United States between 1855 and 1945. In 2008, roughly the same number of non-US residents traveled as tourists to the country by aircraft.
4 ships
38,119 immigrants
50
30
20
10
1905
1910
1918
1930
1940
1945

LZ 127 »Graf Zeppelin« 1928	Airbus A380 2007
Rigid air ship	Jet airliner
236.6 m	72.3 m
20	853
4 days	8 hours

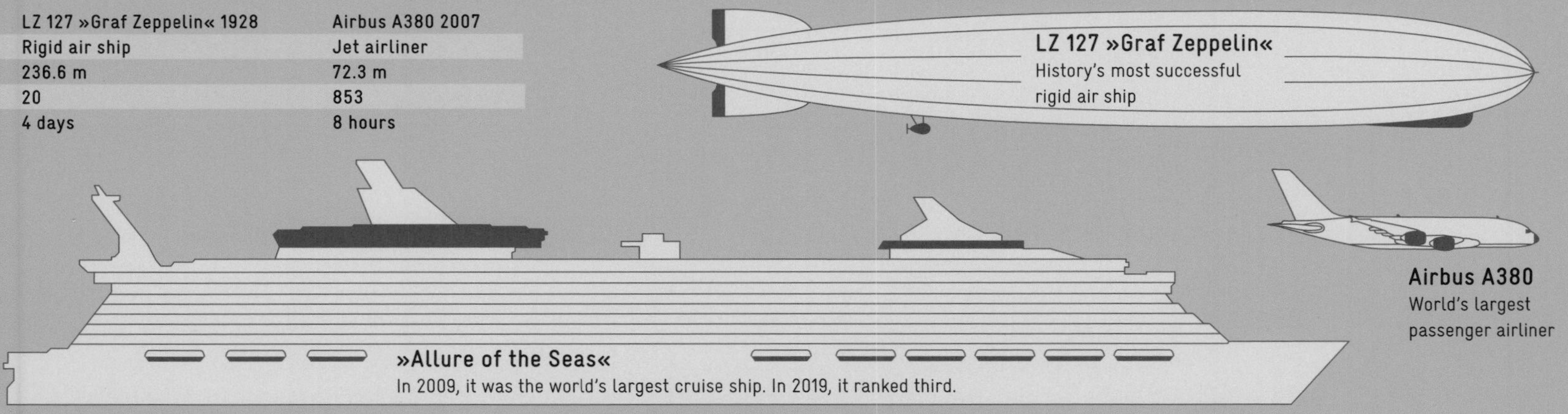
LZ 127 »Graf Zeppelin«
History's most successful rigid air ship
Airbus A380
World's largest passenger airliner
»Allure of the Seas«
In 2009, it was the world's largest cruise ship. In 2019, it ranked third.

THE GREAT WAR 1914 1918

The First World War broke out in 1914. After warfare on a scale never seen before, the political and social structures of old Europe saw their downfall by the end of the war in late 1918. The war led to the rise of two global superpowers: the United States of America and the Soviet Union. At the same time, the seed for further conflicts was planted which eventually led to the Second World War. By mid-1918, 36 states from six continents had joined the war and 17 took part directly in combat. The main theater of war was Europe, but other areas were also involved in military action, such as the Middle East, German colonies in Africa, China and the Pacific.

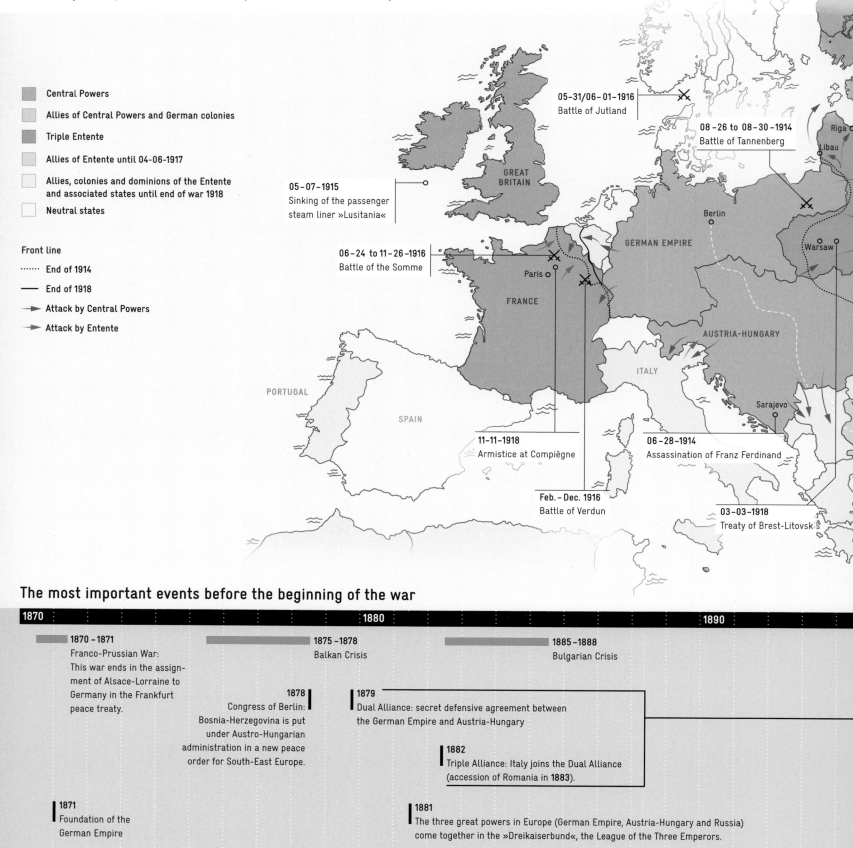

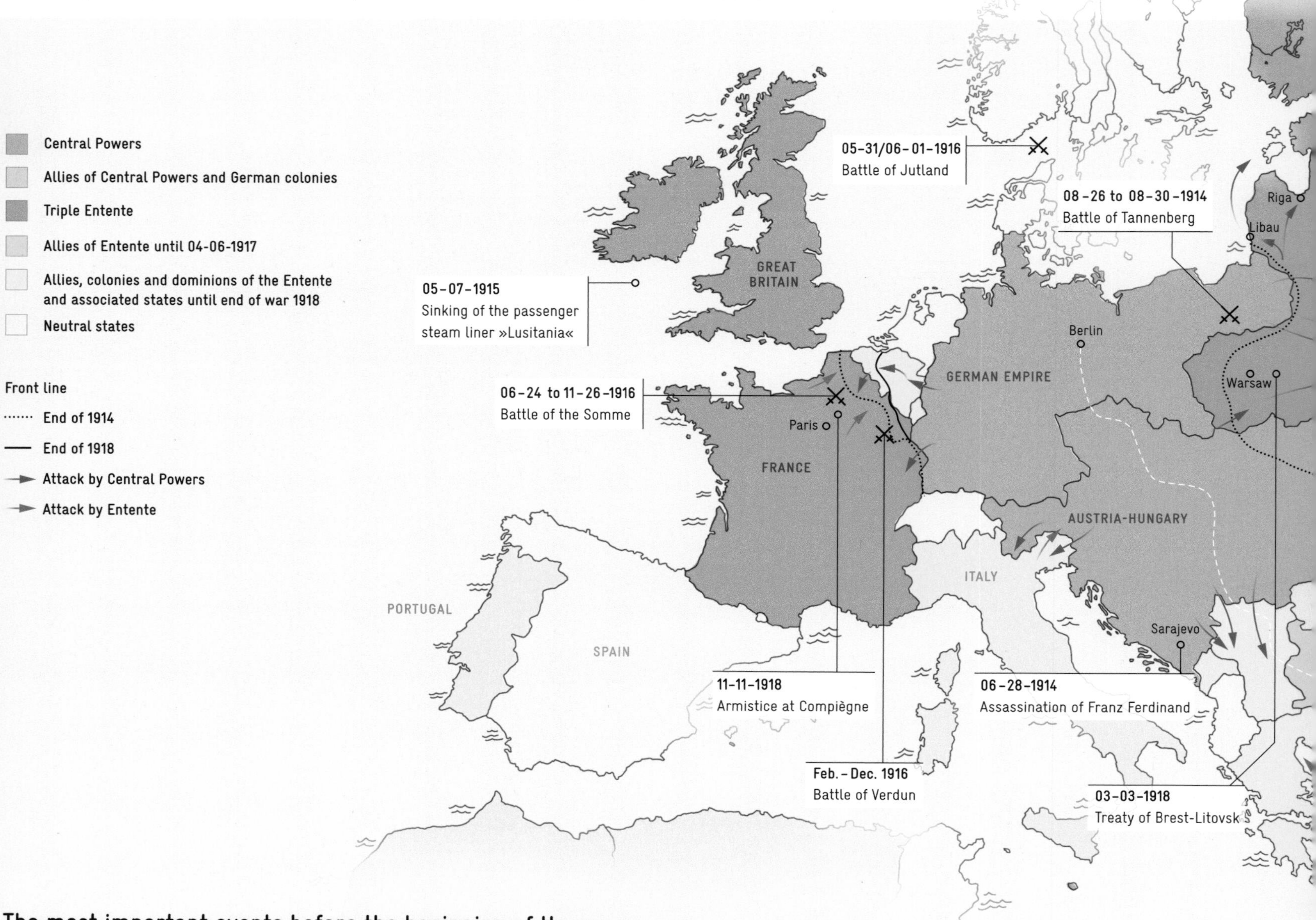
Central Powers
Allies of Central Powers and German colonies
Triple Entente
Allies of Entente until 04-06-1917
Allies, colonies and dominions of the Entente and associated states until end of war 1918
Neutral states
Front line
End of 1914
End of 1918
Attack by Central Powers
Attack by Entente
05-31/06-01-1916
Battle of Jutland
08-26 to 08-30-1914
Battle of Tannenberg
Riga
Libau
05-07-1915
Sinking of the passenger steam liner »Lusitania«
GREAT BRITAIN
Berlin
GERMAN EMPIRE
Warsaw
06-24 to 11-26-1916
Battle of the Somme
Paris
FRANCE
AUSTRIA-HUNGARY
ITALY
PORTUGAL
SPAIN
Sarajevo
11-11-1918
Armistice at Compiègne
06-28-1914
Assassination of Franz Ferdinand
Feb.-Dec. 1916
Battle of Verdun
03-03-1918
Treaty of Brest-Litovsk

The most important events before the beginning of the war

1870 | 1880 | 1890

1870-1871
Franco-Prussian War: This war ends in the assignment of Alsace-Lorraine to Germany in the Frankfurt peace treaty.

1871
Foundation of the German Empire

1875-1878
Balkan Crisis

1878
Congress of Berlin: Bosnia-Herzegovina is put under Austro-Hungarian administration in a new peace order for South-East Europe.

1879
Dual Alliance: secret defensive agreement between the German Empire and Austria-Hungary

1881
The three great powers in Europe (German Empire, Austria-Hungary and Russia) come together in the »Dreikaiserbund«, the League of the Three Emperors.

1882
Triple Alliance: Italy joins the Dual Alliance (accession of Romania in **1883**).

1885-1888
Bulgarian Crisis

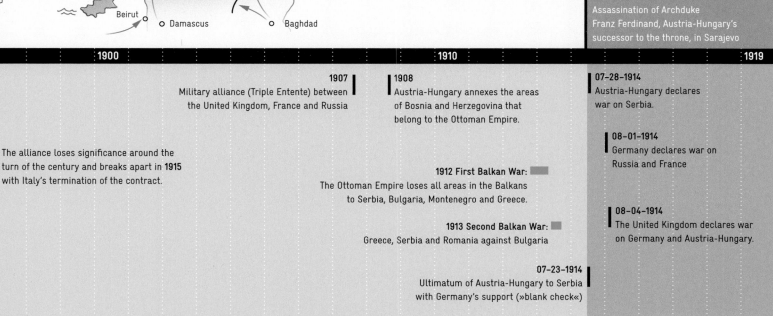

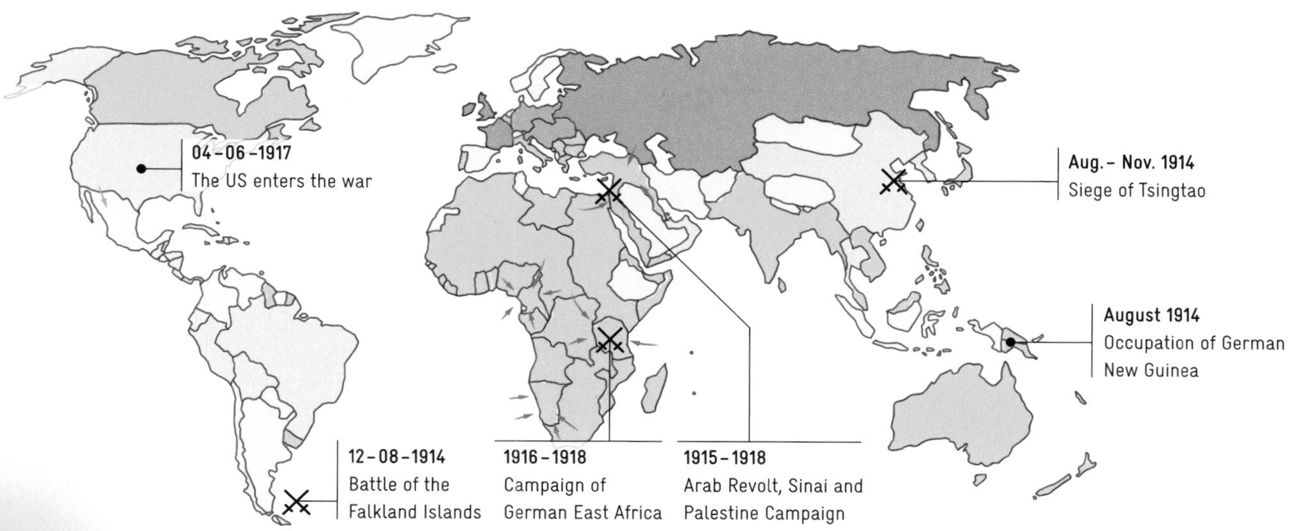
04-06-1917
The US enters the war
Aug.– Nov. 1914
Siege of Tsingtao
August 1914
Occupation of German New Guinea
12-08-1914
Battle of the Falkland Islands
1916-1918
Campaign of German East Africa
1915-1918
Arab Revolt, Sinai and Palestine Campaign

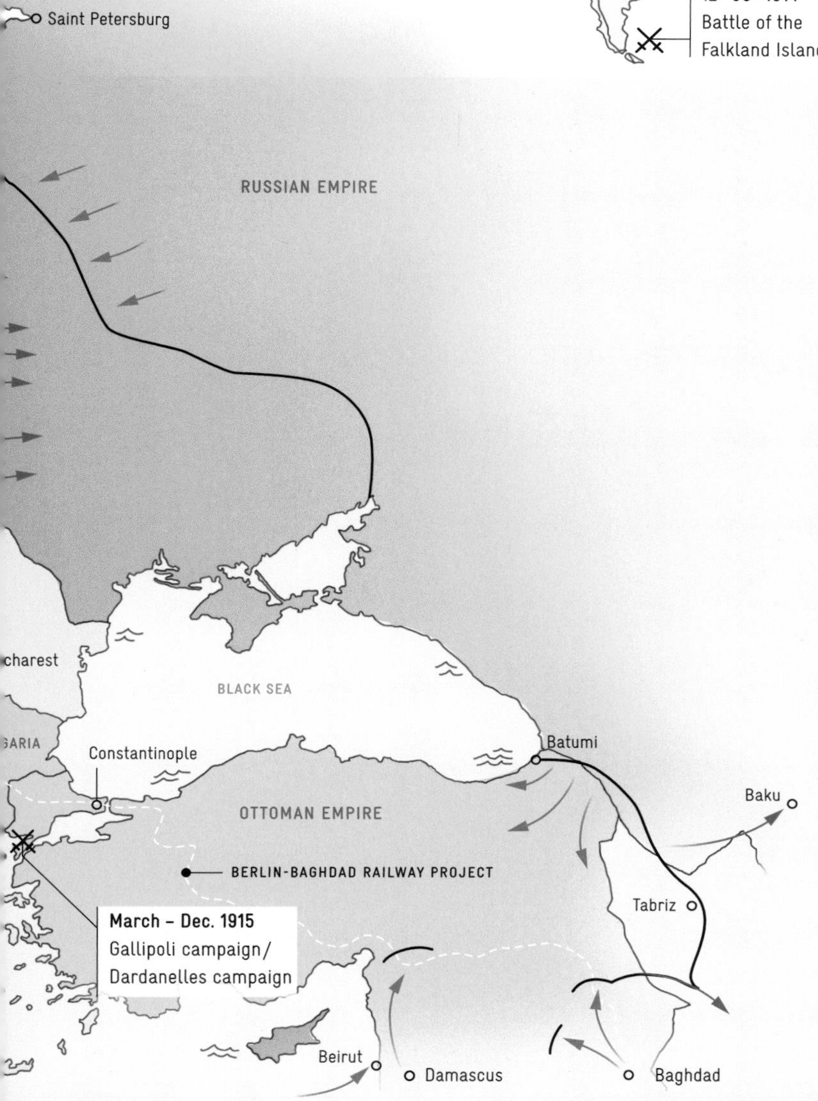
Saint Petersburg
RUSSIAN EMPIRE
charest
BLACK SEA
GARIA
Constantinople
Batumi
OTTOMAN EMPIRE
Baku
BERLIN-BAGHDAD RAILWAY PROJECT
Tabriz
March – Dec. 1915
Gallipoli campaign/
Dardanelles campaign
Beirut
Damascus
Baghdad

The road to war

The series of events that led to the First World War began in the Balkans at the end of the 19th century with the disintegration of the Ottoman Empire. After the Balkan crisis, which was caused in **1875** by separatist movements, the Ottoman Empire had to accept the independence of Serbia, Montenegro and Romania at the Congress of Berlin in **1878**. It also had to allow Austria-Hungary's occupation of Bosnia-Herzegovina against Russia's will. The territorial shifts created constant conflicts during the Bulgarian crisis from **1885 to 1888**, the annexation of Bosnia-Herzegovina through Austria-Hungary in **1908**, as well as the First Balkan War in **1912** and the Second Balkan War in **1913**—while Russia, the protecting power of the Pan-Slav movement, and Austria-Hungary largely remained in the background. In the First Balkan War, the Ottoman Empire lost all areas in the Balkans. In the Second Balkan War, Bulgaria lost almost all territorial gains from the First. The old alliance constellations had shifted on the eve of the First World War: The former »Dreikaiserbund«-partners, Austria-Hungary and Russia, pursued completely opposite interests. Bulgaria and the Ottoman Empire got closer to the Central Powers while other »Dreibund«-partners Italy and Romania leaned towards the Entente, and Serbia was still dreaming of a »Great Serbia«. At the end of the »July Crisis« following the assassination of Franz Ferdinand, Austria-Hungary invaded Serbia on **July 28, 1914**, backed by a German »blank check«. It only took a few days until the German Empire, in support of its ally, declared war on Russia and France and immediately attacked them. The violation of Belgium's neutrality drew Great Britain into action.

06-28-1914
Assassination of Archduke Franz Ferdinand, Austria-Hungary's successor to the throne, in Sarajevo

1900 **1910** **1919**

1907
Military alliance (Triple Entente) between the United Kingdom, France and Russia

1908
Austria-Hungary annexes the areas of Bosnia and Herzegovina that belong to the Ottoman Empire.

→ The alliance loses significance around the turn of the century and breaks apart in **1915** with Italy's termination of the contract.

1912 First Balkan War:
The Ottoman Empire loses all areas in the Balkans to Serbia, Bulgaria, Montenegro and Greece.

1913 Second Balkan War:
Greece, Serbia and Romania against Bulgaria

07-23-1914
Ultimatum of Austria-Hungary to Serbia with Germany's support (»blank check«)

07-28-1914
Austria-Hungary declares war on Serbia.

08-01-1914
Germany declares war on Russia and France

08-04-1914
The United Kingdom declares war on Germany and Austria-Hungary.

LAND WARFARE

The German »Schlieffen Plan« aimed at a quick defeat of France, by attacking from the north, followed by a major attack against Russia. After it failed in September 1914, trench warfare began with front lines hardly moving. The result was senseless destruction and generals who did not differentiate between »technical« and »human« material.

GAS MASKS for people and animals: As a response to the first gas attacks in **1915**, triple-layered filters were developed to protect German soldiers.

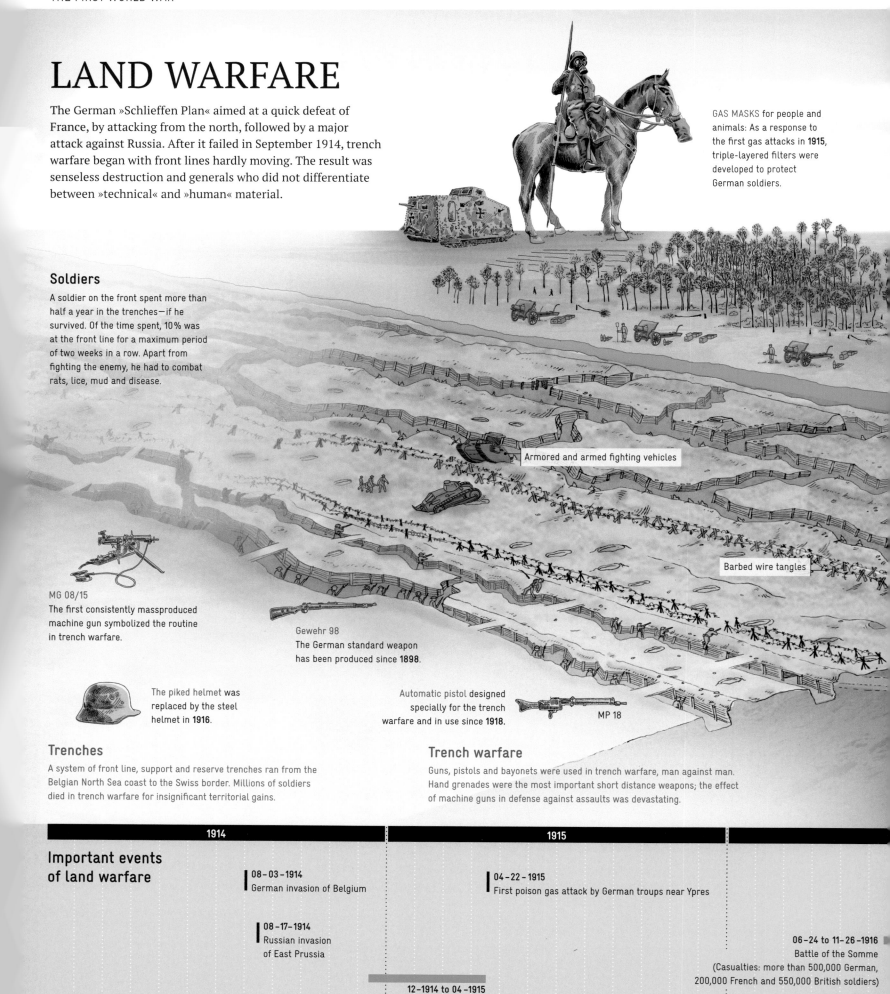

Armored and armed fighting vehicles
Barbed wire tangles

Soldiers

A soldier on the front spent more than half a year in the trenches—if he survived. Of the time spent, 10% was at the front line for a maximum period of two weeks in a row. Apart from fighting the enemy, he had to combat rats, lice, mud and disease.

MG 08/15
The first consistently massproduced machine gun symbolized the routine in trench warfare.

Gewehr 98
The German standard weapon has been produced since **1898**.

The piked helmet was replaced by the steel helmet in **1916**.

Automatic pistol designed specially for the trench warfare and in use since **1918**.

MP 18

Trenches

A system of front line, support and reserve trenches ran from the Belgian North Sea coast to the Swiss border. Millions of soldiers died in trench warfare for insignificant territorial gains.

Trench warfare

Guns, pistols and bayonets were used in trench warfare, man against man. Hand grenades were the most important short distance weapons; the effect of machine guns in defense against assaults was devastating.

1914 | **1915**

Important events of land warfare

08-03-1914
German invasion of Belgium

08-17-1914
Russian invasion of East Prussia

08-26 to 08-30-1914
Battle of Tannenberg

09-05 to 09-12-1914
Battle of the Marne

12-1914 to 04-1915
Battle of the Carpathian Passes

04-22-1915
First poison gas attack by German troups near Ypres

06-23-1915
First battle of the Isonzo (of a total of 12)

06-24 to 11-26-1916
Battle of the Somme
(Casualties: more than 500,000 German, 200,000 French and 550,000 British soldiers)

06-04-1916 to 12-1916
Russian offensive on the Eastern Front

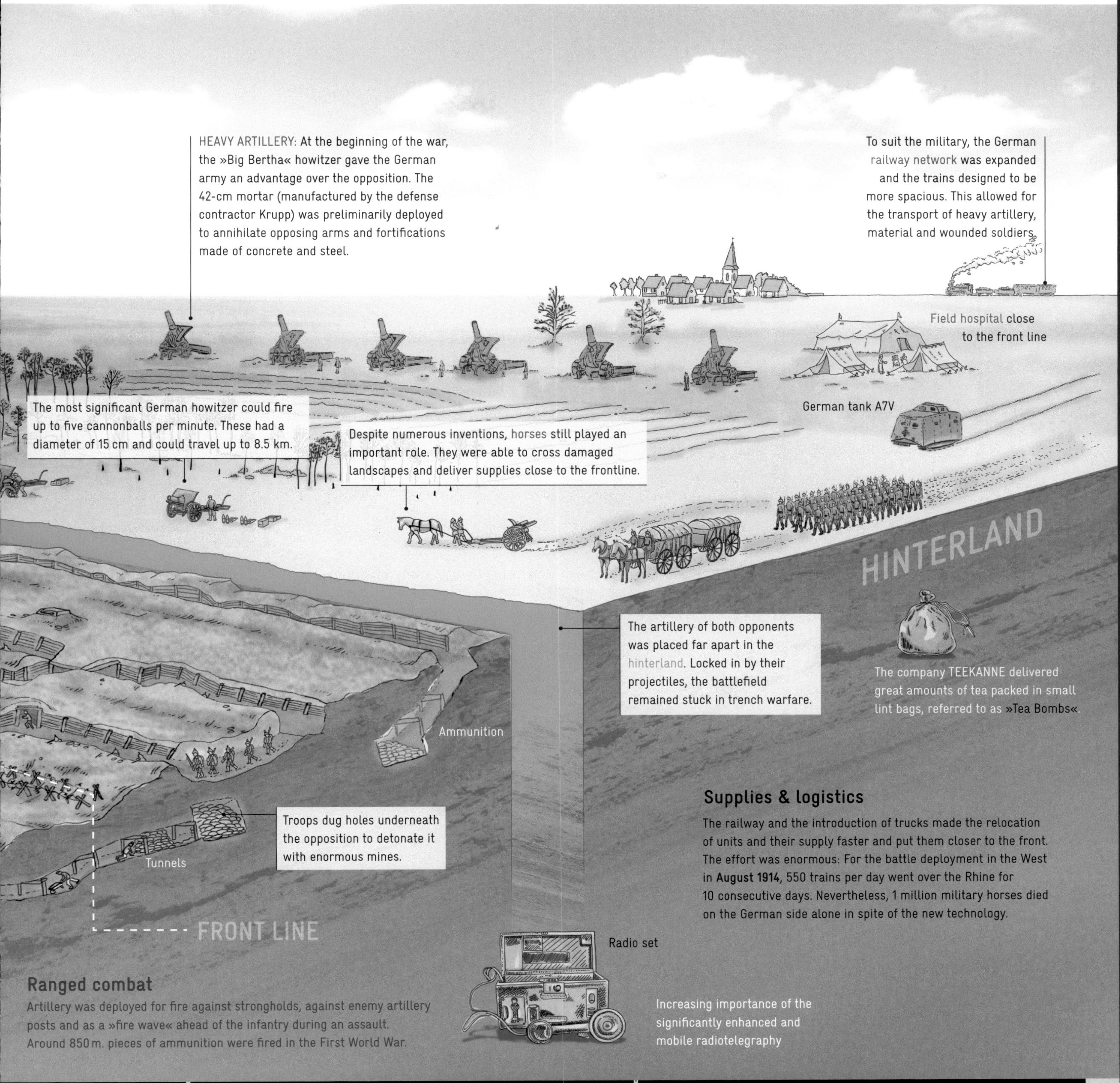
HEAVY ARTILLERY: At the beginning of the war, the »Big Bertha« howitzer gave the German army an advantage over the opposition. The 42-cm mortar (manufactured by the defense contractor Krupp) was preliminarily deployed to annihilate opposing arms and fortifications made of concrete and steel.
To suit the military, the German railway network was expanded and the trains designed to be more spacious. This allowed for the transport of heavy artillery, material and wounded soldiers.
Field hospital close to the front line
German tank A7V
The most significant German howitzer could fire up to five cannonballs per minute. These had a diameter of 15 cm and could travel up to 8.5 km.
Despite numerous inventions, horses still played an important role. They were able to cross damaged landscapes and deliver supplies close to the frontline.
HINTERLAND
The artillery of both opponents was placed far apart in the hinterland. Locked in by their projectiles, the battlefield remained stuck in trench warfare.
The company TEEKANNE delivered great amounts of tea packed in small lint bags, referred to as »Tea Bombs«
Ammunition
Troops dug holes underneath the opposition to detonate it with enormous mines.
Tunnels
FRONT LINE
Radio set
Increasing importance of the significantly enhanced and mobile radiotelegraphy

Supplies & logistics

The railway and the introduction of trucks made the relocation of units and their supply faster and put them closer to the front. The effort was enormous: For the battle deployment in the West in **August 1914**, 550 trains per day went over the Rhine for 10 consecutive days. Nevertheless, 1 million military horses died on the German side alone in spite of the new technology.

Ranged combat

Artillery was deployed for fire against strongholds, against enemy artillery posts and as a »fire wave« ahead of the infantry during an assault. Around 850 m. pieces of ammunition were fired in the First World War.

6 | 1917 | 1918

08-29-1916
Paul von Hindenburg's appointment to Chief of the General Staff and Erich Ludendorff's appointment to Quartermaster General

12-15-1917
Ceasefire of Brest-Litovsk

09-27-1918
Allies' breakthrough at the Siegfried line

09-30-1918
Ceasefire Bulgaria/Entente

09-15-1916
First deployment of tanks by the British army

06-1916
First US troops in France

10-30-1918
Ceasefire Turkey/Entente

02-21-1916 to 12-18-1916
Battle of Verdun (losses: **337,000** German and **362,000** French soldiers)

11-03-1918
Ceasefire Austria-Hungary/Italy

5-20-1916 to 12-1917
Battle of Flanders
(losses: 332,000 British and 217,000 German soldiers)

11-11-1918
Ceasefire of Compiègne
(between the German Empire and Western powers)

NAVAL WARFARE

In contrast to the armament race of the fleet during the pre-war years, naval warfare was not decisive for the outcome of the war. Unrestricted submarine warfare, however, sped up the United State's entry to the war.

The main adversary of the Germans at sea: The Royal Navy

RMS Lusitania

The sinking of this British liner by a German submarine represents the greatest naval loss, in terms of fatalities.

Submarine warfare

As the main weapon in naval warfare in the First World War, submarines replaced large battleships. Their original purpose was merely escorting, but they were soon used to fight battleships and, on the German side, merchant ships—from **1917** in »unrestricted submarine warfare«. The submarine U-35 alone sank 224 merchant ships and two battleships.

As a response to the naval convoys of the British, the Germans changed their strategy of emerging from the water to fire, to shooting submarine torpedoes from underwater. Though this was more efficient, only a few shots per passage were possible.

Felixstowe F.2A

In **1917**, the Felixstowe flying-boats were inaugurated for aerial reconnaissance across the North Sea as well as to attack boats, submarines and airships.

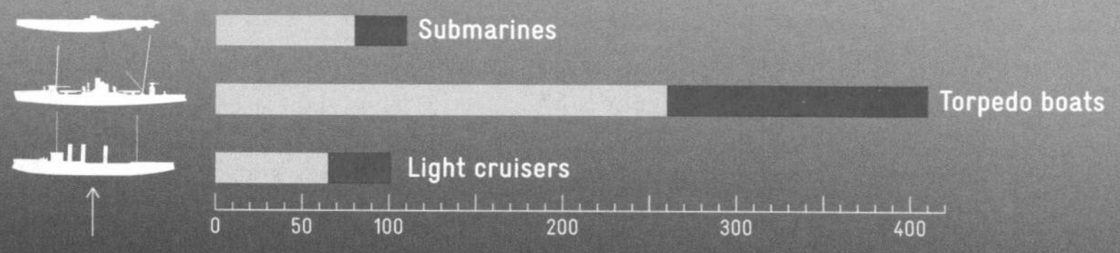

British vs German fleet (at the beginning of WWI)

Great Britain
German Empire
Submarines
Torpedo boats
Light cruisers
0
50
100
200
300
400

A selection of British and German types of warship

Approximately 380 German submarines were deployed, around half of them were destroyed.

Important events of naval warfare

1914

08-01-1914
Great Britain mobilizes its fleet.

08-28-1914
Naval battle between the German and the British fleets

11-02-1914
Great Britain imposes a sea blockade in the North Sea, resulting in a food shortage in the German Empire.

12-08-1914
Naval battle at the Falkland Islands, sinking of the East Asia Squadron

1915

02-04-1915
Germany declares British waters a war zone and launches its submarine warfare against merchant ships.

04-25-1915
British, Australian, New Zealand and French troops land on the Gallipoli peninsula (Ottoman Empire).

05-07-1915
Sinking of the passenger steam liner »Lusitania« by a German submarine (1,200 deaths of which 128 were US citizens); temporary restriction of submarine warfare

1

05-31 to 06-01-1916
Battle of Jutland between 112 German and 150 British warships

Navy

The navies of all war parties relied on large battleships with enormous firepower. Germany and Great Britain shied away from a decisive naval battle, which led to the neutralization of their battle fleets. The British navy only carried out blockades. German cruisers operated overseas. The most well-known fleet was the East Asia squadron.

After German U-boats caused initial heavy losses, the British navy started moving in convoys. Heavily armed military ships surrounded and accompanied transport vessels on their journey.

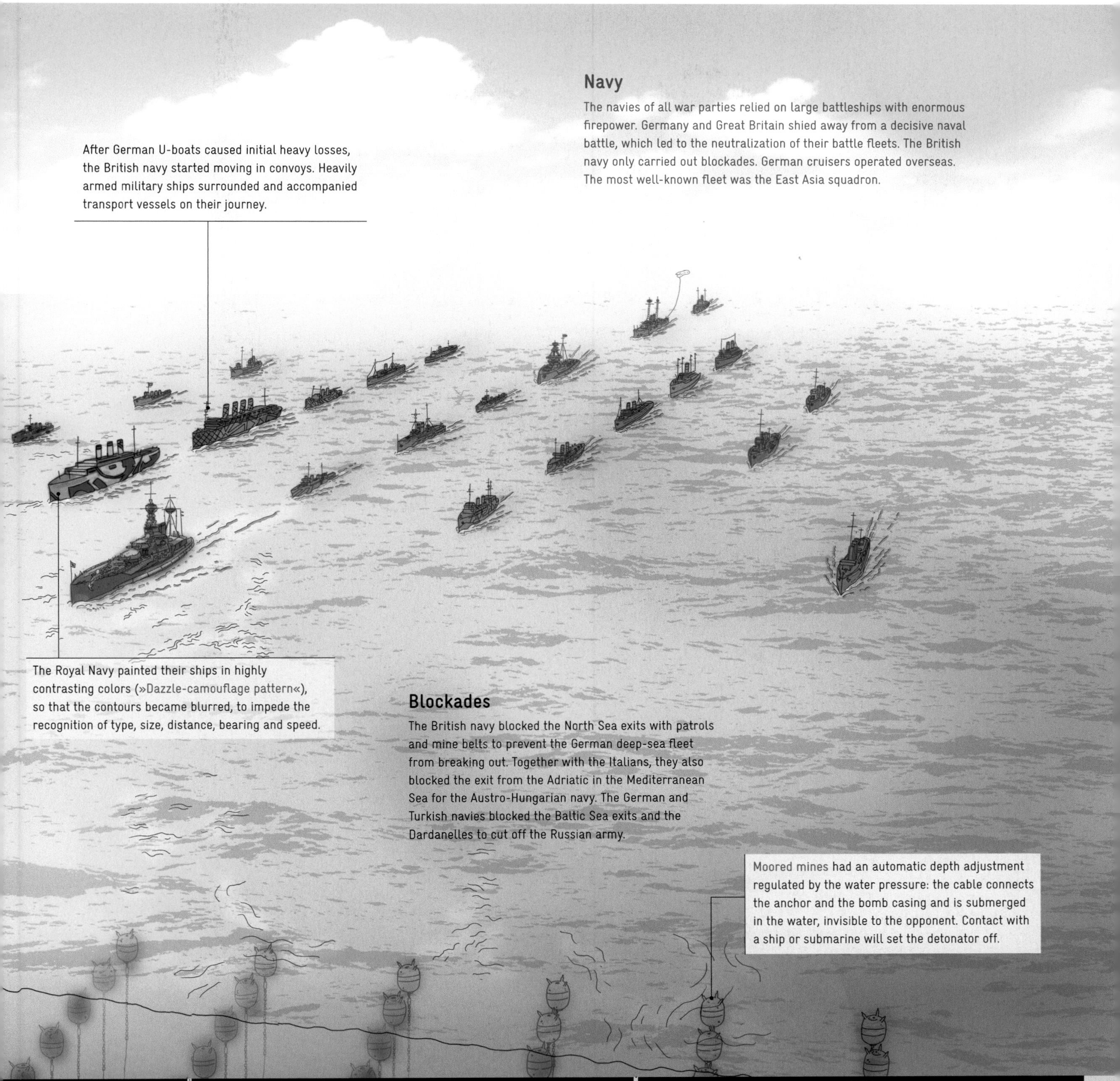

The Royal Navy painted their ships in highly contrasting colors (»Dazzle-camouflage pattern«), so that the contours became blurred, to impede the recognition of type, size, distance, bearing and speed.

Blockades

The British navy blocked the North Sea exits with patrols and mine belts to prevent the German deep-sea fleet from breaking out. Together with the Italians, they also blocked the exit from the Adriatic in the Mediterranean Sea for the Austro-Hungarian navy. The German and Turkish navies blocked the Baltic Sea exits and the Dardanelles to cut off the Russian army.

Moored mines had an automatic depth adjustment regulated by the water pressure: the cable connects the anchor and the bomb casing and is submerged in the water, invisible to the opponent. Contact with a ship or submarine will set the detonator off.

6 | 1917 | 1918

02-01-1917
German Empire declares unrestricted submarine warfare.

from 02-1916
German Empire intensifies submarine warfare.

05-1917
The Allies introduce the convoy system. Casualties through submarines are reduced.

10-28-1918
During ongoing negotiations regarding a ceasefire, the German submarine SM UB-123 sinks the British liner »RMS Leinster« with two torpedoes. 501 out of 771 passengers die. Nine days later the submarine hits a mine. All 36 crew members are dead.

10-28-1918
The order by the German Navy High Command to sail against the British fleet triggers the Kiel sailors' revolt in the North German harbor city

AERIAL WARFARE

Planes became the new weapon of war. Initially only used for reconnaissance, special types were soon constructed for aerial combat, bomb raids and battlefield support.
Apart from the technical changes, there was also a change in the organization—as air forces were established as an independent military branch.

IMMELMANN TURN: Following the attack, the aircraft is pulled back up, enabling a rapid altering of the plane's flight course within a small area. Now facing the same direction as the enemy, the pilot dives down and shoots again.
NOSEDIVE: With high velocity, the enemy aircraft is fired from the front. Ideally, the shooter has the sun on his back, so that the enemy is blinded.
HALF ROLL: To shake off the enemy behind him, the pilot turns the aircraft on its head and pulls back on the control stick.
Before special cannons were developed, weapons like common MGs were used for air defense.

Allocation of air forces (at the beginning of WWI)

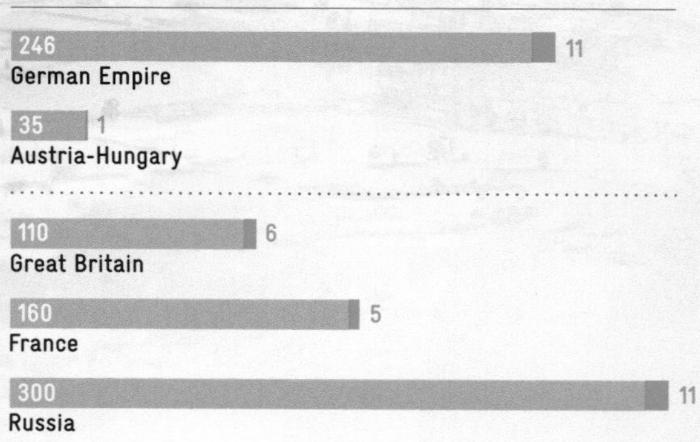
number of planes
number of airships
246
11
German Empire
35
1
Austria-Hungary
110
6
Great Britain
160
5
France
300
11
Russia

Aerial combat

Initially, military pilots fought each other with pistols and guns or rammed the enemy's planes. From May **1915**, however, aerial combat took on a new shape with the introduction of machine guns that could shoot through the propeller. German fighter pilot Max Immelmann developed the first aerial combat tactics, which was to attack coming from the direction of the sun followed by a quick turnaround using the »Immelmann Turn«. Germany put together the first »fighter groups« to exclusively fight enemy planes.

Important events of aerial combat

1914 | 1915 | 1

08-28-1914
First German airship attack (on Antwerp)

10-08-1914
First British aerial attack on Germany

01-19-1915
First German airship attack on Great Britain

05-01-1915
First synchronized machine gun launch by German fighter plane

Beginning of 1916
Formation of German »fighter groups«

Aircraft production/year

Number of planes produced

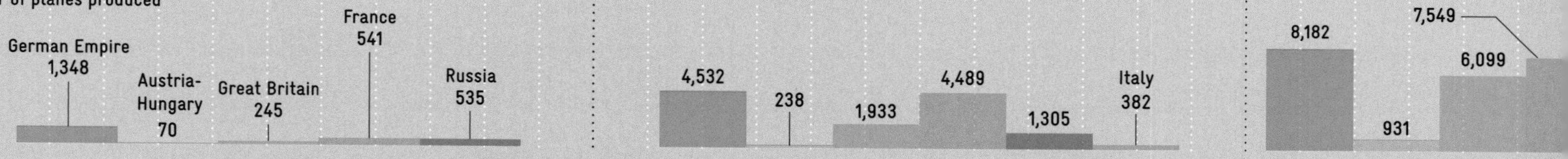
German Empire
1,348
Austria-Hungary
70
Great Britain
245
France
541
Russia
535
4,532
238
1,933
4,489
1,305
Italy
382
8,182
931
7,549
6,099

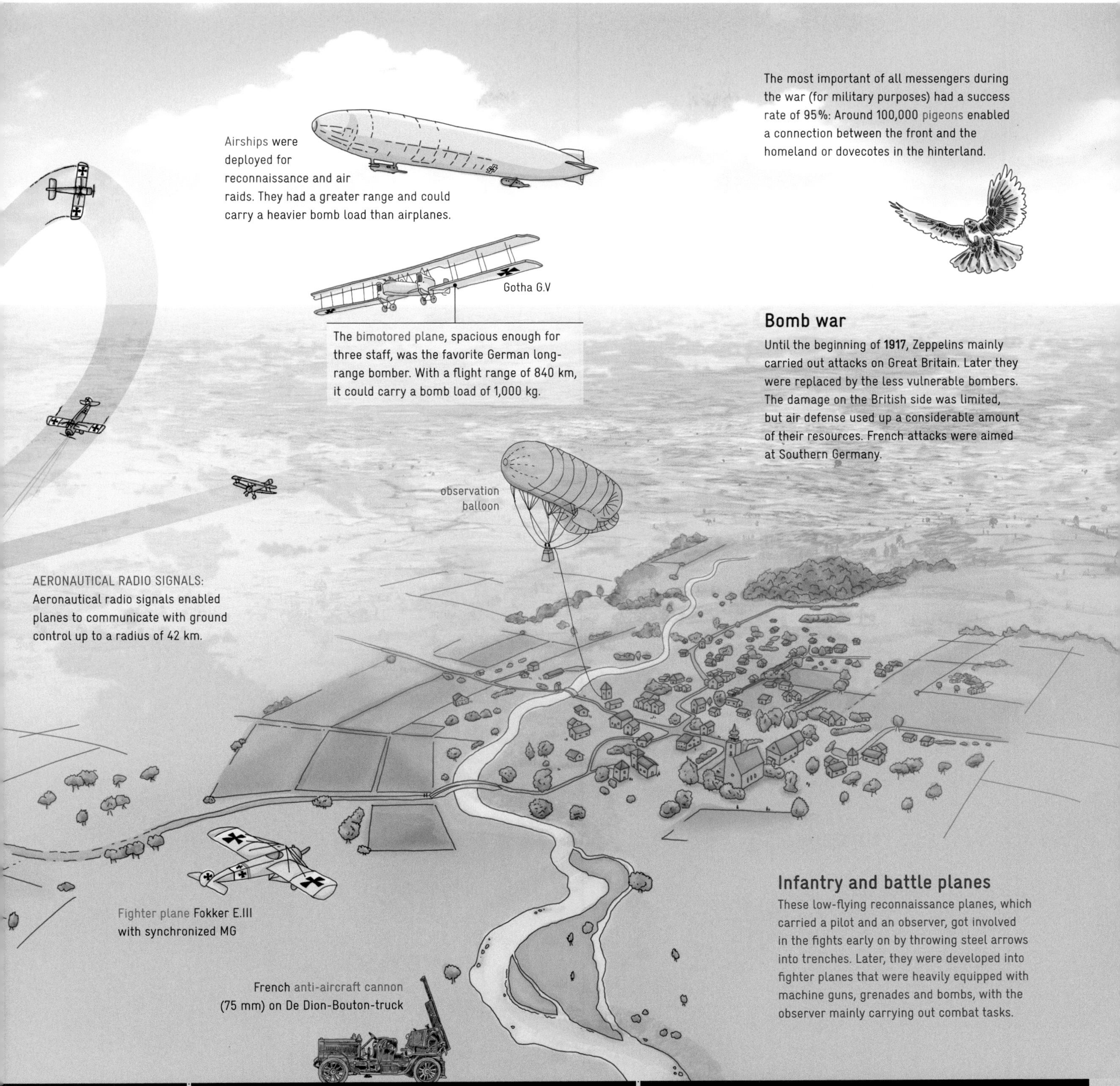
Gotha G.V
observation balloon

Airships were deployed for reconnaissance and air raids. They had a greater range and could carry a heavier bomb load than airplanes.

The most important of all messengers during the war (for military purposes) had a success rate of 95%: Around 100,000 pigeons enabled a connection between the front and the homeland or dovecotes in the hinterland.

The bimotored plane, spacious enough for three staff, was the favorite German long-range bomber. With a flight range of 840 km, it could carry a bomb load of 1,000 kg.

Bomb war

Until the beginning of **1917**, Zeppelins mainly carried out attacks on Great Britain. Later they were replaced by the less vulnerable bombers. The damage on the British side was limited, but air defense used up a considerable amount of their resources. French attacks were aimed at Southern Germany.

AERONAUTICAL RADIO SIGNALS: Aeronautical radio signals enabled planes to communicate with ground control up to a radius of 42 km.

Infantry and battle planes

These low-flying reconnaissance planes, which carried a pilot and an observer, got involved in the fights early on by throwing steel arrows into trenches. Later, they were developed into fighter planes that were heavily equipped with machine guns, grenades and bombs, with the observer mainly carrying out combat tasks.

Fighter plane Fokker E.III with synchronized MG

French anti-aircraft cannon (75 mm) on De Dion-Bouton-truck

1917 **1918**

10-08-1916 Formation of the »German Air Force« as independent force

07-13-1917 Start of daily bombing campaigns on London by German bombers

04-21-1918 Manfred von Richthofen, aka—the Red Baron, WWI's most successful fighter pilot, is killed.

04-01-1918 Establishment of the Royal Air Force

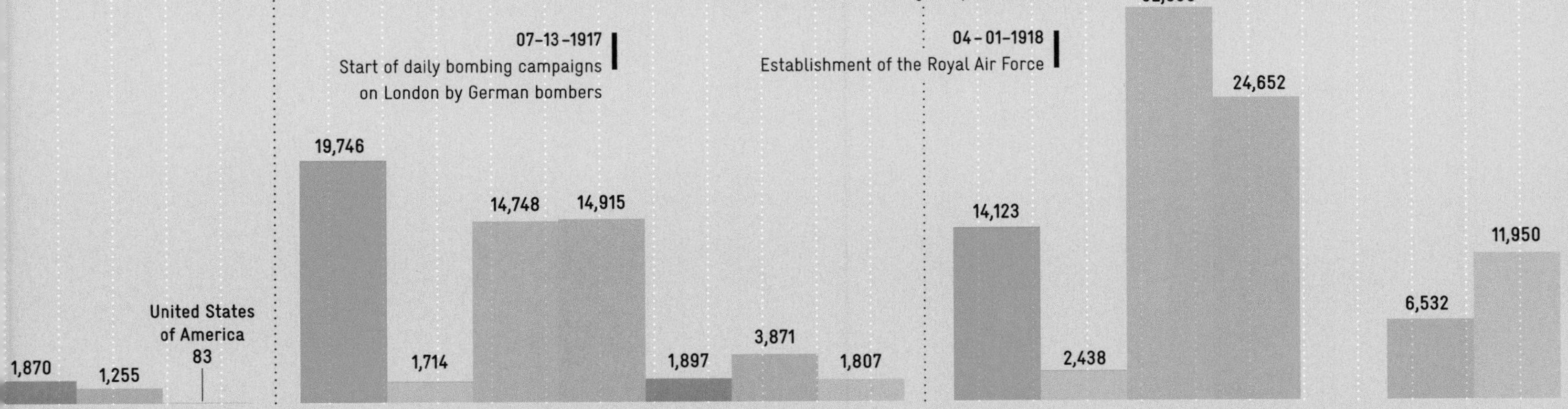
1,870
1,255
United States of America
83
19,746
1,714
14,748
14,915
1,897
3,871
1,807
14,123
2,438
32,036
24,652
6,532
11,950

THE VICTIMS AND THE AFTERMATH

By the end of the war, almost 9 million soldiers had died and about 20 million were injured. About 7 million civilians were killed. The conditions of the Treaty of Versailles fueled feelings of vengeance, which forced the way to the Second World War. Some historians call it a 30-year war between 1914 and 1945, which was only interrupted by a ceasefire.

KEY

- troops
- † soldiers fallen
- % percentage share of soldiers fallen
- 2,500 soldiers fallen

Country	Troops	Soldiers fallen	%
RUSSIA	15,800,000	1,800,000	11.4
OTTOMAN EMPIRE	1,600,000	325,000	20.3
AUSTRIA-HUNGARY	9,000,000	1,460,000	16.2
GERMAN EMPIRE	13,200,000	2,040,000	15.5
BULGARIA	600,000	88,000	14.7
FRANCE	8,100,000	1,330,000	16.4

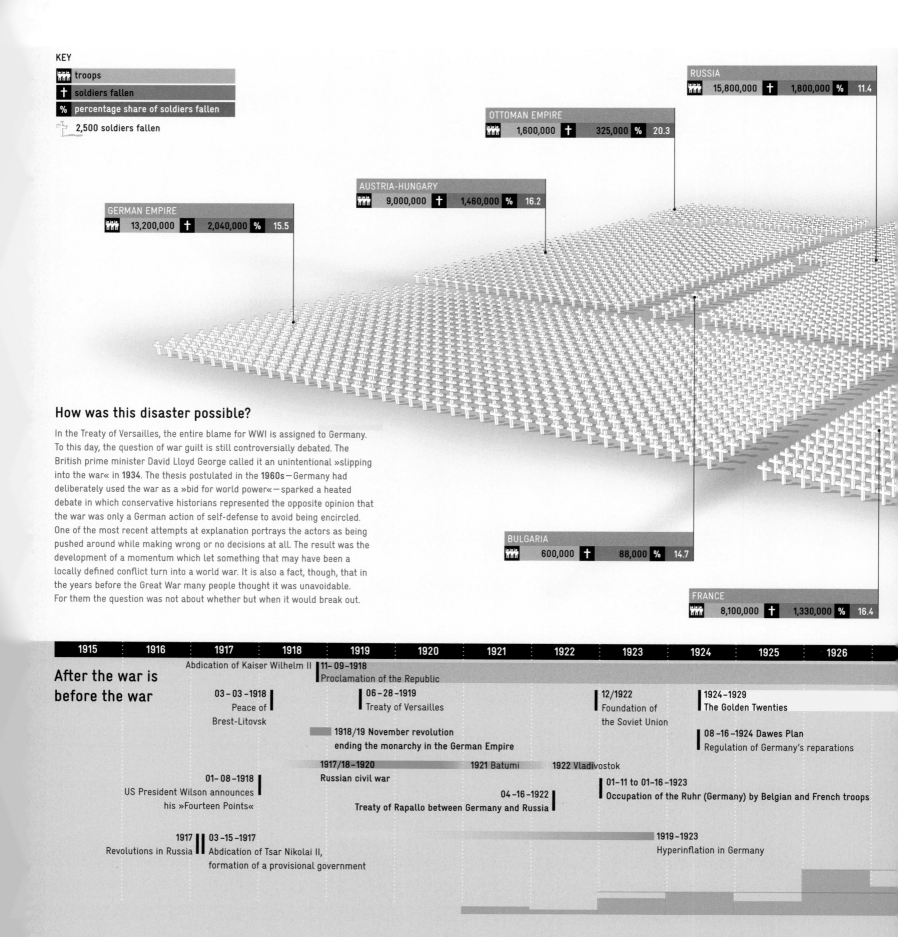

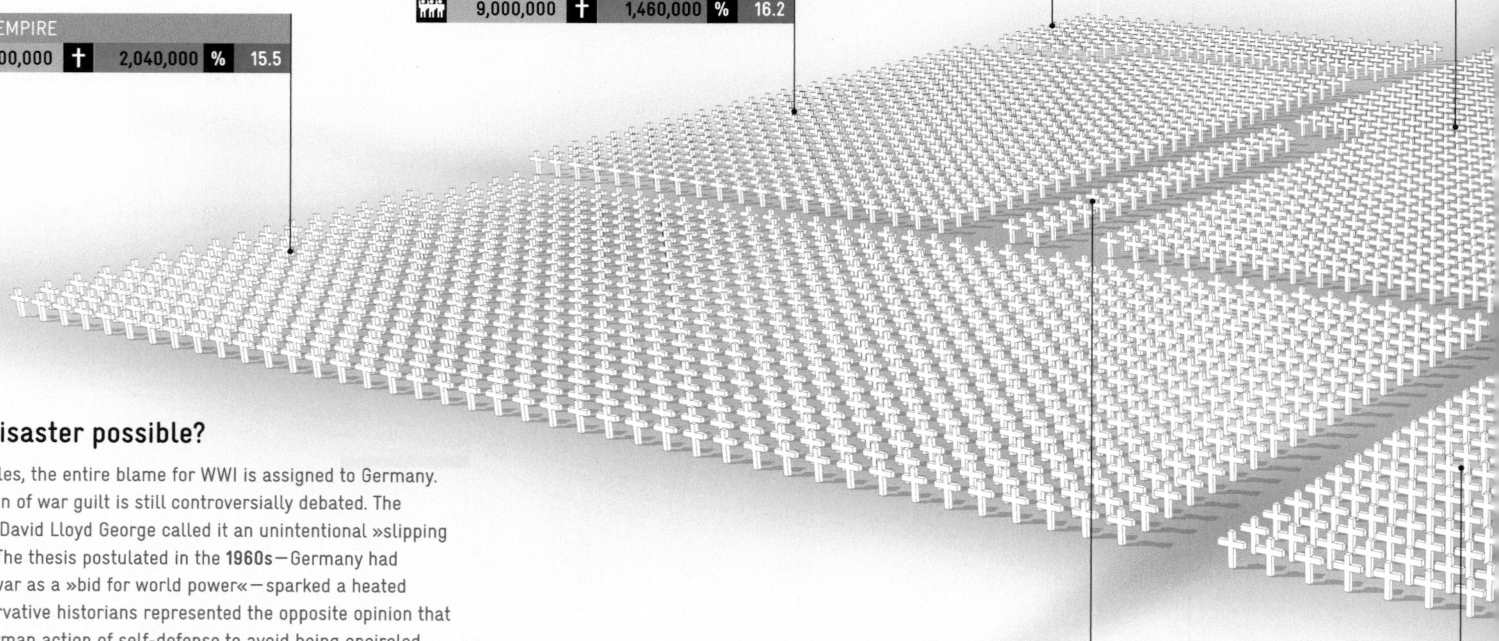

How was this disaster possible?

In the Treaty of Versailles, the entire blame for WWI is assigned to Germany. To this day, the question of war guilt is still controversially debated. The British prime minister David Lloyd George called it an unintentional »slipping into the war« in **1934**. The thesis postulated in the **1960s**—Germany had deliberately used the war as a »bid for world power«—sparked a heated debate in which conservative historians represented the opposite opinion that the war was only a German action of self-defense to avoid being encircled. One of the most recent attempts at explanation portrays the actors as being pushed around while making wrong or no decisions at all. The result was the development of a momentum which let something that may have been a locally defined conflict turn into a world war. It is also a fact, though, that in the years before the Great War many people thought it was unavoidable. For them the question was not about whether but when it would break out.

After the war is before the war

1915 | 1916 | 1917 | 1918 | 1919 | 1920 | 1921 | 1922 | 1923 | 1924 | 1925 | 1926

- Abdication of Kaiser Wilhelm II — **11-09-1918** Proclamation of the Republic
- **03-03-1918** Peace of Brest-Litovsk
- **06-28-1919** Treaty of Versailles
- **12/1922** Foundation of the Soviet Union
- **1924-1929** The Golden Twenties
- **1918/19 November revolution** ending the monarchy in the German Empire
- **08-16-1924 Dawes Plan** Regulation of Germany's reparations
- **1917/18-1920** Russian civil war — 1921 Batumi — 1922 Vladivostok
- **01-08-1918** US President Wilson announces his »Fourteen Points«
- **01-11 to 01-16-1923** Occupation of the Ruhr (Germany) by Belgian and French troops
- **04-16-1922** Treaty of Rapallo between Germany and Russia
- **1917** Revolutions in Russia
- **03-15-1917** Abdication of Tsar Nikolai II, formation of a provisional government
- **1919-1923** Hyperinflation in Germany

LIVING VICTIMS: The war left more than 20 million disabled with physical and psychological conditions, some of which were not even known then. The gravity of the soldiers' and civilians' mutilations was a surgical challenge and the study of prostheses officially became a part of medical science.

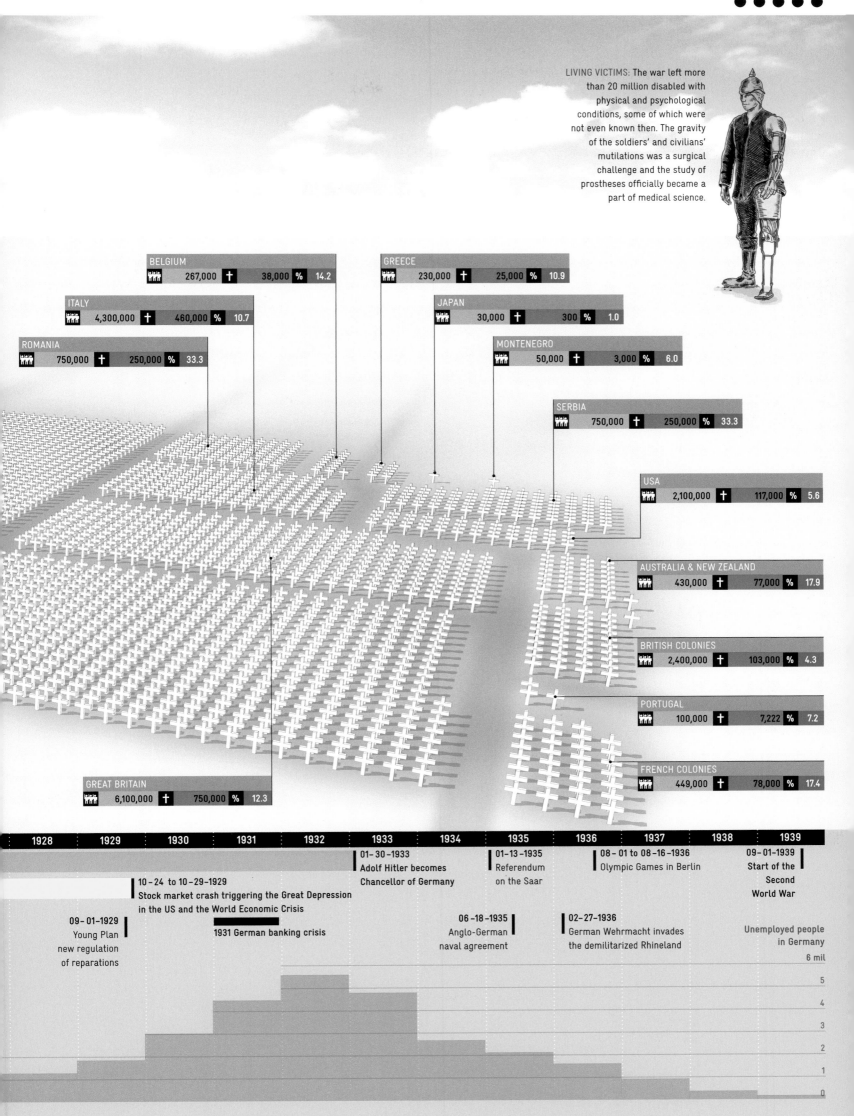

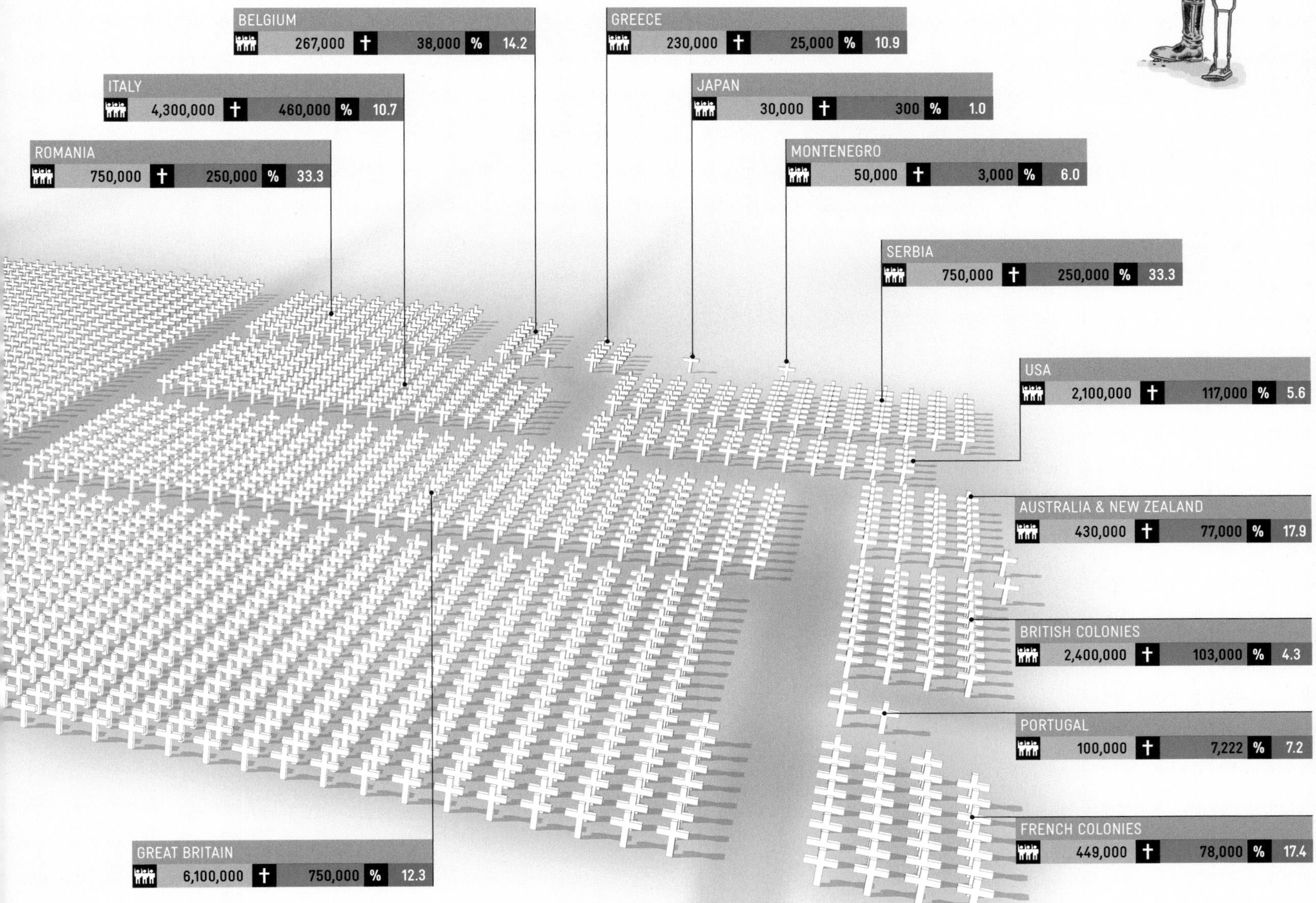
BELGIUM 267,000 38,000 % 14.2
ITALY 4,300,000 460,000 % 10.7
ROMANIA 750,000 250,000 % 33.3
GREECE 230,000 25,000 % 10.9
JAPAN 30,000 300 % 1.0
MONTENEGRO 50,000 3,000 % 6.0
SERBIA 750,000 250,000 % 33.3
USA 2,100,000 117,000 % 5.6
AUSTRALIA & NEW ZEALAND 430,000 77,000 % 17.9
BRITISH COLONIES 2,400,000 103,000 % 4.3
PORTUGAL 100,000 7,222 % 7.2
FRENCH COLONIES 449,000 78,000 % 17.4
GREAT BRITAIN 6,100,000 750,000 % 12.3

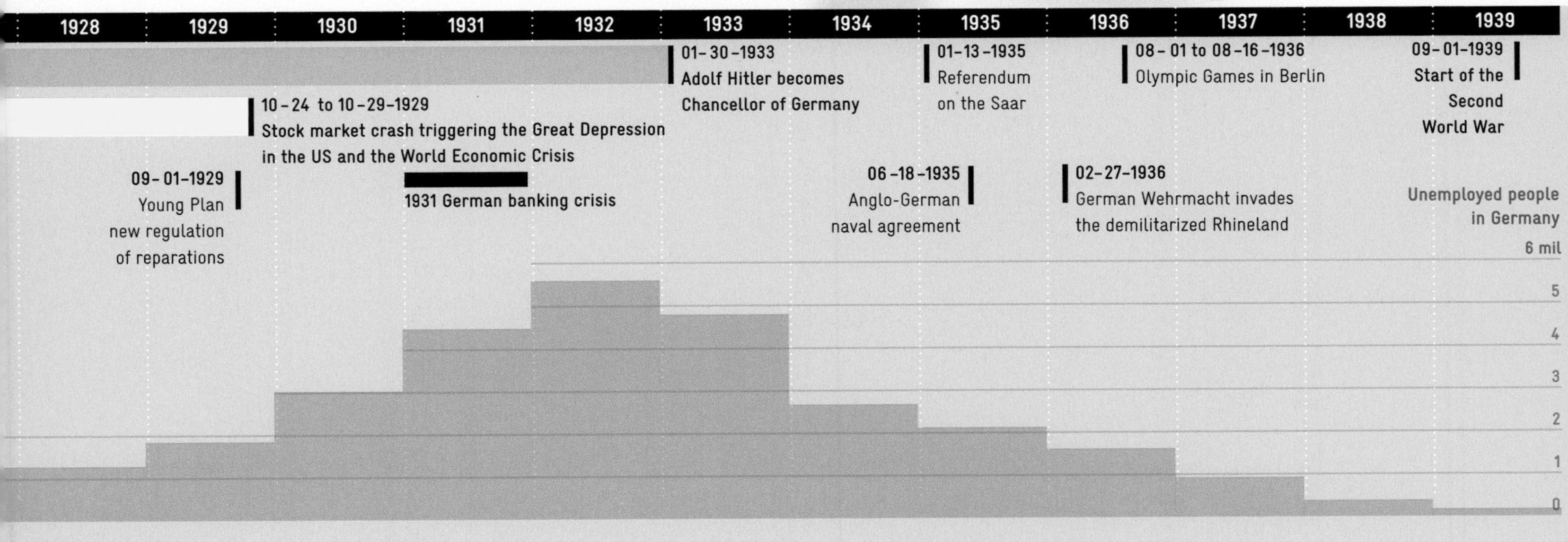
1928 1929 1930 1931 1932 1933 1934 1935 1936 1937 1938 1939
01-30-1933 Adolf Hitler becomes Chancellor of Germany
01-13-1935 Referendum on the Saar
08-01 to 08-16-1936 Olympic Games in Berlin
09-01-1939 Start of the Second World War
10-24 to 10-29-1929 Stock market crash triggering the Great Depression in the US and the World Economic Crisis
09-01-1929 Young Plan new regulation of reparations
1931 German banking crisis
06-18-1935 Anglo-German naval agreement
02-27-1936 German Wehrmacht invades the demilitarized Rhineland
Unemployed people in Germany
6 mil
5
4
3
2
1
0

DISSECTING OPERATION VALKYRIE

In the final year of the Nazi Regime, a group of Wehrmacht officers and police started carrying out Operation Valkyrie on **July 20, 1944**. The operartion was an assassination attempt on Adolf Hitler. The German armed forces representatives saw the war as lost and believed that removing the Führer was the only way to secure Germany's future. Other motives included bringing an end to the Regime's crimes against humanity.

Operation Valkyrie failed. The officers, believing Hitler to be dead, triggered the second half of the plan, which included setting up the state secret police–the SS–as the organization responsible for Hitler's death. The final step was to arrest the heads of the SS and leaders of the Nazi party (NSDAP) in order to pave the way for a new government. But as the radio announced that Hitler had survived the attack, the perpetrators realized they had failed. The officers leading the attempted military coup were arrested and executed on July 21, 1944.

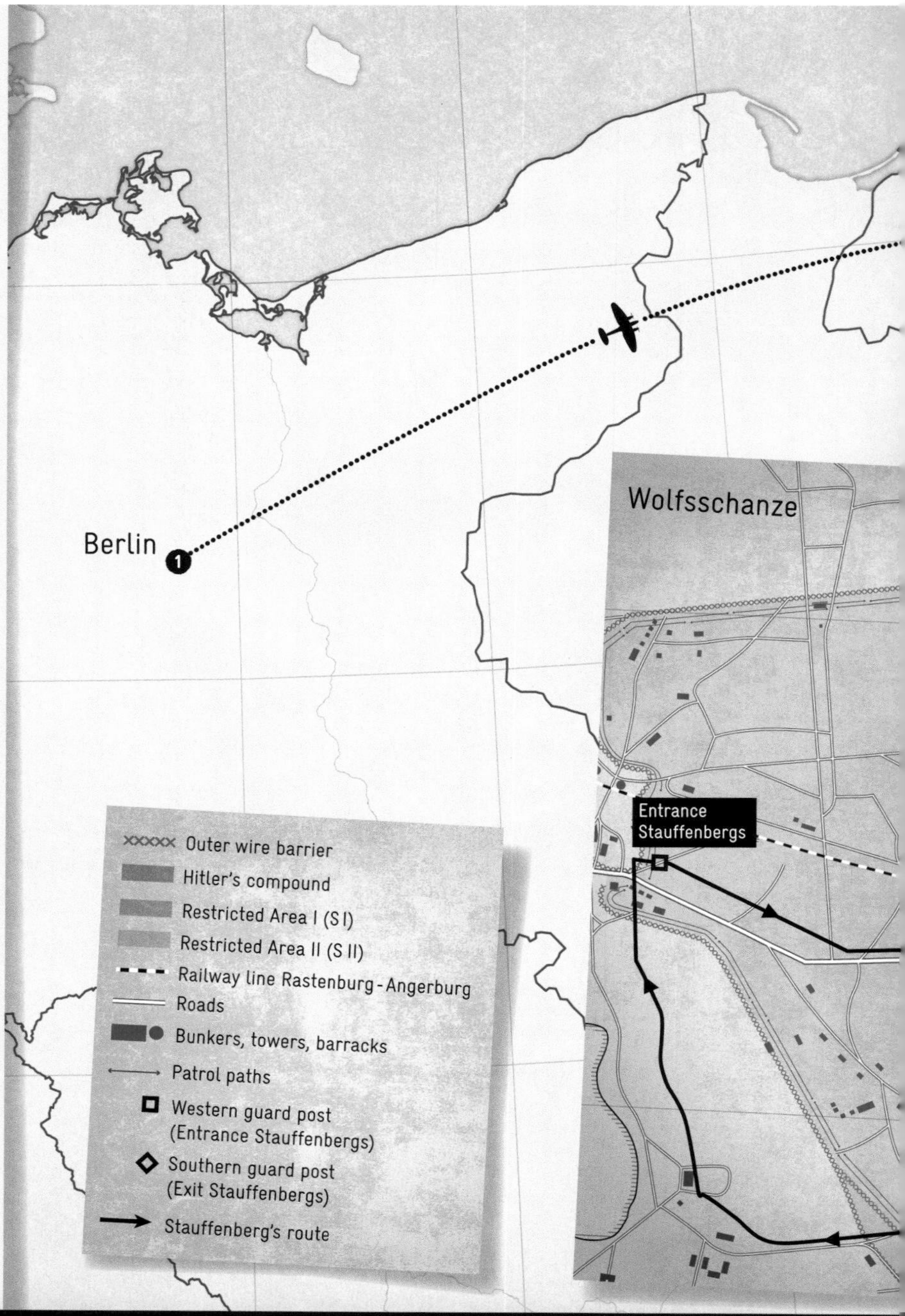
Berlin
1
Wolfsschanze
Entrance Stauffenbergs
Outer wire barrier
Hitler's compound
Restricted Area I (S I)
Restricted Area II (S II)
Railway line Rastenburg - Angerburg
Roads
Bunkers, towers, barracks
Patrol paths
Western guard post (Entrance Stauffenbergs)
Southern guard post (Exit Stauffenbergs)
Stauffenberg's route

THE ASSASSINATION ATTEMPT'S SEQUENCE OF EVENTS

Rangsdorf Airport (1) — Colonel Graf von Stauffenberg and his adjutant Senior lieutenant von Haeften head off to the Führer's headquarters Wolfschanze (Wolf's Lair) near Rastenburg in East Prussia (now Poland). From the airport (2) they drive towards Wolfschanze and pass the western guard post. Stauffenberg has breakfast with Cavalry Captain von Möllendorf and other officers in Restricted Area II (3), after which a meeting of staff takes place in the Chief of the Wehrmacht operations staff's barracks (4). Stauffenberg reports to the supreme command of the armed forces, Field Marshal Wilhelm Keitel (5). Under the pretext of having to freshen up and change shirts, Stauffenberg and Haeften go to the bedroom of Keitel's adjutant. There, Stauffenberg activates the explosive's time fuse. They are disturbed by Staff Sergeant Vogel, so they are only able to activate one of the two explosive devices (6). Stauffenberg hurries to the conference, which is 400 meters away. Keitel introduces him to Hitler to whom he is supposed to provide a progress report later (7). In the crowded room it is impossible to put the bag in close proximity to Hitler. Therefore, he places the bag next to the conference table's leg and leaves the room pretending to have to make a phone call. He hurries to Lieutenant Colonel Sander's room, where Haeften waits for him. He also meets co-conspirator General Fellgiebel there. Sander orders a car (8). At 12:42, the bomb

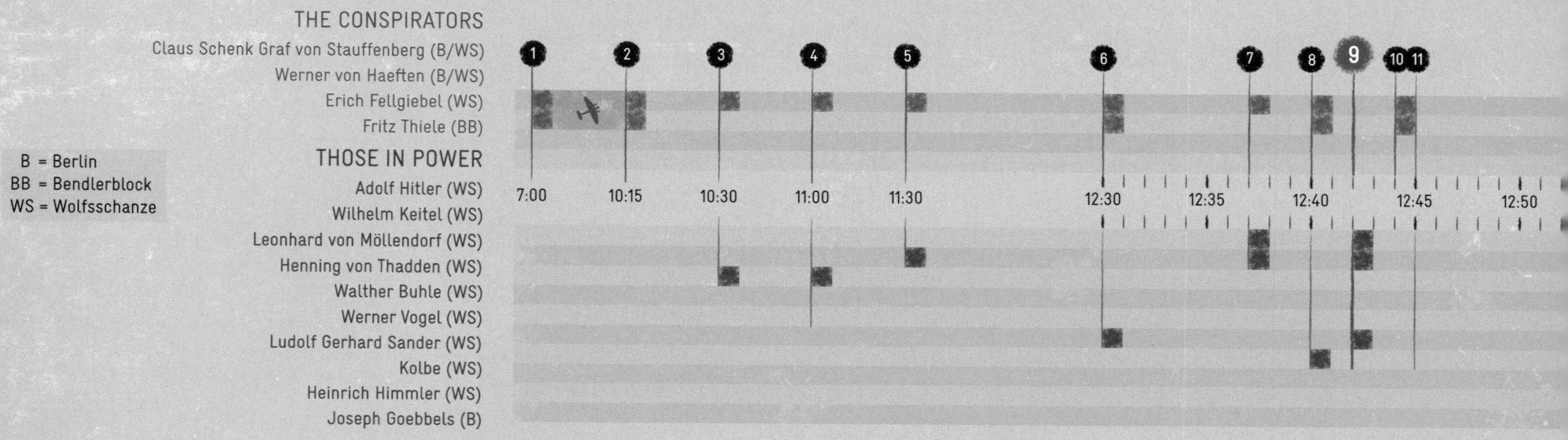
THE CONSPIRATORS
Claus Schenk Graf von Stauffenberg (B/WS)
Werner von Haeften (B/WS)
Erich Fellgiebel (WS)
Fritz Thiele (BB)
THOSE IN POWER
Adolf Hitler (WS)
Wilhelm Keitel (WS)
Leonhard von Möllendorf (WS)
Henning von Thadden (WS)
Walther Buhle (WS)
Werner Vogel (WS)
Ludolf Gerhard Sander (WS)
Kolbe (WS)
Heinrich Himmler (WS)
Joseph Goebbels (B)
B = Berlin
BB = Bendlerblock
WS = Wolfsschanze
1 2 3 4 5 6 7 8 9 10 11
7:00 10:15 10:30 11:00 11:30 12:30 12:35 12:40 12:45 12:50

Wolfsschanze
2
Front line between the 19 and 21 July 1944

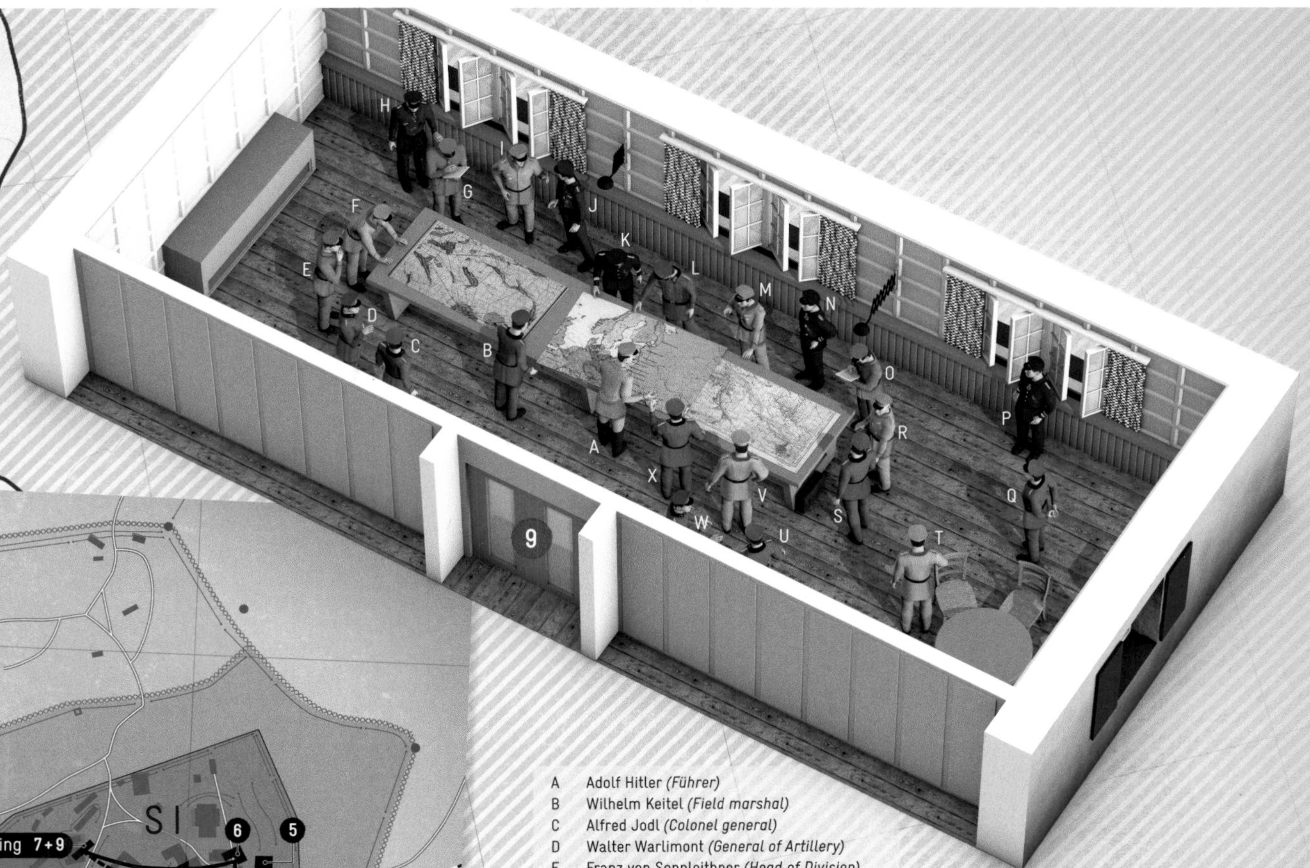

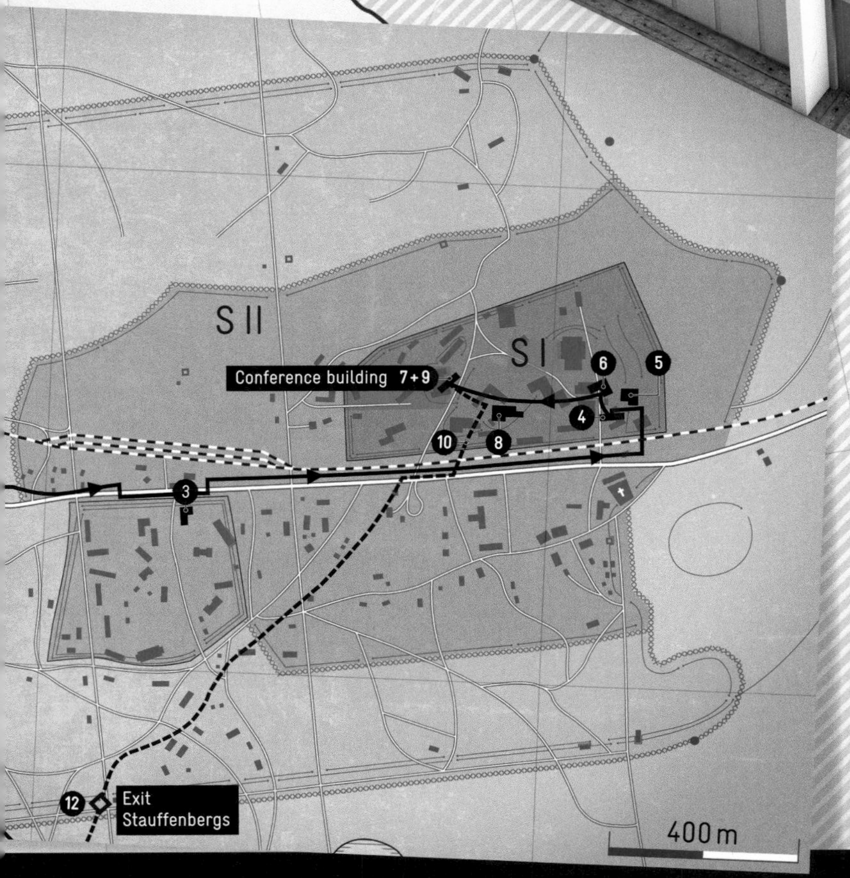
S II
S I
Conference building 7+9
6
5
4
10
8
3
12
Exit Stauffenbergs
400 m

A Adolf Hitler *(Führer)*
B Wilhelm Keitel *(Field marshal)*
C Alfred Jodl *(Colonel general)*
D Walter Warlimont *(General of Artillery)*
E Franz von Sonnleithner *(Head of Division)*
F Herbert Büchs *(Major general staff)*
G Heinz Buchholz *(Stenographer)*
H Hermann Fegelein *(SS Lieutenant General)*
I Nicolaus von Below *(Colonel)*
J Otto Günsche *(SS Major)*
K Hans-Erich Voß *(Rear Admiral)*
L Walter Scherff *(Major General)*
M Ernst John von Freyend *(Major)*
N Heinz Aßmann *(Captain)*
O Heinrich Berger *(Stenographer)* ✝
P Karl-Jesko von Puttkamer *(Rear Admiral)*
Q Walter Buhle *(General)*
R Heinrich Borgmann *(Lieutenant Colonel)*
S Rudolf Schmundt *(Lieutenant General)* ✝
T Heinz Waizenegger *(Lieutenant Colonel)*
U Karl Bodenschatz *(General)*
V Heinz Brandt *(Colonel)* ✝
W Günther Korten *(General)* ✝
X Adolf Heusinger *(Lieutenant General)*

explodes and brings all conference participants to the floor (9). Four people die, the rest are lightly to severely wounded. Stauffenberg watches the explosion from a 200 meters distance. He and Haeften leave Restricted Area I (10). Later, the alarm is activated for all restricted areas (11). They then drive to the southern exterior guard post where Staff Sergeant Kolbe refuses to let them pass. Möllendorf authorizes their departure over the phone (12).

On the way to the airport Haeften throws a second bomb out of the car (13). Fellgiebel declares a news blackout which however does not affect the SS's news communication line and Goebbels learns about the attempted assassination shortly after 13:00 (14). Fellgiebel contacts Lieutenant General Thiele, the Head of the Armed Forces' communications in Berlin, and reports the failure of the assassination and that Hitler is only lightly injured (15). Himmler, Supreme

Commander of the SS, arrives at Wolfsschanze (16) and gives the order to collect information about the assassination attempt. Stauffenberg's quick disappearance is noticed and he becomes a suspect. Himmler orders his arrest at the airport in Rangsdorf (17).

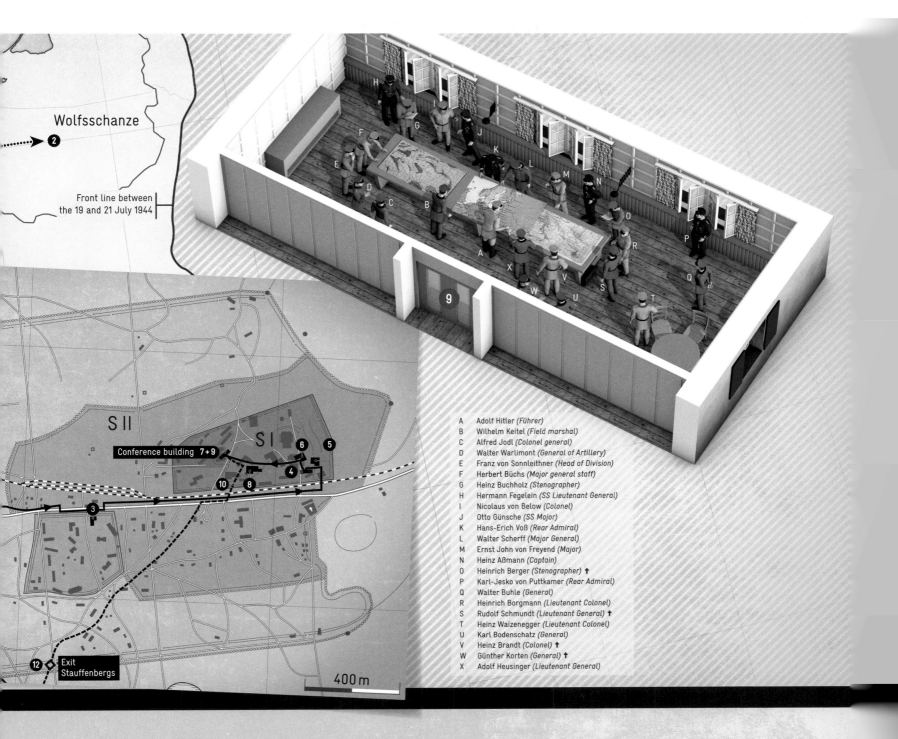

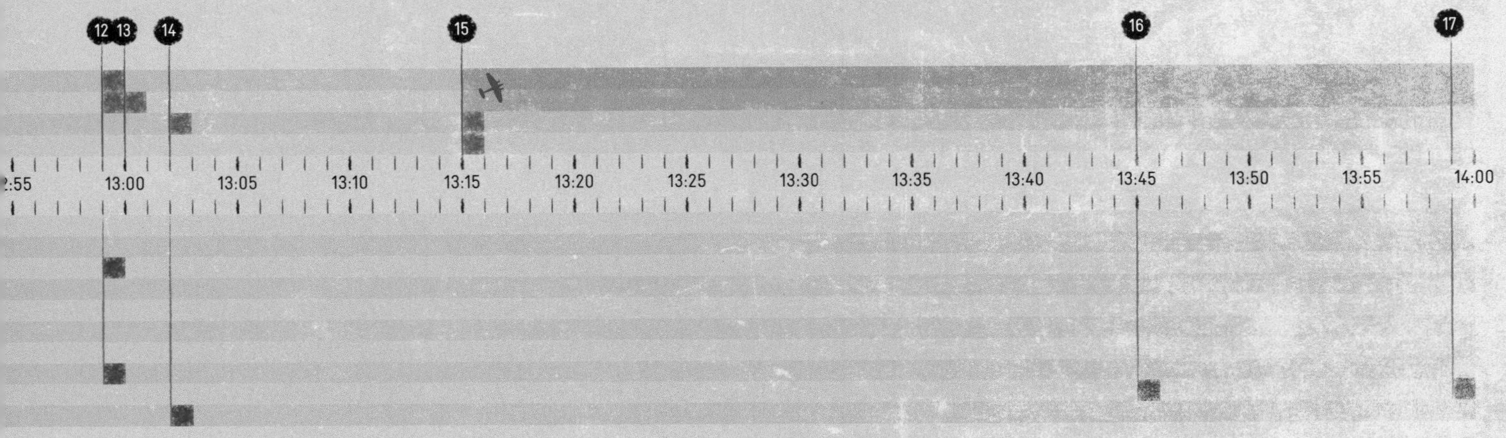
12
13
14
15
16
17
:55
13:00
13:05
13:10
13:15
13:20
13:25
13:30
13:35
13:40
13:45
13:50
13:55
14:00

There are 2 million people in West Berlin. We have to get them supplies!
If we forcibly open the border, it's an act of war.
Or the alternative is that we give up West Berlin.
We have to negotiate with the Soviets.

Harry S. Truman, US President

George Marshall, US Secretary of State

Lucius Clay, US Military Governor

June 24, 1948 - September 30, 1949

THE BERLIN AIRLIFT

After World War II, Germany was divided into four zones and Berlin into four sectors. West Berlin, made up of the British, French and American sectors, was enclosed by Soviet territory. Three days after the Western powers introduced a new currency, the Deutschmark, as an economic reform in their three sectors, the Soviet Union reacted by blocking access into its sector by land as well as water. West Berlin was completely isolated from West Germany.

52

If we give up West Berlin, we have lost our own victory.
We're staying!

Without knowing how long the blockade would last, the western powers decided to conduct an airlift.

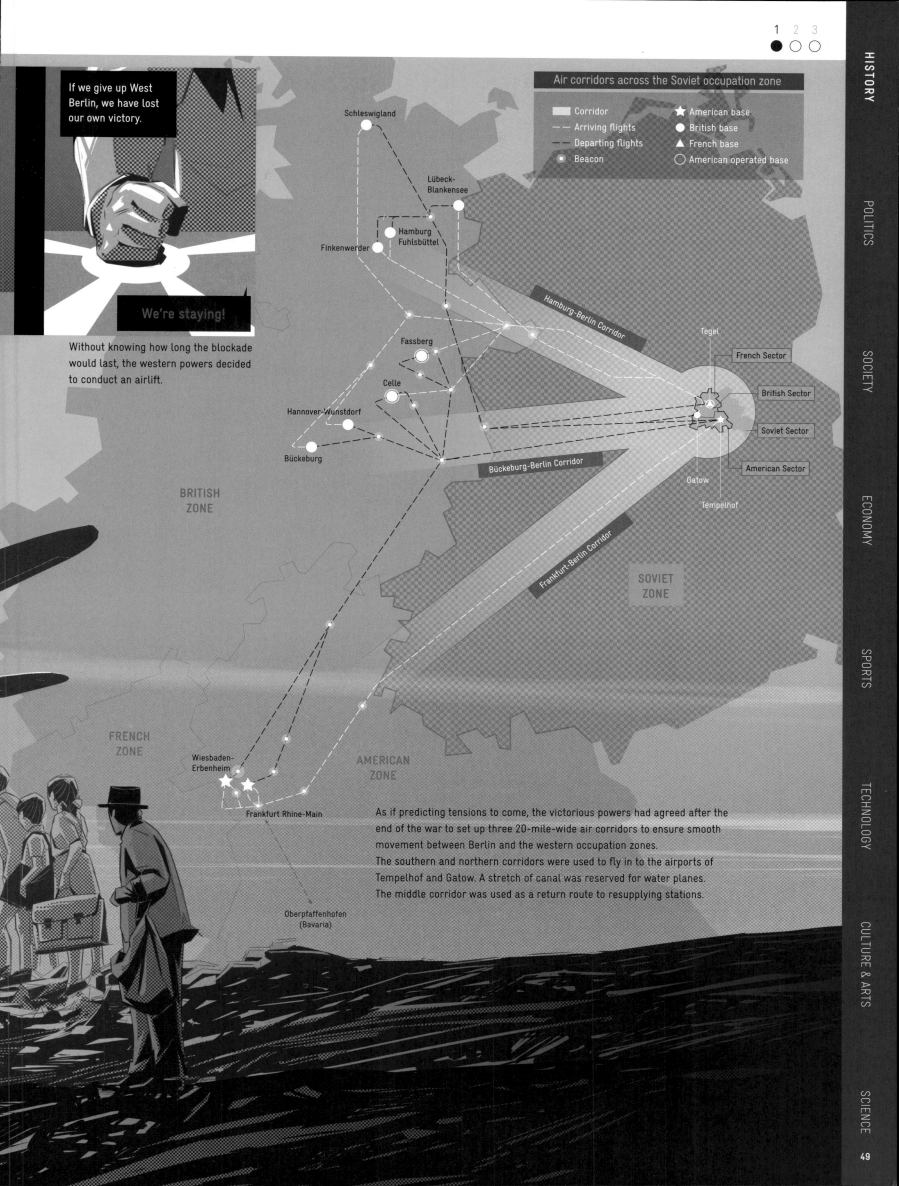

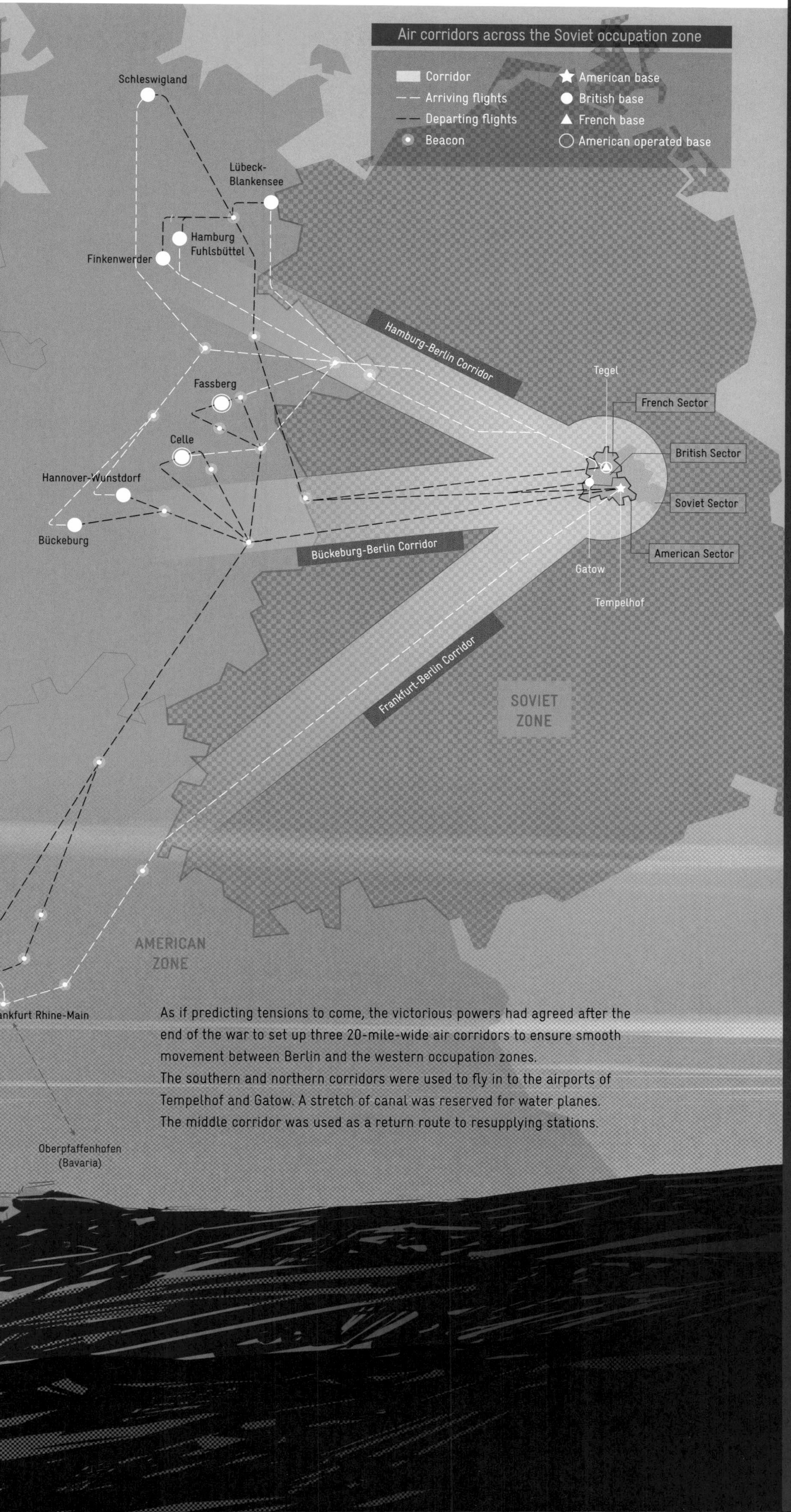
Air corridors across the Soviet occupation zone
Corridor
Arriving flights
Departing flights
Beacon
American base
British base
French base
American operated base
Schleswigland
Lübeck-Blankensee
Hamburg Fuhlsbüttel
Finkenwerder
Hamburg-Berlin Corridor
Fassberg
Celle
Hannover-Wunstdorf
Bückeburg
Bückeburg-Berlin Corridor
Tegel
French Sector
British Sector
Soviet Sector
American Sector
Gatow
Tempelhof
BRITISH ZONE
SOVIET ZONE
Frankfurt-Berlin Corridor
FRENCH ZONE
AMERICAN ZONE
Wiesbaden-Erbenheim
Frankfurt Rhine-Main
Oberpfaffenhofen (Bavaria)

As if predicting tensions to come, the victorious powers had agreed after the end of the war to set up three 20-mile-wide air corridors to ensure smooth movement between Berlin and the western occupation zones.
The southern and northern corridors were used to fly in to the airports of Tempelhof and Gatow. A stretch of canal was reserved for water planes.
The middle corridor was used as a return route to resupplying stations.

Western air traffic control (GCA)
No Western air traffic control contact
3 minutes
around 150 meters
52
Illustration not to scale

To guarantee supplies to West Berlin, planes flew continuously at record pace. New radar systems helped navigate even in poor visibility and pilots reported their times and positions to other planes via a checkpoint with radio beacon. With this system, pilots were able to keep to precise scheduling and avoid collision.
Once inside the Soviet Zone, pilots had no beacon or radio contact for exactly 40 minutes. Flying by compass, the pilot took care not to leave the corridor until reaching transmission range for the ground control station at Tempelhof.

Disruptive maneuvers, which ranged from firing rockets and flares to causing radio interference and light disruption, were ongoing.

Soviet disturbing maneuvers during the airlift

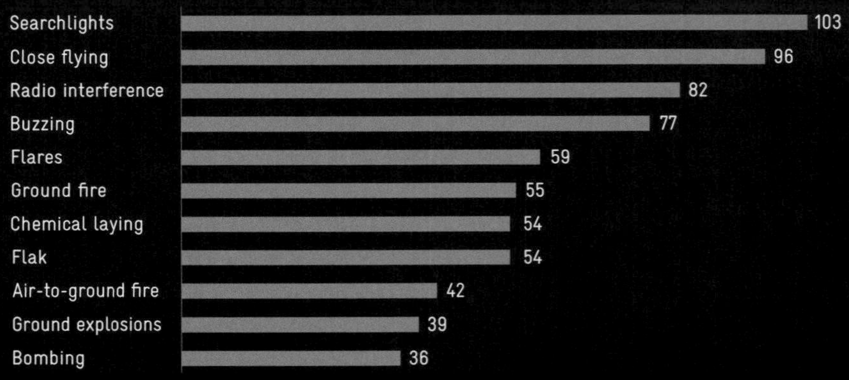
Searchlights 103
Close flying 96
Radio interference 82
Buzzing 77
Flares 59
Ground fire 55
Chemical laying 54
Flak 54
Air-to-ground fire 42
Ground explosions 39
Bombing 36

You're flying over the glide path. Now 50 feet too high. Increase your sink rate. Azimuth is good. Three miles from touchdown. You're continuing, closer to the glide path, falling at 550 feet per minute. Your azimuth is good. You're on the glide path, two miles from touchdown. Cleared for landing by the tower. One and a half miles from touchdown. Your azimuth is good. Flying slightly under the glide path, you're 25 feet too high, adjust your sink rate.

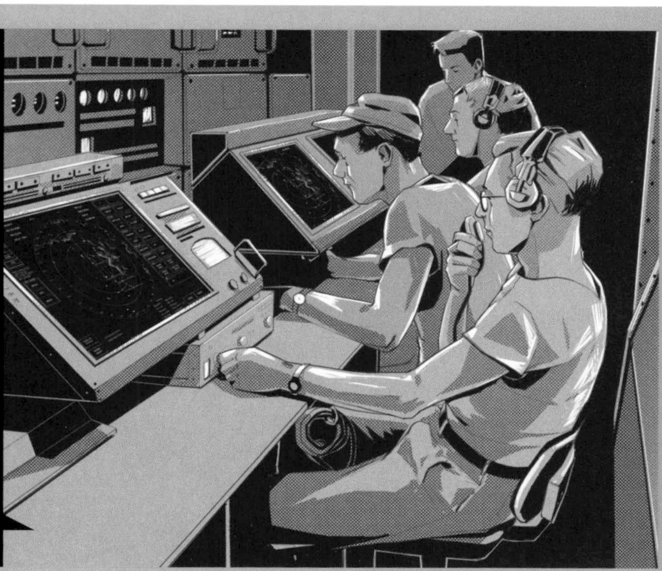

When visibility was poor, pilots needed to land using the Ground Controlled Approach (GCA), in which the GCA station directed pilots to the runway on a radar screen. Twenty percent of all landings were controlled this way.

To ensure safety in the Berlin skies, each airport had fixed routes for landing and takeoff. In addition to the standard routes to the west, there were alternative routes to the east of each airfield. Altitudes, directions and times were clearly set for each section of the routes. Each pilot had only one landing attempt. If they failed, the machine had to fly directly back with the payload. This was more efficient than disrupting the clock.

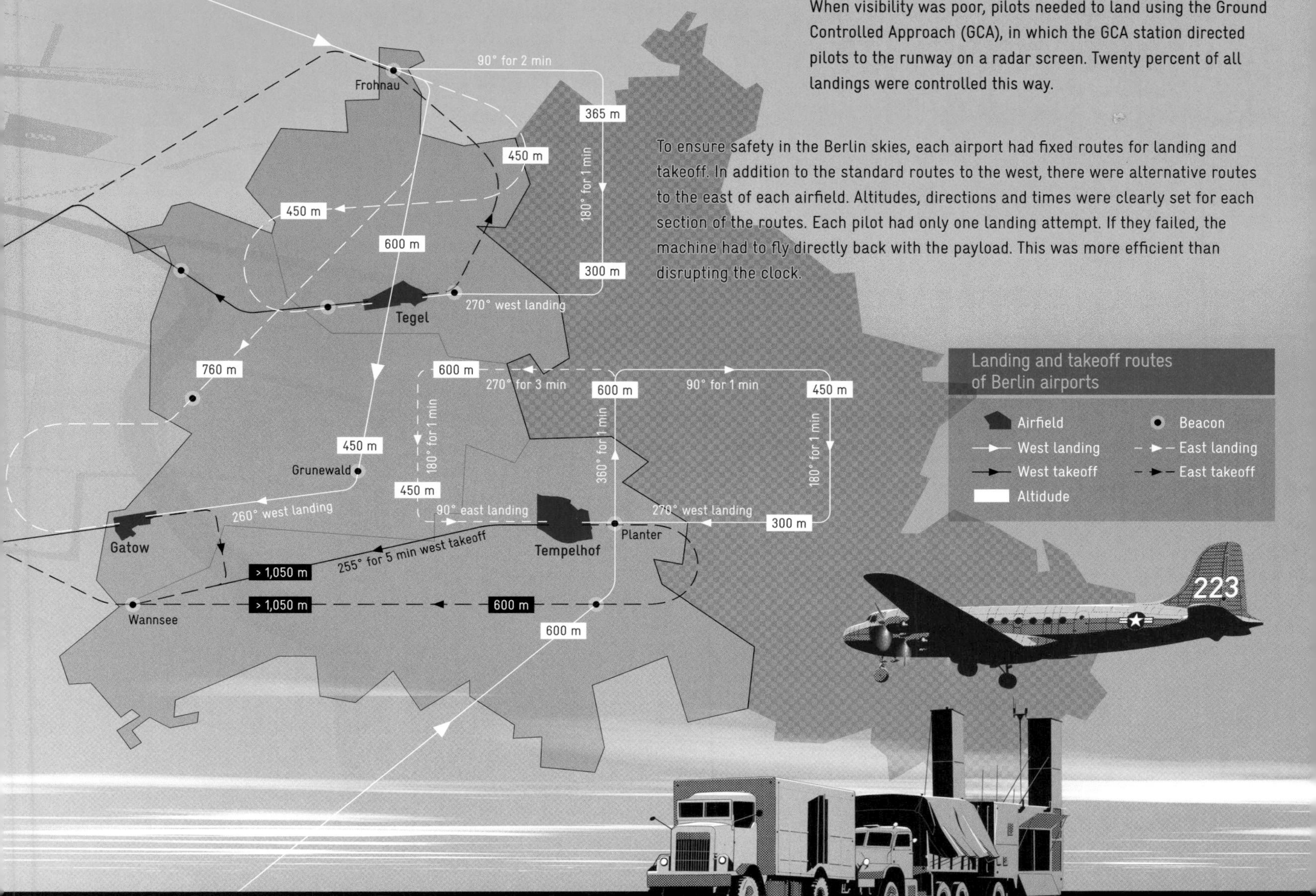

Landing and takeoff routes of Berlin airports
Airfield
Beacon
West landing
East landing
West takeoff
East takeoff
Altidude
Frohnau
90° for 2 min
365 m
450 m
180° for 1 min
450 m
600 m
300 m
270° west landing
Tegel
760 m
600 m
270° for 3 min
600 m
90° for 1 min
450 m
180° for 1 min
360° for 1 min
180° for 1 min
450 m
Grunewald
450 m
260° west landing
90° east landing
270° west landing
300 m
Gatow
Tempelhof
Planter
> 1,050 m
255° for 5 min west takeoff
> 1,050 m
600 m
Wannsee
600 m
223

Workhorses

▮ = 10 aircraft | loading weight | maximum speed

Aircraft	Number	Loading weight	Maximum speed
Douglas C-54 Skymaster/R5D	380	37.4 t	365 km/h
Douglas C-47 Skytrain/Dakota	170	15.0 t	297 km/h
Avro York	42	31.1 t	365 km/h
Handley Page Hastings	24	36.3 t	552 km/h

More Aircraft in Use

Tanker Aircrafts 30

Handley Page Halton 24.7 t
Avro 691 Lancastrian 29.5 t

Special transport 11

Fairchild C-82 Packet 24,5 t
Douglas C-74 Globemaster I 77.8 t

Flying boats 11

Short S.25 Sunderland 29.5 t
Consolidated PBY-6A Catalina 16.1 t

Other 13

Avro 689 Tudor 2 36.3 t
Bristol Type 170 Freighter/Wayfarer 20.0 t

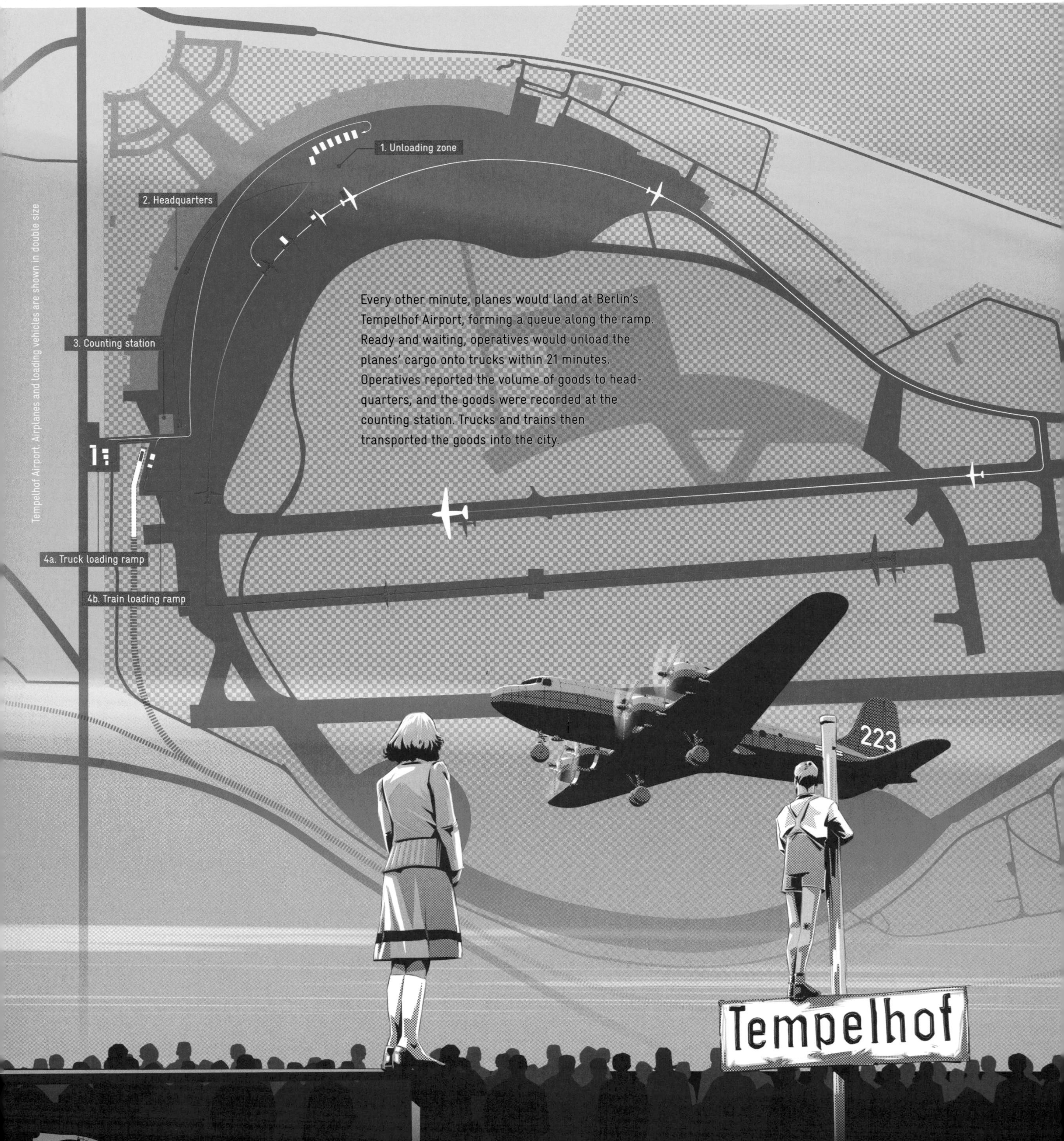
1. Unloading zone
2. Headquarters
3. Counting station
4a. Truck loading ramp
4b. Train loading ramp
223
Tempelhof

Tempelhof Airport. Airplanes and loading vehicles are shown in double size

Every other minute, planes would land at Berlin's Tempelhof Airport, forming a queue along the ramp. Ready and waiting, operatives would unload the planes' cargo onto trucks within 21 minutes. Operatives reported the volume of goods to headquarters, and the goods were recorded at the counting station. Trucks and trains then transported the goods into the city.

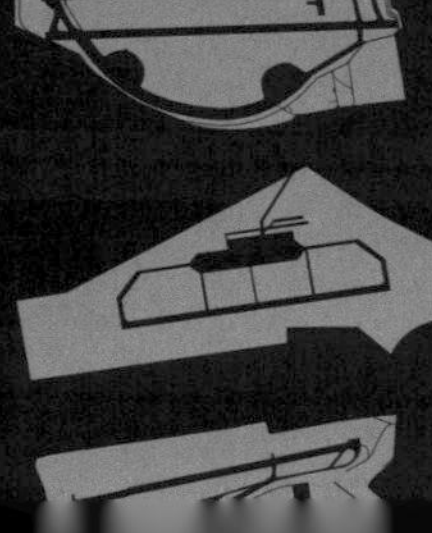

	Flights and landings (Total: 277,569)		Goods transported (Total in tons: 2,109,667)		Average unloading time in min
Tempelhof	39%	109,176	42%	903,167 t	21 min
Tegel	19%	52,780	24%	499,216 t	11 min
Gatow	42%	115,612	34%	707,284 t	15 min

Airlift memorial
Berlin-Tempelhof,
Frankfurt a. M., Celle

Number of US & UK airlift flights

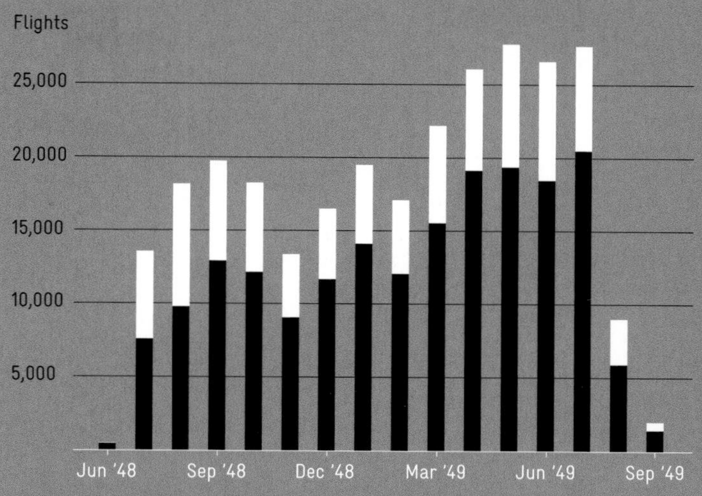
US
UK
Flights
25,000
20,000
15,000
10,000
5,000
Jun '48
Sep '48
Dec '48
Mar '49
Jun '49
Sep '49

Daily tonnage during the airlift

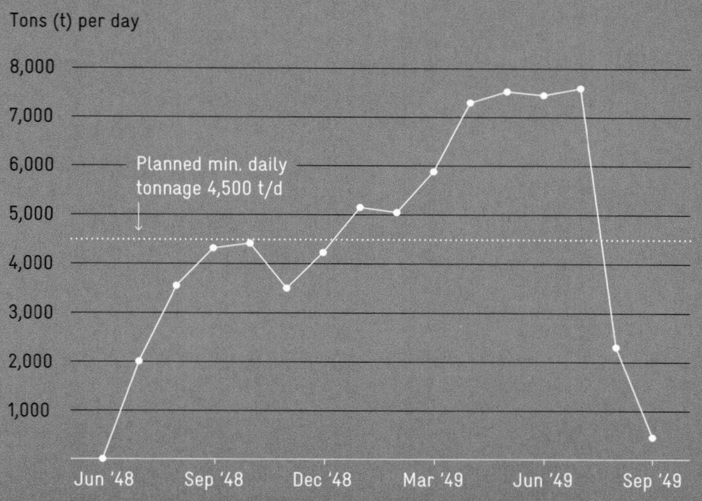
Tons (t) per day
8,000
7,000
6,000
5,000
4,000
3,000
2,000
1,000
Planned min. daily
tonnage 4,500 t/d
Jun '48
Sep '48
Dec '48
Mar '49
Jun '49
Sep '49

Total imports, in tons

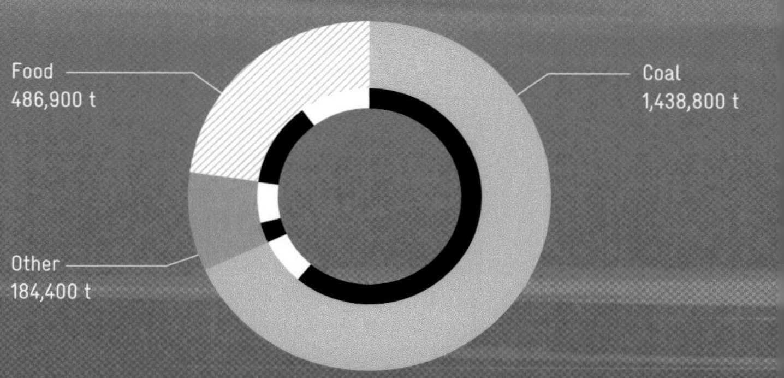
US
UK
Food
486,900 t
Coal
1,438,800 t
Other
184,400 t

Amount of Passenger Import and Export during the Airlift

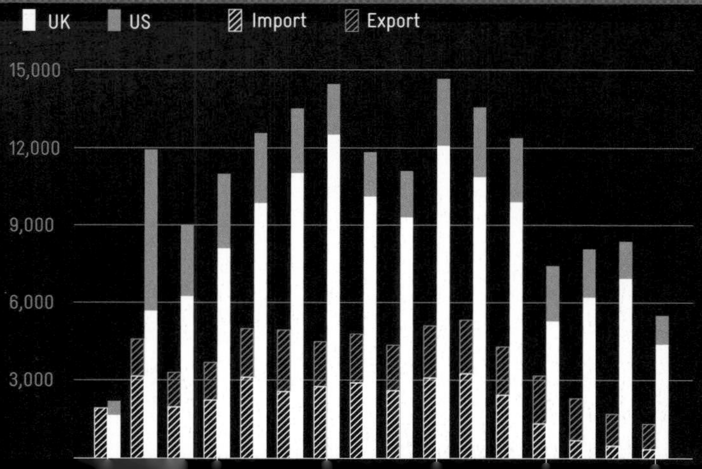
UK
US
Import
Export
15,000
12,000
9,000
6,000
3,000

After a relentless 14 months, compounded by problems in their own economy, the Soviet Union lifted the total blockade on May 12, 1949. The western allies continued delivering supplies by air.

On September 30, 1949, the airlift officially ended. The western powers had demonstrated their will to stay in West Berlin, but the Cold War was just beginning.

TRAPPED IN THE SUEZ CANAL

In 1967, Egypt and Israel went to war, making the Suez Canal the front line. The global shipping passage was brought to a standstill – with 14 ships caught in the middle as eyewitnesses. This is the story of 14 ships that took nearly 8 years to complete a 12-hour journey and the crews that turned boredom into adventure and a war zone into a front line of seafarer solidarity.

1 The morning of June 5, 1967, a convoy of 14 cargo ships entered the Suez Canal, expecting the passage through Egypt to take 12 to 16 hours.

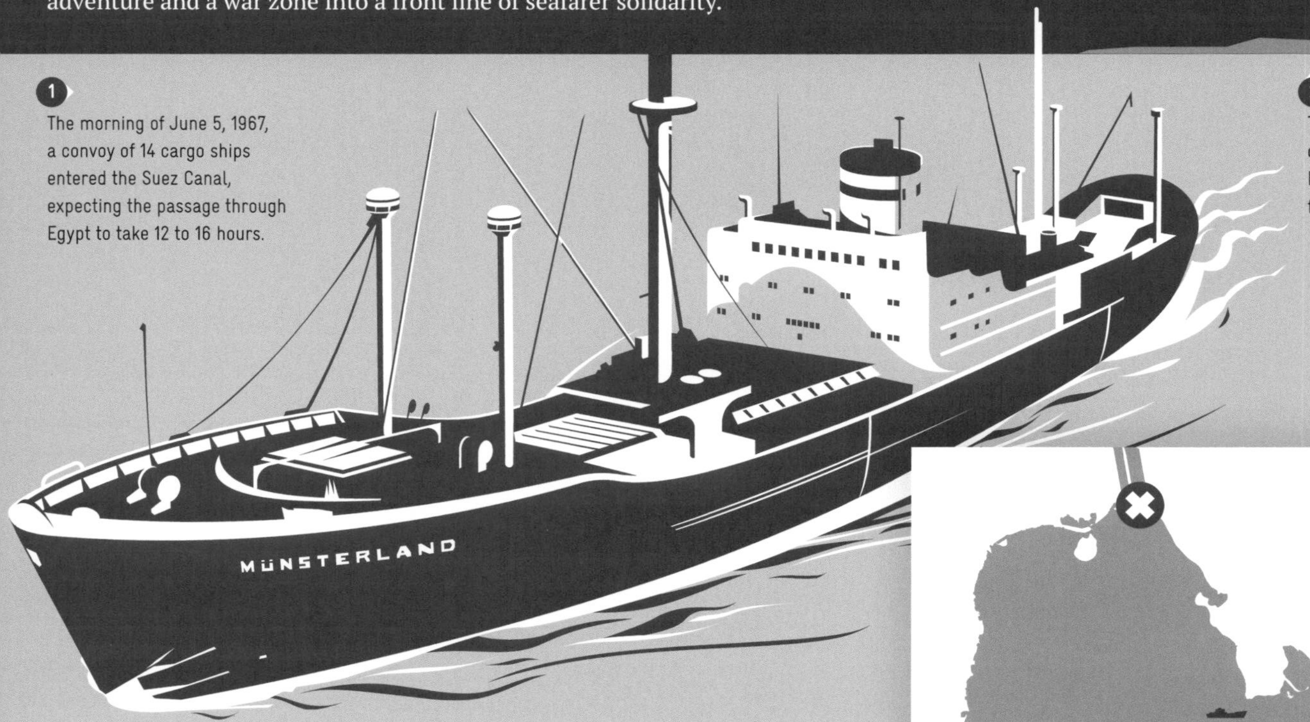
MÜNSTERLAND

2 Then the bombing started. This was the beginning of the Six-Day War between Egypt and Israel. Despite a cease-fire signed after six days of fighting, bombing went on for two weeks.

3 The ships were stranded in the Great Bitter Lake between two fronts.

As Egyptian authorities assured the captains they could continue sailing in a few days, Egyptian authorities blocked each end of the bypass. The ships were trapped and would stay there for another eight years.

Instead, Egyptian forces strategically blocked the lake's exits by sinking a dredger at the northern end and a ship at the southern end. The cargo ships were now trapped in the Great Bitter Lake. No one knew then that this blockade would last for another eight years.

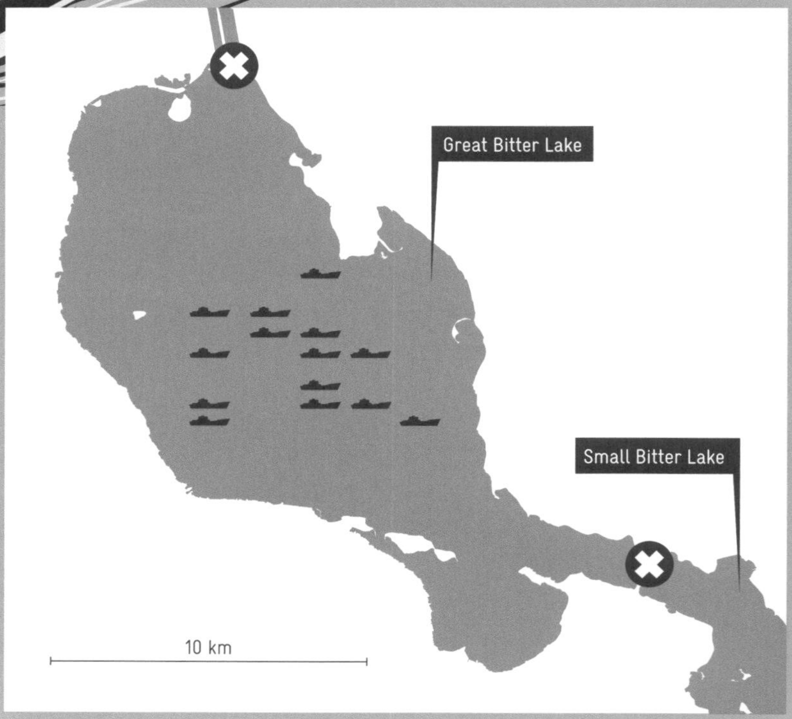
Great Bitter Lake
Small Bitter Lake
10 km

4 There were 14 ships in the Great Bitter Lake. Winds covered the vessels in yellow sand and the crew dubbed themselves the »Yellow Fleet«. To reduce maintenance costs, the ships organized themselves into 3 groups, christening the fleets with names combining the vessel names. Sailors were sent home, skeleton crews were formed to keep the ships from sinking. These teams consisted of 10 people including 1 captain, 2 engineers, 2 engineer assistants, 1 electrical engineer, 1 carpenter, 2 merchant seamen and 1 cook. All were swapped out every 6 months and accompanied by 2 Egyptian soldiers. 2 of the 14 ships, the »Vasil Levski« and »African Glen« chose not to join the collective.

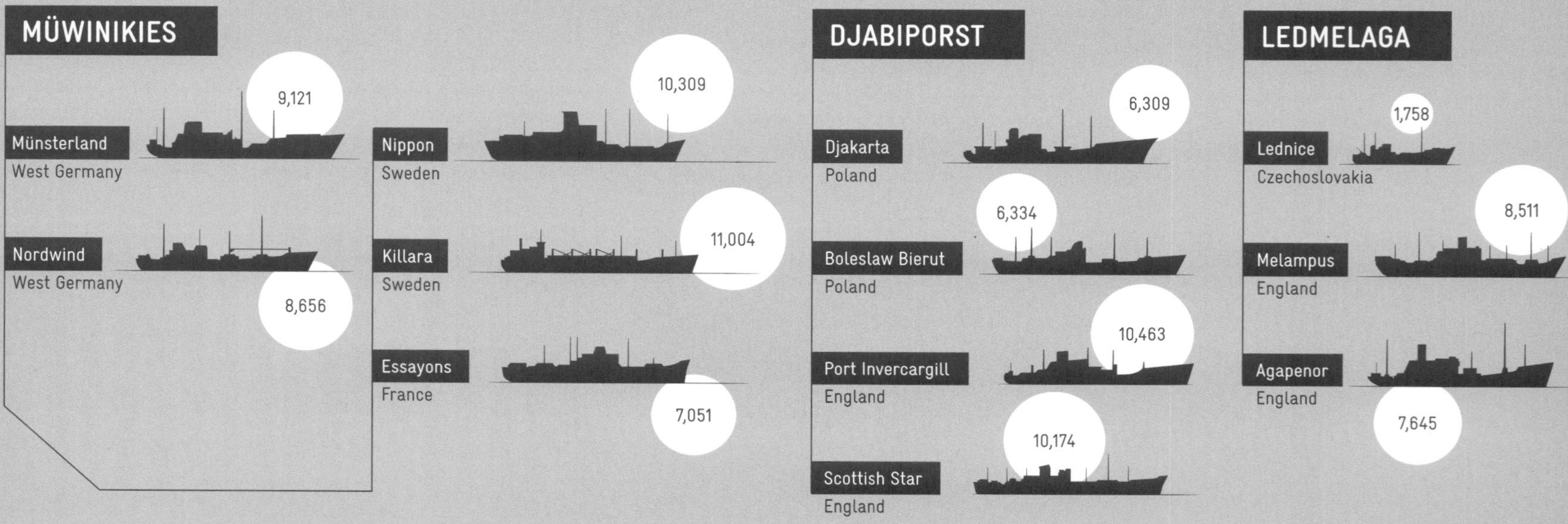
MÜWINIKIES
Münsterland
West Germany
9,121
Nordwind
West Germany
8,656
Nippon
Sweden
10,309
Killara
Sweden
11,004
Essayons
France
7,051
DJABIPORST
Djakarta
Poland
6,309
Boleslaw Bierut
Poland
6,334
Port Invercargill
England
10,463
Scottish Star
England
10,174
LEDMELAGA
Lednice
Czechoslovakia
1,758
Melampus
England
8,511
Agapenor
England
7,645

6

The Suez Canal is the shortest shipping route between Asia and Europe and is among the most important straits worldwide. Its sudden closure was a dramatic and unexpected shock for global trade.

Ships were now forced to travel the longer and more expensive route around the African continent. Higher transport costs drove up the price of goods. Certain countries saw a doubling of their shipping distances, resulting in substantial changes in trade partnerships.

Countries in Southeast Asia and eastern Africa were hit especially hard. A ship from Mumbai heading to Lisbon now had to sail 9,700 nautical miles (NM) rather than the 5,300 NM possible before the Suez Canal's closure.

5

The Suez Canal was the frontline of the crisis. Egyptian troops were on the west bank while Israeli troops occupied the east bank. The Great Bitter Lake was right in the middle of the conflict zone.

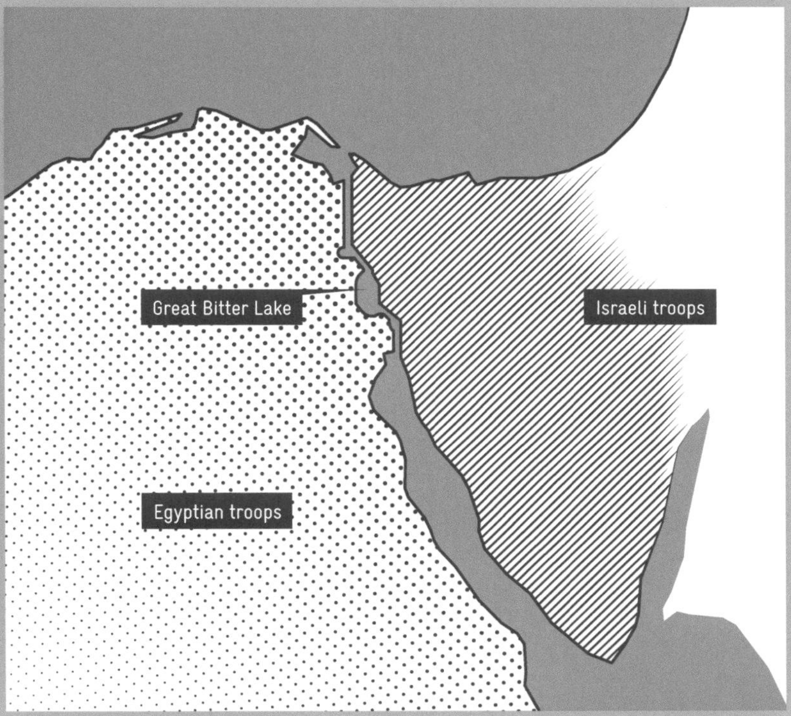
Great Bitter Lake
Israeli troops
Egyptian troops

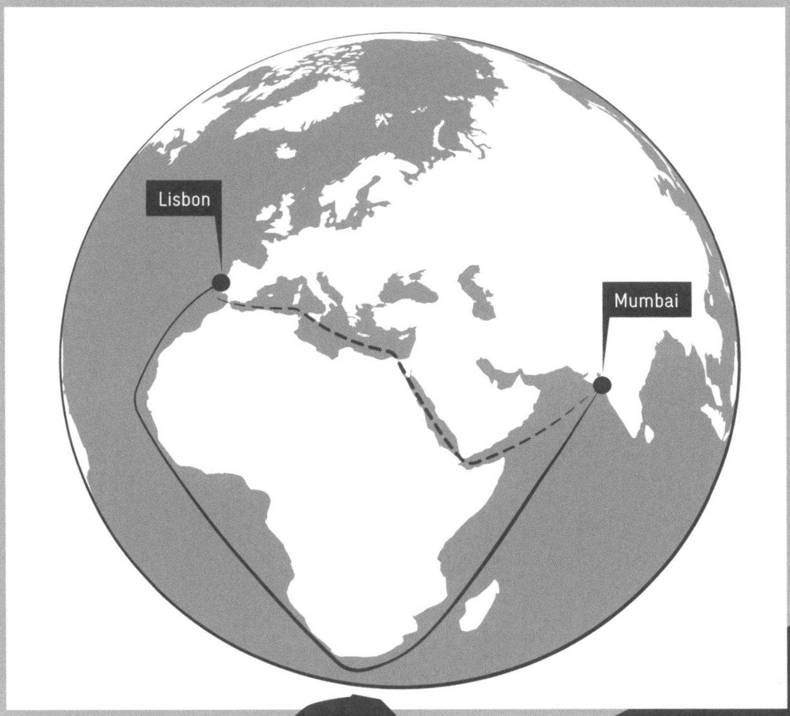
Lisbon
Mumbai

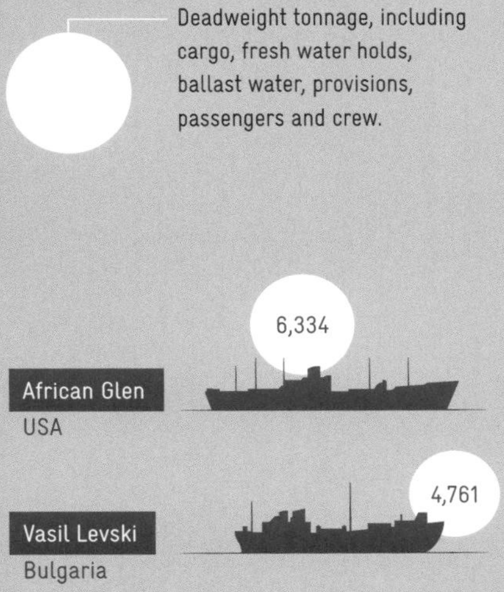
Deadweight tonnage, including cargo, fresh water holds, ballast water, provisions, passengers and crew.
6,334
African Glen
USA
4,761
Vasil Levski
Bulgaria

7

The crews that were unable to travel supported each other with much-needed camaraderie. These isolated eyewitnesses of many years of tension around the Sinai Peninsula formed the Great Bitter Lake Association.

8

The shipping companies turned to their cargo—especially those carrying foodstuffs—to sustain sailors for some time.

9

Church services were held every Sunday and collective meals were regularly prepared, supported by a vegetable garden grown on the deck of France's MS Essayons. Even Christmas was celebrated together on the decks.

10

They sent postcards and letters from these adventures to loved ones at home. Often bearing unique »postage stamps« created on board, these missives have become widely sought collector's items among stamp collectors.

11

The shipmen also kept fit on board. Competitive sporting events ranged from rescue boat regattas to swimming or soccer tournaments, and even a Bitter Lake Olympic Games in 1968. Medals were awarded for various events, with the Polish team taking the year's crown.

12

After a long series of negotiations with the Egyptian government, 12 German sailors were allowed to visit Cairo and the pyramids.

13

Six years after the Six-Day War, the Arab world sought revenge for their 1967 loss. The Yom Kippur War began on October 6, 1973. This time, the Egyptians had also enlisted Syria to fight with them against Israel. Israel was completely surprised by the attack, launched on the holiest day in Judaism. It took days for the Israelis to regain their positions before advancing against the Arab armies.

14

Superpower pressure on the warring parties led to a ceasefire agreement on October 25, unanimously passed as Resolution 340 in the United Nations Security Council. After years of standstill, the canal, including the Great Bitter Lake, was a stagnant cesspool of equipment and artillery.

15

After the troops were recalled, naval units began freeing the canal from mines and war wreckage. They removed 3 sand dams, excavators filled with cement, 20 semi trucks, at least 8 tanks and more than 100 small boats and barges clogging the waterway. A further 750,000 mines were removed from the banks. The clean-up took almost two years. During this time, German engineers were working on getting the MS Münsterland and the MS Nordwind ready for the passage home.

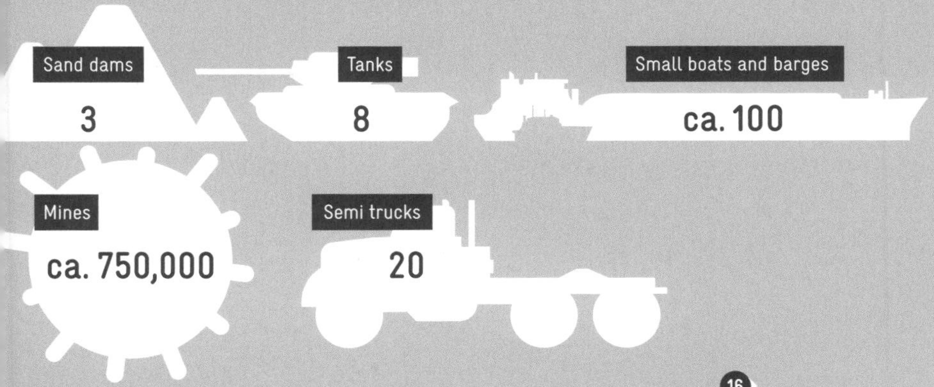
Sand dams
3
Tanks
8
Small boats and barges
ca. 100
Mines
ca. 750,000
Semi trucks
20

16

On June 5, 1975, the day finally arrived for the Yellow Fleet's seamen to say goodbye to the Great Bitter Lake—and to one another.

17

The German ships were the only ones to return to their ports under their own power. When they came home, around 30,000 spectators greeted them as they reached the Kiel Canal. Even today, the story of the Yellow Fleet remains one of the most moving episodes of seafaring history—not only for its exceptionalism, but also for the beacon of optimism, camaraderie and mutual support in the face of an apparently hopeless situation shown by its formidable sailing crews.

»MY GOD, I'VE BEEN HIT«

John F. Kennedy is on his election campaign tour through the USA. Cheering crowds welcome the President in Dallas, Texas, when he turns onto Elm Street in his limousine. At 12:30 pm, three shots ring out. Fatally hit, the President slumps, and Texas governor John Connally is also seriously wounded. Kennedy's death triggers shock and horror all over the world. Even today, more than 55 years later, his assassination provides a lot of fuel for conspiracy theories.

November 22, 1963 · Dealey Plaza in Dallas, Texas · 12:30 pm

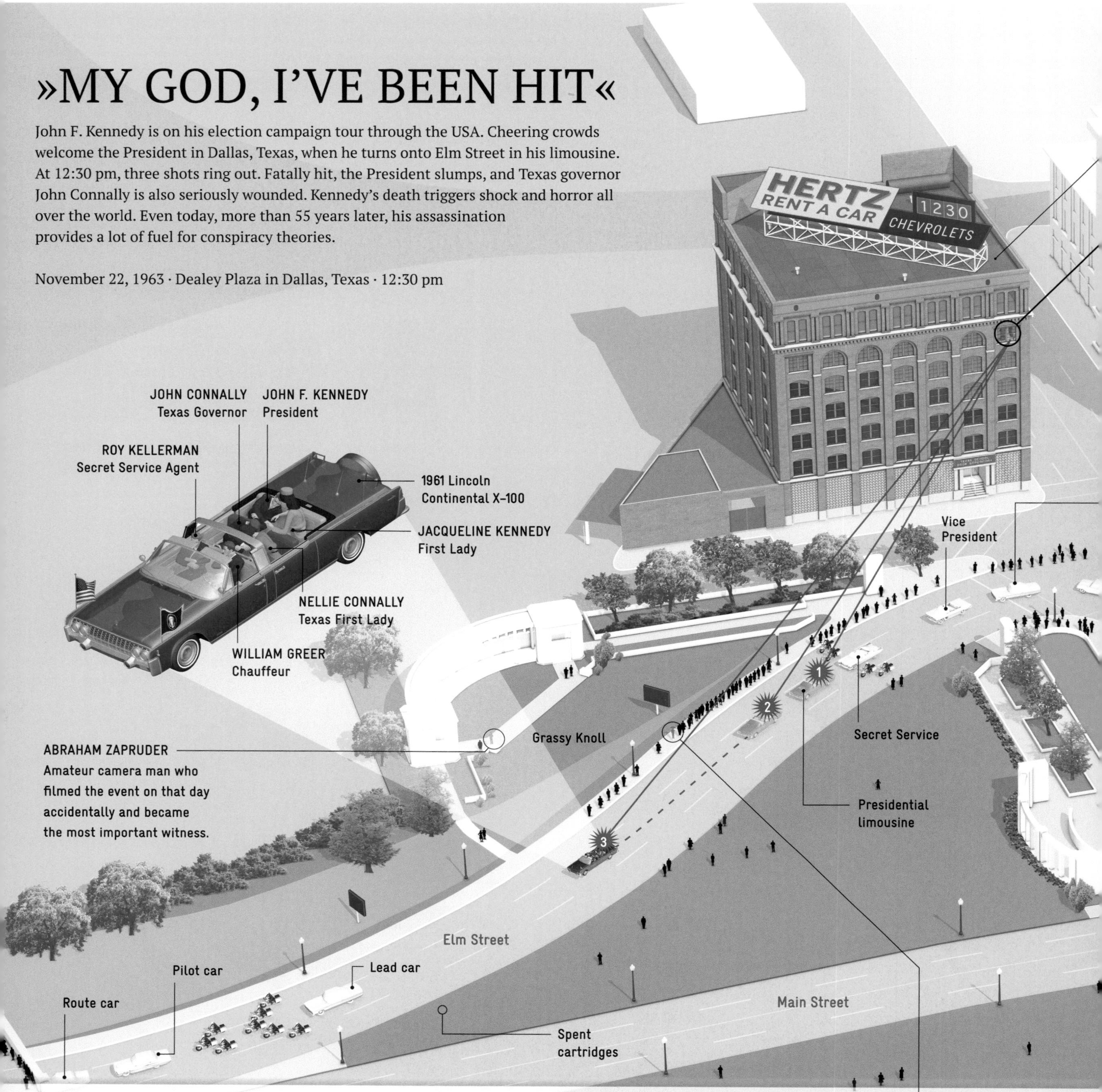
HERTZ
RENT A CAR
1230
CHEVROLETS
JOHN CONNALLY
Texas Governor
JOHN F. KENNEDY
President
ROY KELLERMAN
Secret Service Agent
1961 Lincoln
Continental X-100
JACQUELINE KENNEDY
First Lady
NELLIE CONNALLY
Texas First Lady
WILLIAM GREER
Chauffeur
Vice
President
ABRAHAM ZAPRUDER
Amateur camera man who filmed the event on that day accidentally and became the most important witness.
Grassy Knoll
Secret Service
Presidential
limousine
1
2
3
Elm Street
Main Street
Pilot car
Lead car
Route car
Spent
cartridges

Food for conspiracy theories. Even more than 55 years later there are still unanswered questions.

Was there a shot from the front?

Several hundred spectators made statements that differed from the official report of the Warren Commission. 50 witnesses were convinced they heard shots coming from the Grassy Knoll and therefore from the front.

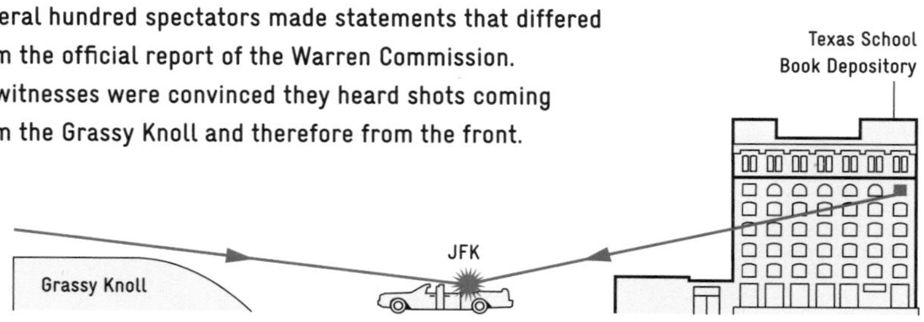
Texas School
Book Depository
JFK
Grassy Knoll

Did the »umbrella man« play a role?

On this sunny day, one single spectator holds an opened umbrella at the roadside. As the Lincoln approaches, the man lifts the umbrella high above his head. A signal for another shooter?

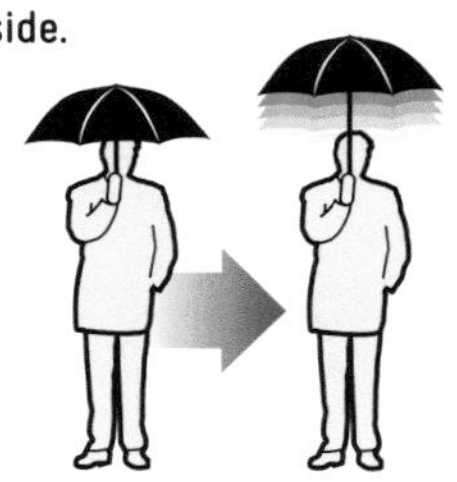

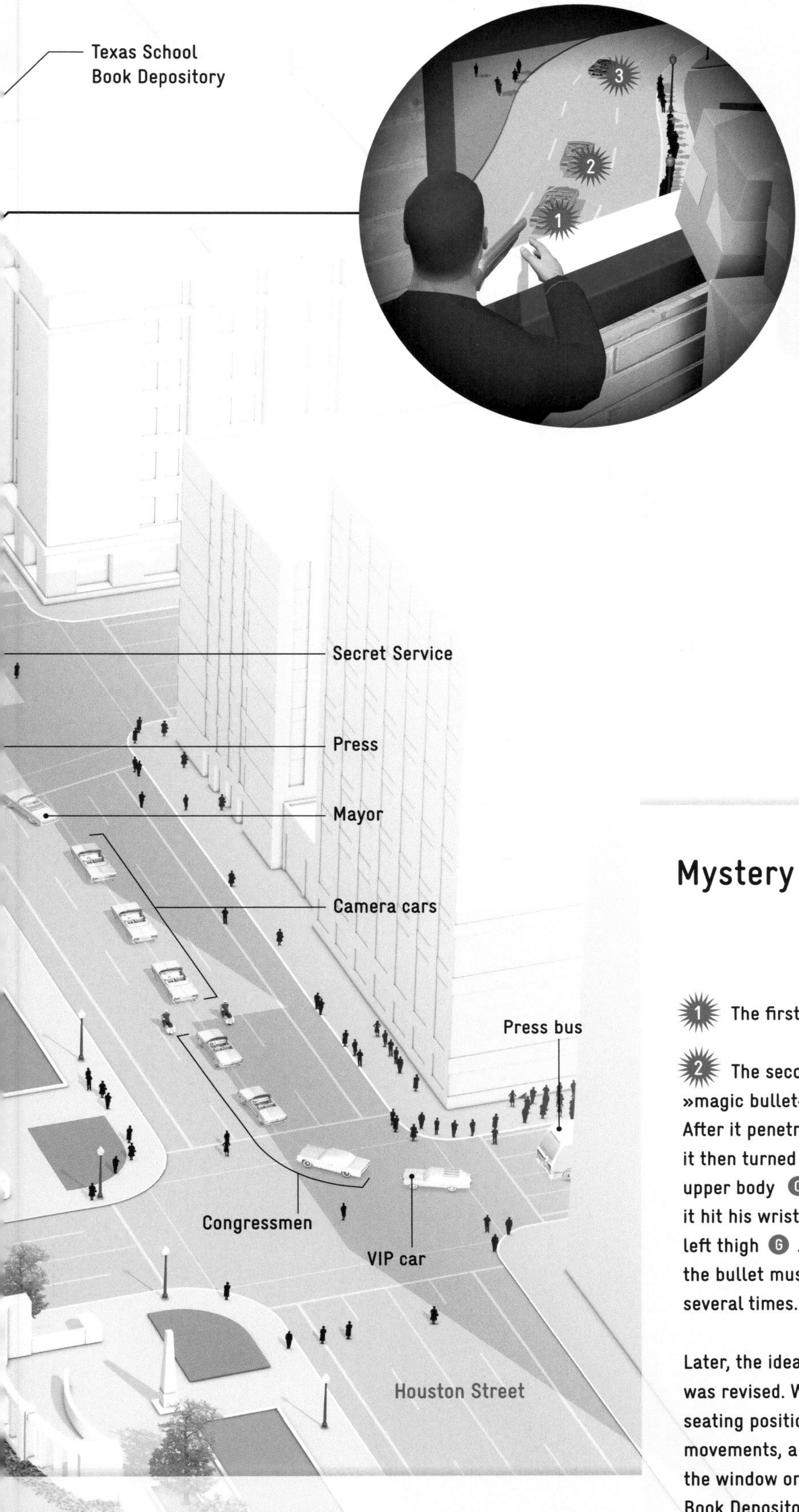
Texas School
Book Depository
Secret Service
Press
Mayor
Camera cars
Press bus
Congressmen
VIP car
Houston Street

Death of an assassin

Lee Harvey Oswald was the main suspect in Kennedy's assassination. The case seemed clear: According to the Warren Commission, he fired from a window on the fifth floor of the »Texas School Book Depository« at the President who was passing in front of the building with his convoy. Behind a pile of book boxes, police found a repeater with rifle scope and three empty bullet casings. Jack Ruby, who supposedly had connections to the Mafia, shot Lee Harvey Oswald only two days after his arrest when Oswald was transferred to the state prison. Oswald was murdered even before charges were brought against him.

The persons shown represent the questioned witnesses.

Three or four shots?

81% of the witnesses reported hearing three shots. But recordings made by the motorcycle police officer's radio contact between Kennedy's escort and the police station led investigators to conclude there was a 95% likelihood that a fourth shot was fired.

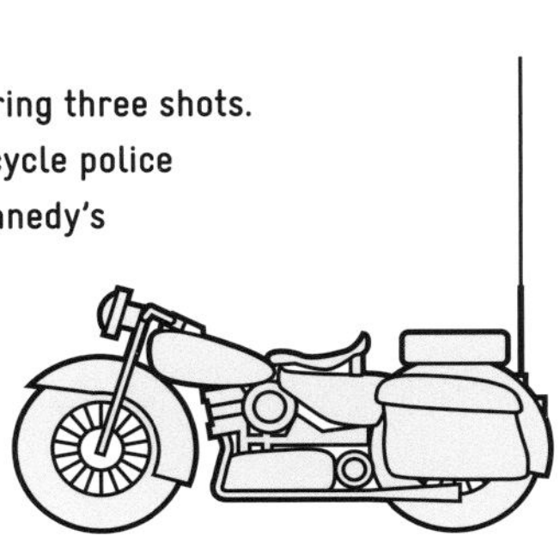

Mystery of the »magic bullet«

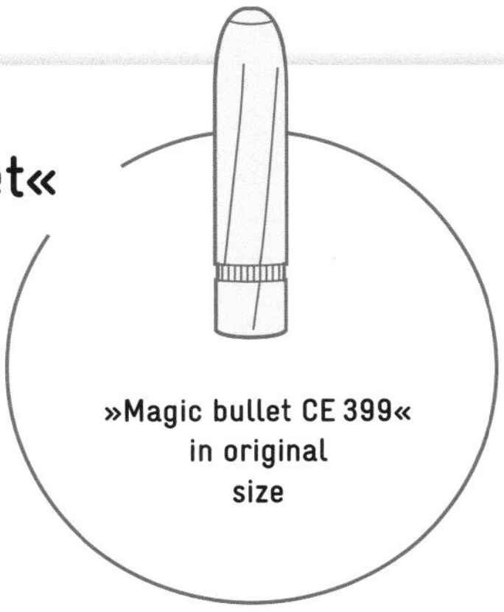
»Magic bullet CE 399«
in original
size

(1) The first bullet missed its target.

(2) The second bullet, also called the »magic bullet«, caused seven injuries: After it penetrated Kennedy's neck (A) (B), it then turned right, then left and hit Connally's upper body (C) (D). After another right turn, it hit his wrist (E) (F) and got stuck in his left thigh (G). To cause all these injuries, the bullet must have changed its direction several times.

Later, the idea of the uncontrolled bullet was revised. With revised seating heights, seating positions and Connally's head movements, a straight shooting line from the window on the »Texas School Book Depository's« fifth floor seems possible. But this latest view still does not provide an explanation for the intactness of the bullet.

(3) The third shot fatally hits Kennedy in the back of his head.

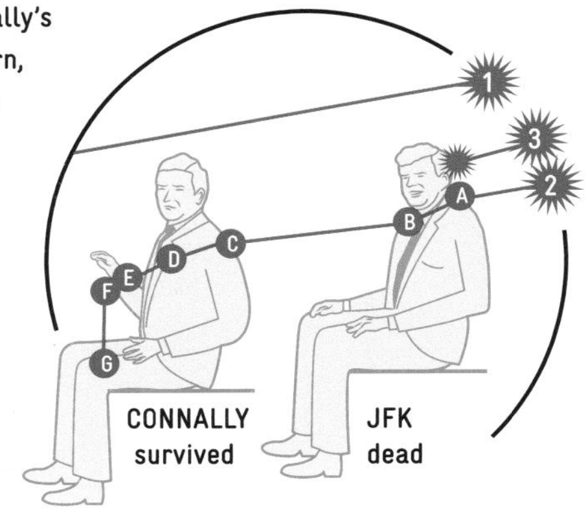
CONNALLY
survived
JFK
dead

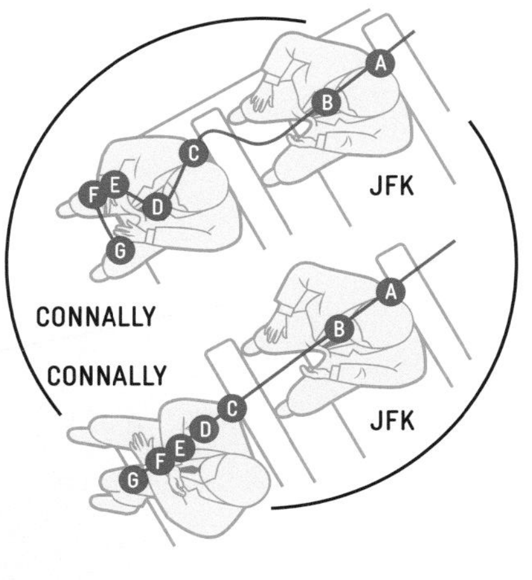
JFK
CONNALLY
CONNALLY
JFK

THE GREAT TRAIN ROBBERY

August 8, 1963, 3 a.m.: In a spectacular raid on the mail train of Britain's Royal Mail en route from Glasgow to London, a 17-member gang steals the impressive sum of £2,631,684 in just 15 minutes—without a shot being fired. Before that, in November 1962, a raid is made on the wages of the airline »BOAC« at London airport. The perpetrators overwhelm the couriers and steal £62,500. At least five, maybe six, of the Royal Mail train robbers are involved in the attack and secure the funding for the largest train robbery of all time.

1 Roger Cordrey covers the green railway signal from the gallery above the tracks with a glove. With a battery, he powers the red signal. John Daly changes the signal 1,400 meters north to yellow. Roy James cuts the telephone wires leading to the surrounding farms.

2 The mail train comes to a stop at the Sears Crossing signal. Stoker David Whitby runs for a distance telephone. On his way, two masked men attack him.

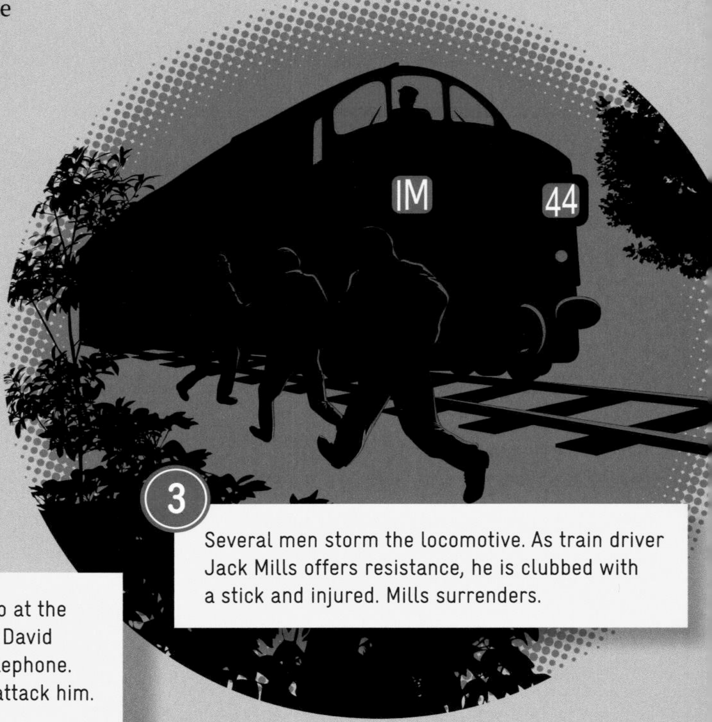

3 Several men storm the locomotive. As train driver Jack Mills offers resistance, he is clubbed with a stick and injured. Mills surrenders.

4 Two men disengage the coupling at the back of the second carriage.

5 Now, the engine has to be moved 1,200 meters further to Bridego Bridge. A retired engine driver hired for this job fails. Mills is forced to set the locomotive with the two remaining cars in motion.

6 Leader Bruce Reynolds and his brother-in-law John Daly follow the train in a Land Rover on the parallel country road.

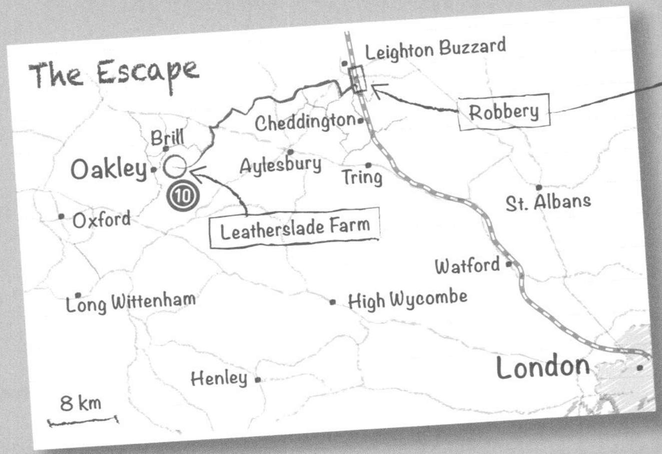

7 At Bridego Bridge the track meets the road. The train stops. Charlie Wilson and seven robbers storm the second wagon. They overwhelm the postal workers and break the lock on the rear of the wagon. More than 120 mail bags with money await them.

8 The robbers create a chain from the river bank to the bridge. In a matter of minutes, they load 108 sacks out of the train car into two Landrovers and a truck.

9 After 15 minutes, the robbery is over. Mills and Whitby are locked in with the postal workers—for 30 minutes none of them are allowed to move. The gang leaves for Leatherslade Farm near Oakley. The radio is tuned to police radio.

The Robbery

100 m

Main Line
Glasgow–London

↓ Bruce Reynolds

Minor Signal
①

Redborough Farm

↓ John Daly

Train →

Signal Bridge
Sears Crossing

④
↓ Roger Cordrey
↓ Bill Jennings
↓ Jimmy White

Ronald Biggs ↓
Gordon Goody ↓
Jim Hussey ↓ ③
↓ Roy James

Charlie Wilson ↓
Tommy Wisbey ↓
Frank Munroe ↓

↓ Alf Thomas
↓ Robert Welch

B 488

Escape Route to
Leatherslade Farm

↓ to London

Trucks, two Landrovers

Rowden Farm

Bridego Bridge

↓ to Mentmore

⑧

After 45 minutes, just as the vehicles arrive at Leatherslade Farm, the police radio comes to life. »You will not believe it, but they have just stolen a train!«

Within months, the police detains 12 of the 17 gang members. They left many fingerprints and other traces in their hideout, Leatherslade Farm.

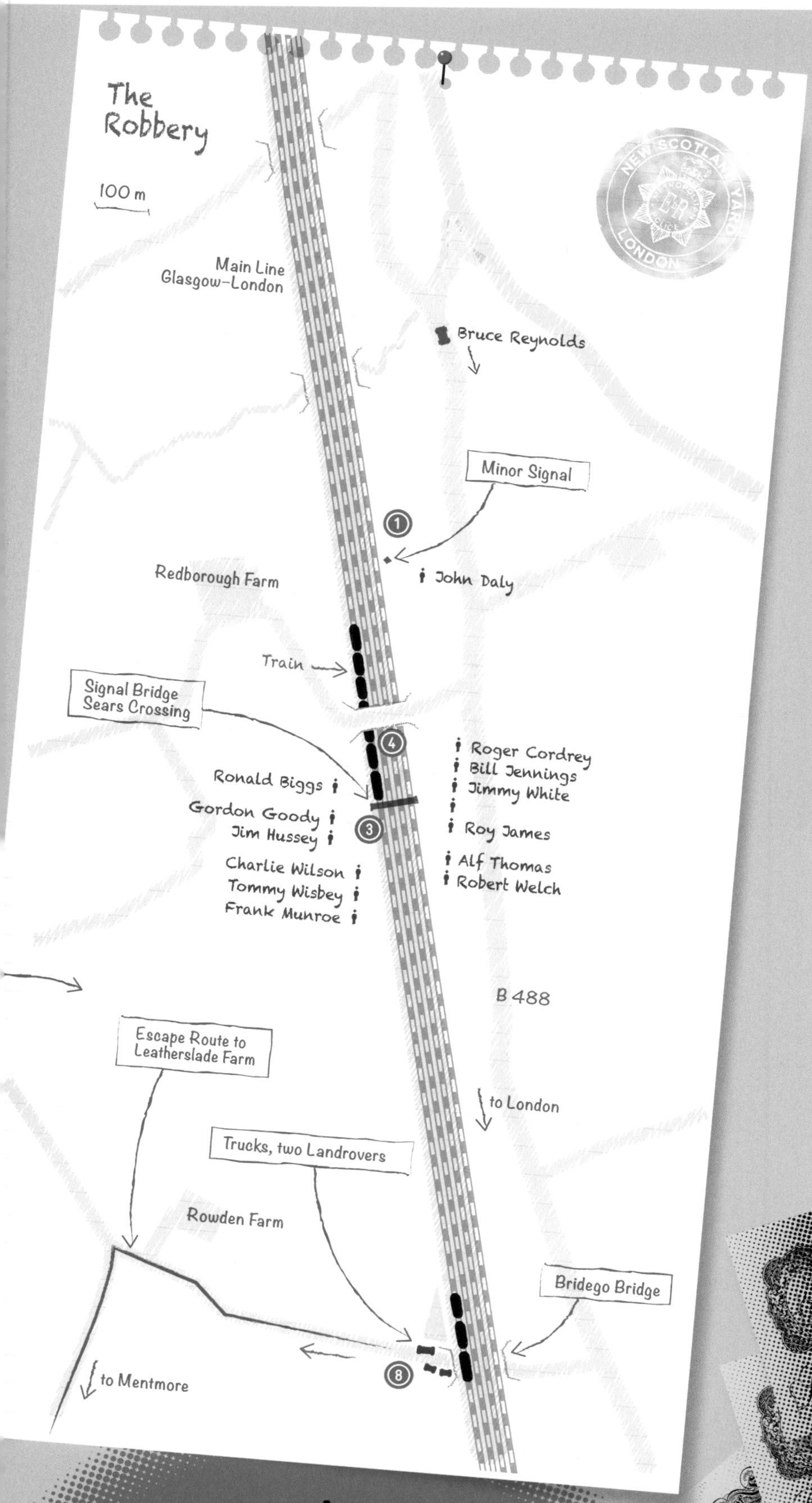

Where's the cash?
10 gangsters blow the whistle

TOTAL STOLEN:
£ 2,631,684

Present day values around 40M pounds or 48M Euro

£4000	spent in prison
£12,850	to accomplices
£111,500	lost or stolen
£168,400	escape
£180,100	legal expenses
£231,500	money in safe deposit
£322,873	expenditure
£339,153	found by police
£81,684	bribes
£1,179,624	remaining share

£2,631,684

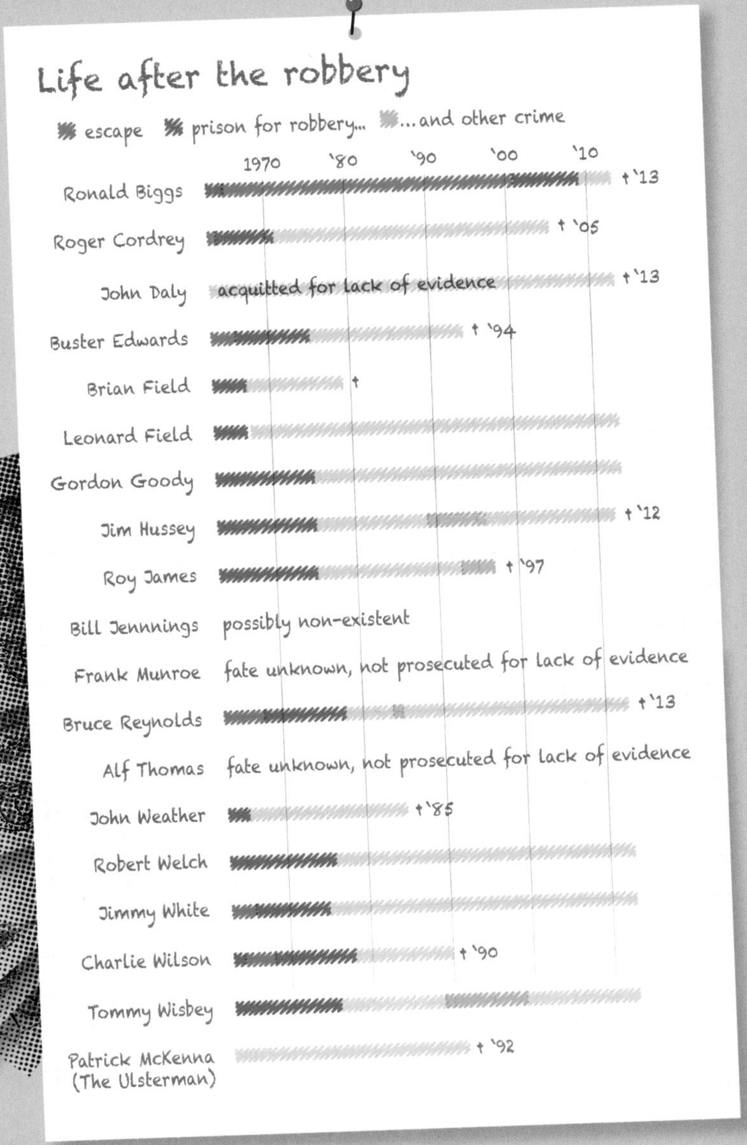

Life after the robbery

▨ escape ▨ prison for robbery... ▨ ...and other crime

1970 '80 '90 '00 '10

Ronald Biggs ▨▨▨▨▨ † '13
Roger Cordrey ▨▨▨ † '05
John Daly — acquitted for lack of evidence † '13
Buster Edwards ▨▨ † '94
Brian Field ▨ †
Leonard Field ▨
Gordon Goody ▨▨
Jim Hussey ▨▨ † '12
Roy James ▨▨▨ † '97
Bill Jennings — possibly non-existent
Frank Munroe — fate unknown, not prosecuted for lack of evidence
Bruce Reynolds ▨▨▨ † '13
Alf Thomas — fate unknown, not prosecuted for lack of evidence
John Weather ▨ † '85
Robert Welch ▨▨
Jimmy White ▨▨
Charlie Wilson ▨▨ † '90
Tommy Wisbey ▨▨
Patrick McKenna
(The Ulsterman) ▨ † '92

ATTACK ON THE WORLD TRADE CENTER

The images of two planes crashing into the World Trade Center on September 11, 2001, has been seared into our collective memory. In the four attacks, 2,996 people lost their lives, including 343 firefighters, 72 police officers and 19 terrorists. More than 6,000 people were injured and an estimated $10 billion in damage was caused.

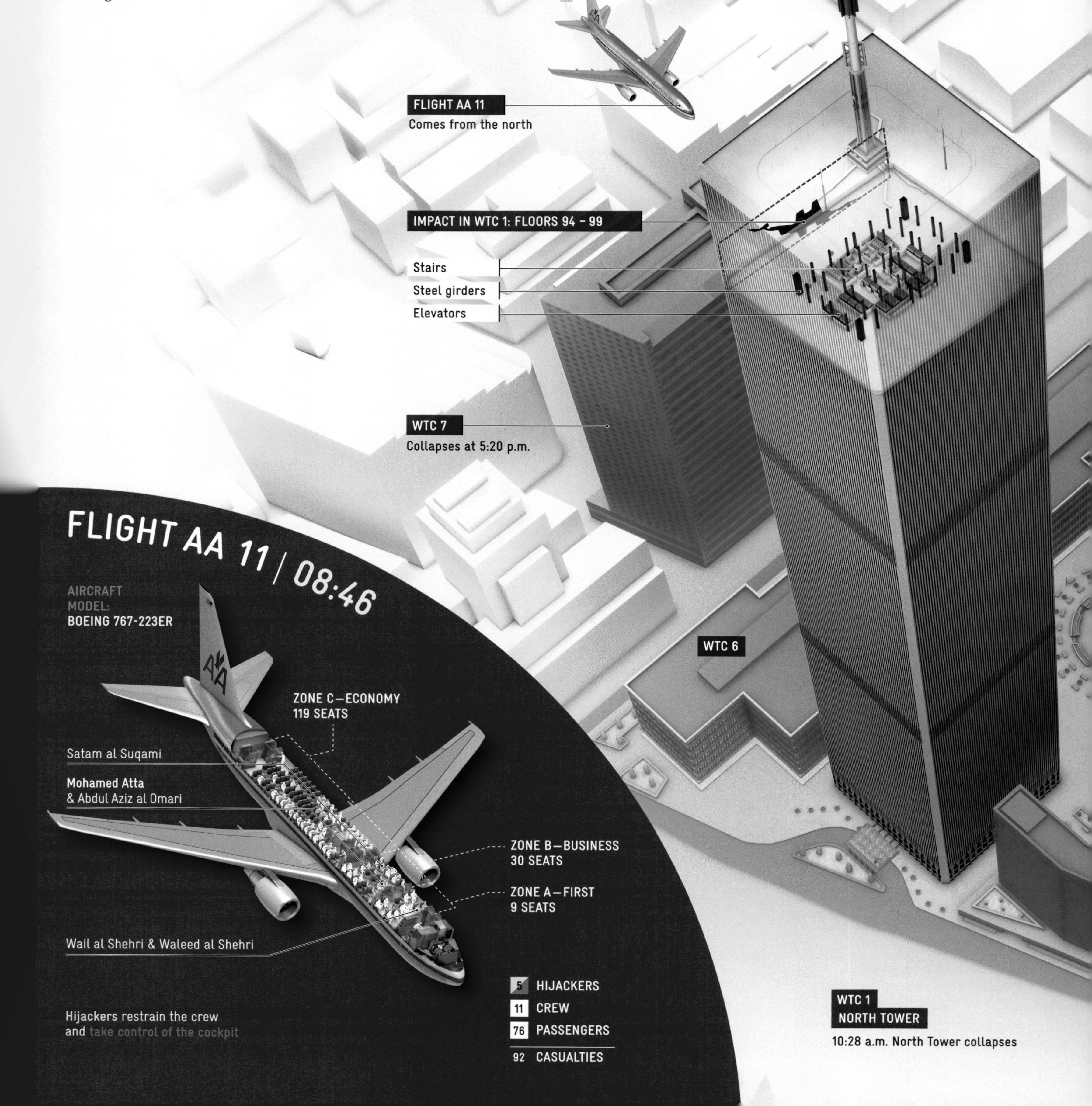
FLIGHT AA 11
Comes from the north
IMPACT IN WTC 1: FLOORS 94 - 99
Stairs
Steel girders
Elevators
WTC 7
Collapses at 5:20 p.m.
WTC 6
WTC 1
NORTH TOWER
10:28 a.m. North Tower collapses
FLIGHT AA 11 / 08:46
AIRCRAFT MODEL:
BOEING 767-223ER
ZONE C—ECONOMY
119 SEATS
Satam al Suqami
Mohamed Atta
& Abdul Aziz al Omari
ZONE B—BUSINESS
30 SEATS
ZONE A—FIRST
9 SEATS
Wail al Shehri & Waleed al Shehri
Hijackers restrain the crew and take control of the cockpit
5 HIJACKERS
11 CREW
76 PASSENGERS
92 CASUALTIES

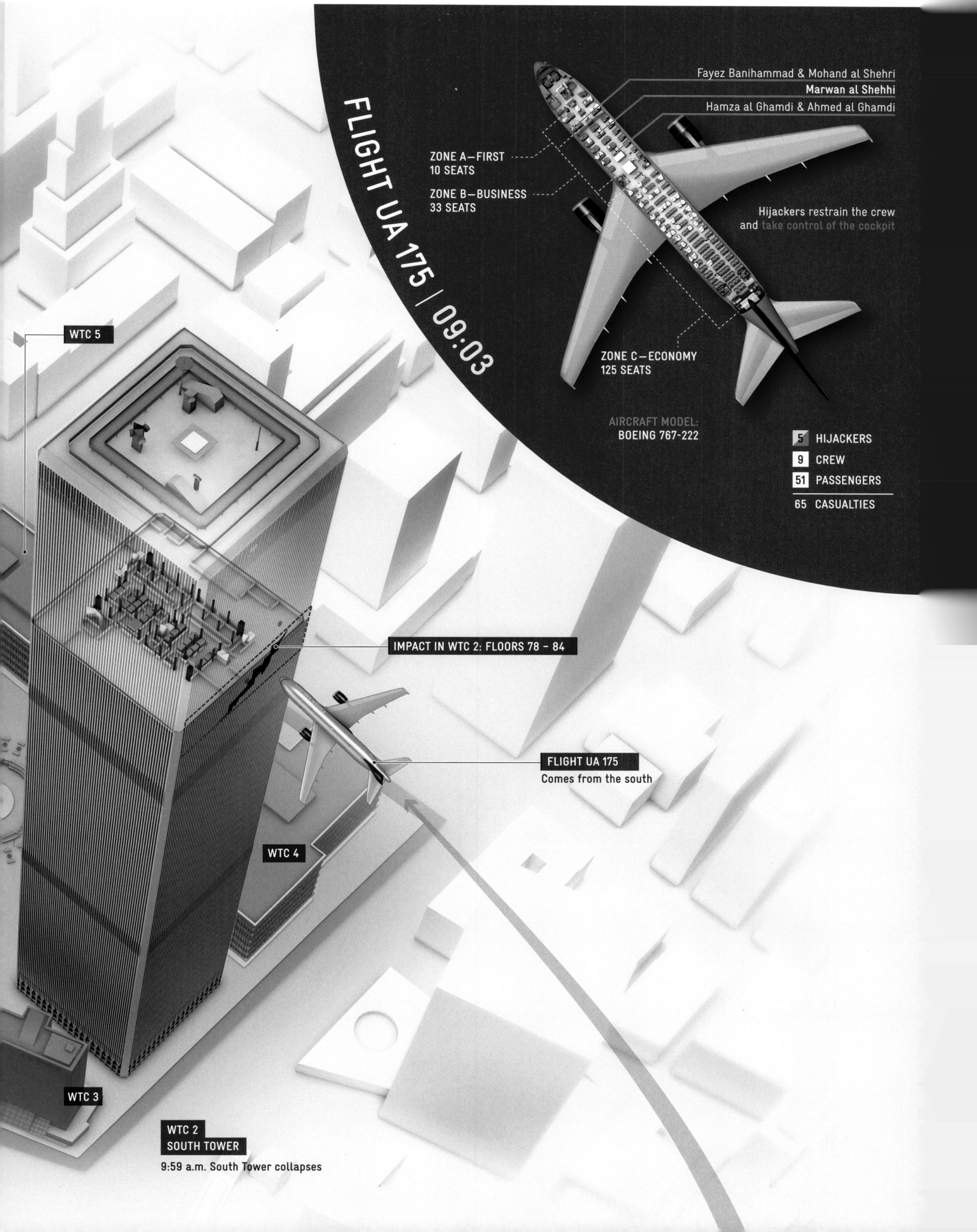
FLIGHT UA 175 | 09:03
Fayez Banihammad & Mohand al Shehri
Marwan al Shehhi
Hamza al Ghamdi & Ahmed al Ghamdi
ZONE A—FIRST
10 SEATS
ZONE B—BUSINESS
33 SEATS
Hijackers restrain the crew and take control of the cockpit
ZONE C—ECONOMY
125 SEATS
AIRCRAFT MODEL:
BOEING 767-222
5 HIJACKERS
9 CREW
51 PASSENGERS
65 CASUALTIES
WTC 5
IMPACT IN WTC 2: FLOORS 78 - 84
FLIGHT UA 175
Comes from the south
WTC 4
WTC 3
WTC 2
SOUTH TOWER
9:59 a.m. South Tower collapses

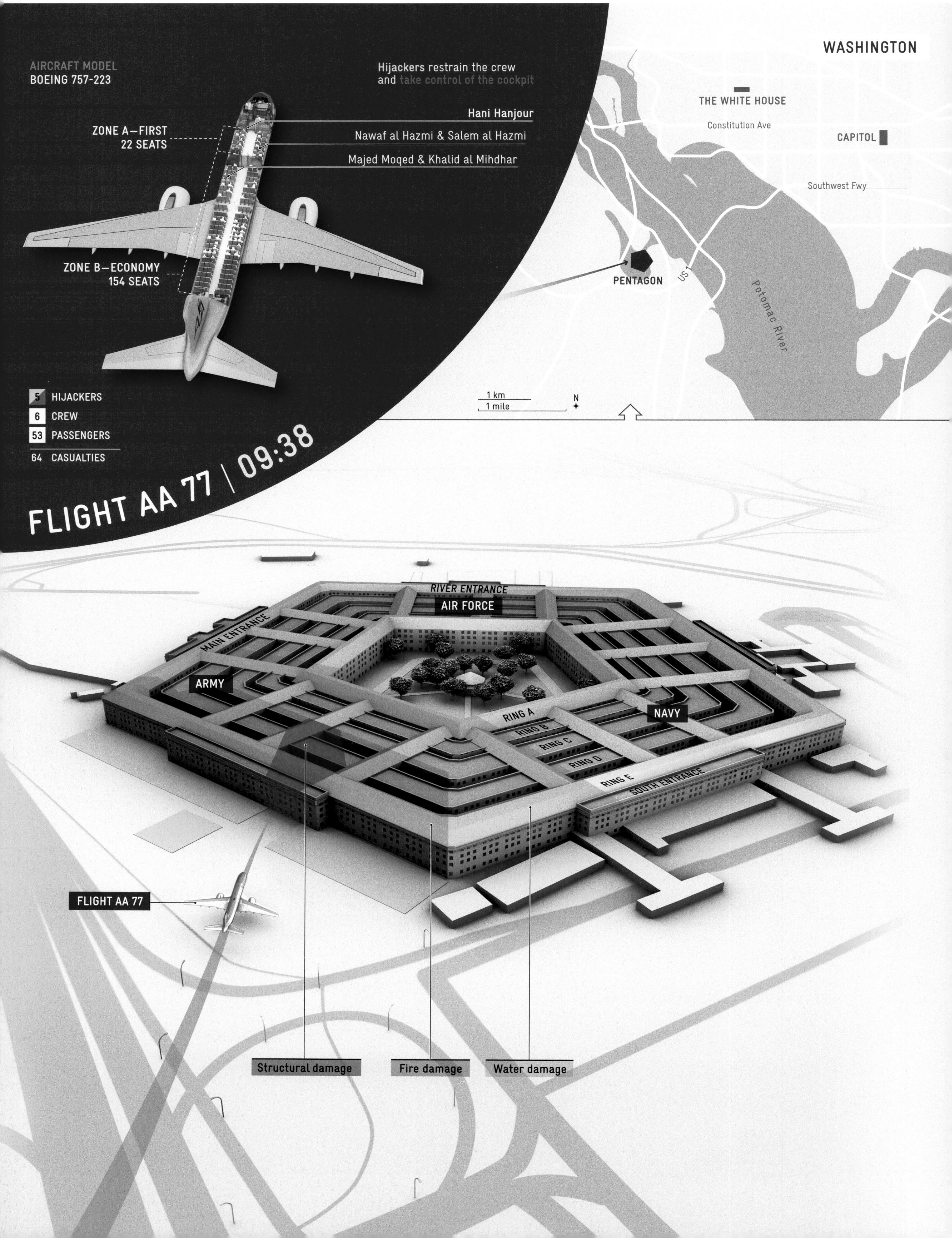
FLIGHT AA 77 | 09:38
AIRCRAFT MODEL
BOEING 757-223
Hijackers restrain the crew
and take control of the cockpit
ZONE A—FIRST
22 SEATS
ZONE B—ECONOMY
154 SEATS
Hani Hanjour
Nawaf al Hazmi & Salem al Hazmi
Majed Moqed & Khalid al Mihdhar
5 HIJACKERS
6 CREW
53 PASSENGERS
64 CASUALTIES
WASHINGTON
THE WHITE HOUSE
Constitution Ave
CAPITOL
Southwest Fwy
PENTAGON
US 1
Potomac River
1 km
1 mile
N
RIVER ENTRANCE
AIR FORCE
MAIN ENTRANCE
ARMY
NAVY
RING A
RING B
RING C
RING D
RING E
SOUTH ENTRANCE
FLIGHT AA 77
Structural damage
Fire damage
Water damage

ATTACK ON THE PENTAGON AND THE HEROES OF UA93

Half an hour after the planes crashed into the WTC, Flight AA77 hit its target, the Pentagon. All 64 people on board as well as 125 people in the US Department of Defense headquaters were killed. It is suspected that the fourth plane, UA93, targeted the White House, but the passengers were able to overpower the highjackers and crashed the plane into a field. None of the 40 passengers and four terrorists survived. Their actions, however, saved countless lives.

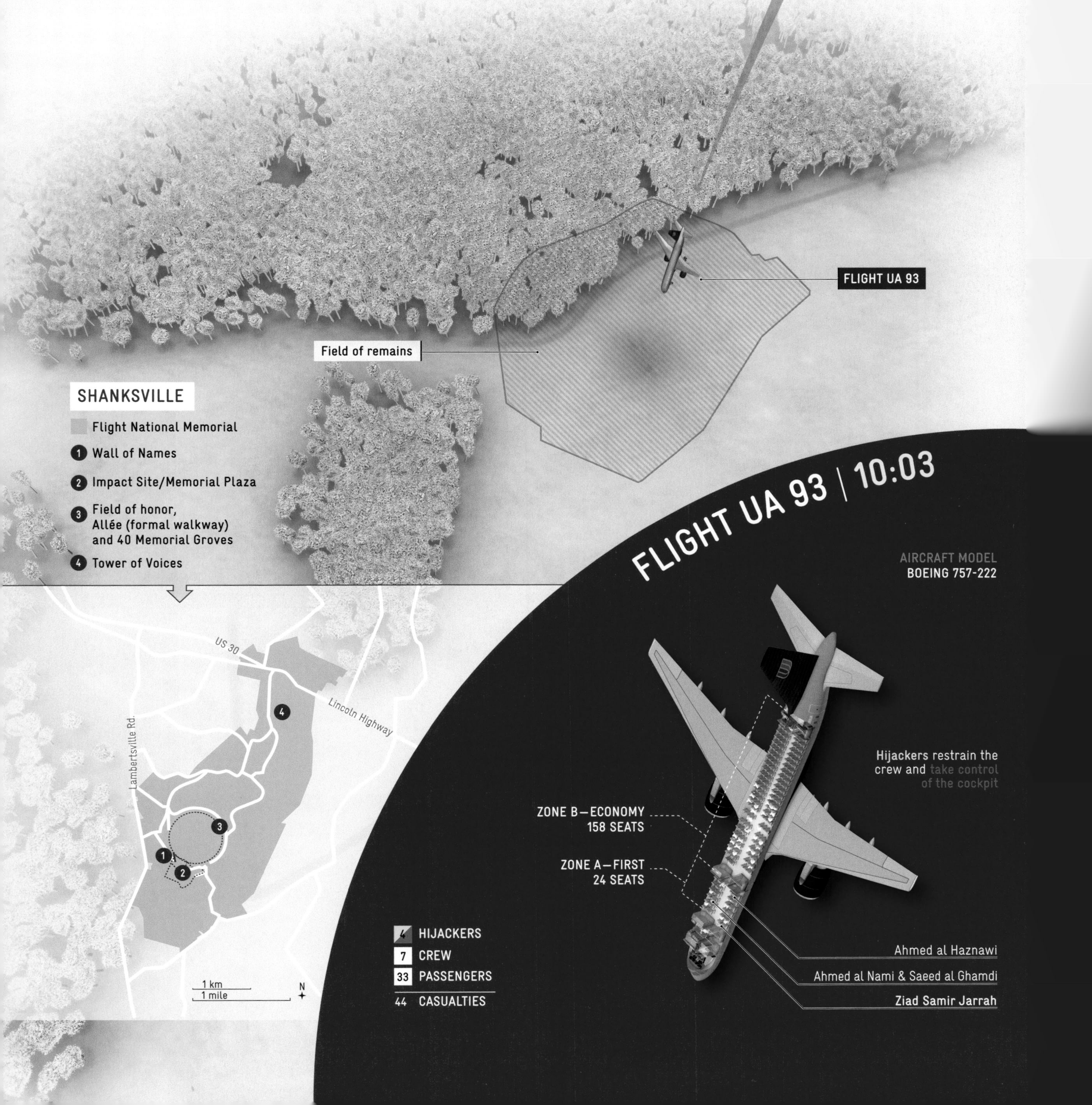

FLIGHT UA 93
Field of remains
SHANKSVILLE
Flight National Memorial
1 Wall of Names
2 Impact Site/Memorial Plaza
3 Field of honor, Allée (formal walkway) and 40 Memorial Groves
4 Tower of Voices
US 30
Lincoln Highway
Lambertsville Rd.
1 km
1 mile
N
FLIGHT UA 93 | 10:03
AIRCRAFT MODEL
BOEING 757-222
Hijackers restrain the crew and take control of the cockpit
ZONE B—ECONOMY
158 SEATS
ZONE A—FIRST
24 SEATS
4 HIJACKERS
7 CREW
33 PASSENGERS
44 CASUALTIES
Ahmed al Haznawi
Ahmed al Nami & Saeed al Ghamdi
Ziad Samir Jarrah

TRACING THE TERRORISTS

The World Trade Center attacks were two years in the making. Each participant made their way to the United States via various pathways and set up a life for themselves with a single goal in mind.

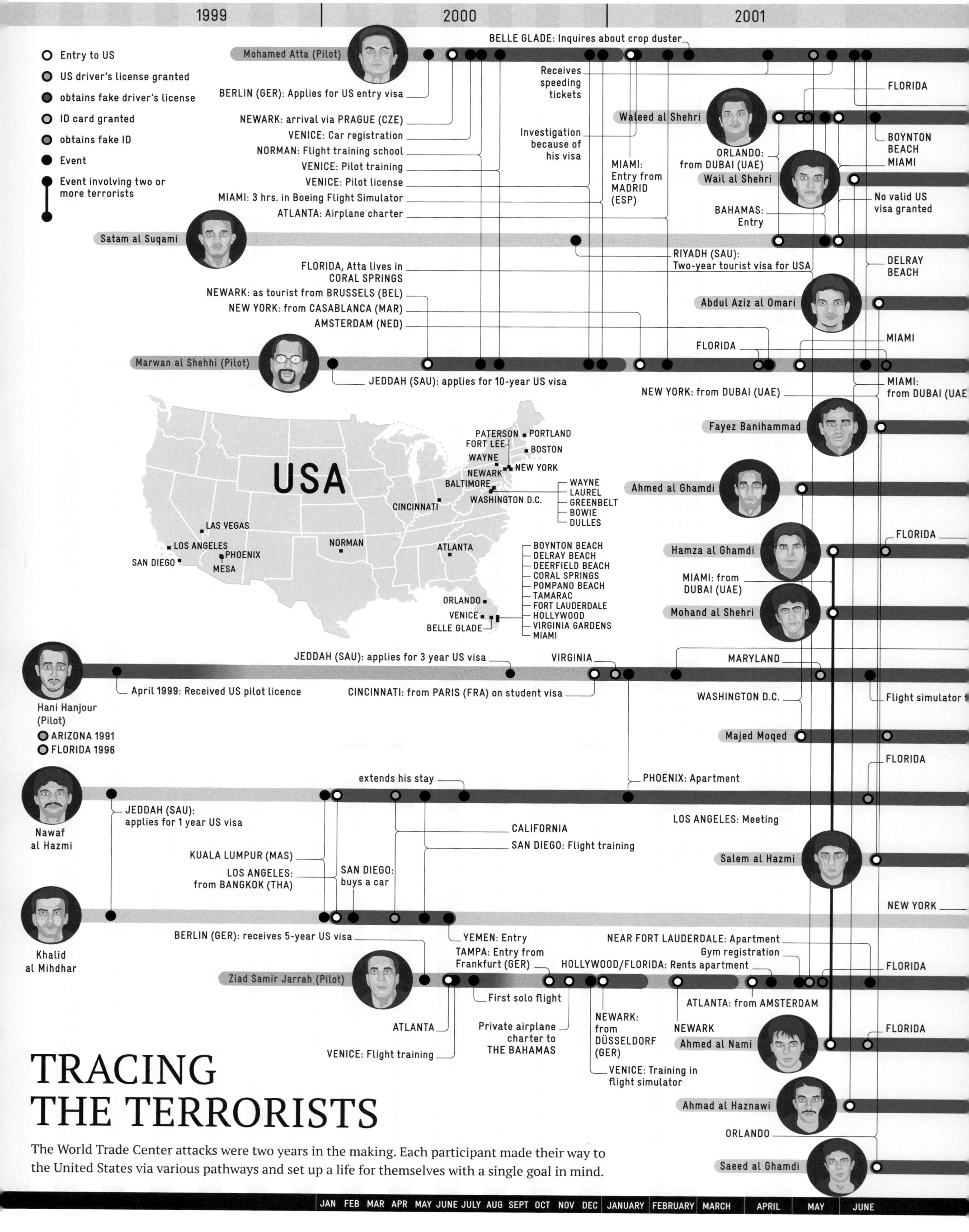

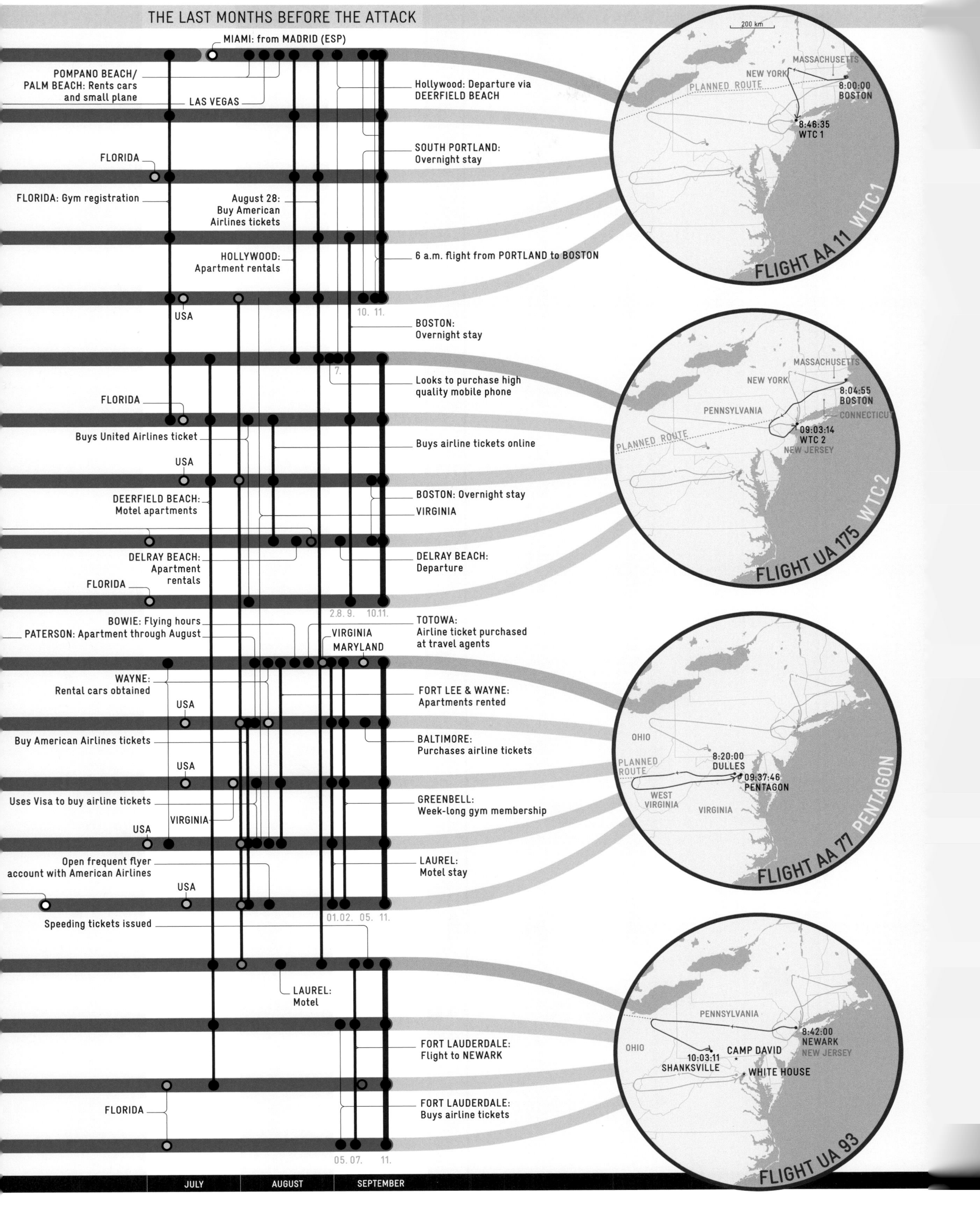
THE LAST MONTHS BEFORE THE ATTACK
MIAMI: from MADRID (ESP)
POMPANO BEACH/ PALM BEACH: Rents cars and small plane
LAS VEGAS
Hollywood: Departure via DEERFIELD BEACH
FLORIDA
SOUTH PORTLAND: Overnight stay
FLORIDA: Gym registration
August 28: Buy American Airlines tickets
HOLLYWOOD: Apartment rentals
6 a.m. flight from PORTLAND to BOSTON
USA
10. 11.
BOSTON: Overnight stay
7.
Looks to purchase high quality mobile phone
FLORIDA
Buys United Airlines ticket
Buys airline tickets online
USA
DEERFIELD BEACH: Motel apartments
BOSTON: Overnight stay
VIRGINIA
DELRAY BEACH: Apartment rentals
DELRAY BEACH: Departure
FLORIDA
2.8. 9. 10.11.
BOWIE: Flying hours
PATERSON: Apartment through August
TOTOWA: Airline ticket purchased at travel agents
VIRGINIA
MARYLAND
WAYNE: Rental cars obtained
FORT LEE & WAYNE: Apartments rented
USA
Buy American Airlines tickets
BALTIMORE: Purchases airline tickets
USA
Uses Visa to buy airline tickets
GREENBELL: Week-long gym membership
VIRGINIA
USA
Open frequent flyer account with American Airlines
LAUREL: Motel stay
USA
01.02. 05. 11.
Speeding tickets issued
LAUREL: Motel
FORT LAUDERDALE: Flight to NEWARK
FLORIDA
FORT LAUDERDALE: Buys airline tickets
05. 07. 11.
JULY
AUGUST
SEPTEMBER
200 km
MASSACHUSETTS
NEW YORK
PLANNED ROUTE
8:00:00 BOSTON
8:46:35 WTC 1
FLIGHT AA 11 WTC1
MASSACHUSETTS
NEW YORK
8:04:55 BOSTON
PENNSYLVANIA
CONNECTICUT
09:03:14 WTC 2
PLANNED ROUTE
NEW JERSEY
FLIGHT UA 175 WTC2
OHIO
8:20:00 DULLES
PLANNED ROUTE
09:37:46 PENTAGON
WEST VIRGINIA
VIRGINIA
FLIGHT AA 77 PENTAGON
PENNSYLVANIA
8:42:00 NEWARK
NEW JERSEY
OHIO
10:03:11 SHANKSVILLE
CAMP DAVID
WHITE HOUSE
FLIGHT UA 93

TERROR IN NUMBERS

The number of terrorist attacks around the world is gradually increasing. The worst attacks were undoubtedly the ones against the United States of America on September 11, 2001. This was the spark that ignited »Operation Enduring Freedom«, the wars in Afghanistan and Iraq. Our graphic shows the victims of terror as well as the fatalities (soldiers) from the subsequent wars.

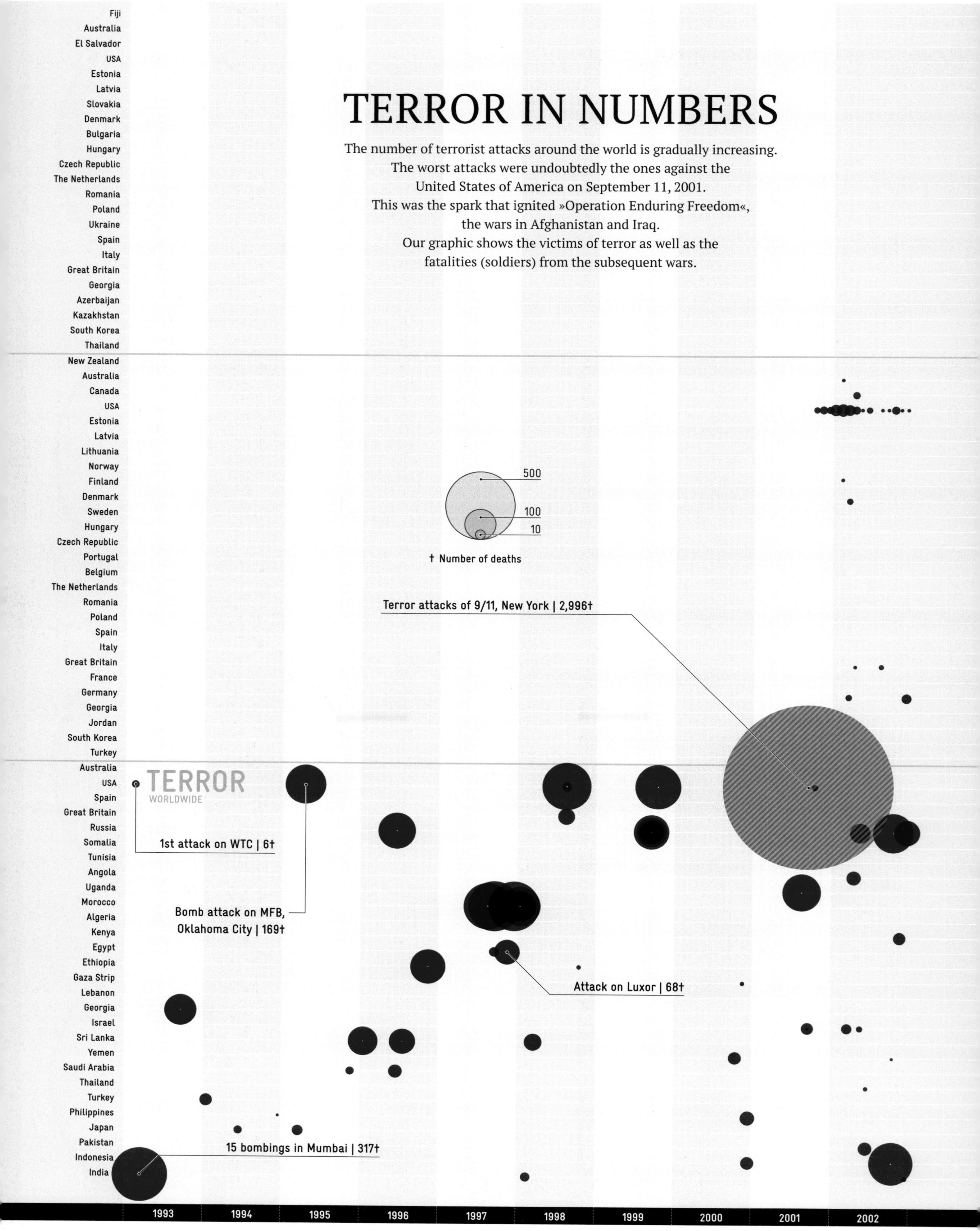
Fiji
Australia
El Salvador
USA
Estonia
Latvia
Slovakia
Denmark
Bulgaria
Hungary
Czech Republic
The Netherlands
Romania
Poland
Ukraine
Spain
Italy
Great Britain
Georgia
Azerbaijan
Kazakhstan
South Korea
Thailand
New Zealand
Australia
Canada
USA
Estonia
Latvia
Lithuania
Norway
Finland
Denmark
Sweden
Hungary
Czech Republic
Portugal
Belgium
The Netherlands
Romania
Poland
Spain
Italy
Great Britain
France
Germany
Georgia
Jordan
South Korea
Turkey
Australia
USA
Spain
Great Britain
Russia
Somalia
Tunisia
Angola
Uganda
Morocco
Algeria
Kenya
Egypt
Ethiopia
Gaza Strip
Lebanon
Georgia
Israel
Sri Lanka
Yemen
Saudi Arabia
Thailand
Turkey
Philippines
Japan
Pakistan
Indonesia
India
500
100
10
† Number of deaths
Terror attacks of 9/11, New York | 2,996†
TERROR
WORLDWIDE
1st attack on WTC | 6†
Bomb attack on MFB, Oklahoma City | 169†
Attack on Luxor | 68†
15 bombings in Mumbai | 317†
1993
1994
1995
1996
1997
1998
1999
2000
2001
2002

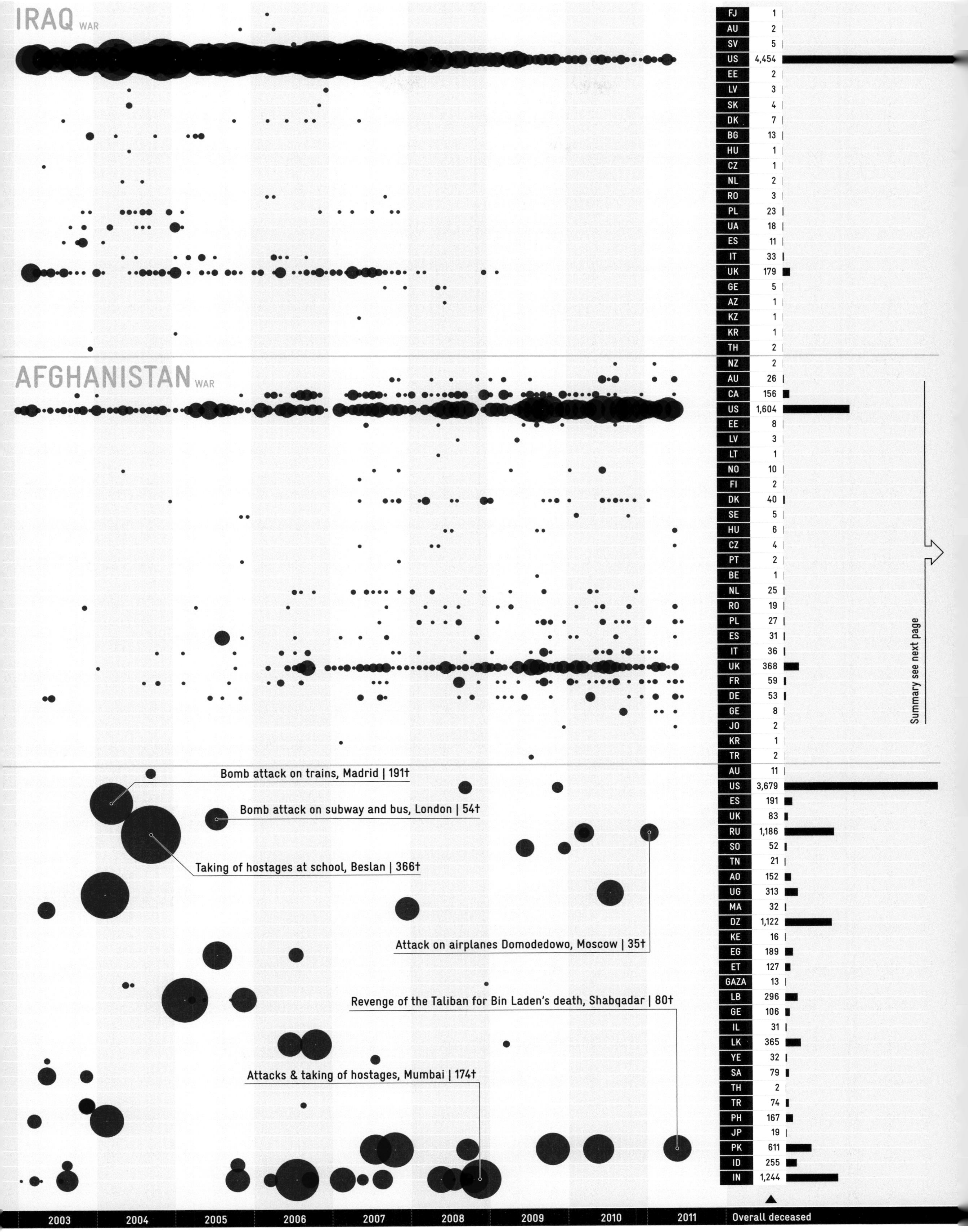
IRAQ WAR
FJ 1
AU 2
SV 5
US 4,454
EE 2
LV 3
SK 4
DK 7
BG 13
HU 1
CZ 1
NL 2
RO 3
PL 23
UA 18
ES 11
IT 33
UK 179
GE 5
AZ 1
KZ 1
KR 1
TH 2
AFGHANISTAN WAR
NZ 2
AU 26
CA 156
US 1,604
EE 8
LV 3
LT 1
NO 10
FI 2
DK 40
SE 5
HU 6
CZ 4
PT 2
BE 1
NL 25
RO 19
PL 27
ES 31
IT 36
UK 368
FR 59
DE 53
GE 8
JO 2
KR 1
TR 2
Summary see next page
Bomb attack on trains, Madrid | 191†
Bomb attack on subway and bus, London | 54†
Taking of hostages at school, Beslan | 366†
Attack on airplanes Domodedowo, Moscow | 35†
Revenge of the Taliban for Bin Laden's death, Shabqadar | 80†
Attacks & taking of hostages, Mumbai | 174†
AU 11
US 3,679
ES 191
UK 83
RU 1,186
SO 52
TN 21
AO 152
UG 313
MA 32
DZ 1,122
KE 16
EG 189
ET 127
GAZA 13
LB 296
GE 106
IL 31
LK 365
YE 32
SA 79
TH 2
TR 74
PH 167
JP 19
PK 611
ID 255
IN 1,244
2003
2004
2005
2006
2007
2008
2009
2010
2011
Overall deceased

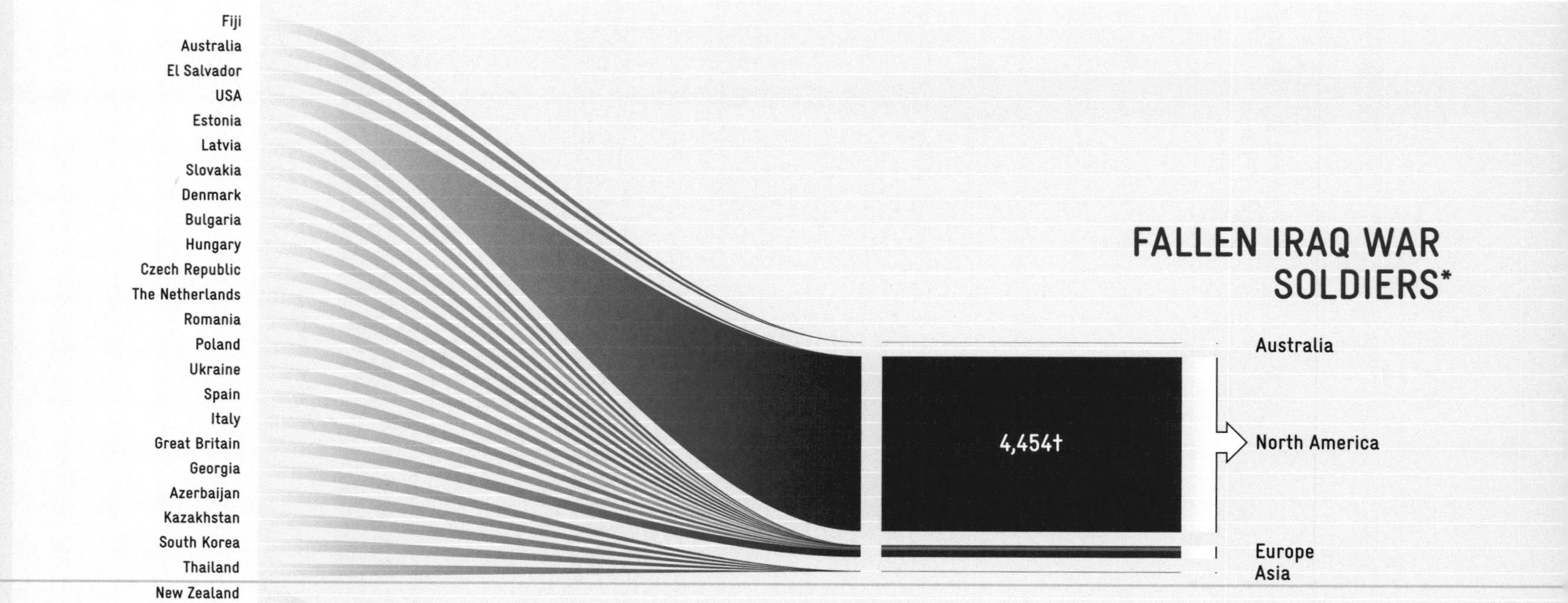
FALLEN IRAQ WAR SOLDIERS*
Fiji
Australia
El Salvador
USA
Estonia
Latvia
Slovakia
Denmark
Bulgaria
Hungary
Czech Republic
The Netherlands
Romania
Poland
Ukraine
Spain
Italy
Great Britain
Georgia
Azerbaijan
Kazakhstan
South Korea
Thailand
4,454†
Australia
North America
Europe
Asia

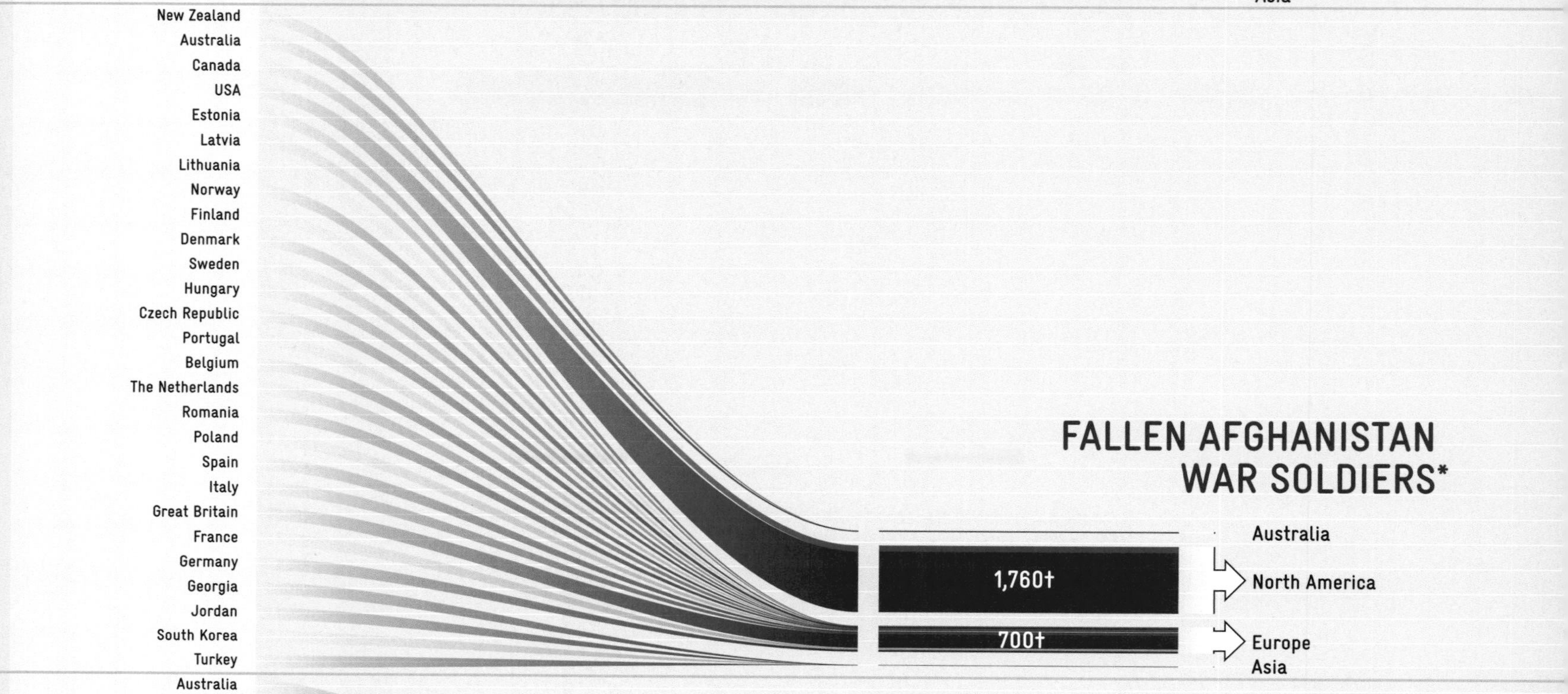
FALLEN AFGHANISTAN WAR SOLDIERS*
New Zealand
Australia
Canada
USA
Estonia
Latvia
Lithuania
Norway
Finland
Denmark
Sweden
Hungary
Czech Republic
Portugal
Belgium
The Netherlands
Romania
Poland
Spain
Italy
Great Britain
France
Germany
Georgia
Jordan
South Korea
Turkey
1,760†
700†
Australia
North America
Europe
Asia

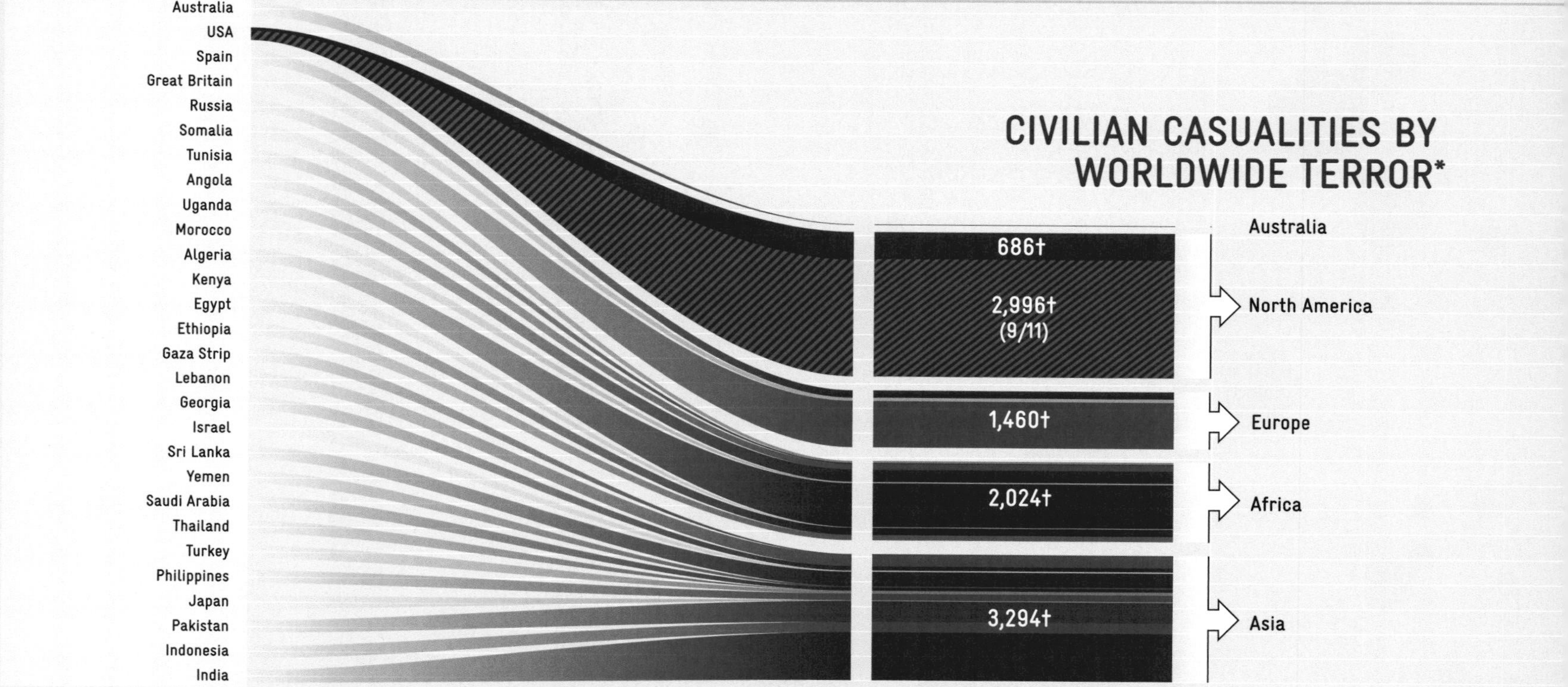
CIVILIAN CASUALITIES BY WORLDWIDE TERROR*
Australia
USA
Spain
Great Britain
Russia
Somalia
Tunisia
Angola
Uganda
Morocco
Algeria
Kenya
Egypt
Ethiopia
Gaza Strip
Lebanon
Georgia
Israel
Sri Lanka
Yemen
Saudi Arabia
Thailand
Turkey
Philippines
Japan
Pakistan
Indonesia
India
686†
2,996† (9/11)
1,460†
2,024†
3,294†
Australia
North America
Europe
Africa
Asia

* All figures represent the status until 2011.

WHO PAYS THE PRICE OF WAR

Soldiers sign up for the military knowing there is a chance they will not come home intact from the front lines. But civilians can do nothing but hope for a miss when rockets start firing.

In the first decade of the 2000s, wars were carried out on several fronts, but no one paid more dearly than the people in the wrong place at the wrong time.

50,000†

CIVILIAN CASUALITIES IN THE IRAQ WAR*

THE NUMBER OF CIVILIAN CASUALTIES IS TAKEN FROM A VARIETY OF SOURCES AND IS TO BE SEEN AS A VALUATION. OTHER SOURCES ESTIMATE MUCH HIGHER NUMBERS.

16,000†

CIVILIAN CASUALITIES IN THE AFGHANISTAN WAR*

THE NUMBER OF CIVILIAN CASUALTIES IS TAKEN FROM A VARIETY OF SOURCES AND IS TO BE SEEN AS A VALUATION.

THE NEW WORLD TRADE CENTER

On the day of the attacks, the Mayor of New York City, Rudy Giuliani, proclaimed, »We will rebuild. We're going to come out of this stronger than before, politically stronger, economically stronger. The skyline will be made whole again.« One year later the Lower Manhattan Development Corporation (LMDC) announced a design study for the World Trade Center site. On February 27, 2003, the architect Daniel Libeskind and his studio officially won the competition to be the master planner for the World Trade Center redesign. Though Libeskind designed the site, the individual buildings and skyscrapers were in the end designed by different architects.

541 m
2 TWO WORLD TRADE CENTER
403 m
7 SEVEN WORLD TRADE CENTER
417 m
228 m
THE ONE WORLD OBSERVATORY
is the highest viewing platform in New York. In just 47 seconds, the SkyPod lift takes you up the many floors to the 360-degree viewing platform, from where you can see far across the city.
1 ONE WORLD TRADE CENTER
A RONALD O. PERELMAN PERFORMING ARTS CENTER
NORTH MEMORIAL

LOCATION

Location of the WTC's site in Lower Manhattan

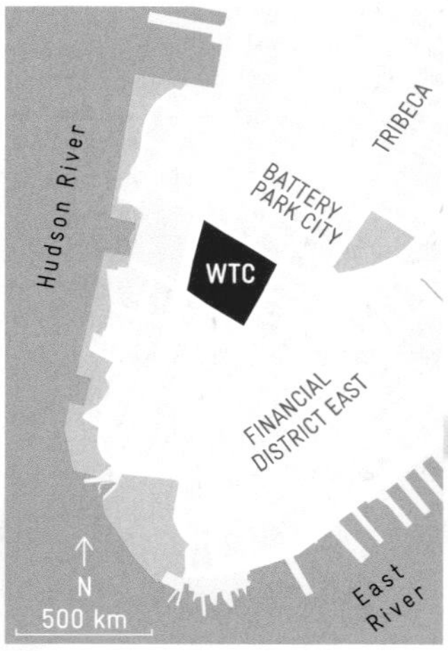
Hudson River
TRIBECA
BATTERY PARK CITY
WTC
FINANCIAL DISTRICT EAST
East River
N
500 km

FACTS OF ONE WTC

Architect	Skidmore, Owings & Merrill LLP
Rental areas	271,629 m²
Floors	105 ↑ ground B1–B5 ↓
Cost	$3.9 bil.

MORE THAN A WALL

On August 13, 1961, the German Democratic Republic (GDR) sealed off the borders to West Berlin. What started as a temporary wall, a few kilometers in length of barbed wire, ended as an extensive structure with many different components: walls, fences, bunkers, vehicle ditches, watchtowers, dog runs, patrol roads and vehicle traps. During the 28 years it stood, the border wall was constantly upgraded and perfected by the GDR.

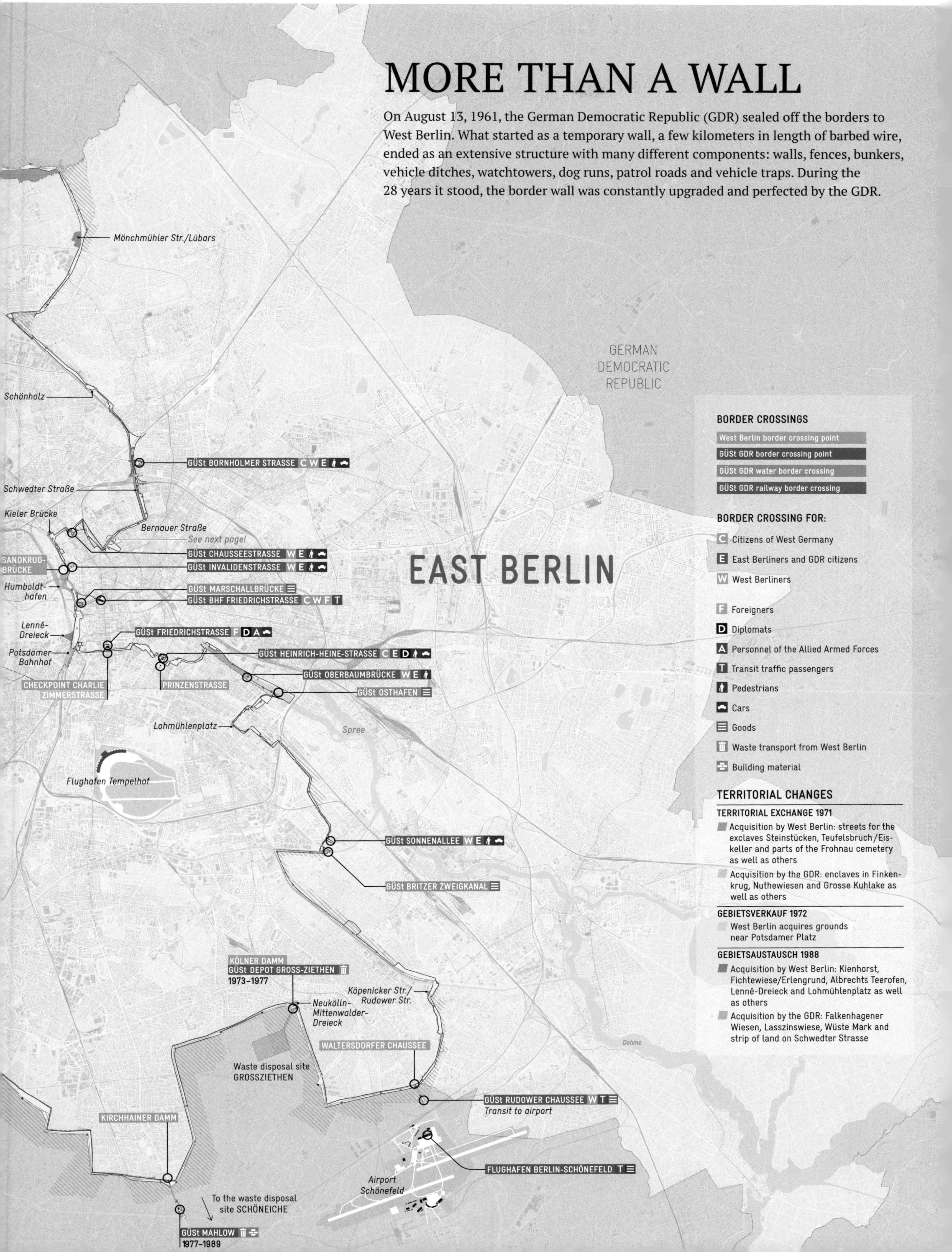

GERMAN DEMOCRATIC REPUBLIC
EAST BERLIN
Mönchmühler Str./Lübars
Schönholz
GÜSt BORNHOLMER STRASSE C W E
Schwedter Straße
Kieler Brücke
Bernauer Straße
See next page!
GÜSt CHAUSSEESTRASSE W E
SANDKRUG-BRÜCKE
GÜSt INVALIDENSTRASSE W E
Humboldt-hafen
GÜSt MARSCHALLBRÜCKE
GÜSt BHF FRIEDRICHSTRASSE C W F T
Lenné-Dreieck
GÜSt FRIEDRICHSTRASSE F D A
Potsdamer Bahnhof
GÜSt HEINRICH-HEINE-STRASSE C E D
CHECKPOINT CHARLIE
ZIMMERSTRASSE
PRINZENSTRASSE
GÜSt OBERBAUMBRÜCKE W E
GÜSt OSTHAFEN
Lohmühlenplatz
Spree
Flughafen Tempelhof
GÜSt SONNENALLEE W E
GÜSt BRITZER ZWEIGKANAL
KÖLNER DAMM
GÜSt DEPOT GROSS-ZIETHEN
1973–1977
Köpenicker Str./ Rudower Str.
Neukölln-Mittenwalder-Dreieck
WALTERSDORFER CHAUSSEE
Waste disposal site GROSSZIETHEN
GÜSt RUDOWER CHAUSSEE W T
Transit to airport
KIRCHHAINER DAMM
FLUGHAFEN BERLIN-SCHÖNEFELD T
Airport Schönefeld
To the waste disposal site SCHÖNEICHE
GÜSt MAHLOW
1977–1989
Dahme
BORDER CROSSINGS
West Berlin border crossing point
GÜSt GDR border crossing point
GÜSt GDR water border crossing
GÜSt GDR railway border crossing
BORDER CROSSING FOR:
C Citizens of West Germany
E East Berliners and GDR citizens
W West Berliners
F Foreigners
D Diplomats
A Personnel of the Allied Armed Forces
T Transit traffic passengers
Pedestrians
Cars
Goods
Waste transport from West Berlin
Building material
TERRITORIAL CHANGES
TERRITORIAL EXCHANGE 1971
Acquisition by West Berlin: streets for the exclaves Steinstücken, Teufelsbruch/Eiskeller and parts of the Frohnau cemetery as well as others
Acquisition by the GDR: enclaves in Finkenkrug, Nuthewiesen and Grosse Kuhlake as well as others
GEBIETSVERKAUF 1972
West Berlin acquires grounds near Potsdamer Platz
GEBIETSAUSTAUSCH 1988
Acquisition by West Berlin: Kienhorst, Fichtewiese/Erlengrund, Albrechts Teerofen, Lenné-Dreieck and Lohmühlenplatz as well as others
Acquisition by the GDR: Falkenhagener Wiesen, Lasszinswiese, Wüste Mark and strip of land on Schwedter Strasse

STAGES OF EXPANSION

The border between East and West Berlin ran along Bernauer Strasse, through the middle of a vibrant residential neighborhood. The buildings, as well as the cross street Ackerstrasse and a cemetery, were located on the East Berlin side, while the street itself, including both sidewalks, belonged to West Berlin. The border fortifications became more elaborate over time and existing buildings were integrated into the border security. A wide border strip was created in 1965. The apartment buildings along Bernauer Strasse were torn down and the remains of their facades became part of the border wall. Over the years, more modern obstacles and surveillance elements were incorporated and made the border strip increasingly invincible.

1962

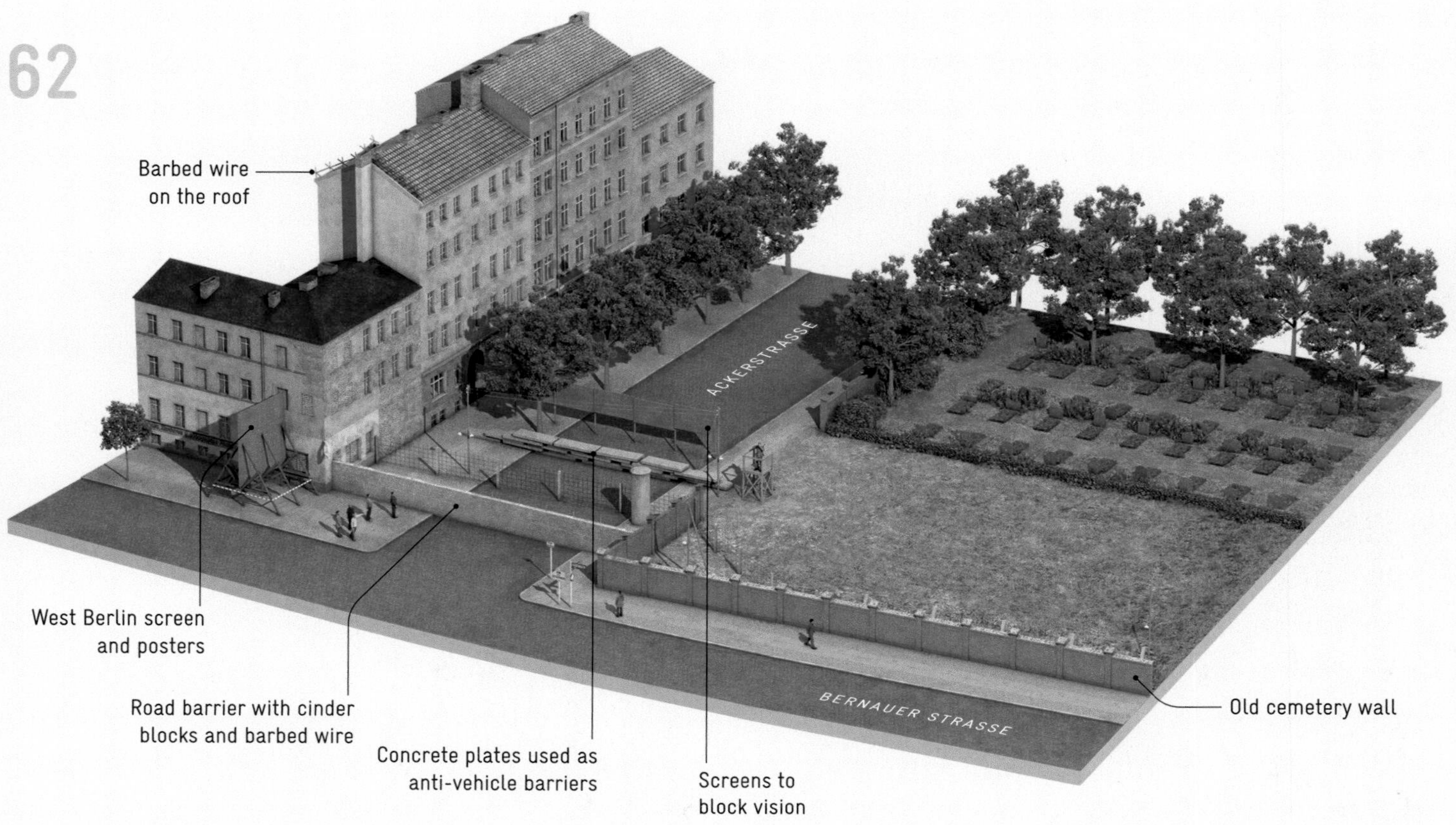
Barbed wire
on the roof
ACKERSTRASSE
West Berlin screen
and posters
Road barrier with cinder
blocks and barbed wire
Concrete plates used as
anti-vehicle barriers
Screens to
block vision
BERNAUER STRASSE
Old cemetery wall

1966

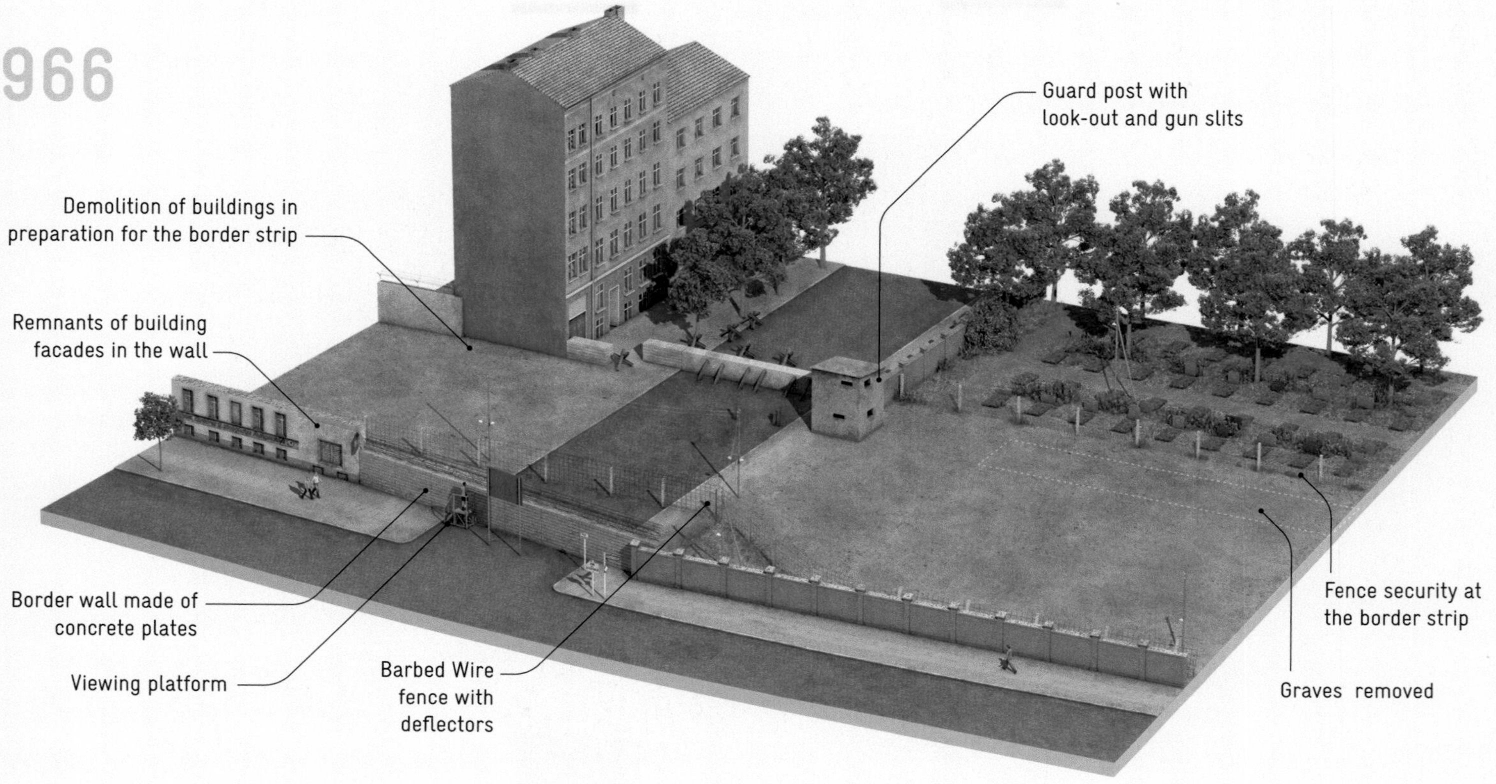
Guard post with
look-out and gun slits
Demolition of buildings in
preparation for the border strip
Remnants of building
facades in the wall
Border wall made of
concrete plates
Viewing platform
Barbed Wire
fence with
deflectors
Fence security at
the border strip
Graves removed

3 THREE WORLD TRADE CENTER
329 m
298 m
4 FOUR WORLD TRADE CENTER
B TRANSPORTATION HUB
46 m high and 19 m below
C NATIONAL SEPTEMBER 11 MUSEUM
5 FIVE WORLD TRADE CENTER
SOUTH MEMORIAL
D NATIONAL SEPTEMBER 11 MEMORIAL

THE CONSTRUCTION

The financial crisis has delayed the construction of the new WTC. It is not sure yet, whether all buildings will be built at the planned height.

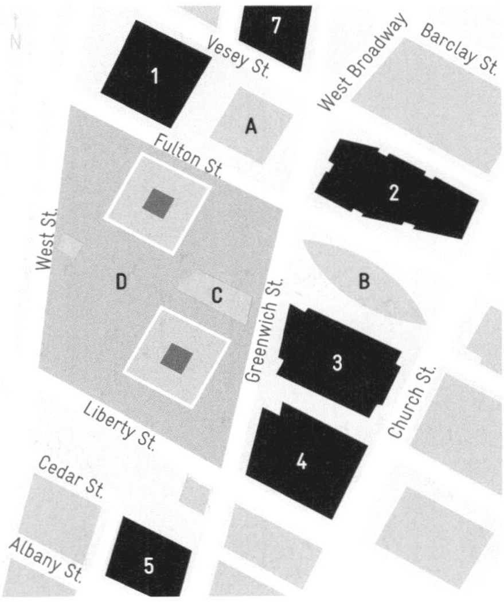

- **1** Opened in 2014
- **2** Will open in 2022
- **3** Opened in 2018
- **4** Opened in 2013
- **5** Construction on hold
- **7** Opened in 2006

- **A** **Performing Arts Center** will open in 2021
- **B** **Transportation hub** opened in 2016
- **C** **National September 11 Museum** opened in 2014
- **D** **National September 11 Memorial** opened in 2011

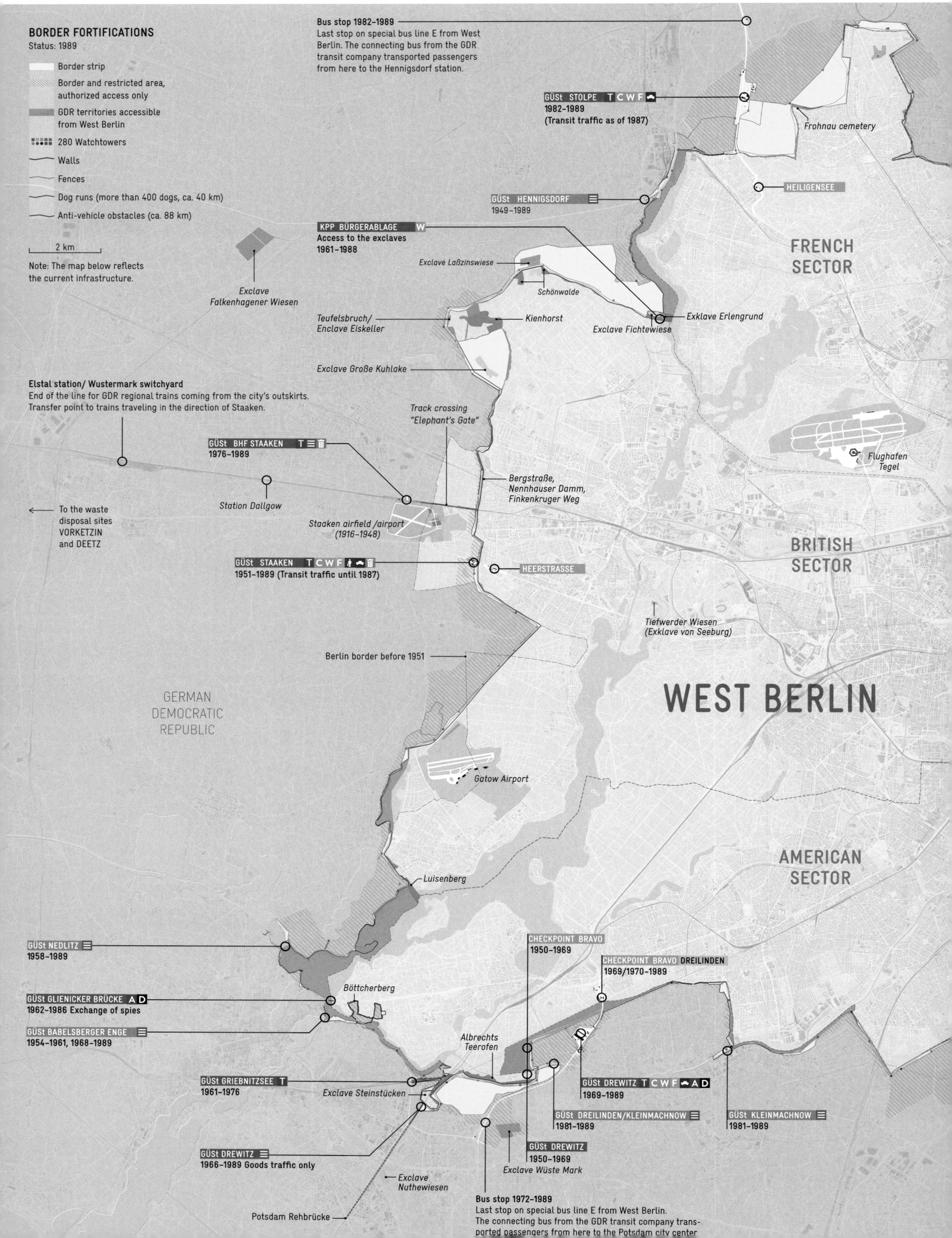
BORDER FORTIFICATIONS
Status: 1989
Border strip
Border and restricted area, authorized access only
GDR territories accessible from West Berlin
280 Watchtowers
Walls
Fences
Dog runs (more than 400 dogs, ca. 40 km)
Anti-vehicle obstacles (ca. 88 km)
2 km
Note: The map below reflects the current infrastructure.
Bus stop 1982–1989
Last stop on special bus line E from West Berlin. The connecting bus from the GDR transit company transported passengers from here to the Hennigsdorf station.
GÜSt STOLPE T C W F
1982–1989
(Transit traffic as of 1987)
Frohnau cemetery
HEILIGENSEE
GÜSt HENNIGSDORF
1949–1989
KPP BÜRGERABLAGE W
Access to the exclaves
1961–1988
FRENCH SECTOR
Exclave Laßzinswiese
Schönwalde
Exclave Falkenhagener Wiesen
Teufelsbruch/ Enclave Eiskeller
Kienhorst
Exklave Erlengrund
Exclave Fichtewiese
Exclave Große Kuhlake
Elstal station/ Wustermark switchyard
End of the line for GDR regional trains coming from the city's outskirts. Transfer point to trains traveling in the direction of Staaken.
Track crossing "Elephant's Gate"
GÜSt BHF STAAKEN T
1976–1989
Flughafen Tegel
Bergstraße, Nennhauser Damm, Finkenkruger Weg
Station Dallgow
To the waste disposal sites VORKETZIN and DEETZ
Staaken airfield /airport (1916–1948)
BRITISH SECTOR
GÜSt STAAKEN T C W F
1951–1989 (Transit traffic until 1987)
HEERSTRASSE
Tiefwerder Wiesen (Exklave von Seeburg)
Berlin border before 1951
WEST BERLIN
GERMAN DEMOCRATIC REPUBLIC
Gatow Airport
AMERICAN SECTOR
Luisenberg
CHECKPOINT BRAVO
1950–1969
CHECKPOINT BRAVO DREILINDEN
1969/1970–1989
GÜSt NEDLITZ
1958–1989
Böttcherberg
GÜSt GLIENICKER BRÜCKE A D
1962–1986 Exchange of spies
GÜSt BABELSBERGER ENGE
1954–1961, 1968–1989
Albrechts Teerofen
GÜSt GRIEBNITZSEE T
1961–1976
Exclave Steinstücken
GÜSt DREWITZ T C W F A D
1969–1989
GÜSt DREILINDEN/KLEINMACHNOW
1981–1989
GÜSt KLEINMACHNOW
1981–1989
GÜSt DREWITZ
1966–1989 Goods traffic only
GÜSt DREWITZ
1950–1969
Exclave Wüste Mark
Exclave Nuthewiesen
Potsdam Rehbrücke
Bus stop 1972–1989
Last stop on special bus line E from West Berlin.
The connecting bus from the GDR transit company transported passengers from here to the Potsdam city center

Berlin Wall Foundation

The **Berlin Wall Memorial** on Bernauer Strasse is the main memorial site of the wall and is managed by the **Berlin Wall Foundation**. The graphics on these pages have been created in cooperation with the Foundation as part of an infographic poster exhibition, which was shown until September 2017:
www.berliner-mauer-gedenkstaette.de/en/understanding-the-border-910.html

The Memorial is open Tuesday to Sunday,
10 a.m. – 6 p.m. at Bernauer Strasse 119.

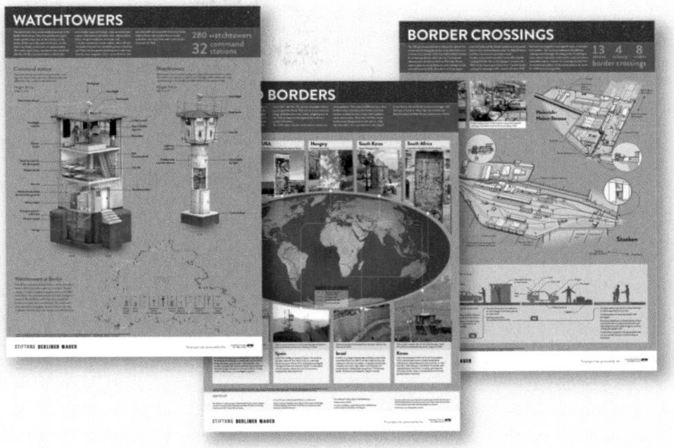

1971

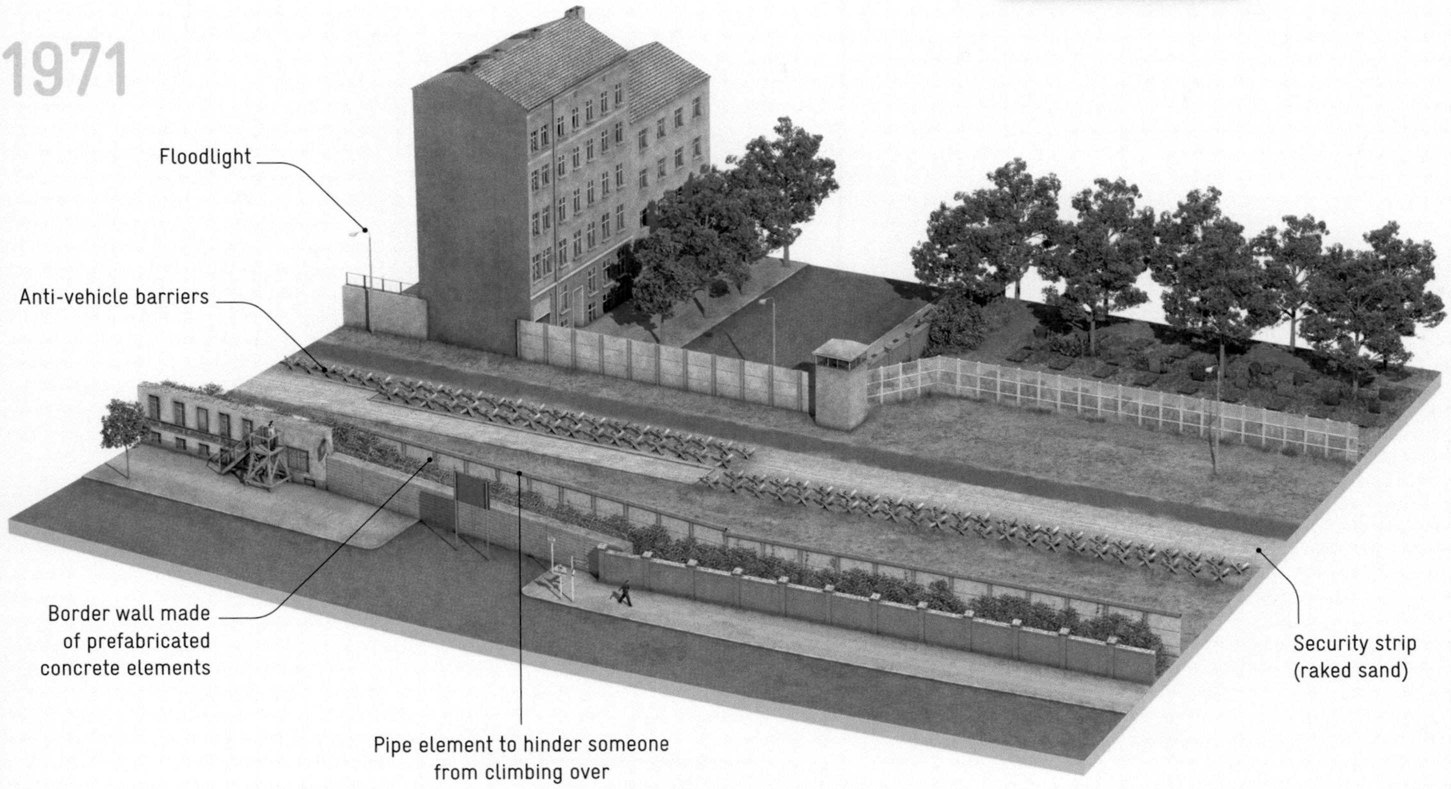
Floodlight
Anti-vehicle barriers
Border wall made of prefabricated concrete elements
Pipe element to hinder someone from climbing over
Security strip (raked sand)

1986

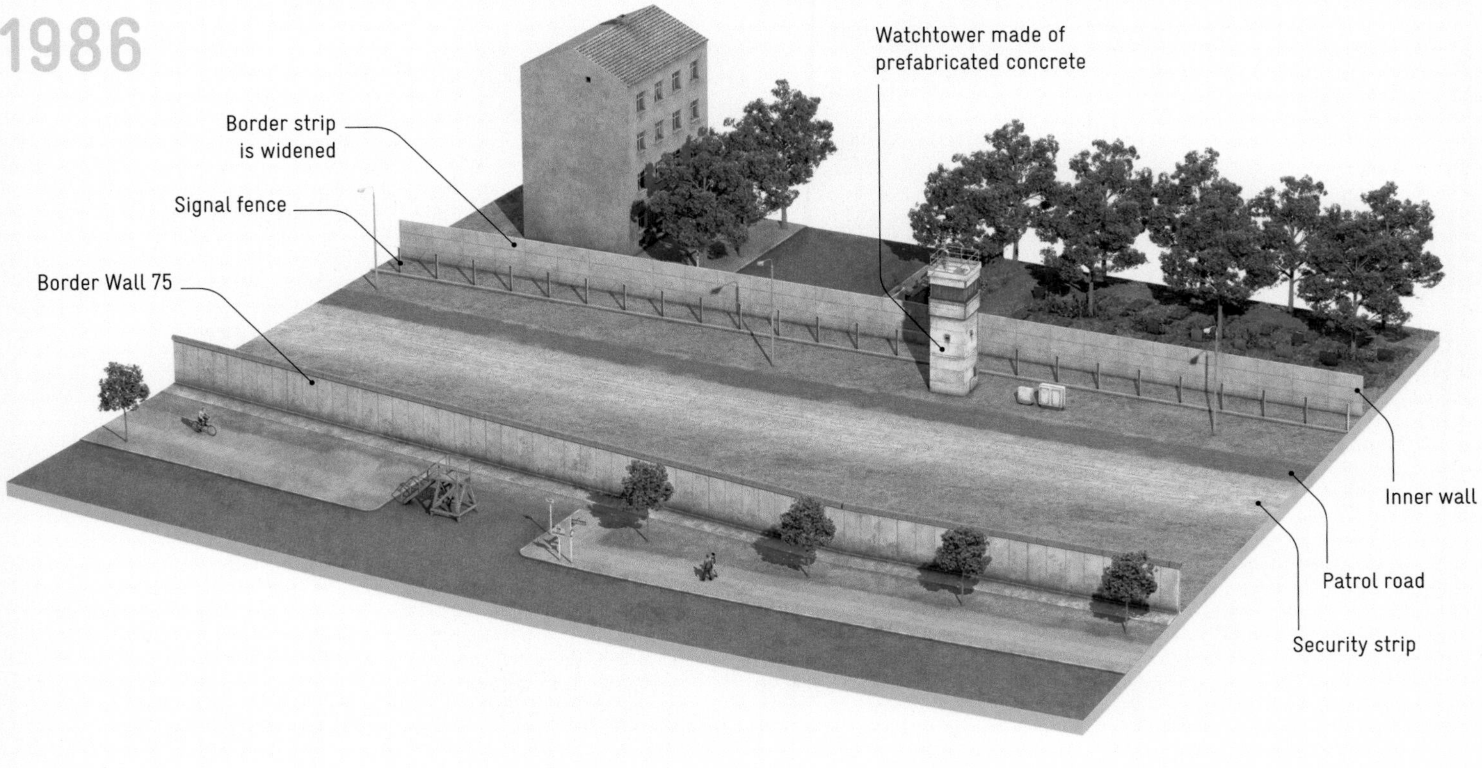
Watchtower made of prefabricated concrete
Border strip is widened
Signal fence
Border Wall 75
Inner wall
Patrol road
Security strip

WATCHTOWERS

The watchtowers were an essential component of the border fortifications. They were positioned to give border guards a clear view of their section of the border all the way to the next watchtower. Thoughout the inner-city border, towers were set approximately 250 meters apart. A telecommunication system connected every watchtower with the command station in the border unit's segment. Information and orders were collected there before being forwarded to the border unit.

From the watchtowers, border soldiers observed both the border strip and the surrounding areas in the East and West. Like the guards patrolling the border strip, they too were assigned to duty in pairs. Routine duty was often dull and uneventful. But many border soldiers feared the moment that an escape took place since they were under orders to shoot people who fled.

Command station

The watchtowers that served as command stations were larger than the normal watchtowers. There was always an officer and soldier on duty on the upper level.

Height 8.5 meters
(edge of roof)

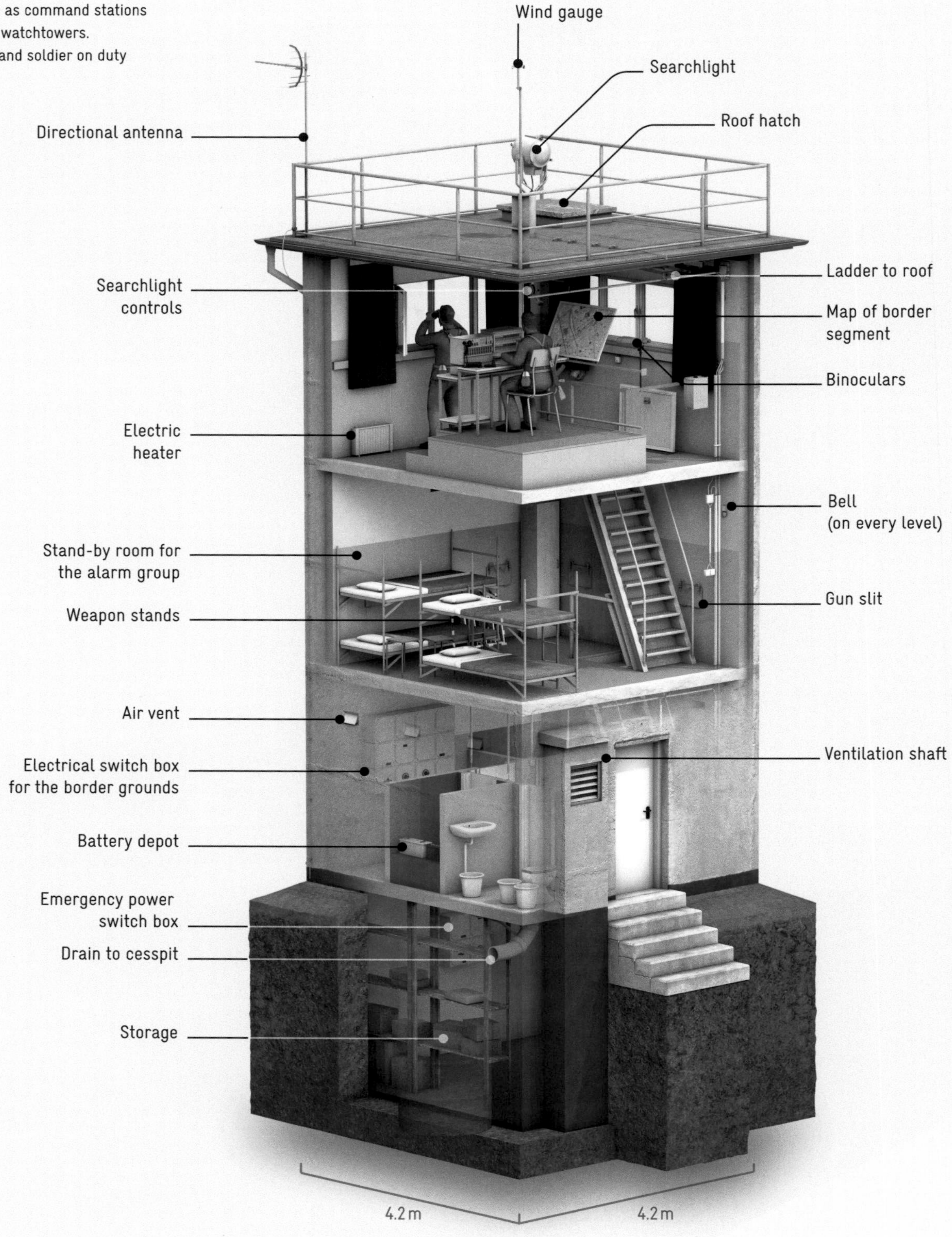
Wind gauge
Searchlight
Roof hatch
Directional antenna
Searchlight controls
Ladder to roof
Map of border segment
Binoculars
Electric heater
Bell (on every level)
Stand-by room for the alarm group
Weapon stands
Gun slit
Air vent
Electrical switch box for the border grounds
Ventilation shaft
Battery depot
Emergency power switch box
Drain to cesspit
Storage
4.2 m
4.2 m

Watchtowers in Berlin

The GDR erected the first watchtowers on the border to West Berlin in 1952. These were usually wood structures. The construction of watchtowers had changed several times by 1989. In the 1960s, the towers were either wood, steel or stone constructions. By the 1970s, watchtowers were erected with round turrets made of concrete elements. The round towers were replaced by a rectangular structure with a two-by-two meter base. Some older watchtowers, however, remained in use.

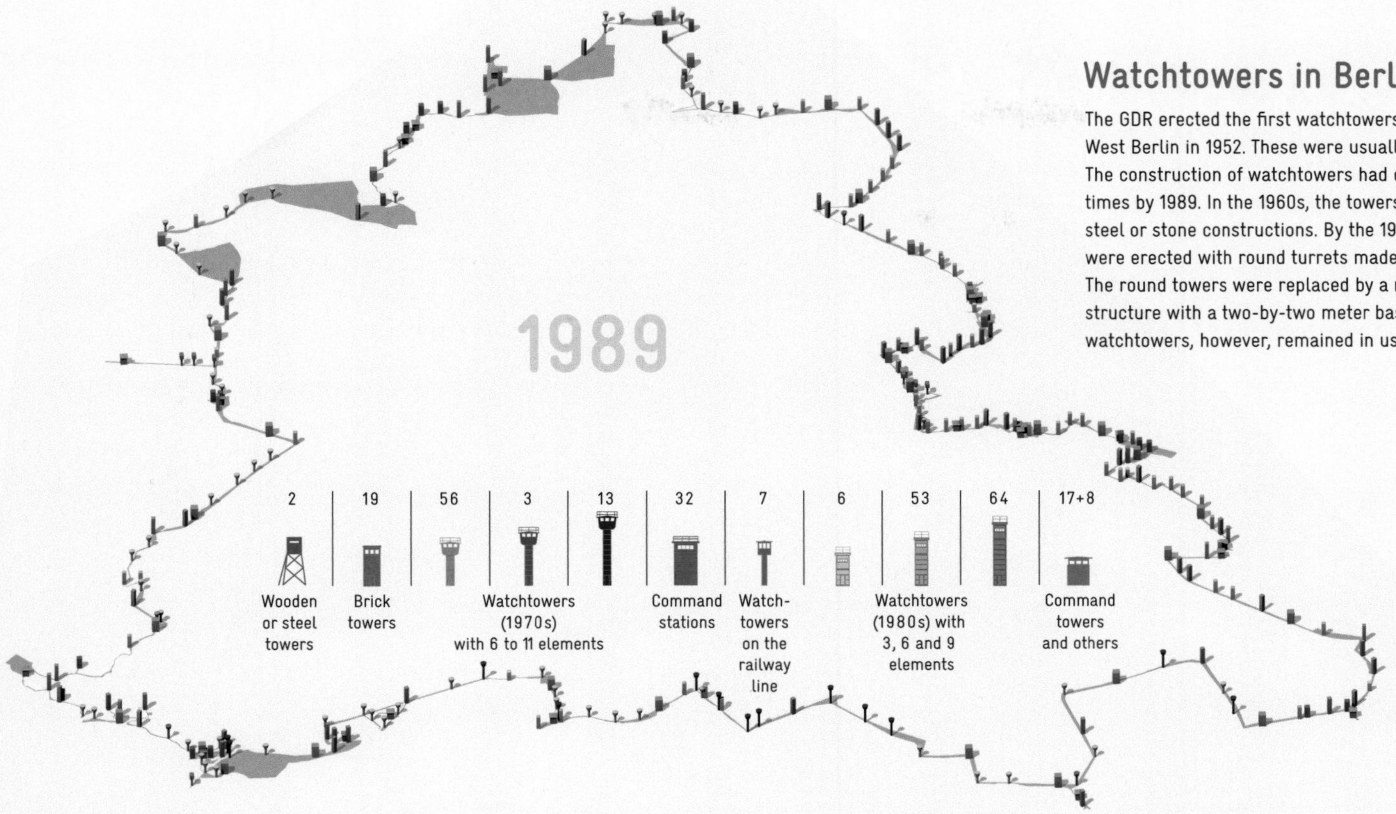

1989
2
Wooden or steel towers
19
Brick towers
56
3
13
Watchtowers (1970s) with 6 to 11 elements
32
Command stations
7
Watch-towers on the railway line
6
53
64
Watchtowers (1980s) with 3, 6 and 9 elements
17+8
Command towers and others

Watchtowers

Watchtowers were connected to the power supply and communications system. Two soldiers were stationed at each tower. The height of the watchtowers could vary depending on the number of prefabricated concrete elements used.

Height 9.4 meters
(tip of roof)

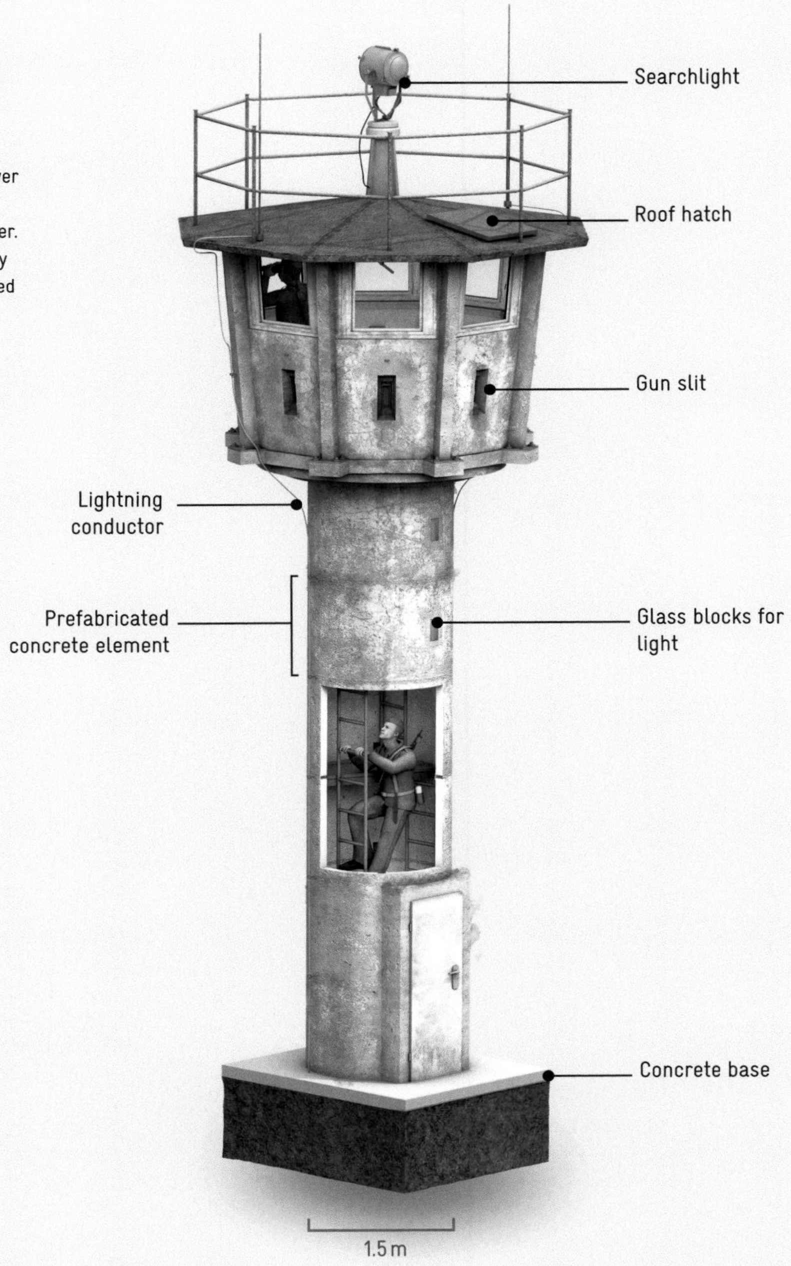

Searchlight
Roof hatch
Gun slit
Lightning conductor
Prefabricated concrete element
Glass blocks for light
Concrete base
1.5 m

WITHOUT A TRACE

On June 1, 2009, Air France Flight 447 crashed into the Atlantic Ocean on its journey from Rio de Janeiro to Paris. The wreckage of the A330 was first found nearly two years later in May 2011, when the flight recorder, cockpit voice recorder and 50 bodies were recovered from the ocean floor. The investigation found that human error was responsible for the 228 lives lost.

!(FPL-AFR447-IS
-A332/H-SGIJPRWY/SD
-SBGL2200
-N0481F350 DCT AWAKE UZ10 FLIRT/M082F350 UZ10 NTL UN873
INTOL/M082F350 UN873 SALPU/M082F370 UN873 ORARO/M082F370 UN873
ISOKA/N0471F370 UN873 LIMAL/N0466F390 UN873 SAMAR/N0468F380 UN873
BAROK/N0465F400 DCT PORTA UN873 MOKOR UN741 NTS/N0484F280 UN741 KEPER
UT182 ROMLO/N0483F270
-LFPG1034 LFPO
-EET/SBBS0028 SBRE0050 SBAO0302 GOOO0349 GVSC0512 GCCC0606 LIMAL0643
GMMM0731 LPPC0816 LECM0851 LFRR0930 LFFF1004 RIF/ZMR UN976 DGO UL176
SSN UP181 ENSAC SOLSO DIRAX LFBD REG/FGZCP SEL/CPHQ DAT/SV DOF/090531
SRC/RQP ORGN/SBGLYOYX)

Planned flight plan of flight AF447 and its alternate route to Europe

By looking at the flight plan and which waypoints the crew reached, authorities could estimate where the flight crashed and use the data to locate the wreckage. But to find out how the tragedy happened, more digging was needed.

Last known whereabouts

At 01:45 UTC, the aircraft experienced turbulence. It left Brazilian Atlantic radar surveillance at 01:49 UTC and flew straight into a heavy thunderstorm front. Shortly after, at 01:52 UTC, the captain woke the second co-pilot and said that he would be taking his place. After a attending a briefing between the two co-pilots, the captain left to rest at 02:01 UTC. So at the time of the crash, the plane was being flown by two co-pilots.

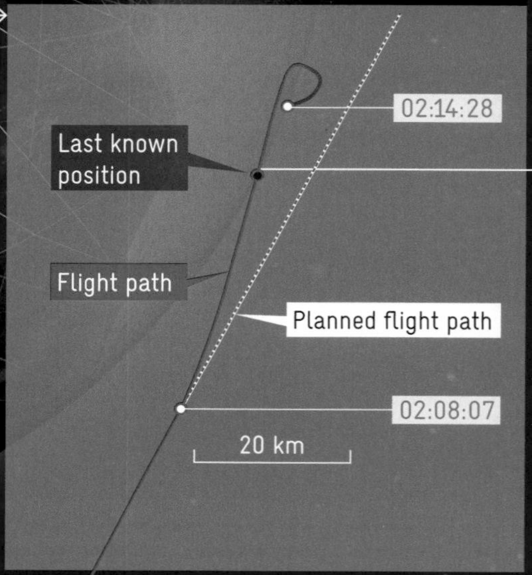

Departure from Rio de Janeiro

The Airbus A330-203 operated by Air France departed from Rio de Janeiro Galeão-Antônio Carlos Jobim International Airport as scheduled on May 31, 2009 at 19:29 local time (22:29 UTC). It was scheduled to arrive at Charles de Gaulle Airport in Paris at 09:03 UTC the following day with an estimated flight time of 10 hours and 34 minutes. The crew consisted of nine people in the cabin and three on the flight deck. Among the 216 passengers, there were 126 men, 82 women and eight children. The pilot and co-pilot were in the cockpit. The third flight crew member, a second co-pilot, was resting for the first three and a half hours of the flight.

The route

Like cars on highways, airplanes stick to planned routes that are mapped out around the globe. The crew on AF447 had a detailed plan with set waypoints, to make the crossing from Rio de Janeiro to Paris.

→ **INTOL** is the last waypoint of the Brazilian air traffic control. At 01:35 UTC, flight AF447 passed over the INTOL waypoint, 565 kilometers away from NATAL on Brazil's northeastern coast, three hours and six minutes after departure. This was the last voice contact the crew made.

The accident

At around 02:08 UTC, the crew changed course by 12 degrees to the left, presumably to avoid returns detected by the weather radar. At 02:10 UTC, the speed measurements were incorrect and some automatic systems disconnected, probably caused by ice crystals obstructing the Pitot tubes that measure velocity.
On May 27, 2011, the French Bureau of Enquiry and Analysis (BEA) for Civil Aviation Safety released some information in advance about the last minutes of the flight. The new details were investigated with the help of the rescued flight data recorders.

The last minutes of the disaster

The French BEA published the last sound recordings from the cockpit, which were taken from the flight data recorder.

1 Autopilot disengaged, aircraft climbs to 38,000ft (11,560m)

2 Stall warning triggered and the aicraft stalled

3 Descent lasted 3min 30s, during which the aircraft remained stalled. The angle of attack increased and remained above 35° degrees. Engines were operating and always responded to crew commands.

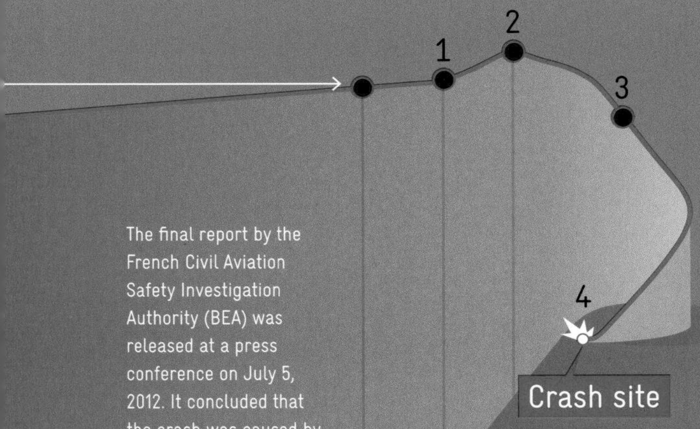

The final report by the French Civil Aviation Safety Investigation Authority (BEA) was released at a press conference on July 5, 2012. It concluded that the crash was caused by human error on the part of the co-pilots who mishandled the missing Pitot tube readings.

4 Last recorded values were a pitch attiitude of 16.2° nose-up, a roll angle of 5.3° left and a rate of descent of -10.912 ft/min

Translated Transcript (PIC: Captain, PF: Pilot Flying, PNF: Pilot monitoring):

Time	*Source*	
02:00:33	PF	Well a bit of turbulence which you just saw... we will ... we should find it again before, in fact we are in the cloud layer unfortunately as we can not climb too much for the moment because of the temperatue which is sinking less than expected. This is reducing the REC MAX for us a little lower to go for 37 *(FL370)*
02:06:44	PF	The ITC, there it is between SALPU and TASIL
02:06:54	PF	Minus 42, we are not going to use the anti ice it is still there
02:07	PF	You see we are really on the limit of the cloud layer.
02:08:07	PNF	Can you maybe turn a bit to the left? I agree that we are in manual, right?
02:08:19	PNF	What I call manual means we are not in managed mode *(Nav)*
02:09:54	PNF	Here, I'll reduce the speed a bit for you.
02:10:03	PF	Do you want to switch to Ignition Start?
02:10:06	PF	I have control
02:10:09	PF	Ignition Start
02:10:11	PNF	What is this?
02:10:14	PF	We don't have a good... We don't have a good indication of ....
02:10:17	PNF	We have lost the speeds, engine thrust A T H R engine lever thrust
02:10:18	PF	... speed
02:10:22	PNF	Alternate Law Protections
02:10:24	PNF	Wait, we are about to loose
02:10:25	PNF	Wing Anti-Ice
02:10:27	PNF	Watch your speed, Watch your speed
	PF	Ok, ok, I will descend back
	PNF	You are stabilizing
	PF	Yeah
	PNF	You are descending back
02:10:33	PNF	According to the three you are climbing, now you are descending.
02:10:35	PF	Agreed
02:10:36	PNF	You are at... descend back
	PF	It is going, we are descending back
02:10:39	PNF	I'll put you on A T T *(*) (Selecteur ATT /HDG is put in position F/O on 3)*
02:10:42	PF	We are, yes we are in climb
02:10:49	PNF	Where is he, eh?
02:10:56	PF	TOGA
02:11	PNF	Try to use the lateral controls as few as possible hey!
02:11:03	PF	I am in TOGA
02:11:06	PNF	... is he coming or not
02:11:21	PNF	We have certainly the engines, what is happening?
02:11:32	PF	I don't have control of the aircraft, I don't have control of the aircraft at all
02:11:38	PNF	Command to the left *(taking control)*
02:11:41	PF	I have the impression that we have speed.... *(we are in speed)*
02:11:43	PIC	Hey, what are you doing?
	PNF	What is happening, I don't know, I don't know what is happening
02:11:53	PIC	Ok, take, take this
02:11:58	PF	have a problem, I have no more vertical speed here
	PIC	Agreed
	PF	I have no indication at all.
02:12:04	PF	I have the impression that we have a crazy speed, no, what do you think? *[Speedbrakes are deployed]**
02:12:07	PNF	NO, don't extend them! Certainly not.
02:12:13	PNF	What do you think, what doyou think, what do we have to do?
02:12:15	PIC	I don't know, it descends.
02:12:10	PF	Here, that is good, we have wings level, no it doesn't want.
	PIC	Wings to level, the horizon, the backup horizon.
	PNF	The horizon *(secondary)*
02:12:26	PNF	The speed?
02:12:27	PNF	You are climbing,
	VS	Stall Stall
	PNF	You are descending, descending descending
02:12:30	PF	I am descending?
	PNF	Descend!
02:12:32	PIC	No, you are climbing
02:12:33	PF	Here, I am climbing, okay, right so lets descend *(or okay we are descending) (unclear)*
02:12:42	PF	OK, we are in TOGA
02:12:42	PF	On the altitude where are we?
02:12:44	PIC	this is not possible
02:12:45	PF	On alti*(tude)* we are where?
02:12:45	PNF	What do you mean on altitude?
	PF	Yes, yes, yes, I am descending there, no?
	PNF	Yes, you are descending.
	PIC	Hey, you are in.... put the wings level,
	PNF	Put the wings level!
	PF	That is what I am trying to do
	PIC	Put the wings level
02:12:59	PF	I am at the limit of, with the warping
	PIC	The rudder
02:13:25	PF	What, how is it that we are continuing to descend at the limit there?
02:13:28	PNF	Try to find what you can do with the controls up there, The primaries e.t.c.
02:13:32	PF	At level 100
02:13:36	PF	9,000 ft
02:13:38	PIC	Carefull with the rudder!
02:13:39	PNF	Climb, climb. Climb, climb
02:13:40	PF	But I am at the limit of the nose since a while
	PIC	No, no, no, don't climb
	PNF	So descend
02:13:45	PNF	So, give me the controls, to me the controls.
	PF	Go ahead, you have the controls, we are still on TOGA
02:14:05	PIC	Careful, you are nose high *(cabres?)*
	PNF	I am nose high?
	PF	Well, we need to, we are at 4,000 ft
02:14:18	PIC	Go, Pull
	PF	Go, Pull pullpull
02:14:26	PIC	Ten degrees pitch

*at 02:12:04 the transcript mentions the speedbrakes have been deployed. The FDR graphics as well as the remainder of the report do not mention at all whether the speedbrakes have been extended or not.

PEOPLE ON THE RUN

Europe is facing a crucial test. In 2015, more than a million people risked fleeing to Europe while only a few countries were willing to take in large numbers of refugees. It is very hard to provide a precise figure of how many refugees were staying where. German media fueled fears with headlines such as »In 2015, 1.1 million refugees came to Germany.«* But is this figure correct? Many of them were registered several times or traveled on to other countries. Where did the refugees arrive at the end of their journey?

Schengen area
Schengen candidate countries
Refugees' major routes
Connecting or minor routes
Refugee camps
Border fences
Planned border fences
Kirkenes
Storskog
Murmansk
A total of 5,500 people, mainly refugees from the Middle East, entered Norway in the fall of 2015.
FINLAND
St. Petersburg
SWEDEN
Moscow
NORWAY
Stockholm
ESTONIA
RUSSIA
Oslo
LATVIA
LITHUANIA
BELARUS
DENMARK
Copenhagen
POLAND
UKRAINE
from AFGHANISTAN and PAKISTAN
NETHER-LANDS
Hamburg
Berlin
GERMANY
Amsterdam
CZECH R.
SLOVAKIA
GREAT BRITAIN
Cologne
Black Sea
London
Calais
BELGIUM
Frankfurt
ROMANIA
Luxembourg
AUSTRIA
HUNGARY
Munich
Freilassing
TURKEY
Paris
SLOVENIA
SERBIA
BULGARIA
Istanbul
Ankara
SWITZER-LAND
CROATIA
BOSNIA & HERZEG.
KOSOVO
SYRIA
Baghdad
Milan
NORTH MACED.
IRAQ
Thessaloniki
FRANCE
ALBANIA
L
Genua
B
M
N
O
P
R
S
K
ITALY
J
Athens
Rome
D
GREECE
H
Crete
C
Mediterranean Sea
Alexandria
E
F
G
Madrid
Tunis
EGYPT
PORTUGAL
SPAIN
Benghazi
Algiers
Lisbon
ALGERIA
Tripoli
TUNISIA
LIBYA
A
MOROCCO
from NIGERIA
from ERITREA, SOMALIA & SUDAN

A RECONSTRUCTION OF THE REFUGEE FLOWS TO EUROPE IN 2015

We have compiled the most trustworthy sources, compared them and put them together in a graphic.
Research shows that there are significantly fewer people staying in Germany than commonly believed.

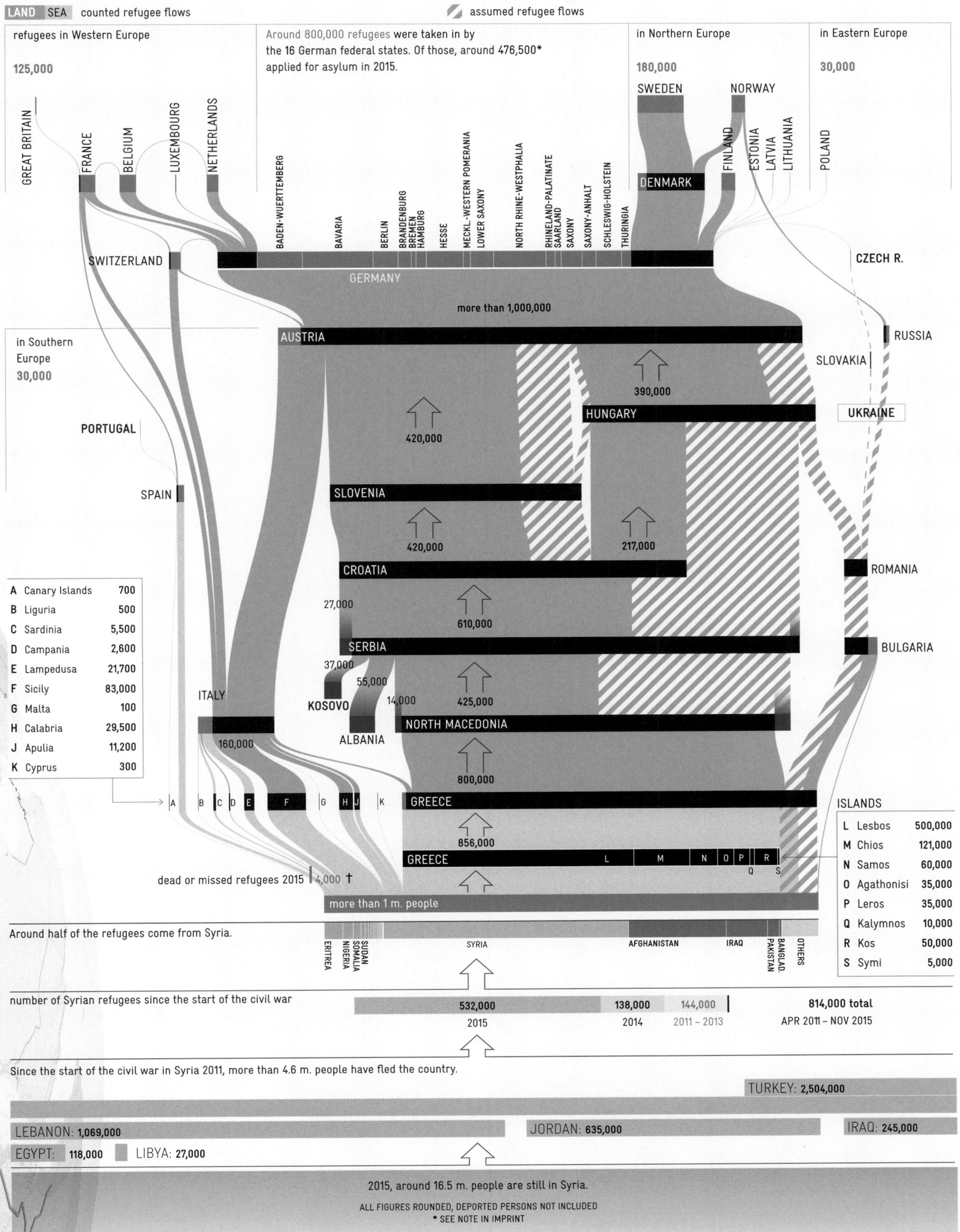
LAND SEA counted refugee flows
assumed refugee flows
refugees in Western Europe
125,000
GREAT BRITAIN
FRANCE
BELGIUM
LUXEMBOURG
NETHERLANDS
Around 800,000 refugees were taken in by the 16 German federal states. Of those, around 476,500* applied for asylum in 2015.
BADEN-WUERTTEMBERG
BAVARIA
BERLIN
BRANDENBURG
BREMEN
HAMBURG
HESSE
MECKL.-WESTERN POMERANIA
LOWER SAXONY
NORTH RHINE-WESTPHALIA
RHINELAND-PALATINATE
SAARLAND
SAXONY
SAXONY-ANHALT
SCHLESWIG-HOLSTEIN
THURINGIA
in Northern Europe
180,000
SWEDEN
NORWAY
DENMARK
FINLAND
ESTONIA
LATVIA
LITHUANIA
in Eastern Europe
30,000
POLAND
SWITZERLAND
GERMANY
CZECH R.
more than 1,000,000
AUSTRIA
RUSSIA
in Southern Europe
30,000
SLOVAKIA
390,000
PORTUGAL
420,000
HUNGARY
UKRAINE
SPAIN
SLOVENIA
420,000
217,000
CROATIA
ROMANIA
A Canary Islands 700
B Liguria 500
C Sardinia 5,500
D Campania 2,600
E Lampedusa 21,700
F Sicily 83,000
G Malta 100
H Calabria 29,500
J Apulia 11,200
K Cyprus 300
27,000
610,000
SERBIA
BULGARIA
37,000
55,000
ITALY
KOSOVO
14,000
425,000
ALBANIA
NORTH MACEDONIA
160,000
800,000
A B C D E F G H J K
GREECE
ISLANDS
856,000
L Lesbos 500,000
M Chios 121,000
N Samos 60,000
O Agathonisi 35,000
P Leros 35,000
Q Kalymnos 10,000
R Kos 50,000
S Symi 5,000
GREECE
L M N O P R
Q S
dead or missed refugees 2015
4,000 †
more than 1 m. people
Around half of the refugees come from Syria.
ERITREA
NIGERIA
SOMALIA
SUDAN
SYRIA
AFGHANISTAN
IRAQ
PAKISTAN
BANGLAD.
OTHERS
number of Syrian refugees since the start of the civil war
532,000
2015
138,000
2014
144,000
2011 – 2013
814,000 total
APR 2011 – NOV 2015
Since the start of the civil war in Syria 2011, more than 4.6 m. people have fled the country.
TURKEY: 2,504,000
LEBANON: 1,069,000
JORDAN: 635,000
IRAQ: 245,000
EGYPT: 118,000
LIBYA: 27,000
2015, around 16.5 m. people are still in Syria.
ALL FIGURES ROUNDED, DEPORTED PERSONS NOT INCLUDED
* SEE NOTE IN IMPRINT

PRIPYAT **UKRAINE**

51° 24′N, 30° 3′O

Pripyat was founded in **1970** as a housing estate for the workers of the first Ukrainian nuclear power plant. People lived in this city for only 16 years.

7.9 km²
47,500
1900
1950
1970
1986

April 26, the Chernobyl disaster struck. It took 36 hours to evacuate the city from its almost **50,000** inhabitants. Today, Pripyat is within Chernobyl's restricted zone. It will be uninhabitable for at least another 300 years.

DOEL **BELGIUM**

51° 19′N, 4° 15′ O

The Doel district of the town of Beveren once had two and a half thousand inhabitants and is located between a nuclear power plant and the Antwerp harbor.

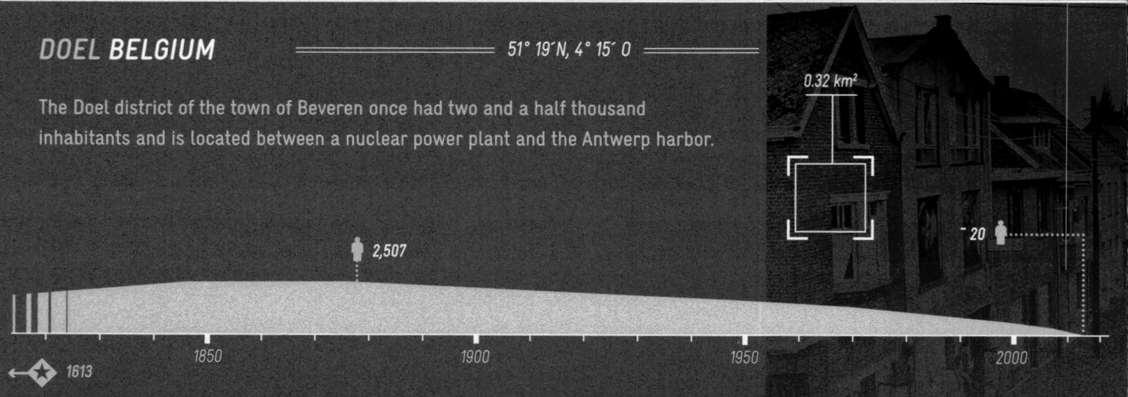
0.32 km²
20
2,507
1613
1850
1900
1950
2000

After **1998**, Doel's fate was sealed. The plan is for it to make way for a harbor basin. Since then, around one thousand people have left their homes and the signs of depopulation are clearly visible. Only around **20** people live in Doel now and firmly refuse to leave their homes behind.

AGDAM **AZERBAIJAN**

39° 59′N, 46° 55′O

Agdam is located in a region of the Nagorna-Karabakh conflict. For almost 100 years, Christian Armenians and Muslim Azerbaijanis have been fighting over the fertile land.

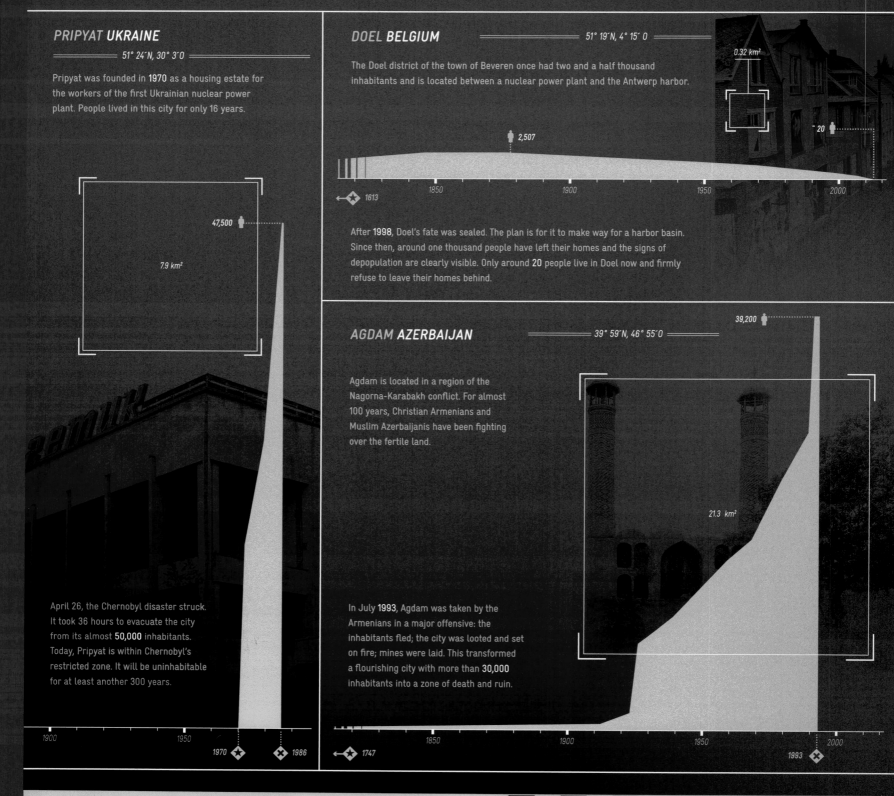

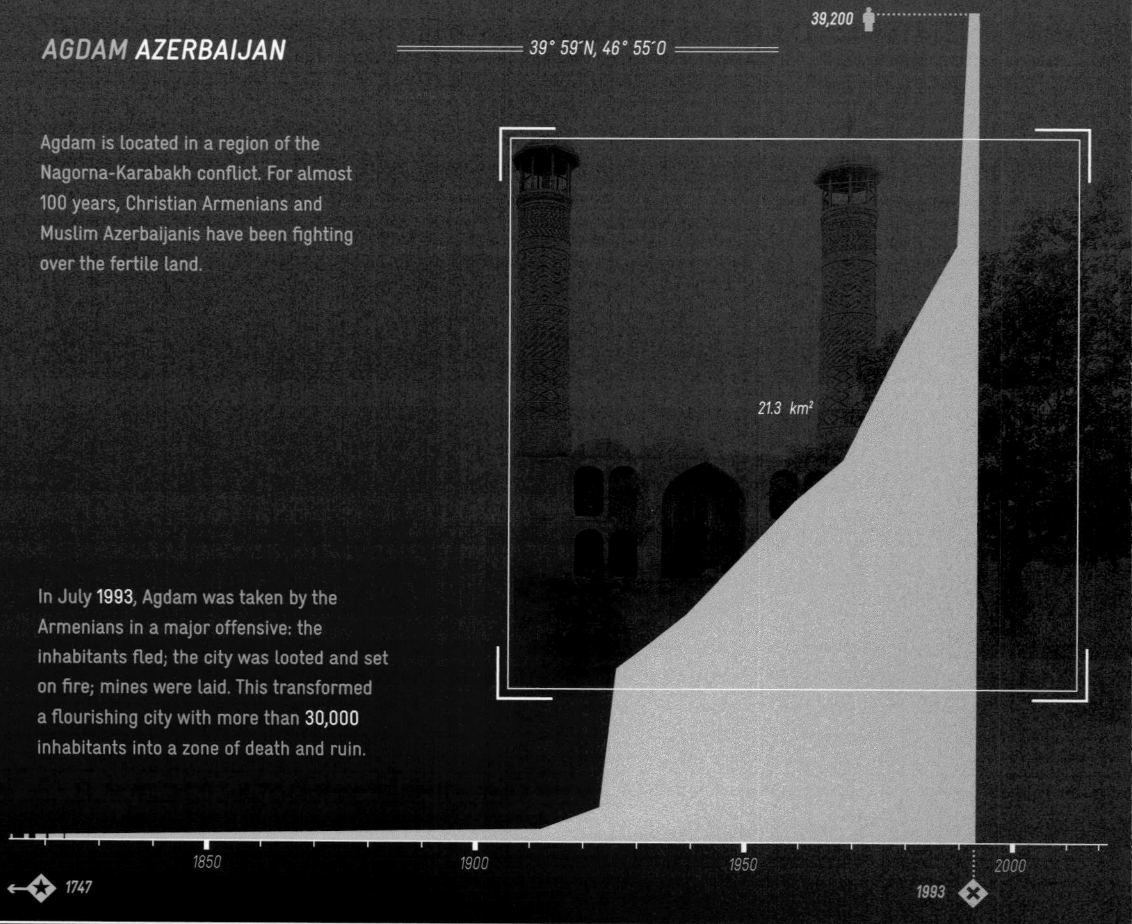
39,200
21.3 km²
1747
1850
1900
1950
2000
1993

In July **1993**, Agdam was taken by the Armenians in a major offensive: the inhabitants fled; the city was looted and set on fire; mines were laid. This transformed a flourishing city with more than **30,000** inhabitants into a zone of death and ruin.

ABANDONED CITIES

When a whole population leaves a city, it is mostly due to dramatic reasons: natural disasters, wars or economic constraints force citizens out of their homes — what is left are deserted ghost towns. Depopulation progresses very differently, depending on the causes. Consequently, every city leaves an individual footprint depending on its size and history.

SEWELL ***CHILE*** — *34° 5′ S, 70° 23′ W*

In **1905**, Braden Copper Company bought the El Teniente copper mine in the Andes. To start with, the miners lived in small camps around the mine until the camps were all combined in 1915 to form the mining city Sewell. It seemed like paradise because all of the basic products and services such as electricity, water, schools, food and healthcare were provided for free to the miners.

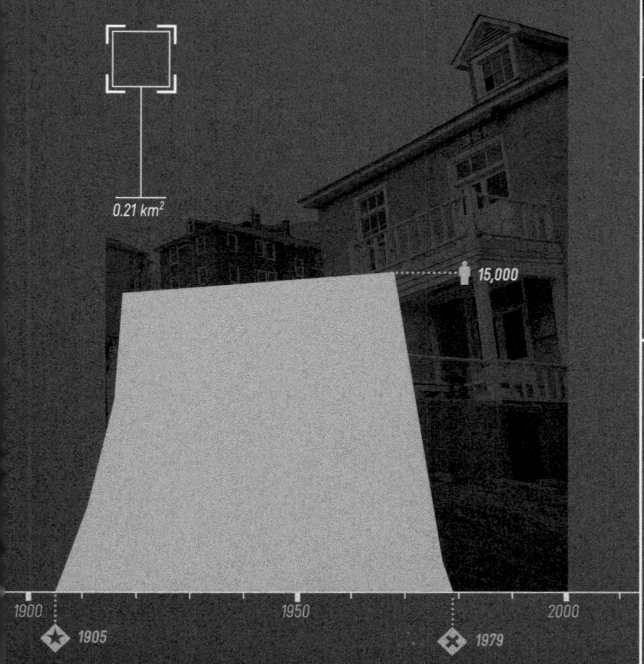
0.21 km²
15,000
1900
1950
2000
1905
1979

The mine became a state company in **1971** and copper the most important source of income for Chile. The mine was greatly enlarged and the miners were gradually resettled from Sewell to the bigger city Rangacua. Today, Sewell is a ghost town with colorful roofs. It is a UNESCO heritage site and a clear example of globalization processes in industrial history.

0.063 km²

HASHIMA ***JAPAN*** — *32° 37′N, 129° 44′O*

At the end of the 19th century, a coal mine was built on the island which originally measured **120 × 320** meters. The Mitsubishi group, which bought the island in **1890**, constantly expanded the area with excavation material to a size of **6.3** hectares by **1931**. During its heyday, around **5,000** people could live there.
This resulted in the largest ever measured population density—almost six times as high as in today's Tokyo.

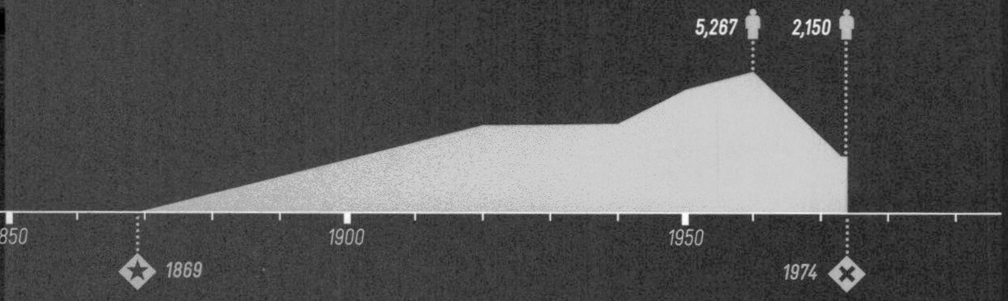
5,267
2,150
1850
1900
1950
1869
1974

The closure of the plants happened very abruptly. It only took three months from the closure to a complete exodus from the island. Today, Hashima is an industrial ruin which is slowly being developed for tourism.

POGGIOREALE ***ITALY*** — *37° 46′N, 13° 2′O*

The Poggioreale estate was developed in **1624** at the foot of Mount Castelazzo. In **1968**, it was badly damaged in an earthquake and so its inhabitants left. Today, the ruins with their morbid charm are a popular tourist attraction.

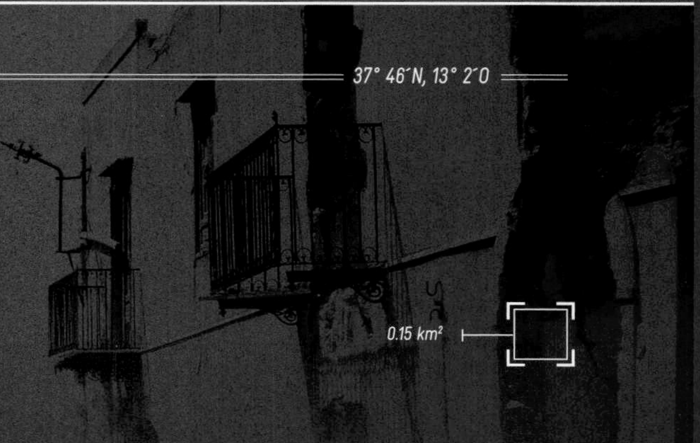
0.15 km²

The new Poggioreale estate was constructed only a few kilometers southeast of the original location and has around **1,500** citizens today.

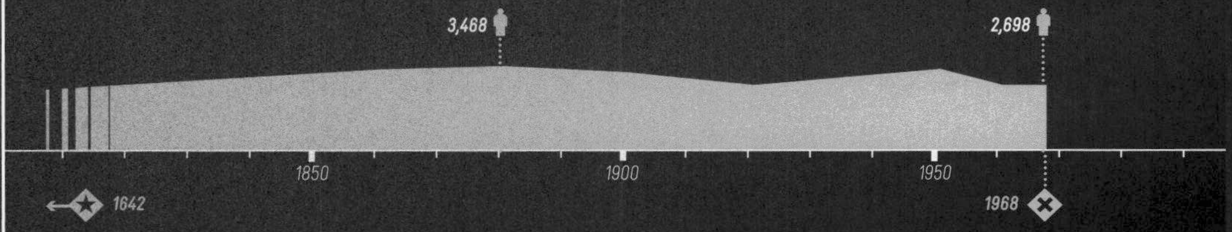
3,468
2,698
1850
1900
1950
1642
1968

Area

Foundation

Decline

Population

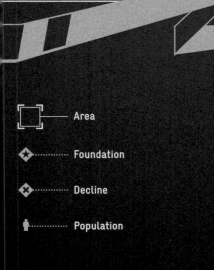

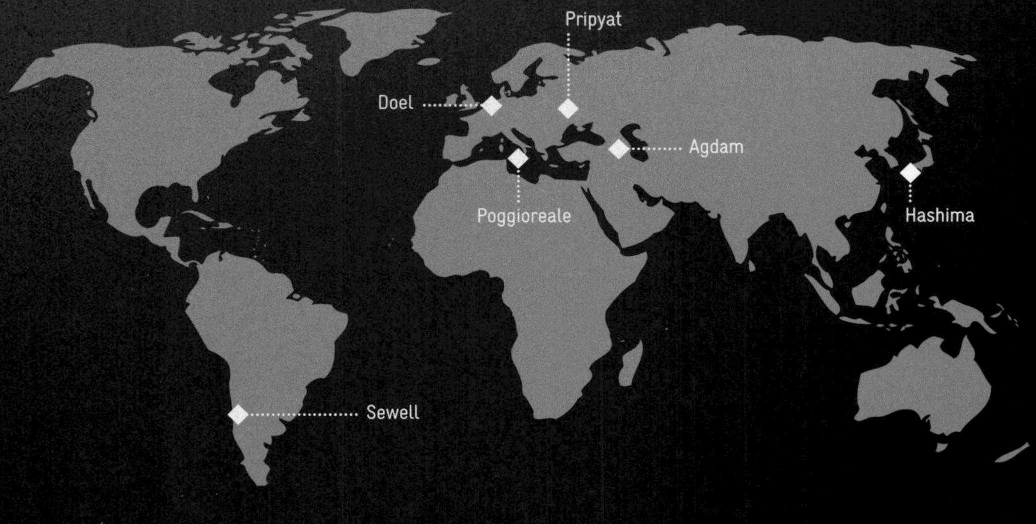
Pripyat
Doel
Agdam
Poggioreale
Hashima
Sewell

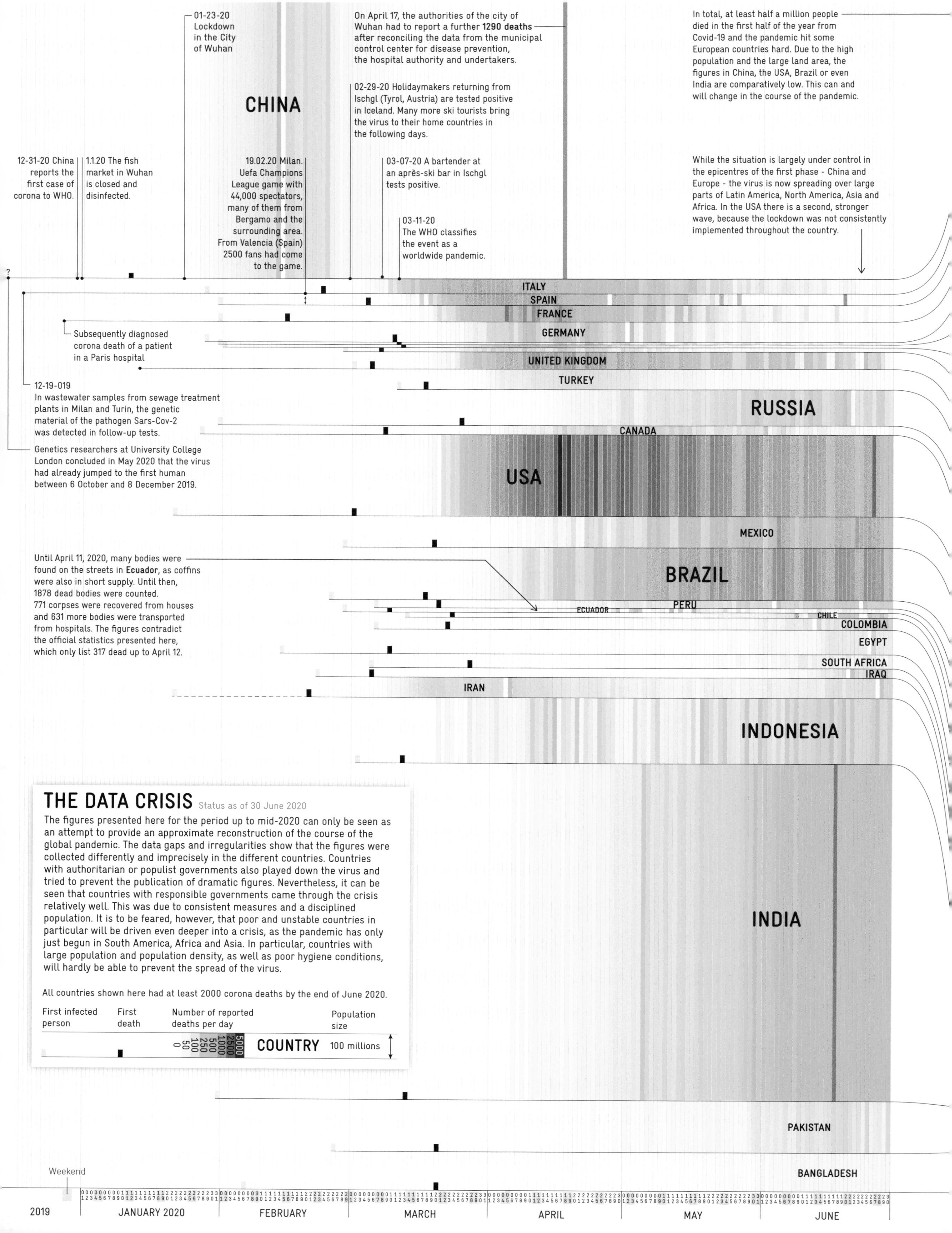
01-23-20 Lockdown in the City of Wuhan
CHINA
On April 17, the authorities of the city of Wuhan had to report a further **1290 deaths** after reconciling the data from the municipal control center for disease prevention, the hospital authority and undertakers.
02-29-20 Holidaymakers returning from Ischgl (Tyrol, Austria) are tested positive in Iceland. Many more ski tourists bring the virus to their home countries in the following days.
In total, at least half a million people died in the first half of the year from Covid-19 and the pandemic hit some European countries hard. Due to the high population and the large land area, the figures in China, the USA, Brazil or even India are comparatively low. This can and will change in the course of the pandemic.
12-31-20 China reports the first case of corona to WHO.
1.1.20 The fish market in Wuhan is closed and disinfected.
19.02.20 Milan. Uefa Champions League game with 44,000 spectators, many of them from Bergamo and the surrounding area. From Valencia (Spain) 2500 fans had come to the game.
03-07-20 A bartender at an après-ski bar in Ischgl tests positive.
03-11-20 The WHO classifies the event as a worldwide pandemic.
While the situation is largely under control in the epicentres of the first phase - China and Europe - the virus is now spreading over large parts of Latin America, North America, Asia and Africa. In the USA there is a second, stronger wave, because the lockdown was not consistently implemented throughout the country.
?
ITALY
SPAIN
FRANCE
Subsequently diagnosed corona death of a patient in a Paris hospital
GERMANY
UNITED KINGDOM
TURKEY
12-19-019 In wastewater samples from sewage treatment plants in Milan and Turin, the genetic material of the pathogen Sars-Cov-2 was detected in follow-up tests.
RUSSIA
CANADA
Genetics researchers at University College London concluded in May 2020 that the virus had already jumped to the first human between 6 October and 8 December 2019.
USA
MEXICO
Until April 11, 2020, many bodies were found on the streets in **Ecuador**, as coffins were also in short supply. Until then, 1878 dead bodies were counted. 771 corpses were recovered from houses and 631 more bodies were transported from hospitals. The figures contradict the official statistics presented here, which only list 317 dead up to April 12.
BRAZIL
ECUADOR
PERU
CHILE
COLOMBIA
EGYPT
SOUTH AFRICA
IRAQ
IRAN
INDONESIA
INDIA
PAKISTAN
BANGLADESH
Weekend
2019
JANUARY 2020
FEBRUARY
MARCH
APRIL
MAY
JUNE

THE DATA CRISIS

Status as of 30 June 2020

The figures presented here for the period up to mid-2020 can only be seen as an attempt to provide an approximate reconstruction of the course of the global pandemic. The data gaps and irregularities show that the figures were collected differently and imprecisely in the different countries. Countries with authoritarian or populist governments also played down the virus and tried to prevent the publication of dramatic figures. Nevertheless, it can be seen that countries with responsible governments came through the crisis relatively well. This was due to consistent measures and a disciplined population. It is to be feared, however, that poor and unstable countries in particular will be driven even deeper into a crisis, as the pandemic has only just begun in South America, Africa and Asia. In particular, countries with large population and population density, as well as poor hygiene conditions, will hardly be able to prevent the spread of the virus.

All countries shown here had at least 2000 corona deaths by the end of June 2020.

	Deaths per 1m. population	Total cases per 1m. population
WORLD	66	1,360
CHINA	3	58
ITALY	575	3,979
SPAIN	606	6,338
FRANCE	457	2,525
GERMANY	108	2,337
SWEDEN	531	6,890
BELGIUM	841	5,300
NETHERLANDS	357	2,934
U. KINGDOM	644	4,606
TURKEY	61	2,370
RUSSIA	64	4,439
CANADA	228	2,761
USA	393	8,244
MEXICO	210	1,711
BRAZIL	281	6,626
PERU	293	8,650
ECUADOR	257	3,199
CHILE	298	14,615
COLOMBIA	66	1,923
EGYPT	29	668
SOUTH AFRICA	45	2,550
IRAQ	48	1,221
IRAN	129	2,711
INDONESIA	11	206
INDIA	13	424
PAKISTAN	19	948
BANGLADESH	11	883

A VIRUS CHANGES THE WORLD

Never before has the earth experienced anything like this – it took just a few weeks for the global pandemic to bring our lives to a standstill. Various statistics are available to help us gauge its impact on our lives. The hunger for data of both business and institutions, coupled with the technical possibilities, has enabled us to present you some interesting charts. The economic consequences will keep us busy for years, or even decades. As these charts demonstrate most impressively, however, crises also produce winners.

The willingness of consumers to spend is declining.

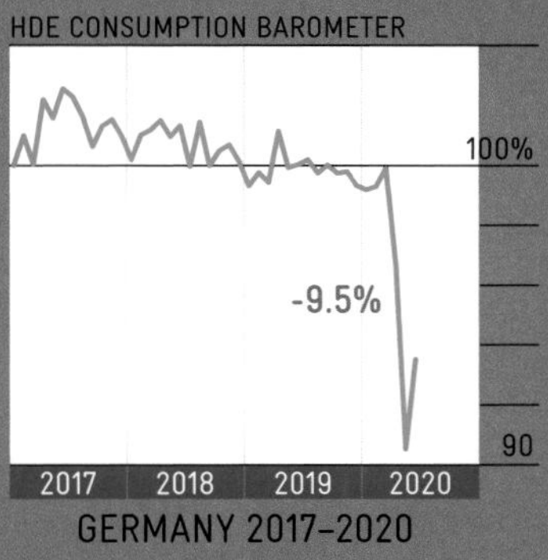

HDE CONSUMPTION BAROMETER
100%
-9.5%
90
2017 2018 2019 2020
GERMANY 2017–2020

Manufacturers of hygiene products are among the winners.

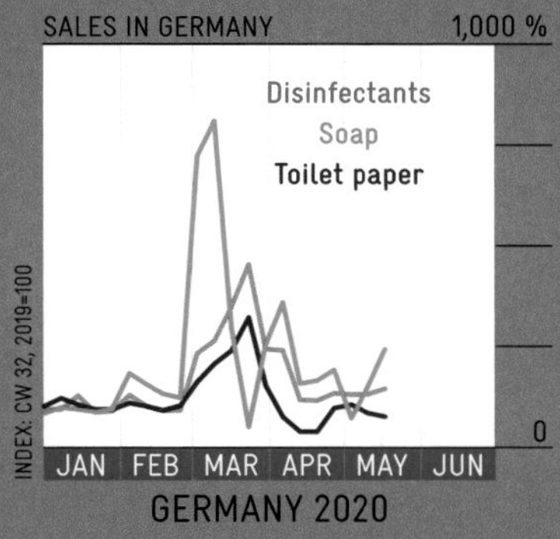

SALES IN GERMANY
1,000 %
Disinfectants
Soap
Toilet paper
INDEX: CW 32, 2019=100
0
JAN FEB MAR APR MAY JUN
GERMANY 2020

Americans stock up on weapons.

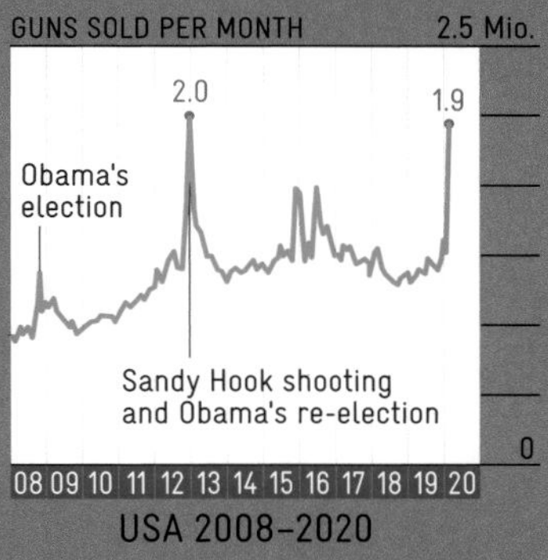

GUNS SOLD PER MONTH
2.5 Mio.
2.0
1.9
Obama's election
Sandy Hook shooting and Obama's re-election
0
08 09 10 11 12 13 14 15 16 17 18 19 20
USA 2008–2020

Boredom at home: Streaming services are thriving

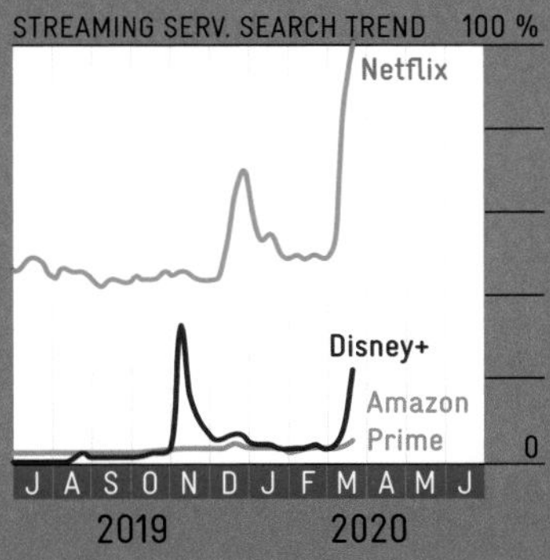

STREAMING SERV. SEARCH TREND
100 %
Netflix
Disney+
Amazon Prime
0
J A S O N D J F M A M J
2019 2020

Home office and home schooling: Video conferencing is booming

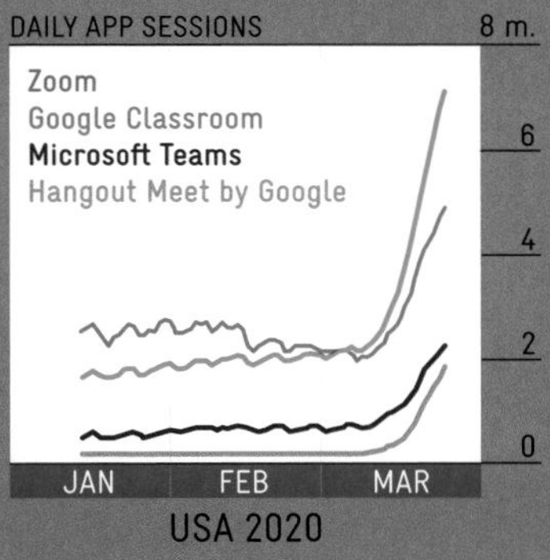

DAILY APP SESSIONS
8 m.
Zoom
Google Classroom
Microsoft Teams
Hangout Meet by Google
6
4
2
0
JAN FEB MAR
USA 2020

Electricity demand in northern Italy declines

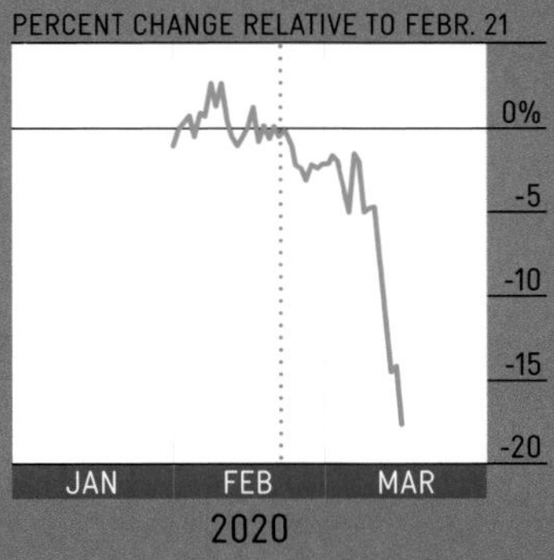

PERCENT CHANGE RELATIVE TO FEBR. 21
0%
-5
-10
-15
-20
JAN FEB MAR
2020

In April, worldwide air traffic almost comes to a standstill.

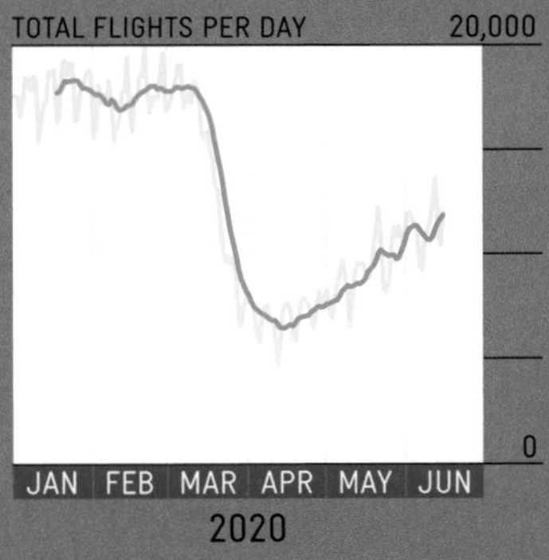

TOTAL FLIGHTS PER DAY
20,000
0
JAN FEB MAR APR MAY JUN
2020

Tourism no longer takes place worldwide.

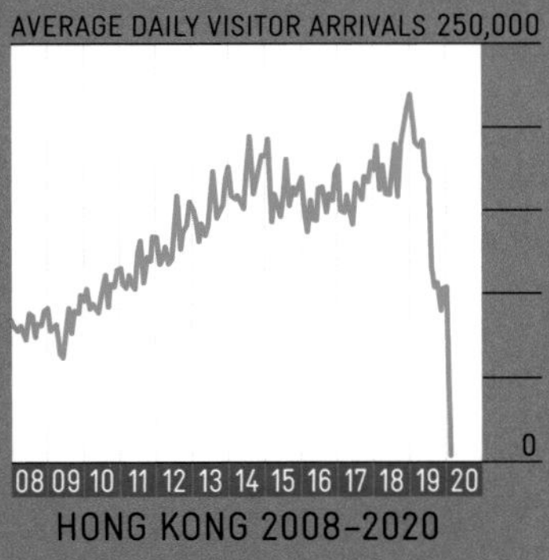

AVERAGE DAILY VISITOR ARRIVALS
250,000
0
08 09 10 11 12 13 14 15 16 17 18 19 20
HONG KONG 2008–2020

People stay at home and hardly move at all.

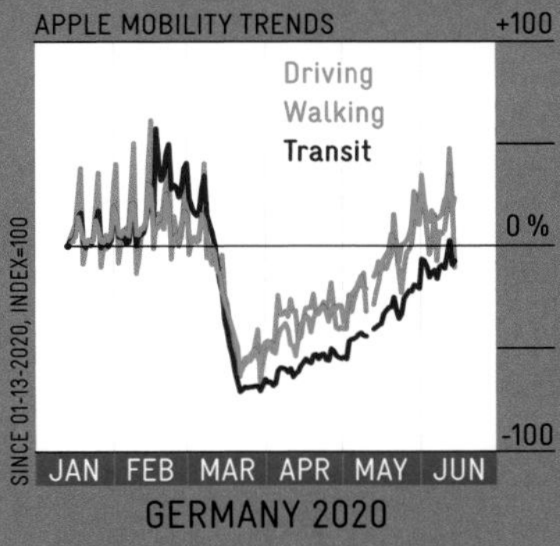

APPLE MOBILITY TRENDS
+100
Driving
Walking
Transit
0 %
-100
SINCE 01-13-2020, INDEX=100
JAN FEB MAR APR MAY JUN
GERMANY 2020

The production of CORONA beer is discontinued in Mexico.

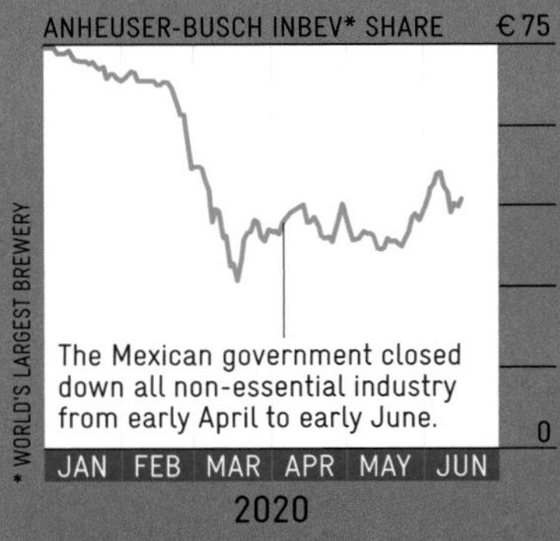

ANHEUSER-BUSCH INBEV* SHARE
€ 75
The Mexican government closed down all non-essential industry from early April to early June.
0
* WORLD'S LARGEST BREWERY
JAN FEB MAR APR MAY JUN
2020

The stock markets go into a tailspin.

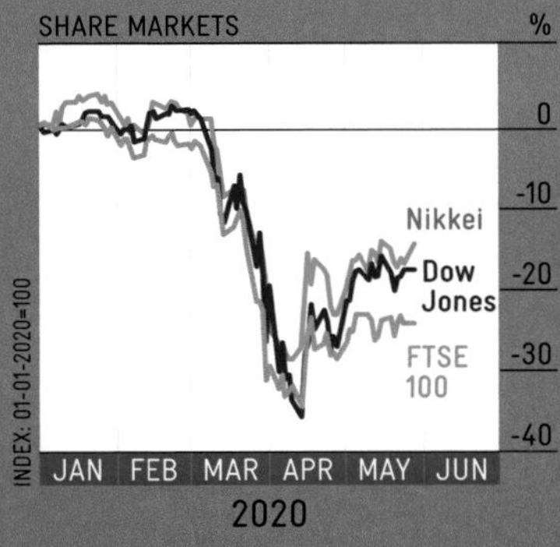

SHARE MARKETS
%
0
-10
-20
-30
-40
Nikkei
Dow Jones
FTSE 100
INDEX: 01-01-2020=100
JAN FEB MAR APR MAY JUN
2020

Many people lose their jobs and their existence.

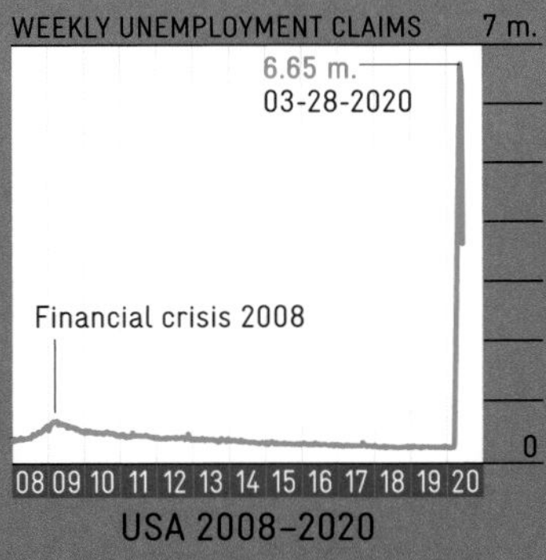

WEEKLY UNEMPLOYMENT CLAIMS
7 m.
6.65 m.
03-28-2020
Financial crisis 2008
0
08 09 10 11 12 13 14 15 16 17 18 19 20
USA 2008–2020

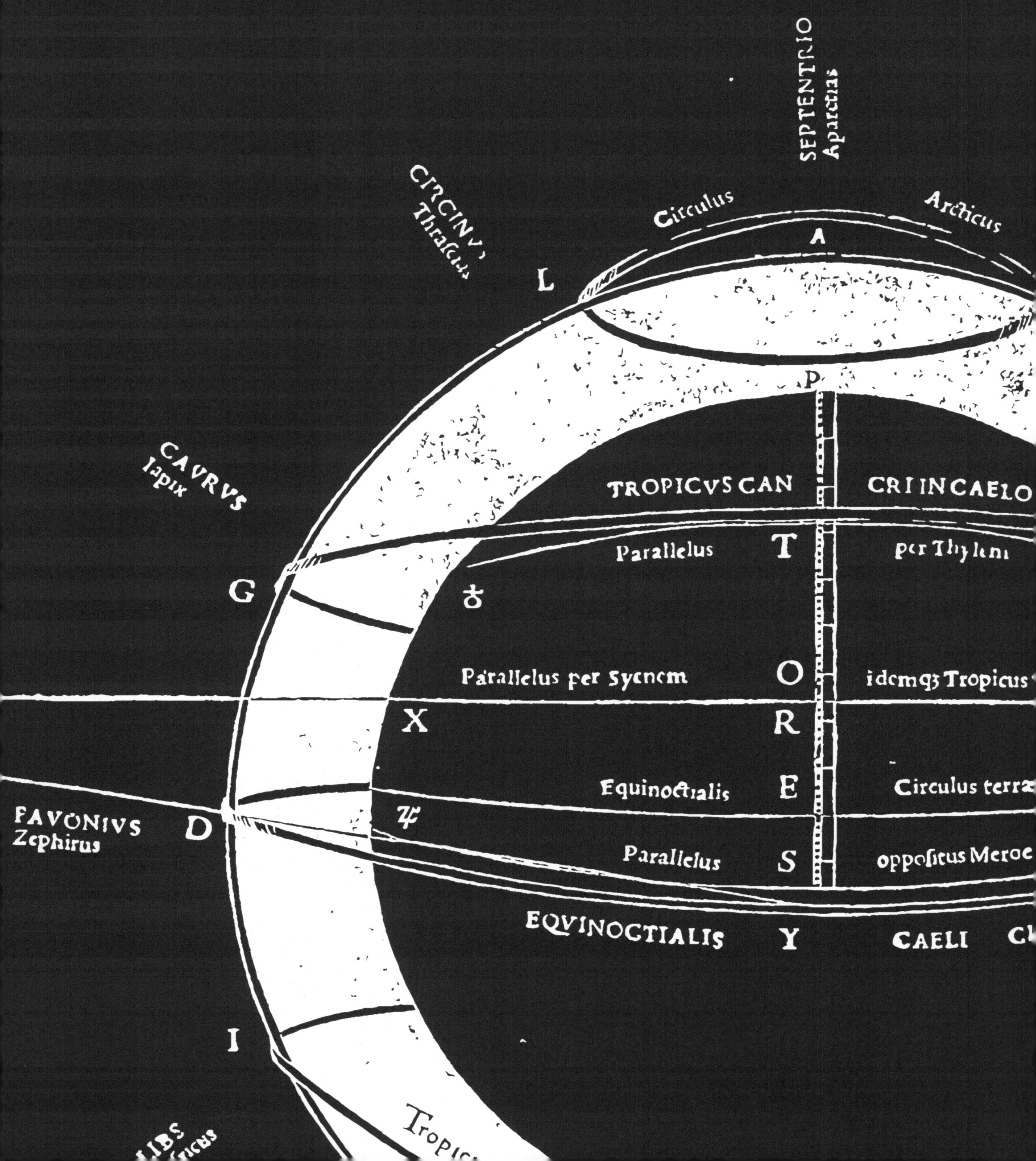

SEPTENTRIO
Aparctias
CIRCINVS
Thrascias
Circulus
Arcticus
A
L
P
CAVRVS
Iapix
TROPICVS CAN
CRI IN CAELO
Parallelus
T
G
Parallelus per Sycnem
O
idemq3 Tropicus
X
R
Equinoctialis
E
Circulus terrae
FAVONIVS
Zephirus
D
Parallelus
S
oppositus Meroe
EQVINOCTIALIS
Y
CAELI
I
LIBS
Tropic

POLITICS

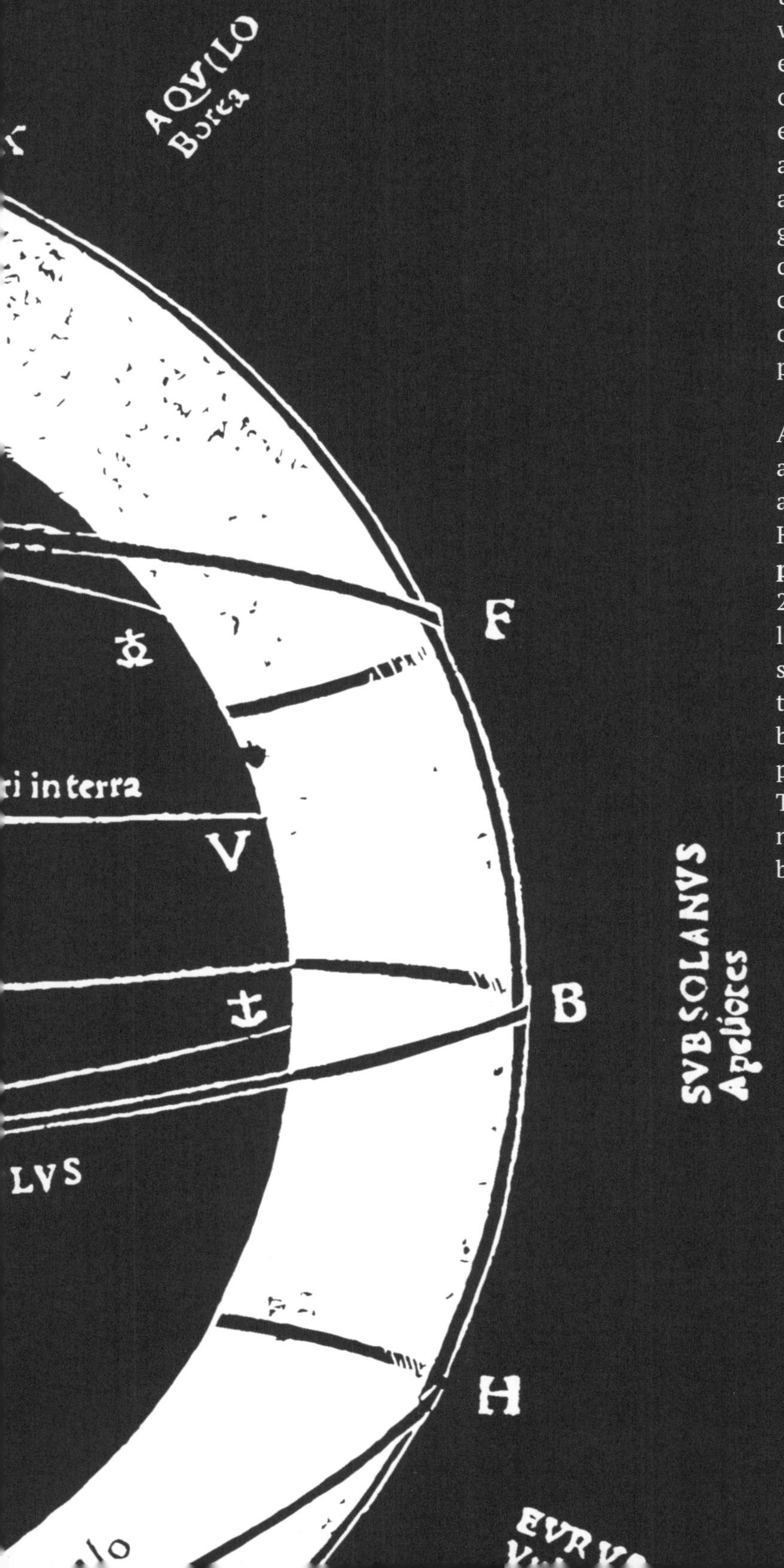

In journalism infographics have long been used in accounting for the state of the world. Political journalism, in particular, employs maps to locate issues beyond our individual spatial recognition. Be it election results or military conflicts, maps are used in politics to analyze and set an agenda. Since the Enlightenment, geographic charts have also been paired with diagrams to form thematic maps. These can link space to often invisible conditions and processes and allow the display of population density or the flow of goods.

A common feature of modern maps is accuracy, which was pioneered by the ancient Greek **Claudius Ptolemy**.
He defined latitude and introduced **map projections** of the spherical Earth in the 2nd century AD. The illustration to the left, taken from a Renaissance publication, shows the construction of such a projection. Today, digitalization blurs the line between the globe and the planar map produced with interactive tools.
The everyday user can easily find the next restaurant or concert hall, but borders and conflicts persist.

DEGREES OF DEMOCRACY

The Economist's »Democracy Index« measures and categorizes the state of democracy in 167 countries. A full democracy usually has the following features: free and fair elections; political pluralism; respect of civil liberties and human rights; protection of minority rights; functioning government with an effective system of checks and balances; equality before the law and an independent judiciary as well as free and diverse media.

POPULATION

Only a small percentage of the population live in countries with full democracies. A large number live in flawed democracies, like India, or authoritarian regimes, like China.

While the population in the two most populous countries is almost equal, there are big differences when it comes to the average annual birth rates. In China, like in the US, there are on average 12.49 births per 1,000 habitants, which is a small number compared to the 19.55 and 21.14 in India and Bangladesh respectively.

LAND MASS

When scaling countries according to their land masses, it is evident that half of the Earth's land mass belongs to full or flawed democracies, and that half of the population lives under these government systems. But still 40 % of the Earth's land mass is controlled by authoritarian regimes.

Although almost equal in terms of population, India and China differ in terms of territory. This indicates a large difference in population density. While in China, there are 146 people per square kilometer of land, in India there are 441. For the United States the number is 35, and in Bangladesh it is 1,237 – one of the highest densities in the world.

ECONOMY

When scaling countries according to their gross domestic product (GDP), it's clear that full democracies have a bigger share of the world's economy than corresponds to their population or land mass. While democracy might be one indicator for economic productivity, other factors such as historical and geographic conditions and the market system must also be taken into account.

While economic heavyweights China and the US match up to each other in absolute numbers, comparing the numbers per capita would draw a different picture. The GDP per capita is $ 55,800 in the United States, but only $ 14,100 in China, $ 6,200 in India, and a mere $ 3,600 in Bangladesh.

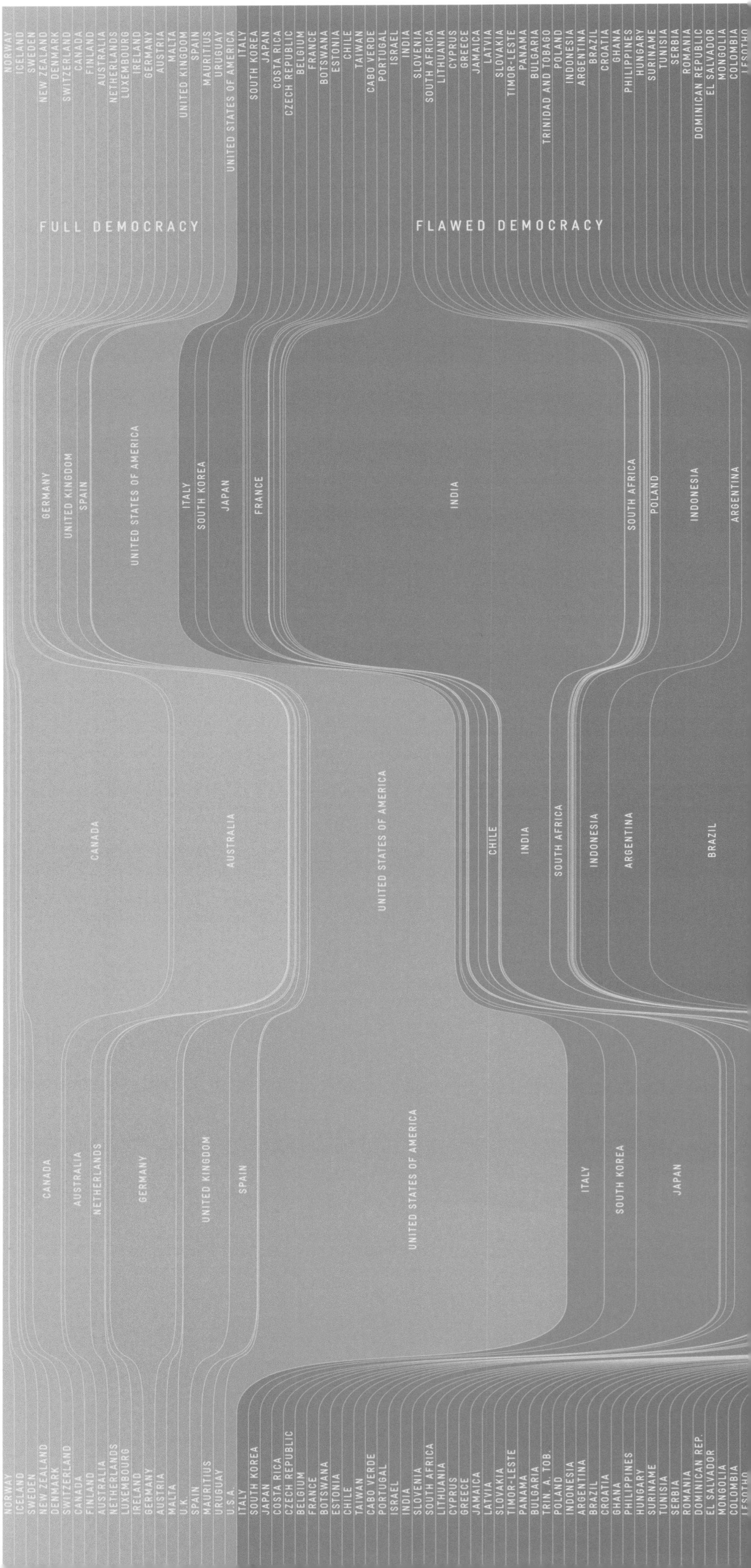

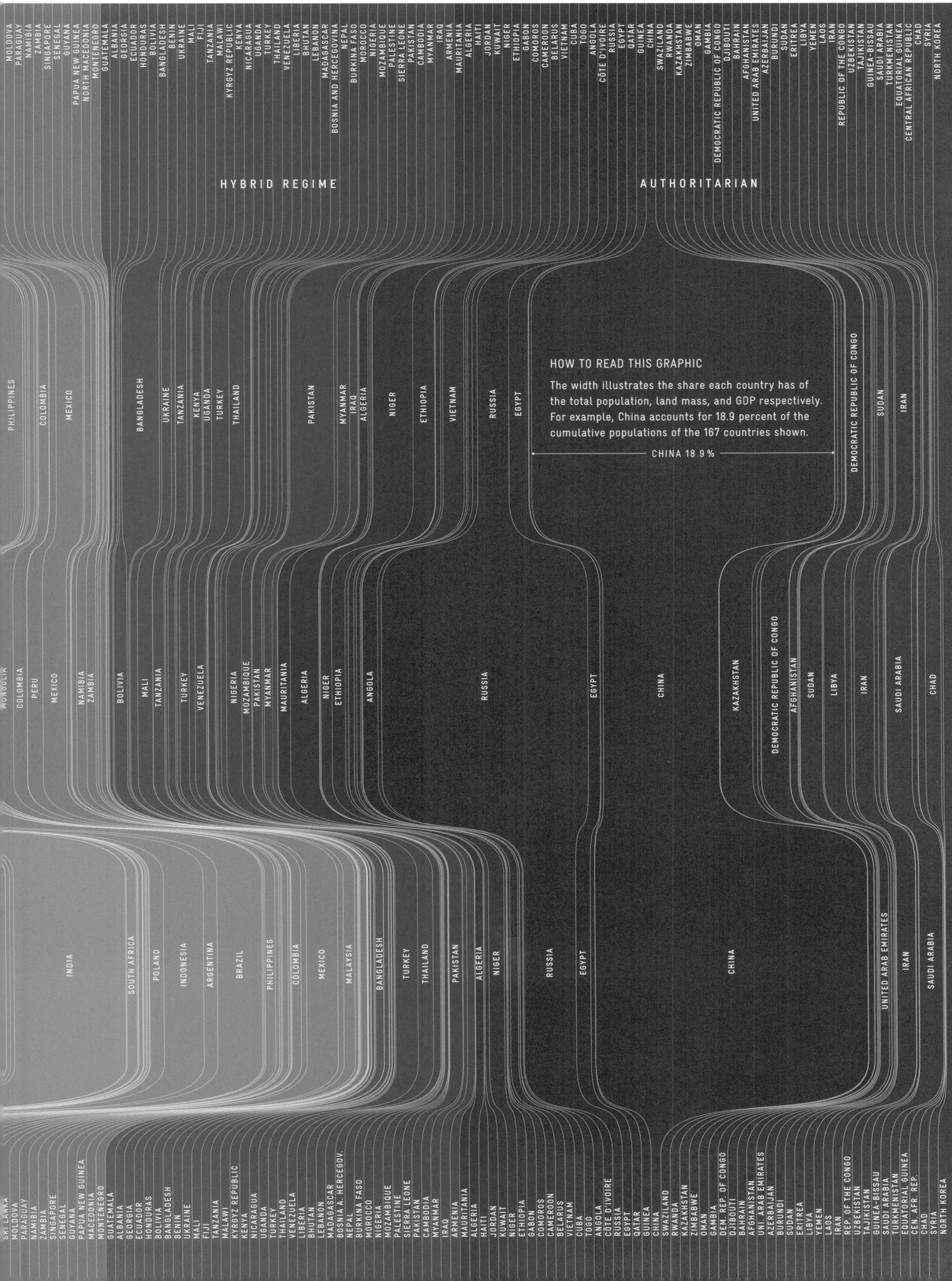

HYBRID REGIME
AUTHORITARIAN
HOW TO READ THIS GRAPHIC
The width illustrates the share each country has of the total population, land mass, and GDP respectively. For example, China accounts for 18.9 percent of the cumulative populations of the 167 countries shown.
CHINA 18.9 %

COLD PEACE

The Antarctic Treaty was signed on December 1, 1959.
Since then – 140 years after the exploration of Antarctica – the treaty has regulated the peaceful coexistence of different social systems on the continent. It is of great political and scientific importance.

The ANTARCTIC TREATY allows independent and trouble-free scientific exchange for the participating nations and saves the environment from pollution. It is administered and updated by a council, which is in session every other year. This is a summary of its content.

ART. 1
The Antarctic may only be used for peaceful purposes.

ART. 2
Research and scientific cooperation between member states is unrestricted.

ART. 3
There is a free and easy exchange of information and personnel between member states.

ART. 4
Territorial claims must not be established nor discussed.

ART. 5
Nuclear weapons testing and disposal of nuclear waste is prohibited.

ART. 6
Main subject of the treaty is land and frozen surfaces south of 60 degrees latitude.

ART. 7
Member states nominate observers who get free access to territories, establishments and equipment.

ART. 8
Researchers and observers are under the jurisdiction of their respective country of origin.

ART. 9 – 14
These Articles serve the purpose of maintenance, improvement and administration of the treaty.

The TREATY was developed in Washington D.C. during the International Geophysical Year of 1957/58. One of the main reasons for it was the unresolved ownership claims of the various nations in Antarctica.

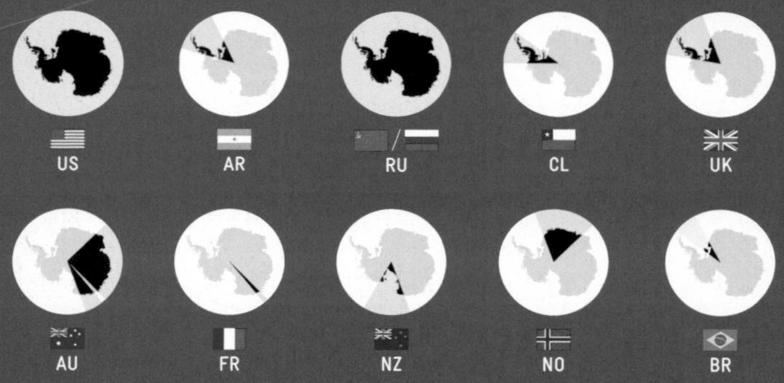
US
AR
RU
CL
UK
AU
FR
NZ
NO
BR

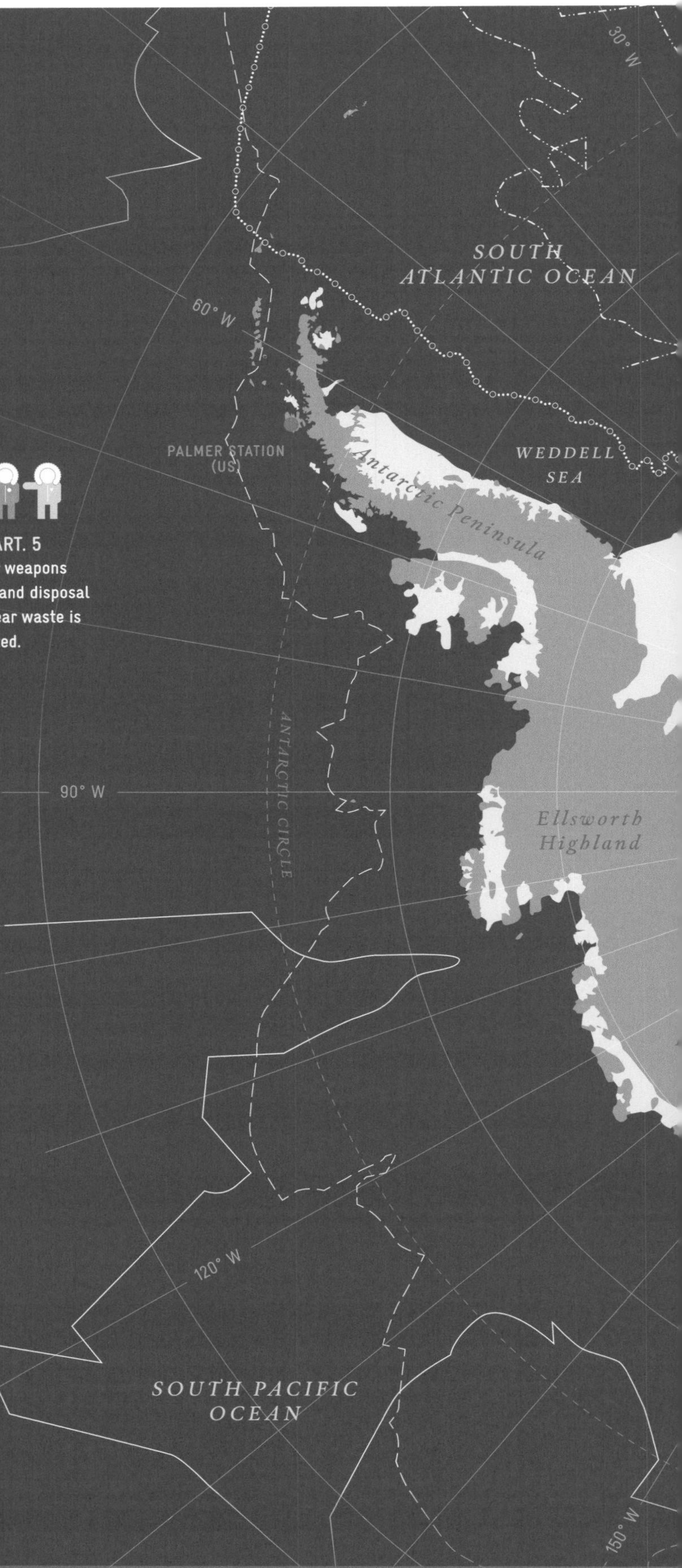
30° W
SOUTH ATLANTIC OCEAN
60° W
PALMER STATION (US)
WEDDELL SEA
Antarctic Peninsula
ANTARCTIC CIRCLE
90° W
Ellsworth Highland
120° W
SOUTH PACIFIC OCEAN
150° W

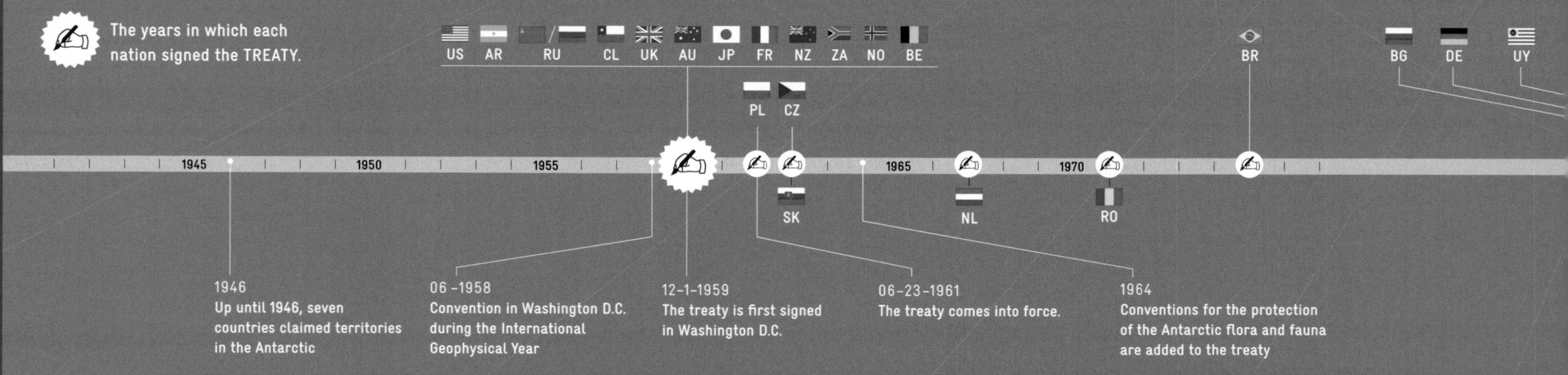
The years in which each nation signed the TREATY.
US AR RU CL UK AU JP FR NZ ZA NO BE
PL CZ
BR
BG DE UY
1945
1950
1955
1965
1970
SK
NL
RO
1946
Up until 1946, seven countries claimed territories in the Antarctic
06 -1958
Convention in Washington D.C. during the International Geophysical Year
12-1-1959
The treaty is first signed in Washington D.C.
06-23-1961
The treaty comes into force.
1964
Conventions for the protection of the Antarctic flora and fauna are added to the treaty

RACING TO THE END OF THE WORLD

In 1911, the Norwegian Roald Amundsen and his team were the first people to reach the South Pole. They won the race for glory just a month before Robert Falcon Scott from Great Britain and his team also reached the most southern point in the world. Unfortunately they didn't survive the arduous journey back and died in the cold. For a long time people tried to fathom out the Antarctic. James Cook was the first to circuit the continent in 1773/74 and established it as an exploration destination.

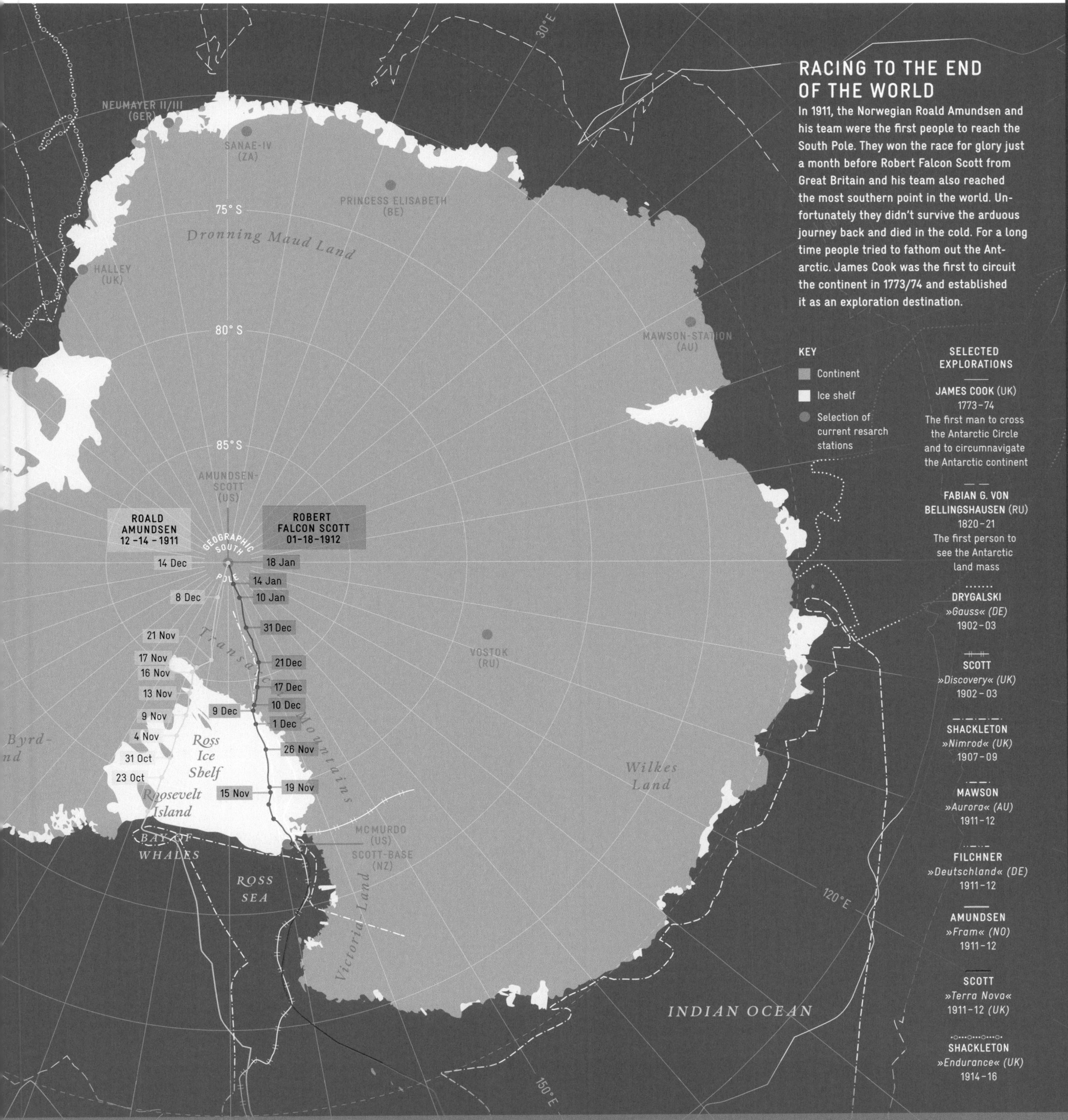
NEUMAYER II/III (GER)
SANAE-IV (ZA)
PRINCESS ELISABETH (BE)
HALLEY (UK)
MAWSON-STATION (AU)
VOSTOK (RU)
AMUNDSEN-SCOTT (US)
MCMURDO (US)
SCOTT-BASE (NZ)
30° E
75° S
80° S
85° S
120° E
150° E
Dronning Maud Land
Wilkes Land
Victoria Land
Transantarctic Mountains
Ross Ice Shelf
Roosevelt Island
BAY OF WHALES
ROSS SEA
INDIAN OCEAN
GEOGRAPHIC SOUTH POLE
ROALD AMUNDSEN 12-14-1911
ROBERT FALCON SCOTT 01-18-1912
14 Dec
8 Dec
21 Nov
17 Nov
16 Nov
13 Nov
9 Nov
4 Nov
31 Oct
23 Oct
18 Jan
14 Jan
10 Jan
31 Dec
21 Dec
17 Dec
10 Dec
9 Dec
1 Dec
26 Nov
19 Nov
15 Nov

KEY

- Continent
- Ice shelf
- Selection of current resarch stations

SELECTED EXPLORATIONS

JAMES COOK (UK)
1773–74
The first man to cross the Antarctic Circle and to circumnavigate the Antarctic continent

FABIAN G. VON BELLINGSHAUSEN (RU)
1820–21
The first person to see the Antarctic land mass

DRYGALSKI
»Gauss« (DE)
1902–03

SCOTT
»Discovery« (UK)
1902–03

SHACKLETON
»Nimrod« (UK)
1907–09

MAWSON
»Aurora« (AU)
1911–12

FILCHNER
»Deutschland« (DE)
1911–12

AMUNDSEN
»Fram« (NO)
1911–12

SCOTT
»Terra Nova«
1911–12 *(UK)*

SHACKLETON
»Endurance« (UK)
1914–16

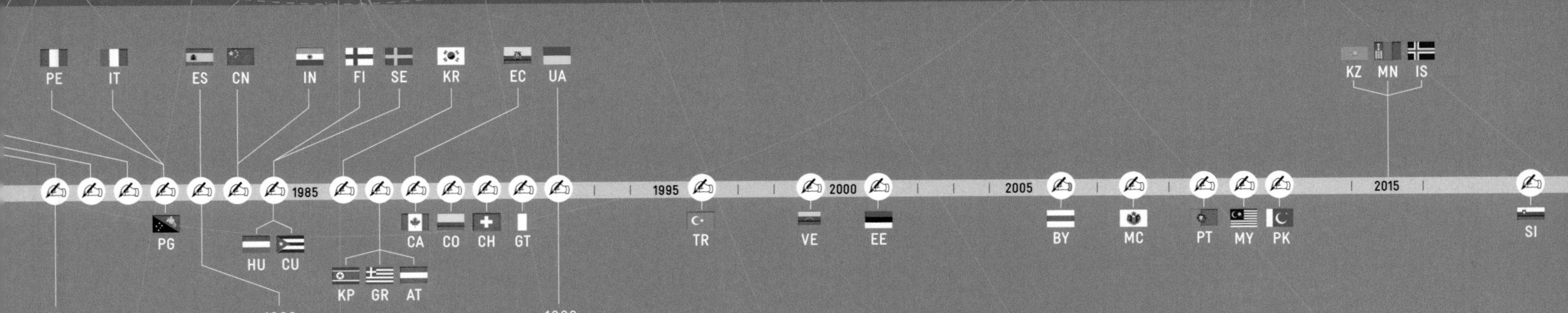
PE
IT
ES
CN
IN
FI
SE
KR
EC
UA
KZ
MN
IS
1985
1995
2000
2005
2015
PG
HU
CU
KP
GR
AT
CA
CO
CH
GT
TR
VE
EE
BY
MC
PT
MY
PK
SI

1978
Conventions for the protection of the Antarctic seals are added to the treaty

1982
Conventions for the conservation of the Antarctic marine living resources are added to the treaty

1992
A protocol prohibits the mining of mineral resources in the Antarctic

PUTIN'S ARCTIC AMBITIONS

Russia is laying claim to a huge region of the Arctic seafloor, including the North Pole. Vladimir Putin is currently investing billions to expand civil and military constructions within the territory – to the horror of other Arctic nations. What's behind this power struggle in the Arctic Circle?

Who owns the North Pole?

The disputed territory in the Arctic Ocean lies outside territorial waters (the exclusive economic zone). Nations who want to lay claim to this territory have to prove to the UN that the region belongs to their own continental shelf. Russia is claiming the North Pole as its own. It's all a question of the Lomonosov Ridge and whether this is an extension of the Russian mainland. On the other hand, Denmark regards the area as part of Greenland. What's more, Norway, Canada and the USA all lay claim to this 'no man's land'. As a result, the Arctic nations are strengthening their military presence in the region, and none more so than Russia.

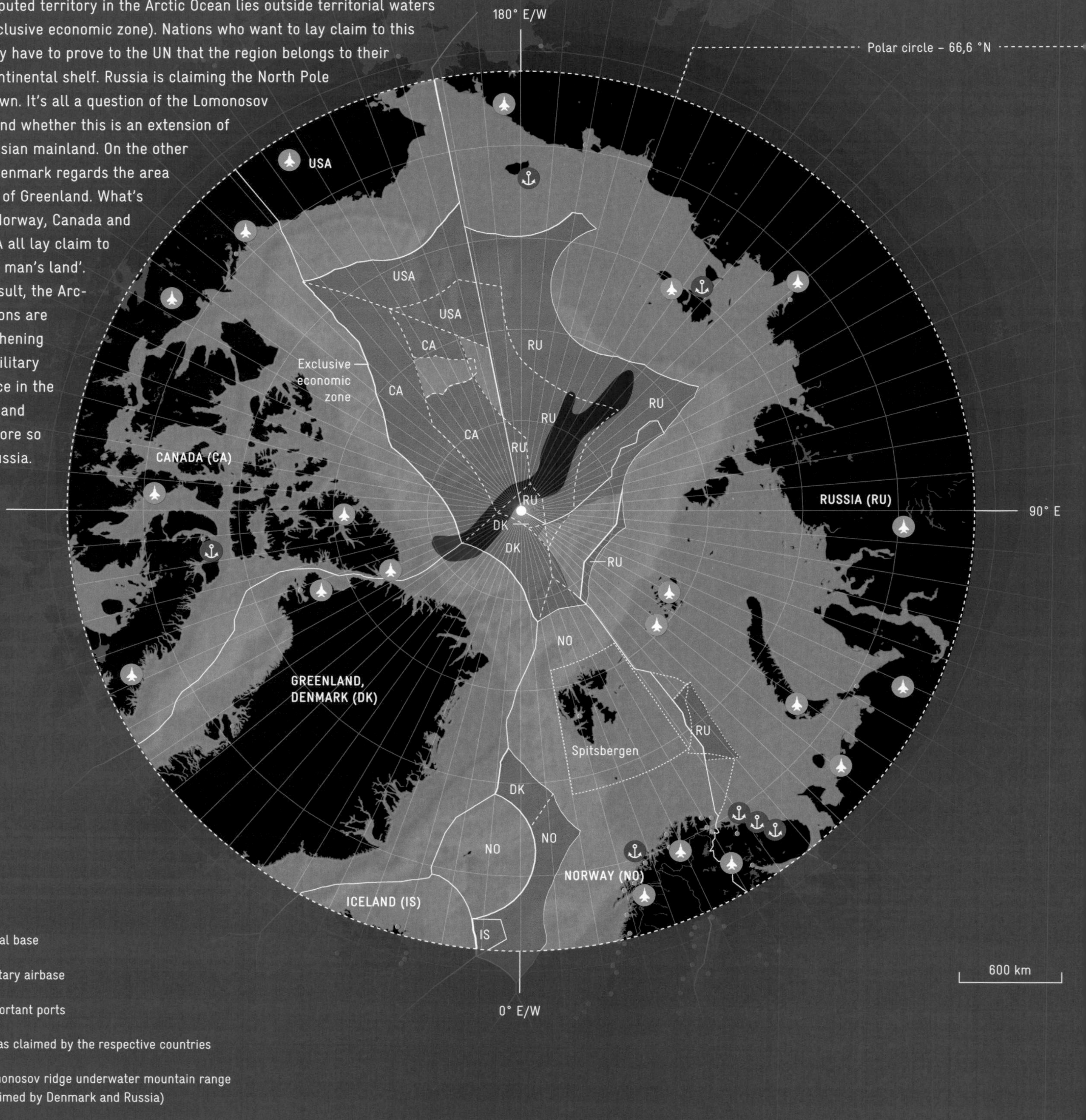

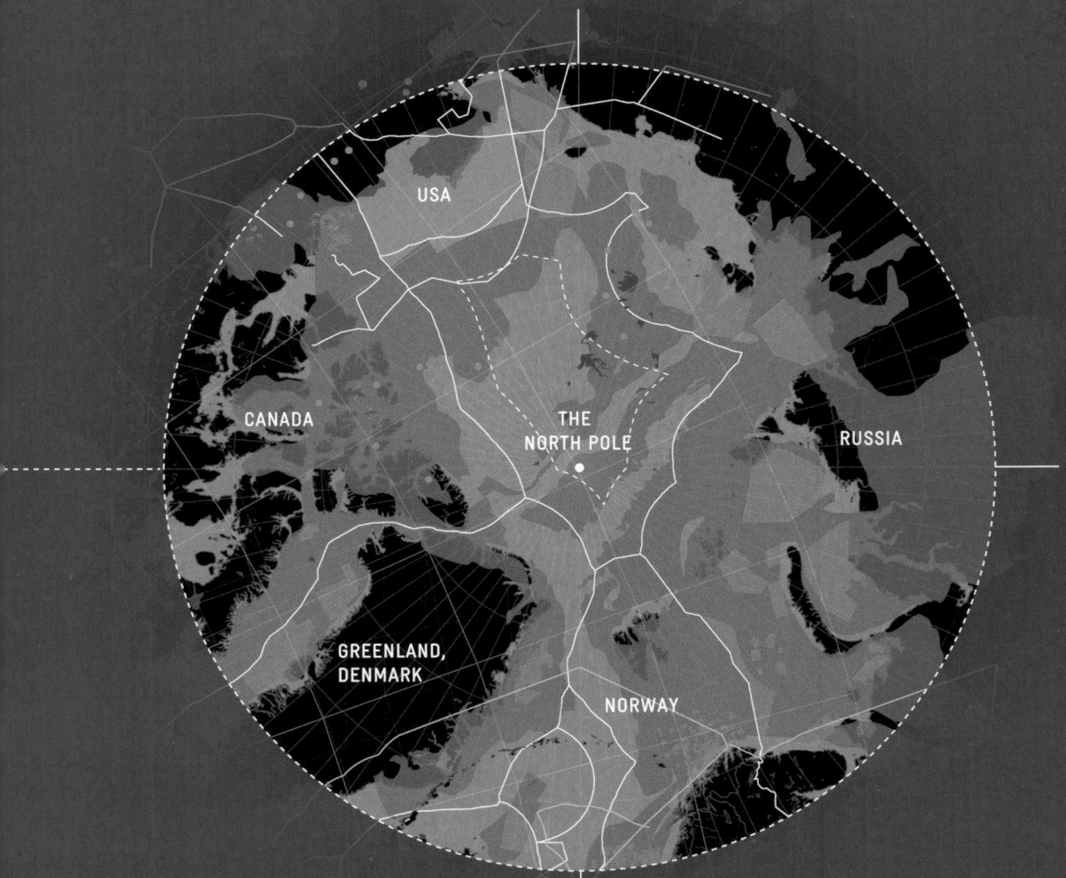

Allocated licenses to operate

Future licenses to operate

Oil and natural gas deposits

Vast deposits of oil and gas

It is estimated that 15 % of the world's oil and up to 30 % of its gas lies under the Arctic Ocean. Nations have already issued comprehensive drilling and production licenses inside their exclusive economic zones and now it's a matter of securing the rights to the no man's land around the North Pole. The former Russian Prime Minister Dmitry Medvedev describes the use of these resources as the key to securing energy for the whole of Russia.

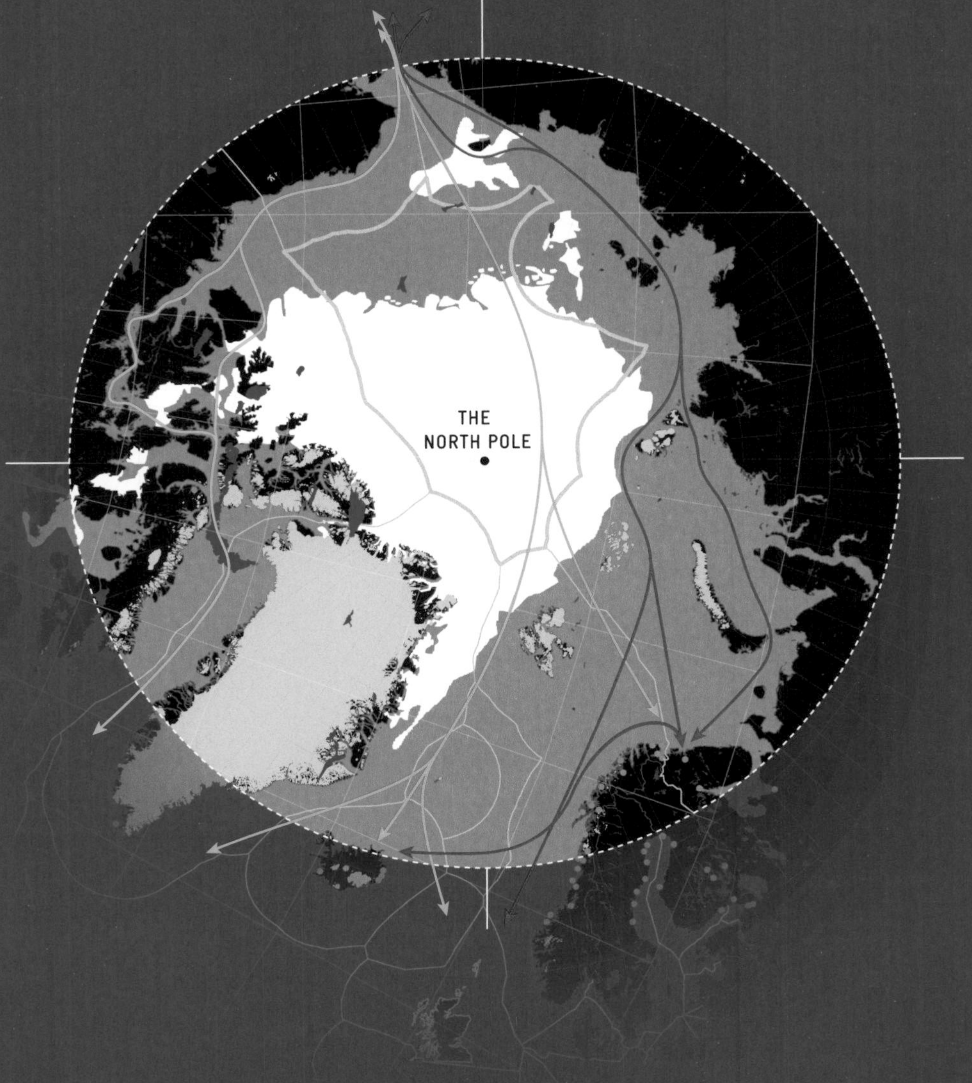

Northwest passage

Transpolar sea route

Northeast passage

Important ports

Glacier

Expanse of sea ice as per September 16, 2012

Shortcuts

In winter, most of the Arctic is covered by glaciers or several meters of thick sea ice. Yet global warming means that more ice melts in summer, freeing up shipping routes and significantly shortening the path from Asia to Europe and from Europe to the west coast of the USA. A ship traveling from Seattle to Rotterdam via the Northwest Passage takes 25 % less time than a ship passing through the Panama Canal. Even more time could be saved if the polar ice caps were to completely melt in summer, which could occur as soon as 2050.

HEAD TO HEAD

In 227 years, Americans have voted for 45 presidents in 58 elections. The nation has had to cope with crises, wars and disasters, and many of them have influenced the presidential elections. No other democratic election attracts so much global attention.

Hard Times

The election happens after the voting

The president and his deputy are not directly elected by the people, but by the Electoral College, the electors (see below). Formally they are not bound to the vote of the citizens - they could also vote differently than their voters.

In November, the nation votes

As the voters do not directly determine the President, it may be that the candidate with the most votes does not win the election.

A growing nation

As the number of states grew, so did the number of Electoral College votes. There are currently 538.

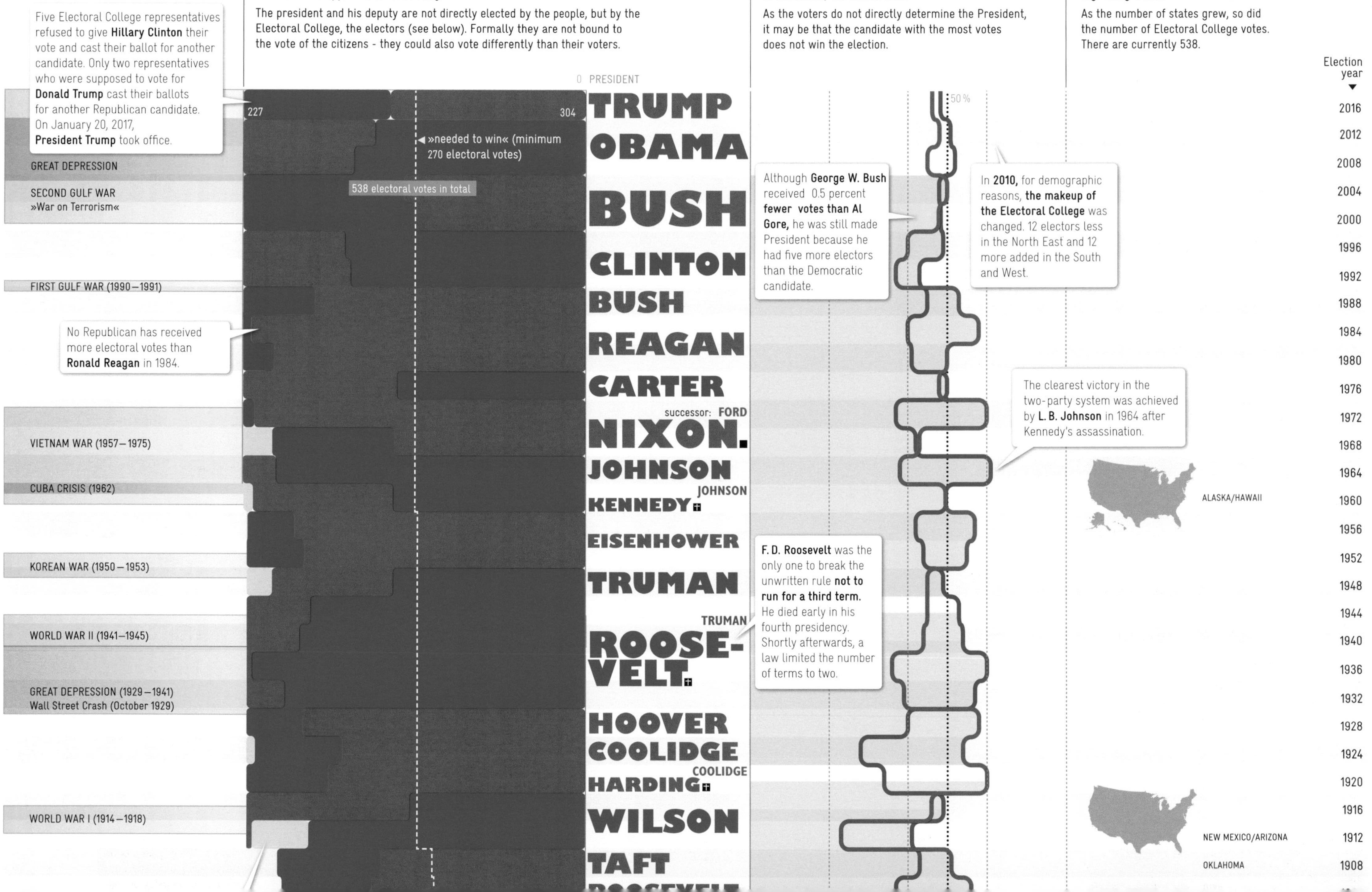

Five Electoral College representatives refused to give **Hillary Clinton** their vote and cast their ballot for another candidate. Only two representatives who were supposed to vote for **Donald Trump** cast their ballots for another Republican candidate. On January 20, 2017, **President Trump** took office.
GREAT DEPRESSION
SECOND GULF WAR »War on Terrorism«
FIRST GULF WAR (1990–1991)
No Republican has received more electoral votes than **Ronald Reagan** in 1984.
VIETNAM WAR (1957–1975)
CUBA CRISIS (1962)
KOREAN WAR (1950–1953)
WORLD WAR II (1941–1945)
GREAT DEPRESSION (1929–1941) Wall Street Crash (October 1929)
WORLD WAR I (1914–1918)
0 PRESIDENT
227
304
◄»needed to win« (minimum 270 electoral votes)
538 electoral votes in total
TRUMP
OBAMA
BUSH
CLINTON
BUSH
REAGAN
CARTER
successor: FORD
NIXON
JOHNSON
JOHNSON
KENNEDY
EISENHOWER
TRUMAN
TRUMAN
ROOSE-VELT
HOOVER
COOLIDGE
COOLIDGE
HARDING
WILSON
TAFT
50 %
Although **George W. Bush** received 0.5 percent **fewer votes than Al Gore,** he was still made President because he had five more electors than the Democratic candidate.
In **2010,** for demographic reasons, **the makeup of the Electoral College** was changed. 12 electors less in the North East and 12 more added in the South and West.
The clearest victory in the two-party system was achieved by **L. B. Johnson** in 1964 after Kennedy's assassination.
F. D. Roosevelt was the only one to break the unwritten rule **not to run for a third term.** He died early in his fourth presidency. Shortly afterwards, a law limited the number of terms to two.
ALASKA/HAWAII
NEW MEXICO/ARIZONA
OKLAHOMA
Election year
2016
2012
2008
2004
2000
1996
1992
1988
1984
1980
1976
1972
1968
1964
1960
1956
1952
1948
1944
1940
1936
1932
1928
1924
1920
1916
1912
1908

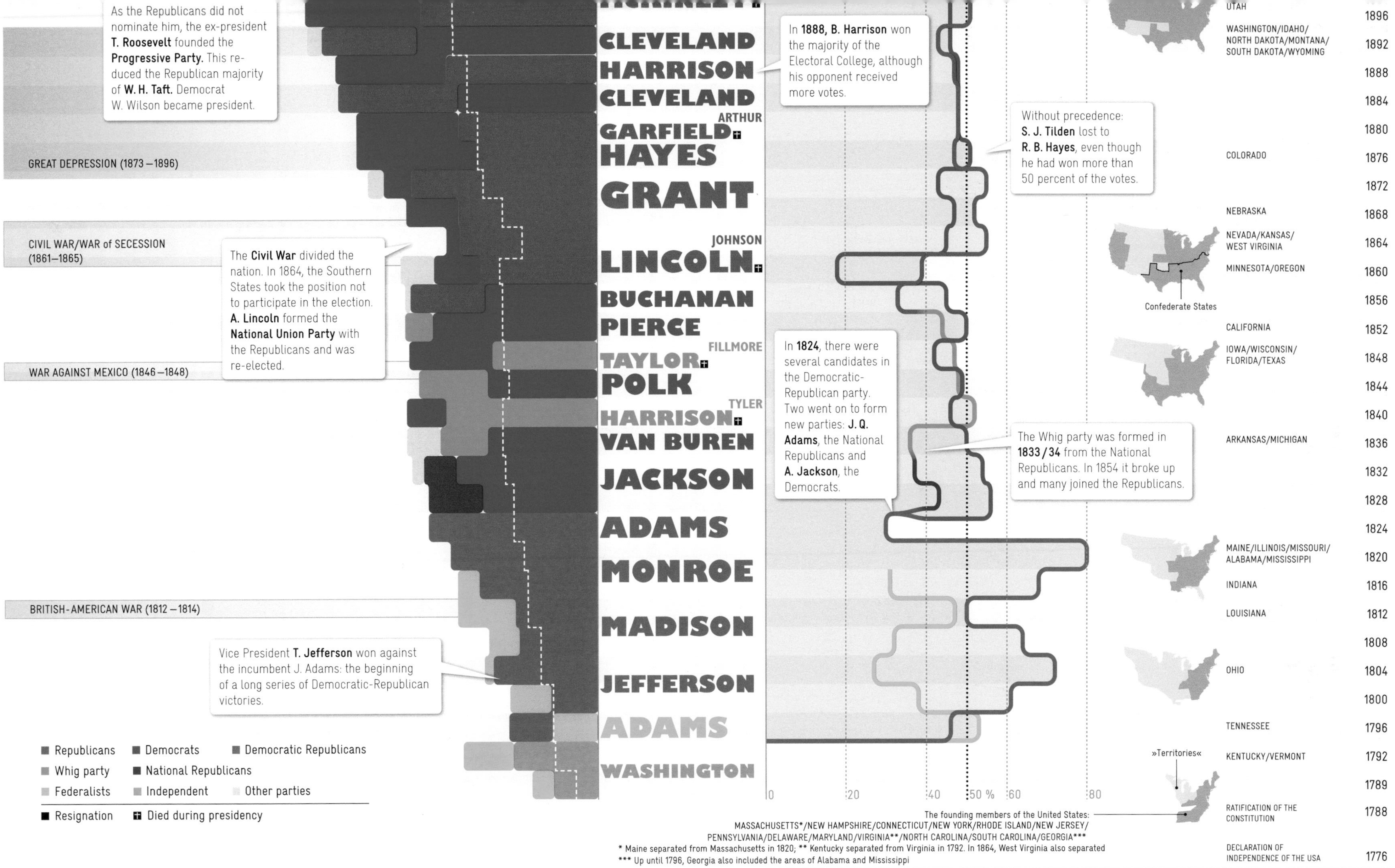

As the Republicans did not nominate him, the ex-president **T. Roosevelt** founded the **Progressive Party.** This reduced the Republican majority of **W. H. Taft.** Democrat W. Wilson became president.
GREAT DEPRESSION (1873 – 1896)
CIVIL WAR/WAR of SECESSION (1861–1865)
The **Civil War** divided the nation. In 1864, the Southern States took the position not to participate in the election. **A. Lincoln** formed the **National Union Party** with the Republicans and was re-elected.
WAR AGAINST MEXICO (1846 – 1848)
BRITISH-AMERICAN WAR (1812 – 1814)
Vice President **T. Jefferson** won against the incumbent J. Adams: the beginning of a long series of Democratic-Republican victories.
Republicans
Democrats
Democratic Republicans
Whig party
National Republicans
Federalists
Independent
Other parties
Resignation
Died during presidency
CLEVELAND
HARRISON
CLEVELAND
ARTHUR
GARFIELD
HAYES
GRANT
JOHNSON
LINCOLN
BUCHANAN
PIERCE
FILLMORE
TAYLOR
POLK
TYLER
HARRISON
VAN BUREN
JACKSON
ADAMS
MONROE
MADISON
JEFFERSON
ADAMS
WASHINGTON
In **1888, B. Harrison** won the majority of the Electoral College, although his opponent received more votes.
Without precedence: **S. J. Tilden** lost to **R. B. Hayes**, even though he had won more than 50 percent of the votes.
In **1824**, there were several candidates in the Democratic-Republican party. Two went on to form new parties: **J. Q. Adams**, the National Republicans and **A. Jackson**, the Democrats.
The Whig party was formed in **1833 / 34** from the National Republicans. In 1854 it broke up and many joined the Republicans.
0
20
40
50 %
60
80
UTAH
WASHINGTON/IDAHO/NORTH DAKOTA/MONTANA/SOUTH DAKOTA/WYOMING
COLORADO
NEBRASKA
NEVADA/KANSAS/WEST VIRGINIA
MINNESOTA/OREGON
Confederate States
CALIFORNIA
IOWA/WISCONSIN/FLORIDA/TEXAS
ARKANSAS/MICHIGAN
MAINE/ILLINOIS/MISSOURI/ALABAMA/MISSISSIPPI
INDIANA
LOUISIANA
OHIO
TENNESSEE
»Territories«
KENTUCKY/VERMONT
RATIFICATION OF THE CONSTITUTION
DECLARATION OF INDEPENDENCE OF THE USA
1896
1892
1888
1884
1880
1876
1872
1868
1864
1860
1856
1852
1848
1844
1840
1836
1832
1828
1824
1820
1816
1812
1808
1804
1800
1796
1792
1789
1788
1776
The founding members of the United States:
MASSACHUSETTS*/NEW HAMPSHIRE/CONNECTICUT/NEW YORK/RHODE ISLAND/NEW JERSEY/PENNSYLVANIA/DELAWARE/MARYLAND/VIRGINIA**/NORTH CAROLINA/SOUTH CAROLINA/GEORGIA***
* Maine separated from Massachusetts in 1820; ** Kentucky separated from Virginia in 1792. In 1864, West Virginia also separated
*** Up until 1796, Georgia also included the areas of Alabama and Mississippi

THE ELECTORAL SYSTEM OF THE UNITED STATES

Many think that the US presidential election appears complicated. The procedure, however, has a long tradition and has worked for 200 years without computers.

Public Vote

Voters cast their votes not for the candidate himself, but choose an elector from his political camp.

»The winner takes all«

In most states, the electors are delegated according to the majority principle: The winner takes all.

Next stop: Washington, D. C.

In the past, the electors went independently on the dangerous journey to Washington. The elections weren't held until two months later.

The Electoral College

All electors vote for the president. Due to the electoral system a candidate losing by a percentage can still win.

The inauguration

On the January 20, the president is sworn into office and takes the White House for four years.

Electors A
Electors B
A
B
President A
President B

HOME OF THE SITTING PRESIDENT

One of the most powerful addresses in the world: 1600 Pennsylvania Avenue NW. The White House welcomes nearly 2 million visitors every year to see its 132 rooms and 35 bathrooms. George Washington, who selected the location together with city planner Pierre L'Enfant, oversaw its construction and his successor, John Adams, was the first president to move in. Since then, it has been the seat of the government and the home of the sitting president.

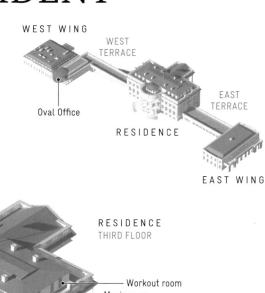

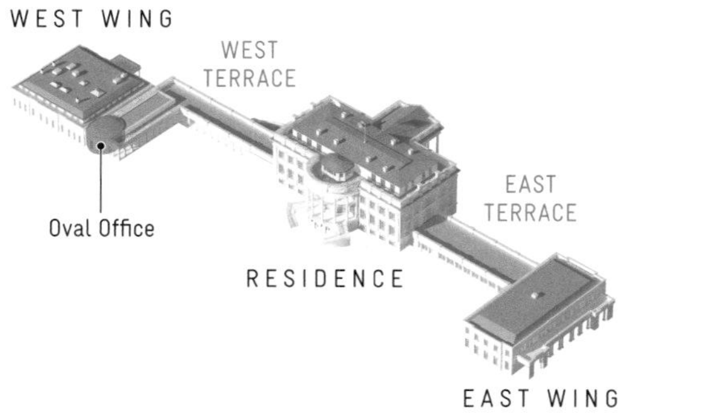

WEST WING
WEST TERRACE
Oval Office
RESIDENCE
EAST TERRACE
EAST WING

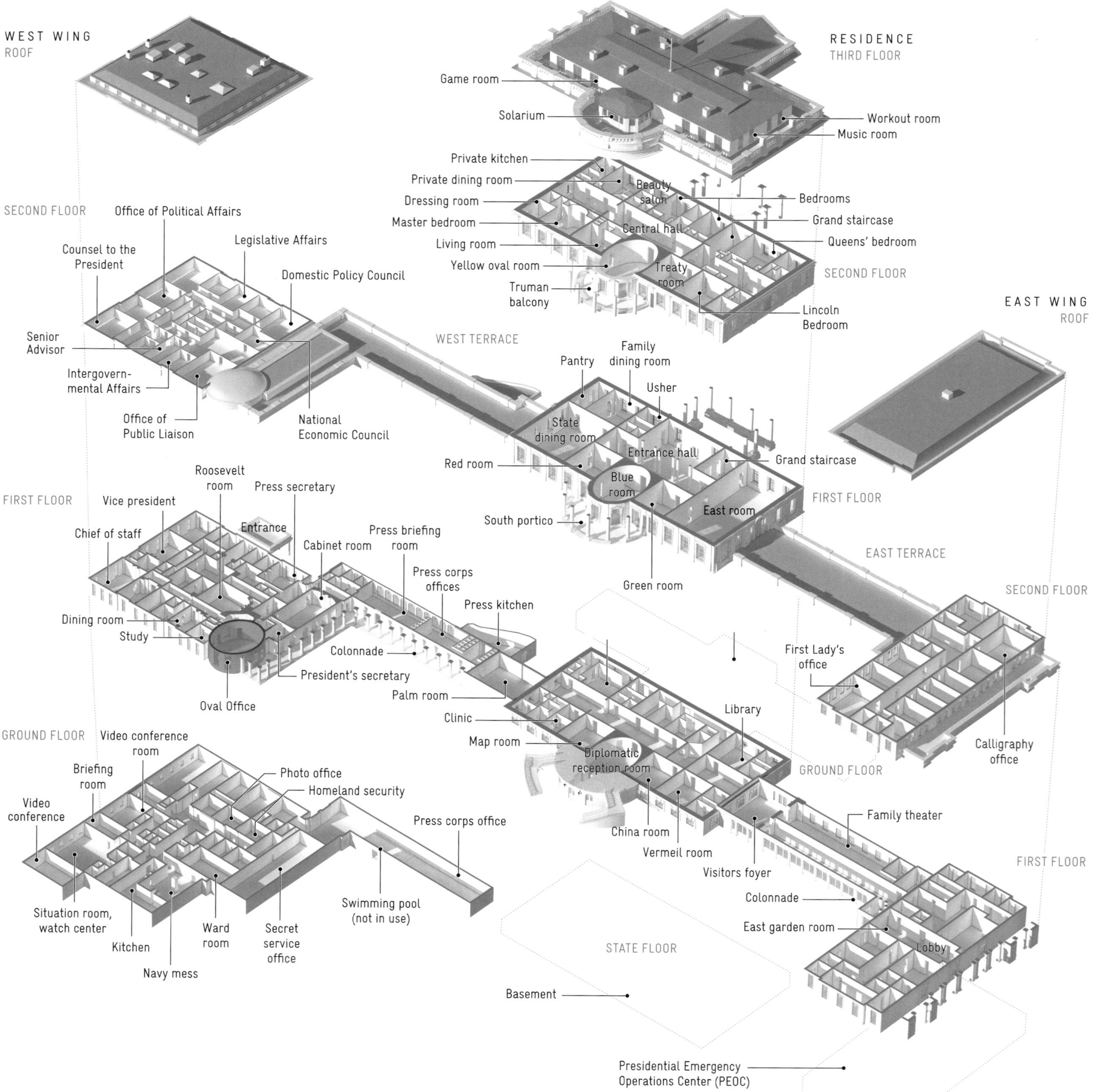

WEST WING
ROOF
SECOND FLOOR
Office of Political Affairs
Counsel to the President
Legislative Affairs
Domestic Policy Council
Senior Advisor
Intergovernmental Affairs
Office of Public Liaison
National Economic Council
FIRST FLOOR
Roosevelt room
Press secretary
Vice president
Chief of staff
Entrance
Cabinet room
Press briefing room
Press corps offices
Press kitchen
Dining room
Study
Colonnade
President's secretary
Oval Office
Palm room
GROUND FLOOR
Video conference room
Briefing room
Video conference
Photo office
Homeland security
Press corps office
Situation room, watch center
Kitchen
Navy mess
Ward room
Secret service office
Swimming pool (not in use)
RESIDENCE
THIRD FLOOR
Game room
Solarium
Workout room
Music room
Private kitchen
Private dining room
Dressing room
Master bedroom
Living room
Yellow oval room
Truman balcony
Beauty salon
Central hall
Treaty room
Bedrooms
Grand staircase
Queens' bedroom
SECOND FLOOR
Lincoln Bedroom
WEST TERRACE
Pantry
Family dining room
Usher
State dining room
Entrance hall
Grand staircase
Red room
Blue room
East room
FIRST FLOOR
South portico
Green room
EAST TERRACE
Clinic
Map room
Diplomatic reception room
Library
China room
Vermeil room
GROUND FLOOR
Visitors foyer
STATE FLOOR
Basement
Presidential Emergency Operations Center (PEOC)
EAST WING
ROOF
SECOND FLOOR
First Lady's office
Calligraphy office
Family theater
FIRST FLOOR
Colonnade
East garden room
Lobby

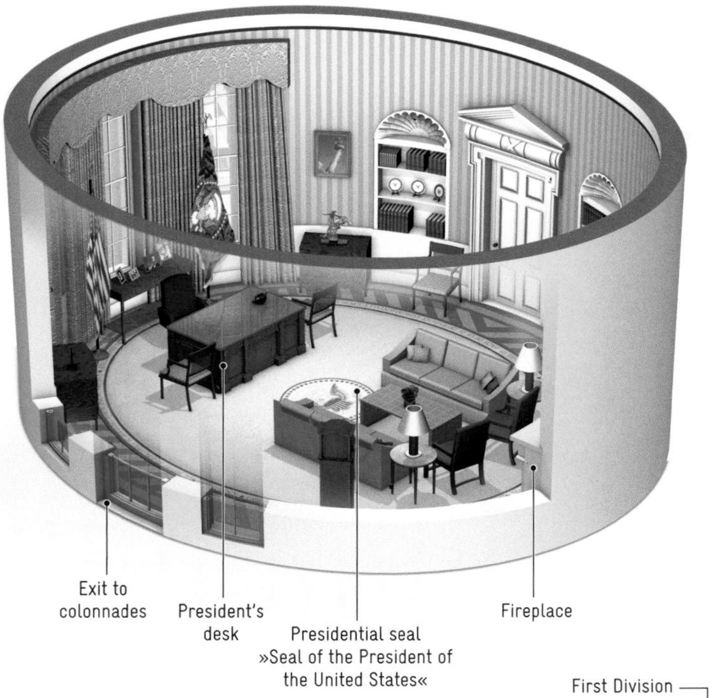
Exit to colonnades
President's desk
Presidential seal »Seal of the President of the United States«
Fireplace

Chamber of power

In the look of Barack Obama's office – each president applies changes to the room's design. The Oval Office has become associated in Americans' minds with the presidency itself. Several presidents have addressed the nation from the Oval Office on occasion:

1962 Kennedy presenting news of the Cuban Missile Crisis

1974 Nixon announcing his resignation from office

1986 Ronald Reagan following the Space Shuttle Challenger disaster

2001 George W. Bush in the wake of the September 11 attacks

White House Facts

Architect	**James Hoban**
Start of Construction	**October 13, 1792**
Measures (residence)	**52 m x 26 m x 18 m**
Floor space (residence)	**5,109 m²**
Area	**45,750 m²**
Rooms	**132**
Of which are bathrooms	**35**
Annual Visitors	**1,825,000**
Value	**$308 million**

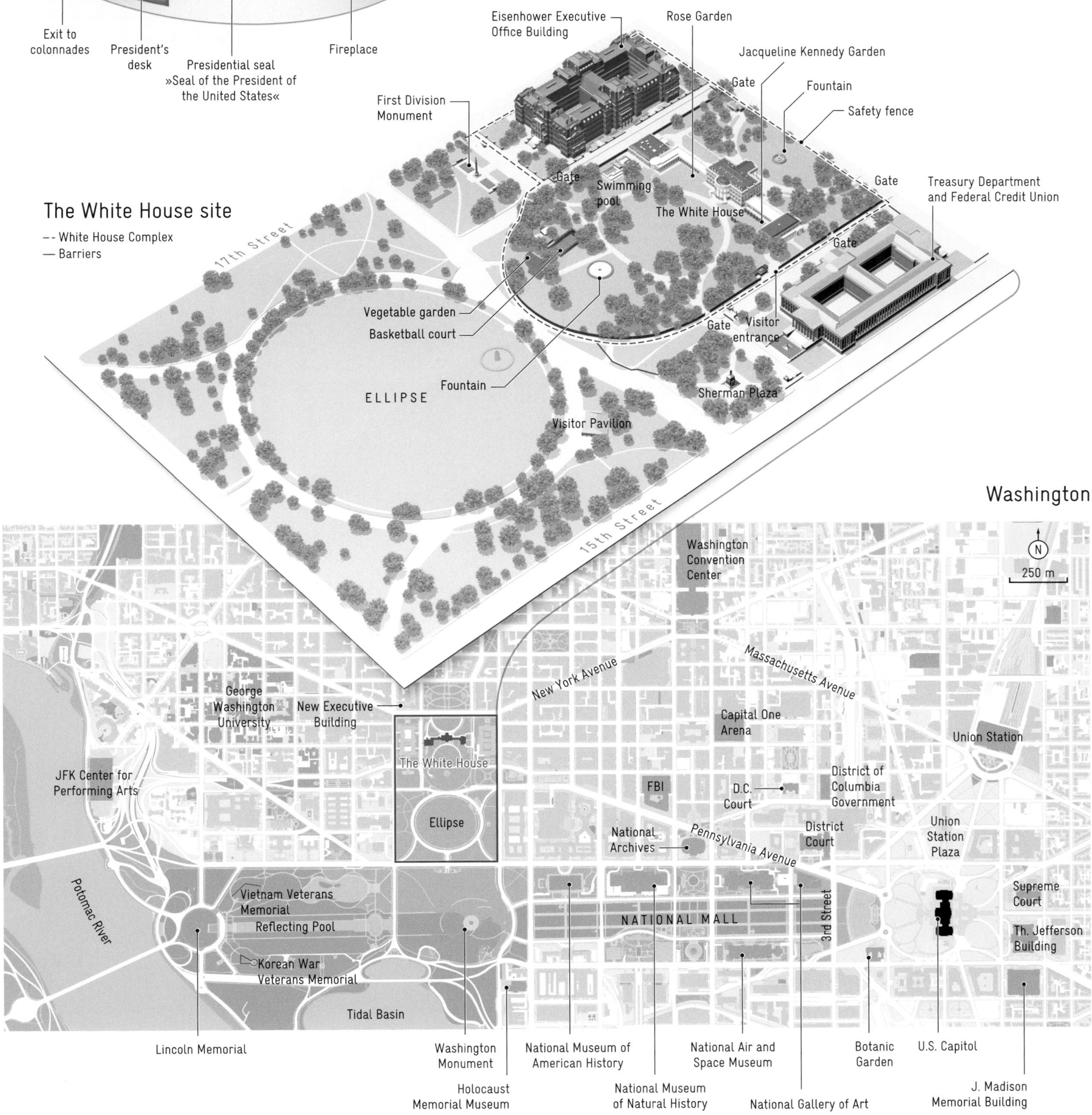
The White House site
-- White House Complex
— Barriers
Eisenhower Executive Office Building
Rose Garden
Jacqueline Kennedy Garden
Gate
Fountain
Safety fence
First Division Monument
Gate
Swimming pool
The White House
Gate
Treasury Department and Federal Credit Union
Gate
17th Street
Vegetable garden
Basketball court
Gate
Visitor entrance
Fountain
ELLIPSE
Sherman Plaza
Visitor Pavilion
15th Street
Washington
250 m
Washington Convention Center
Massachusetts Avenue
New York Avenue
George Washington University
New Executive Building
Capital One Arena
Union Station
The White House
JFK Center for Performing Arts
FBI
D.C. Court
District of Columbia Government
Ellipse
National Archives
Pennsylvania Avenue
District Court
Union Station Plaza
Potomac River
Vietnam Veterans Memorial
Reflecting Pool
NATIONAL MALL
3rd Street
Supreme Court
Th. Jefferson Building
Korean War Veterans Memorial
Tidal Basin
Lincoln Memorial
Washington Monument
National Museum of American History
National Air and Space Museum
Botanic Garden
U.S. Capitol
Holocaust Memorial Museum
National Museum of Natural History
National Gallery of Art
J. Madison Memorial Building

On January 20, 2017, Donald Trump was sworn in as the 45th president of the USA. He has given conflicting messages regarding his stance on nuclear weapons.
It's a horror to use nuclear weapons.
Nuclear is just the power, the devastation is very important to me.

The »doomsday clock« in the journal »Bulletin of the Atomic Scientists« shows how vulnerable we are to a catastrophe from nuclear weapons, climate change, and new technologies (the apocalypse is at midnight). After the election of Donald Trump in November 2016, the clock was set to 23:57:30 for the first time since the Cuban conflict in 1962. That poses an urgent question: How easy is it for a US president to deploy nuclear weapons?

TWO AND A HALF MINUTES TO MIDNIGHT

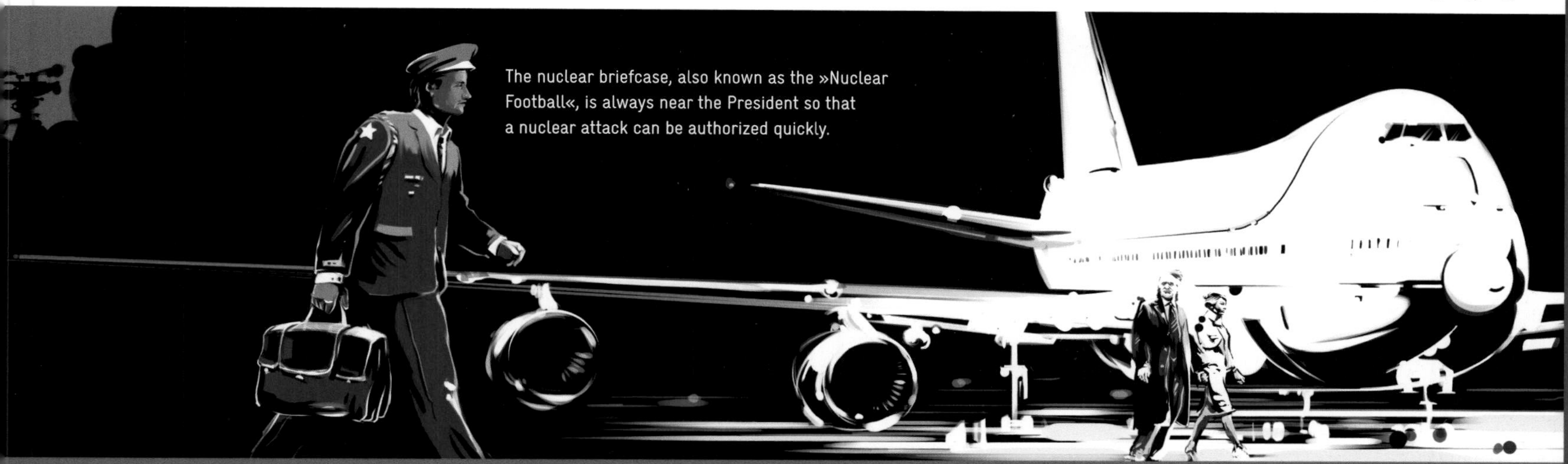
The nuclear briefcase, also known as the »Nuclear Football«, is always near the President so that a nuclear attack can be authorized quickly.

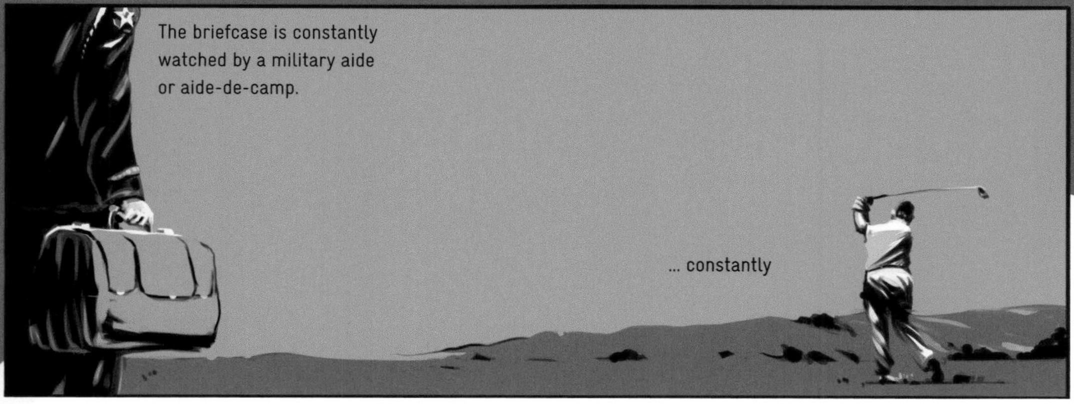
The briefcase is constantly watched by a military aide or aide-de-camp.
... constantly

The »nuclear football« was created during **Dwight D. Eisenhower's** administration to react to a nuclear attack as quickly as possible.

To keep each other in check, since the end of WWII, the USA and the Soviet Union have expanded their nuclear arsenals. In 2010, Russia had 12,000 active nuclear warheads while the USA had 5,000. A further 4,000 American warheads are in working order but dismantled. All other nuclear powers combined have less than 1,000 **nuclear warheads**.

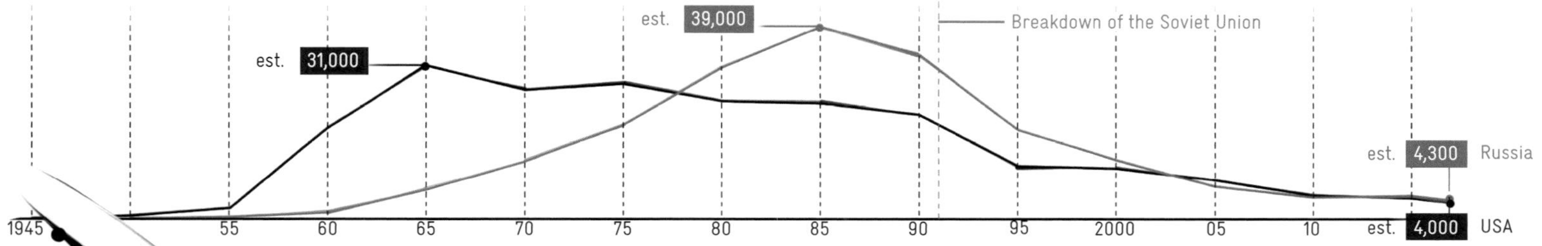
est. 39,000
Breakdown of the Soviet Union
est. 31,000
est. 4,300 Russia
1945
55
60
65
70
75
80
85
90
95
2000
05
10
est. 4,000 USA

Currently eight nations are known to have nuclear weapons: USA, Russia, United Kingdom, France, China, Israel, India and Pakistan. Besides President Trump, the Russian and the French presidents have nuclear briefcases that they can use to call for a nuclear attack within minutes.
Russian president
French president
The British system is unique. There are four »letters of last resort« hand-written by the prime minister located in a safe onboard the four ballistic missile submarines. They contain the orders on the action to be taken if the British government is destroyed.
American president

The nuclear briefcase is opened after receiving an alert of a nuclear attack (which could also be a false alarm) or if the president decides to strike first.

»LAUNCH ON WARNING« STRATEGY

If the »Launch on Warning« strategy goes into effect, all designated steps have to be followed within a certain time frame so that the attack can be started before the enemy destroys the missile launch sites. A Russian attack is seen to be the most likely reason for the Americans to use the nuclear briefcase.

1 Midnight in Washington.
Russian nuclear warheads are fired.

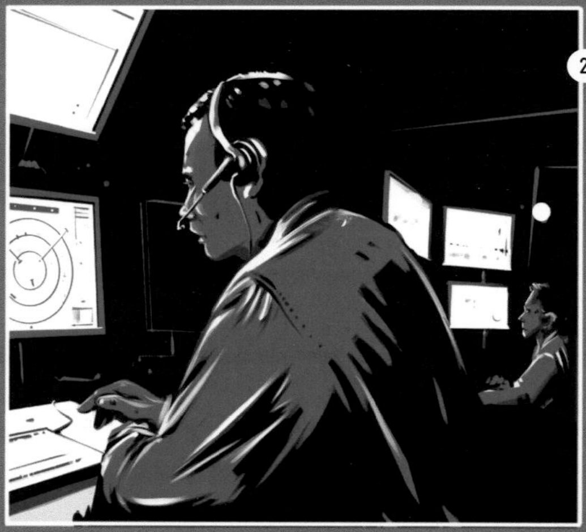

2 00:03
Three minutes later, signals from satellites and ground radars arrive at the Northern American Aerospace Defence Command (NORAD) in Colorado.

3 00:04
NORAD informs the National Security Advisor. It is his responsibility to assess the situation within three minutes and decide if he should contact the White House.
In 1979, the US National Security Advisor Zbigniew Brzezinski received a phone call in the middle of the night informing him that the Soviets had launched a missile attack on the US. Just a few seconds before the three-minute deadline it became clear that it was a false alarm.

4 00:07
The White House is alerted.
Activation of the nuclear briefcase!

In the oval office...
The military aide that protects the nuclear briefcase instructs the president of all possible nuclear counterattacks.

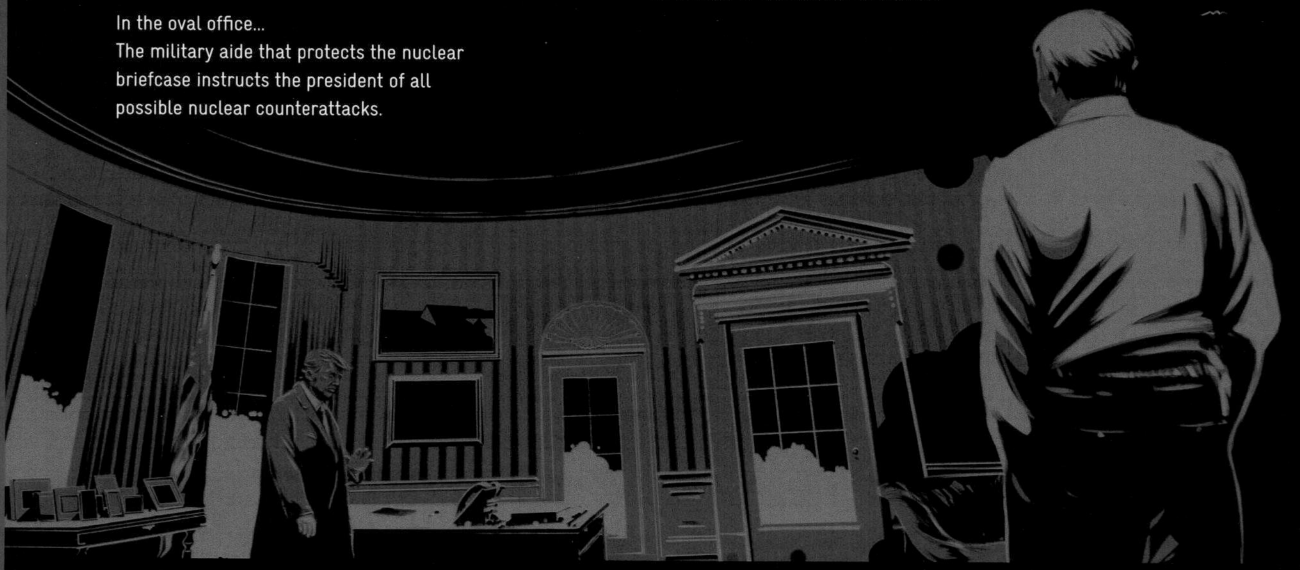

The source for this briefing is the »Black Book«.

The leather briefcase that travels with the president is opened and inside is a metal case.

5 **00:08**

It is a misconception that there is a red button inside the nuclear briefcase. In reality there are two manuals, one satellite telephone and a list of coded attack instructions – the GO CODES.

The so-called »biscuit« is always carried by the US President. This plastic card contains the »Gold Codes« used by the president to identify himself during a phone call with the Pentagon to order an attack.

The »Biscuit« was misplaced after Ronald Reagan's attempted assassination. Jimmy Carter once accidentally sent his to the laundry. Bill Clinton once lost his completely.

»Go Codes« are coded commands for different attack options.

Satellite telephone

Two emergency manuals: the »Black Book« describes the different attack options and the»Emergency Procedures White House«gives protocols of what the government should do.

6 **00:12**

The president has only two minutes to decide the fate of mankind. After the decision, a sequence of events begins, and ends with the nuclear missiles being launched.

After this decision is made there is no turning back.

Every attack option included in the »Black Book« is coded with a »Go Code«, which has about 150 characters.

A) »Gold Code« (Identification of the president)
B) »Go Code« (a coded command to attack)
A) »Gold Code« confirmed
B) »Go Code« confirmed

7 **00:14**

When the president decides on one of the options from the Black Book, a secure phone call with a satellite phone to the Pentagon is established.

An unusual two-man principle is applied:
the Secretary of Defense must jointly authenticate every command but he has no veto power. If he disagrees with a command, the president can in theory dismiss him immediately.

8 **00:19**

Everything else happens within the military command chain. The Missile Launch Control Centers have three minutes to receive and decode the Emergency Action Message.

9 **00:22**

After decoding the message, it takes about two minutes to complete the launch sequence and fire the nuclear warheads.

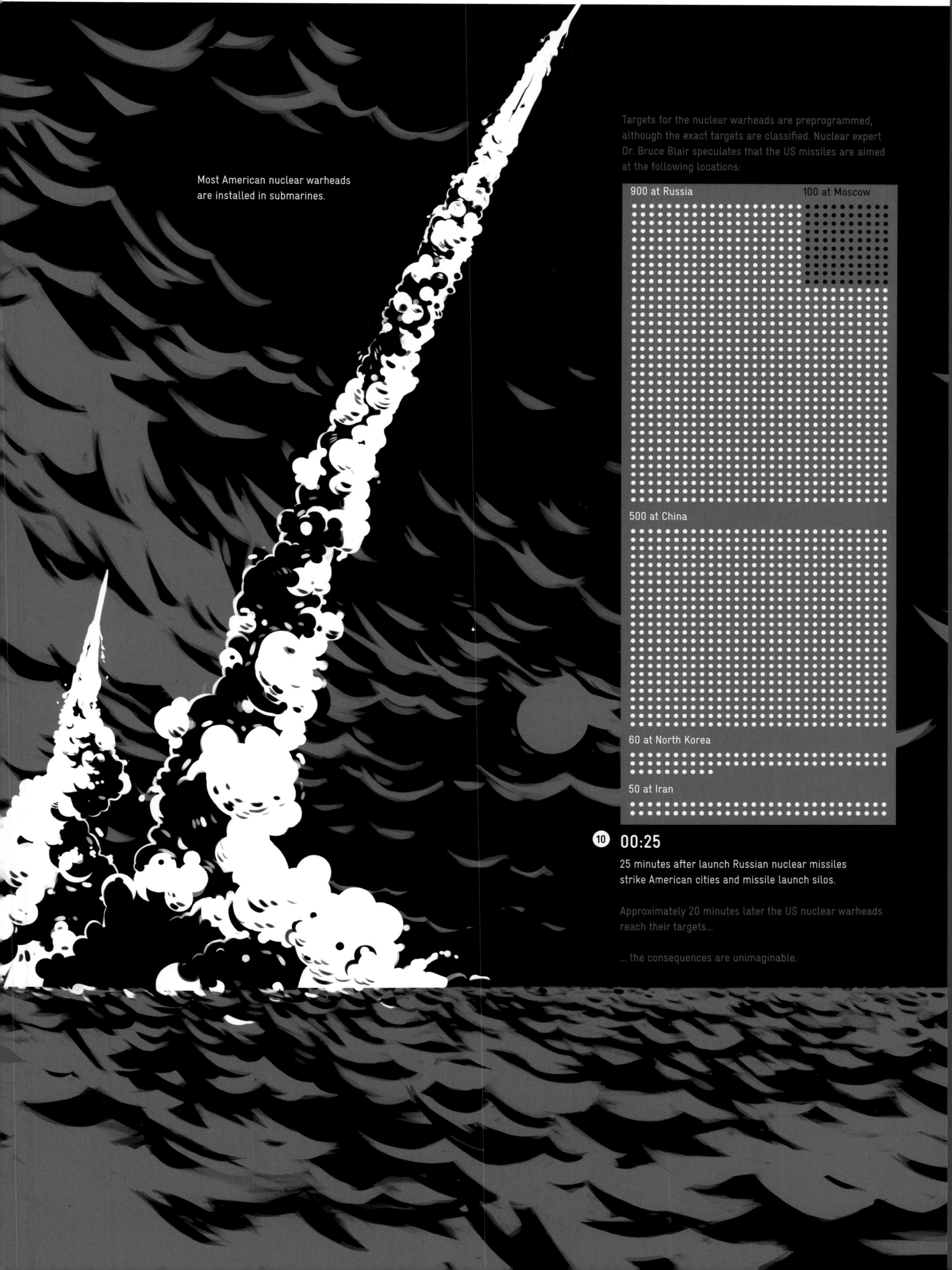

Most American nuclear warheads are installed in submarines.

Targets for the nuclear warheads are preprogrammed, although the exact targets are classified. Nuclear expert Dr. Bruce Blair speculates that the US missiles are aimed at the following locations:

900 at Russia
100 at Moscow
500 at China
60 at North Korea
50 at Iran

10 **00:25**

25 minutes after launch Russian nuclear missiles strike American cities and missile launch silos.

Approximately 20 minutes later the US nuclear warheads reach their targets...

... the consequences are unimaginable.

THE US EMBASSY IN THE HEART OF BERLIN

It doesn't get more exclusive than having the Brandenburg Gate as your next door neighbor and the Reichstag building only a few feet away. The USA opened their embassy at Pariser Platz 2 on July 4, 2008, their national holiday. The building is more a fortress than an embassy; a beautified high security block made from reinforced concrete and bulletproof glass, with retractable bollards and a security fence. Plans for the 83 million euro building with a 14,000 square meter floor space were radically revised after the September 11 terrorist attack in 2001. There's no longer any underground parking, instead the base of the building is made from a meter-thick concrete slab. The construction site was sealed off as if it were in Baghdad and even German site supervisors weren't allowed to enter. Construction managers from German subcontractors were refused access to the third and fourth floors; whatever is in there remains an American secret.

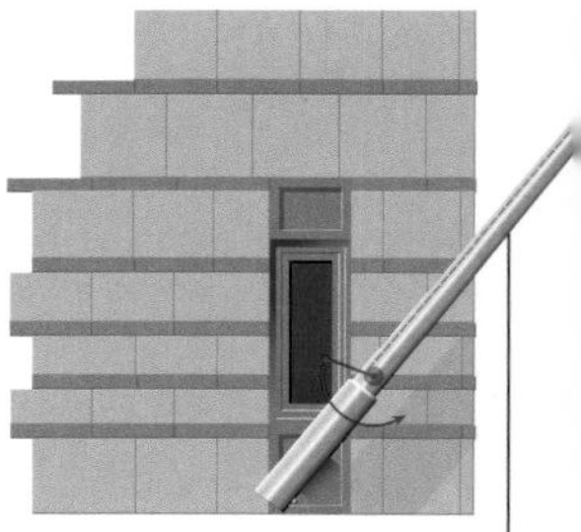

THE BUILDINGS AT PARISER PLATZ

UNTER DEN LINDEN 75–77
Proprietor: Fundus Fonds-Verwaltungen
Use: the Adlon Hotel, Kempinski

WILHELMSTRASSE 70/71
Proprietor: Foreign & Commonwealth Office
Use: British Embassy

WILHELMSTRASSE 72
Proprietor: Fundus Fonds-Verwaltungen
Use: Adlon residence, Adlon Hotel extension

UNTER DEN LINDEN 78
Proprietor: Fa. Stoffel
Use: residential building and business premises

UNTER DEN LINDEN 80
Proprietor: ABG Allg. Bauträger GmbH + Co (German private limited company)
Use: residential building and business premises

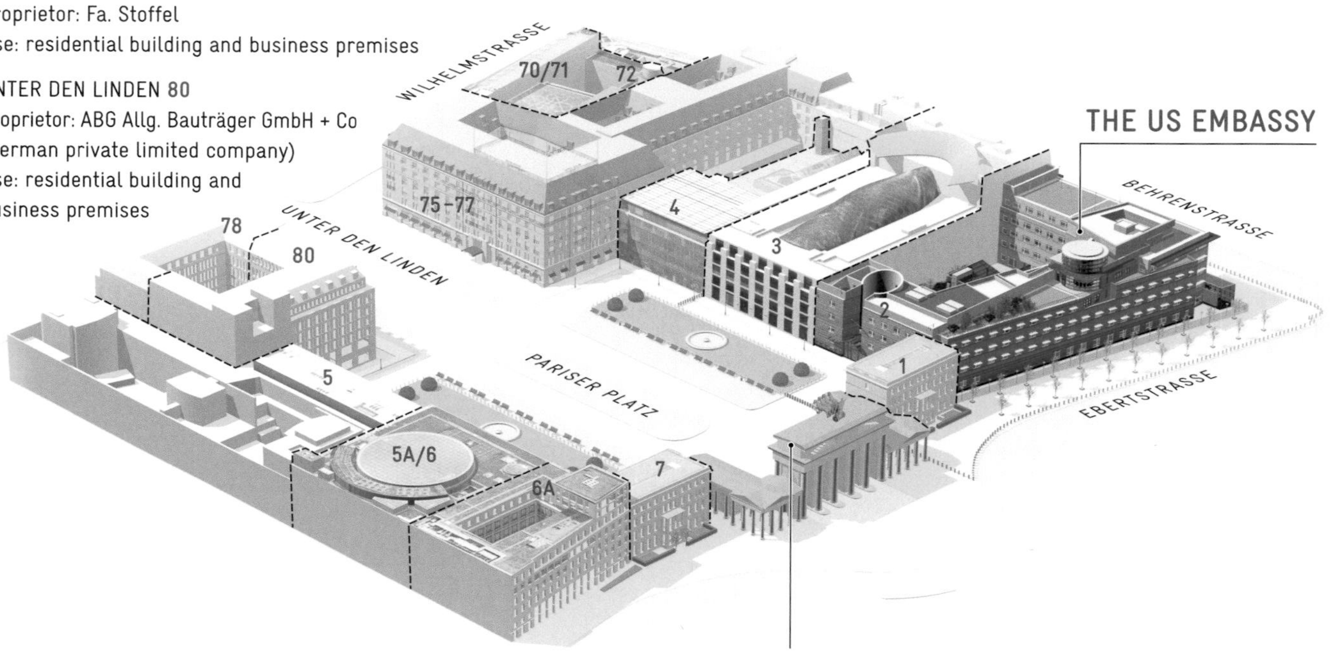

PARISER PLATZ 1 »Haus Sommer«
Proprietor: Rheinische Hypothekenbank
Use: business premises and exhibition building

THE BRANDENBURG GATE
Proprietor: The City of Berlin

PARISER PLATZ 2
Proprietor: United States of America
Use: US Embassy

PARISER PLATZ 3
Proprietor: Grundbesitz GmbH & Co. »Bau« KG
Use: DZ bank, residential and office building

PARISER PLATZ 4
Proprietor: State of Berlin
Use: Academy of Arts

PARISER PLATZ 5
Proprietor: The Republic of France
Use: French Embassy

PARISER PLATZ 5A/6
Proprietor: Dresdner Bank AG
Use: representative office of the Dresdner Bank

PARISER PLATZ 6A
Proprietor: Rheinische Hypothekenbank
Use: business premises and exhibition building

PARISER PLATZ 7 »Haus Liebermann«
Proprietor: Quandt Grundbesitz
Use: business premises and exhibition building

MAIN LOBBY
Next to a bald eagle made from Meissen porcelain, the preamble to the US constitution is written in the stone: »We the people of the United States, ...«

HIDDEN DOOR
The function of this door remains a mystery. It's possible that the state reception uses it as an additional entrance for security personnel. Things such as the red carpet, which are required at a welcome reception, can be carried through this door.

BUILDING NAME on the façade

EMBASSY OF THE UNITED STATES OF AMERICA

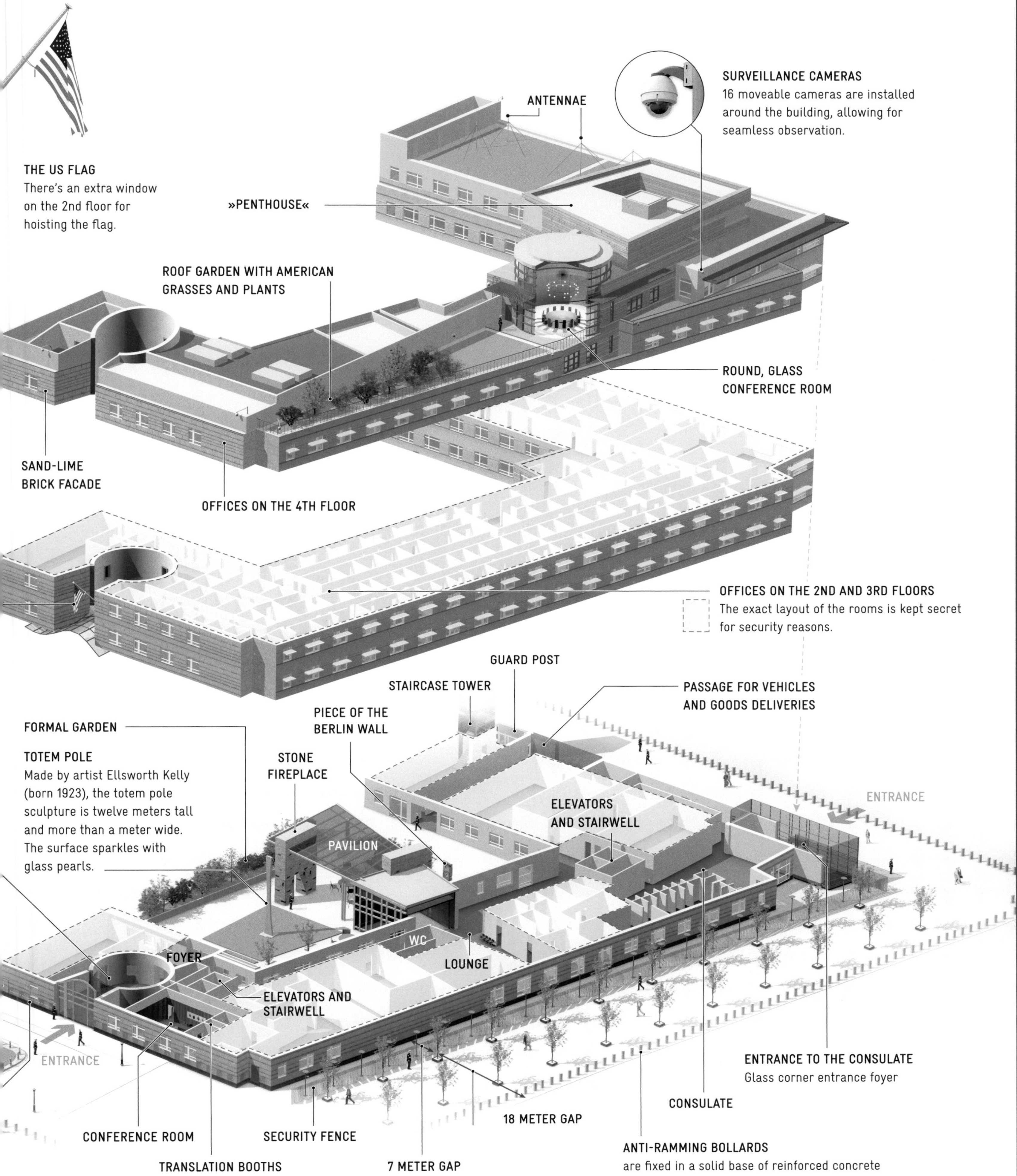
THE US FLAG
There's an extra window on the 2nd floor for hoisting the flag.
ANTENNAE
»PENTHOUSE«
SURVEILLANCE CAMERAS
16 moveable cameras are installed around the building, allowing for seamless observation.
ROOF GARDEN WITH AMERICAN GRASSES AND PLANTS
ROUND, GLASS CONFERENCE ROOM
SAND-LIME BRICK FACADE
OFFICES ON THE 4TH FLOOR
OFFICES ON THE 2ND AND 3RD FLOORS
The exact layout of the rooms is kept secret for security reasons.
GUARD POST
STAIRCASE TOWER
PASSAGE FOR VEHICLES AND GOODS DELIVERIES
PIECE OF THE BERLIN WALL
FORMAL GARDEN
TOTEM POLE
Made by artist Ellsworth Kelly (born 1923), the totem pole sculpture is twelve meters tall and more than a meter wide. The surface sparkles with glass pearls.
STONE FIREPLACE
PAVILION
ELEVATORS AND STAIRWELL
ENTRANCE
WC
LOUNGE
FOYER
ELEVATORS AND STAIRWELL
ENTRANCE
ENTRANCE TO THE CONSULATE
Glass corner entrance foyer
CONSULATE
18 METER GAP
CONFERENCE ROOM
SECURITY FENCE
TRANSLATION BOOTHS
7 METER GAP
ANTI-RAMMING BOLLARDS
are fixed in a solid base of reinforced concrete

ONE OF A KIND

The European Union is a unique organization. It is the only community in which sovereign states bundle resources and powers to increase their role on the world stage. By committing to this supranationality, states voluntarily waive their complete autonomy. The EU is not only a world player in a political sense: its territory extends from the Indian Ocean to the Caribbean.

EUROPEAN UNION

EU

28
States

513
million citizens

EUROZONE

1 EURO

19
States

338
million citizens

All EU states are part of the Economic and Monetary Union. Here, the introduction of the EURO is obligatory as soon as the so-called convergence criteria are fulfilled. Denmark, Sweden and Great Britain have negotiated an »opt-out« option for the EURO currency obligation.

KEY
- EU Member States
- Outermost Regions (full EU members + EURO)
- Overseas Countries and Territories (associated with EU)
- EU missions in the world: Civilian, Military
- Global diplomatic EU representations

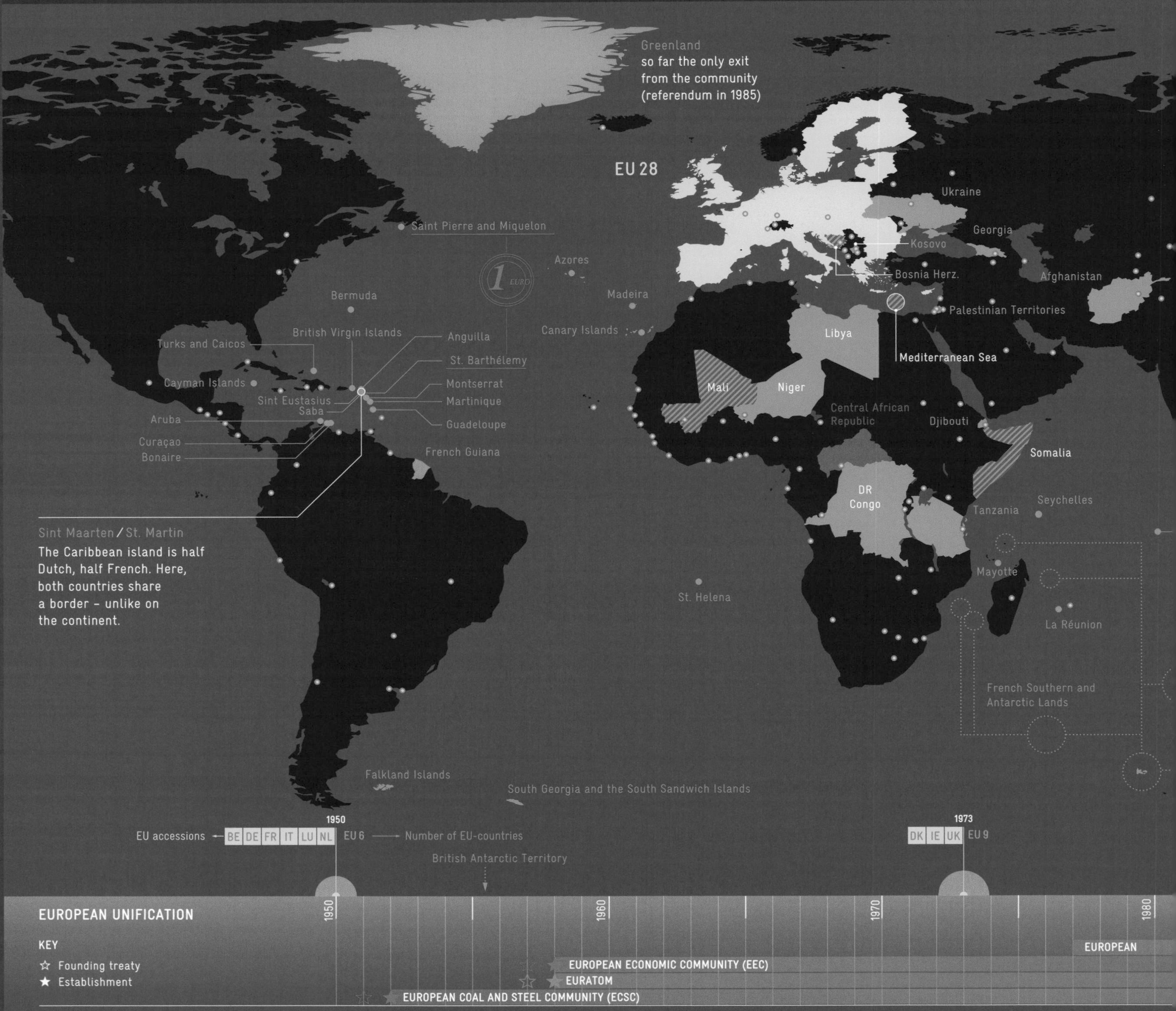
Greenland
so far the only exit from the community (referendum in 1985)
EU 28
Ukraine
Georgia
Kosovo
Bosnia Herz.
Afghanistan
Palestinian Territories
Libya
Mediterranean Sea
Mali
Niger
Central African Republic
Djibouti
Somalia
DR Congo
Tanzania
Seychelles
Mayotte
La Réunion
French Southern and Antarctic Lands
St. Helena
Saint Pierre and Miquelon
Azores
Madeira
Canary Islands
Bermuda
Turks and Caicos
British Virgin Islands
Anguilla
St. Barthélemy
Montserrat
Martinique
Guadeloupe
Cayman Islands
Sint Eustasius
Saba
Aruba
Curaçao
Bonaire
French Guiana
Sint Maarten / St. Martin
The Caribbean island is half Dutch, half French. Here, both countries share a border – unlike on the continent.
Falkland Islands
South Georgia and the South Sandwich Islands
British Antarctic Territory
1950
EU accessions
BE DE FR IT LU NL
EU 6
Number of EU-countries
1973
DK IE UK
EU 9
EUROPEAN UNIFICATION
KEY
Founding treaty
Establishment
1950
1960
1970
1980
EUROPEAN
EUROPEAN ECONOMIC COMMUNITY (EEC)
EURATOM
EUROPEAN COAL AND STEEL COMMUNITY (ECSC)

SCHENGEN AREA

Some EU-countries are not part of the Schengen area, but four non-EU countries chose to become members of the club.

- IS Iceland
- LI Liechtenstein
- NO Norway
- CH Switzerland

Schengen Area
European Union
Eurozone

Schengen Area, European Union, Eurozone	European Union, Eurozone	European Union, Schengen Area	European Union
AT Austria BE Belgium DE Germany EE Estonia ES Spain FI Finland FR France GR Greece IT Italy LT Lithuania LU Luxembourg LV Latvia MT Malta NL Netherlands PT Portugal SI Slovenia SK Slovakia	CY Cyprus IE Ireland	CZ Czech Republic HU Hungary PL Poland	BG Bulgaria DK Denmark HR Croatia RO Romania SE Sweden UK United Kingdom

Four non-EU countries have their own EURO coins. They have monetary agreements with the EU.

1 EURO

- AD Andorra
- MC Monaco
- SM San Marino
- VA Vatican

The European Parliament and Commission operate in all EU countries and have delegates across the globe.

British Indian Ocean Territory
Wallis and Futuna
New Caledonia
French Polynesia
Pitcairn Islands

How far could the EU expand?

Theoretically, there are no geographical limits. Candidate countries only have to meet the so-called **Copenhagen criteria**

- Institutionally stable democracy
- Functioning market economy
- Assumption of all EU obligations

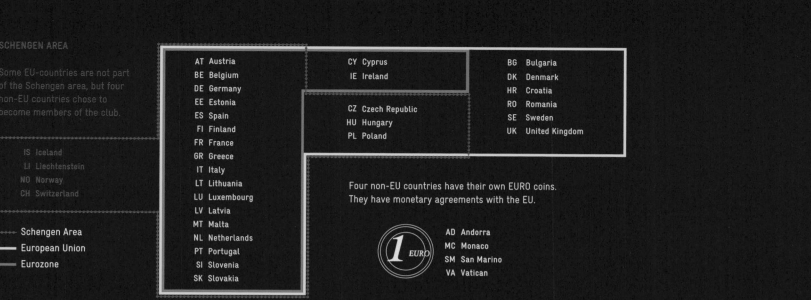

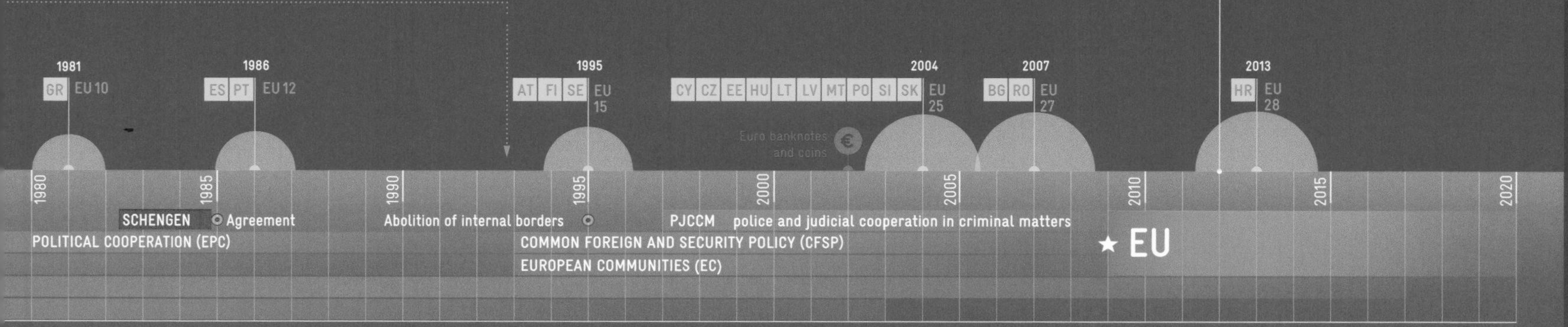
2012 Nobel Peace Prize
1981
GR EU 10
1986
ES PT EU 12
1995
AT FI SE EU 15
2004
CY CZ EE HU LT LV MT PO SI SK EU 25
2007
BG RO EU 27
2013
HR EU 28
Euro banknotes and coins
1980
1985
1990
1995
2000
2005
2010
2015
2020
SCHENGEN Agreement
Abolition of internal borders
PJCCM police and judicial cooperation in criminal matters
POLITICAL COOPERATION (EPC)
COMMON FOREIGN AND SECURITY POLICY (CFSP)
EUROPEAN COMMUNITIES (EC)
★ EU

AXIS OF COMPLEXITY

Today, the European Union is a highly complex structure. Seven institutions form its core. Their positions and functions are defined in the EU treaties, which have a constitutional status. The institutions are bundled in the three »EU capitals« – Brussels, Luxembourg and Strasbourg – that form an axis in the heart of Europe. A decentralized EU-wide network of agencies with specific areas of responsibility supports them and the member states.

THE INSTITUTIONS

- President of institution
- Council presidency (6-months rota)
- Places of work

EUROGROUP MEMBERS

- A Heads of state and government
- B Economic and Monetary Affairs Commissioner
- C Eurozone ministers of finance and economics
- D ECB President

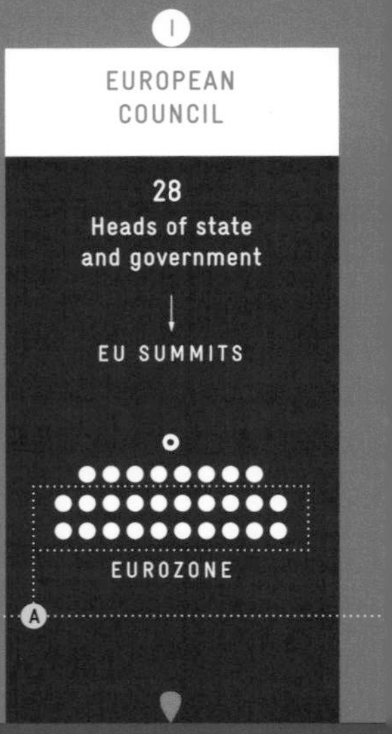
I
EUROPEAN COUNCIL
28
Heads of state and government
EU SUMMITS
EUROZONE
A

A DECENTRALIZED NETWORK OF SPECIALIZED AGENCIES

KEY ☆ EU agency • Brussels • Luxembourg • Strasbourg

The institutions are bundled in three »EU capital cities«. A decentralized EU-wide network made of agencies with specific areas of responsibility supports them and the member states.

EUROPOL
coordinates the collaboration between European police authorities.
FRONTEX
secures the external borders of the Schengen area.
THE HAGUE
STOCKHOLM
HELSINKI
TALLINN
RIGA
VILNIUS
COPENHAGEN
BRUSSELS
DUBLIN
LONDON
COLOGNE
FRANKFURT
WARSAW
VALENCIENNES
PRAGUE
PARIS
STRASBOURG
ANGERS
LUXEMBOURG
VIENNA
BUDAPEST
LJUBLJANA
TURIN
PARMA
BILBAO
VIGO
MADRID
BARCELONA
THESSALONIKI
LISBON
ALICANTE
ATHENS
VALLETTA
HERAKLION
F4E (Fusion for Energy)
researches the feasibility of nuclear fusion (EU contribution to the ITER project).
ENISA
ensures cyber security.

CAPITAL CITIES

EU institutions provide prestige and are an important economic factor for a city.

KEY

- Population
- ★ Institutions ☆ Interinstitutional EU bodies
- EU Jobs · Indirect jobs · Temporary jobs

BRUSSELS ★★★★★ 7 ☆☆☆☆☆☆☆☆☆☆☆☆☆☆ 14

1,175,000

40,000

26,400

- 20,000 Lobbyists
- 5,400 Diplomats
- 1,000 Accredited journalists

LUXEMBOURG ★★★★★ 5 ☆☆☆☆☆☆☆☆ 8

110,000

9,500 = 2.5 % of total workforce

STRASBOURG ★→ EP headquarters

475,000

- 150 Full-time employees
- 751 Parliamentarians
- + 3,500–8,000 Staff, journalists and lobbyists

Only 150 full-time employees work year-round in Strasbourg – only 12 plenary sessions per year are held here.

TRIPLE-SEAT

Twelve times a year, parliamentarians move from their main work locations to the EP's headquarters together with staff and documents. A merger of all work places could save money but they are fixed in treaties.

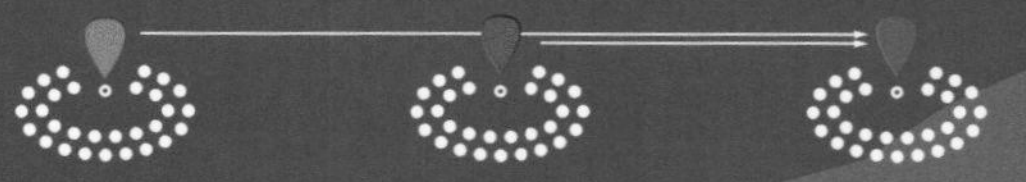

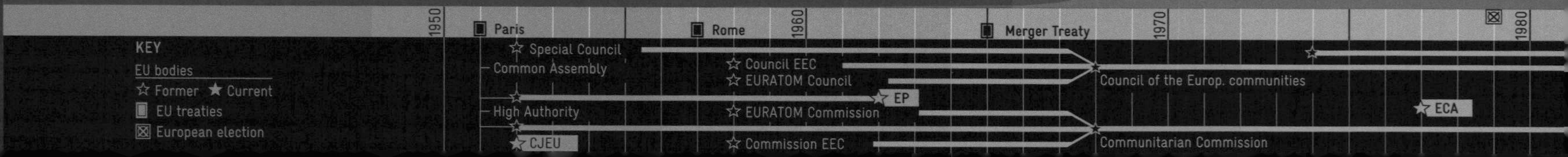
KEY
EU bodies
☆ Former ★ Current
EU treaties
European election
1950
Paris
Rome
1960
Merger Treaty
1970
1980
Special Council
Common Assembly
Council EEC
EURATOM Council
Council of the Europ. communities
EP
High Authority
EURATOM Commission
ECA
CJEU
Commission EEC
Communitarian Commission

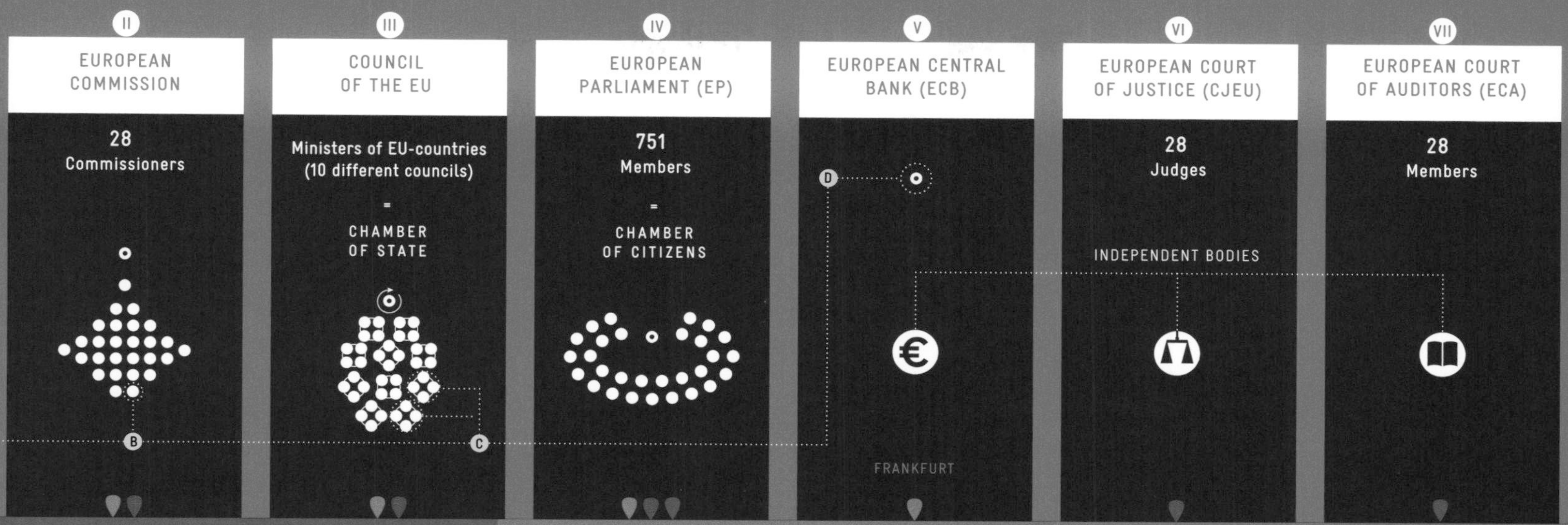
II
EUROPEAN COMMISSION
28 Commissioners
III
COUNCIL OF THE EU
Ministers of EU-countries (10 different councils)
=
CHAMBER OF STATE
IV
EUROPEAN PARLIAMENT (EP)
751 Members
=
CHAMBER OF CITIZENS
V
EUROPEAN CENTRAL BANK (ECB)
FRANKFURT
VI
EUROPEAN COURT OF JUSTICE (CJEU)
28 Judges
VII
EUROPEAN COURT OF AUDITORS (ECA)
28 Members
INDEPENDENT BODIES
B
C
D

POLICY

For which policy areas does the EU hold legislative responsibility?

AREAS WITH EXCLUSIVE RESPONSIBILITY

- MONETARY POLICY (EURO STATES)
- CUSTOMS UNION
- COMPETITION
- TRADE POLICY
- PRESERVATION OF MARITIME BIODIVERSITY

AREAS WITH SHARED RESPONSIBILITY

- JOINT FOREIGN & SECURITY POLICY
- INTERNAL MARKET
- SOCIAL POLICY
- AGRICULTURE
- FISHERIES
- ENVIRONMENT
- DEVELOPMENT & HUMANITARIAN AID
- CONSUMER PROTECTION
- PUBLIC HEALTH SAFETY
- ENERGY
- TRANSEUROPEAN NETWORKS
- ECONOMIC, SOCIAL & TERRITORIAL COHESION
- RESEARCH & DEVELOPMENT
- TRANSPORT
- SPACE
- FREEDOM, SECURITY & JUSTICE

THE INSTITUTIONAL TRIANGLE

How do EU institutions work together? And who else has influence on legislative processes?

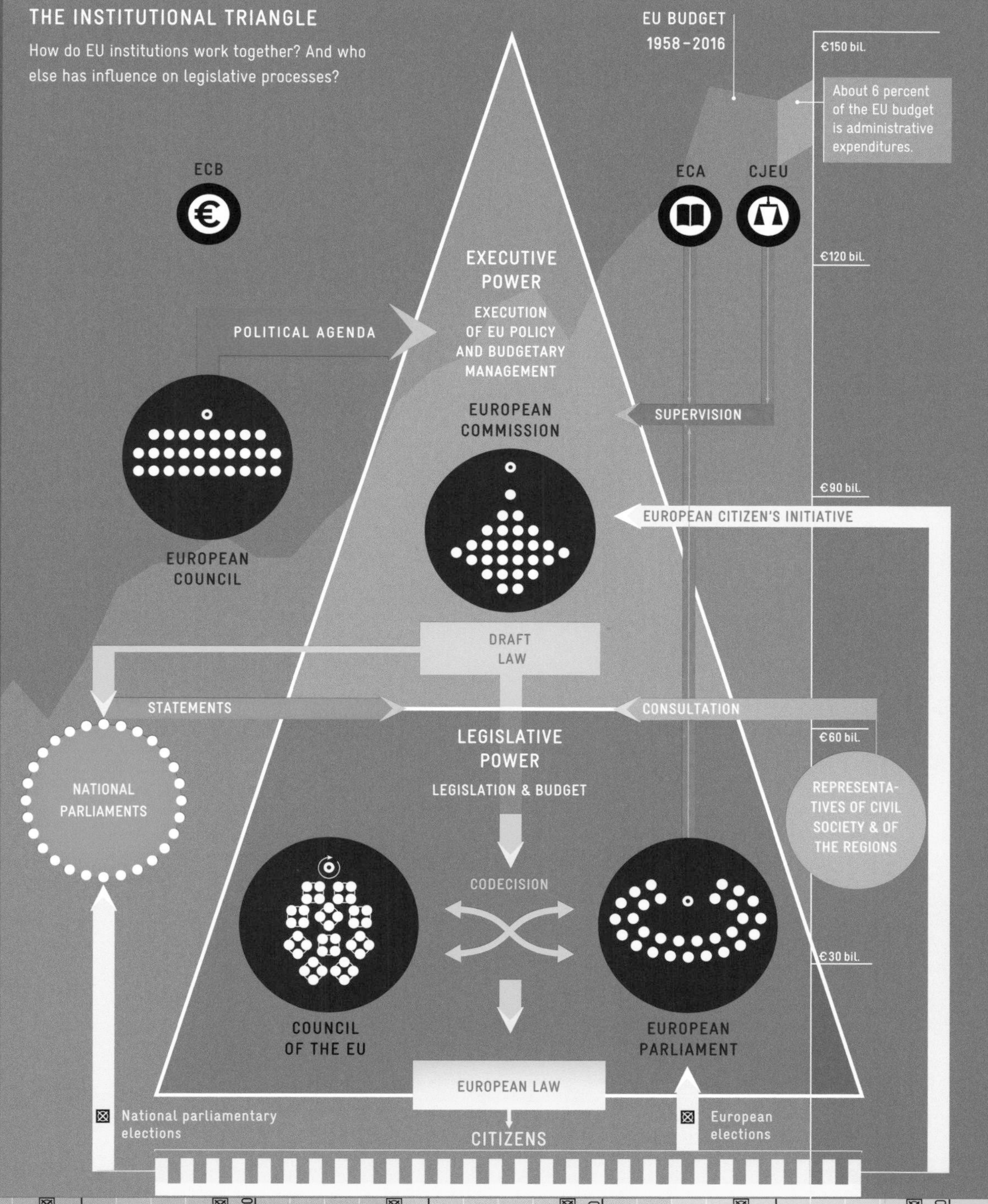
EU BUDGET 1958–2016
€150 bil.
About 6 percent of the EU budget is administrative expenditures.
€120 bil.
€90 bil.
€60 bil.
€30 bil.
ECB
ECA
CJEU
EXECUTIVE POWER
EXECUTION OF EU POLICY AND BUDGETARY MANAGEMENT
POLITICAL AGENDA
EUROPEAN COMMISSION
SUPERVISION
EUROPEAN COUNCIL
EUROPEAN CITIZEN'S INITIATIVE
DRAFT LAW
STATEMENTS
CONSULTATION
NATIONAL PARLIAMENTS
LEGISLATIVE POWER
LEGISLATION & BUDGET
REPRESENTA-TIVES OF CIVIL SOCIETY & OF THE REGIONS
CODECISION
COUNCIL OF THE EU
EUROPEAN PARLIAMENT
EUROPEAN LAW
National parliamentary elections
European elections
CITIZENS

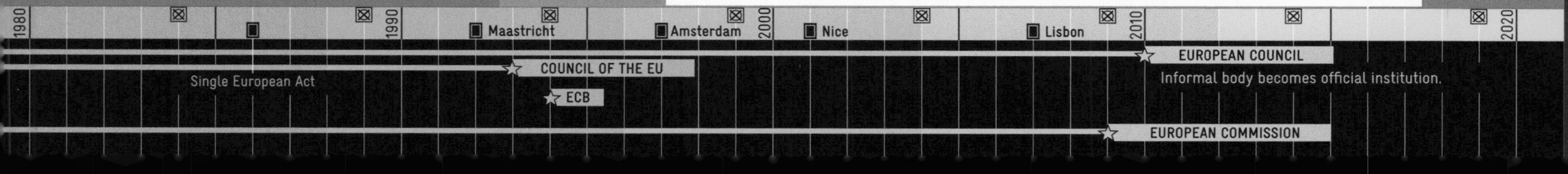
1980
1990
2000
2010
2020
Maastricht
Amsterdam
Nice
Lisbon
Single European Act
COUNCIL OF THE EU
ECB
EUROPEAN COUNCIL
Informal body becomes official institution.
EUROPEAN COMMISSION

HISTORY
POLITICS
SOCIETY
ECONOMY
SPORTS
TECHNOLOGY
CULTURE & ARTS
SCIENCE

U^UNITED^ S^STATES^ OF EUROPE

The EU ranks between the federal system of the United States and a loose cooperation network such as the United Nations. The regional differences and cultural variety within the EU are enormous. Its multilingualism is a treasure but it also makes some things, like labor mobility, more difficult. Could the EU really become the United States of Europe one day?

TRANSLATING FOR THE EU

EU citizens have the right to view EU documents in their respective (official) language. The EP's parliamentarians can make contributions in each of the EU's current 24 official languages. This means 276 potential language pairs for interpreters and translators.

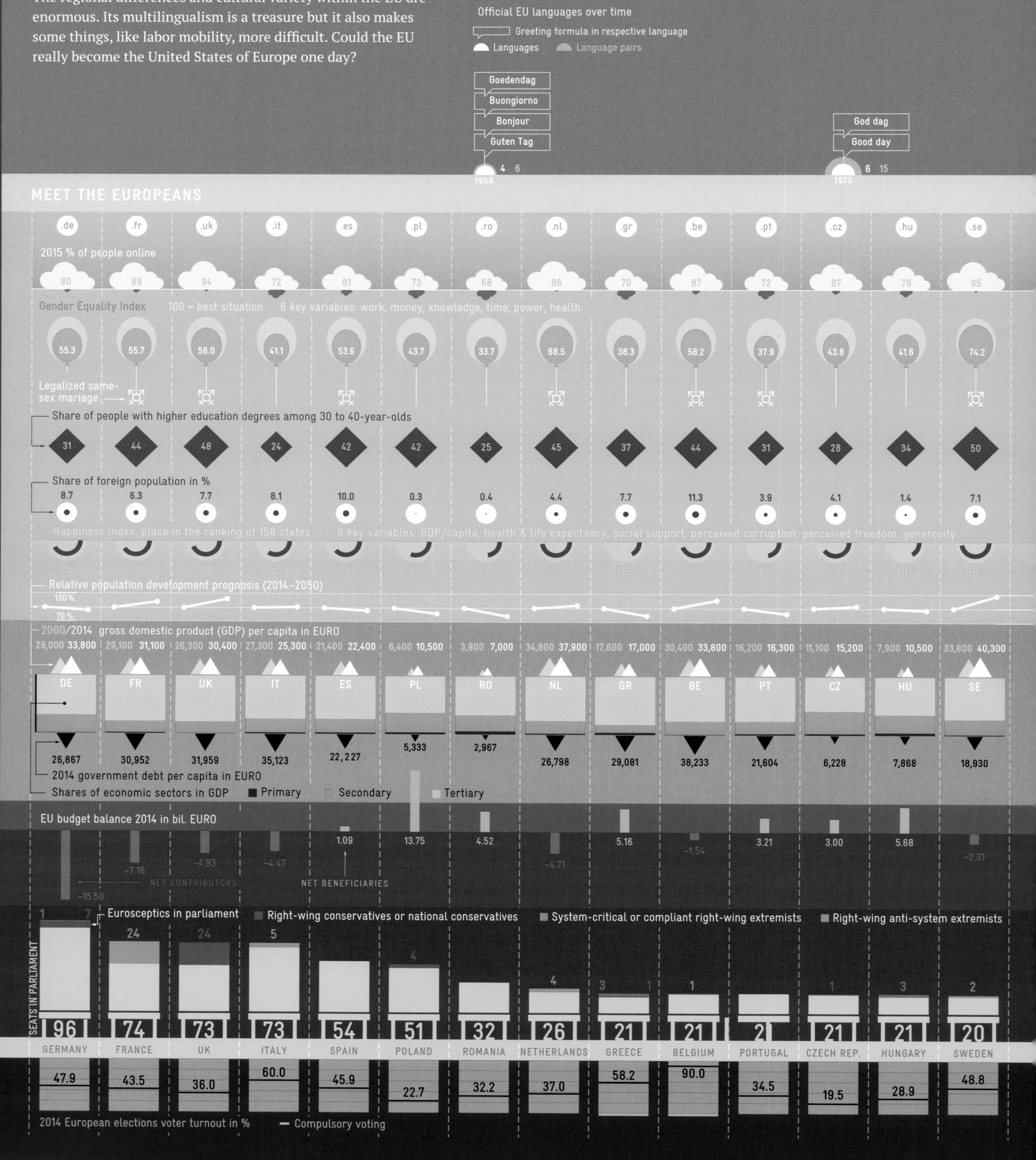
Official EU languages over time
Greeting formula in respective language
Languages
Language pairs
Goedendag
Buongiorno
Bonjour
Guten Tag
4 6
1958
God dag
Good day
6 15
1973
MEET THE EUROPEANS
.de .fr .uk .it .es .pl .ro .nl .gr .be .pt .cz .hu .se
2015 % of people online
90 89 94 72 81 73 68 96 70 87 72 87 79 95
Gender Equality Index 100 = best situation 6 key variables: work, money, knowledge, time, power, health
55.3 55.7 58.0 41.1 53.6 43.7 33.7 68.5 38.3 58.2 37.9 43.8 41.6 74.2
Legalized same-sex mariage
Share of people with higher education degrees among 30 to 40-year-olds
31 44 48 24 42 42 25 45 37 44 31 28 34 50
Share of foreign population in %
8.7 6.3 7.7 8.1 10.0 0.3 0.4 4.4 7.7 11.3 3.9 4.1 1.4 7.1
Happiness Index: place in the ranking of 158 states 6 key variables: GDP/capita, health & life expectancy, social support, perceived corruption, perceived freedom, generosity
26 29 21 50 36 60 86 7 102 19 88 31 104 8
Relative population development prognosis (2014–2050)
130 %
70 %
2000/2014 gross domestic product (GDP) per capita in EURO
29,000 33,800 | 29,100 31,100 | 26,300 30,400 | 27,300 25,300 | 21,400 22,400 | 6,400 10,500 | 3,900 7,000 | 34,800 37,900 | 17,600 17,000 | 30,400 33,800 | 16,200 16,300 | 11,100 15,200 | 7,900 10,500 | 33,800 40,300
DE FR UK IT ES PL RO NL GR BE PT CZ HU SE
26,867 30,952 31,959 35,123 22,227 5,333 2,967 26,798 29,081 38,233 21,604 6,228 7,868 18,930
2014 government debt per capita in EURO
Shares of economic sectors in GDP Primary Secondary Tertiary
EU budget balance 2014 in bil. EURO
−15.50 −7.16 −4.93 −4.47 1.09 13.75 4.52 −4.71 5.16 −1.54 3.21 3.00 5.68 −2.31
NET CONTRIBUTORS
NET BENEFICIARIES
Eurosceptics in parliament
Right-wing conservatives or national conservatives
System-critical or compliant right-wing extremists
Right-wing anti-system extremists
1 7 | 24 | 24 | 5 | | 4 | | 4 | 3 1 | 1 | | 1 | 3 | 2
SEATS IN PARLIAMENT
96 74 73 73 54 51 32 26 21 21 2 21 21 20
GERMANY FRANCE UK ITALY SPAIN POLAND ROMANIA NETHERLANDS GREECE BELGIUM PORTUGAL CZECH REP. HUNGARY SWEDEN
47.9 43.5 36.0 60.0 45.9 22.7 32.2 37.0 58.2 90.0 34.5 19.5 28.9 48.8
2014 European elections voter turnout in %
Compulsory voting

MODELS OF THE FUTURE

How the EU will evolve in the future is not yet known, but here are some theories.

Europe of different speeds

States capable of integration and willing to integrate lead the way.

Europe of concentric circles

Groups of states with differing integration levels.

Federation

Community arrangements of all important policy areas.

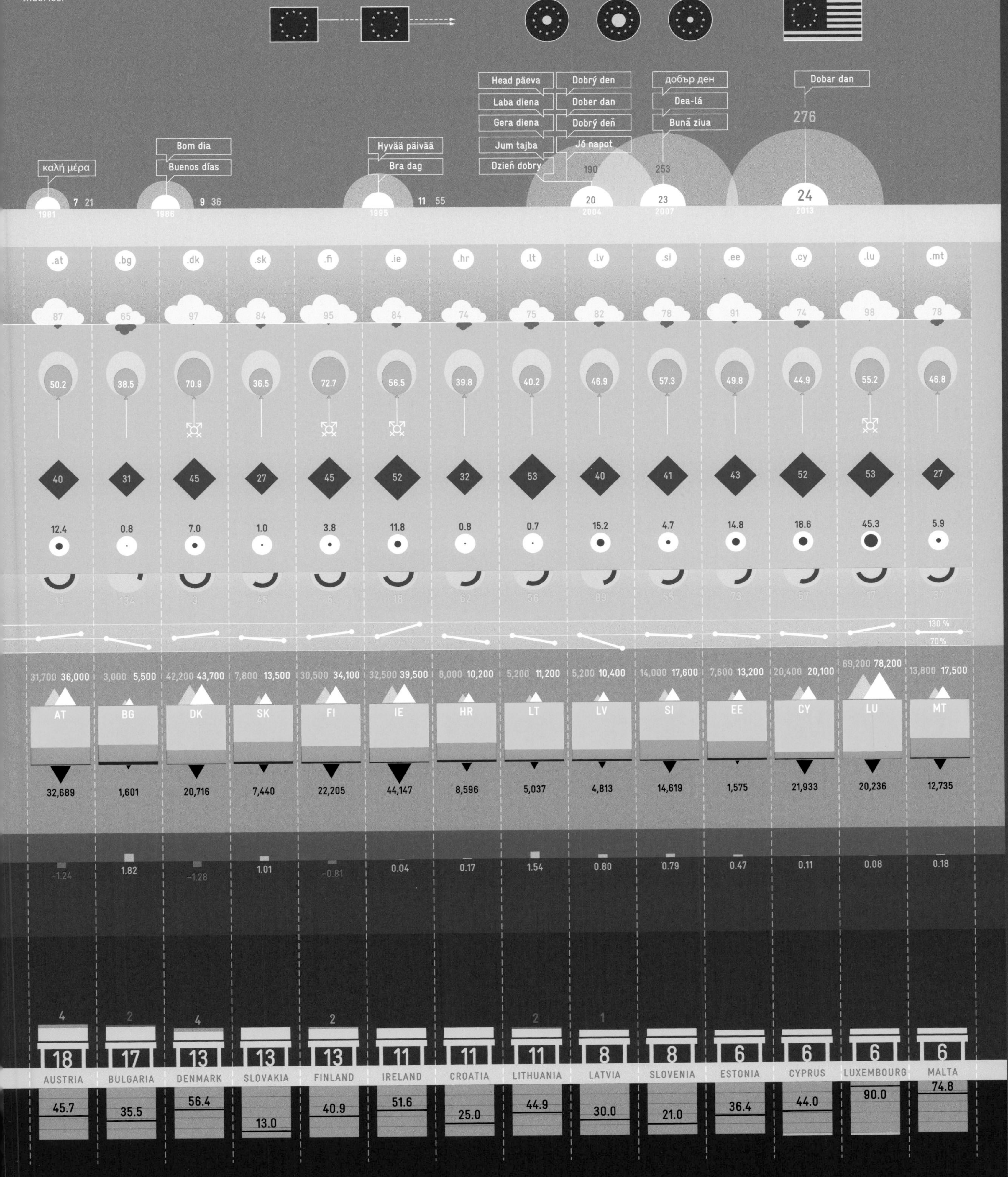
καλή μέρα
7 21
1981
Bom dia
Buenos días
9 36
1986
Hyvää päivää
Bra dag
11 55
1995
Head päeva
Laba diena
Gera diena
Jum tajba
Dzień dobry
Dobrý den
Dober dan
Dobrý deň
Jó napot
190
20
2004
добър ден
Dea-lá
Bună ziua
253
23
2007
Dobar dan
276
24
2013
.at .bg .dk .sk .fi .ie .hr .lt .lv .si .ee .cy .lu .mt
87 65 97 84 95 84 74 75 82 78 91 74 98 78
50.2 38.5 70.9 36.5 72.7 56.5 39.8 40.2 46.9 57.3 49.8 44.9 55.2 46.8
40 31 45 27 45 52 32 53 40 41 43 52 53 27
12.4 0.8 7.0 1.0 3.8 11.8 0.8 0.7 15.2 4.7 14.8 18.6 45.3 5.9
13 134 3 45 5 18 62 56 89 55 73 67 17 37
130 %
70 %
31,700 36,000
3,000 5,500
42,200 43,700
7,800 13,500
30,500 34,100
32,500 39,500
8,000 10,200
5,200 11,200
5,200 10,400
14,000 17,600
7,600 13,200
20,400 20,100
69,200 78,200
13,800 17,500
AT BG DK SK FI IE HR LT LV SI EE CY LU MT
32,689 1,601 20,716 7,440 22,205 44,147 8,596 5,037 4,813 14,619 1,575 21,933 20,236 12,735
−1.24 1.82 −1.28 1.01 −0.81 0.04 0.17 1.54 0.80 0.79 0.47 0.11 0.08 0.18
4 2 4 2 2 1
18 17 13 13 13 11 11 11 8 8 6 6 6 6
AUSTRIA
BULGARIA
DENMARK
SLOVAKIA
FINLAND
IRELAND
CROATIA
LITHUANIA
LATVIA
SLOVENIA
ESTONIA
CYPRUS
LUXEMBOURG
MALTA
45.7 35.5 56.4 13.0 40.9 51.6 25.0 44.9 30.0 21.0 36.4 44.0 90.0 74.8

RESCUING THE RESCUERS

The Euro crisis resulted in countries that had rescued banks needing to be rescued themselves. In response, the member states of the eurozone ratified the European Stability Mechanism (ESM) in 2012. This created a new way of handling bailout packages for member states and led to the stabilization of the euro.

The EU and its aid measures

Greece, Ireland and Portugal were the first countries to benefit from the rescue operation. From the initial funds provided by the Troika (the European Commission, European Central Bank, and the International Monetary Fund), nearly half has been paid to the crisis countries. The new ESM has been active since October 2012. It can lend up to a maximum of €500 billion. After the summer of 2013, it replaced all previous measures. Spain and Cyprus were the next countries to make use of the EU's assistance alongside Greece (Third program).

The role of the ECB

The European Central Bank (ECB) participates strongly in the stabilization of the euro. It first took over the sovereign debts from non-performing countries. A further announcement to buy unlimited government bonds in case of an emergency also reassured the markets. Finally, in the winter of 2011 to 2012, it dealt out low interest credits worth almost a trillion euros to the banks (»BIG BERTHA«).

Bailout measures

Since 2010, there have been a variety of bailout measures to stop ailing EU countries from collapsing.

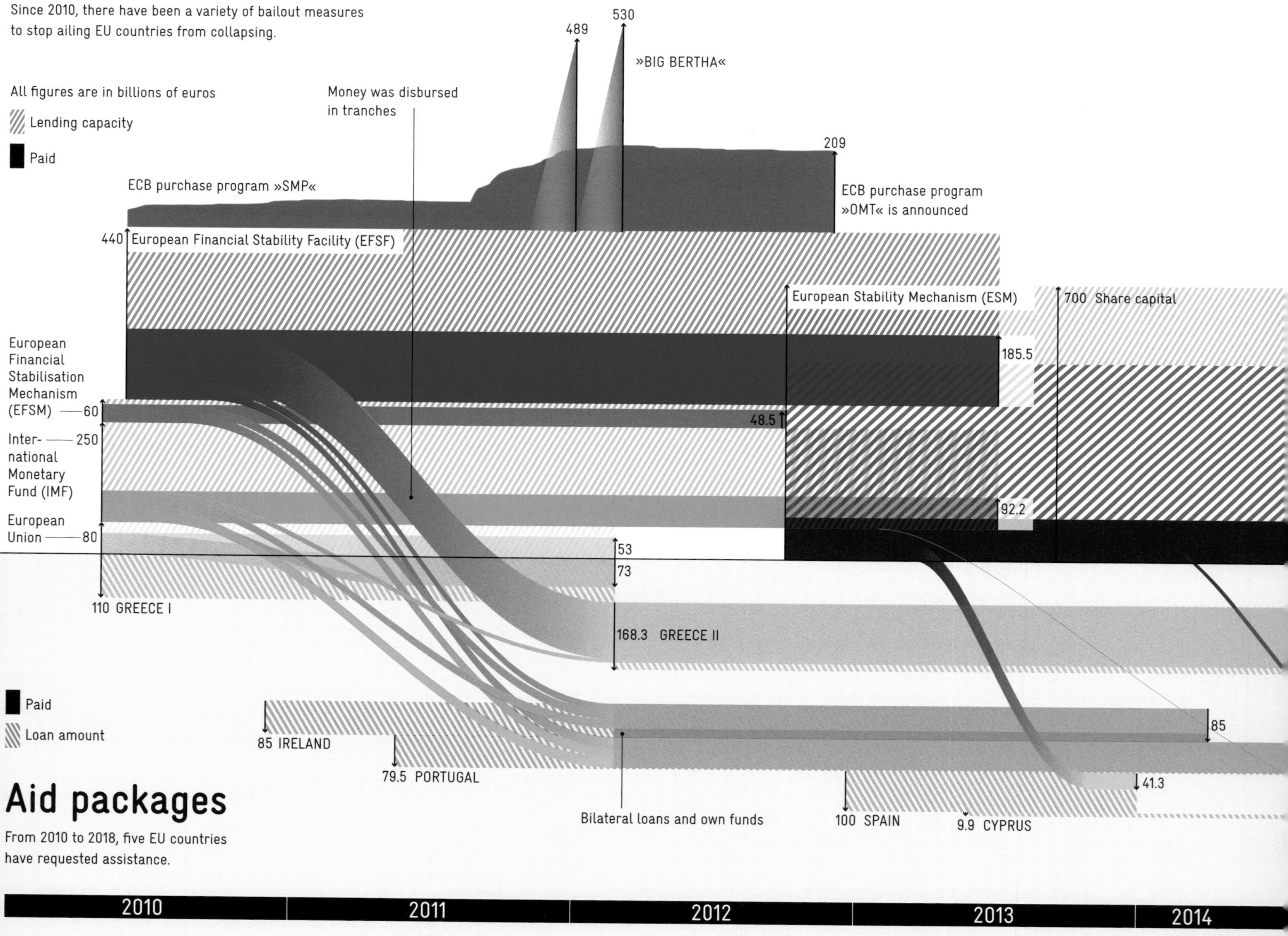
All figures are in billions of euros
Lending capacity
Paid
Money was disbursed in tranches
489
530
»BIG BERTHA«
209
ECB purchase program »SMP«
ECB purchase program »OMT« is announced
440 European Financial Stability Facility (EFSF)
European Stability Mechanism (ESM)
700 Share capital
185.5
European Financial Stabilisation Mechanism (EFSM) 60
International Monetary Fund (IMF) 250
European Union 80
48.5
92.2
53
73
110 GREECE I
168.3 GREECE II
Paid
Loan amount
85 IRELAND
79.5 PORTUGAL
85
41.3
Bilateral loans and own funds
100 SPAIN
9.9 CYPRUS
Aid packages
From 2010 to 2018, five EU countries have requested assistance.
2010
2011
2012
2013
2014

How the ECB stabilized the euro

The M3 money supply in the euro zone shows the success of one European Central Bank (ECB) policy: the deposit facility. This allows commercial banks with liquid funds to make short-term deposits with the ECB.

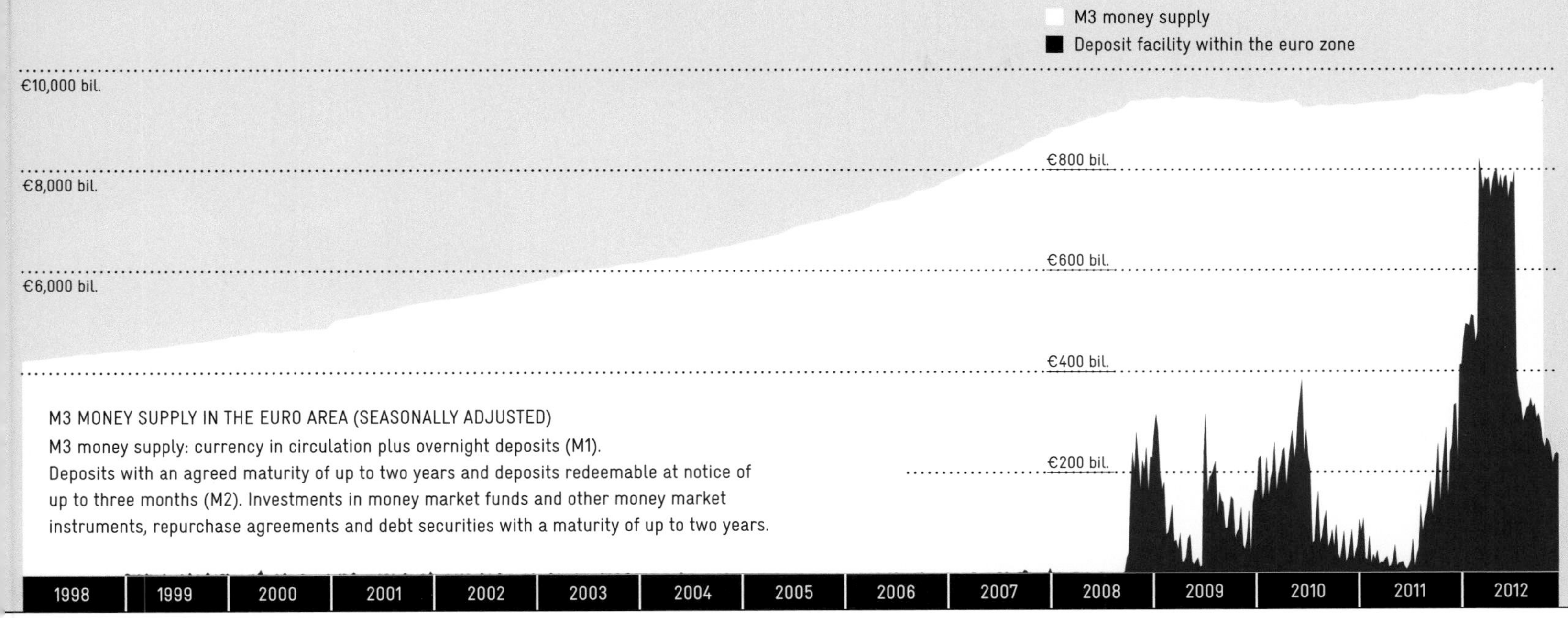

M3 money supply
Deposit facility within the euro zone
€10,000 bil.
€8,000 bil.
€6,000 bil.
€800 bil.
€600 bil.
€400 bil.
€200 bil.
M3 MONEY SUPPLY IN THE EURO AREA (SEASONALLY ADJUSTED)
M3 money supply: currency in circulation plus overnight deposits (M1).
Deposits with an agreed maturity of up to two years and deposits redeemable at notice of up to three months (M2). Investments in money market funds and other money market instruments, repurchase agreements and debt securities with a maturity of up to two years.
1998
1999
2000
2001
2002
2003
2004
2005
2006
2007
2008
2009
2010
2011
2012

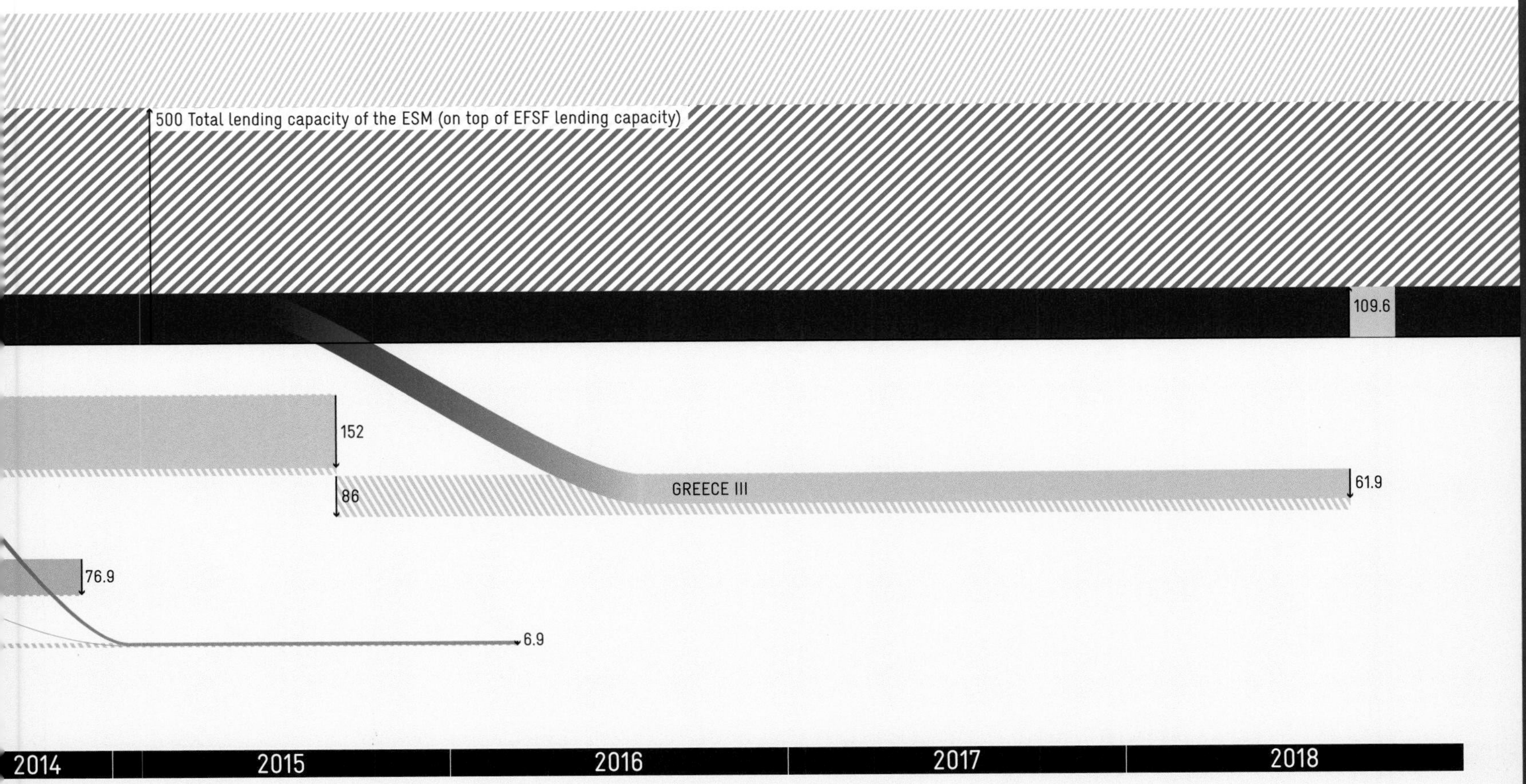

500 Total lending capacity of the ESM (on top of EFSF lending capacity)
109.6
152
86
GREECE III
61.9
76.9
6.9
2014
2015
2016
2017
2018

DIVIDED ISLANDS

Like no other type of landscape, islands stand for a desire for happiness and freedom – and yet they are surrounded by the sea and have fixed limits. It seems grotesque that a state border should exist on an island: Fortunately, divided islands are a rarity.

PACIFIC OCEAN
INDONESIA
49%
ARAFURA SEA
Bandar Seri Begawan
BRUNEI
0.6%
SOUTH CHINA SEA
CELEBES SEA
MALAYSIA
26.8%
Kuching
INDONESIA
72.6%
BORNEO
MAKASSAR STRAIT
Banjarmasin
JAVA SEA
NORTH CHANNEL
UK
17.3%
Belfast
ATLANTIC OCEAN
IRISH SEA
IRELAND
82.7%
Dublin
ST GEORGE'S CHANNEL

Tierra del Fuego

Chile/Argentina

47,992 km²

Border defined by the former colonial administration, in the Boundary Treaty of 1881

Timor

West Timor/East Timor

28,418 km²

Border defined in 1916 between NL and PT colonies

Cyprus

Republic of Cyprus/ Northern Cyprus

9,234 km²

Northern Cyprus occupied since 1974 by Turkey, internationally not accepted

Corocoro

Venezuela / Guyana

690 km²

Both countries claim the island

New Guinea
Indonesia / Papua New Guinea
785,753 km²

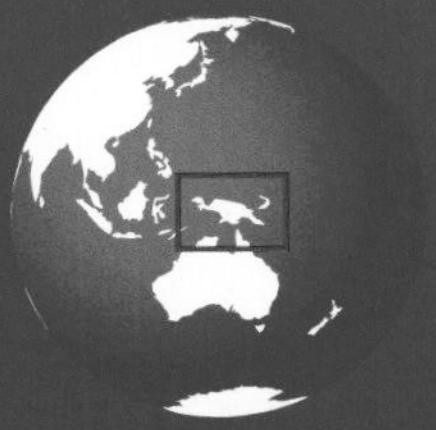

Island divided after DE, UK and NL fortified the territory in 1884

Borneo
Indonesia / Malaysia / Brunei
748,168 km²

Territorial division into three parts between the colonial powers UK, NL and PT

Ireland
Ireland / United Kingdom
81,638 km²

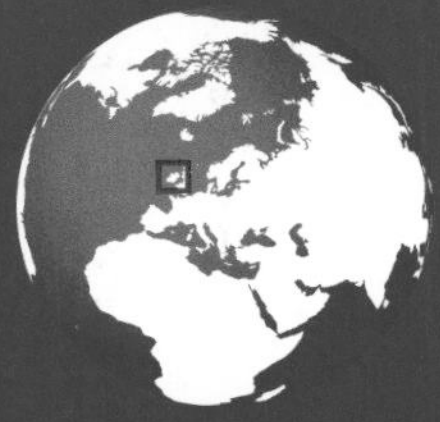

Border defined in the Anglo-Irish Treaty after the Irish War of Independence

Hispaniola
Haiti/Dominican Republic
73,929 km²

This border has been in place since it was colonized by France and Spain in 1776.

Jayapura
BISMARCK SEA
PAPUA NEW GUINEA
51 %
GULF OF PAPUA
NEW GUINEA
Port Moresby
SALOMON SEA
CORAL SEA
HISPANIOLA
ATLANTIC OCEAN
HT
35.2 %
DO
64.8 %
Santo Domingo
Port-au-Prince
CARIBBEAN SEA
TIMOR
Dili
EAST
47.9 %
SAVU SEA
WEST
52.1 %
Kupang
TIMOR SEA
BALTIC SEA
DE
89.5 %
PL
10.5 %
100 km
CELEBES SEA
MY
42.7 %
ID
57.3 %
TIERRA DEL FUEGO
ATLANTIC OCEAN
Porvenir
Rio Grande
CL
57.2 %
AR
42.8 %
PACIFIC OCEAN
Nikosia
42.8 %
NORTHERN CYPRUS
57.2 %
REPUBLIC CYPRUS
MEDITERRANEAN SEA
CYPRUS
ATLANTIC OCEAN
VE
88.7 %
GY
11.3 %
RIO BARIMA (RIVER)

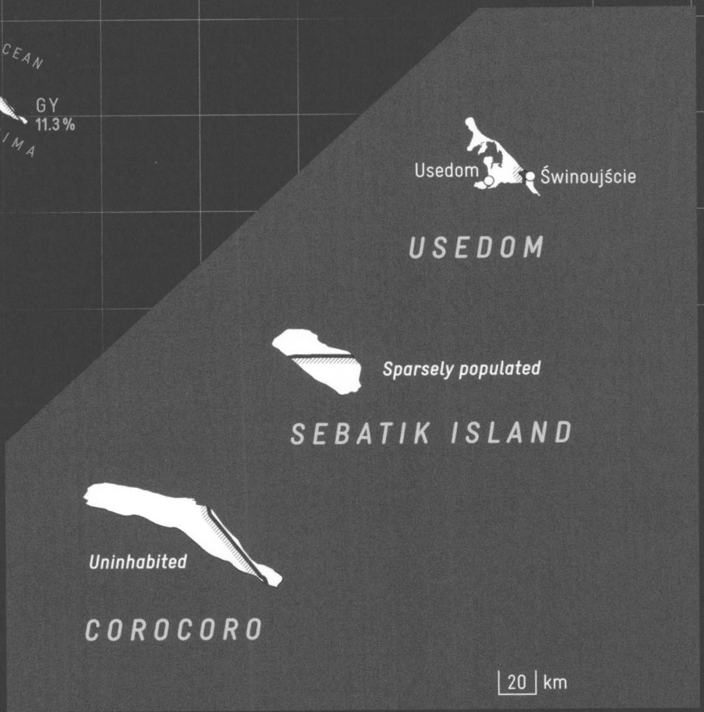
Usedom
Świnoujście
USEDOM
Sparsely populated
SEBATIK ISLAND
Uninhabited
COROCORO
20 km

Sebatik Island
Indonesia / Malaysia
452 km²

Territorial division between the colonial powers UK and NL

Usedom
Germany / Poland
445 km²

Eastern part of the island awarded to Poland in the Treaty of Potsdam in 1945

DISPUTED AREAS

People are strange creatures: they like to maintain boundaries between each other. On a small scale, this is a neighborly dispute over a fence. On a larger scale, two states war over a border. The legal situation gets particularly complicated when it comes to islands. Under Article 55 of the United Nations Convention on the Law of the Sea, each coastal state has a claim to a 200-nautical-mile-wide, exclusive economic zone adjacent to its coast. In this zone, the coastal state has sovereign rights and jurisdiction, particularly the sole right to economic utilization, including fishing. But also on land, there are many different causes that can lead to a dispute, like nuclear power plants operating in border areas.

- States with border disputes
- States free from dispute
- Disputed maritime areas
- Disputed territories
- Disputed borders

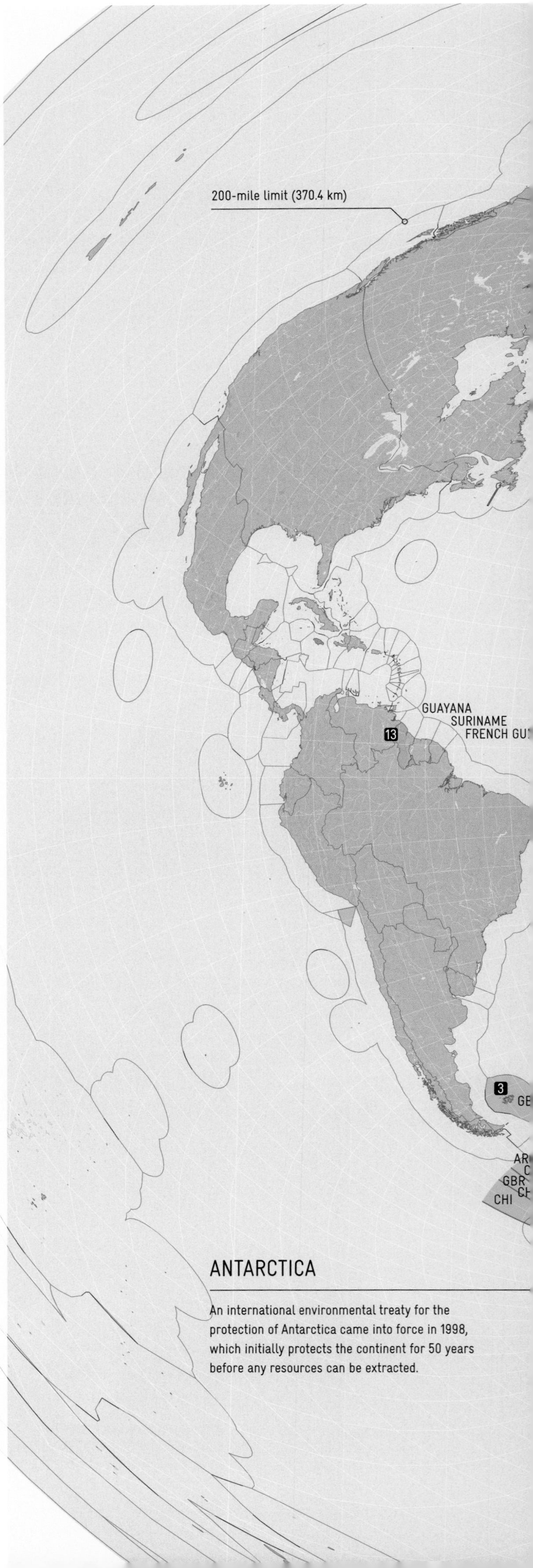

ANTARCTICA

An international environmental treaty for the protection of Antarctica came into force in 1998, which initially protects the continent for 50 years before any resources can be extracted.

A SELECTION OF KNOWN CASES:

1 **Palestine**, claims: Palestine vs. Israel, **Golan Heights**, claims: Syria vs. Israel
2 **Taiwan**, claims: China vs. Republic of China (Taiwan)
3 **Falkland Islands**, claims: Argentina vs. United Kingdom
4 **Cyprus**, claims: Cyprus vs. Turkish Republic of Northern Cyprus
5 **Tibet**, claims: Central Tibetan Administration vs. China
6 **Kosovo**, claims: Serbia vs. Republic of Kosovo
7 **Jammu and Kashmir**, claims: China vs. India vs. Pakistan
8 **Western Sahara**, claims: Marocco vs. Sahrawi Arab Democratic Republic
9 **Liancourt Rocks**, claims: South Korea vs. Japan
10 **Senkaku Islands** (jap.) / **Diaoyu Islands** (chi.), claims: China vs. Japan
11 **Spratly Islands**, claims: Vietnam vs. China vs. Taiwan vs. Malaysia vs. Philippines vs. Brunei
12 **Abyei**, claims: Sudan vs. South-Sudan, **Darfur** (civil war)
13 **Guayana Esequiba**, claims: Venezuela vs. Guayana
14 **Kurile Islands**, claims: Russia vs. Japan
15 **Transnistria**, claims: Transnistria vs. Moldova
16 **Rockall**, claims: United Kingdom vs. Iceland vs. Ireland vs. Danmark
17 **Gibraltar**, claims: Spain vs. United Kingdom
18 **South Georgia and South Sandwich Islands**, claims: Argentina vs. United Kingdom
19 **Abkhazia and South Ossetia**, claims: Georgia vs. Republic of Abkhazia and Republic of South Ossetia
20 **Crimea**, claims: Russia vs. Ukraine

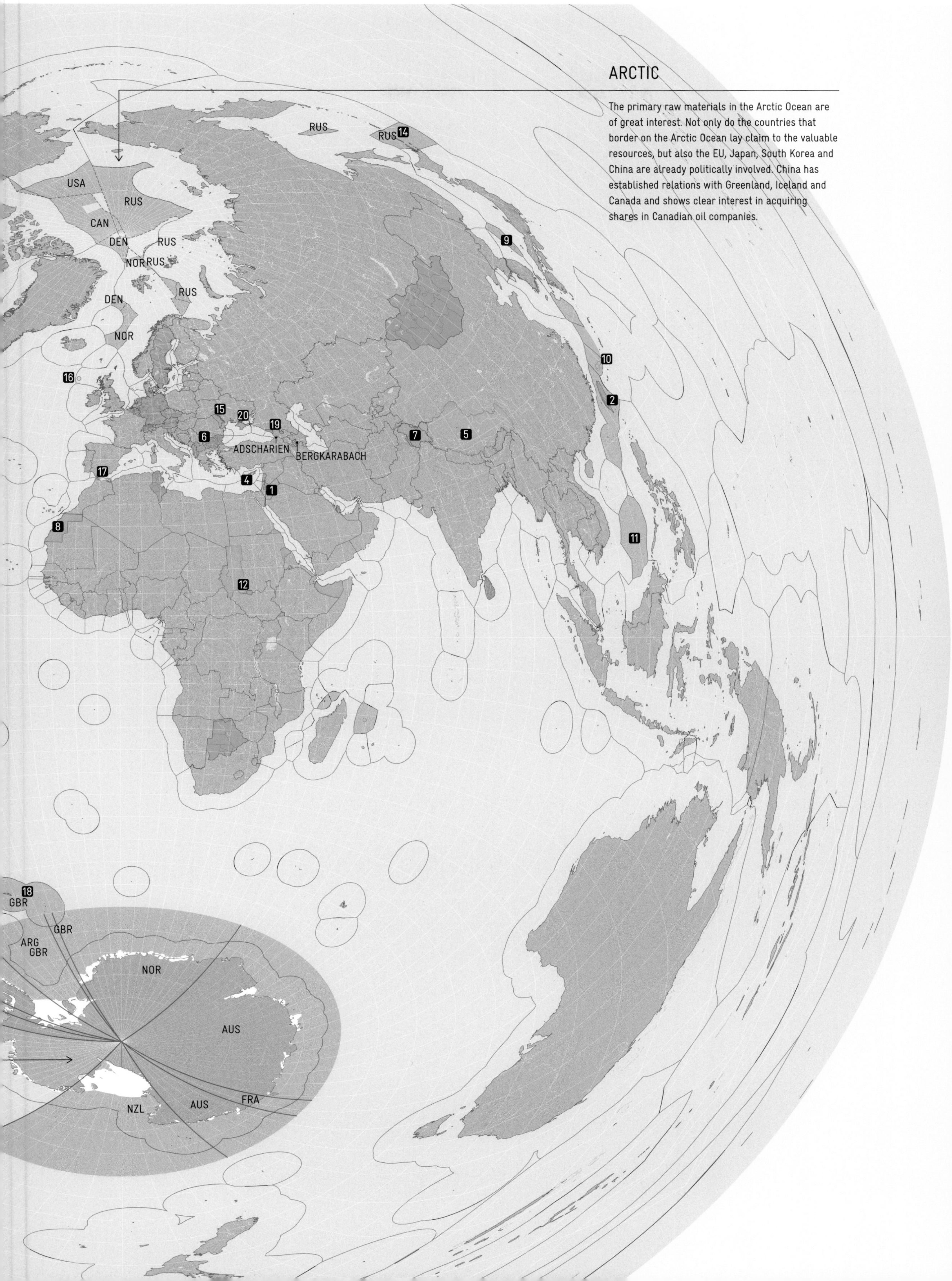

RUS
RUS 14
USA
RUS
CAN
DEN
RUS
NOR RUS
RUS
DEN
NOR
16
15
20
19
6
ADSCHARIEN
BERGKARABACH
7
5
9
10
2
17
4
1
8
11
12
18
GBR
GBR
ARG
GBR
NOR
AUS
NZL
AUS
FRA

ARCTIC

The primary raw materials in the Arctic Ocean are of great interest. Not only do the countries that border on the Arctic Ocean lay claim to the valuable resources, but also the EU, Japan, South Korea and China are already politically involved. China has established relations with Greenland, Iceland and Canada and shows clear interest in acquiring shares in Canadian oil companies.

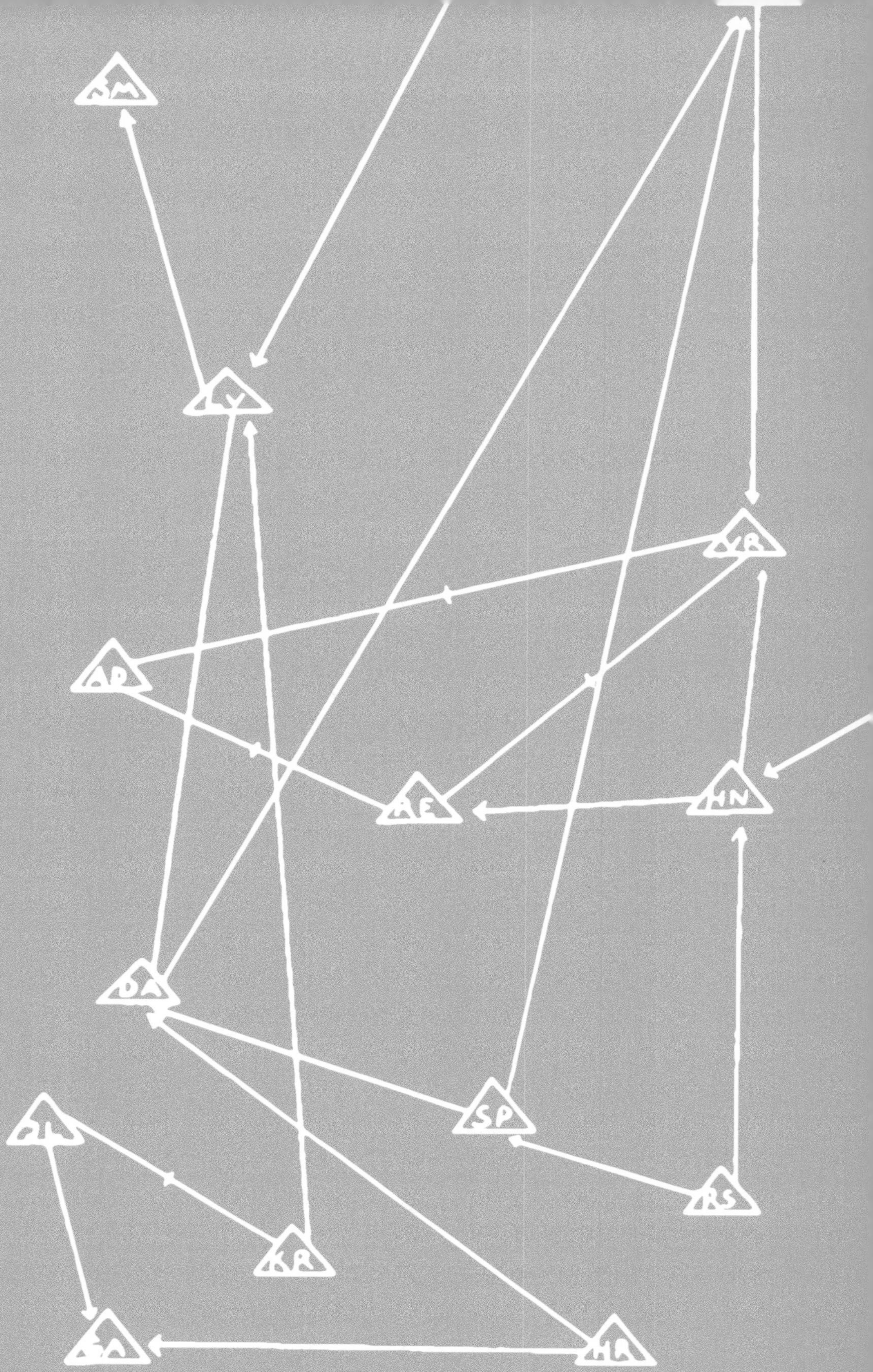
SM
LY
AP
RE
HN
DA
SP
RS
KR
HR

SOCIETY

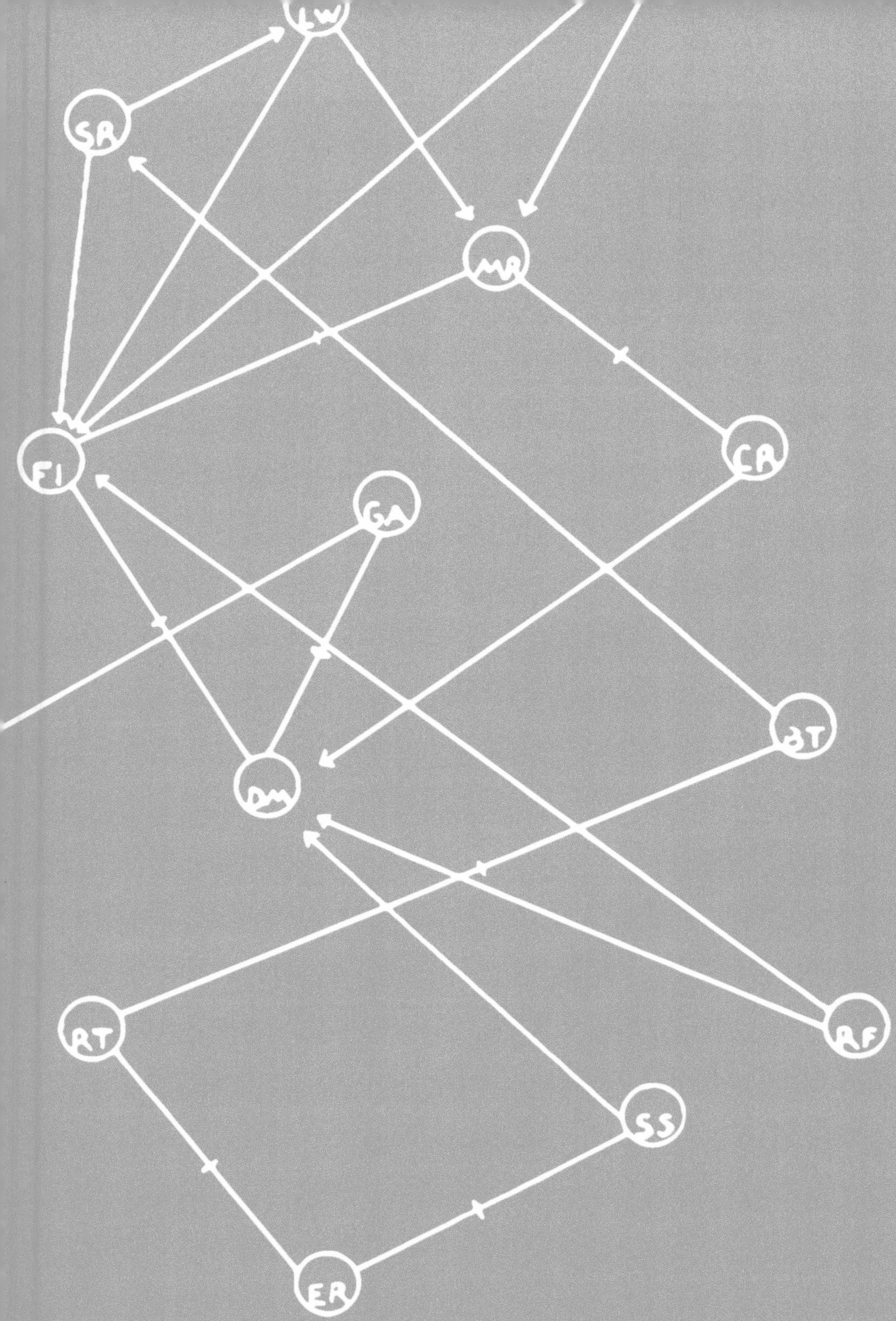

Relationships between people as well as their actions toward one another define societal developments. The larger the group, the more complex the fabric of relationships. For this reason, scientists in the late 19th century began depicting human relationships as graphic networks, which helped clarify their defining connections and influences.

One of the founders of social network analysis, **Jacob L. Moreno** quantitatively measured which roles individuals in a given group play. His 1934 diagram is one of the earliest examples of a **sociogram, or social network visualization**. Using simple symbols, it shows connections within one fifth grade classroom: friendships (arrows) connecting girls (circles) and boys (triangles). Due to their formal structure, network graphics are well suited to clearly depict collaborations, communications, technical connections, and family trees or other relational networks — thereby providing a better basis for understanding and assessment.

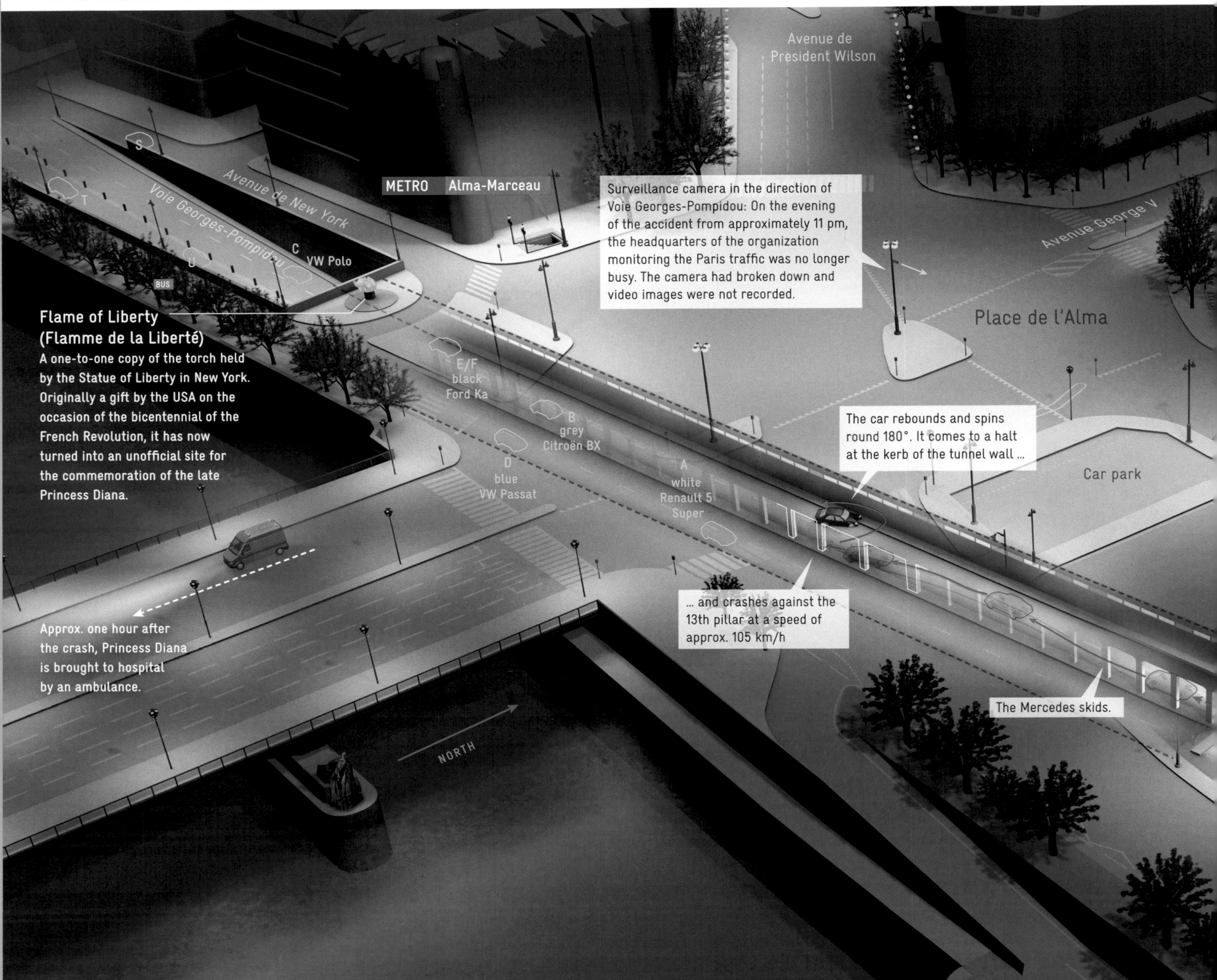
Avenue de President Wilson
METRO Alma-Marceau
Avenue de New York
Voie Georges-Pompidou
C VW Polo
BUS
Surveillance camera in the direction of Voie Georges-Pompidou: On the evening of the accident from approximately 11 pm, the headquarters of the organization monitoring the Paris traffic was no longer busy. The camera had broken down and video images were not recorded.
Avenue George V
Place de l'Alma
Flame of Liberty (Flamme de la Liberté)
A one-to-one copy of the torch held by the Statue of Liberty in New York. Originally a gift by the USA on the occasion of the bicentennial of the French Revolution, it has now turned into an unofficial site for the commemoration of the late Princess Diana.
E/F black Ford Ka
B grey Citroën BX
D blue VW Passat
A white Renault 5 Super
The car rebounds and spins round 180°. It comes to a halt at the kerb of the tunnel wall ...
Car park
... and crashes against the 13th pillar at a speed of approx. 105 km/h
Approx. one hour after the crash, Princess Diana is brought to hospital by an ambulance.
The Mercedes skids.
NORTH

What happened on August 31, 1997?

DEATH OF A PRINCESS

A Mercedes 280 C races into the Place d'Alma tunnel in Paris. Some 23 years later there are still conspiracy theories.

After the accident, dozens of witnesses reported to the Parisian authorities. Their testimonies are very contradictory in parts. This compilation of the most meaningful reports has been derived from the official investigation report from the »Operation Paget«, which was undertaken by the London Police from January 2004 to December 2006 and published online on December 14, 2006.

A Benoît Boura
He enters the tunnel from the opposite direction. He sees flash lights and a motorcycle behind the Mercedes. After the crash, this vehicle passes the wreck slowly then accelerates again.

B Mohammed Medjahdi & Souad Moufakkir
Both hear the squealing of car tires. Looking into their rear mirror, they see the Mercedes slide to the left and crash against the pillar. They are then overtaken by a motorcycle. They see between five and seven cars behind the wreck, but no motorcycles.

C David Laurent & Blanchard family
They overtake a small light fastback, which drives noticeably slowly into the tunnel. Then they overtake a mid-sized car, which then leaves the tunnel behind them. When leaving the tunnel they hear a car horn, screeching brakes and a collision.

D Grigori Rassinier
He drives into the tunnel from the opposite direction. He hears the crash and sees the Mercedes come to a halt. He also sees a motorcycle with one driver appearing out of the smoke.

E Francois Levistre
He enters the Alma Tunnel from the Cours Albert 1er. Together with his wife Roselyn, they drive ahead of the Mercedes and the trailing motorcycles. At the entrance to the tunnel, they are overtaken by a small white car (not a Fiat Uno) at a speed of approx. 80 mph. In his rear view mirror he sees a bright flash and a motorcycle in front of the Mercedes. The Mercedes then starts to roll. They stop at the end of the tunnel for three to five minutes. When they continue their ride they are overtaken by a motorcyclist with a passenger.

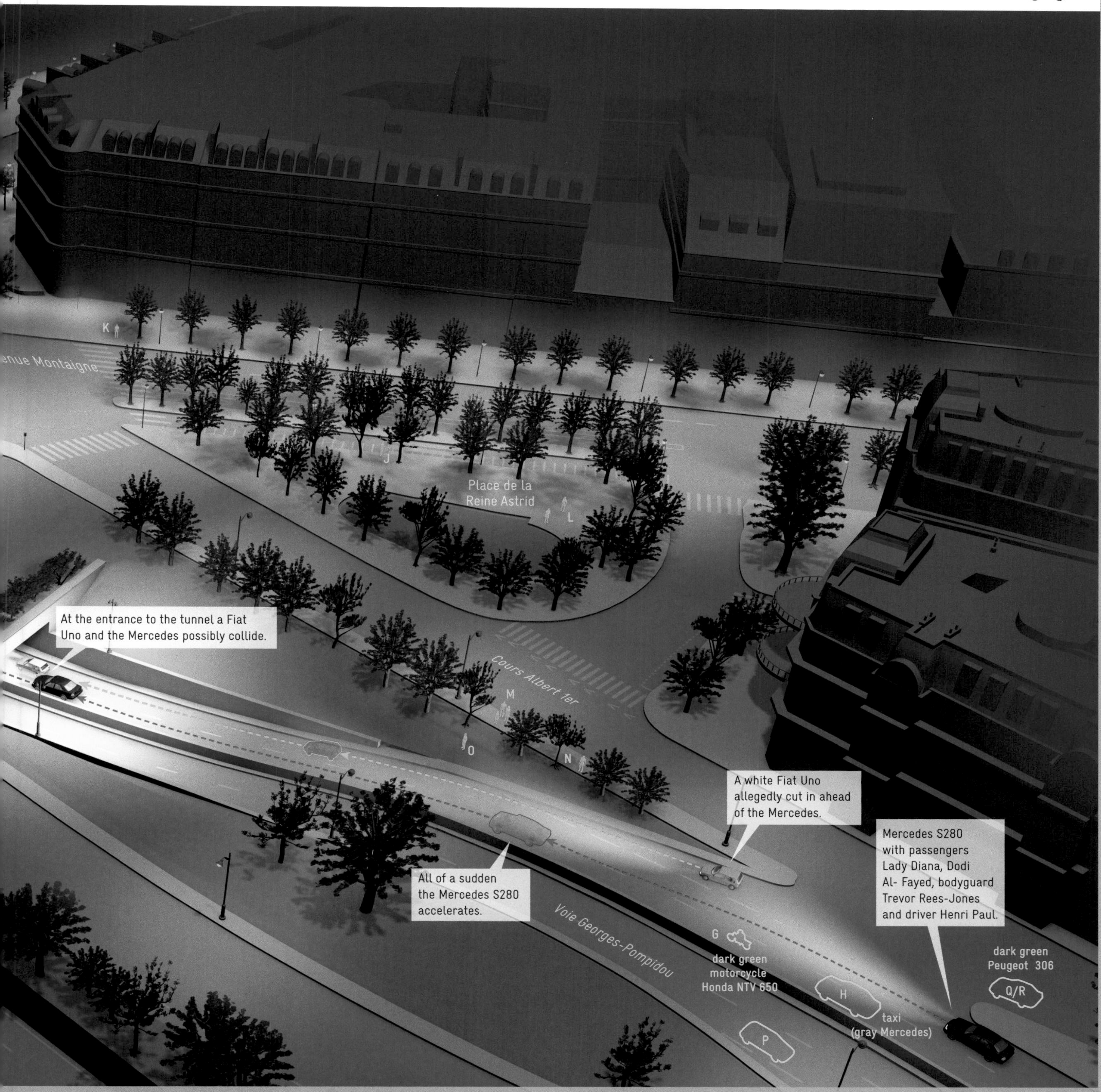
K
enue Montaigne
J
Place de la
Reine Astrid
L
At the entrance to the tunnel a Fiat
Uno and the Mercedes possibly collide.
Cours Albert 1er
M
O
N
A white Fiat Uno
allegedly cut in ahead
of the Mercedes.
Mercedes S280
with passengers
Lady Diana, Dodi
Al- Fayed, bodyguard
Trevor Rees-Jones
and driver Henri Paul.
All of a sudden
the Mercedes S280
accelerates.
Voie Georges-Pompidou
G
dark green
motorcycle
Honda NTV 650
H
taxi
(gray Mercedes)
P
dark green
Peugeot 306
Q/R

F Roselyn Levistre (passenger)
Mrs. Levistre states that she remembers that besides overtaking the Mercedes, they also overtook a second dark car.

G Stephan Darmon
He rides with his motorcycle and Romuad Rat as his passenger behind the Mercedes. After the crash he stops to let R. Rat get off to take photographs, then he panics and drives up to the opposite tunnel entrance. Before entering the tunnel they were followed by another motorcycle, also with a passenger, who stopped at the entrance and took pictures of the wreck and then turned away without passing through the tunnel.

H Brian Anderson
He is the passenger in the taxi that is overtaken by the Mercedes and three motorcycles before entering the tunnel. The motorcycles are closing in on the Mercedes, one of them is attempting to overtake it on its left side. Before the crash, he sees a flashing light.

J Cliffort Gooroovadoo
He stands at the corner of the Place de la Reine Astrid and the Avenue Montaigne when he sees the Mercedes approaching at high speed, followed by one motorcycle with a passenger at a distance of thirty or forty metres. Another dark car drives ahead of the Mercedes at normal speed. After the crash he immediately enters the tunnel where he meets the photographers Christian Martinez and Romuald Rat, plus two or three other persons.

K Olivier Partouche
He watches from the Avenue Montaigne and sees how the Mercedes, trailed by one or several motorcycles, enters the tunnel behind a small, inconspicuous car. He estimates the speed of the Mercedes to be about 90 mph. After the crash he sees flashing lights coming from out of the tunnel.

L Abdelatif Redjil & Belkcem Bouizid
They hear the crash from the Place de la Reine Astrid. On their way to the scene they see a dark car with two passengers slowly leaving the tunnel.

M Catheline family
They see two large cars driving towards the tunnel, hear the sound of a collision and a loud bang. Seconds after the accident they also see a light taxi and a motorcycle. The taxi stops at the tunnel entrance, but the motorcycle drives up to and around the Mercedes.

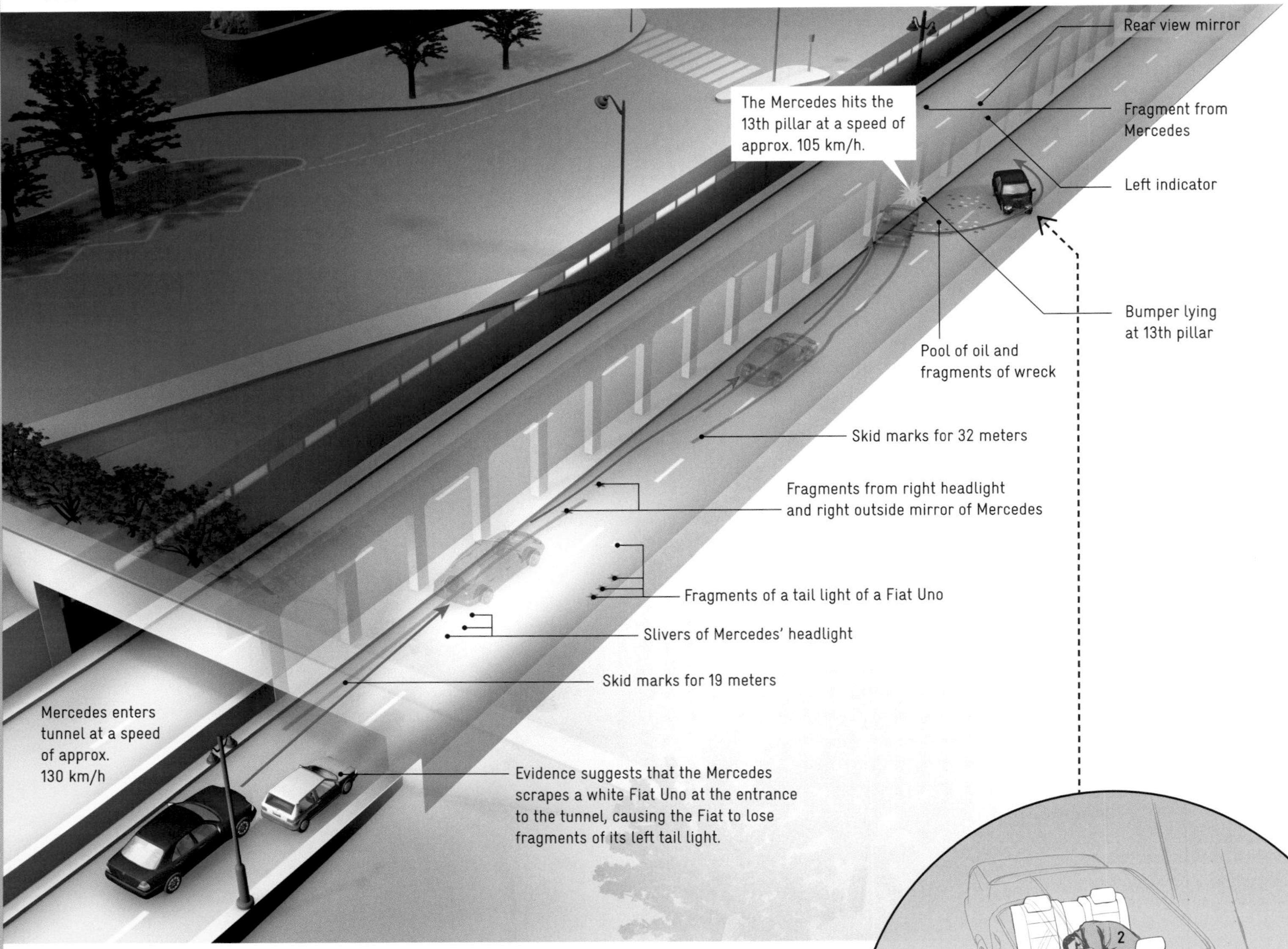
Rear view mirror
The Mercedes hits the 13th pillar at a speed of approx. 105 km/h.
Fragment from Mercedes
Left indicator
Bumper lying at 13th pillar
Pool of oil and fragments of wreck
Skid marks for 32 meters
Fragments from right headlight and right outside mirror of Mercedes
Fragments of a tail light of a Fiat Uno
Slivers of Mercedes' headlight
Skid marks for 19 meters
Mercedes enters tunnel at a speed of approx. 130 km/h
Evidence suggests that the Mercedes scrapes a white Fiat Uno at the entrance to the tunnel, causing the Fiat to lose fragments of its left tail light.

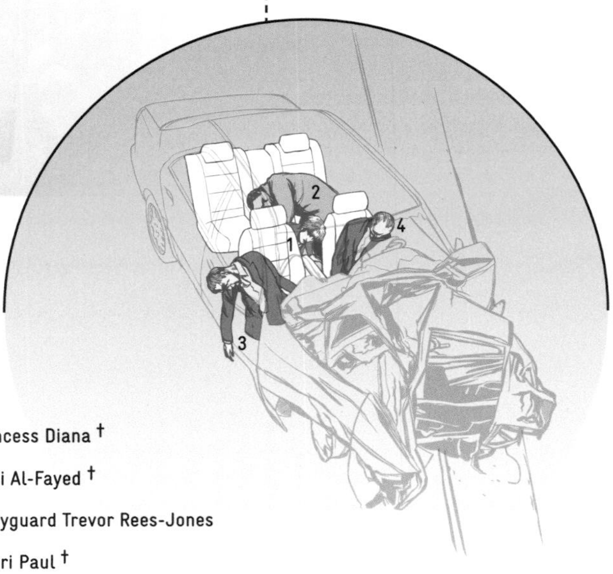

Inside the tunnel: The scene of the accident

What really happened on the night of August 31, 1997, in the Alma tunnel is still unknown today. There are various theories:
The driver, Henri Paul—did he commit suicide? Was he really drunk when he undertook his last duty? Were his blood samples switched? Was there a white Fiat Uno as some witnesses have said? Were there any other vehicles near the car when it drove into the tunnel? Did one of these cars harass the Mercedes and caused it to spin? Was the Mercedes S280 deliberately blinded by a flash in the tunnel? Where were the paparazzi with their motorcycles? Too many questions remain open, providing the conspiracy theorists with enough material. The first of these was Dodi's father, Mohamed Al-Fayed, who is still convinced that his son and the princess were murdered.

1 | Princess Diana †

2 | Dodi Al-Fayed †

3 | Bodyguard Trevor Rees-Jones

4 | Henri Paul †

None of the passengers wore a seatbelt. If they had done so, their survival would have been more likely. The driver, Henri Paul was found to have been taking antidepressants and a drug to control alcohol dependency (Tiapridal). He had a blood alcohol content of 1.75 g/L.

N David Le Ny
He sees the Mercedes overtake a large dark car before the tunnel, and also sees a red limousine and a BMW approx. 300 meters behind the Mercedes. After the accident he notes a motorcycle entering the tunnel.

O Gary Dean
Dean senses the speed of the approaching Mercedes as very high. He sees the car turn on full beam before entering the tunnel, and he does not notice any other flashing lights. He does not see any other vehicle in immediate proximity of the Mercedes.

P Christophe Lascaux
He drives through the tunnel in the opposite direction and sees the Mercedes entering the tunnel at high speed and rolling. It is tailed by two motorcycles. Then he sees flashes and hears a loud bang shortly after the Mercedes has entered the tunnel, then squealing tires and a second bang.

Q Antonio Lopes Borges
He reaches the scene of the accident shortly after the crash. He sees a dark car passing the scene.

R Anna Simao (passenger)
She sees a small white car pass between a pillar and the Mercedes, but she is not sure whether this car left the tunnel or not.

S Georges & Sabine Dauzonne
They watch as a white Fiat Uno drives slowly through the tunnel and stop approx. 30 meters outside it.

T Dr. Frédéric Mailliez & Mark Butt
Both arrive at the scene of the tragedy shortly after the accident. Dr. Mailliez carries his first aid kit and he is the first to give medical treatment to Lady Diana.

U Damien Dalby, Audrey Lemaigre, Sébastien Masseron & Sébastien Pennequin
The group reaches the tunnel after the crash coming from the western side and they notice the tailback and many flashing lights. They see five to six people standing around the Mercedes. Pennequin walks up to the wreck, where he notices a green limousine and its driver, who is making a call with his cellphone, while another man hurries away from the scene of the accident. He helps the police hold the paparazzi away from the accident scene. His brother Dalby hears Diana saying: »Oh my God, oh my God«.

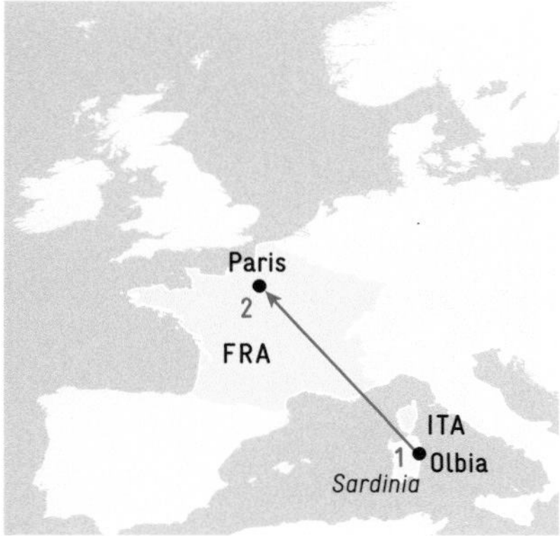
Paris
2
FRA
ITA
1
Olbia
Sardinia

Chain of events

On July 11, 1997, Lady Diana Spencer and her sons William and Harry are hosted by Mohamed Al-Fayed in St. Tropez. On July 14, Dodi Al-Fayed joins the family. Diana and her sons return to London on July 20. Without any attention paid by the press, Diana and Dodi meet in Paris on July 26.

After a short stay in England, they fly to the French and Italian Riviera for a holiday, where a paparazzo takes the first shot of the kissing couple. This holiday ends on August 6, but on August 22, Diana and Dodi continue their holiday on the Riviera.

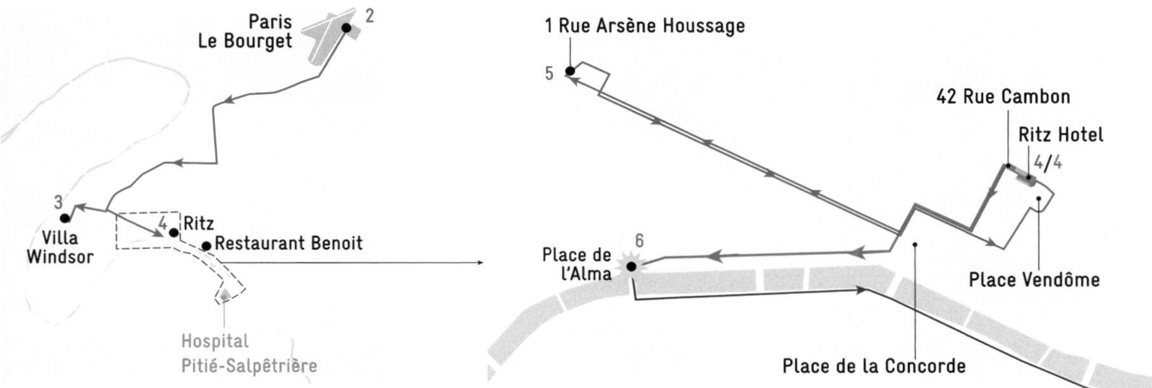
Paris
Le Bourget
2
3
Villa
Windsor
4
Ritz
Restaurant Benoit
Hospital
Pitié-Salpêtrière
1 Rue Arsène Houssage
5
42 Rue Cambon
Ritz Hotel
4/4
Place Vendôme
Place de
l'Alma
6
Place de la Concorde

7 2:06 am
Following the instructions of the emergency physician, the ambulance drives very slowly, to stabilize the injured passengers. It arrives at the hospital about 40 minutes later. The average speed of the ambulance was therefore around 6 mph (10 km/h). The severely injured bodyguard Trevor Rees-Jones is brought to the same hospital.

8 3:55 am
Lady Diana Spencer is officially declared dead.

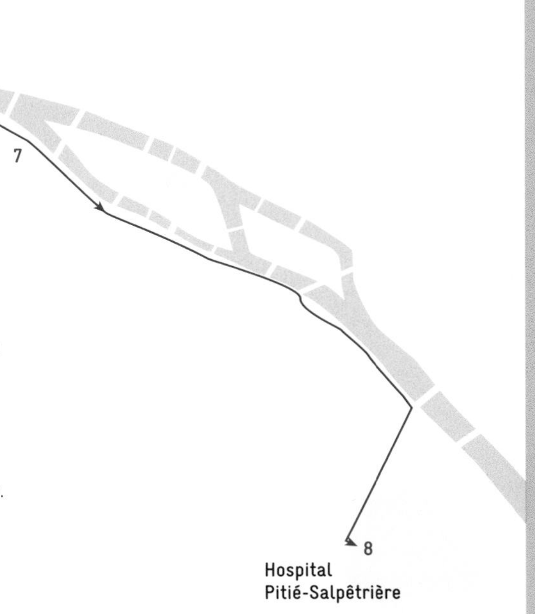
7
8
Hospital
Pitié-Salpêtrière

August 30, 1997

1 1:00 pm, Sardinia
Diana and Dodi depart from Olbia Airport in Al-Fayed's private jet after a holiday spent on the family yacht cruising off the coast of Sardinia.

2 3:20 pm, Paris
Arrival at Le Bourget Airport, Paris, the couple are awaited by six paparazzi and Henri Paul, the Deputy Head of Security at the Ritz Hotel.

3 3:50 pm
On their way to the city they take a detour to the Villa Windsor, which is owned by the Al-Fayeds and is about to be auctioned in the next 10 days.

4 4:20 pm
The couple enters the Ritz through the back entrance to avoid the crowd of photographers waiting in the front.

4 6:30 pm
Dodi enters the Repossi jeweller's shop, also located at Place Vendôme, and chooses a ring for $ 200,000, which he has engraved for Diana.

5 7:15 pm
The couple arrives at Dodi Al-Fayed's Appartment at 1 Rue Arsène Houssaye after they again used the back entrance for their exit.

4 9:51pm
Instead of driving to the Benoit restaurant as planned, Diana and Dodi return to the Ritz and take their dinner in the Imperial Suite.

August 31, 1997

4 12:19 am
Hoping to escape the photographers, the couple leaves again through the back entrance and gets into the Mercedes S280, registered as 688LTV75. There are 10 surveillance cameras on the route to the Place de l'Alma, but none are aligned to catch images of the Mercedes.

6 ca. 12:25 am
The Mercedes enters the tunnel passing under the Place de l'Alma at a high speed and crashes against the 13th pillar, counted from the car's entrance to the tunnel.

6 12:26 am
The Paris Fire Brigade receives an emergency call reporting a serious accident in the Alma Tunnel.

6 12:26 am
First aid administered by Dr. Mailliez

6 12:33 am
Approx. eight minutes after the accident, two policemen arrive at the scene in their patrol car.

6 12:38 am
A fire engine from the fire brigade arrives at the scene.

6 12:41 am
The first ambulance arrives at the scene.

6 01:25 am
After the wreck has been cut open and first medical treatment has taken place, the ambulance with the critically injured Lady Diana Spencer drives from the scene.

Important persons involved

Romuald Rat (36*)
Rat was working for the Gamma photography agency and was one of the first photographers at the scene of the accident. Rat was trained in first aid, felt Diana's pulse and tried to help. He and another seven photographers were later arrested for manslaughter. The proceedings were dismissed in 1999.

James Andanson (54†)
Paris police and, above all, Dodi's father Mohammed Al-Fayed suspected this paparazzo to have caused the accident in his white Fiat Uno. According to Al-Fayed, Andanson was said to have worked for the British Security Service. Andanson supposedly had an alibi for the time period in question. On May 5, 2000 he was found dead in his burnt out BMW in the south of France, allegedly a suicide for familial reasons.

Frédéric Mailliez (46*)
The physician was the first to pass the scene of the accident by pure chance. He called the ambulance and provided first aid.

Bruno Riou (49*)
He was in charge of the emergency team at Pitié-Salpêtrière hospital, where Diana was brought. He announced her death on August 31, 1997.

Trevor Rees-Jones (29*)
Dodi Al-Fayed's bodyguard survived the accident with severe injuries. He resigned from his duties with the Al-Fayed family in 1998. In response to the family's allegation that he is partly responsible for the deaths of Dodi and Diana, he published the book »The Bodyguard's Story« in 2000.

* age at the time of the accident in 1997

BLUE BLOOD

In 2011, everyone caught a little bit of royal wedding fever when Charlene Lynette Wittstock married Prince Albert of Monaco and Catherine Middleton said 'I do' to Prince William, thereby adding two branches to royal family trees. A look back to the year 1660 shows a long trail of royal blue blood.

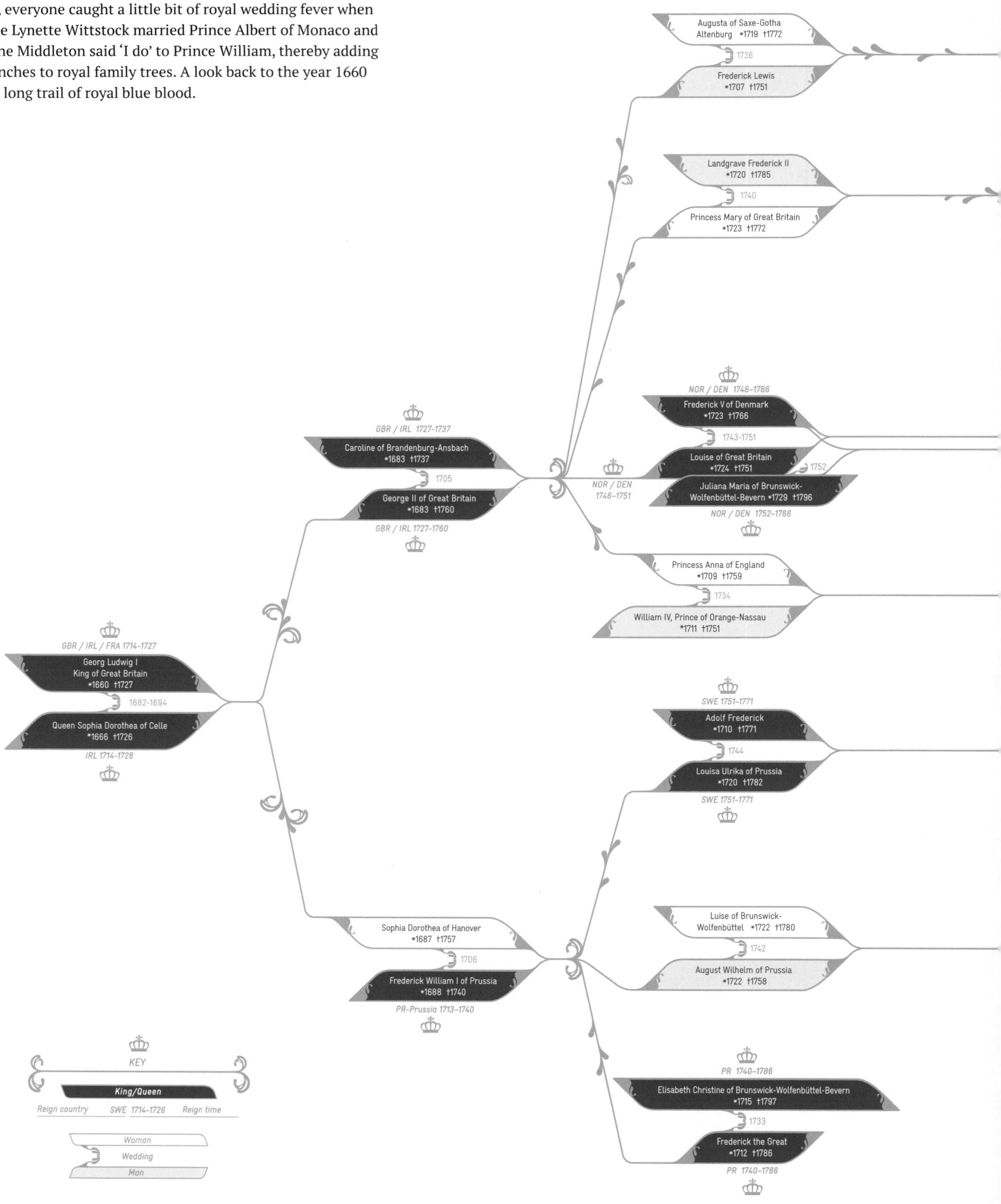

Augusta of Saxe-Gotha Altenburg *1719 †1772
1736
Frederick Lewis *1707 †1751
Landgrave Frederick II *1720 †1785
1740
Princess Mary of Great Britain *1723 †1772
NOR / DEN 1746–1766
Frederick V of Denmark *1723 †1766
1743-1751
Louise of Great Britain *1724 †1751
1752
Juliana Maria of Brunswick-Wolfenbüttel-Bevern *1729 †1796
NOR / DEN 1752–1766
NOR / DEN 1746–1751
GBR / IRL 1727-1737
Caroline of Brandenburg-Ansbach *1683 †1737
1705
George II of Great Britain *1683 †1760
GBR / IRL 1727–1760
Princess Anna of England *1709 †1759
1734
William IV, Prince of Orange-Nassau *1711 †1751
GBR / IRL / FRA 1714-1727
Georg Ludwig I King of Great Britain *1660 †1727
1682-1694
Queen Sophia Dorothea of Celle *1666 †1726
IRL 1714–1726
SWE 1751–1771
Adolf Frederick *1710 †1771
1744
Louisa Ulrika of Prussia *1720 †1782
SWE 1751–1771
Sophia Dorothea of Hanover *1687 †1757
1706
Frederick William I of Prussia *1688 †1740
PR-Prussia 1713–1740
Luise of Brunswick-Wolfenbüttel *1722 †1780
1742
August Wilhelm of Prussia *1722 †1758
PR 1740–1786
Elisabeth Christine of Brunswick-Wolfenbüttel-Bevern *1715 †1797
1733
Frederick the Great *1712 †1786
PR 1740–1786
KEY
King/Queen
Reign country
SWE 1714–1726
Reign time
Woman
Wedding
Man

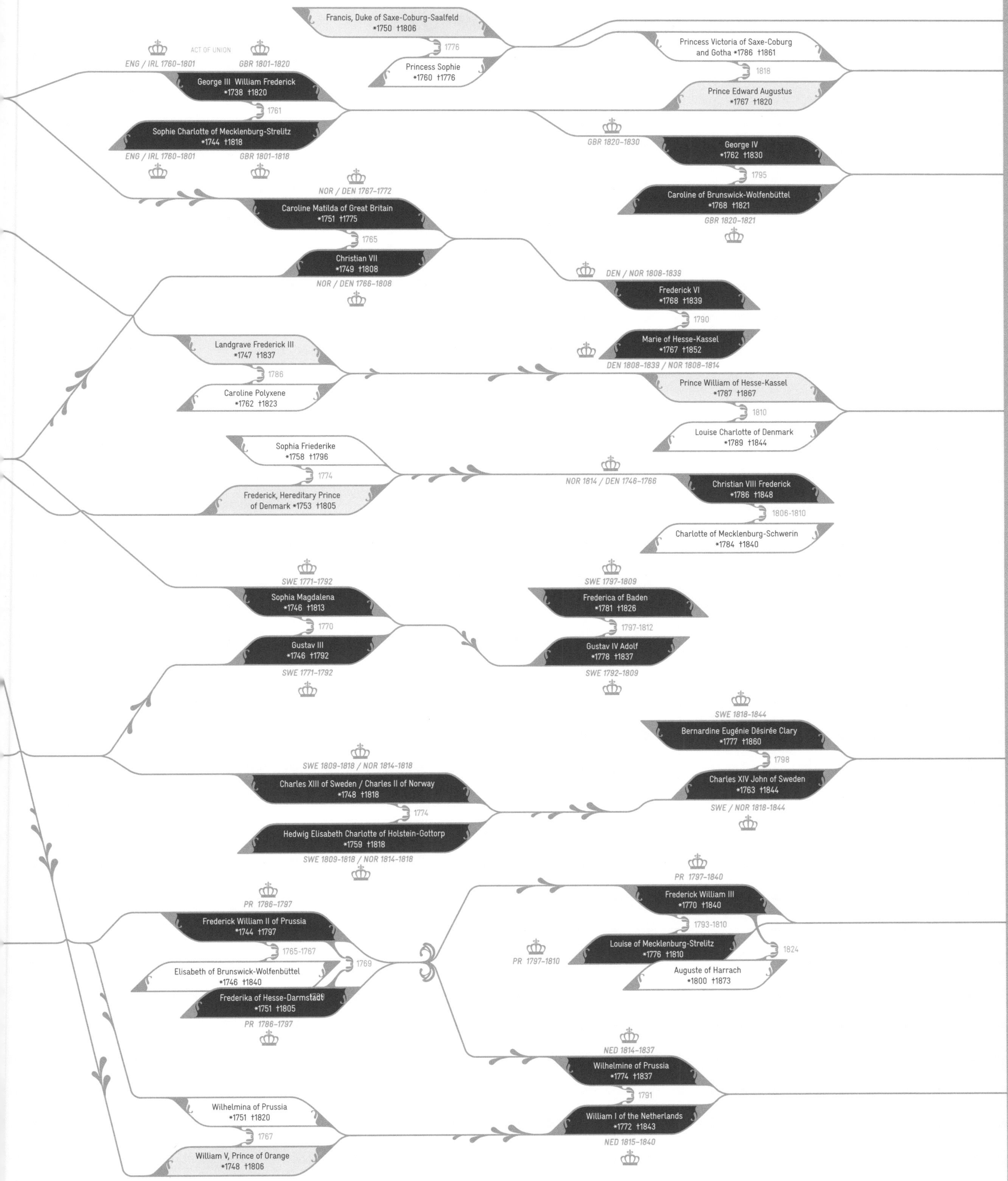
Francis, Duke of Saxe-Coburg-Saalfeld *1750 †1806
1776
Princess Sophie *1760 †1776
Princess Victoria of Saxe-Coburg and Gotha *1786 †1861
1818
Prince Edward Augustus *1767 †1820
ENG / IRL 1760–1801
ACT OF UNION
GBR 1801–1820
George III William Frederick *1738 †1820
1761
Sophie Charlotte of Mecklenburg-Strelitz *1744 †1818
ENG / IRL 1760–1801
GBR 1801–1818
GBR 1820–1830
George IV *1762 †1830
1795
Caroline of Brunswick-Wolfenbüttel *1768 †1821
GBR 1820–1821
NOR / DEN 1767–1772
Caroline Matilda of Great Britain *1751 †1775
1765
Christian VII *1749 †1808
NOR / DEN 1766–1808
DEN / NOR 1808–1839
Frederick VI *1768 †1839
1790
Marie of Hesse-Kassel *1767 †1852
DEN 1808–1839 / NOR 1808–1814
Landgrave Frederick III *1747 †1837
1786
Caroline Polyxene *1762 †1823
Prince William of Hesse-Kassel *1787 †1867
1810
Louise Charlotte of Denmark *1789 †1844
Sophia Friederike *1758 †1796
1774
Frederick, Hereditary Prince of Denmark *1753 †1805
NOR 1814 / DEN 1746–1766
Christian VIII Frederick *1786 †1848
1806-1810
Charlotte of Mecklenburg-Schwerin *1784 †1840
SWE 1771–1792
Sophia Magdalena *1746 †1813
1770
Gustav III *1746 †1792
SWE 1771–1792
SWE 1797–1809
Frederica of Baden *1781 †1826
1797-1812
Gustav IV Adolf *1778 †1837
SWE 1792–1809
SWE 1818–1844
Bernardine Eugénie Désirée Clary *1777 †1860
1798
Charles XIV John of Sweden *1763 †1844
SWE / NOR 1818–1844
SWE 1809–1818 / NOR 1814–1818
Charles XIII of Sweden / Charles II of Norway *1748 †1818
1774
Hedwig Elisabeth Charlotte of Holstein-Gottorp *1759 †1818
SWE 1809–1818 / NOR 1814–1818
PR 1786–1797
Frederick William II of Prussia *1744 †1797
1765-1767
1769
Elisabeth of Brunswick-Wolfenbüttel *1746 †1840
Frederika of Hesse-Darmstadt *1751 †1805
PR 1786–1797
PR 1797–1840
Frederick William III *1770 †1840
1793-1810
1824
PR 1797–1810
Louise of Mecklenburg-Strelitz *1776 †1810
Auguste of Harrach *1800 †1873
NED 1814–1837
Wilhelmine of Prussia *1774 †1837
1791
William I of the Netherlands *1772 †1843
NED 1815–1840
Wilhelmina of Prussia *1751 †1820
1767
William V, Prince of Orange *1748 †1806

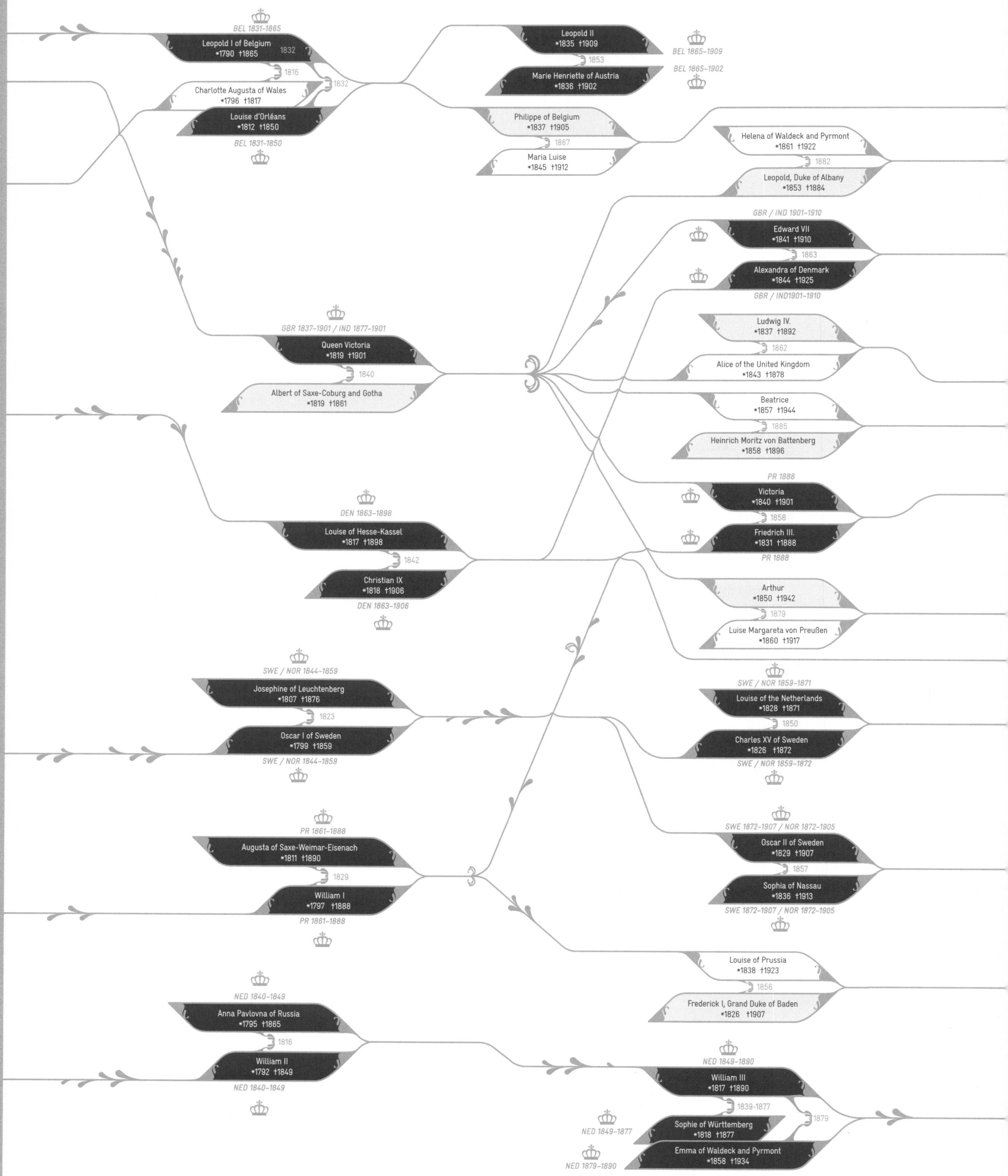

BEL 1831–1865
Leopold I of Belgium
*1790 †1865
1832
1816
Charlotte Augusta of Wales
*1796 †1817
1832
Louise d'Orléans
*1812 †1850
BEL 1831–1850
Leopold II
*1835 †1909
BEL 1865–1909
1853
Marie Henriette of Austria
*1836 †1902
BEL 1865–1902
Philippe of Belgium
*1837 †1905
1867
Maria Luise
*1845 †1912
Helena of Waldeck and Pyrmont
*1861 †1922
1882
Leopold, Duke of Albany
*1853 †1884
GBR / IND 1901–1910
Edward VII
*1841 †1910
1863
Alexandra of Denmark
*1844 †1925
GBR / IND1901–1910
GBR 1837–1901 / IND 1877–1901
Queen Victoria
*1819 †1901
1840
Albert of Saxe-Coburg and Gotha
*1819 †1861
Ludwig IV.
*1837 †1892
1862
Alice of the United Kingdom
*1843 †1878
Beatrice
*1857 †1944
1885
Heinrich Moritz von Battenberg
*1858 †1896
PR 1888
Victoria
*1840 †1901
1858
Friedrich III.
*1831 †1888
PR 1888
DEN 1863–1898
Louise of Hesse-Kassel
*1817 †1898
1842
Christian IX
*1818 †1906
DEN 1863–1906
Arthur
*1850 †1942
1879
Luise Margareta von Preußen
*1860 †1917
SWE / NOR 1844–1859
Josephine of Leuchtenberg
*1807 †1876
1823
Oscar I of Sweden
*1799 †1859
SWE / NOR 1844–1859
SWE / NOR 1859–1871
Louise of the Netherlands
*1828 †1871
1850
Charles XV of Sweden
*1826 †1872
SWE / NOR 1859–1872
PR 1861–1888
Augusta of Saxe-Weimar-Eisenach
*1811 †1890
1829
William I
*1797 †1888
PR 1861–1888
SWE 1872–1907 / NOR 1872–1905
Oscar II of Sweden
*1829 †1907
1857
Sophia of Nassau
*1836 †1913
SWE 1872–1907 / NOR 1872–1905
Louise of Prussia
*1838 †1923
1856
Frederick I, Grand Duke of Baden
*1826 †1907
NED 1840–1849
Anna Pavlovna of Russia
*1795 †1865
1816
William II
*1792 †1849
NED 1840–1849
NED 1849–1890
William III
*1817 †1890
1839–1877
1879
NED 1849–1877
Sophie of Württemberg
*1818 †1877
Emma of Waldeck and Pyrmont
*1858 †1934
NED 1879–1890

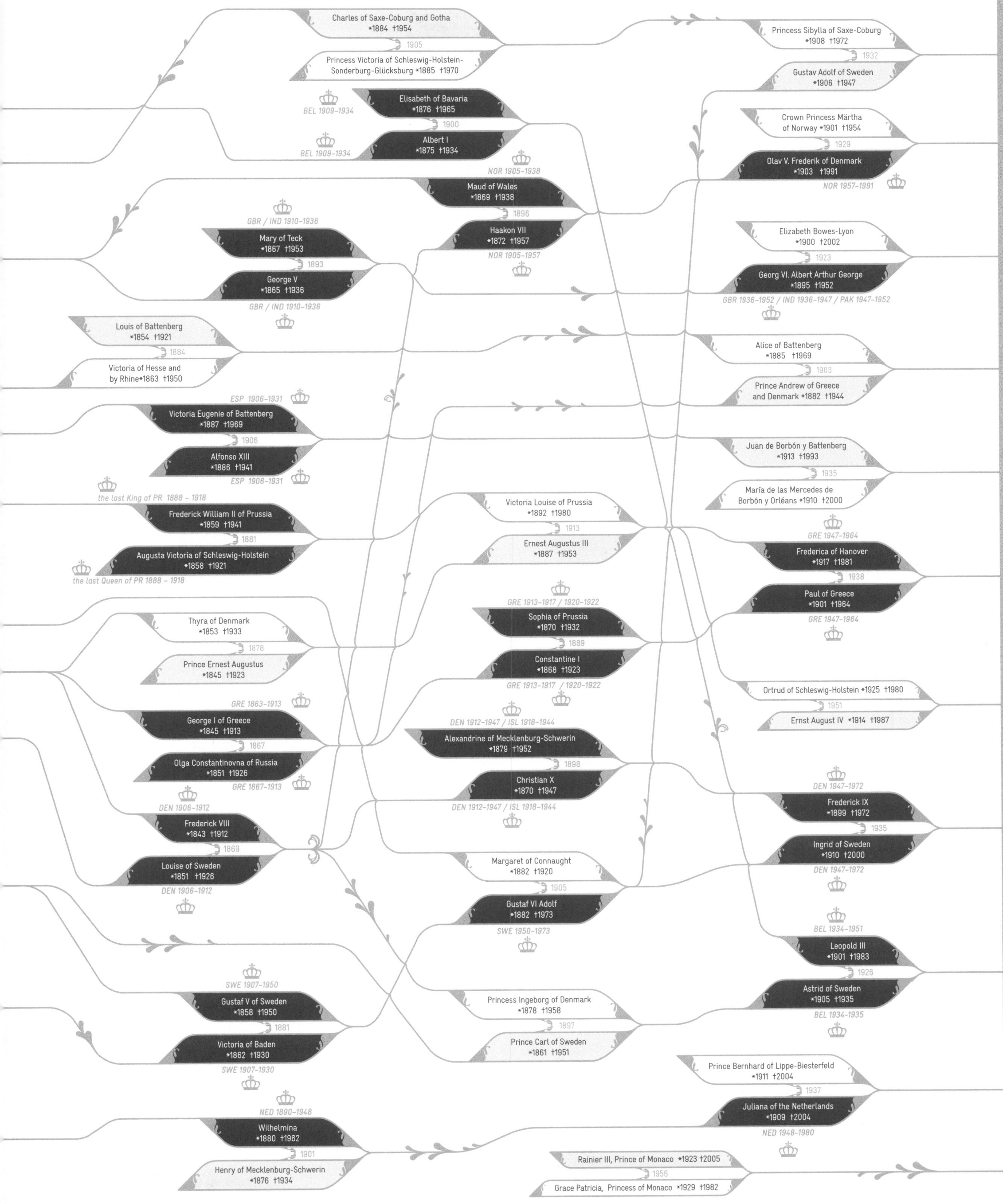
Charles of Saxe-Coburg and Gotha *1884 †1954
1905
Princess Victoria of Schleswig-Holstein-Sonderburg-Glücksburg *1885 †1970
BEL 1909–1934
Elisabeth of Bavaria *1876 †1965
1900
Albert I *1875 †1934
BEL 1909–1934
NOR 1905–1938
Maud of Wales *1869 †1938
1896
Haakon VII *1872 †1957
NOR 1905–1957
GBR / IND 1910–1936
Mary of Teck *1867 †1953
1893
George V *1865 †1936
GBR / IND 1910–1936
Louis of Battenberg *1854 †1921
1884
Victoria of Hesse and by Rhine*1863 †1950
ESP 1906–1931
Victoria Eugenie of Battenberg *1887 †1969
1906
Alfonso XIII *1886 †1941
ESP 1906–1931
the last King of PR 1888 – 1918
Frederick William II of Prussia *1859 †1941
1881
Augusta Victoria of Schleswig-Holstein *1858 †1921
the last Queen of PR 1888 – 1918
Thyra of Denmark *1853 †1933
1878
Prince Ernest Augustus *1845 †1923
GRE 1863–1913
George I of Greece *1845 †1913
1867
Olga Constantinovna of Russia *1851 †1926
GRE 1867–1913
DEN 1906–1912
Frederick VIII *1843 †1912
1869
Louise of Sweden *1851 †1926
DEN 1906–1912
SWE 1907–1950
Gustaf V of Sweden *1858 †1950
1881
Victoria of Baden *1862 †1930
SWE 1907–1930
NED 1890–1948
Wilhelmina *1880 †1962
1901
Henry of Mecklenburg-Schwerin *1876 †1934
Victoria Louise of Prussia *1892 †1980
1913
Ernest Augustus III *1887 †1953
GRE 1913–1917 / 1920–1922
Sophia of Prussia *1870 †1932
1889
Constantine I *1868 †1923
GRE 1913–1917 / 1920–1922
DEN 1912–1947 / ISL 1918–1944
Alexandrine of Mecklenburg-Schwerin *1879 †1952
1898
Christian X *1870 †1947
DEN 1912–1947 / ISL 1918–1944
Margaret of Connaught *1882 †1920
1905
Gustaf VI Adolf *1882 †1973
SWE 1950–1973
Princess Ingeborg of Denmark *1878 †1958
1897
Prince Carl of Sweden *1861 †1951
Princess Sibylla of Saxe-Coburg *1908 †1972
1932
Gustav Adolf of Sweden *1906 †1947
Crown Princess Märtha of Norway *1901 †1954
1929
Olav V. Frederik of Denmark *1903 †1991
NOR 1957–1991
Elizabeth Bowes-Lyon *1900 †2002
1923
Georg VI. Albert Arthur George *1895 †1952
GBR 1936–1952 / IND 1936–1947 / PAK 1947–1952
Alice of Battenberg *1885 †1969
1903
Prince Andrew of Greece and Denmark *1882 †1944
Juan de Borbón y Battenberg *1913 †1993
1935
María de las Mercedes de Borbón y Orléans *1910 †2000
GRE 1947–1964
Frederica of Hanover *1917 †1981
1938
Paul of Greece *1901 †1964
GRE 1947–1964
Ortrud of Schleswig-Holstein *1925 †1980
1951
Ernst August IV *1914 †1987
DEN 1947–1972
Frederick IX *1899 †1972
1935
Ingrid of Sweden *1910 †2000
DEN 1947–1972
BEL 1934–1951
Leopold III *1901 †1983
1926
Astrid of Sweden *1905 †1935
BEL 1934–1935
Prince Bernhard of Lippe-Biesterfeld *1911 †2004
1937
Juliana of the Netherlands *1909 †2004
NED 1948–1980
Rainier III, Prince of Monaco *1923 †2005
1956
Grace Patricia, Princess of Monaco *1929 †1982

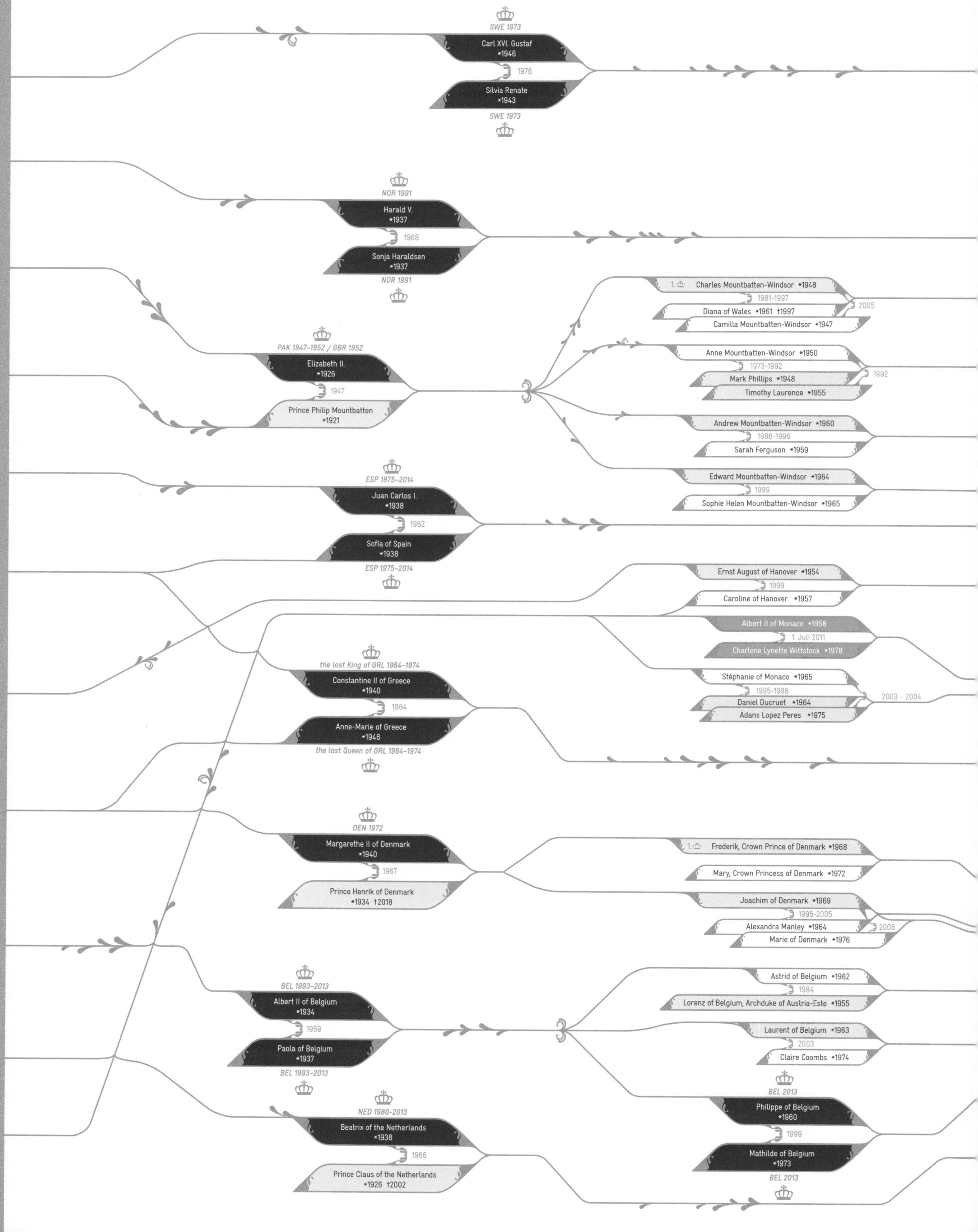
SWE 1973
Carl XVI. Gustaf *1946
1976
Silvia Renate *1943
SWE 1973
NOR 1991
Harald V. *1937
1968
Sonja Haraldsen *1937
NOR 1991
Charles Mountbatten-Windsor *1948
1981-1997
Diana of Wales *1961 †1997
2005
Camilla Mountbatten-Windsor *1947
PAK 1947–1952 / GBR 1952
Elizabeth II. *1926
1947
Prince Philip Mountbatten *1921
Anne Mountbatten-Windsor *1950
1973-1992
Mark Phillips *1948
1992
Timothy Laurence *1955
Andrew Mountbatten-Windsor *1960
1986-1996
Sarah Ferguson *1959
Edward Mountbatten-Windsor *1964
1999
Sophie Helen Mountbatten-Windsor *1965
ESP 1975–2014
Juan Carlos I. *1938
1962
Sofía of Spain *1938
ESP 1975–2014
Ernst August of Hanover *1954
1999
Caroline of Hanover *1957
Albert II of Monaco *1958
1. Juli 2011
Charlene Lynette Wittstock *1978
the last King of GRL 1964–1974
Constantine II of Greece *1940
1964
Anne-Marie of Greece *1946
the last Queen of GRL 1964–1974
Stéphanie of Monaco *1965
1995-1996
Daniel Ducruet *1964
2003 - 2004
Adans Lopez Peres *1975
DEN 1972
Margarethe II of Denmark *1940
1967
Prince Henrik of Denmark *1934 †2018
Frederik, Crown Prince of Denmark *1968
Mary, Crown Princess of Denmark *1972
Joachim of Denmark *1969
1995-2005
Alexandra Manley *1964
2008
Marie of Denmark *1976
BEL 1993–2013
Albert II of Belgium *1934
1959
Paola of Belgium *1937
BEL 1993–2013
Astrid of Belgium *1962
1984
Lorenz of Belgium, Archduke of Austria-Este *1955
Laurent of Belgium *1963
2003
Claire Coombs *1974
BEL 2013
Philippe of Belgium *1960
1999
Mathilde of Belgium *1973
BEL 2013
NED 1980–2013
Beatrix of the Netherlands *1938
1966
Prince Claus of the Netherlands *1926 †2002

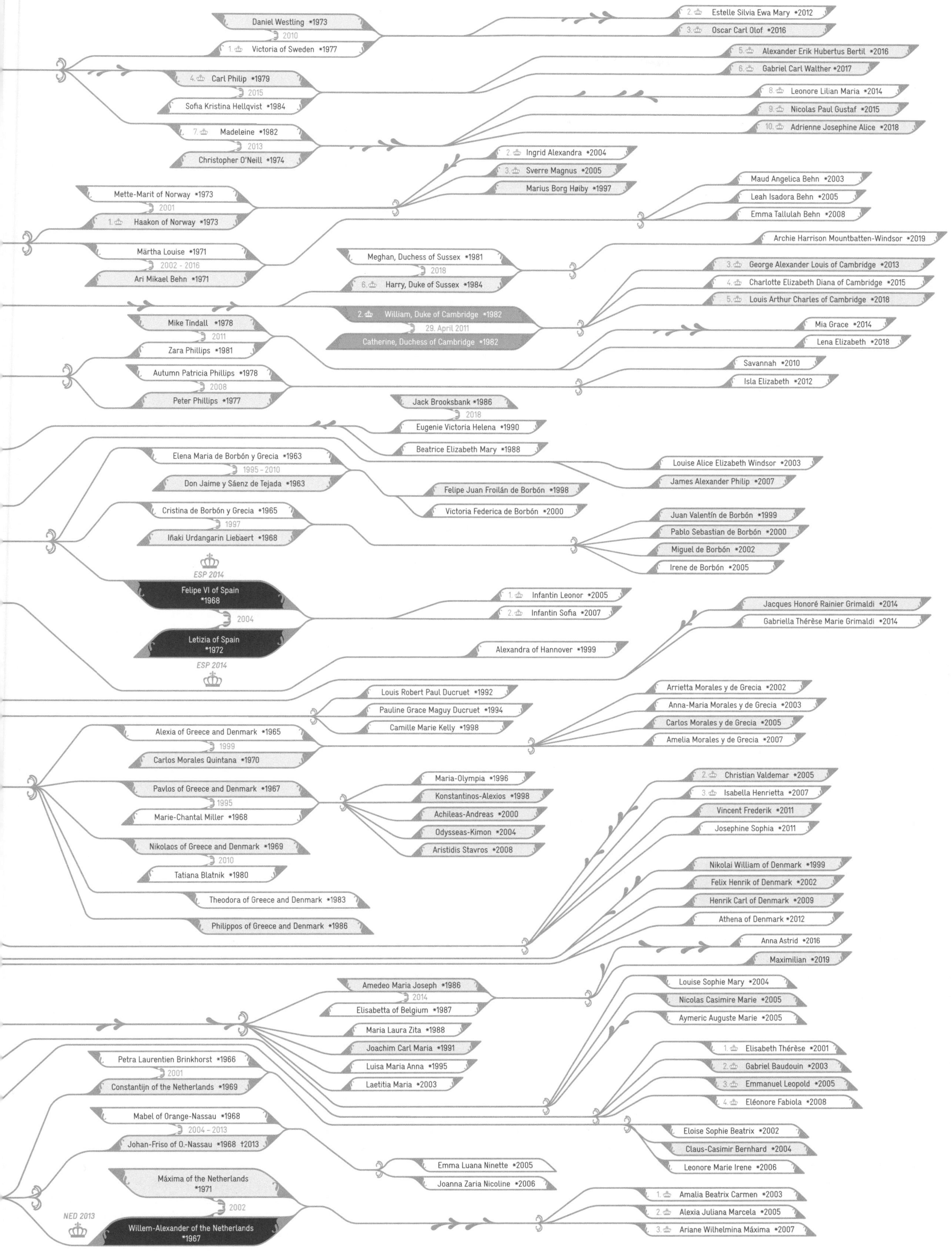
Daniel Westling *1973
2010
1. Victoria of Sweden *1977
2. Estelle Silvia Ewa Mary *2012
3. Oscar Carl Olof *2016
4. Carl Philip *1979
2015
Sofia Kristina Hellqvist *1984
5. Alexander Erik Hubertus Bertil *2016
6. Gabriel Carl Walther *2017
7. Madeleine *1982
2013
Christopher O'Neill *1974
8. Leonore Lilian Maria *2014
9. Nicolas Paul Gustaf *2015
10. Adrienne Josephine Alice *2018
Mette-Marit of Norway *1973
2001
1. Haakon of Norway *1973
2. Ingrid Alexandra *2004
3. Sverre Magnus *2005
Marius Borg Høiby *1997
Märtha Louise *1971
2002 - 2016
Ari Mikael Behn *1971
Maud Angelica Behn *2003
Leah Isadora Behn *2005
Emma Tallulah Behn *2008
Meghan, Duchess of Sussex *1981
2018
6. Harry, Duke of Sussex *1984
Archie Harrison Mountbatten-Windsor *2019
2. William, Duke of Cambridge *1982
29. April 2011
Catherine, Duchess of Cambridge *1982
3. George Alexander Louis of Cambridge *2013
4. Charlotte Elizabeth Diana of Cambridge *2015
5. Louis Arthur Charles of Cambridge *2018
Mike Tindall *1978
2011
Zara Phillips *1981
Mia Grace *2014
Lena Elizabeth *2018
Autumn Patricia Phillips *1978
2008
Peter Phillips *1977
Savannah *2010
Isla Elizabeth *2012
Jack Brooksbank *1986
2018
Eugenie Victoria Helena *1990
Beatrice Elizabeth Mary *1988
Louise Alice Elizabeth Windsor *2003
James Alexander Philip *2007
Elena Maria de Borbón y Grecia *1963
1995 - 2010
Don Jaime y Sáenz de Tejada *1963
Felipe Juan Froilán de Borbón *1998
Victoria Federica de Borbón *2000
Cristina de Borbón y Grecia *1965
1997
Iñaki Urdangarin Liebaert *1968
Juan Valentín de Borbón *1999
Pablo Sebastian de Borbón *2000
Miguel de Borbón *2002
Irene de Borbón *2005
ESP 2014
Felipe VI of Spain *1968
2004
Letizia of Spain *1972
ESP 2014
1. Infantin Leonor *2005
2. Infantin Sofia *2007
Jacques Honoré Rainier Grimaldi *2014
Gabriella Thérèse Marie Grimaldi *2014
Alexandra of Hannover *1999
Louis Robert Paul Ducruet *1992
Pauline Grace Maguy Ducruet *1994
Camille Marie Kelly *1998
Alexia of Greece and Denmark *1965
1999
Carlos Morales Quintana *1970
Arrietta Morales y de Grecia *2002
Anna-Maria Morales y de Grecia *2003
Carlos Morales y de Grecia *2005
Amelia Morales y de Grecia *2007
Pavlos of Greece and Denmark *1967
1995
Marie-Chantal Miller *1968
Maria-Olympia *1996
Konstantinos-Alexios *1998
Achileas-Andreas *2000
Odysseas-Kimon *2004
Aristidis Stavros *2008
2. Christian Valdemar *2005
3. Isabella Henrietta *2007
Vincent Frederik *2011
Josephine Sophia *2011
Nikolaos of Greece and Denmark *1969
2010
Tatiana Blatnik *1980
Theodora of Greece and Denmark *1983
Philippos of Greece and Denmark *1986
Nikolai William of Denmark *1999
Felix Henrik of Denmark *2002
Henrik Carl of Denmark *2009
Athena of Denmark *2012
Anna Astrid *2016
Maximilian *2019
Amedeo Maria Joseph *1986
2014
Elisabetta of Belgium *1987
Louise Sophie Mary *2004
Nicolas Casimire Marie *2005
Aymeric Auguste Marie *2005
Maria Laura Zita *1988
Joachim Carl Maria *1991
Luisa Maria Anna *1995
Laetitia Maria *2003
1. Elisabeth Thérèse *2001
2. Gabriel Baudouin *2003
3. Emmanuel Leopold *2005
4. Eléonore Fabiola *2008
Petra Laurentien Brinkhorst *1966
2001
Constantijn of the Netherlands *1969
Eloise Sophie Beatrix *2002
Claus-Casimir Bernhard *2004
Leonore Marie Irene *2006
Mabel of Orange-Nassau *1968
2004 - 2013
Johan-Friso of O.-Nassau *1968 †2013
Emma Luana Ninette *2005
Joanna Zaria Nicoline *2006
Máxima of the Netherlands *1971
2002
NED 2013
Willem-Alexander of the Netherlands *1967
1. Amalia Beatrix Carmen *2003
2. Alexia Juliana Marcela *2005
3. Ariane Wilhelmina Máxima *2007

WHERE IN THE WORLD IS MS. SPECIMEN?

Crests, medals and guild signs were the ID cards of medieval times. They have now been replaced by other insignia. We have selected certain countries and compared their sample ID cards. Have fun searching the most frequent names or the same birthdays.

BILHETE DE IDENTIDATE
DE CIDADNO NACIONAL

ANGOLA

IDENTITEITSKAART • CARTE D'IDENTITE •
PERSONALAUSWEIS • IDENTITY CARD

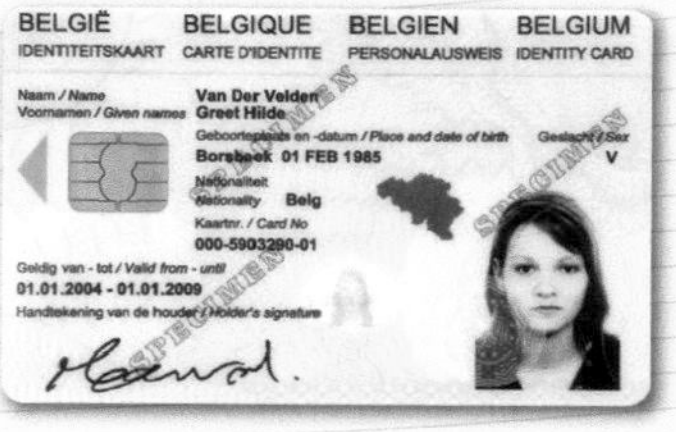

BELGIUM

LIČNA KARTA • OSOBNA ISKAZNICA
ЛИЧНА-КАРТА • CARTE NATIONALE D'IDENTITETE
NATIONAL IDENTITY CARD

BOSNIA AND HERZEGOVINA

中华人民共和国居民身份证

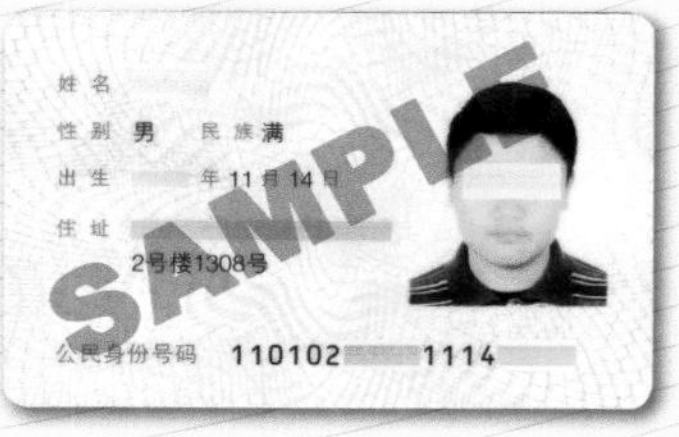

CHINA

ISIKUTUNNISTUS • IDENTITY CARD

ESTONIA

HENKILÖKORTTI • IDENTITETSKORT
IDENTITY CARD

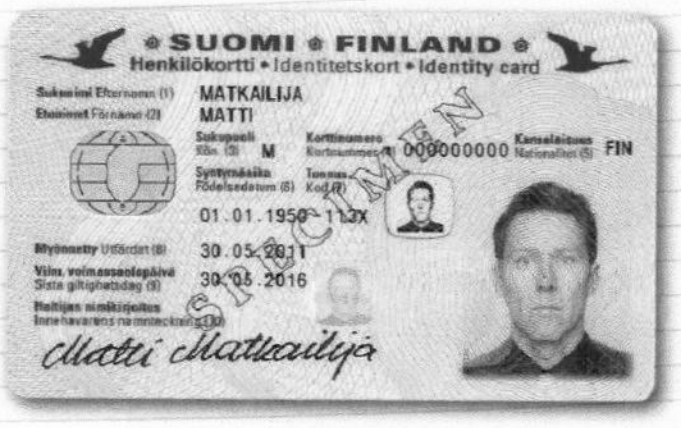

FINLAND

FRANCE

IDENTITY CARD
CARTE D'IDENTITE

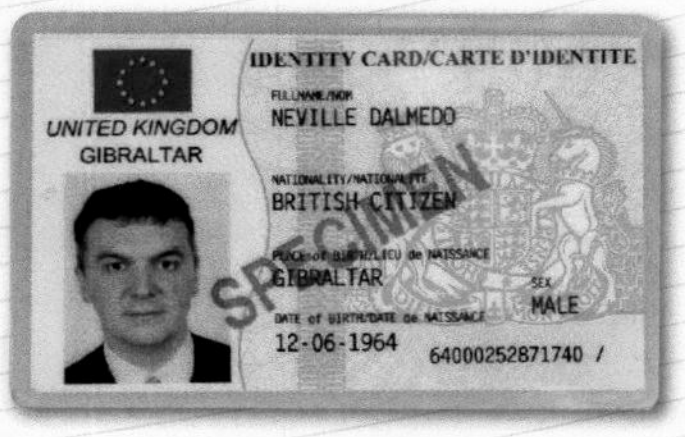

GIBRALTAR

IDENTIFICATION CARD

UNITED KINGDOM

香港永久性居民身份證
HONG KONG PERMANENT IDENTITY CARD

HONG KONG

CARTA DI IDENTITÀ

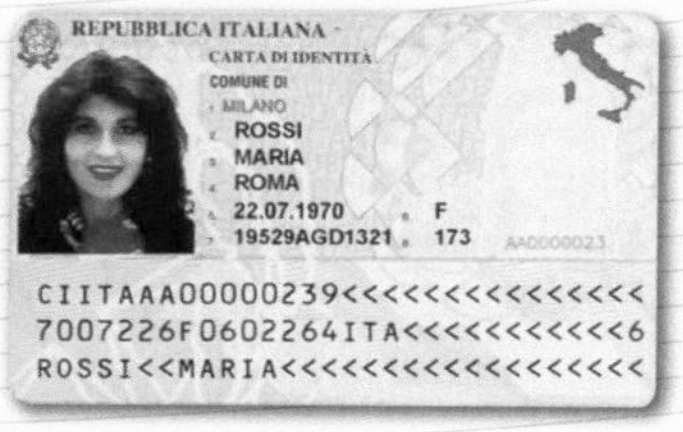

ITALY

PERMANENT RESIDENT CARD
CARTE DE RESIDENT PERMANENT

CANADA

OSOBNA ISKAZNICA
IDENTITY CARD

CROATIA

ASMENS TAPATYBĖS KORTĖLE
PERSONAL IDENTITY CARD

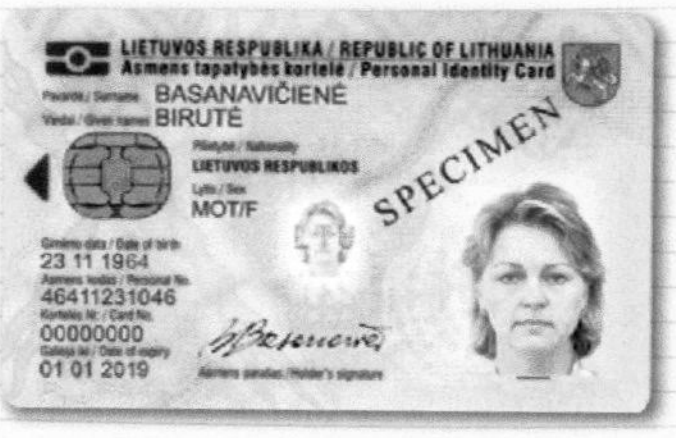

LITHUANIA

РЕСПУБЛИКА МАКЕДОНИЈА
ЛИЧНА-КАРТА

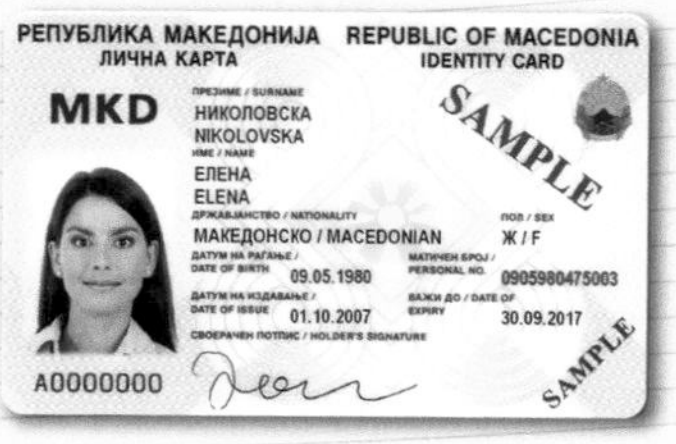

MACEDONIA

KAD PENGENALAN

MALAYSIA

KARTA TA' L-IDENTITÀ

MALTA

MOLDAU

CARTE D'IDENTICÉ
NATIONALITÉ MONEGASQUE

MONACO

NEDERLANDSE IDENTITEITSKAART
IDENTITY CARD • CARTE D'IDENTITÉ

THE NETHERLANDS

GERMANY
PERSONALAUSWEIS

Original size

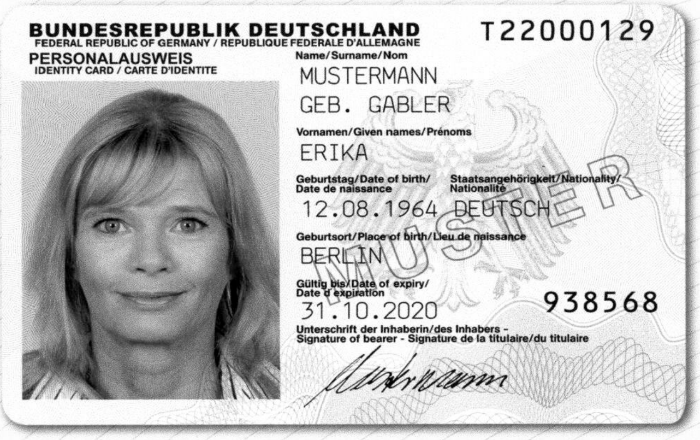
BUNDESREPUBLIK DEUTSCHLAND
FEDERAL REPUBLIC OF GERMANY / REPUBLIQUE FEDERALE D'ALLEMAGNE
T22000129
PERSONALAUSWEIS
IDENTITY CARD / CARTE D'IDENTITE
Name/Surname/Nom
MUSTERMANN
GEB. GABLER
Vornamen/Given names/Prénoms
ERIKA
Geburtstag/Date of birth/Date de naissance
Staatsangehörigkeit/Nationality/Nationalité
12.08.1964 DEUTSCH
Geburtsort/Place of birth/Lieu de naissance
BERLIN
MUSTER
Gültig bis/Date of expiry/Date d'expiration
31.10.2020
938568
Unterschrift der Inhaberin/des Inhabers - Signature of bearer - Signature de la titulaire/du titulaire

UNITED STATES OF AMERICA
PERMANENT RESIDENT

UNITED STATES OF AMERICA
PERMANENT RESIDENT
SPECIMEN TEST V 01 JAN 1920
Surname
SPECIMEN
Given Name
TEST V
USCIS#
000-000-001
Category
RE8
Country of Birth
Utopia
Date of Birth
01 JAN 1920
Sex
F
Card Expires:
08/21/07
Resident Since:
08/21/07
Test V. Specimen

PERSONALAUSWEIS
IDENTITY CARD • CARTE D'IDENTITE

AUSTRIA

قومی شناختی کارڈ برائے پاکستان

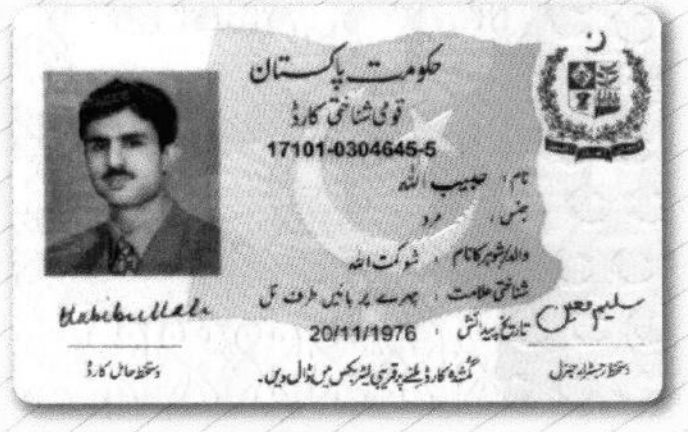

PAKISTAN

REGISTRO NACIONAL DE IDENTIFICAION Y ESTADO CIVIL
DOCUMENTO NATIONAL DE IDENTIDAD

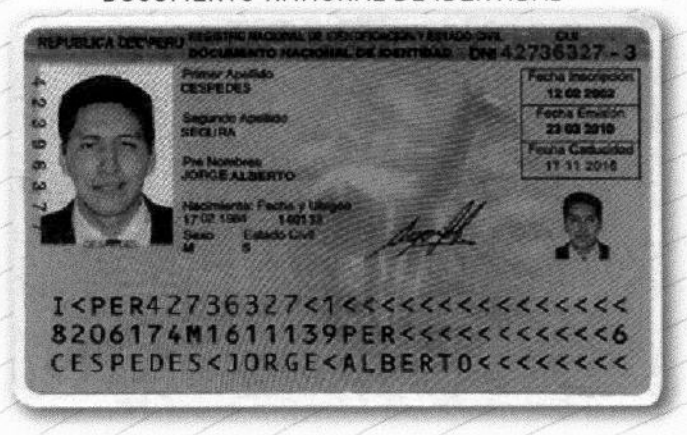

PERU

DOWÓD OSOBISTY
IDENTITY CARD

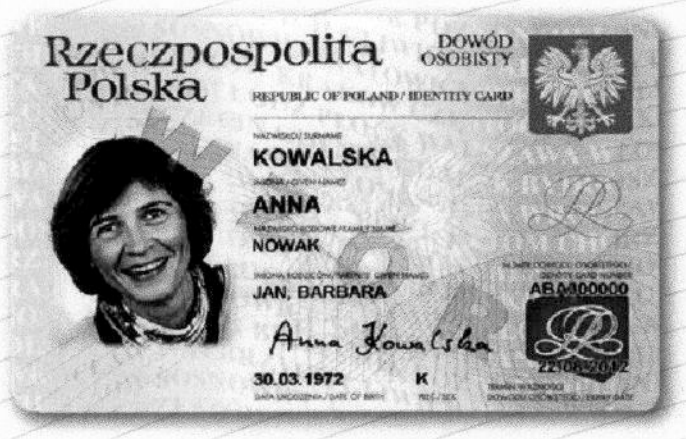

POLAND

CARTÃO DE CIDADÃO
CITIZEN CARD

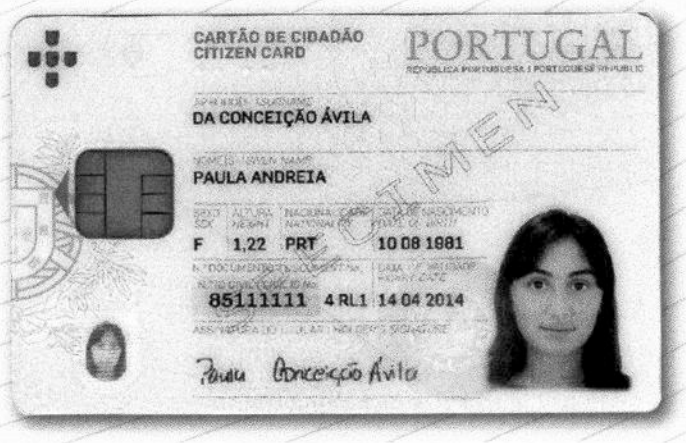

PORTUGAL

ةينطولا ةيوهلا ةقاطب
NATIONAL ID CARD

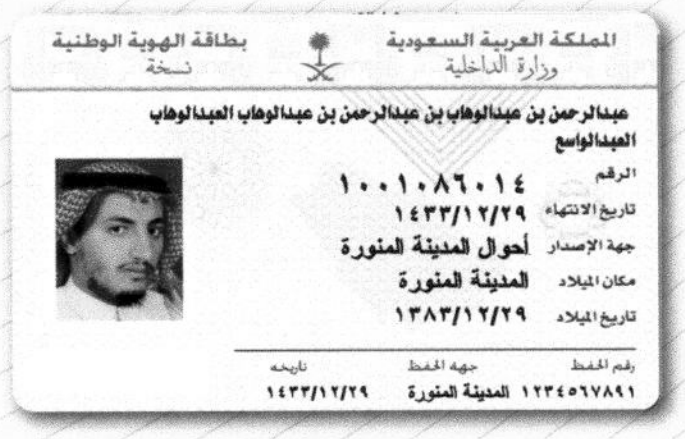

SAUDI ARABIA

IDENTITETSKORT

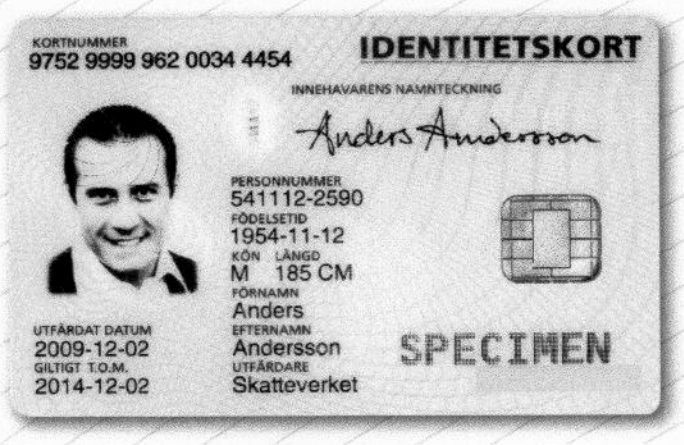

SWEDEN

IDENTITÄTSKARTE • CARTE D ' IDENTITÉ
CARTA D'IDENTITÀ • CARTA D'IDENTITAD
IDENTITY CARD

SWITZERLAND

BULETIN DE IDENTITATE
IDENTITY CARD

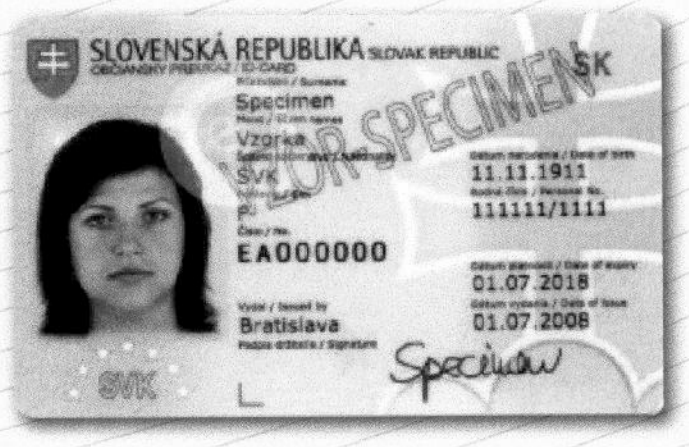

SLOVAKIA

DOWÓD OSOBISTY
REPUBLIC OF POLAND • IDENTITY CARD

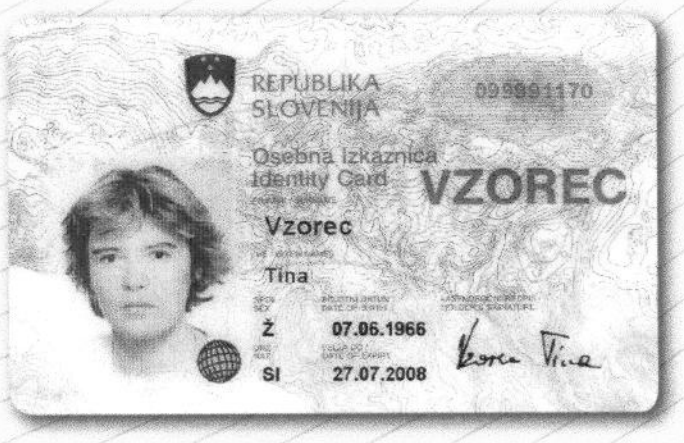

SLOVENIA

DOCUMENTO NACIONAL DE IDENTIDAD

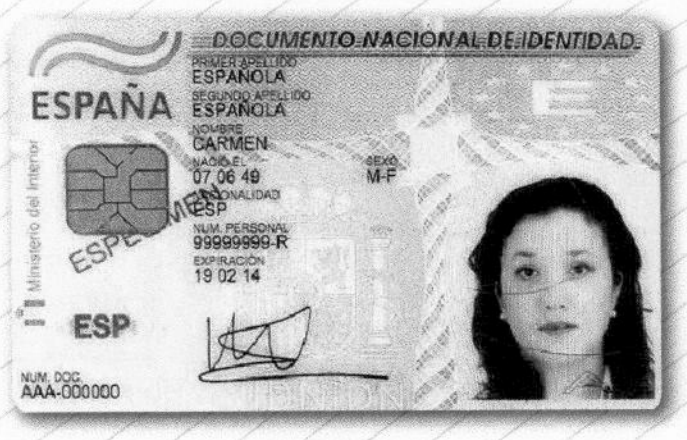

SPAIN

NATIONAL IDENTIFICATION CARD

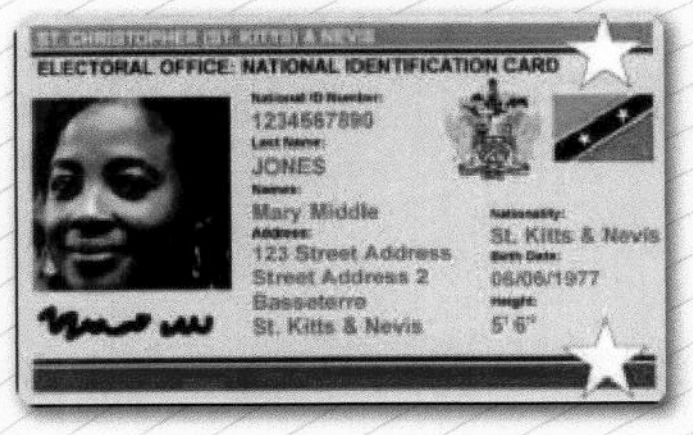

ST. KITTS & NEVIS[(2)]

신분증
IDENTITY CARD

SOUTH KOREA

中華民國國民身份證

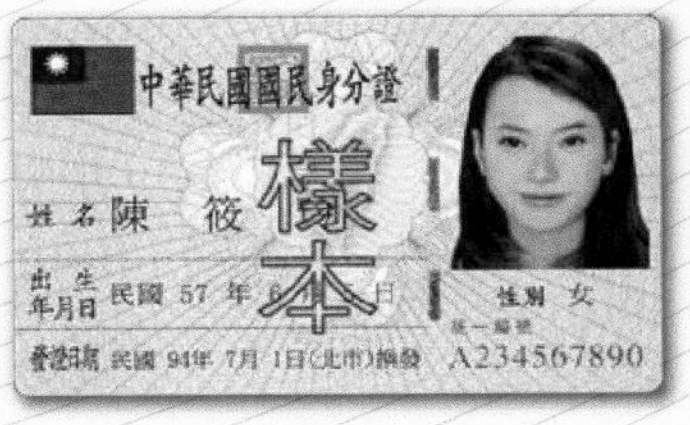

TAIWAN

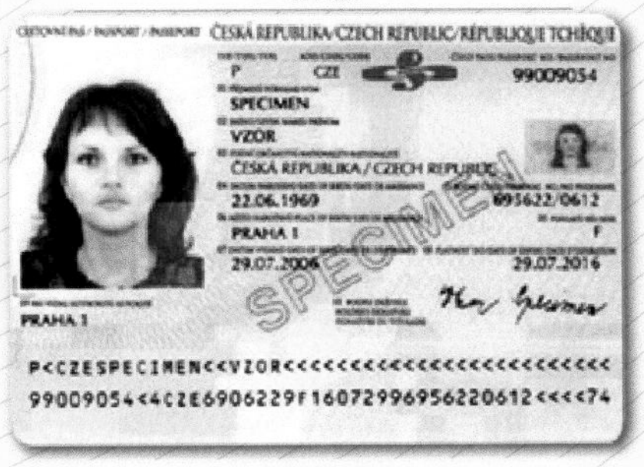

CZECHIA

ETI KIMLIK KARTI
IDENTITY CARD

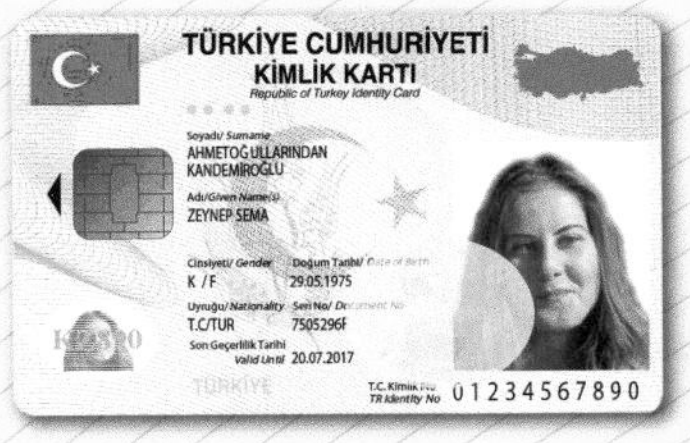

TURKEY

SZEMÉLYAZONOSÍTÓ IGAZOLVÁNY
IDENTITY CARD

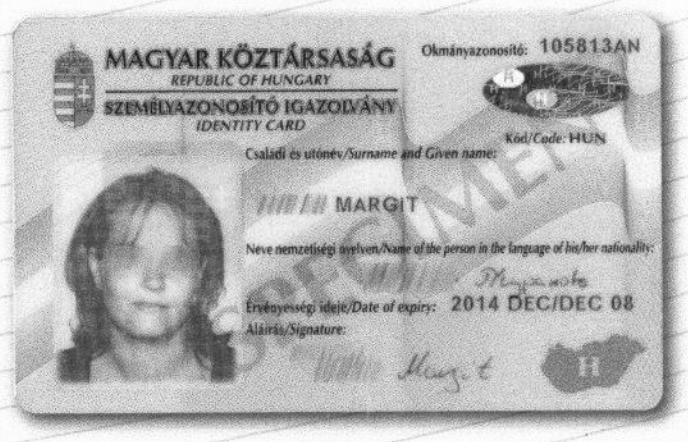

HUNGARY

ةيوه ةقاطب
IDENTITY CARD

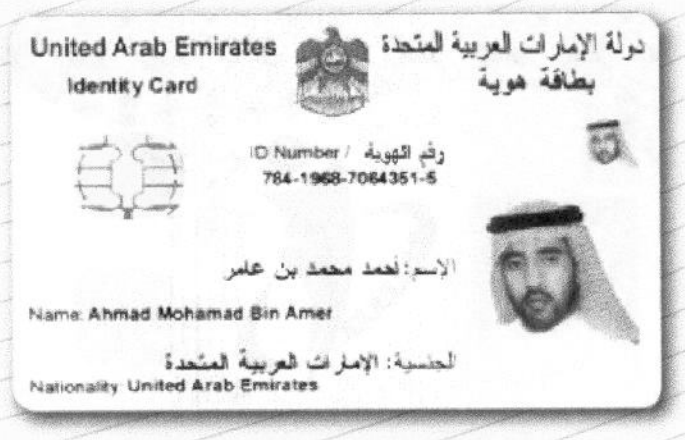

UNITED ARAB EMIRATES

ΔΕΛΤΙΟ ΤΑΥΤΟΤΗΤΑΣ KİMLİK KARTI
IDENTITY CARD

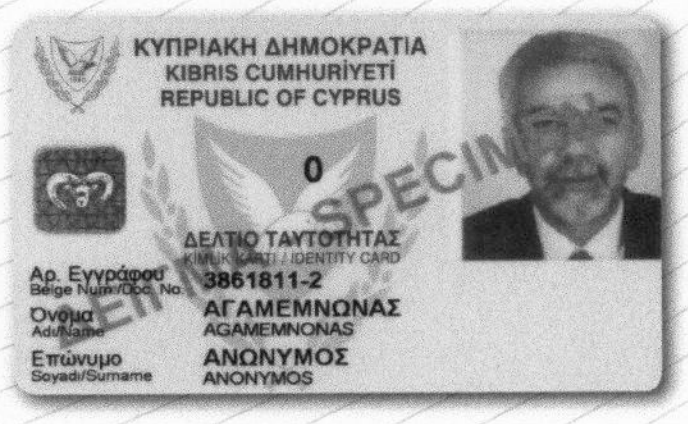

CYPRUS

IDENTITY CARD
CARTE D'IDENTITE

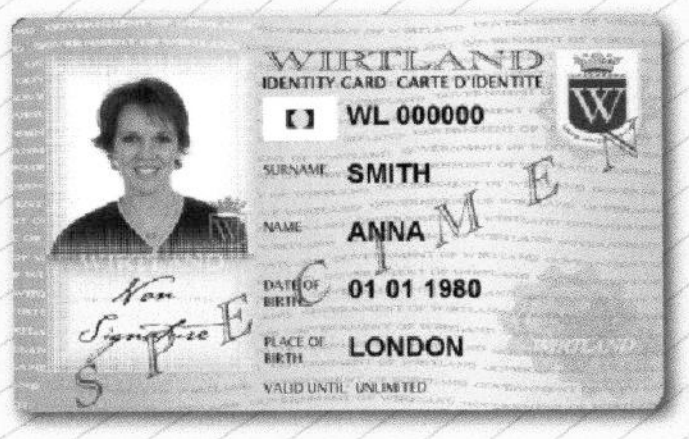

WIRTLAND[(1)]

(1) Internet-based micronation, foundation 2008

(2) Caribbean island state

MS. SPECIMEN

All publications of sample ID cards (see previous two pages) must show fictitious people. Our analysis of the most common names and dates of birth revealed some amazing things.

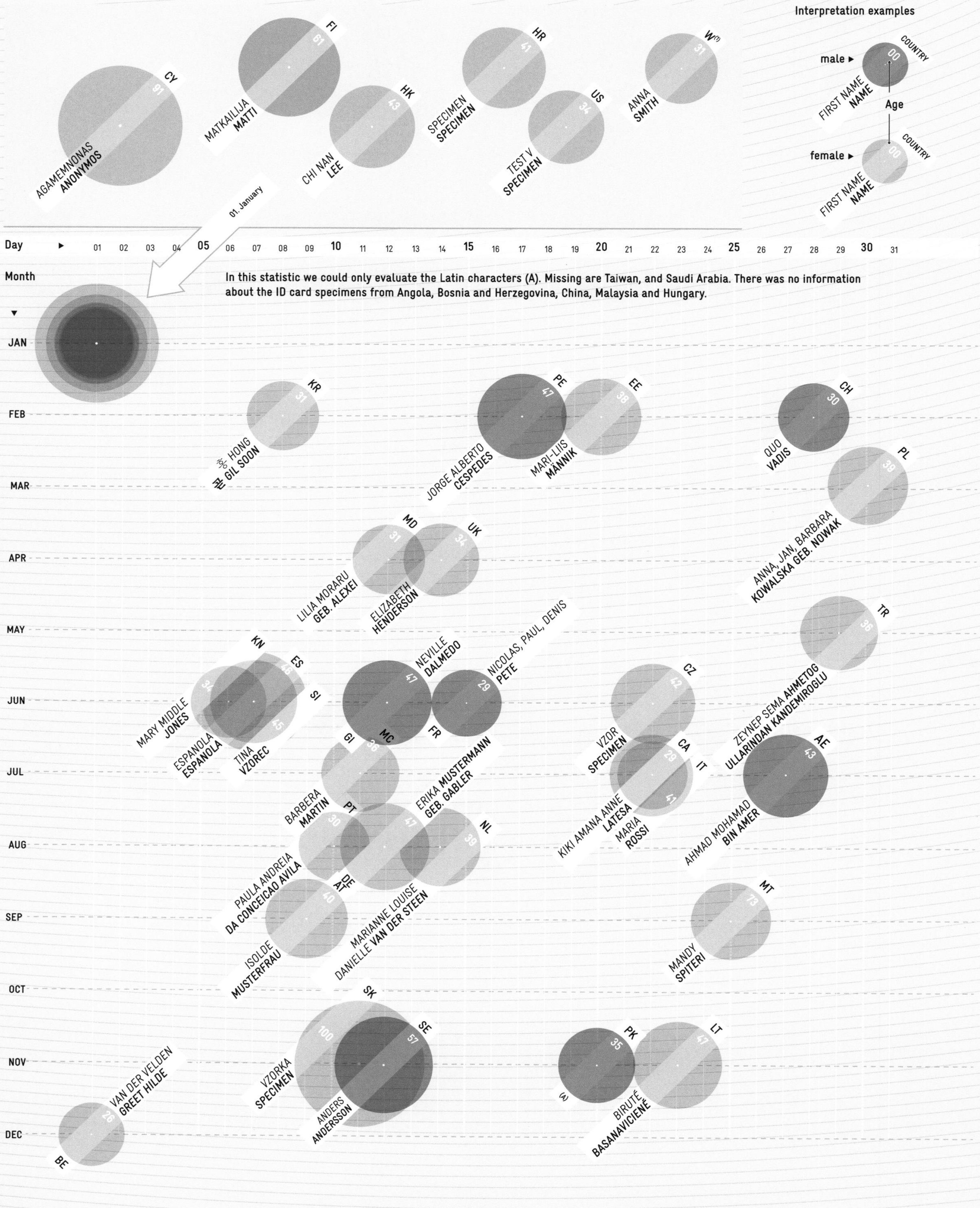

SAMPLE COLLECTION

In the newly established, remote and largely unexplored country of Infographicsland, the authorities aimed to create an ID-Card that contains all available example designs. The black and white image belongs to the lower left corner. Most states do not need a chip and place their sovereign symbol in the upper left corner. The scientific advisory board of Infographicsland did a good job analyzing the most frequent numbers from the examples.

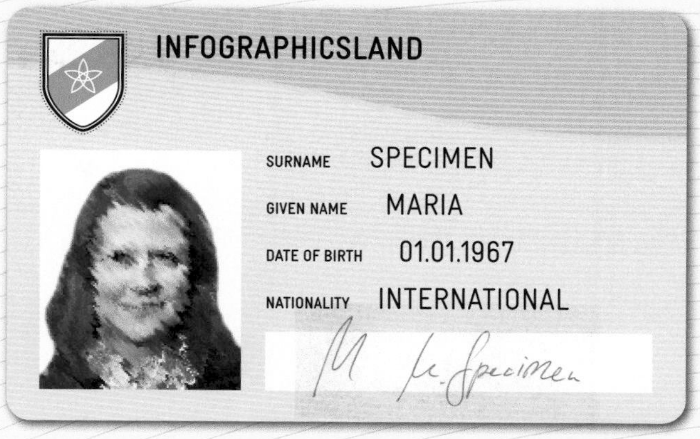
INFOGRAPHICSLAND
SURNAME SPECIMEN
GIVEN NAME MARIA
DATE OF BIRTH 01.01.1967
NATIONALITY INTERNATIONAL

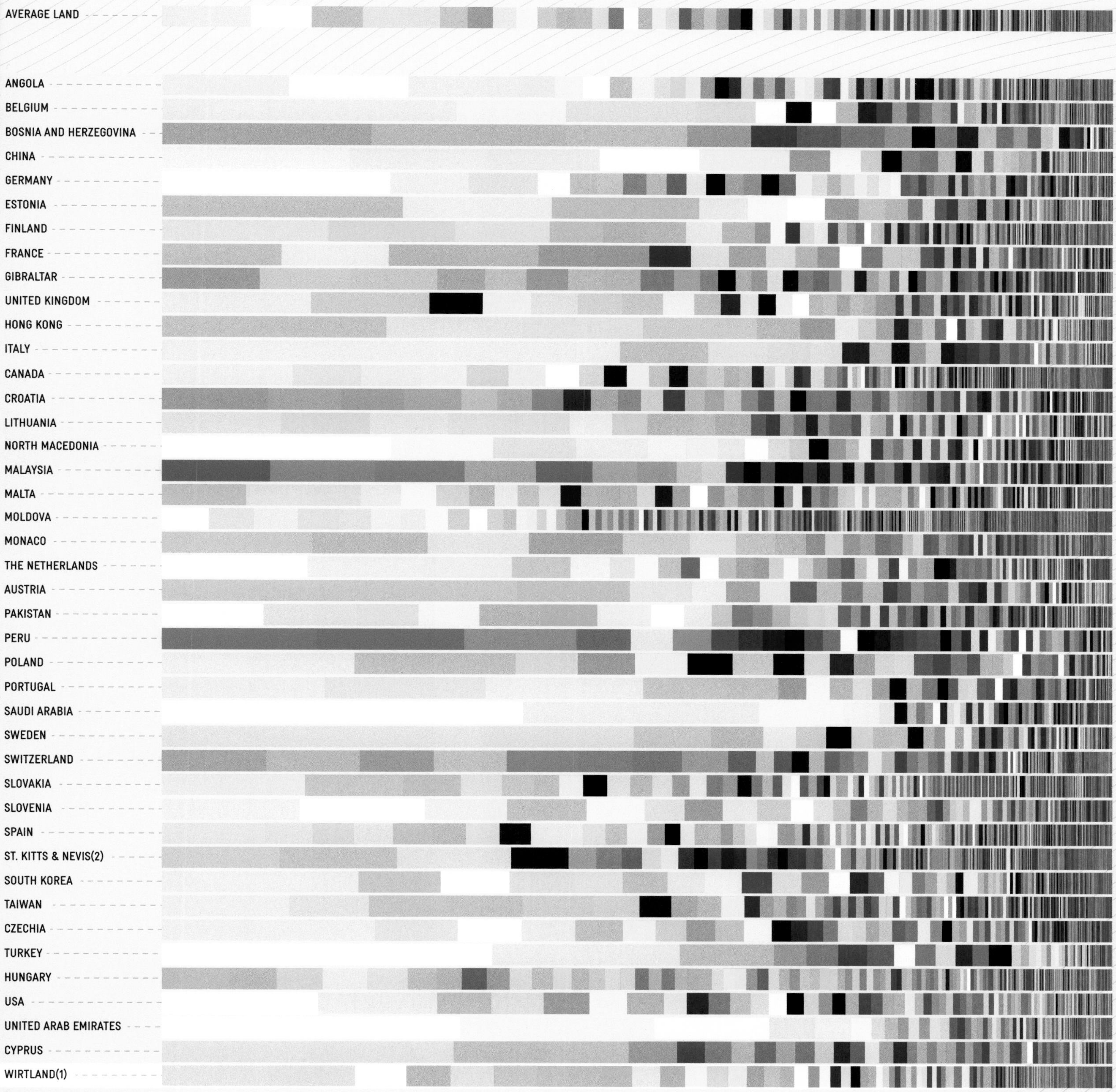
AVERAGE LAND
ANGOLA
BELGIUM
BOSNIA AND HERZEGOVINA
CHINA
GERMANY
ESTONIA
FINLAND
FRANCE
GIBRALTAR
UNITED KINGDOM
HONG KONG
ITALY
CANADA
CROATIA
LITHUANIA
NORTH MACEDONIA
MALAYSIA
MALTA
MOLDOVA
MONACO
THE NETHERLANDS
AUSTRIA
PAKISTAN
PERU
POLAND
PORTUGAL
SAUDI ARABIA
SWEDEN
SWITZERLAND
SLOVAKIA
SLOVENIA
SPAIN
ST. KITTS & NEVIS(2)
SOUTH KOREA
TAIWAN
CZECHIA
TURKEY
HUNGARY
USA
UNITED ARAB EMIRATES
CYPRUS
WIRTLAND(1)

(1) Internet-based micronation, foundation 2008
(2) Caribbean island state

WHO'S WHO

People know what to call their close relatives, but what do you call family relations that you are not a direct descendent of? There are six systematic kinship systems described in Henry Lewis Morgan's 1871 book »Systems of Consanguinity and Affinity of the Human Family«. Of those, western societies are best modeled after the Eskimo kin terms. This system does not differentiate relatives from the mother's or the father's side and does not take into account the children of or marriage between relatives. This graphic reflects that ordering principle.

FEMALE **MALE**

PARENTAL DESCENT

SIBLINGS

2 **Degree of relationship ⟶ defines how closely related one person is to another. It is not identical with the legal definition.**

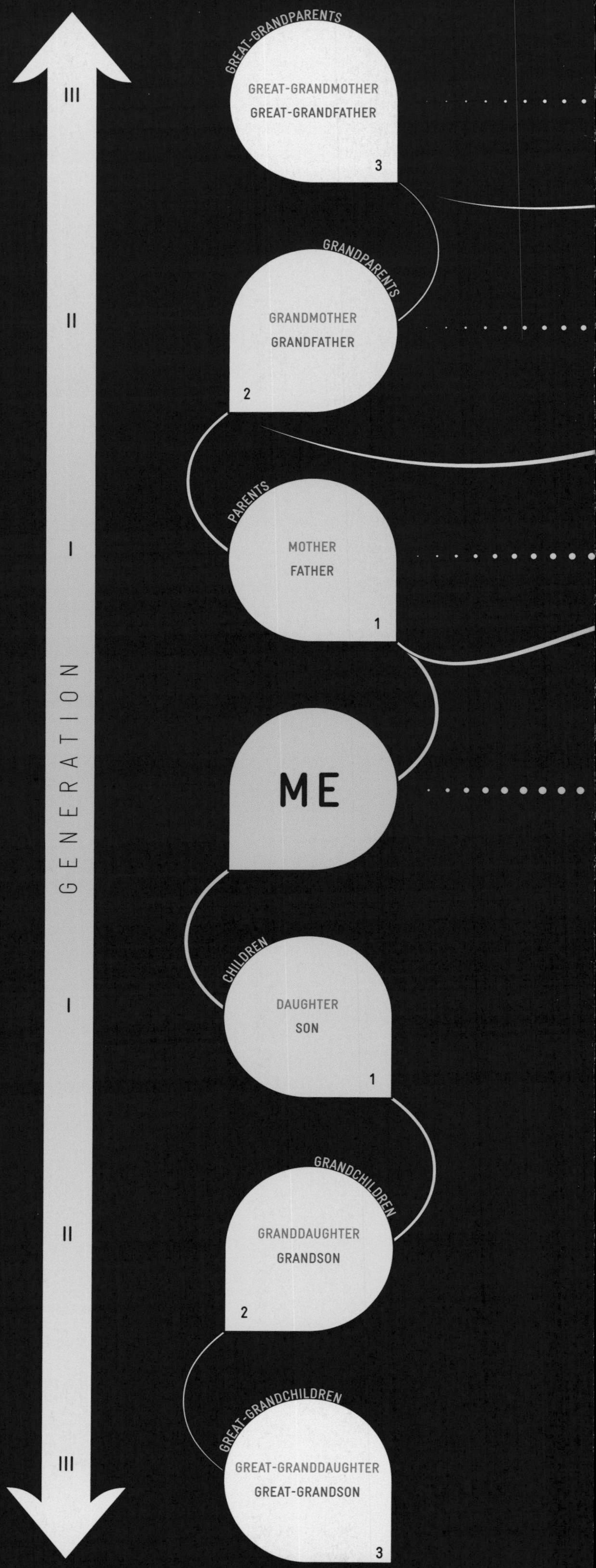
GENERATION
III
II
I
I
II
III
GREAT-GRANDPARENTS
GREAT-GRANDMOTHER
GREAT-GRANDFATHER
3
GRANDPARENTS
GRANDMOTHER
GRANDFATHER
2
PARENTS
MOTHER
FATHER
1
ME
CHILDREN
DAUGHTER
SON
1
GRANDCHILDREN
GRANDDAUGHTER
GRANDSON
2
GREAT-GRANDCHILDREN
GREAT-GRANDDAUGHTER
GREAT-GRANDSON
3

PARENTS
Direct ancestors

HALF-SIBLINGS
Children of mother or father with a different partner

STEP-SIBLINGS
Children of the parent's new partner

CHILDREN
Direct descendants

AUNTS/UNCLES
Parent's siblings and their partners

COUSINS
Nieces and nephews of own parents

NIECES/NEPHEWS
Children of siblings or children of brothers- and sisters-in-law

BROTHERS- and SISTERS-IN-LAW
Partner of sister or brother and siblings of own partner

GRAND-
Family relationship with a distance of two generations

GREAT-
Family relationship with a distance of three generations

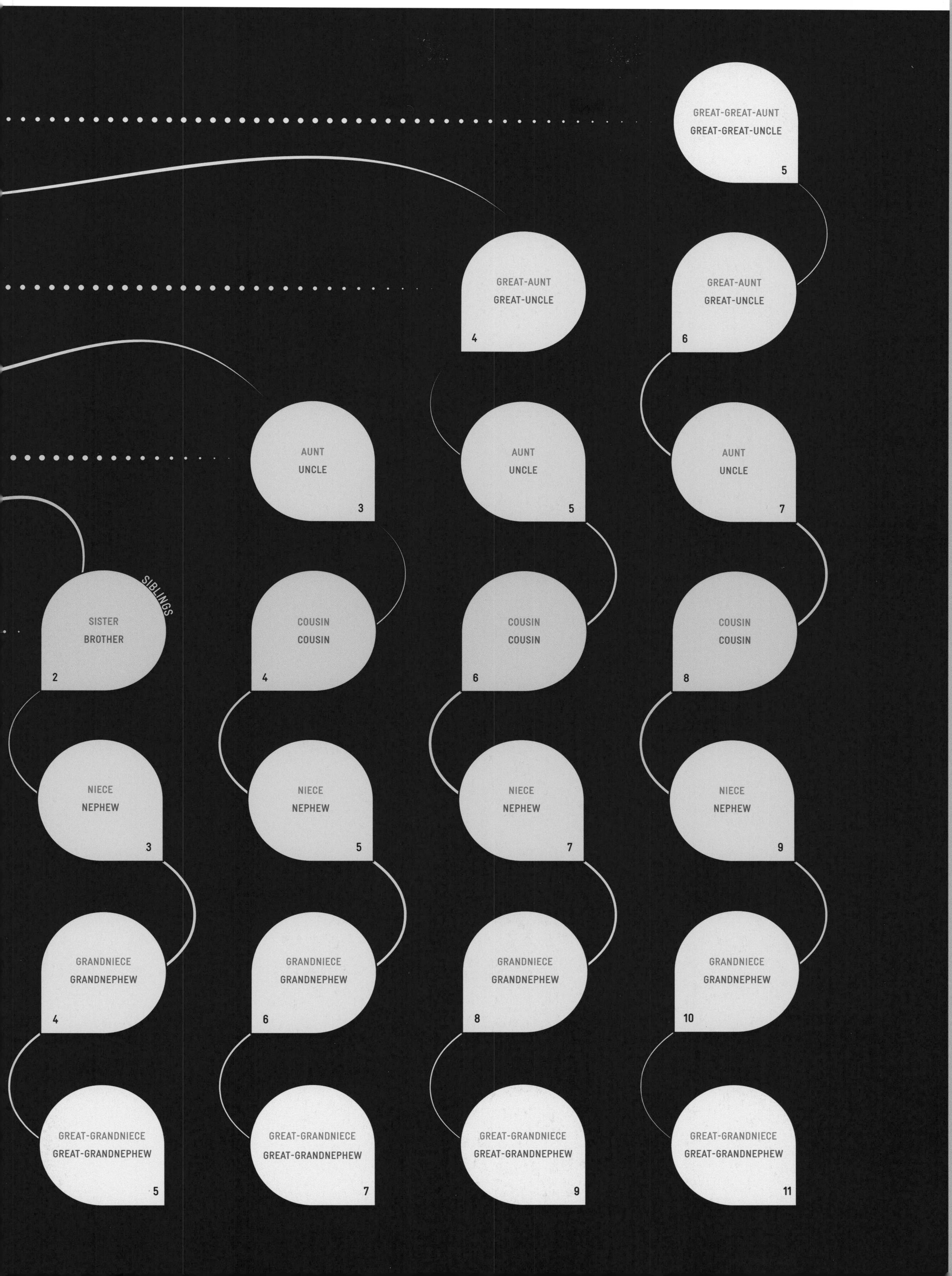
GREAT-GREAT-AUNT
GREAT-GREAT-UNCLE
5
GREAT-AUNT
GREAT-UNCLE
4
GREAT-AUNT
GREAT-UNCLE
6
AUNT
UNCLE
3
AUNT
UNCLE
5
AUNT
UNCLE
7
SIBLINGS
SISTER
BROTHER
2
COUSIN
COUSIN
4
COUSIN
COUSIN
6
COUSIN
COUSIN
8
NIECE
NEPHEW
3
NIECE
NEPHEW
5
NIECE
NEPHEW
7
NIECE
NEPHEW
9
GRANDNIECE
GRANDNEPHEW
4
GRANDNIECE
GRANDNEPHEW
6
GRANDNIECE
GRANDNEPHEW
8
GRANDNIECE
GRANDNEPHEW
10
GREAT-GRANDNIECE
GREAT-GRANDNEPHEW
5
GREAT-GRANDNIECE
GREAT-GRANDNEPHEW
7
GREAT-GRANDNIECE
GREAT-GRANDNEPHEW
9
GREAT-GRANDNIECE
GREAT-GRANDNEPHEW
11

CHRISTIANITY WORLDWIDE

Since 1970, Islam, Hinduism and Buddhism have overtaken Christianity as the fastest growing religions in the world. In fact, all the major religions—aside from Christianity—are growing faster than the global population. The numbers of believers has doubled, as has the number of people on earth. Atheists and Agnostics, however, have not seen a rise: In 1970, they made up 19.2% of the world's population; today, it's only 10.7%.

	1970 (3,696 million)	2020 (7,656 million)
CHRISTIANS	**1,229 MILLION**	**2,551 MILLION**
MUSLIMS	**557.2 MILLION**	**1,800 MILLION**
HINDUS	**463.2 MILLION**	**1,060 MILLION**
BUDDHISTS	**235 MILLION**	**540.2 MILLION**
ATHEISTS AND AGNOSTICS	**708.1 MILLION**	**814.4 MILLION**
OTHER	**503.5 MILLION**	**890.4 MILLION**

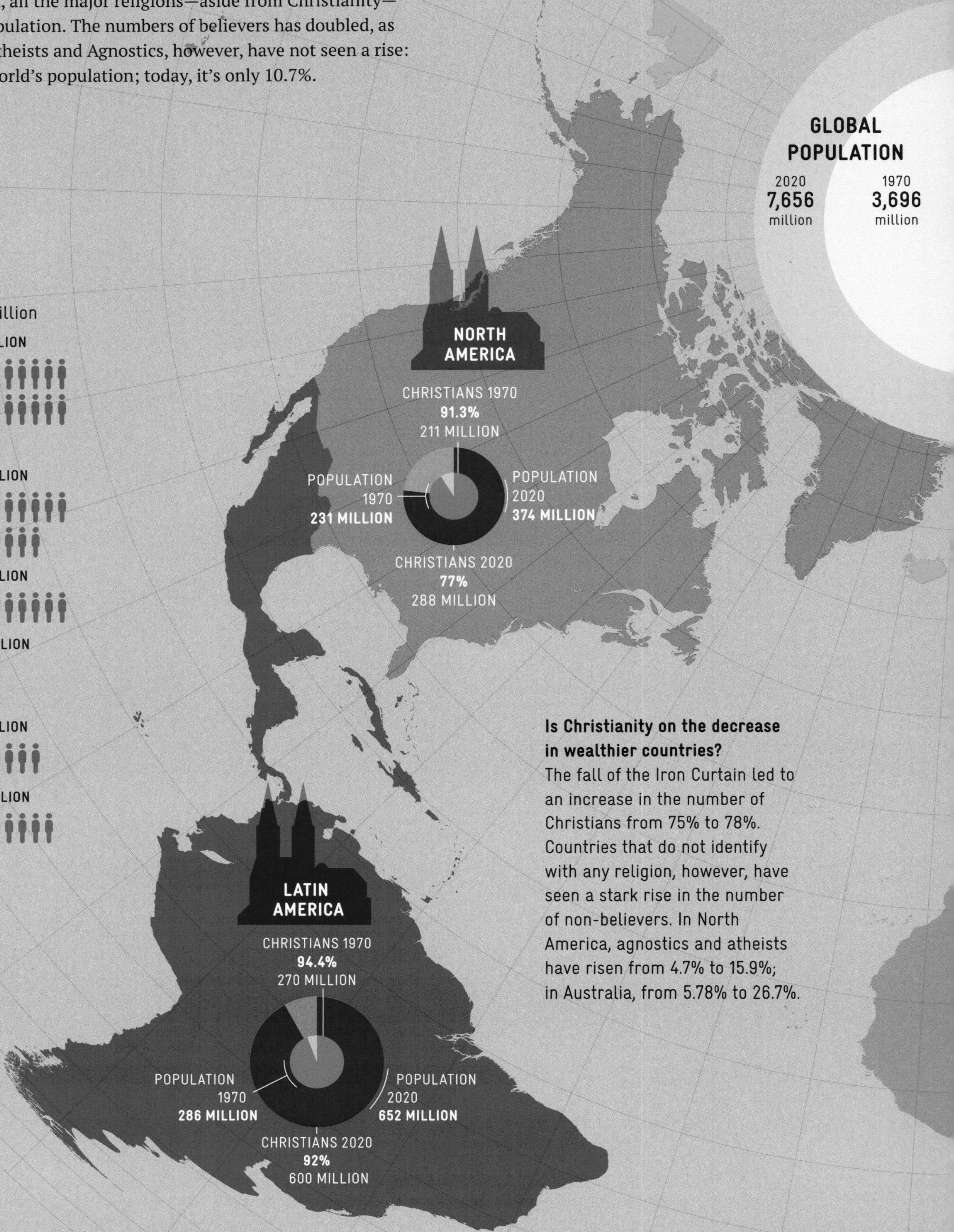
GLOBAL POPULATION
2020
7,656
million
1970
3,696
million
NORTH AMERICA
CHRISTIANS 1970
91.3%
211 MILLION
POPULATION 1970
231 MILLION
POPULATION 2020
374 MILLION
CHRISTIANS 2020
77%
288 MILLION
LATIN AMERICA
CHRISTIANS 1970
94.4%
270 MILLION
POPULATION 1970
286 MILLION
POPULATION 2020
652 MILLION
CHRISTIANS 2020
92%
600 MILLION

Is Christianity on the decrease in wealthier countries?

The fall of the Iron Curtain led to an increase in the number of Christians from 75% to 78%. Countries that do not identify with any religion, however, have seen a stark rise in the number of non-believers. In North America, agnostics and atheists have risen from 4.7% to 15.9%; in Australia, from 5.78% to 26.7%.

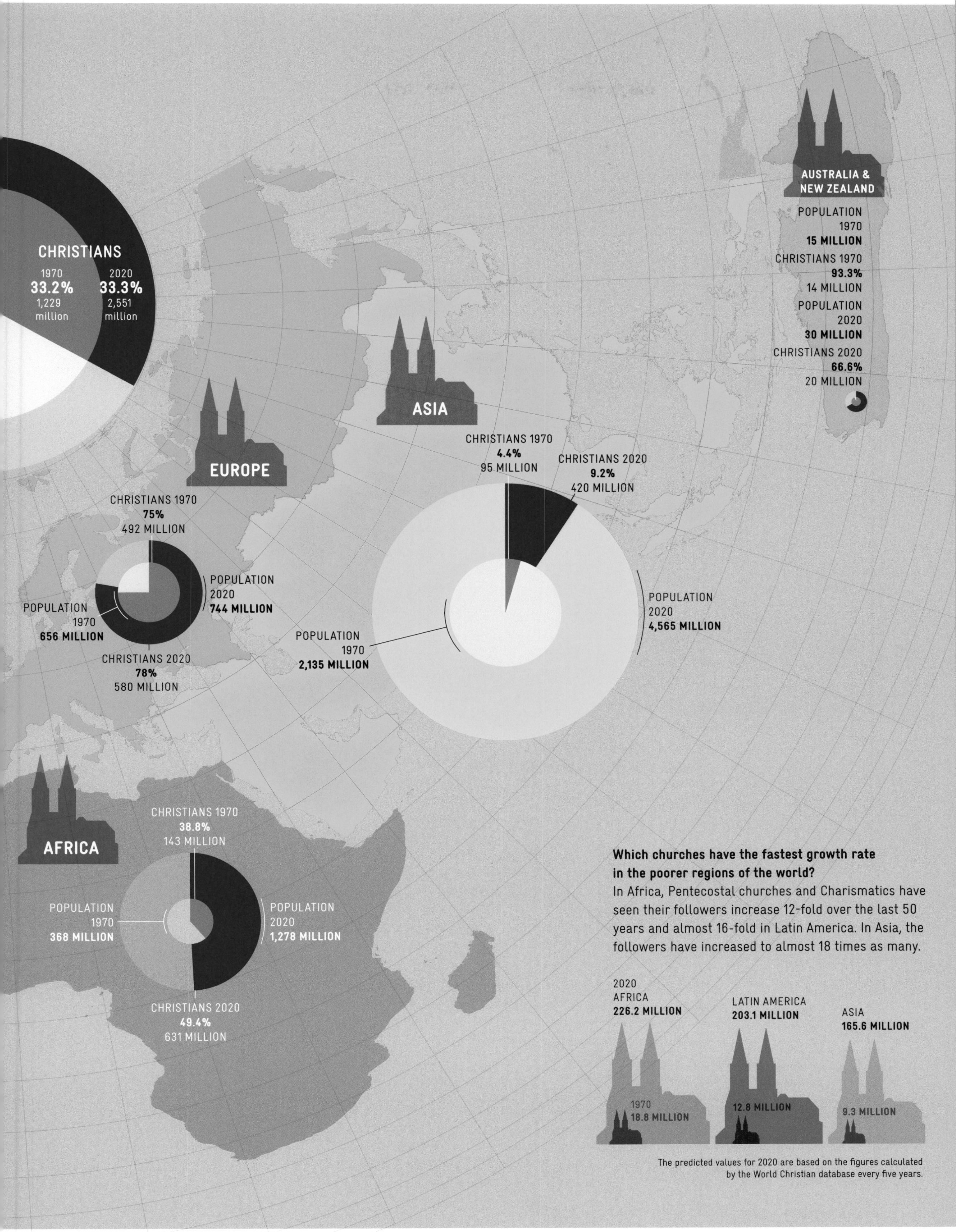
CHRISTIANS
1970
33.2%
1,229 million
2020
33.3%
2,551 million
AUSTRALIA & NEW ZEALAND
POPULATION 1970
15 MILLION
CHRISTIANS 1970
93.3%
14 MILLION
POPULATION 2020
30 MILLION
CHRISTIANS 2020
66.6%
20 MILLION
ASIA
CHRISTIANS 1970
4.4%
95 MILLION
CHRISTIANS 2020
9.2%
420 MILLION
POPULATION 1970
2,135 MILLION
POPULATION 2020
4,565 MILLION
EUROPE
CHRISTIANS 1970
75%
492 MILLION
POPULATION 2020
744 MILLION
POPULATION 1970
656 MILLION
CHRISTIANS 2020
78%
580 MILLION
AFRICA
CHRISTIANS 1970
38.8%
143 MILLION
POPULATION 1970
368 MILLION
POPULATION 2020
1,278 MILLION
CHRISTIANS 2020
49.4%
631 MILLION
2020
AFRICA
226.2 MILLION
1970
18.8 MILLION
LATIN AMERICA
203.1 MILLION
12.8 MILLION
ASIA
165.6 MILLION
9.3 MILLION

Which churches have the fastest growth rate in the poorer regions of the world?
In Africa, Pentecostal churches and Charismatics have seen their followers increase 12-fold over the last 50 years and almost 16-fold in Latin America. In Asia, the followers have increased to almost 18 times as many.

The predicted values for 2020 are based on the figures calculated by the World Christian database every five years.

THE WORLD IN 1500

Around the beginning of the early modern period, the largest metropolises were not to be found in Europe, nor was Europe the center of the world. Great empires existed in Asia, Africa as well as in Central and South America. They boasted well-organized social and administrative structures, rich cultures and sometimes very advanced technology. China was a pioneer in the sciences and led expeditions with huge treasure ships. The Great Wall was built against the Mongols. Different raw materials in the various regions of the world provided the basis for close economic relations and even for offshore trade. Architecture still standing from this time testifies to a period of cultural diversity.

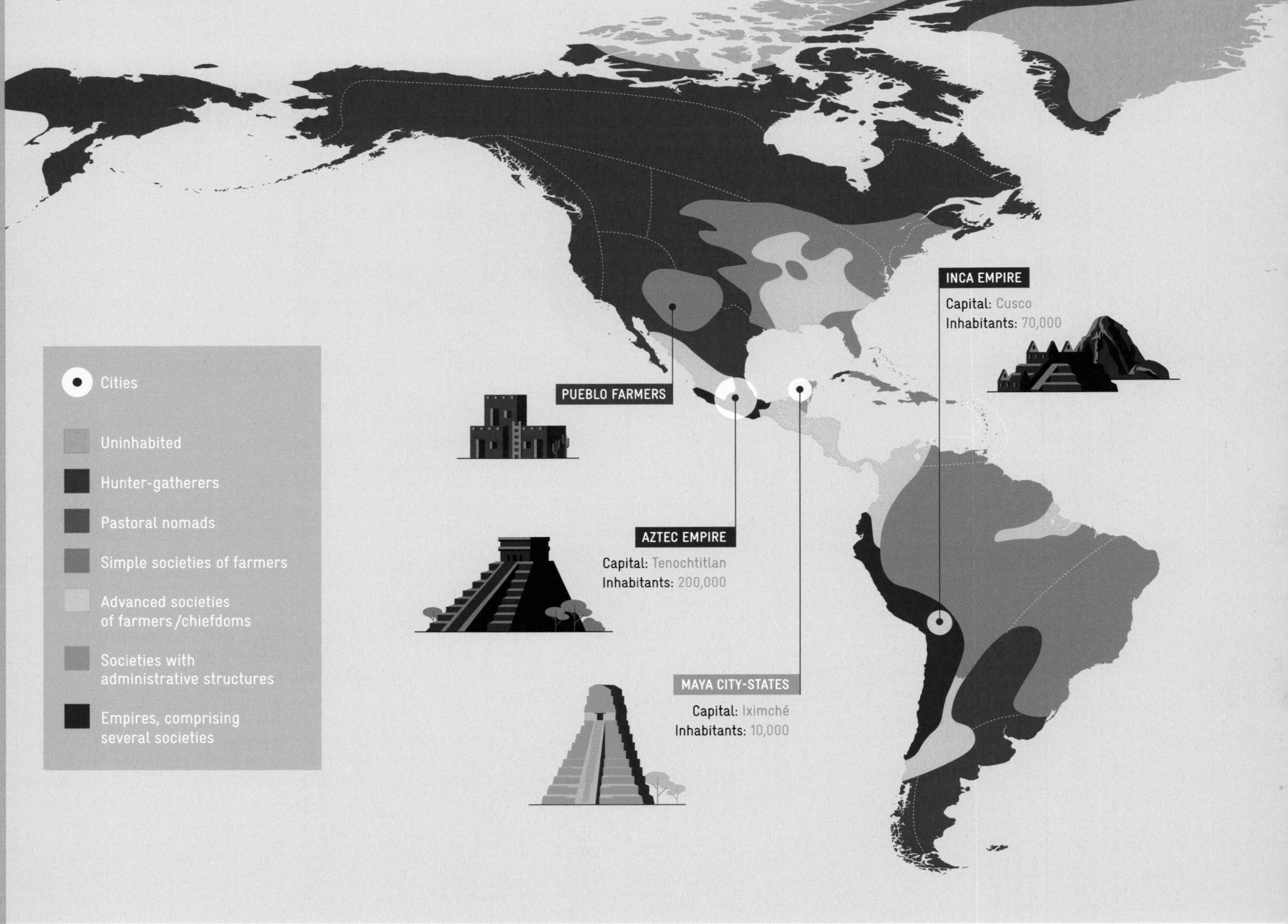
Cities
Uninhabited
Hunter-gatherers
Pastoral nomads
Simple societies of farmers
Advanced societies of farmers/chiefdoms
Societies with administrative structures
Empires, comprising several societies
PUEBLO FARMERS
INCA EMPIRE
Capital: Cusco
Inhabitants: 70,000
AZTEC EMPIRE
Capital: Tenochtitlan
Inhabitants: 200,000
MAYA CITY-STATES
Capital: Iximché
Inhabitants: 10,000

Why did Europe become the leading power?

Around 1500, there were a number of empires that were on a similar or even higher level than Europe in various fields (such as technology, science, culture or economics).
Europe, however, became a global player in the long term because of its highly diverse geography, which, unlike Asia, lacks the vast plains that can be controlled by equestrian peoples. Conversely, Europe has many navigable rivers and contains mountain ranges and large forests with different climates.

It is surrounded by sea, and is therefore difficult to conquer. These geographical conditions have ensured that no central government could develop here. Instead, the European continent was shaped by the rivalry of several sovereigns. The various goods stimulated a flourishing trade; technical and scientific progress was triggered by competition.
It is because of these factors that Europe became the source of power in the world.

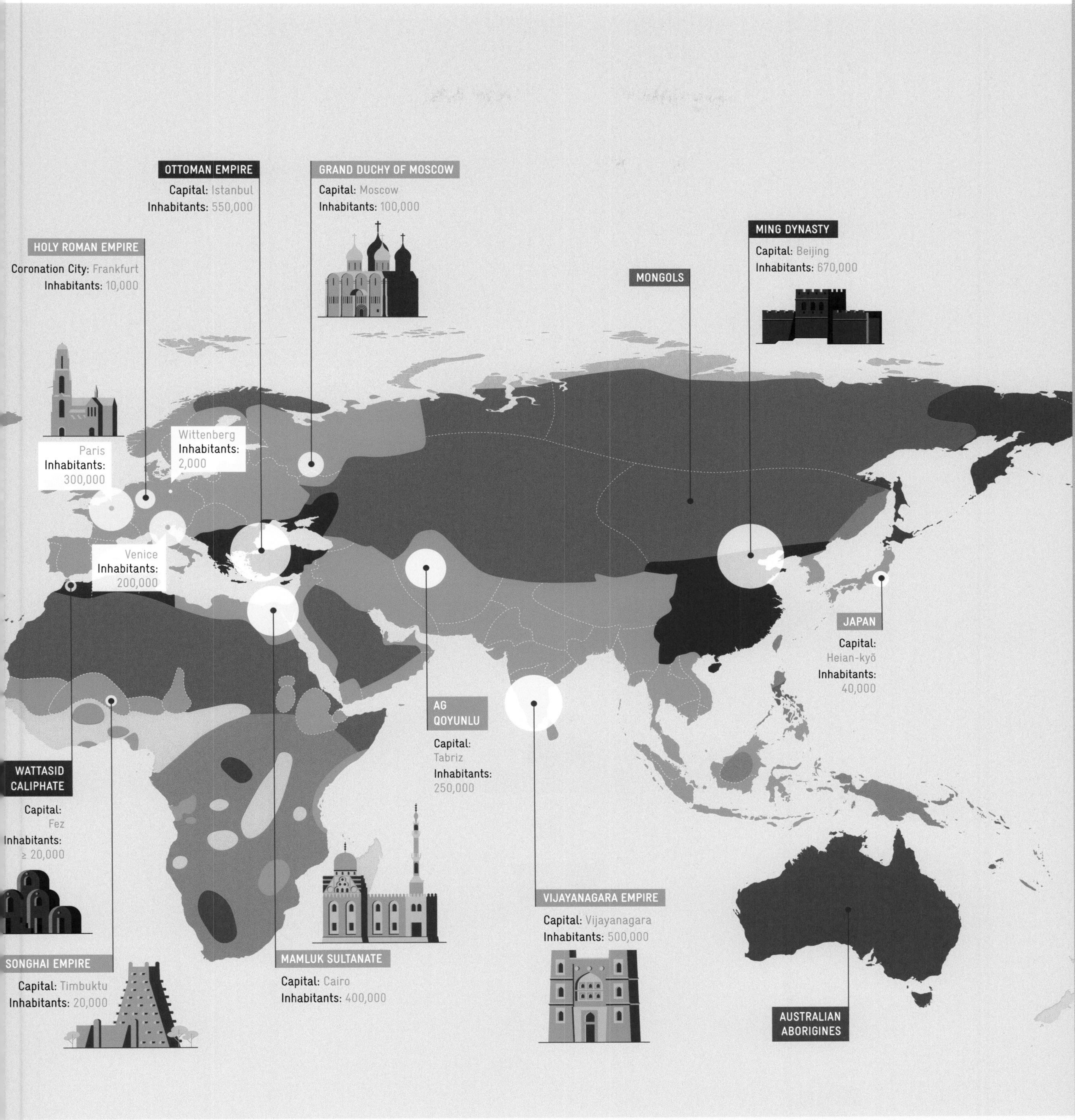
OTTOMAN EMPIRE
Capital: Istanbul
Inhabitants: 550,000
GRAND DUCHY OF MOSCOW
Capital: Moscow
Inhabitants: 100,000
HOLY ROMAN EMPIRE
Coronation City: Frankfurt
Inhabitants: 10,000
MING DYNASTY
Capital: Beijing
Inhabitants: 670,000
MONGOLS
Wittenberg
Inhabitants:
2,000
Paris
Inhabitants:
300,000
Venice
Inhabitants:
200,000
JAPAN
Capital:
Heian-kyō
Inhabitants:
40,000
AG
QOYUNLU
Capital:
Tabriz
Inhabitants:
250,000
WATTASID
CALIPHATE
Capital:
Fez
Inhabitants:
≥ 20,000
VIJAYANAGARA EMPIRE
Capital: Vijayanagara
Inhabitants: 500,000
SONGHAI EMPIRE
Capital: Timbuktu
Inhabitants: 20,000
MAMLUK SULTANATE
Capital: Cairo
Inhabitants: 400,000
AUSTRALIAN
ABORIGINES

NUMBER OF TROOPS AROUND 1550

Spain
France
England
Inca
Ming Dynasty
100,000
200,000
300,000
400,000

SHIPBUILDING

»Santa Maria« (1480 –1492)		Treasure ship »Baochuan« (1405 –1433)
Christopher Columbus	Captain	Admiral Zheng He
23 meters	Length	130 meters
7 meters	Width	48 meters

MONEY STORIES

After the discovery of America, trade was enhanced by precious metal imports from the territories conquered by the Spanish. Around the year 1500, there were about 500 mints in the Holy Roman Empire. Stock exchanges and lending banks began to form. The Fuggers, with their fortune of five million thalers, organized the papal cash flow from the European dioceses to Rome, lending money and sponsoring the Swiss Guard. Crop failures, inflation and price increases led to social unrest. The hardship heightened apocalyptic expectations among the population; the sale of religious indulgences flourished. Part of the money made from—essentially—selling forgiveness was used for the construction of the Basilica of Saint Peter in Rome. Sales of indulgences had previously been used to finance the construction of hospitals and churches.

THE SALE OF INDULGENCES UNDER CARDINAL ALBERT OF BRANDENBURG

LIABILITIES

I. **Lending business**
Albert of Brandenburg borrows tens of thousands of guilders from the Fuggers' banking business.

II. **Agreement**
In exchange for a fee, the Pope makes Albert of Brandenburg head of several dioceses. The Pope authorizes Albert to organize the sale of indulgences in his territories.

III. **Debt settlement**
Albert pays off his debts to the Fuggers with the revenue from indulgences.

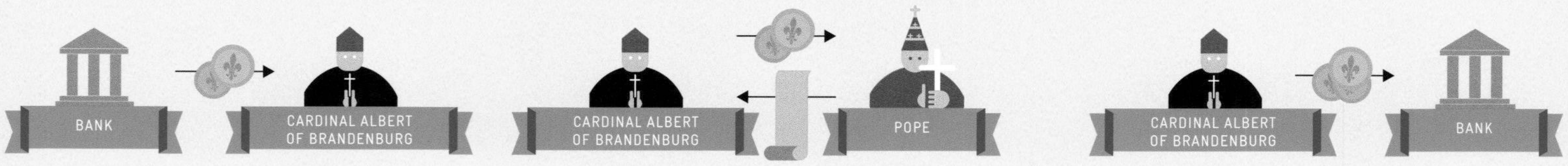
BANK
CARDINAL ALBERT OF BRANDENBURG
CARDINAL ALBERT OF BRANDENBURG
POPE
CARDINAL ALBERT OF BRANDENBURG
BANK

TRADE

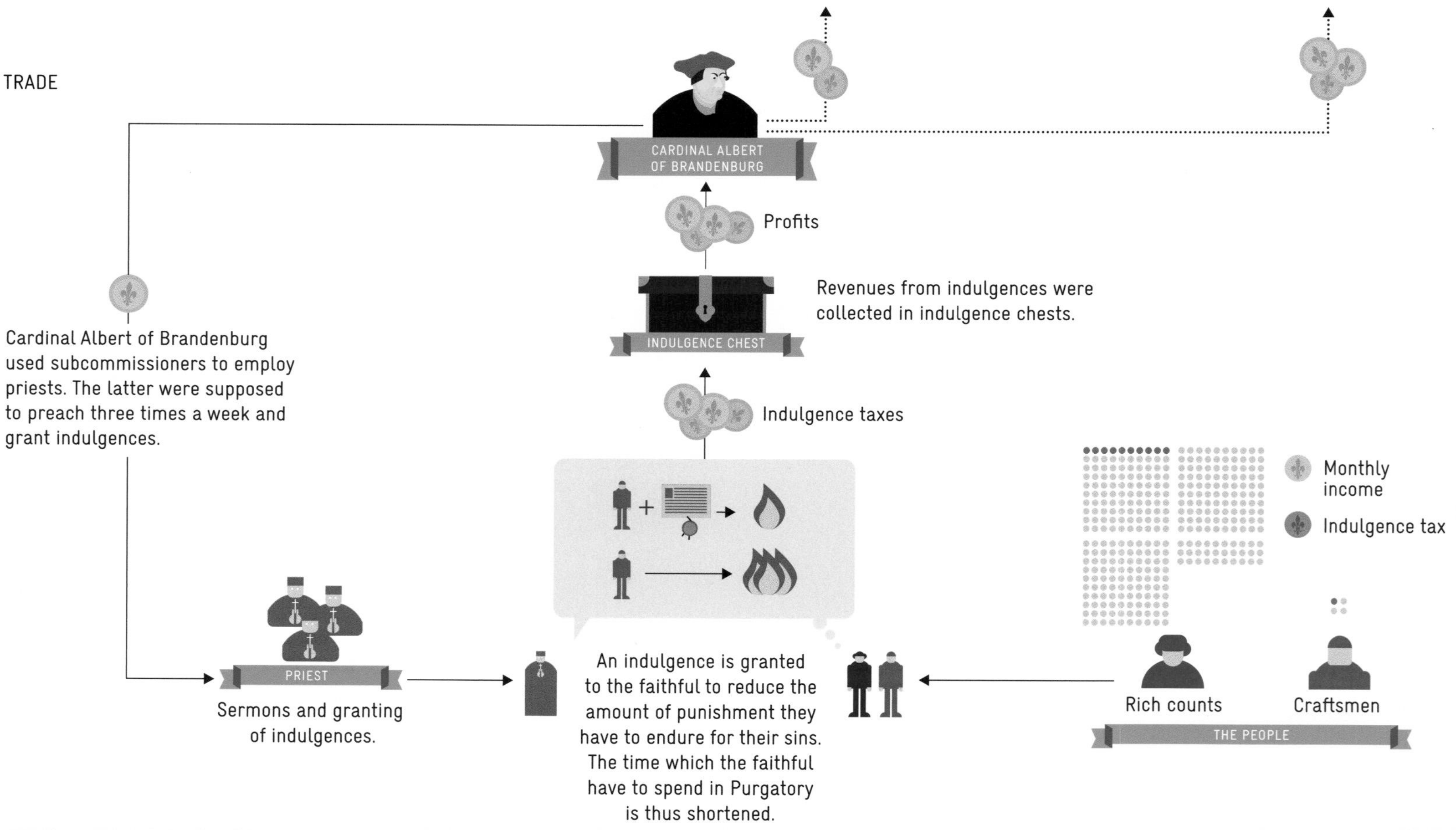
CARDINAL ALBERT OF BRANDENBURG
Profits
Revenues from indulgences were collected in indulgence chests.
INDULGENCE CHEST
Indulgence taxes
Cardinal Albert of Brandenburg used subcommissioners to employ priests. The latter were supposed to preach three times a week and grant indulgences.
PRIEST
Sermons and granting of indulgences.
An indulgence is granted to the faithful to reduce the amount of punishment they have to endure for their sins. The time which the faithful have to spend in Purgatory is thus shortened.
Monthly income
Indulgence tax
Rich counts
Craftsmen
THE PEOPLE

TRANSLATION OF THE BIBLE

During the European Reformation, the Bible was translated into several different languages, changing the linguistic landscape forever. These books were analogous translations of the original Greek and Hebrew texts, which also defined the book's intention. These translations then determined the national language for each country and even introduced new words to the conversation.
William Tyndale's English translation of the New Testament from 1525 was one of the most important pieces of work that emerged from this period. Tyndale's translation coined the phrase: The spirit is willing, but the flesh is weak, which echoed Martin Luther's work in the Book of Matthew.
The quote below, from Matthew 10:29-30 is also taken from Tyndale's translation.

Translation of the New Testament 1521–1522
DECEMBER 1521 AT THE WARTBURG
SOURCES: GREEK ORIGINAL LATIN VULGATE
THIS STILL DOES NOT SOUND QUITE RIGHT, MARTIN!
Melanchthon
I HAVE ILLUSTRATED THE BIBLE AND AM ALSO GOING TO PUBLISH IT.
Cranach
Workshop Melchior Lotter
The New Testament by Martin Luther 1st Edition 3,000 Copies
THE TRANSLATION IS FINISHED IN SEPTEMBER 1522. THE SECOND REVISED EDITION IS ALREADY PUBLISHED IN DECEMBER.
"ARE NOT TWO SPAROWES SOLDE FOR A FARTHINGE? AND NONE OF THEM DOTHE LYGHT ON THE GROUNDE WITH OUT YOURE FATHER. AND NOW ARE ALL THE HEERIS OF YOURE HEEDIS NUMBERED..."
Inn
Reader
Offer: Luther Bible 1½ Guilders
WITHOUT A COVER THE BOOKS COULD BE ROLLED UP. TUCKED AWAY IN A KEG, THEY WERE PROTECTED FROM MOISTURE AND DIRT DURING TRANSPORT.
Book fair
ONLY AT THE BOOKBINDER'S DID THE BOOKS GET THEIR COVER.

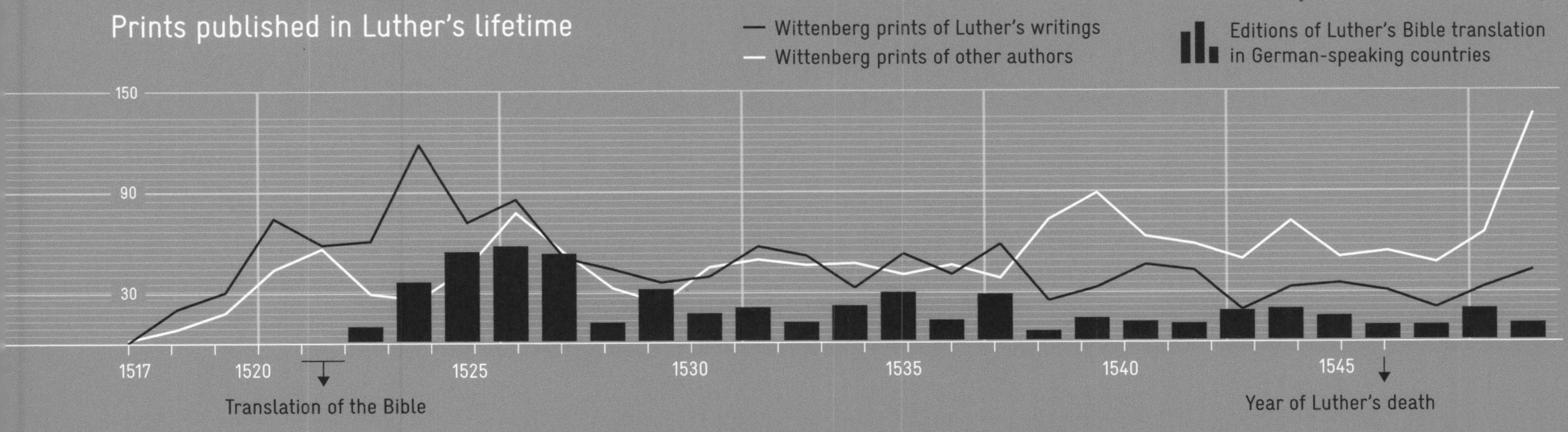
Prints published in Luther's lifetime
— Wittenberg prints of Luther's writings
— Wittenberg prints of other authors
Editions of Luther's Bible translation in German-speaking countries
150
90
30
1517
1520
1525
1530
1535
1540
1545
Translation of the Bible
Year of Luther's death

REFORMATION NETWORKS

In as far as existing data allows it, this diagram shows all correspondents of the major Reformation protagonists pictured here. Although many letters have been lost, it is clear that the main reformers were prolific correspondents. Around 4,300 letters by Luther and around 7,500 by Philipp Melanchthon have been preserved. Each had his own circle of correspondents, with only about 30 joint addressees, including, as important branch points, Johannes Bugenhagen, Justus Jonas and the emperor. Melanchthon had a significantly greater number of correspondents than Luther.

Ulrich von Hutten was well-integrated into the Reformation network—unlike Thomas Müntzer, who appears more as an outsider.

They had hardly any contact with representatives of the Catholic Church (Pope, cardinals), who had their own (Catholic) correspondents. The artists were networked with imperial politicians and reformers alike, but wrote comparatively few letters. Only seven letters by Lucas Cranach the Elder have survived.

Further research will be necessary to build a more complete image of the Reformation networks.

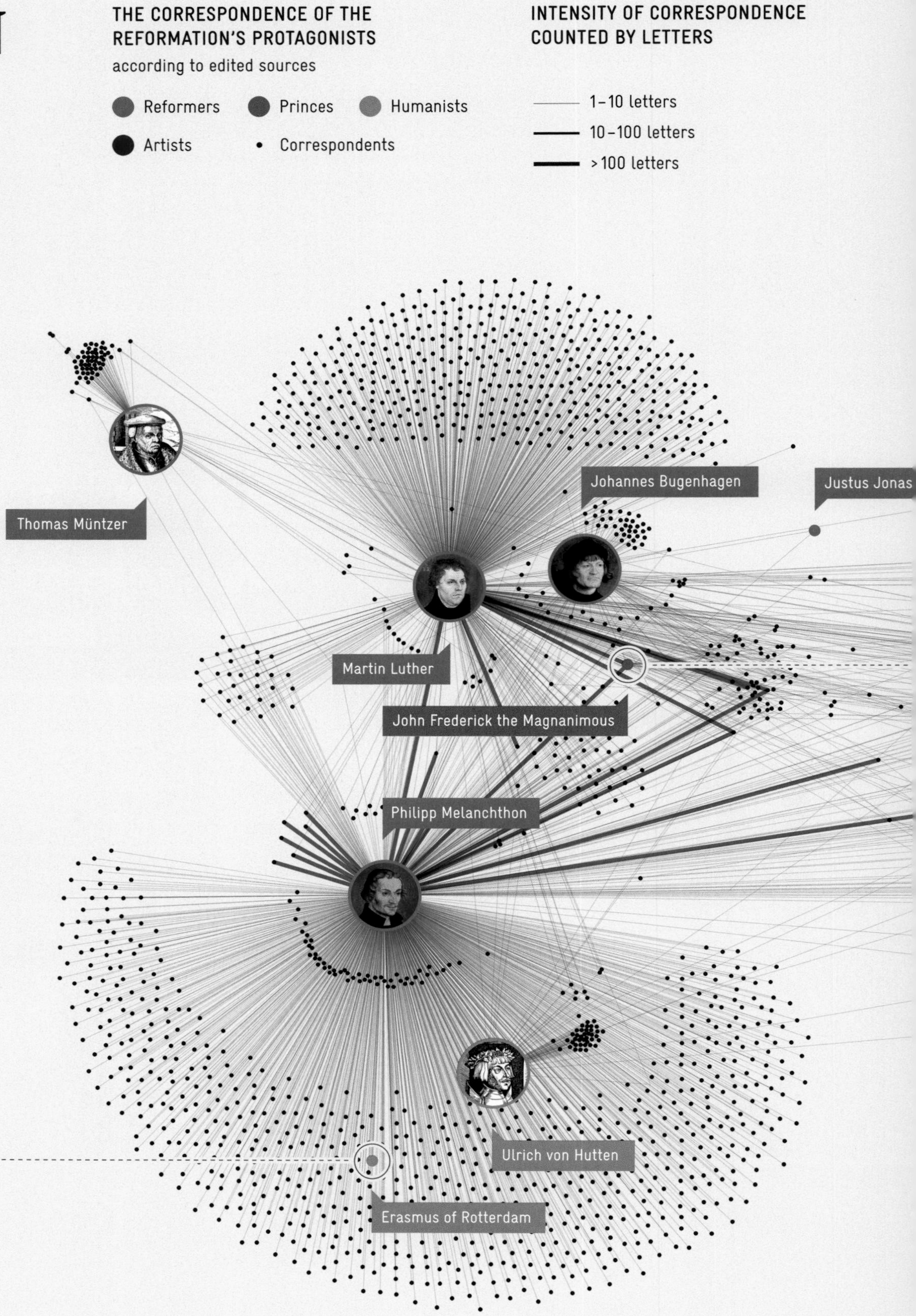
THE CORRESPONDENCE OF THE REFORMATION'S PROTAGONISTS
according to edited sources
Reformers
Princes
Humanists
Artists
Correspondents
INTENSITY OF CORRESPONDENCE COUNTED BY LETTERS
1–10 letters
10–100 letters
> 100 letters
Thomas Müntzer
Johannes Bugenhagen
Justus Jonas
Martin Luther
John Frederick the Magnanimous
Philipp Melanchthon
Ulrich von Hutten
Erasmus of Rotterdam

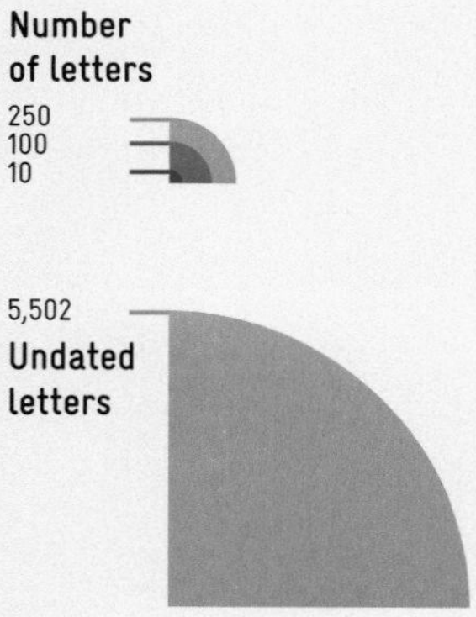
Number of letters
250
100
10
5,502
Undated letters

ERASMUS OF ROTTERDAM

Erasmus of Rotterdam, the most important humanist of his time, left 150 books and more than 2,000 letters when he died. There seems to have been little contact with the reformers: Erasmus only wrote four letters to Melanchthon, and eleven to Luther, receiving seven and two letters respectively from them in response.

THE KEY PEOPLE OF THE SCHMALKALDIC LEAGUE

John Frederick the Magnanimous and Philip of Hesse, the leaders of the Protestant imperial princes, served as a bridge between the reformers and imperial politicians.

ELISABETH OF ROCHLITZ

Elisabeth of Rochlitz (actually Elisabeth of Hesse), the sister of Philip of Hesse, appears as an inconspicuous correspondent of Maurice of Saxony. However, she had a lively correspondence with many princes not pictured here.

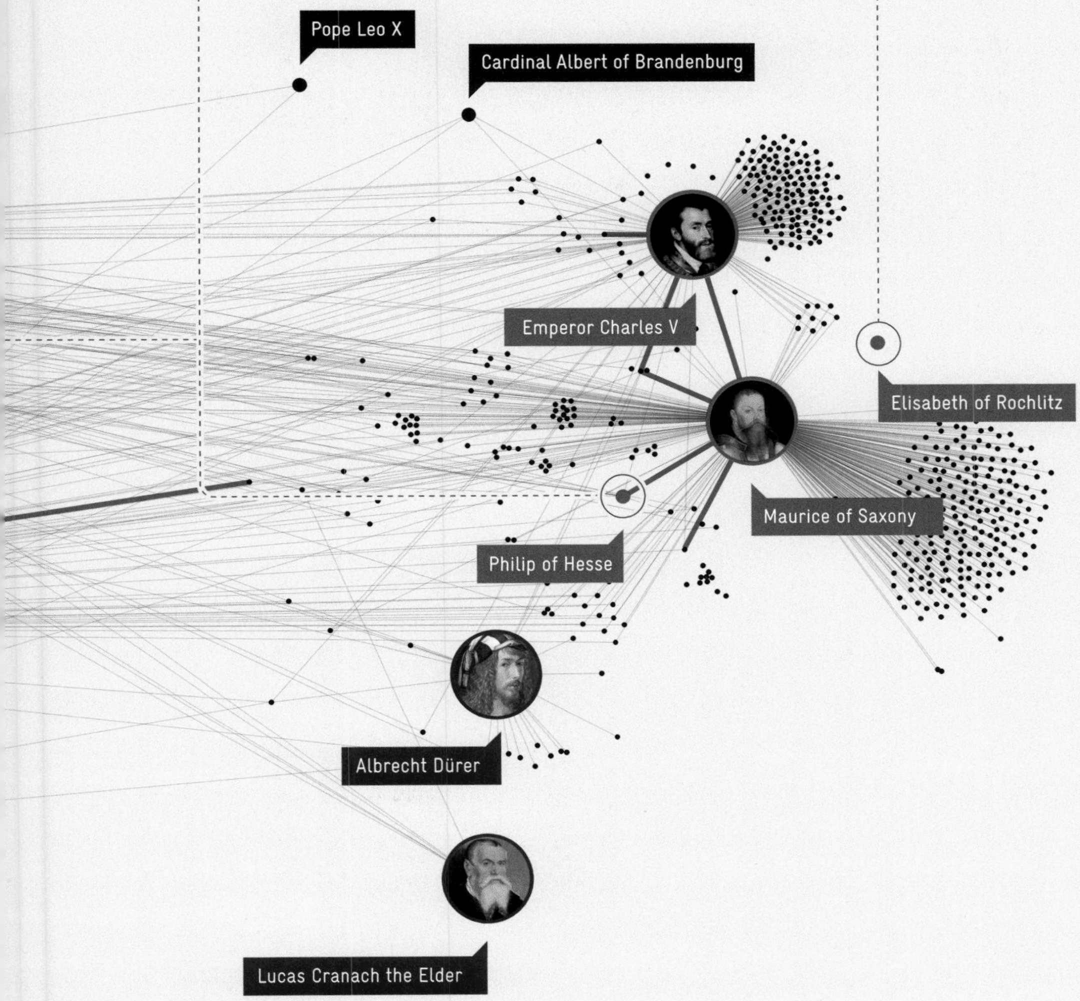
Pope Leo X
Cardinal Albert of Brandenburg
Emperor Charles V
Elisabeth of Rochlitz
Maurice of Saxony
Philip of Hesse
Albrecht Dürer
Lucas Cranach the Elder

Number of letters

250
100
10

CHRONOLOGICAL SEQUENCE OF CORRESPONDENCE

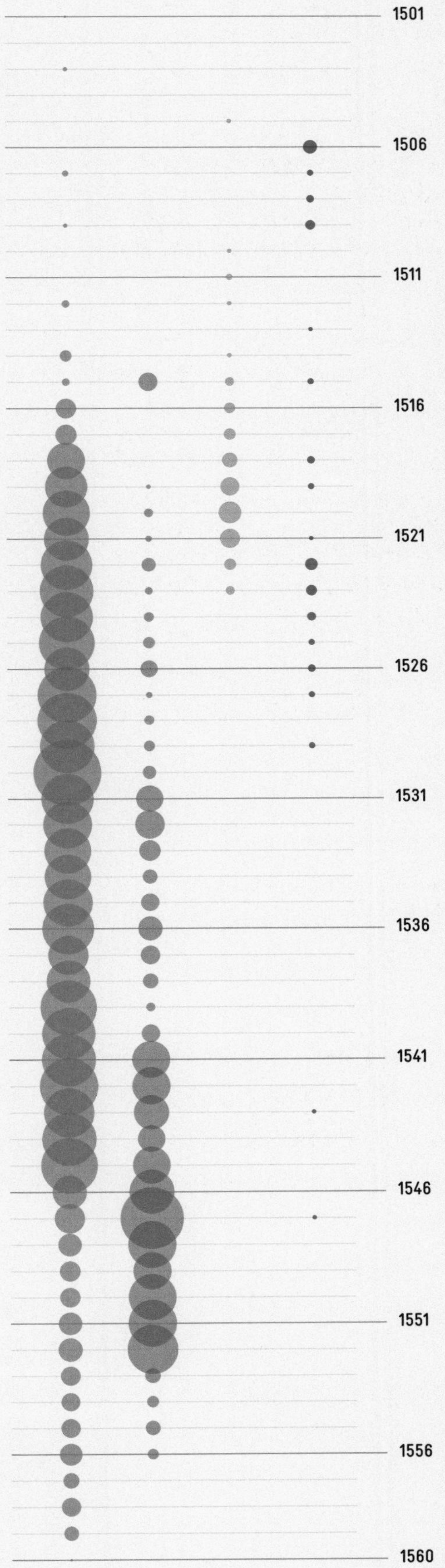
1501
1506
1511
1516
1521
1526
1531
1536
1541
1546
1551
1556
1560

CHRONOLOGICAL DISTRIBUTION

Many of the letters were not dated by the senders. Despite this lack of clarity, an interesting picture emerges from the dated letters. The reformers' correspondences have been preserved evenly, with a significant decline after Luther's death (1546).

Most of the preserved letters from politicians date from the time of the Schmalkaldic War between Emperor Charles V and the Protestant princes (1546/47).

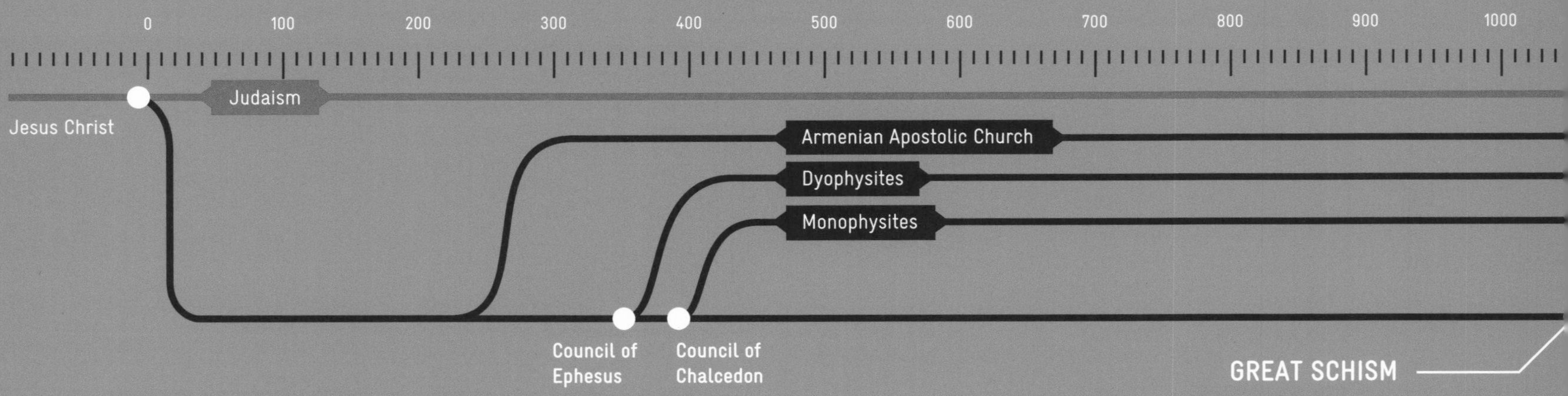

A council doctrine made up of mostly Bishops decide the doctrine and structure of each church.

A schism is the split-up of a religious community.

THE DEVELOPMENT OF CHRISTIANITY

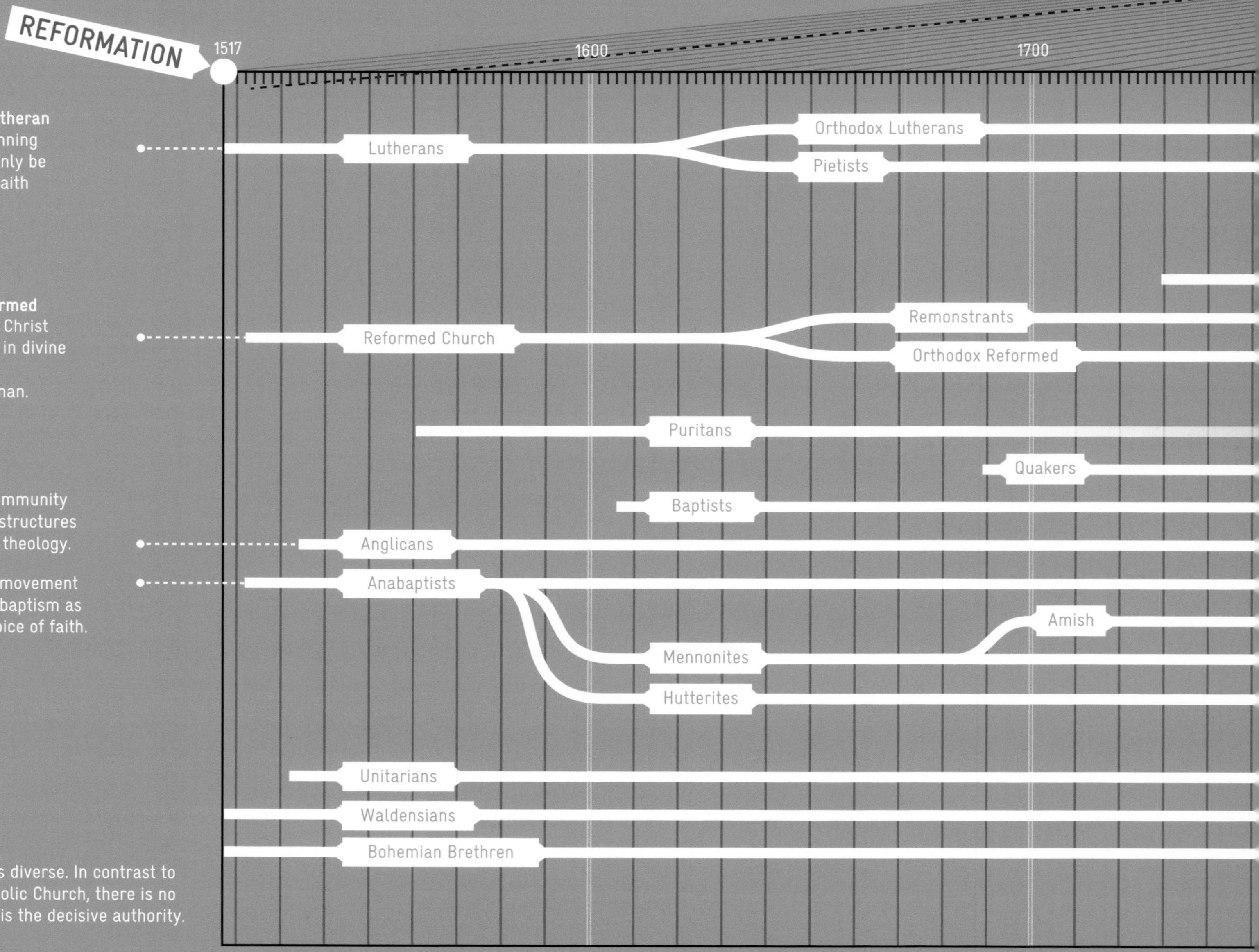
REFORMATION
1517
1600
1700
Lutherans
Orthodox Lutherans
Pietists
Reformed Church
Remonstrants
Orthodox Reformed
Puritans
Quakers
Baptists
Anglicans
Anabaptists
Amish
Mennonites
Hutterites
Unitarians
Waldensians
Bohemian Brethren

According to **Lutheran** tradition, the sinning individual can only be saved through faith in Jesus Christ.

Within the **Reformed** tradition, Jesus Christ reveals himself in divine election and his covenant with man.

The **Anglican** community unites Catholic structures with Protestant theology.

The **Anabaptist** movement practices adult baptism as a deliberate choice of faith.

Protestantism is diverse. In contrast to the Roman Catholic Church, there is no Pope. The Bible is the decisive authority.

Christianity
From the beginnings until 2020 AD

The Protestants
1517 AD–2020 AD

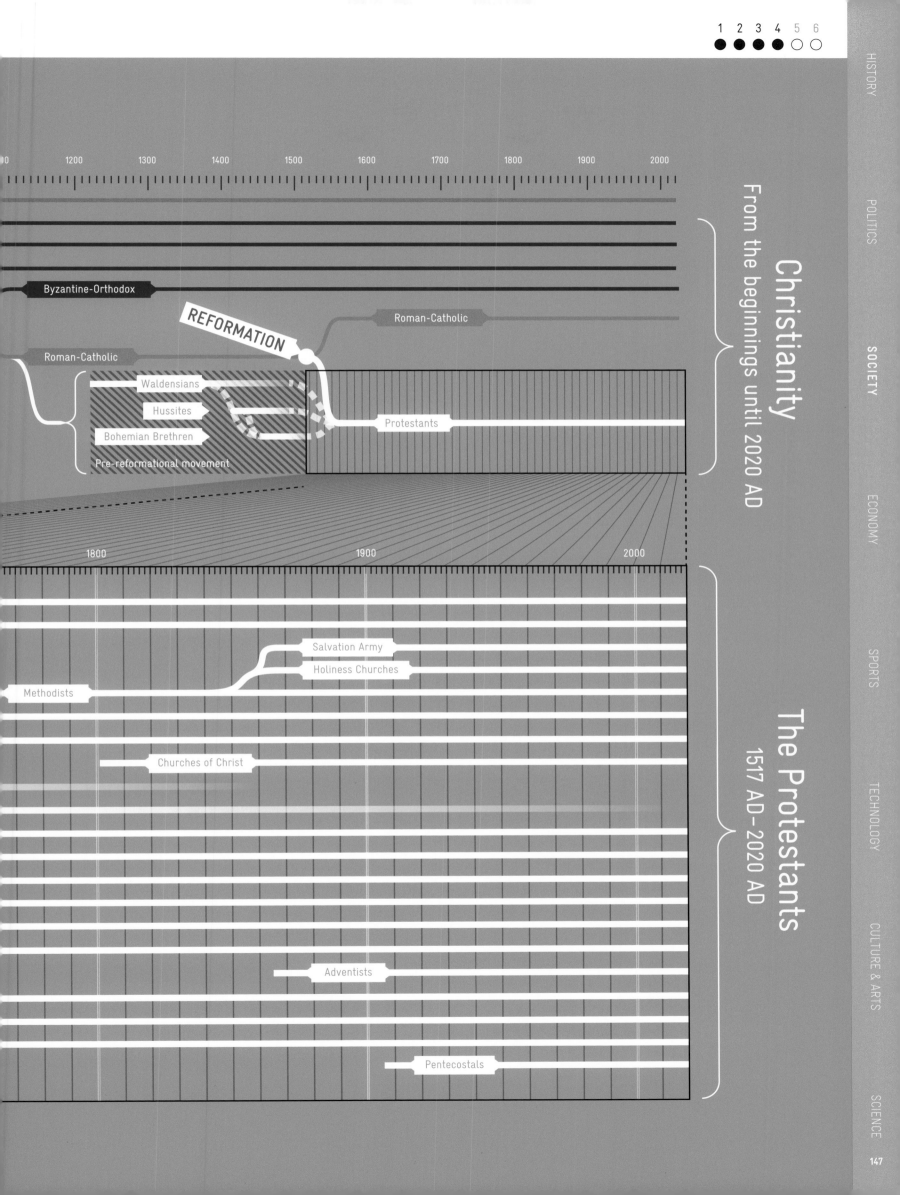

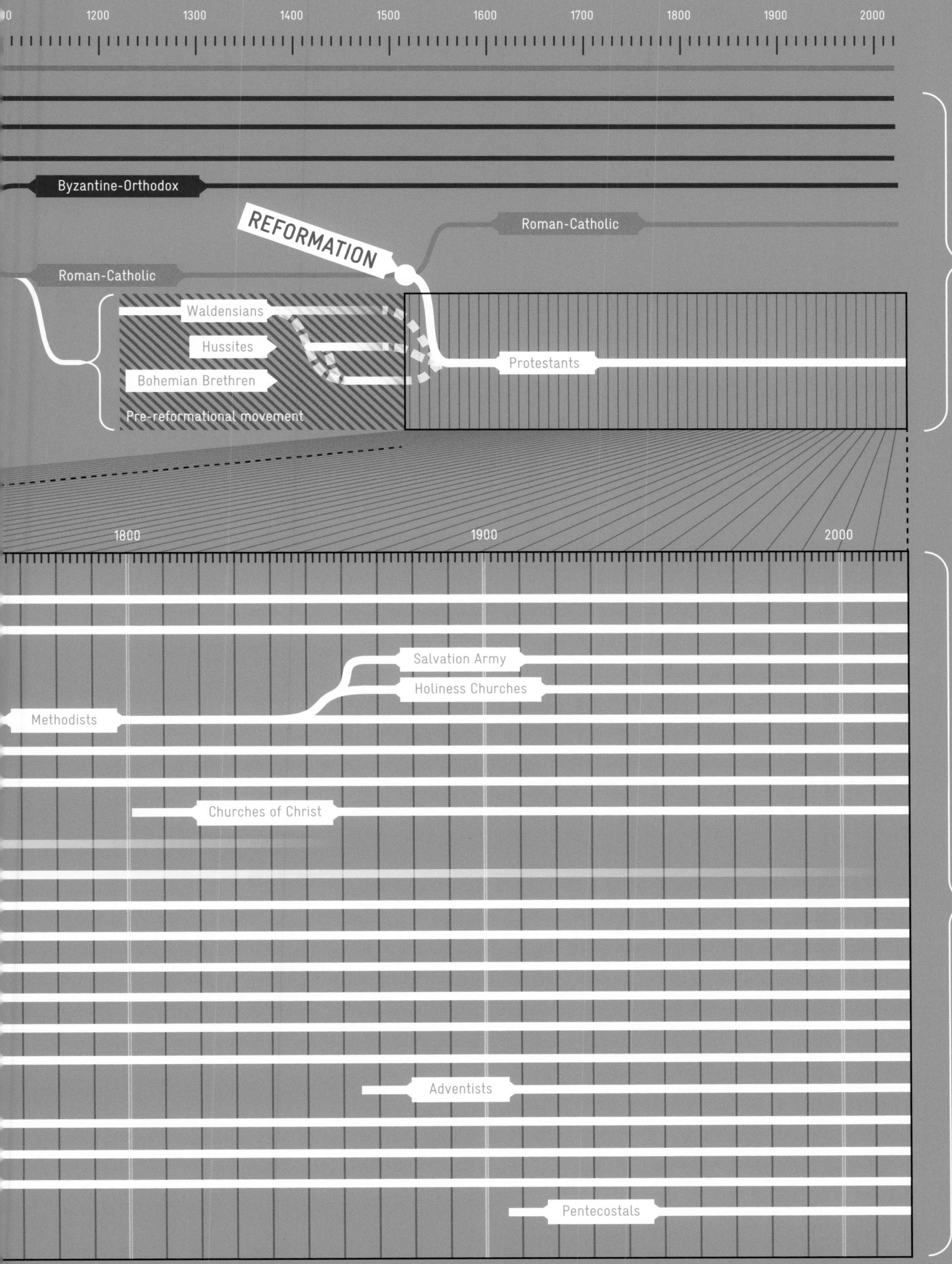

MARTIN LUTHER AND HIS TIME

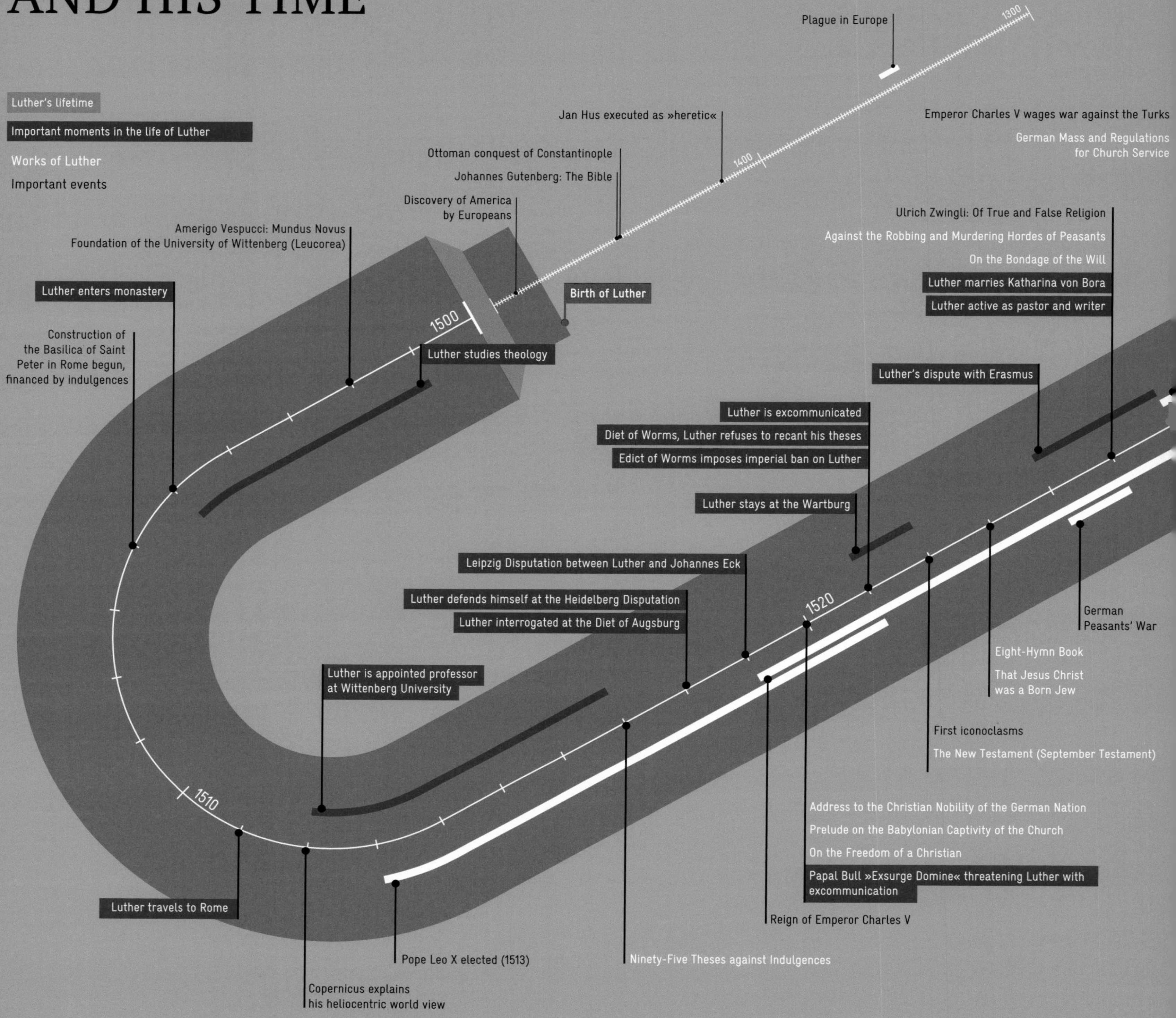
Luther's lifetime
Important moments in the life of Luther
Works of Luther
Important events
1300
Plague in Europe
Jan Hus executed as »heretic«
1400
Ottoman conquest of Constantinople
Johannes Gutenberg: The Bible
Discovery of America by Europeans
Amerigo Vespucci: Mundus Novus
Foundation of the University of Wittenberg (Leucorea)
Birth of Luther
1500
Luther enters monastery
Luther studies theology
Construction of the Basilica of Saint Peter in Rome begun, financed by indulgences
1510
Luther travels to Rome
Copernicus explains his heliocentric world view
Pope Leo X elected (1513)
Luther is appointed professor at Wittenberg University
Ninety-Five Theses against Indulgences
Luther defends himself at the Heidelberg Disputation
Luther interrogated at the Diet of Augsburg
Leipzig Disputation between Luther and Johannes Eck
1520
Reign of Emperor Charles V
Address to the Christian Nobility of the German Nation
Prelude on the Babylonian Captivity of the Church
On the Freedom of a Christian
Papal Bull »Exsurge Domine« threatening Luther with excommunication
Luther is excommunicated
Diet of Worms, Luther refuses to recant his theses
Edict of Worms imposes imperial ban on Luther
Luther stays at the Wartburg
First iconoclasms
The New Testament (September Testament)
Eight-Hymn Book
That Jesus Christ was a Born Jew
German Peasants' War
Luther's dispute with Erasmus
Ulrich Zwingli: Of True and False Religion
Against the Robbing and Murdering Hordes of Peasants
On the Bondage of the Will
Luther marries Katharina von Bora
Luther active as pastor and writer
Emperor Charles V wages war against the Turks
German Mass and Regulations for Church Service

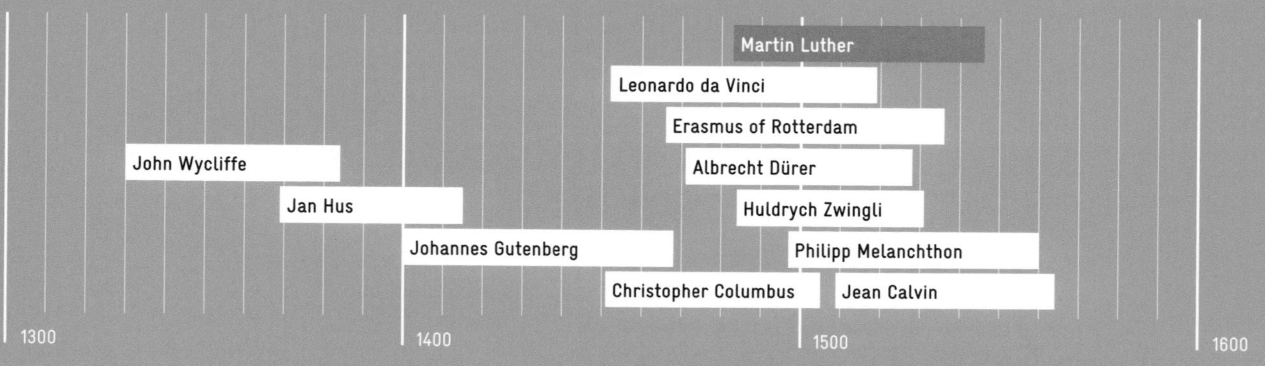
Martin Luther
Leonardo da Vinci
Erasmus of Rotterdam
John Wycliffe
Albrecht Dürer
Jan Hus
Huldrych Zwingli
Johannes Gutenberg
Philipp Melanchthon
Christopher Columbus
Jean Calvin
1300
1400
1500
1600

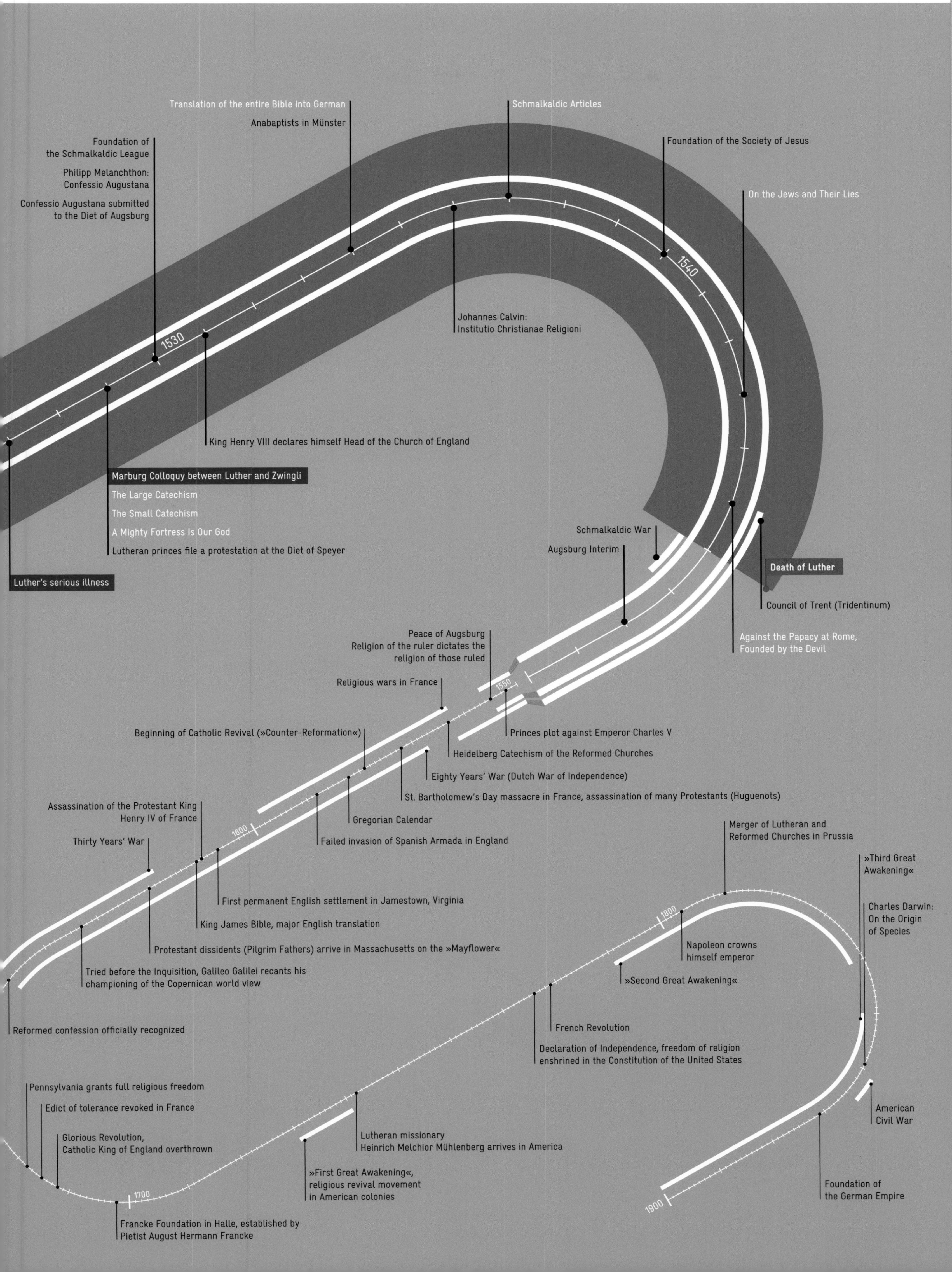
Luther's serious illness
Marburg Colloquy between Luther and Zwingli
The Large Catechism
The Small Catechism
A Mighty Fortress Is Our God
Lutheran princes file a protestation at the Diet of Speyer
Foundation of
the Schmalkaldic League
Philipp Melanchthon:
Confessio Augustana
Confessio Augustana submitted
to the Diet of Augsburg
1530
King Henry VIII declares himself Head of the Church of England
Translation of the entire Bible into German
Anabaptists in Münster
Johannes Calvin:
Institutio Christianae Religioni
Schmalkaldic Articles
Foundation of the Society of Jesus
1540
On the Jews and Their Lies
Against the Papacy at Rome,
Founded by the Devil
Death of Luther
Council of Trent (Tridentinum)
Schmalkaldic War
Augsburg Interim
Peace of Augsburg
Religion of the ruler dictates the
religion of those ruled
1550
Princes plot against Emperor Charles V
Religious wars in France
Heidelberg Catechism of the Reformed Churches
Beginning of Catholic Revival (»Counter-Reformation«)
Eighty Years' War (Dutch War of Independence)
St. Bartholomew's Day massacre in France, assassination of many Protestants (Huguenots)
Gregorian Calendar
Failed invasion of Spanish Armada in England
1600
Assassination of the Protestant King
Henry IV of France
First permanent English settlement in Jamestown, Virginia
King James Bible, major English translation
Thirty Years' War
Protestant dissidents (Pilgrim Fathers) arrive in Massachusetts on the »Mayflower«
Tried before the Inquisition, Galileo Galilei recants his
championing of the Copernican world view
Reformed confession officially recognized
Pennsylvania grants full religious freedom
Edict of tolerance revoked in France
Glorious Revolution,
Catholic King of England overthrown
1700
Francke Foundation in Halle, established by
Pietist August Hermann Francke
»First Great Awakening«,
religious revival movement
in American colonies
Lutheran missionary
Heinrich Melchior Mühlenberg arrives in America
Declaration of Independence, freedom of religion
enshrined in the Constitution of the United States
French Revolution
»Second Great Awakening«
1800
Napoleon crowns
himself emperor
Merger of Lutheran and
Reformed Churches in Prussia
»Third Great
Awakening«
Charles Darwin:
On the Origin
of Species
American
Civil War
Foundation of
the German Empire
1900

MARTIN LUTHER KING

Civil rights leader Martin Luther King and Martin Luther share the same name.

But how similar are these two great figures of world history? Here's a juxtaposition of the most important stages in the lives of the two men.

King claims to have had a vision of God in Montgomery in 1957, which encouraged him in his fight against racism.

AWAKENING

Luther tells of an awakening experience when reading Romans, which goes down in history as the »Tower Experience«

King was a Baptist minister.
In his theology, he did not make any reference to Martin Luther. Important impulses came from the philosophy of Mahatma Gandhi and theologian Walter Rauschenbusch.

THEOLOGY

Luther's theology was based on his findings in the Bible. Faith in Christ is sufficient for attaining salvation; good works are not necessary for this purpose. Luther rejected believers' baptism, as practiced by Anabaptists.

The young Mike King Jr. was renamed Martin Luther King Jr. by his own father. When visiting East Berlin in 1964, he declared: »I come to you not altogether as a stranger, for the name that I happen to have is a name so familiar to you, so familiar to Germany, and so familiar to the world, and I am happy that my parents decided to name me after the great Reformer.«

THE NAME MARTIN LUTHER

In 1517, the Reformer changed his name from Luder to Luther. He called himself »Eleutherius«, the free one, adopting the »th« for his name.

Martin Luther

I have a dream

The day before his death, King said that he had seen the promised land.

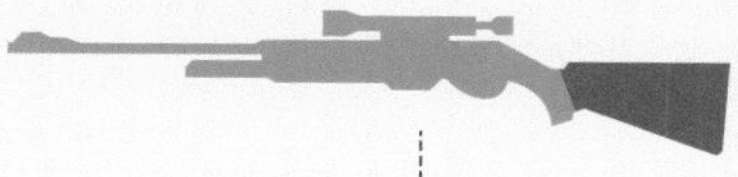

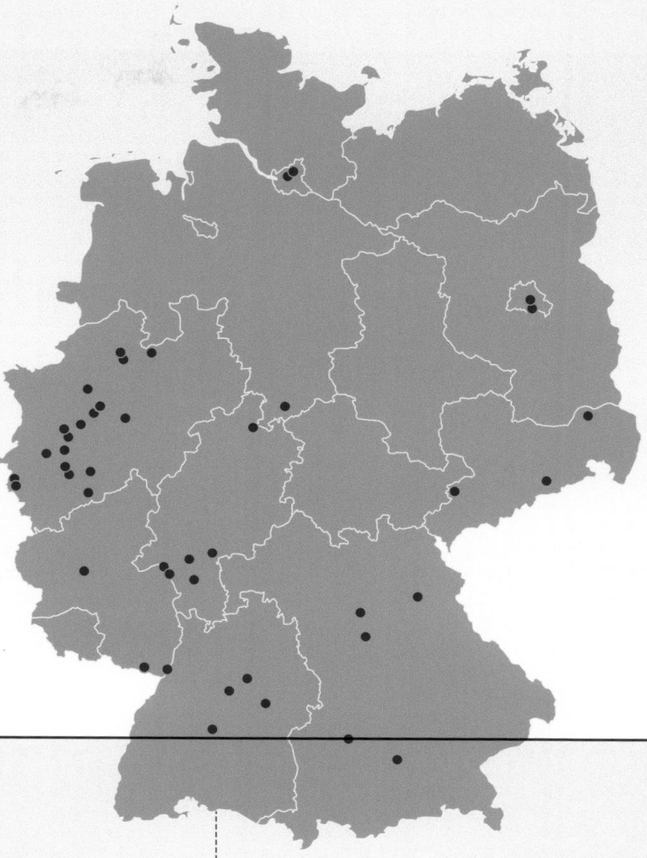

»I have a Dream«
1963, Washington, D.C.

King was shot by a white racist in 1968.

In Germany, 71 institutions are named after Martin Luther King.

MOST FAMOUS QUOTE

DEATH

AFTERLIFE

»Here I stand, I can do no other.«
1521 Worms, Germany

Luther died in his hometown of Eisleben in 1546, probably from a stroke.

In 1883, the 400th anniversary of Luther was celebrated. A copy of the Luther statue in Worms was made, shipped to the US and erected in Washington, D.C.

Here I stand ...

The quote was put into Luther's mouth after his interrogation at the Diet of Worms in 1521.

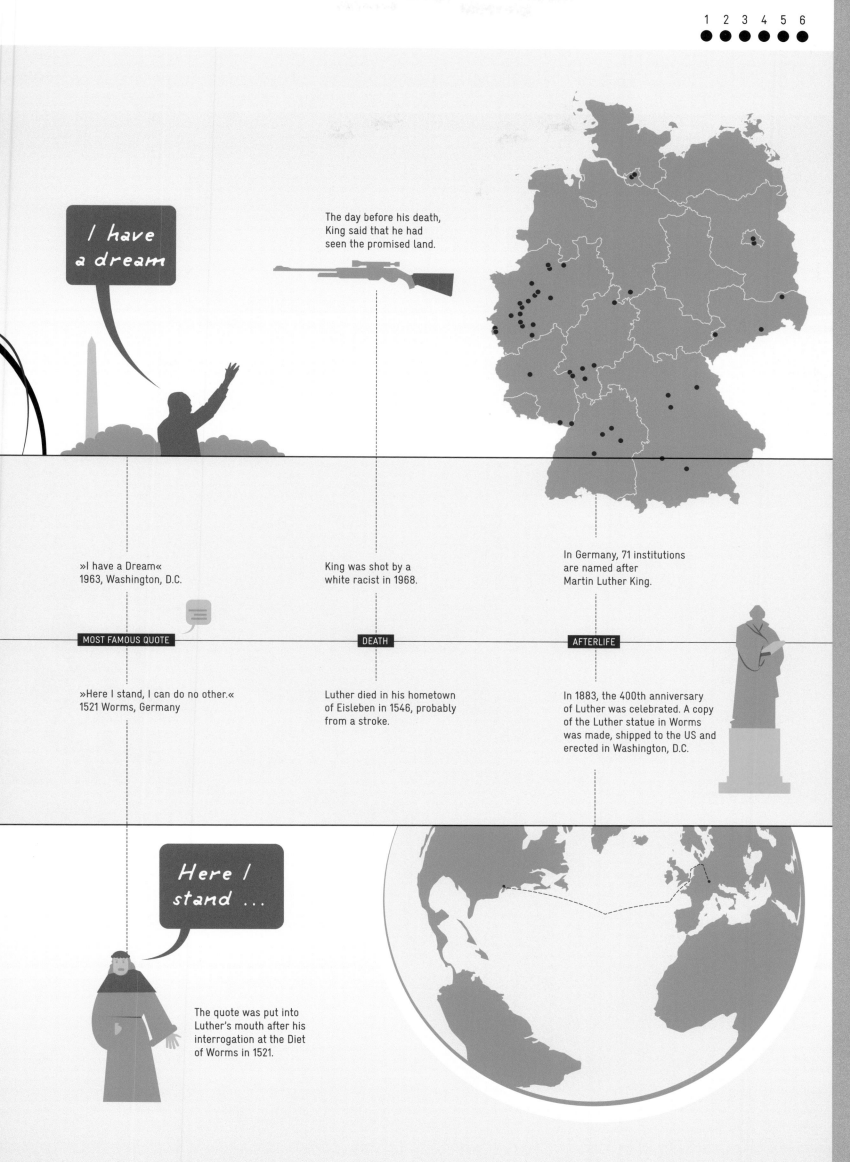

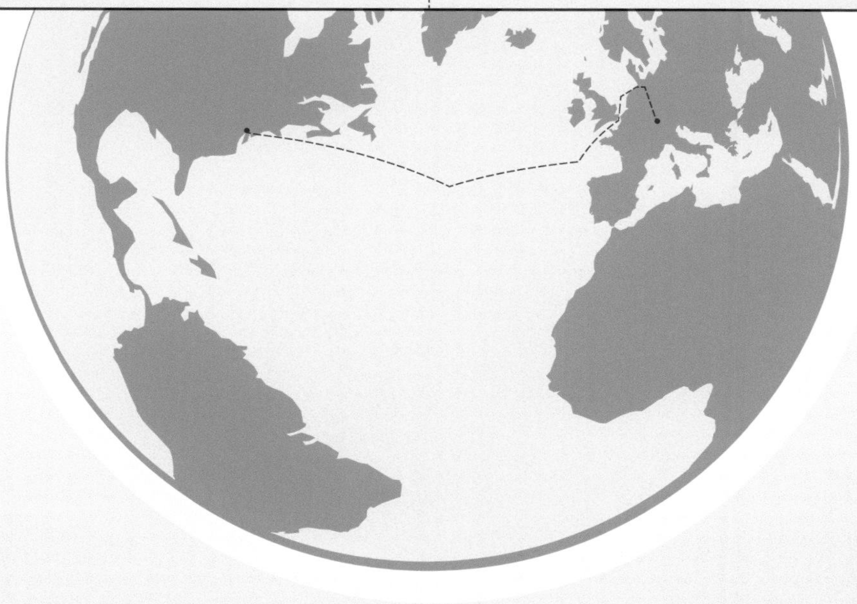

ISLAMIC DISPUTE

The conflict in Iraq and Syria is more than just a war between countries– it's also a war between Sunni and Shiite muslims. This separation of Islam into two dominant branches goes all the way back to the dispute over who would be the successor of the Prophet Muhammad. In the Middle East, power politics, culture and history all play an equally important role as separate beliefs, even to this day.

Map as per a template from Dr. Michael Izady: http://gulf2000.columbia.edu/maps.shtml

Sunnites | Shiites | Wahhabites | Ibadites | Christians | Jews | Other | Sparsely populated or unpopulated area

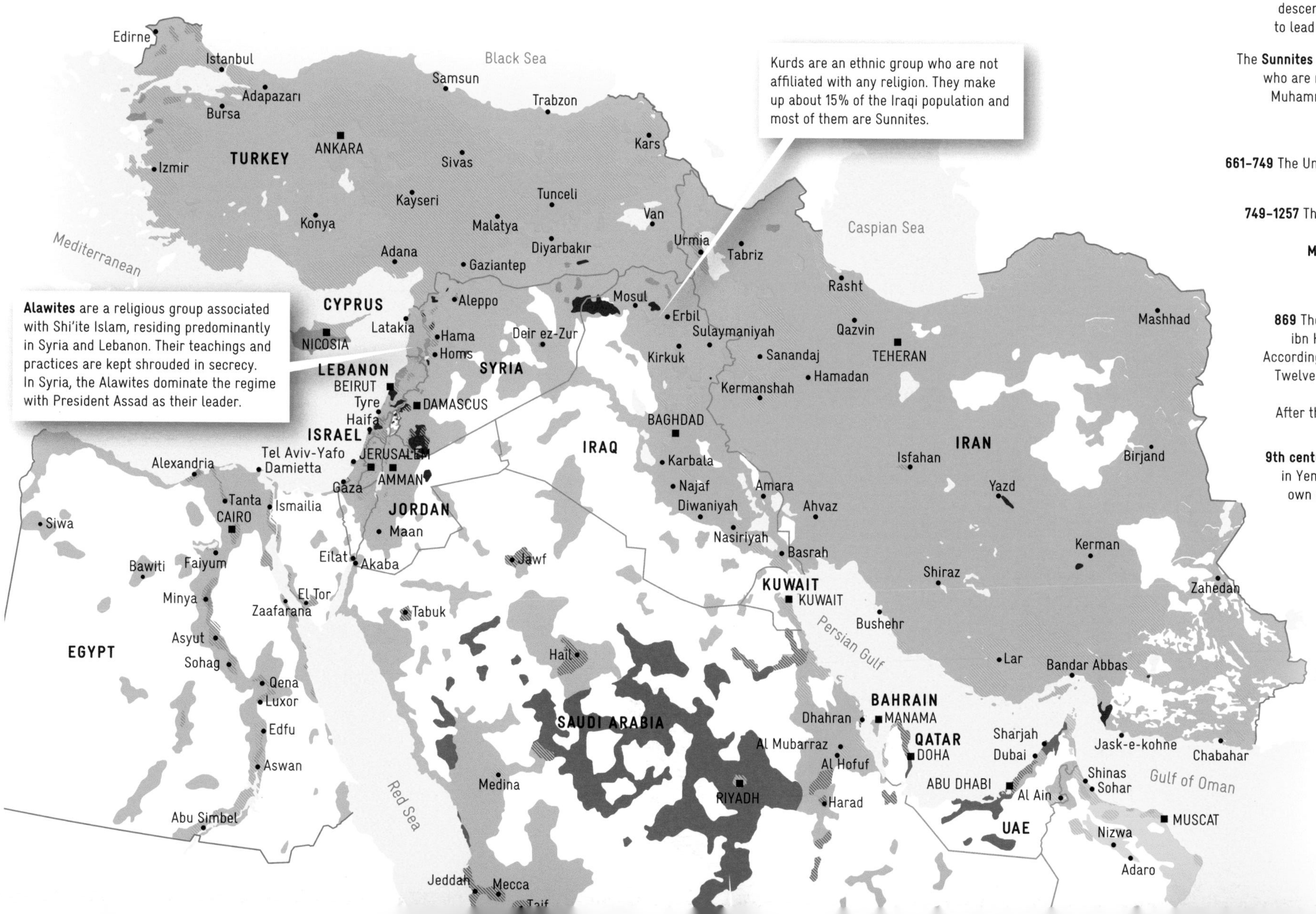

Kurds are an ethnic group who are not affiliated with any religion. They make up about 15% of the Iraqi population and most of them are Sunnites.

Alawites are a religious group associated with Shi'ite Islam, residing predominantly in Syria and Lebanon. Their teachings and practices are kept shrouded in secrecy. In Syria, the Alawites dominate the regime with President Assad as their leader.

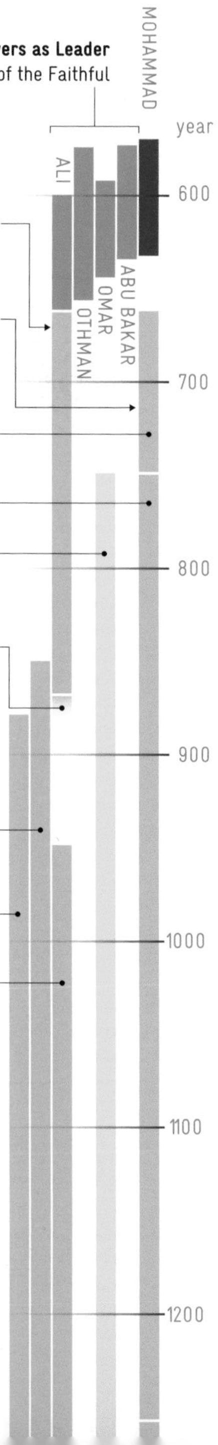
MOHAMMAD
ABU BAKAR
OMAR
OTHMAN
ALI
year
600
700
800
900
1000
1100
1200

Mohammad's **first four followers as Leader** of the Faithful

The **Shiites** believe only descendants of Ali are allowed to lead the Muslims (»Imams«)

The **Sunnites** also accept descendants who are more distantly related to Muhammad as the Leader of the Faithful (»Caliphs«)

661–749 The Umayyad Caliphate has its capital in Damascus

749–1257 The Abbasid Caliphate has its capital in Bagdad

Middle of the 8th century Ibadis emerge, who are neither Sunni or Shias

869 The 12th Imam Muhammad ibn Hassan al-Mahdi is born. According to the teachings of the Twelve Shia, he enters a period of Occultation. After this period, he will return and save the world.

9th century Zaydi Shia is formed in Yemen, which developed its own concept of the Imamate.

Late 9th century Alawites emerge.

10th century Shiite teachings are developed.

1257–1517 Mamluk Sultanate has

Muslims around the world
Total of 1.6 billion people

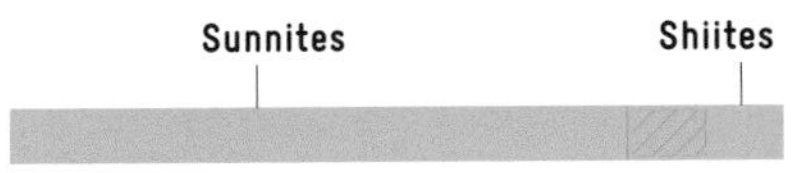

Abha
Dhahran
Najran
Jizan
Sa'dah
SANA
Ma'rib
Al Hudaydah
Shabwah
YEMEN
Al Mukalla
Mocha
Taizz
Lahij
Aden
Gulf of Aden
OMAN
Salalah
Arabian Sea

Wahhabism is the state religion of Saudi Arabia and is orientated toward fundamentalism. The Wahhabis think of their religion as a particularly pure form of Islam.

The **Ibadi teachings** originate from the middle of the 8th century. They believe that any devout Muslim can be Leader of the Faithful. The Ibadis make up a small minority.

What is the difference between the Sunnites and the Shiites?

Proportion of followers in the Middle East

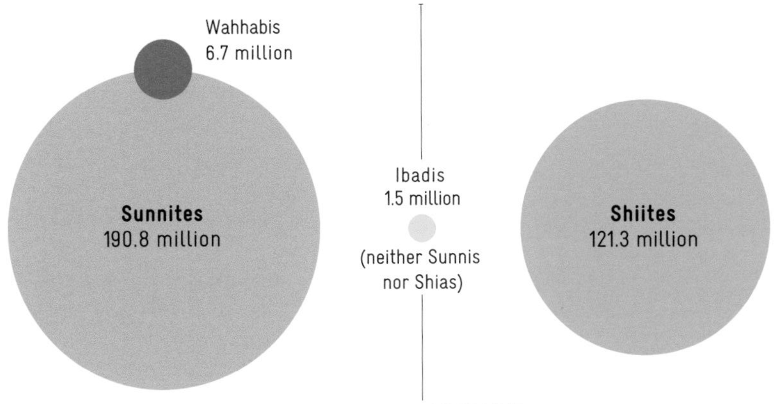

Wahhabis
6.7 million
Sunnites
190.8 million
Ibadis
1.5 million
(neither Sunnis nor Shias)
Shiites
121.3 million

MUSLIM LEADERSHIP

Sunnites	Shiites
The term 'Sunnis or Sunnites' stems from the Arabic word 'Sunna', meaning tradition. The story of Muhammad has been passed down from generation to generation. For the Sunnites, the Leader of the Faithful (»Caliph«) must belong to the line of prophets. He is fallible.	The term 'Shias or Shiites' comes from the Arabic 'Shiat Ali', meaning the Party of Ali. Only direct descendants of Muhammad are allowed to be the Leader of the Faithful (»Imam«). They are not fallible. As the prophet did not bear a son, his nephew and son-in-law Ali was the only rightful caliph.

ROLE OF THE DIVINE

Sunnites	Shiites
The legal opinion (»Fatwa«) of a Sunnite scholar is not binding.	The opinion of a Shiite scholar is binding for every follower who has joined the school of said scholar.

DENOMINATIONS

Sunnites	Shiites
There are four different schools of jurisprudence (Hanafi, Maliki, Shafi'i, Hanbali). The most important, most fundamental denominations are Wahhabis and Salafis.	Most Shiites belong to the »Twelver Shia«. They believe that the 12th Imam entered a period of Occultation, hiding himself in order to return as the »Mahdi« (Messiah). Other denominations are: Zaidi, Ismaili and Alawites.

POLITICS

Sunnites	Shiites
Sunnites have historically been the dominant force, but there have been eras of dialogue and peaceful coexistence.	The Shiites were mainly considered politically abstinent. There were, however, Shias states and dynasties, that have occasionally governed the Sunnis.

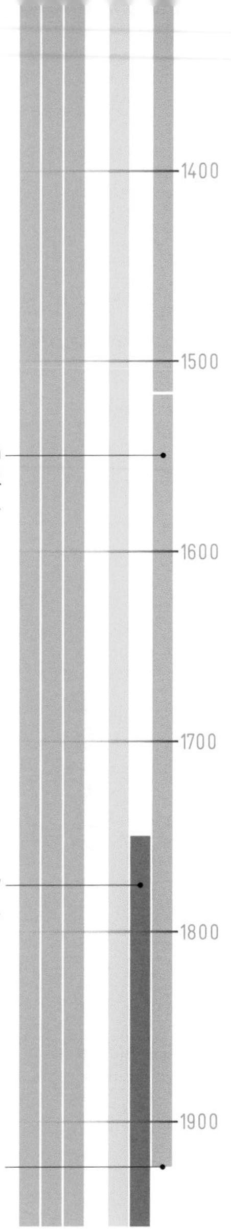

1400
1500
1600
1700
1800
1900

1517–1924 The Ottoman Caliphate has its capital in Istanbul.

Middle of the 18th century Wahhabis emerge.

1924 The caliphate is abolished.

Other religions in the Middle East

Number of followers

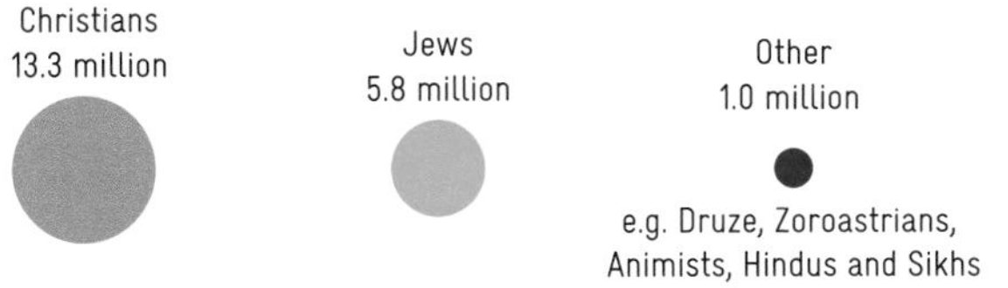

Christians
13.3 million
Jews
5.8 million
Other
1.0 million
e.g. Druze, Zoroastrians, Animists, Hindus and Sikhs

Shiite-Sunnite conflicts in the modern era

1979	IRAN	Islamic revolution and establishment of Shiite theocracy; from 1980 to 1988 war against Iraq
1975–1990	LEBANON	Civil war, triggered through tensions between Sunnis and Shias
since 2004	IRAQ	Sunni jihadists start a terror campaign against Shiites to spark a civil war
since 2004	YEMEN	Armed conflict between Shiite Houthi rebels and the Sunni national government; still simmering today
since 2012	SYRIA	Rebellion against the Assad Regime run by the Alawites leads to increasingly more conflict between Sunnites and Shiites
2014	IRAQ	The Sunni terrorist organization Isis deliberately fuels the ongoing conflict between Sunnites and Shiites

THE HAJJ

The annual Hajj to Mecca, known as the Hajj, is one of the Five Pillars of Islam that the faithful must complete at least once in their lifetime as part of their duty to Allah. They can also do the Hajj on behalf of someone else. Pilgrims wear white garments called Ihram as they embark on one of three different paths to Mecca.

The first is the Hajj al-Tamattu, which includes the Umrah, or »minor pilgrimage« as well as the Hajj (Arabic for pilgrimage). The third path, the Hajj al-Qiran, is not usually performed today. The Hajj al-Ifrad is the only form of this pilgrimage that does not require an animal sacrifice. The sacrifice does not have to be committed by the pilgrims, but can be done on their behalf. People then butcher the animals and donate the meat to feed the hungry.

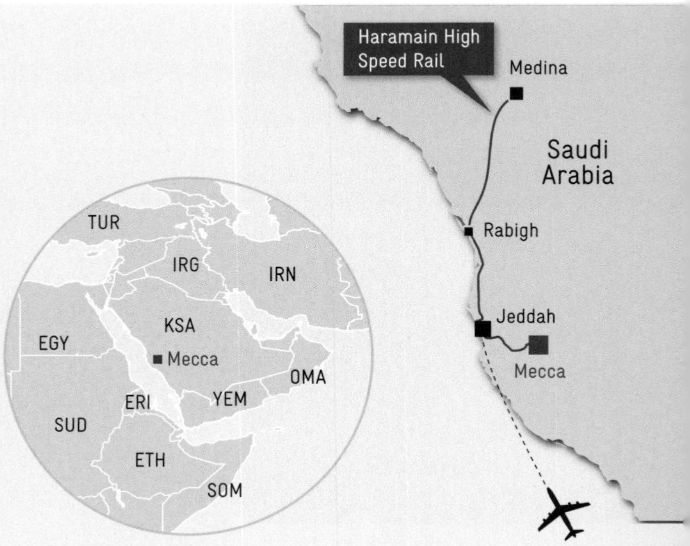
Haramain High Speed Rail
Medina
Saudi Arabia
Rabigh
Jeddah
Mecca
TUR
IRG
IRN
EGY
KSA
Mecca
OMA
ERI
YEM
SUD
ETH
SOM

ARRIVAL

More than 2 million people attend the Hajj every year. Most travel to Jeddah by plane. The Haramain High Speed Rail connects Jeddah to Mecca to ensure speedy and safe passage. The railway will also provide a connection to Medina, the second holiest city of Islam.

ORDER OF EVENTS

A preset series of actions must be followed to do the pilgrimage correctly. These start on the 8th day of the last month of the Islamic calender called »DHU AL-HIJJAH«:

8TH DHU AL-HIJJAH (1ST DAY)

- Entering the consecration/ putting on the pilgrim's garment
- Arrival Tawaf (circling the Kabaa seven times)
- Rushing back and forth between the rocks Safa and Marwah seven times
- Spending the night at Mina

9TH DHU AL-HIJJAH (2ND DAY)

- Lingering and praying close to Mount Arafat until sunset
- Collecting 70 small pebbles for the stoning ceremony from mountain Muzdalifah
- Spending the night in the open air close to Muzdalifah

10TH DHU AL-HIJJAH (3RD DAY)

- Stoning of the pillar Al-Aqaba from the Jamaraat Bridge
- Sacrificing an animal
- Shaving the head (men) or cutting the hair (women)
- Returning to Mecca for Tawaf al-Hajj
- Again moving back and forth between the rocks Safa and Marwah seven times
- Spending the night at Mina

FROM 11TH TO 13TH DHU AL-HIJJAH (4TH TO 6TH DAY)

- Staying in Mina up to three days for stoning all pillars three times
- Farewell Tawaf called Tawaf al-Wadaa

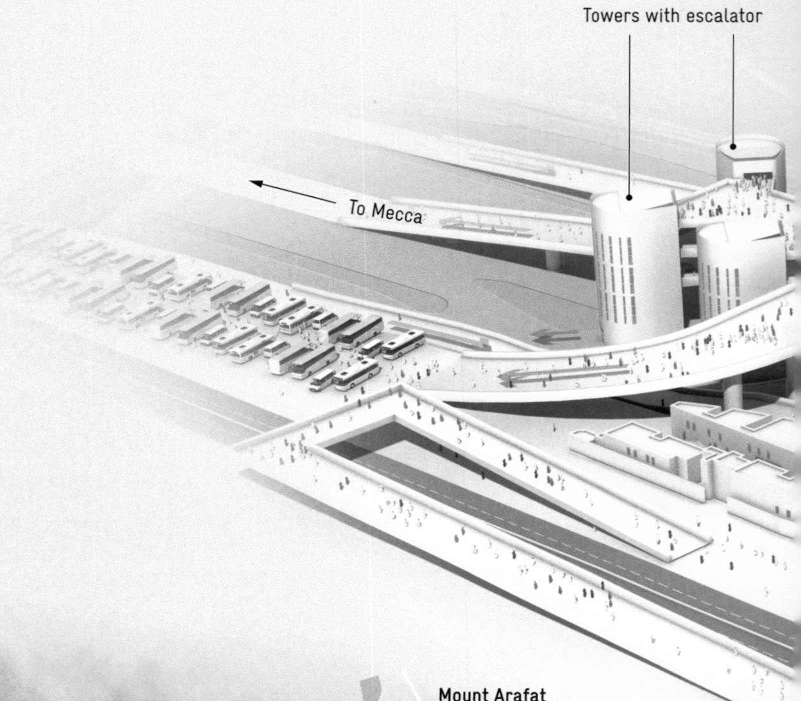
Towers with escalator
To Mecca

THE PILGRIMAGE ROUTE

Mina Mosque
Slaughterhouse
MINA
Jamaraat Bridge
Tent City
Al-Khaif Mosque
Mount Arafat »Mount of Mercy«
ARAFAT
Muzdalifah
Namira Mosque
Main pilgrimage route and sidewalk
Mecca
N
1 km

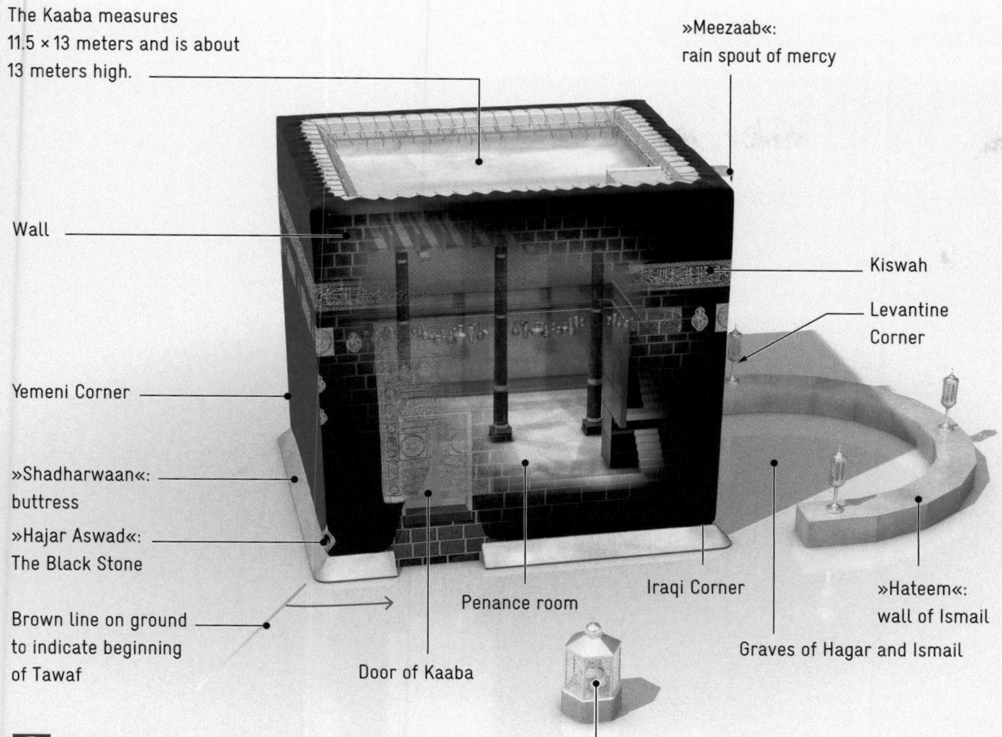
The Kaaba measures
11.5 × 13 meters and is about
13 meters high.
»Meezaab«:
rain spout of mercy
Wall
Kiswah
Levantine
Corner
Yemeni Corner
»Shadharwaan«:
buttress
»Hajar Aswad«:
The Black Stone
Penance room
Iraqi Corner
»Hateem«:
wall of Ismail
Brown line on ground
to indicate beginning
of Tawaf
Door of Kaaba
Graves of Hagar and Ismail
Station of Ibrahim

»KAABA« – HOUSE OF GOD

In Islam, the »Kaaba« (cube) is regarded as the first place of worship, which was first built by the first man and prophet Adam.

THE RITUAL WALKING IN MECCA

The performance of the »Sa'i« (search, ritual walking) serves to commemorate Hagar's (Abraham's wife) search for water for her son and God's mercy in answering prayers. You have to walk 7 times back and forth between the stones Marwa and Safa, 450 m away.

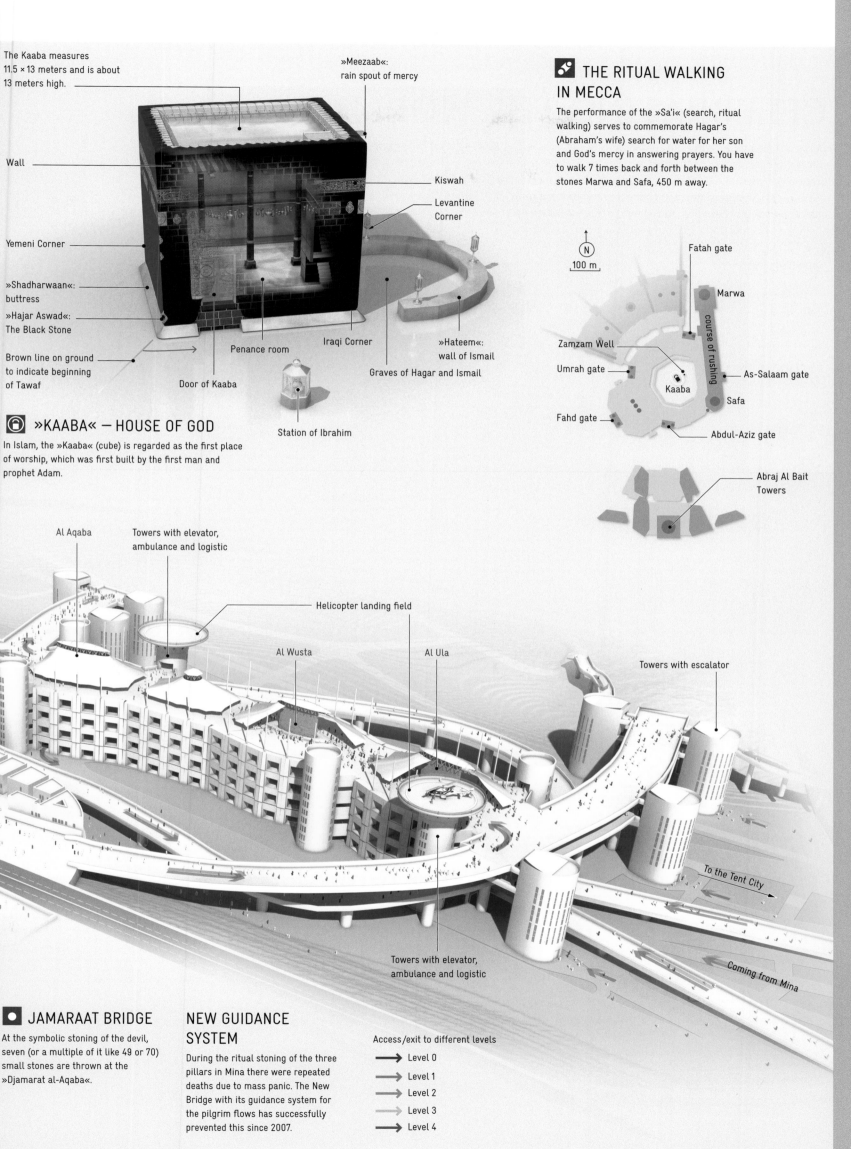

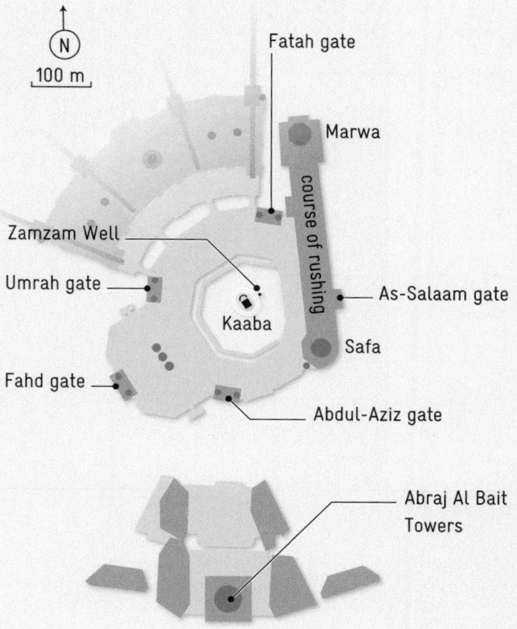
N
100 m
Fatah gate
Marwa
course of rushing
Zamzam Well
Umrah gate
As-Salaam gate
Kaaba
Safa
Fahd gate
Abdul-Aziz gate
Abraj Al Bait
Towers

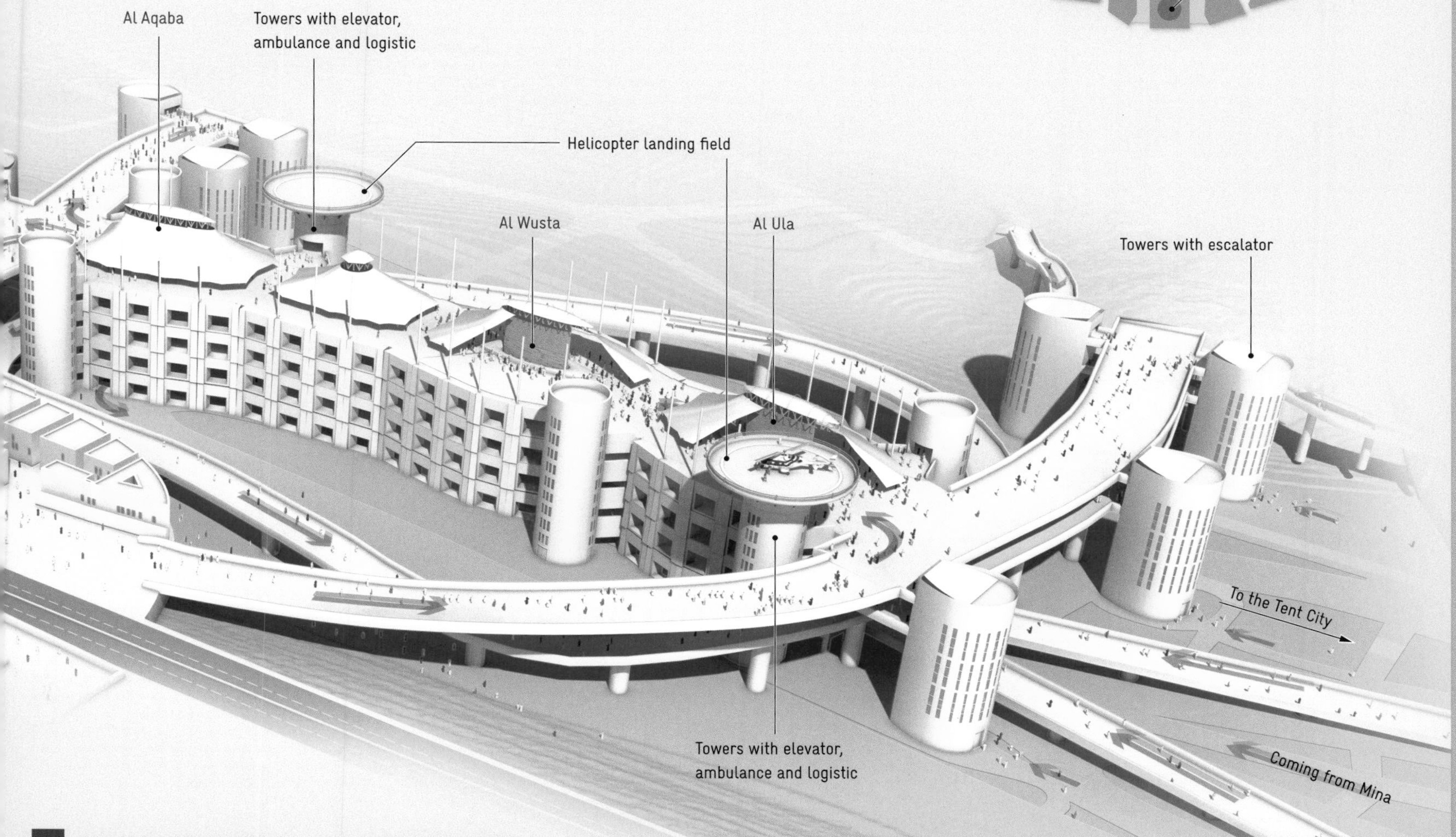
Al Aqaba
Towers with elevator,
ambulance and logistic
Helicopter landing field
Al Wusta
Al Ula
Towers with escalator
To the Tent City
Towers with elevator,
ambulance and logistic
Coming from Mina

JAMARAAT BRIDGE

At the symbolic stoning of the devil, seven (or a multiple of it like 49 or 70) small stones are thrown at the »Djamarat al-Aqaba«.

NEW GUIDANCE SYSTEM

During the ritual stoning of the three pillars in Mina there were repeated deaths due to mass panic. The New Bridge with its guidance system for the pilgrim flows has successfully prevented this since 2007.

Access/exit to different levels

- → Level 0
- → Level 1
- → Level 2
- → Level 3
- → Level 4

CELEBRATING THE WORLD

Being able to predict what the seasons will bring became a survival skill for humans as we evolved into an agricultural society. Calendars followed suit, becoming precise systems of order to organize around the seasons. The Georgian calendar—which is oriented by the Earth's orbit around the sun—has prevailed as the global standard. But many holidays are still calculated with older calendar systems that are oriented by the moon's orbit and phases.

KEY
(selection of holidays)

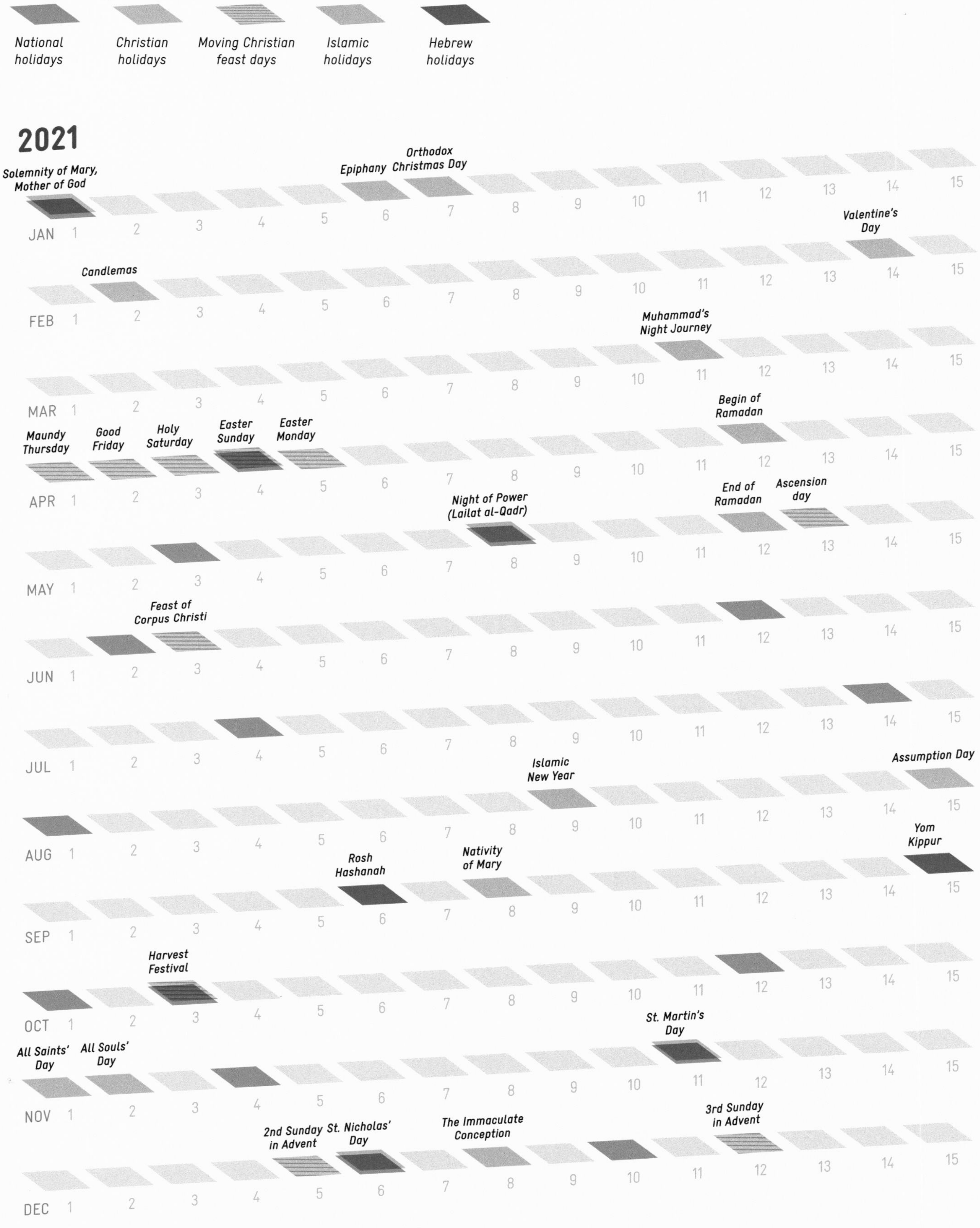

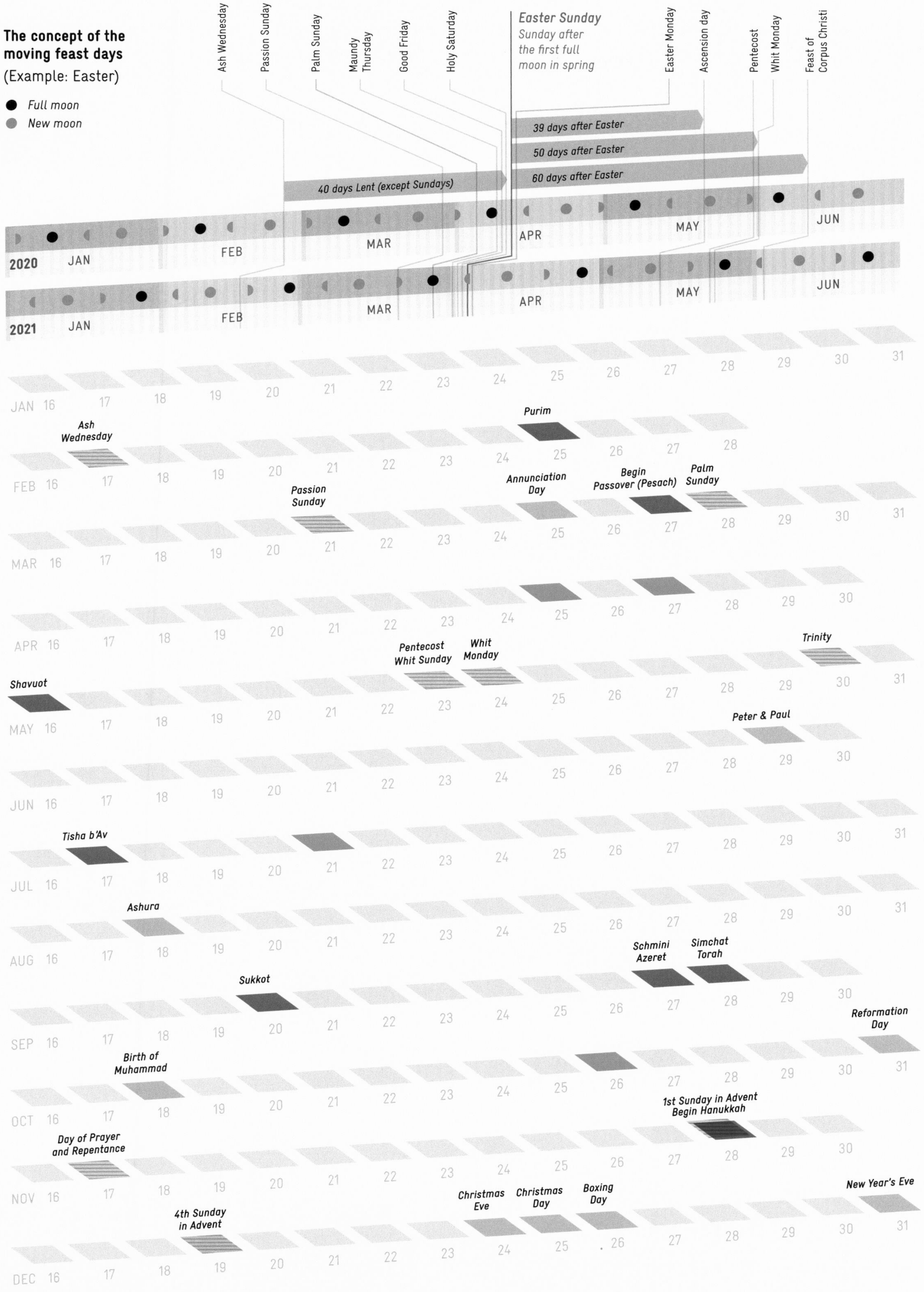
The concept of the moving feast days
(Example: Easter)
Full moon
New moon
Ash Wednesday
Passion Sunday
Palm Sunday
Maundy Thursday
Good Friday
Holy Saturday
Easter Sunday
Sunday after the first full moon in spring
Easter Monday
Ascension day
Pentecost
Whit Monday
Feast of Corpus Christi
39 days after Easter
50 days after Easter
60 days after Easter
40 days Lent (except Sundays)
2020
2021
JAN
FEB
MAR
APR
MAY
JUN
Ash Wednesday
Purim
Passion Sunday
Annunciation Day
Begin Passover (Pesach)
Palm Sunday
Pentecost Whit Sunday
Whit Monday
Trinity
Shavuot
Peter & Paul
Tisha b'Av
Ashura
Schmini Azeret
Simchat Torah
Sukkot
Reformation Day
Birth of Muhammad
1st Sunday in Advent Begin Hanukkah
Day of Prayer and Repentance
Christmas Eve
Christmas Day
Boxing Day
New Year's Eve
4th Sunday in Advent
JAN
FEB
MAR
APR
MAY
JUN
JUL
AUG
SEP
OCT
NOV
DEC

THE FUTURE IS FEMALE

Worldwide, birth rates are falling. In 1960, women had an average of five children. By 2016, the global fertility rate had dropped to 2.4 children per woman and it's still declining. At the same time, the sex ratio shifted significantly towards men. Today, for every 100 women between age zero and 24, there are 107 men. This means there are 104 million women »missing« in this age group.

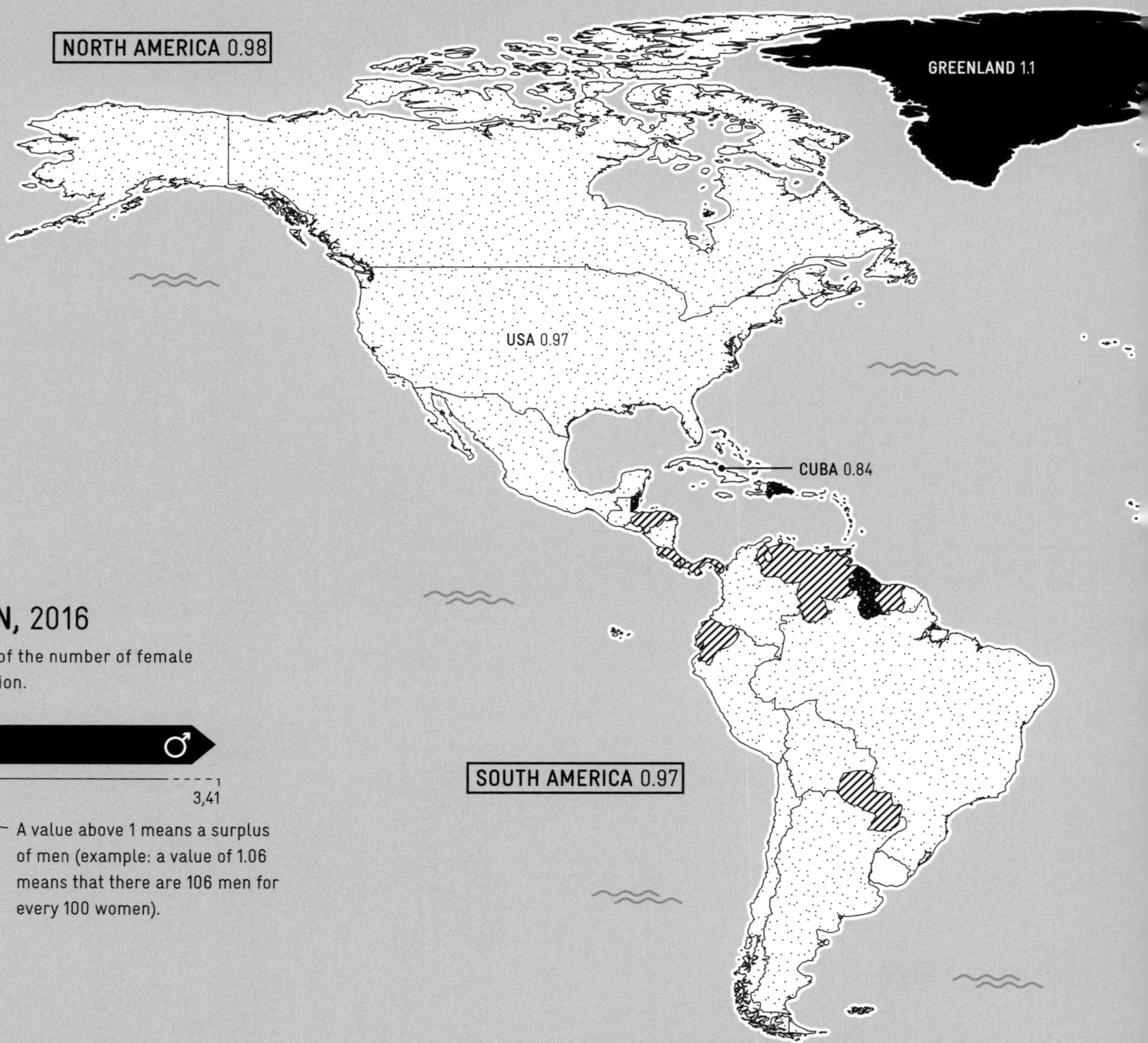
NORTH AMERICA 0.98
GREENLAND 1.1
USA 0.97
CUBA 0.84
SOUTH AMERICA 0.97

SEX RATIO OF TOTAL POPULATION, 2016

The gender distribution (sex ratio) describes the ratio of the number of female members to the number of male members in a population.

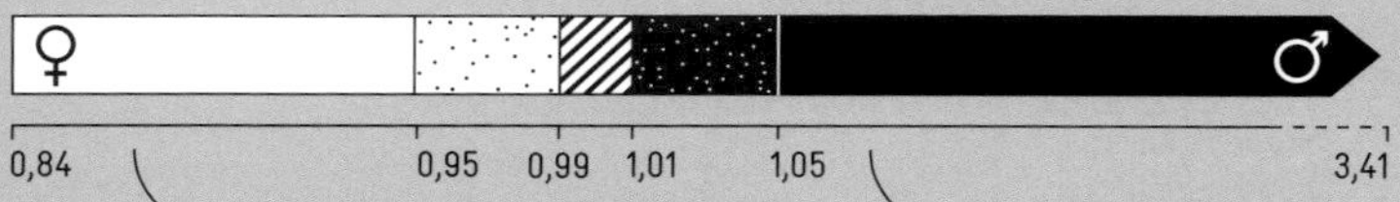
♀
♂
0,84
0,95
0,99
1,01
1,05
3,41

A value below 1 means a surplus of women (example: a value of 0.97 means that there are 97 men for every 100 women).

A value above 1 means a surplus of men (example: a value of 1.06 means that there are 106 men for every 100 women).

SEX RATIO AT BIRTH OVER TIME

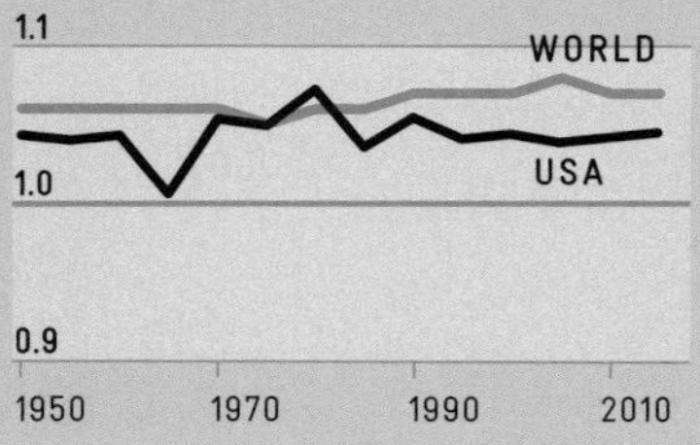
1.1
WORLD
1.0
USA
0.9
1950
1970
1990
2010

The sex ratios at birth within large population groups are very steady. For a long time, on average 106 boys were born for every 100 girls; a sex ratio of 1.06. Since the '90s it has risen to 1.07.

INDIA

Around 80 % of the Indian population is Hindu. The bride has to bring a substantial dowry into the marriage and therefore having a daughter means risking poverty. To escape this financial burden, the sex of the child is determined with prenatal diagnostics and girls are often aborted.

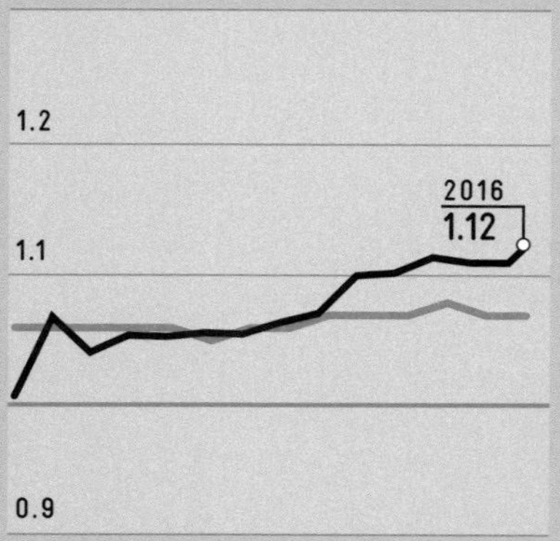
1.2
2016
1.12
1.1
0.9

LIECHTENSTEIN

The highest infant sex ratio worldwide in 2016 was a statistical anomaly. With just under 38,000 inhabitants, Liechtenstein is the 7th-least populated country in the world—only 300–400 children are born every year. Liechtenstein's longterm sex ratio of 1.07 is similar to the worldwide average.

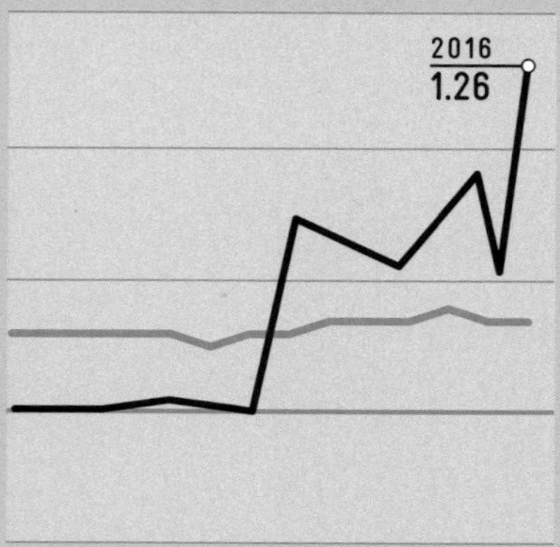
2016
1.26

ARMENIA

A distinct culture of lineage holders prevails here. The pressure to give birth to a boy is enormous, also because the fertility rate is continuously decreasing. There is hardly any prenatal sex selection, but if the first two or three children are only girls, many parents start to select boys.

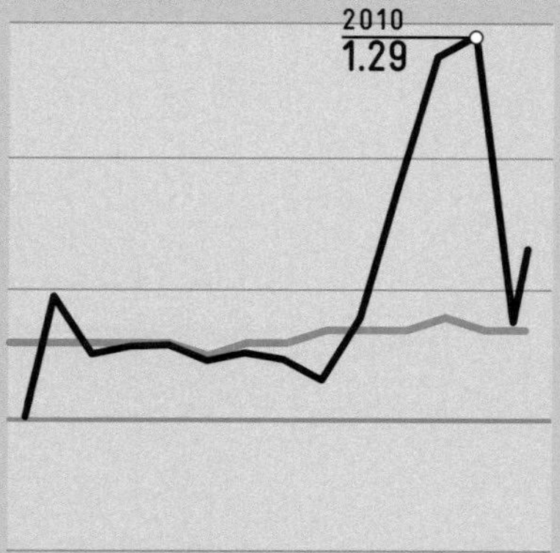
2010
1.29

CUBA

Radioactivity affects sex chromosomes. After the Chernobyl reactor catastrophe in 1986 the sex ratio in Russia and Europe increased for a short time, but in Cuba it increased for over 10 years. Some scientists hypothesized that this long-term increase was related to food imports (powdered milk and cereals) from Russia.

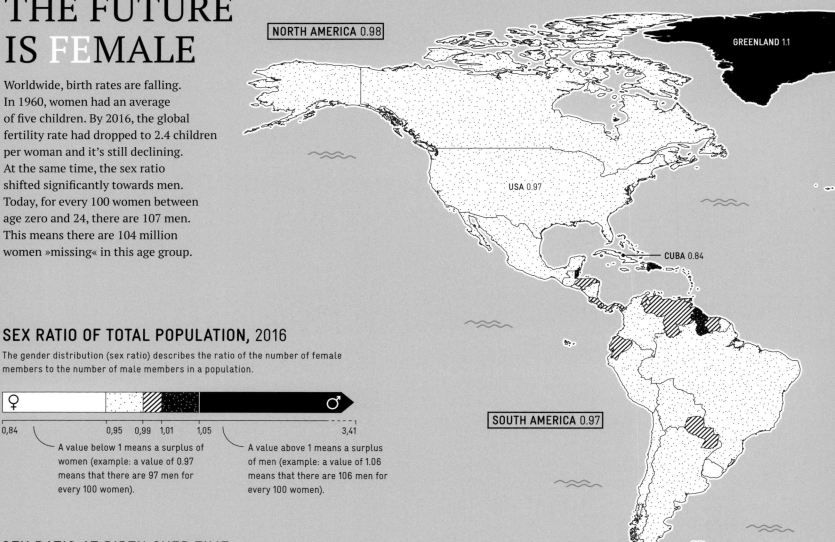

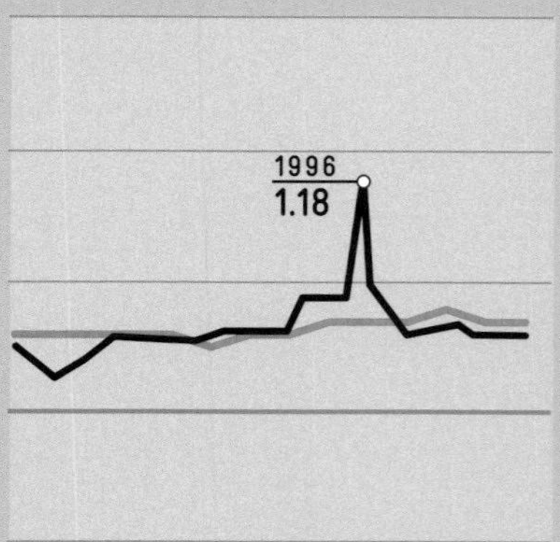
1996
1.18

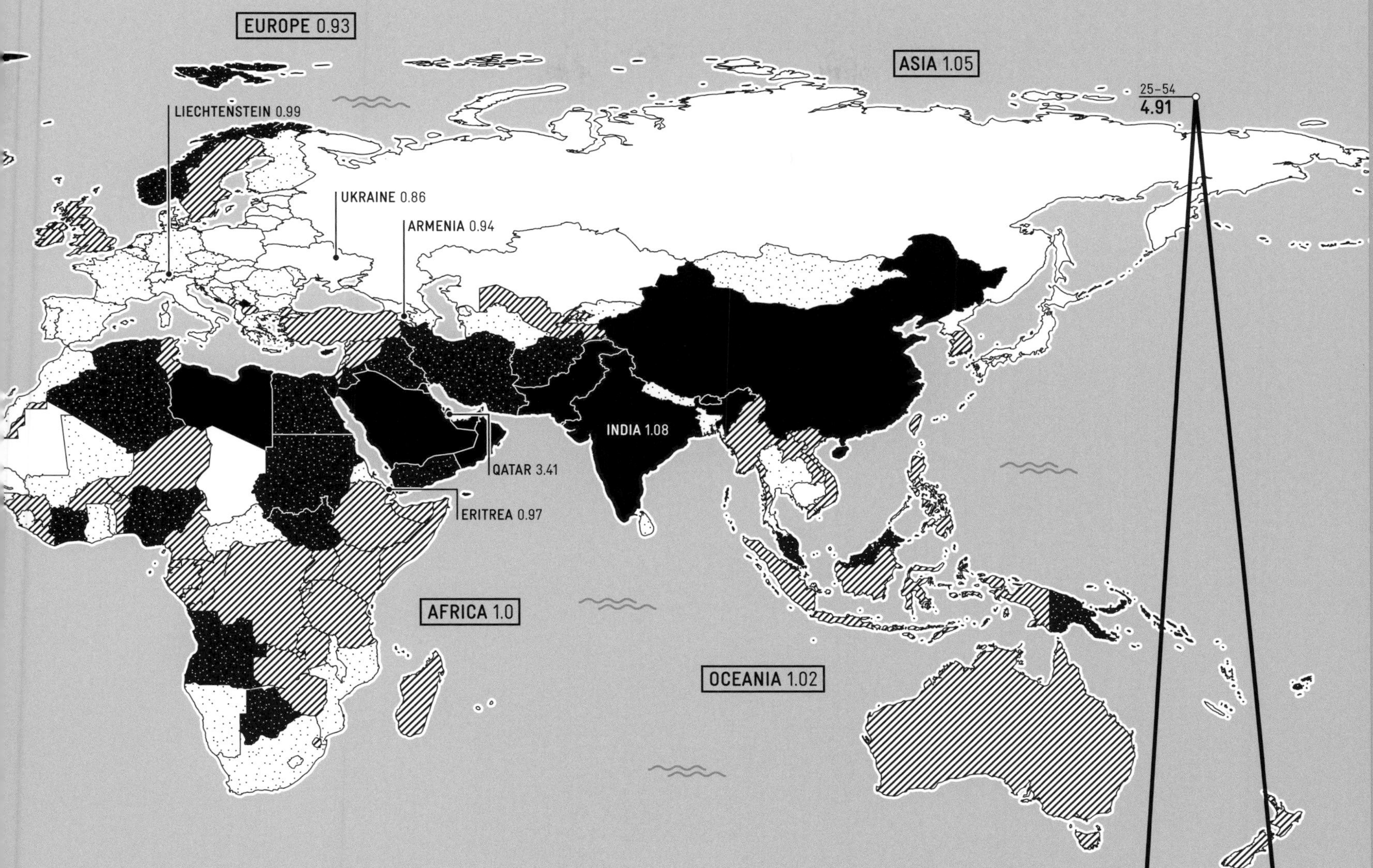
EUROPE 0.93
ASIA 1.05
LIECHTENSTEIN 0.99
UKRAINE 0.86
ARMENIA 0.94
25–54
4.91
INDIA 1.08
QATAR 3.41
ERITREA 0.97
AFRICA 1.0
OCEANIA 1.02

SEX RATIO BY AGE GROUPS, 2016

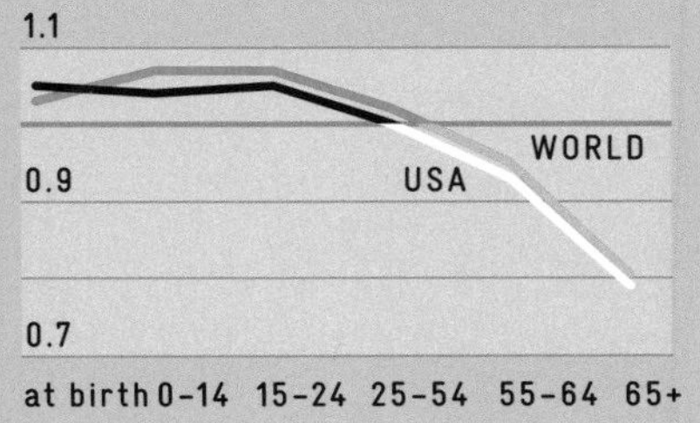
1.1
0.9
0.7
WORLD
USA
at birth 0–14 15–24 25–54 55–64 65+

With age, the sex ratio shifts towards women because men have a shorter life expectancy. In the age group of 65 and over, there is an average of only 80 men for every 100 women.

UKRAINE

In this former Soviet Republic a lot of men were coal miners. Poor working conditions and alcoholism decreased life expectancy notably. This phenomenon of an above-average surplus of women over 65 can also be observed in the Baltic States.

ERITREA

The proportion of men in the 15–24 age group in the East African country is 7.5 % below the world average. In 2016, out of every 1,000 Eritreans, 14.7 emigrate, mostly young men. In Germany three quarters of refugees in this age group are men.

GREENLAND

After WWII many qualified Danish workers moved to this arctic island to help modernize their former colony. They often married and returned home with a Greenlandic wife then.

QATAR

81 % of all Qataris are foreigners. With 18.2 migrants for every 1,000 inhabitants, the country has the highest net migration rate in the world. Young men, predominantly from India and Pakistan, come to Qatar to work and provide for their families back home. The men often stay for decades.

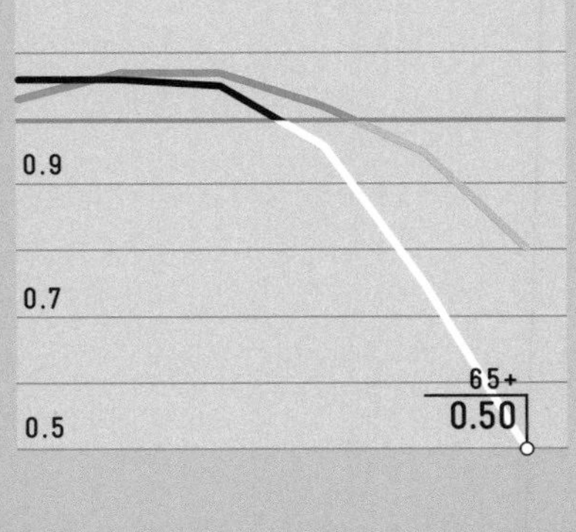
1.2
0.9
0.7
0.5
65+
0.50

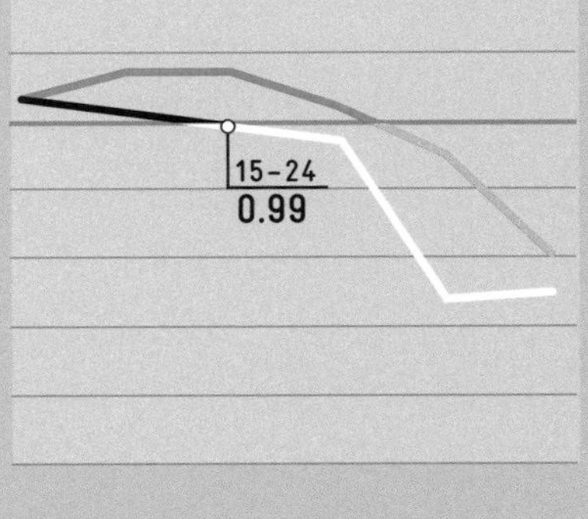
15–24
0.99

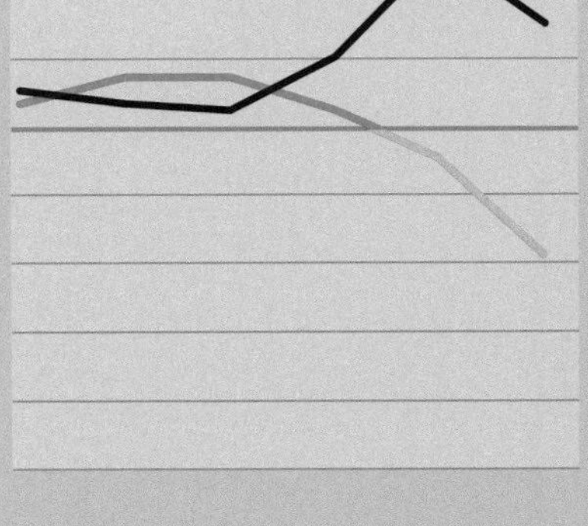
55–64
1.26

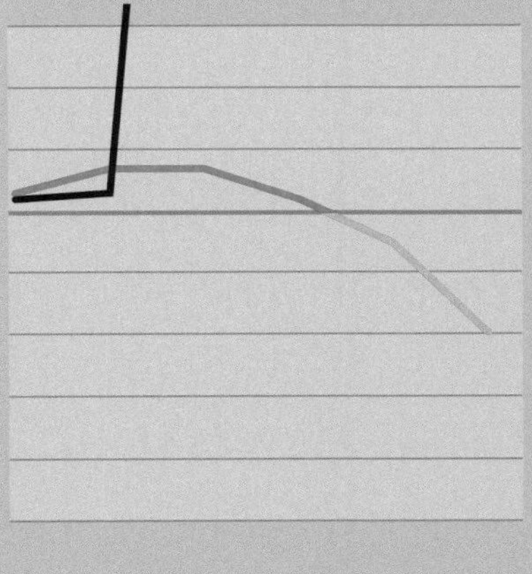

SEX@WORK

Over 40 million people in Germany are employed. According to the Federal Statistical Office's microcensus, the proportion of men and women is almost equal. However, looking at specific fields the differences become more apparent. What influences career choices—requirements, traditions or stereotypes?

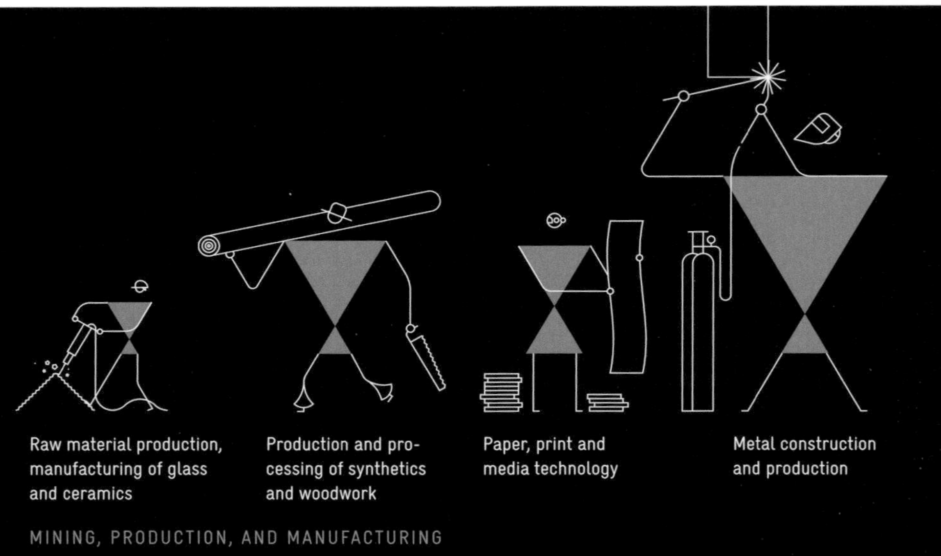
Raw material production, manufacturing of glass and ceramics
Production and processing of synthetics and woodwork
Paper, print and media technology
Metal construction and production
MINING, PRODUCTION, AND MANUFACTURING

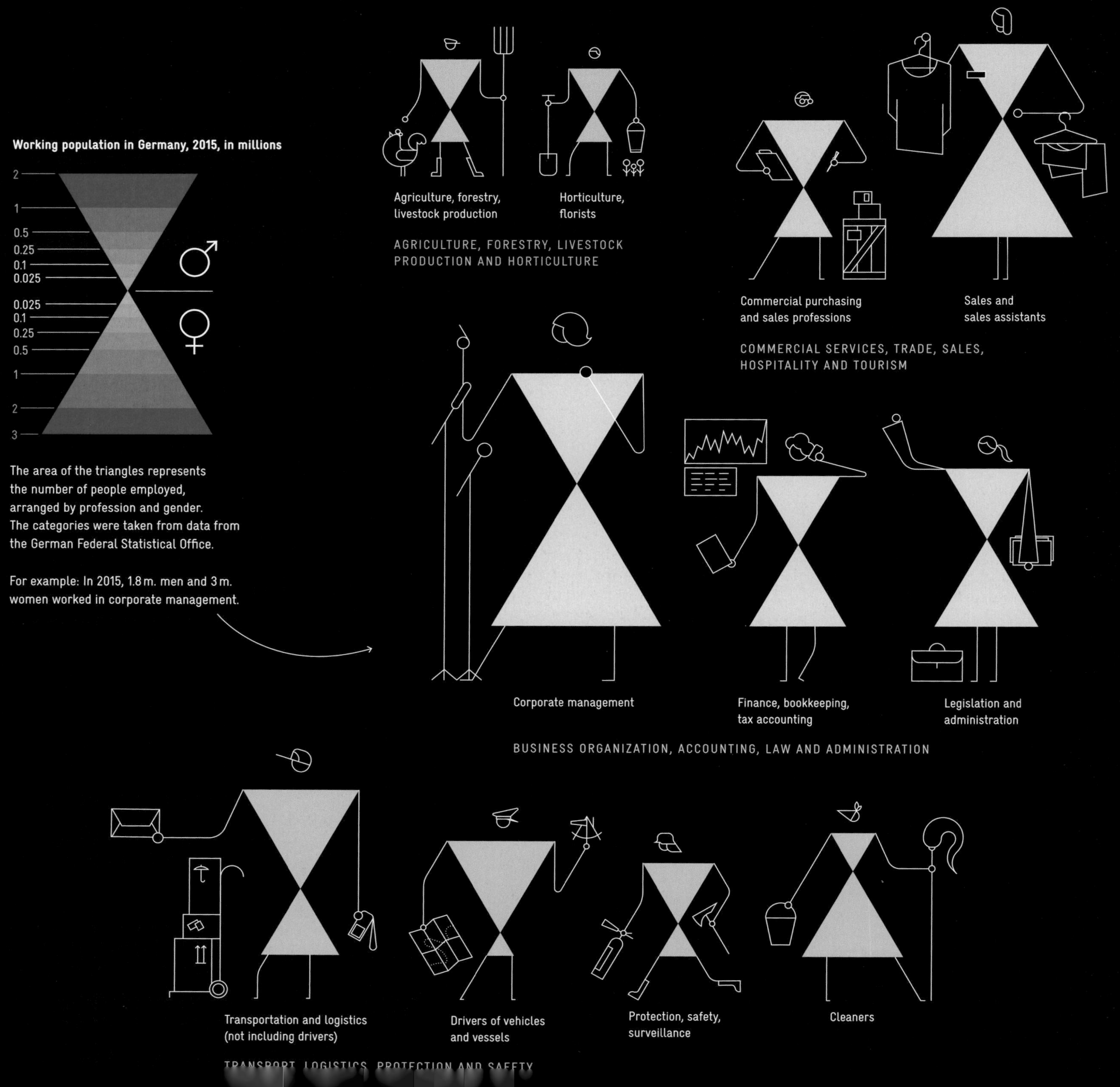
Working population in Germany, 2015, in millions
2
1
0.5
0.25
0.1
0.025
♂
0.025
0.1
0.25
0.5
1
2
3
♀
The area of the triangles represents the number of people employed, arranged by profession and gender. The categories were taken from data from the German Federal Statistical Office.
For example: In 2015, 1.8 m. men and 3 m. women worked in corporate management.
Agriculture, forestry, livestock production
Horticulture, florists
AGRICULTURE, FORESTRY, LIVESTOCK PRODUCTION AND HORTICULTURE
Commercial purchasing and sales professions
Sales and sales assistants
COMMERCIAL SERVICES, TRADE, SALES, HOSPITALITY AND TOURISM
Corporate management
Finance, bookkeeping, tax accounting
Legislation and administration
BUSINESS ORGANIZATION, ACCOUNTING, LAW AND ADMINISTRATION
Transportation and logistics (not including drivers)
Drivers of vehicles and vessels
Protection, safety, surveillance
Cleaners
TRANSPORT, LOGISTICS, PROTECTION AND SAFETY

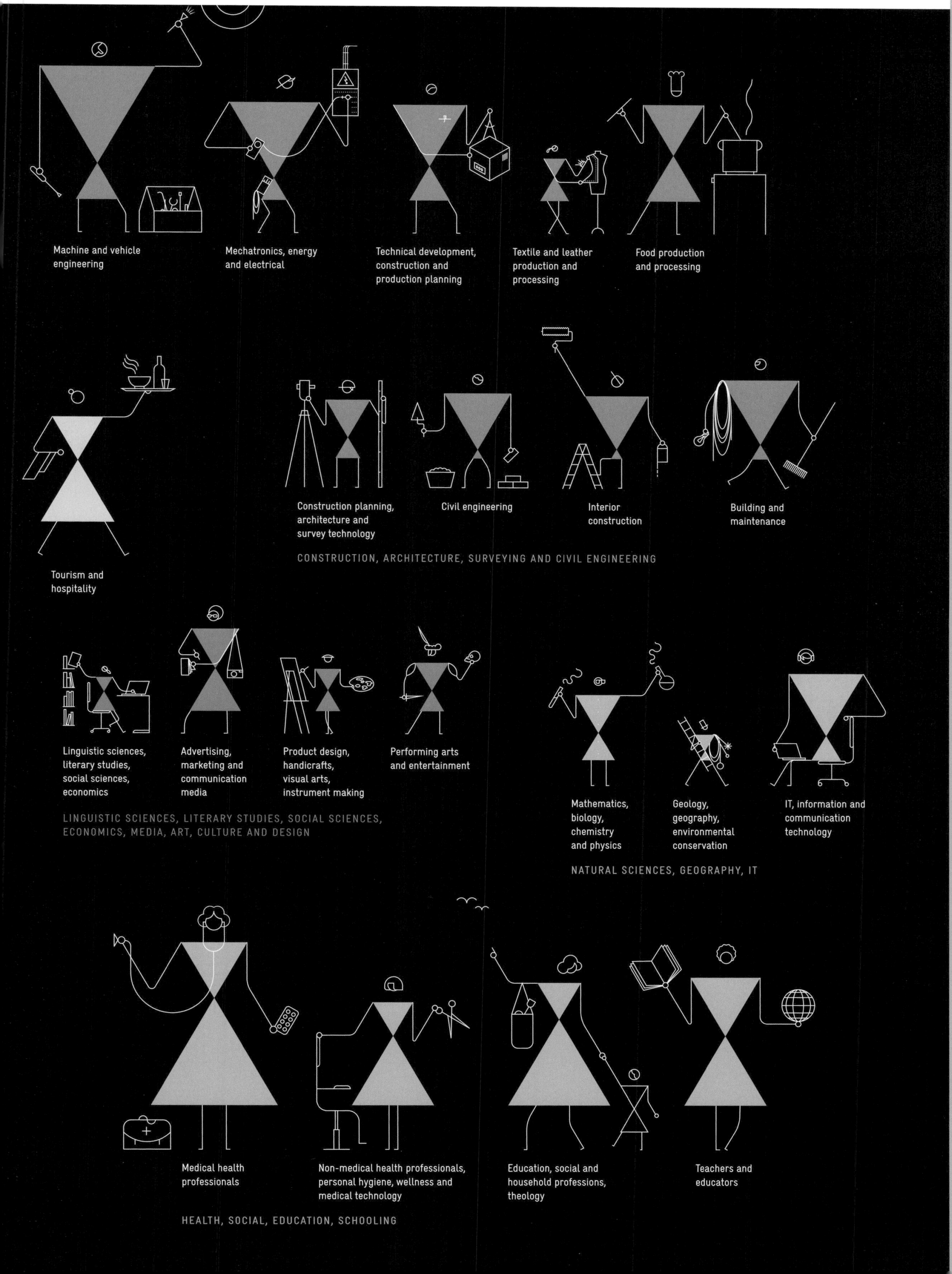
Machine and vehicle engineering
Mechatronics, energy and electrical
Technical development, construction and production planning
Textile and leather production and processing
Food production and processing
Tourism and hospitality
Construction planning, architecture and survey technology
Civil engineering
Interior construction
Building and maintenance
CONSTRUCTION, ARCHITECTURE, SURVEYING AND CIVIL ENGINEERING
Linguistic sciences, literary studies, social sciences, economics
Advertising, marketing and communication media
Product design, handicrafts, visual arts, instrument making
Performing arts and entertainment
LINGUISTIC SCIENCES, LITERARY STUDIES, SOCIAL SCIENCES, ECONOMICS, MEDIA, ART, CULTURE AND DESIGN
Mathematics, biology, chemistry and physics
Geology, geography, environmental conservation
IT, information and communication technology
NATURAL SCIENCES, GEOGRAPHY, IT
Medical health professionals
Non-medical health professionals, personal hygiene, wellness and medical technology
Education, social and household professions, theology
Teachers and educators
HEALTH, SOCIAL, EDUCATION, SCHOOLING

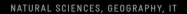

WELCOME TO THE 27 CLUB

»Now he's gone and joined that stupid club« was Wendy O'Connor's statement when she heard her son, Nirvana founder Kurt Cobain, had died. A quarter century after its first member was inaugurated into the 27 Club, the group had a name and a legend was born.

Brian Jones 1942 • 1969

»Jones was perhaps more of a Rolling Stone than any of the others,« wrote Greil Marcus in Rolling Stone magazine. Sex (with ensuing paternity suits), drugs and rock'n'roll all marked the Rolling Stones' founding guitarist. Today he has another distinction: as the pioneering member of the 27 Club. Jones was found dead in his swimming pool in Hartfield, Sussex, on July 3, 1969, at the age of 27. A month earlier, the band asked him to leave, saying his drug and alcohol use was becoming a problem.

Janis Joplin 1943 • 1970

»Maybe I won't last as long as other singers ...« said the singer herself. On October 4, 1970, singer Janis Joplin joined the 27 Club, just weeks after Hendrix. She was found with a broken nose and holding US$4.50 in her hand. But despite the rumors her condition inspired, the coroner said she died of a heroin overdose.

Jimi Hendrix 1942 • 1970

»In rock guitar, there are but two eras—before Hendrix and after Hendrix,« wrote Andy Aledort in his book about the rock legend. The limits of his talent were never known. He died on September 18, 1970 after asphyxiating on his own vomit after mixing sleeping pills and red wine.

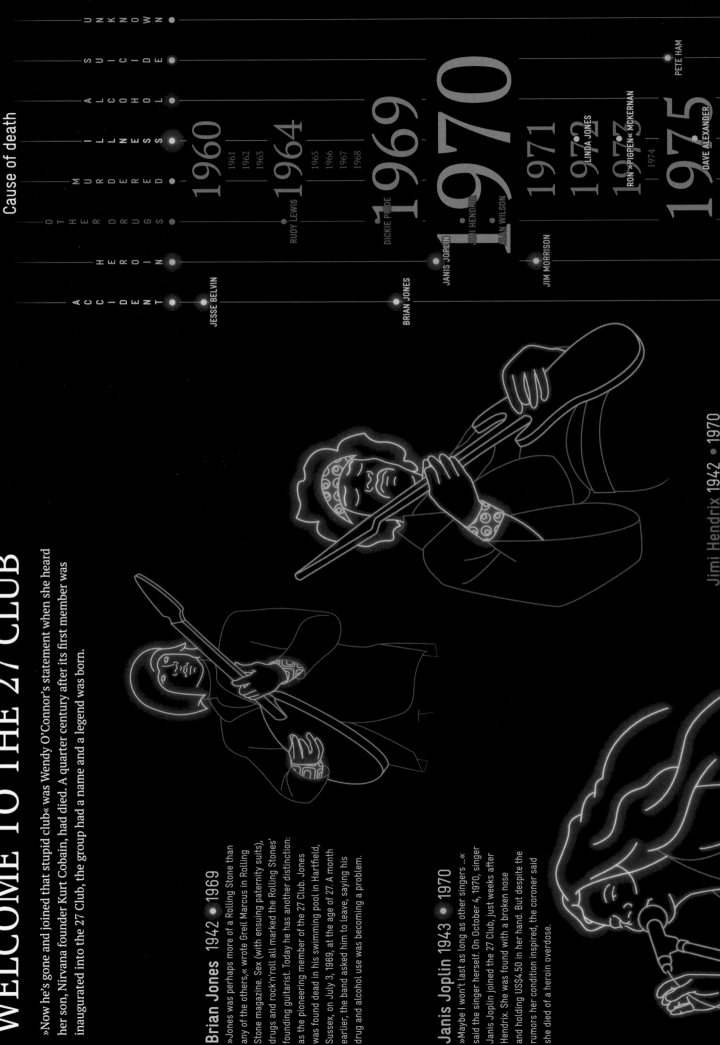

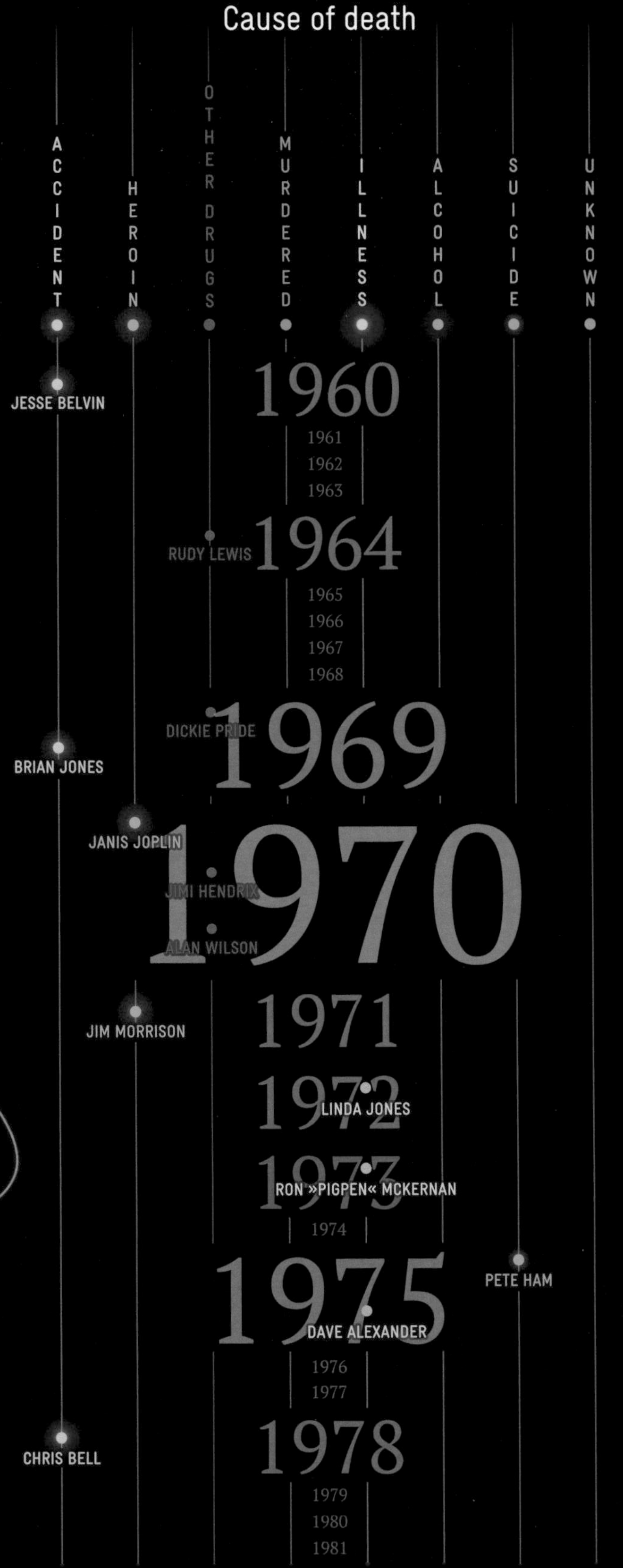
Cause of death
ACCIDENT
HEROIN
OTHER DRUGS
MURDERED
ILLNESS
ALCOHOL
SUICIDE
UNKNOWN
1960
JESSE BELVIN
1961
1962
1963
1964
RUDY LEWIS
1965
1966
1967
1968
1969
DICKIE PRIDE
BRIAN JONES
1970
JANIS JOPLIN
JIMI HENDRIX
ALAN WILSON
1971
JIM MORRISON
1972
LINDA JONES
1973
RON »PIGPEN« MCKERNAN
1974
1975
PETE HAM
DAVE ALEXANDER
1976
1977
1978
CHRIS BELL
1979
1980
1981

Jim Morrison 1943 • 1971

»He'd have no regard for his physical body. He just abused it,« said a former secretary for the Doors. Yet lead singer Morrison's death certificate cites »natural causes« on July 3, 1971. The self-titled Lizard King was in Paris when he died, recovering from an excessive life in Los Angeles. His death was rumored for days before it became official, with his manager saying Morrison's loved ones wanted to avoid the circus that Joplin and Hendrix's death had caused.

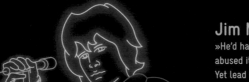

Kurt Cobain 1967 • 1994

»Hey, man, that really scared everybody. And I don't want you to die« Nirvana drummer Dave Grohl told Kurt Cobain. The lead singer and godfather of grunge had just overdosed in Italy, but survived. Later his widow Courtney Love would say it was his first suicide attempt. A month later, on April 5, 1994, while high on drugs, he shot himself.

Amy Winehouse 1982 • 2011

»Sadly, she was all too aware of the 27 Club and was never scared to join it,« a friend of Winehouse told the Daily Mirror. The crooner did just that on July 27, 2011, making the 27 Club relevant for a new generation. She was just as famous for her voice as her party girl reputation. When she died, she had a blood alcohol level of .416, which was enough to repress her breathing.

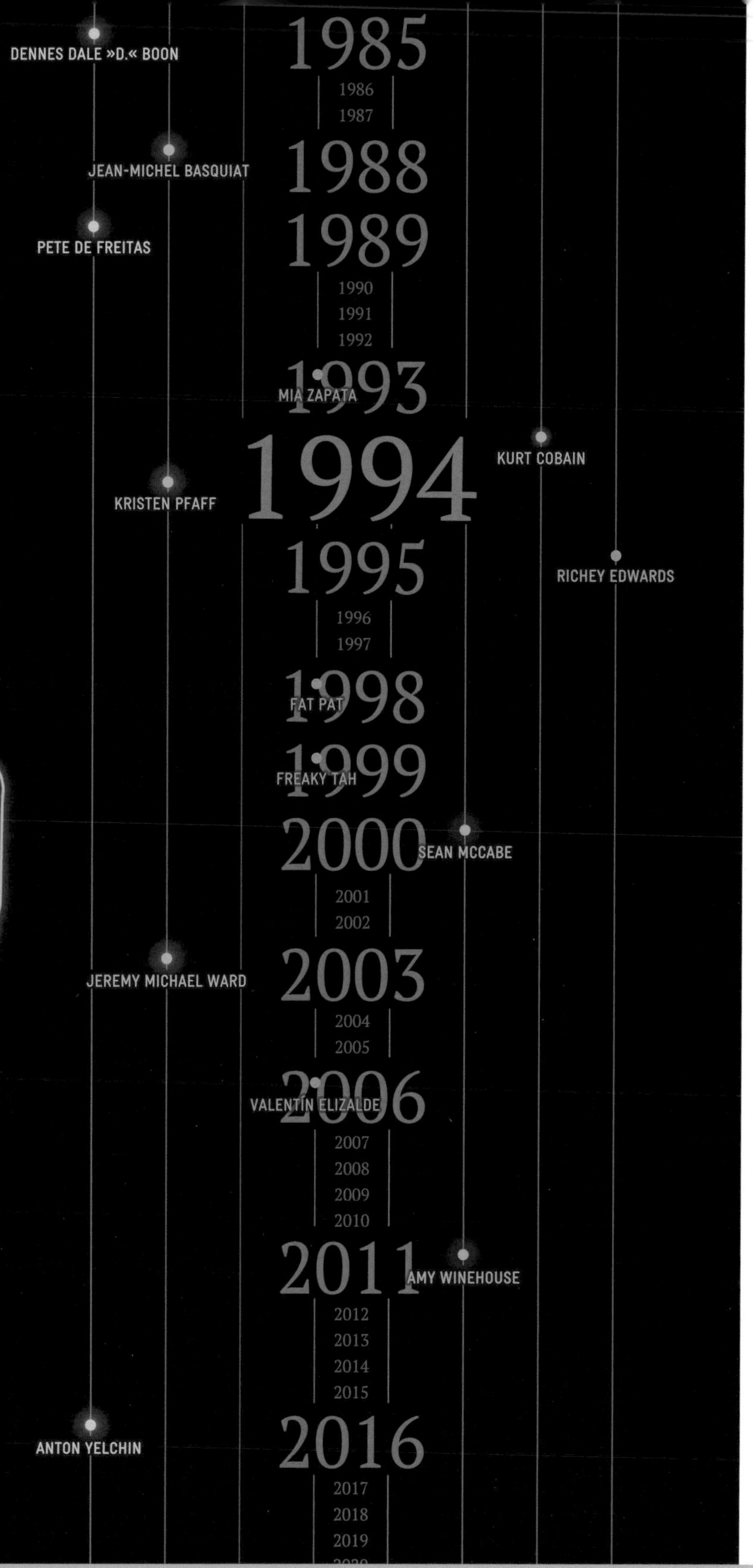

1985
DENNES DALE »D.« BOON
1986
1987
1988
JEAN-MICHEL BASQUIAT
1989
PETE DE FREITAS
1990
1991
1992
1993
MIA ZAPATA
1994
KURT COBAIN
KRISTEN PFAFF
1995
RICHEY EDWARDS
1996
1997
1998
FAT PAT
1999
FREAKY TAH
2000
SEAN MCCABE
2001
2002
2003
JEREMY MICHAEL WARD
2004
2005
2006
VALENTIN ELIZALDE
2007
2008
2009
2010
2011
AMY WINEHOUSE
2012
2013
2014
2015
2016
ANTON YELCHIN
2017
2018
2019

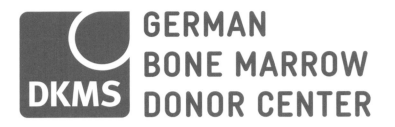

GERMAN BONE MARROW DONOR CENTER

Mechtild Harf was diagnosed with leukemia in 1990—her only chance of survival was a stem cell donation. In those days, only 3,000 donors were registered in Germany and Mechtild died from her disease. Her husband, Dr. Peter Harf, founded the DKMS together with family and friends in 1991. Since then, the DKMS has worked on one vision: eliminating blood cancer.

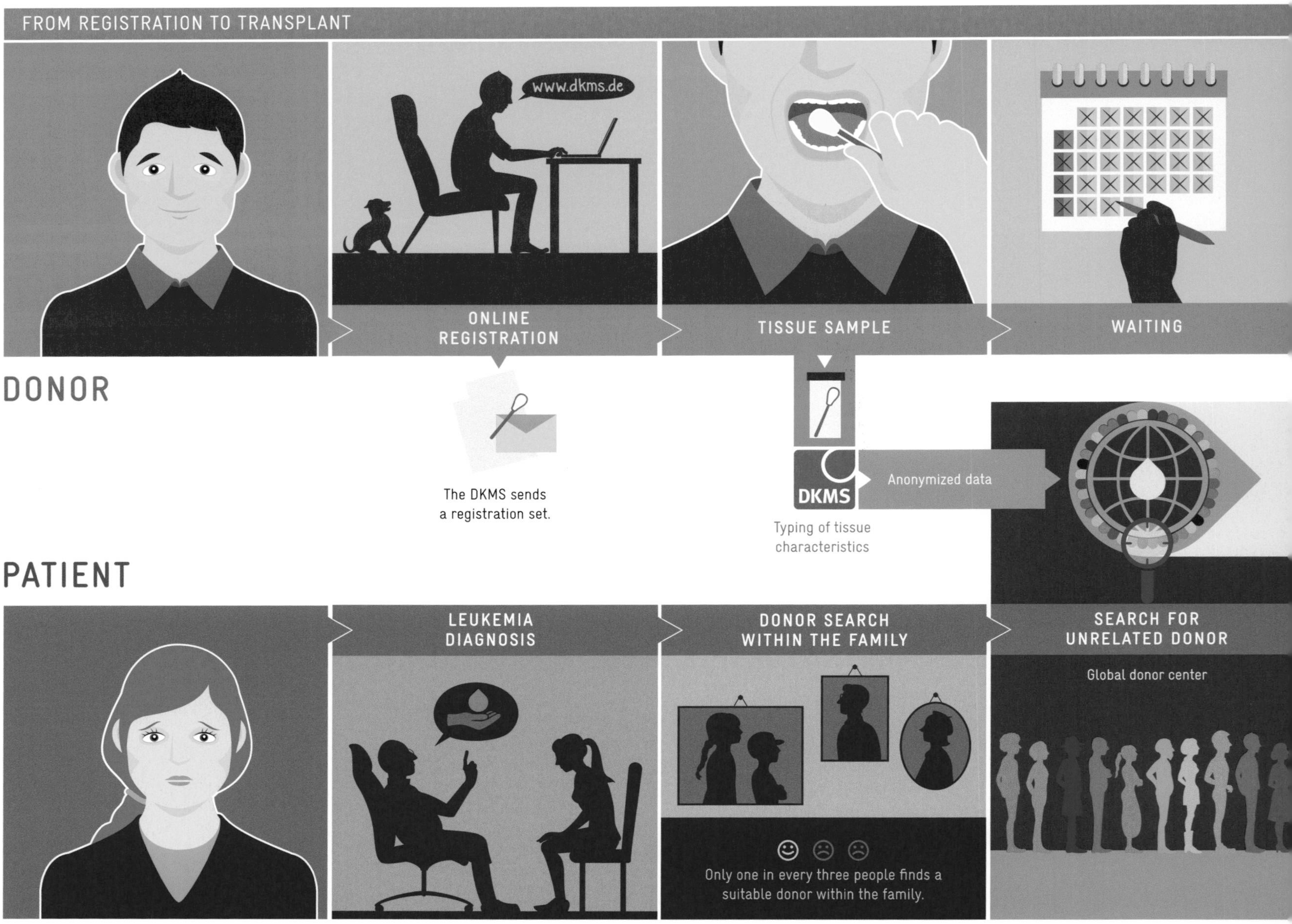
FROM REGISTRATION TO TRANSPLANT
www.dkms.de
ONLINE REGISTRATION
TISSUE SAMPLE
WAITING
DONOR
The DKMS sends a registration set.
DKMS
Anonymized data
Typing of tissue characteristics
PATIENT
LEUKEMIA DIAGNOSIS
DONOR SEARCH WITHIN THE FAMILY
SEARCH FOR UNRELATED DONOR
Global donor center
Only one in every three people finds a suitable donor within the family.

GOOD REASONS FOR A STEM CELL DONATION

EVERY **15** MINUTES
a patient is given a leukemia diagnosis in Germany.

1 IN **10**
leukemia patients in Germany does not find a suitable donor.

MORE THAN **9** M.
donors make the DKMS the largest stem cell donation center in the world, but many more donors are still needed!

To help leukemia patients all over the world, the DKMS is also active in the US, the UK, Spain and Poland. Any healthy person between the age of 17 and 55 can register as a donor. The DKMS also needs monetary donations. The mere registration of a new donor costs the DKMS €35. In the battle against leukemia, every euro counts.

WHAT IS LEUKEMIA?

Non-functioning white blood cells are formed in abundance and suppress healthy blood cells. Immune defense, oxygen transport and blood coagulation are impaired.

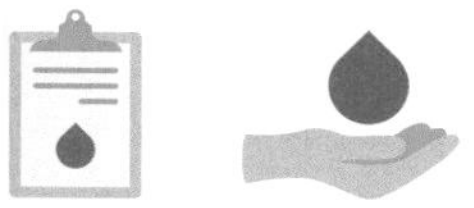

Leukemia diagnosis:
a stem cell transplant is often the only chance of survival.

Tissue characteristics exist in more than 10,000 manifestations, which makes the search for a »genetic twin« extremely difficult.

WHICH STEM CELLS?

Stem cells in the bone marrow are responsible for the blood's formation of new cells. These then build the blood's main components.

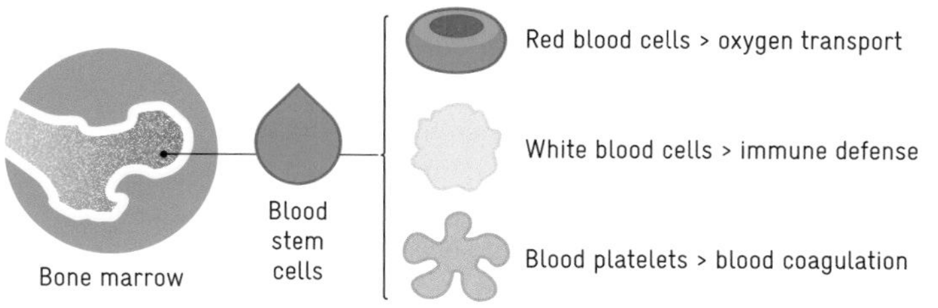

Bone marrow
Blood stem cells
Red blood cells > oxygen transport
White blood cells > immune defense
Blood platelets > blood coagulation

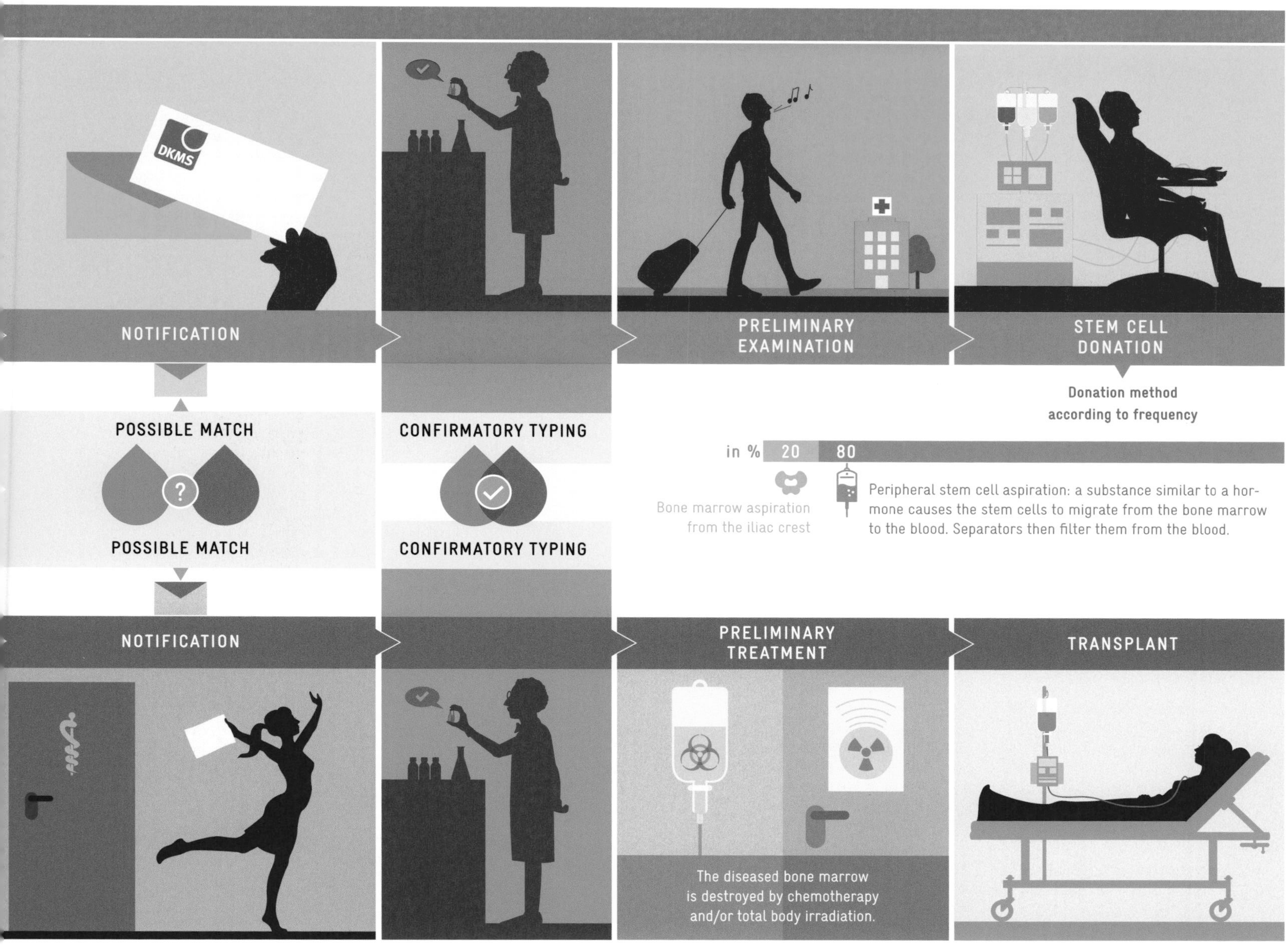

DKMS
NOTIFICATION
PRELIMINARY EXAMINATION
STEM CELL DONATION
Donation method according to frequency
in % 20 80
Bone marrow aspiration from the iliac crest
Peripheral stem cell aspiration: a substance similar to a hormone causes the stem cells to migrate from the bone marrow to the blood. Separators then filter them from the blood.
POSSIBLE MATCH
CONFIRMATORY TYPING
POSSIBLE MATCH
CONFIRMATORY TYPING
NOTIFICATION
PRELIMINARY TREATMENT
TRANSPLANT
The diseased bone marrow is destroyed by chemotherapy and/or total body irradiation.

www.dkms.de

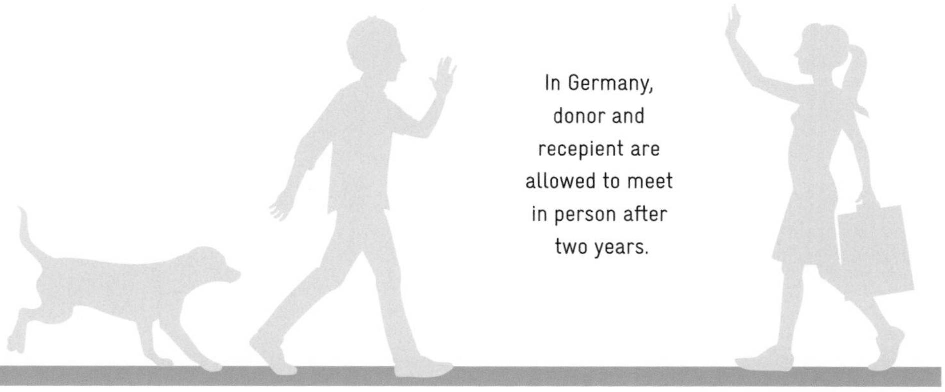

In Germany, donor and recepient are allowed to meet in person after two years.

LOVE AROUND THE WORLD

»Roses are red
Violets are Blue
St. Valentine lost his head
Because they said 'I do'.«

Legend has it that on February 14, 259 AD, the Roman emperor Claudius II beheaded the bishop who would later be canonized as St. Valentine.
His crime was presiding over the weddings of soldiers that were forbidden to be married by the emperor. These secret newlyweds were given bouquets from the bishop's own garden.
Today, Valentine's Day is derided as a commercial holiday that is nonetheless celebrated by billions of lovers around the world. In France, couples meet for romantic meals while Italians spend a weekend away. In China, nothing can compare with cosmetic surgery, which is a popular gift for the day. In Germany, 73 percent see Valentine's Day as pointless, but that's only because they think every day should be a day of love.

How many men between 25 and 34 are married?

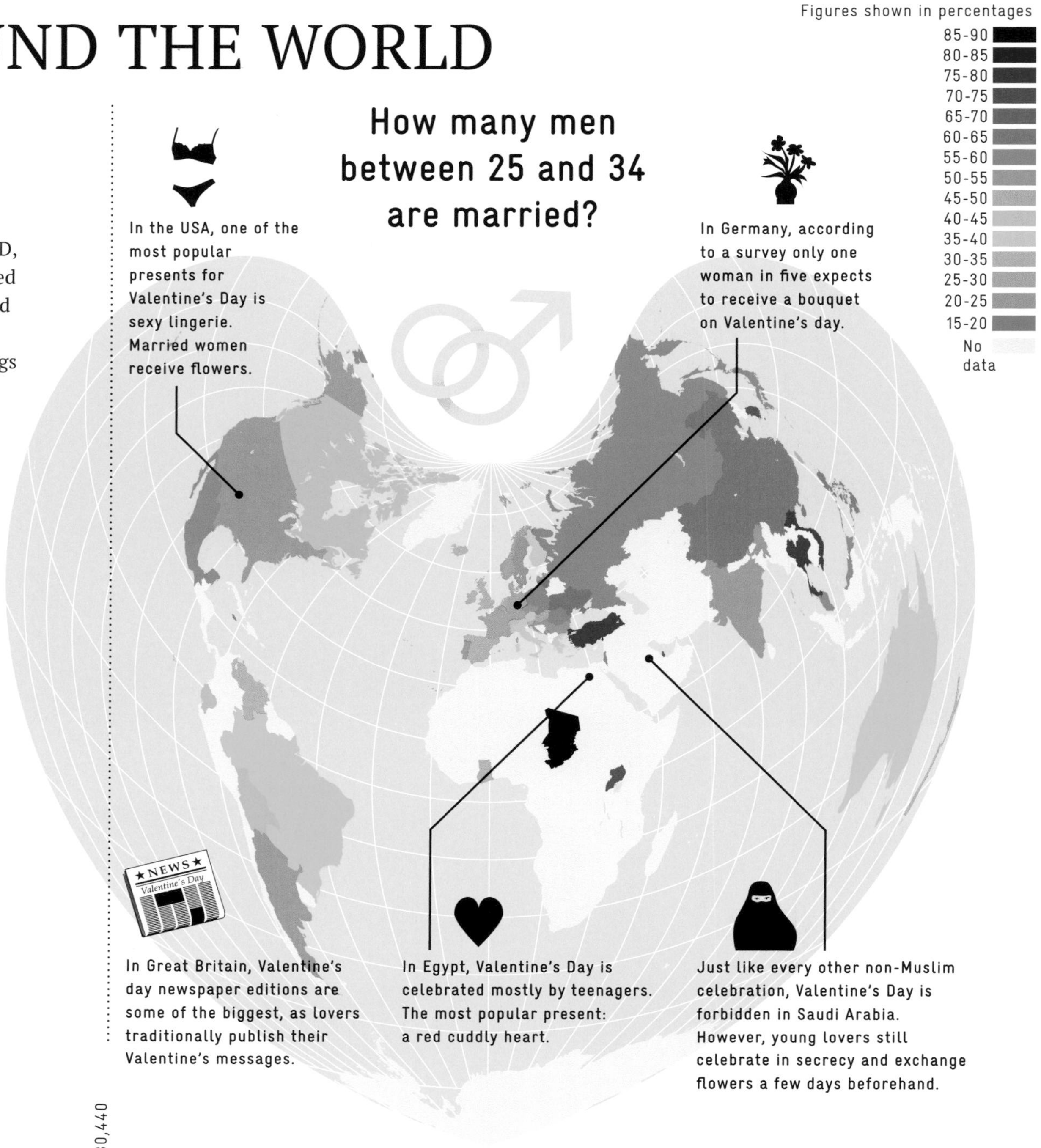
Figures shown in percentages
85-90
80-85
75-80
70-75
65-70
60-65
55-60
50-55
45-50
40-45
35-40
30-35
25-30
20-25
15-20
No data
In the USA, one of the most popular presents for Valentine's Day is sexy lingerie. Married women receive flowers.
In Germany, according to a survey only one woman in five expects to receive a bouquet on Valentine's day.
★NEWS★ Valentine's Day
In Great Britain, Valentine's day newspaper editions are some of the biggest, as lovers traditionally publish their Valentine's messages.
In Egypt, Valentine's Day is celebrated mostly by teenagers. The most popular present: a red cuddly heart.
Just like every other non-Muslim celebration, Valentine's Day is forbidden in Saudi Arabia. However, young lovers still celebrate in secrecy and exchange flowers a few days beforehand.

WAR OF THE ROSES

It's not all about tulips. When it comes to exporting the flowers of love, the Netherlands are in first place.

(IMPORT AND EXPORT OF ROSES IN 2018, AMOUNT IN DOLLARS)

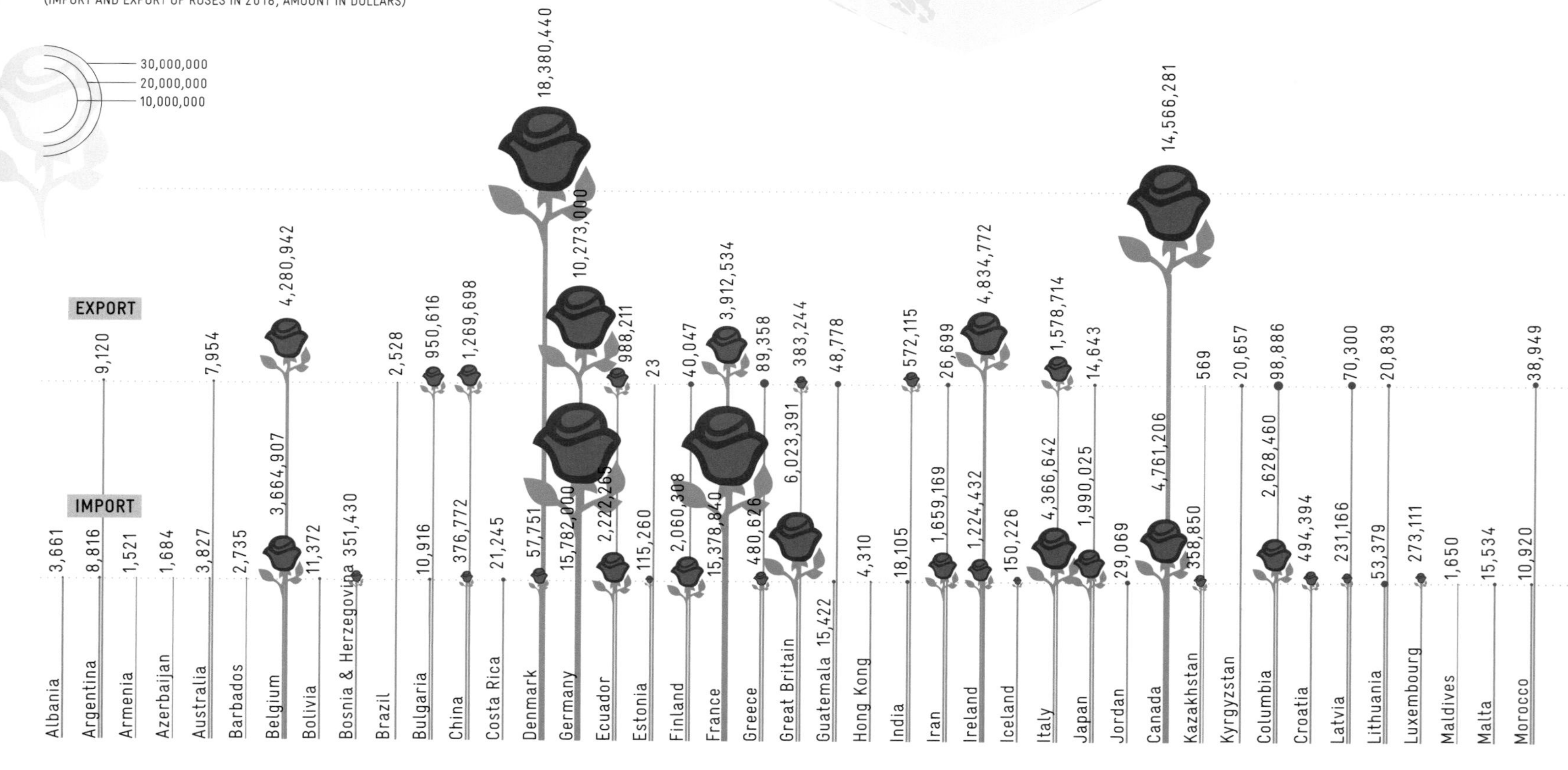
30,000,000
20,000,000
10,000,000
EXPORT
IMPORT

Country	Export	Import
Albania		3,661
Argentina	9,120	8,816
Armenia		1,521
Azerbaijan		1,684
Australia	7,954	3,827
Barbados		2,735
Belgium	4,280,942	3,664,907
Bolivia		11,372
Bosnia & Herzegovina		351,430
Brazil	2,528	
Bulgaria	950,616	10,916
China	1,269,698	376,772
Costa Rica		21,245
Denmark	18,380,440	57,751
Germany	10,273,000	15,782,000
Ecuador	988,211	2,222,265
Estonia	23	115,260
Finland	40,047	2,060,308
France	3,912,534	15,378,840
Greece	89,358	480,626
Great Britain	383,244	6,023,391
Guatemala	48,778	15,422
Hong Kong		4,310
India	572,115	18,105
Iran	26,699	1,659,169
Ireland	4,834,772	1,224,432
Iceland		150,226
Italy	1,578,714	4,366,642
Japan	14,643	1,990,025
Jordan		29,069
Canada	14,566,281	4,761,206
Kazakhstan	569	358,850
Kyrgyzstan	20,657	
Columbia	98,886	2,628,460
Croatia		494,394
Latvia	70,300	231,166
Lithuania	20,839	53,379
Luxembourg		273,111
Maldives		1,650
Malta		15,534
Morocco	38,949	10,920

How many women between 25 and 34 are married?

In Finland, February 14 is celebrated as the rather more innocent »Friendship Day« and cards can be sent anonymously to anyone you think is nice.

In Japan it's the women who give gifts on Valentine's Day. Fine dark chocolate is particularly popular. Gifts are given to partners, colleagues and managers. March 14 is »White Day« where the men return the favor with… white chocolate!

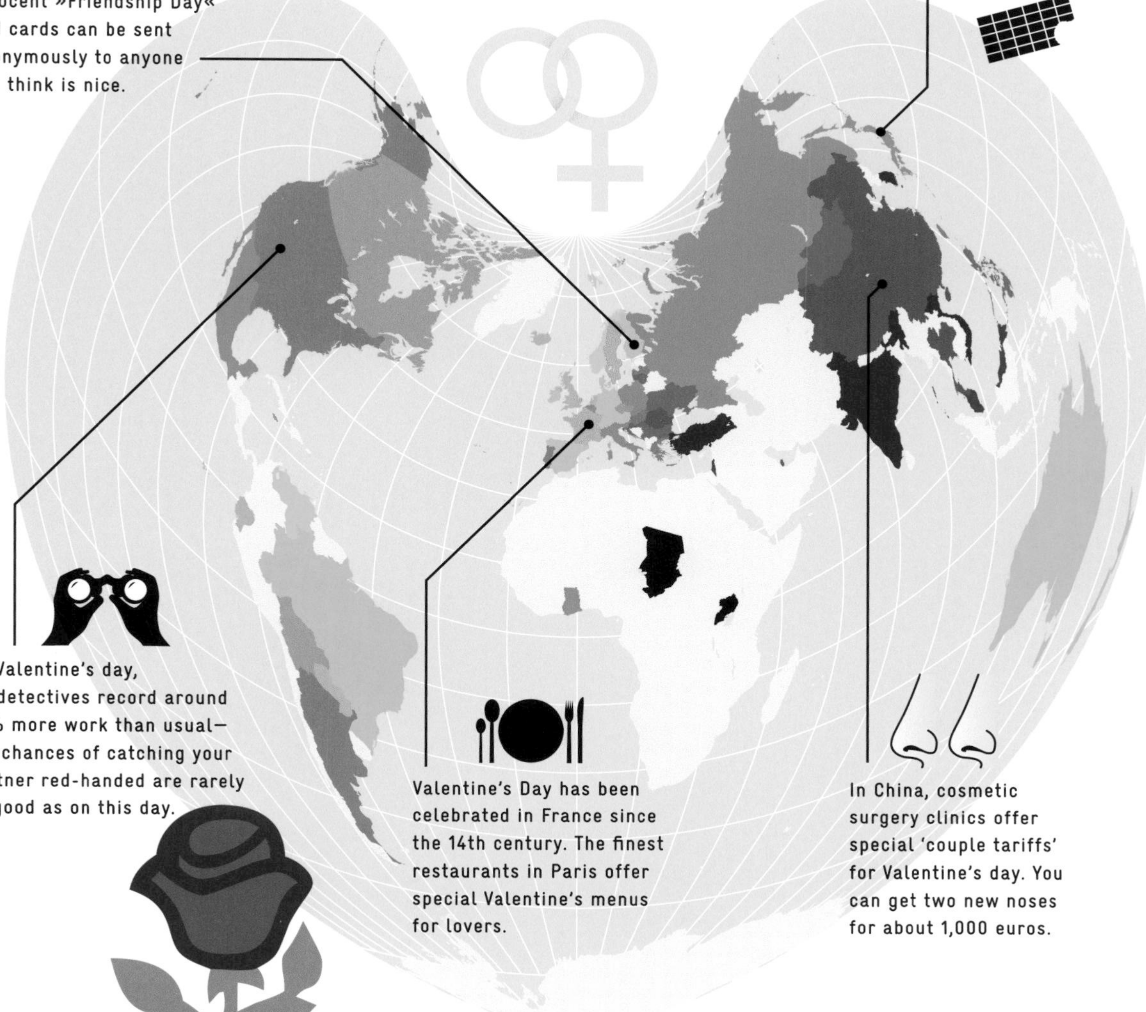

On Valentine's day, US detectives record around 25% more work than usual—the chances of catching your partner red-handed are rarely as good as on this day.

Valentine's Day has been celebrated in France since the 14th century. The finest restaurants in Paris offer special Valentine's menus for lovers.

In China, cosmetic surgery clinics offer special 'couple tariffs' for Valentine's day. You can get two new noses for about 1,000 euros.

SURVEY:
How many times do you have sex per year? Worldwide average: 103 times (2005)

THE WILD ONES…

1. Greece (138 times)
2. Croatia (134)
3. Serbia and Montenegro (128)*
4. Bulgaria (127)
5. Czech Republic, France (120)

24. Germany (104)

… AND THE PRUDES

1. Japan (45 times)
2. Singapore (73)
3. India (75)
4. Indonesia (77)
5. Hong Kong (78)

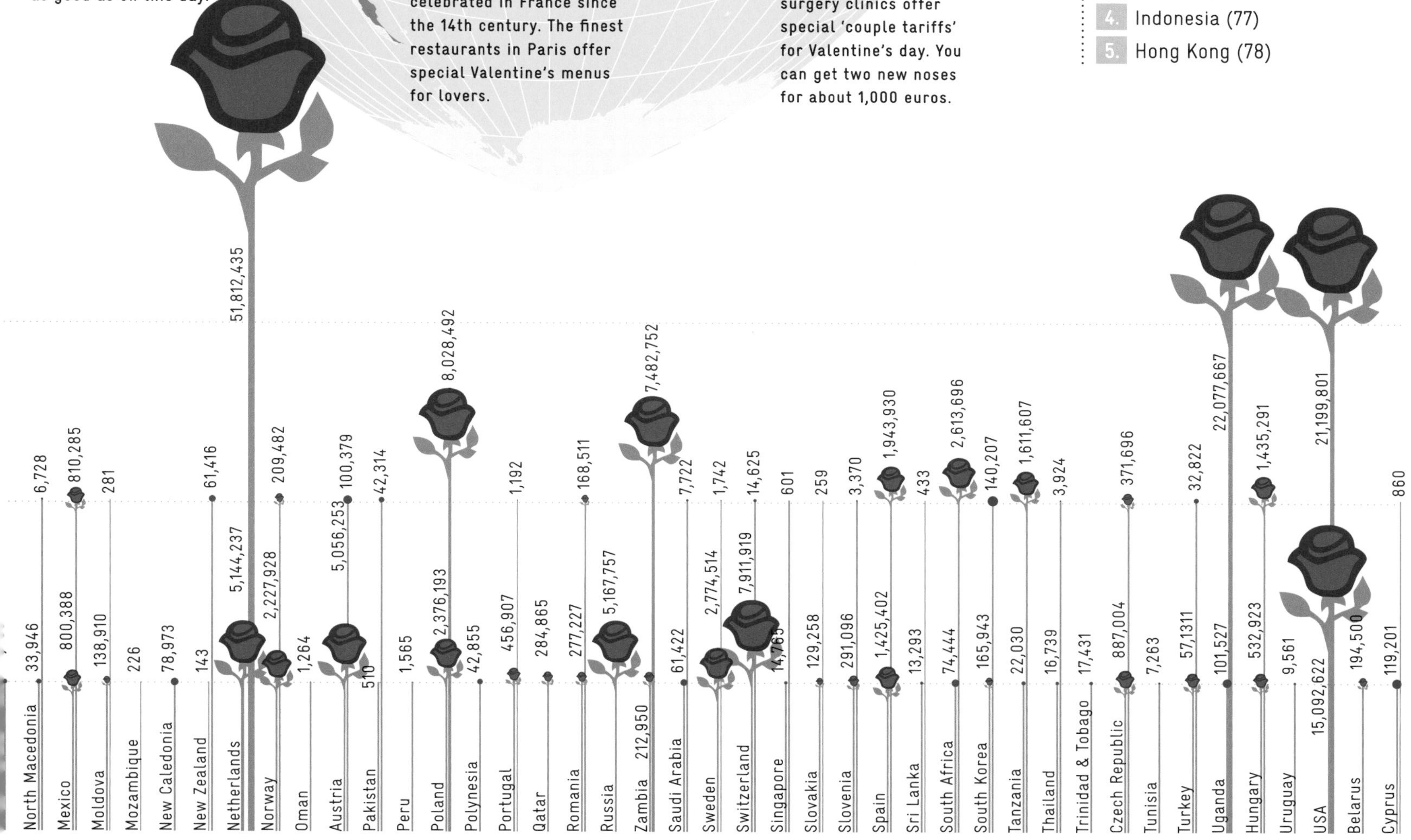
51,812,435
North Macedonia 33,946 6,728
Mexico 800,388 810,285
Moldova 138,910 281
Mozambique 226
New Caledonia 78,973
New Zealand 143 61,416
Netherlands 5,144,237
Norway 2,227,928 209,482
Oman 1,264
Austria 5,056,253 100,379
Pakistan 510 42,314
Peru 1,565
Poland 2,376,193 8,028,492
Polynesia 42,855
Portugal 456,907 1,192
Qatar 284,865
Romania 277,227 168,511
Russia 5,167,757
Zambia 212,950 7,482,752
Saudi Arabia 61,422 7,722
Sweden 2,774,514 1,742
Switzerland 7,911,919 14,625
Singapore 14,765 601
Slovakia 129,258 259
Slovenia 291,096 3,370
Spain 1,425,402 1,943,930
Sri Lanka 13,293 433
South Africa 74,444 2,613,696
South Korea 165,943 140,207
Tanzania 22,030 1,611,607
Thailand 16,739 3,924
Trinidad & Tobago 17,431
Czech Republic 887,004 371,696
Tunisia 7,263
Turkey 57,1311 32,822
Uganda 101,527 22,077,667
Hungary 532,923 1,435,291
Uruguay 9,561
USA 15,092,622 21,199,801
Belarus 194,500
Cyprus 119,201 860

*Serbia and Montenegro is no longer a single country as Montenegro gained its independence in 2006.

DÍA DE MUERTOS

This traditional celebration blends Mexico's ancient mythologies with European Catholic traditions, brought together with all the fundamental elements of Mexican culture: family, food, music, arts and a strong sense of community. The day commemorates the dead's transitory return to the place of the living. In Mexico, people welcome their lost loved ones with an altar known as »La Ofrenda«. Most are in the home, but there are still some villages where this offering is made at the tomb in the cemetery.

1
NOVEMBER
2
NOVEMBER

The first day is for remembering children while the second is for remembering adults.

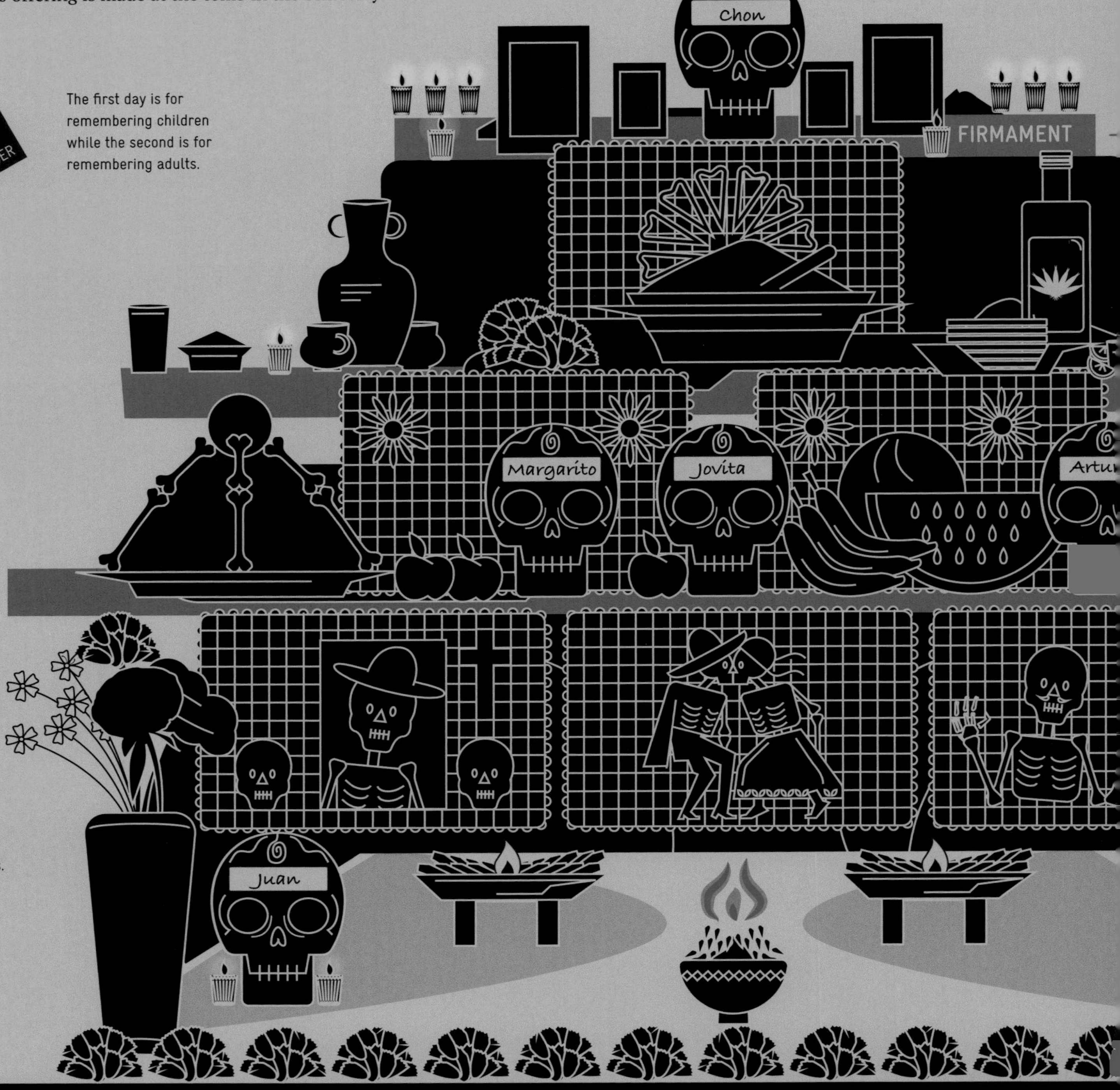
Chon
FIRMAMENT
Margarito
Jovita
Juan

The elements of the altar are there to appeal to the senses. It symbolizes the connection between ancestors in the worlds of the living and the dead.

THE ESSENCIALS FOR BRIDGING LIFE AND DEATH

FOOD AND DRINK

Favorite dishes are prepared to appeal to the senses of smell and taste. Drinks, cigarettes, fruit, tortillas, sweets, coffee and other traditional celebration foods are displayed on the altar.

PAN DE MUERTO

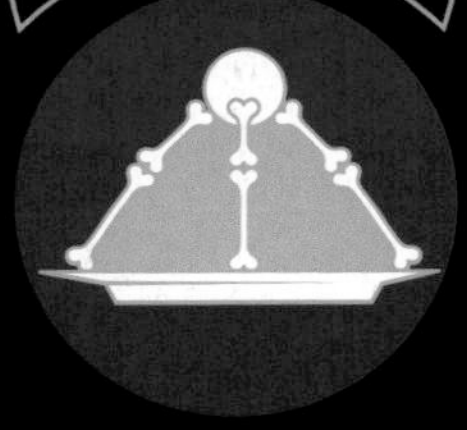

A bread flavored with orange and butter is a traditional food for the festival. It's shaped to represent the bones of the deceased.

WATER

Visitors are sure to be thirsty after their long journey from the underworld, so water is provided.

CALAVERITAS

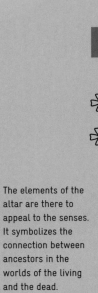

Jovita

Edible chocolate and sugar skulls are decorated with the names of loved ones.

UNIVERSE REPRESENTATION

The »universe« according to Mesoamerican Civilizations is represented in three levels.

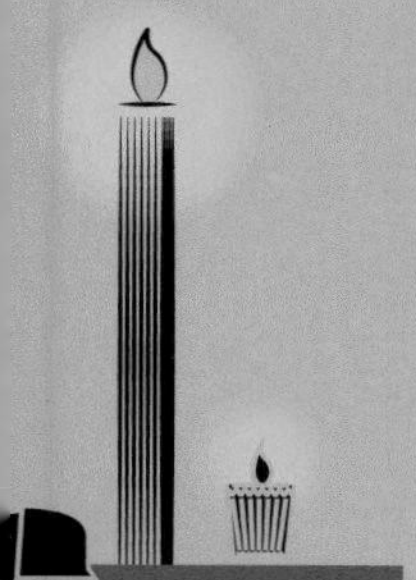

EARTH

UNDERWORLD

The journey to eternity was called »Mictlán« and divided into nine levels. The description was found in the old Codices.

Lupe

Coatlicue, Aztec Goddess of Life and Death

The name *Coatlicue* means *Serpant Skirt* in the Aztec language. She is a monolite dedicated to life and death. The Anthropology Museum in Mexico is home to a huge example of a *Coatlicue* figure.

The Aztec Universe was full of beliefs and traditions. Before the Spanish conquest, Mexican civilizations believed in a diverse range of gods and goddesses and made human sacrifices to honor them.

2.40 m

Her face is composed of two fanged serpents

Her necklace is made up of hands, hearts and a skull. Aztecs believed she fed on corpses, just as the Earth consumes all that dies.

Aztec means »the people of the sun«. The ancient civilization founded Tenochtitlán—the modern Mexico City.

Her fingers and toes are clawed.

Traditional Day of the Dead flowers and their meaning

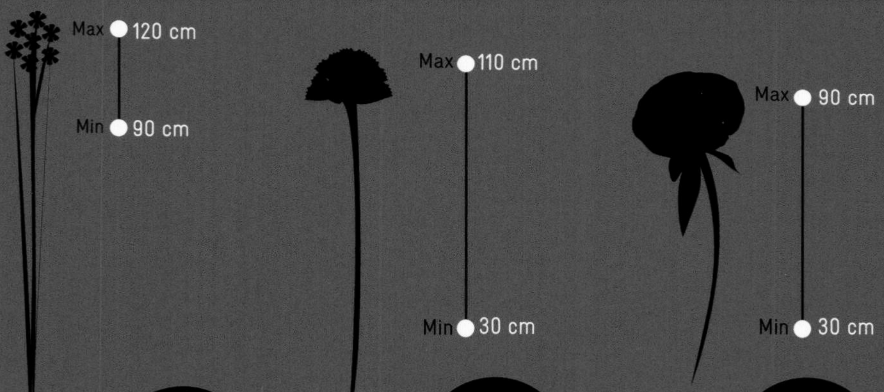

Max 120 cm
Min 90 cm
Max 110 cm
Min 30 cm
Max 90 cm
Min 30 cm

»Nube«
Gypsphilia muralis
These flowers are placed as an offering for deceased children.

»Cempasúchil«
Tagetes Erecta
Aztec Marigold lights the path for the dead souls to visit their living loved ones.

»Terciopelo«
Celosia Cristata
Represents the blood of Christ as an ode to Catholic beliefs and mourning.

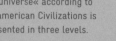

COPAL
As incense turns to smoke, it represents the journey from life to death.

SALT
Salt is laid out to keep the visitor's soul pure and uncorrupted by the

PICTURES OR OBJECTS
Loved ones' photographs and treasures are set out for the senses of sight

PAPEL PICADO
Eyes are further drawn to La Ofrenda by colorful tissue paper cutouts.

CANDLES
Candles light the way as part of the remembrance and

The Day of the Dead was declared to be an Intangible Cultural Heritage of Humanity by UNESCO in 2003.

LOTTO

If you want to win the lottery you only need luck, not brains. For 400 years humans have played the lottery – initially to bet on which candidate would get voted into office, today with the hope of winning millions. Many myths persist that a certain system will increase one's odds, but there is only ever one guaranteed winner – the state.

ONE WORLD – ONE LOTTERY?

Not even close. Even though a few lotteries cross country borders, and some national lotteries are more popular than ever, like the Spanish Christmas lottery El Gordo, lottery systems are very different. Within the lottery systems the number of choices varies: lotteries range from 3 out of 10, 7 out of 55 and even 6 out of 90. Our world map shows 19 different lottery systems where you can choose 6 numbers. On each continent there are clear preferences. Brazil loves 6 out of 59 while North America, Europe and Africa prefer 6 out of 49.

HOW THE GERMANS BET

Today around 10 million people regularly play the lottery. Many play by following a specific system, and yet statistically every one of the 13,983,816 (49!/(6!×43!)) number combinations have the same probability of 0.0000000715 (1/13,983,816) to get drawn. However, there is a difference in how much you can win. And since some number combinations are more popular with players than others, the winnings sometimes have to be split among many people.

The Italian word **lotto** originates from the old high German word hlioz, meaning oracle. A »lot« comes from old English.

This heat map shows the frequency of **single numbers** within a game from a total of 6,803,090 bets placed.

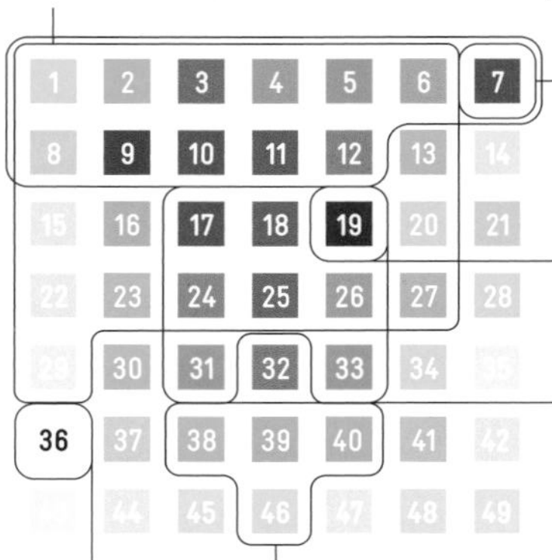

Numbers from 1 to 31 are contained in birthdays and months.

The lucky number 7 is one of the most popular numbers to bet.
The number 19 is often selected—because of birthdays in the 1900s.
Numbers in the middle are selected more often than numbers on the edges.

The number 36 is the least popular number.

Many people pick numbers that are arranged in a geometric pattern. This means the jackpot with these numbers has to be shared between many betters.

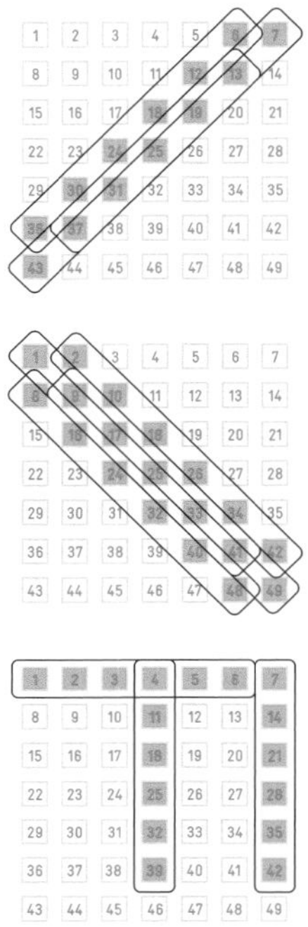

THE HISTORY OF THE LOTTERY

The story starts in Italy at the beginning of the 17th century.

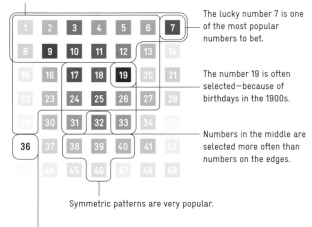

Legend has it that senators were voted into office by lottery. The names of 90 candidates were placed in an urn and five names were drawn randomly.
Genoa, 1620

Pick 6 from: 36 37 38 39 40 41 42 43 44 45 46 47 48 49 50 51 52 53 54 55 56 57 58 59 60 90

Calgary

Canadian Tom Christ won 40 million CAD (€27.4 million) in the Canadian lottery 6 out of 49 in 2013 and then donated the entire amount to healthcare organizations and other causes. His argument: He already had enough money.

ALL DRAWINGS AT A GLANCE

The first lottery with 6 out of 49 was in Hamburg, Germany at 4pm on October 9, 1955. The first winning numbers (3, 12, 13, 16, 23, 41) were drawn by the orphan Elvira Hahn. Since then, the lottery has been played every Saturday–roughly 3,200 times.

Out of all 13,983,816 possible combinations of six numbers, only 0.04% have been drawn; yet four number combinations have been drawn twice.

Five consecutive numbers have only been drawn twice.

This heat map shows the frequency of **drawn numbers** in all drawings (without the bonus number).

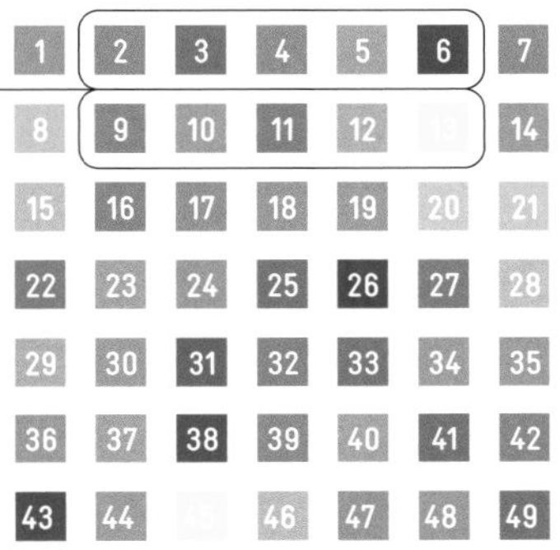
1 2 3 4 5 6 7
8 9 10 11 12 14
15 16 17 18 19 20 21
22 23 24 25 26 27 28
29 30 31 32 33 34 35
36 37 38 39 40 41 42
43 44 46 47 48 49

The number 13 was only drawn 619 times. The most-drawn number was 26, at 738 times.

THE LOTTERY IN GERMANY

Until the 1950s there were moral concerns against playing the lottery; it was banned between 1862 and 1945. In those days, government circles saw the lottery as »the attempt to quickly get a lot of money without honest work«.

The lottery tax today is 16.7% of the stake. With a stake of €4 billion (2015), a few hundred million euros are going straight to the federal budget every year.

4, 26, 31, 40, 48, 49 – With this number combination the first German millionaire was crowned on September 2, 1956. The winner got exactly 1,043,364.50 German marks. In relation to the inflation rate that would be equivalent to 2,465,070 euros today.

Clever businessmen turned this selection process into a betting opportunity. Whoever predicted the senators drawn during the »Lotto di Genova« received a prize.

In short order, names were replaced by numbers and the number lottery 1 out of 90 was born. Whoever correctly predicted the five numbers drawn received the winnings.

60 YEARS OF THE GERMAN LOTTERY

STAKE PER DRAWING BY WEEKDAY

The picture of the jackpot of all 6 out of 49 lotteries shows both small and large patterns. Overall the jackpot has risen steadily. With the addition of a Wednesday lottery in December 2000, the graph splits into a Sunday lottery (which was on Saturdays until 1967) and the Wednesday lottery jackpot.

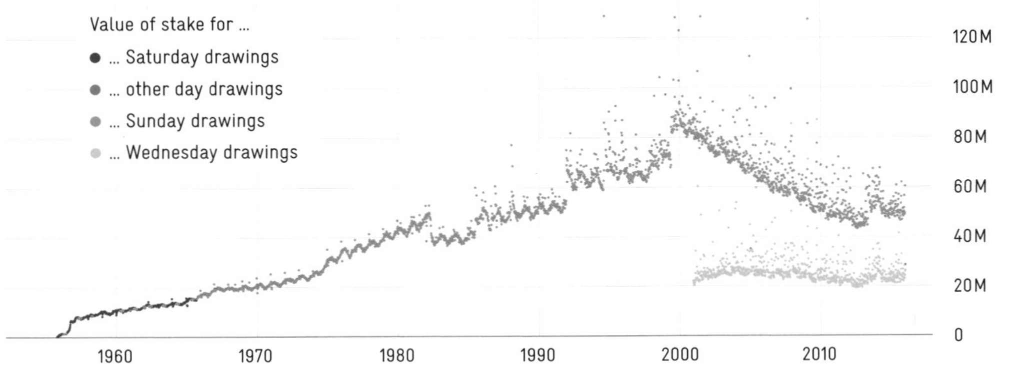

STAKE PER DRAWING WITH »LOTTO AM MITTWOCH«

The format of »Lotto am Mittwoch« (»Lottery on Wednesdays«, not to be confused with the regular Wednesday drawings) existed from April 28, 1982, until June 26, 2013. We can see a rise and fall in the jackpot of regular Lotto during that period.

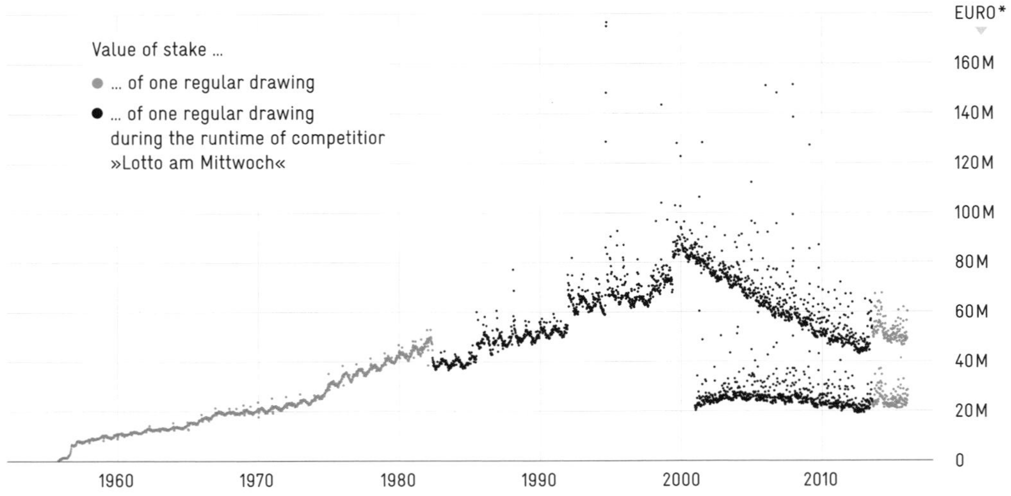

STAKE PER DRAWING BY WINNING CLASS

With the introduction of further prize categories, distinctive phases of stakes become visible. In the beginning, only four prize categories existed (3, 4, 5 and 6 winning numbers). Shortly after the bonus number and the super number were added, the chance to win a high sum with a few numbers made the lottery more attractive. The combination of 6 winning numbers and a super number, plus the reintroduction of three and four winning numbers with a super number in 1999, especially increased the stakes.

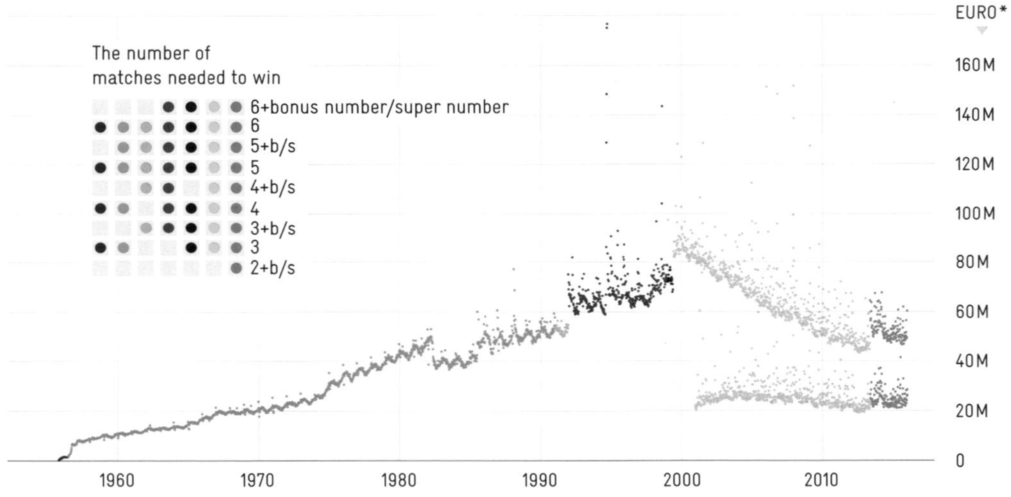

* DM converted to euro

From Genoa the number lottery quickly spread throughout Italy and Europe.
Lottery as a source of income was quickly nationalized. During lean times the winnings financed ornate public buildings and the military.

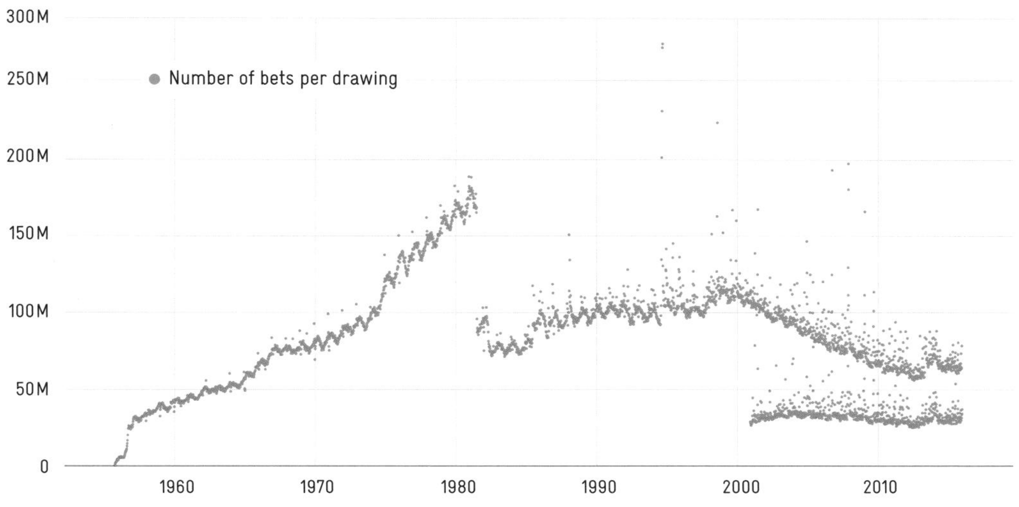

NUMBER OF BETS

If we divide the jackpot by the price for a single game we get the number of bets. Besides a decline in the number of bets from the turn of the millennium, there is a very abrupt drop around 1981.

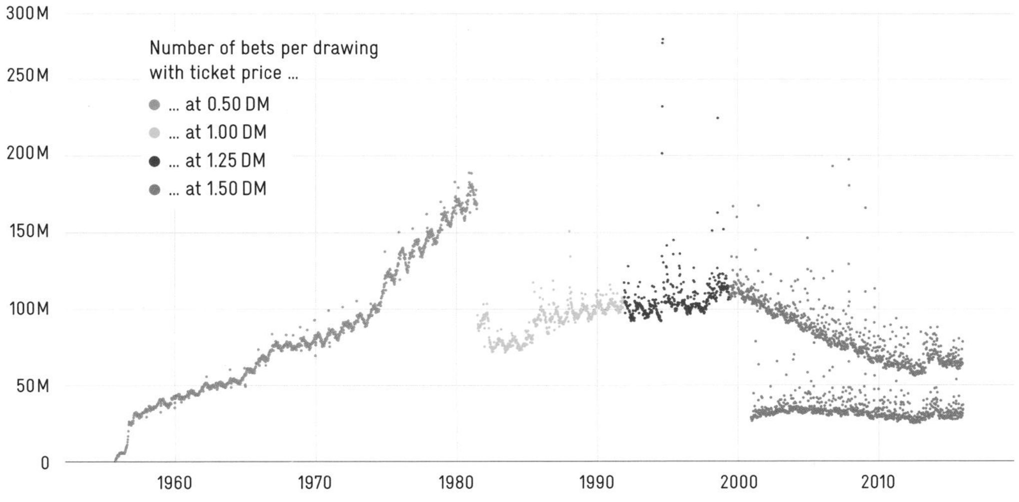

RISING PRICES, FALLING STAKES

If we color the prizes according to the price of a lottery ticket we can see the reason for the sudden decline in the amount of bets: a price increase. The first increase for a lottery ticket, in 1981 (from DM 0.50 to DM 1) shows a dramatic impact. The chances of winning per invested DM were cut in half. However, the increase to DM 1.25 in 1991 and to DM 1.50 in 1999, didn't have such dramatic consequences.

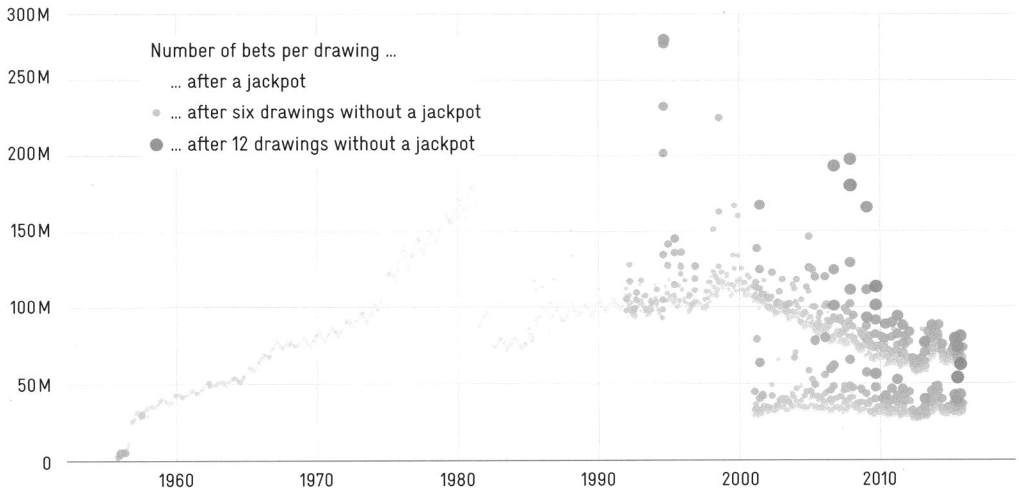

EVERYBODY HOPES TO CRACK THE JACKPOT

The lotteries with exceptionally high numbers of bets represent the chase to win the jackpot. As long as no one wins the jackpot, more people invest in the game in the hope of winning a record sum. Once the jackpot is claimed, the numbers return to normal.

On January 11, 1953, the Berlin Lottery introduced a modified version of the Genoese lottery »5 out of 90«. In 1955, the states of Hamburg, North Rhine-Westphalia, and Schleswig-Holstein founded the North West lottery, where there is still a 6 out of 49 lottery.
But social projects were also financed.
Between 1862 and 1945, playing the lottery in Germany was not allowed—to protect the gambling-crazy population from financial loss.
When the lottery launched on October 9, 1955, the first number drawn was
13

GERMAN AUTOBAHN

Think of a roadtrip through Germany and you're already thinking of what speeds you might reach when driving on its famous Autobahn. Almost 13,000 kilometers of road is webbed across the country, connecting north to south and east to west. Today it's a vital part of Germany's infrastructure, but it is also a vital part of Germany's dark past.

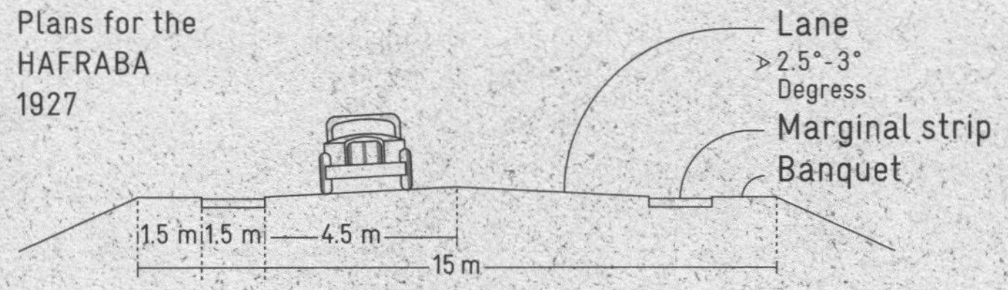
Plans for the HAFRABA 1927
Lane
> 2.5°-3° Degress
Marginal strip
Banquet
1.5 m
1.5 m
4.5 m
15 m

The construction plan for the very first section of the German Autobahn. It is supposed to connect Hamburg, Frankfurt and Basle, yet it has still not been completed.

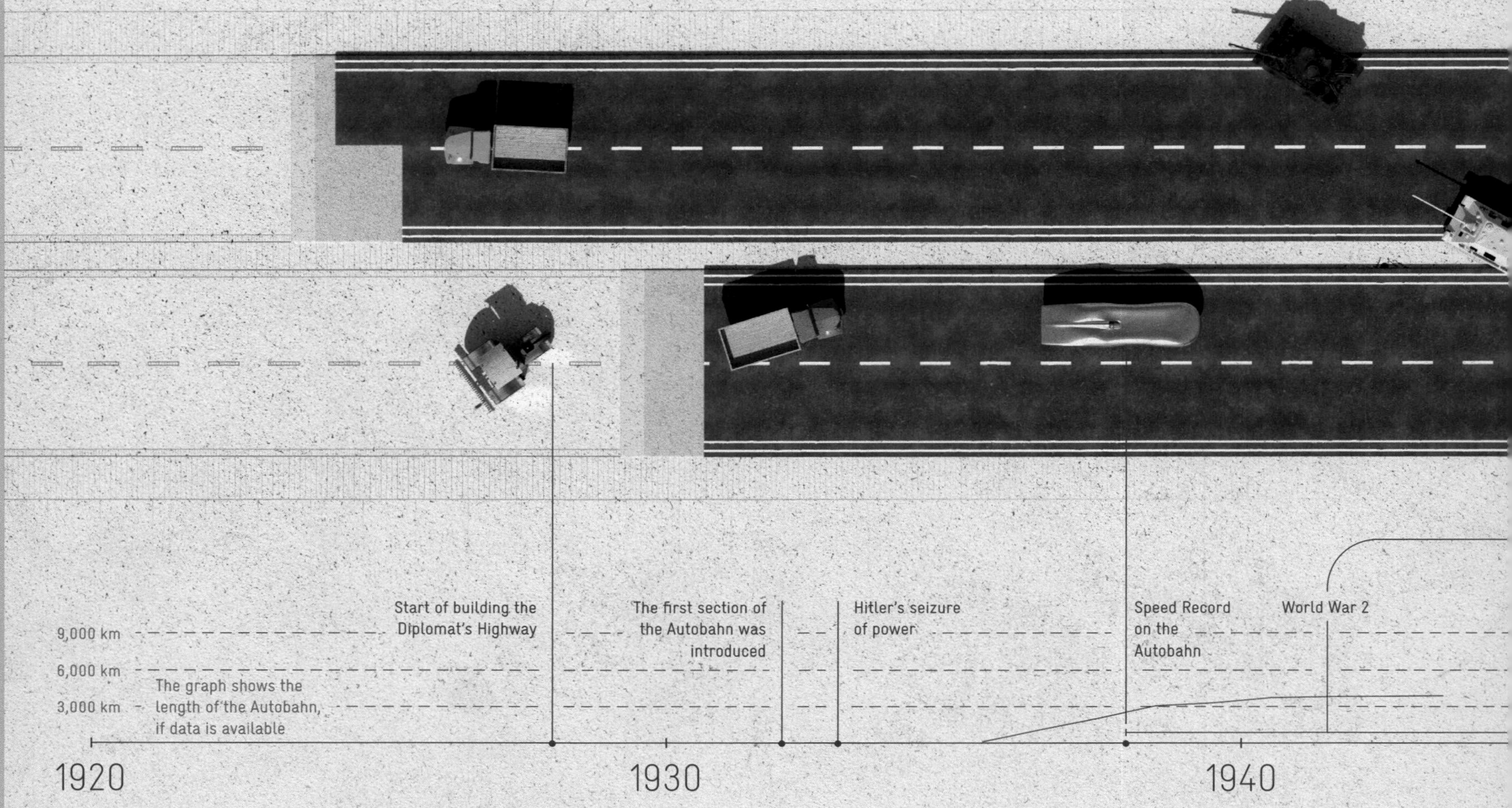
Start of building the Diplomat's Highway
The first section of the Autobahn was introduced
Hitler's seizure of power
Speed Record on the Autobahn
World War 2
9,000 km
6,000 km
3,000 km
The graph shows the length of the Autobahn, if data is available
1920
1930
1940

Hafraba

In the 1920s, cars puttered along increasingly crowded roads. Cities started developing cooperations to connect through-roads unhindered by intersections. The most ambitious of these was the HaFraBa connecting **Hamburg, Frankfurt and Basle**. However the National Socialists, led by Adolf Hitler, and the Communists campaigned against this project that would »only serve the wealthy of the country«.

Adenauer

However, the mayor of Cologne, Konrad Adenauer, opened a small stretch of such road in 1932. The **A555** was known as the **Diplomat's Speedway** and it served officials commuting between **Bonn and Cologne**.

Hitler

Despite his initial opposition, once in power, Hitler introduced plans to build what he called the **»Reichsbahn«**. However the first roads linked **Berlin to southern Bavaria** where Hitler's summer home was, as well as connecting the country east to west.
It became a **massive state infrastructure project**, employing thousands of people across the country and helping Germany undergo an economic recovery.

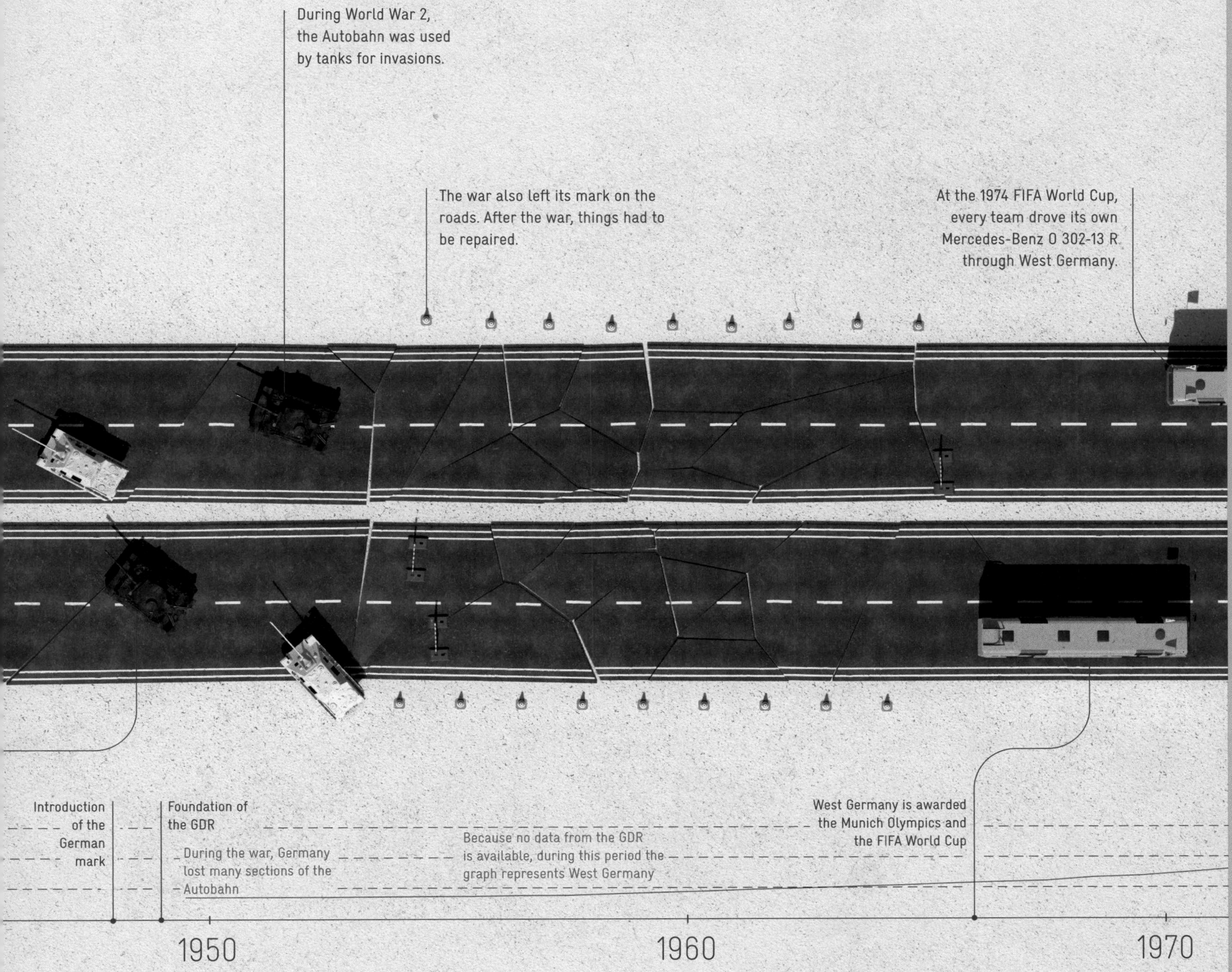
During World War 2, the Autobahn was used by tanks for invasions.
The war also left its mark on the roads. After the war, things had to be repaired.
At the 1974 FIFA World Cup, every team drove its own Mercedes-Benz O 302-13 R through West Germany.
Introduction of the German mark
Foundation of the GDR
During the war, Germany lost many sections of the Autobahn
Because no data from the GDR is available, during this period the graph represents West Germany
West Germany is awarded the Munich Olympics and the FIFA World Cup
1950
1960
1970

War

As Germany went to war, the infrastructure was in place to facilitate the **invasion into Poland and France**. But as more men were sent to the fronts, workers for continuing the building of these roads were hard to find. Hitler's Inspector General for Reichsautobahnen, Fritz Todt, then **continued the construction** through forced labor programs.

Wirtschaftswunder

The economy was in ruins as the aftermath of the war left **Germany divided** between the Soviet and Allied forces. Construction and **repairs were at a standstill**. When the Allied governments agreed to currency reform, introducing the German mark, people in West Germany started getting back to work—and going there by car.

Sports Events

Just 20 years after being a country in ruins, West Germany was awarded two major sporting events: **the 1972 Munich Olympics and 1974 FIFA World Cup**. The committees that take the decisions carefully weigh up transportation infrastructure or plans to improve it before selecting a host. As far as Munich was concerned, the roads had to accommodate visitors to the Olympic Sites. In addition, the **roads had to connect the nine host cities** for the football tournament across western Germany.

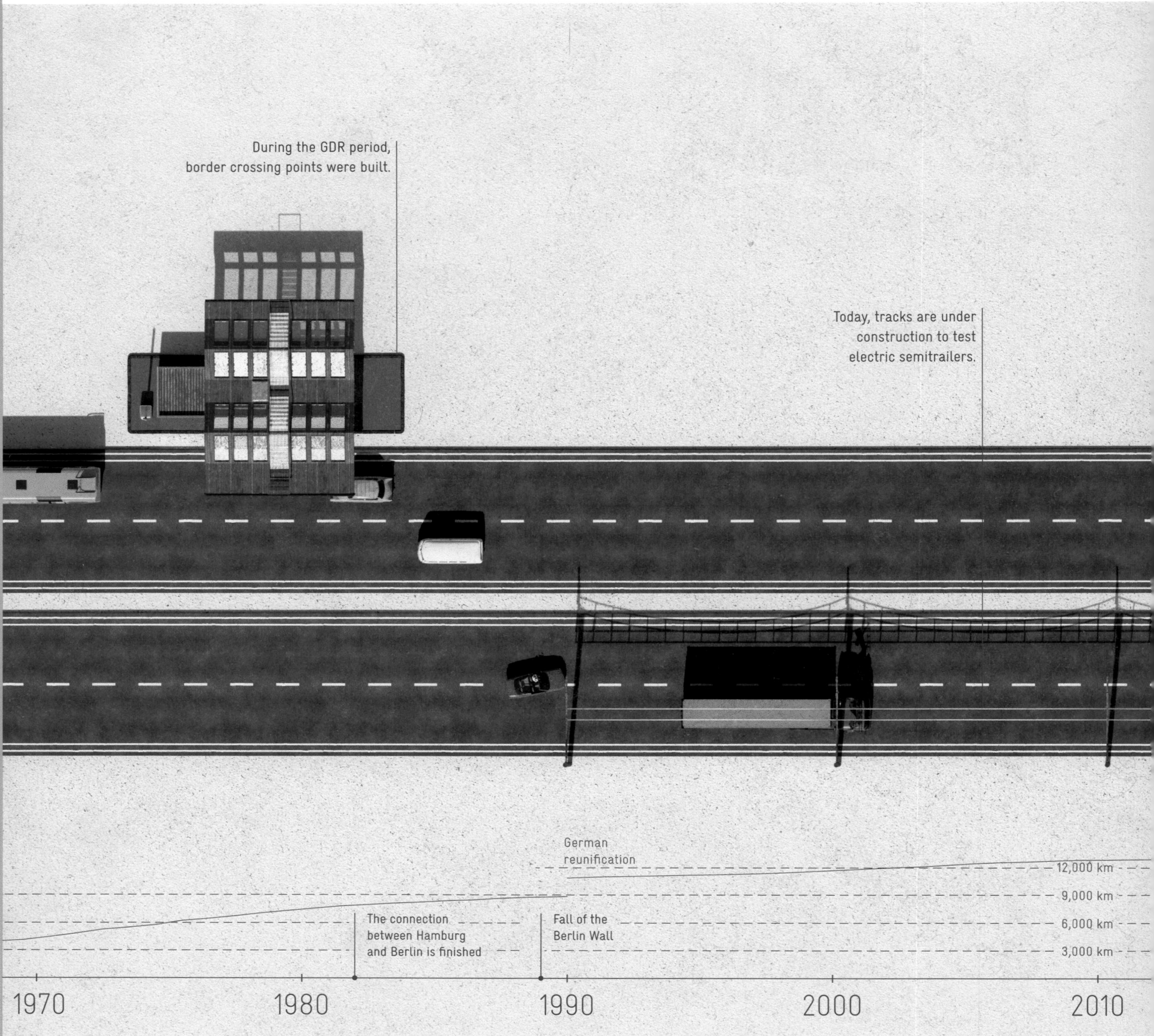
During the GDR period,
border crossing points were built.
Today, tracks are under
construction to test
electric semitrailers.
German
reunification
12,000 km
9,000 km
6,000 km
3,000 km
The connection
between Hamburg
and Berlin is finished
Fall of the
Berlin Wall
1970
1980
1990
2000
2010

Connecting west to west through the east

In the 1980s, West Germany began **connecting Hamburg to East Germany**, but in order to connect the port city with West Berlin, an **agreement** had to be made to build through the connecting territory. The Federal Transportation Minster, Otto Arndt of the German Democratic Republic, gave his western colleague Werner Dollinger the permits to build the 34 kilometers of road. Although the road was in East Germany, West Germany paid the bill.

2 become 1

When the Berlin Wall fell in 1989, it precipitated the end of the East German republic and caused a **major infrastructural challenge**. Autobahns in the East had a speed limit of 100 kilometers per hour—the top speed of the car most East Germans had access to, the Trabant. **Roads were in poor shape**, built in concrete slabs. The cost of creating a newly unified country that felt like one ensured that only a limited budget was available for creating new roads.

Charging into the future

Today, cars are as much a symbol of Germany as a deeply integrated part of its culture. To support this car-crazed nation, **the roadways have to be constantly improved** to handle the growing number of cars on the road—and their ever-increasing speed.

The Autobahn today

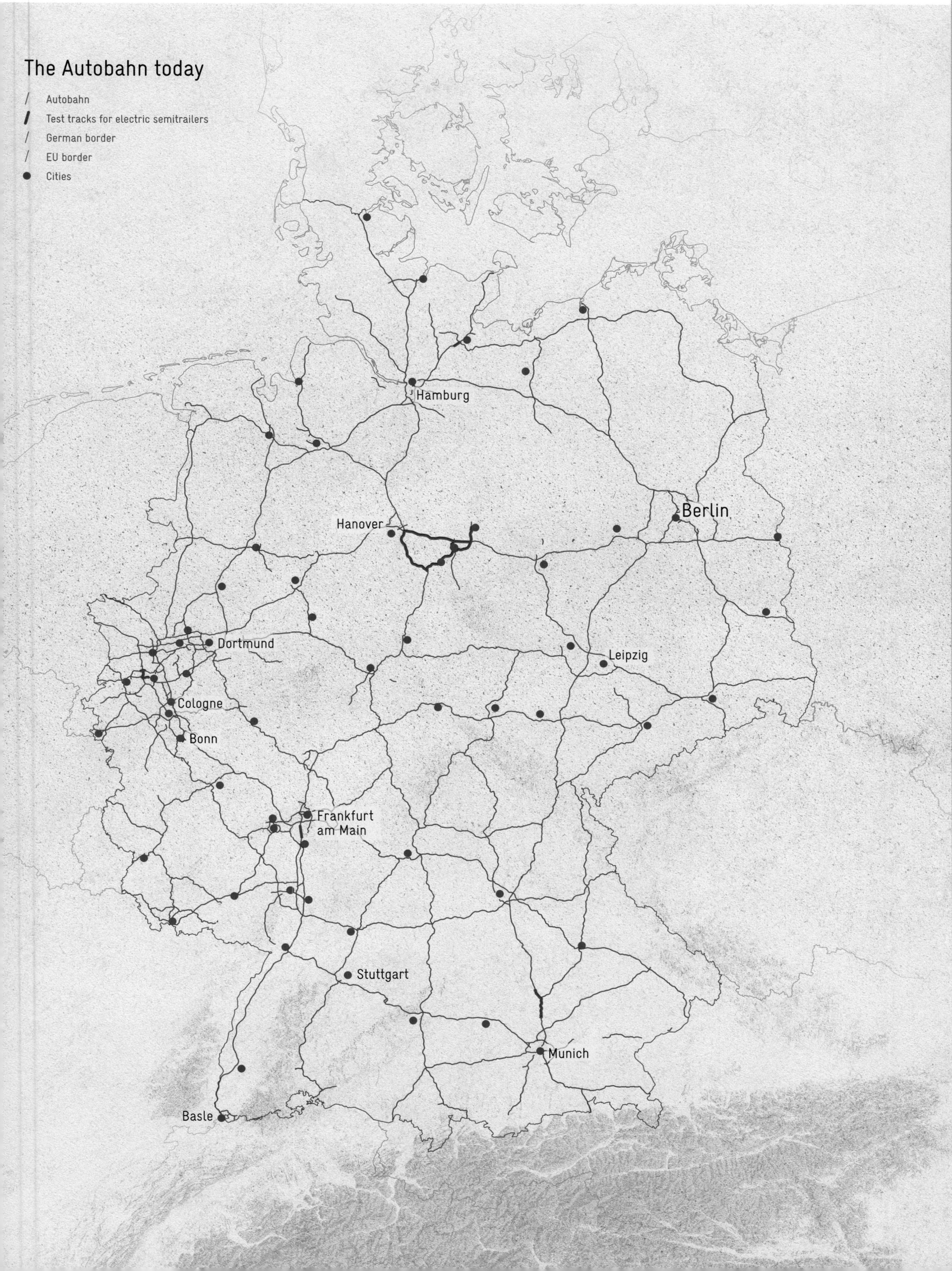
Autobahn
Test tracks for electric semitrailers
German border
EU border
Cities
Hamburg
Berlin
Hanover
Dortmund
Leipzig
Cologne
Bonn
Frankfurt am Main
Stuttgart
Munich
Basle

SPEED AND DEATH

A look at the speed limits and other rules governing vehicular velocity in various countries.

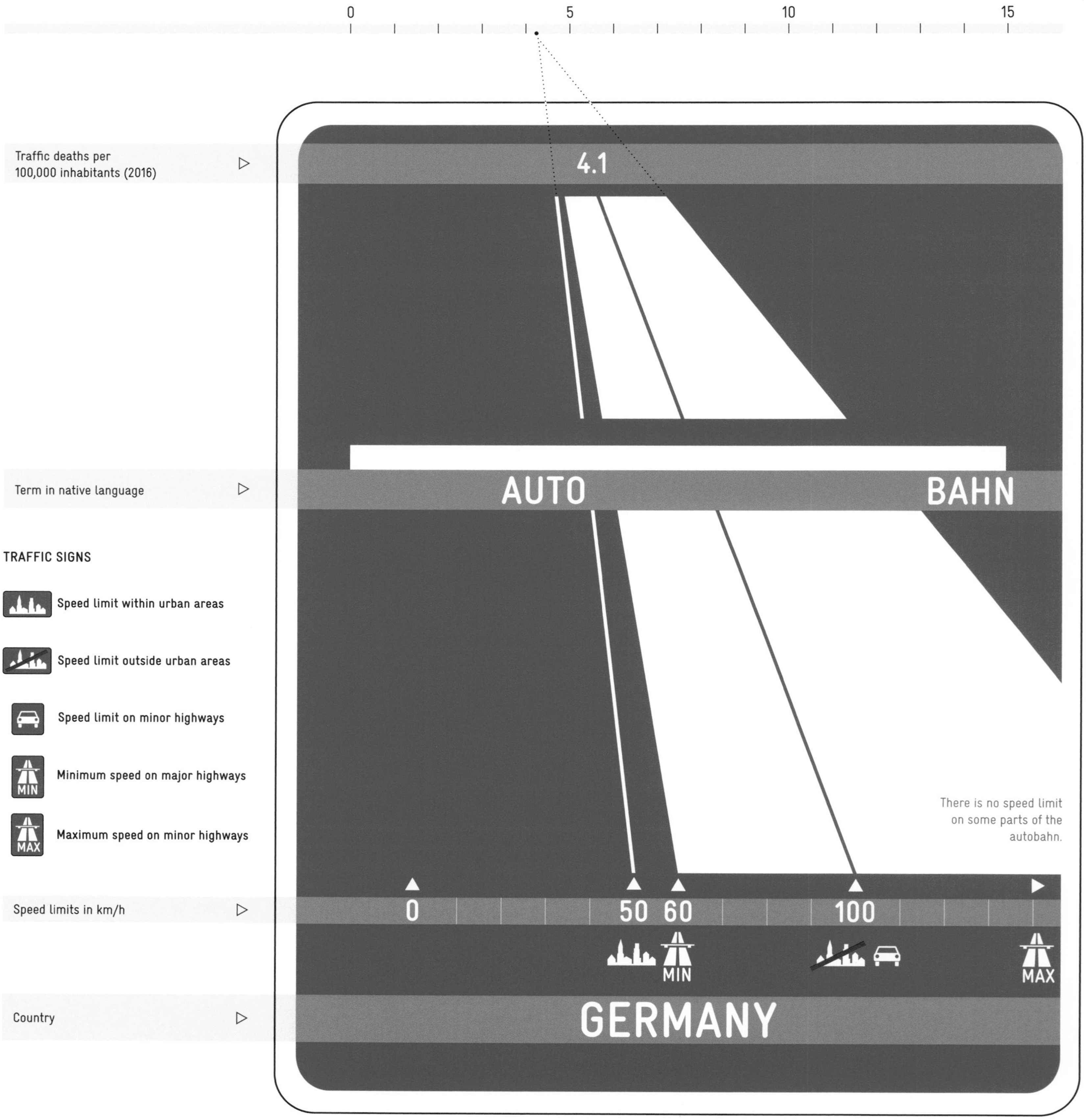
0
5
10
15
Traffic deaths per 100,000 inhabitants (2016)
4.1
Term in native language
AUTO
BAHN
TRAFFIC SIGNS
Speed limit within urban areas
Speed limit outside urban areas
Speed limit on minor highways
MIN
Minimum speed on major highways
MAX
Maximum speed on minor highways
There is no speed limit on some parts of the autobahn.
Speed limits in km/h
0
50
60
100
MIN
MAX
Country
GERMANY

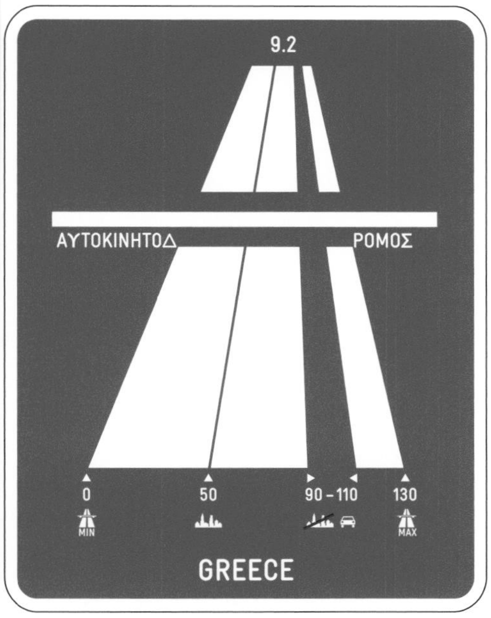

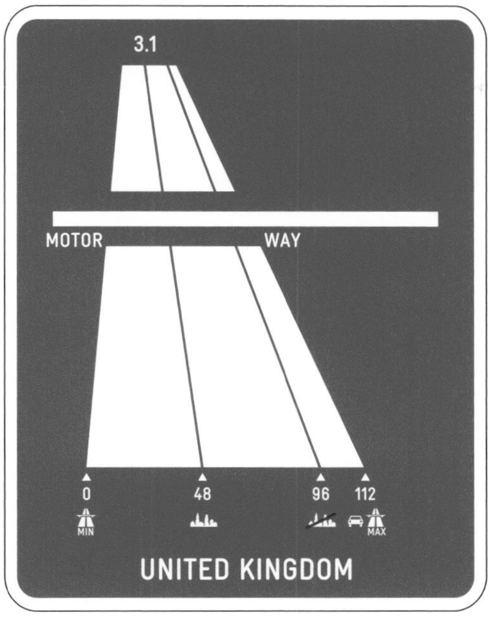

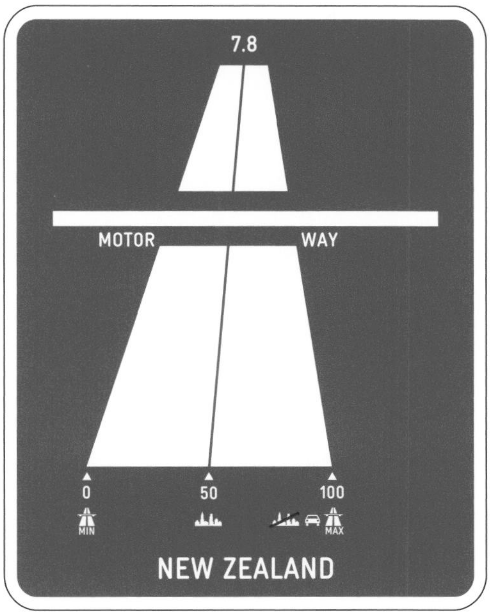

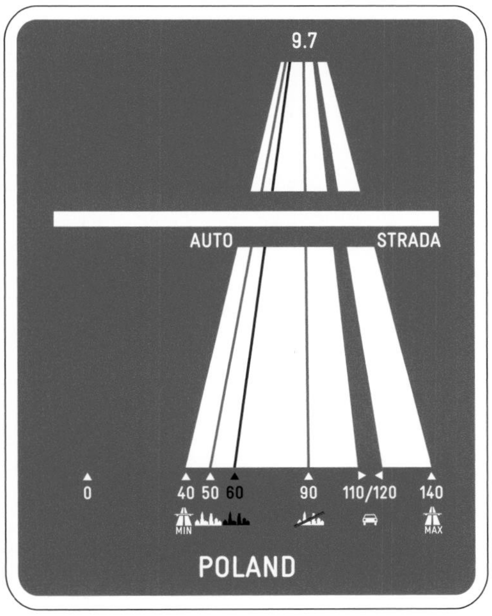

—— at night

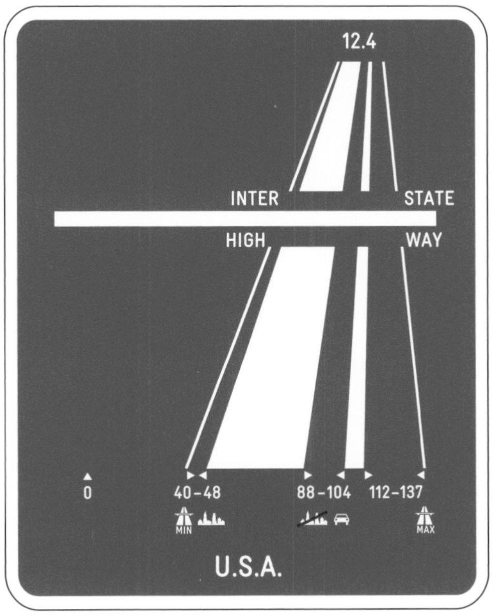

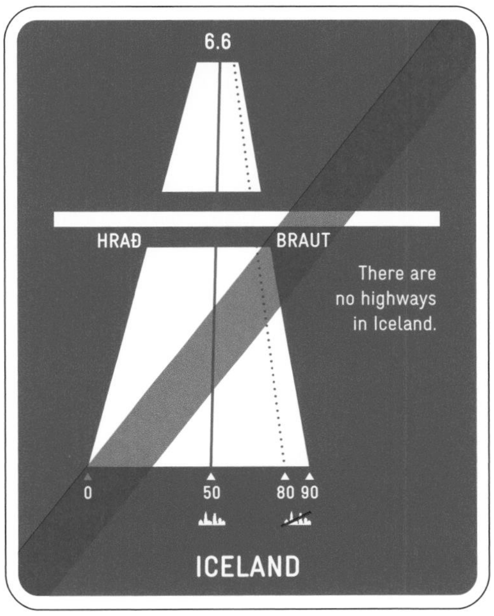

······· on gravel roads

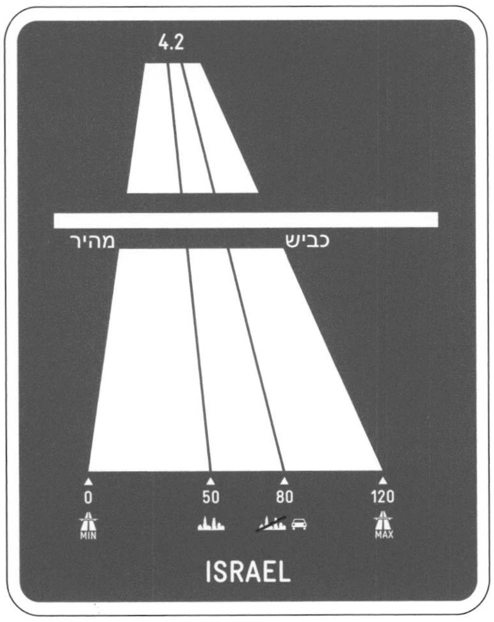

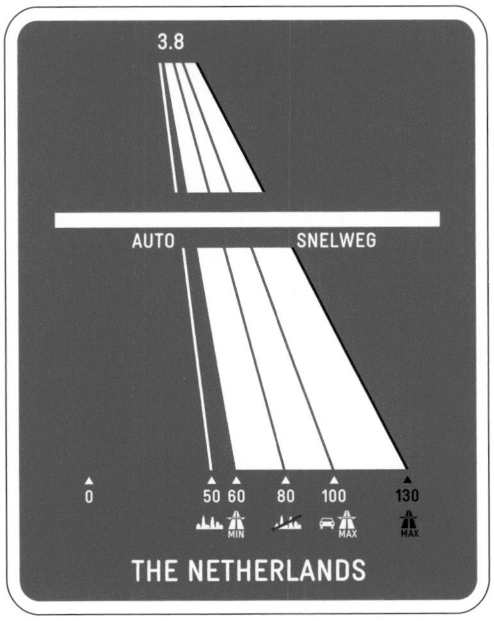

—— at night

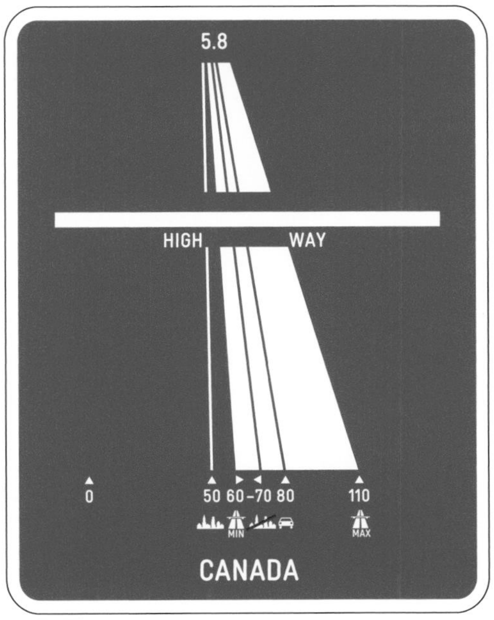

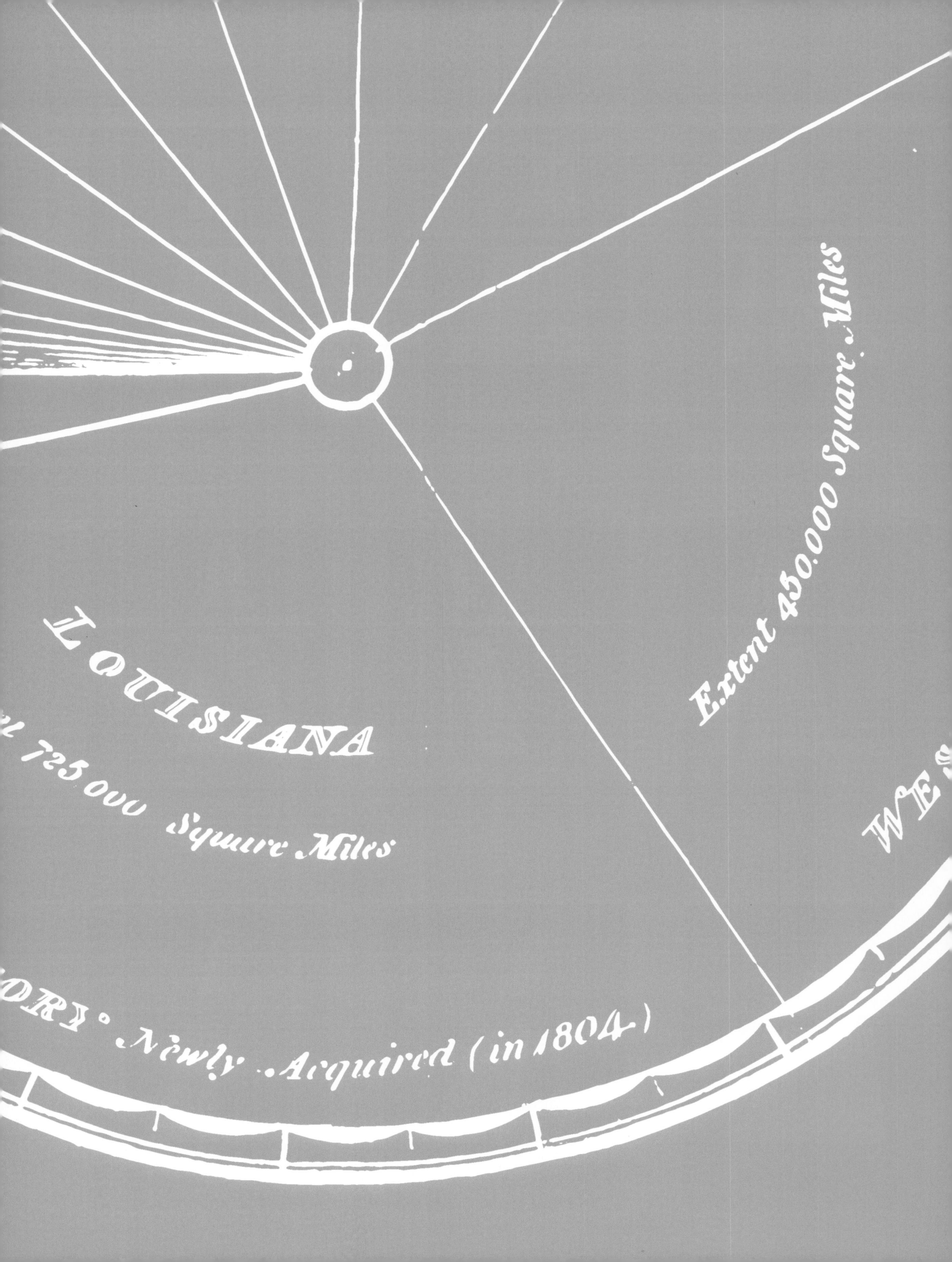

LOUISIANA
725.000 Square Miles
Extent 450.000 Square Miles
Newly Acquired (in 1804)

ECONOMY

Challenges such as war, plague, famine, and migration led kings as early as the 17th century to manage their resources and population with the help of statistical tables. This data provided the foundation for population and economic policy in absolutist states and later established the scientific roots of the field of macroeconomics. Monarchs received those numbers and figures translated into simplified, abstract, graphical forms — one basis for their political decision making.

William Playfair was one of the first to convert economic data into infographics. He is considered the inventor of both the pie chart and the bar graph. **The oldest known pie chart** is a Playfair affair, from 1801. He also edited this 1805 graphic, »Statistical Representation of the U.S.A.,« which shows the areas of different US states.

Today, pie charts and bar graphs are among the most common infographic formats and are generated handily in any popularly available spreadsheet software.

LET'S ADD IT ALL UP

The gross domestic product describes how productive a national economy is. It's calculated from the total value of goods and services that are produced in a national economy in a year. Dividing it by the size of the population yields an important factor (GDP per capita) for comparing a country's prosperity.

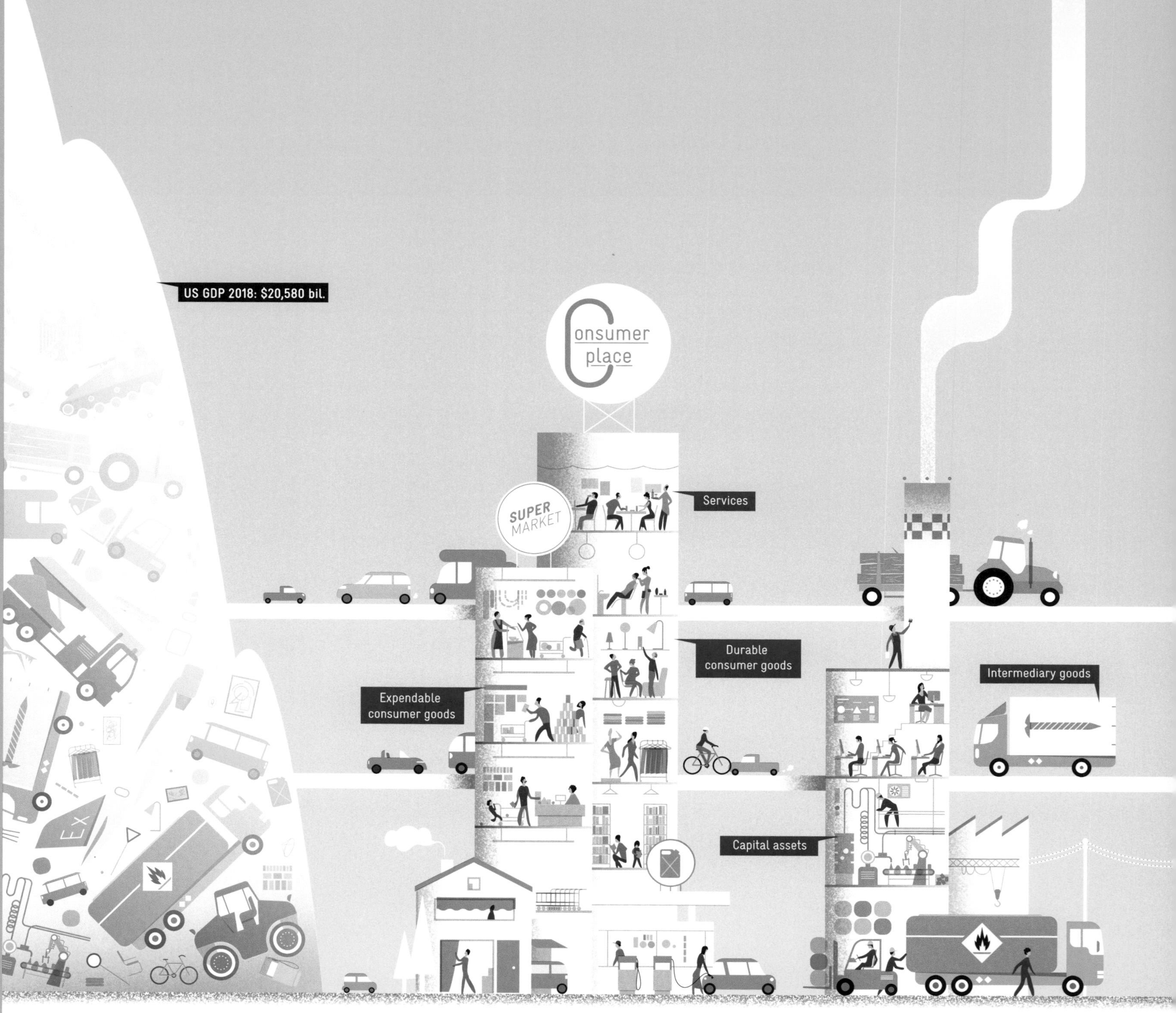
US GDP 2018: $20,580 bil.
Consumer place
SUPER MARKET
Services
Durable consumer goods
Expendable consumer goods
Intermediary goods
Capital assets

$$GDP_m = C + I +$$

Gross domestic product at market prices equals...

... private consumer spending ...

... plus private investments ...

$$G + (Ex - Im)$$

… and government expenditures (public consumption, government investments, social transfers, grants, transfer to interstate organizations) …

… taking into account net exports, meaning the difference between exports and imports.

THE FEDERAL DEBT OF THE USA

This graphic is normally used in the media – because it is so beautifully dramatic. Generally, the media prefer to show just the debt and omit the GDP. Even worse, the graphic has a linear scale that distorts the representation of large changes.

The U.S. national debt was more than $22 trillion in 2019, which is greater than the economic output of the entire country.

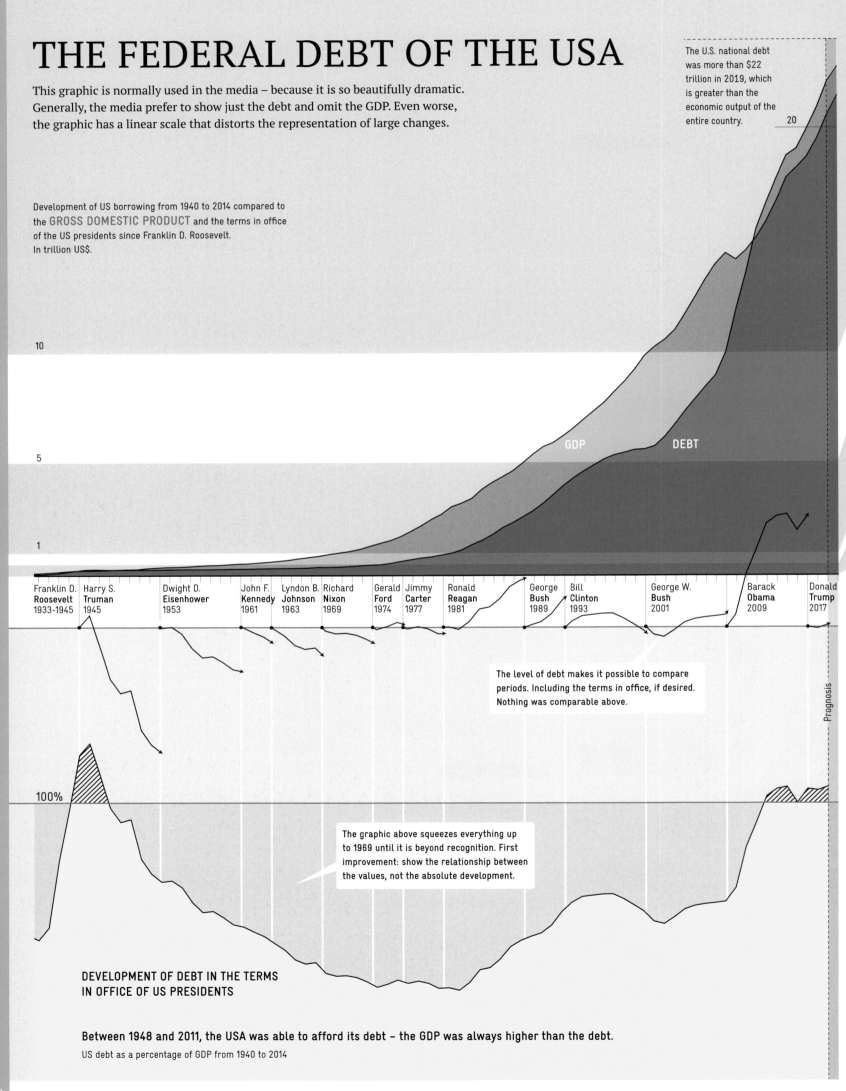

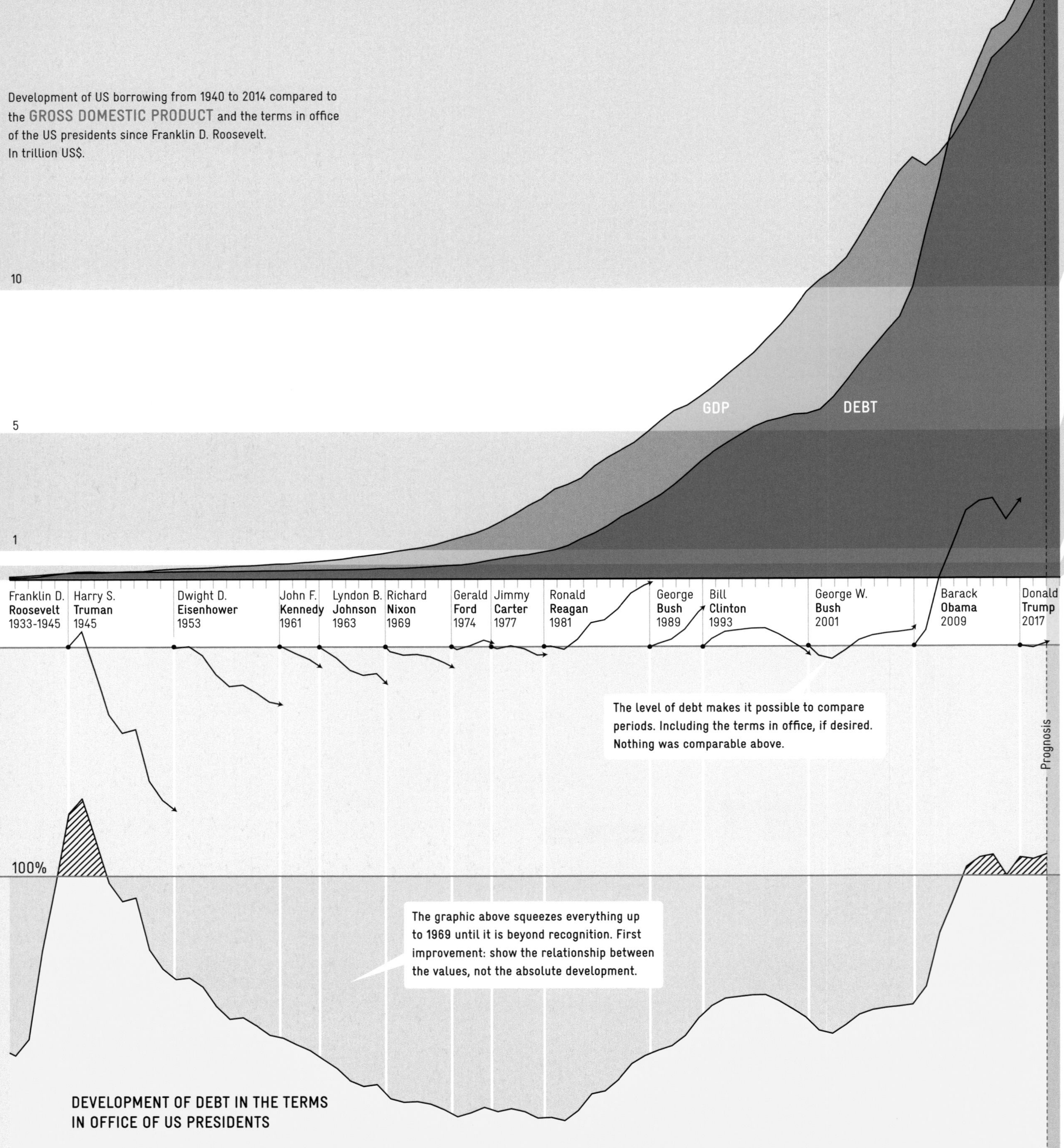
20
Development of US borrowing from 1940 to 2014 compared to the GROSS DOMESTIC PRODUCT and the terms in office of the US presidents since Franklin D. Roosevelt. In trillion US$.
10
5
1
GDP
DEBT
Franklin D. Roosevelt 1933-1945
Harry S. Truman 1945
Dwight D. Eisenhower 1953
John F. Kennedy 1961
Lyndon B. Johnson 1963
Richard Nixon 1969
Gerald Ford 1974
Jimmy Carter 1977
Ronald Reagan 1981
George Bush 1989
Bill Clinton 1993
George W. Bush 2001
Barack Obama 2009
Donald Trump 2017
The level of debt makes it possible to compare periods. Including the terms in office, if desired. Nothing was comparable above.
Prognosis
100%
The graphic above squeezes everything up to 1969 until it is beyond recognition. First improvement: show the relationship between the values, not the absolute development.
DEVELOPMENT OF DEBT IN THE TERMS IN OFFICE OF US PRESIDENTS

Between 1948 and 2011, the USA was able to afford its debt – the GDP was always higher than the debt.

US debt as a percentage of GDP from 1940 to 2014

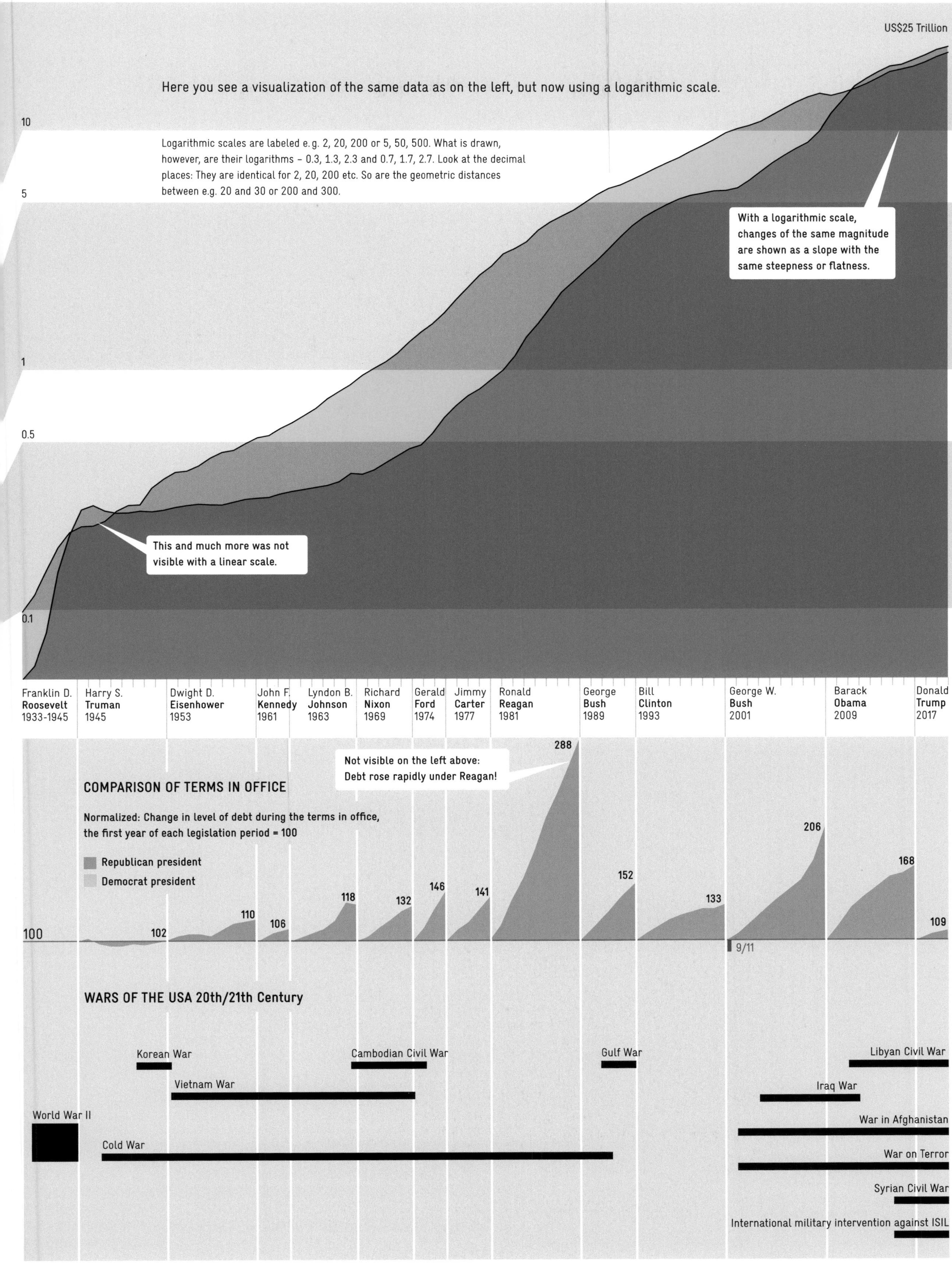
US$25 Trillion
Here you see a visualization of the same data as on the left, but now using a logarithmic scale.
10
Logarithmic scales are labeled e.g. 2, 20, 200 or 5, 50, 500. What is drawn, however, are their logarithms – 0.3, 1.3, 2.3 and 0.7, 1.7, 2.7. Look at the decimal places: They are identical for 2, 20, 200 etc. So are the geometric distances between e.g. 20 and 30 or 200 and 300.
5
With a logarithmic scale, changes of the same magnitude are shown as a slope with the same steepness or flatness.
1
0.5
This and much more was not visible with a linear scale.
0.1
Franklin D. Roosevelt 1933-1945
Harry S. Truman 1945
Dwight D. Eisenhower 1953
John F. Kennedy 1961
Lyndon B. Johnson 1963
Richard Nixon 1969
Gerald Ford 1974
Jimmy Carter 1977
Ronald Reagan 1981
George Bush 1989
Bill Clinton 1993
George W. Bush 2001
Barack Obama 2009
Donald Trump 2017
COMPARISON OF TERMS IN OFFICE
Normalized: Change in level of debt during the terms in office, the first year of each legislation period = 100
Republican president
Democrat president
Not visible on the left above: Debt rose rapidly under Reagan!
100
102
110
106
118
132
146
141
288
152
133
206
168
109
9/11
WARS OF THE USA 20th/21th Century
Korean War
Cambodian Civil War
Gulf War
Libyan Civil War
Vietnam War
Iraq War
World War II
War in Afghanistan
Cold War
War on Terror
Syrian Civil War
International military intervention against ISIL

WORLD ECONOMY ADMINISTRATION

Some economists believe nothing and no one can restrain global capitalism. A network of international organizations and alliances believes otherwise—and has created an international regulatory framework whose powerful member organizations often mutually reinforce one another's power.

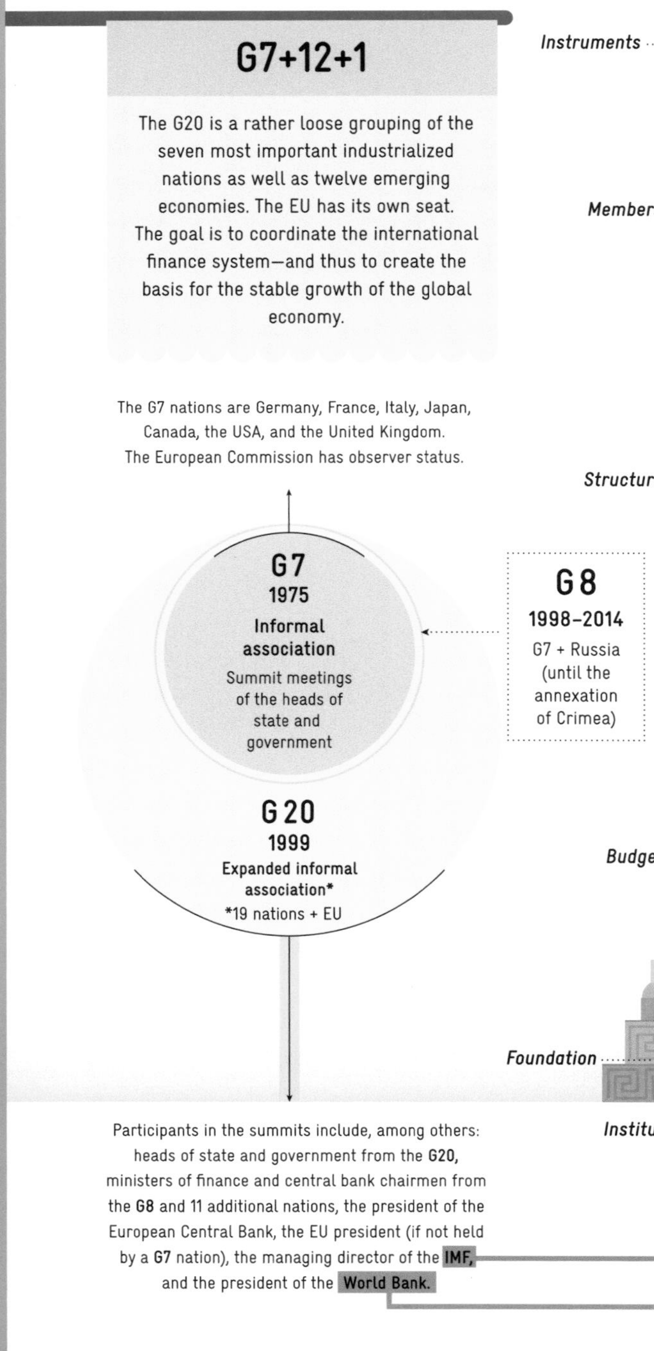

G7+12+1
The G20 is a rather loose grouping of the seven most important industrialized nations as well as twelve emerging economies. The EU has its own seat. The goal is to coordinate the international finance system—and thus to create the basis for the stable growth of the global economy.
The G7 nations are Germany, France, Italy, Japan, Canada, the USA, and the United Kingdom. The European Commission has observer status.
G7
1975
Informal association
Summit meetings of the heads of state and government
G8
1998–2014
G7 + Russia (until the annexation of Crimea)
G20
1999
Expanded informal association*
*19 nations + EU
Participants in the summits include, among others: heads of state and government from the G20, ministers of finance and central bank chairmen from the G8 and 11 additional nations, the president of the European Central Bank, the EU president (if not held by a G7 nation), the managing director of the IMF, and the president of the World Bank.

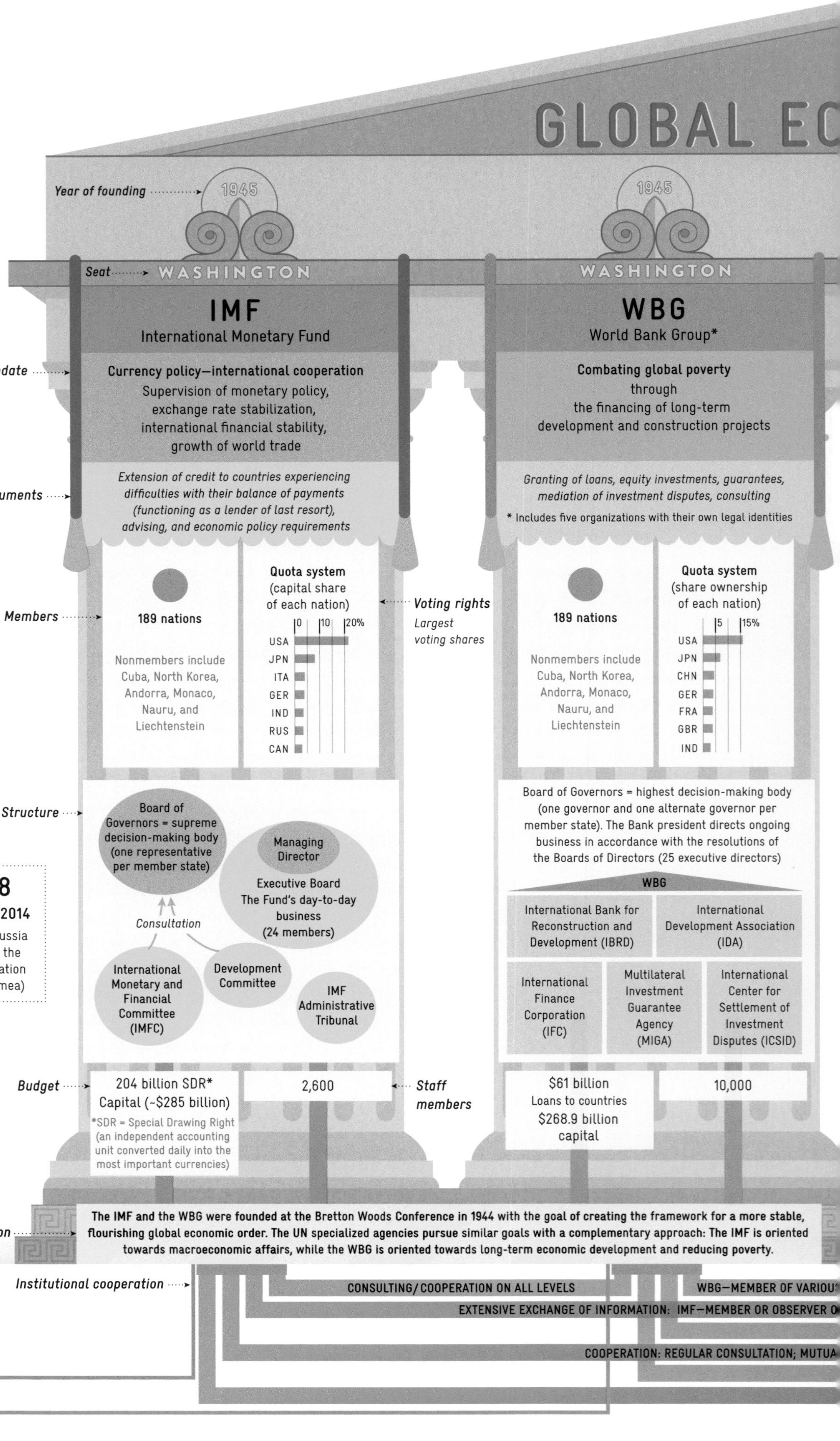

GLOBAL EC
Year of founding
1945
Seat
WASHINGTON
IMF
International Monetary Fund
Mandate
Currency policy—international cooperation
Supervision of monetary policy, exchange rate stabilization, international financial stability, growth of world trade
Instruments
Extension of credit to countries experiencing difficulties with their balance of payments (functioning as a lender of last resort), advising, and economic policy requirements
Members
189 nations
Nonmembers include Cuba, North Korea, Andorra, Monaco, Nauru, and Liechtenstein
Quota system (capital share of each nation)
0
10
20%
USA
JPN
ITA
GER
IND
RUS
CAN
Voting rights
Largest voting shares
Structure
Board of Governors = supreme decision-making body (one representative per member state)
Managing Director
Executive Board
The Fund's day-to-day business
(24 members)
Consultation
International Monetary and Financial Committee (IMFC)
Development Committee
IMF Administrative Tribunal
Budget
204 billion SDR*
Capital (~$285 billion)
*SDR = Special Drawing Right (an independent accounting unit converted daily into the most important currencies)
2,600
Staff members
1945
WASHINGTON
WBG
World Bank Group*
Combating global poverty
through
the financing of long-term development and construction projects
Granting of loans, equity investments, guarantees, mediation of investment disputes, consulting
* Includes five organizations with their own legal identities
189 nations
Nonmembers include Cuba, North Korea, Andorra, Monaco, Nauru, and Liechtenstein
Quota system (share ownership of each nation)
5
15%
USA
JPN
CHN
GER
FRA
GBR
IND
Board of Governors = highest decision-making body (one governor and one alternate governor per member state). The Bank president directs ongoing business in accordance with the resolutions of the Boards of Directors (25 executive directors)
WBG
International Bank for Reconstruction and Development (IBRD)
International Development Association (IDA)
International Finance Corporation (IFC)
Multilateral Investment Guarantee Agency (MIGA)
International Center for Settlement of Investment Disputes (ICSID)
$61 billion
Loans to countries
$268.9 billion capital
10,000
Foundation
The IMF and the WBG were founded at the Bretton Woods Conference in 1944 with the goal of creating the framework for a more stable, flourishing global economic order. The UN specialized agencies pursue similar goals with a complementary approach: The IMF is oriented towards macroeconomic affairs, while the WBG is oriented towards long-term economic development and reducing poverty.
Institutional cooperation
CONSULTING/COOPERATION ON ALL LEVELS
WBG—MEMBER OF VARIOU
EXTENSIVE EXCHANGE OF INFORMATION; IMF—MEMBER OR OBSERVER O
COOPERATION: REGULAR CONSULTATION; MUTUA

NOMIC ADMINISTRATION

OECD
1961 · PARIS

Organization for Economic Cooperation and Development

Advancement of democracy and market economics
Forum for the sharing of experience and the development of collaborative solutions

Recommendations, standards and guidelines, agreements and occasional legally binding treaties as well

34 nations* + European Commission
* The EU nations Bulgaria, Croatia, Cyprus, Latvia, Lithuania, Malta, and Romania do not have membership

One country, one vote
Decisions by mutual consent (except in isolated cases)

Council= decision-making body
Strategic direction and oversight

Committees
Discussion and technical work

Secretariat
Data collection, analysis, and proposals

363 million euros
Budget and agenda are determined on a two-year basis.

2,500

Successor to the Organization for European Economic Cooperation and the 1948 Marshall Plan for the rebuilding of Europe

WTO
1995 · GENEVA

World Trade Organization

Global trade and economic relations
Liberalization of international trade and multilateral trade rules

General Agreement on Tariffs and Trade (GATT)
General Agreement on Trade in Services (GATS)
Trade-related Aspects of Intellectual Property Rights (TRIPS)

161 nations + EU
The EU is a member in its own right along with each EU member state.

One country, one vote
Although a simple majority is sufficient, in actual fact, decisions are reached by consensus as a matter of principle.

Director General
Secretariat

General Council of economic and trade ministers = highest decision-making body (at least every two years)

Ongoing business

The ambassadors and delegates meet regularly in Geneva.

General Council
Dispute Settlement Body
Trade Policy Review Body

197,500,000 Swiss francs

634

Successor organization of the General Agreement on Tariffs and Trade (GATT), which was intended to lower tariffs between trading partners and simplify trade after the Second World War

FSB
2009 · BASEL

Financial Stability Board

Global financial stability
Risk evaluation, formation and coordination of guidelines, monitoring of implementation, compendium of financial standards

Guidelines are not legally binding, but rather rely on moral persuasion and mutual pressure
Association under Swiss law

24 countries* + 12 organizations**
*G20 + Hong Kong, the Netherlands, Singapore, Spain, and Switzerland
**The ECB, European Commission, IMF, OECD, and World Bank, among others

No formal distribution of voting rights
Decisions by consensus

Plenary = decision-making body 69 representatives

Steering Committee: *Operational activity*

4 standing committees
Assessment of Vulnerabilities (SCAV)
Budget and Resources (SCBR)
Supervisory and Regulatory Cooperation (SRC)
Standards Implementation (SCSI)

12,285,000 Swiss francs
Majority of donations from the Bank for International Settlements (BIS)

24

Successor organization of the Financial Stability Forum (FSF), started by G20 nations at the peak of the financial crisis

---

No substantive consultation or cooperation

OECD COMMITTEES
OECD–INFLUENCE ON WTO NEGOTIATIONS
VARIOUS OECD COMMITTEES
OECD–MEMBER OF FSB
REGULAR CONSULTATION AND COOPERATION
OBSERVER STATUS IN VARIOUS COMMITTEES; PARTICIPATION IN VARIOUS MEETINGS
WBG–MEMBER OF FSB
IMF–MEMBER OF FSB

ON FIRE!

Fossil fuels made the Industrial Revolution—and today's mobile society—possible. Nuclear power was once reputed to be a futuristic source of clean energy. Today coal, gas, oil, and uranium satisfy over 90% of the global hunger for energy. And now we know: Along with the blessings of economic growth and prosperity, they brought the curse of climate change, meltdowns, and long-term storage of toxic waste. Taking stock of the situation is necessary before a switch to alternative energy sources is possible.

Energy resources by region, 2015
in exajoules (EJ)

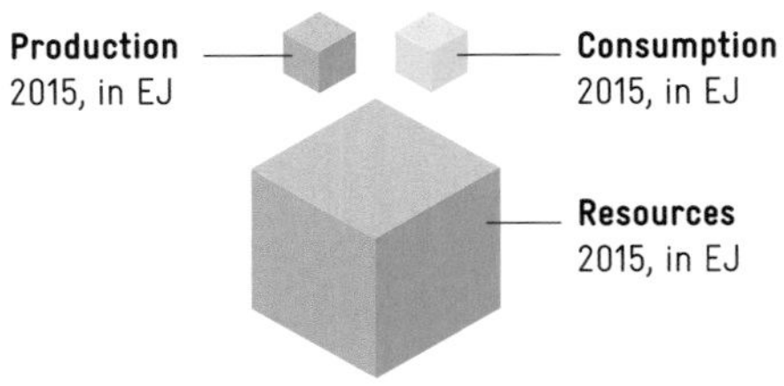
Production
2015, in EJ
Consumption
2015, in EJ
Resources
2015, in EJ

URANIUM

The radioactive metal was discovered in 1789 by the German chemist Martin Heinrich Klaproth. The first nuclear power plant came online in 1954 in the Russian city of Obninsk. Today, there are just over 450 nuclear power plants operating around the world.

OIL

As far back as classical antiquity, oil was used as a building material and as fuel for lamps, but it has been systematically extracted and processed in refineries only since the middle of the nineteenth century.

NATURAL GAS

Highly flammable methane is the main component of natural gas. China was already using it 2,000 years ago for salt production. Among fossil fuels, natural gas is the most environmentally friendly.

COAL

Lignite and anthracite are plentiful around the world and can be mined relatively inexpensively—unfortunately. Coal converted to energy is responsible for the greatest amount of CO_2 emissions by far.

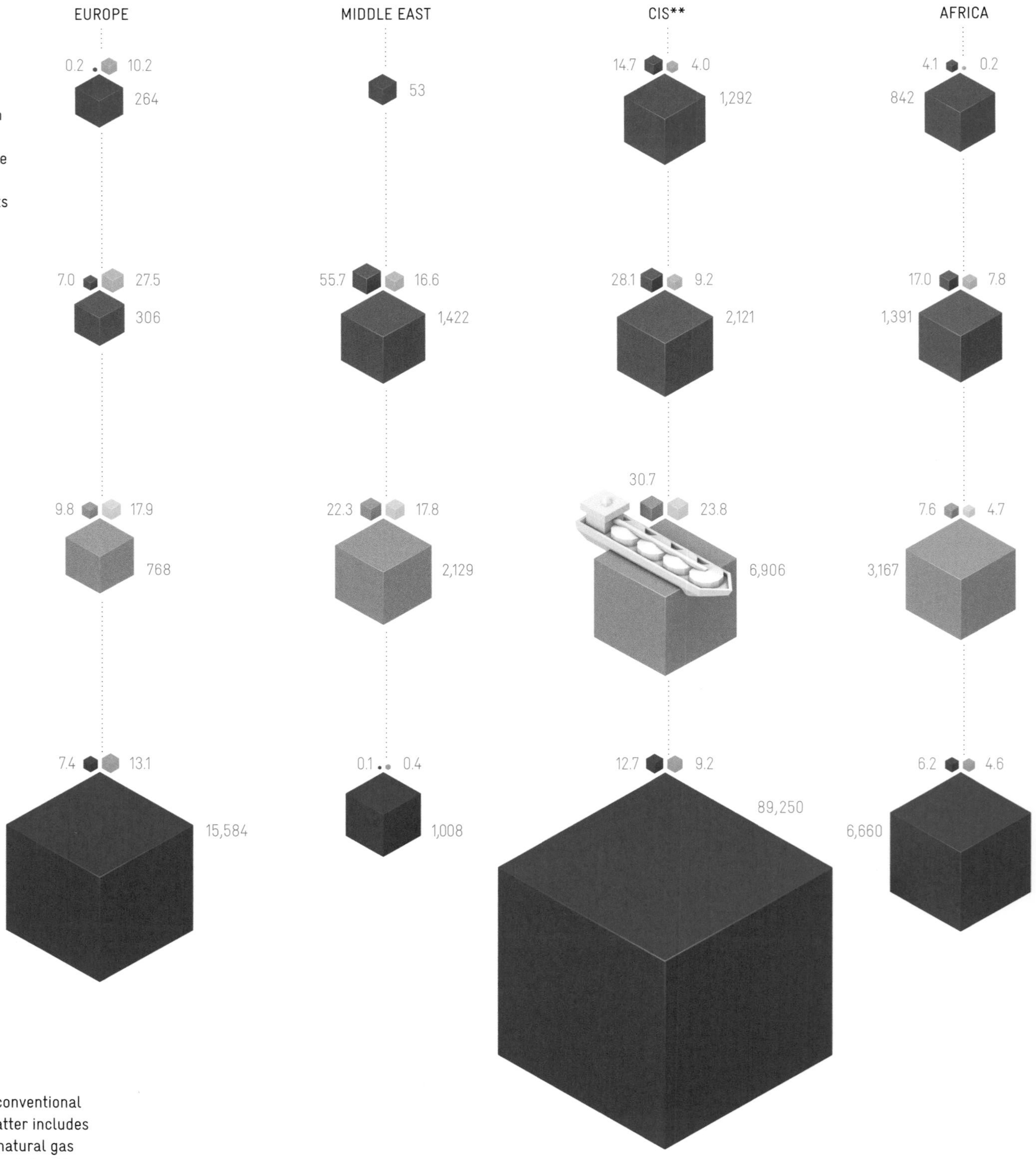
EUROPE
MIDDLE EAST
CIS**
AFRICA
0.2
10.2
264
53
14.7
4.0
1,292
4.1
0.2
842
7.0
27.5
306
55.7
16.6
1,422
28.1
9.2
2,121
17.0
7.8
1,391
9.8
17.9
768
22.3
17.8
2,129
30.7
23.8
6,906
7.6
4.7
3,167
7.4
13.1
15,584
0.1
0.4
1,008
12.7
9.2
89,250
6.2
4.6
6,660

We include oil and natural gas from conventional and non-conventional deposits. The latter includes oil from tar sands and shale oil, and natural gas deposits that can be tapped only through fracking. Coal includes lignite and anthracite.

* Preliminary values; rounding differences are possible
** Commonwealth of Independent States (Russia et al.)

The world's primary energy consumption in 2013 was **567.5 exajoules.**

The US had a primary energy consumption of **102.9 exajoules.***

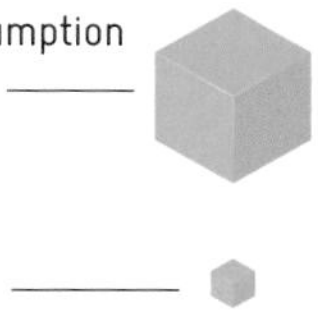

What is primary energy consumption?

Strictly speaking, according to physics, energy cannot be consumed, but only transformed. Nevertheless, economists use this definition: The primary energy consumption of an economy is derived from the final energy consumption and the losses incurred in the production of the energy used (that is, transformed).

How much energy is in an exajoule?

In order to be able to compare the depicted fossil fuels, we illustrate their energy content in exajoules. A joule is equivalent to the work performed by a human heartbeat. An exajoule, in turn, corresponds to a quintillion joules (a one followed by eighteen zeroes)—the work of 340 million human hearts over a lifetime.

US Energy Consumption by Energy Source 2017, in percent

Petroleum
Natural gas
Coal
Renewables
Nuclear power
37
29
11.8
11
9

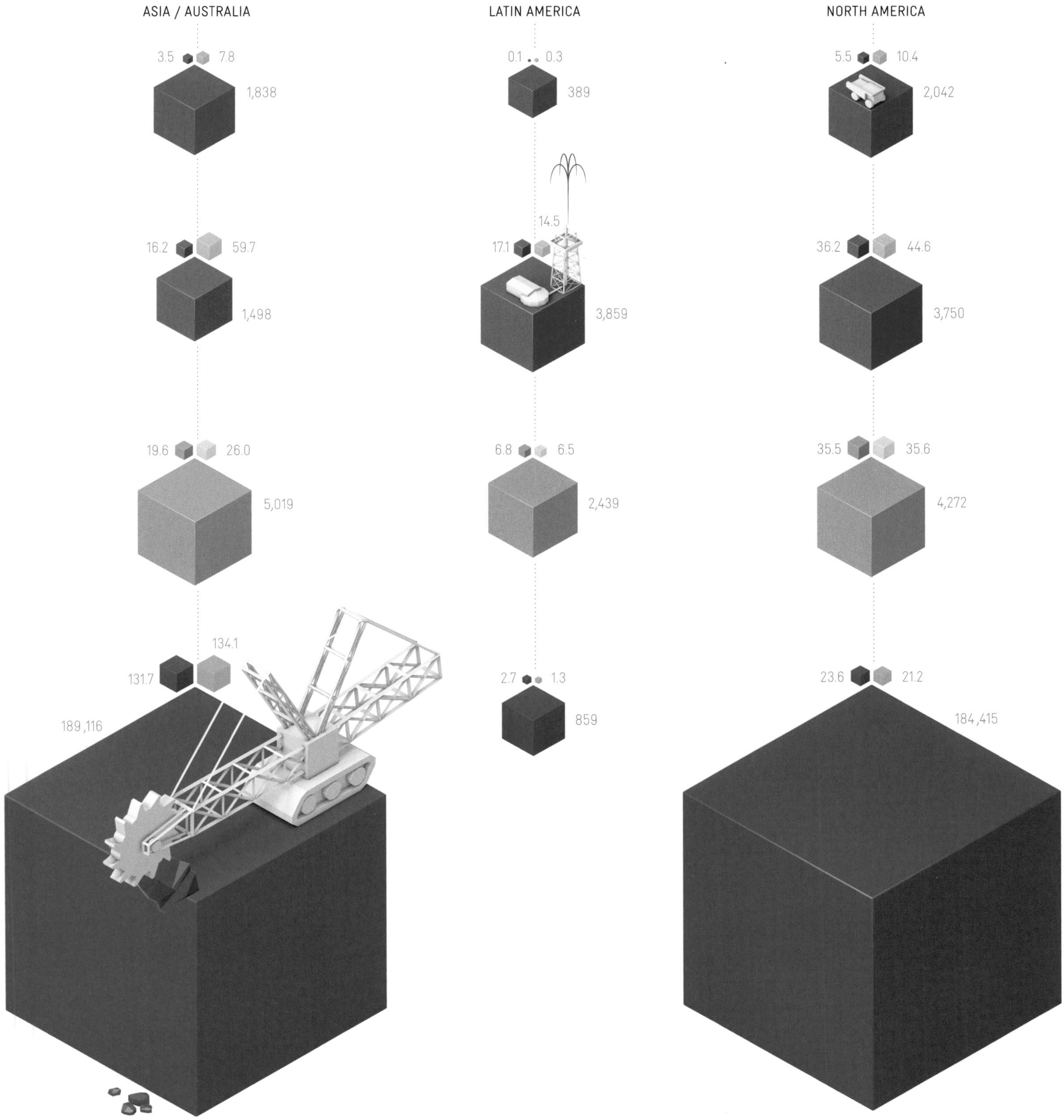

ASIA / AUSTRALIA
3.5
7.8
1,838
16.2
59.7
1,498
19.6
26.0
5,019
131.7
134.1
189,116
LATIN AMERICA
0.1
0.3
389
14.5
17.1
3,859
6.8
6.5
2,439
2.7
1.3
859
NORTH AMERICA
5.5
10.4
2,042
36.2
44.6
3,750
35.5
35.6
4,272
23.6
21.2
184,415

WHERE'S THE GAS?

When people talk about fracking, they assume the drilling happens in their backyard. This infographic features a sequence of layers typically found in northern Germany. Modern drill holes extend several kilometers underground. Research shows that the potential for natural gas reserves is unequally distributed around the globe.

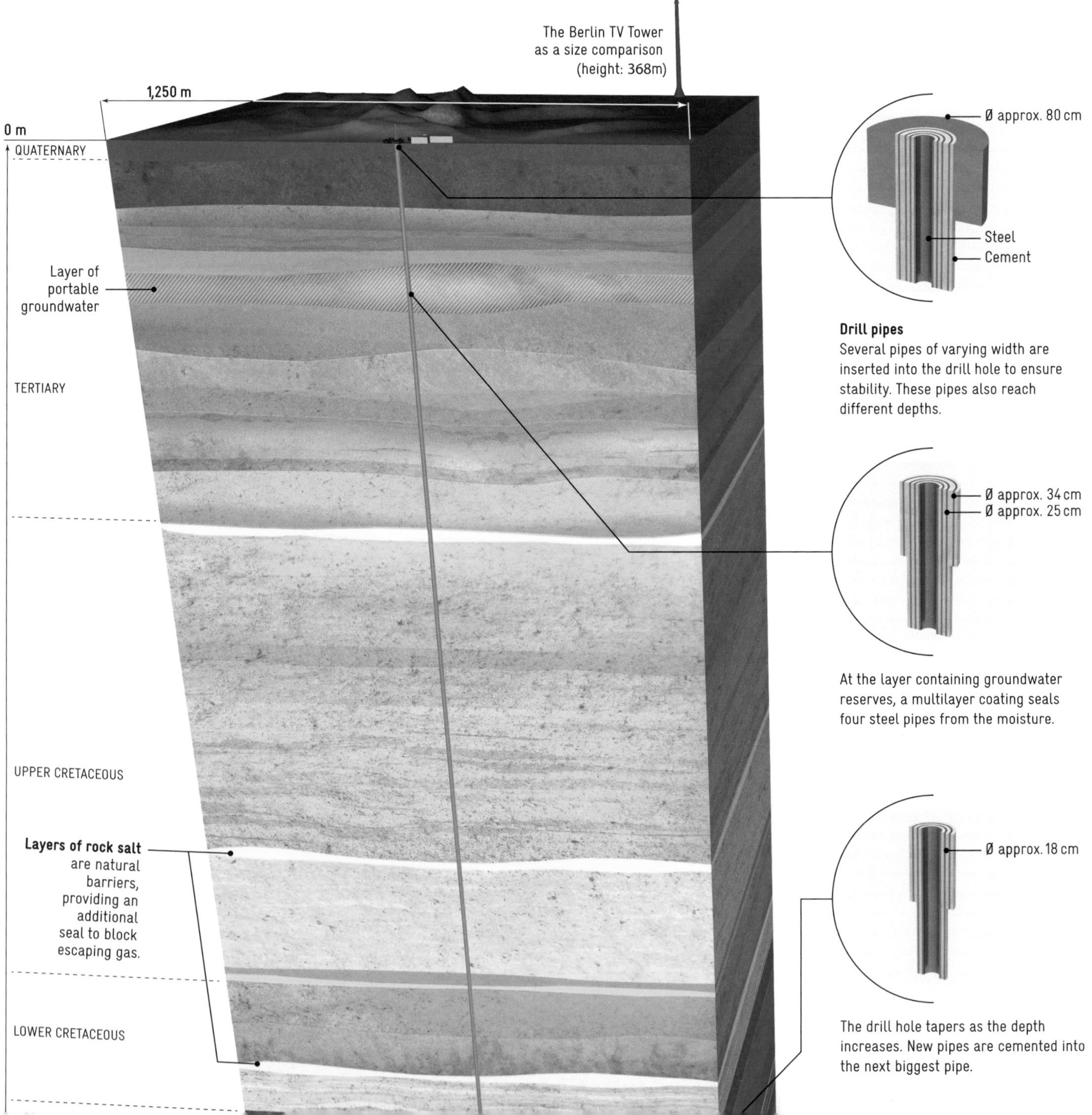
The Berlin TV Tower
as a size comparison
(height: 368m)
1,250 m
0 m
QUATERNARY
Layer of portable groundwater
TERTIARY
UPPER CRETACEOUS
Layers of rock salt are natural barriers, providing an additional seal to block escaping gas.
LOWER CRETACEOUS
Ø approx. 80 cm
Steel
Cement
Drill pipes
Several pipes of varying width are inserted into the drill hole to ensure stability. These pipes also reach different depths.
Ø approx. 34 cm
Ø approx. 25 cm
At the layer containing groundwater reserves, a multilayer coating seals four steel pipes from the moisture.
Ø approx. 18 cm
The drill hole tapers as the depth increases. New pipes are cemented into the next biggest pipe.

Distribution of natural gas reserves around the globe

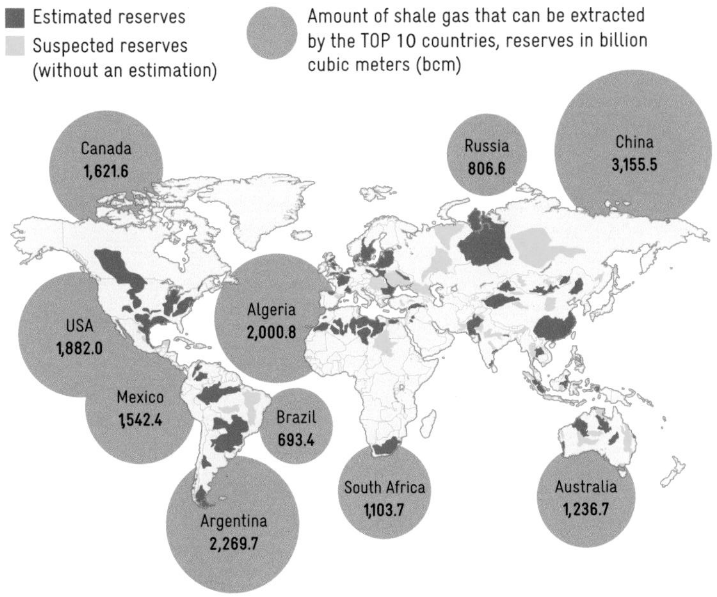
Estimated reserves
Suspected reserves (without an estimation)
Amount of shale gas that can be extracted by the TOP 10 countries, reserves in billion cubic meters (bcm)
Canada 1,621.6
USA 1,882.0
Mexico 1,542.4
Argentina 2,269.7
Brazil 693.4
Algeria 2,000.8
South Africa 1,103.7
Russia 806.6
China 3,155.5
Australia 1,236.7

The largest potential shale gas reserves in Europe

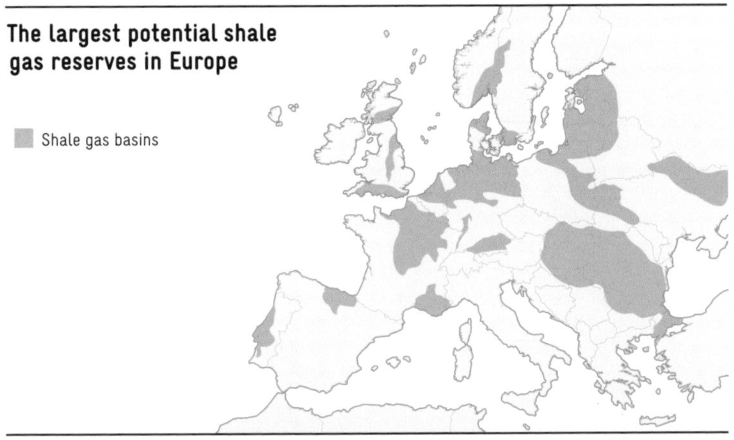
Shale gas basins

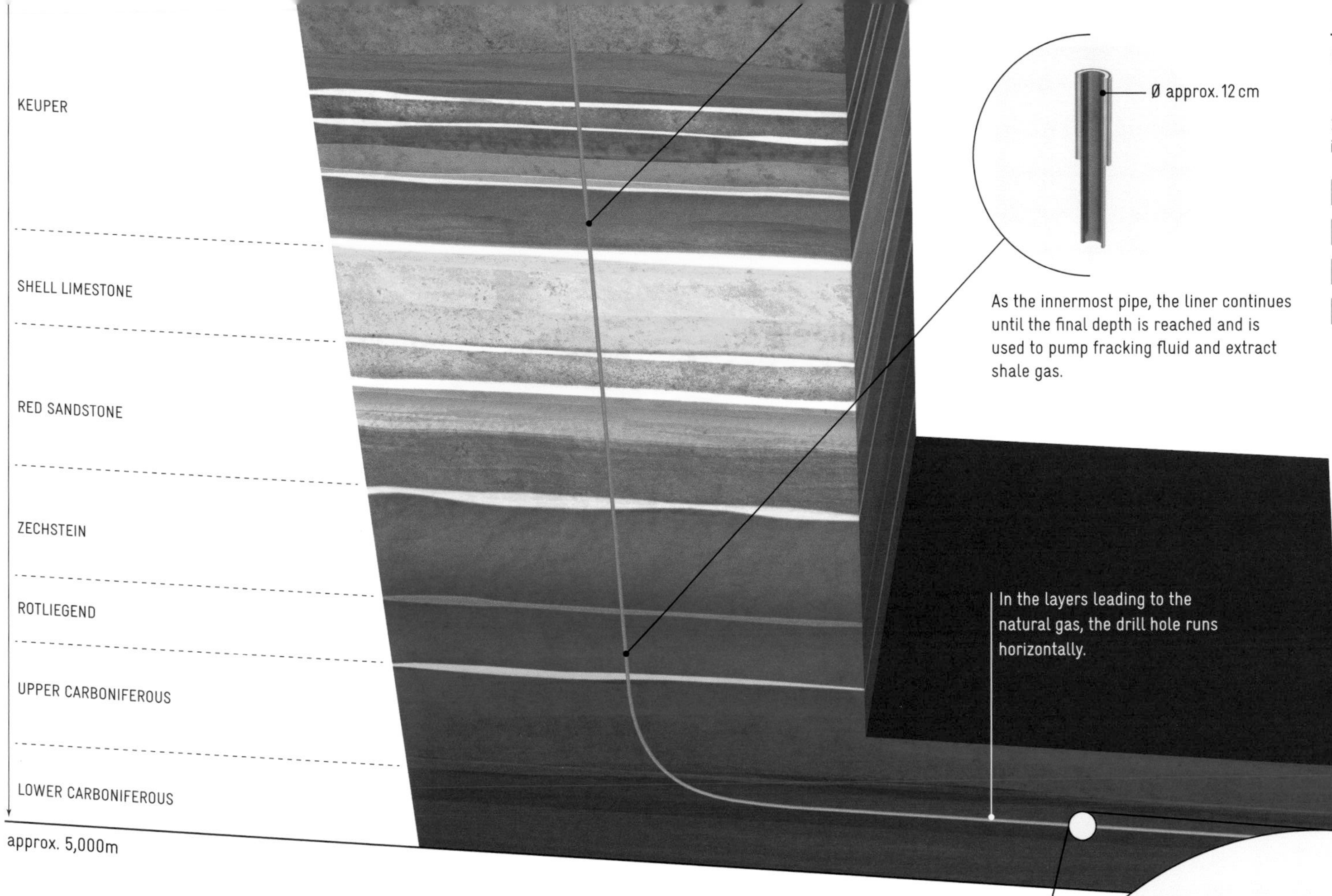

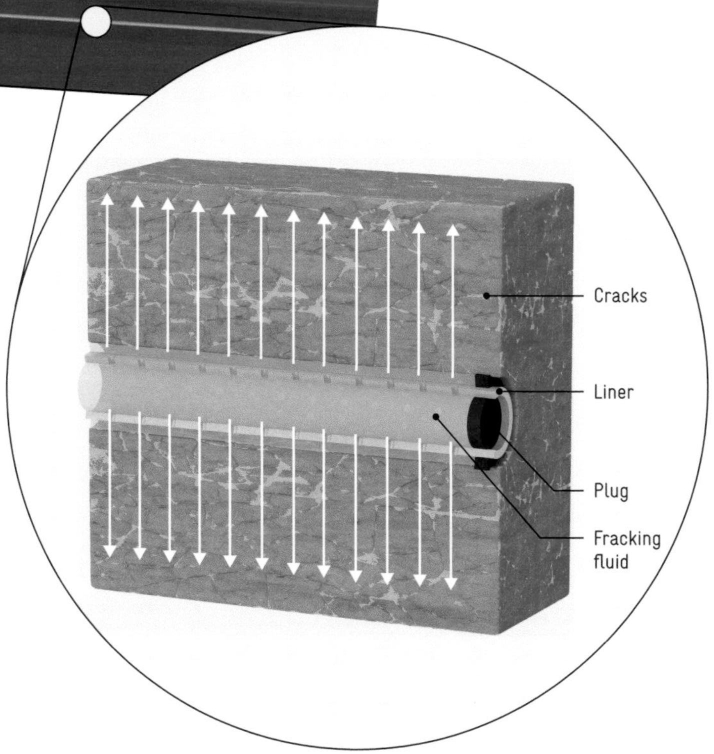

Shale gas in Germany

- Regions with potential shale gas reserves
- Areas granted mining permission to search for shale gas, among others

Hamburg
Berlin
Bremen Hanover Leipzig
Cologne
Frankfurt
Stuttgart
Munich

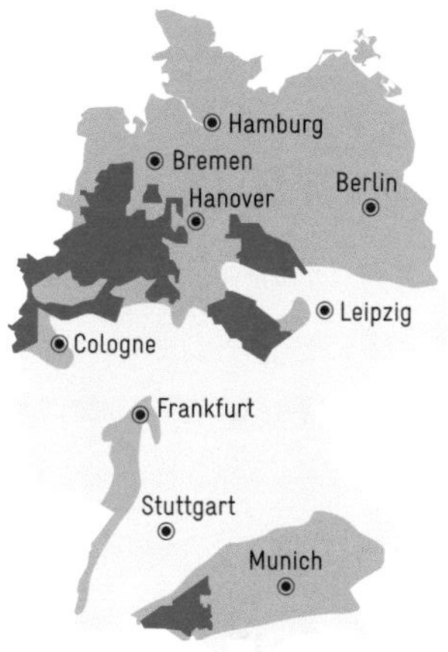

Natural gas extraction
2011, in bcm

World
Germany
3,276.2
11.9

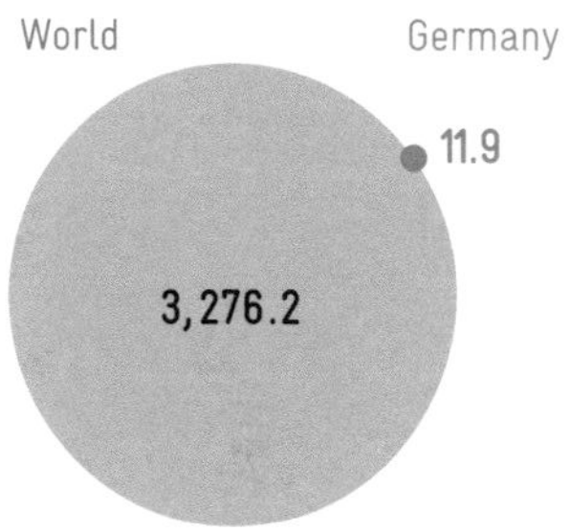

Natural gas consumption
2010, in bcm

World
Germany
3,249.0
95.9

Comparison of significant natural gas resources in Europe

2010, in billion cubic meters (bcm), including shale gas and coal bed methane

Poland 5,536
France 5,302
Norway 4,351
827 Germany

Under high pressures the fluid is pressed into the rock, creating cracks in the sediment. The fluid contains proppants designed to keep cracks open.

Cracks
Liner
Plug
Fracking fluid

Ø approx. 12 cm

As the innermost pipe, the liner continues until the final depth is reached and is used to pump fracking fluid and extract shale gas.

In the layers leading to the natural gas, the drill hole runs horizontally.

KEUPER

SHELL LIMESTONE

RED SANDSTONE

ZECHSTEIN

ROTLIEGEND

UPPER CARBONIFEROUS

LOWER CARBONIFEROUS

approx. 5,000 m

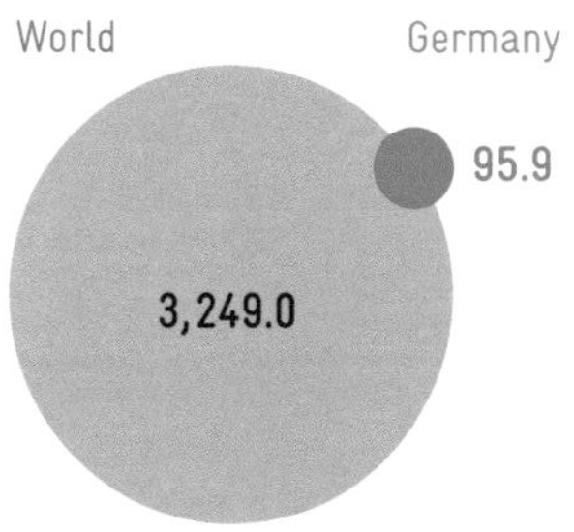

Composition of new fracking fluids for shale gas

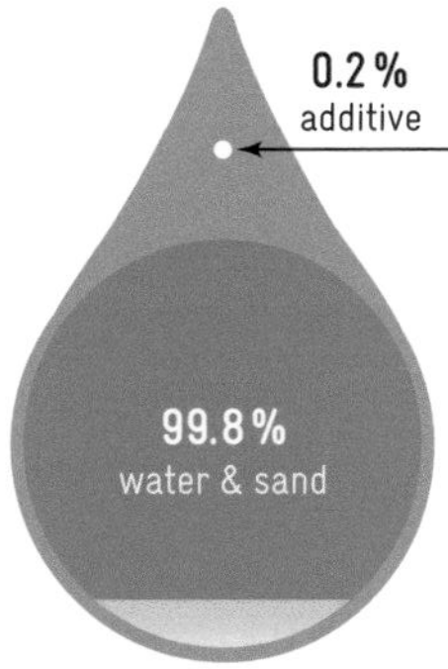

The new generation of fluids contains considerably less

31% Butyldiglycol (friction reducing agent)

69% Choline Chloride (stabilizing agent)

Butyldiglycol is a solvent used in many coatings, resins and household detergents.

Choline chloride is used in some pharmaceutical compounds and as an additive in the animal feed industry.

0.2% additive

99.8% water & sand

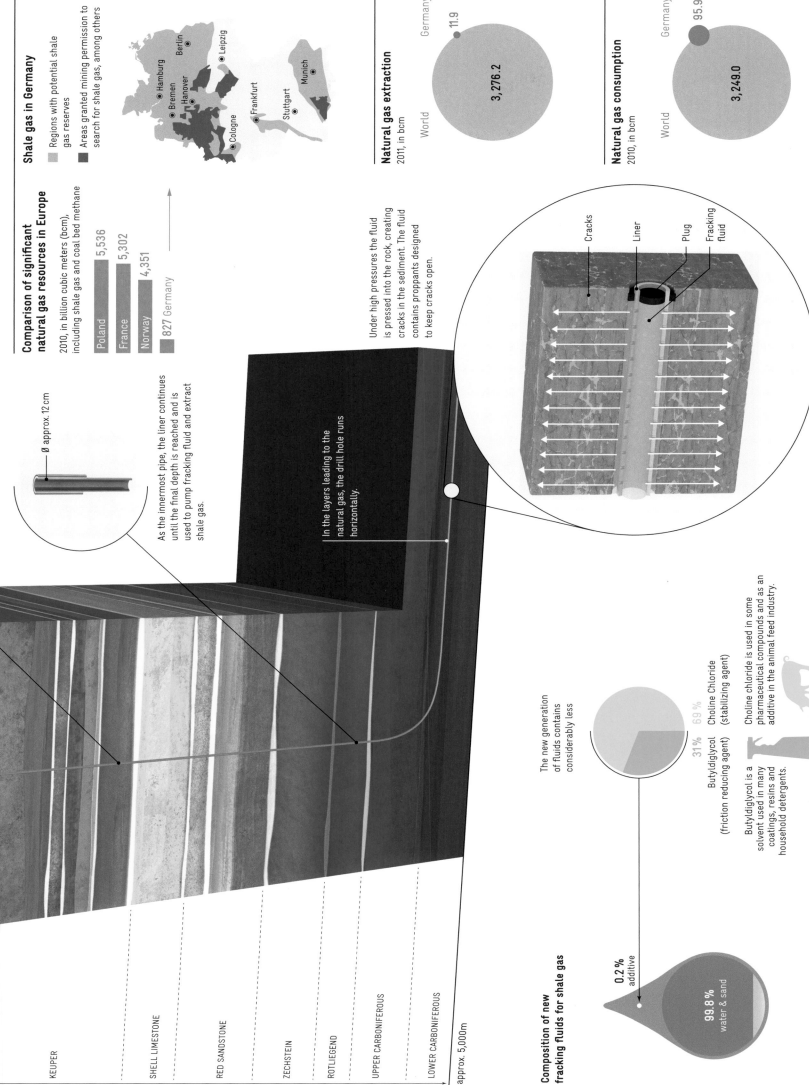

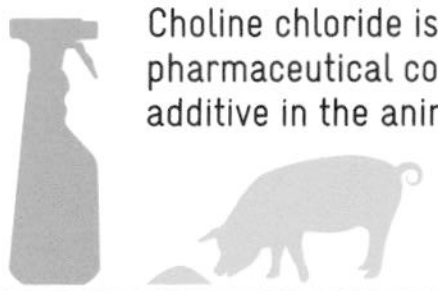

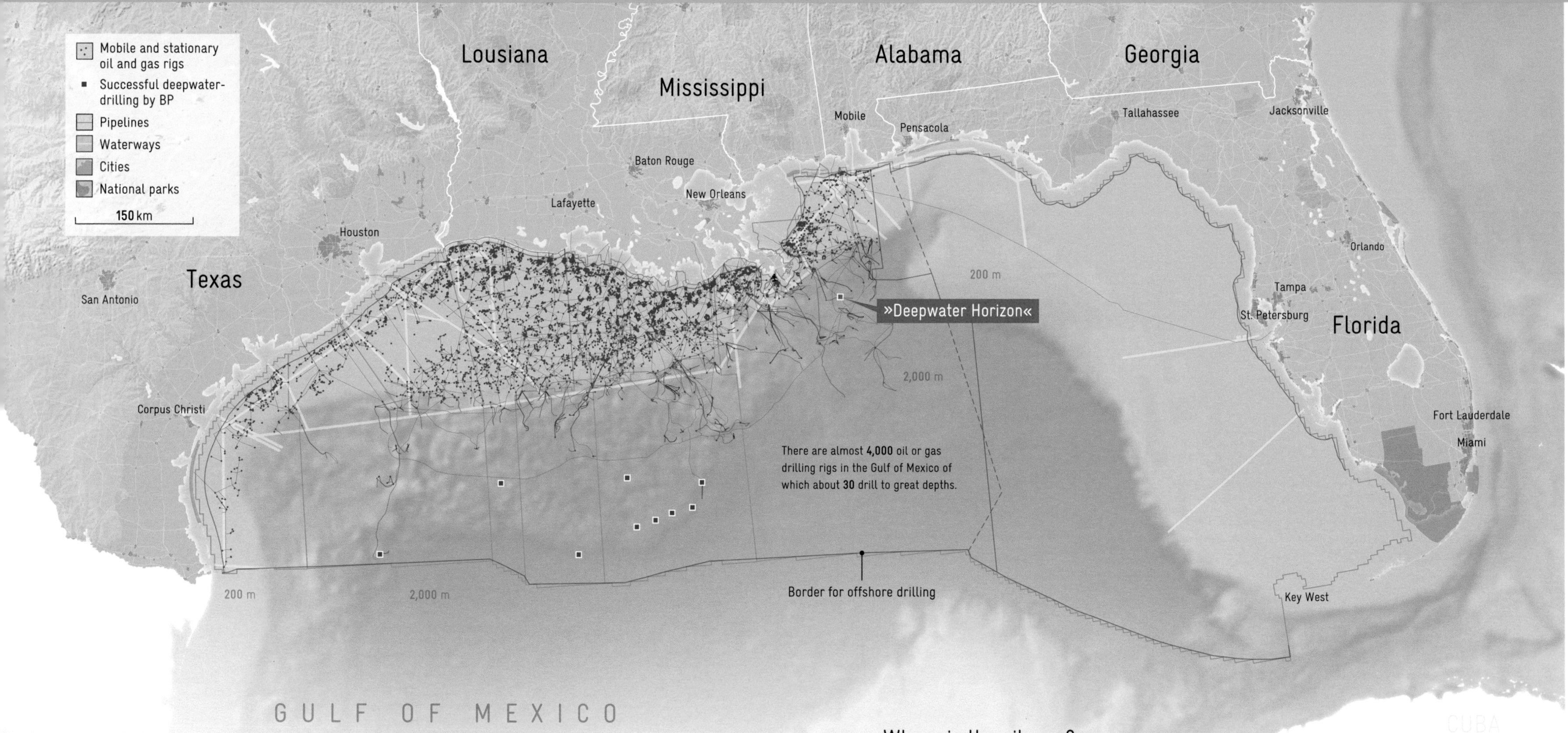
Mobile and stationary oil and gas rigs
Successful deepwater-drilling by BP
Pipelines
Waterways
Cities
National parks
150 km
Lousiana
Mississippi
Alabama
Georgia
Texas
Florida
Mobile
Pensacola
Tallahassee
Jacksonville
Baton Rouge
New Orleans
Lafayette
Houston
San Antonio
Corpus Christi
Orlando
Tampa
St. Petersburg
Fort Lauderdale
Miami
Key West
»Deepwater Horizon«
200 m
2,000 m
There are almost 4,000 oil or gas drilling rigs in the Gulf of Mexico of which about 30 drill to great depths.
Border for offshore drilling
GULF OF MEXICO
CUBA

Where is the oil now?

According to information from the US supervisory authority, only a quarter of the oil that leaked from the well still remains in the ocean.

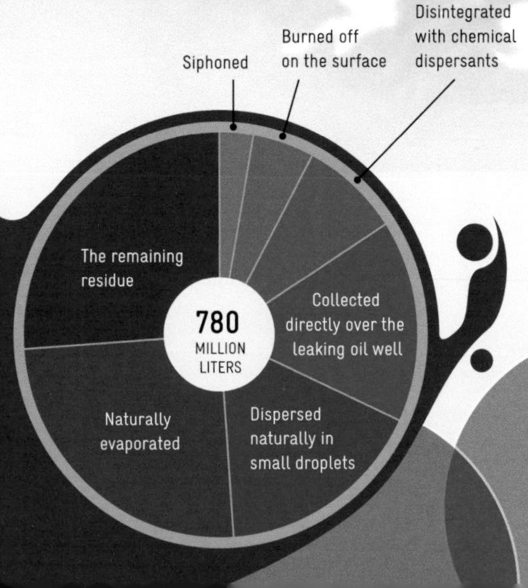
Siphoned
Burned off on the surface
Disintegrated with chemical dispersants
Collected directly over the leaking oil well
Dispersed naturally in small droplets
Naturally evaporated
The remaining residue
780 MILLION LITERS

Tragic accidents in numbers

Never has so much oil spilled uncontrollably into the environment as it did after the disaster on the »Deepwater Horizon«.

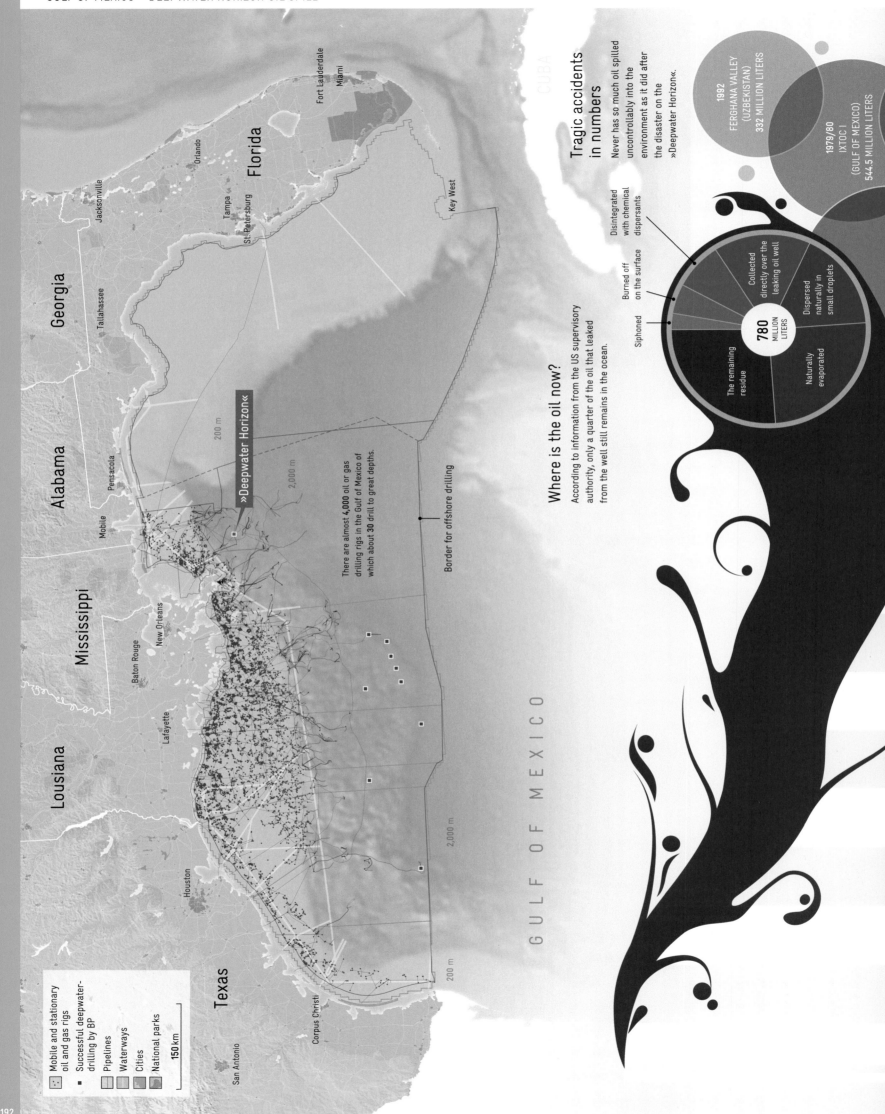

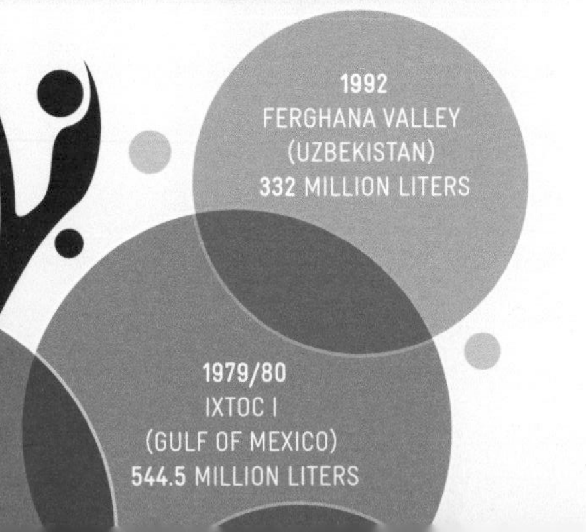
1992
FERGHANA VALLEY
(UZBEKISTAN)
332 MILLION LITERS
1979/80
IXTOC I
(GULF OF MEXICO)
544.5 MILLION LITERS

1991
GULF WAR
(PERSIAN GULF)
636 MILLION LITERS
1979
ATLANTIC EMPRESS/
AEGEAN CAPTAIN
(THE CARIBBEAN)
335 MILLION LITERS

ALL'S WELL THAT ENDS WELL?

For the time being, the well that burst open after the Deepwater Horizon explosion on the Gulf of Mexico seafloor is sealed. Yet thousands of oil rigs continue to operate, many drilling to great depths. The oil spill timeline demonstrates how poorly companies are prepared for emergencies.

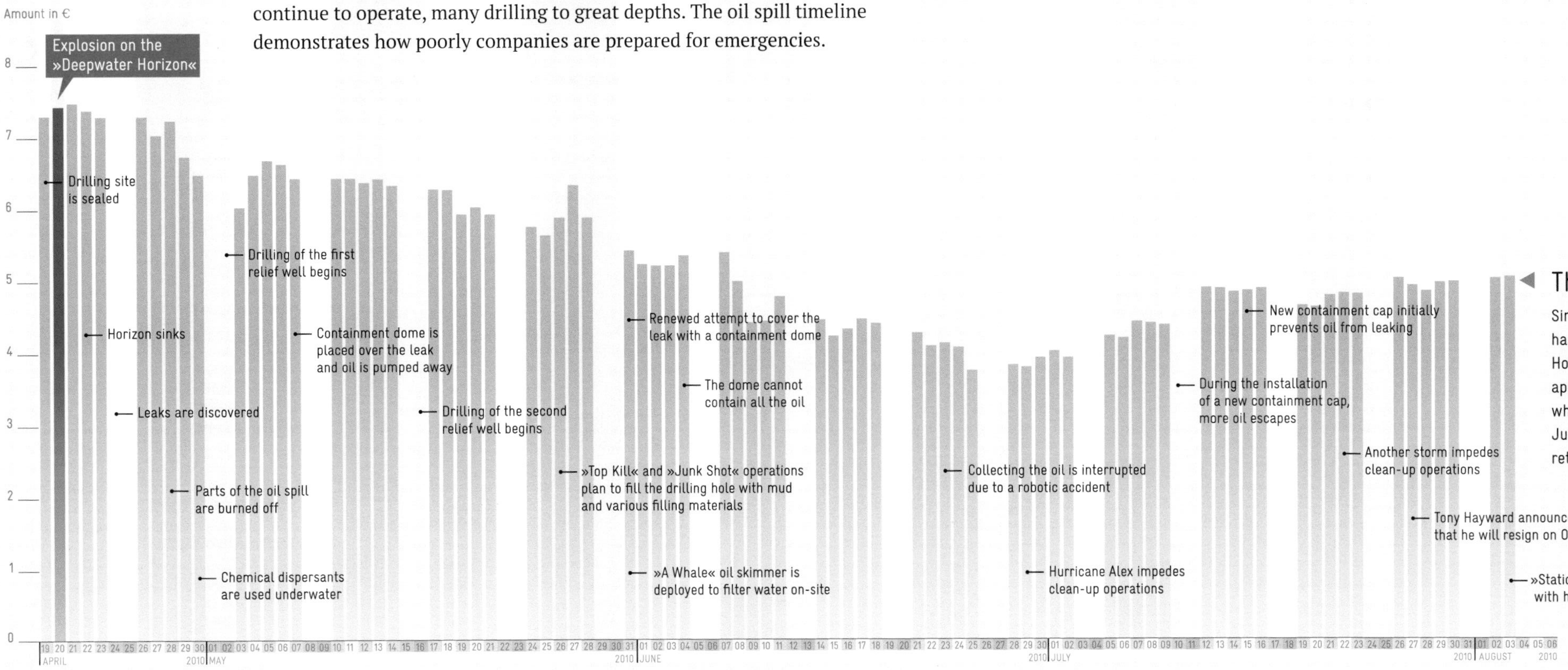
Amount in €
8
7
6
5
4
3
2
1
0
Explosion on the »Deepwater Horizon«
Drilling site is sealed
Horizon sinks
Leaks are discovered
Parts of the oil spill are burned off
Chemical dispersants are used underwater
Drilling of the first relief well begins
Containment dome is placed over the leak and oil is pumped away
Drilling of the second relief well begins
»Top Kill« and »Junk Shot« operations plan to fill the drilling hole with mud and various filling materials
Renewed attempt to cover the leak with a containment dome
The dome cannot contain all the oil
»A Whale« oil skimmer is deployed to filter water on-site
Collecting the oil is interrupted due to a robotic accident
Hurricane Alex impedes clean-up operations
During the installation of a new containment cap, more oil escapes
New containment cap initially prevents oil from leaking
Another storm impedes clean-up operations
Tony Hayward announces that he will resign on October 1, 2010
»Static Kill« seals the oil well with heavy drilling mud
APRIL 2010
MAY 2010
JUNE 2010
JULY 2010
AUGUST 2010

The BP Stock

Since the accident, the stock has lost 30% of its value. However, the downturn appears to be over: anyone who bought BP shares in June can now enjoy a healthy return of 40%.

KEY FIGURES

2009 turnover	€195,000,000,000
Deposit in US funds to pay damages for victims of the oil spill	€16,300,000,000
Gas stations worldwide	24,000
Gas stations in Germany (total)	2,513
Number of customers per day	13,000,000
Liters of oil extracted per day	365,670,648

2009 profit	€12,647,000,000
First half of 2009	
Costs per barrel of oil	€40.75
Profit	€5,242,600,000
First half of 2010	
Costs per barrel of oil	€57.05
Loss	- €8,354,900,000
Employees worldwide	80,300

4. BP is the fourth largest fast-food chain in Germany, the other places are occupied by:
1. MCDONALD'S
2. BURGER KING
3. NORDSEE

4. According to Fortune (07/2010), BP is the fourth largest company according to turnover, the other places are occupied by:
1. WAL-MART
2. ROYAL DUTCH SHELL
3. EXXON MOBIL

THE TOP 5 OIL GIANTS

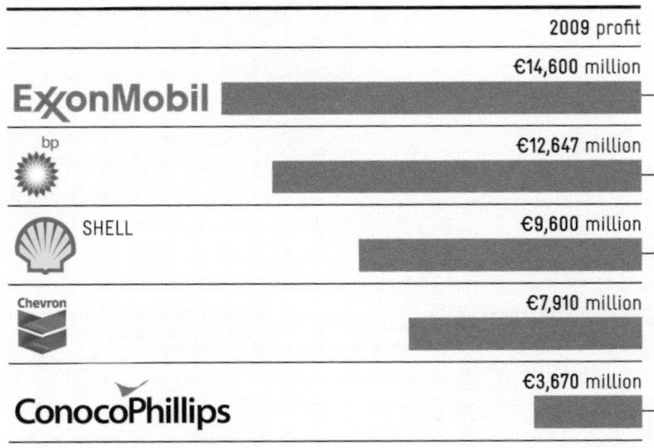
2009 profit
ExxonMobil
€14,600 million
bp
€12,647 million
SHELL
€9,600 million
Chevron
€7,910 million
ConocoPhillips
€3,670 million

OIL COMPANY GAS STATIONS IN GERMANY

Amount of gas stations in Germany, excluding motorway gas stations and purely biodiesel and rest stop gas fueling stations
Total: 14,410 (Others: 5,364)

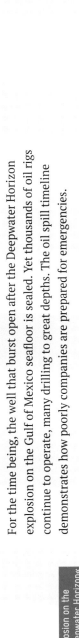

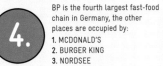

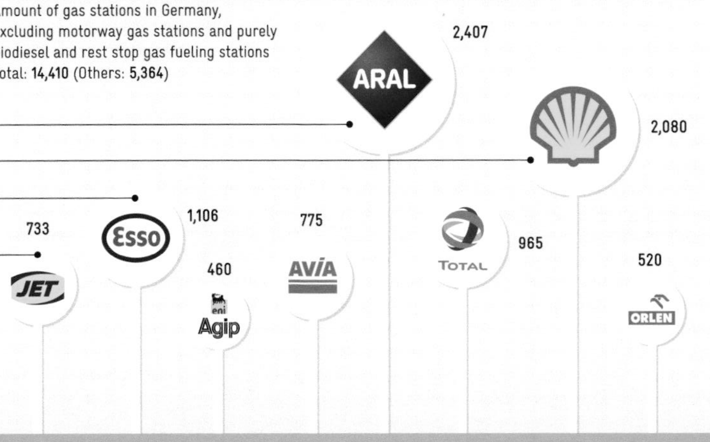
ARAL
2,407
2,080
Esso
1,106
JET
733
Agip
460
AVIA
775
TOTAL
965
ORLEN
520

THE PRICE AND PROFITS OF OIL

The price of oil can make or break a country's future. When the price is right, the oil flows—and the money flows with it into the state coffers. But calculating its profit margins is a tricky business: Each country has its own challenges when it comes to extracting this valuable resource. The situation is complicated by global events that can influence the value—and a government's future.

EXTRACTION

It is becoming increasingly difficult to extract oil from the remaining reserves. Each well creates its own challenges, and these affect the price of production. **They include:**

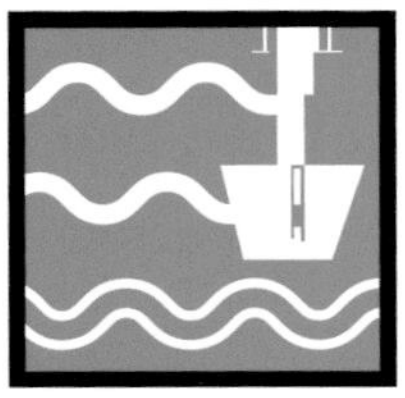

DISCOVERY AND EXPLORATION

INFRASTRUCTURE AND DEVELOPMENT

EXTRACTION OPERATIONAL AND MAINTENANCE COST

ADMINISTRATIVE LOGISTICAL EXPENSES SUCH AS ROYALTIES AND TAXES

The sum of these variables means oil-producing states need to sell oil at a certain price to balance their budgets and continue production.

This is the

BREAK-EVEN POINT.

The higher the profit required, between the pure production and the break-even price, the more dependent a country is on its oil.

INFLUENCING THE PRICE OF OIL (1979-2019)

There are various types of oil, each with its own benchmark pricing. The two most common grades are Brent Crude from Europe and West Texas Intermediate (WTI) from the USA.

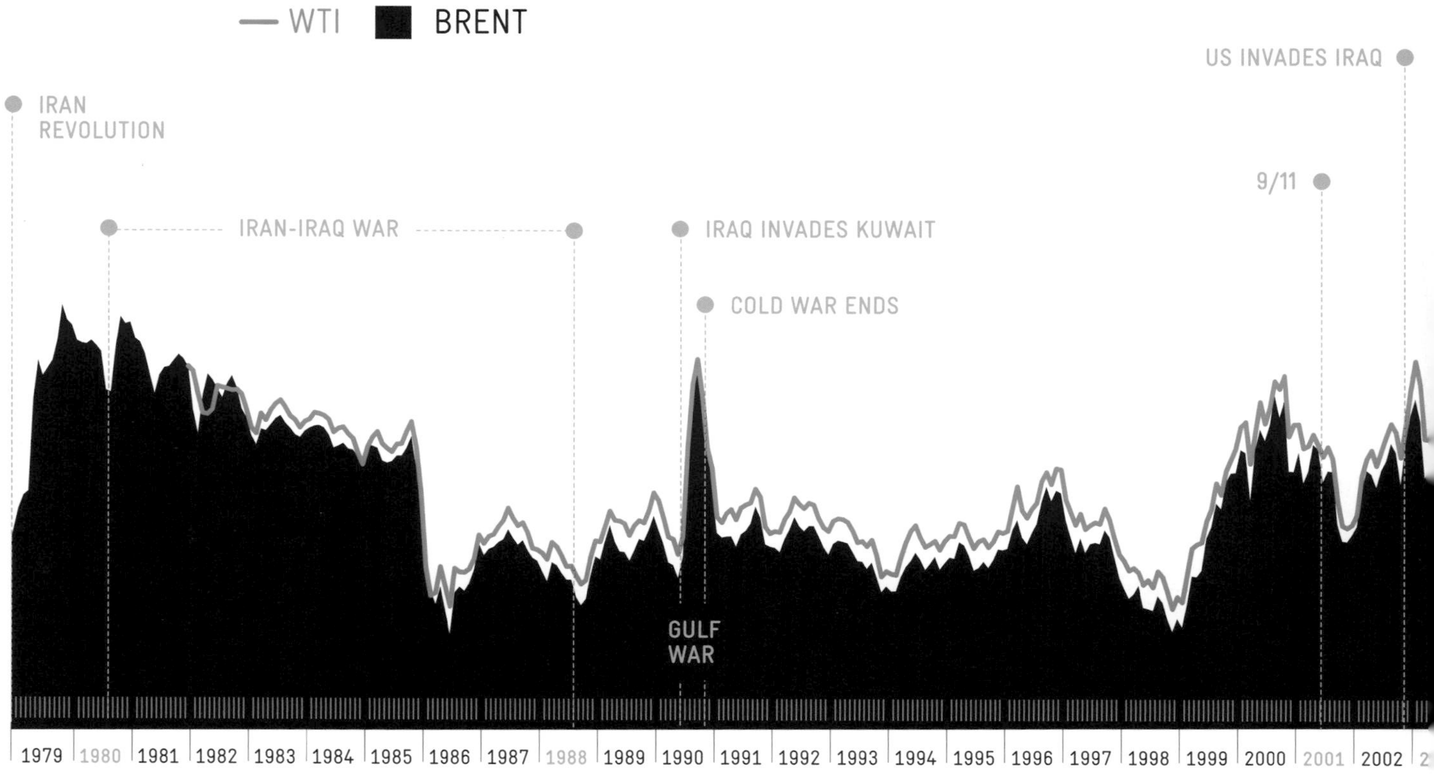

— WTI
BRENT
IRAN REVOLUTION
IRAN-IRAQ WAR
IRAQ INVADES KUWAIT
COLD WAR ENDS
GULF WAR
9/11
US INVADES IRAQ
1979
1980
1981
1982
1983
1984
1985
1986
1987
1988
1989
1990
1991
1992
1993
1994
1995
1996
1997
1998
1999
2000
2001
2002

DOMESTIC CONDITIONS AFFECT THE PRICE OF OIL, HERE ARE SIX REASONS WHY:

GEOPOLITICS

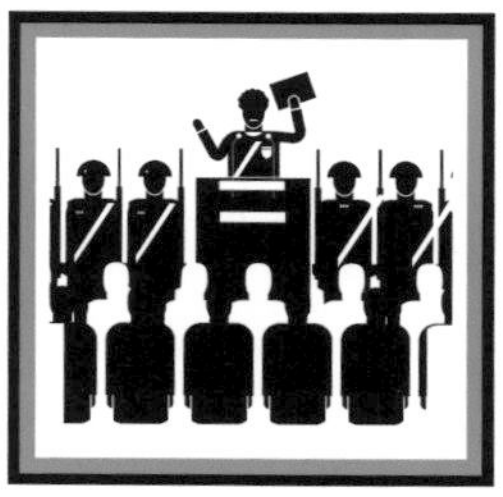

Government-mandated cuts in production result in job losses and anti-government sentiment. This can lead to site attacks and higher security costs.

TECHNOLOGY

The latest innovations make exploration more efficient, saving costs, but also require an investment. Not all countries that rely on oil can afford this investment.

MONEY

The oil industry is dependent on private and public investment. If these decline due to the market situation, less funds are available for oil production.

OPEC STATUS

The Organization of the Petroleum Exporting Countries (OPEC) regulates oil production and prices to ensure regular supplies and fair returns for investors.

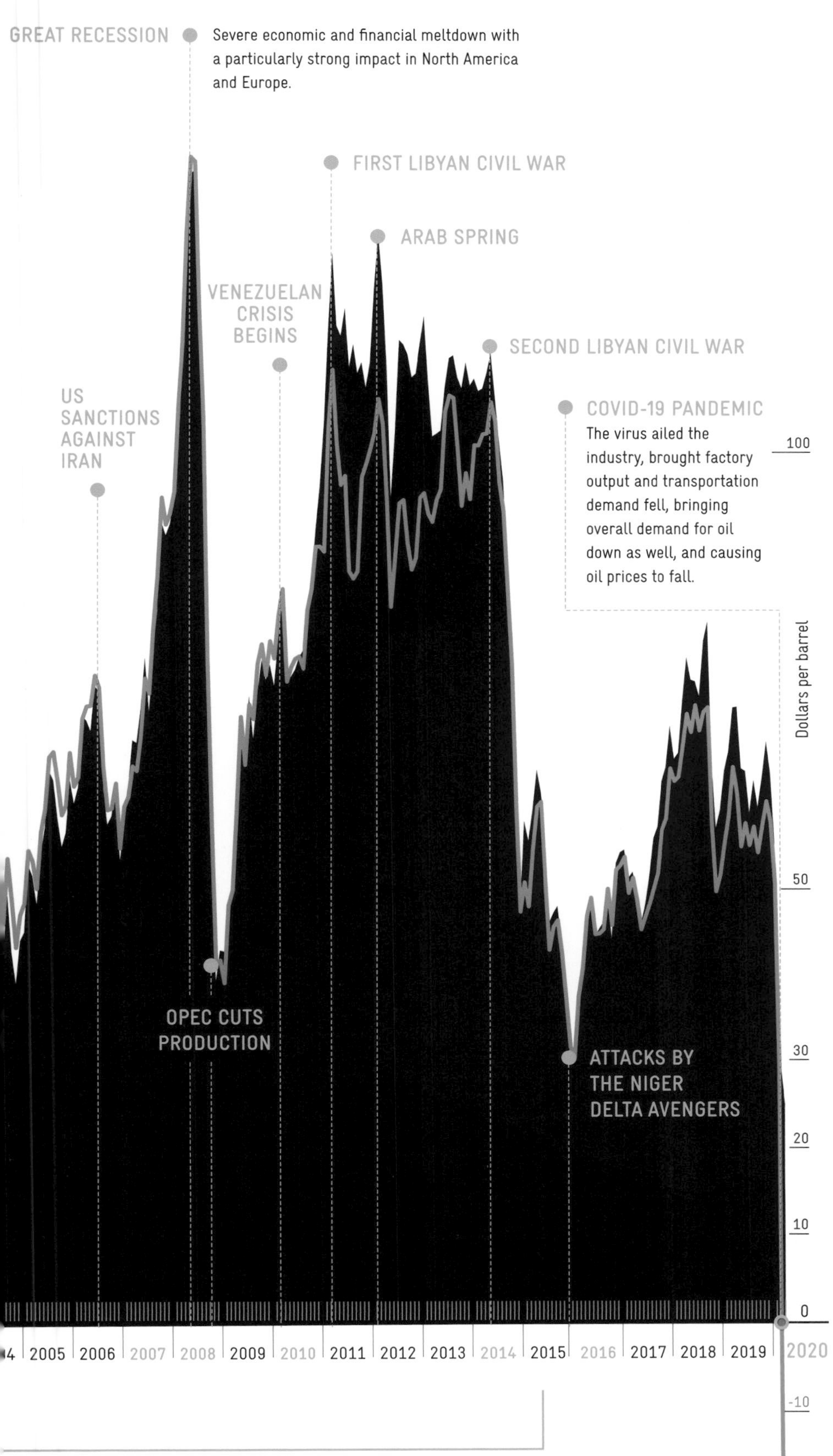

GREAT RECESSION
Severe economic and financial meltdown with a particularly strong impact in North America and Europe.
FIRST LIBYAN CIVIL WAR
ARAB SPRING
VENEZUELAN CRISIS BEGINS
SECOND LIBYAN CIVIL WAR
US SANCTIONS AGAINST IRAN
COVID-19 PANDEMIC
The virus ailed the industry, brought factory output and transportation demand fell, bringing overall demand for oil down as well, and causing oil prices to fall.
OPEC CUTS PRODUCTION
ATTACKS BY THE NIGER DELTA AVENGERS
Dollars per barrel
100
50
30
20
10
0
-10
-20
-30
-40
4
2005
2006
2007
2008
2009
2010
2011
2012
2013
2014
2015
2016
2017
2018
2019
2020

REFINERIES

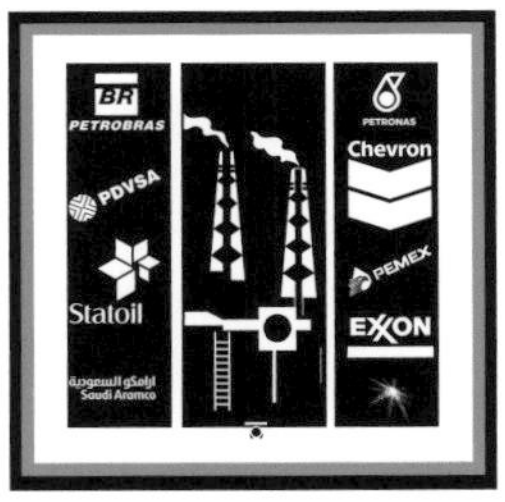

Crude oil requires refining before it is ready to market. The type of oil also impacts the cost of refining the product.

ENVIRONMENT

The weather can also change the price of oil, for example when hurricanes and natural disasters take down platforms or force refineries to shut down due to power failures.

HISTORIC PLUNGE

On April 20, 2020, the WTI crashed below zero, closing the day at **-$37** per barrel. Brent closed at 25.5 dollars per barrel.

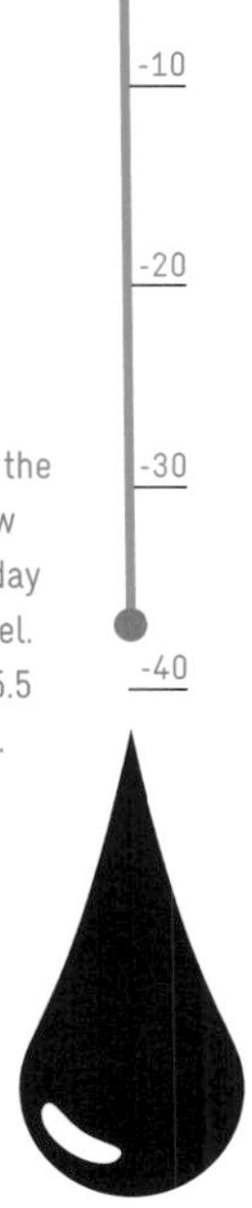

OIL PRODUCERS AROUND THE WORLD

(Dollars per barrel, comparative cases before the COVID-19 pandemic)

- ● BREAK-EVEN POINT
- ○ COSTS OF PRODUCTION
- -- BENCHMARK* (05-02-2019)

NIGERIA

Africa's top oil producer has a high breakeven price as its oil deposits are difficult to access, it has an inefficient government and lacks technology. Political movements also routinely damage oil sites.

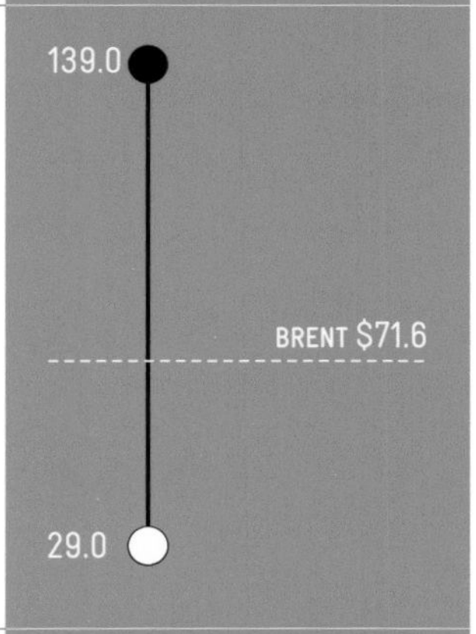

139.0
BRENT $71.6
29.0

NORWAY

The Scandanavian producer makes profits even at low market prices as its deposits are easily accessible. Production costs are further reduced with access to technology and taxes are relatively low on production costs.

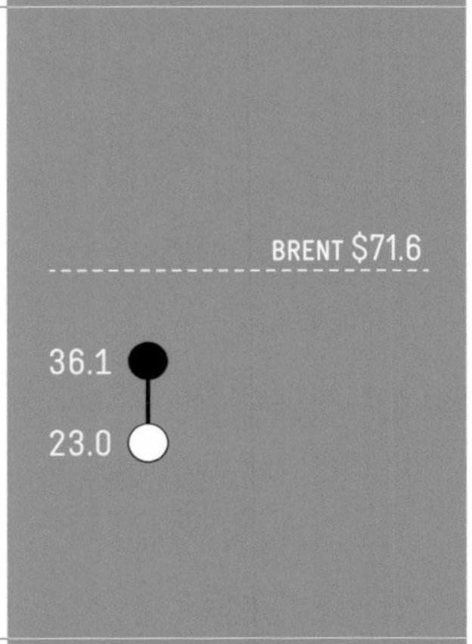

BRENT $71.6
36.1
23.0

VENEZUELA

Political unrest and a failing economy leaves oil as one of the country's only ways to fund its national budget. It accounts for 96% of its exports and makes up 40% of government revenues, leaving its survival in the hands of the market.

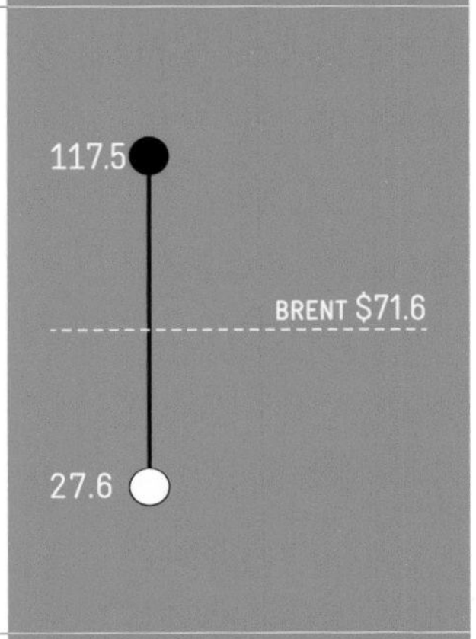

117.5
BRENT $71.6
27.6

MIDDLE EAST

Saudi Arabia, Iraq and Iran can easily access their huge oil reserves and have stable production capacities, resulting in a low break-even point. However, due to the fragile political situation and vulnerability to external influences, oil production in this region still carries risks.

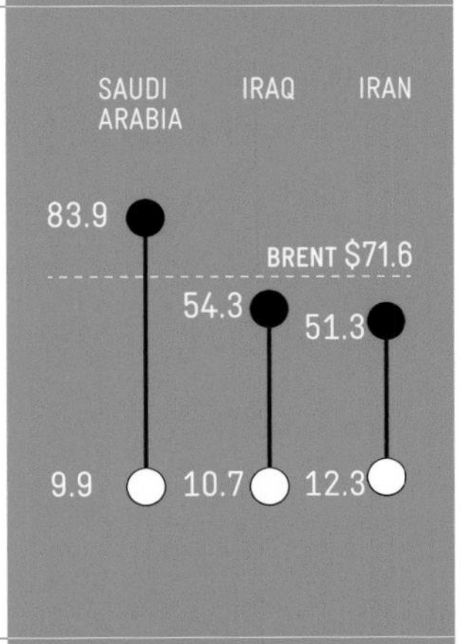

SAUDI ARABIA
IRAQ
IRAN
83.9
BRENT $71.6
54.3
51.3
9.9
10.7
12.3

USA

A vast geography leads to a vast difference in oil production costs. However, the average of all these costs means that oil extraction tends to break even at a lower price.

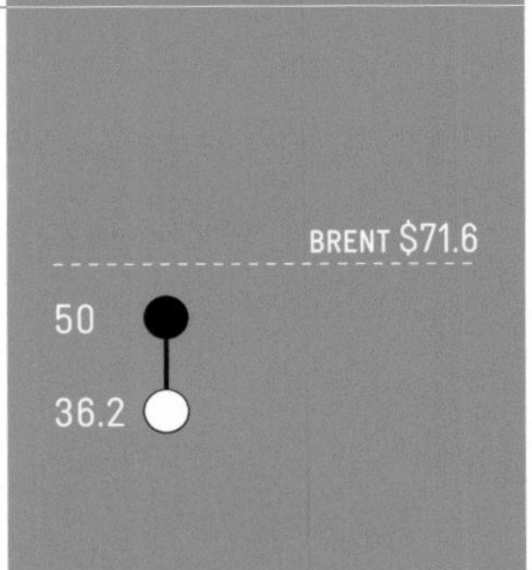

BRENT $71.6
50
36.2

*BRENT CRUDE

GOLD

The last Great Depression saw an increase in the demand for gold as investors preferred to save their funds in hard assets.

Gold reserves in tons (December 2019)

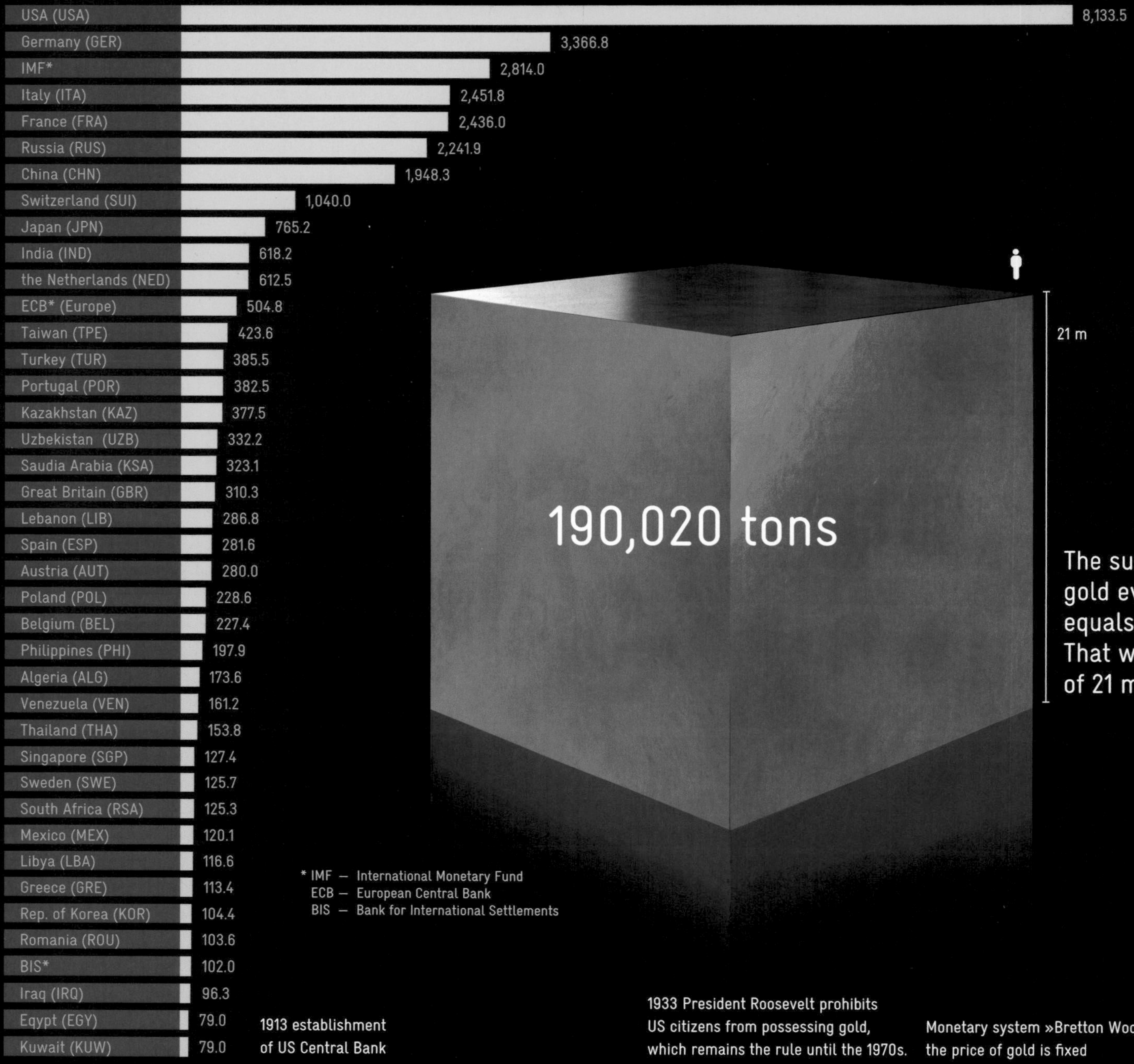
USA (USA) 8,133.5
Germany (GER) 3,366.8
IMF* 2,814.0
Italy (ITA) 2,451.8
France (FRA) 2,436.0
Russia (RUS) 2,241.9
China (CHN) 1,948.3
Switzerland (SUI) 1,040.0
Japan (JPN) 765.2
India (IND) 618.2
the Netherlands (NED) 612.5
ECB* (Europe) 504.8
Taiwan (TPE) 423.6
Turkey (TUR) 385.5
Portugal (POR) 382.5
Kazakhstan (KAZ) 377.5
Uzbekistan (UZB) 332.2
Saudia Arabia (KSA) 323.1
Great Britain (GBR) 310.3
Lebanon (LIB) 286.8
Spain (ESP) 281.6
Austria (AUT) 280.0
Poland (POL) 228.6
Belgium (BEL) 227.4
Philippines (PHI) 197.9
Algeria (ALG) 173.6
Venezuela (VEN) 161.2
Thailand (THA) 153.8
Singapore (SGP) 127.4
Sweden (SWE) 125.7
South Africa (RSA) 125.3
Mexico (MEX) 120.1
Libya (LBA) 116.6
Greece (GRE) 113.4
Rep. of Korea (KOR) 104.4
Romania (ROU) 103.6
BIS* 102.0
Iraq (IRQ) 96.3
Egypt (EGY) 79.0
Kuwait (KUW) 79.0
190,020 tons
21 m

The sum of all gold ever mined equals 190,020 tons. That would be a cube of 21 m edge length.

* IMF – International Monetary Fund
ECB – European Central Bank
BIS – Bank for International Settlements

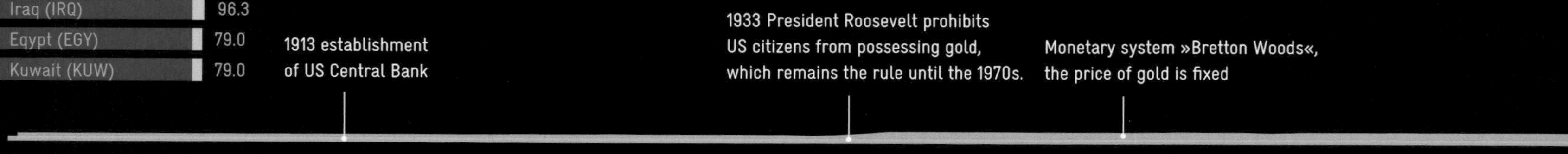
1913 establishment of US Central Bank
1933 President Roosevelt prohibits US citizens from possessing gold, which remains the rule until the 1970s.
Monetary system »Bretton Woods«, the price of gold is fixed

Gold mining since 1900 in tons

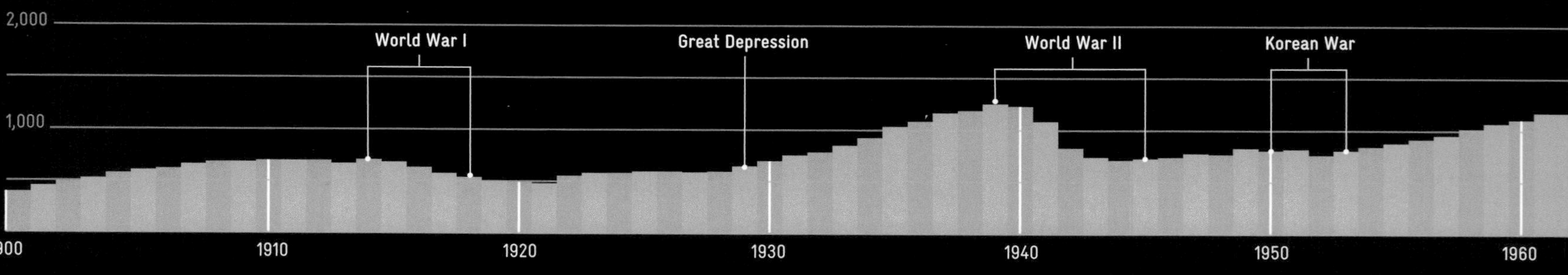
2,000
1,000
World War I
Great Depression
World War II
Korean War
1900
1910
1920
1930
1940
1950
1960

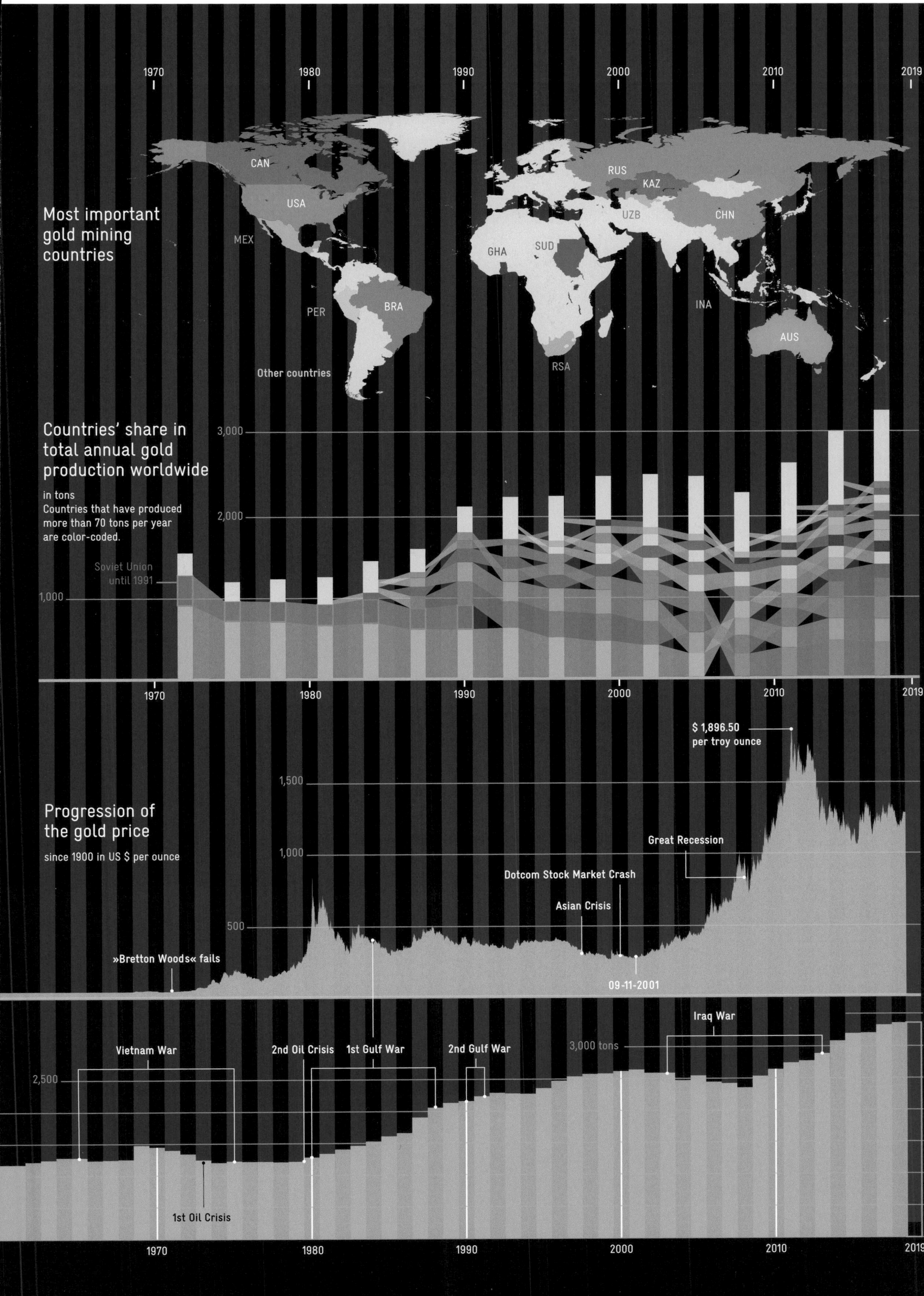

1970
1980
1990
2000
2010
2019
Most important gold mining countries
CAN
USA
MEX
PER
BRA
Other countries
GHA
SUD
RSA
RUS
KAZ
UZB
CHN
INA
AUS
Countries' share in total annual gold production worldwide
in tons
Countries that have produced more than 70 tons per year are color-coded.
Soviet Union until 1991
3,000
2,000
1,000
$ 1,896.50 per troy ounce
Progression of the gold price
since 1900 in US $ per ounce
1,500
1,000
500
Great Recession
Dotcom Stock Market Crash
Asian Crisis
»Bretton Woods« fails
09-11-2001
Iraq War
Vietnam War
2nd Oil Crisis
1st Gulf War
2nd Gulf War
3,000 tons
2,500
1st Oil Crisis

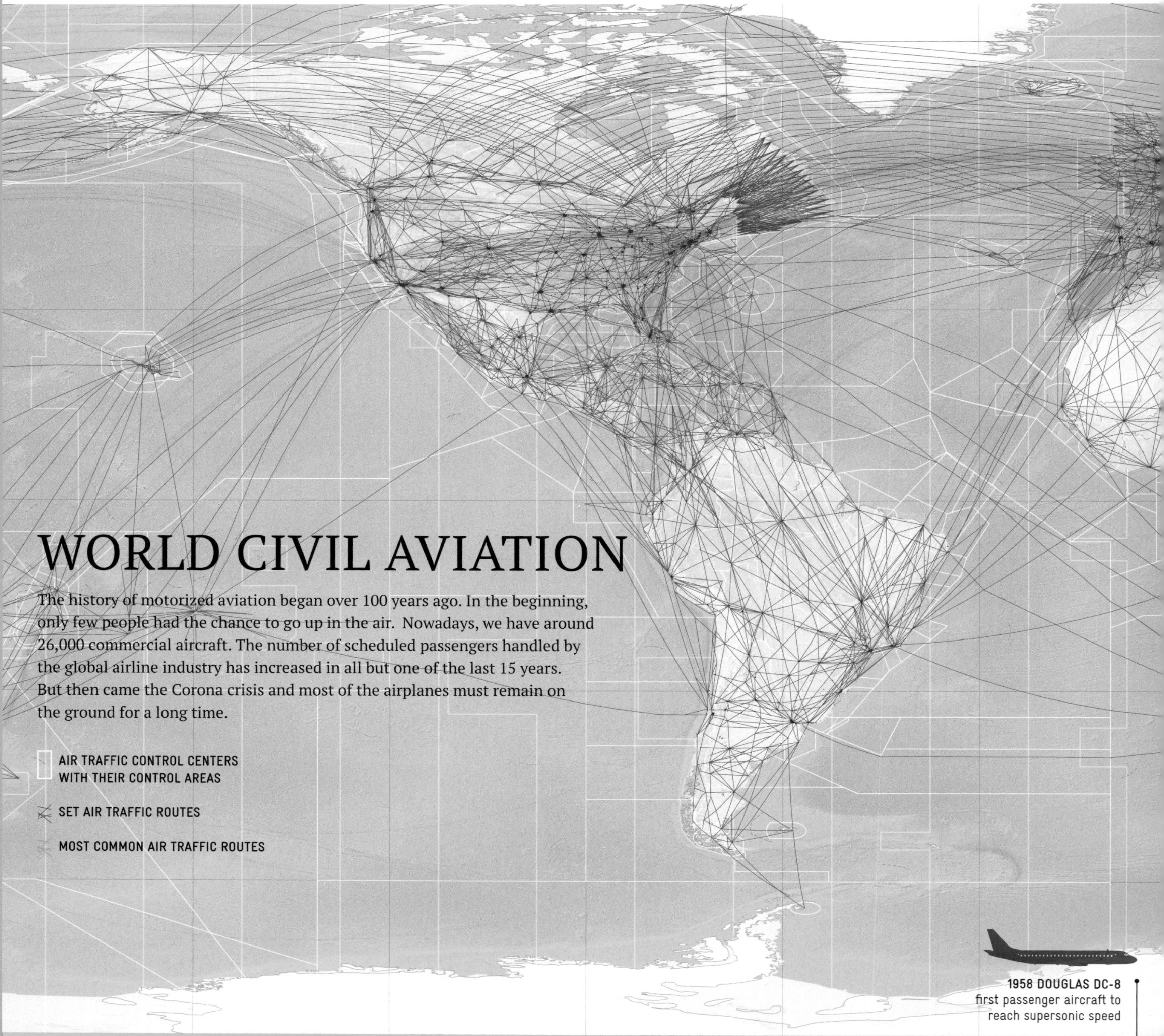
AIR TRAFFIC CONTROL CENTERS
WITH THEIR CONTROL AREAS
SET AIR TRAFFIC ROUTES
MOST COMMON AIR TRAFFIC ROUTES

WORLD CIVIL AVIATION

The history of motorized aviation began over 100 years ago. In the beginning, only few people had the chance to go up in the air. Nowadays, we have around 26,000 commercial aircraft. The number of scheduled passengers handled by the global airline industry has increased in all but one of the last 15 years. But then came the Corona crisis and most of the airplanes must remain on the ground for a long time.

Time flies

IMPORTANT MILESTONES IN CIVIL AVIATION

»Revenue Passenger Kilometers (RPK)« is the unit of measurement for transport performance, in billion km

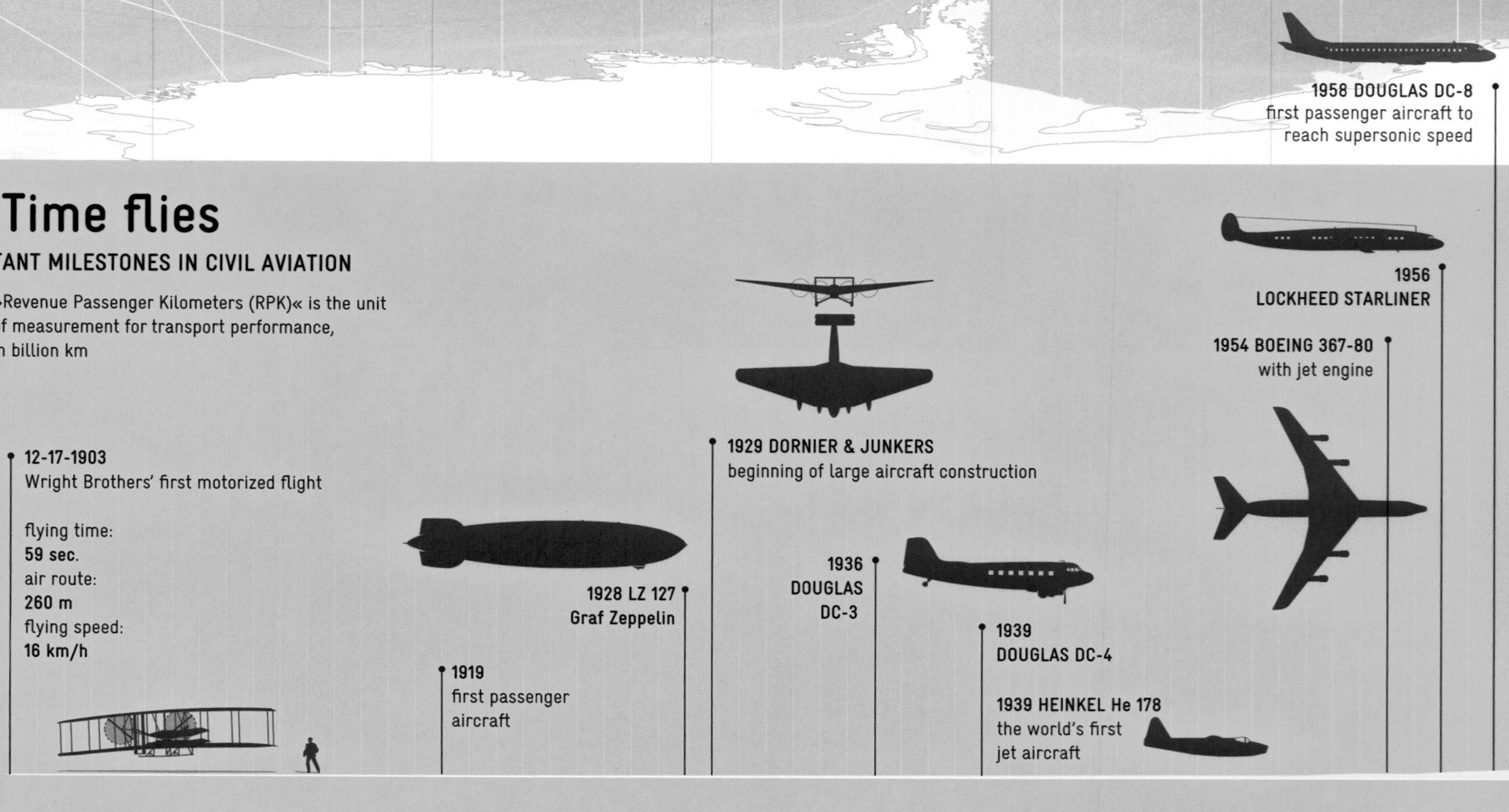
12-17-1903
Wright Brothers' first motorized flight
flying time:
59 sec.
air route:
260 m
flying speed:
16 km/h
1919
first passenger
aircraft
1928 LZ 127
Graf Zeppelin
1929 DORNIER & JUNKERS
beginning of large aircraft construction
1936
DOUGLAS
DC-3
1939
DOUGLAS DC-4
1939 HEINKEL He 178
the world's first
jet aircraft
1954 BOEING 367-80
with jet engine
1956
LOCKHEED STARLINER
1958 DOUGLAS DC-8
first passenger aircraft to
reach supersonic speed

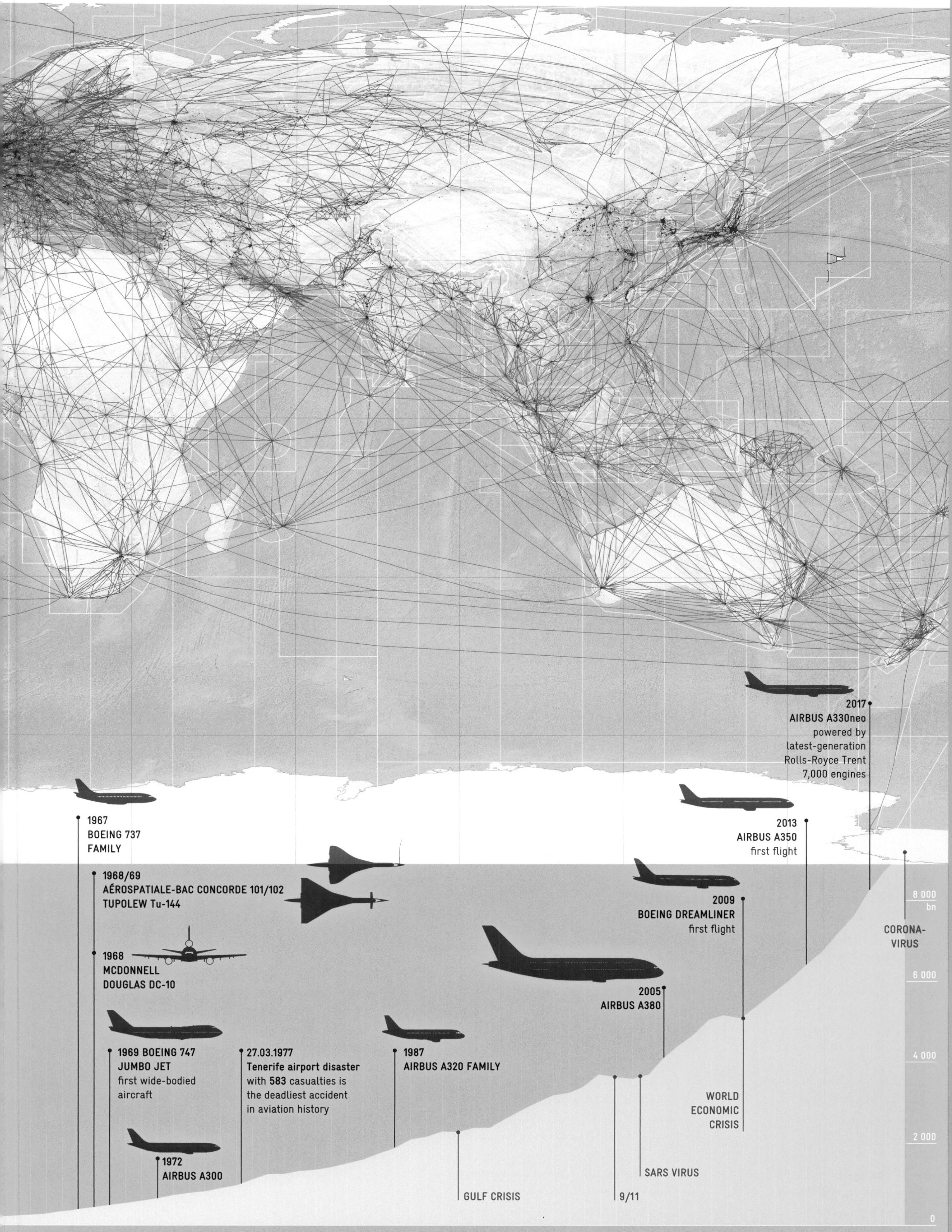
2017
AIRBUS A330neo
powered by
latest-generation
Rolls-Royce Trent
7,000 engines
1967
BOEING 737
FAMILY
2013
AIRBUS A350
first flight
1968/69
AÉROSPATIALE-BAC CONCORDE 101/102
TUPOLEW Tu-144
2009
BOEING DREAMLINER
first flight
8 000
bn
CORONA-
VIRUS
1968
MCDONNELL
DOUGLAS DC-10
6 000
2005
AIRBUS A380
1969 BOEING 747
JUMBO JET
first wide-bodied
aircraft
27.03.1977
Tenerife airport disaster
with 583 casualties is
the deadliest accident
in aviation history
1987
AIRBUS A320 FAMILY
4 000
WORLD
ECONOMIC
CRISIS
2 000
1972
AIRBUS A300
SARS VIRUS
GULF CRISIS
9/11
0

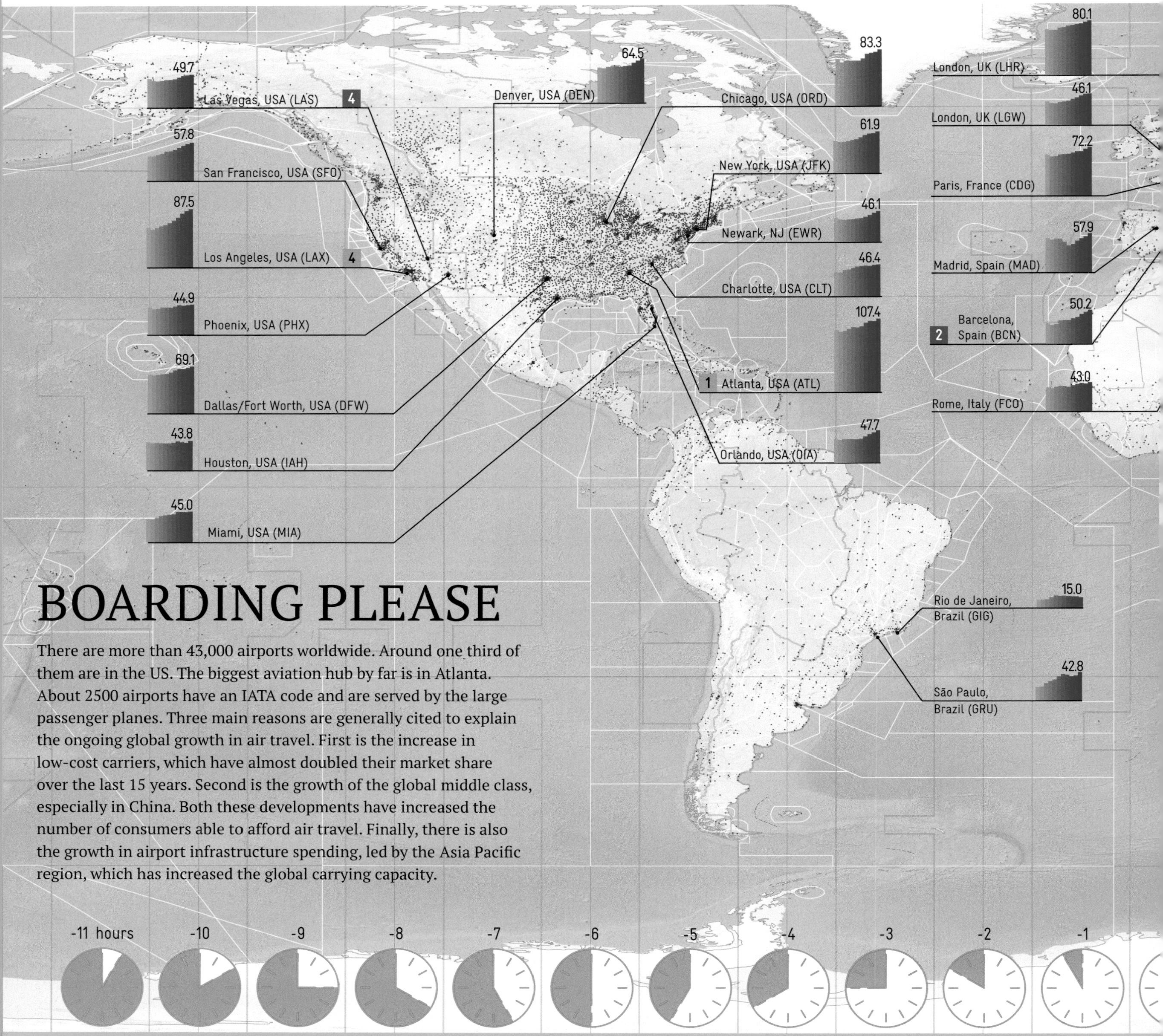

49.7
Las Vegas, USA (LAS) 4
57.8
San Francisco, USA (SFO)
87.5
Los Angeles, USA (LAX) 4
44.9
Phoenix, USA (PHX)
69.1
Dallas/Fort Worth, USA (DFW)
43.8
Houston, USA (IAH)
45.0
Miami, USA (MIA)
64.5
Denver, USA (DEN)
83.3
Chicago, USA (ORD)
61.9
New York, USA (JFK)
46.1
Newark, NJ (EWR)
46.4
Charlotte, USA (CLT)
107.4
1 Atlanta, USA (ATL)
47.7
Orlando, USA (OIA)
80.1
London, UK (LHR)
46.1
London, UK (LGW)
72.2
Paris, France (CDG)
57.9
Madrid, Spain (MAD)
50.2
2 Barcelona, Spain (BCN)
43.0
Rome, Italy (FCO)
15.0
Rio de Janeiro, Brazil (GIG)
42.8
São Paulo, Brazil (GRU)
-11 hours
-10
-9
-8
-7
-6
-5
-4
-3
-2
-1

BOARDING PLEASE

There are more than 43,000 airports worldwide. Around one third of them are in the US. The biggest aviation hub by far is in Atlanta. About 2500 airports have an IATA code and are served by the large passenger planes. Three main reasons are generally cited to explain the ongoing global growth in air travel. First is the increase in low-cost carriers, which have almost doubled their market share over the last 15 years. Second is the growth of the global middle class, especially in China. Both these developments have increased the number of consumers able to afford air travel. Finally, there is also the growth in airport infrastructure spending, led by the Asia Pacific region, which has increased the global carrying capacity.

Your destination

THE WORLD'S BUSIEST AIRPORTS

	IATA-code	airport	passengers dealt with 2018 (in millions)
1	ATL	ATLANTA, USA	107.40
2	PEK	BEIJING, CHINA	101.00
3	DXB	DUBAI, UAE	89.10
4	LAX	LOS ANGELES CA, USA	87.50
5	HND	TOKYO, JAPAN	87.10
6	ORD	CHICAGO, USA	83.30
7	LHR	LONDON, UK	80.10
8	HKG	HONG KONG, HKG	74.50
9	PVG	SHANGHAI, CHINA	74.00
10	CDG	PARIS, FRANCE	72.20
11	AMS	AMSTERDAM, NETHERLANDS	71.10
12	DEL	DELHI, INDIA	69.90
13	CAN	GUANGZHOU, CHINA	69.80
14	FRA	FRANKFURT, GERMANY	69.50
15	DFW	DALLAS/FORT WORTH TX, USA	69.10

LONDON and NEW YORK in comparison

HEATHROW	80.1
GATWICK	46.0
STANSTED	27.9
LUTON	16.7
LONDON CITY	4.8
SOUTHEND	1.4
London metropolitan area	176.9
JFK	61.9
NEWARK	46.1
LAGUARDIA	30.1
New York metropolitan area	137.7

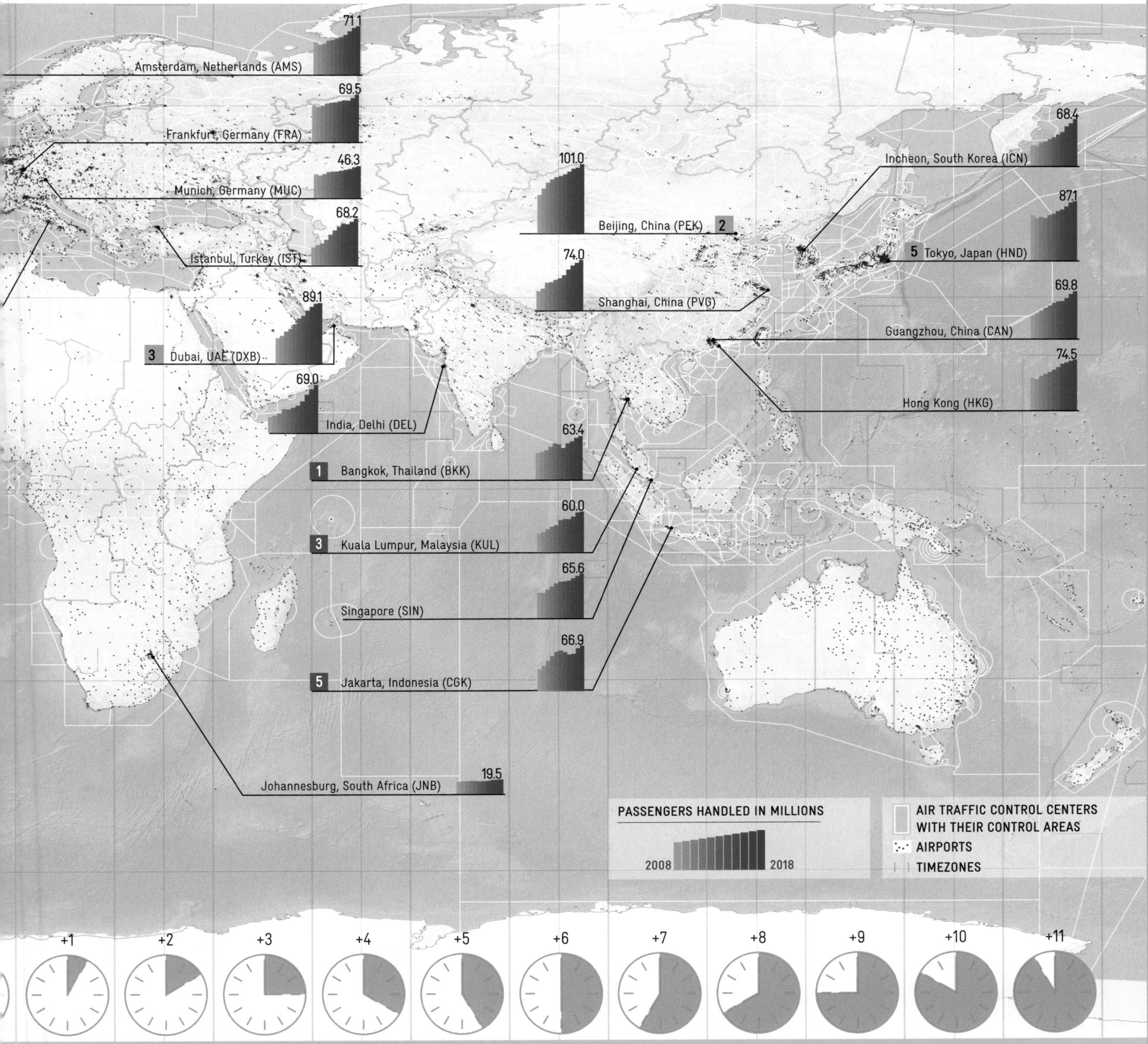
71.1
Amsterdam, Netherlands (AMS)
69.5
Frankfurt, Germany (FRA)
46.3
Munich, Germany (MUC)
68.2
Istanbul, Turkey (IST)
89.1
3 Dubai, UAE (DXB)
69.0
India, Delhi (DEL)
101.0
Beijing, China (PEK) 2
74.0
Shanghai, China (PVG)
68.4
Incheon, South Korea (ICN)
87.1
5 Tokyo, Japan (HND)
69.8
Guangzhou, China (CAN)
74.5
Hong Kong (HKG)
63.4
1 Bangkok, Thailand (BKK)
60.0
3 Kuala Lumpur, Malaysia (KUL)
65.6
Singapore (SIN)
66.9
5 Jakarta, Indonesia (CGK)
19.5
Johannesburg, South Africa (JNB)
PASSENGERS HANDLED IN MILLIONS
2008
2018
AIR TRAFFIC CONTROL CENTERS WITH THEIR CONTROL AREAS
AIRPORTS
TIMEZONES
+1
+2
+3
+4
+5
+6
+7
+8
+9
+10
+11

THE LARGEST AIRPORTS FOR LOW-COST CARRIERS

	IATA-code	airport	LCC capacity
1	DMK	BANGKOK DON MUEANG, THAILAND	951,088
2	BCN	BARCELONA EL PRAT, SPAIN	898,778
3	KUL	KUALA LUMPUR, MALAYSIA	773,264
4	LAS	LAS VEGAS McCARRAN, USA	742,634
5	CGK	JAKARTA SOEKARMO-HATTA, INDONESIA	707,780
6	DEL	DELHI INDIRA GANDHI, INDIA	699,913
7	LGW	LONDON GATWICK, UK	657,766
8	DEN	DENVER, USA	654,320
9	STN	LONDON STANSTED, UK	631,758
10	PMI	PALMA DE MALLORCA AIRPORT	605,957
11	MCO	ORLANDO, USA	569,910
12	BLR	BANGALORE KEMPEGOWDA, INDIA	563,165
13	FLL	FORT LAUDERDALE-HOLLYWOOD, USA	536,718
14	MNL	MANILA NINOY AQUINO, PHILIPPINES	517,590
15	MEX	MEXICO CITY, MEXICO	509,901

A question of time

THE LONGEST WALKS TO THE GATE

IATA-code	airport	max. distance from entrance to gate in km
PEK	BEJING, CHINA	3.20
ATL	ATLANTA, USA	2.10
ZRH	ZURICH, SWITZERLAND	2.00
LGW	LONDON GATWICK, UK	1.80
ICN	SEOUL, SOUTH KOREA	1.70
HKG	HONG KONG, HKG	1.60
LHR	LONDON HEATHROW, UK	1.20
AMS	AMSTERDAM, NETHERLANDS	1.00
FRA	FRANKFURT, GERMANY	1.00
MAN	MANCHESTER AIRPORT, UK	0.90
DXB	DUBAI INT. AIRPORT, UAE	0.89
STN	LONDON STANSTED, UK	0.77
TXL	BERLIN TEGEL, GERMANY	0.31

ENJOY YOUR FLIGHT!

Not all aircraft seats are equally comfortable, quiet and safe. A lot depends on the type of aircraft as well as on the interior design, which is different for each airline. But a few rules of thumb can be applied to all of them as can be seen on this floor plan of a typical jet. Here you will find some useful considerations when selecting your seat the next time you get on an airplane:

Perfect climate

The humidity on board is only 10 to 20 percent, which is a little too low for some but any more would damage the aircraft's electrical systems. The air pressure in the cabin at cruising altitude is as low as outside at an altitude of 2,100 meters. The temperature for passengers to feel comfortable is usually 23 degrees Celsius.

Standing room

For years, there have been rumors about the introduction of standing room. But should it happen, the fight for the best seats might get even worse. There's no ideal seat for all passengers, only a compromise of advantages and disadvantages, as perceived by individuals.

The best seats

It is louder near the kitchen. There is more leg room at emergency exits—directly in front of them the seatbacks can't be folded back. Right at the back, there's a risk of smells from the toilet.

good seats   seats with disadvantages   bad seats

Leg room

Squeezing more seats into a plane leaves passengers cramped, but gives airlines an opportunity to upsell customers for more leg room.

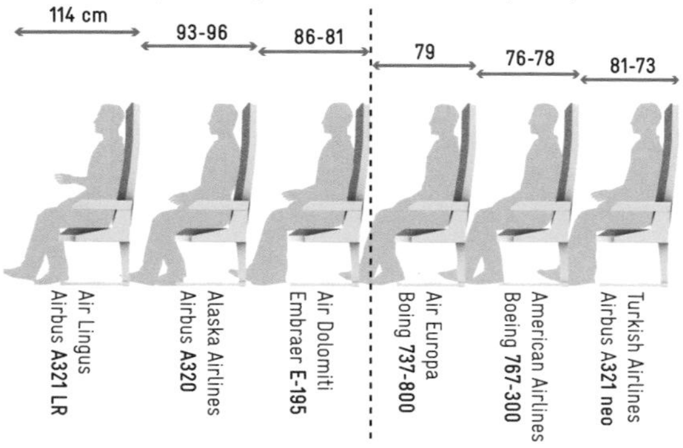

Three spacious airplanes*
Three cramped airplanes*
114 cm
93-96
86-81
79
76-78
81-73
Air Lingus Airbus A321 LR
Alaska Airlines Airbus A320
Air Dolomiti Embraer E-195
Air Europa Boing 737-800
American Airlines Boeing 767-300
Turkish Airlines Airbus A321 neo

Warming up

Each person on board emits around 70 watts of thermal output and each small screen 20 to 30 watts. The cabin needs to be cooled, and economy class needs more cooling than business class due to the higher concentration of passengers. That's why there can be a draft in the transition area.

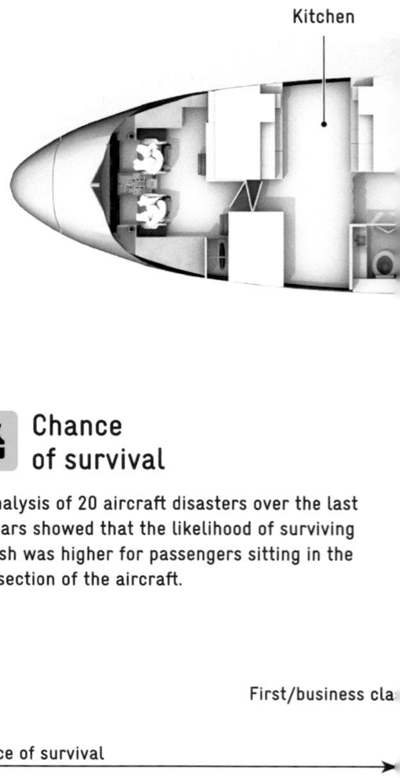

Kitchen
First/business cla
Chance of survival

Heating

Modern aircrafts are divided up into 8 to 15 temperature zones that can be individually regulated.

Airborne substances

The most common volatile organic compound in the cabin is alcohol, at 70 to 90 percent. It evaporates off alcoholic drinks served on board.

Chance of survival

An analysis of 20 aircraft disasters over the last 30 years showed that the likelihood of surviving a crash was higher for passengers sitting in the rear section of the aircraft.

Take a seat

SEAT PITCH 2020 (centimeters)

Generous seating (TOP 3)			Compact seating (TOP 3)		
Economy/Economy Plus (short-haul)					
114.3	106.7	96.5	76.2	73.7	71.1
Business/First (short-haul)					
185.4	157.5	152.4	83.8	76.2	73.7
Economy Class (long-haul)					
116.8	96.5	94.0	76.2	73.7	71.1
Premium Economy Class (65% less expensive than a Business Class fare)					
152.4	114.3	106.7	94.0	91.4	88.9
Business (long-haul)					
221.0	208.2	206.7	91.4	86.4	78.7
First (long-haul)					
226.0	215.9	213.4	99.0	96.5	94.0

The air up here

AIR CIRCULATION

Cool air is distributed into the cabin from above. The floor under the aisle seats is therefore a little bit cooler than under the window seats where the air is sucked up again. This ensures that the air is completely renewed around 20 times per hour. 40 to 50 percent of the air from the air conditioning system is fresh air. Filters remove 99.98 percent of all particles between 0.001 and 100 micrometers in size – the air is as clean as in an operating room.

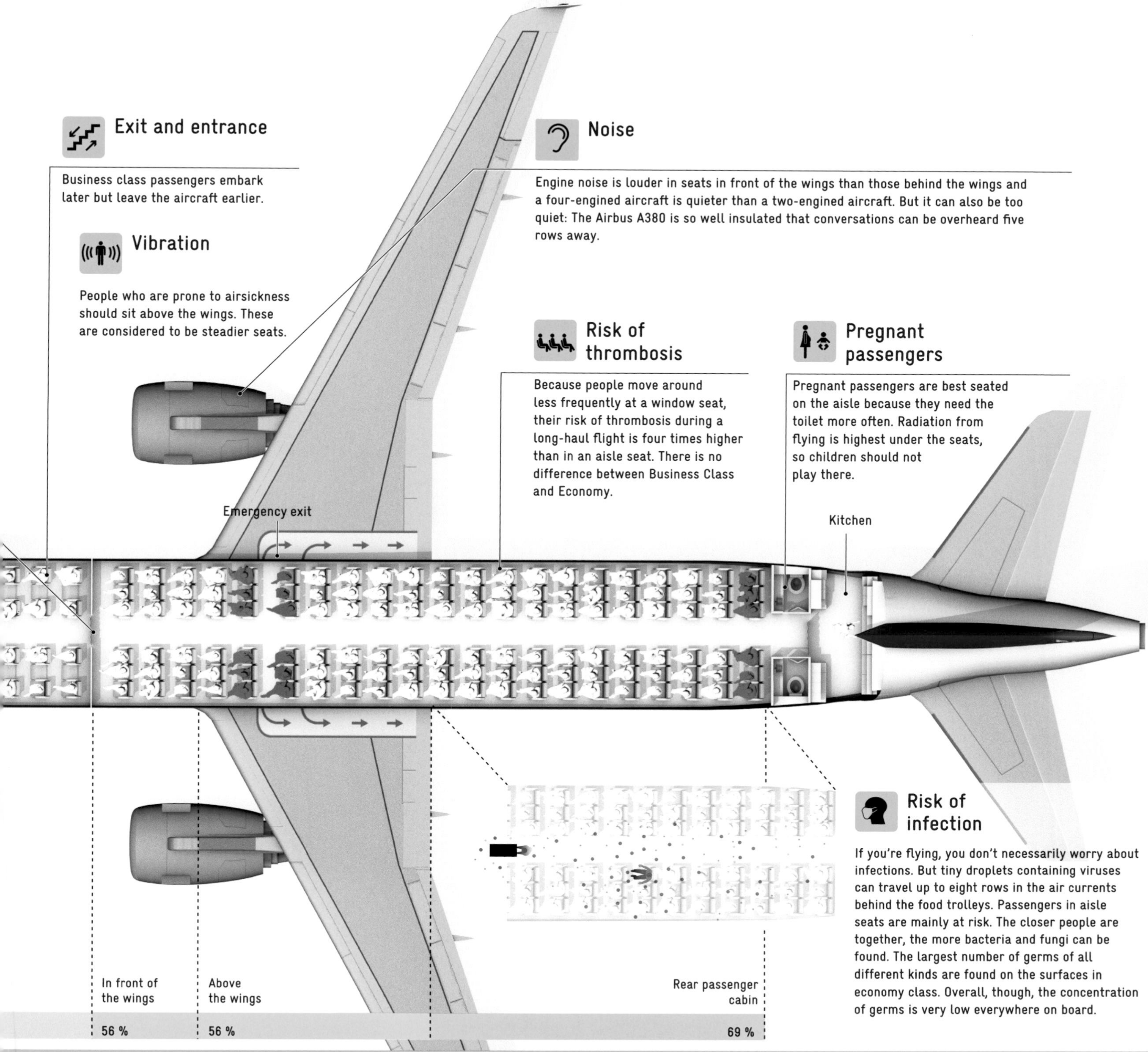
Emergency exit
Kitchen
In front of the wings
56 %
Above the wings
56 %
Rear passenger cabin
69 %

Exit and entrance

Business class passengers embark later but leave the aircraft earlier.

Vibration

People who are prone to airsickness should sit above the wings. These are considered to be steadier seats.

Noise

Engine noise is louder in seats in front of the wings than those behind the wings and a four-engined aircraft is quieter than a two-engined aircraft. But it can also be too quiet: The Airbus A380 is so well insulated that conversations can be overheard five rows away.

Risk of thrombosis

Because people move around less frequently at a window seat, their risk of thrombosis during a long-haul flight is four times higher than in an aisle seat. There is no difference between Business Class and Economy.

Pregnant passengers

Pregnant passengers are best seated on the aisle because they need the toilet more often. Radiation from flying is highest under the seats, so children should not play there.

Risk of infection

If you're flying, you don't necessarily worry about infections. But tiny droplets containing viruses can travel up to eight rows in the air currents behind the food trolleys. Passengers in aisle seats are mainly at risk. The closer people are together, the more bacteria and fungi can be found. The largest number of germs of all different kinds are found on the surfaces in economy class. Overall, though, the concentration of germs is very low everywhere on board.

Baggage collection

MISHANDLED LUGGAGE IN THE AIRLINE INDUSTRY

Year	Number of scheduled passengers boarded from 2011 to 2018 (in billions)	Total number of bags mishandled from 2011 to 2018 (in millions)	Average rate of mishandled bags 2011-2018 (per 1,000 passengers)
2018	4.4	24.8	5.69
2017	4.1	22.7	5.57
2016	3.8	21.6	5.73
2015	3.6	23.3	6.53
2014	3.3	24.3	7.3
2013	3.1	21.8	6.96
2012	3.0	26.3	8.83
2011	2.9	25.3	8.99

Causes of delayed bags in air travel 2018

- 2.5 % LOST / STOLEN
- 17 % DAMAGED
- 78 % DELAYED

REASONS:

- 46 % Transfer mishandling
- 16 % Ticketing error/bag switch/Security/other
- 16 % Failed to load
- 9 % Airport/customs/weather/Space-weight restriction
- 5 % Arrival mishandling
- 5 % Tagging error
- 3 % Loading error

GATEAWAY TO THE WORLD

Commercial air travel has a reputation for being a safe way to travel. Since 2017, more than four billion passengers have been flying annually on nearly 40 million scheduled flights. Moreover, both these figures have seen significant increases every year since 2009. At the same time, the number of fatalities from commercial air travel accidents has been decreasing on average (although, sadly, some years are worse than others).

THE WORLD'S 20 LARGEST AIRLINES

by capacity Available Seat Kilometers (ASKs), 2018

20. QANTAS Group
1920 • oneworld

19. Cathay Pacific Airways
1946 • oneworld

18. Hainan Airlines Group
1993 • No affiliated alliance

17. Singapore Airlines
1947 (Malayan Airways) • Star Alliance

16. Aeroflot Group
1923 • SkyTeam

15. Air Canada
1937 • Star Alliance

14. Turkish Airlines
1933 • Star Alliance

13. Ryanair
1985 • No affiliated alliance

12. Qatar Airlines
1993 • oneworld

11. China Eastern A.
1988 • SkyTeam

10. Southwest Airlines
1967 • No affiliated alliance

9. Air China Group
1988 • SkyTeam

8. Air France
1933 • SkyTeam

7. China Southern
1988 • SkyTeam

6. IAG Group
1974 • oneworld

5. Lufthansa
1955 • Star Alliance

Dangerous rides

WHAT'S THE SAFEST MODE OF TRANSPORT?

There will probably never be a complete answer to this question because the different results depend on the sources and how the numbers are interpreted. Here's an example: Most plane crashes happen during take off or landing, whereas a car driver faces ever-present danger. If the kilometers per traveling person are the reference value in relation to traffic casualties, the result is worse for the car driver. We have nevertheless decided to use this statistic because there are trusted sources available. According to these statistics, the aircraft is indeed the safest mode of transport.

123 **Number of times you would have to orbit the earth** before having a very high likelihood of a fatal crash

123 **Circle size = fatal casualties** according to the mode of transport **per one billion person-kilometers** in Germany

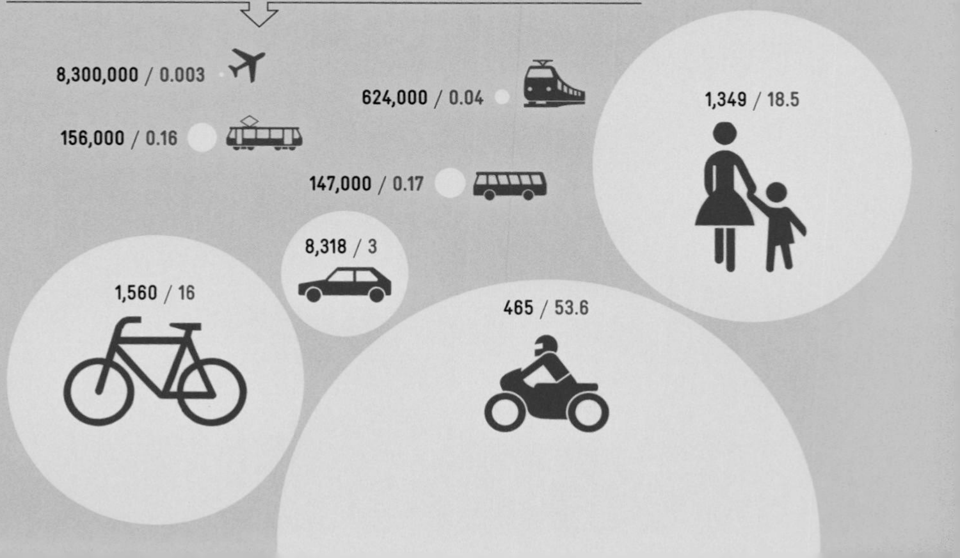
8,300,000 / 0.003
624,000 / 0.04
156,000 / 0.16
147,000 / 0.17
1,349 / 18.5
8,318 / 3
1,560 / 16
465 / 53.6

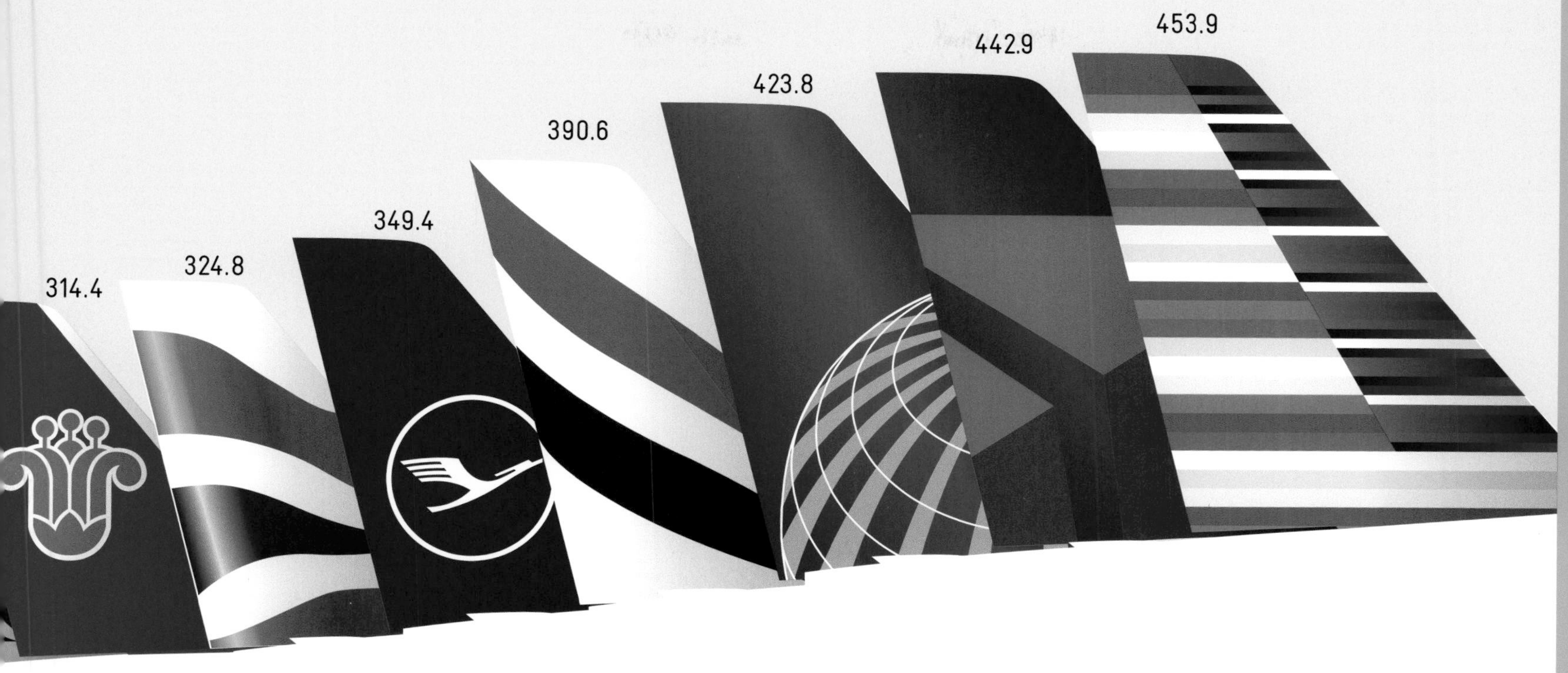

	4. Emirates Group	3. Delta Airlines	2. United Airlines/ United Continental	1. American Airlines Group
	1985	1928 2008: + Northwest Airlines • SkyTeam	1926 (Varney Air Lines) 2011: + Continental Airlines • Star Alliance	1934, 2001: + Trans World Airlines 1984: + American Eagle 2015 + AMR Corporation and US Airways • oneworld
BASE	Dubai, V.A.E.	Atlanta, USA	Chicago Base, USA	Dallas/Fort Worth, USA
FLEET SIZE	270	898	758	935
DESTINATIONS	158	325	342	350
EMPLOYEES	103,363	86,564	92,000	128,900
PASSENGERS	58.6 million	192.5 million	158.3 million	203.7 million
REVENUE	$27.88 in billion US dollars	$44.4 in billion US dollars	$41.3 in billion US dollars	$44.54 in billion US dollars

Calm skies ahead

THE SAFEST AIRLINES

rank/ code/ airline, country			JACDEC RISK INDEX 2019** SAFE=100%
1	FIN	FINNAIR, FINLAND	93.91%
2	TG	SCOOT TIGAIR, SINGAPORE	93.60%
3	NAX	NORWEGIAN AIR SHUTTLE, NORWAY	93.48%
4	UAE	EMIRATES, EMIRATES	93.39%
5	AEA	AIR EUROPA, SPAIN	93.03%
6	TRA	TRANSAVIA, NL	92.78%
7	ETD	ETIHAD AIRWAYS, UAE	92.70%
8	VIR	VIRGIN ATLANTIC AIRWAYS, UK	92.48%
9	KLM	KLM-ROYAL DUTCH AIRLINES, NL	92.33%
10	JST	JETSTAR AIRWAYS, AUSTRALIA	92.31%
11	CPA	CATHAY PACIFIC AIRWAYS, HONG KONG	92.23%
12	EVA	EVA AIR, TAIWAN	92.13%
13	VLG	VUELING AIRLINES, SPAIN	92.03%
14	EZY	EASYJET, UK	91.85%
15	JBU	JETBLUE AIRWAYS, USA	91.71%

Air alliance

ALLIANCES IN COMPARISON

	MEMBERS	FLEET	HEADQUARTERS	PER YEAR (2018) flights 17.65 million	seats 2.55 million	revenue 508.5*
oneworld (SINCE 1999)	13	3,560	NEW YORK, USA	4.6	649.03	142.4
SkyTeam (SINCE 2000)	19	3,937	AMSTERDAM, NL	6.1	917.78	152.9
Star Alliance (SINCE 1997)	26	4,657	FRANKFURT/MAIN, DE	6.8	982.06	213.2

*in billion U.S. dollars

DUEL IN THE SKY

There are around 80,000 flights every day worldwide and the airlines have around 26,000 planes of different types at their disposal. By far the most important commercial aircraft manufacturing companies are Boeing and Airbus. Together, they control around 65 percent of the market.

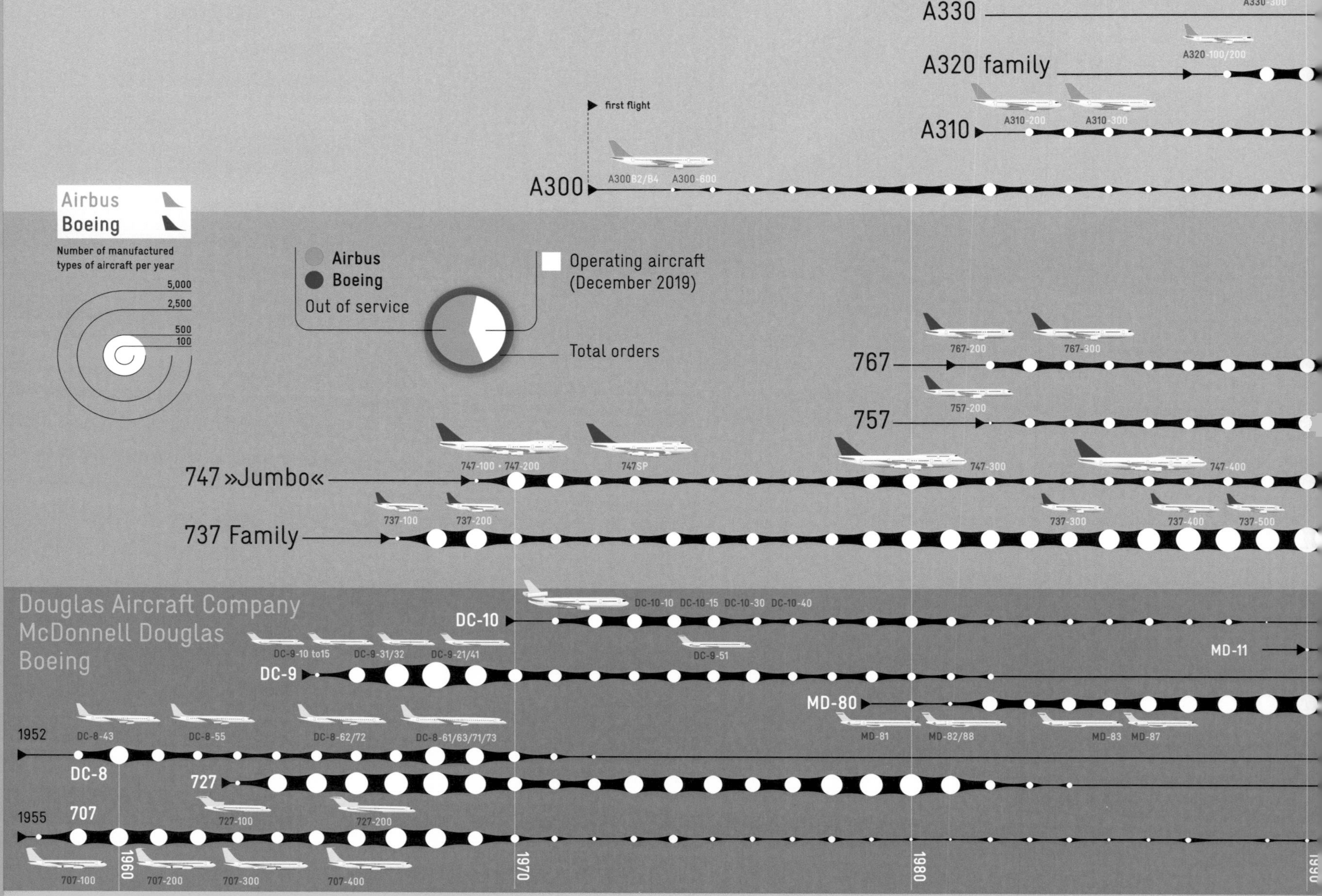
A340
A340-300
A330
A330-300
A320 family
A320-100/200
A310
A310-200
A310-300
first flight
A300
A300B2/B4
A300-600
Airbus
Boeing
Number of manufactured types of aircraft per year
5,000
2,500
500
100
Airbus
Boeing
Out of service
Operating aircraft (December 2019)
Total orders
767
767-200
767-300
757
757-200
747 »Jumbo«
747-100 · 747-200
747SP
747-300
747-400
737 Family
737-100
737-200
737-300
737-400
737-500
Douglas Aircraft Company
McDonnell Douglas
Boeing
DC-10
DC-10-10 DC-10-15 DC-10-30 DC-10-40
MD-11
DC-9
DC-9-10 to15
DC-9-31/32
DC-9-21/41
DC-9-51
MD-80
MD-81
MD-82/88
MD-83 MD-87
1952
DC-8
DC-8-43
DC-8-55
DC-8-62/72
DC-8-61/63/71/73
727
727-100
727-200
1955
707
707-100
707-200
707-300
707-400
1960
1970
1980
1990

Takeoff

CIVIL COMMERCIAL AIRCRAFT WORLDWIDE

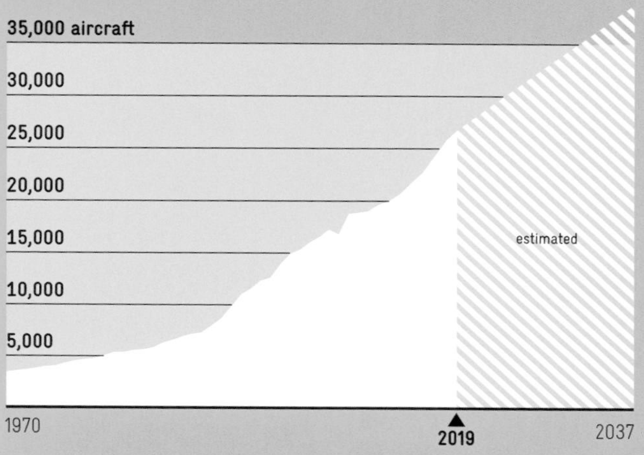
35,000 aircraft
30,000
25,000
20,000
15,000
10,000
5,000
estimated
1970
2019
2037

Duel on the ground

AIRCRAFT DELIVERIES BY MANUFACTURER, GLOBAL AIRCRAFT FLEET 1998-2018

Number of delivered jets (Passenger jets, including combi and quick change)

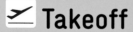

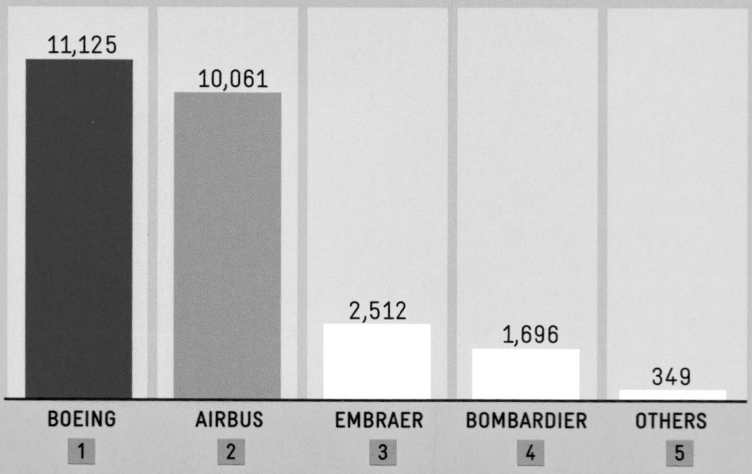
11,125
10,061
2,512
1,696
349
BOEING
1
AIRBUS
2
EMBRAER
3
BOMBARDIER
4
OTHERS
5

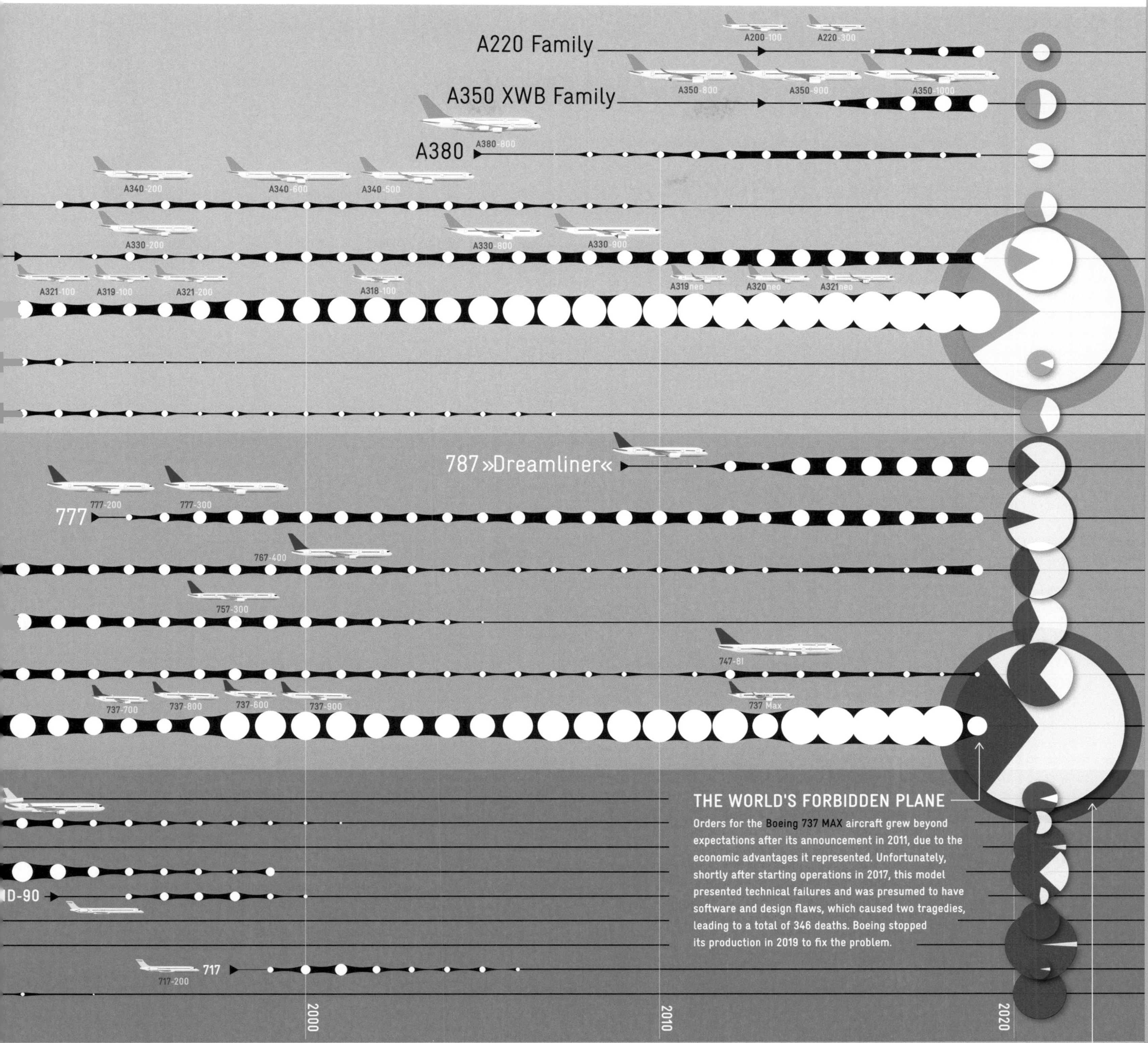

A220 Family
A200-100
A220-300
A350 XWB Family
A350-800
A350-900
A350-1000
A380
A380-800
A340-200
A340-600
A340-500
A330-200
A330-800
A330-900
A321-100
A319-100
A321-200
A318-100
A319neo
A320neo
A321neo
787 »Dreamliner«
777
777-200
777-300
767-400
757-300
747-81
737-700
737-800
737-600
737-900
737 Max
D-90
717
717-200
2000
2010
2020
THE WORLD'S FORBIDDEN PLANE
Orders for the Boeing 737 MAX aircraft grew beyond expectations after its announcement in 2011, due to the economic advantages it represented. Unfortunately, shortly after starting operations in 2017, this model presented technical failures and was presumed to have software and design flaws, which caused two tragedies, leading to a total of 346 deaths. Boeing stopped its production in 2019 to fix the problem.
Due to the Corona crisis, the two aircraft manufacturers are also experiencing severe turmoil. Many orders will have to be cancelled.

Boeing, Airbus and the others

TYPES OF AIRCRAFT ON MAINLINE ROUTES 2018

	manufacturer, aircraft	total number
1	AIRBUS A320 FAMILY	7,132
2	BOEING 737 NEXT GENERATION	6,373
3	BOEING 777	1,422
4	AIRBUS A330	1,269
5	BOEING 737 CLASSIC/ORIGINAL	818
6	BOEING 767	740
7	BOEING 787	696
8	BOEING 757	669
9	BOEING 717/MD-80/90/DC-9	516
10	BOEING 747	475

TYPES OF AIRCRAFT ON REGIONAL ROUTES 2018

	manufacturer, aircraft	total number
1	**EMBRAER** E-JETS	1,358
2	**ATR** 42/72	994
3	**BOMBARDIER** CRJ700/900/1000	775
4	**EMBRAER** ERJ 145 FAMILY	531
5	**BOMBARDIER** CRJ100/2000	515
6	**BOMBARDIER** Q400	506
7	**BEECHCRAFT** 1900-100/200/300	420
8	**BOMBARDIER** DASH 8-100/200/300	374
9	**DE HAVILLAND CANADA** DHC-6 TWIN OTTER	330
10	**SAAB** 340	215

SHIPPED BY AIR FREIGHT

Urgently needed spare parts, medical samples and important documents are transported quickly and reliably from A to B via air—but urgent transport requires complex logistics. As of July 2019, the worldwide fleet of MD-11s totals 118 aircraft in commercial service, with cargo operators FedEx Express (55), UPS Airlines (37), Lufthansa Cargo (12), Western Global Airlines (11) and other operators with fewer aircraft.

THE TANK SYSTEM

An MD-11 has 5 tanks: two in the wings, two in the main body and one at the rear. The front tanks are filled with up to 67 tons of fuel and the rear tank is also filled. Six computers control the fueling system, known as KCC, which is also used by the US Air Force in their tanker aircraft.

The computers make sure fuel is pumped to the right places in line with the requirements set by the trim. These demands change constantly throughout the flight due to continuous fuel consumption.

The tank of an MD-11 can be filled with a maximum of 117.3 tons of kerosene. When fully laden with cargo, the plane uses up 2 tons of fuel during the journey from the parking position to the runway alone.

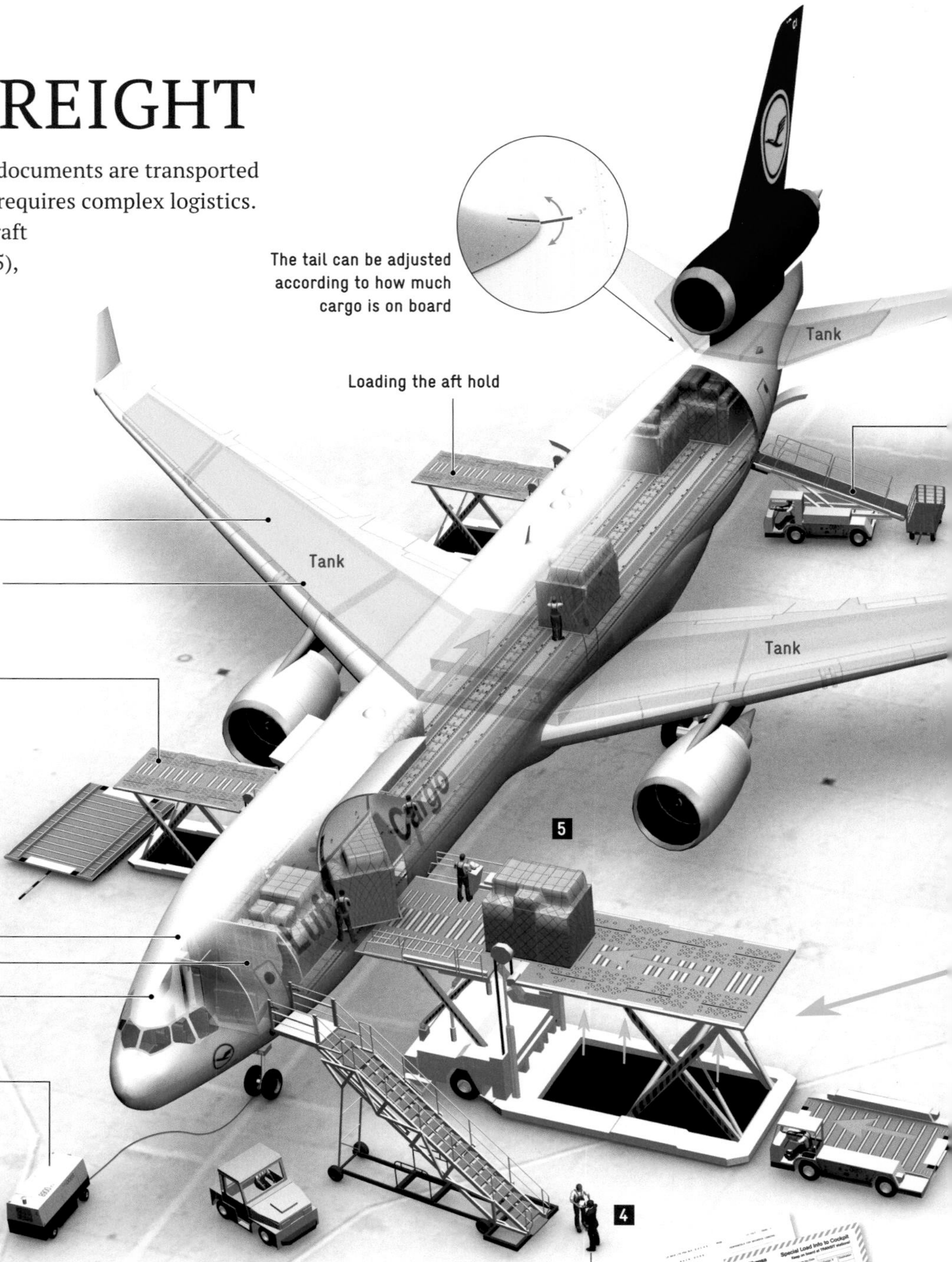
The tail can be adjusted according to how much cargo is on board
Loading the aft hold
Tank
Tank
Tank
The tank is filled after cargo has been loaded onto the plane
Loading the forward hold
Toilet
Safety net
Cockpit
Battery car to power the aircraft
5
4

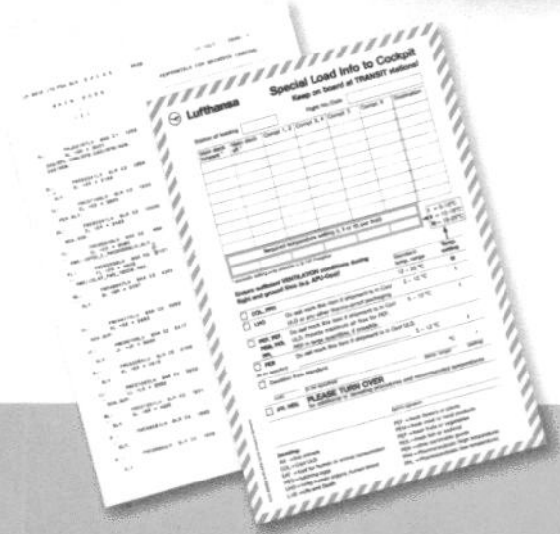

Pre-Logistics

WHAT HAPPENS BEFORE THE PLANE IS LOADED WITH CARGO?

1 Shipments are delivered to the plane in Frankfurt from the most diverse range of places: standard freight cargo, perishables, post, express, valuable cargo, animals and freight that comes straight from Cargo City South as BUP (Bulk Unitization Programme) – they all come from their own department within the airport.

2 The computer calculates and designs the correct placement of the aircraft according to the specifications and creates a loading plan.

3 The loadmaster checks that the loading schedule is accurate and issues the Notification to the Captain (NoTOC). This details the required temperatures for certain shipments, live freight or dangerous goods on board. Knowing if the shipment is corrosive or explosive is critically important if the fire brigade is called in case of emergency.

4 The pilot receives a loading plan and a notification to the captain (NoTOC). After he signs the NoTOC, the aircraft check with the co-pilot can begin.

5 The plane is loaded with cargo using a pallet and container loader – in other words, the freight makes its way to the plane on a built-in elevator (see right for details of the loading sequence). The pallets are then loaded onto the plane in their respective positions using muscle power. Loading on the main deck is aided by rollers on the floor equipped with electric motors.

6 After two hours and 30 minutes, the plane leaves its parking position and rolls towards the runway – this is the typical »turnaround time« for an MD-11 at Lufthansa Cargo.

Cross-section

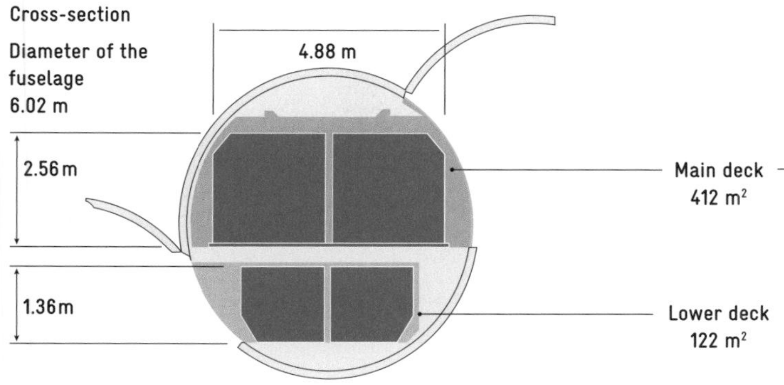
Diameter of the fuselage 6.02 m
4.88 m
2.56 m
1.36 m
Main deck
412 m²
Lower deck
122 m²

Lengthways

Size of the door on the main deck: W 3.55 m × H 2.56 m

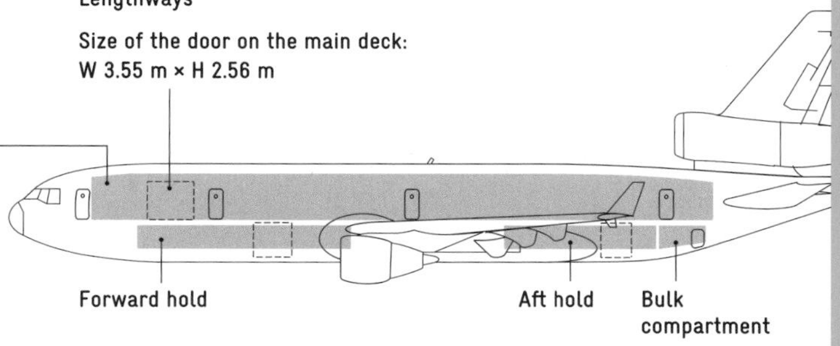
Forward hold
Aft hold
Bulk compartment

Loading the bulk compartment

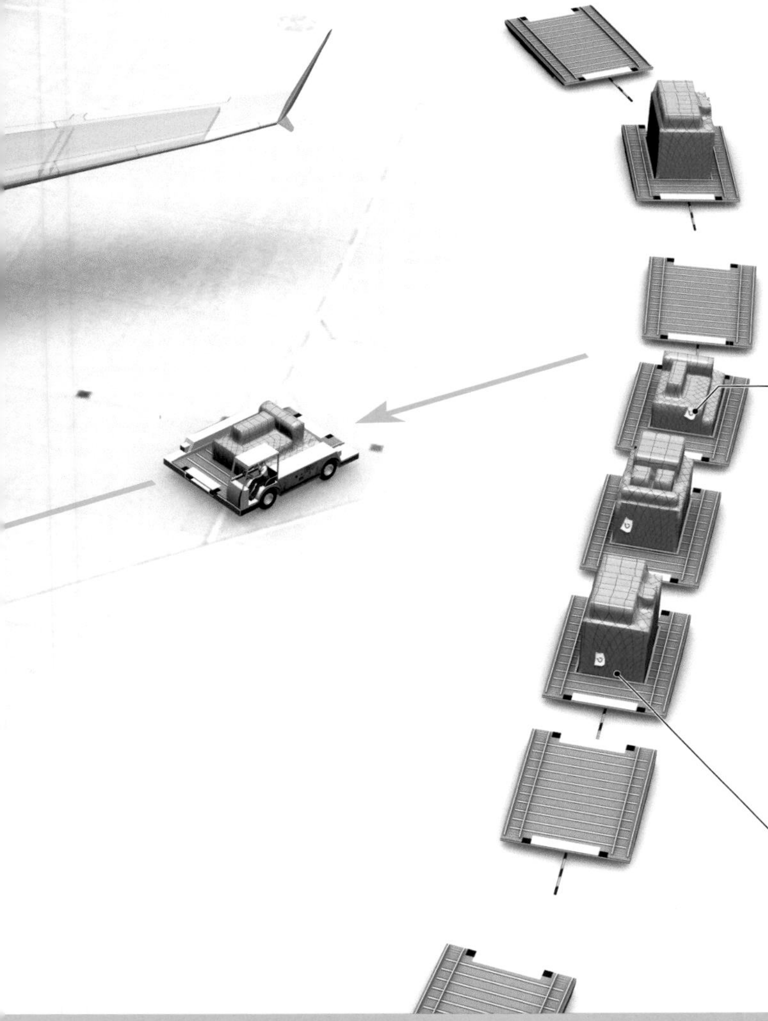

MD-11 F Facts

Maiden flight	10/01/1990*
Total constructed	200
Length	61.60 m
Wingspan	51.80 m
Height	17.60 m
Wing surface area	338.90 m²
Winglet height	2.71 m
Unladen weight	114.10 t
Max. landing weight	222.90 t
Cargo load capacity	95.10 t
Engines	3
Max. weight for lift off	286 t

*as a passenger aircraft

AWB number, pallets and container ID

Lufthansa
Unit Load Device
ID Code:

The Air Waybill (AWB) is the shipment's ticket. It can be one unit or thousands of single units. Each pallet and each container also have their own ID code.

PAJ22187 LH MAA C1 1258

Type of pallet — Airline — Destination (Madras) — Weight in kg

ID Code

Logistics

THE LOADING SEQUENCE

A

LOADING THE FRONT

The first row of the main deck and the forward hold are loaded with cargo.

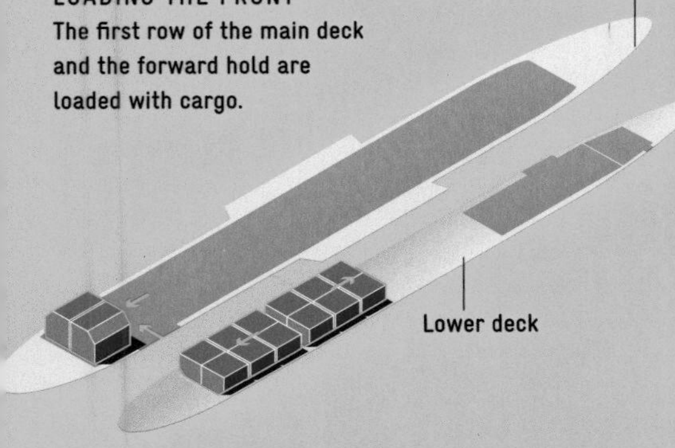
Main deck
Lower deck

B

FILLING THE MAIN DECK

The entire upper deck is filled with cargo. The pallets to be located at the rear of the plane are loaded first.

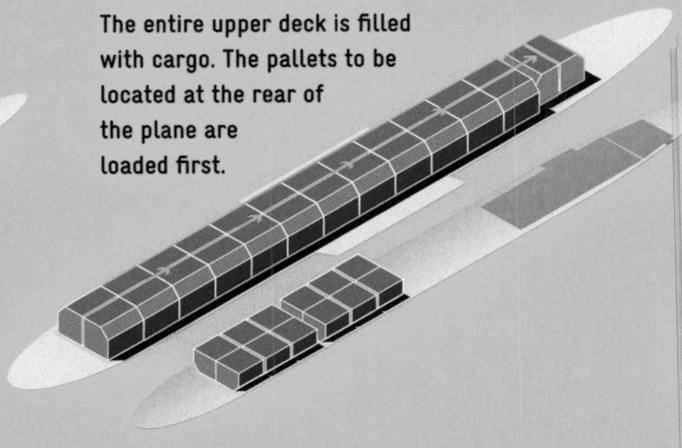

C

LOADING THE BACK

Once all pallets are filled with cargo, it is ready to take off!

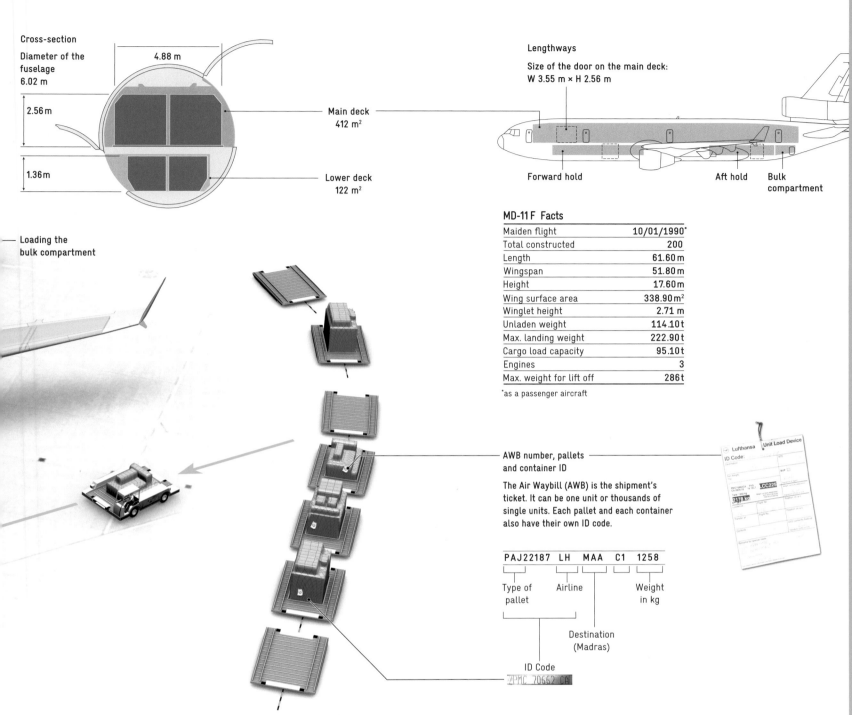

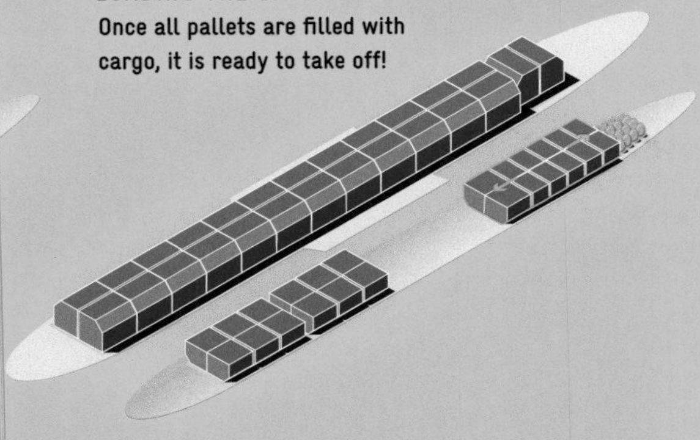

HISTORY POLITICS SOCIETY ECONOMY SPORTS TECHNOLOGY CULTURE & ARTS SCIENCE

150 YEARS OF SIEMENS & ZEISS

They are two of Germany's best known entrepreneurs: Carl Zeiss and Werner von Siemens were born three months apart in 1816. They went on to build companies that were successful beyond their lifetimes and have become two of Germany's best-known exporters. Their legacies, however, took different paths. The sons of the Siemens family took over the founder's business philosophy and the management of the company itself. As for Zeiss, Ernst Abbe, one of the company's partners, transformed it into the Carl Zeiss Foundation, thereby guaranteeing the founder's enduring legacy.

Siemens

INDUSTRY SECTORS

- Energy
- Industry / automation
- Health sector
- Mobility
- Communication
- Light
- Consumer goods

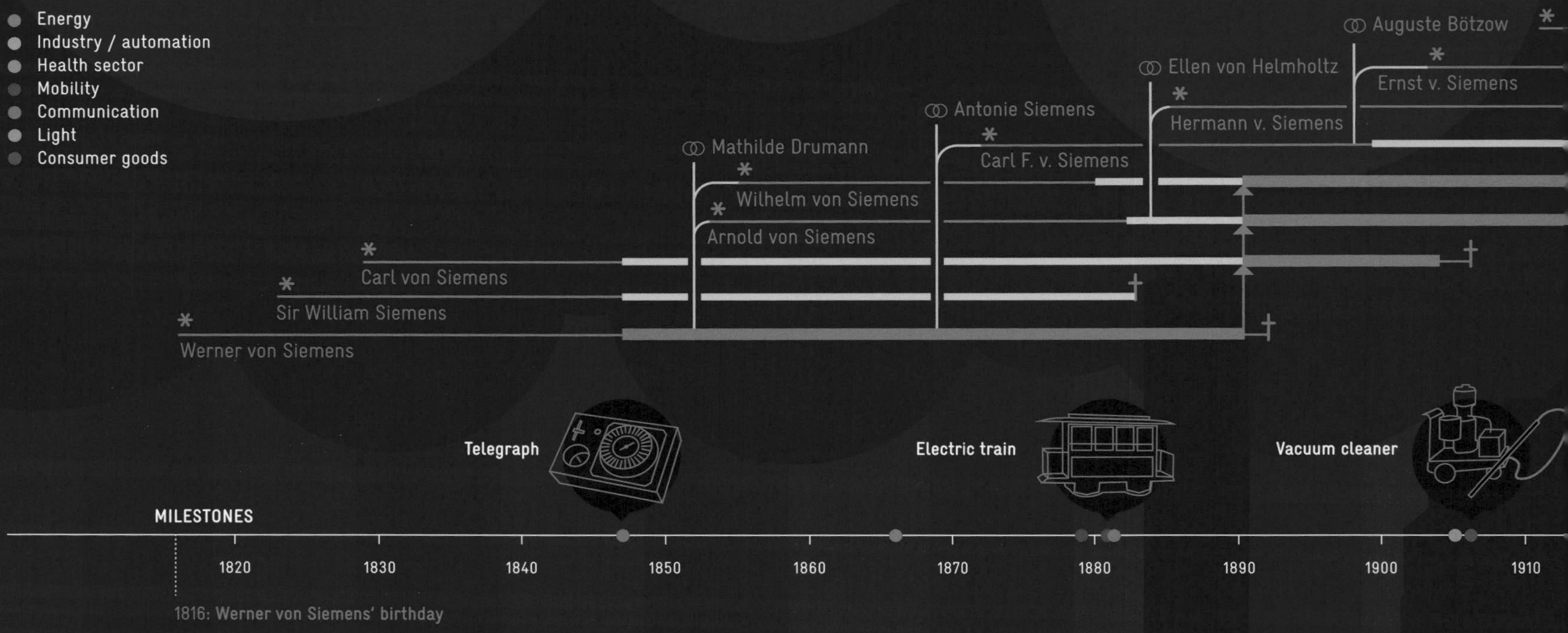
Auguste Bötzow
Ernst v. Siemens
Ellen von Helmholtz
Hermann v. Siemens
Antonie Siemens
Carl F. v. Siemens
Mathilde Drumann
Wilhelm von Siemens
Arnold von Siemens
Carl von Siemens
Sir William Siemens
Werner von Siemens
Telegraph
Electric train
Vacuum cleaner
MILESTONES
1820
1830
1840
1850
1860
1870
1880
1890
1900
1910
1816: Werner von Siemens' birthday

The Zeiss company was transformed into the Carl Zeiss Foundation by partner Ernst Abbe. His aim was to transfer the founding father's vision to the future.

Zeiss

INDUSTRY SECTORS

- Lenses
- Microscopy
- Binoculars
- Photo and cinema lenses
- Industrial metrology
- Semiconductor technology
- Medical technology
- Planetariums

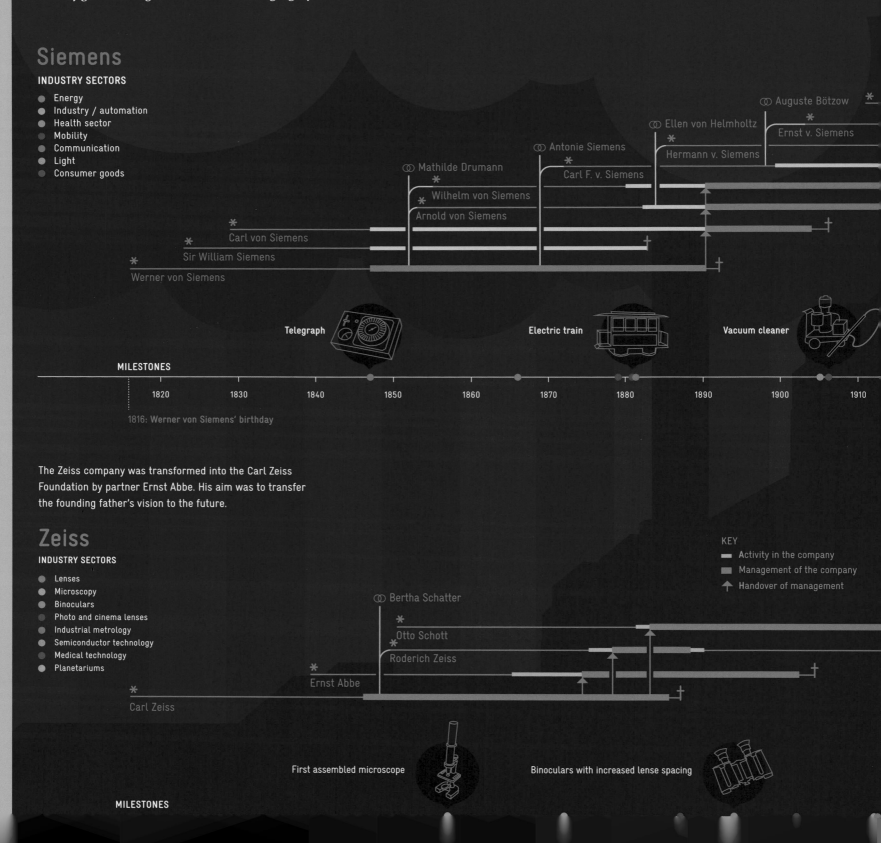

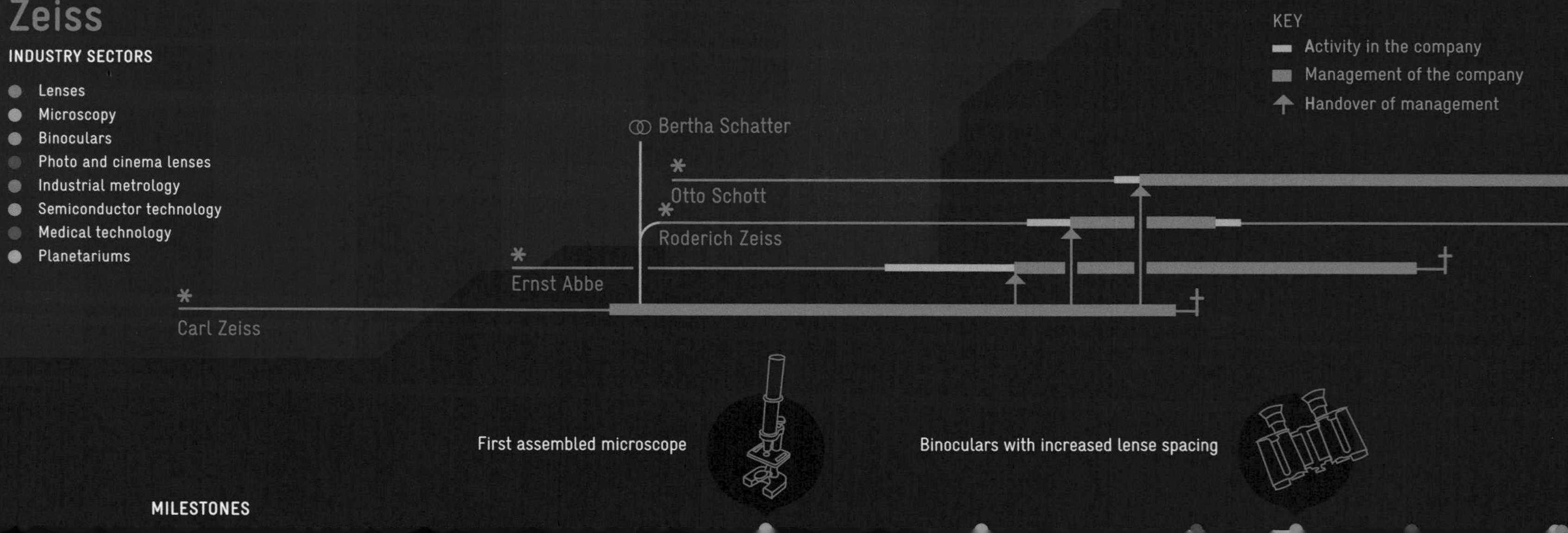
KEY
Activity in the company
Management of the company
Handover of management
Bertha Schatter
Otto Schott
Roderich Zeiss
Ernst Abbe
Carl Zeiss
First assembled microscope
Binoculars with increased lense spacing
MILESTONES

THE MITTELSTAND

Family-controlled companies are the driving force behind Germany's »mittelstand« (mid-sized businesses). Many can already look back on more than a century of success. Their long-term strategy provides stability, even during difficult economic times.

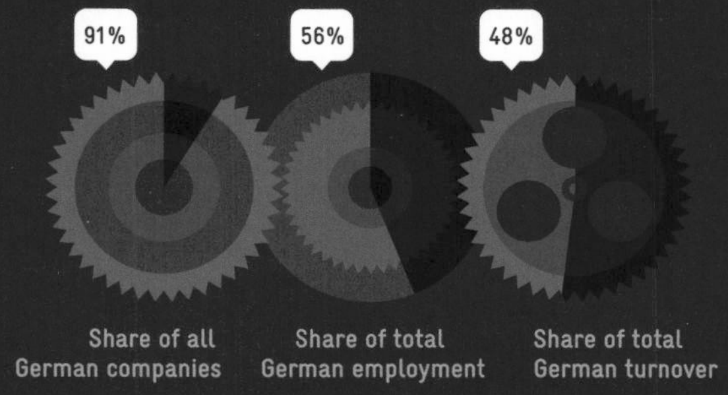

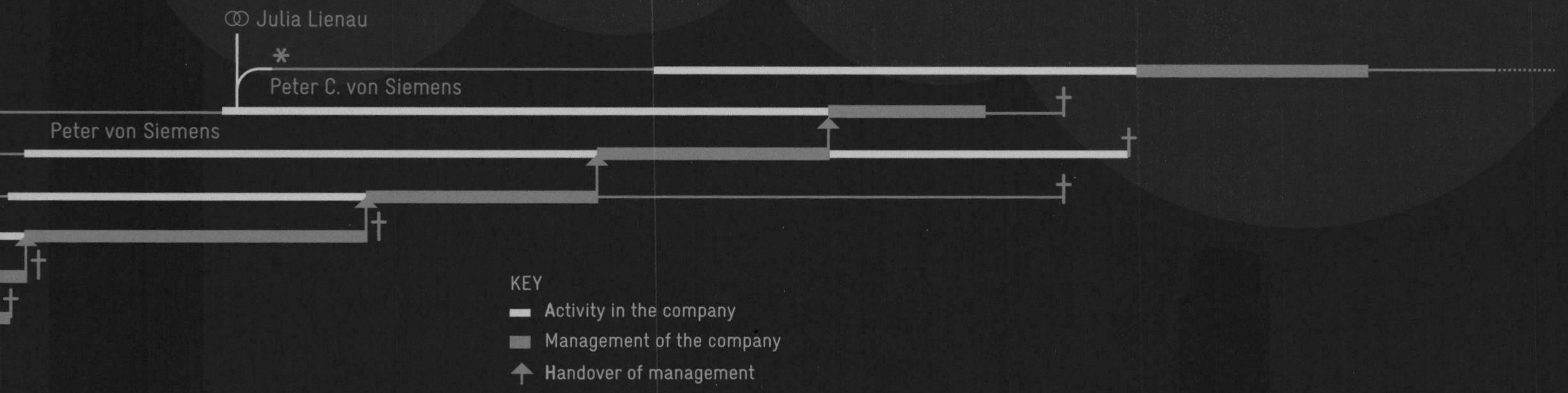

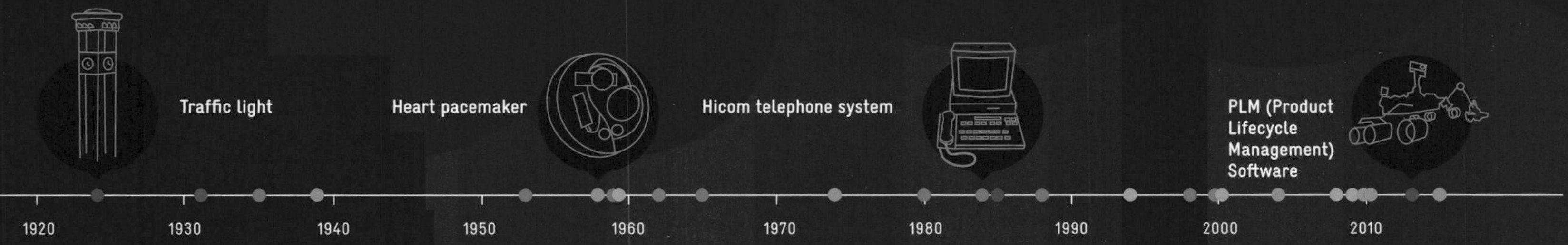

SUCCESSION PLANNING IN LARGE COMPANIES

Around 40 of the 100 largest mittelstand companies in Germany are holding companies. These are generally set up in a way that protects the company from inheritance and succession disputes.

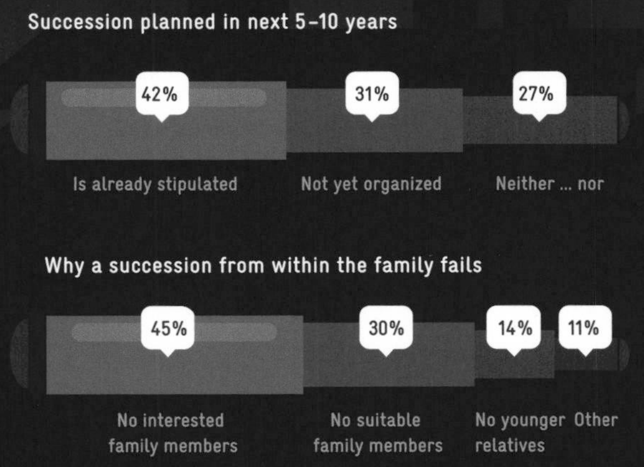

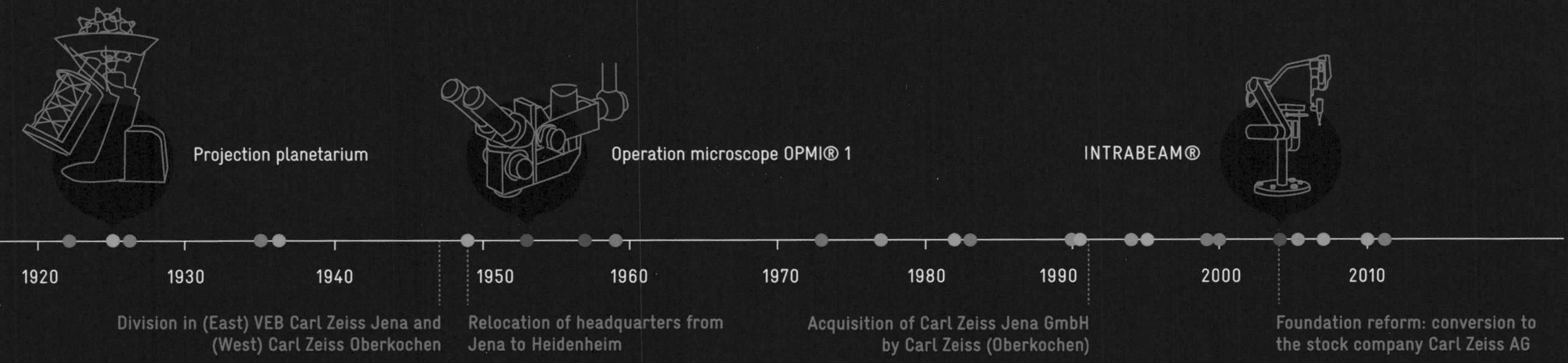

HISTORY OF NESTLÉ

Nestlé is the world's largest food company—and yet its production methods attract criticism throughout the world. Founder Henri Nestlé—born Heinrich Nestle in 1814—pioneered the mass production of food. Today, the Swiss group represents the legacy of his life's work.

1814

Heinrich Nestle is born in **Frankfurt** on August 10. He is the 11th of a middle-class family's **14 children**. His father is a master glazier, whose family originates from Württemberg. The name Nestle means »small nest«, a motif that is also found in the family's crest and nowadays in the group's logo.

HEINRICH NESTLE AND NESTLÉ TODAY

Today, the Nestlé **German headquarters** is located in Heinrich Nestle's home town. His products have been available in Germany since 1874.

AFTER 1833

Nestle is a chemist's assistant and emigrates to the French-speaking part of Switzerland. He flees the repressive politics of his home town. Nestle's circle of friends also consists of Liberals who openly protest about the political situation in Frankfurt.

1839

Nestle passes the chemist's assistant admission exam in Switzerland. He changes his name to Henri Nestlé. He is interested in chemical experiments. His workplace is the **»Pharmacie Centrale«** in **Vevey**.

1843

Nestlé acquires an **industrial estate** in Vevey and founds his own company. His products include alcoholic drinks, oils, mineral water and lemonades with **carbonic acid**. Later, he stops beverage production.

1849

Nestlé sets up his own chemical laboratory. He reorganizes his business due to an economic crisis in 1857. Apart from fertilizers, he only produces **liquid gas**, which he developed himself. He provides the gas for Vevey's **city lights** from 1857.

The Nestlé Group is the target of many protests for their practices, including:

Marketing **baby formula** in a way that lowers the likelihood of mothers choosing to breastfeed.

Upsetting the ecological balance at **water sources**.

Insufficiently labelling **genetically modified food**.

Sourcing from **cocoa plantations** that enslave their workers.

Today, the group invests in pharmaceutical food. »Nestlé Health Science«, **with its headquarters in Vevey,** aims to develop products that will prevent and treat chronic illnesses. Nestlé wants to open new markets by positioning itself as a health and wellness group.

Revenue of respective Nestlé branches 2016 in bll. Swiss Francs

15.0 *Nutrition and healthcare*

Today, Nestlé sells drinks again. The Nestlé Waters branch controls production sites in 36 countries from its **Paris headquarters**. Instant coffee – a Nestlé invention from 1938 – makes up the largest share of revenue earned by beverages. The company receives constant criticism for its privatization of water sources and work conditions on coffee plantations.

27.2 *Powdered and liquid beverages; water products*

Today, the group researches and develops products at its **research headquarters** in Lausanne and employs more than 5,000 people worldwide in this field. More than €1 bn is invested to develop and improve products. In 2011, the animal welfare group Peta accused Nestlé of conducting unnecessary animal testing in its research.

1863

Vevey builds a central gas works that makes it **independent** from Nestlé's supplies. The company owner now has to come up with new products to create revenue.

1866

American brothers George and Charles Page found the **»Anglo-Swiss Condensed Milk Company«** in **Cham**, which becomes a strong competitor to Nestlé. Apart from condensed milk, Nestlé also sells milk powder from 1878 onwards – at that time, the most important source of income for the company. The fierce competition only ends in 1905 with the merger of the two companies.

1867

Using modern production methods, Nestlé develops a long-lasting substitute food for children, a milk powder called **»children's flour«**. It quickly becomes successful as a way of fighting malnutrition and is marketed as a remedy to illness.

1874

Henri Nestlé and his wife Clémentine become official citizens of the city of Vevey. He sells his company for a million Swiss Francs and a **coach** and moves to an **estate in Glion** near Montreux for his retirement. The Nestlé company continues to expand as a stock company.

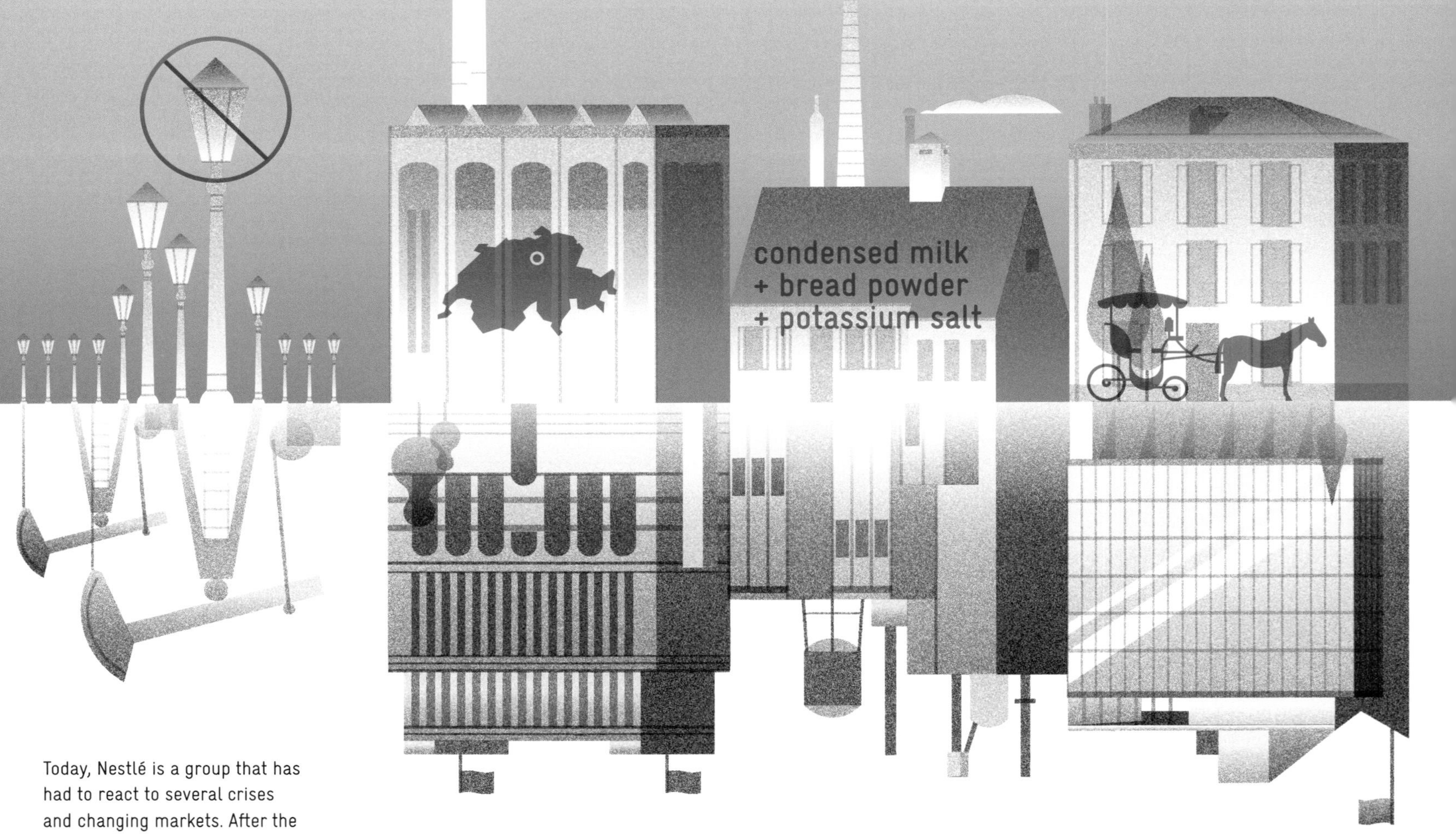
condensed milk
+ bread powder
+ potassium salt

Today, Nestlé is a group that has had to react to several crises and changing markets. After the **oil crisis in 1973**, for example, Alcon, a producer of eye care products,* was taken over by Nestlé. During growth periods, the business continues to expand, for example, with its move into the pet food business through the acquisition of Ralston Purina in 2001.

12.1 *PetCare*

Nestlé, nowadays the world's largest food producer, fights for market share with other global companies such as **Unilever**.

The biggest competitors, revenue in $bil. (2016)

Nestlé	90.8
PepsiCo	62.8
Unilever	58.3
Mondelez	25.9
Danone	24.3

Today, the Nestlé group has significantly expanded its business with baby and toddler food by acquiring other companies such as the US company **Gerber**.
Other milk products, like ice cream, contribute considerably to its turnover.

14.3 *Milk products and ice cream*

Today, there are an estimated 250,000 shareholders who hold 3.2 bil. shares worth 322 m. Swiss Francs. According to Swiss law, they remain anonymous.
It is not clear which important shareholders have a say at the **headquarters in Vevey.**

* completely sold again in 2010

1875
Daniel Peter, Henri Nestlé's neighbor, is one of the first people to industrially produce milk chocolate. His success is shown by the steadily growing **share capital.** In 1901, he founds his **chocolate factory** in the Swiss city of Orbe. The company starts collaborating with Nestlé in 1904.

1875
Nestlé's children's flour is now sold in 18 countries. More than one million tins leave the factory per year. The product is distributed by agents and supplied directly to individual buyers. It is mainly shipped by **train.**

1886
Julius Maggi, who owns **mills in Zurich,** Kemptthal and Schaffhausen invents a soup concentrate and seasoning made out of **legumes.**
He, too, founds a pioneering industrial food production company in Switzerland.

1890
Henri Nestlé dies aged 76 on July 7. His wife stays in Montreux until her death in 1900. They had no children. Directly after Nestlé's death, the **Montreux market hall** is constructed and funded with his money. It is one of his many foundations.

Today, the Nestlé group does business in 194 countries. It owns production sites in 86 countries and employs 339,000 people. It often gains market access by buying local brands – it claims its portfolio is comprised of more than 8,000 companies. Unions accuse Nestlé of tolerating the violation of labor laws in unstable countries.

Factories by geographic area (2016)

Americas	158
Europe, Middle East, North Africa	151
Asia, Oceania, Africa	109

Today, chocolate is no longer produced in Orbe, although Nestlé runs modern production and **research sites** there. Sweets continue to be an important revenue generator for the company. It also owns many brands and factories in this business sector.

8.8 *Confectionery*

Today, Maggi is part of Nestlé. The merger with Maggi, which had suffered after the Second World War, took place in 1947 and complements Nestlé's range of milk products, instant coffee and chocolate. Today, Maggi is run from its **headquarters in Cham,** Switzerland.

12.1 *Prepared dishes and cooking aids*

Today, one of the Nestlé group's **former administration buildings** in Vevey is home to an exhibition about the company's history and its founder.

GLOBALIZATION'S BOTTLENECK

The Panama Canal was built in 1914, largely financed by the USA, which controlled the waterway until 1999. For 50 years, this route has functioned as one of the most important for global trade. But as the container ships that dominate those trade routes are getting increasingly bigger, the channels have to be expanded. New canals, such as the Nicaragua Canal, are in the works.

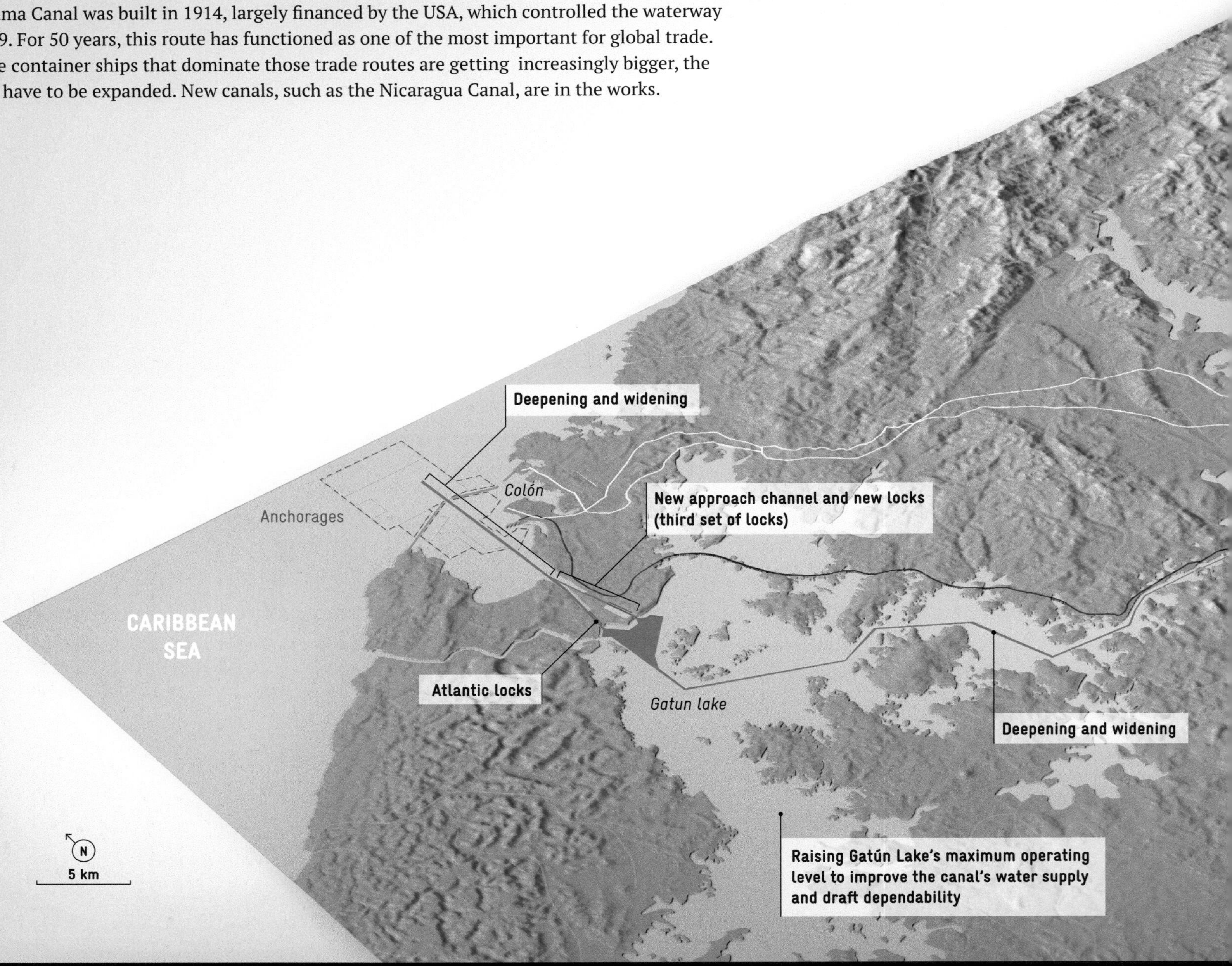
Deepening and widening
Colón
Anchorages
New approach channel and new locks (third set of locks)
CARIBBEAN SEA
Atlantic locks
Gatun lake
Deepening and widening
Raising Gatún Lake's maximum operating level to improve the canal's water supply and draft dependability
N
5 km

NICARAGUA CANAL

Construction time	unfinished
Length	**278 km**
Planned construction costs	US$ ~ **40 bil.**

In July 2012, the Nicaraguan parliament approved a draft law for the construction of the Nicaragua Canal. Around a year later, in July 2013, a 100-year-concession was granted to the HK Nicaragua Canal Development Investment Co., Ltd. consortium (»HKND Group« Hong Kong). HKND will hold 49 % of the shares while the State of Nicaragua is the majority shareholder with 51%. A train connection, pipeline, two harbors and airport are also part of the program. Construction has, however, not yet started.

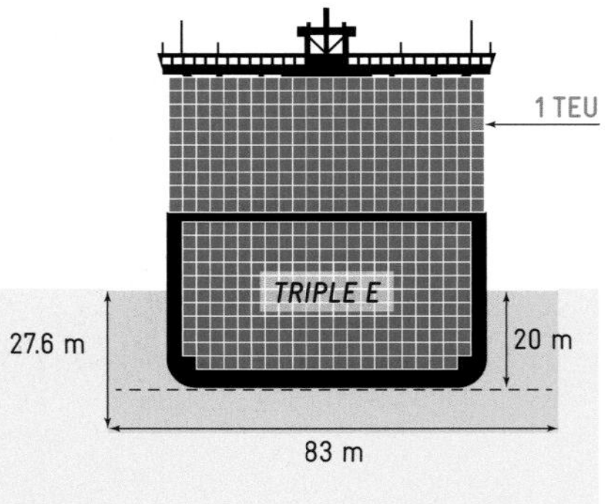
1 TEU
TRIPLE E
27.6 m
20 m
83 m

Maximum ship size

Container	**18,270 TEU***
Capacity	**400,000 t**

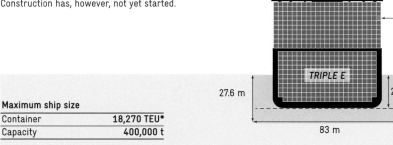

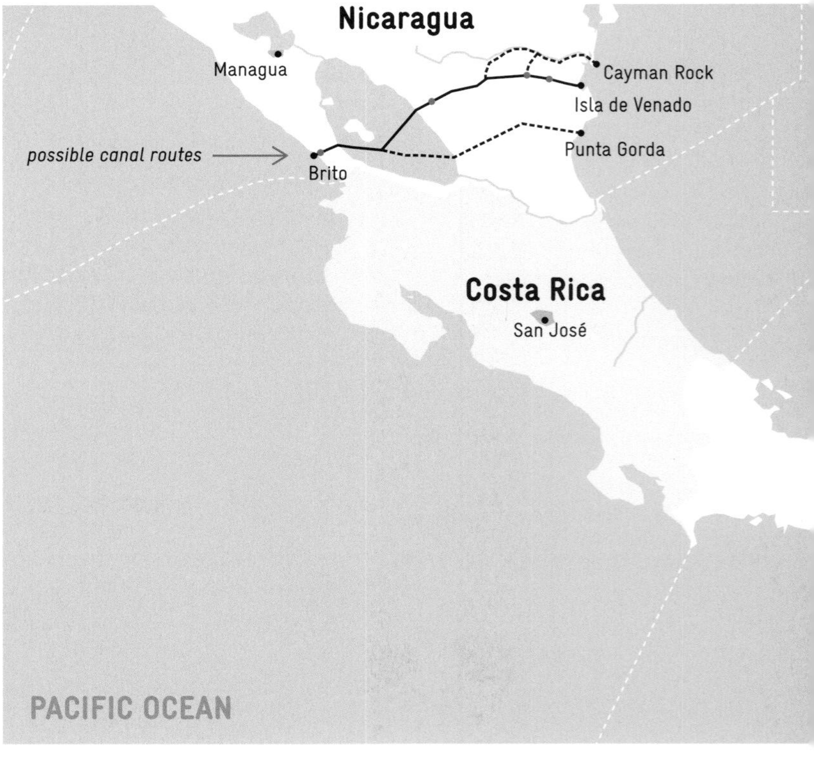
Nicaragua
Managua
Cayman Rock
Isla de Venado
possible canal routes
Brito
Punta Gorda
Costa Rica
San José
PACIFIC OCEAN

The three most important waterways in comparison

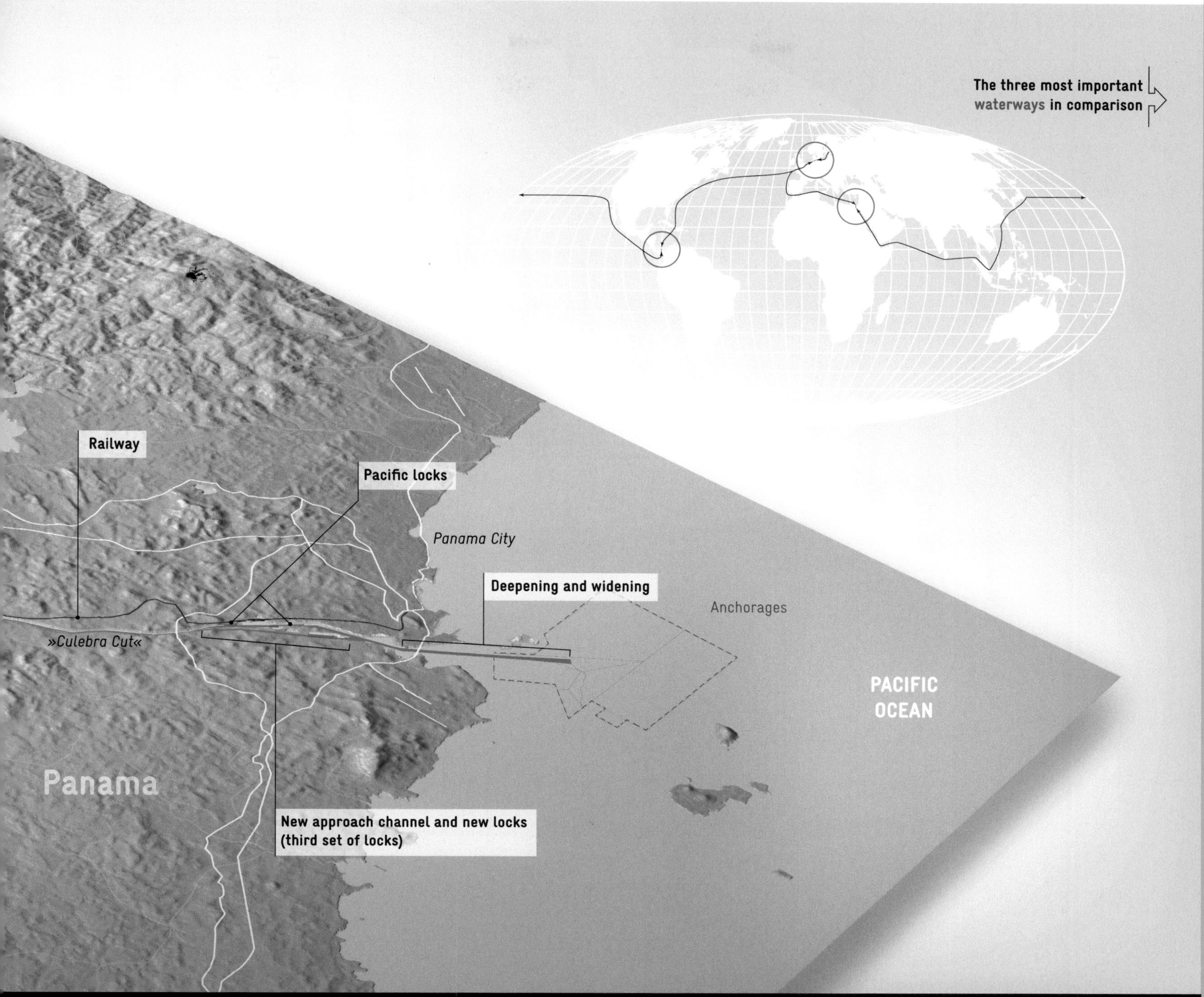
Railway
Pacific locks
Panama City
Deepening and widening
Anchorages
»Culebra Cut«
PACIFIC OCEAN
Panama
New approach channel and new locks (third set of locks)

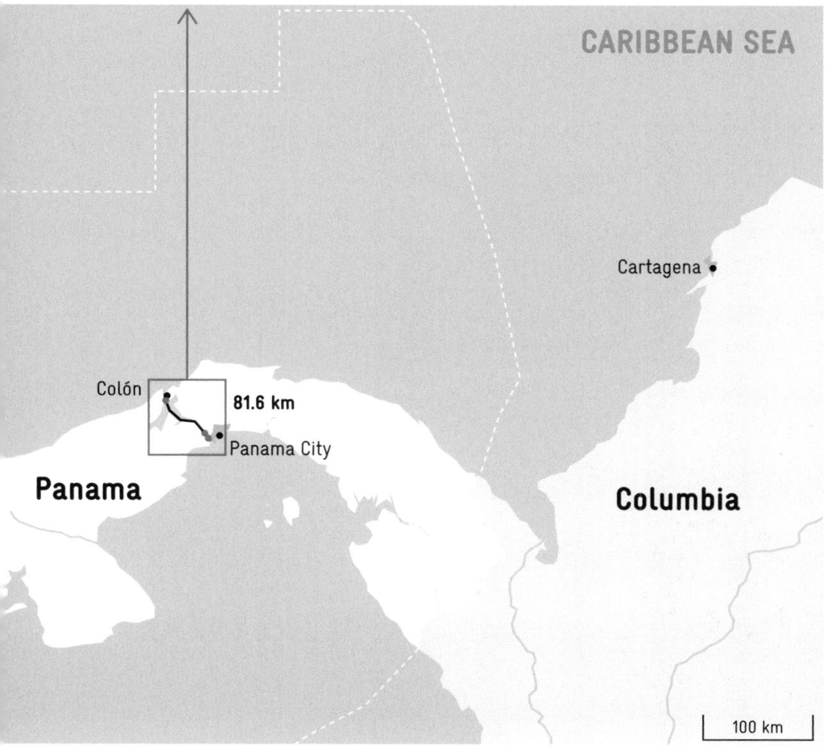
CARIBBEAN SEA
Cartagena
Colón
81.6 km
Panama City
Panama
Columbia
100 km

POST PANAMA CANAL

Construction time	2007–2016
Length	81.6 km
Expansion costs	€5.25 bil.

The expansion of the 100-year-old canal allows the passage of many ships. The canal's permitted maximum capacity per container ship was nearly tripled after the expansion program—from 5,000 TEU to 14,600 TEU.

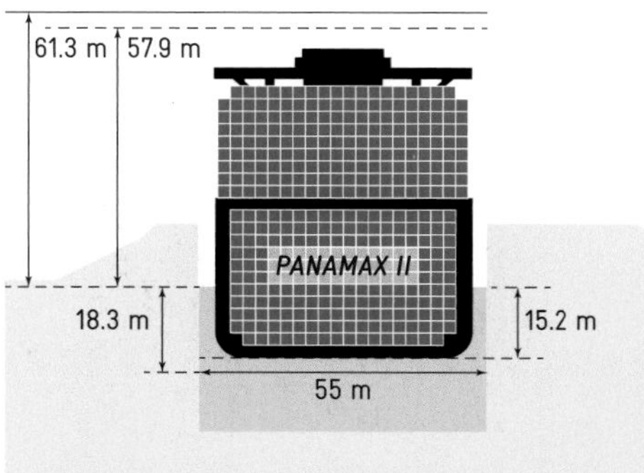
61.3 m
57.9 m
PANAMAX II
18.3 m
15.2 m
55 m
NEW LOCKS

Maximum ship size	
Beam	49.00 m
Height	57.90 m
Length	366.00 m
Container	14,600 TEU*
Capacity	200,000 t

* 1 TEU = Container measuring 20 • 8 • 8.5 ft

PANAMA CANAL

Built	1904–1914
Length	81.6 km
Tolls 2019	US$ 2.59 bil.

Duration per canal passage	20–30 h
Daily canal passages (2018)	ø 37
Revenues per transit (2018)	US$ ø 187,749

Old maximum ship size

Beam	32.31 m
Height	57.90 m
Length	294.13 m
Container	5,000 TEU*
Capacity	80,000 t

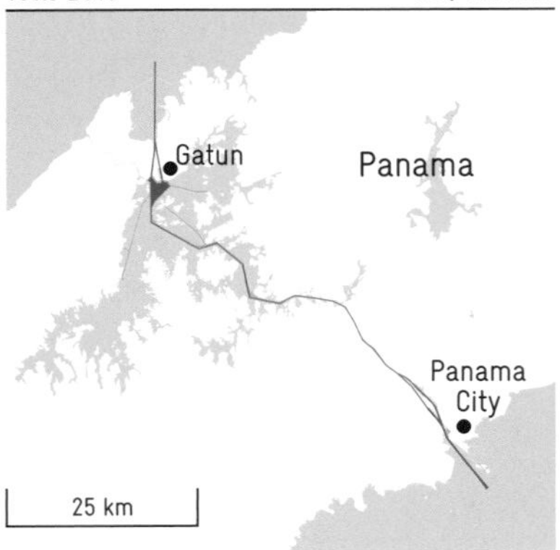

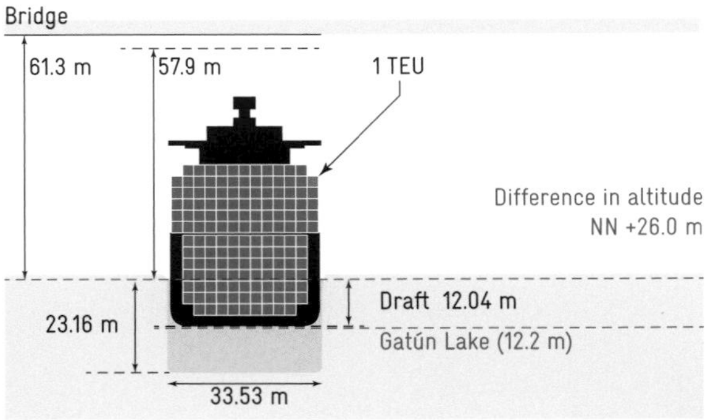
Bridge
61.3 m
57.9 m
1 TEU
Difference in altitude
NN +26.0 m
Draft 12.04 m
23.16 m
Gatún Lake (12.2 m)
33.53 m

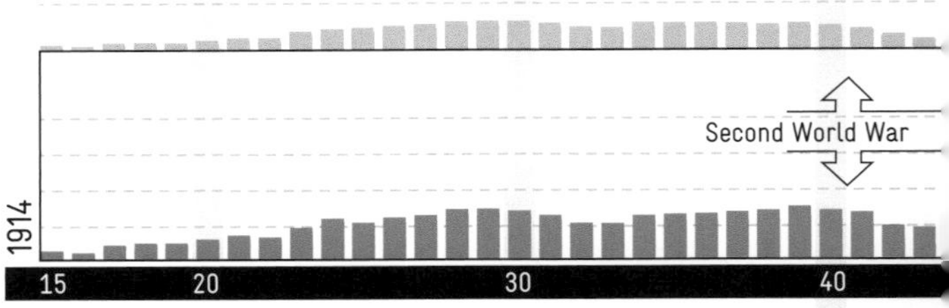
Second World War
1914
15
20
30
40

KIEL CANAL

Built	1887–1895
Length	98.6 km
Tolls 2016	US$ 24.8 m.

Duration per canal passage	7–9 h
Daily canal passages (2018)	ø 82
Revenues per transit (2016)	US$ ø 846

Maximum ship size

Beam	32.5 m
Height	40.0 m
Length	235 m

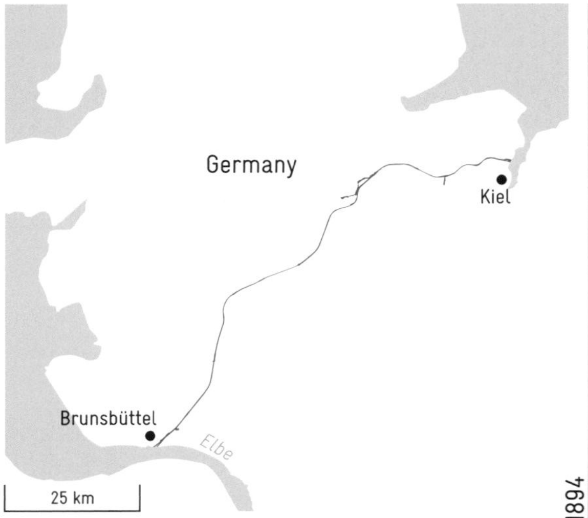
Germany
Kiel
Brunsbüttel
Elbe
25 km

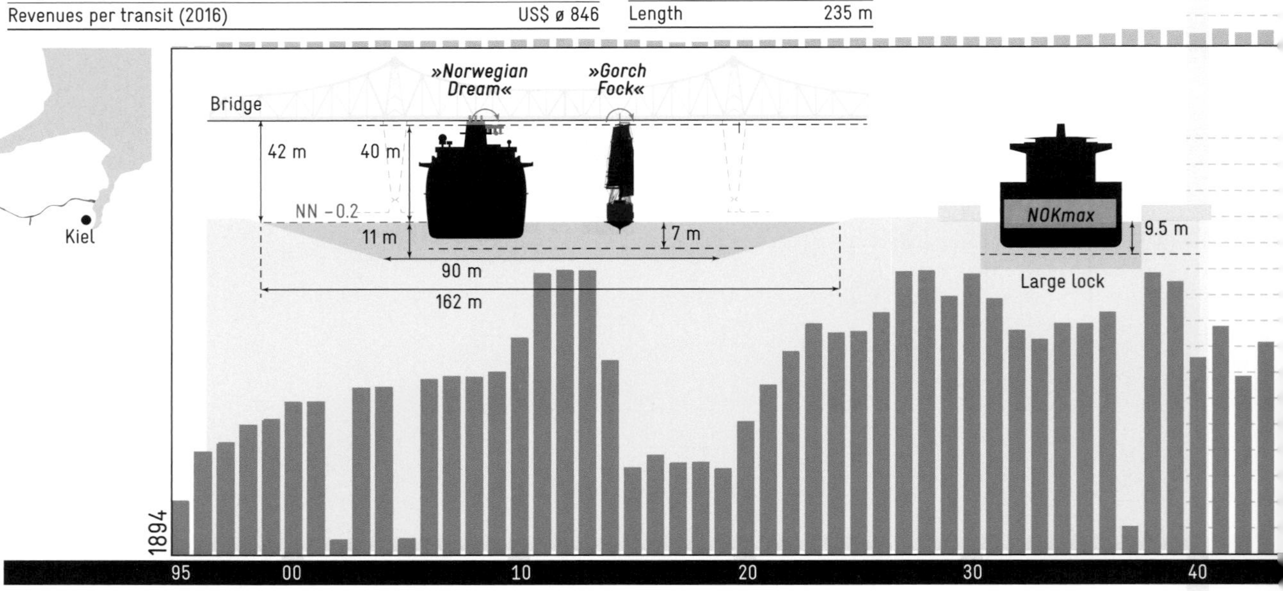
Bridge
»Norwegian Dream«
»Gorch Fock«
42 m
40 m
NN –0.2
11 m
7 m
90 m
162 m
NOKmax
9.5 m
Large lock
1894
95
00
10
20
30
40

SUEZ CANAL

Built	04-25-1859 – 11-17-1869
Length	193.3 km
Tolls 2019	US$ 5.8 bil.

Duration per canal passage	11 h
Daily canal passages (2018)	~49 (max.: 98)
Revenues per transit (2018)	US$ ø 302,630

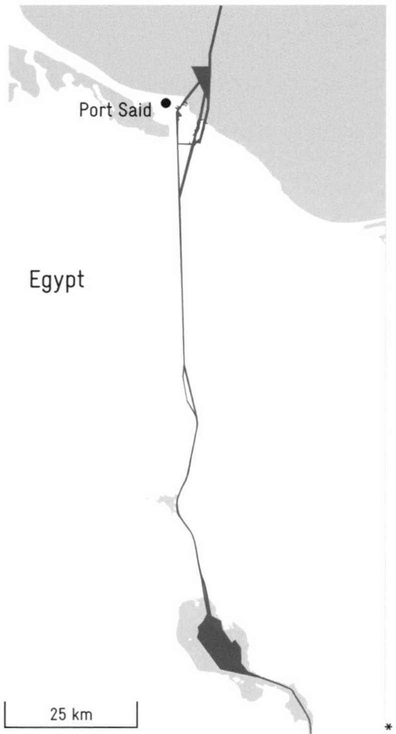

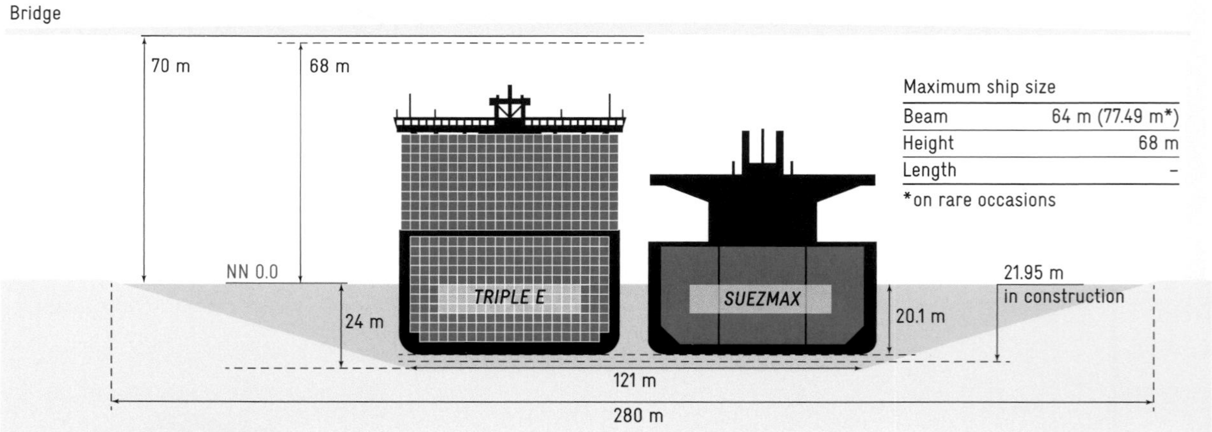
Bridge
70 m
68 m
NN 0.0
24 m
TRIPLE E
SUEZMAX
20.1 m
21.95 m
in construction
121 m
280 m

Maximum ship size

Beam	64 m (77.49 m*)
Height	68 m
Length	–

*on rare occasions

* 1 TEU = Container measuring 20 • 8 • 8.5 ft

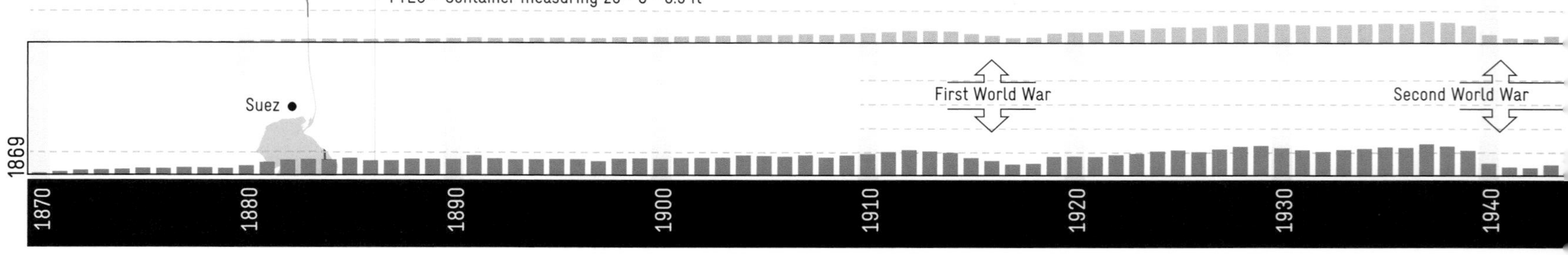
First World War
Second World War
1869
1870
1880
1890
1900
1910
1920
1930
1940

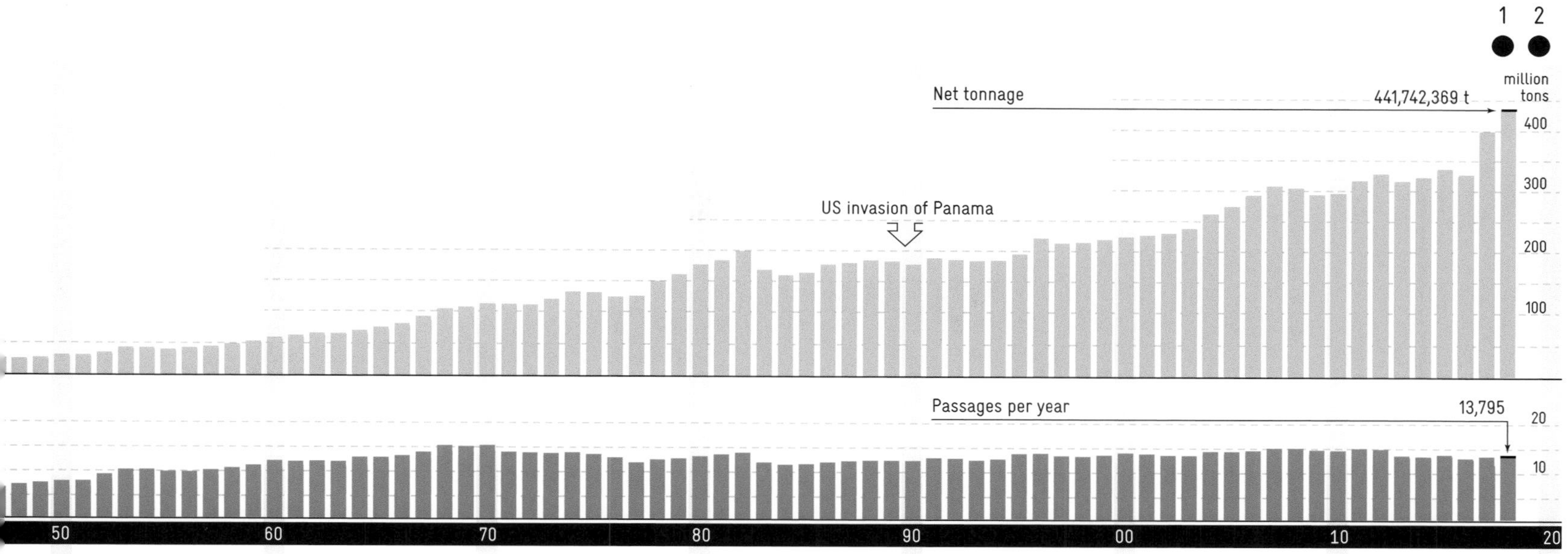
1
2
million tons
Net tonnage
441,742,369 t
400
300
US invasion of Panama
200
100
Passages per year
13,795
20
10
50
60
70
80
90
00
10
20

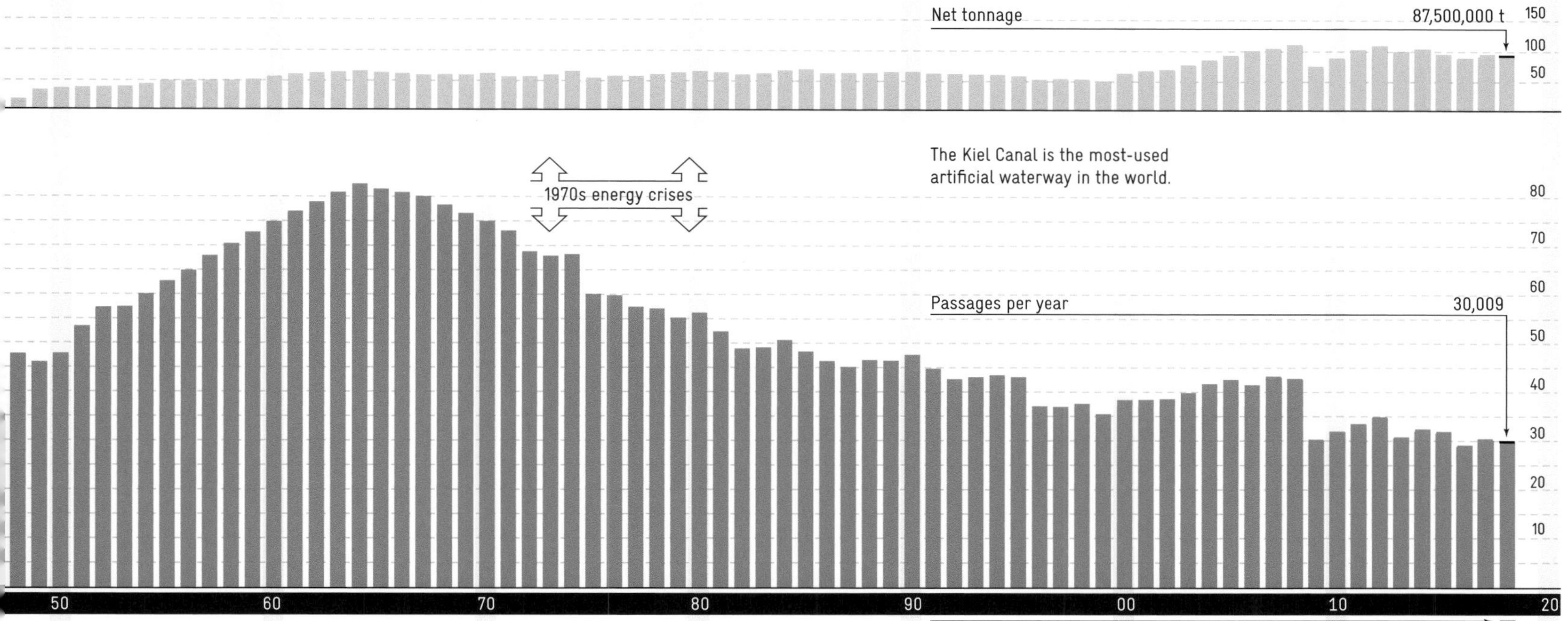
Net tonnage
87,500,000 t
150
100
50
The Kiel Canal is the most-used artificial waterway in the world.
1970s energy crises
80
70
60
Passages per year
30,009
50
40
30
20
10
50
60
70
80
90
00
10
20

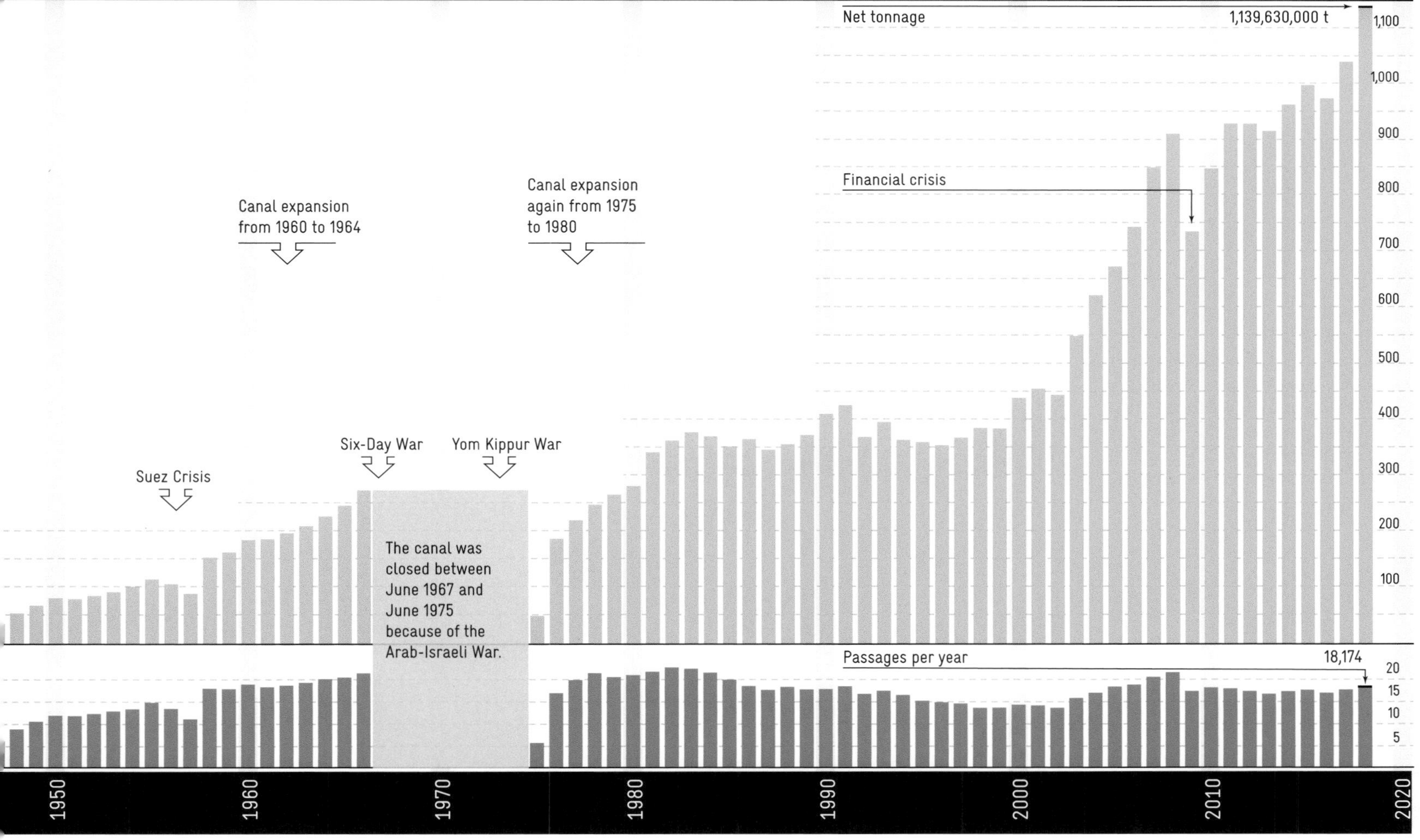
Net tonnage
1,139,630,000 t
1,100
1,000
900
Financial crisis
800
Canal expansion from 1960 to 1964
Canal expansion again from 1975 to 1980
700
600
500
400
Six-Day War
Yom Kippur War
Suez Crisis
300
200
The canal was closed between June 1967 and June 1975 because of the Arab-Israeli War.
100
Passages per year
18,174
20
15
10
5
1950
1960
1970
1980
1990
2000
2010
2020

MOTOR OF GLOBALIZATION

Container ships, invented in the 1960s, paved the way for global trade. The lead ship of the Triple-E class (EEE–Economy of scale, Energy efficiency, Environmentally improved) is the »Mærsk Mc-Kinney Møller«, the world's longest operating container ship. In 2019, however, the MSC Megamax-24 had the highest maximum TEU of 23,500.

THE ASIA-EUROPE ROUTE

Trade with China requires container cargo capacity to increase. The Triple-E class is designed for the routes between Asia and Europe. Because of their size, Triple-E vessels can only dock in a few particularly large harbors.

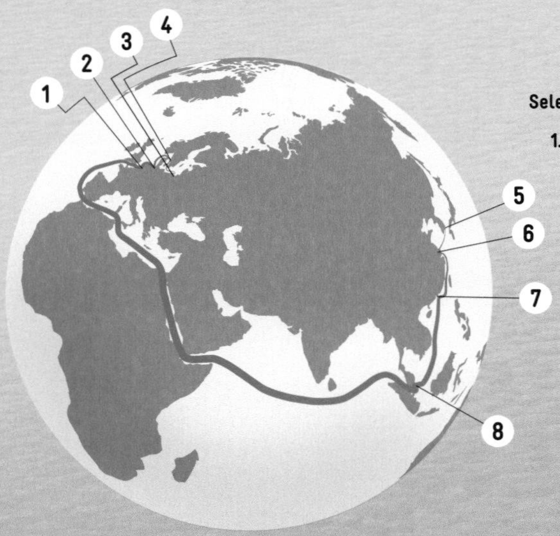

Selection of accessible ports:

1. Rotterdam (NL)
2. Bremerhaven (DE)
3. Gdansk (PL)
4. Gothenburg (SE)
5. Busan (KR)
6. Shanghai (CN)
7. Yantian (CN)
8. Tanjung Pelepas (MY)

TECHNICAL DATA

Length	**400 m** // 1,312 ft
Width	**59 m** // 194 ft
Draft	**14.5 m** // 48 ft
Speed	**25 kn** (46 km/h)
Capacity	**18,270 TEU* Container**
Launch	**02-24-2013**

* TEU = twenty-foot equivalent unit

»Megablock«

Bridge of the
22-member crew
MÆRSK MC-KINNEY MØLLER
Ballast water

PAPER-THIN GIANT

The Triple-E class's outer wall is made of a 4-cm-thin steel layer. If the ship were the size of a car, the layer would be thinner than paper. An exact loading plan is a vital requirement to protect the ship from breaking apart. On rough seas, the bending between bow and stern can be up to 3 meters.

EFFICIENT USE OF SPACE

The U-shaped hull of the »Mærsk Mc-Kinney Møller« holds most of the load. In contrast to its predecessor, the »Emma Maersk«, the broad hull is optimized for slower, more energy-efficient speeds.

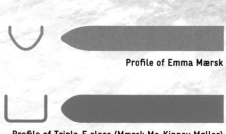

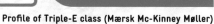

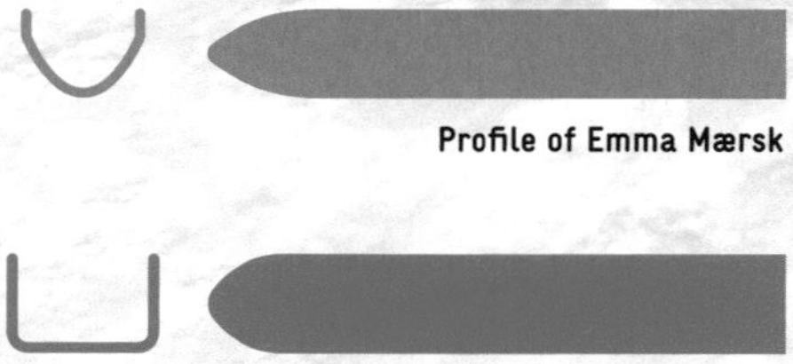

Profile of Emma Mærsk

Profile of Triple-E class (Mærsk Mc-Kinney Møller)

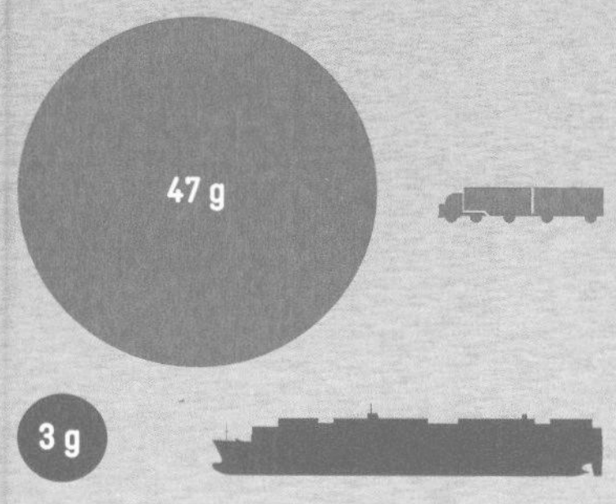

47 g
3 g

HOW MUCH IS 18,000 CONTAINERS?

A truck convoy transporting all these containers while keeping a safe distance of 40 m between them would be more than 500 km long, which is roughly the distance between Bremerhaven and Frankfurt (Main). They could hold up to 111 million pairs of shoes or 182 million iPads.

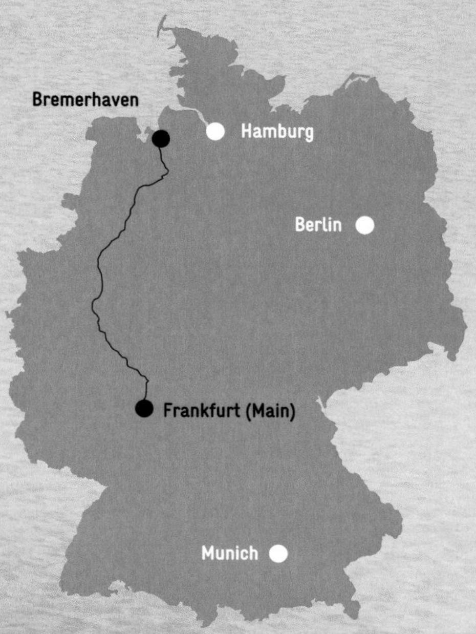

Bremerhaven
Hamburg
Berlin
Frankfurt (Main)
Munich

LESS AIR POLLUTION

The steel giant saves up to 50 % carbon dioxide per standard container in contrast to older ships. The CO_2 emissions for the transport of one ton for one kilometer are, on average, 16 times lower than transportation by truck.

»Two-island« design: The wider gap between the bridge and chimneys creates more stowage.
MAE
LINE
24 »megablocks« form the steel hull.
The hull's shape allows for as many as 23 rows of containers across its width.

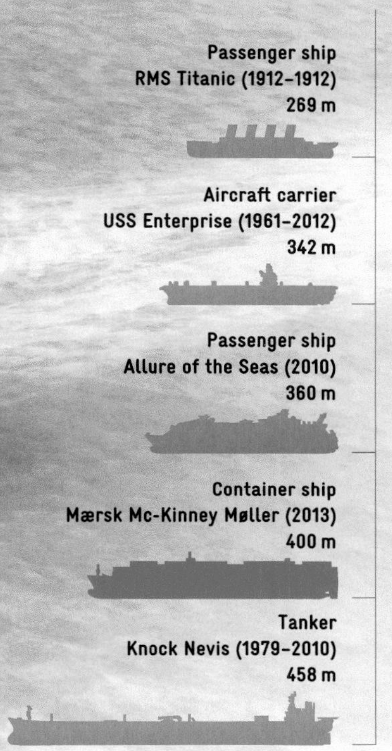

Passenger ship
RMS Titanic (1912–1912)
269 m
Aircraft carrier
USS Enterprise (1961–2012)
342 m
Passenger ship
Allure of the Seas (2010)
360 m
Container ship
Mærsk Mc-Kinney Møller (2013)
400 m
Tanker
Knock Nevis (1979–2010)
458 m

MAXIMUM CAPACITY LOAD RECORDS

The carrying capacity is the economically relevant unit for the specification of cargo vessels. It measures the difference between the water displacement of a fully-loaded and an unloaded ship. It is defined in »tons deadweight« (tdw). While the development of tankers largely came to an end in the 1980s, the boom of container ships is still in full progress.

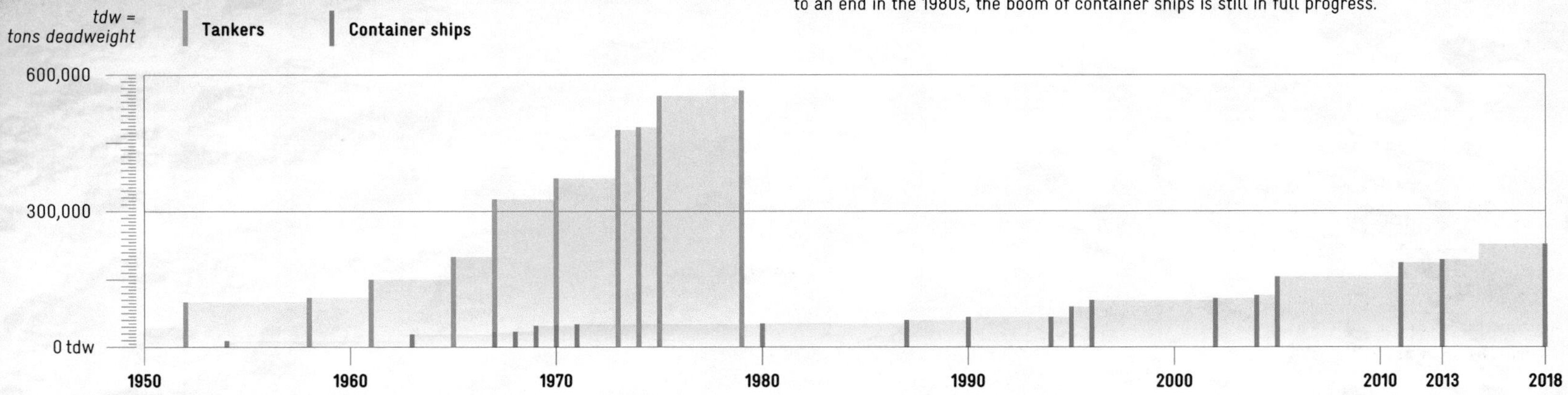

tdw = tons deadweight
Tankers
Container ships
600,000
300,000
0 tdw
1950
1960
1970
1980
1990
2000
2010
2013
2018

THE JEANS BUSINESS

In 1873, Levi Strauss and Jacob W. Davis patented »blue jeans.«
Even back then, American jeans makers imported cloth from Europe.
The rugged workman's trousers were pioneers of globalization.
They became brand icons, the expression of an attitude towards life,
and an example of a highly unequal global distribution of value creation.

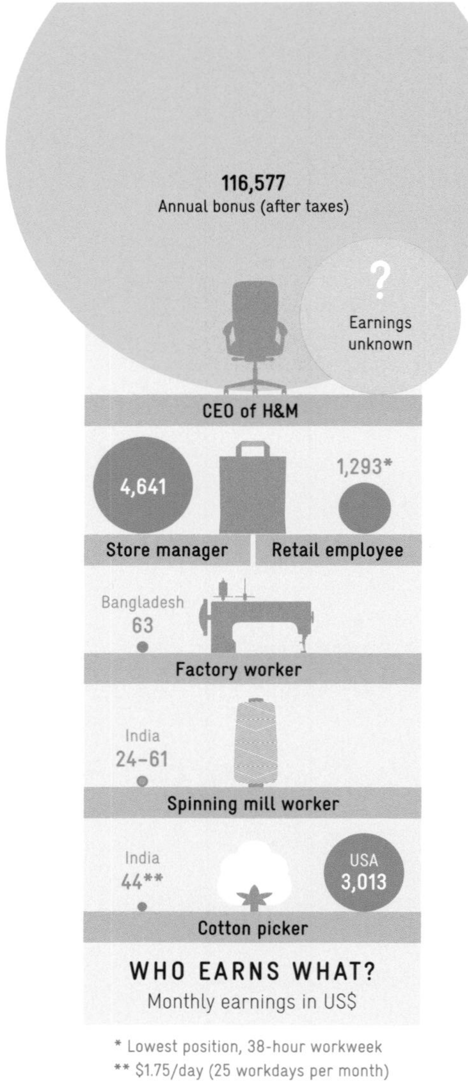
116,577
Annual bonus (after taxes)
?
Earnings unknown
CEO of H&M
4,641
1,293*
Store manager
Retail employee
Bangladesh
63
Factory worker
India
24–61
Spinning mill worker
India
44**
USA
3,013
Cotton picker
WHO EARNS WHAT?
Monthly earnings in US$
* Lowest position, 38-hour workweek
** $1.75/day (25 workdays per month)

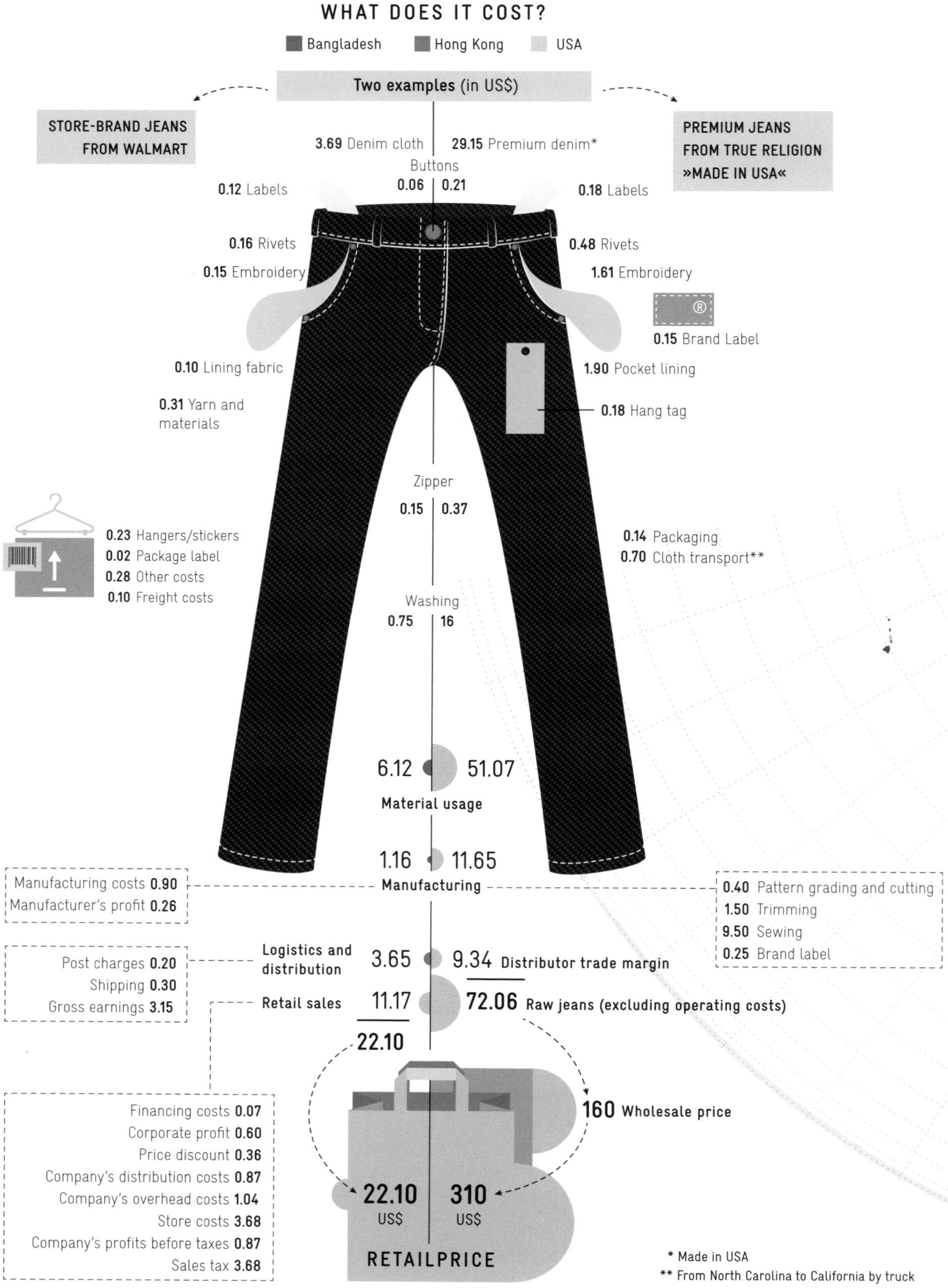
WHAT DOES IT COST?
Bangladesh
Hong Kong
USA
Two examples (in US$)
STORE-BRAND JEANS FROM WALMART
PREMIUM JEANS FROM TRUE RELIGION »MADE IN USA«
3.69 Denim cloth
29.15 Premium denim*
Buttons
0.06 | 0.21
0.12 Labels
0.18 Labels
0.16 Rivets
0.48 Rivets
0.15 Embroidery
1.61 Embroidery
0.15 Brand Label
0.10 Lining fabric
1.90 Pocket lining
0.31 Yarn and materials
0.18 Hang tag
Zipper
0.15 | 0.37
0.23 Hangers/stickers
0.02 Package label
0.28 Other costs
0.10 Freight costs
0.14 Packaging
0.70 Cloth transport**
Washing
0.75 | 16
6.12
51.07
Material usage
1.16
11.65
Manufacturing
Manufacturing costs 0.90
Manufacturer's profit 0.26
0.40 Pattern grading and cutting
1.50 Trimming
9.50 Sewing
0.25 Brand label
Logistics and distribution
3.65
9.34 Distributor trade margin
Post charges 0.20
Shipping 0.30
Gross earnings 3.15
Retail sales
11.17
72.06 Raw jeans (excluding operating costs)
22.10
160 Wholesale price
Financing costs 0.07
Corporate profit 0.60
Price discount 0.36
Company's distribution costs 0.87
Company's overhead costs 1.04
Store costs 3.68
Company's profits before taxes 0.87
Sales tax 3.68
22.10 US$
310 US$
RETAILPRICE
* Made in USA
** From North Carolina to California by truck

Raw materials and accessories
Operations in the manufacturing process
Sales activities
31,000 miles
+ 4,000 miles
Shipped to Africa
Sale at used-clothing markets

WHAT IS MADE WHERE?

A pair of jeans travels halfway around the world before it ends up in a clothing store. Many of them take this route:

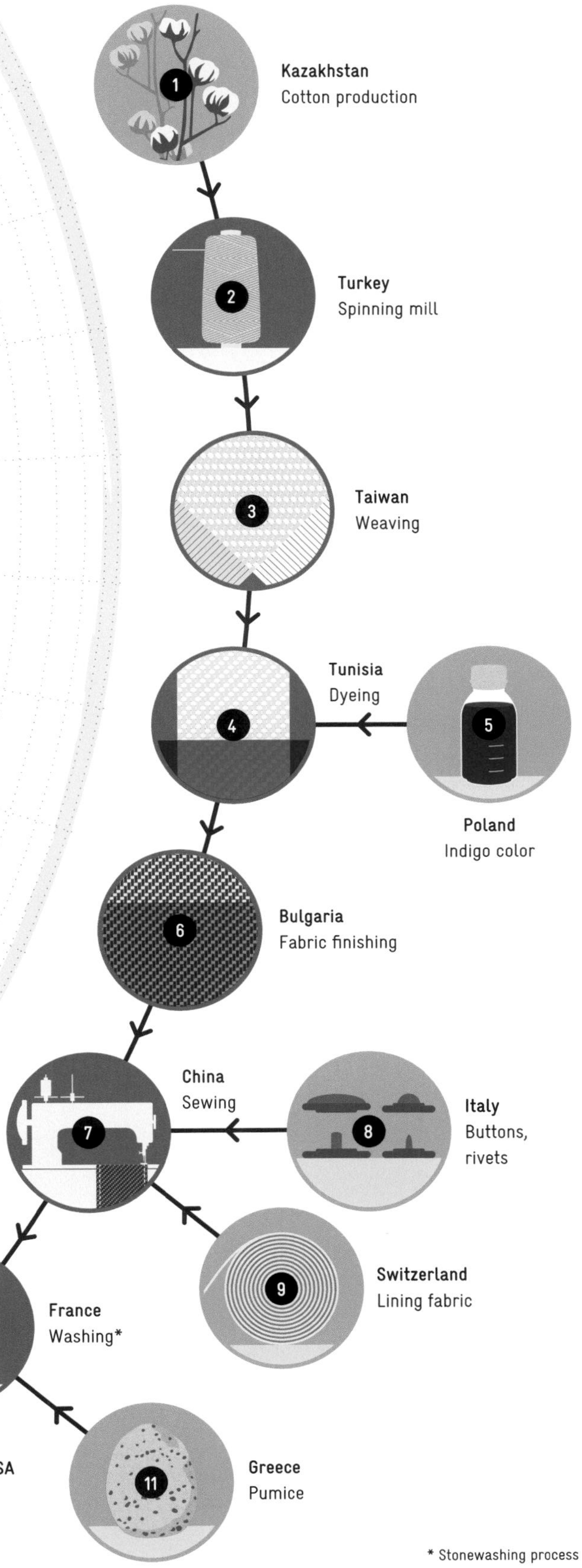
Kazakhstan
Cotton production
Turkey
Spinning mill
Taiwan
Weaving
Tunisia
Dyeing
Poland
Indigo color
Bulgaria
Fabric finishing
China
Sewing
Italy
Buttons, rivets
Switzerland
Lining fabric
France
Washing*
Greece
Pumice
Europe and USA
Distribution

* Stonewashing process

IS EVERYTHING SUPER IN THE SUPERMARKET?

Why do all grocery stores feel the same? A lot of research goes into their configuration—determining everything from the fact that customers prefer to make their rounds counterclockwise to which shelf configuration will increase sales.

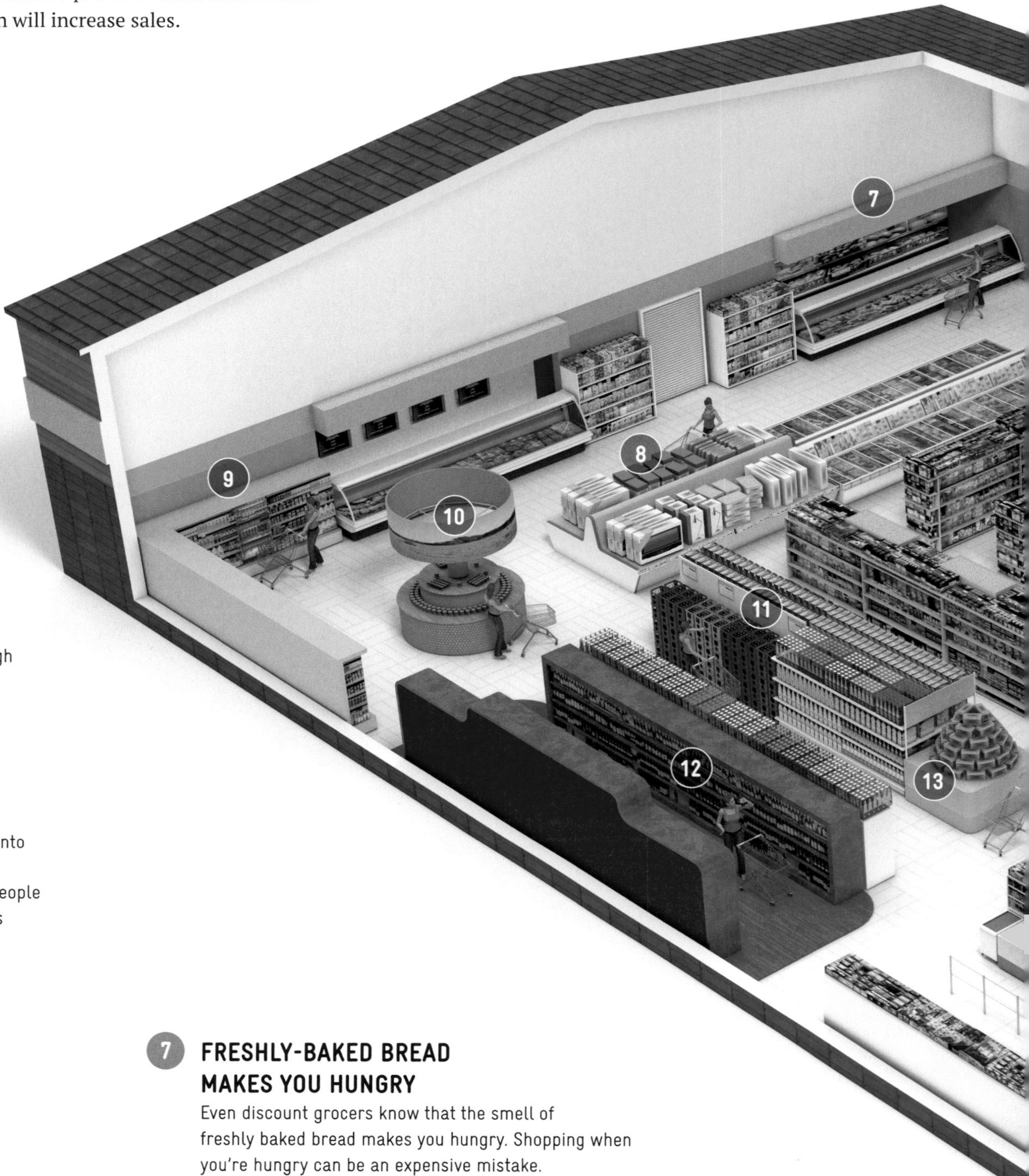

1 SIZE MATTERS

You're not getting smaller – grocery carts are getting bigger. With a big cart, the average customer is likely to buy 40% more.

2 NO WAY BACK

Automatic barriers don't do much to stop thieves, but are an effective way to send shoppers on a pre-determined journey through the aisles.

3 A MEANINGFUL START

Fruit and vegetables entice more customers into the store, stimulating the senses. In turn, the whole shopping atmosphere is boosted and people are more inclined to make impulse purchases thoughout their shop.

4 BREAKFAST ALLIANCE

Coffee is placed near jam and crackers, as they sell better together than on their own.

5 SHELVING FUNNELS SALES

Products with high profit margins are placed on shelves at the end of the aisles (so-called »end caps«). The customer's eye tends to wander here regularly.

6 AT EYE LEVEL

Shelves at eye level are expensive, not just for customers, but also for brand manufacturers. They often have to pay stores high placement fees to have the most lucrative spot.

7 FRESHLY-BAKED BREAD MAKES YOU HUNGRY

Even discount grocers know that the smell of freshly baked bread makes you hungry. Shopping when you're hungry can be an expensive mistake.

8 THE SALE AISLE

Temporary offers in the middle aisle always suggest that is where you can find a good deal. Sometimes it's even true.

9 THE LONG JOURNEY TO THE MILK

Bread and butter can often be found at the rear of the store. On the long way there, you have plenty of opportunities to make impulse purchases.

10 COMPLIMENTARY CHEESE

Free samples often end up being expensive whether the cheese tastes good or not. A quick taste can make shoppers feel guilty and obligated to buy.

11 BRAND MARKERS

Name brand items like Coca Cola can all be found in the middle of the aisle so we can get our bearings in terms of price and location.

12 A SHOP WITHIN A SHOP

Shelves of cosmetics or wine are often presented as another world. This makes shoppers re-think their expected pricing level.

13 SPECIAL OFFERS

Competitive prices entice thrifty customers into store, signaling just one thing: save money! Now they no longer have to pay attention to price.

14 TANTRUM ALLEY

We don't just keep our children quiet with a treat at the till, but we also reward ourselves for the great achievement of having completed our shopping.

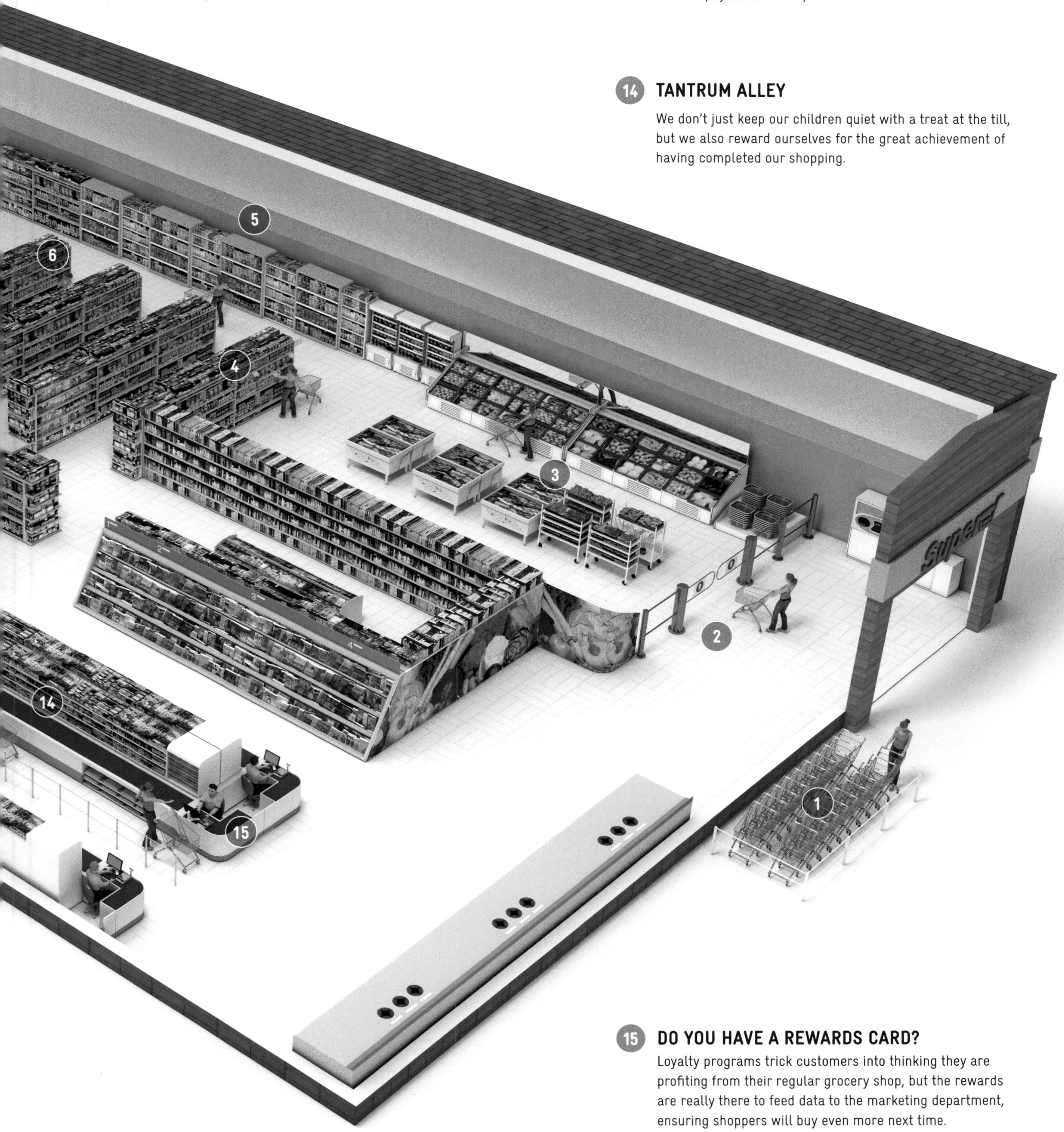

15 DO YOU HAVE A REWARDS CARD?

Loyalty programs trick customers into thinking they are profiting from their regular grocery shop, but the rewards are really there to feed data to the marketing department, ensuring shoppers will buy even more next time.

TUTTI FRUTTI

In Germany, consumers are treated to a full range of fruit and vegetables in well-stocked supermarkets all year. The acreage for fruit, vegetables and cereals has become an extremely important competitive factor in the global market. But where does it all come from? During the course of a year, as much as 50 percent of vegetables and 80 percent of fruit is imported. Apples from New Zealand or bananas from Ecuador travel a long way from farms to German dinner tables.

- Apples
- Bananas
- Oranges
- Tangerines, clementines, other crossings
- Table grapes
- Melons
- Watermelons
- Strawberries
- Nectarines
- Pears, quinces
- Pineapples
- Raspberries
- Sweet cherries
- Sour cherries
- Peaches
- Kiwis
- Apricots
- Plums, sloes
- Lemons, limes
- Shaddocks/pomelo, grapefruits
- Papayas
- Guavas, mangos

THE MOST POPULAR FRUITS IN GERMANY, IN %

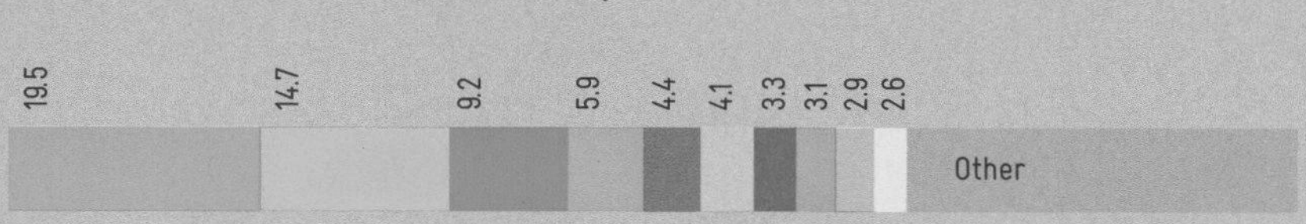
19.5
14.7
9.2
5.9
4.4
4.1
3.3
3.1
2.9
2.6
Other

In the countries surrounding the Mediterranean sea, an average of 700 grams of fruit and vegetables per person are eaten per day. In Germany, however, people are satisfied with 250 grams. Among the EU-27 countries, only Estonia, Finland, Ireland and Lithuania are behind Germany in fruit and vegetable consumption.

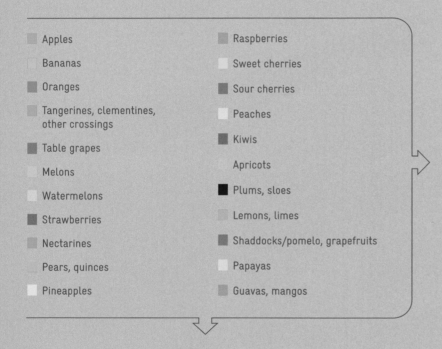

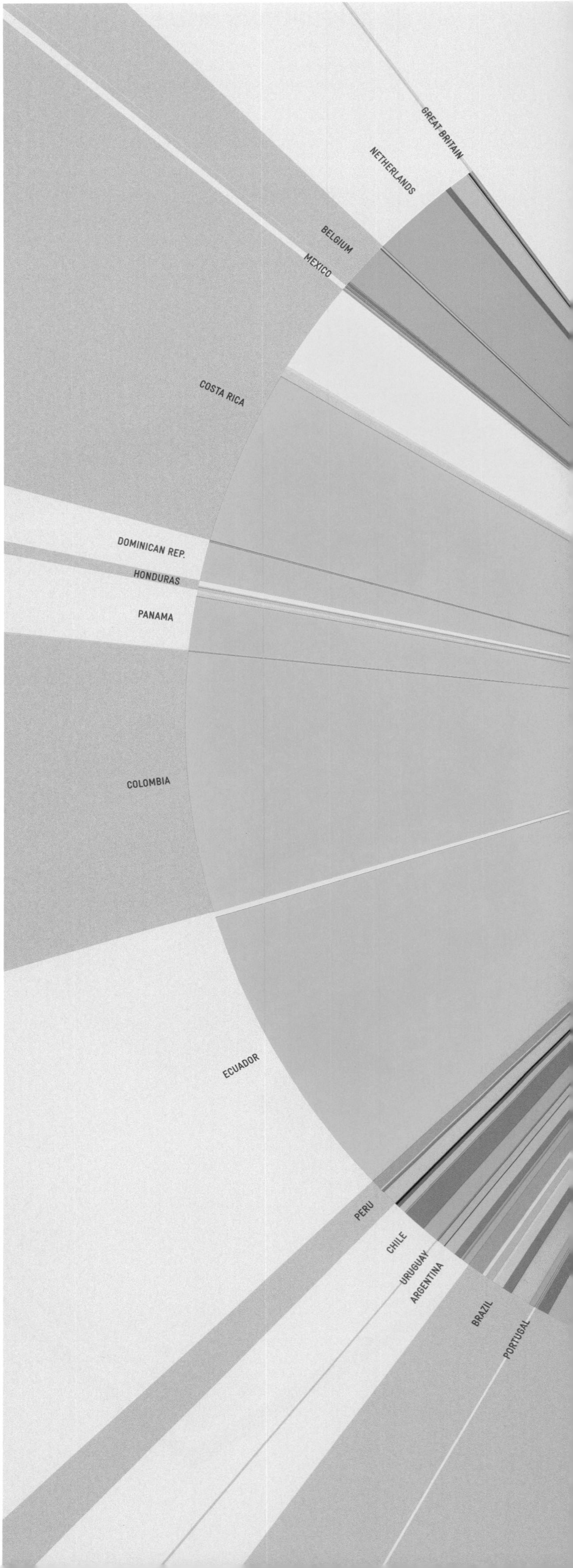

WHERE DOES FRUIT COME FROM?

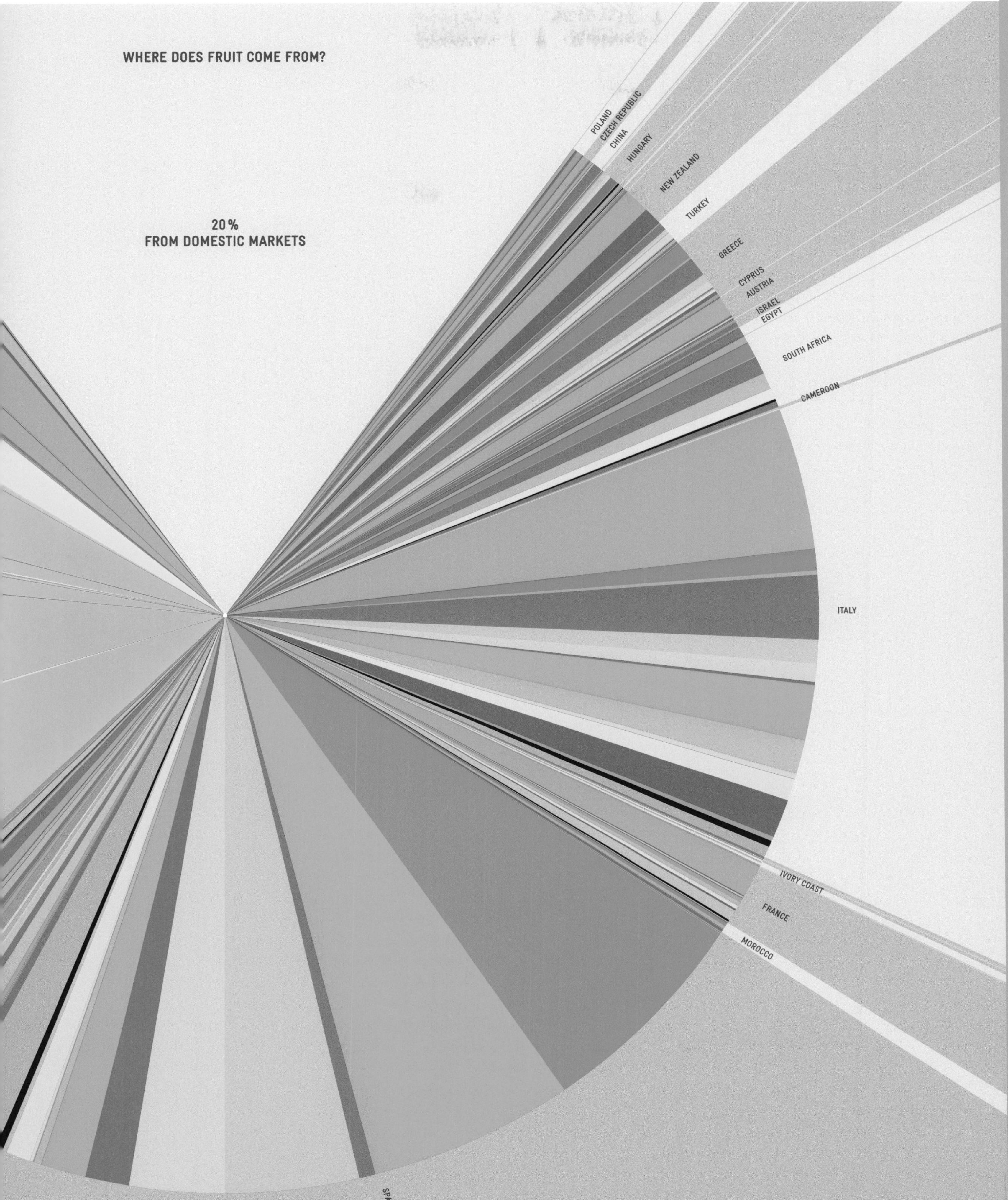

20 %
FROM DOMESTIC MARKETS
POLAND
CZECH REPUBLIC
CHINA
HUNGARY
NEW ZEALAND
TURKEY
GREECE
CYPRUS
AUSTRIA
ISRAEL
EGYPT
SOUTH AFRICA
CAMEROON
ITALY
IVORY COAST
FRANCE
MOROCCO
SPAIN

The graph refers to selected types of fruit from 90 countries (2011).

FABULOUSLY RICH – THE MODERN UNICORNS

The spiraled horn of one of the rarest mystical creatures symbolizes power and progress. In 2013, venture capitalist Aileen Lee applied the symbolism to economics in her article »Welcome To The Unicorn Club: Learning from Billion-Dollar Startups«. Venture capital investments can transform an idea into a multi-billion dollar company. These were the highest-valued »unicorn« startups in 2016—but as value is driven by investment, this can put these companies on the same level as established industrial giants.

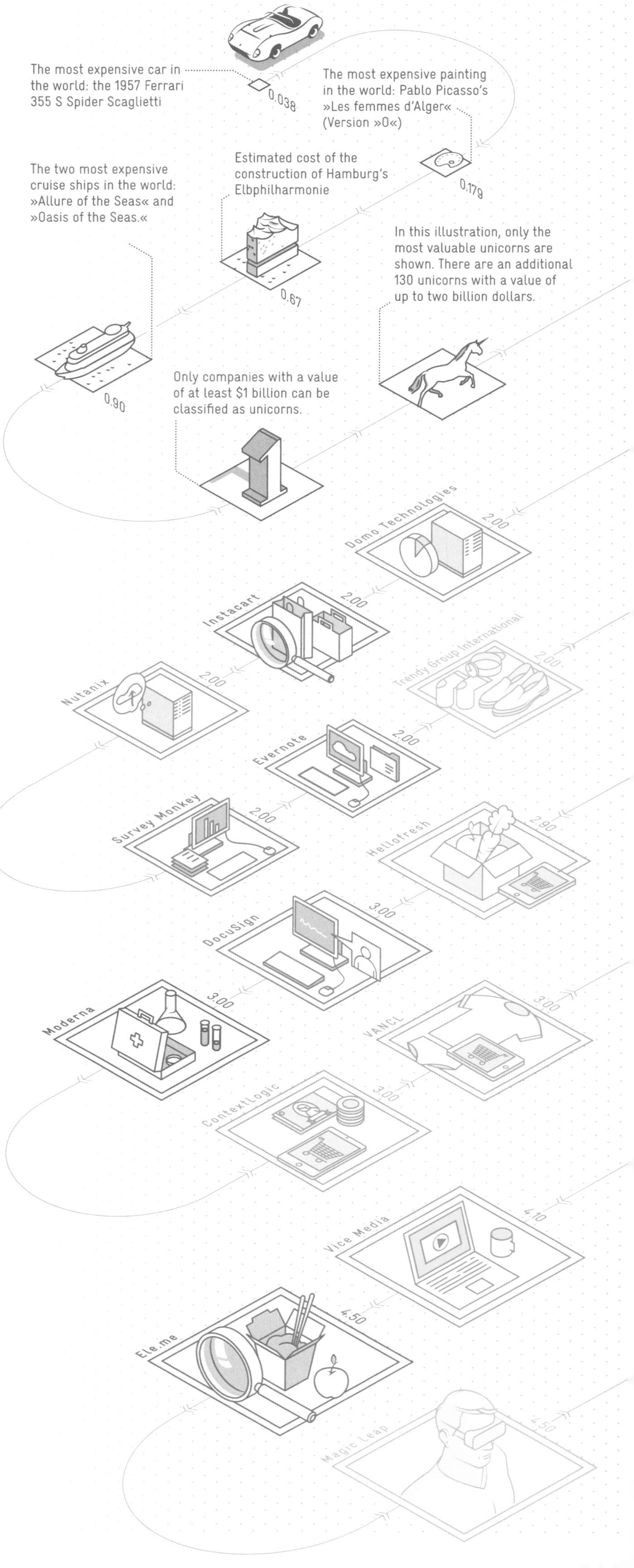
The most expensive car in the world: the 1957 Ferrari 355 S Spider Scaglietti
0.038
The most expensive painting in the world: Pablo Picasso's »Les femmes d'Alger« (Version »0«)
0.179
The two most expensive cruise ships in the world: »Allure of the Seas« and »Oasis of the Seas.«
Estimated cost of the construction of Hamburg's Elbphilharmonie
0.67
In this illustration, only the most valuable unicorns are shown. There are an additional 130 unicorns with a value of up to two billion dollars.
0.90
Only companies with a value of at least $1 billion can be classified as unicorns.
Domo Technologies
2.00
Instacart
2.00
Trendy Group International
2.00
Nutanix
2.00
Evernote
2.00
Survey Monkey
2.00
Hellofresh
2.90
DocuSign
3.00
Moderna
3.00
VANCL
3.00
ContextLogic
3.00
Vice Media
4.10
Ele.me
4.50
Magic Leap
4.50

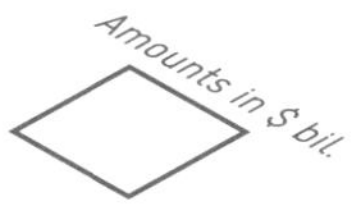
Amounts in $ bil.

Amounts in comparison

Data from September 2016

Colors and symbols shown indicate different industries.

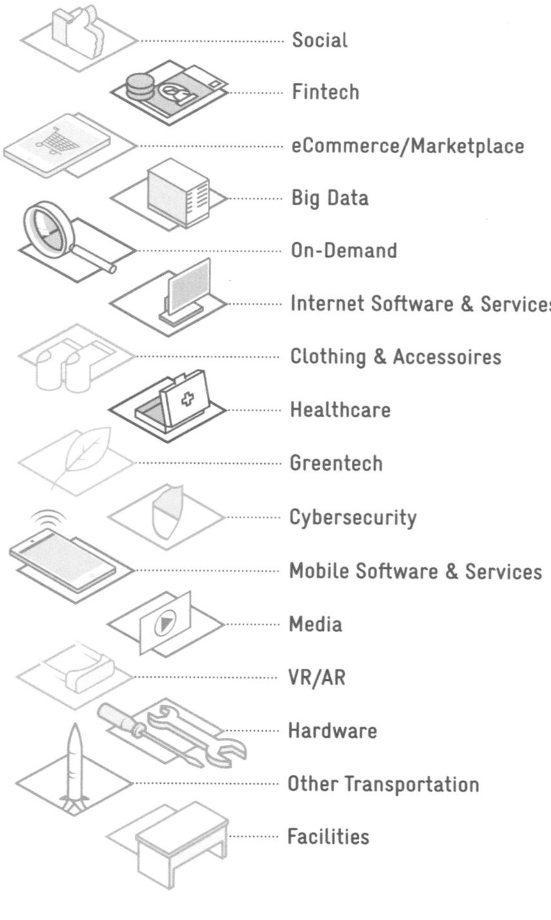
Social
Fintech
eCommerce/Marketplace
Big Data
On-Demand
Internet Software & Services
Clothing & Accessoires
Healthcare
Greentech
Cybersecurity
Mobile Software & Services
Media
VR/AR
Hardware
Other Transportation
Facilities

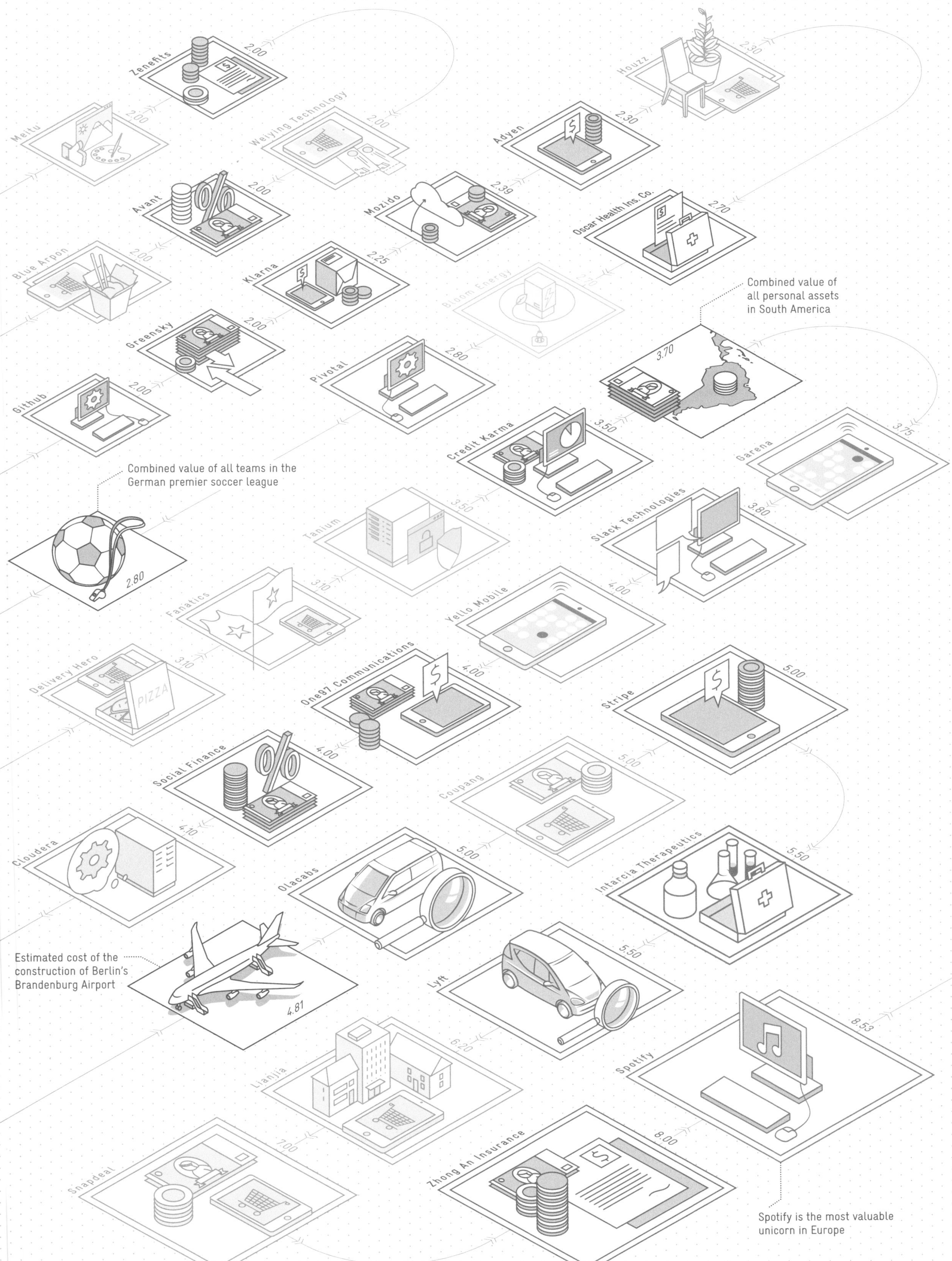

Zenefits
2.00
Meitu
2.00
Weiying Technology
2.00
Houzz
2.30
Adyen
2.30
Avant
2.00
Mozido
2.39
Oscar Health Ins. Co.
2.70
Blue Apron
2.00
Klarna
2.25
Bloom Energy
Combined value of all personal assets in South America
Greensky
2.00
Pivotal
2.80
3.70
Github
2.00
Credit Karma
3.50
Garena
3.75
Combined value of all teams in the German premier soccer league
Tanium
3.50
Slack Technologies
3.80
2.80
Fanatics
3.10
Yello Mobile
4.00
Delivery Hero
3.10
PIZZA
One97 Communications
4.00
Stripe
5.00
Social Finance
4.00
Coupang
5.00
Cloudera
4.10
Olacabs
5.00
Intarcia Therapeutics
5.50
Estimated cost of the construction of Berlin's Brandenburg Airport
Lyft
5.50
4.81
Lianjia
6.20
Spotify
8.53
Snapdeal
7.00
Zhong An Insurance
8.00
Spotify is the most valuable unicorn in Europe

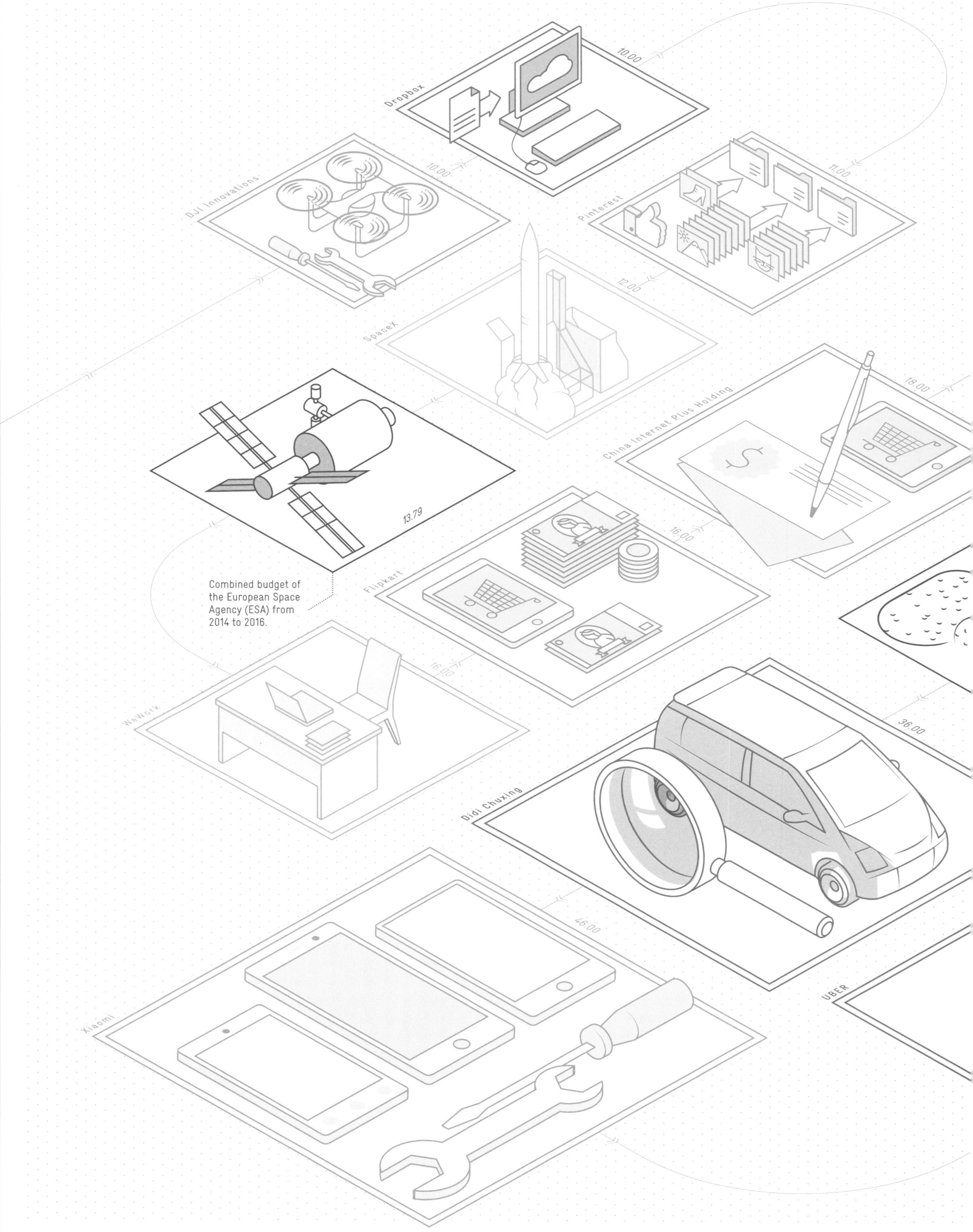
Dropbox
10.00
DJI Innovations
10.00
Pinterest
11.00
SpaceX
12.00
13.79
Combined budget of the European Space Agency (ESA) from 2014 to 2016.
China Internet Plus Holding
18.00
Flipkart
16.00
WeWork
16.00
Didi Chuxing
36.00
Xiaomi
46.00
UBER

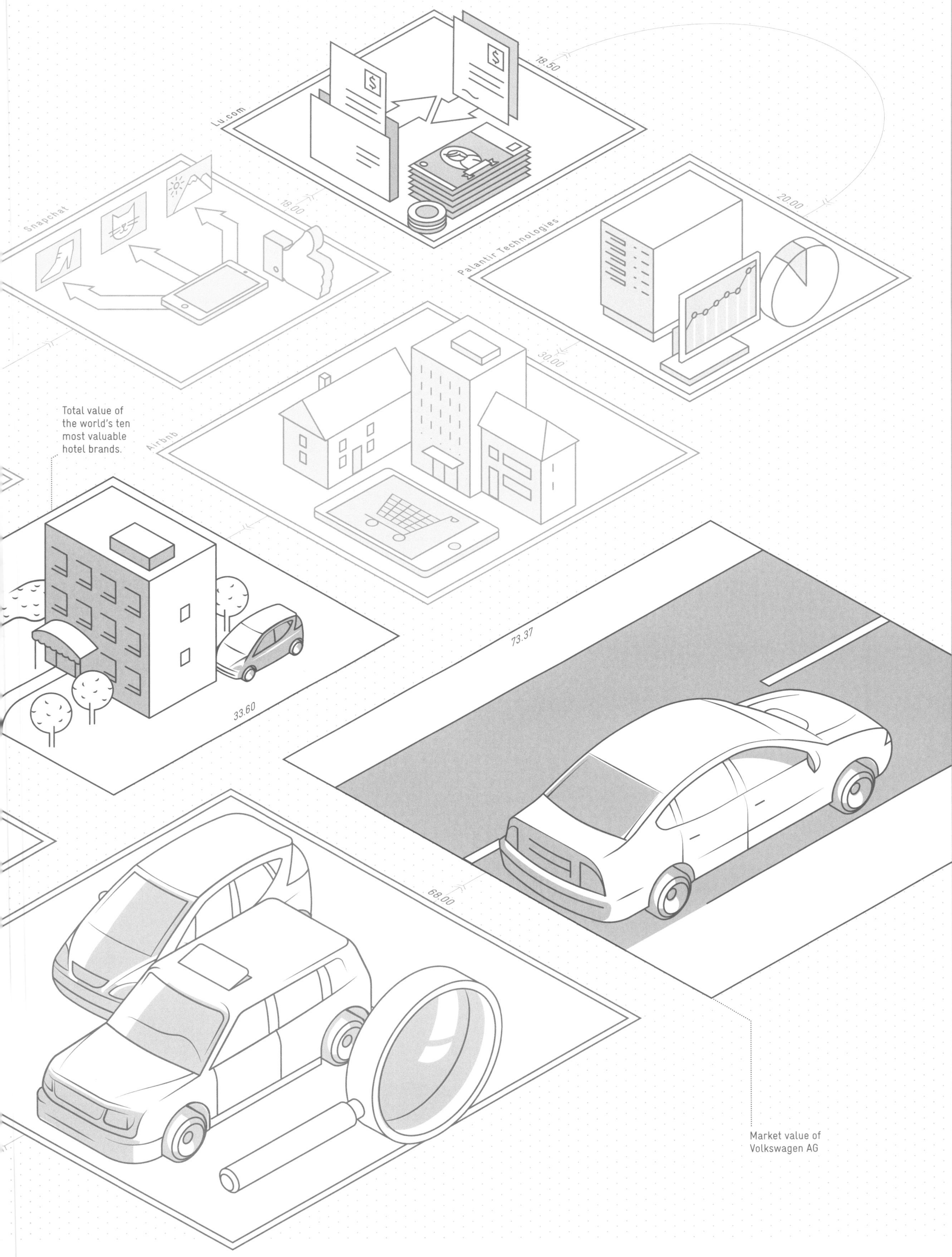
Lu.com
18.50
Snapchat
18.00
Palantir Technologies
20.00
30.00
Airbnb
Total value of the world's ten most valuable hotel brands.
33.60
73.37
68.00
Market value of Volkswagen AG

VALLEY OF THE FUTURE

Silicon Valley is the world's most important location for IT and high-tech industries. In 1939, William Hewlett and David Packard finished their degrees at Stanford University and founded Hewlett-Packard in a garage in Palo Alto with just $538 in initial capital investment. Since then, this valley between San Francisco and San José has been a mecca for business founders who want to change the world. Stanford University is still an important training ground and catalyst for young entrepreneurs. Venture capital firms and private investors provide the capital to launch these companies.

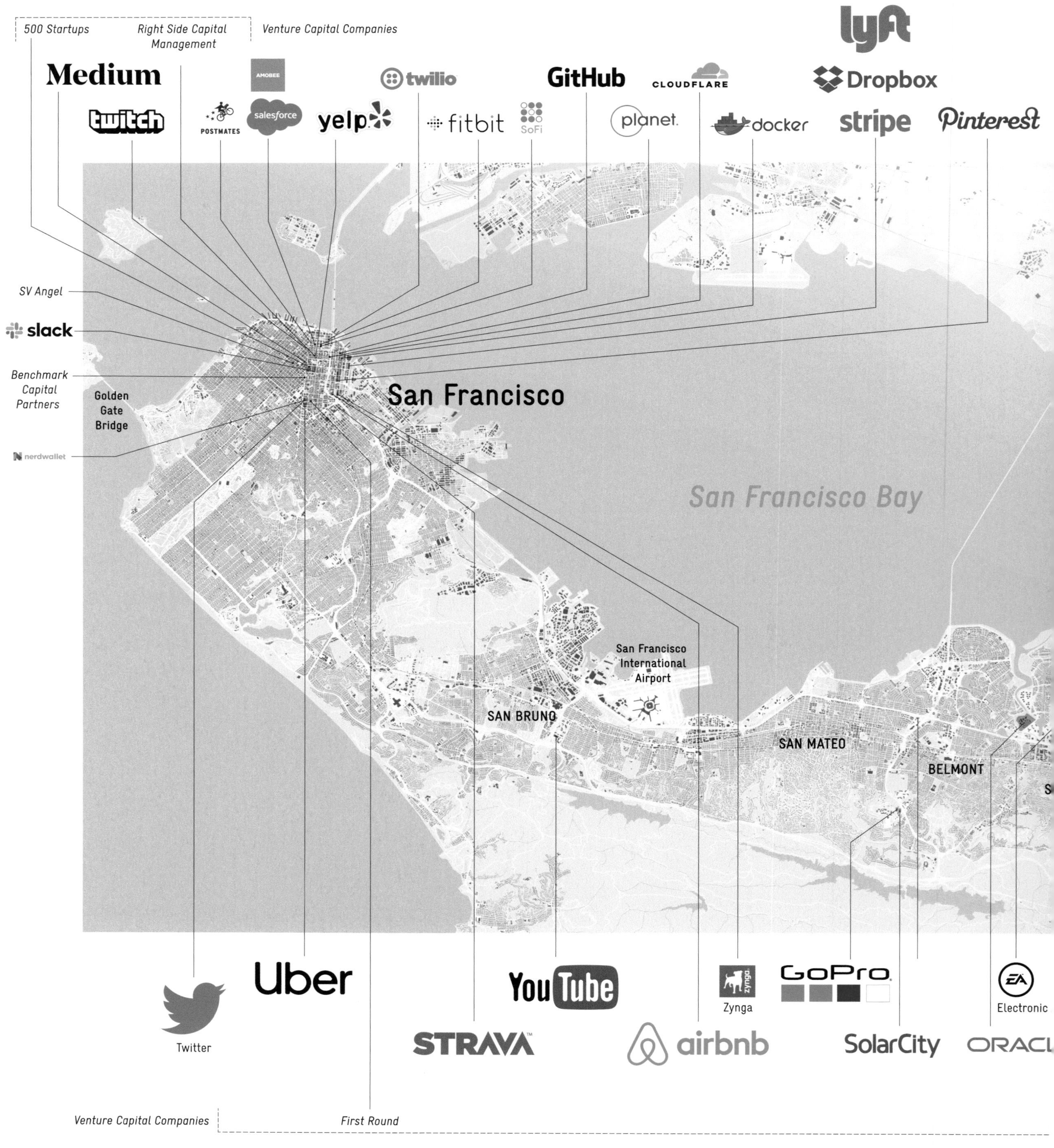

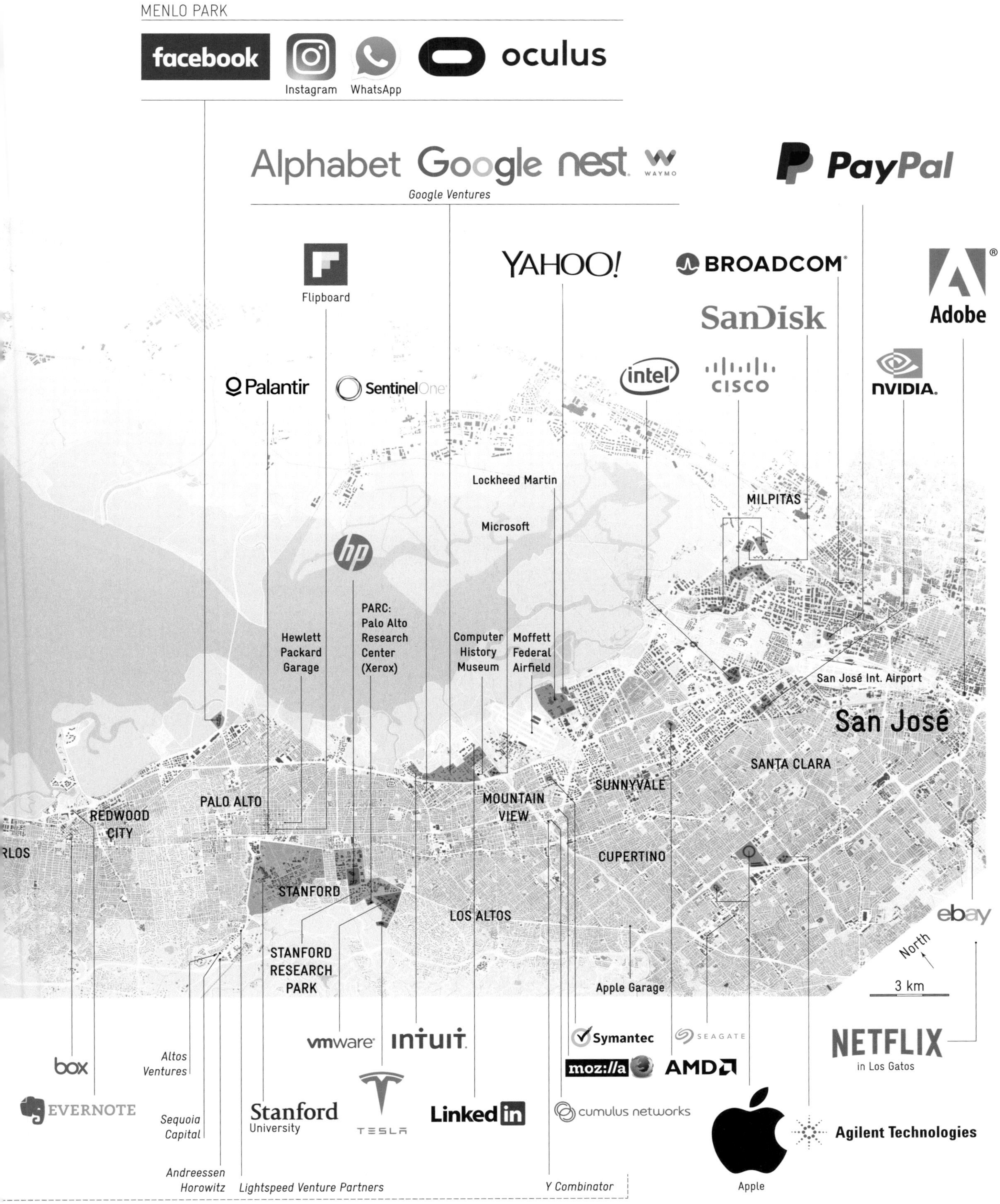
MENLO PARK
facebook
Instagram
WhatsApp
oculus
Alphabet
Google
nest
WAYMO
Google Ventures
PayPal
Flipboard
YAHOO!
BROADCOM
SanDisk
Adobe
Palantir
SentinelOne
intel
CISCO
NVIDIA
Lockheed Martin
MILPITAS
Microsoft
PARC: Palo Alto Research Center (Xerox)
Hewlett Packard Garage
Computer History Museum
Moffett Federal Airfield
San José Int. Airport
San José
SANTA CLARA
SUNNYVALE
MOUNTAIN VIEW
PALO ALTO
REDWOOD CITY
RLOS
CUPERTINO
STANFORD
LOS ALTOS
STANFORD RESEARCH PARK
Apple Garage
ebay
North
3 km
box
Altos Ventures
vmware
intuit
Symantec
SEAGATE
NETFLIX
in Los Gatos
moz://a
AMD
EVERNOTE
Sequoia Capital
Stanford University
TESLA
LinkedIn
cumulus networks
Agilent Technologies
Andreessen Horowitz
Lightspeed Venture Partners
Y Combinator
Apple

TO BE DISRUPTED

When does an innovation become disruptive? The term disruption refers to an innovation that changes the way we live in a profound way. It is a gamechanger, at once creative and destructive. This graphic shows a snapshot of innovations and disruptions in 2014. It is based on a concept developed jointly by Cisco and GDI*. A variety of experts faced the challenge of identifying today's innovations that will become tomorrow's disruptions.

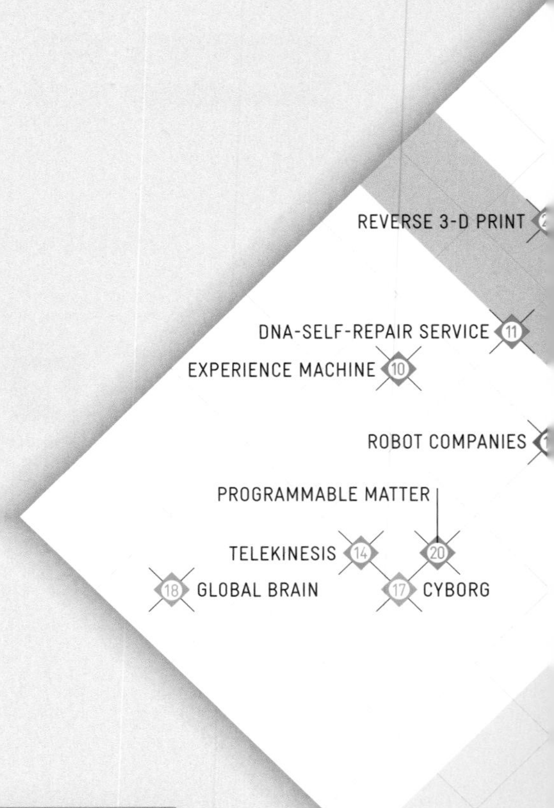

REVERSE 3-D PRINT
DNA-SELF-REPAIR SERVICE 11
EXPERIENCE MACHINE 10
ROBOT COMPANIES
PROGRAMMABLE MATTER
TELEKINESIS 14
20
18 GLOBAL BRAIN
17 CYBORG

*Concept: Cisco, GDI Gottlieb Duttweiler Institute (stages based upon Pyramid of Technology model by Van Mensvoort, 2014)

ONLINE VERSION: **http://www.gdi.ch/i2d**

HOW TO READ

The map depicts innovations ◆ along two dimensions: mindset and technology. Along these, each innovation faces challenges, going through several phases, to eventually be considered disruptive. A tipping point is reached when a SHIFT in paradigm occurs, when a significant technological obstacle is overcome or barriers in people's minds start to disintegrate.

- ◆ Former disruptions
- ◆ Expanding human capabilities
- ◆ Organizational breakthroughs
- ◆ Redefining physical movement
- ◆ Redefining the concept of mankind
- ◆ Redefining physical infrastructure

THE INTERNET AS A FORMER DISRUPTION

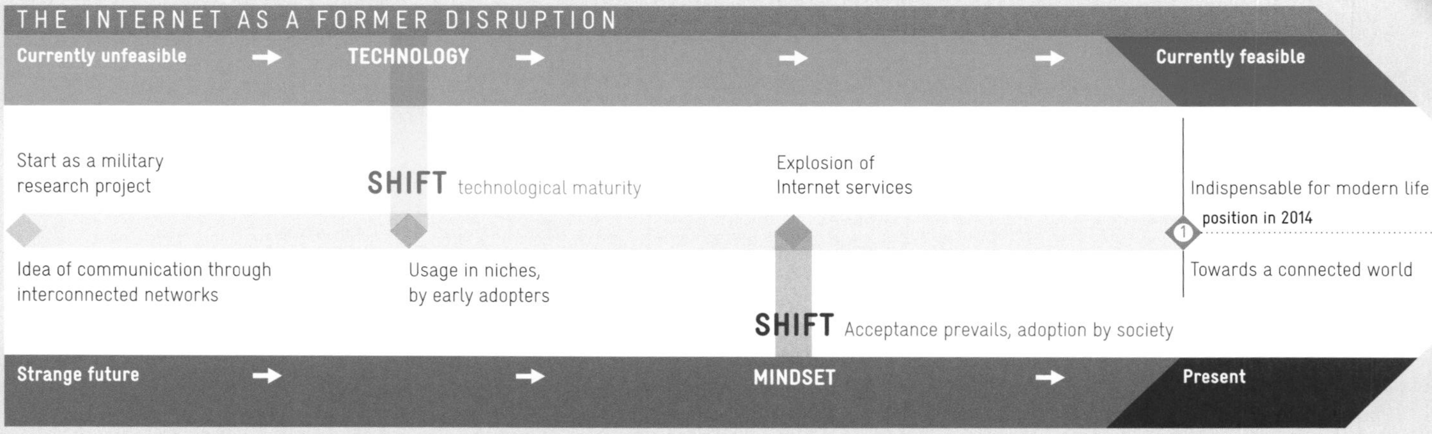

Currently unfeasible → TECHNOLOGY → → → Currently feasible
Start as a military research project
SHIFT technological maturity
Explosion of Internet services
Indispensable for modern life
position in 2014
1
Idea of communication through interconnected networks
Usage in niches, by early adopters
Towards a connected world
SHIFT Acceptance prevails, adoption by society
Strange future → → MINDSET → Present

THE DISRUPTIONS

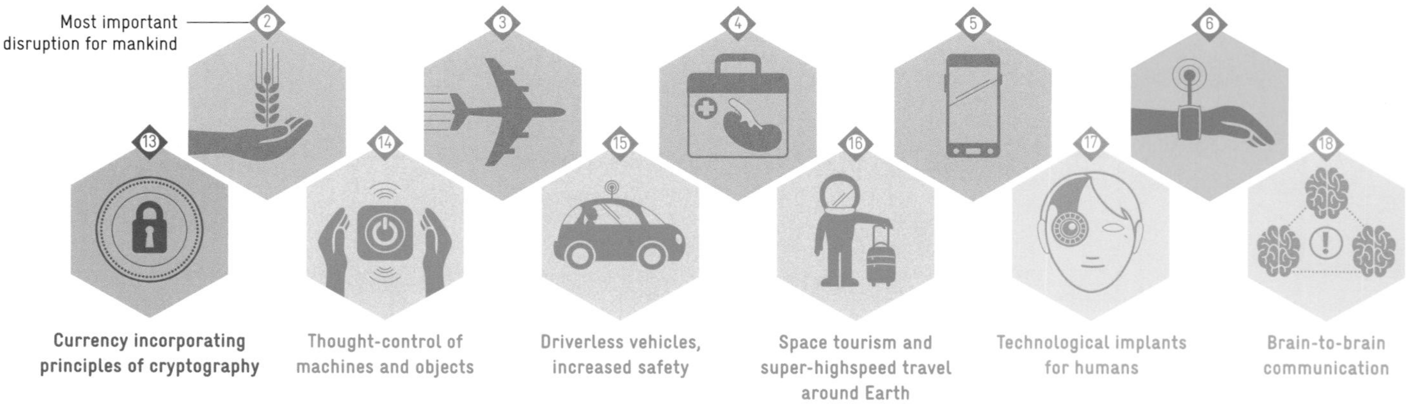

Agriculture
Air travel
Organ transplantation
Smartphones
Wearables
Most important disruption for mankind
2
3
4
5
6
13
14
15
16
17
18
Currency incorporating principles of cryptography
Thought-control of machines and objects
Driverless vehicles, increased safety
Space tourism and super-highspeed travel around Earth
Technological implants for humans
Brain-to-brain communication

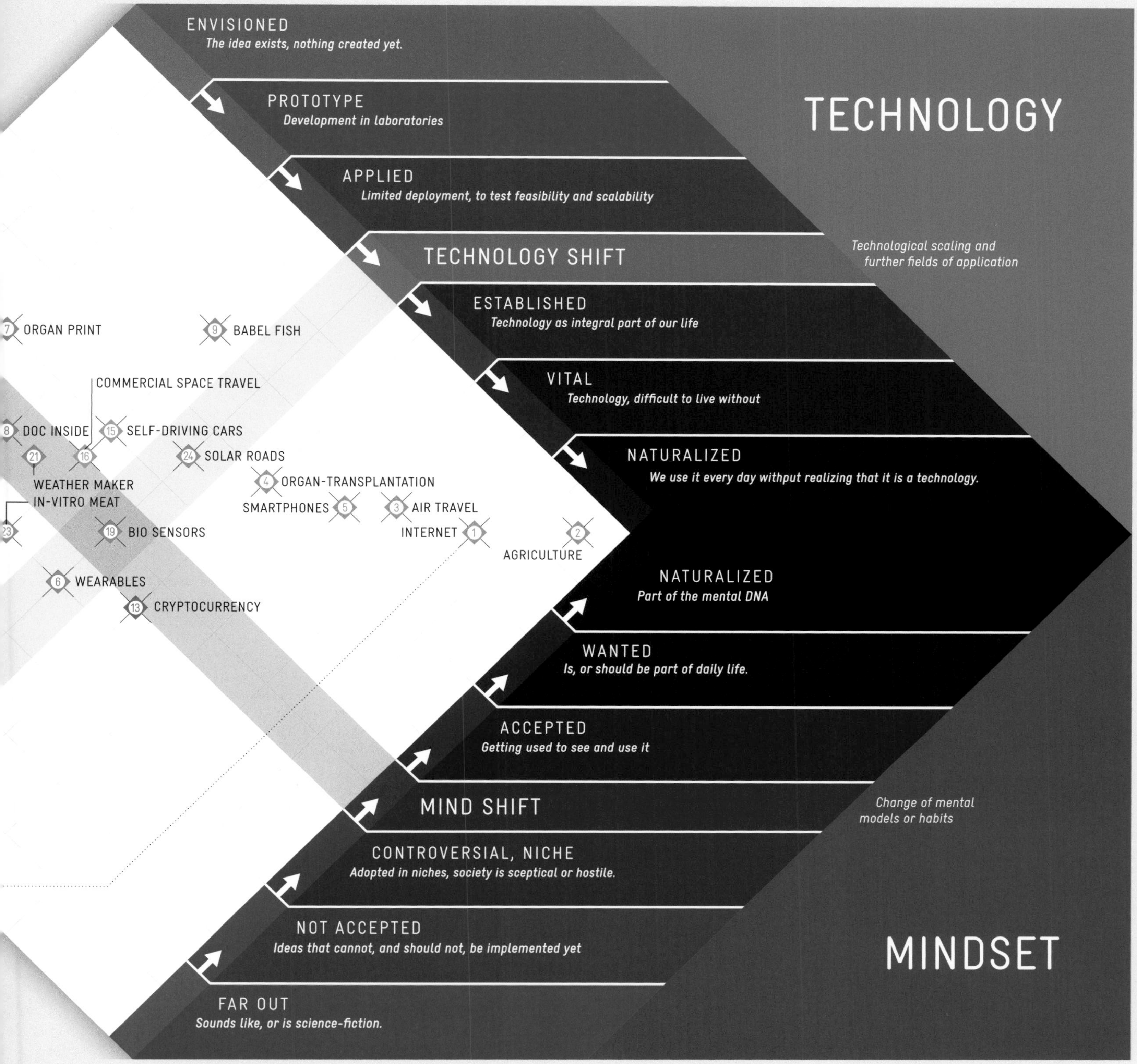

ENVISIONED
The idea exists, nothing created yet.
PROTOTYPE
Development in laboratories
APPLIED
Limited deployment, to test feasibility and scalability
TECHNOLOGY SHIFT
ESTABLISHED
Technology as integral part of our life
VITAL
Technology, difficult to live without
NATURALIZED
We use it every day withput realizing that it is a technology.
TECHNOLOGY
Technological scaling and further fields of application
NATURALIZED
Part of the mental DNA
WANTED
Is, or should be part of daily life.
ACCEPTED
Getting used to see and use it
MIND SHIFT
Change of mental models or habits
CONTROVERSIAL, NICHE
Adopted in niches, society is sceptical or hostile.
NOT ACCEPTED
Ideas that cannot, and should not, be implemented yet
FAR OUT
Sounds like, or is science-fiction.
MINDSET
7 ORGAN PRINT
9 BABEL FISH
COMMERCIAL SPACE TRAVEL
8 DOC INSIDE
15 SELF-DRIVING CARS
21
16
24 SOLAR ROADS
WEATHER MAKER
IN-VITRO MEAT
4 ORGAN-TRANSPLANTATION
SMARTPHONES 5
3 AIR TRAVEL
23
19 BIO SENSORS
INTERNET 1
2
AGRICULTURE
6 WEARABLES
13 CRYPTOCURRENCY

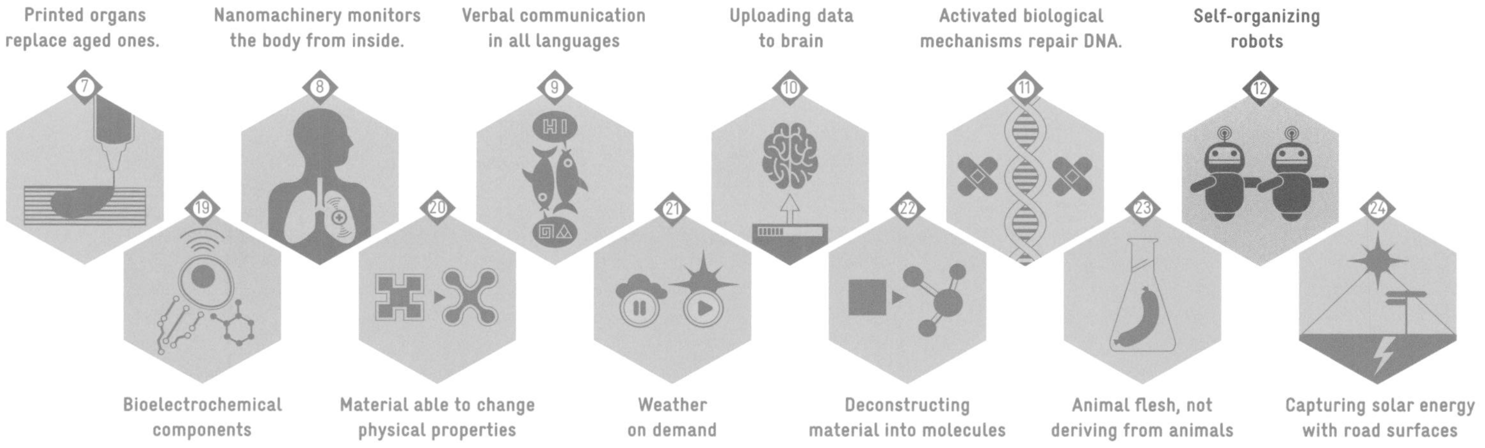

Printed organs replace aged ones. 7
Nanomachinery monitors the body from inside. 8
Verbal communication in all languages 9
HI
Uploading data to brain 10
Activated biological mechanisms repair DNA. 11
Self-organizing robots 12
19 Bioelectrochemical components
20 Material able to change physical properties
21 Weather on demand
22 Deconstructing material into molecules
23 Animal flesh, not deriving from animals
24 Capturing solar energy with road surfaces

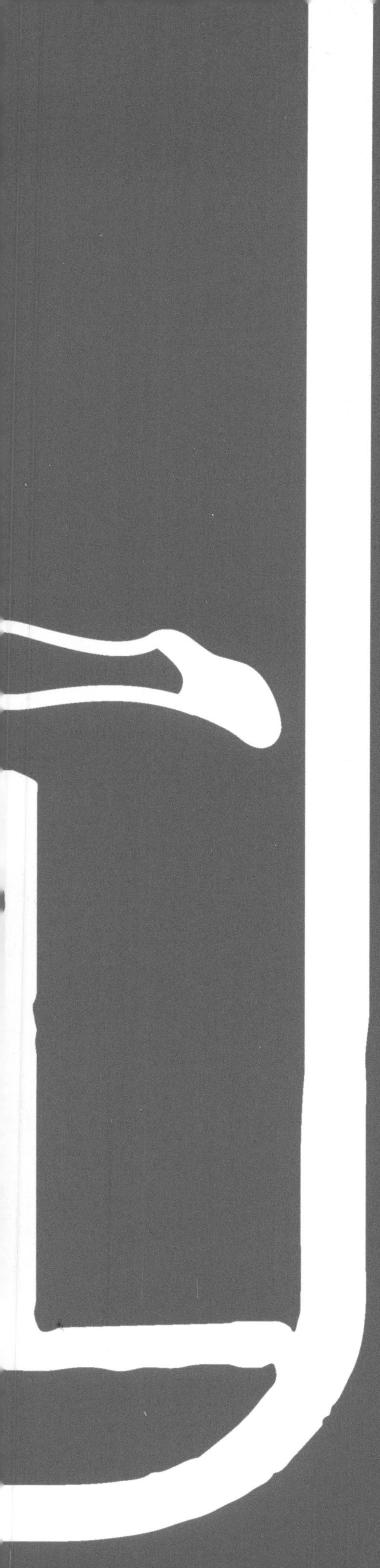

SPORTS

International sporting competitions require forms of communication that can cross any language barrier. The most famous example is the Olympic Games. As early as 1912, 1924, and 1936, iconographic illustrations represented specific types of sports. But it was **the London Olympic Games in 1948** that were the first to have a continuous sign system. Here you see **the pictogram for track and field**.

The 1964 Tokyo Games developed a modern system encompassing typography, colors, and symbols. Otl Aicher took this system even further for the 1972 Munich Games. These pictograms were influenced by Isotype, an international pictorial language of standardized, abstracted symbols created by Otto Neurath and Gerd Arntz in the 1920s. Following the principles of maximum reduction and minimum specificity, pictograms appeal to a wide variety of viewers and convey information at a single glance. Pervasive examples are the obligatory standards for pictograms regulating universal signage in public facilities from the US Department of Transportation (DOT) and the International Organization for Standardization (ISO).

ANCIENT OLYMPIC GAMES

The first Olympic Games were held in 776 BC to honor Zeus, the ruler of all Greek gods of Olympus. What we know today about that tournament comes from a winner's list written by Hippis of Elis, the second century travel stories of Pausanias and archaeological excavations that date back to 1875. The games stopped when the Roman emperor Theodosius issued a ban in 394 AD. Today the ruins continue to be a place of inspiration and an important site in ancient Greece.

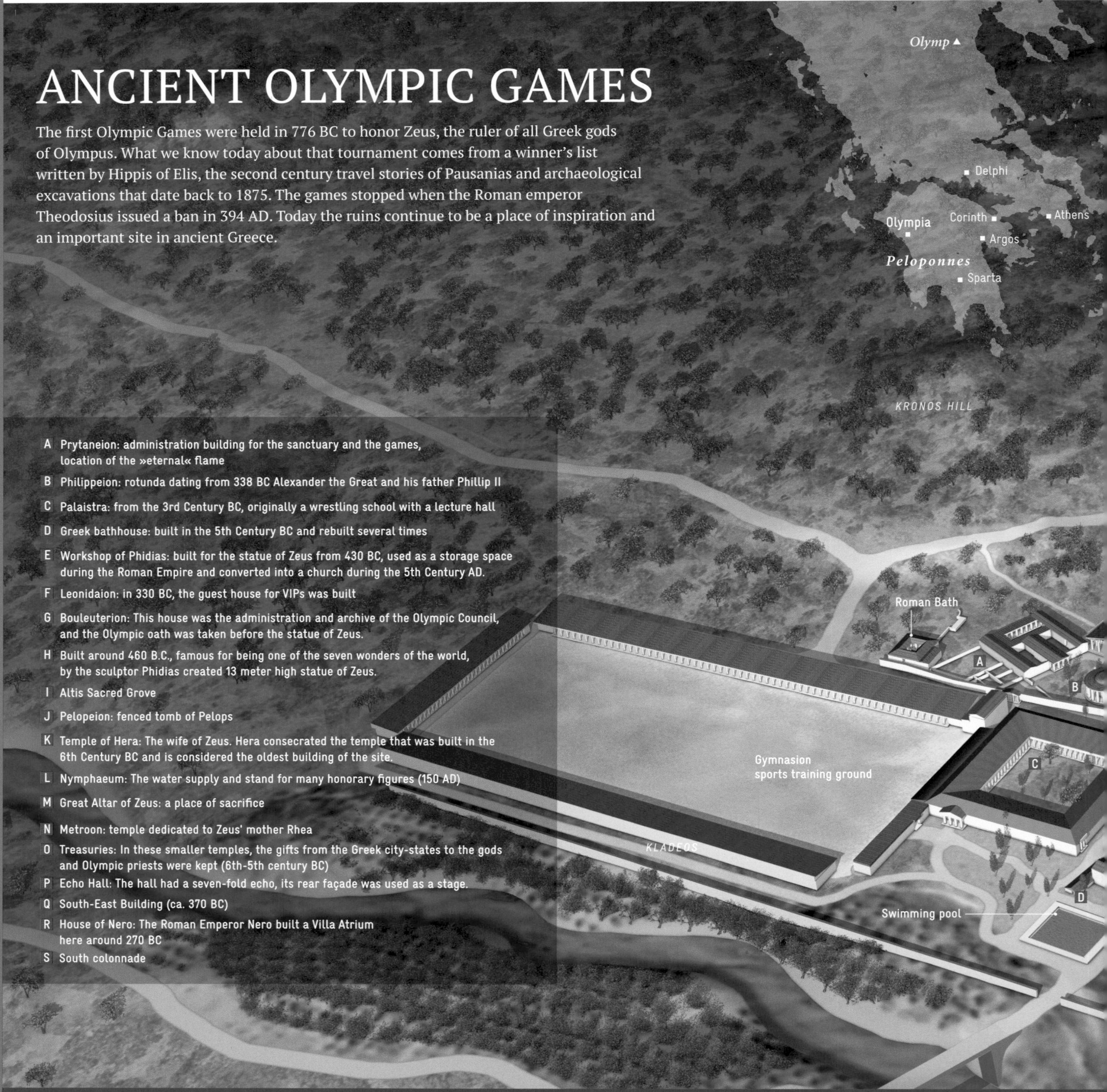

Olymp
Delphi
Olympia
Corinth
Athens
Argos
Peloponnes
Sparta
KRONOS HILL
Roman Bath
A
B
C
D
Gymnasion
sports training ground
KLADEOS
Swimming pool

- **A** Prytaneion: administration building for the sanctuary and the games, location of the »eternal« flame
- **B** Philippeion: rotunda dating from 338 BC Alexander the Great and his father Phillip II
- **C** Palaistra: from the 3rd Century BC, originally a wrestling school with a lecture hall
- **D** Greek bathhouse: built in the 5th Century BC and rebuilt several times
- **E** Workshop of Phidias: built for the statue of Zeus from 430 BC, used as a storage space during the Roman Empire and converted into a church during the 5th Century AD.
- **F** Leonidaion: in 330 BC, the guest house for VIPs was built
- **G** Bouleuterion: This house was the administration and archive of the Olympic Council, and the Olympic oath was taken before the statue of Zeus.
- **H** Built around 460 B.C., famous for being one of the seven wonders of the world, by the sculptor Phidias created 13 meter high statue of Zeus.
- **I** Altis Sacred Grove
- **J** Pelopeion: fenced tomb of Pelops
- **K** Temple of Hera: The wife of Zeus. Hera consecrated the temple that was built in the 6th Century BC and is considered the oldest building of the site.
- **L** Nymphaeum: The water supply and stand for many honorary figures (150 AD)
- **M** Great Altar of Zeus: a place of sacrifice
- **N** Metroon: temple dedicated to Zeus' mother Rhea
- **O** Treasuries: In these smaller temples, the gifts from the Greek city-states to the gods and Olympic priests were kept (6th-5th century BC)
- **P** Echo Hall: The hall had a seven-fold echo, its rear façade was used as a stage.
- **Q** South-East Building (ca. 370 BC)
- **R** House of Nero: The Roman Emperor Nero built a Villa Atrium here around 270 BC
- **S** South colonnade

Olympic Games of Antiquity

The ancient Olympic Games lasted five days, and the winners were honored on the sixth. The Games were held every four years during the summer, the period of four years was called Olympia. The athletes, first only Greeks, and later participants from other countries of the ancient world, took part in several disciplines. The winners were awarded an olive tree branch after the race. Women could not participate in the games and could only watch if they were not married.

A RUNNING

Short run; 629 ft (192 m)
Double run; 1260 ft (384 m)
Weapons run; 1,260 ft (384 m)
Long distance run; 2.5 mi (4 km)

B WRESTLING

The wrestling allows all over body handles without ground fighting. The winner was the one who threw his opponent three times.

C BOXING

The hands were wrapped in leather straps. There was no time limit and the bout carried on until one of the two submitted.

D TOTAL COMBAT

Spectators loved this ancient discipline, one of the toughest in the games. All swings, kicks and punches were allowed. A win occurred when one of the opponents submitted.

E THE PENTATHLON

Five competitions: includes discus, long jump, javelin, running and wrestling. The decision about the final victory was often taken in wrestling, since only a small percentage of the participants could qualify for it.

F CHARIOT RACE

The highlight of the festivities: there were races for teams of two and four horses. The Olympic champion was the aristocratic owner not the charioteer.

Hippodrome: the horse and chariot races were held here from about 680 B.C.
Turning column
Stadium III: The competition venue was rebuilt twice. The grandstand had a capacity of 20,000 spectators. The Priestess of Demeter (goddess of fertility) had a place at the right altar.
Target column with the statue of Hippodamia
Start
A B C D E
Demeter Altar
Tribune
Referee
Underpass
Referee lodge
Finish line
Tribune
Dolphin
O
P
R
L
N
Q
F
Column of Nike
Roman gate
Eagle
M
Altis I
K
J
S
G
H
Starting gates for horse racing
As a start signal the dolphin fell to the ground, and the eagle rose up
South Hall (360-350 BC)
Festival road
E
Heroon
F
Theokoleon (House of Priests of Olympia)

Olympic sports in the modern era

continuously · irregularly

1 Badminton	14 Athletics	27 Tennis	40 Castling
2 Baseball	15 Modern Pentathlon	28 Table tennis	41 Jeu de Paume
3 Basketball	16 Cycling	29 Triathlon	42 Motorboat
4 Beach volleyball	17 Horse riding	30 Gymnastics	43 Rackets
5 Archery	18 Wrestling freestyle	31 Volleyball	44 Figure skating
6 Boxing	19 Wrestling, Greco-Roman	32 Water polo	45 Tug of war
7 Fencing	20 Rowing	33 Water jump	46 Ice hockey
8 Soccer	21 Swimming	34 Cricket	47 Karate*
9 Weightlifting	22 Sailing	35 Croquet	48 Skateboarding*
10 Handball	23 Softball	36 Golf	49 Climbing*
11 Hockey	24 Shooting	37 Polo	50 Surfing*
12 Judo	25 Synchronized swimming	38 Rugby	
13 Canoeing	26 Taekwondo	39 Lacrosse	

* from 2020

Sports listed on following pages

BEIJING'S OLYMPIC STADIUMS

The 2008 Summer Games were an undisputed spectacle where host country China pulled out all the stops. From a showstopping Opening Ceremony to the eye-catching sports facilities, Beijing wowed the world as it hosted more than 10,000 athletes from around the world. Total cost to the country: a mere $6.8 billion.

»WATER CUBE«
National Aquatics Center

Design	PTW Architects
Length × Width × Height	177 × 177 × 31 m
Capacity (Olympic Games)	17,000
Capacity (permanent)	6,000
Construction Costs	circa $140 m.

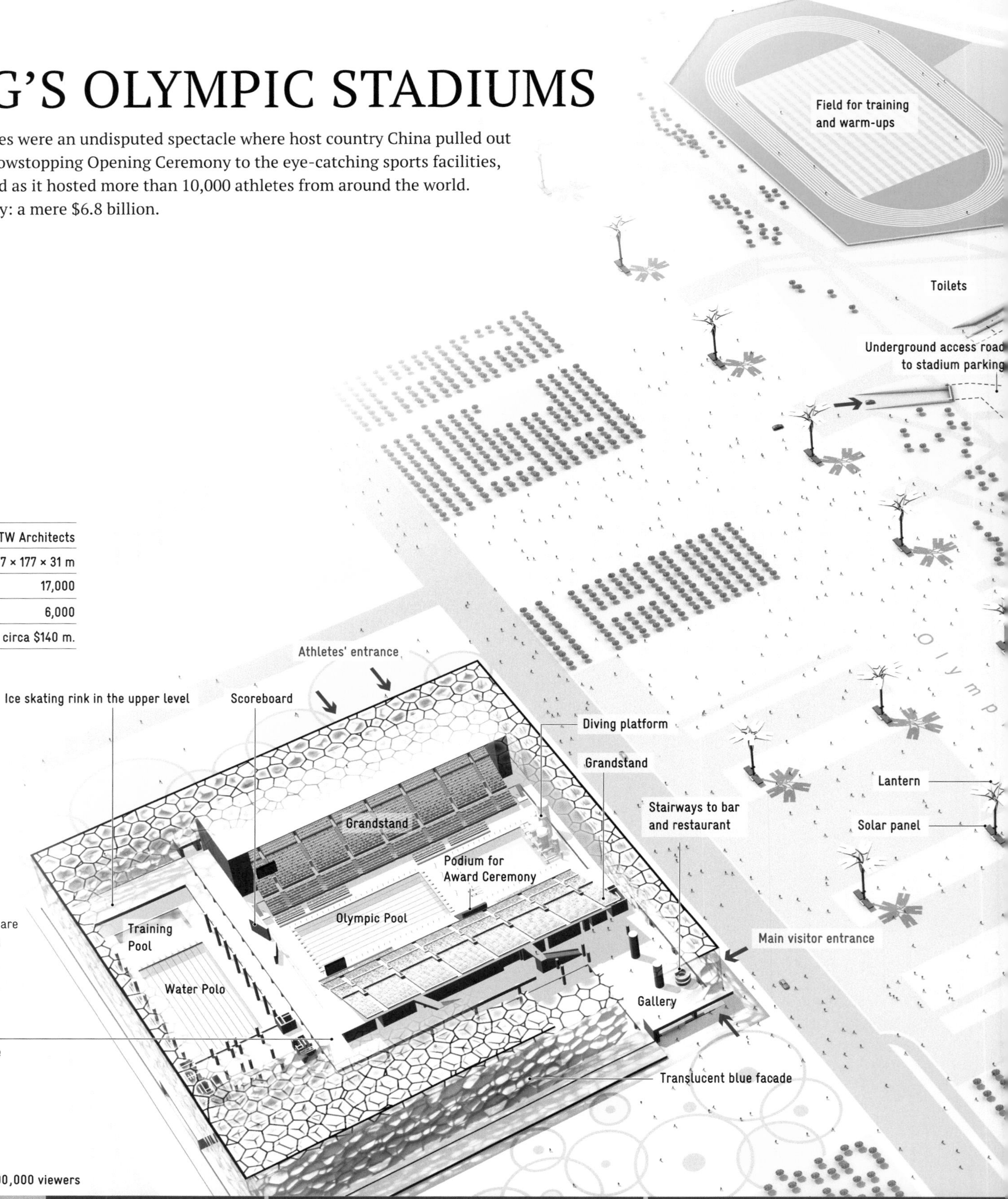

Field for training and warm-ups
Toilets
Underground access road to stadium parking
Athletes' entrance
Ice skating rink in the upper level
Scoreboard
Diving platform
Grandstand
Grandstand
Stairways to bar and restaurant
Lantern
Solar panel
Podium for Award Ceremony
Olympic Pool
Training Pool
Water Polo
Main visitor entrance
Gallery
Public concourse
Translucent blue facade

The walls of the Aquatic Center are made of roughly 3,000 cushions with a laminated polymer membrane skin, which imitates the appearance of water.

up to 1,000 athletes · 100,000 viewers

	I. Athens 1896 GRE	II. Paris 1900 FRA	III. St. Louis 1904 USA
SPORTS	7 9 14 16 19 21 24 27 30	5 7 8 14 16 17 20 21 22 24 27 30 32 34 35 36 37 38	2 5 6 7 8 9 14 16 18 20 21 27 30 32 33 36 39 40
NUMBER OF ATHLETES	Men 265 Women 0	1,617 20	676 6
NUMBER OF NATIONS	12	25	12
VIEWERS	approx. 312,000	200,000	250,000

First Olympic Games of modern times. | The first time women took part: in two sports, golf and tennis. | The last time combined with a national competition.

»Bird's Nest«
National Stadium

Design	Herzog & de Meuron
Length × Width × Height	320 × 297 × 69.2 m
Capacity (Olympic Games)	91,000
Capacity (permanent)	80,000
Construction costs	circa $540 m.
Start Construction Work	December 23, 2003
Steel Frame (Roof)	45,000 t

While arranged in a decorative fashion, each of the »Bird's Nest's« steel beams are a necessary structural element. The entire steel structure is welded together to form a single structure weighing 45,000 tonnes and is supported by 24 steel columns, which weigh 1,000 tonnes each.

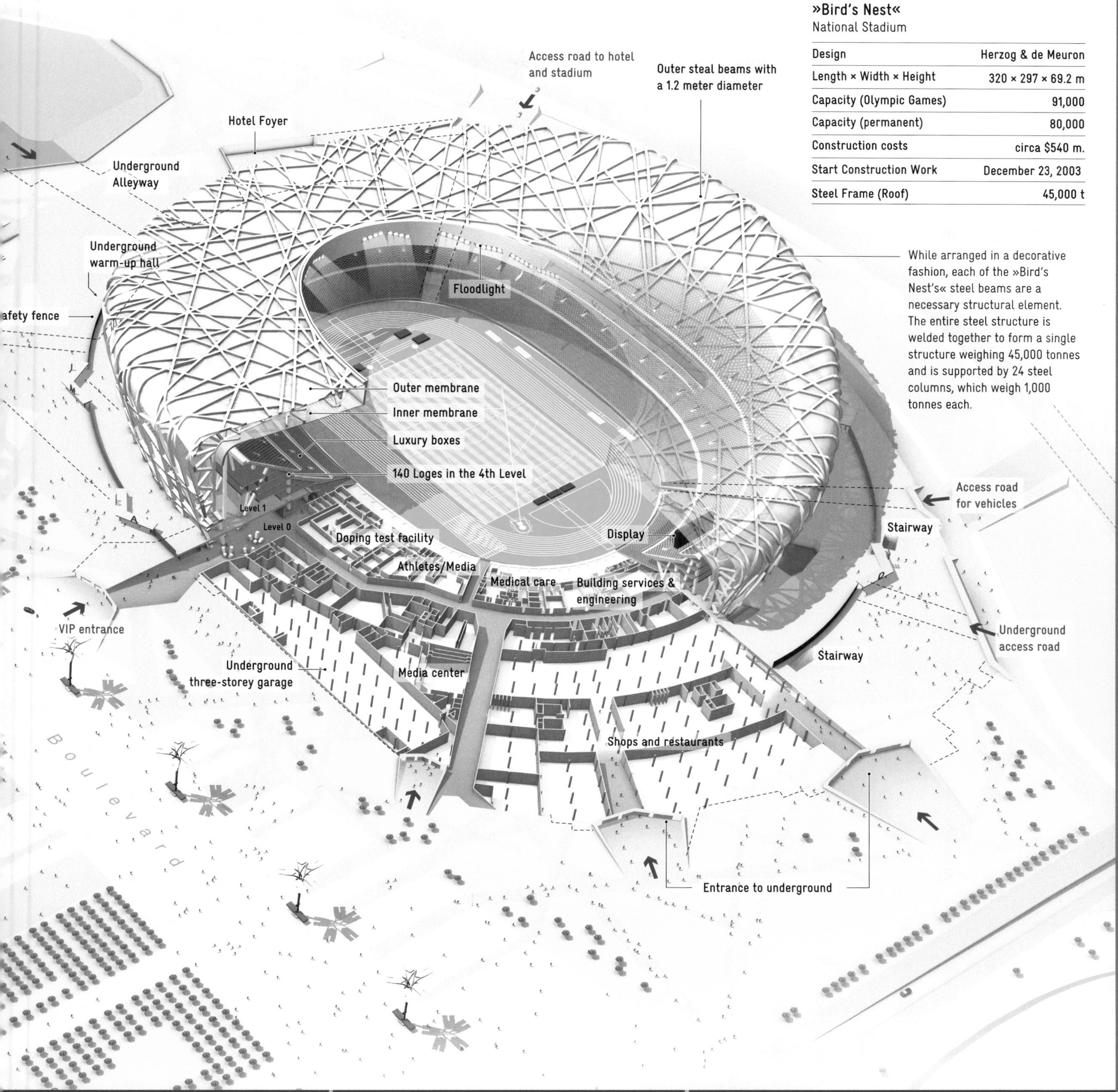
Access road to hotel and stadium
Outer steal beams with a 1.2 meter diameter
Hotel Foyer
Underground Alleyway
Underground warm-up hall
afety fence
Floodlight
Outer membrane
Inner membrane
Luxury boxes
140 Loges in the 4th Level
Level 1
Level 0
Doping test facility
Athletes/Media
Medical care
Building services & engineering
Display
Access road for vehicles
Stairway
Underground access road
Stairway
VIP entrance
Underground three-storey garage
Media center
Shops and restaurants
Boulevard
Entrance to underground

Athens 1906 GRE

7 8 9 14 16 19 20 21 24 27 30 33

883
20

19

ca. 300,000

Olympic Games held to celebrate ten-year anniversary.

IV. London 1908 ENG

5 6 7 8 11 14 16 18 19 20 21 22 24 27 30 32 33 37 38 39 41 42 43

2,005
42

22

300,000

For the first time with 24 sports, setting new standards.

V. Stockholm 1912 SWE

7 8 14 15 16 17 19 20 21 22 24 27 30 32 33 45

2,377
53

28

327,000

Gold for tug of war went to the team from Sweden.

The city silhouettes show the current view.

FASTER, HIGHER, STRONGER

When Her Majesty the Queen, as Head of State, proclaims the Games open by saying: »I declare the Games of London celebrating the 30th Olympiad of the modern era, open,« the spectators start to cheer. The Olympic arena is not only a functional building, it also provides a close emotional link to the Games.

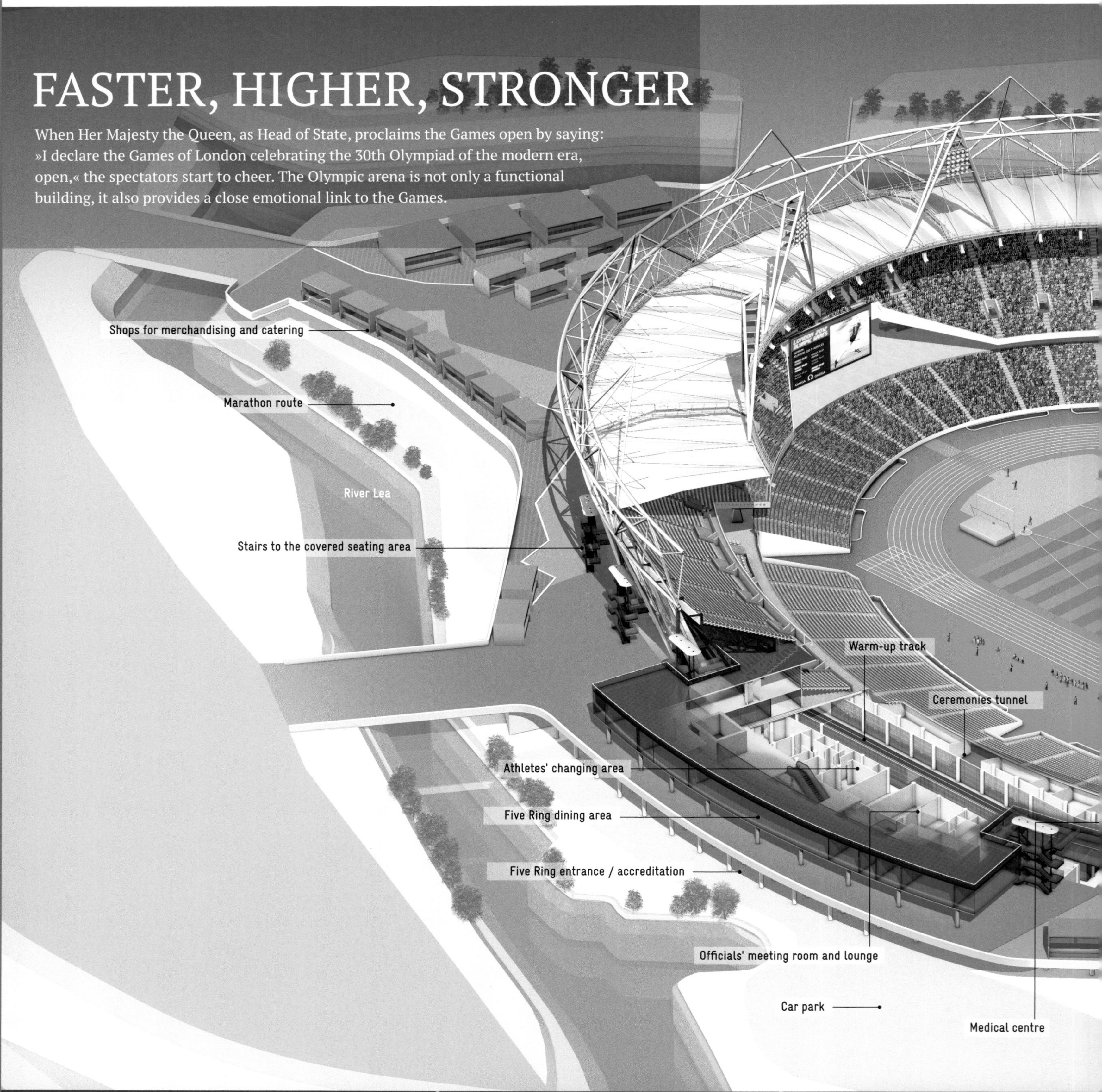
Shops for merchandising and catering
Marathon route
River Lea
Stairs to the covered seating area
Warm-up track
Ceremonies tunnel
Athletes' changing area
Five Ring dining area
Five Ring entrance / accreditation
Officials' meeting room and lounge
Car park
Medical centre

VI. Berlin 1916 GER

Not held because of the First World War

VII. Antwerp 1920 BEL

5 6 7 8 9 11 14 15 16 17 18 19 20 21 22 24 27 30 32 33 38 46 44 37 38 45

Men 2,591
Women 77

25

350,000

Germany was not allowed to participate.

VIII: Paris 1924 FRA

6 7 8 9 14 15 16 17 18 19 20 21 22 24 27 30 32 33 37 38

2,937
139

44

612,000

Germany was not allowed to participate.

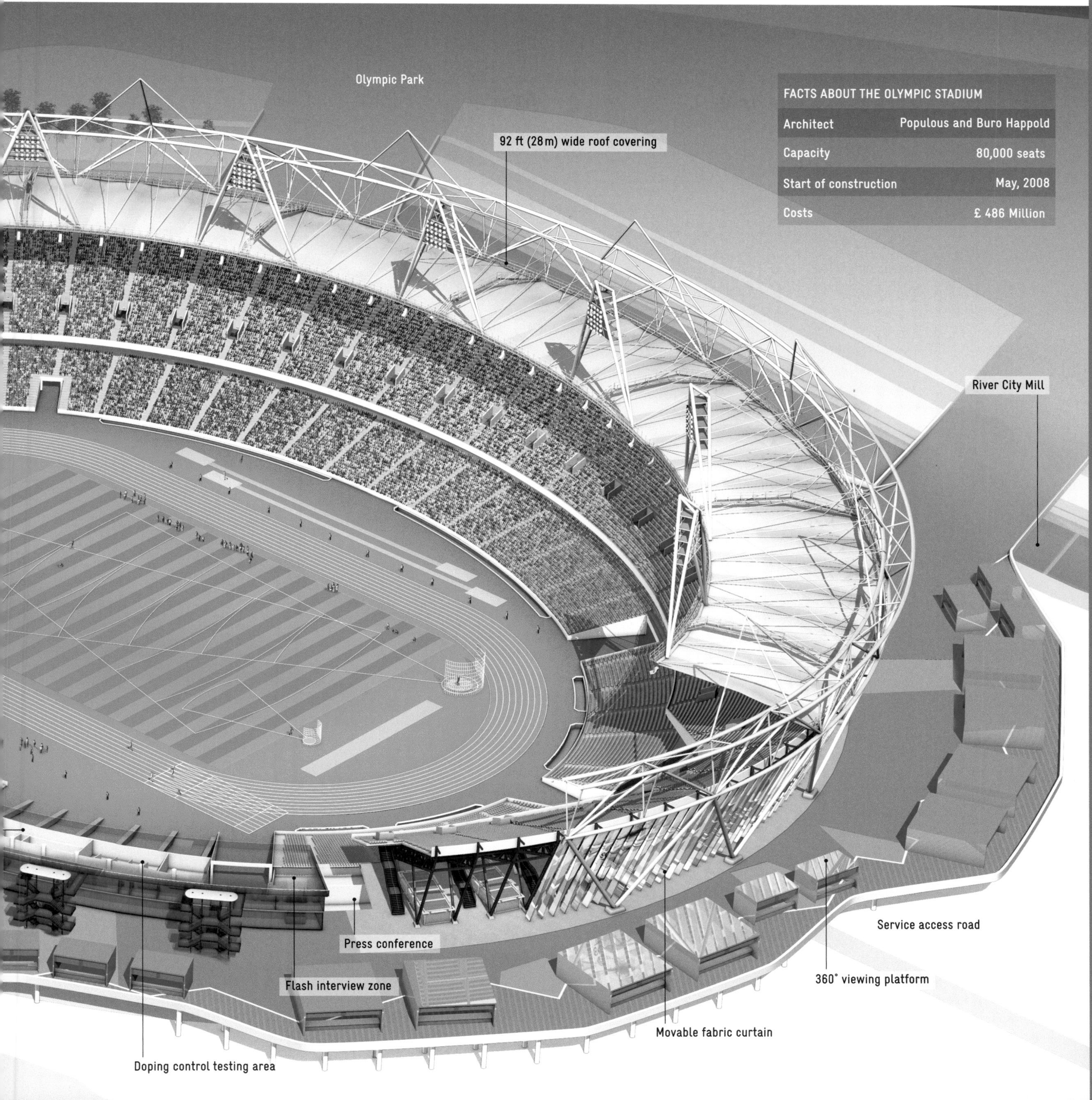
Olympic Park
92 ft (28 m) wide roof covering
River City Mill
Service access road
360° viewing platform
Movable fabric curtain
Press conference
Flash interview zone
Doping control testing area

FACTS ABOUT THE OLYMPIC STADIUM	
Architect	Populous and Buro Happold
Capacity	80,000 seats
Start of construction	May, 2008
Costs	£ 486 Million

IX. Amsterdam 1928 NED

6 7 8 9 11 14 15 16 17 18 19 20 21 22 30 32 33

2,610
278

46

666,000

Women were allowed to compete in athletics for the first time.

X. Los Angeles 1932 USA

6 7 9 11 14 15 16 17 18 19 20 21 22 24 30 32 33

1,204
126

37

1,248,000

The US athletes won 41 gold medals.

XI. Berlin 1936 GER

3 6 7 8 9 10 11 13 14 15 16 17 18 19 20 21 22 24 30 32 33 37

Men 3,634
Women 328

3,770,000

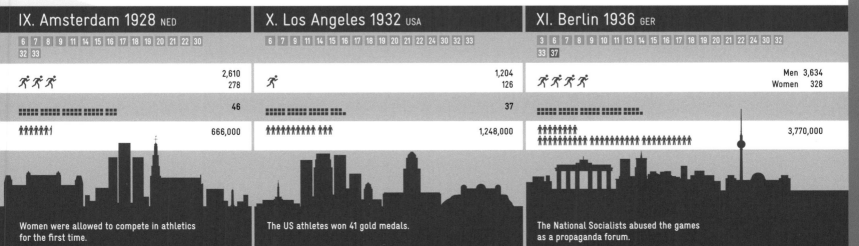

The National Socialists abused the games as a propaganda forum.

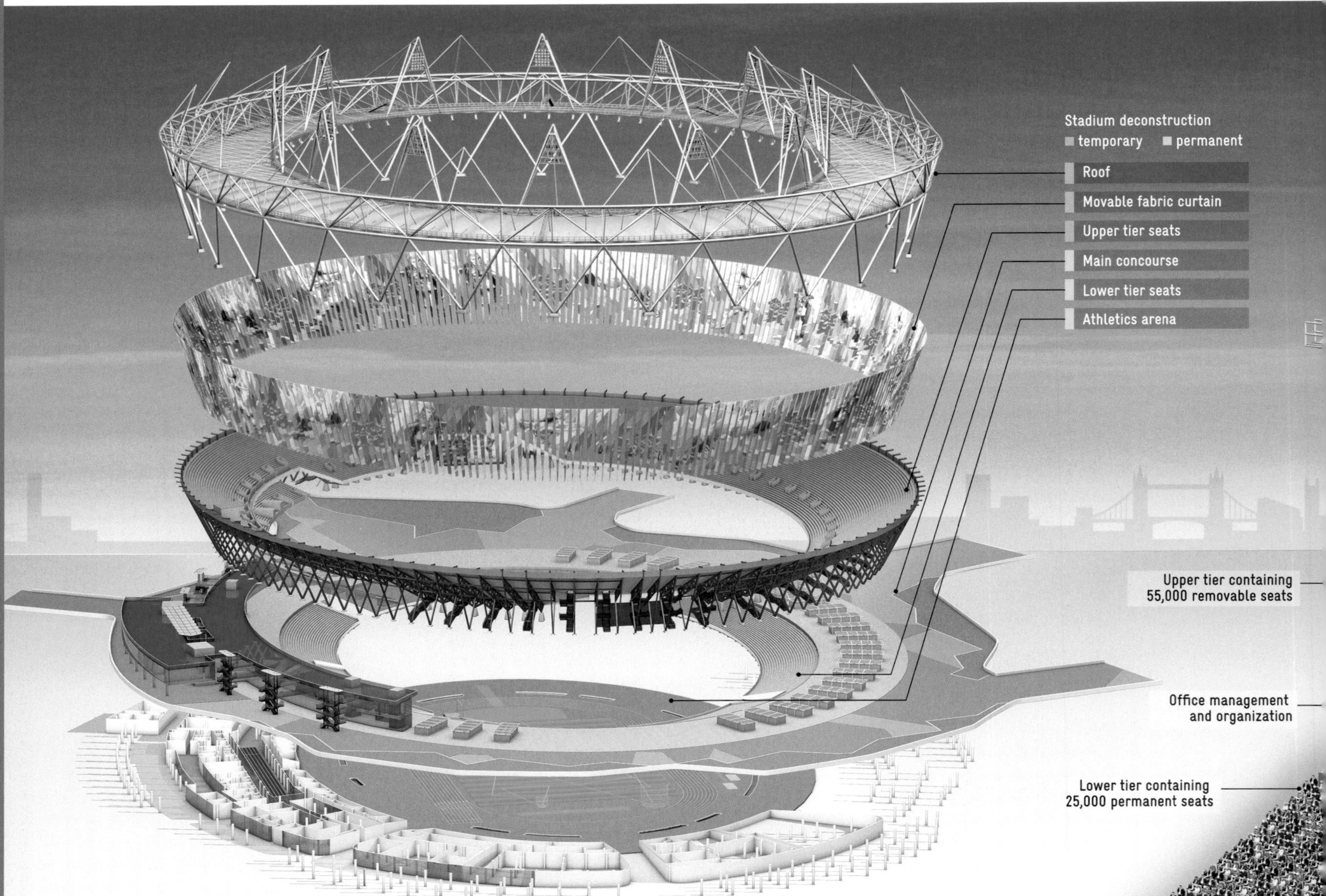
Stadium deconstruction
temporary
permanent
Roof
Movable fabric curtain
Upper tier seats
Main concourse
Lower tier seats
Athletics arena
Upper tier containing
55,000 removable seats
Office management
and organization
Lower tier containing
25,000 permanent seats

The stadium over time

Once the Olympic Games were over, an 80,000 seat arena could not be operated at a profit. The London Stadium has been redeveloped at a significant cost and now hosts Premier League football, athletics tournaments and other sporting events.

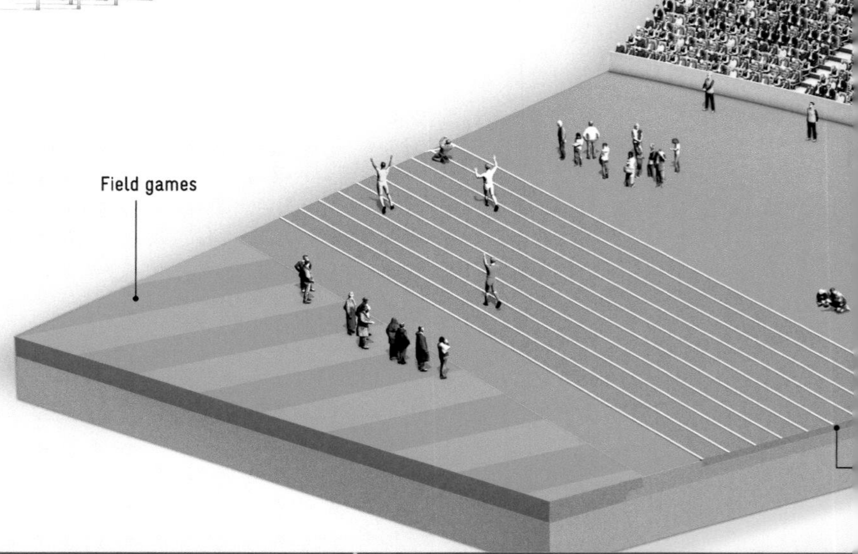
Field games

XII. Helsinki, Tokyo 1940 FIN, JPN

XIII. London 1944 ENG

Not held because of the Second World War

XIV. London 1948 ENG

3 6 7 8 9 11 13 14 15 16 17 18 19 20 21 22 24 30 32 33

Men	3,766
Women	355
	59
	1,247,000

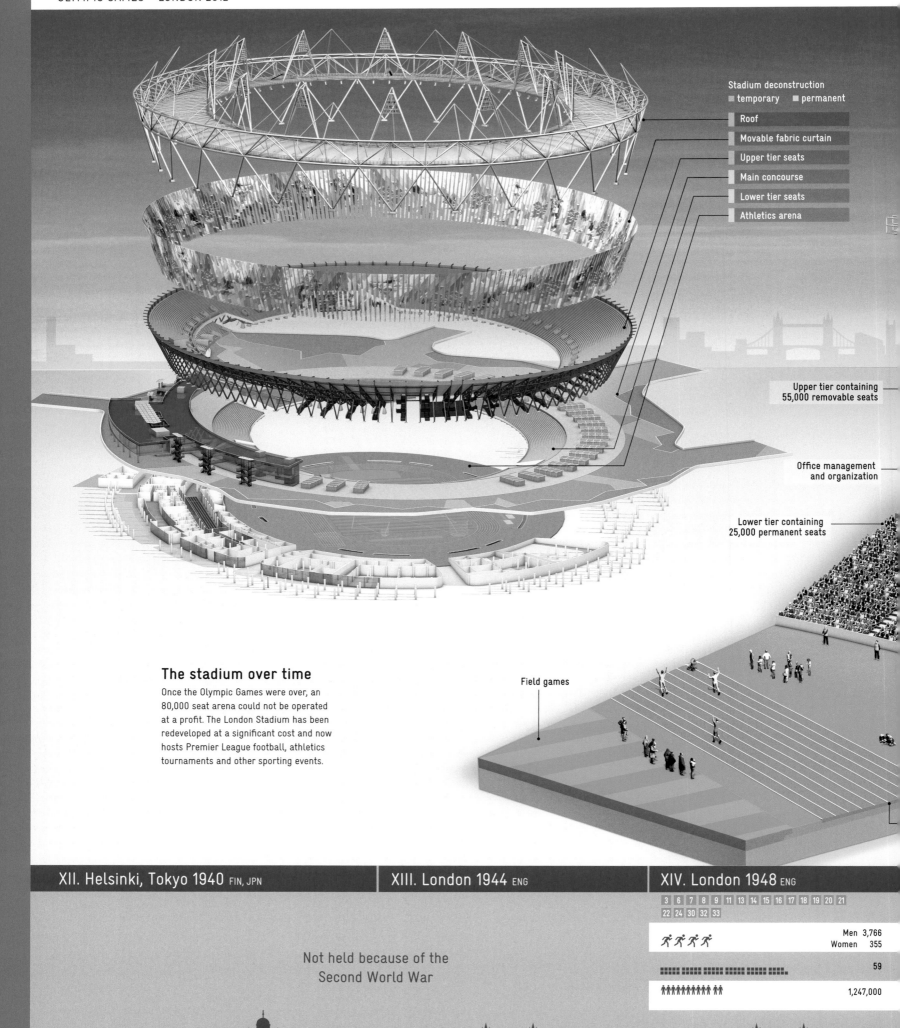

Germany was not allowed to participate.

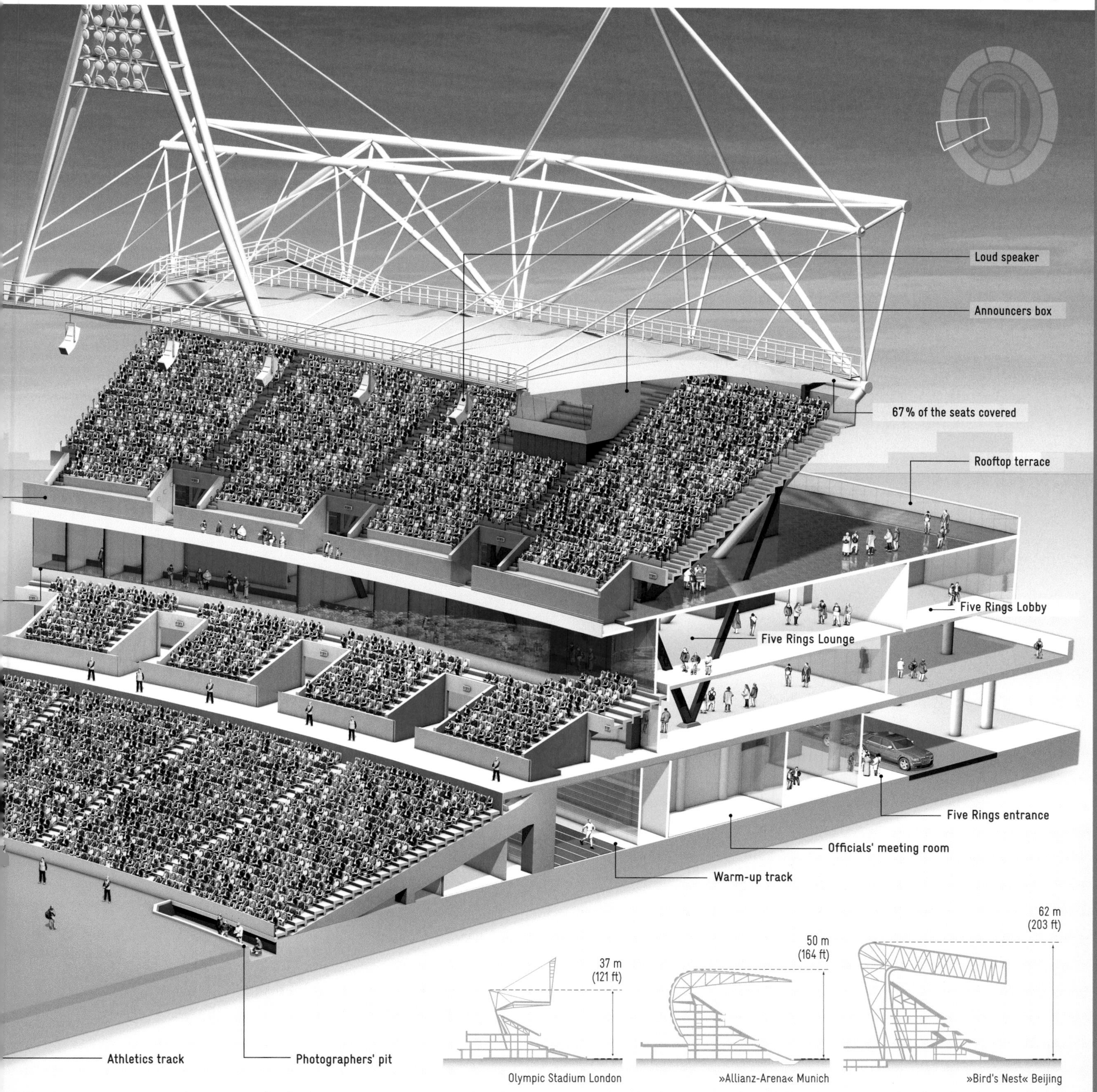
Loud speaker
Announcers box
67 % of the seats covered
Rooftop terrace
Five Rings Lobby
Five Rings Lounge
Five Rings entrance
Officials' meeting room
Warm-up track
Athletics track
Photographers' pit
37 m
(121 ft)
Olympic Stadium London
50 m
(164 ft)
»Allianz-Arena« Munich
62 m
(203 ft)
»Bird's Nest« Beijing

XV. Helsinki 1952 FIN

3 6 7 8 9 11 13 14 15 16 17 18 19 20 21 22 24 30 32 33

4,361
516

67

1,377,000

First time USSR participated.

XVI. Melbourne 1956 AUS

3 6 7 8 9 11 13 14 15 16 17 18 19 20 21 22 24 30 32 33

2,909
382

70

1,507,000

Due to to strict quarantine regulations in Australia, the equestrian events were held in Stockholm.

XVII. Rome 1960 ITA

3 6 7 8 9 11 13 14 15 16 17 18 19 20 21 22 24 30 32 33

Men 4,727
Women 611

82

1,436,000

For the second time the USSR leads medal table.

SHOT PUT

Could you throw a TV over eleven cars?

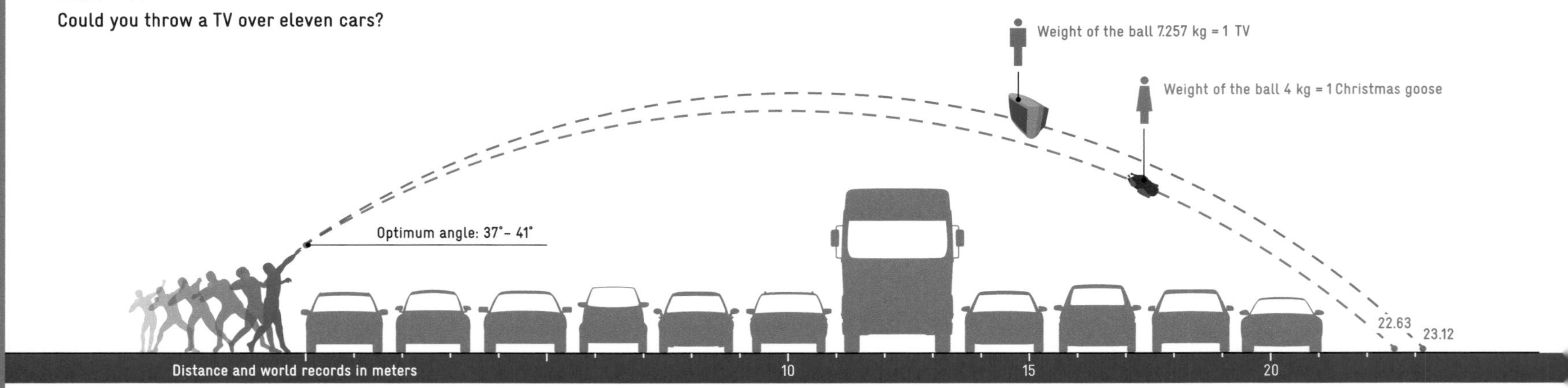
Weight of the ball 7.257 kg = 1 TV
Weight of the ball 4 kg = 1 Christmas goose
Optimum angle: 37°– 41°
22.63
23.12
Distance and world records in meters
10
15
20

PARTICIPATION IS EVERYTHING?

Taking part in the Olympic Games means a great deal to athletes. He gives everything for the maximum success. For years he trains to increase his performance—pushing it to the very limits of what is possible. To gain an impression of what a world record means, a few are shown figuratively.

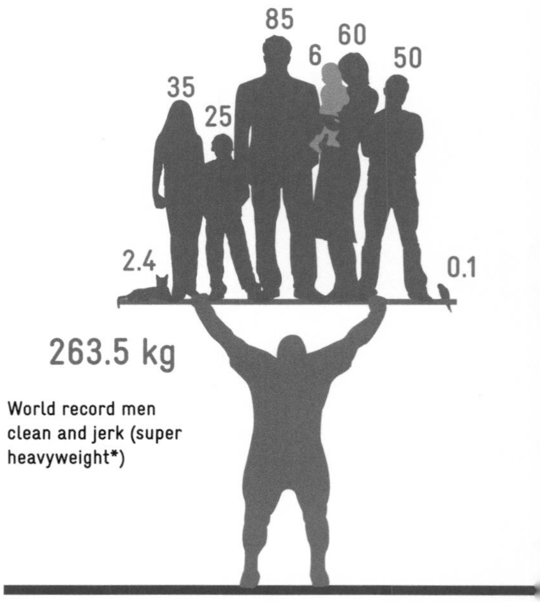
85
6
60
50
35
25
2.4
0.1
263.5 kg
World record men clean and jerk (super heavyweight*)

WEIGHTLIFTING

You need to lift a whole family for a gold medal

DRESSAGE

Horses with integrated navigation

WALK
TROT
CANTER

The ride of Isabell Werth (2004) in the dressage arena

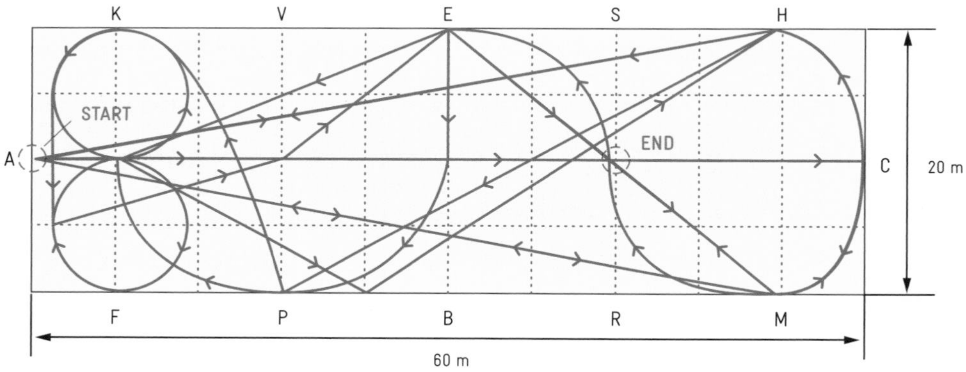
K
V
E
S
H
START
END
A
C
20 m
F
P
B
R
M
60 m

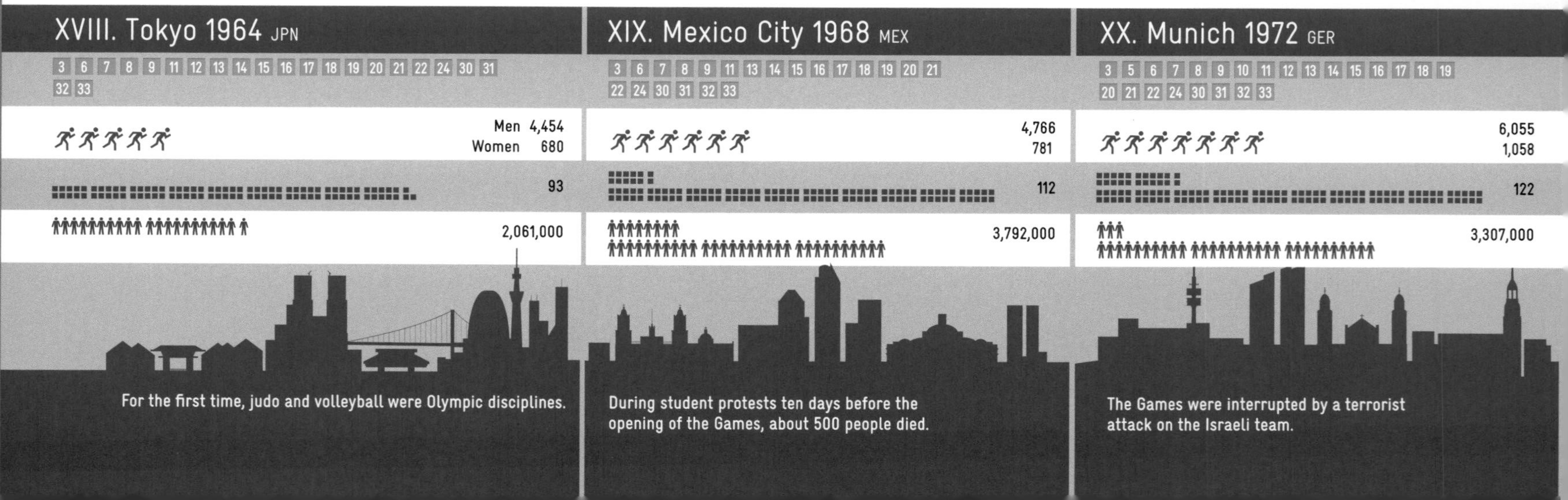
XVIII. Tokyo 1964 JPN
3 6 7 8 9 11 12 13 14 15 16 17 18 19 20 21 22 24 30 31 32 33
Men 4,454
Women 680
93
2,061,000
For the first time, judo and volleyball were Olympic disciplines.
XIX. Mexico City 1968 MEX
3 6 7 8 9 11 13 14 15 16 17 18 19 20 21 22 24 30 31 32 33
4,766
781
112
3,792,000
During student protests ten days before the opening of the Games, about 500 people died.
XX. Munich 1972 GER
3 5 6 7 8 9 10 11 12 13 14 15 16 17 18 19 20 21 22 24 30 31 32 33
6,055
1,058
122
3,307,000
The Games were interrupted by a terrorist attack on the Israeli team.

ARCHERY
More accurate than Robin Hood

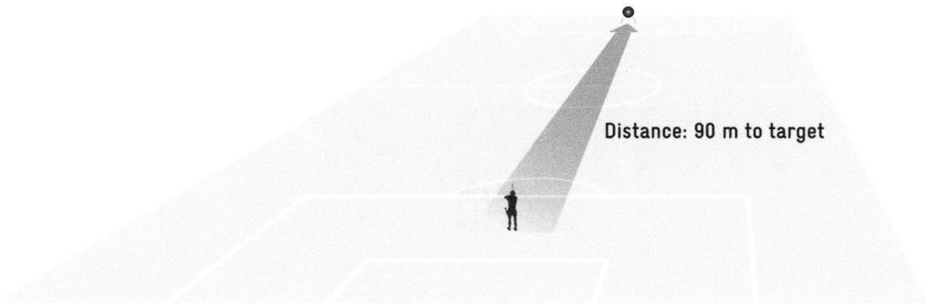
Distance: 90 m to target

Olympic round: 2 times 36 arrows in a knock-out competition

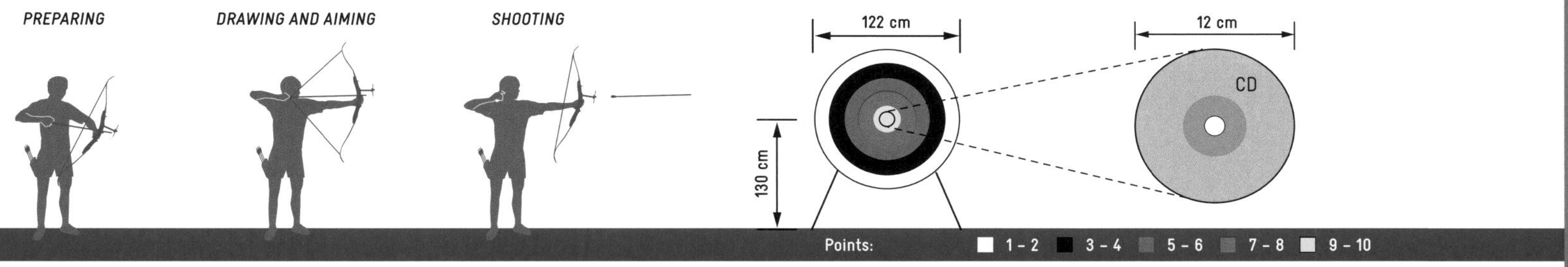
PREPARING
DRAWING AND AIMING
SHOOTING
122 cm
12 cm
CD
130 cm
Points:
1 - 2
3 - 4
5 - 6
7 - 8
9 - 10

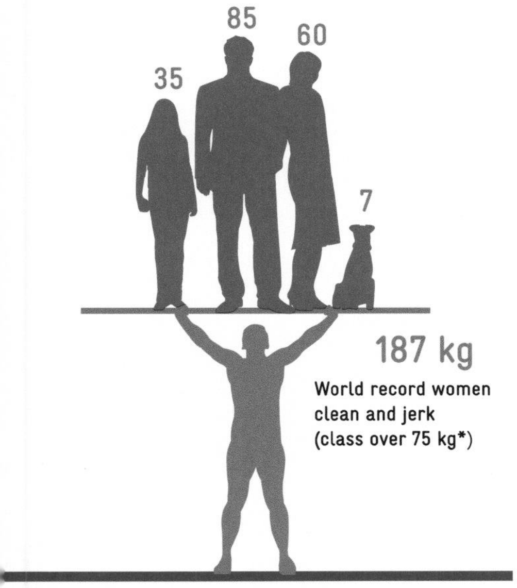
35
85
60
7
187 kg
World record women clean and jerk (class over 75 kg*)

* Weight class: up to 56, 62, 69, 77, 85, 94, 105, over 105 kg

* Weight class: up to 48, 53, 58, 63, 69, 75, über 75 kg

LONG JUMP
One jump over two cars

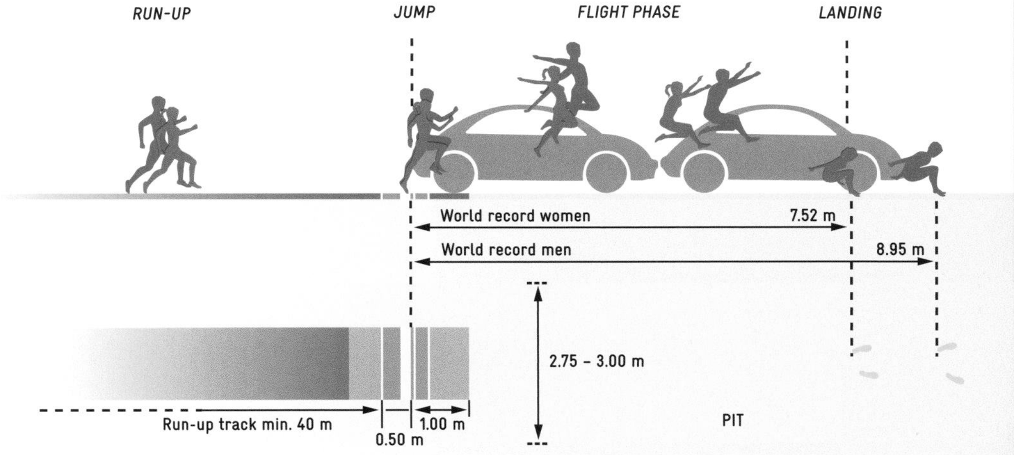
RUN-UP
JUMP
FLIGHT PHASE
LANDING
World record women
7.52 m
World record men
8.95 m
2.75 – 3.00 m
Run-up track min. 40 m
0.50 m
1.00 m
PIT

100 METER FREESTYLE
As fast as penguins

World record (average speed): men 7.56 km/h

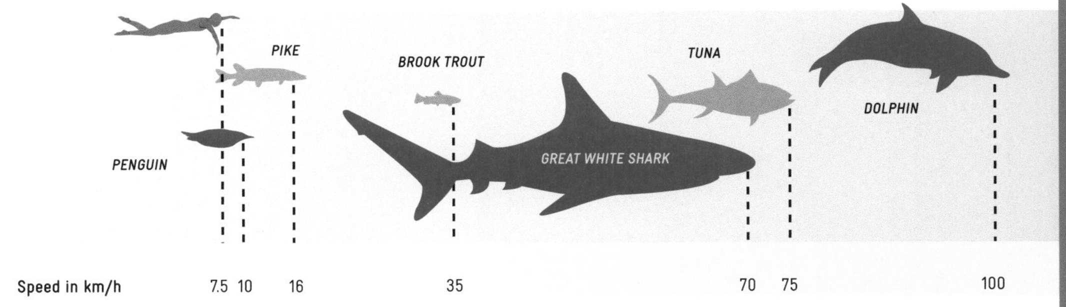
PIKE
BROOK TROUT
TUNA
DOLPHIN
PENGUIN
GREAT WHITE SHARK
Speed in km/h
7.5
10
16
35
70
75
100

XXI. Montreal 1976 CAN

3 5 6 7 8 9 10 11 12 13 14 15 16 17 18 19 20 21 22 24 30 31 32 33

4,794
1,261

92

3,187,000

The host country Canada did not win any gold medals.

XXII. Moscow 1980 RUS

3 5 6 7 8 9 10 11 12 13 14 15 16 17 18 19 20 21 22 24 30 31 32 33

4,135
1,120

80

5,268,000

42 countries boycotted the Games because of the invasion of Afghanistan by the USSR.

XXIII. Los Angeles 1984 USA

3 5 6 7 8 9 10 11 12 13 14 15 16 17 18 19 20 21 22 24 25 30 31 32 33

Men 5,235
Women 1,558

140

5,018,000

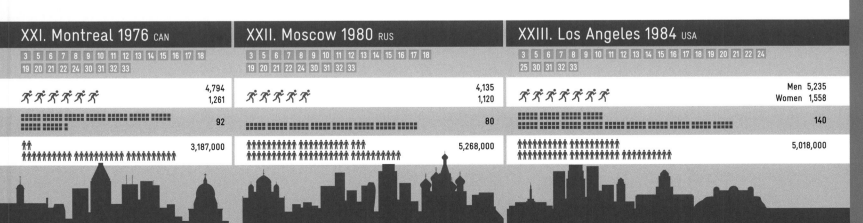

The Eastern Bloc countries boycotted the Games and organize the »competitions of friendship«

HIGHER, FASTER, FURTHER

In the hunt for medals, athletes continue to break records. Time and again you think that the human body has reached its limits. Some records stand for decades, but then someone comes along who can do it just that little bit better. The chart shows the evolution of records in selected Olympic disciplines and highlights those that were set during the Games.

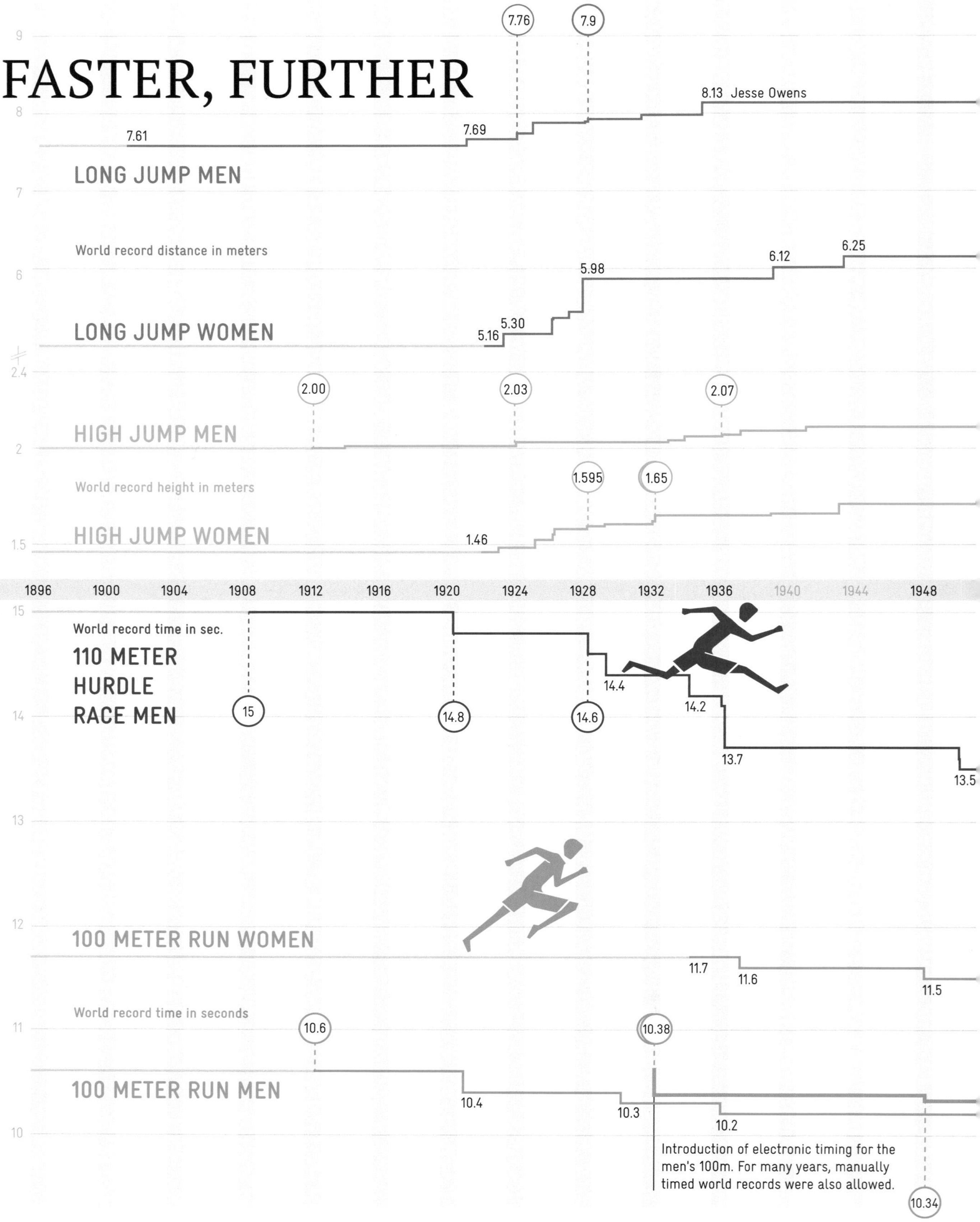
LONG JUMP MEN
7.61
7.69
7.76
7.9
8.13 Jesse Owens
World record distance in meters
LONG JUMP WOMEN
5.16
5.30
5.98
6.12
6.25
HIGH JUMP MEN
2.00
2.03
2.07
World record height in meters
HIGH JUMP WOMEN
1.46
1.595
1.65
YEAR
1896 1900 1904 1908 1912 1916 1920 1924 1928 1932 1936 1940 1944 1948
World record time in sec.
110 METER HURDLE RACE MEN
15
14.8
14.6
14.4
14.2
13.7
13.5
100 METER RUN WOMEN
11.7
11.6
11.5
World record time in seconds
100 METER RUN MEN
10.6
10.4
10.3
10.38
10.2
10.34
Introduction of electronic timing for the men's 100m. For many years, manually timed world records were also allowed.

7.76 World record set during the Olympic Games

Manually measured value

Electronically measured value

XXIV. Seoul 1988 KOR

3 5 6 7 8 9 10 11 12 13 14 15 16 17 18 19 20 21 22 24 25 27 28 30 31 32 33

Men 6,245
Women 2,197

159

3,306,000

Tennis and table tennis were added to the Olympic disciplines.

XXV. Barcelona 1992 ESP

1 2 3 5 6 7 8 9 10 11 12 13 14 15 16 17 18 19 20 21 22 24 25 27 28 30 31 32 33

6,648
2,705

169

3,033,000

First time a unified all-German team participated.

XXVI. Atlanta 1996 USA

1 2 3 4 5 6 7 8 9 10 11 12 13 14 15 16 17 18 19 20 21 22 23 24 25 27 28 30 31 32 33

6,822
3,513

197

8,384,000

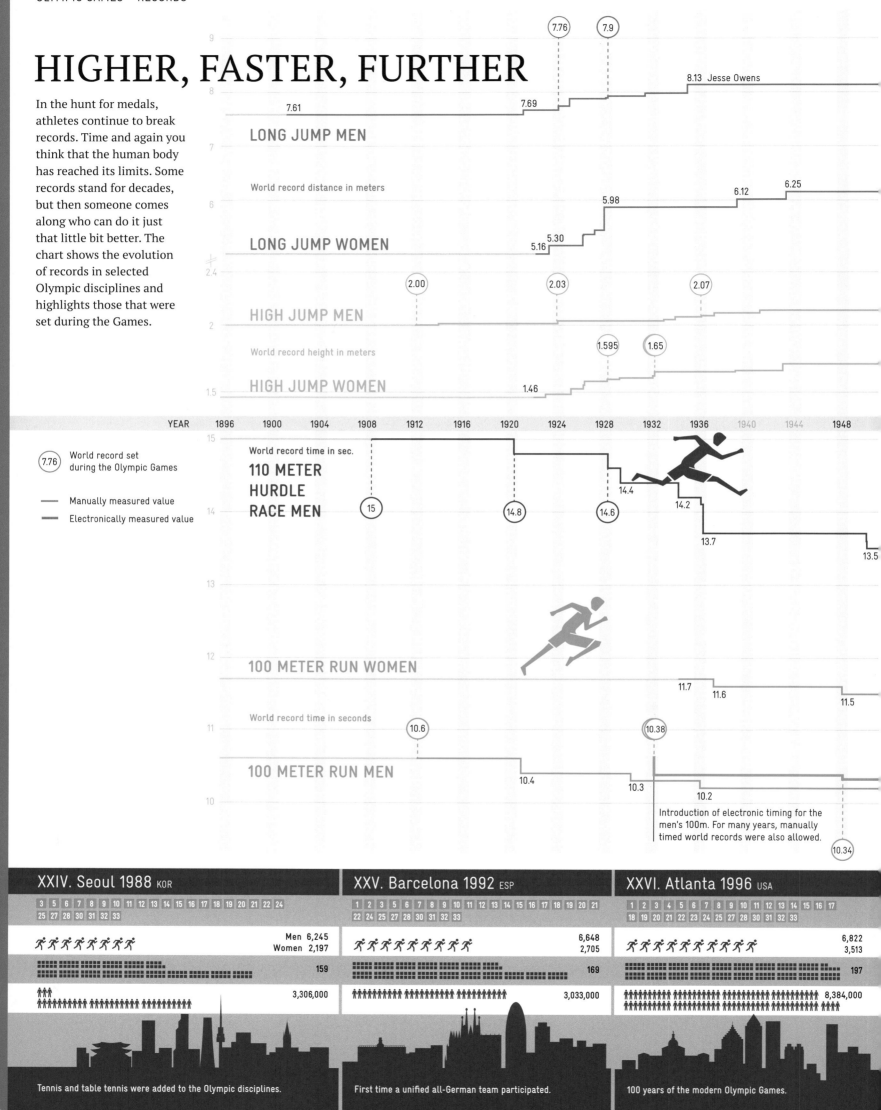

100 years of the modern Olympic Games.

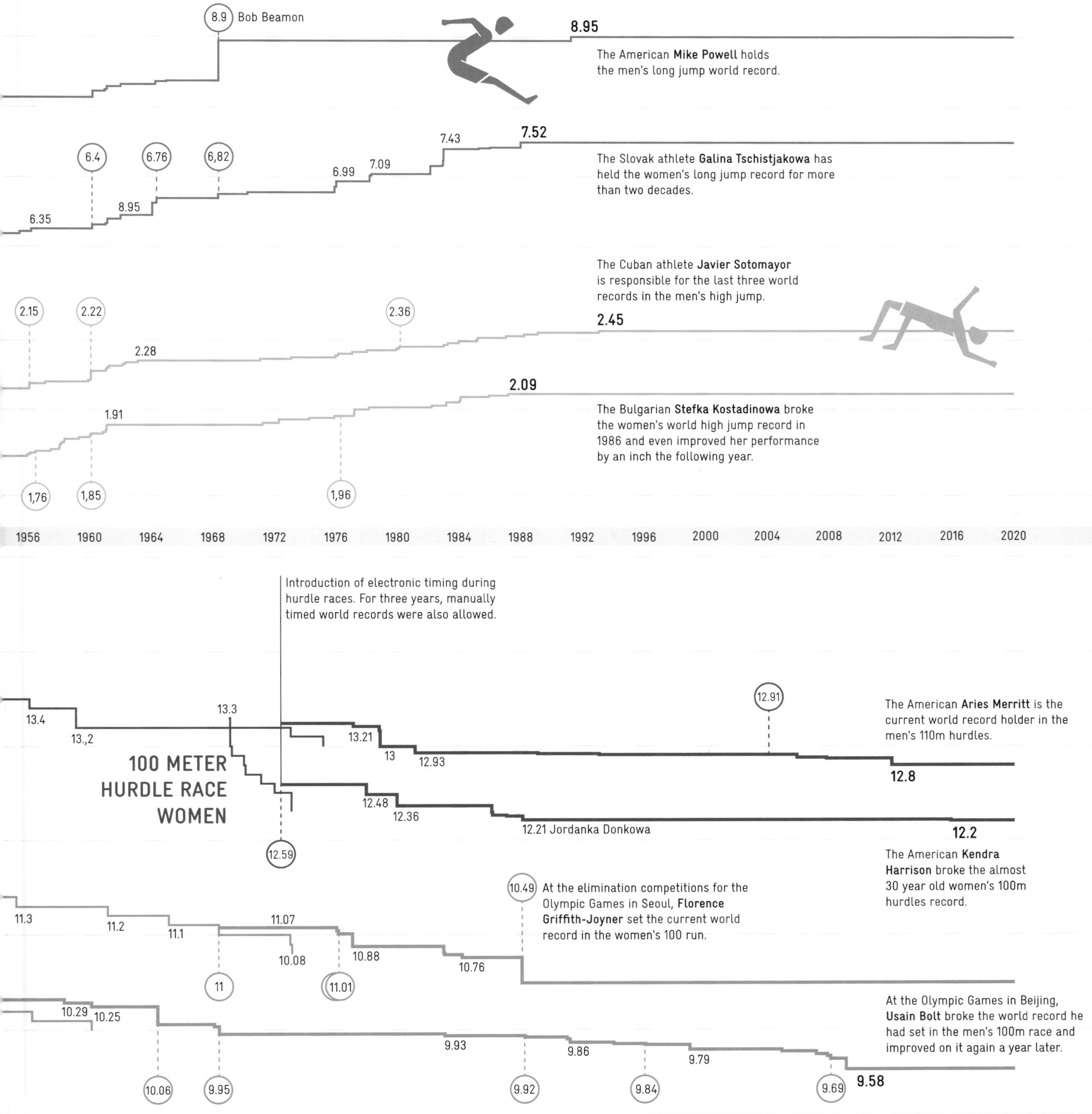

8.9 Bob Beamon
8.95
The American **Mike Powell** holds the men's long jump world record.
6.4
6.76
6,82
7.43
7.52
6.99
7.09
8.95
6.35
The Slovak athlete **Galina Tschistjakowa** has held the women's long jump record for more than two decades.
The Cuban athlete **Javier Sotomayor** is responsible for the last three world records in the men's high jump.
2.15
2.22
2.36
2.45
2.28
2.09
1.91
The Bulgarian **Stefka Kostadinowa** broke the women's world high jump record in 1986 and even improved her performance by an inch the following year.
1,76
1,85
1,96
1956 1960 1964 1968 1972 1976 1980 1984 1988 1992 1996 2000 2004 2008 2012 2016 2020
Introduction of electronic timing during hurdle races. For three years, manually timed world records were also allowed.
12.91
The American **Aries Merritt** is the current world record holder in the men's 110m hurdles.
13.4
13.3
13.,2
13.21
13
12.93
100 METER HURDLE RACE WOMEN
12.8
12.48
12.36
12.21 Jordanka Donkowa
12.2
12.59
The American **Kendra Harrison** broke the almost 30 year old women's 100m hurdles record.
10.49
At the elimination competitions for the Olympic Games in Seoul, **Florence Griffith-Joyner** set the current world record in the women's 100 run.
11.3
11.2
11.1
11.07
10.08
10.88
10.76
11
11.01
At the Olympic Games in Beijing, **Usain Bolt** broke the world record he had set in the men's 100m race and improved on it again a year later.
10.29
10.25
9.93
9.86
9.79
10.06
9.95
9.92
9.84
9.69
9.58

XXVII. Sydney 2000 AUS

1 2 3 4 5 6 7 8 9 10 11 12 13 14 15 16 17 18 19 20 21 22 23 24 25 26 27 28 29 30 31 32 33

6,838
4,287

200

6,700,000

Inclusion of taekwondo, triathlon and trampoline.

XXVIII. Athens 2004 GRE

1 2 3 4 5 6 7 8 9 10 11 12 13 14 15 16 17 18 19 20 21 22 23 24 25 26 27 28 29 30 31 32 33

6,296
4,329

202

3,800,000

The Games returned to their roots: 6 golds for Greece.

XXIX. Beijing 2008 CHN

1 2 3 4 5 6 7 8 9 10 11 12 13 14 15 16 17 18 19 20 21 22 23 24 25 26 27 28 29 30 31 32 33

Men 6,305
Women 4,637

204

6,500,000

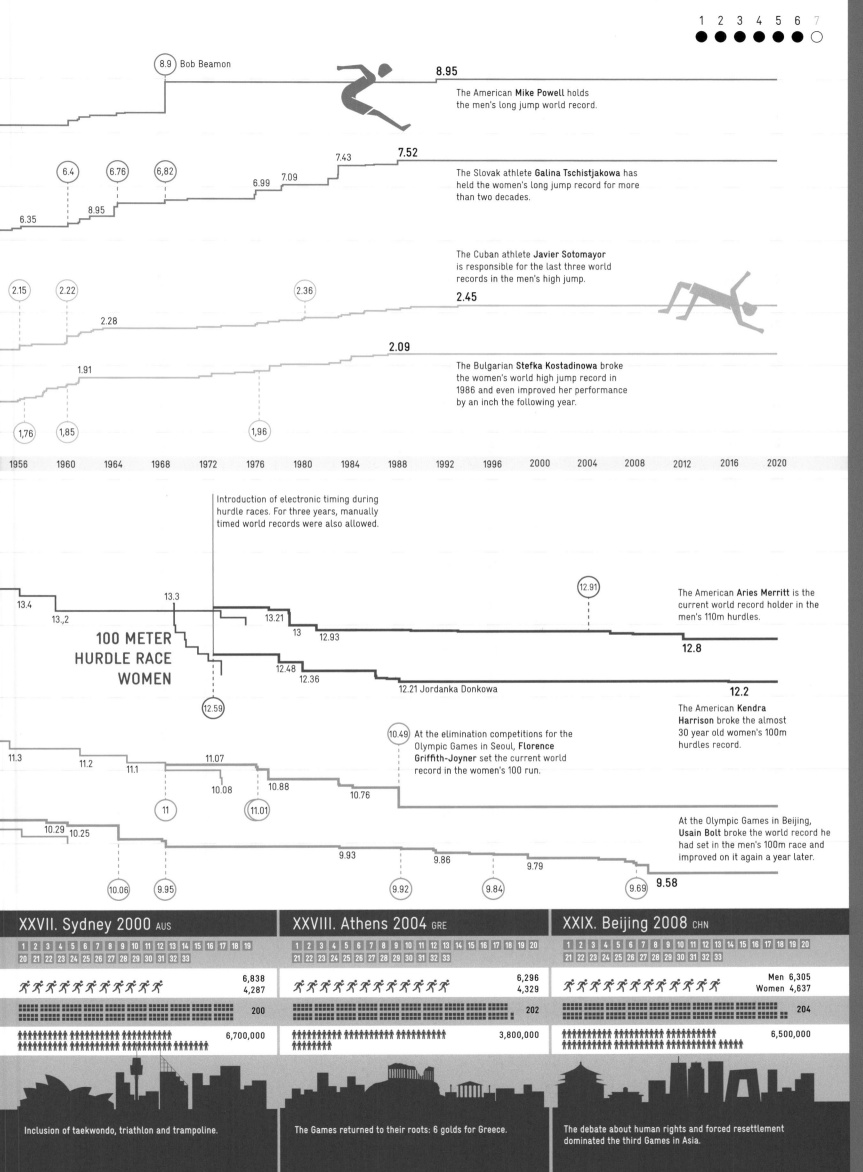

The debate about human rights and forced resettlement dominated the third Games in Asia.

BREAD & CIRCUSES

The vision of Baron Pierre de Coubertin, the founder of the IOC, was to revitalize the Ancient Olympic Games in order to bring peoples and nations closer together. Nevertheless, the games are all about business too. It is therefore preferable to hold them in countries with a profitable infrastructure. They are never held in Africa despite there being enough applicants.

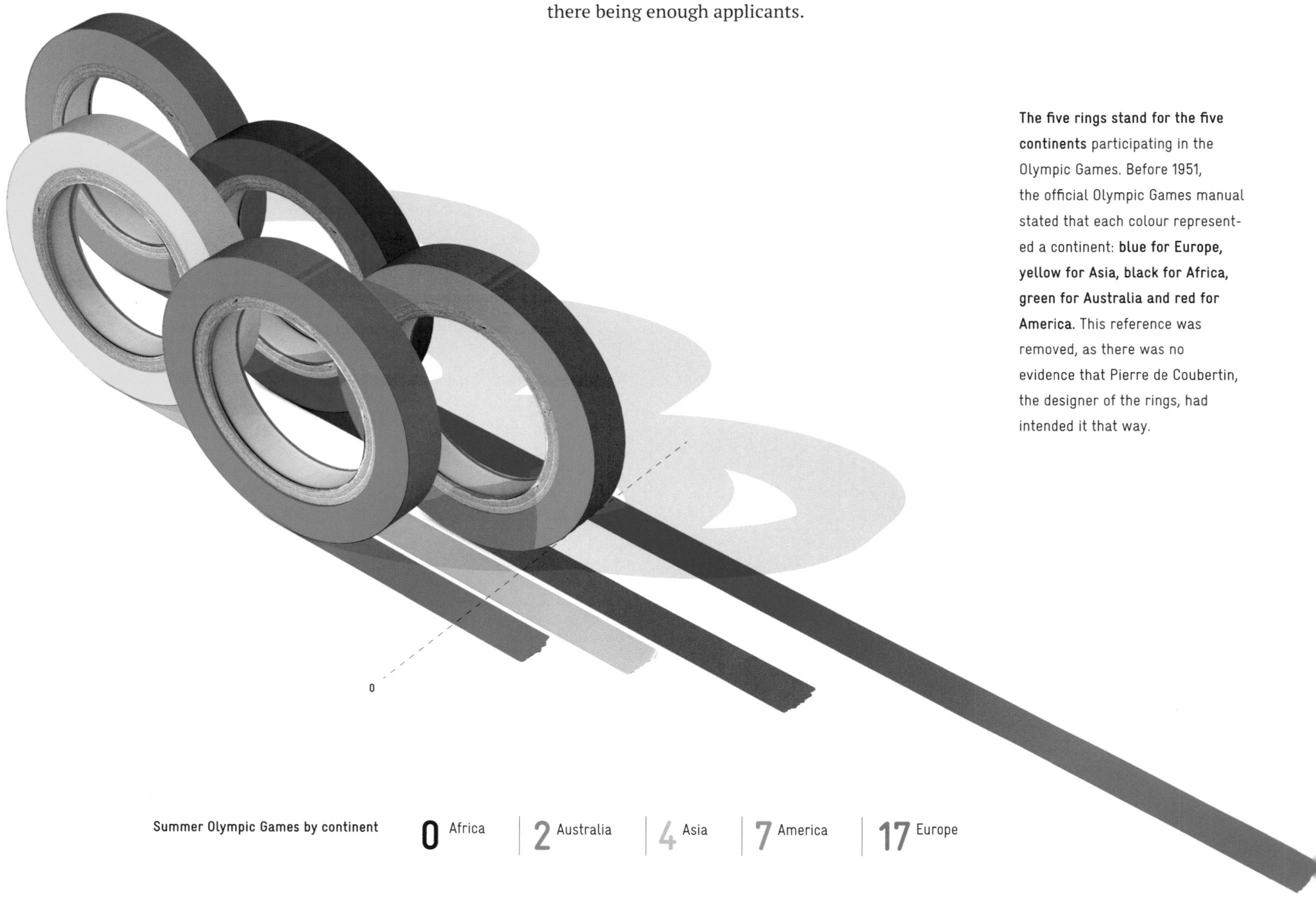

The five rings stand for the five continents participating in the Olympic Games. Before 1951, the official Olympic Games manual stated that each colour represented a continent: **blue for Europe, yellow for Asia, black for Africa, green for Australia and red for America.** This reference was removed, as there was no evidence that Pierre de Coubertin, the designer of the rings, had intended it that way.

Summer Olympic Games by continent

0 Africa | 2 Australia | 4 Asia | 7 America | 17 Europe

1890 1900 1910 1920 1930 1940

1 — Berlin 1936

1 — London 1948

2 — Helsinki 1952

XXX. London 2012 ENG

1 3 5 6 7 8 9 10 11 12 13 14 15 16 17 18 20 21 22 24
25 26 27 28 29 30 31 32 33

Men 5,864
Women 4,656

204

8,200,000

XXXI. Rio de Janeiro 2016 BRA

1 3 4 5 6 7 8 9 10 11 12 13 14 15 16 17 18 19 20 21 22
24 25 26 27 28 29 30 31 32 33 36 38

6,181
5,057

207

6,200,000

XXXII. Tokyo 2020 JPN

postponed to 2021
due to COVID 19 pandemic

takes place from July 23
to August 8, 2021

Revenues in numbers

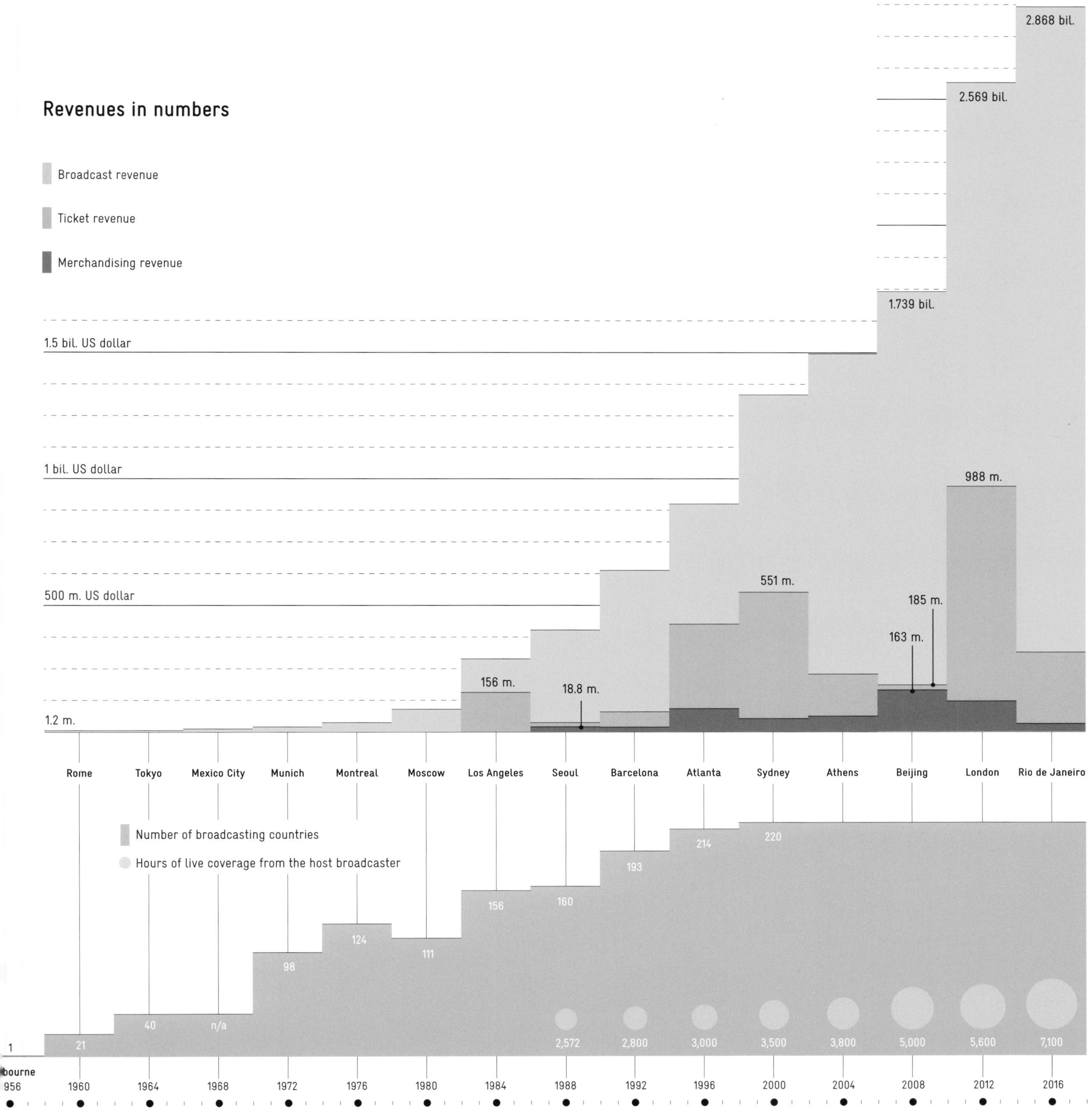

Broadcast revenue
Ticket revenue
Merchandising revenue
1.5 bil. US dollar
1 bil. US dollar
500 m. US dollar
1.2 m.
156 m.
18.8 m.
551 m.
163 m.
185 m.
1.739 bil.
988 m.
2.569 bil.
2.868 bil.
Rome
Tokyo
Mexico City
Munich
Montreal
Moscow
Los Angeles
Seoul
Barcelona
Atlanta
Sydney
Athens
Beijing
London
Rio de Janeiro
Number of broadcasting countries
Hours of live coverage from the host broadcaster
1
21
40
n/a
98
124
111
156
160
193
214
220
2,572
2,800
3,000
3,500
3,800
5,000
5,600
7,100
bourne
956
1960
1964
1968
1972
1976
1980
1984
1988
1992
1996
2000
2004
2008
2012
2016

Facts and figures Rio de Janeiro 2016

12,000 Olympic torchbearers passed through all 26 Brazilian states

3,604 Apartments in Rio's Olympic Village (11,000 athletes and 6,000 coaches were housed there)

2,488 Olympic medals (812 gold, 812 silver, 864 bronze) have been awarded to athletes in Rio

250,000kg Food served each day

450,000 Condoms were distributed to athletes

3.2 billion global audience reach

7,100 hours of content provided to the rights-holding Broadcasters

REGATTA SAILING

Regattas originated in Venice where gondoliers raced each other every year through the city's canals. The original meaning of the word »regatta« is unknown. Today, the term is also used in sailing. Regattas can last just hours or many months. Smaller boats without a keel normally compete in multiple laps through a triangular course.

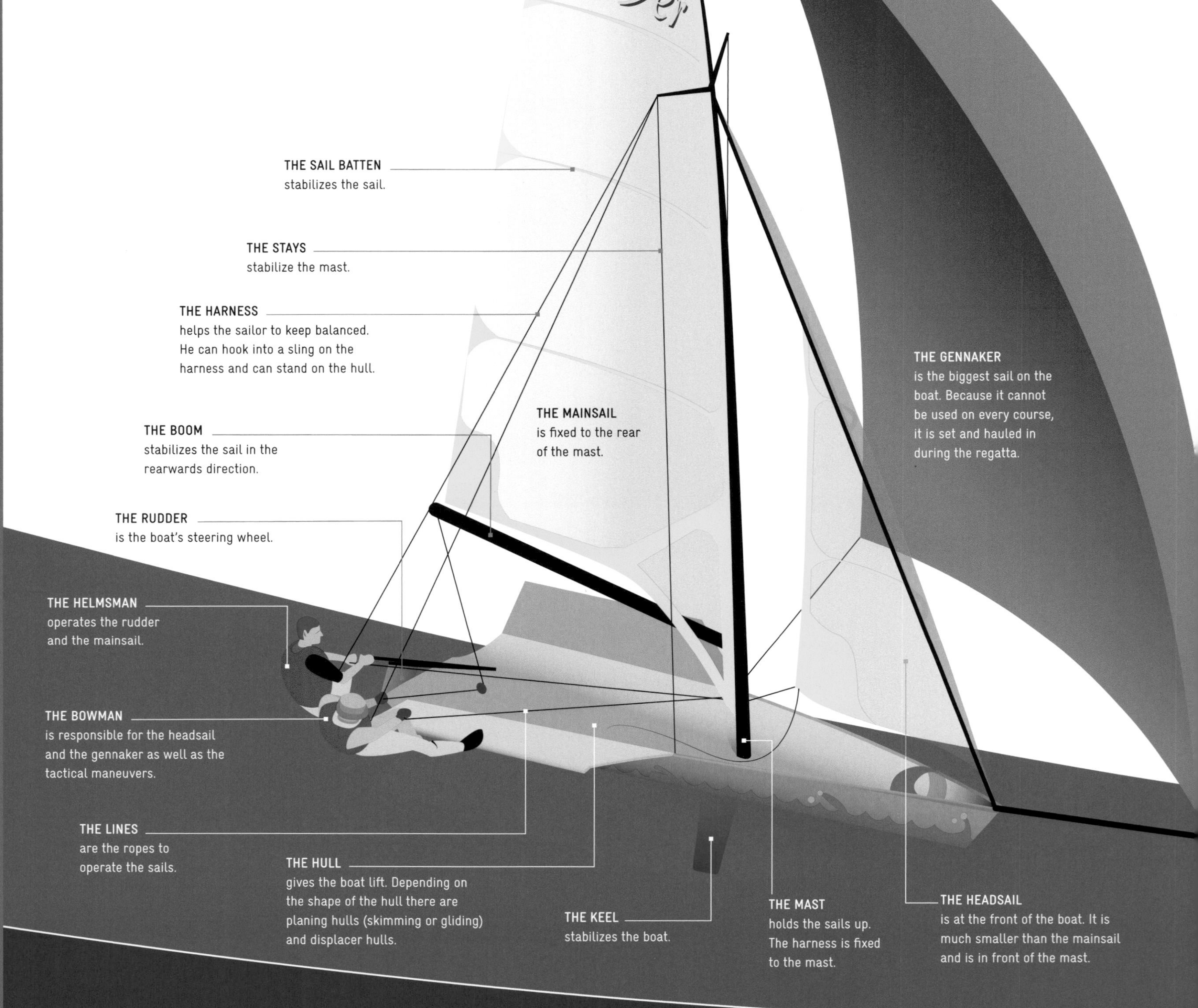
49er
THE SAIL BATTEN
stabilizes the sail.
THE STAYS
stabilize the mast.
THE HARNESS
helps the sailor to keep balanced. He can hook into a sling on the harness and can stand on the hull.
THE BOOM
stabilizes the sail in the rearwards direction.
THE RUDDER
is the boat's steering wheel.
THE MAINSAIL
is fixed to the rear of the mast.
THE GENNAKER
is the biggest sail on the boat. Because it cannot be used on every course, it is set and hauled in during the regatta.
THE HELMSMAN
operates the rudder and the mainsail.
THE BOWMAN
is responsible for the headsail and the gennaker as well as the tactical maneuvers.
THE LINES
are the ropes to operate the sails.
THE HULL
gives the boat lift. Depending on the shape of the hull there are planing hulls (skimming or gliding) and displacer hulls.
THE KEEL
stabilizes the boat.
THE MAST
holds the sails up. The harness is fixed to the mast.
THE HEADSAIL
is at the front of the boat. It is much smaller than the mainsail and is in front of the mast.

OLYMPIC BOAT TYPES

Pictured are the classes of boats that started at the Olympic Games in Rio de Janeiro in 2016. The yardstick is a method to compare the performance of different classes of boats. The general rule is: the smaller the number, the faster the boat.

	LASER RADIAL	LASER STANDARD	FINN DINGHY
Designed:	1970	1970	1949
Sail area:	5.7 m^2	7.06 m^2	10.0 m^2
Yardstick:	114	113	112
Crew:			

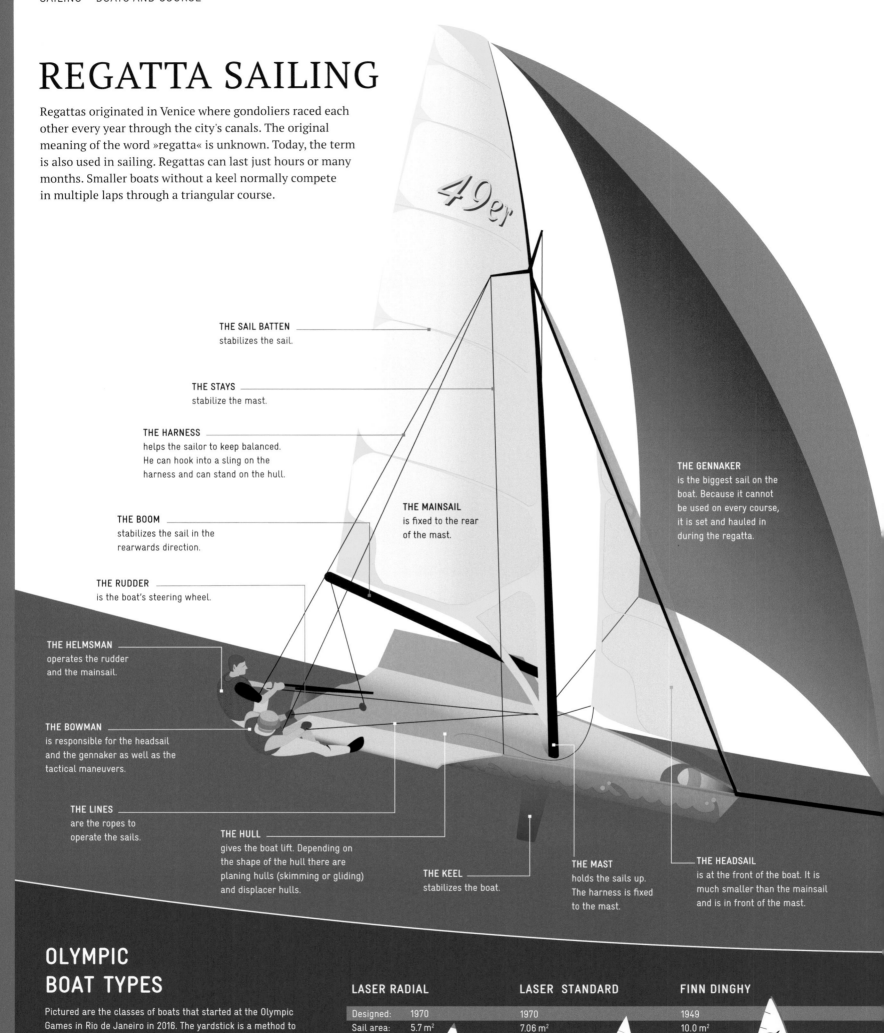

THE REGATTA COURSE

The regatta course is the race course where the boats sail. One of the most common regatta courses is the Olympic triangle made of three marked canister buoys that the competitors have to circle. Race control is responsible for overseeing the race and making sure that each participant follows the course.

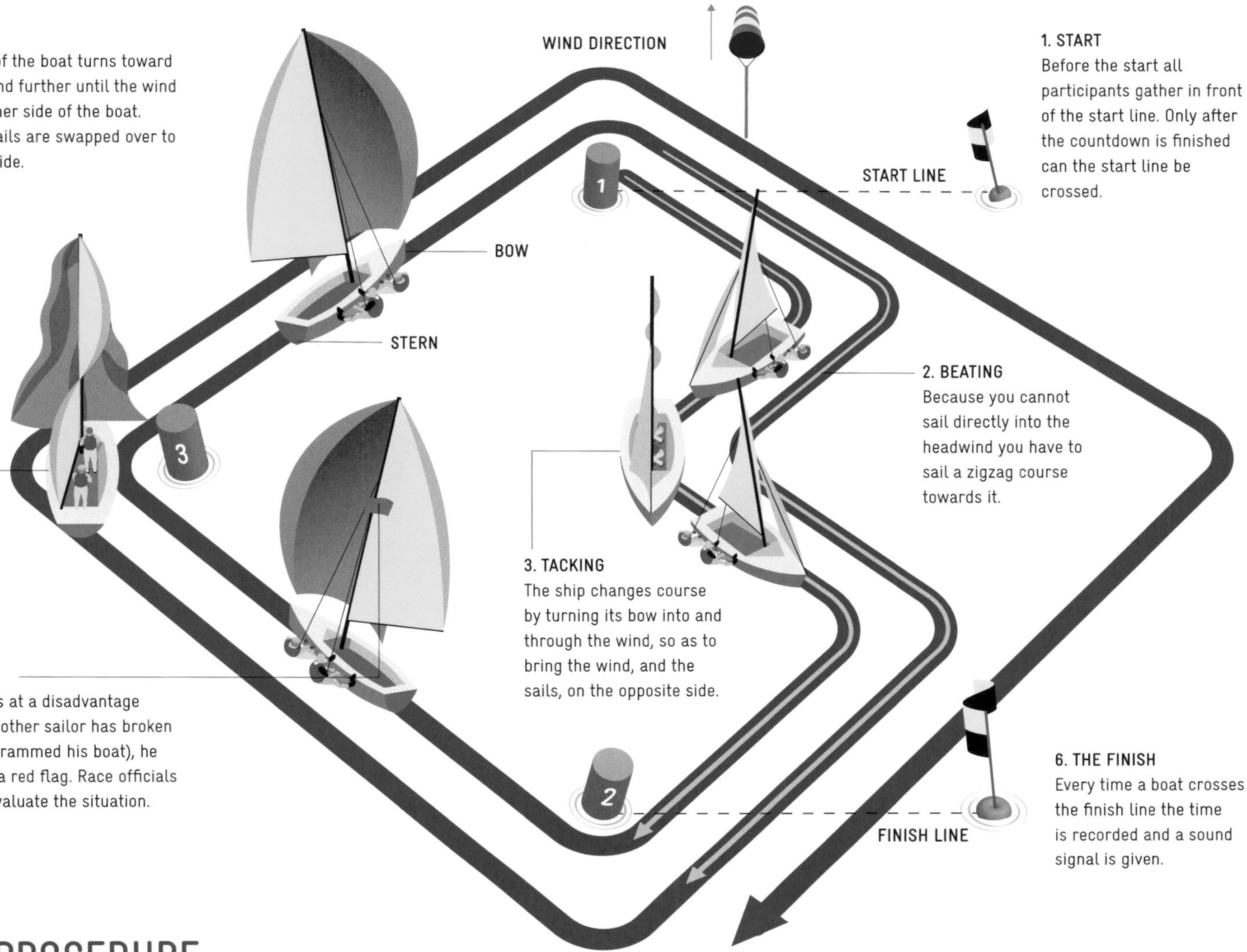

1. START
Before the start all participants gather in front of the start line. Only after the countdown is finished can the start line be crossed.

2. BEATING
Because you cannot sail directly into the headwind you have to sail a zigzag course towards it.

3. TACKING
The ship changes course by turning its bow into and through the wind, so as to bring the wind, and the sails, on the opposite side.

4. PROTEST
If a sailor is at a disadvantage because another sailor has broken a rule (e.g. rammed his boat), he can signal a red flag. Race officials will then evaluate the situation.

5. JIBING
The stern of the boat turns toward the wind and further until the wind hits the other side of the boat. Then the sails are swapped over to the other side.

6. THE FINISH
Every time a boat crosses the finish line the time is recorded and a sound signal is given.

THE PROCEDURE

THE REGATTA OFFICE
is responsible for the regatta. It manages the organization of the event, announcements and overall administration.

RACE CONTROL
is responsible for the execution of the race on water. They place the buoys, oversee the start, penalize any rule breakers and determine the winner.

WORLD OF SAILING
»WOS« is the institution that sets the competition rules.

REGISTRATION
Weeks or months before the regatta, the participants have to register. With some regattas (e.g. the America's Cup) teams challenge others to participate.

THE HELMSMAN BRIEFING
Before each regatta, the sailors discuss the race procedure. All the sailors meet for the helmsman briefing.

THE START
Race control conducts the start that follows a certain pattern.

THE FINISH
The finish times are recorded. In regattas with mixed boat types, points are calculated using the yardstick system.

THE AWARD CEREMONY
The fastest sailor is honored. The most celebrated regattas are the Olympic Games and the America's Cup.

470ER
1963
12.7 m²
103
2 regattas

49ER FX
2012
19.6 m²
(not determined)

49ER
1995
21.2 m²
82

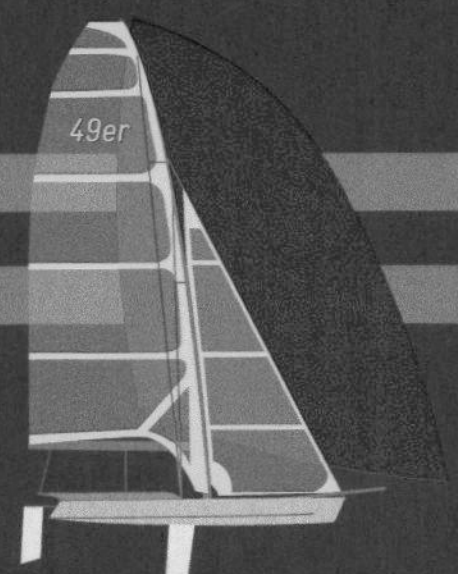

NACRA 17
2011
20.1 m²
(not determined)

REGATTA COMPETITION RULES

Regatta races follow certain rules. If crew don't obey these rules, they are penalized. Penalties can even be imposed during races. After severe offenses (e.g. a penalty is ignored) crews can be disqualified.

WIND DIRECTION

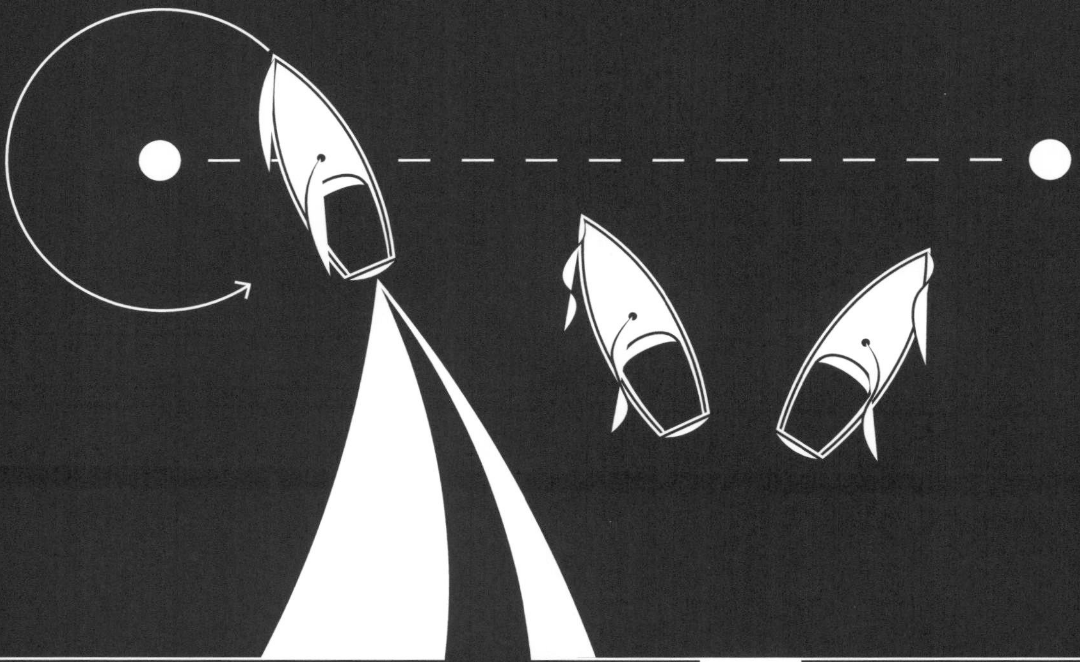

JUMP START

If a boat crosses the starting line too early, it has to cross it again by going around the outside of the race marker.

PORT TACK BEFORE STARBOARD TACK

The white boat is sailing windward with wind coming from starboard (right) side. It has the sails on »port tack« (left), and therefore has the right of way.

AN OVERTAKING VESSEL MUST KEEP CLEAR

When a boat is much faster than the other it can overtake leeward or windward but it must stay clear of the vessel it overtakes.

Leeward means towards the wind and windward is in the direction of the wind.

LEEWARD

WINDWARD

LEEWARD BEFORE WINDWARD

If two boats are on collision course and sailing on the same tack, then the boat sailing leeward has the right of way (the white one).

TOUCHING A RACE MARKER

Touching race markers during the regatta is not allowed. If it does happen, the crew is not disqualified but has to complete a full circle by tacking and jibing.

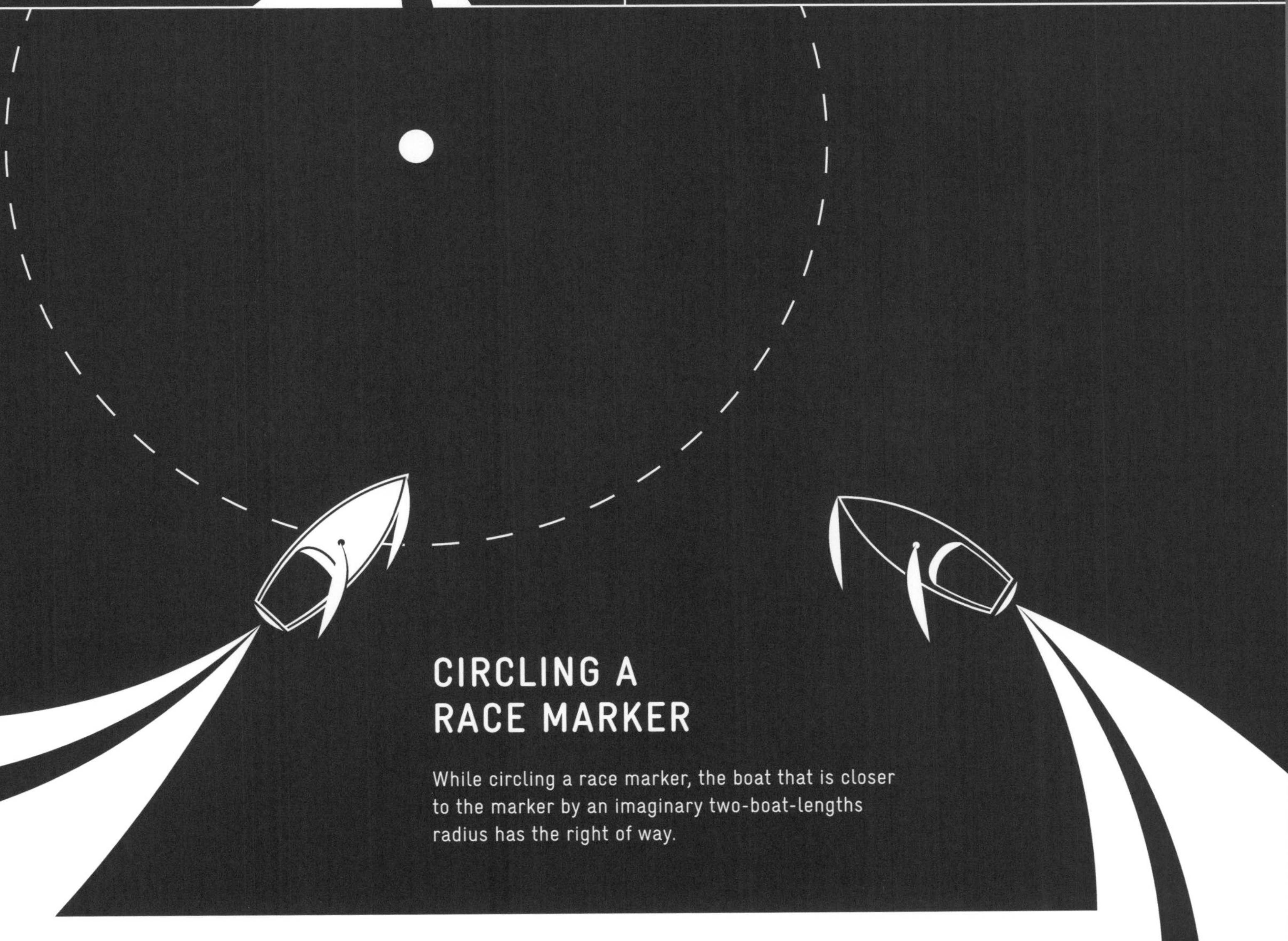

CIRCLING A RACE MARKER

While circling a race marker, the boat that is closer to the marker by an imaginary two-boat-lengths radius has the right of way.

WORLD OF STADIUMS

One of the most famous buildings marking the start of civilization is the Colosseum in Rome, built in 80 AD. Spectator sports have changed since then, but cities are still constructed themselves around these vast arenas of entertainment. Today's stadiums are designed and outfitted for individual sports as fans from all walks of life pack the seats to the rafters to cheer for their home team.

The Indianapolis Speedway is the largest stadium in the US with 257,325 seats.
USE OF STADIUMS
Soccer
Football | Rugby
Basketball
Hockey
Baseball
Bullfighting
Cricket
Car racing
Equestrian sports
Other
CAPACITIES
150
257,325

The graphic shows a selection of 7,258 stadiums and their construction date.

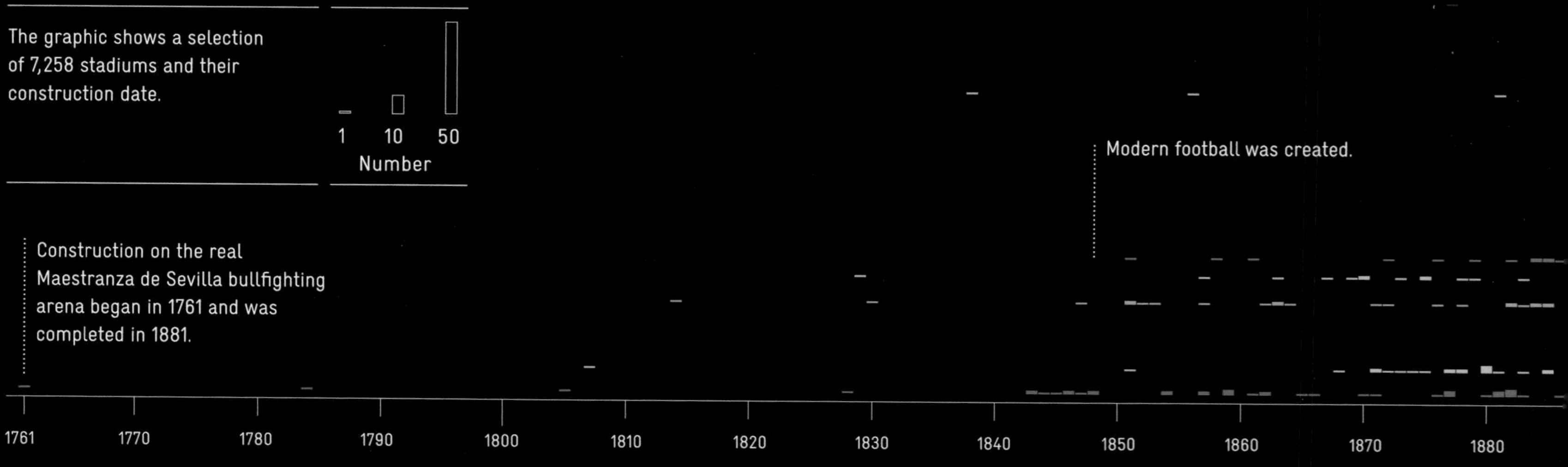
1
10
50
Number
Construction on the real Maestranza de Sevilla bullfighting arena began in 1761 and was completed in 1881.
Modern football was created.
1761
1770
1780
1790
1800
1810
1820
1830
1840
1850
1860
1870
1880

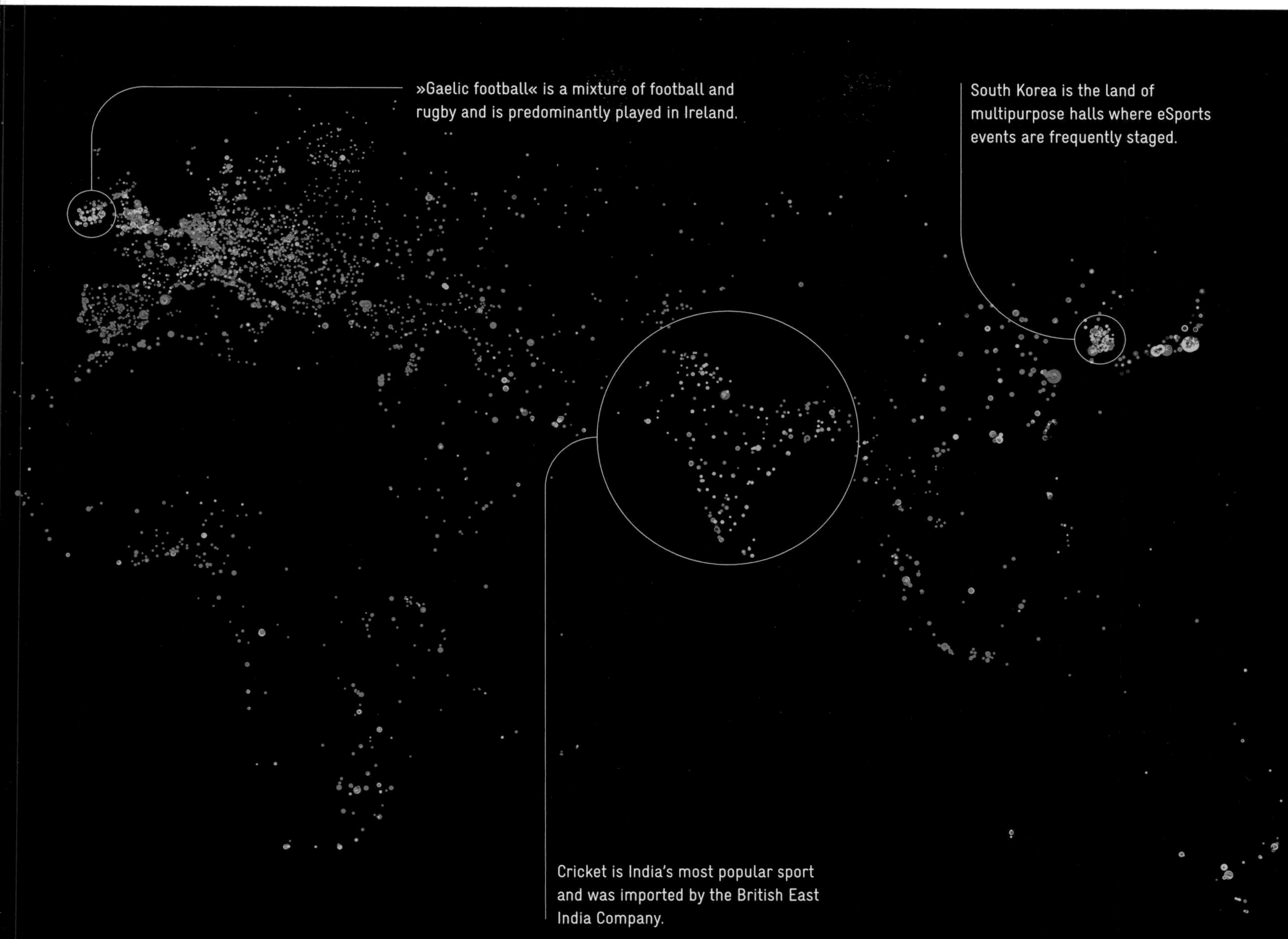
»Gaelic football« is a mixture of football and rugby and is predominantly played in Ireland.
South Korea is the land of multipurpose halls where eSports events are frequently staged.
Cricket is India's most popular sport and was imported by the British East India Company.

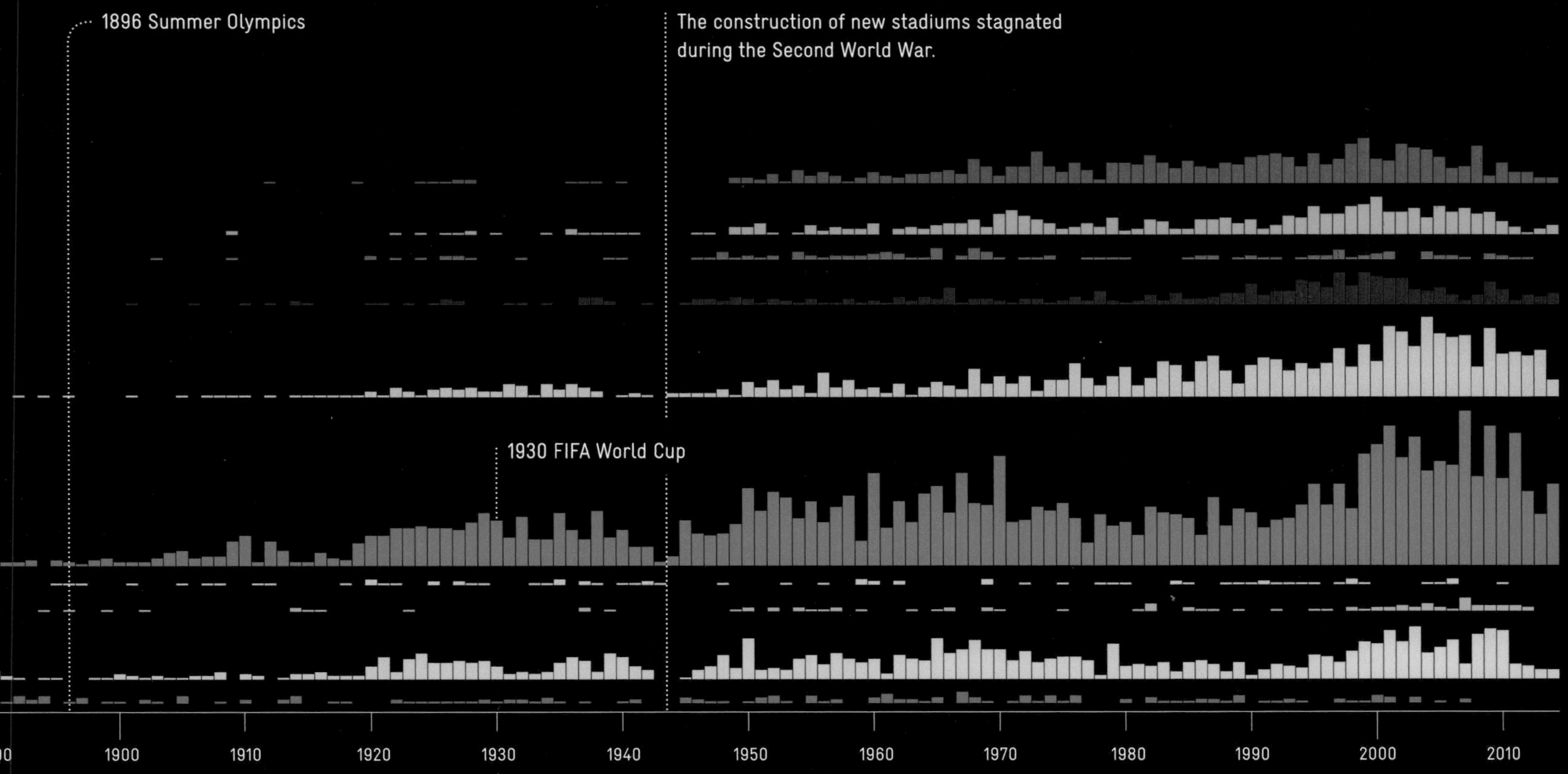
1896 Summer Olympics
The construction of new stadiums stagnated during the Second World War.
1930 FIFA World Cup
1900
1910
1920
1930
1940
1950
1960
1970
1980
1990
2000
2010

FC BAYERN MÜNCHEN
SV WERDER BREMEN
HAMBURGER SV
VFB STUTTGART
BORUSSIA DORTMUND
BORUSSIA MÖNCHENGLADBACH
FC SCHALKE 04
1. FC KÖLN
1. FC KAISERSLAUTERN
EINTRACHT FRANKFURT
BAYER 04 LEVERKUSEN
VFL BOCHUM
HERTHA BSC
1. FC NÜRNBERG
MSV DUISBURG
HANNOVER 96
KARLSRUHER SC
FORTUNA DÜSSELDORF
TSV 1860 MÜNCHEN
EINTRACHT BRAUNSCHWEIG
VFL WOLFSBURG
ARMINIA BIELEFELD
SC FREIBURG
KFC UERDINGEN 05
F.C. HANSA ROSTOCK
1. FSV MAINZ 05
SV WALDHOF MANNHEIM
KICKERS OFFENBACH
ROT-WEISS ESSEN
FC ST. PAULI
TSG 1899 HOFFENHEIM
FC ENERGIE COTTBUS
ALEMANNIA AACHEN
SG WATTENSCHEID 09
1. FC SAARBRÜCKEN
SG DYNAMO DRESDEN
SC ROT-WEIß OBERHAUSEN
WUPPERTALER SV
BORUSSIA NEUNKIRCHEN
FC 08 HOMBURG
SPVGG UNTERHACHING
STUTTGARTER KICKERS
FC AUGSBURG
SV DARMSTADT 98
TENNIS BORUSSIA BERLIN
SSV ULM 1846
SC FORTUNA KÖLN
SC PREUßEN 06 MÜNSTER
SPVGG GREUTHER FÜRTH
BLAU-WEIß 90 BERLIN
VFB LEIPZIG
SC TASMANIA 1900 BERLIN

1963 – 2013

JOY DIVISIÓN

There is no photo or video recording of the first goal scored in the newly founded German Soccer League. In 1963, 23-year-old Dortmund striker Timo Konietzka scored that goal just 58 seconds into the match against Bremen. Journalists hadn't yet taken their seats. Things have come a long way since then. The opening game of the 50th anniversary season of the DFB (Deutsche Fussball Bund) 2012/2013 season was broadcast live in more than 200 countries. Stadiums welcome around 13 million fans each year. A total of 52 clubs have played in the Premier League. Bayern Munich dominates the league, with 23 titles, ending the 50th DFB season as league champions, cup winners and Champions League winners.

The graphic shows all end-of-season placings from 1963 to 2013.

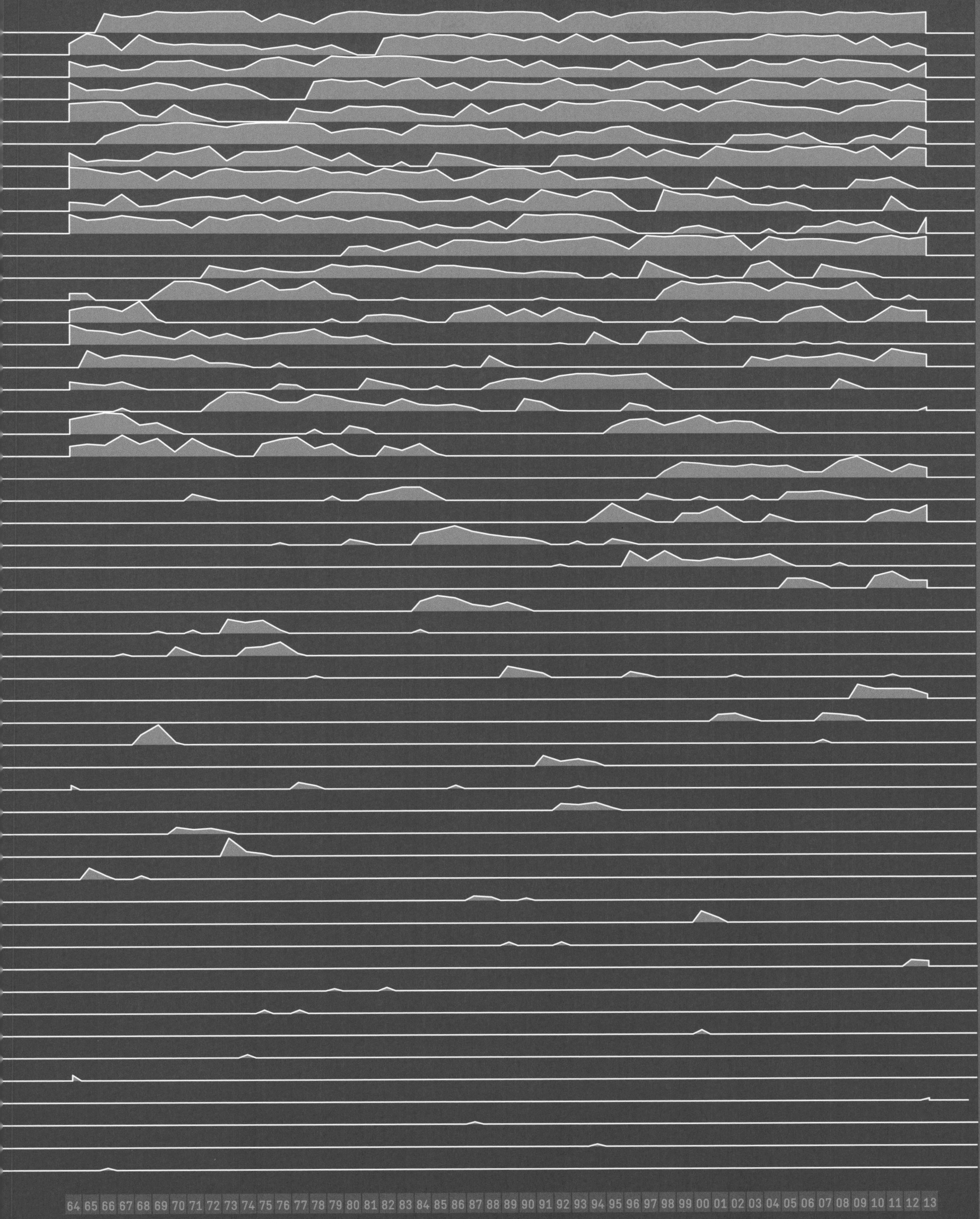
64 65 66 67 68 69 70 71 72 73 74 75 76 77 78 79 80 81 82 83 84 85 86 87 88 89 90 91 92 93 94 95 96 97 98 99 00 01 02 03 04 05 06 07 08 09 10 11 12 13

ETERNAL LEAGUE TABLE

HIGHEST VALUE LOWEST VALUE

		WINS	CHAMPIONS	2ND	YEARS	MATCHES	GOALS	GOAL DIFFERENCE	POINTS	Ø-POINTS
1.	FC BAYERN MUNICH	936	22	10	48	1,636	3,510:1,861	1,649	3,186	1.95
2.	SV WERDER BREMEN	717	4	7	49	1,662	2,834:2,360	474	2,564	1.54
3.	HAMBURGER SV	701	3	5	50	1,696	2,759:2,377	382	2,561	1.51
4.	VFB STUTTGART	692	3	2	48	1,628	2,760:2,325	435	2,474	1.52
5.	BORUSSIA DORTMUND	669	5	3	46	1,560	2,706:2,241	465	2,416	1.55
6.	BORUSSIA MÖNCHENGLADBACH	608	5	2	45	1,534	2,620:2,259	361	2,237	1.46
7.	FC SCHALKE 04	597		6	45	1,526	2,253:2,199	54	2,174	1.42
8.	1. FC KÖLN	593	2	5	43	1,458	2,459:2,170	289	2,140	1.47
9.	1. FC KAISERSLAUTERN	575	2	1	44	1,492	2,348:2,344	4	2,094	1.40
10.	EINTRACHT FRANKFURT	552			44	1,492	2,376:2,313	63	2,031	1.36
11.	BAYER 04 LEVERKUSEN	485		5	34	1,160	1,933:1,559	374	1,786	1.54
12.	VFL BOCHUM	356			34	1,160	1,602:1,887	-285	1,374	1.18
13.	HERTHA BSC	372		1	30	1,012	1,466:1,559	-93	1,372	1.36
14.	1. FC NÜRNBERG	336	1		31	1,050	1,365:1,656	-291	1,273	1.21
15.	MSV DUISBURG	296		1	28	948	1,291:1,520	-229	1,147	1.21
16.	HANNOVER 96	265			25	846	1,193:1,432	-239	1,010	1.19
17.	KARLSRUHER SC	241			24	812	1,093:1,408	-315	953	1.17
18.	FORTUNA DÜSSELDORF	245			23	786	1,160:1,386	-226	950	1.21
19.	TSV 1860 MÜNCHEN	238	1	1	20	672	1,022:1,059	-37	884	1.32
20.	EINTRACHT BRAUNSCHWEIG	236	1		20	672	908:1,026	-118	878	1.31
21.	VFL WOLFSBURG	201	1		16	544	813:814	-1	741	1.36
22.	ARMINIA BIELEFELD	153			16	544	645:883	-238	598	1.10
23.	SC FREIBURG	150			14	476	603:756	-153	565	1.19
24.	KFC UERDINGEN 05	138			14	476	644:844	-200	543	1.14
25.	F.C. HANSA ROSTOCK	124			12	412	492:621	-129	479	1.16
26.	1. FSV MAINZ 05	78			7	238	307:335	-28	301	1.26
27.	SV WALDHOF MANNHEIM	71			7	238	299:378	-79	285	1.20
28.	KICKERS OFFENBACH	77			7	238	368:486	-118	282	1.18
29.	ROT-WEISS ESSEN	61			7	238	346:483	-137	262	1.10
30.	FC ST. PAULI	58			8	272	296:485	-189	254	0.93
31.	TSG 1899 HOFFENHEIM	55			5	170	240:255	-15	212	1.25
32.	FC ENERGIE COTTBUS	56			6	204	211:338	-127	211	1.03
33.	ALEMANNIA AACHEN	43		1	4	136	186:270	-84	157	1.15
34.	SG WATTENSCHEID 09	34			4	140	186:248	-62	150	1.07
35.	1. FC SAARBRÜCKEN	32			5	166	202:336	-134	144	0.87
36.	SG DYNAMO DRESDEN	33			4	140	132:211	-79	140	1.00
37.	SC ROT-WEIß OBERHAUSEN	36			4	136	182:281	-99	139	1.02
38.	WUPPERTALER SV	25			3	102	136:200	-64	102	1.00
39.	BORUSSIA NEUNKIRCHEN	25			3	98	109:223	-114	93	0.95
40.	FC 08 HOMBURG	21			3	102	103:200	-97	90	0.88
41.	SPVGG UNTERHACHING	20			2	68	75:101	-26	79	1.16
42.	STUTTGARTER KICKERS	20			2	72	94:132	-38	77	1.07
43.	FC AUGSBURG	16			2	68	69:100	-31	71	1.04
44.	SV DARMSTADT 98	12			2	68	86:157	-71	54	0.79
45.	TENNIS BORUSSIA BERLIN	11			2	68	85:174	-89	49	0.72
46.	SSV ULM 1846	9			1	34	36:62	-26	35	1.03
47.	SC FORTUNA KÖLN	8			1	34	46:79	-33	33	0.97
48.	SC PREUßEN 06 MÜNSTER	7			1	30	34:52	-18	30	1.00
49.	SPVGG GREUTHER FÜRTH	4			1	34	26:60	-34	21	0.62
50.	BLAU-WEIß 90 BERLIN	3			1	34	36:76	-40	21	0.62
51.	VFB LEIPZIG	3			1	34	32:69	-37	20	0.59
52.	SC TASMANIA 1900 BERLIN	2			1	34	15:108	-93	10	0.29

THE MOST COMMON RESULTS

FINAL SCORE / NUMBER OF MATCHES

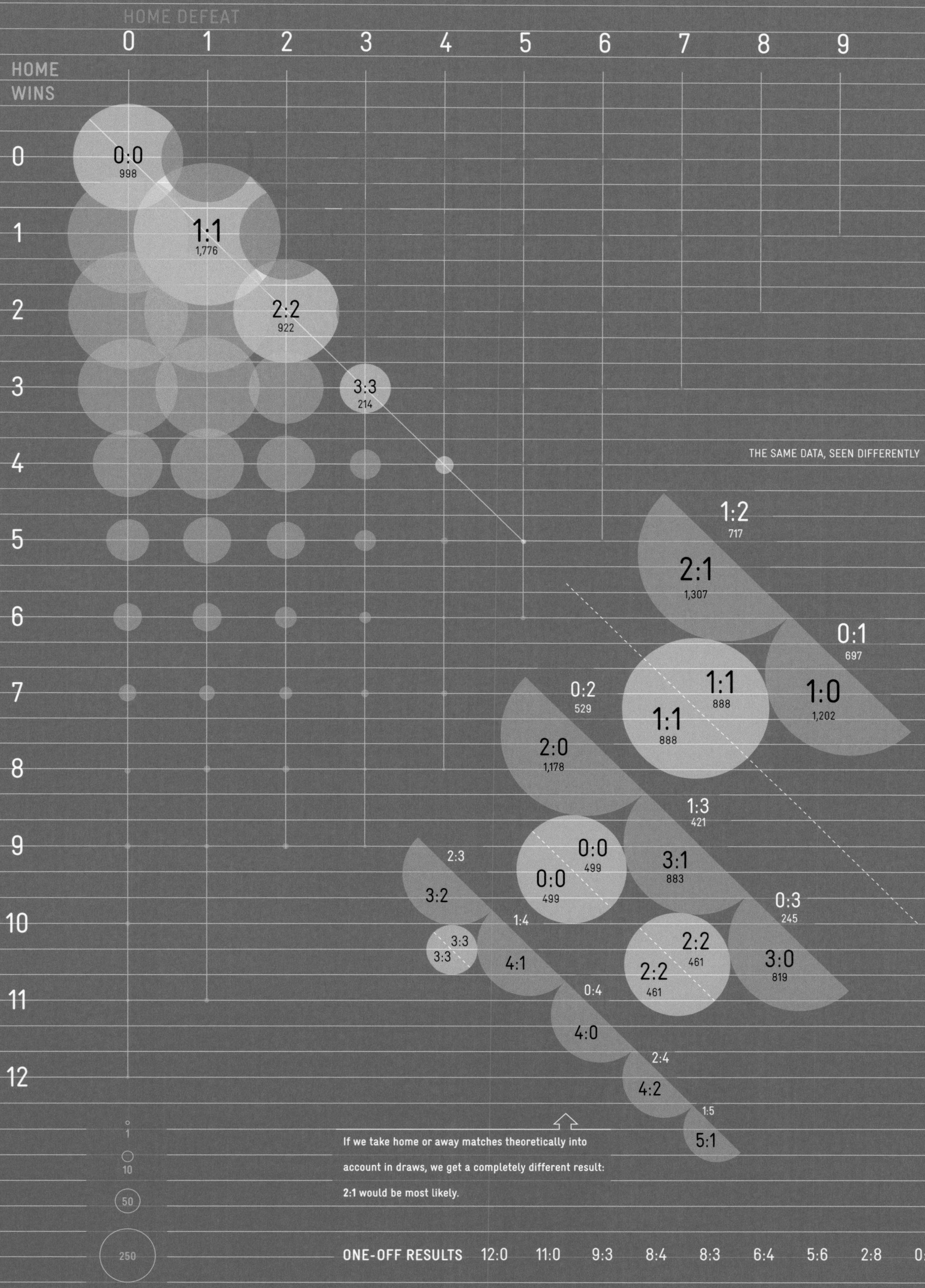
HOME DEFEAT
0 1 2 3 4 5 6 7 8 9
HOME WINS
0 1 2 3 4 5 6 7 8 9 10 11 12
0:0 998
1:1 1,776
2:2 922
3:3 214
THE SAME DATA, SEEN DIFFERENTLY
1:2 717
2:1 1,307
0:1 697
1:0 1,202
1:1 888
1:1 888
0:2 529
2:0 1,178
1:3 421
3:1 883
0:0 499
0:0 499
2:3
3:2
0:3 245
3:0 819
1:4
4:1
3:3
3:3
2:2 461
2:2 461
0:4
4:0
2:4
4:2
1:5
5:1
1
10
50
250

If we take home or away matches theoretically into account in draws, we get a completely different result: 2:1 would be most likely.

ONE-OFF RESULTS 12:0 11:0 9:3 8:4 8:3 6:4 5:6 2:8 0:9

TRANSFER CALLIGRAPHY

Soccer is by far the sport in which the highest transfer fees are paid. The current record holder is Neymar with € 222 million. In the graph below, the width of the strokes symbolizes the fees paid for the player in question. The numbered dots indicate the club to which they were transfered.

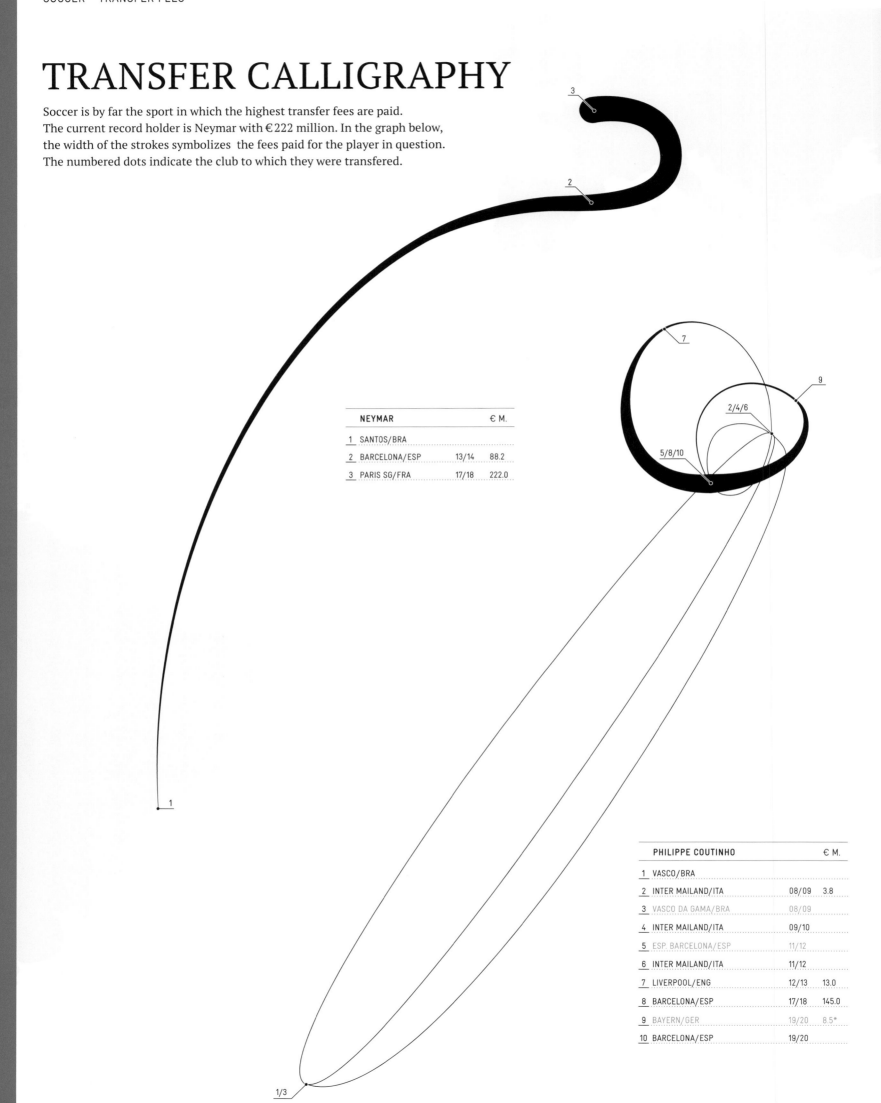

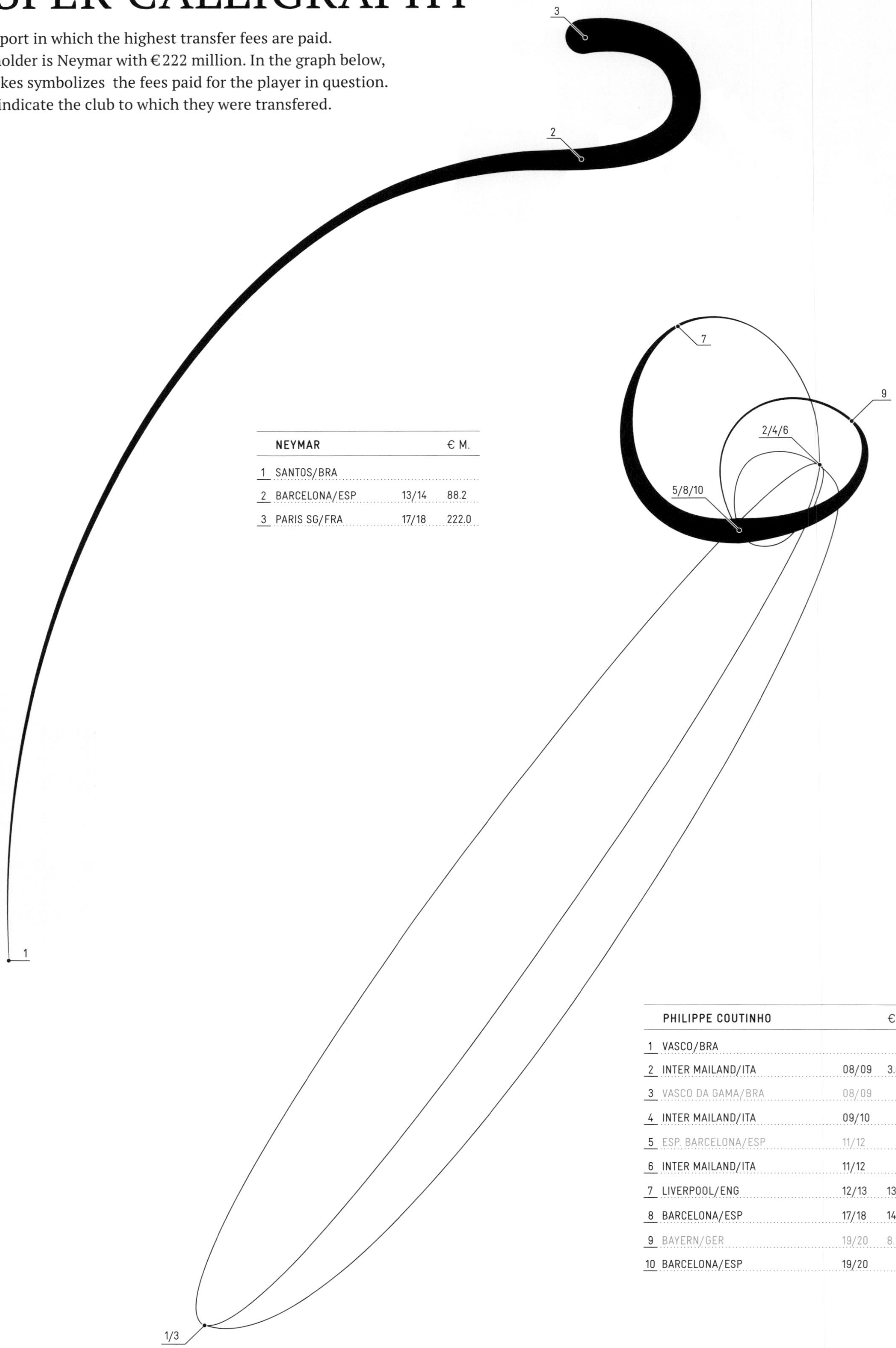

	NEYMAR		€ M.
1	SANTOS/BRA		
2	BARCELONA/ESP	13/14	88.2
3	PARIS SG/FRA	17/18	222.0

	PHILIPPE COUTINHO		€ M.
1	VASCO/BRA		
2	INTER MAILAND/ITA	08/09	3.8
3	VASCO DA GAMA/BRA	08/09	
4	INTER MAILAND/ITA	09/10	
5	ESP. BARCELONA/ESP	11/12	
6	INTER MAILAND/ITA	11/12	
7	LIVERPOOL/ENG	12/13	13.0
8	BARCELONA/ESP	17/18	145.0
9	BAYERN/GER	19/20	8.5*
10	BARCELONA/ESP	19/20	

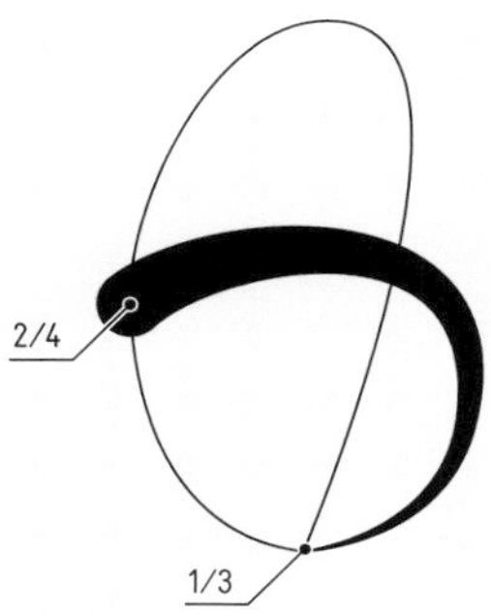

KEY

	PLAYER'S NAME		€ M.
1	FIRST CLUB/COUNTRY		
2	SECOND CLUB/COUNTRY	Season	Transfer fee

* LENT, lending fee

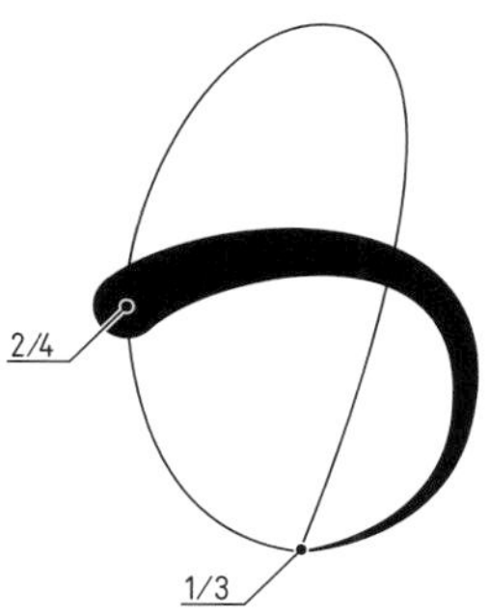

	KYLIAN MBAPPÉ		€ M.
1	AS MONACO /MCO		
2	PSG/FRA	17/18	35.0*
3	AS MONACO /MCO	17/18	
4	PSG/FRA	18/19	145.0

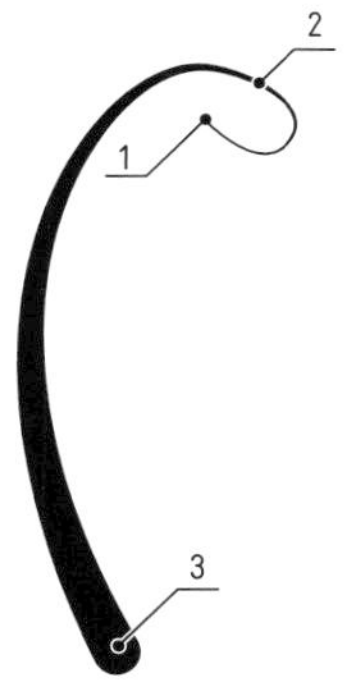

	GARETH BALE		€ M.
1	SOUTHAMPTON/ENG		
2	TOTTENHAM/ENG	07/08	14.7
3	REAL MADRID/ESP	13/14	101.0

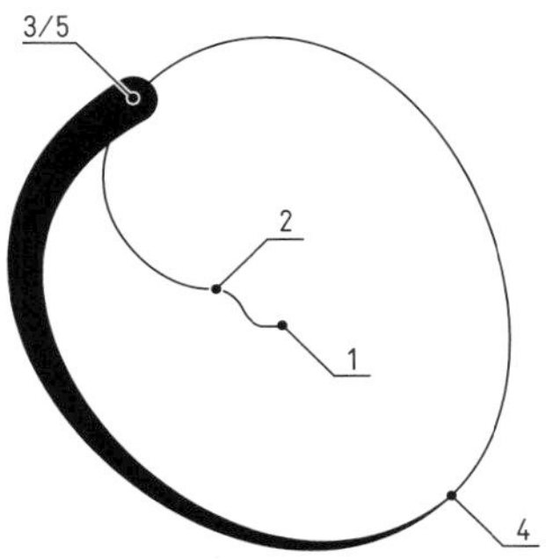

	PAUL POGBA		€ M.
1	US TORCY/FRA		
2	LE HAVRE/FRA	07/08	
3	MANCHESTER UNITED/ENG	09/10	
4	JUVENTUS TURIN/ITA	16/17	
5	MANCHESTER UNITED/ENG	16/17	105.0

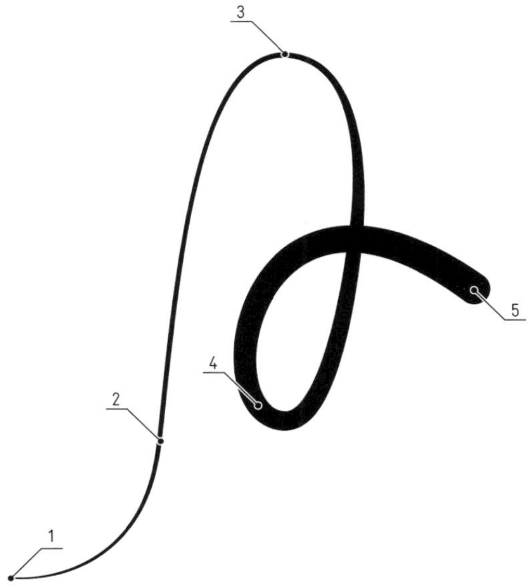

	CRISTIANO RONALDO		€ M.
1	NACIONAL /POR		
2	SPORTING/POR	97/98	
3	MANCHESTER UNITED/ENG	03/04	19.0
4	REAL MADRID/ESP	09/10	94.0
5	JUVENTUS TURIN/ITA	18/19	117.0

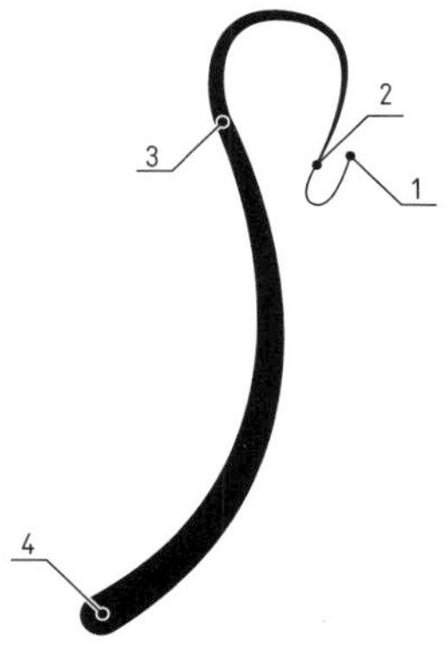

	EDEN HAZARD		€ M.
1	TUBIZE/BEL		
2	LOSC LILLE/FRA	05/06	
3	CHELSEA/ENG	12/13	35.0
4	REAL MADRID/ESP	19/20	100.0

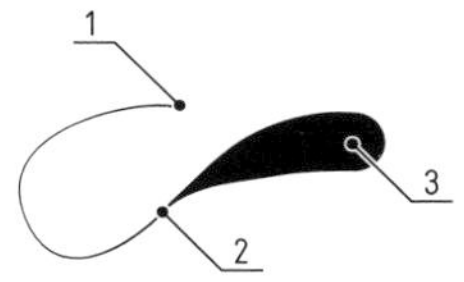

	JOÃO FÉLIX		€ M.
1	PORTO/POR		
2	BENFICA/POR	15/16	
3	ATLETICO MADRID/ESP	19/20	126.0

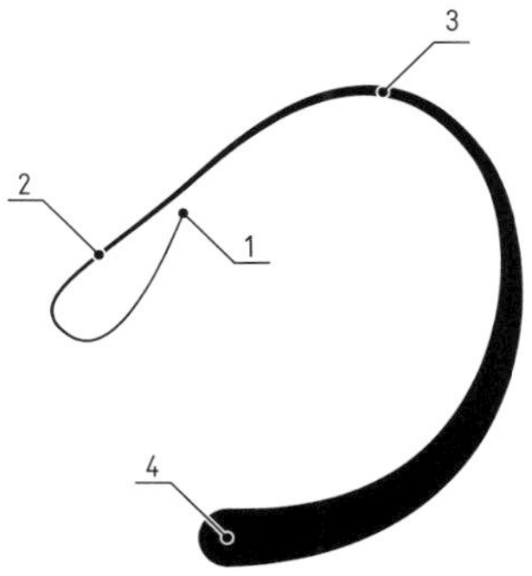

	OUSMANE DEMBÉLÉ		€ M.
1	EVREUX FC/FRA		
2	STADE RENNES/FRA	10/11	
3	BORUSSIA DORTMUND/GER	16/17	15.0
4	BARCELONA/ESP	17/18	125.0

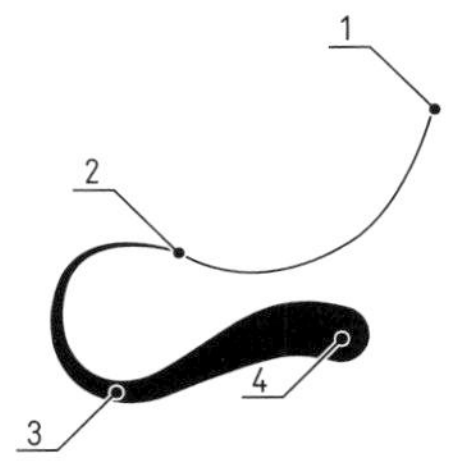

	ANTOINE GRIEZMANN		€ M.
1	MACONNAIS/FRA		
2	REAL SOCIEDAD/FRA	05/06	
3	ATLETICO MADRID/ESP	14/15	54.0
4	BARCELONA/ESP	19/20	120.0

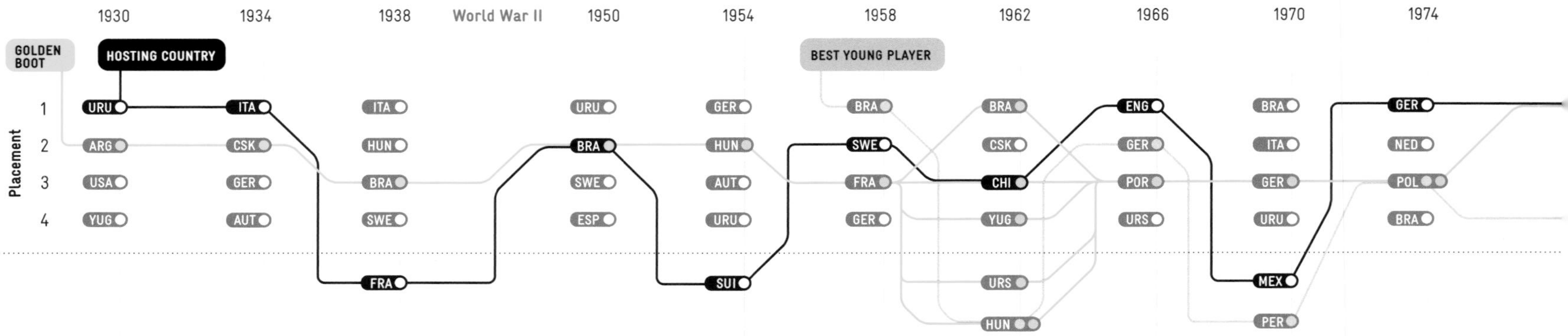

FEVER PITCH

The history of the soccer World Cup in facts and figures

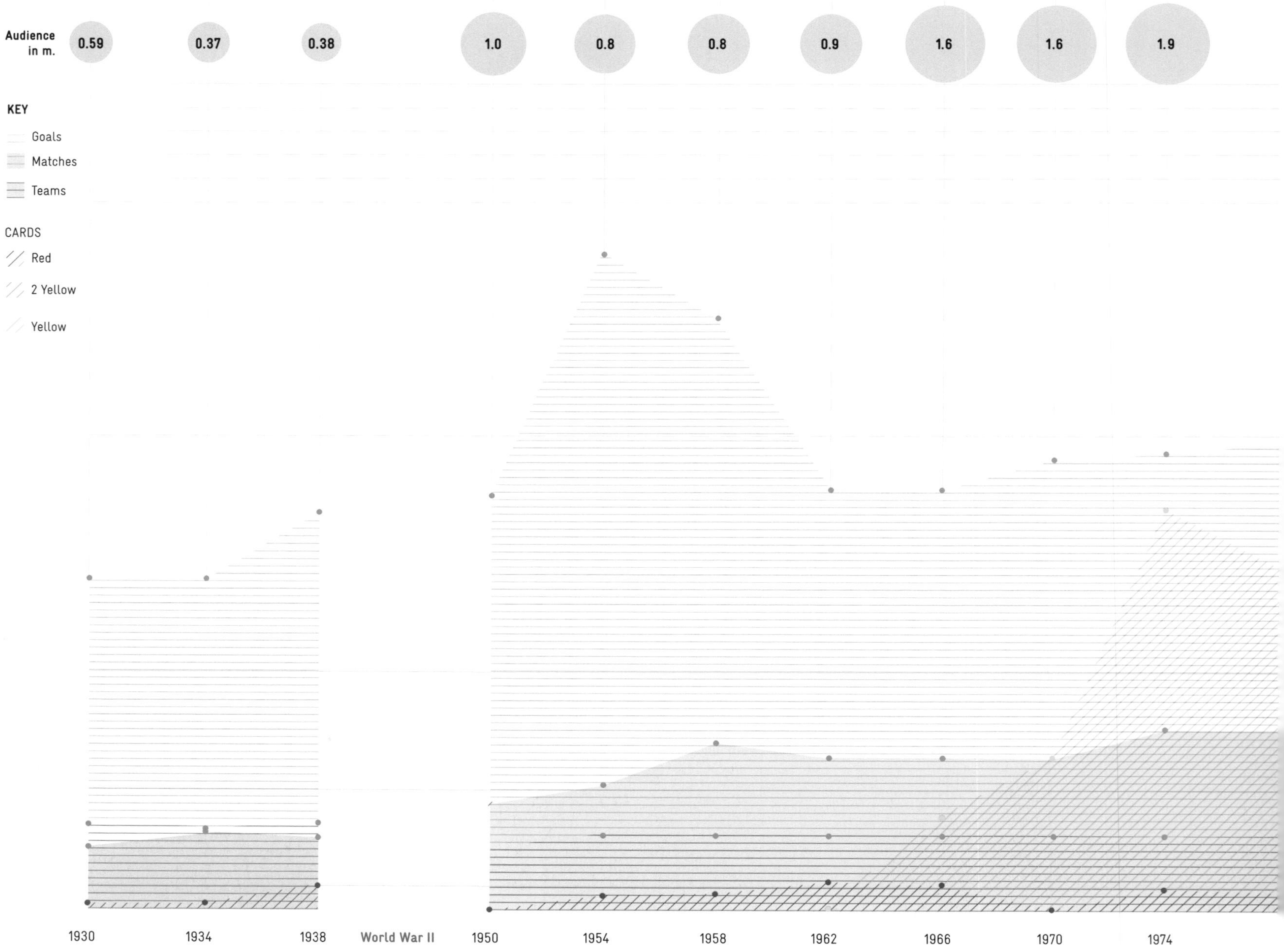

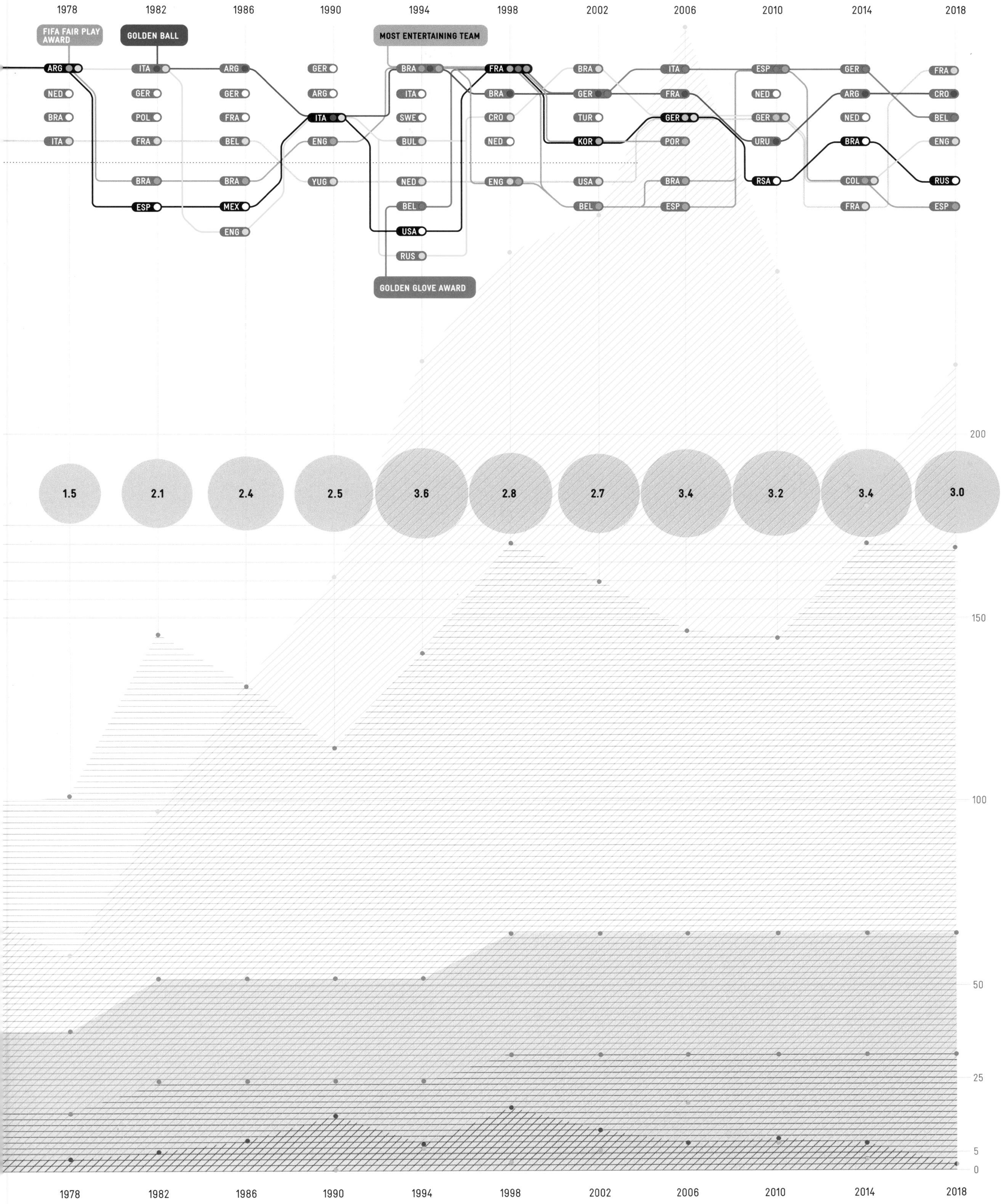

1978
1982
1986
1990
1994
1998
2002
2006
2010
2014
2018
FIFA FAIR PLAY AWARD
GOLDEN BALL
MOST ENTERTAINING TEAM
GOLDEN GLOVE AWARD
ARG
NED
BRA
ITA
ITA
GER
POL
FRA
BRA
ESP
ARG
GER
FRA
BEL
BRA
MEX
ENG
GER
ARG
ITA
ENG
YUG
BRA
ITA
SWE
BUL
NED
BEL
USA
RUS
FRA
BRA
CRO
NED
ENG
BRA
GER
TUR
KOR
USA
BEL
ITA
FRA
GER
POR
BRA
ESP
ESP
NED
GER
URU
RSA
GER
ARG
NED
BRA
COL
FRA
FRA
CRO
BEL
ENG
RUS
ESP
1.5
2.1
2.4
2.5
3.6
2.8
2.7
3.4
3.2
3.4
3.0
200
150
100
50
25
5
0

THE WORLD'S HIGHEST MOUNTAINS

Reaching the peak of all fourteen 8000ers is the dream of every mountaineer — but only a few have mangaed it so far.
Most people try to climb Mount Everest and even though it is the highest mountain, it is not the one with the highest death rate.

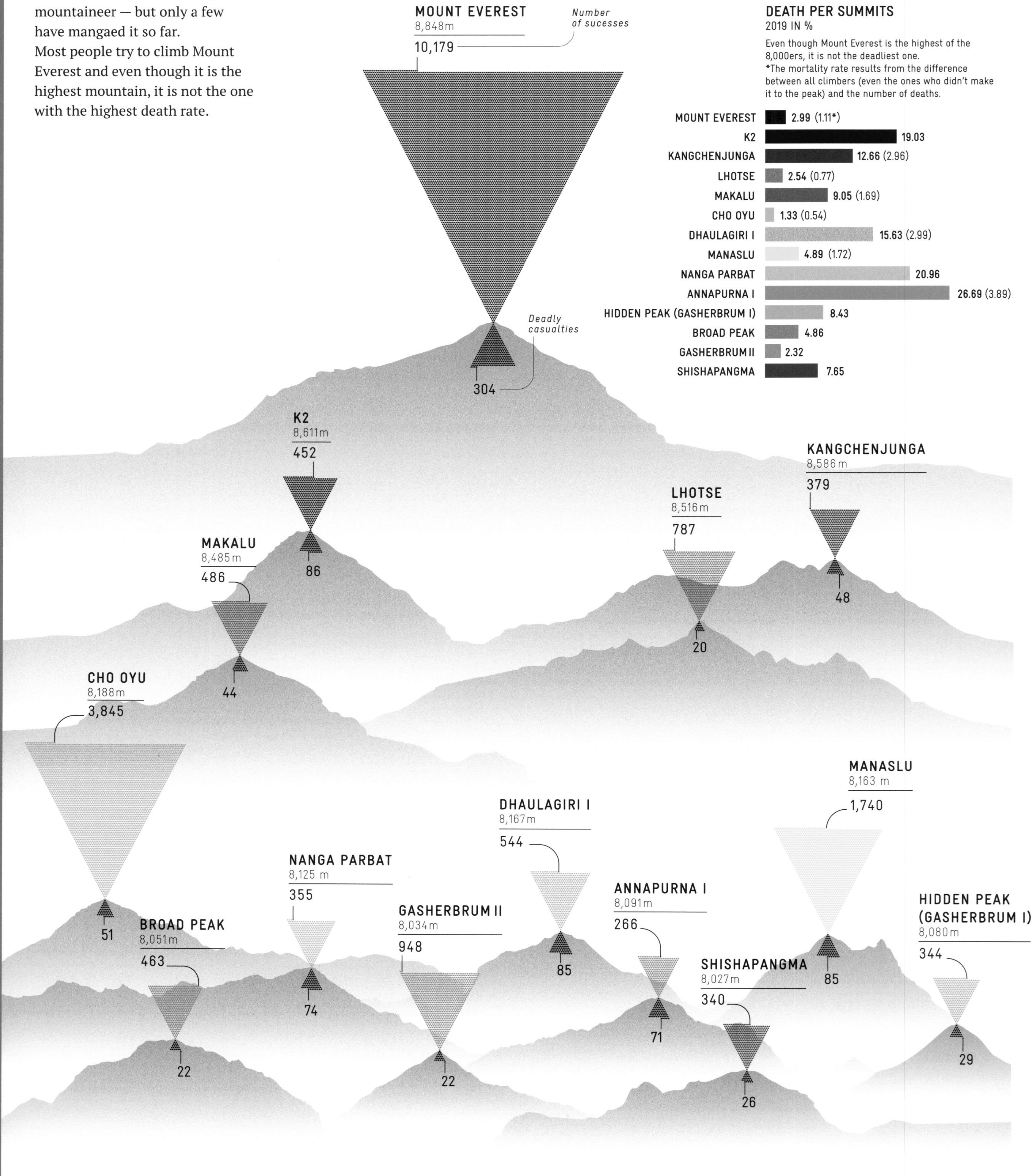
MOUNT EVEREST
8,848m
10,179
Number of sucesses
Deadly casualties
304
DEATH PER SUMMITS
2019 IN %
Even though Mount Everest is the highest of the 8,000ers, it is not the deadliest one.
*The mortality rate results from the difference between all climbers (even the ones who didn't make it to the peak) and the number of deaths.
MOUNT EVEREST 2.99 (1.11*)
K2 19.03
KANGCHENJUNGA 12.66 (2.96)
LHOTSE 2.54 (0.77)
MAKALU 9.05 (1.69)
CHO OYU 1.33 (0.54)
DHAULAGIRI I 15.63 (2.99)
MANASLU 4.89 (1.72)
NANGA PARBAT 20.96
ANNAPURNA I 26.69 (3.89)
HIDDEN PEAK (GASHERBRUM I) 8.43
BROAD PEAK 4.86
GASHERBRUM II 2.32
SHISHAPANGMA 7.65
K2
8,611m
452
86
KANGCHENJUNGA
8,586m
379
48
LHOTSE
8,516m
787
20
MAKALU
8,485m
486
44
CHO OYU
8,188m
3,845
51
MANASLU
8,163 m
1,740
85
DHAULAGIRI I
8,167m
544
85
NANGA PARBAT
8,125 m
355
74
ANNAPURNA I
8,091m
266
71
HIDDEN PEAK (GASHERBRUM I)
8,080m
344
29
BROAD PEAK
8,051m
463
22
GASHERBRUM II
8,034m
948
22
SHISHAPANGMA
8,027m
340
26

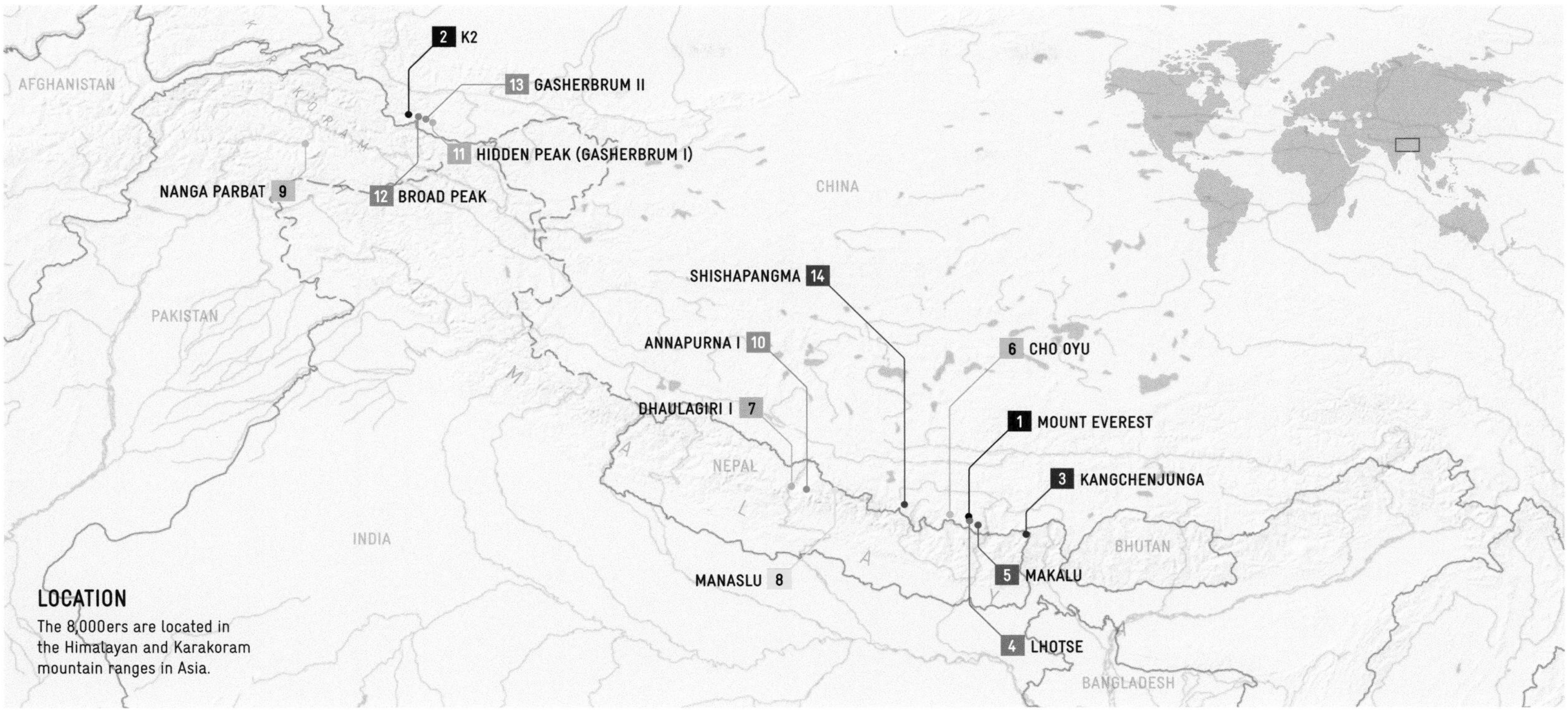
2 K2
13 GASHERBRUM II
11 HIDDEN PEAK (GASHERBRUM I)
12 BROAD PEAK
NANGA PARBAT 9
AFGHANISTAN
PAKISTAN
CHINA
INDIA
NEPAL
BHUTAN
BANGLADESH
SHISHAPANGMA 14
ANNAPURNA I 10
DHAULAGIRI I 7
6 CHO OYU
1 MOUNT EVEREST
3 KANGCHENJUNGA
5 MAKALU
4 LHOTSE
MANASLU 8

LOCATION

The 8,000ers are located in the Himalayan and Karakoram mountain ranges in Asia.

FIRST ASCENTS

10 ANNAPURNA I
Louis Lachenal **FRA**, Maurice Herzog **FRA**

1 MOUNT EVEREST
Edmund Hillary **NZL**, Tenzing Norgay **NEP**

9 NANGA PARBAT
Hermann Buhl **AUT**

2 K2
Achille Compagnoni **ITA**, Lino Lacedelli **ITA**

6 CHO OYU
Josef Jöchler **AUT**, Herbert Tichy **AUT**, Pasang Dawa Lama **NEP**

3 KANGCHENJUNGA
George Band **GBR**, Joe Brown **GBR**

5 MAKALU
Lionel Terray **FRA**, Jean Couzy **FRA**

4 LHOTSE
Fritz Luchsinger **SUI**, Ernst Reiss **SUI**

8 MANASLU
Gyalzen Norbu **NEP**, Toshio Imanishi **JPN**

13 GASHERBRUM II
Fritz Moravec **AUT**, Josef Larch **AUT**, Hans Willenpart **AUT**

12 BROAD PEAK
Hermann Buhl **AUT**, Kurt Diemberger **AUT**, Marcus Schmuck **AUT**, Fritz Wintersteller **AUT**

11 HIDDEN PEAK (GASHERBRUM I)
Peter K. Schoening **USA**, Andrew J. Kauffman **USA**

7 DHAULAGIRI I
Kurt Diemberger **AUT**, Albin Schelbert **AUT**, Nawang Dorje **NEP**, Nima Dorje **NEP**, Ernst Forrer **SUI**, Peter Diener **GER**

14 SHISHAPANGMA
Hsu Ching, Chang Chun-yen, Wang Fuzhou, Chen San, Cheng Tien-liang, Wu Tsung-yue, Sodnam Doji, Migmar Trashi, Doji, Yonten, alle **CHN**

ASCENTS OF ALL 8,000ERS**

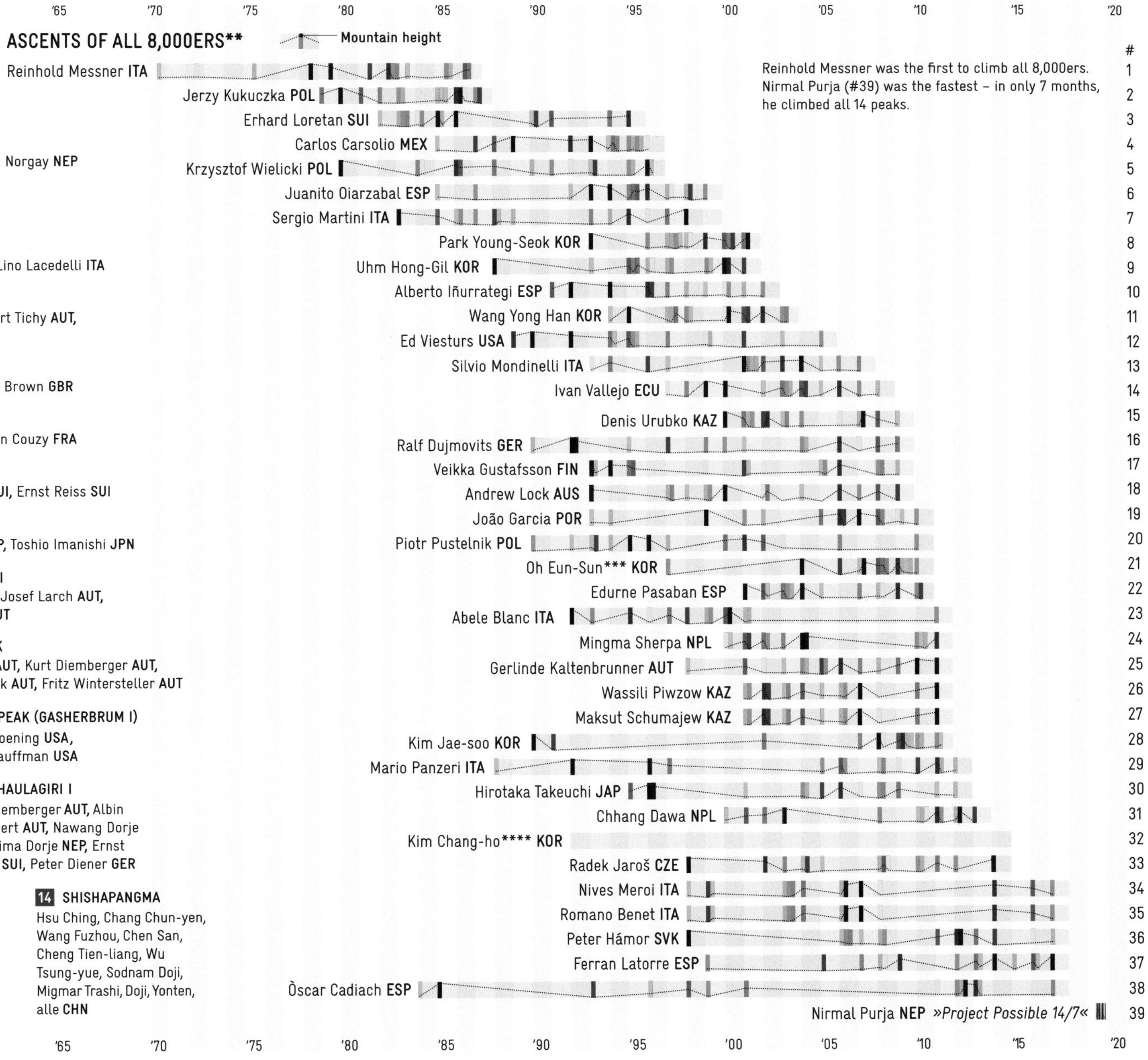
'50 '55 '60 '65 '70 '75 '80 '85 '90 '95 '00 '05 '10 '15 '20
Mountain height
#
Reinhold Messner was the first to climb all 8,000ers. Nirmal Purja (#39) was the fastest – in only 7 months, he climbed all 14 peaks.
Reinhold Messner ITA 1
Jerzy Kukuczka POL 2
Erhard Loretan SUI 3
Carlos Carsolio MEX 4
Krzysztof Wielicki POL 5
Juanito Oiarzabal ESP 6
Sergio Martini ITA 7
Park Young-Seok KOR 8
Uhm Hong-Gil KOR 9
Alberto Iñurrategi ESP 10
Wang Yong Han KOR 11
Ed Viesturs USA 12
Silvio Mondinelli ITA 13
Ivan Vallejo ECU 14
Denis Urubko KAZ 15
Ralf Dujmovits GER 16
Veikka Gustafsson FIN 17
Andrew Lock AUS 18
João Garcia POR 19
Piotr Pustelnik POL 20
Oh Eun-Sun*** KOR 21
Edurne Pasaban ESP 22
Abele Blanc ITA 23
Mingma Sherpa NPL 24
Gerlinde Kaltenbrunner AUT 25
Wassili Piwzow KAZ 26
Maksut Schumajew KAZ 27
Kim Jae-soo KOR 28
Mario Panzeri ITA 29
Hirotaka Takeuchi JAP 30
Chhang Dawa NPL 31
Kim Chang-ho**** KOR 32
Radek Jaroš CZE 33
Nives Meroi ITA 34
Romano Benet ITA 35
Peter Hámor SVK 36
Ferran Latorre ESP 37
Òscar Cadiach ESP 38
Nirmal Purja NEP »Project Possible 14/7« 39
'50 '55 '60 '65 '70 '75 '80 '85 '90 '95 '00 '05 '10 '15 '20

** only the first ascents of the main peaks are shown, regardless of the use of oxygen
*** the legitimacy of Oh Eun-Sun's achievements is a much disputed topic (a few more climbers have reached the top in questionable ways, but they are not shown here).
**** no further information available

1 Mountains of Data

All of the existing data relating to the number and timing of summit ascents have enabled us to create a 3D-model which shows the growth of tourism and peak season in one picture. Our calendar starts in July in order to emphasize the peak season in May.

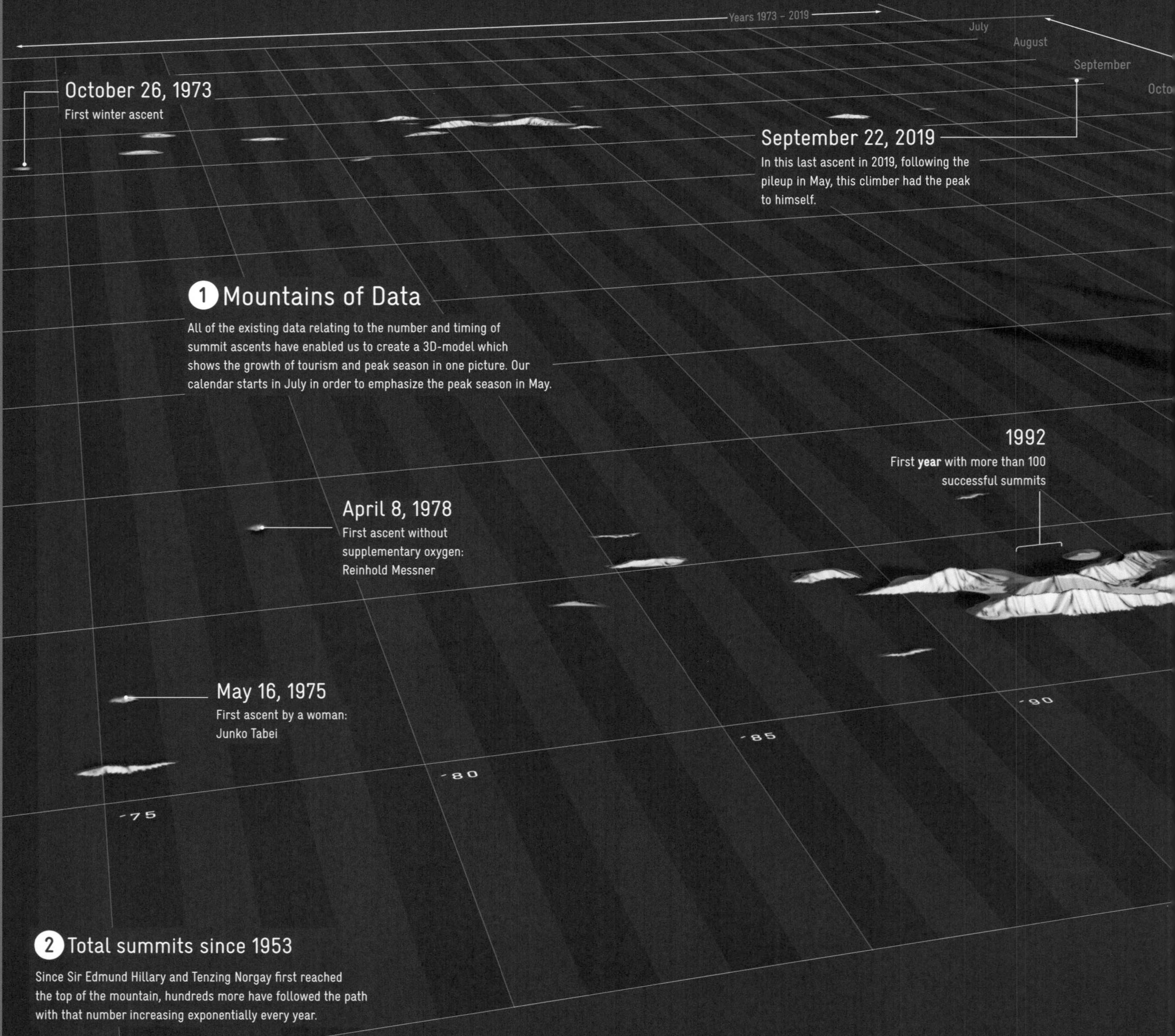
Years 1973 – 2019
July
August
September
October 26, 1973
First winter ascent
September 22, 2019
In this last ascent in 2019, following the pileup in May, this climber had the peak to himself.
1992
First **year** with more than 100 successful summits
April 8, 1978
First ascent without supplementary oxygen: Reinhold Messner
May 16, 1975
First ascent by a woman: Junko Tabei
-75
-80
-85
-90

2 Total summits since 1953

Since Sir Edmund Hillary and Tenzing Norgay first reached the top of the mountain, hundreds more have followed the path with that number increasing exponentially every year.

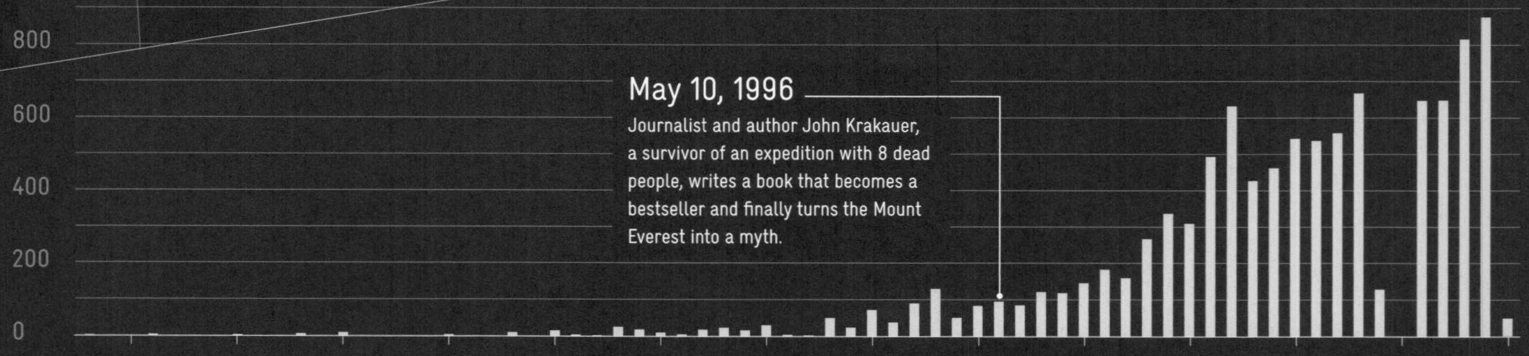
800
600
400
200
0
May 10, 1996
Journalist and author John Krakauer, a survivor of an expedition with 8 dead people, writes a book that becomes a bestseller and finally turns the Mount Everest into a myth.

TO THE TOP OF THE WORLD

Climbing all 8,848 meters of Mount Everest was once considered an impossible feat. But in 1953 the impossible had become possible. Today, the tallest peak in the world has become a destination for any thrillseeker who can afford it.

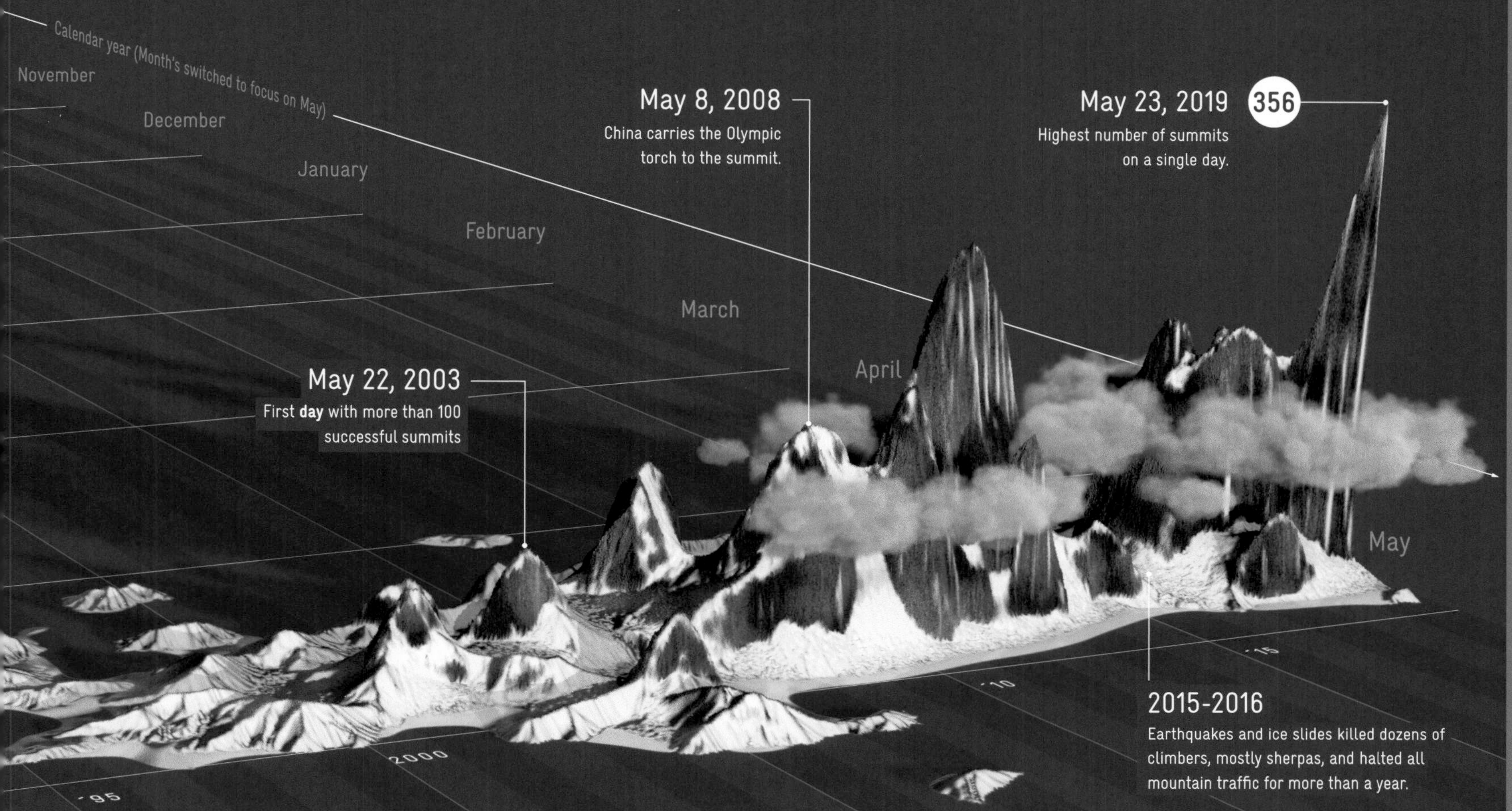

3 Peak season

In any year, the period in which the wind, temperature and precipitation are manageable is very short. The optimal time is at the end of May and nearly all successful summits over time have used this window.

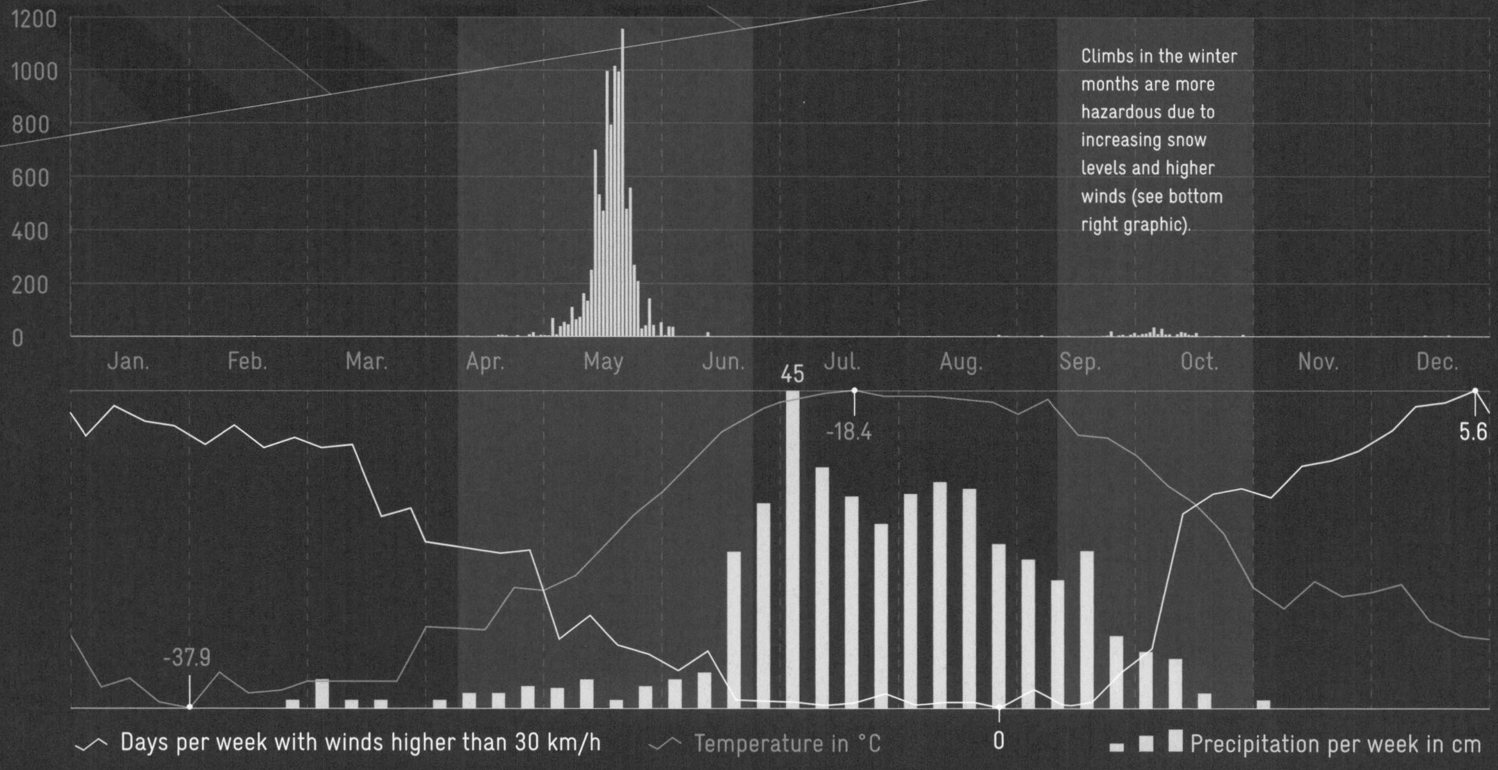

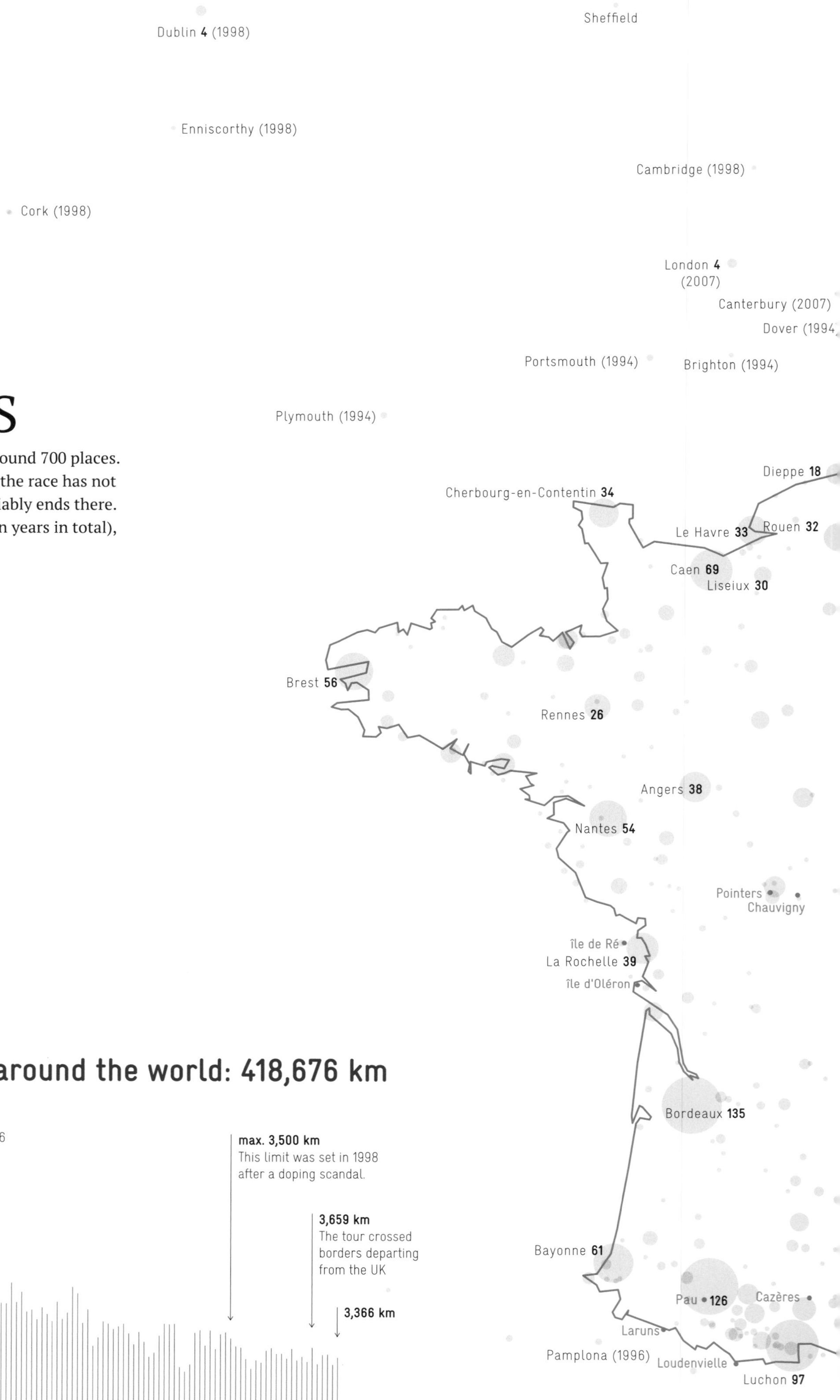
Dublin 4 (1998)
Sheffield
Enniscorthy (1998)
Cambridge (1998)
Cork (1998)
London 4 (2007)
Canterbury (2007)
Dover (1994)
Portsmouth (1994)
Brighton (1994)
Plymouth (1994)
Dieppe 18
Cherbourg-en-Contentin 34
Le Havre 33
Rouen 32
Caen 69
Liseiux 30
Brest 56
Rennes 26
Angers 38
Nantes 54
Pointers
Chauvigny
île de Ré
La Rochelle 39
île d'Oléron
Bordeaux 135
Bayonne 61
Pau 126
Cazères
Laruns
Pamplona (1996)
Loudenvielle
Luchon 97

106 RACES IN 117 YEARS

Since 1903, the route has passed through around 700 places. Paris has always been a part of it– although the race has not always started in »the city of light«, it invariably ends there. During World War I and World War II (eleven years in total), there was no touring.

In 106 races 10.4 times around the world: 418,676 km

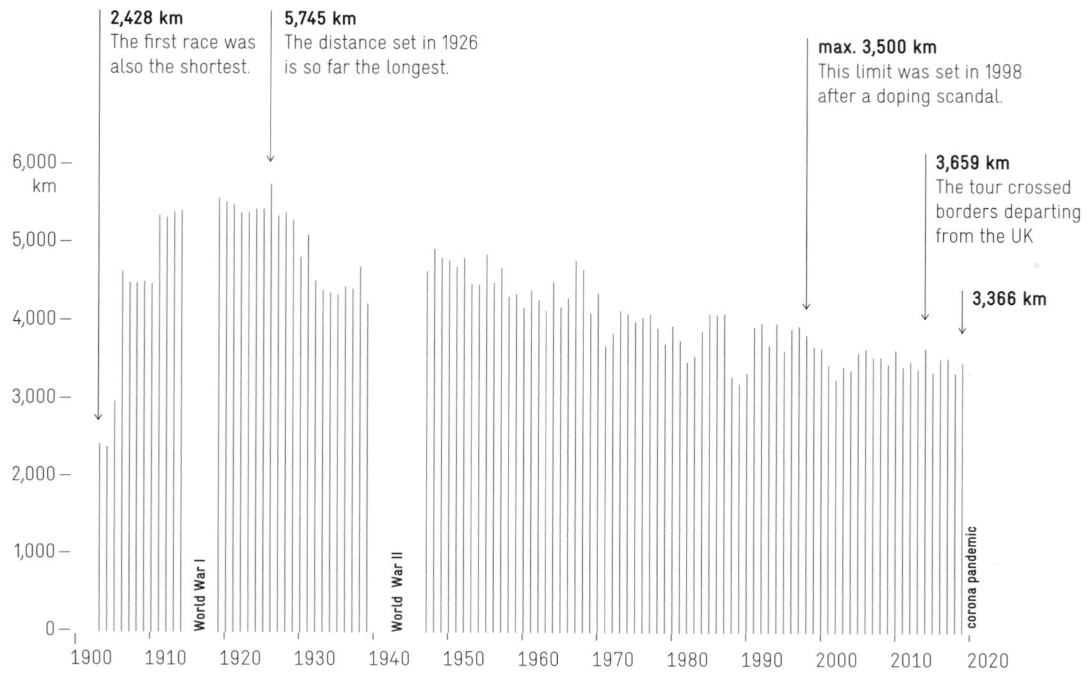
2,428 km
The first race was also the shortest.
5,745 km
The distance set in 1926 is so far the longest.
max. 3,500 km
This limit was set in 1998 after a doping scandal.
3,659 km
The tour crossed borders departing from the UK
3,366 km
6,000 – km
5,000 –
4,000 –
3,000 –
2,000 –
1,000 –
0 –
World War I
World War II
corona pandemic
1900
1910
1920
1930
1940
1950
1960
1970
1980
1990
2000
2010
2020

Outside French borders

The Tour de France first left French territory in **1907** – for Metz, which at the time still was German. Since then, the Tour de France has passed through many European cities, including London, Amsterdam and the then-divided Berlin.

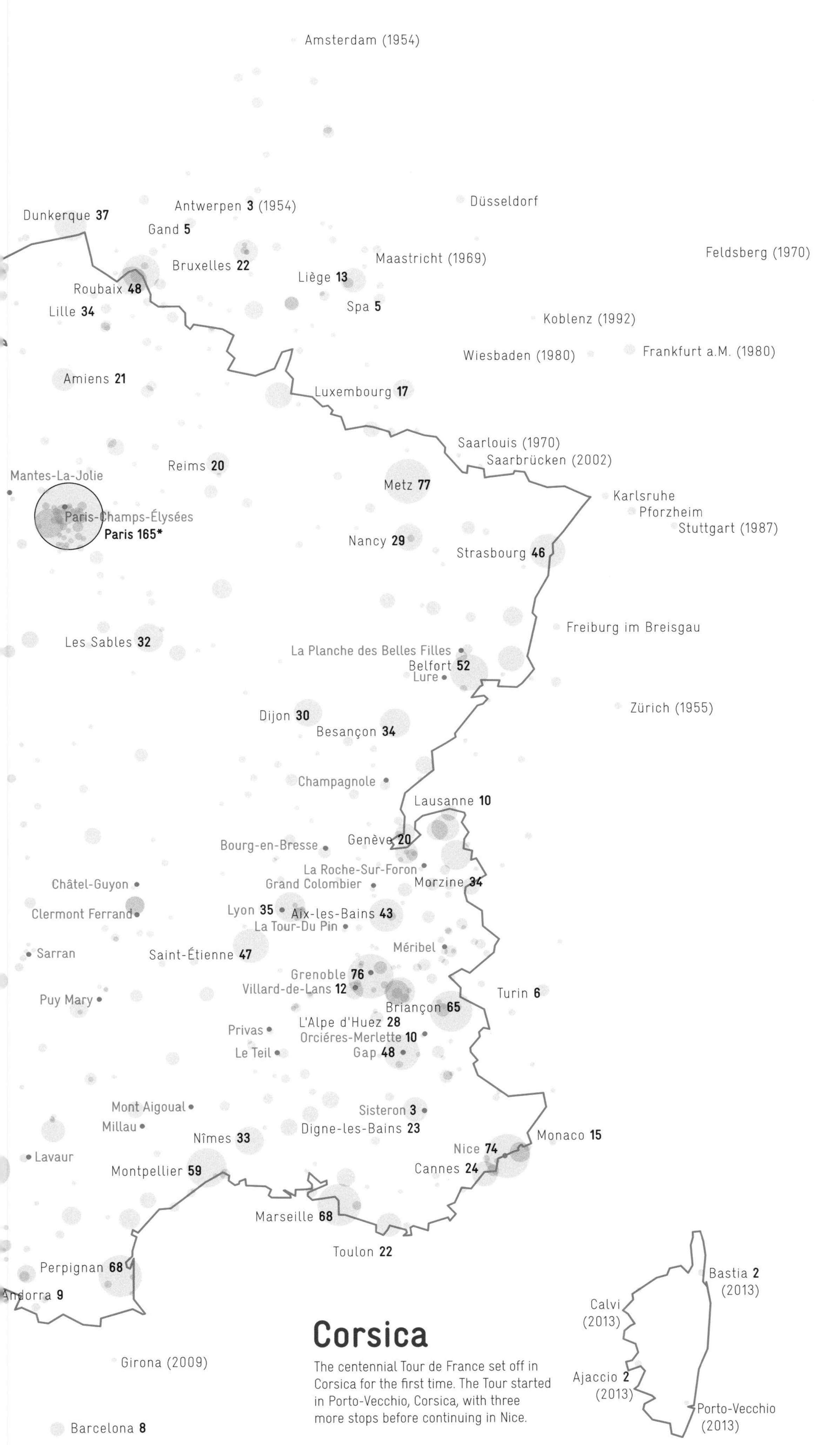

Berlin **6** (1987)
Amsterdam (1954)
Dunkerque **37**
Antwerpen **3** (1954)
Gand **5**
Düsseldorf
Bruxelles **22**
Maastricht (1969)
Feldsberg (1970)
Roubaix **48**
Liège **13**
Spa **5**
Lille **34**
Koblenz (1992)
Wiesbaden (1980)
Frankfurt a.M. (1980)
Amiens **21**
Luxembourg **17**
Saarlouis (1970)
Saarbrücken (2002)
Mantes-La-Jolie
Reims **20**
Metz **77**
Karlsruhe
Pforzheim
Paris-Champs-Élysées
Paris **165***
Stuttgart (1987)
Nancy **29**
Strasbourg **46**
Freiburg im Breisgau
Les Sables **32**
La Planche des Belles Filles
Belfort **52**
Lure
Zürich (1955)
Dijon **30**
Besançon **34**
Champagnole
Lausanne **10**
Bourg-en-Bresse
Genève **20**
La Roche-Sur-Foron
Châtel-Guyon
Grand Colombier
Morzine **34**
Clermont Ferrand
Lyon **35**
Aix-les-Bains **43**
La Tour-Du Pin
Méribel
Sarran
Saint-Étienne **47**
Grenoble **76**
Villard-de-Lans **12**
Turin **6**
Puy Mary
Briançon **65**
L'Alpe d'Huez **28**
Privas
Orciéres-Merlette **10**
Le Teil
Gap **48**
Mont Aigoual
Sisteron **3**
Millau
Digne-les-Bains **23**
Nîmes **33**
Monaco **15**
Lavaur
Nice **74**
Montpellier **59**
Cannes **24**
Marseille **68**
Toulon **22**
Perpignan **68**
Andorra **9**
Girona (2009)
Barcelona **8**
Bastia **2** (2013)
Calvi (2013)
Ajaccio **2** (2013)
Porto-Vecchio (2013)

Corsica

The centennial Tour de France set off in Corsica for the first time. The Tour started in Porto-Vecchio, Corsica, with three more stops before continuing in Nice.

NUMBER OF TIMES TOWN STAGES WERE INCLUDED IN A TOUR

(Counting the city or village of start and finish since 1903 to 2020)

• **Town Stages for 2020**

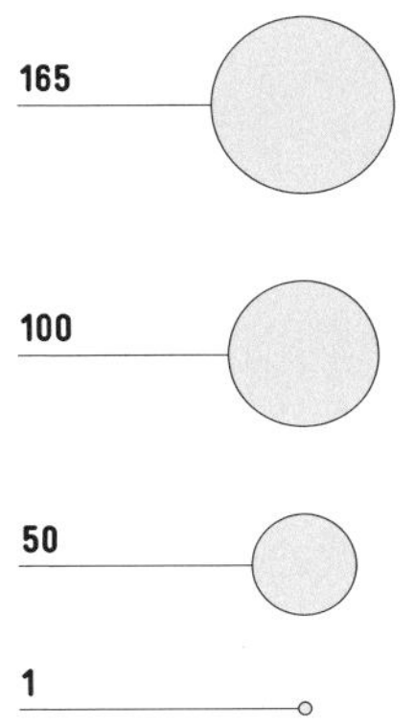

165
100
50
1

* Including the stages between areas:
- Paris (140)
- Paris Champs-Élysées (15)
- Le Touquet-Paris-Plage (5)
- Disneyland-Paris (4)
- Sèvres - Grand Paris Seine Ouest (1)

2300 STAGES

Around France and Europe between 1903-2020

TOUR OF DECEPTION

The Tour de France is the most famous and most gruelling bicycle race in the world. For many athletes, only the yellow jersey matters and they will do anything to get it. The Tour's reputation has been tarnished over the years by one doping scandal after another. Others win by dropping nails on the road, slipping sleeping pills into competitors' food, changing wheels without authorization, finding sneaky short cuts and pushing teammates. Athletes are stretched to the limit—as can be seen in the drop-out rates.

- Doping during the Tour de France
- Convicted of doping at some point in their career
- Suspected doping
- Other aids during the tour
- Victim of sabotage
- Placement denied

One Tour racer, Henri Pelissier, pulled a vial of cocaine from his jersey in front of journalists, stating: »the only way we can keep going ...«

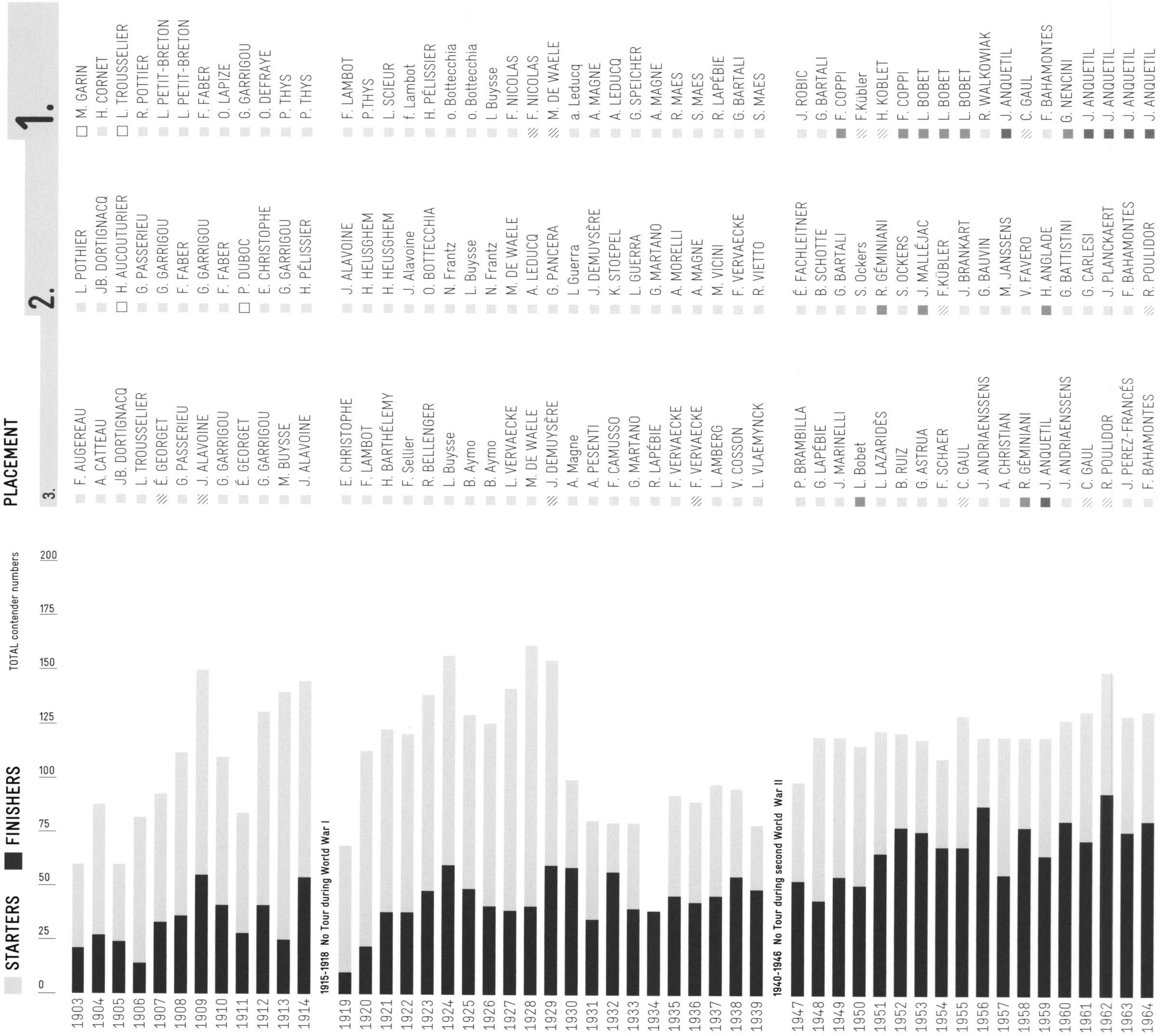

The top 5 doping methods in cycling

What exactly was taken by some athletes, and in what quantities, will probably remain a mystery. These are the most common doping agents used in the endurance sport of cycling.

Stimulants
Amphetamine,
Ephedrin

Act on the central nervous system and increase motoric activity.

Anabolic steroids
Testosterone,
Steroids

Affects metabolism: The protein structure in the muscles is increased and the percentage of body fat decreased.

Erythropoietin (EPO)

The hormone stimulates the production of red blood cells to increase the oxygenation in muscles.

Blood doping

Increases the red blood cells that carry oxygen to the muscles and organs. This may deliver a performance boost of up to 15%.

Agents that disguise doping
Probenecid

Substances that reduce the traceability of doping products, but have no performance-enhancing effect themselves.

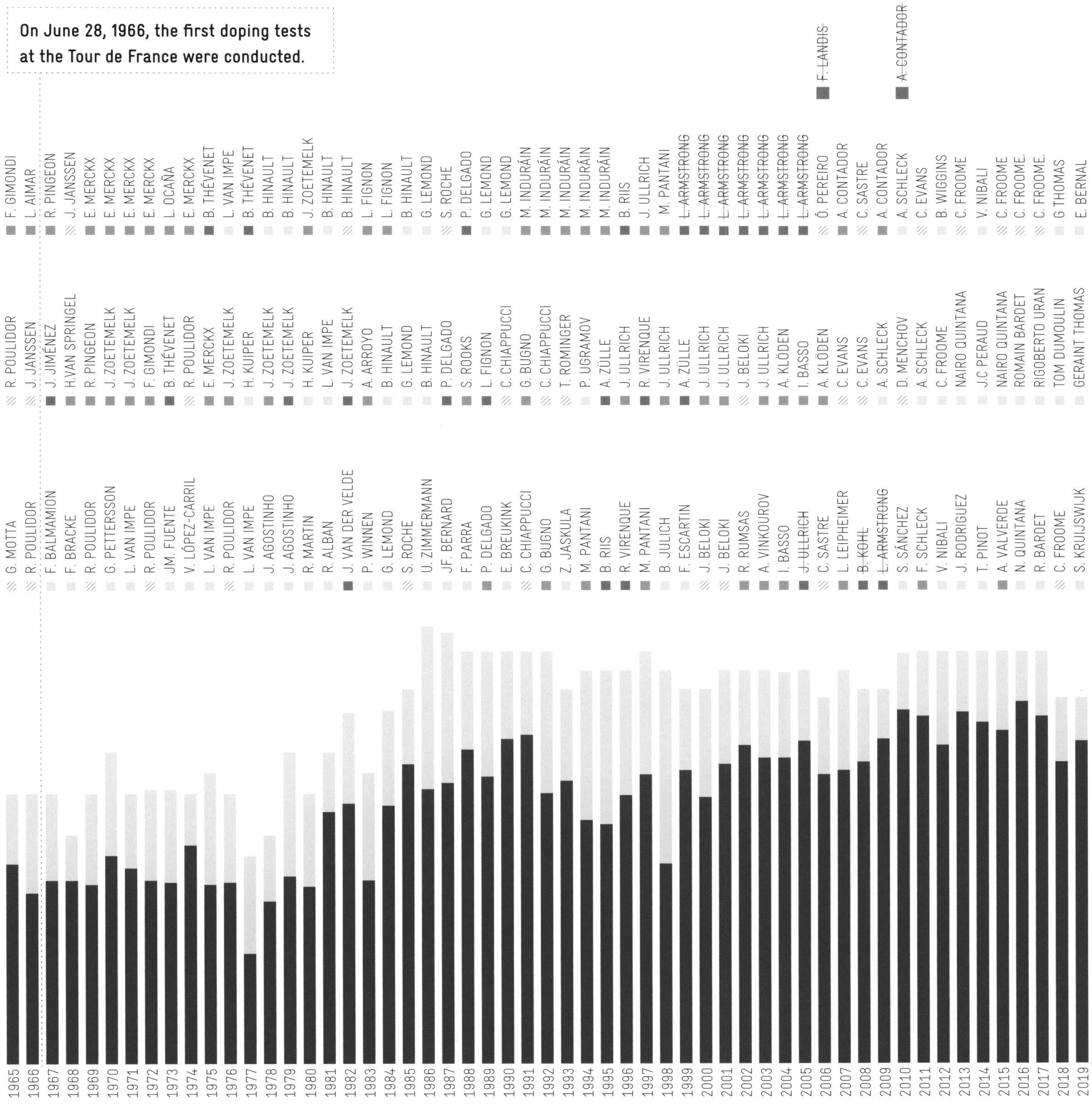

COURSES AND ELEVATION CHARTS
sorted by speed of event
as of Jan 2020

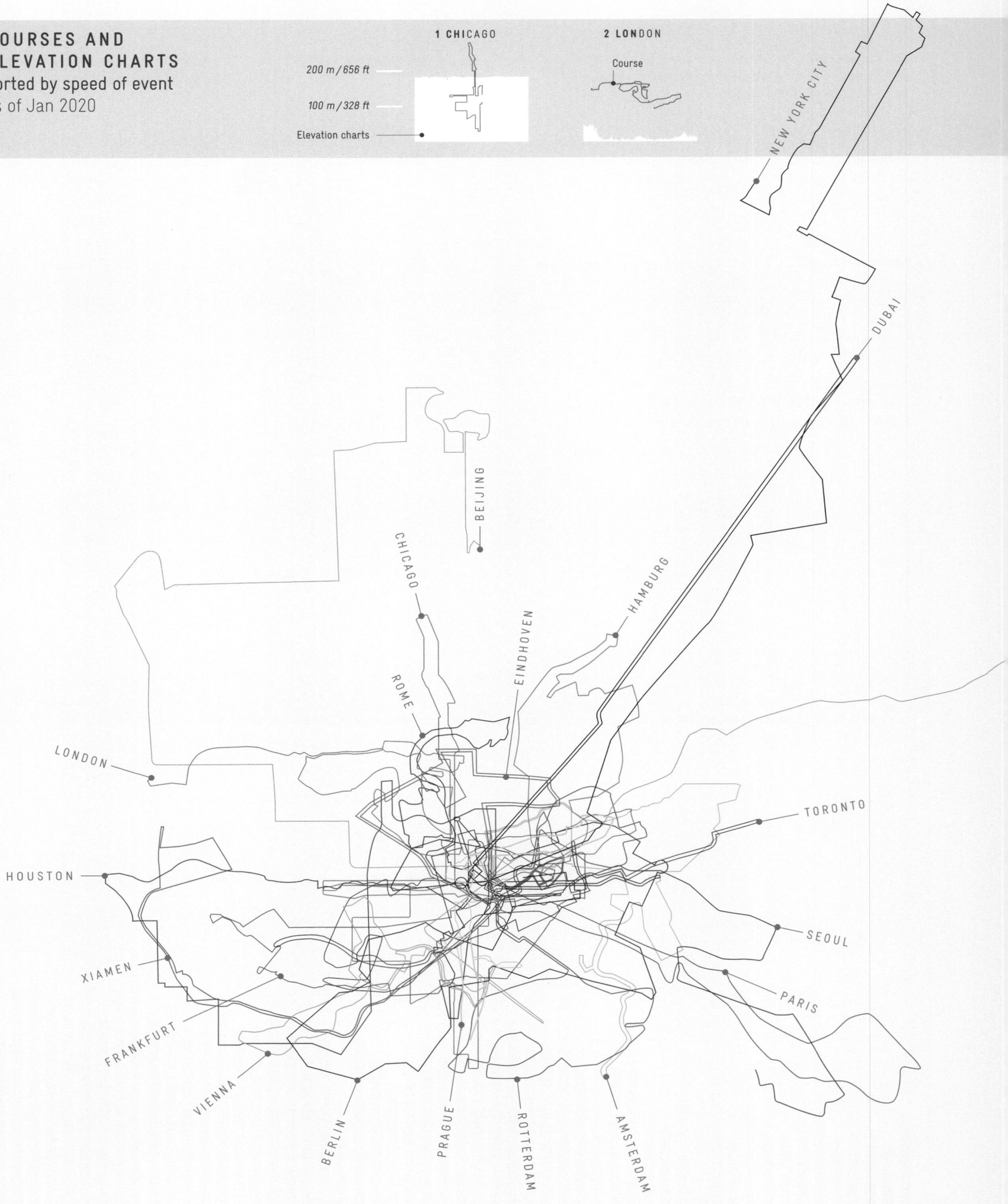
1 CHICAGO
2 LONDON
200 m / 656 ft
100 m / 328 ft
Elevation charts
Course
NEW YORK CITY
DUBAI
BEIJING
CHICAGO
HAMBURG
EINDHOVEN
ROME
LONDON
TORONTO
HOUSTON
SEOUL
XIAMEN
PARIS
FRANKFURT
VIENNA
BERLIN
PRAGUE
ROTTERDAM
AMSTERDAM
N

COURSES
From the starting line

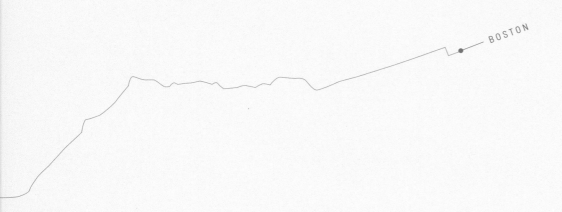

3 BERLIN
4 DUBAI
5 BOSTON
6 ROTTERDAM
7 FRANKFURT
8 SEOUL

BOSTON

THE FASTEST 843,900 METERS IN THE WORLD

The 20 fastest marathon events in the world* determined by the total of their minimum record times for men and women.

*As of January 2020; except for championships

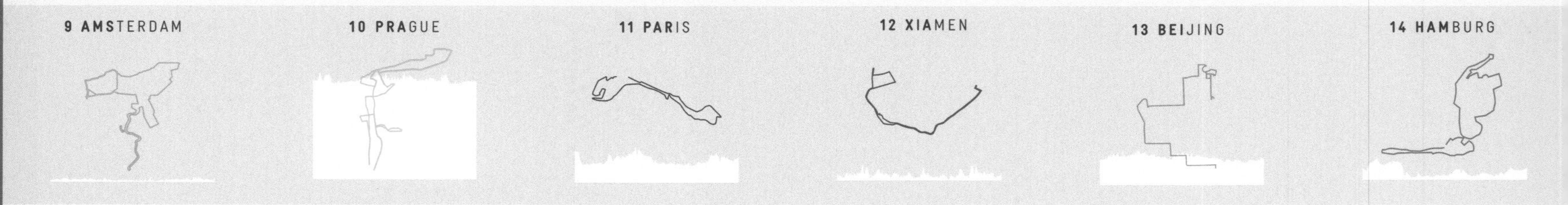
9 AMSTERDAM
10 PRAGUE
11 PARIS
12 XIAMEN
13 BEIJING
14 HAMBURG

THE RACE CONDITIONS

Month and average temperature of the race

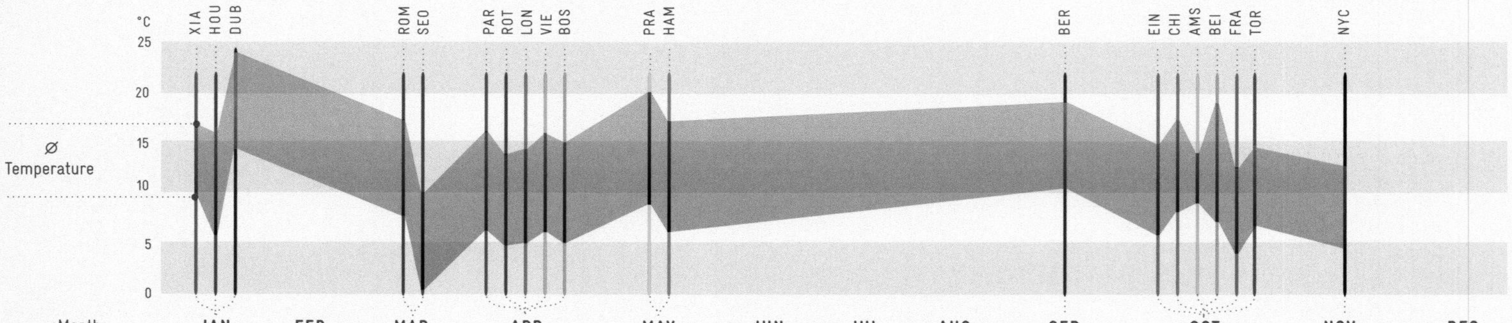
°C
25
20
15
10
5
0
Ø
Temperature
XIA HOU DUB
ROM SEO
PAR ROT LON VIE BOS
PRA HAM
BER
EIN CHI AMS BEI FRA TOR
NYC

Month	JAN	FEB	MAR	APR	MAY	JUN	JUL	AUG	SEP	OCT	NOV	DEC
Number of worldwide marathons per month Ø	17	22	25	36	32	16	9	18	28	54	44	26

THE EVOLUTION

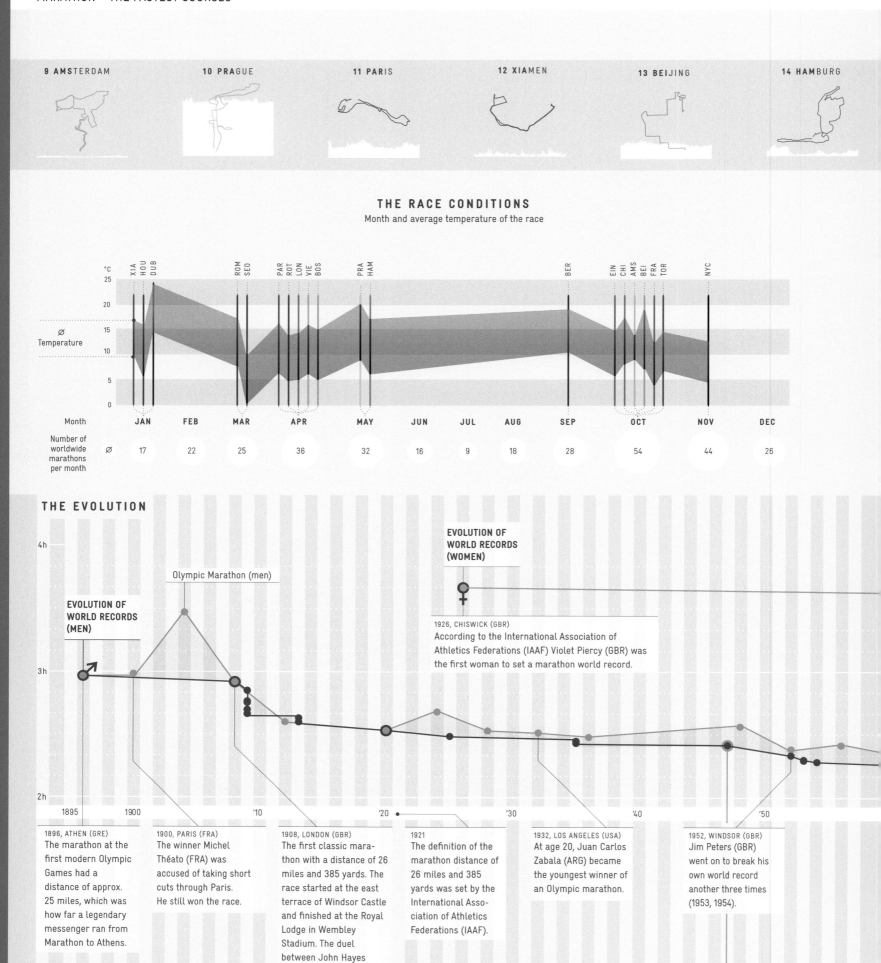

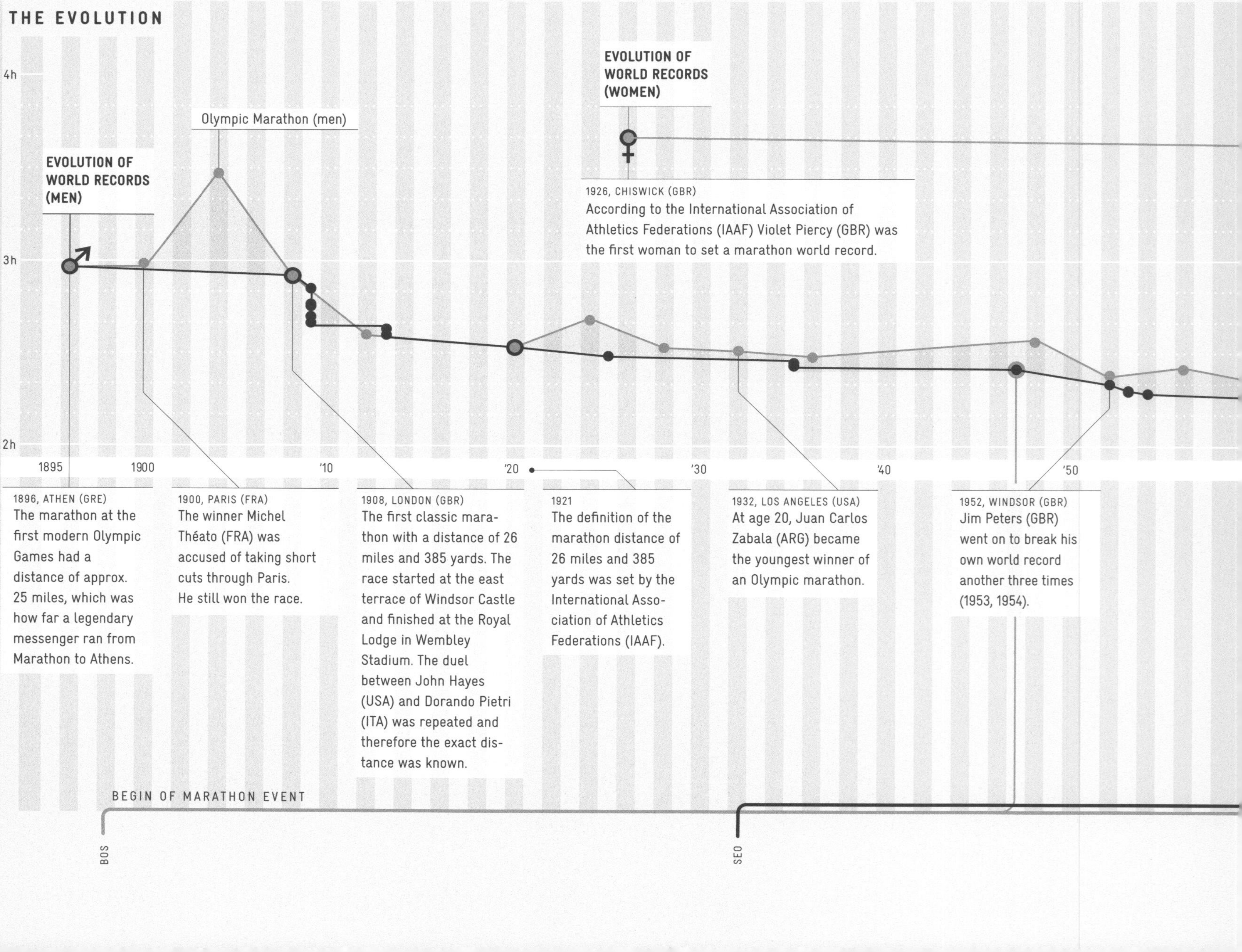
4h
3h
2h
1895
1900
'10
'20
'30
'40
'50
Olympic Marathon (men)
EVOLUTION OF WORLD RECORDS (MEN)
EVOLUTION OF WORLD RECORDS (WOMEN)
1926, CHISWICK (GBR)
According to the International Association of Athletics Federations (IAAF) Violet Piercy (GBR) was the first woman to set a marathon world record.
1896, ATHEN (GRE)
The marathon at the first modern Olympic Games had a distance of approx. 25 miles, which was how far a legendary messenger ran from Marathon to Athens.
1900, PARIS (FRA)
The winner Michel Théato (FRA) was accused of taking short cuts through Paris. He still won the race.
1908, LONDON (GBR)
The first classic marathon with a distance of 26 miles and 385 yards. The race started at the east terrace of Windsor Castle and finished at the Royal Lodge in Wembley Stadium. The duel between John Hayes (USA) and Dorando Pietri (ITA) was repeated and therefore the exact distance was known.
1921
The definition of the marathon distance of 26 miles and 385 yards was set by the International Association of Athletics Federations (IAAF).
1932, LOS ANGELES (USA)
At age 20, Juan Carlos Zabala (ARG) became the youngest winner of an Olympic marathon.
1952, WINDSOR (GBR)
Jim Peters (GBR) went on to break his own world record another three times (1953, 1954).
BEGIN OF MARATHON EVENT
BOS
SEO

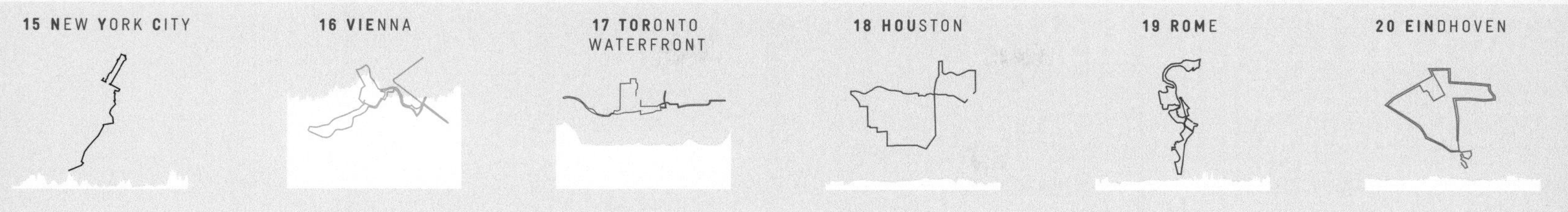
15 NEW YORK CITY
16 VIENNA
17 TORONTO WATERFRONT
18 HOUSTON
19 ROME
20 EINDHOVEN

PARTICIPATION

Participants and fees 2010/11 (starters only shown when known)

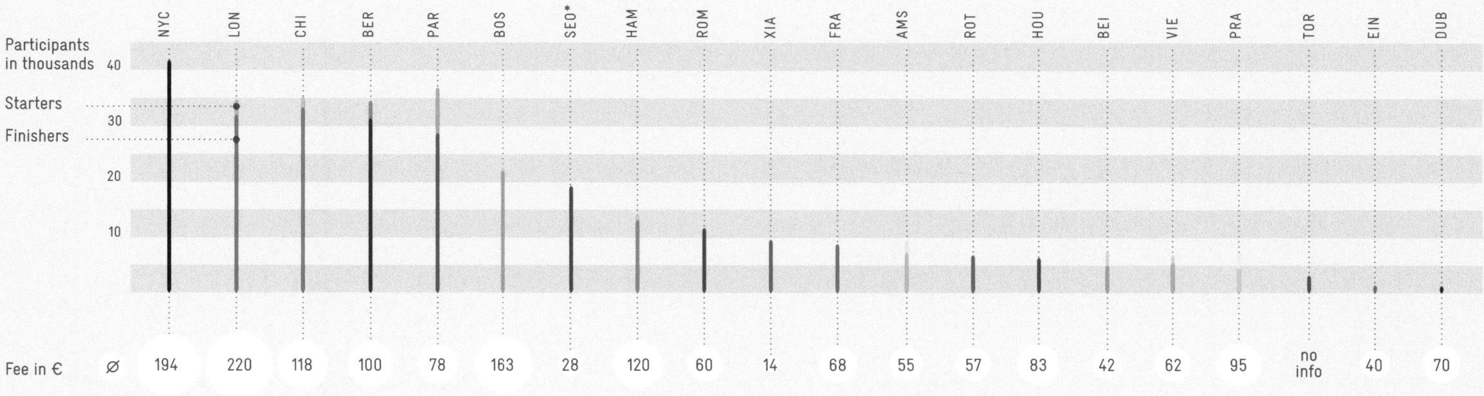
NYC
LON
CHI
BER
PAR
BOS
SEO*
HAM
ROM
XIA
FRA
AMS
ROT
HOU
BEI
VIE
PRA
TOR
EIN
DUB
Participants in thousands
40
Starters
30
Finishers
20
10
Fee in €
ø
194
220
118
100
78
163
28
120
60
14
68
55
57
83
42
62
95
no info
40
70

* Average number of runners, no exact data available

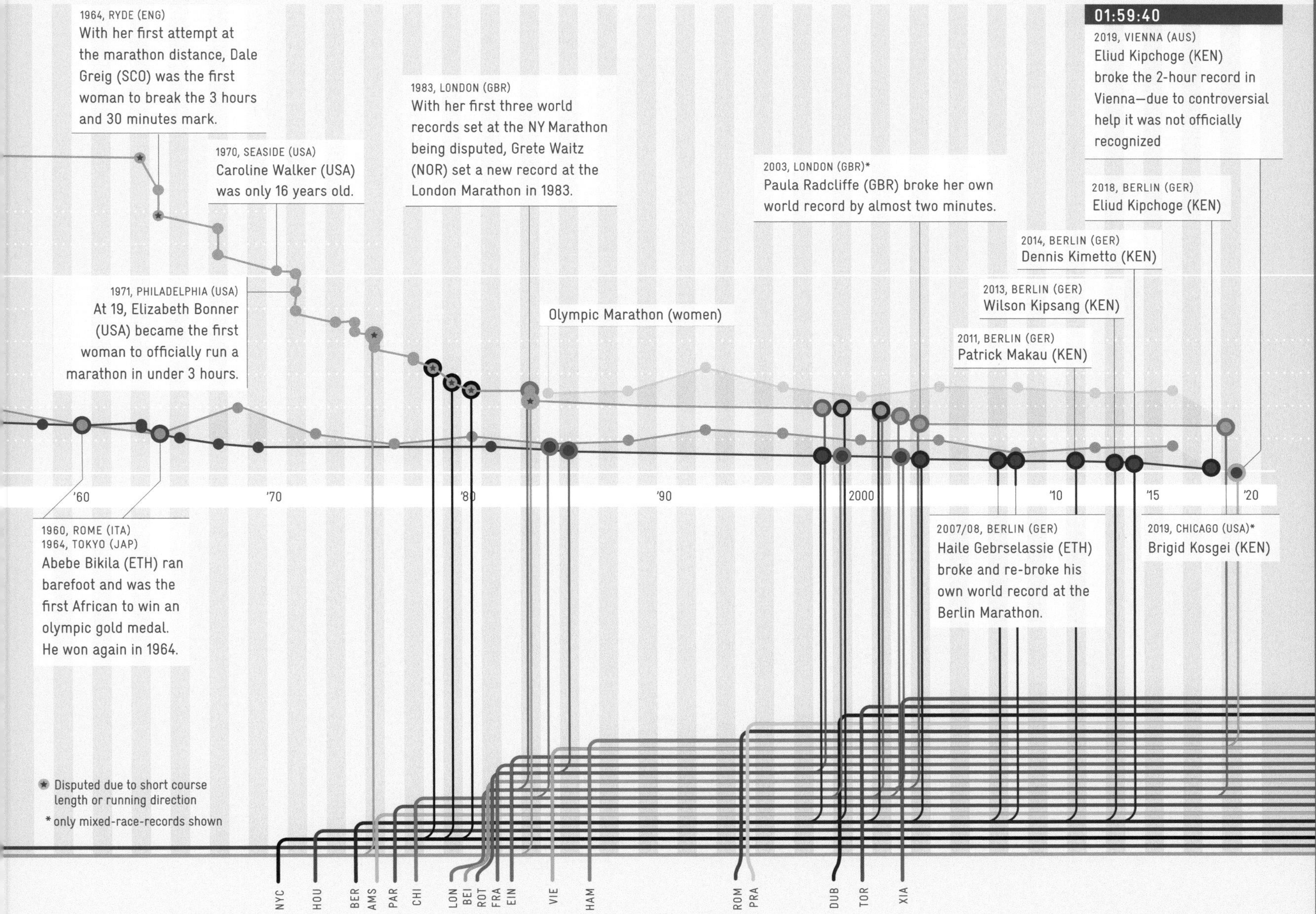
1964, RYDE (ENG)
With her first attempt at the marathon distance, Dale Greig (SCO) was the first woman to break the 3 hours and 30 minutes mark.
1970, SEASIDE (USA)
Caroline Walker (USA) was only 16 years old.
1983, LONDON (GBR)
With her first three world records set at the NY Marathon being disputed, Grete Waitz (NOR) set a new record at the London Marathon in 1983.
01:59:40
2019, VIENNA (AUS)
Eliud Kipchoge (KEN) broke the 2-hour record in Vienna—due to controversial help it was not officially recognized
2003, LONDON (GBR)*
Paula Radcliffe (GBR) broke her own world record by almost two minutes.
2018, BERLIN (GER)
Eliud Kipchoge (KEN)
2014, BERLIN (GER)
Dennis Kimetto (KEN)
2013, BERLIN (GER)
Wilson Kipsang (KEN)
2011, BERLIN (GER)
Patrick Makau (KEN)
1971, PHILADELPHIA (USA)
At 19, Elizabeth Bonner (USA) became the first woman to officially run a marathon in under 3 hours.
Olympic Marathon (women)
'60
'70
'80
'90
2000
'10
'15
'20
1960, ROME (ITA)
1964, TOKYO (JAP)
Abebe Bikila (ETH) ran barefoot and was the first African to win an olympic gold medal. He won again in 1964.
2007/08, BERLIN (GER)
Haile Gebrselassie (ETH) broke and re-broke his own world record at the Berlin Marathon.
2019, CHICAGO (USA)*
Brigid Kosgei (KEN)
Disputed due to short course length or running direction
* only mixed-race-records shown
NYC
HOU
BER
AMS
PAR
CHI
LON
BEI
ROT
FRA
EIN
VIE
HAM
ROM
PRA
DUB
TOR
XIA

ESPORTS IS HERE

For a long time, computer games were regarded as a leisure activity for children and adolescents. However, these private network parties have developed into professional tournaments which promise huge amounts of prize money, fill entire stadiums and have made schools offer eSports classes.

TOURNAMENT FIREWORKS

In the last five years alone, there were eight eSports tournaments with top prize money that exceeded 10 million U.S. dollars. Numerous tournaments with smaller prize money offer an additional income and can facilitate entry to a professional sports career. In total, more than 220 million U.S. dollars in prize money were distributed in 2019 alone.

Tournaments according to time and prize money. Each game is represented by a color in the graphic below.

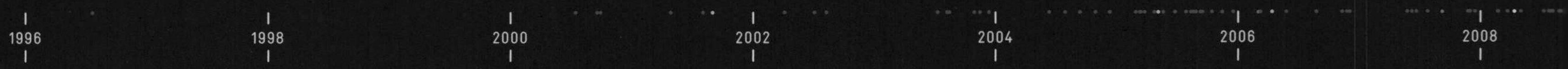
1996
1998
2000
2002
2004
2006
2008

PRIZE EXPLOSION

The total monthly prize money demonstrates the phases of popularity the top game series run through. New versions can reinvigorate a title. New tournaments take place even before the official game release. As a result, a title already gains fame in the development phase and can be marketed early-on via eSport events.

Prize money per month according to games series

US$ 30 m.
10 m.
100,000

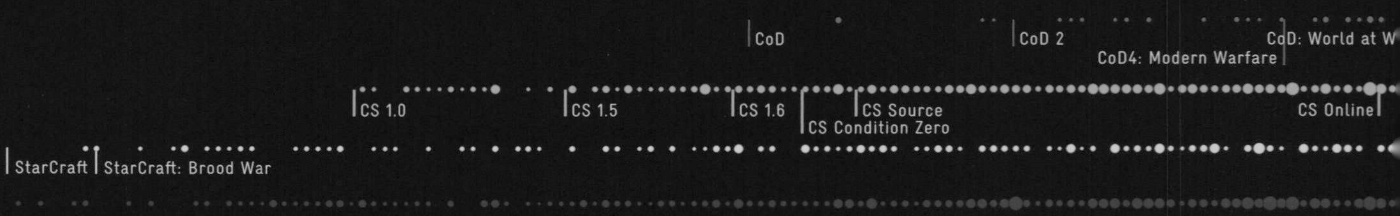
CoD
CoD 2
CoD4: Modern Warfare
CoD: World at W
CS 1.0
CS 1.5
CS 1.6
CS Source
CS Condition Zero
CS Online
StarCraft
StarCraft: Brood War

EVERGREENS VS NEWCOMERS

Successful titles can dominate a whole genre. »Super Smash Bros. Ultimate« took over 40% of the fighting game events. In the »First Person Shooter« genre, »Counterstrike« and »Call of Duty« constitute the most successful events for years. Whereas in the new genre »Battle Royale«, the top games »Fortnite« and »PlayerUnknown's Battlegrounds« try to increase their communitiy size with high prize pools.

Number of tournaments per year according to genre

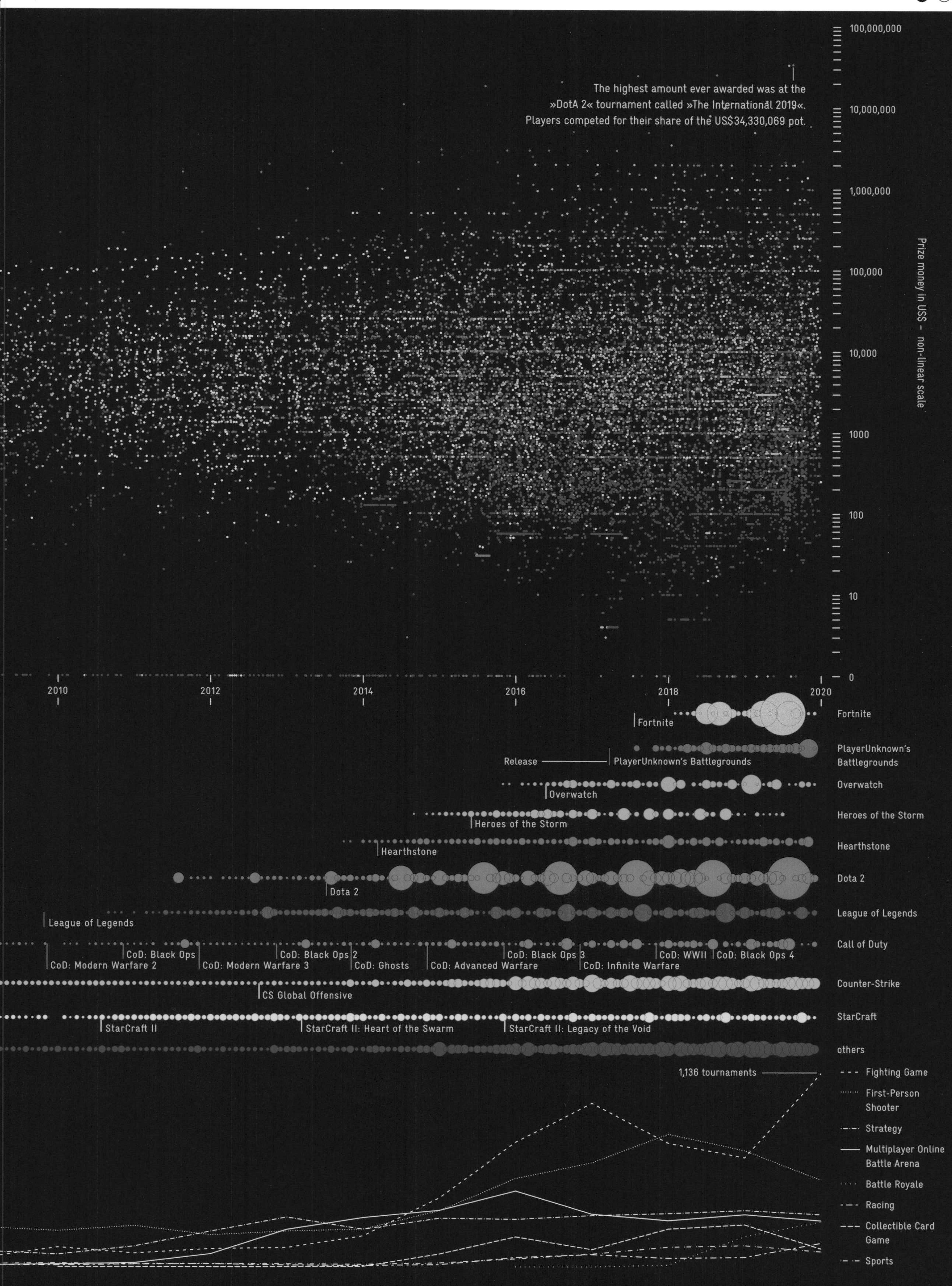
The highest amount ever awarded was at the »DotA 2« tournament called »The International 2019«. Players competed for their share of the US$34,330,069 pot.
100,000,000
10,000,000
1,000,000
100,000
10,000
1000
100
10
0
Prize money in US$ – non-linear scale
2010
2012
2014
2016
2018
2020
Fortnite
Release
PlayerUnknown's Battlegrounds
Overwatch
Heroes of the Storm
Hearthstone
Dota 2
League of Legends
CoD: Black Ops
CoD: Modern Warfare 2
CoD: Black Ops 2
CoD: Modern Warfare 3
CoD: Ghosts
CoD: Advanced Warfare
CoD: Black Ops 3
CoD: Infinite Warfare
CoD: WWII
CoD: Black Ops 4
CS Global Offensive
StarCraft II
StarCraft II: Heart of the Swarm
StarCraft II: Legacy of the Void
Fortnite
PlayerUnknown's Battlegrounds
Overwatch
Heroes of the Storm
Hearthstone
Dota 2
League of Legends
Call of Duty
Counter-Strike
StarCraft
others
1,136 tournaments
Fighting Game
First-Person Shooter
Strategy
Multiplayer Online Battle Arena
Battle Royale
Racing
Collectible Card Game
Sports

ESPORTS IS EVERYWHERE

Thanks to the internet and a low entry barrier, eSports and their athletes are no longer just a marginal phenomenon. Spectator numbers of live streams and public events are rising wherever »Pro's« are celebrated as stars. They can earn their living as influencers and streamers, or as professional tournament athletes. Teams are usually supported by big sponsors, mostly from the hardware industry. Even traditional soccer clubs are starting to form their own eSport teams.

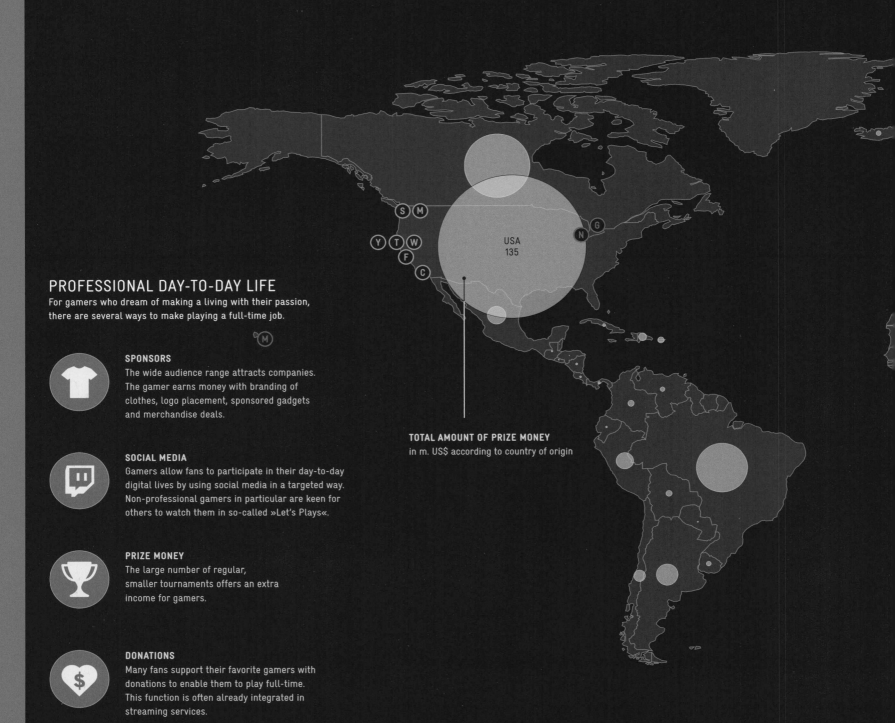

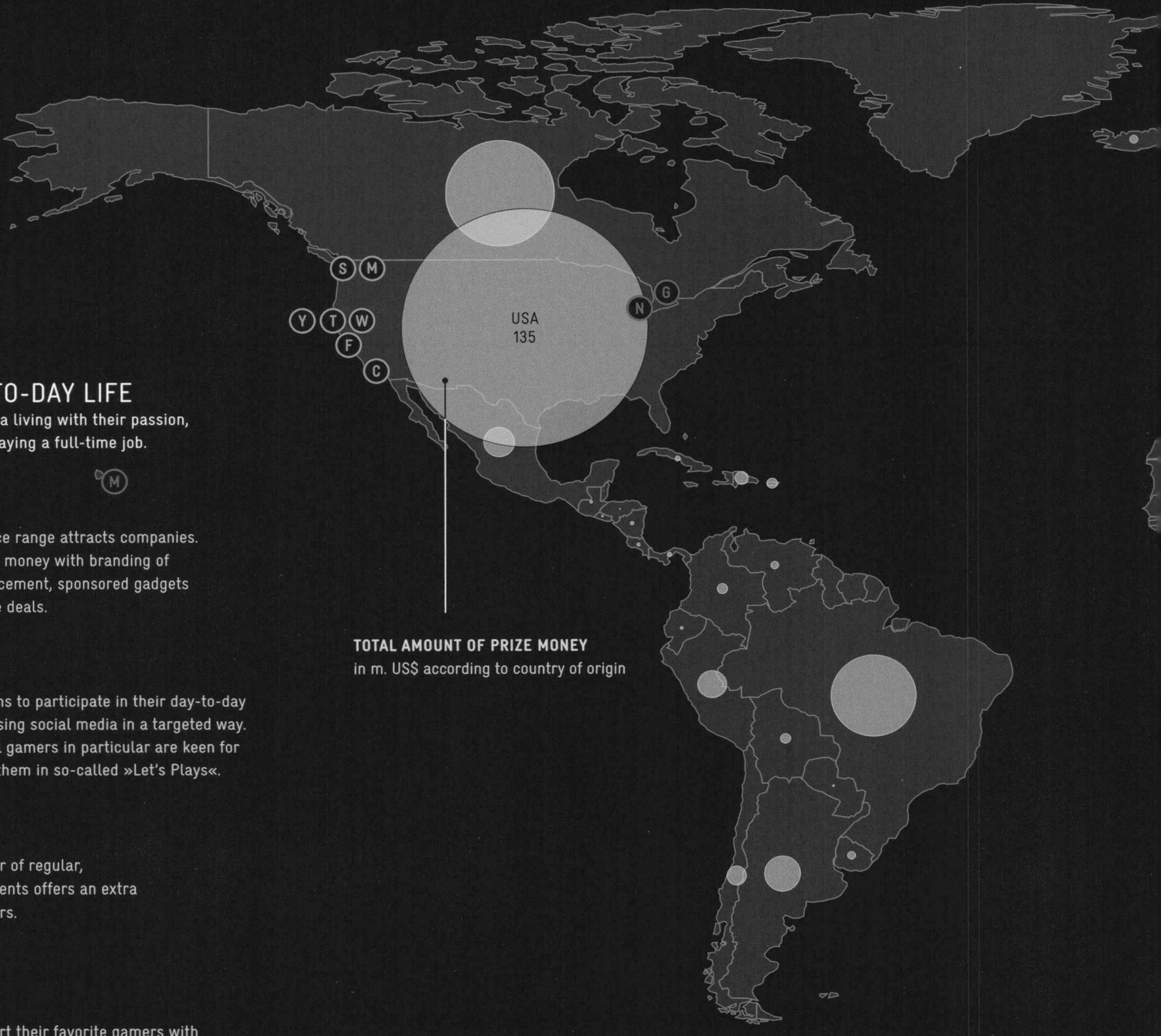

TOTAL AMOUNT OF PRIZE MONEY
in m. US$ according to country of origin

PROFESSIONAL DAY-TO-DAY LIFE

For gamers who dream of making a living with their passion, there are several ways to make playing a full-time job.

SPONSORS
The wide audience range attracts companies. The gamer earns money with branding of clothes, logo placement, sponsored gadgets and merchandise deals.

SOCIAL MEDIA
Gamers allow fans to participate in their day-to-day digital lives by using social media in a targeted way. Non-professional gamers in particular are keen for others to watch them in so-called »Let's Plays«.

PRIZE MONEY
The large number of regular, smaller tournaments offers an extra income for gamers.

DONATIONS
Many fans support their favorite gamers with donations to enable them to play full-time. This function is often already integrated in streaming services.

POPULAR GAMERS WITH MORE THAN 20 MILLION FOLLOWERS

Olajide William ›KSI‹ Olatunji
20.9 m. followers – ***1993**

Daniel Robert ›DanTDM‹ Middleton
22.4 m. followers – ***1991**

Evan ›VanossGaming‹ Fong
24.5 m. followers – ***1992**

Samuel ›VEGETTA777‹ de Luque
28.6 m. followers – ***1989**

Rubén Doblas ›ElrubiusOMG‹ Gundersen
39.92 m. followers – ***1990**

>20 m.

STREAMED ENTERTAINMENT

Millions of spectators follow eSports world championships, small tournaments and private gaming via live streaming from their homes or smart devices. The most popular platforms to do this are Twitch and Youtube. Amazon beat Google to snap up Twitch in 2015 for US$970 million.

HOW DOES TWITCH EARN MONEY?

ADVERTISING

Hardware manufacturers as well as companies like Coca-Cola, HBO and Red Bull broadcast their advertising within the streams or on websites.

SUBSCRIPTIONS

In order to hide advertising or to get special emoticons, users pay between US$4.99 to US$24.99 per month. With these options, the viewer has the ability to support their favorites.

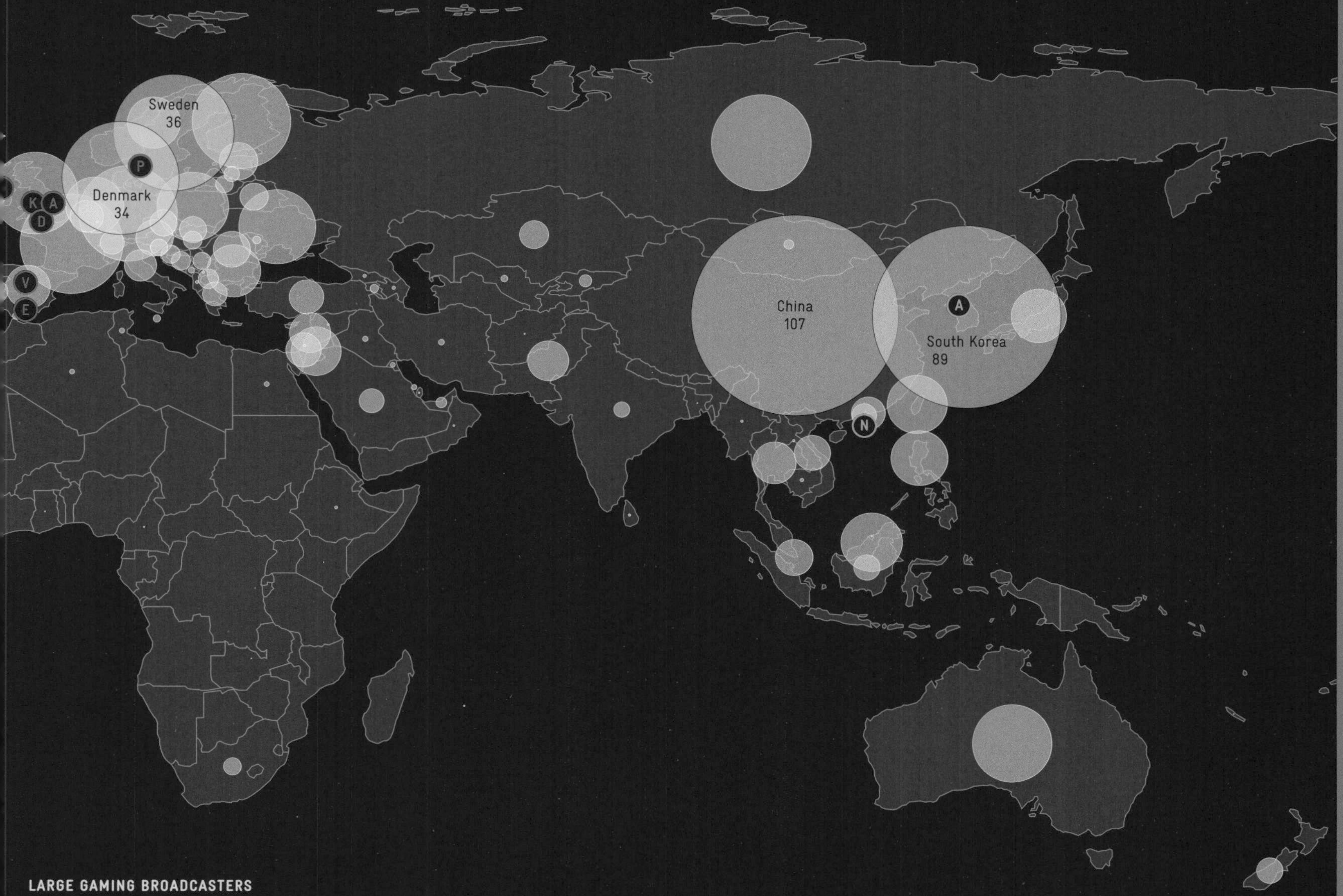
Sweden
36
P
Denmark
34
K
A
D
V
E
China
107
A
South Korea
89
N

LARGE GAMING BROADCASTERS

- (A) **AfreecaTV** *Seongnam, KOR*
- (M) **mixer** *Redmond, USA*
- (T) **Twitch** *San Francisco, USA*
- (C) **Smashcast.tv** *Los Angeles, USA*
- (Y) **youtube** *San Francisco, USA*
- (F) **facebook** *Menlo Park, USA*
- (N) **Nonolive** *Hong Kong, HKG*
- (W) **Twitter** *San Francisco, USA*
- (S) **steamtv** *Bellevue, USA*

TECHNOLOGY

Technologies never stop developing. This makes it even more important to explain how they work as quickly and clearly as possible. As infographics can illustrate technical complexity abstractly and pictorially, they are especially good at conveying technological applications and operations.

Decades before Leonardo da Vinci, in the first half of the 15th century, the wood carver and engineer **Mariano di Jacopo, also known as Taccola**, drew this **dolly with a hoist**. He published two extensive treatises with technical diagrams of machines and created the first exploded view drawing. An exploded view drawing shows an object's components either displayed a short distance from one another or positioned in space. This remains a popular graphic format to illustrate how objects or technologies are built and how they work. One popular alternative to exploded views are sectional drawings.

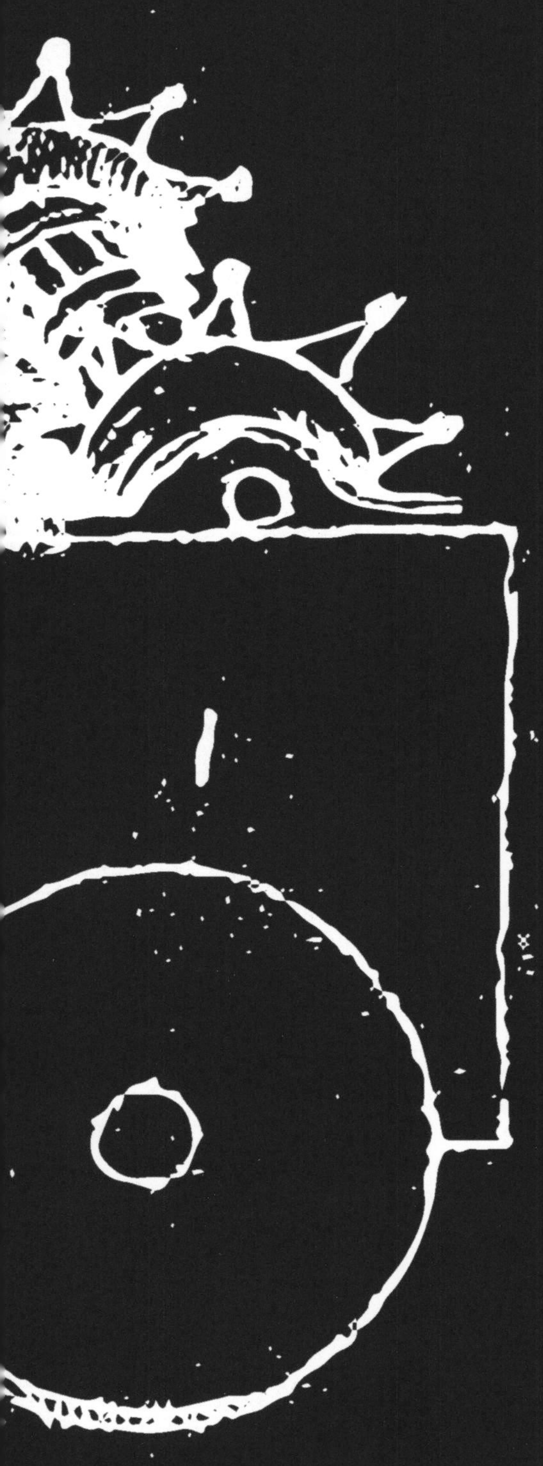

BACK TO THE FUTURE

Electric cars are hailed as the vehicle of the future, but they are not a new invention. Developing emission-free vehicles goes back to the 19th century and the advent of the automobile.

START

1881
G. TROUVÉ
Tricycle, probably the first functional electric car
12 km/h (7.5 mph)

1882
W. E. AYRTON & J. PERRY
Tricycle, similar to the model of G. Trouvé
14 km/h (9 mph)

1890
W. MORRISON
The first successful electric car
12 km/h (7.5 mph)

1895
DEY-GRISWOLD & CO. ELECTRIC PHAETON
Car with electric motor and hydraulic drive
50 km/h (30 mph) record

1899
C. JENATZ LA JAMAIS CONTENTE
Electric racing car
105 km/h (65 mph) record

1890
The Morrison Electric

The first successful electric car
speeds up to
12 km/h (7.5 mph)

1882
Ayrton & Perry Electric Tricycle

One of the first electric cars
speeds up to
14 km/h (9 mph)

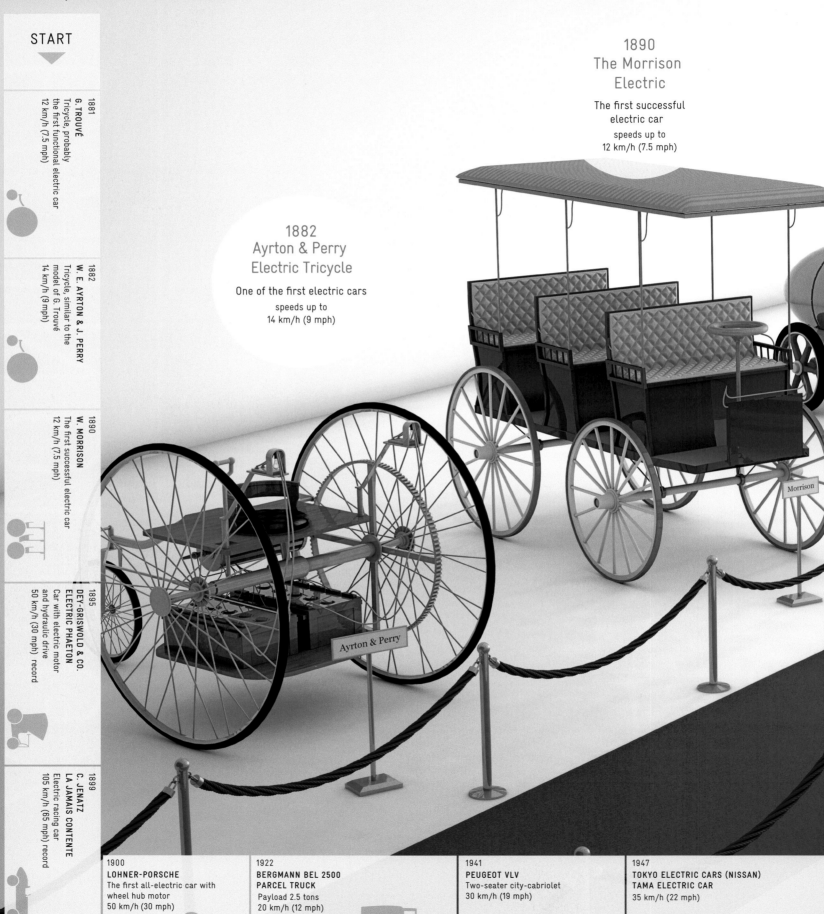

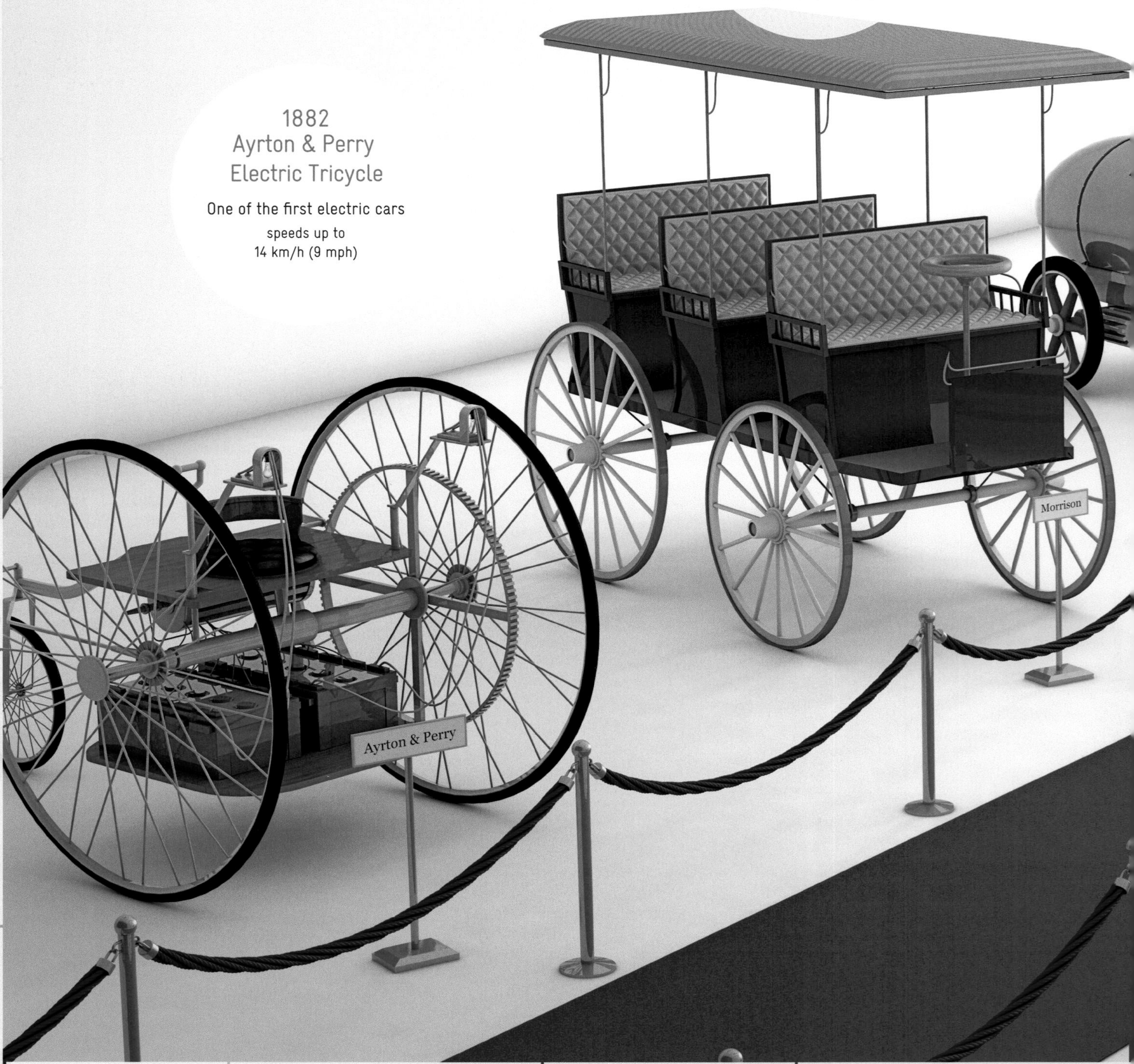

1900
LOHNER-PORSCHE
The first all-electric car with wheel hub motor
50 km/h (30 mph)

1922
BERGMANN BEL 2500 PARCEL TRUCK
Payload 2.5 tons
20 km/h (12 mph)

1941
PEUGEOT VLV
Two-seater city-cabriolet
30 km/h (19 mph)

1947
TOKYO ELECTRIC CARS (NISSAN) TAMA ELECTRIC CAR
35 km/h (22 mph)

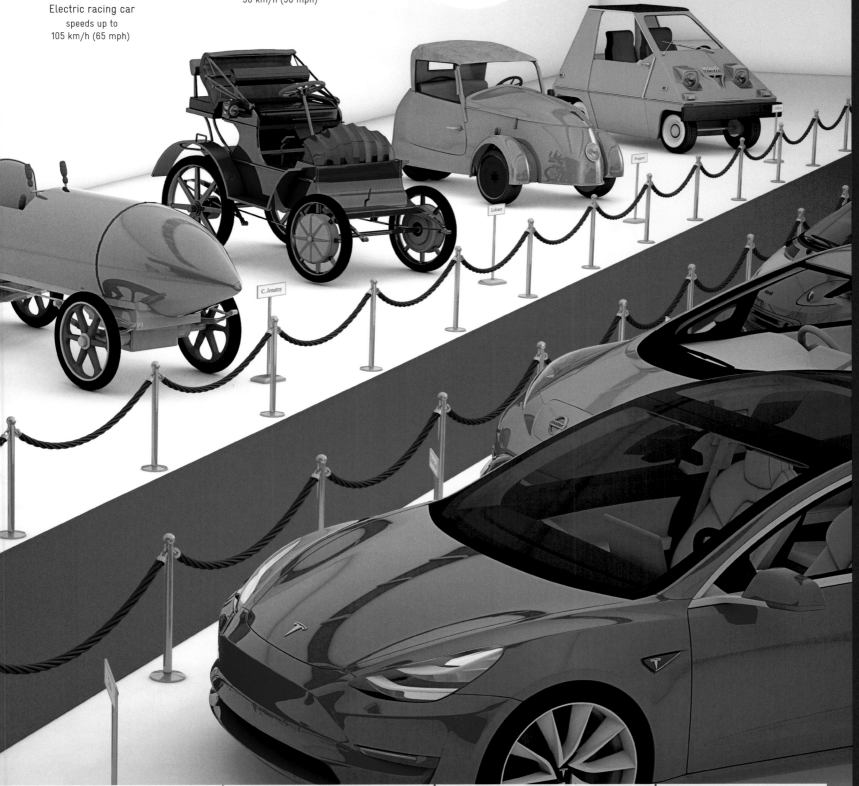

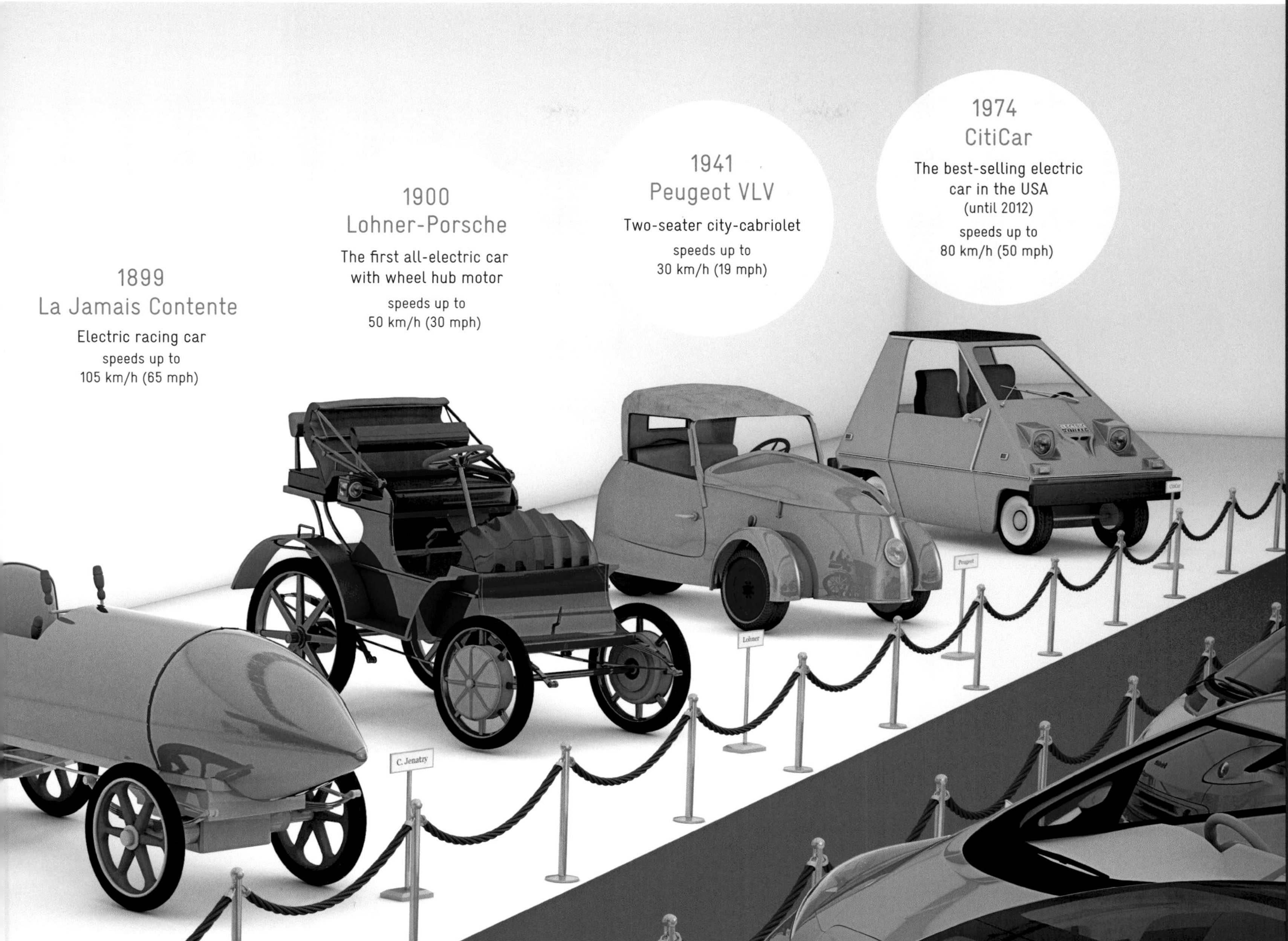
1899
La Jamais Contente
Electric racing car
speeds up to
105 km/h (65 mph)
1900
Lohner-Porsche
The first all-electric car
with wheel hub motor
speeds up to
50 km/h (30 mph)
1941
Peugeot VLV
Two-seater city-cabriolet
speeds up to
30 km/h (19 mph)
1974
CitiCar
The best-selling electric
car in the USA
(until 2012)
speeds up to
80 km/h (50 mph)
C. Jenatzy
Lohner

1974
SEBRING-VANGUARD INC.
CITICAR
The best-selling electric car in the USA
(until 2012)
80 km/h (50 mph)

1974
L. SCHIMMELPENNINK
WITKAR
Electric rental car for Amsterdam;
precursor of the Car2go
30 km/h (19 mph)

1970er
FORD TRANSIT
MILKFLOAT
Used mainly in Great Britain
25 km/h (15 mph)

1981
SINCLAIR C5
C. SINCLAIR / HOOVER
With additional pedals
25 km/h (15 mph)

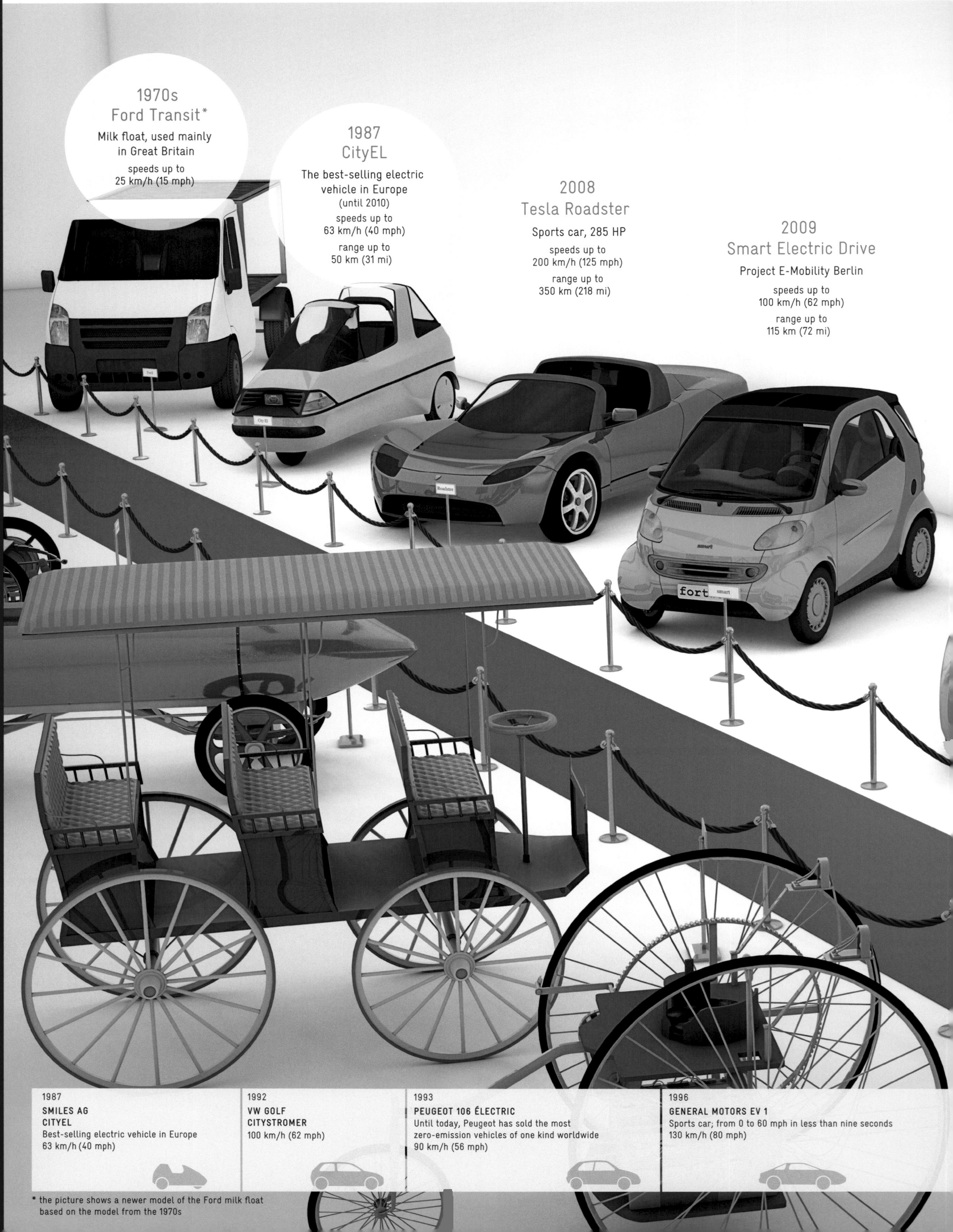

1970s
Ford Transit*
Milk float, used mainly in Great Britain
speeds up to 25 km/h (15 mph)

1987
CityEL
The best-selling electric vehicle in Europe (until 2010)
speeds up to 63 km/h (40 mph)
range up to 50 km (31 mi)

2008
Tesla Roadster
Sports car, 285 HP
speeds up to 200 km/h (125 mph)
range up to 350 km (218 mi)

2009
Smart Electric Drive
Project E-Mobility Berlin
speeds up to 100 km/h (62 mph)
range up to 115 km (72 mi)

1987
SMILES AG
CITYEL
Best-selling electric vehicle in Europe
63 km/h (40 mph)

1992
VW GOLF
CITYSTROMER
100 km/h (62 mph)

1993
PEUGEOT 106 ÉLECTRIC
Until today, Peugeot has sold the most zero-emission vehicles of one kind worldwide
90 km/h (56 mph)

1996
GENERAL MOTORS EV 1
Sports car; from 0 to 60 mph in less than nine seconds
130 km/h (80 mph)

* the picture shows a newer model of the Ford milk float based on the model from the 1970s

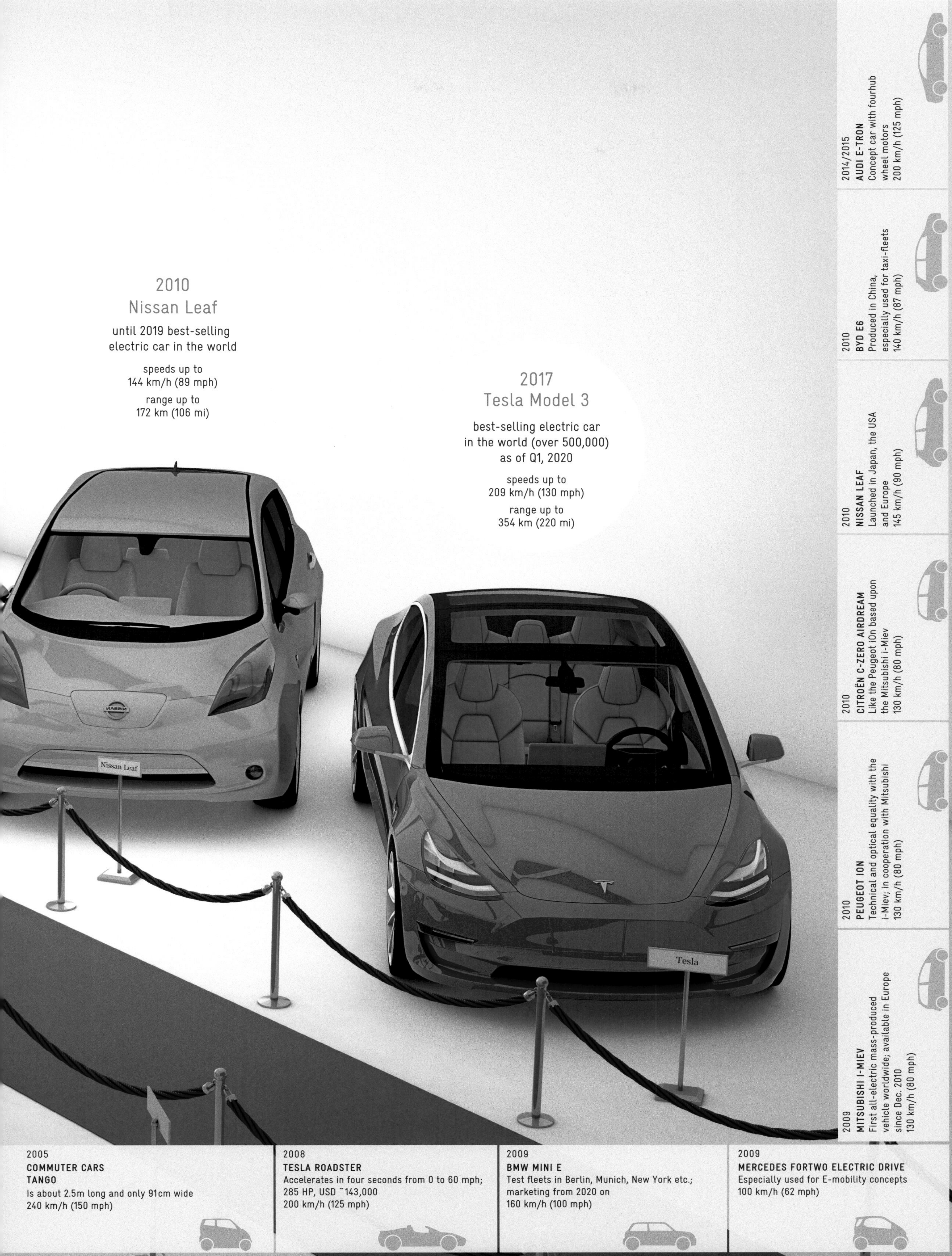

2010
Nissan Leaf

until 2019 best-selling
electric car in the world

speeds up to
144 km/h (89 mph)

range up to
172 km (106 mi)

2017
Tesla Model 3

best-selling electric car
in the world (over 500,000)
as of Q1, 2020

speeds up to
209 km/h (130 mph)

range up to
354 km (220 mi)

2005
COMMUTER CARS TANGO
Is about 2.5m long and only 91cm wide
240 km/h (150 mph)

2008
TESLA ROADSTER
Accelerates in four seconds from 0 to 60 mph;
285 HP, USD ~143,000
200 km/h (125 mph)

2009
BMW MINI E
Test fleets in Berlin, Munich, New York etc.;
marketing from 2020 on
160 km/h (100 mph)

2009
MERCEDES FORTWO ELECTRIC DRIVE
Especially used for E-mobility concepts
100 km/h (62 mph)

2009
MITSUBISHI I-MIEV
First all-electric mass-produced
vehicle worldwide; available in Europe
since Dec. 2010
130 km/h (80 mph)

2010
PEUGEOT ION
Technical and optical equality with the
i-Miev; in cooperation with Mitsubishi
130 km/h (80 mph)

2010
CITROËN C-ZERO AIRDREAM
Like the Peugeot iOn based upon
the Mitsubishi i-Miev
130 km/h (80 mph)

2010
NISSAN LEAF
Launched in Japan, the USA
and Europe
145 km/h (90 mph)

2010
BYD E6
Produced in China,
especially used for taxi-fleets
140 km/h (87 mph)

2014/2015
AUDI E-TRON
Concept car with fourhub
wheel motors
200 km/h (125 mph)

A SPARK OF BRILLIANCE

He is one of the most important inventors of the 19th Century: In 1892, Rudolf Diesel filed a patent for a »Method of an Apparatus for Converting Heat into Work«, now known simply as the »diesel engine«. On September 29, 1913, the engineer died on a sea journey from Antwerp, Belgium, to London.

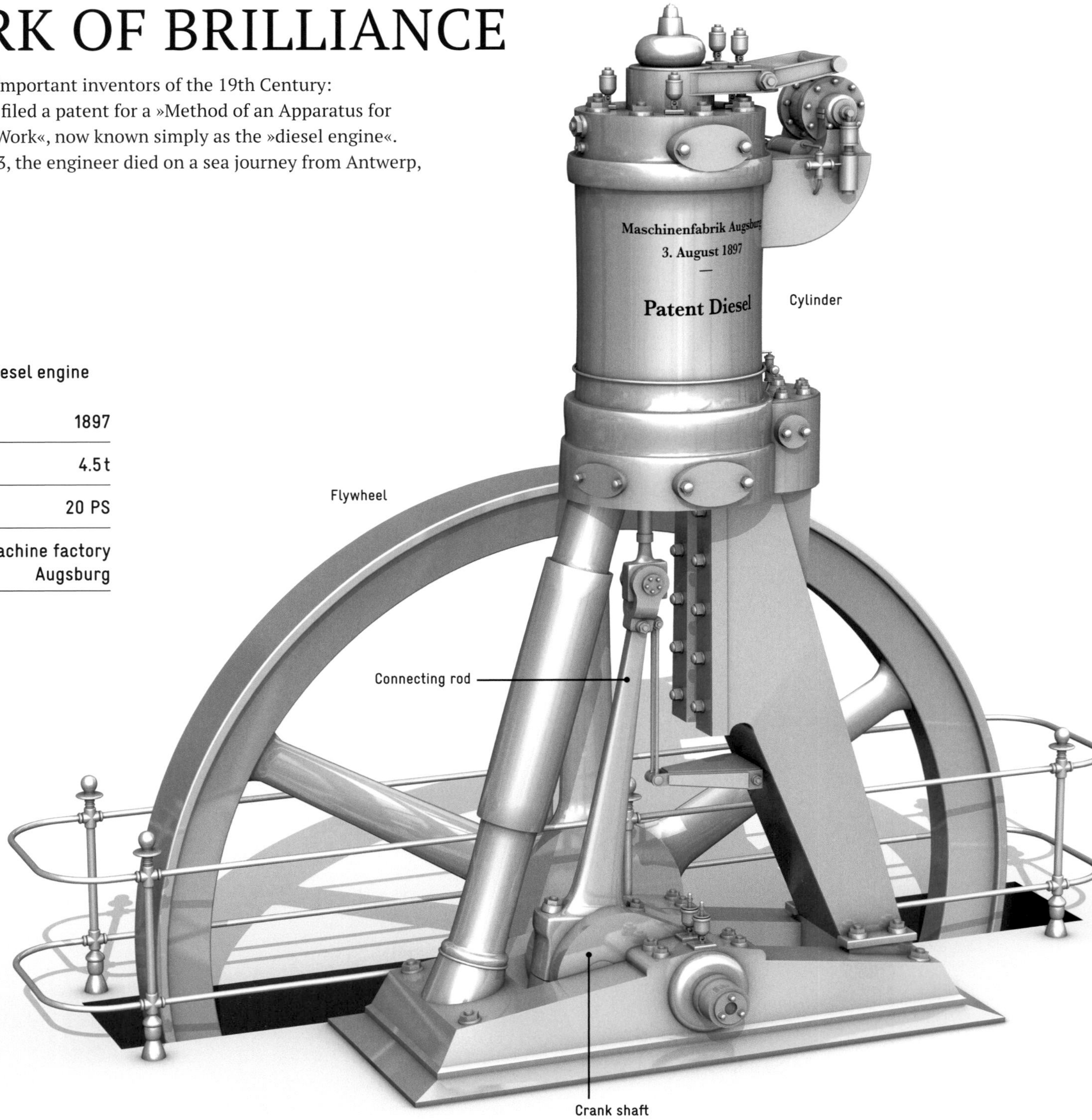
Maschinenfabrik Augsburg
3. August 1897
Patent Diesel
Cylinder
Flywheel
Connecting rod
Crank shaft

The first functioning diesel engine

Year of construction	1897
Weight	4.5 t
Power	20 PS
Location	machine factory Augsburg

Diesel vs. Otto

Ignition

The concept of the diesel engine is based on a simple idea: Air is heated by compression and explodes as a result of the increased pressure.

Spark ignition

The compression in gasoline engines is weaker. A spark plug is required for ignition.

Refining of crude oil

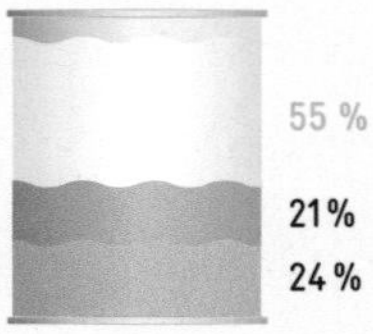
55 %
21 %
24 %

Flammable temperature

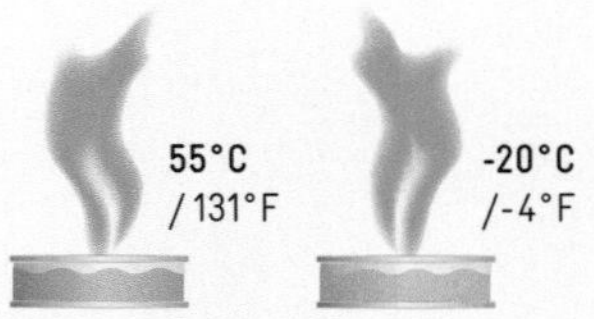
55 °C / 131 °F
-20 °C / -4 °F

Weight of one liter

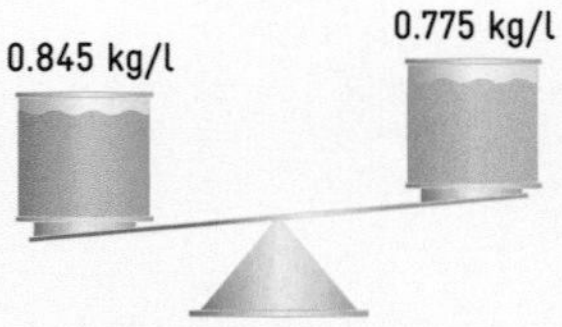
0.845 kg/l
0.775 kg/l

Carbon emissions

2.65 kg/l
2.36 kg/l

The four beats of ignition

The engine's operation can be divided into four beats. Each beat represents a single upward or downward movement of the piston.

What causes the knocking?

The main cause is the ignition delay. The timing interaction between compression, injection, and combustion causes the engine, for a short time, to work against the piston.

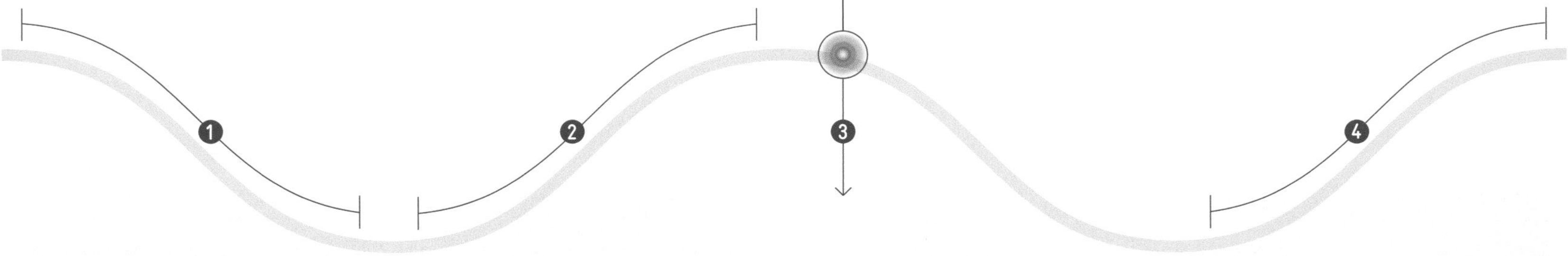

1 Induction

The downward motion of the piston sucks pure air in through the open intake valve.

2 Compression

The air is compressed and heats up. At the top of the compression stroke, fuel is injected.

3 Power

The heat ignites the fuel so that it expands to exert force on the piston.

4 Exhaust

The momentum of the piston pushes the exhaust air out of the cylinder and the process starts again.

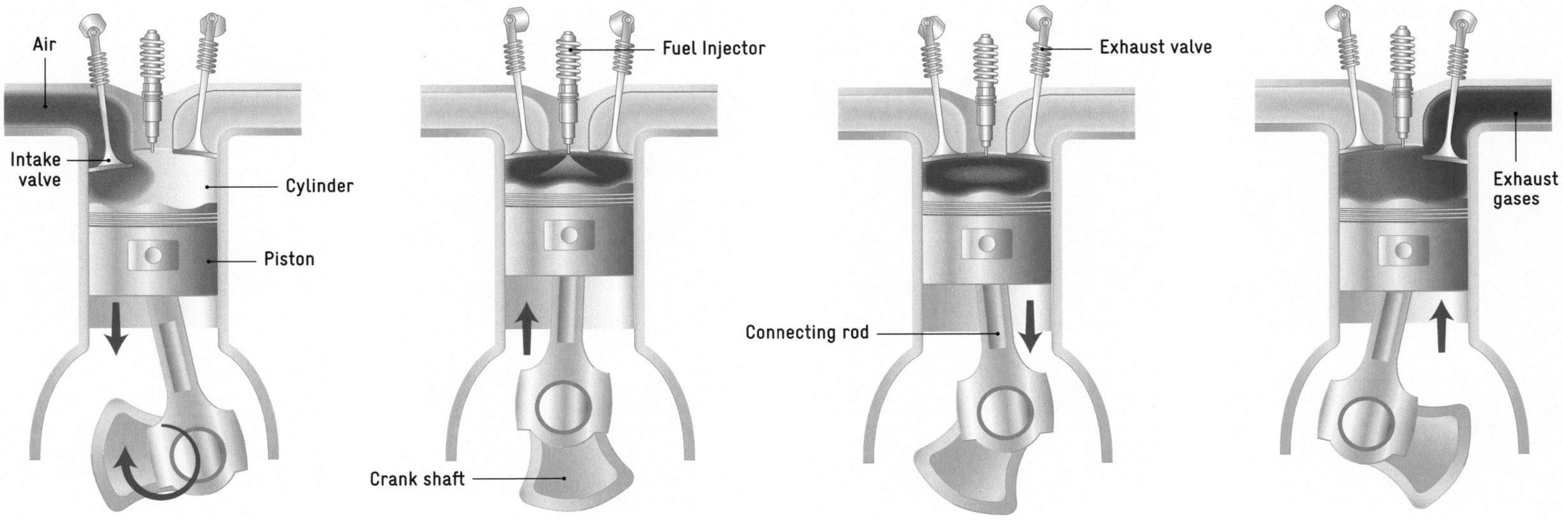

Air
Intake valve
Cylinder
Piston
Fuel Injector
Crank shaft
Exhaust valve
Connecting rod
Exhaust gases

Milestones

Turbocharger 1905

A turbine is driven by the exhaust gases. A connected compressor increases the volume of air entering the combustion chamber.

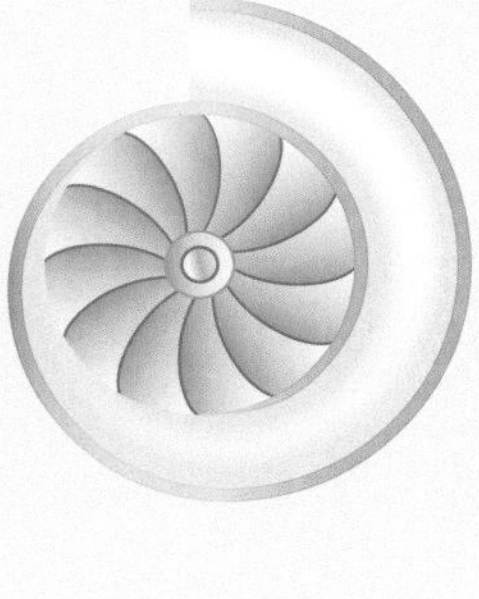

Fuel injector 1909

In contrast to the pre-chamber or swirl chamber injection, the finely atomized fuel is injected directly into the combustion chamber.

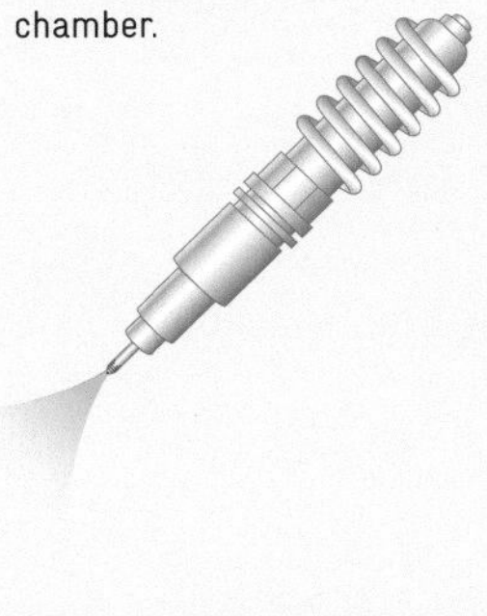

Particulate filter 1985

Initially developed for the military purpose of camouflage. Used in passenger cars from the mid-80s on, now almost all vehicles have these filters.

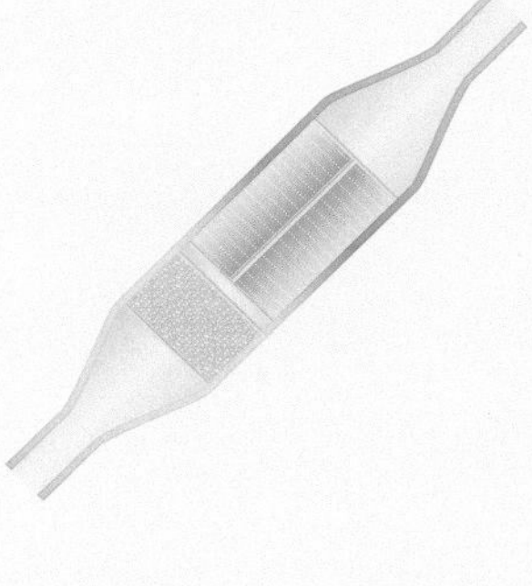

Common Rail 1993

Using an electronic pump, all fuel injection nozzles are brought to a high pressure level.

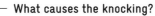

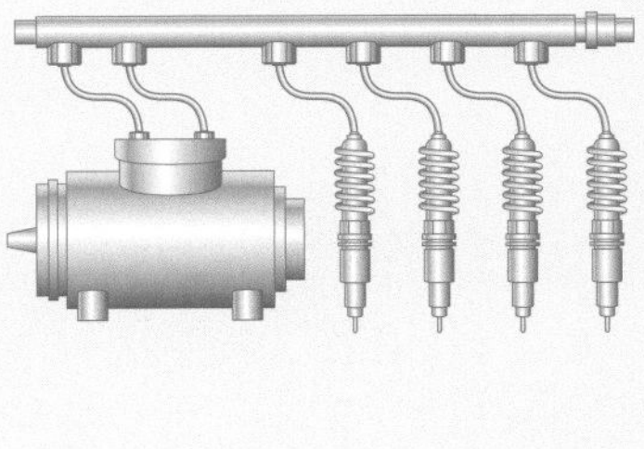

THE BEETLE

It's hard to think of a more iconic car than the VW Beetle. Designed as a robust and affordable family car, it is now treasured by collectors the world over. The prototype was built in 1935 and mass production began in 1945.

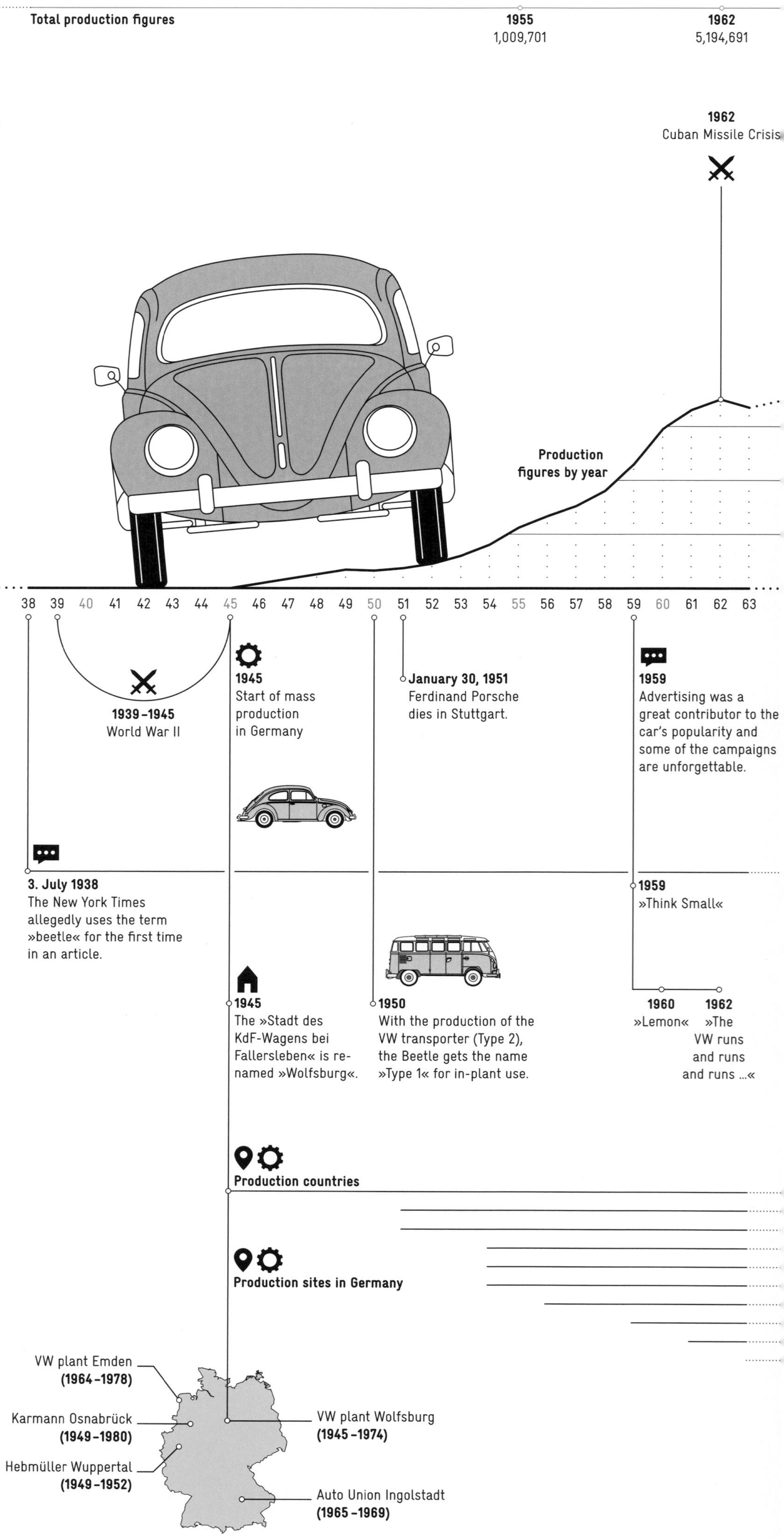
Total production figures
1955
1,009,701
1962
5,194,691
1962
Cuban Missile Crisis
Production figures by year
38 39 40 41 42 43 44 45 46 47 48 49 50 51 52 53 54 55 56 57 58 59 60 61 62 63
1939–1945
World War II
1945
Start of mass production in Germany
January 30, 1951
Ferdinand Porsche dies in Stuttgart.
1959
Advertising was a great contributor to the car's popularity and some of the campaigns are unforgettable.
3. July 1938
The New York Times allegedly uses the term »beetle« for the first time in an article.
1959
»Think Small«
1945
The »Stadt des KdF-Wagens bei Fallersleben« is re-named »Wolfsburg«.
1950
With the production of the VW transporter (Type 2), the Beetle gets the name »Type 1« for in-plant use.
1960
»Lemon«
1962
»The VW runs and runs and runs ...«
Production countries
Production sites in Germany
VW plant Emden
(1964–1978)
Karmann Osnabrück
(1949–1980)
Hebmüller Wuppertal
(1949–1952)
VW plant Wolfsburg
(1945–1974)
Auto Union Ingolstadt
(1965–1969)

1925
Béla Barényi creates the first design that serves as the basis for the Beetle's construction. The authorship (VW Type1) is recognized in court in 1955.

1930
Ferdinand Porsche sets up his first construction office.

1931
Porsche constructs a prototype of a small car for the Zündapp-Werke GmbH, the Porsche Type 12.

1933
A midsize prototype follows for the NSU D-Rad Vereinigte Fahrzeugwerke AG (Porsche Type 32).

June 22, 1934
Porsche and the Reich's Association of the Automobile Industry sign a contract for the construction of the »Volkswagen«.

July 3, 1935
Type 60 prototypes (internally called V1) are built in the garage of Porsche's private residence.

1937
The Porsche Type 60 (VW 30) pre-series is manufactured at Daimler-Benz.

1938
The pre-series VW 38, the official »KdF-Wagen« (strength through joy) is built.

May 26, 1938
Adolf Hitler, an enthusiastic car fan, lays the foundation stone at the Volkswagen plant near Fallersleben. The plan is to start mass production a year later.

July 1, 1938
In the the vicinity of the plant, the »Stadt des KdF-Wagens bei Fallersleben« is founded. Today the city is called Wolfsburg.

1939
World War II prevents mass production because the plant has to produce millitary vehicles for the Wehrmacht.

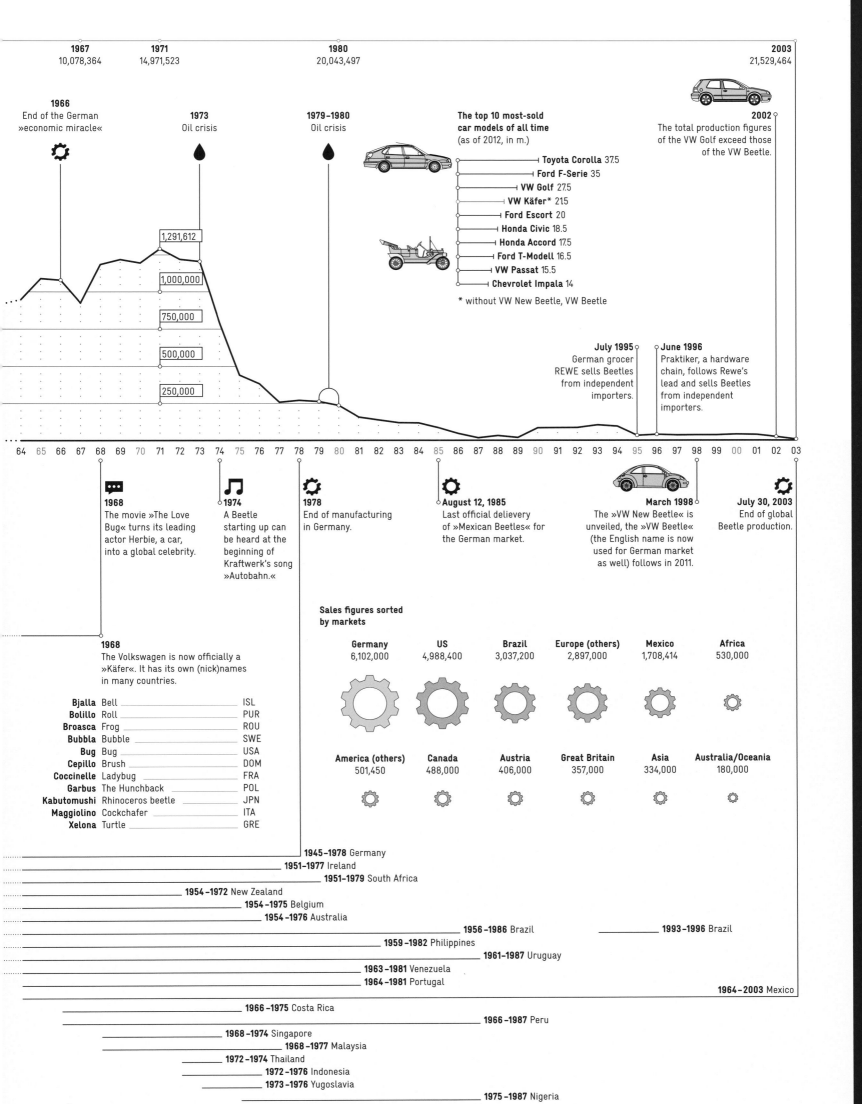

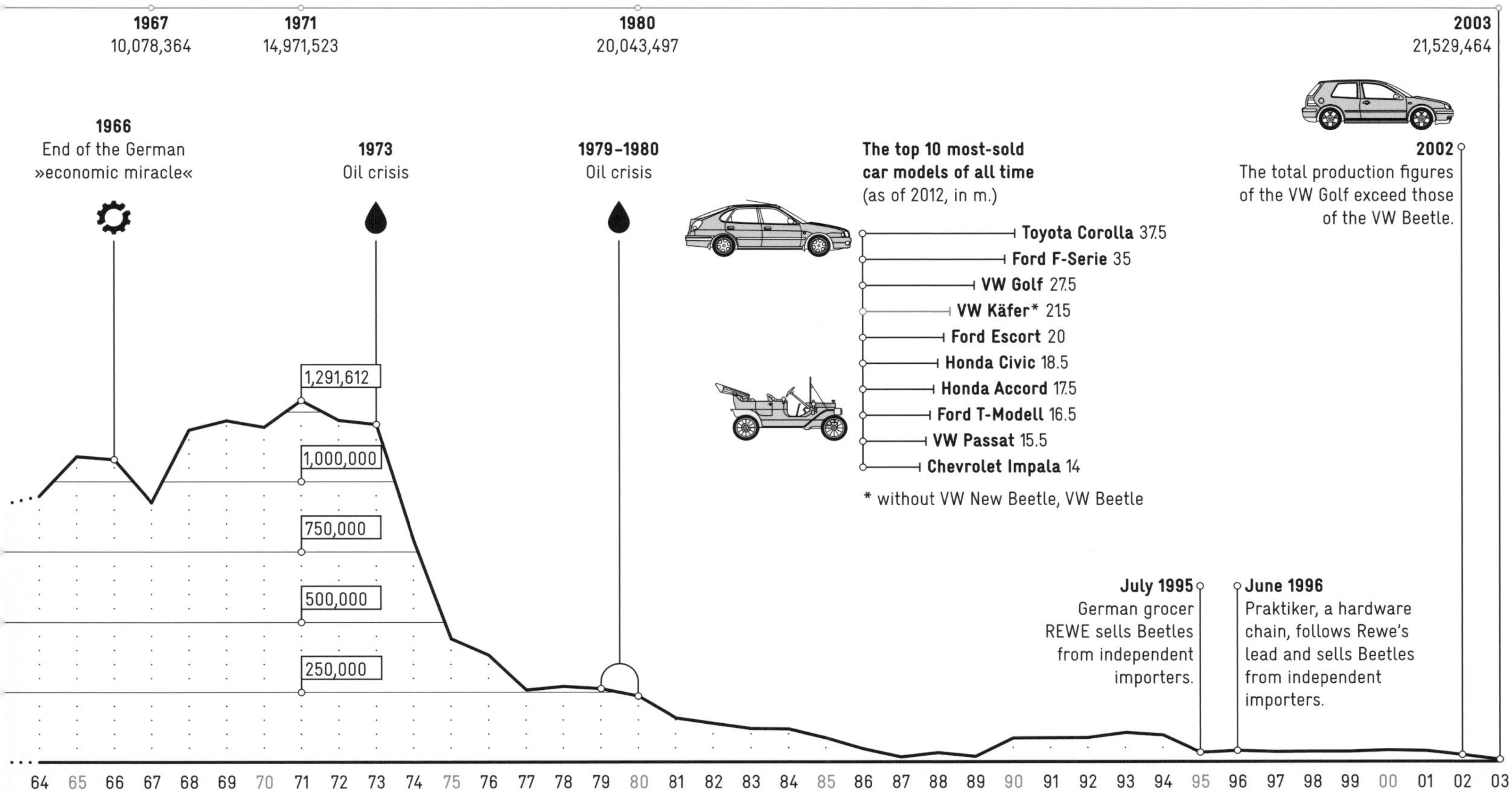
1967
10,078,364
1971
14,971,523
1980
20,043,497
2003
21,529,464
1966
End of the German »economic miracle«
1973
Oil crisis
1979–1980
Oil crisis
The top 10 most-sold car models of all time
(as of 2012, in m.)
Toyota Corolla 37.5
Ford F-Serie 35
VW Golf 27.5
VW Käfer* 21.5
Ford Escort 20
Honda Civic 18.5
Honda Accord 17.5
Ford T-Modell 16.5
VW Passat 15.5
Chevrolet Impala 14
* without VW New Beetle, VW Beetle
2002
The total production figures of the VW Golf exceed those of the VW Beetle.
1,291,612
1,000,000
750,000
500,000
250,000
July 1995
German grocer REWE sells Beetles from independent importers.
June 1996
Praktiker, a hardware chain, follows Rewe's lead and sells Beetles from independent importers.
64 65 66 67 68 69 70 71 72 73 74 75 76 77 78 79 80 81 82 83 84 85 86 87 88 89 90 91 92 93 94 95 96 97 98 99 00 01 02 03

1968
The movie »The Love Bug« turns its leading actor Herbie, a car, into a global celebrity.

1974
A Beetle starting up can be heard at the beginning of Kraftwerk's song »Autobahn.«

1978
End of manufacturing in Germany.

August 12, 1985
Last official delievery of »Mexican Beetles« for the German market.

March 1998
The »VW New Beetle« is unveiled, the »VW Beetle« (the English name is now used for German market as well) follows in 2011.

July 30, 2003
End of global Beetle production.

1968
The Volkswagen is now officially a »Käfer«. It has its own (nick)names in many countries.

Bjalla	Bell	ISL
Bolillo	Roll	PUR
Broasca	Frog	ROU
Bubbla	Bubble	SWE
Bug	Bug	USA
Cepillo	Brush	DOM
Coccinelle	Ladybug	FRA
Garbus	The Hunchback	POL
Kabutomushi	Rhinoceros beetle	JPN
Maggiolino	Cockchafer	ITA
Xelona	Turtle	GRE

Sales figures sorted by markets

Market	Sales
Germany	6,102,000
US	4,988,400
Brazil	3,037,200
Europe (others)	2,897,000
Mexico	1,708,414
Africa	530,000
America (others)	501,450
Canada	488,000
Austria	406,000
Great Britain	357,000
Asia	334,000
Australia/Oceania	180,000

1945–1978 Germany
1951–1977 Ireland
1951–1979 South Africa
1954–1972 New Zealand
1954–1975 Belgium
1954–1976 Australia
1956–1986 Brazil
1993–1996 Brazil
1959–1982 Philippines
1961–1987 Uruguay
1963–1981 Venezuela
1964–1981 Portugal
1964–2003 Mexico
1966–1975 Costa Rica
1966–1987 Peru
1968–1974 Singapore
1968–1977 Malaysia
1972–1974 Thailand
1972–1976 Indonesia
1973–1976 Yugoslavia
1975–1987 Nigeria

BICYCLE REVOLUTION

The bicycle revolution spun into gear with Karl Drais who created the »running machine«, a first in wheeled self-propelled mobility. The bicycle's key development stages happened in quick succession. Bikes made at the start of the 20th century closely resemble bikes we ride today.

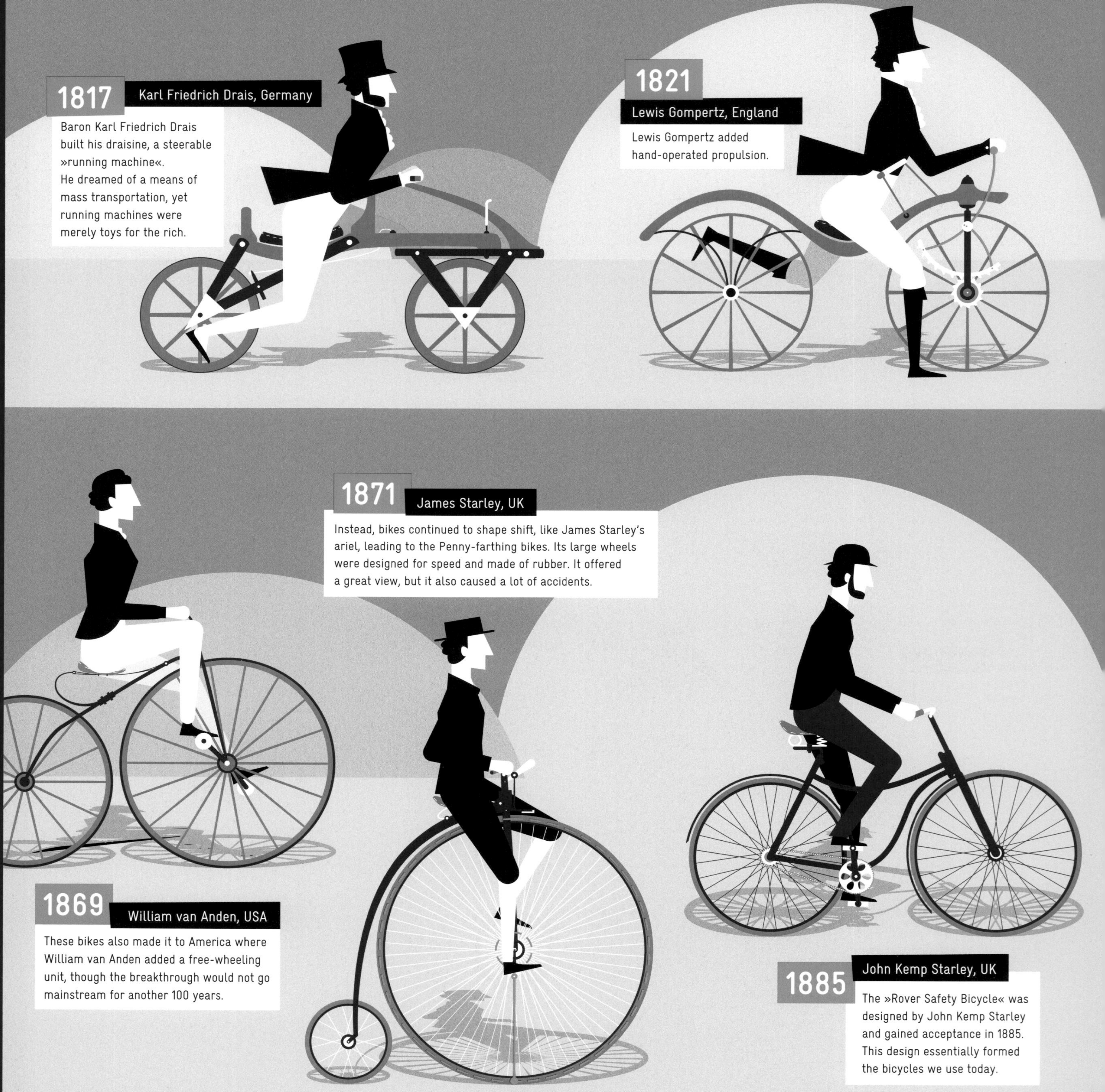

1817 Karl Friedrich Drais, Germany

Baron Karl Friedrich Drais built his draisine, a steerable »running machine«. He dreamed of a means of mass transportation, yet running machines were merely toys for the rich.

1821 Lewis Gompertz, England

Lewis Gompertz added hand-operated propulsion.

1869 William van Anden, USA

These bikes also made it to America where William van Anden added a free-wheeling unit, though the breakthrough would not go mainstream for another 100 years.

1871 James Starley, UK

Instead, bikes continued to shape shift, like James Starley's ariel, leading to the Penny-farthing bikes. Its large wheels were designed for speed and made of rubber. It offered a great view, but it also caused a lot of accidents.

1885 John Kemp Starley, UK

The »Rover Safety Bicycle« was designed by John Kemp Starley and gained acceptance in 1885. This design essentially formed the bicycles we use today.

1853

Philipp Moritz Fischer, Germany

It took a generation until pedals were added by Philipp Fischer.

1863

Pierre Michaux, France

10 years later, Frenchman Pierre Michaux made the velocipede, and the first popular bike despite the bone-rattling ride.

1963

BMX

The nimble BMX bikes (bicycle motocross) came into existence in the USA, with beaded edge tires, small wheels and high handlebars. The 1982 film E.T. triggered a boom in BMX sales among teenagers.

1974

Mountain Bike

Three Californians named Joe Breeze, Charles Kelly and Gary Fisher made old bikes with lugged tires as off-road bikes. The mountain bike was created.

1903

Racing Bike

As people found new ways to enjoy bicycles, the form continued to change. Racing bikes developed with the popularity of races like the Tour de France.

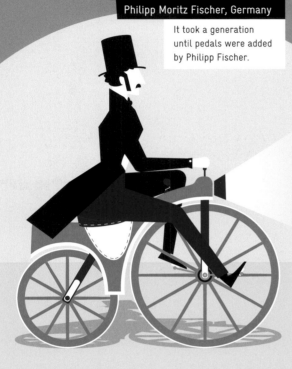

1928
where derailleur gears first featured in 1937, nine years after their invention.

DONT WALK

Green and red icons have been safely ushering pedestrians across the street since the mid-19th century and have since evolved into many shapes and forms. Appreciate their diversity in our selection from all over the world!

GERMANY (FORMER GDR)

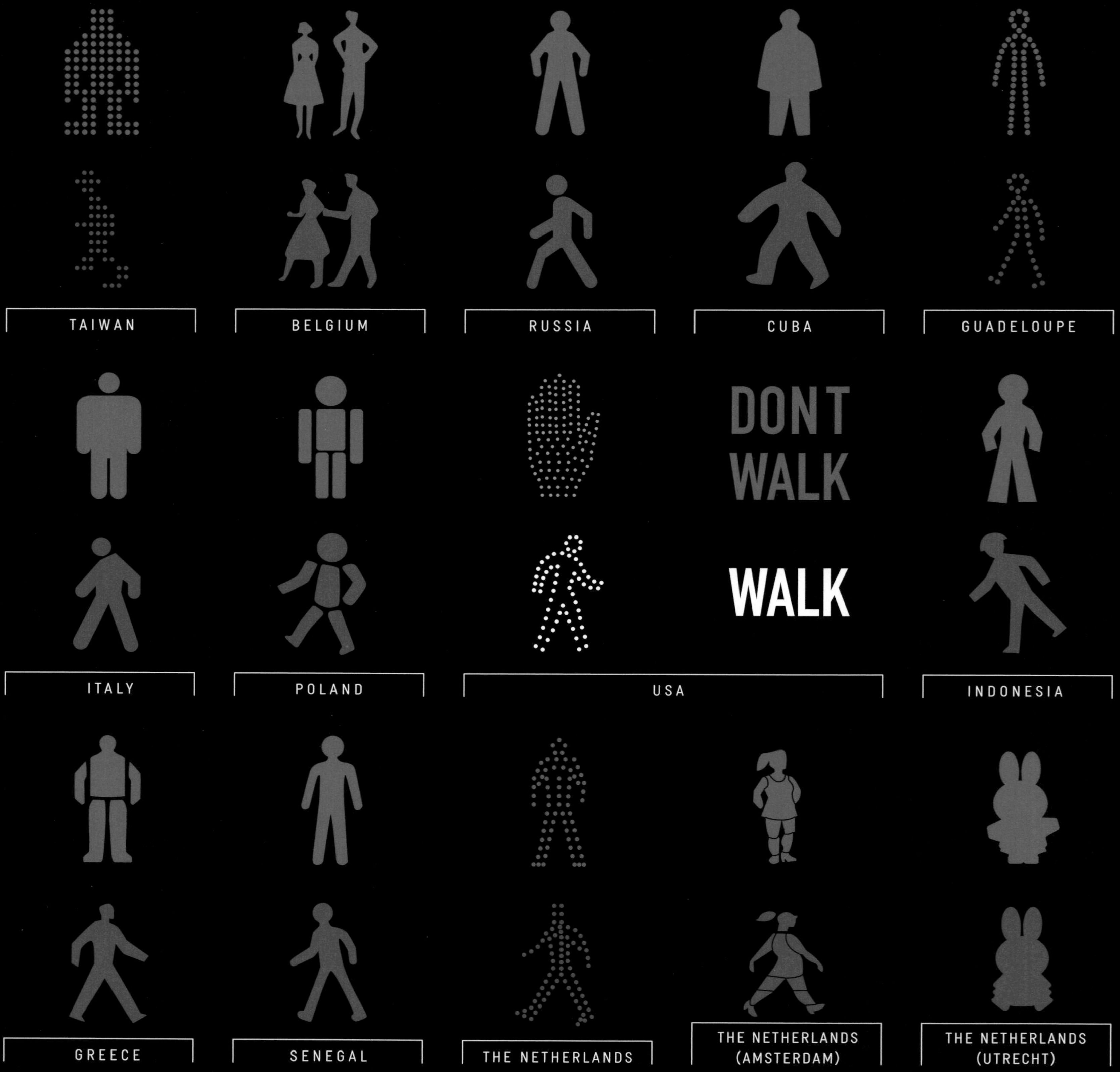
TAIWAN
BELGIUM
RUSSIA
CUBA
GUADELOUPE
DONT
WALK
WALK
ITALY
POLAND
USA
INDONESIA
GREECE
SENEGAL
THE NETHERLANDS
THE NETHERLANDS (AMSTERDAM)
THE NETHERLANDS (UTRECHT)

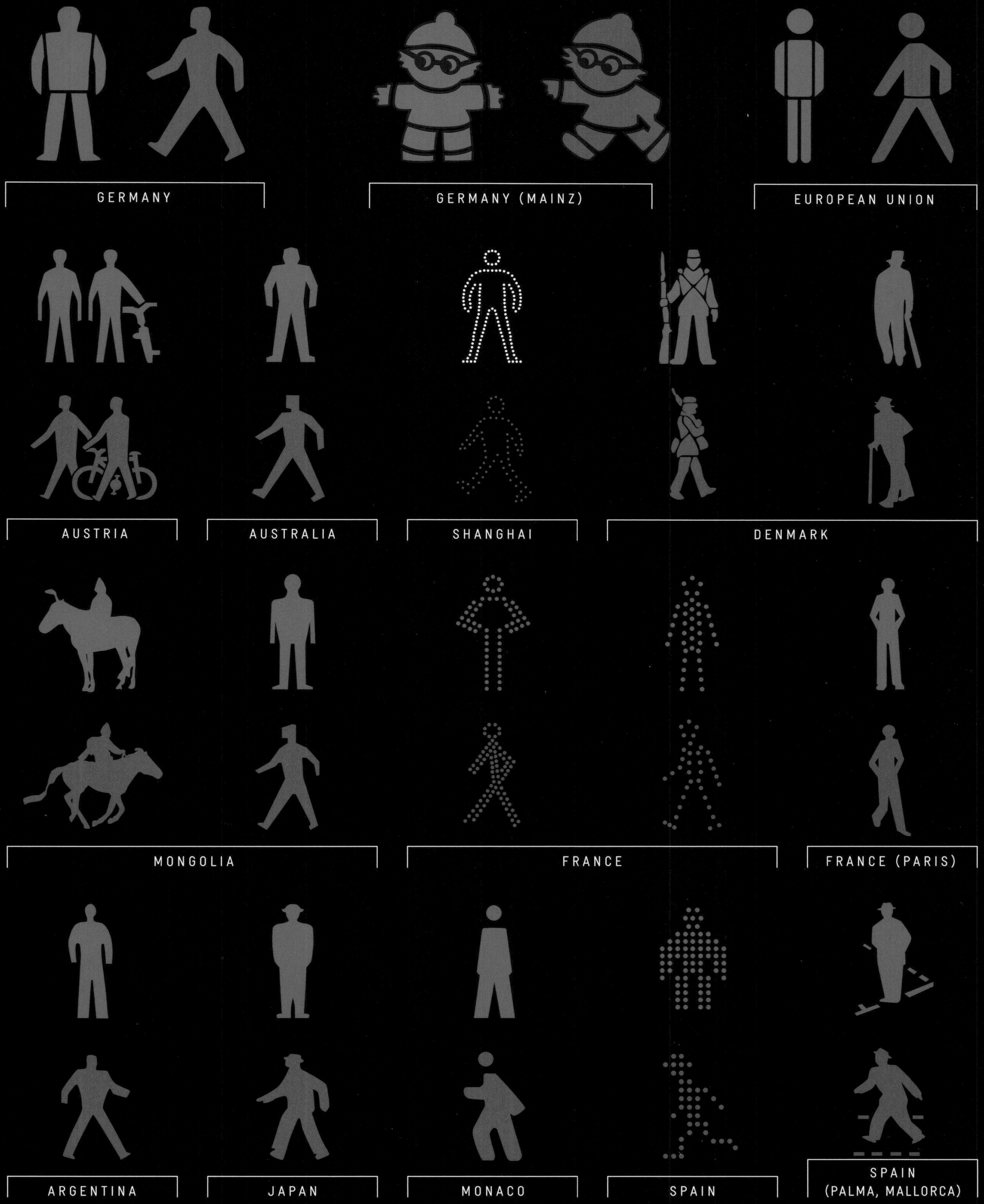
GERMANY
GERMANY (MAINZ)
EUROPEAN UNION
AUSTRIA
AUSTRALIA
SHANGHAI
DENMARK
MONGOLIA
FRANCE
FRANCE (PARIS)
ARGENTINA
JAPAN
MONACO
SPAIN
SPAIN (PALMA, MALLORCA)

CROSSING TIME

Have you ever wondered when the first traffic light characters were invented and where the red-and-green color scheme comes from? Today, these signals are ubiquitous and come in multiple shapes and characters. But life wasn't always so easy for the pedestrian ...

Walk like a pedestrian

As long as people were just on foot, there was no need for traffic lights. They shared the street with each other and people could easily move around each other.

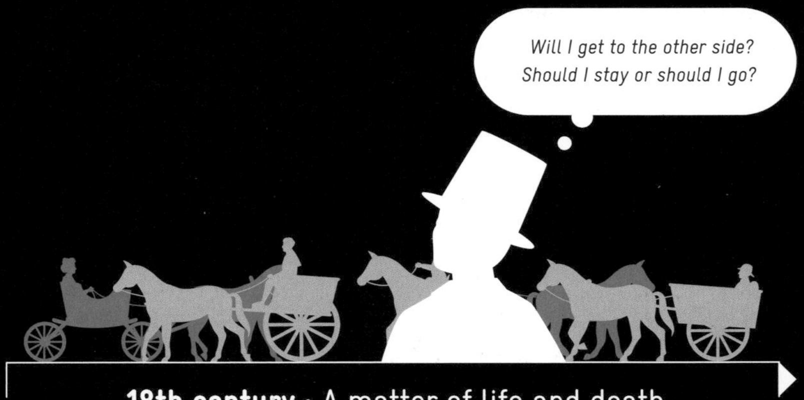
Will I get to the other side?
Should I stay or should I go?

18th century · A matter of life and death

Industrialization—and the urbanization that came with it—made streets increasingly crowded by a chaotic flow of horse-drawn traffic. Accidents happened frequently and pedestrians gambled with their lives with every step they took in the streets.

1866 · An enlightened idea

British railroad engineer John Peake Knight proposed to implement the same system used in railroads to make London streets safer for pedestrians. His idea included using the same red-green color scheme that had told trains when to stop and go since the 1830s.

If I stay it will be double

First light

The first electric lights for pedestrians were undocumented, but as they started to appear, they kept the red-green color scheme. But relying on the same signals as car drivers was becoming a risk. Something had to be done.

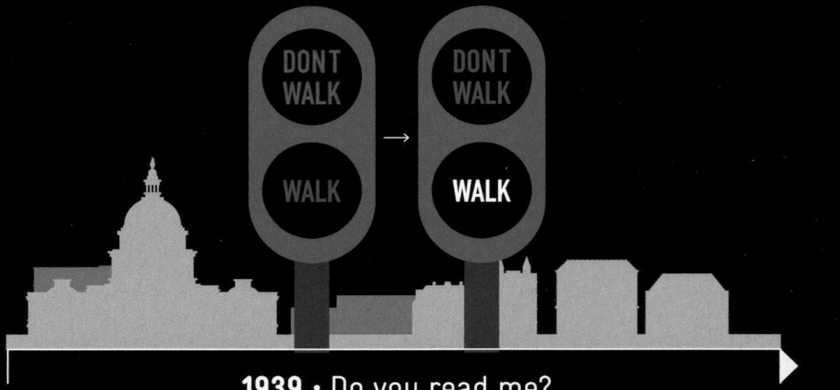

1939 · Do you read me?

Before pictograms took over the streets, typography told people when to walk and when to stay. These signs debuted in Washington DC, USA. They were a success and soon appeared at street corners throughout America. To keep things simple, the apostrophe was dropped.

Can't wait to see him dance

1999 · Let's dance

The first animated traffic light system was placed in Taipei, Taiwan. The faster the little green man goes, the closer the light is to turning red. Today, this concept is used in other countries, including Spain, Mexico and China.

Exactly who I'm supposed to be

2000 · Gender equality

A small Dutch town introduced a female counterpart to the red and green men. The traffic light woman is nicknamed Sofie. Today, Sofie helps people cross streets in other Dutch towns. Although female icons appear in other countries, they remain a curiosity.

Iconic silhouettes

The first pedestrians created pictographic representations of themselves, but it would be thousands of years before similar icons would be ushering people across the street.

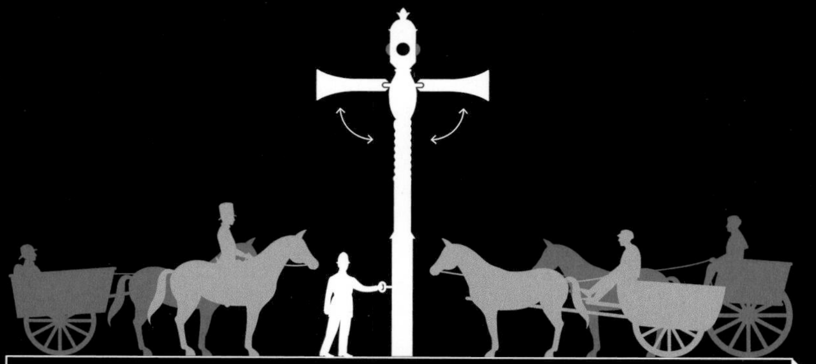

1868 · Give it some gas

It took two years for Knight to see his idea realized. The design combined a railway semaphore signal to control traffic by day and red-green gas lights by night. Pedestrians did not have their own signal, but the controlled traffic still allowed them to cross the streets safely.

These fancy new motor vehicles are a menace to the streets! If I go there will be trouble ...

1914 · New light

The advent of electricity sped up the evolution of traffic lights. The first regular electric traffic signal was installed at Euclid Avenue and East 105th Street in Cleveland, USA. Red-green lights were still used as indicators.

1950s · Icons hit the street

Pictograms experienced a renaissance in the 1950s and were soon used for pedestrian-oriented traffic lights, like these above left, which were first seen in West Germany. Eastern Germany introduced its famous »Ampelmännchen« in the 70s.

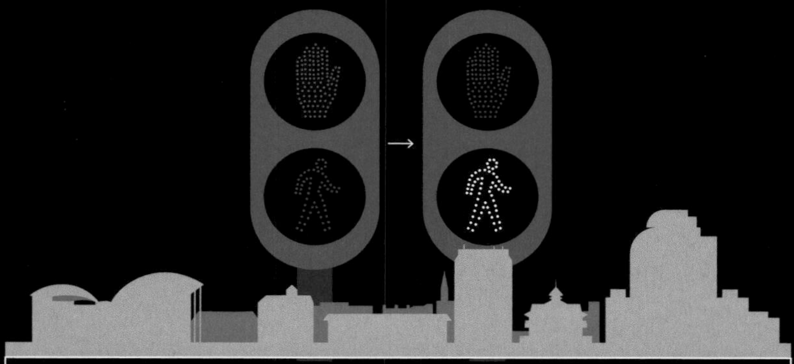

1996 · Let's count down

Countdown timers were first introduced in Hampton, Virginia, USA and have been a mandatory feature at all larger American intersections. They have further decreased the number of accidents.

In German, you would be called a »smombie« (combination of smartphone and zombie)

2016 · Smombie lights

Augsburg in Germany has started testing in-ground lights for pedestrians glued to their phones. The lights start to flash as soon as the regular pedestrian traffic light turns red. Several other cities are testing ways to solve the problem of texting while walking.

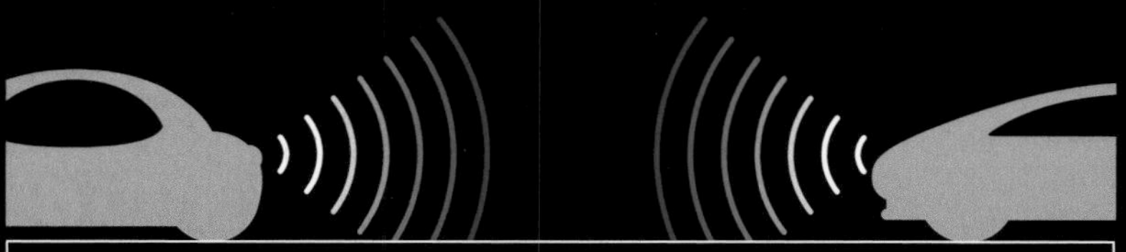

The future · Autonomous intersections

The MIT predicts that once all cars on the road are autonomous smart cars, intersections will operate similarly to air traffic control towers. However, this is unlikely to happen until all conventional cars are off the road. So until then, red means stop and green means go.

THE TUBE

On January 10, 1863, the first subway in the world was opened in London. Due to the many commuters that clogged up the streets of the city, the construction of a new railway line was urgently needed. The new line was supposed to connect the mainline terminus stations on the outskirts of the city with each other. The decision was made to build an underground railway line so as not to destroy the cityscape. It was built along existing main roads, so no buildings had to be demolished.

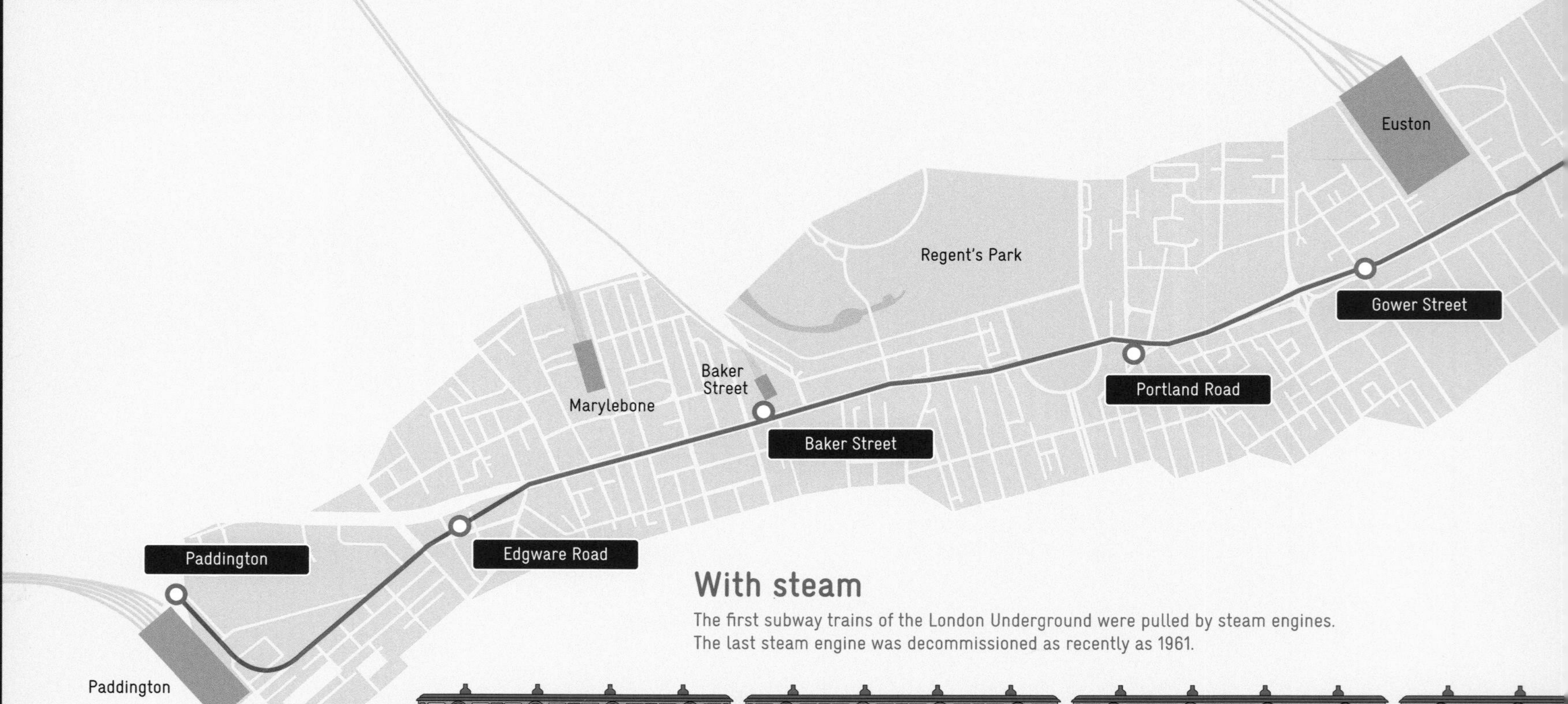
Euston
Regent's Park
Gower Street
Portland Road
Baker Street
Marylebone
Baker Street
Edgware Road
Paddington
Paddington

With steam

The first subway trains of the London Underground were pulled by steam engines. The last steam engine was decommissioned as recently as 1961.

The history of the London Underground map

The Underground maps were not always as simple as today's presentations. The main design that changed how present-day drafters design subway plans around the world goes back to draftsman Harry Beck in 1933.

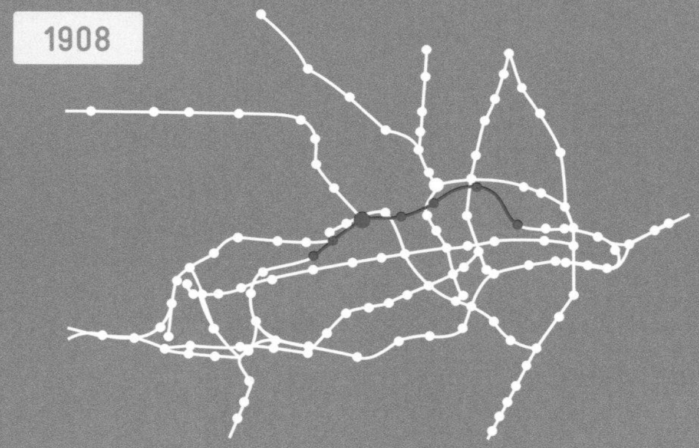
1908

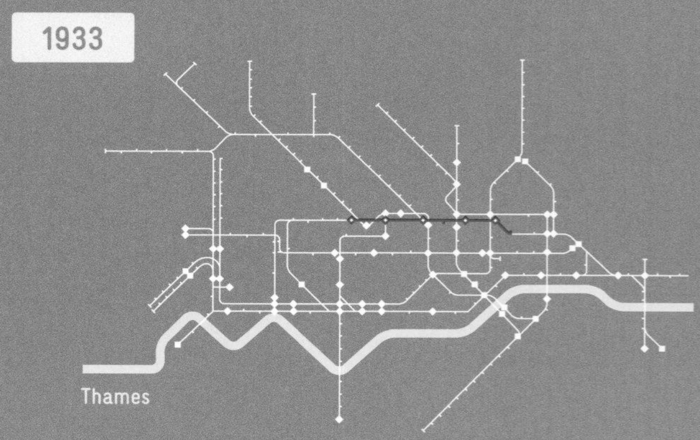
1933
Thames

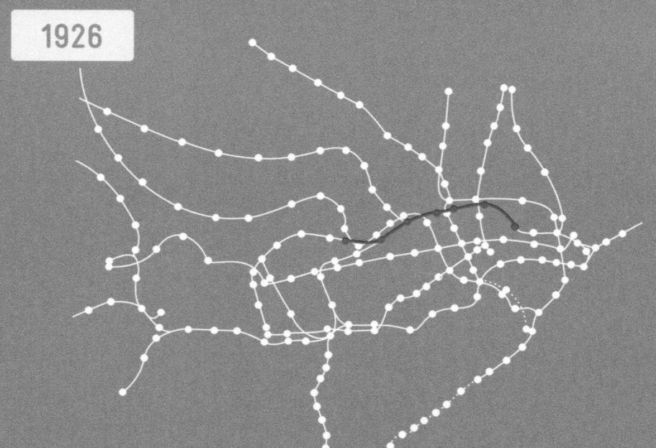
1926

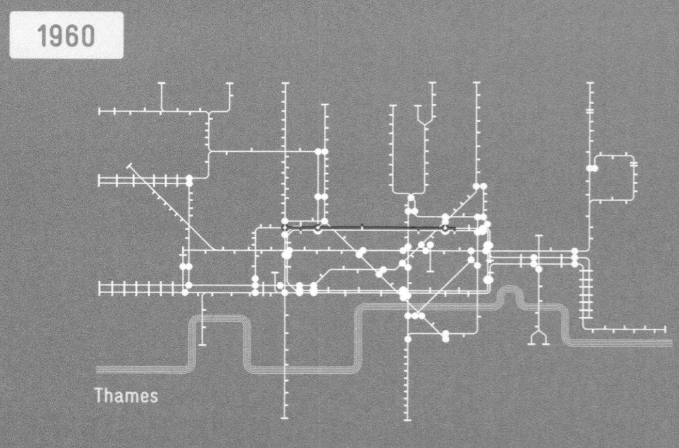
1960
Thames

Total length of the line	6.04 km
Total travelling time	18 min.
Stops	7
Passengers on the first day	30,000

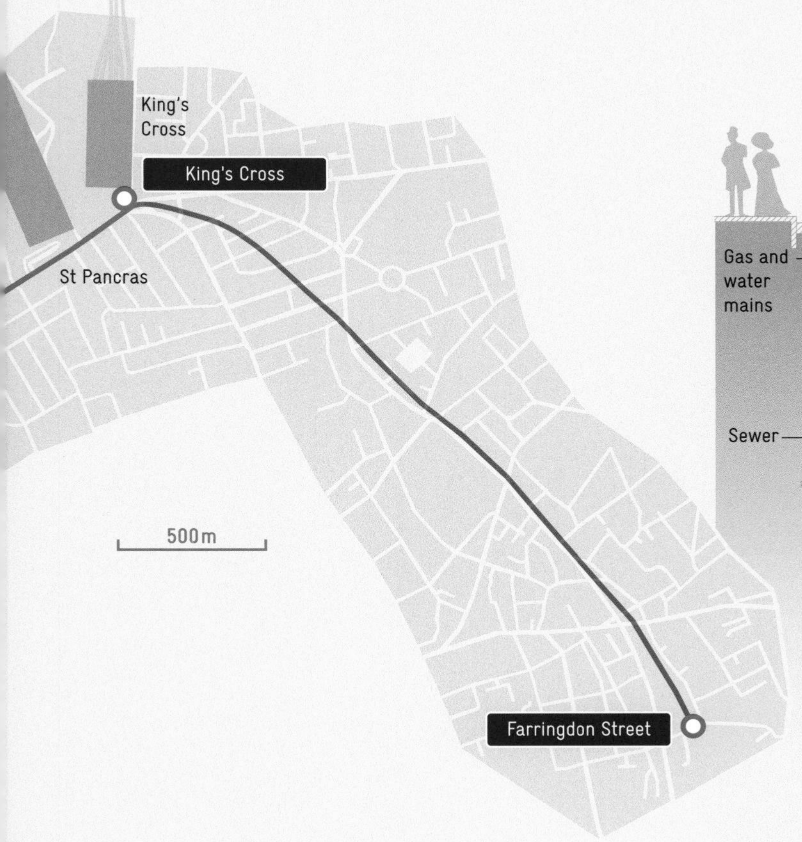
King's Cross
King's Cross
St Pancras
500m
Farringdon Street

Cut-and-cover

In 1860, there was only one way to dig a subterranean tunnel large enough to take a steam engine: dig a trench and then cover it up again (the Cut-and-cover method). Later, after the advent of electric locomotives, the simpler tunnelling shield method could be used. This allowed for a much deeper tunnel, thus creating the tubes.

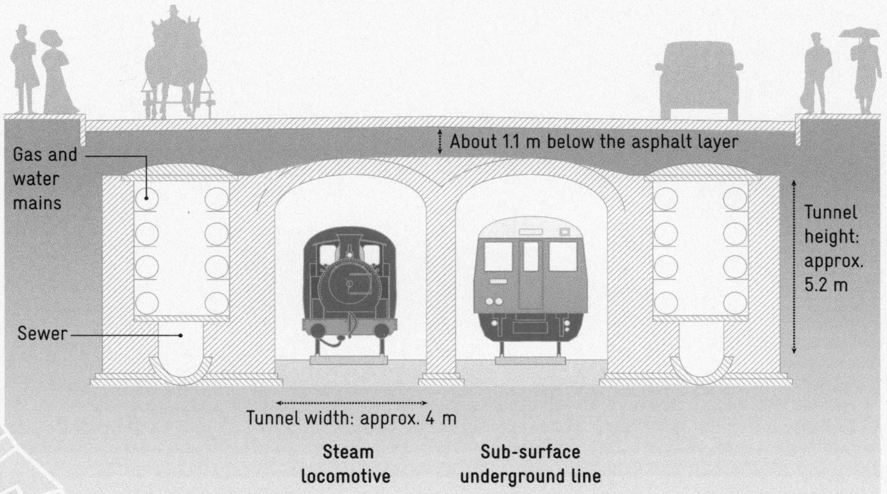
About 1.1 m below the asphalt layer
Gas and water mains
Sewer
Tunnel height: approx. 5.2 m
Tunnel width: approx. 4 m
Steam locomotive
Sub-surface underground line

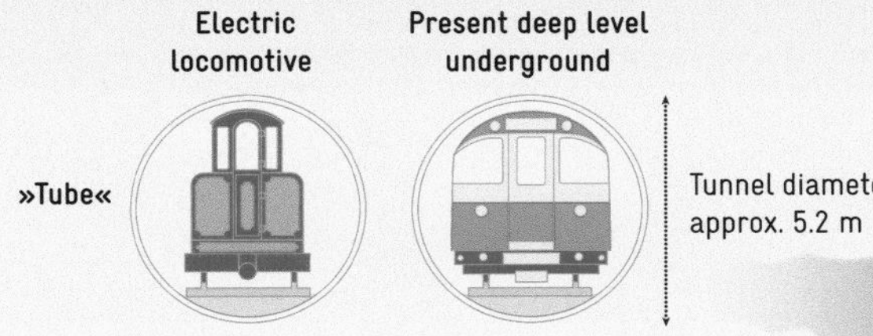
Electric locomotive
Present deep level underground
»Tube«
Tunnel diameter: approx. 5.2 m

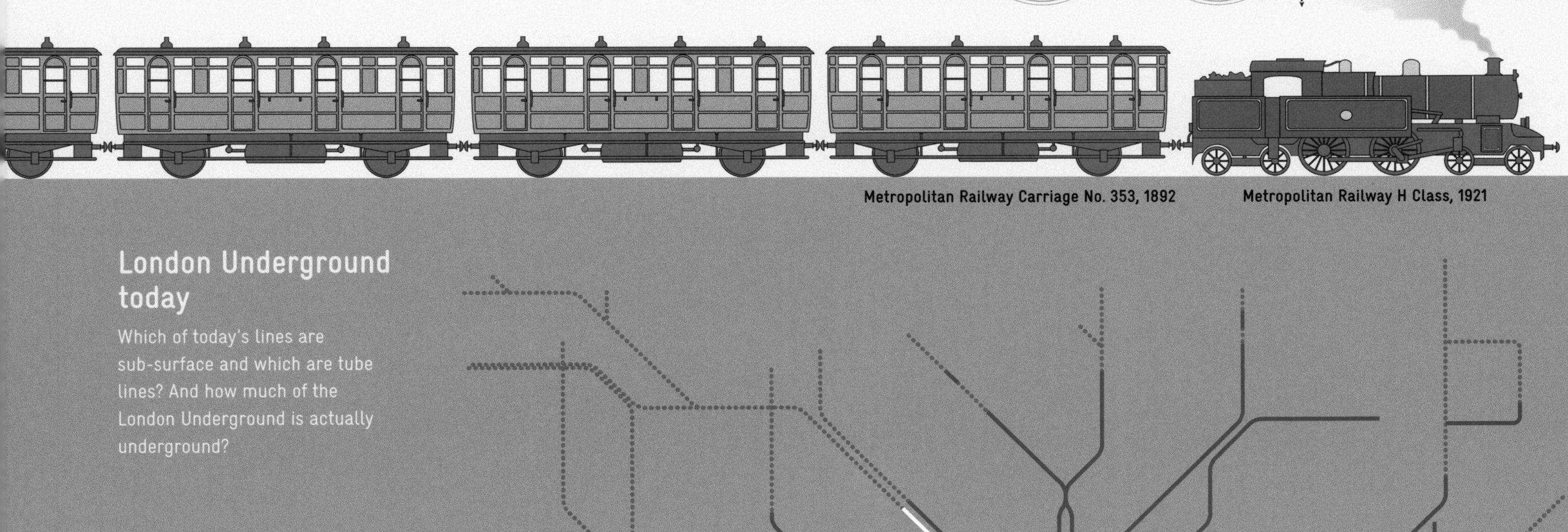
Metropolitan Railway Carriage No. 353, 1892
Metropolitan Railway H Class, 1921

London Underground today

Which of today's lines are sub-surface and which are tube lines? And how much of the London Underground is actually underground?

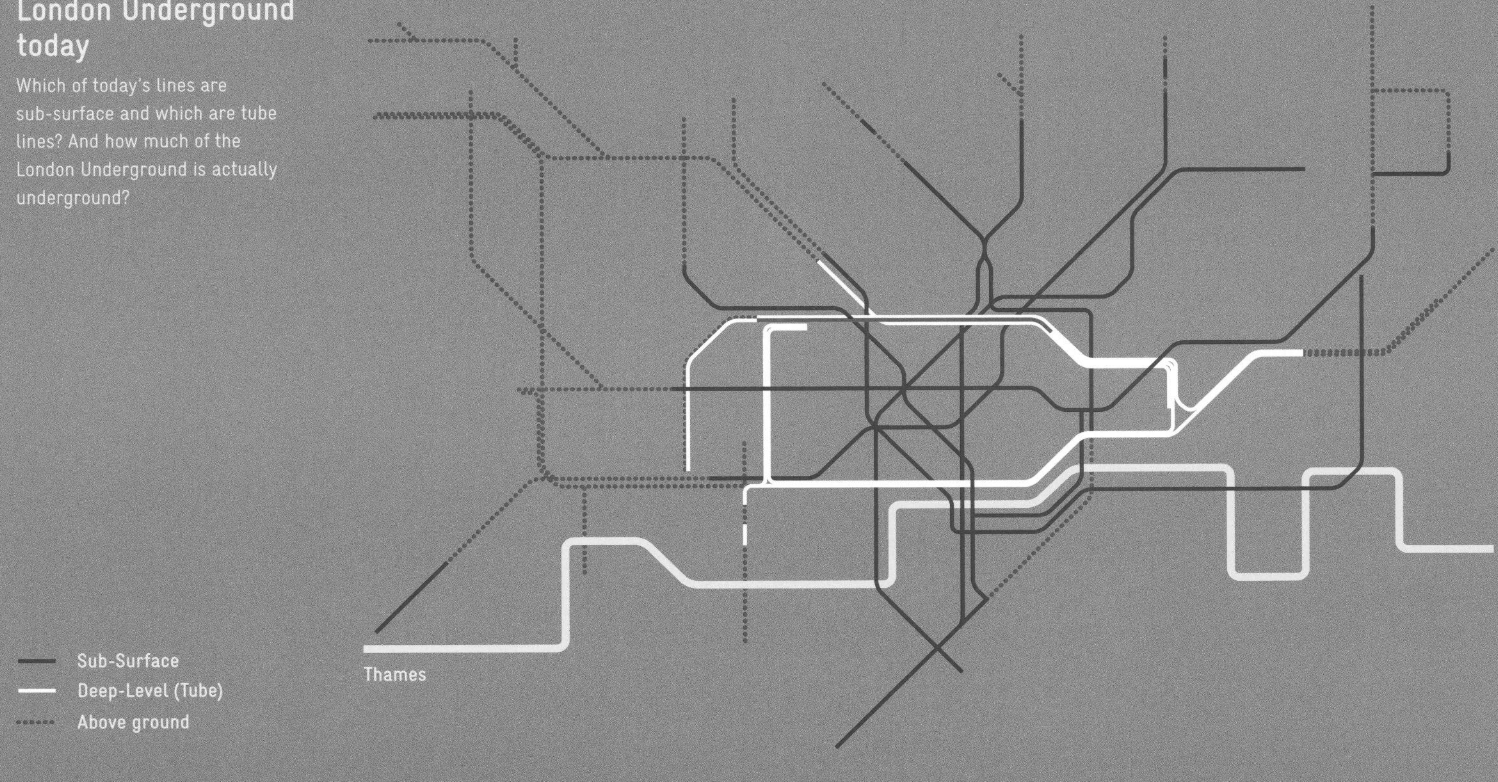
Thames
Sub-Surface
Deep-Level (Tube)
Above ground

THE MILLENNIUM HOLE

Switzerland made transport history 135 years ago with the construction of the longest tunnel in the Alps: the Gotthard Tunnel. Since 1999, the Swiss Alps have been cracked open, drilled through and excavated for a new record. In 2016, the longest and deepest railway tunnel in the world was opened: the Gotthard Base Tunnel.

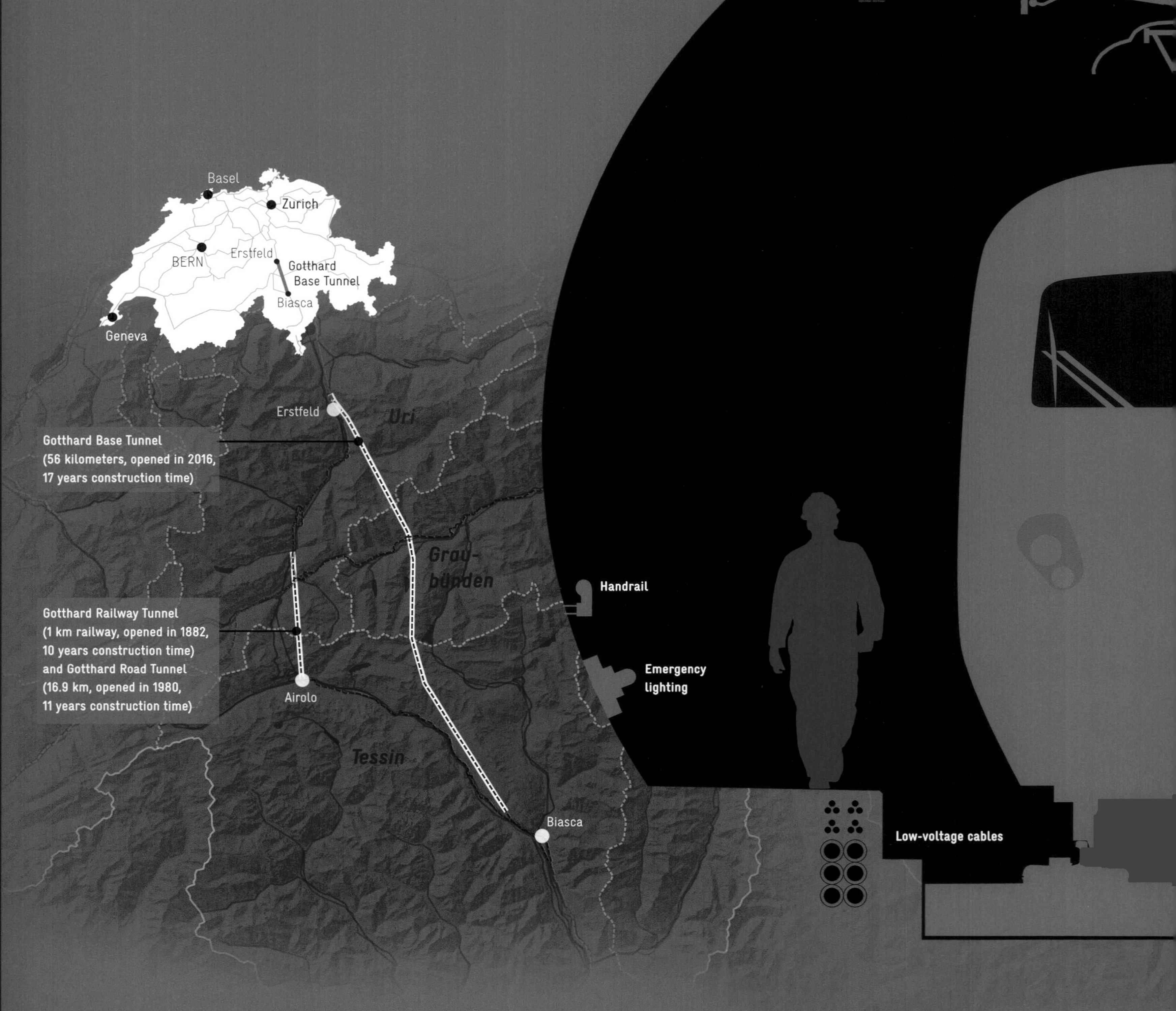

Basel
Zurich
BERN
Erstfeld
Gotthard Base Tunnel
Biasca
Geneva
Erstfeld
Uri
Gotthard Base Tunnel (56 kilometers, opened in 2016, 17 years construction time)
Grau-bünden
Gotthard Railway Tunnel (1 km railway, opened in 1882, 10 years construction time) and Gotthard Road Tunnel (16.9 km, opened in 1980, 11 years construction time)
Airolo
Tessin
Biasca
Handrail
Emergency lighting
Low-voltage cables

LONGITUDINAL PROFILE GOTTHARD BASE TUNNEL

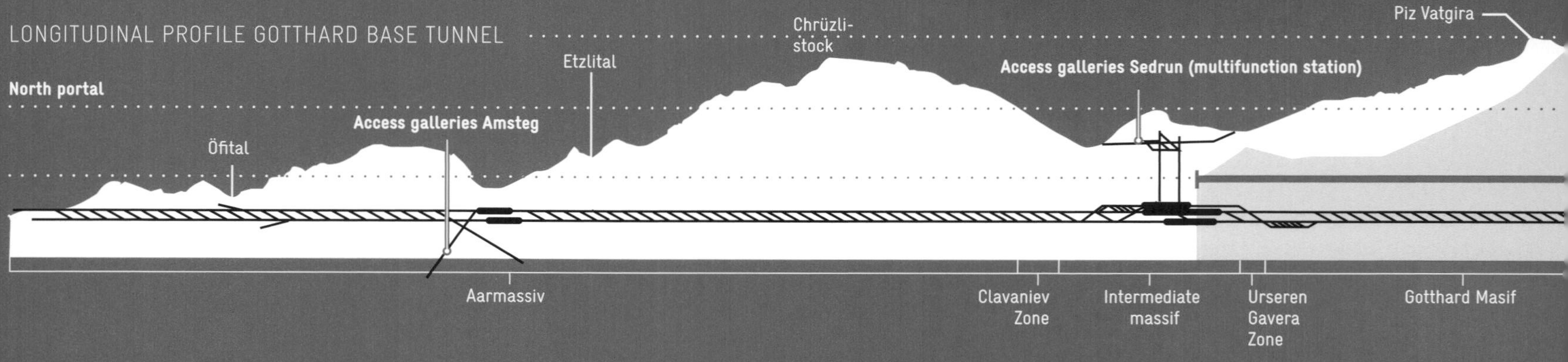

North portal
Öfital
Access galleries Amsteg
Etzlital
Chrüzli-stock
Access galleries Sedrun (multifunction station)
Piz Vatgira
Aarmassiv
Clavaniev Zone
Intermediate massif
Urseren Gavera Zone
Gotthard Masif

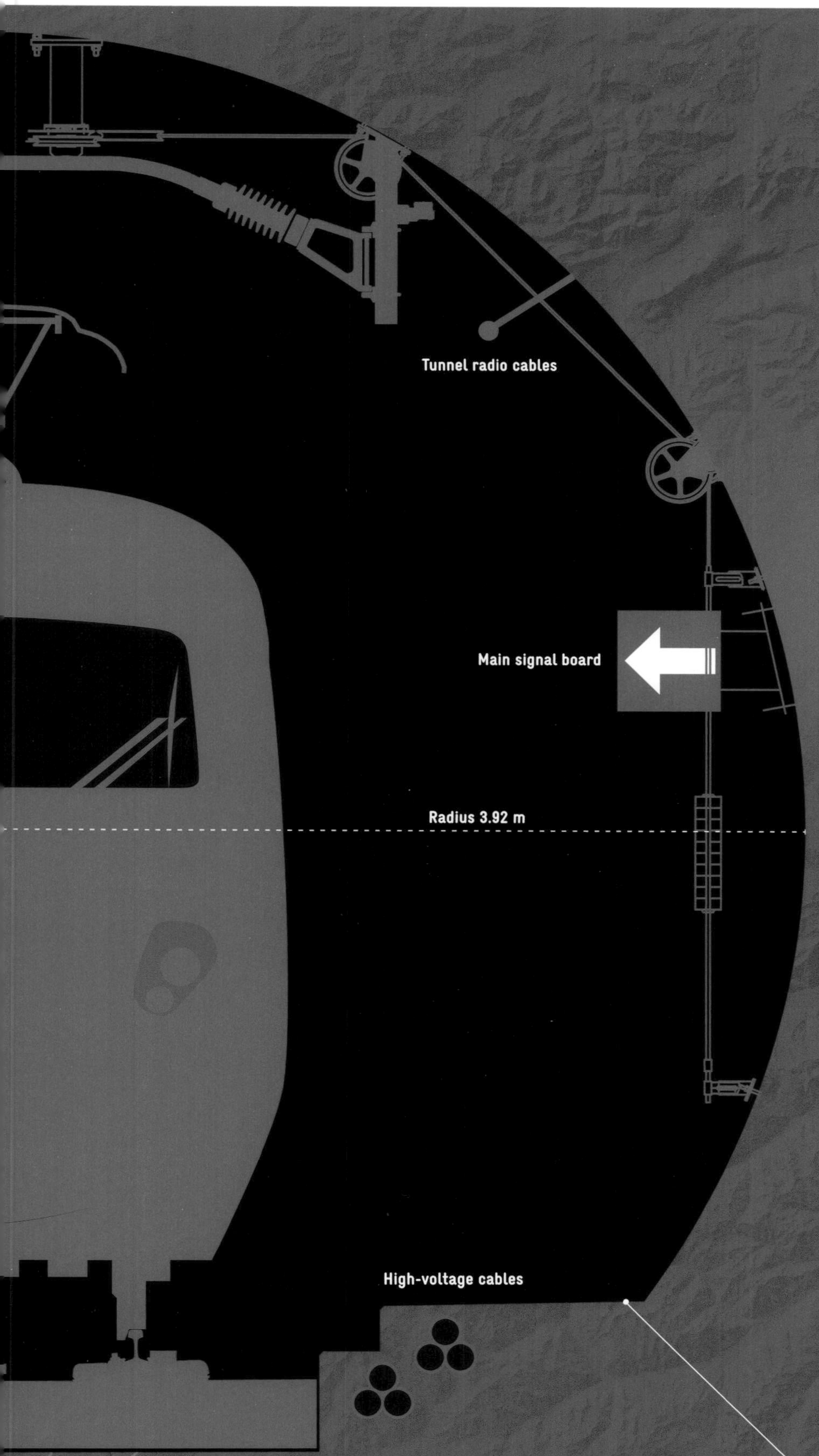
Tunnel radio cables
Main signal board
Radius 3.92 m
High-voltage cables

Data and facts about the Gotthard Base Tunnel

First outline of a Gotthard Base Tunnel in 1947 by engineer C. E. Gruner

Original break-through schedule missed by 8 cm horizontally and 1 cm vertically

Around CHF 18.2 bil. estimated total cost

2,600 people involved in construction

13.3 m. m³ excavated material (> 5 Cheops pyramids)

2,300 meter max. rock overburden

Railway tunnels worldwide in length

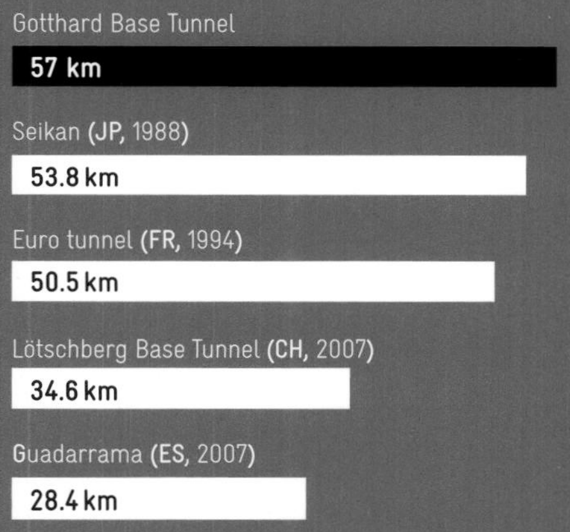
Gotthard Base Tunnel
57 km
Seikan (JP, 1988)
53.8 km
Euro tunnel (FR, 1994)
50.5 km
Lötschberg Base Tunnel (CH, 2007)
34.6 km
Guadarrama (ES, 2007)
28.4 km

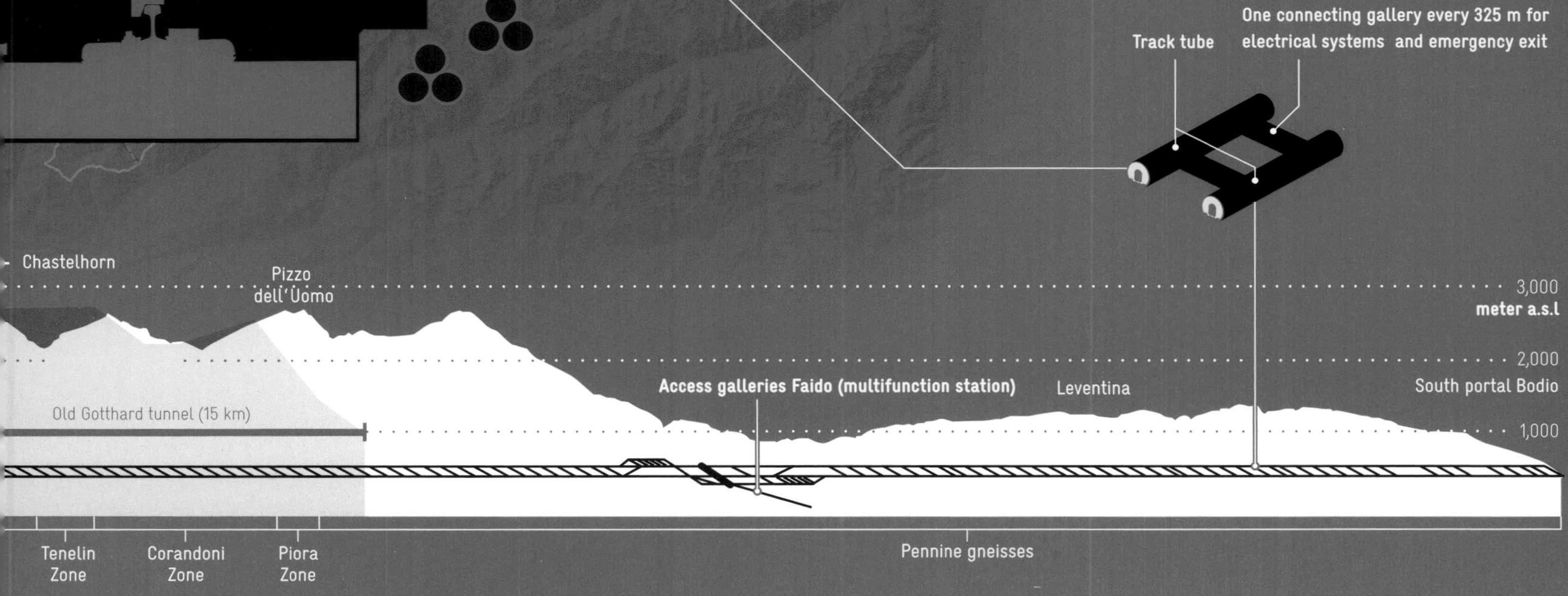
Track tube
One connecting gallery every 325 m for electrical systems and emergency exit
Chastelhorn
Pizzo dell'Uomo
3,000 meter a.s.l
2,000
1,000
Old Gotthard tunnel (15 km)
Access galleries Faido (multifunction station)
Leventina
South portal Bodio
Tenelin Zone
Corandoni Zone
Piora Zone
Pennine gneisses

PLANING OR DISPLACING?

The way a hull is shaped is one of the most important features of a ship: it determines the speed, passenger comfort, storage capacity and price, as well as how much energy it consumes. There are generally two types—the sporty planing hull or the comfortable displacement hull.

A SWIFTER JOURNEY—THE PLANING HULL

Planing hulls can overcome their own self-created wave system. The flat lines of the underwater ship body displaces the wake in good time. They are swift, agile and cool.

SPEED > HULL SPEED

U-RIB

Seaworthy cruisers designed for long journeys or expeditions are built with this classic shape of displacement hull. The u-rib offers a lot of space below deck and it also saves fuel.

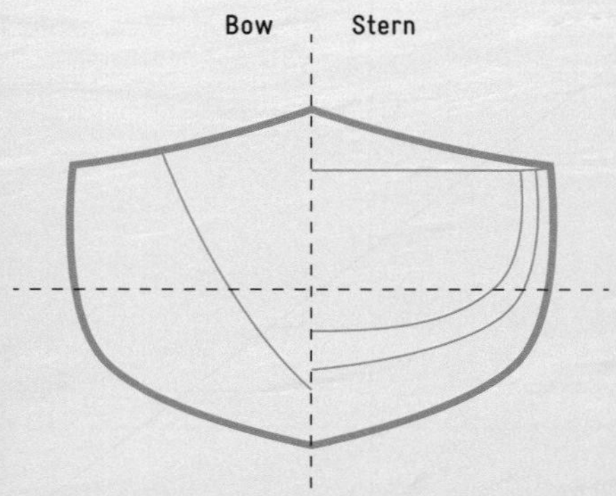

POWER BOAT

With this semi-planing hull, the bow wave is absorbed by the concave area of the hull. As a result, the hull speed can be vastly exceeded without the ship planing. That's perfect for large, comfortable yachts that also need to be fast.

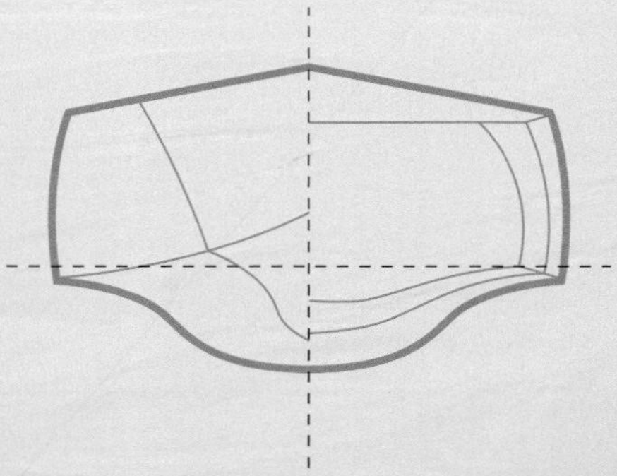

FLAT V-RIB

This shape means the ship handles in a very sporty manner. The ships are exceptionally fast, start to plane early, yet make for a rough journey as they cut through waves. The rear end is very flat, providing little directional stability. Therefore, the V-rib is more suited to calmer seas.

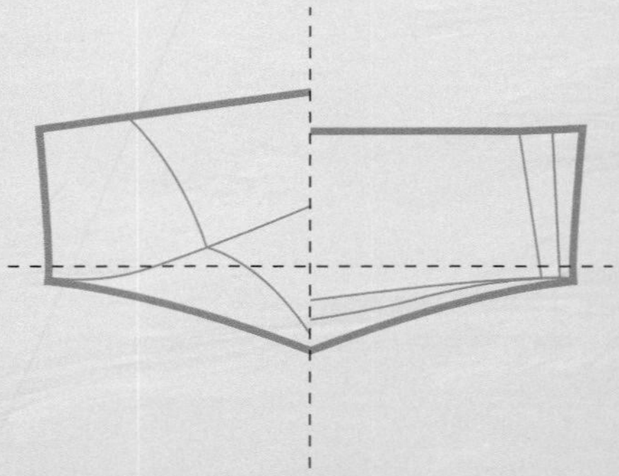

A GENTLE JOURNEY THROUGH THE WAVES—THE DISPLACEMENT HULL

Displacement hulls don't go beyond their hull speed. They are caught between their bow waves and wake. They are thus more stable, more cost-effective and more comfortable.

Hull and bow sit deeper underwater.
Wake
Bow wave
Hull
SPEED = HULL SPEED

CONCAVE V-RIB

Many regard this classic hull shape as the definition of great aesthetics. It is still very popular, despite its rather poor handling when seas are rough. What's more, the concave V-rib has been experiencing a veritable renaissance in recent years.

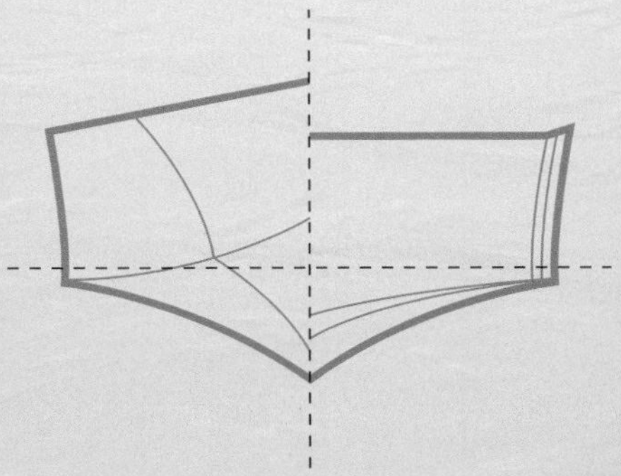

CONVEX V-RIB

This hull is a further development of the concave form and is often found on today's fast boats. The waves behave very well with a convex-shaped hull, as the boat is able to cut through them more smoothly.

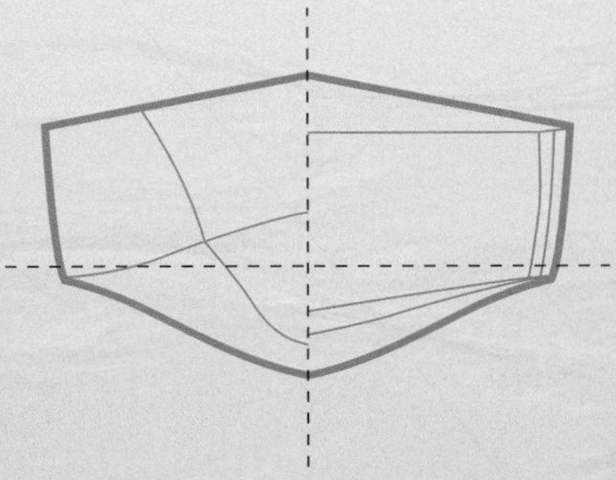

MODERN PLANING HULL

This planing hull is employed on fast off-shore boats, due to their powerful engines. This shape has proven itself to be very seaworthy—however strong turbulence at the stern slows the ship down during long journeys.

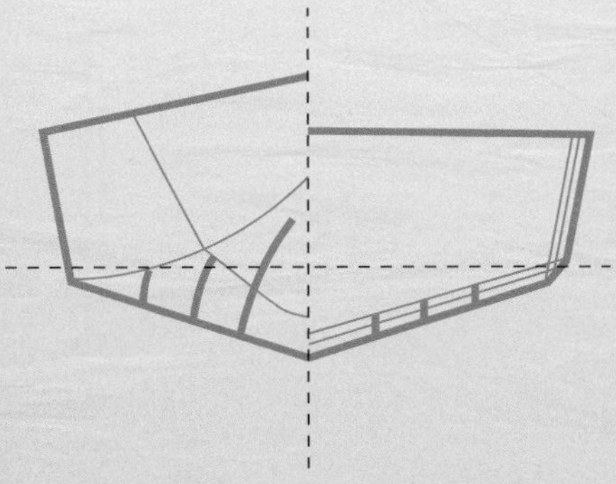

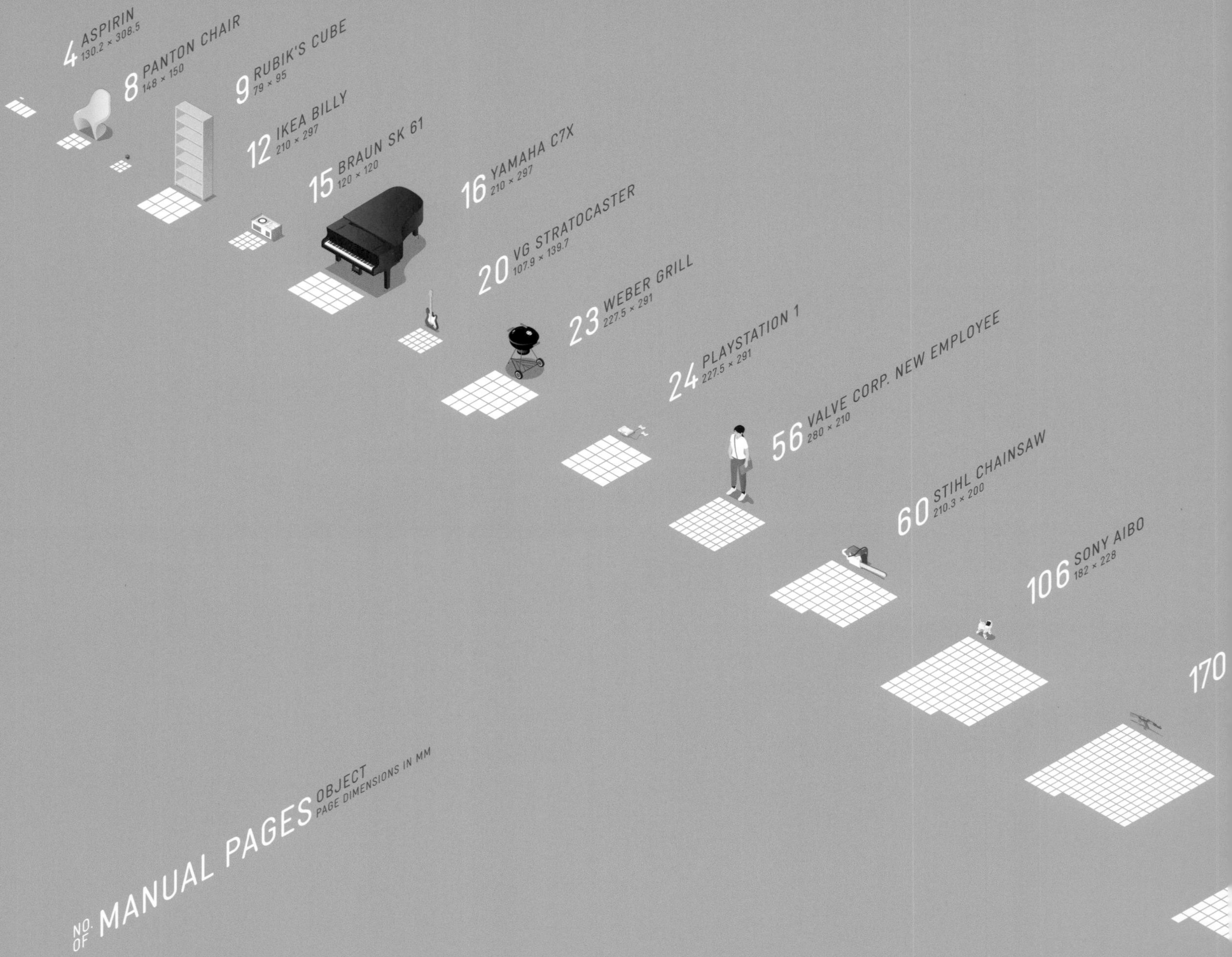

PAPER PLAINS

Some study them thoroughly, others like to hide them deep down in drawers. Manuals are the silent and often essential companions to products. Here we show the printed versions in direct relation to their product. Every manual page is pictured to scale and gives an idea of the scope of the manuals.

9 Since 1980, Erno Rubik's **cube** has confounded players all over the world. The manual explains the challenge in one sentence; the remaining pages contain hints.

15 The **radio and record player** SK61 was designed by Hans Gugelot and Dieter Rams in 1962. Its simple and functional design is mirrored in the square manual, colored black, white, and red.

20 In 1954, Fender showed that **electric guitars** don't have to look like acoustic ones. The VG Stratocaster offered five different models in 2006—one of which can simulate an acoustic guitar.

56 **Valve** develops computer and console games like Half-Life and Portal. The company has a flat management structure. With a touch of irony, their »Handbook for **new employees**« explains how new recruits can find their way within this flat hierarchy.

60 In 1926, Andreas Stihl developed the first electric **chainsaw**. Recent gasoline models used in forestry have a cutting length of up to 75 cm. Thoughtfully, the manual contains numerous warnings.

106 According to its manual, the Japanese **robot dog** Aibo can be trained in many ways. However, in 2006 the manufacturer decided to decommission the electrical pet and ended its production after corporate restructuring.

228 At a length of 90 cm and with over 3,000 pieces, the Star Wars spaceship is one of the largest **Lego models**. To keep the manual manageable, the instructions come in a three-ring binder.

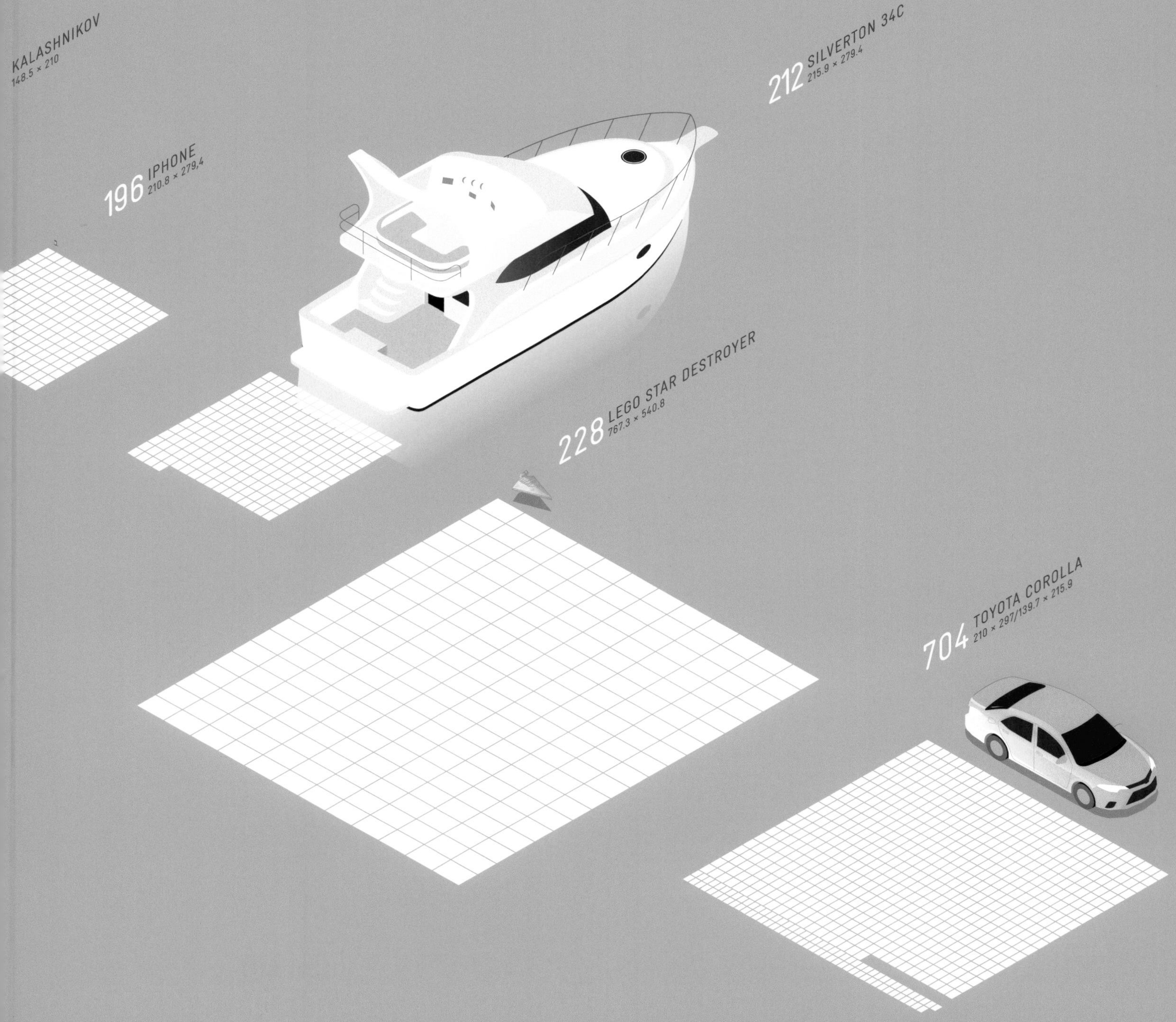
KALASHNIKOV
148.5 × 210
196 IPHONE
210.8 × 279.4
212 SILVERTON 34C
215.9 × 279.4
228 LEGO STAR DESTROYER
767.3 × 540.8
704 TOYOTA COROLLA
210 × 297/139.7 × 215.9

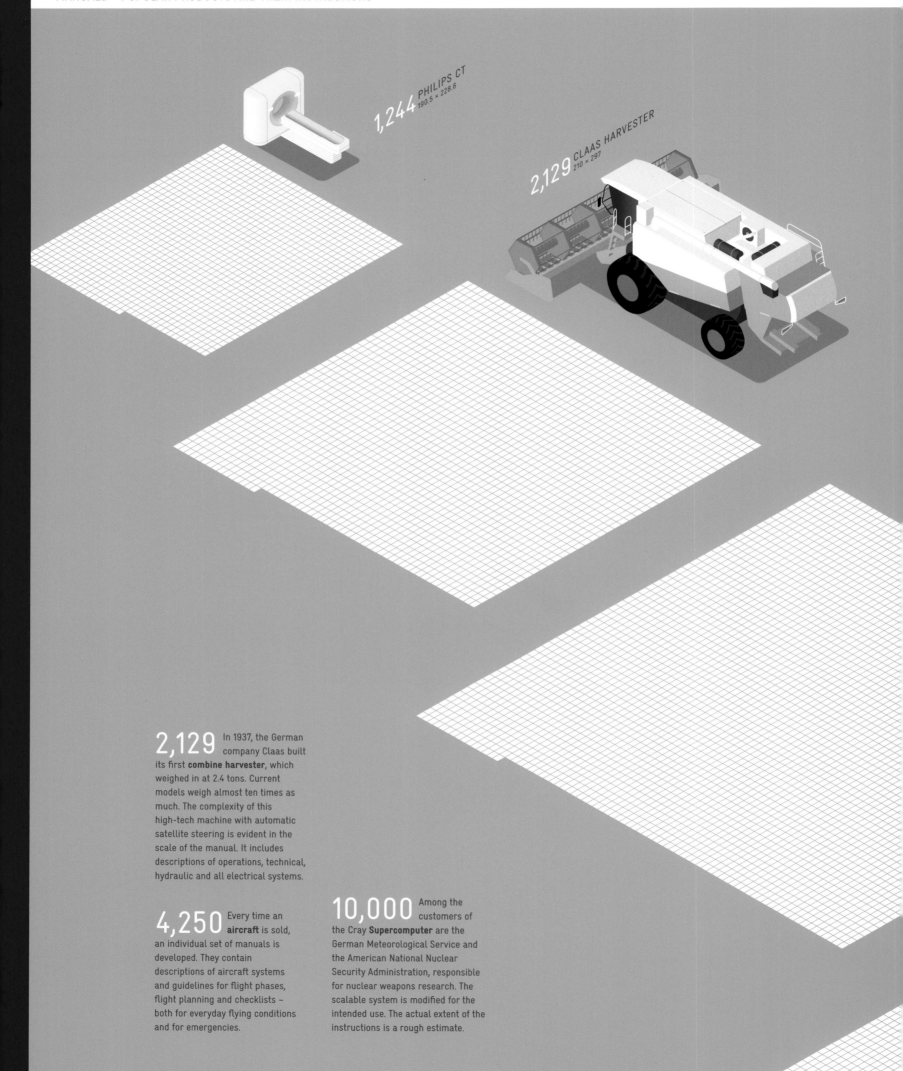

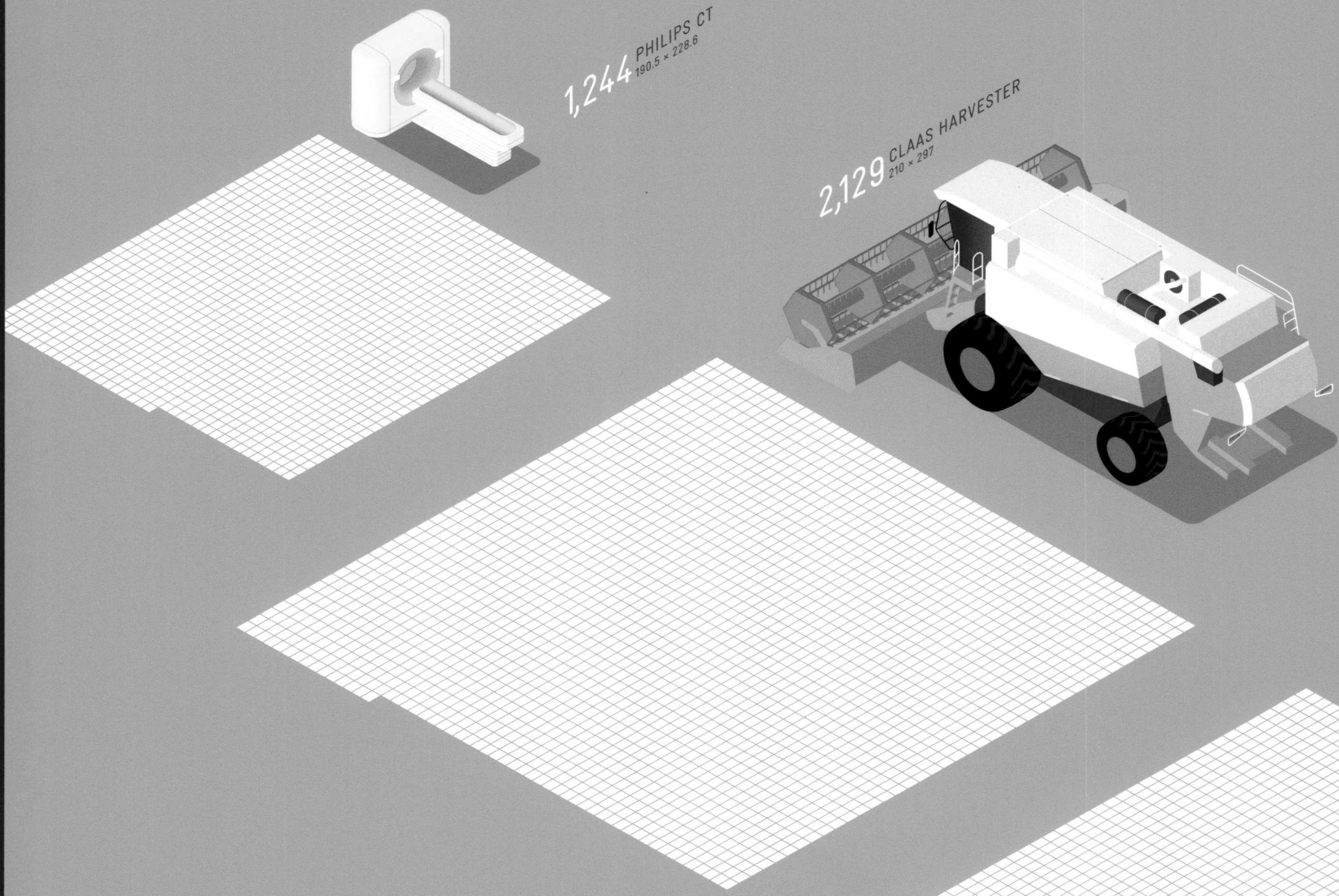
1,244 PHILIPS CT
190.5 × 228.6
2,129 CLAAS HARVESTER
210 × 297

2,129 In 1937, the German company Claas built its first **combine harvester**, which weighed in at 2.4 tons. Current models weigh almost ten times as much. The complexity of this high-tech machine with automatic satellite steering is evident in the scale of the manual. It includes descriptions of operations, technical, hydraulic and all electrical systems.

4,250 Every time an **aircraft** is sold, an individual set of manuals is developed. They contain descriptions of aircraft systems and guidelines for flight phases, flight planning and checklists – both for everyday flying conditions and for emergencies.

10,000 Among the customers of the Cray **Supercomputer** are the German Meteorological Service and the American National Nuclear Security Administration, responsible for nuclear weapons research. The scalable system is modified for the intended use. The actual extent of the instructions is a rough estimate.

* digital content converted to 210 x 297 mm pages

4,250 BOEING 747
136.9 × 211.7
10,000 CRAY XC
210 × 297*

PLENTY OF THRUST

Lift, resistance, weight are forces that all come together to determine thrust—the driving force that lifts a plane into the air. Modern aircraft use turbofans located under the wings to achieve this effect.

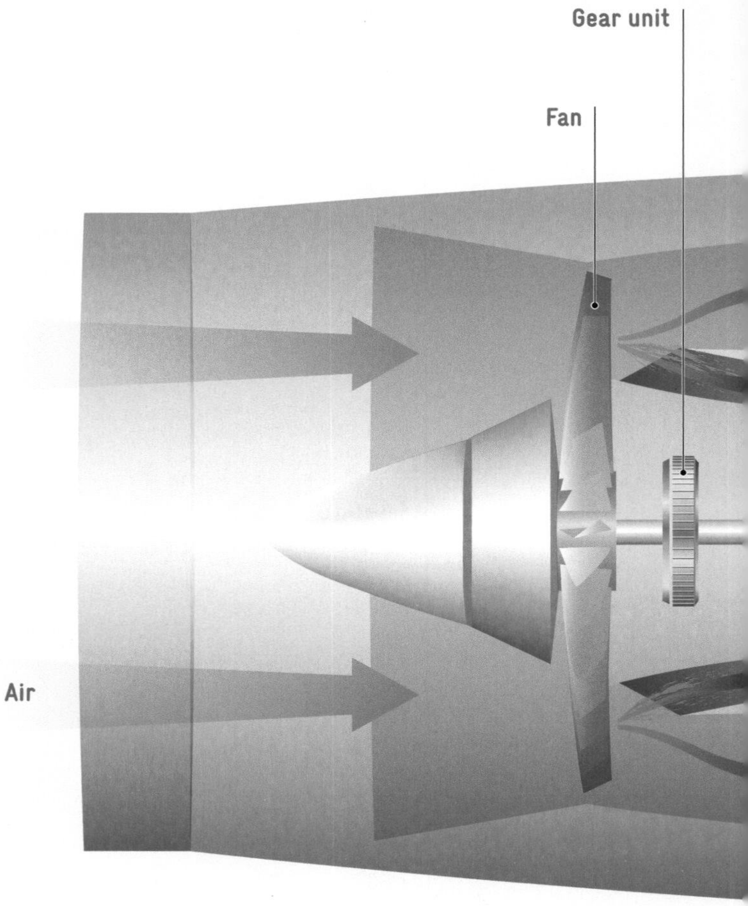

What is thrust?

Thrust is a driving force. It pushes the aircraft forward and accelerates it.

Low-pressure shaft **High-pressure shaft**

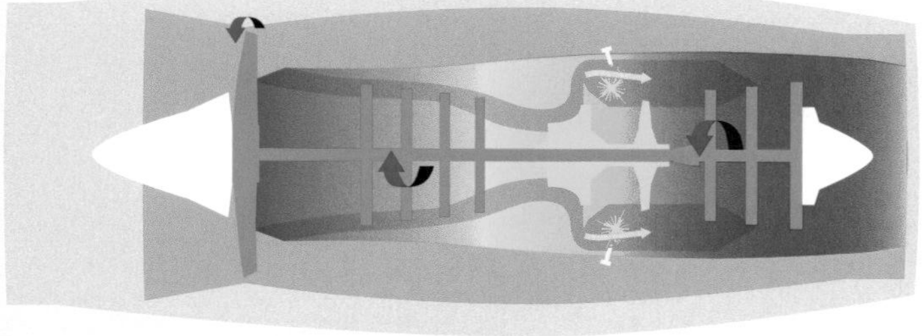

1 STARTING THE ENGINES

Typically, air or electric starters are used to set the high-pressure shaft in motion. Air is compressed and heats up. Fuel is injected and ignites with the mix of hot air. This sets the low-pressure shaft and fan in motion, turning in the opposite direction to the high-pressure shaft.

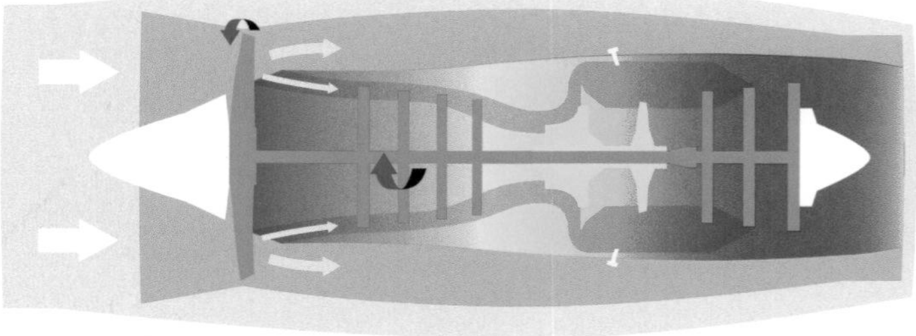

1 2 SUCKING IN AIR AND SEPARATING THE AIR FLOW

The fan sucks in air. The air is divided into two streams. The majority goes into the external air flow (bypass flow) to cool down the combustion chamber and provide noise insulation. The remaining air flow streams into the inner engine.

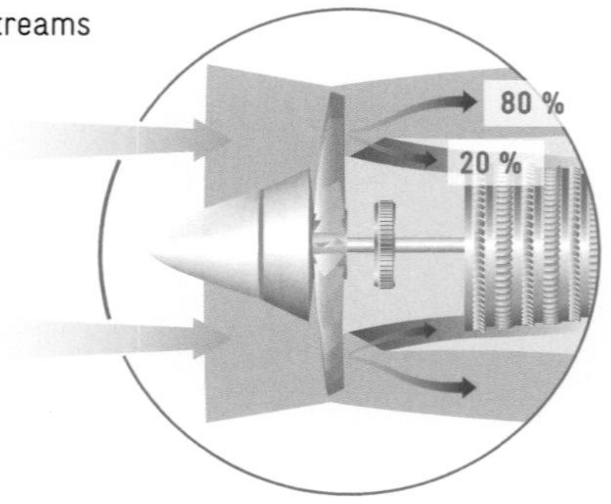

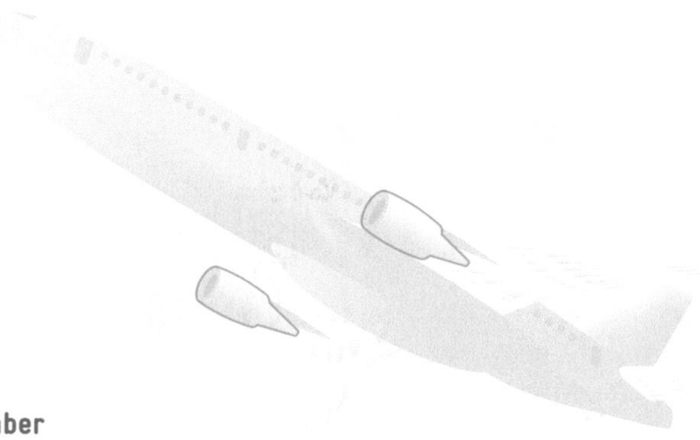

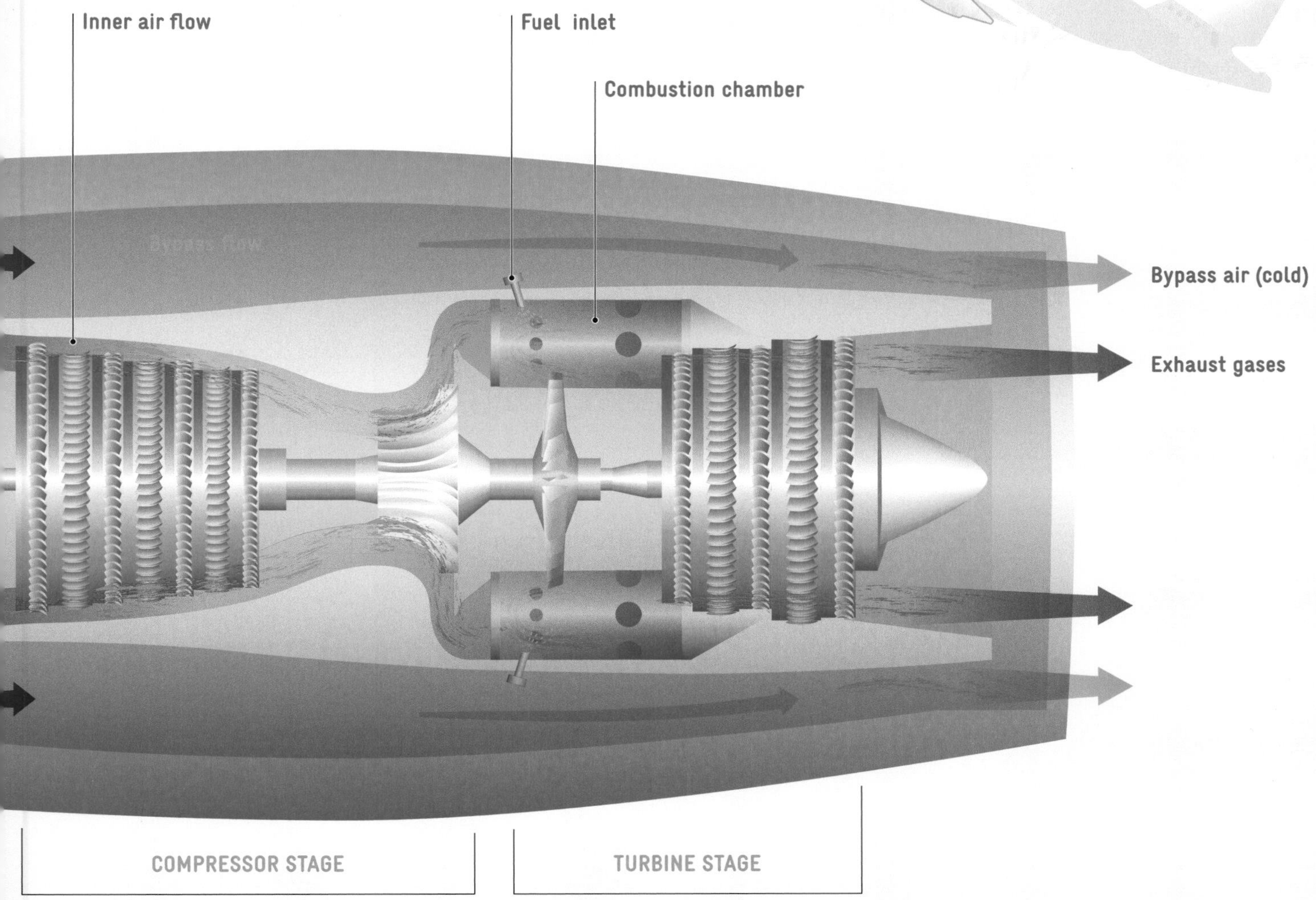

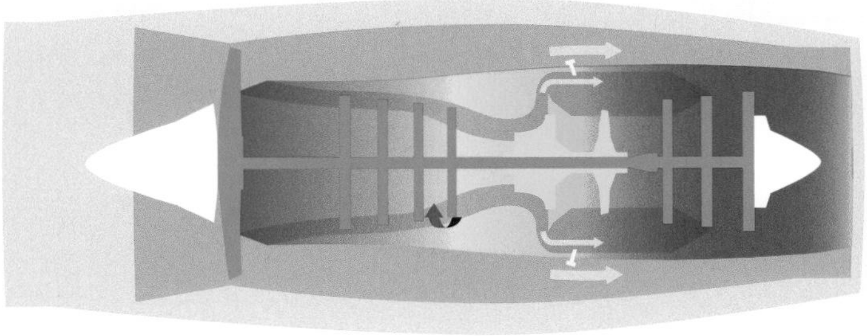

1 2 3 **COMPRESSING THE AIR**

The compressor consists of alternating steady blade wheels (guide wheels) and rotating blade wheels (compressor blades). The air is compressed, causing the temperature and pressure to rise.

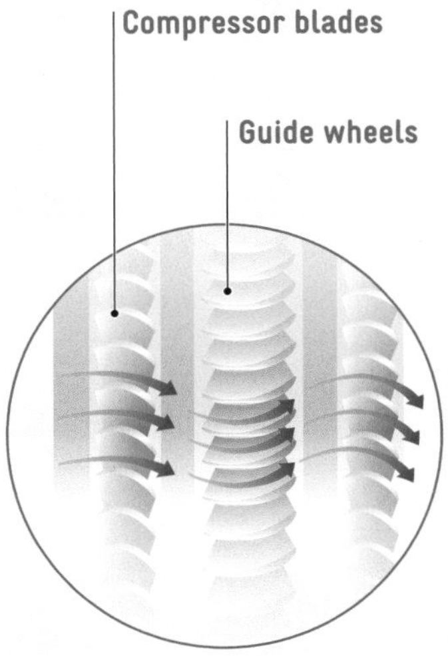

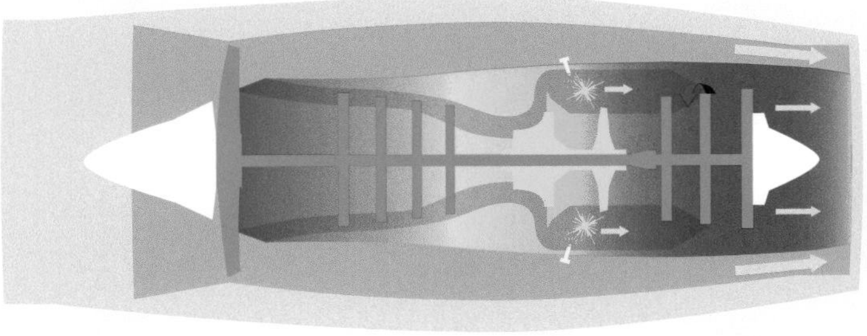

1 2 3 4 **FUEL SUPPLY**

Kerosene is injected into the combustion chambers through the fuel inlets. The hot air stream is mixed with the fuel and continually ignited. This causes hot exhaust gases, which expand explosively. The flow of exhaust gas drives the turbine, air is sucked in by the fan. But most of the thrust isn't provided by the hot exhaust gases. Actually, the main driving force comes from the flow of bypass air. The aircraft picks up enough speed to create sufficient lift for takeoff.

OUT OF CONTROL

On March 11, 2011, Japan was struck by an earthquake, 129 kilometers off the coast and 24 kilometers below the ocean floor. It measured 9.0 on the moment magnitude scale, and is therefore considered the most powerful one known to have hit the country. A tsunami followed the quake soon afterwards. In the region Fukushima-Daiichi, it reached heights of up to 14 meters (46 ft). These unimaginably powerful natural forces changed the lives of people in the affected areas drastically. The third disaster, caused by the first two, is the nuclear catastrophe which occurred at the Fukushima Daiichi power plant.This catastrophe, and the one at Chernobyl, are the most devastating accidents in the history of nuclear power plants. These graphics give an insight into the plant's functional principles and security systems.

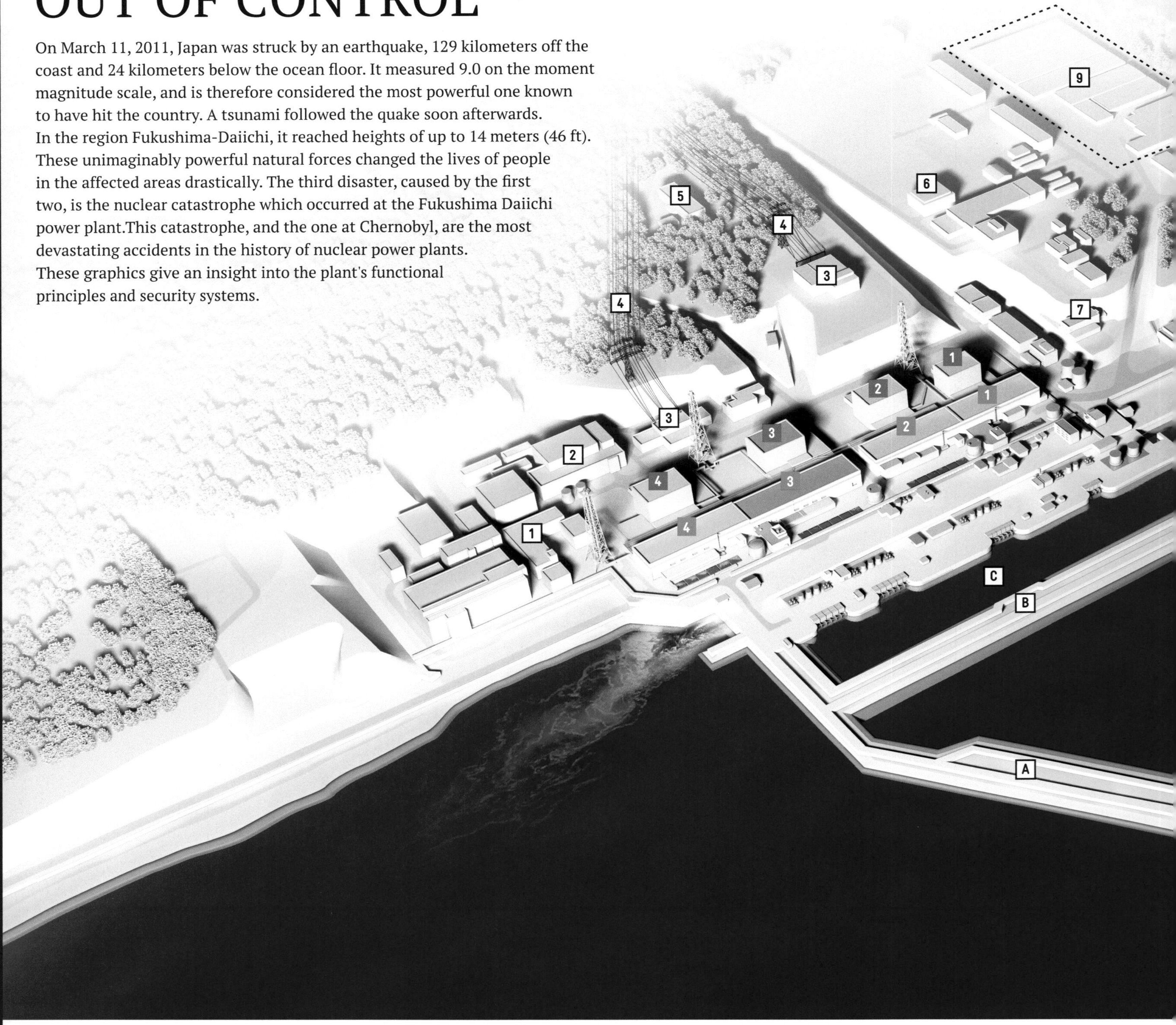

THE NORMAL OPERATION

Normal operation: High pressure steam from the reactor drives turbines that generate electricity. Sea water runs through a condenser, cooling the low pressure steam from the turbine so it becomes water again. The cold water is re-used for cooling the reactor.

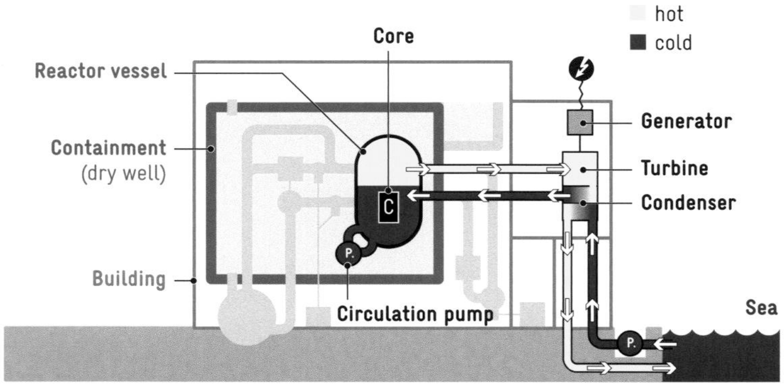

EMERGENCY SHUTDOWN AND RESIDUAL HEAT REMOVAL

The turbines are taken out of the system relatively quickly. The output power from the core is reduced by inserting the control rods. But the core continues producing decay heat that needs to be removed. A pump conveys the steam to the heat exchangers. The pump is driven by a motor that receives its power from diesel generators.

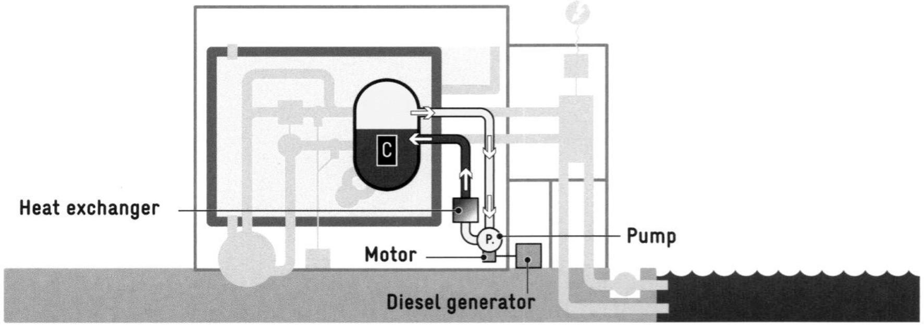

10
3
6
5
6
5
9
C
8
D
E
1 - 6 Reactor buildings
1 - 6 Turbine buildings
1 Centralized Radiation Waste Treatment Facility
2 Common Spent Fuel Storage Facility
3 Extra-High Voltage Switching Yard
4 275 kV Transmission line
5 Large Maintenance Equipment Building
6 Crisis center
7 Administration Office
8 Cask Storage Facility
9 Radioactive Solid Waste Storage Facility
10 500 kV Transmission line
A South Breakwater
B East Breakwater
C Intake Canal
D Wharf
E North Breakwater

EMERGENCY CORE-COOLING SYSTEM

If the system with the heat exchangers and the diesel generators is not functional, the Reactor Core Isolation Cooling sets in. The steam is transferred to a steam suppression pool where it becomes water. While being transferred, the steam drives a turbine that pumps cooling water back to the reactor vessel.

The motor-driven valves require AC power to keep open. The source may be external or, temporarily, on-site batteries. At the Fukushima Daiichi Nuclear Power Plant, this system also failed after the batteries ran empty and there was no other power source.

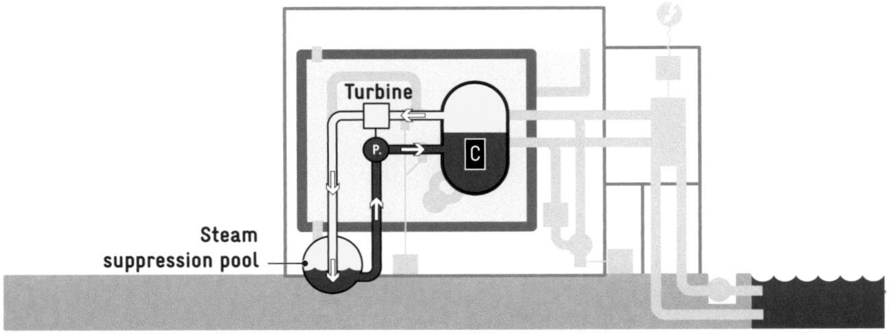

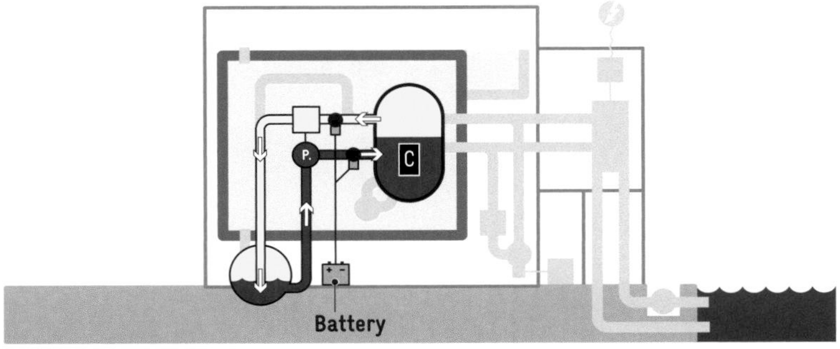

DAMAGE LIMITATION

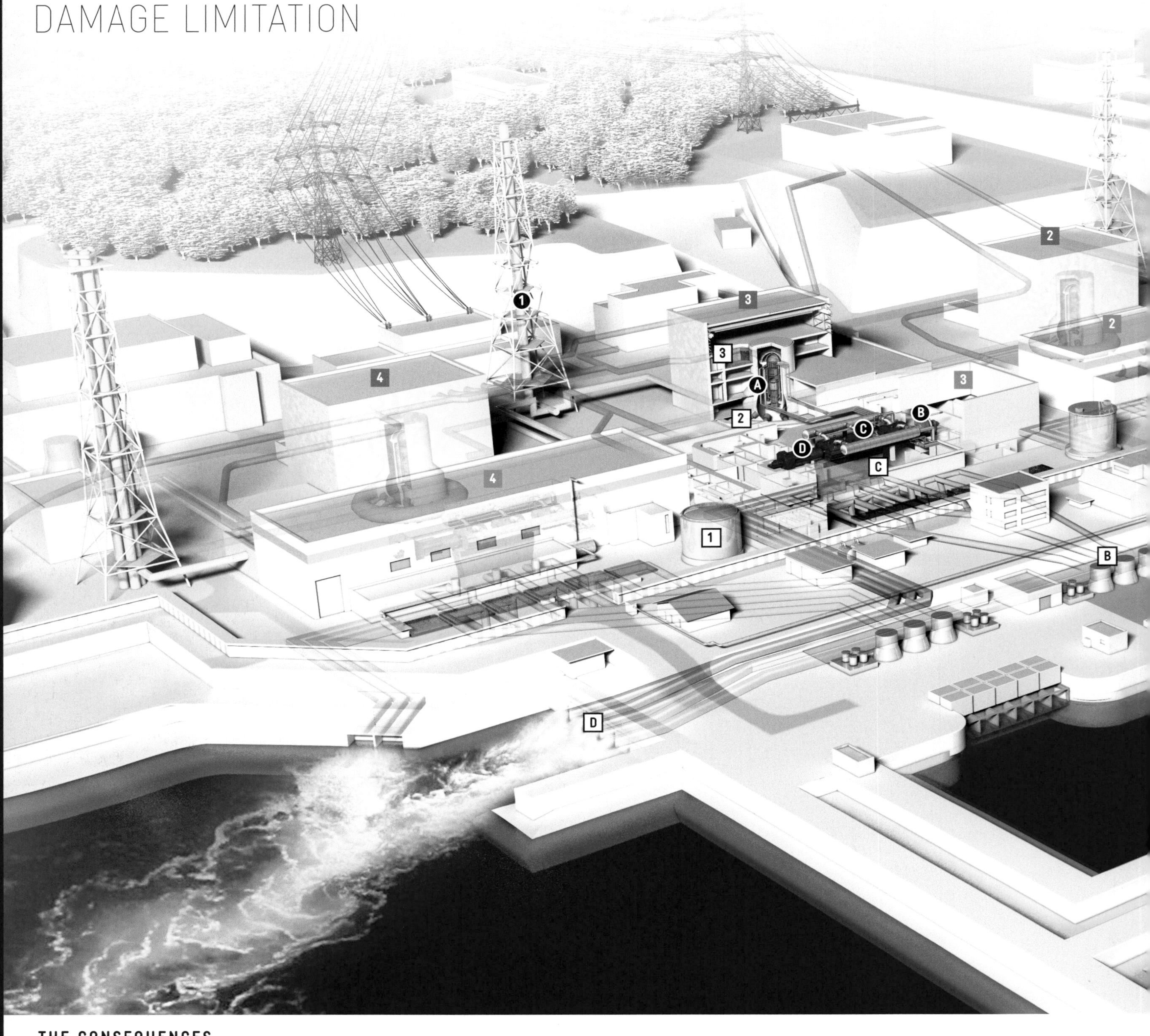

THE CONSEQUENCES

The valves close as there is no AC power supply. To lower the rising pressure inside the reactor vessel, the steam is vented directly into the steam suppression pool. Water stops being pumped back, the level of cooling water inside the reactor drops.

Without coolant, the core starts to melt down. The Zircaloy cladding of the fuel rods reacts with the steam, releasing hydrogen. To relieve the increasing pressure, the steam suppression pool is vented – first into the dry well, later into the service floor of the building. The gas mixture in reactor buildings 1 and 3 eventually explodes, severely damaging the structure of the building.

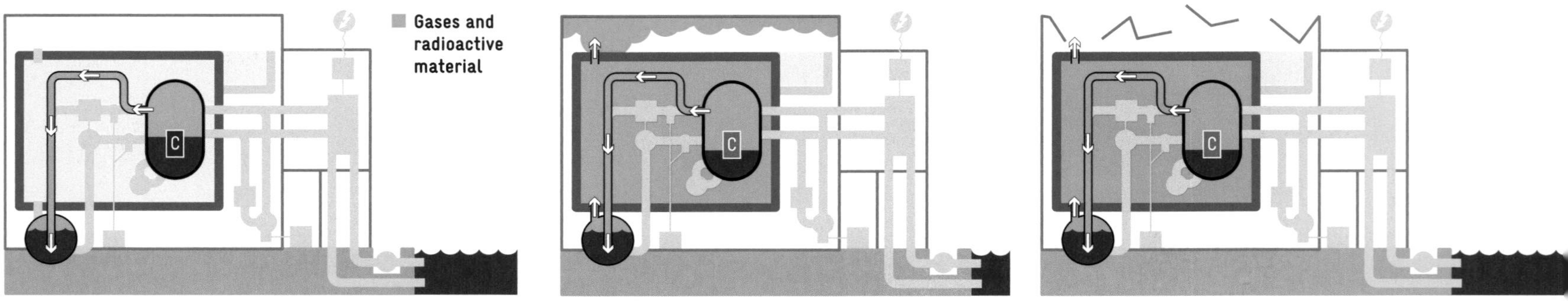

General

1 - 6 Reactor building

1 - 6 Turbine building

❶ Chimney ❷ Oil Tank

Energy cycle of the reactor

Ⓐ Reactor

Ⓑ High Pressure Turbine

Ⓒ Turbine

Ⓓ Generator

Cooling water cycle for the reactor

1 Fresh Water Tank

2 Pressure Suppression Chamber

3 Spent Fuel Pool

Cooling water cycle for the condenser

A Cooling Water Inlet

B Water Pump

C Condenser

D Cooling Water Outlet

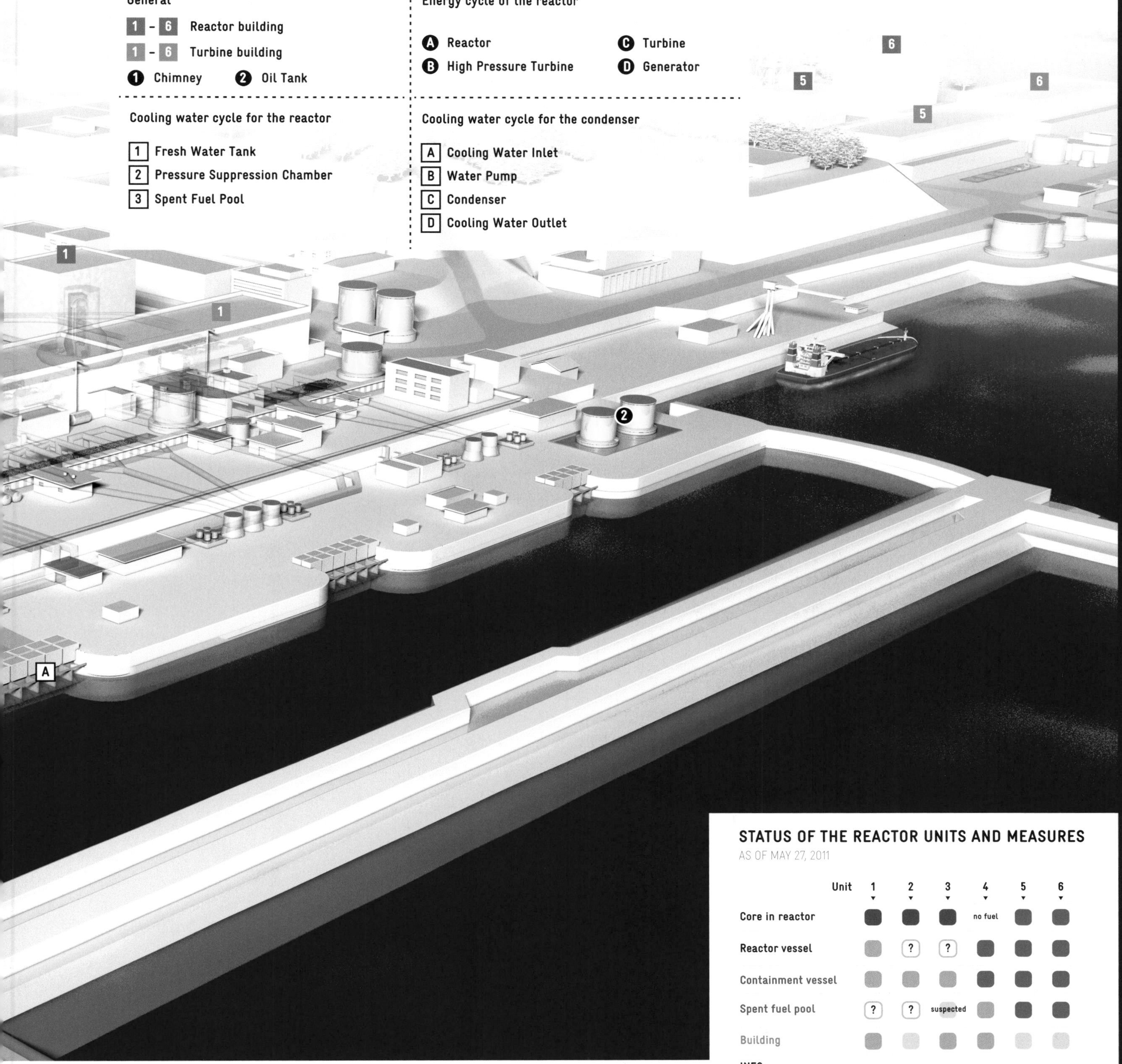

STATUS OF THE REACTOR UNITS AND MEASURES

AS OF MAY 27, 2011

Unit	1	2	3	4	5	6
Core in reactor	Core melt	Core melt	Core melt	no fuel	Not damaged	Not damaged
Reactor vessel	Damaged	?	?	Not damaged	Not damaged	Not damaged
Containment vessel	Damaged	Damaged	Damaged	Not damaged	Not damaged	Not damaged
Spent fuel pool	?	?	suspected	Damaged	Not damaged	Not damaged
Building	Damaged	Partial damage	Damaged	Damaged	Partial damage	Partial damage
INES Level	7	7	7	3	-	-

Core melt · Damaged · Partial damage · Not damaged · ? Unknown status

External cooling

Unit	1	2	3	4	5	6
Reactor vessel	Water injection	Water injection	Water injection	Not necessary	Not necessary	Not necessary
Containment vessel	Water injection	Planned injection	Planned injection	Not necessary	Not necessary	Not necessary
Spent fuel pool	Water spray	Water injection	Water spray / Water injection	Water spray / Water injection	Not necessary	Not necessary

Not necessary · Water injection · Water spray · Planned injection

In unit 2, the steam suppression pool is damaged due to the high pressure and releases gas, contaminated water and fission products into the plant.

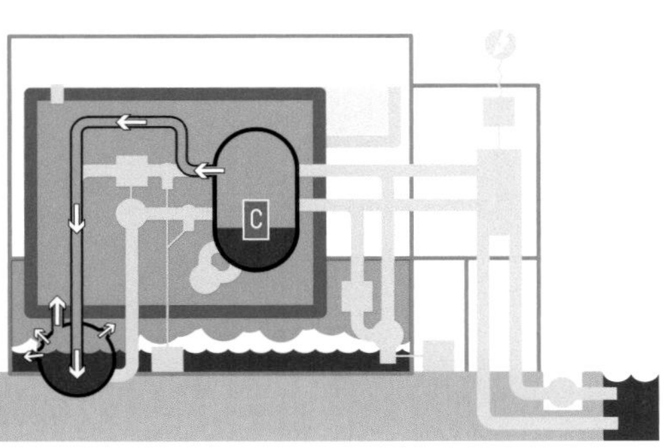

In unit 4, the fuel rods are in the spent fuel tank. This is damaged during the earthquake and leaks water, causing a meltdown. What follows is an explosion of the gas mixture.

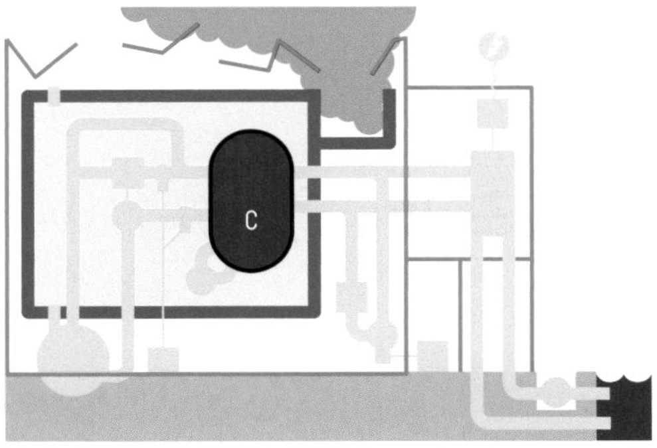

BUSINESS AS USUAL

In 2020, nine years after the Fukushima disaster, more than 100 nuclear plants are still scheduled all over the world. This chronology of global nuclear reactors is a snapshot of all commercial power plants in 2013. There are more, but they are not always in operation—like research reactors. The transition from low capacity reactors—many of which have already shut down—to more powerful ones becomes visible in our diagram. The 1970s and 1980s are the decades in which the technology boomed, especially in the Western world. The end of the time line shows China's hunger for energy. By the start of 2020, this country alone has 43 reactors at the planning stage.

1954» OBNINSK RU **1956»** ARGONNE US CALDER HALL GB 1 **1957»** CALDER HALL GB 2 SANTA SUSANA US SHIPPINGPORT US VALLECITOS US
MARCOULE FR G3 **1961»** YANKEE ROWE US **1962»** BERKELEY GB 1 2 BR3 PWR BE BRADWELL GB A B DOUNREAY GB INDIAN POINT US
1964» AGESTA SE BELOYARSK RU 1 BONUS US CHINON FR 1 EBR US II ELK RIVER US GARIGLIANO IT HUNTERSTON GB A1 A2 LATINA IT
1966» CHINON FR 3 ENRICO FERMI US 1 KARLSRUHE DE PATHFINDER US RHEINSBERG DE SIZEWELL GB A1 A2 TOKAI JP 1 **1967»** CHOOZ FR
OLDBURY GB 2 SAN ONOFRE US 1 WINFRITH GB **1969»** BELOYARSK RU 2 BEZNAU CH 1 GKN DODEWAARD NL JOSE CABRERA ES 1 JUELICH DE
1970» MARVIKEN SE [2] BILIBINO RU 1 DRESDEN US 2 GROSSWELZHEIM DE MIHAMA JP 1 NOVOVORONEZH RU 2 POINT BEACH US 1 R. E. GINNA US
PICKERING CA 1 2 SANTA MARIA DE GARONA ES ST. LAURENT FR A2 WYLFA GB 1 **1972»** BOHUNICE A SK 1 BUGEY FR 1 GENTILLY CA 1 KARACHI PK
STADE DE SURRY US 1 TURKEY POINT US 3 VANDELLOS ES 1 VERMONT YANKEE US WYLFA GB 2 **1973»** BN-350 AKTAU KZ BORSSELE NL
SURRY US 2 TURKEY POINT US 4 ZION US 1 **1974»** CRYSTAL RIVER US 4 [2] ARKANSAS NUCLEAR ONE US 1 ATUCHA AR 1 BROWNS FERRY US 1 COOPER US
PEACH BOTTOM US 2 3 PHENIX FR PRAIRIE ISLAND US 2 SHIMANE JP 1 TAKAHAMA JP 1 THREE MILE ISLAND US 1 ZION US 2 **1975»** WNP US
DUANE ARNOLD US 1 FITZPATRICK US GENKAI JP 1 GREIFSWALD DE 2 HATCH US 1 KOLA RU 2 KOZLODUY BG 2 MILLSTONE US 2 OSKARSHAMN SE
FUKUSHIMA DAIICHI JP 3 HAMAOKA JP 1 HINKLEY POINT GB B2 HUNTERSTON GB B1 INDIAN POINT US 3 LENINGRAD RU 2 MIHAMA JP 3 NECKARWESTHEIM DE
BRUNSBÜTTEL DE BRUNSWICK US 1 CALVERT CLIFFS US 2 CRYSTAL RIVER US 3 FARLEY US 1 FESSENHEIM FR 1 HUNTERSTON GB B2 IKATA JP 1 KNK DE
DAVIS BESSE US 1 DONALD COOK US 2 FESSENHEIM FR 2 FUKUSHIMA DAIICHI JP 4 5 GREIFSWALD DE 3 HAMAOKA JP 2 HINKLEY POINT GB B1 KORI KR
FORT ST VRAIN US FUGEN JP FUKUSHIMA DAIICHI JP 6 GOESGEN CH GREIFSWALD DE 4 HATCH US 2 ISAR DE 1 KURSK RU 2 OHI JP 1
FORSMARK SE 1 GRAVELINES FR 1 2 LENINGRAD RU 3 NORTH ANNA US 2 PHILIPPSBURG DE 1 TRICASTIN FR 1 2 **1981»** TRICASTIN FR 4 [2] BELOYARS
KOZLODUY BG 3 KUOSHENG TW 1 LENINGRAD RU 4 LOVIISA FI 2 MCGUIRE US 1 NOVOVORONEZH RU 5 RAJASTHAN IN 2 RINGHALS SE 3 ROVNO UA 1 SALE
FUKUSHIMA DAINI JP 1 GRAFENRHEINFELD DE IKATA JP 2 KOLA RU 3 KOZLODUY BG 4 OLKILUOTO FI 2 SEQUOYAH US 2 **1983»** CLINCH RIVER US
PICKERING CA 5 POINT LEPREAU CA RINGHALS SE 4 SAN ONOFRE US 2 SMOLENSK RU 1 SOUTH UKRAINE UA 1 ST. LAURENT FR B1 B2 ST. LUCIE US
MIDLAND US 1 [2] 2 [2] ODESSA UA 2 [1] ALMARAZ ES 2 ASCO ES 1 BRUCE CA 6 CALLAWAY US 1 CHERNOBYL UA 4 CHINON FR B1 B2 COLUMBIA US
LASALLE US 1 2 LEIBSTADT CH MAANSHAN TW 1 MCGUIRE US 2 ONAGAWA JP 1 PAKS HU 2 PICKERING CA 6 SAN ONOFRE US 3 SENDAI JP 1 VIRG
CRUAS FR 2 4 DIABLO CANYON US 1 DOEL BE 4 DUKOVANY CZ 1 DUNGENESS GB B2 FORSMARK SE 3 FUKUSHIMA DAINI JP 3 GRAND GULF US 1 GRAVELIN
OSKARSHAMN SE 3 PALUEL FR 1 2 PHILIPPSBURG DE 2 PICKERING CA 7 SENDAI JP 2 SHOREHAM US SMOLENSK RU 2 SOUTH UKRAINE UA 2 SUSQUEHANNA
BALAKOVO RU 1 BROKDORF DE BRUCE CA 7 CATAWBA US 2 DIABLO CANYON US 2 DUKOVANY CZ 2 3 4 FLAMANVILLE FR 1 HOPE CREEK US 1 KALPAKKAM
ST. ALBAN FR 1 SUPER-PHENIX FR YONGGWANG KR 1 ZAPOROZHE UA 2 **1987»** SOUTH UKRAINE UA 4 [1] HAMAOKA JP 3 BEAVER VALLEY US
MUELHEIM-KARLICH DE PAKS HU 4 PERRY US 1 ROVNO UA 3 SHEARON HARRIS US 1 ST. ALBAN FR 2 THTR-300 DE TSURUGA JP 2 VOGTLE US
CATTENOM FR 2 CHINON FR B4 EMSLAND DE ENRICO FERMI US 2 ISAR DE 2 KHMELNITSKI UA 1 KOZLODUY BG 5 NINE MILE POINT US 2 NOGENT FR
BALAKOVO RU 3 BELLEVILLE FR 2 DUNGENESS GB B1 GREIFSWALD DE 5 HARTLEPOOL GB 1 2 HEYSHAM GB A1 A2 B1 B2 NECKARWESTHEIM DE
1990» GREIFSWALD DE 6 [2] 7 [2] 8 [2] TEMELIN CZ 3 [2] 4 [2] COMANCHE PEAK US 1 DARLINGTON CA 2 KASHIWAZAKI KARIWA JP 2 5 LAGUNA VERDE MX
SINPO KP 1 2 STENDAL DE 1 TOMARI JP 2 **1992»** CATTENOM FR 4 DARLINGTON CA 1 NARORA IN 2 PENLY FR 2 **1993»** KURSK RU 6 [2] BALAKO
OHI JP 4 SHIKA JP 1 STENDAL DE 2 **1994»** GORKY RU 1 [2] 2 [2] PERRY US 2 [2] DAYA BAY CN 1 2 GENKAI JP 3 GOLFECH FR 2 IKATA JP
1996» CERNAVODA RO 1 KASHIWAZAKI KARIWA JP 6 STENDAL DE 3 WATTS BAR US 1 YONGGWANG KR 4 ZAPOROZHE UA 6 **1997»** GENKAI JP
2000» JURAGUA CU 1 2 CHASMA PK 1 CHOOZ FR B1 B2 KAIGA IN 1 2 MOCHOVCE SK 2 RAJASTHAN IN 3 4 **2001»** ANGRA BR 2 ROSTOV RU
QINSHAN CN 5 **2004»** KALININ RU 3 KHMELNITSKI UA 2 QINSHAN CN 3 ROVNO UA 4 ULCHIN KR 5 **2005»** SHIMANE JP 3 [1] HIGASHI-DORI (TOHOKU) JP
TIANWAN CN 2 **2009»** TOMARI JP 3 **2010»** CEFR CN BUSHEHR IR 1 LING AO II CN 1 QINSHAN CN 6 RAJASTHAN IN 5 6 ROSTOV RU
SHIN-KORI KR 1 2 WOLSONG KR 5 **2012»** KUDANKULAM IN 2 KAIGA IN 5 6 NOVOVORONEZH II RU 1 HONGYANHE CN 1 TIANWAN CN 3 XIAOMOSHA
2013» FANGJIASHAN CN 1 LENINGRAD II RU 1 ROSTOV RU 3 HONGYANHE CN 2 SANMEN CN 1 TIANWAN CN 4 YANGJIANG CN 1 BELENE BG 1 BELOYAR
HONGYANHE CN 3 4 SANMEN CN 2 TAISHAN CN 1 YANGJIANG CN 2 BELENE BG 2 CHANGJIANG CN 1 FLAMANVILLE FR 3 FUQING CN 2 NING
HONGYANHE CN 5 6 PENGZE CN 1 2 SHANDONG SHIDAOWAN CN TAISHAN CN 2 TAOHUAJIANG CN 1 XIANNING CN 1 2 YANGJIANG CN
LENINGRAD II RU 2 3 NOVOVORONEZH II RU 2 ROSTOV RU 4 WUHU CN 1 2 YANGJIANG CN 4 HIGASHI-DORI (TOHOKU) JP 2 CERNAVODA RO 3
YANGJIANG CN 5 6 BRAKA AE 1 BELLEFONTE US 1 FUKUSHIMA DAIICHI JP 8 HIGASHI-DORI (TEPCO) JP 1 PENLY FR 3 TSURUGA JP 3 **2018»** TAOHUAJIAN
SHIN-KORI KR 6 SOUTH URALS RU 2 **2020»** KAMINOSEKI JP 2 SHIN ULCHIN KR 3 BELLEFONTE US 2 **2021»** SHIN ULCHIN KR 4 BRAKA AE

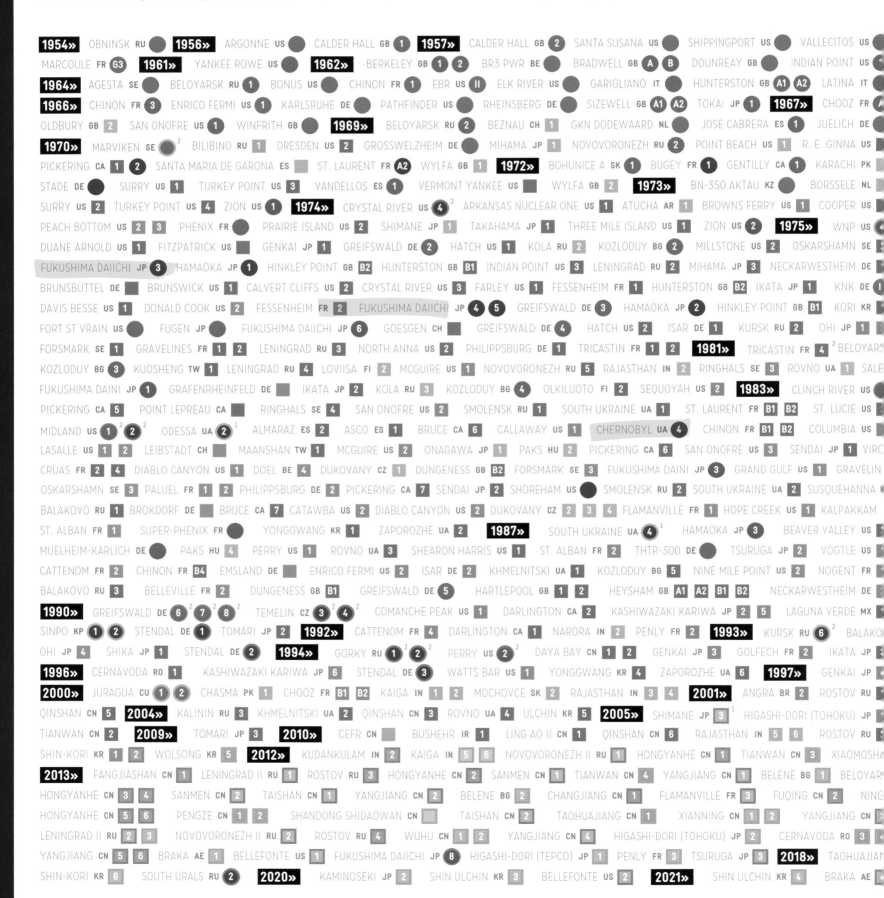

2001» Date of (planned) commission

1 Date of (planned) construction start

2 Date of cancellation

Capacity

100 500 1,000 MW

not yet operating ▸

operating ▸

No longer operating ▸

planned

under construction or about to be commissioned

construction suspended

cancelled or suspended indefinitely

Interpretation examples

1993» DARLINGTON CA 3 4 ▸ The reactors 3 and 4 of the Darlington site in Canada have a capacity of between 500 and 1,000 Megawatt and were commissioned in 1993.

2021» BRAKA AE 4 ▸ Planned commission of Reactor No. 4 in Braka, United Arab Emirates, is 2021. It is supposed to deliver over 1,000 MW.

1993» BALAKOVO RU 6 ▸ The construction of reactor 6 in the russian site Balakovo was suspended in 1993. A capacity of 500 to 1,000 MW was planned.

reactors where incidents with serious consequences happened are highlighted

958» CALDER HALL GB 3 **1959»** CALDER HALL GB 4 CHAPELCROSS GB 1 2 3 MARCOULE FR G2 **1960»** CHAPELCROSS GB 4 DRESDEN US 1
AHL DE ROLPHTON CA **1963»** BIG ROCK POINT US CAROLINAS US HALLAM US HUMBOLDT BAY US PIQUA US WINDSCALE GB
1965» CHINON FR 2 DUNGENESS GB A1 A2 HINKLEY POINT GB A1 A2 JPDR JP II NOVO MELEKES RU TRAWSFYNYDD GB 1 2 TRINO VERCELLESE IT
L FR 4 GUNDREMMINGEN DE A OLDBURY GB 1 PEACH BOTTOM US 1 **1968»** DOUGLAS POINT CA HADDAM NECK US LINGEN DE LUCENS CH
ACROSSE US NINE MILE POINT US 1 NOVOVORONEZH RU 1 OBRIGHEIM DE OYSTER CREEK US ST. LAURENT FR A1 TARAPUR IN 1 2
SURUGA JP 1 **1971»** BEZNAU CH 2 DRESDEN US 3 FUKUSHIMA DAIICHI JP 1 H. B. ROBINSON US 2 MILLSTONE US 1 MONTICELLO US PALISADES US
AINE YANKEE US MIHAMA JP 2 MUEHLEBERG CH NOVOVORONEZH RU 3 OSKARSHAMN SE 1 PICKERING CA 3 PILGRIM US 1 POINT BEACH US 2
OLA RU 1 NIEDERAICHBACH DE NOVOVORONEZH RU 4 OCONEE US 1 PICKERING CA 4 PRAIRIE ISLAND US 1 QUAD CITIES US 1 2 RAJASTHAN IN 1
ORT CALHOUN US 1 FUKUSHIMA DAIICHI JP 2 GREIFSWALD DE 1 INDIAN POINT US 2 KEWAUNEE US KOZLODUY BG 1 LENINGRAD RU 1 OCONEE US 2 3
ARSEBAECK SE 1 BIBLIS DE A BILIBINO RU 2 BROWNS FERRY US 2 BRUNSWICK US 2 CALVERT CLIFFS US 1 DOEL BE 1 2 DONALD COOK US 1
ANCHO SECO US RINGHALS SE 2 TAKAHAMA JP 2 TIHANGE BE 1 WURGASSEN DE **1976»** BEAVER VALLEY US 1 BILIBINO RU 3 DOUNREAY GB
INGHALS SE 1 ST. LUCIE US 1 TROJAN US **1977»** BARSEBAECK SE 2 BIBLIS DE B BILIBINO RU 4 BROWNS FERRY US 3 BRUCE CA 1 2
URSK RU 1 LOVIISA FI 1 SALEM US 1 **1978»** TULLNERFELD AT 2 AKTASH UA 1 1 WNP US 1 1 BRUCE CA 3 CHERNOBYL UA 1 CHIN SHAN TW 1
ORTH ANNA US 1 THREE MILE ISLAND US 2 TOKAI JP 2 **1979»** ARMENIA AM 1 BRUCE CA 4 BUGEY FR 2 3 4 CHERNOBYL UA 2 CHIN SHAN TW 2
LKILUOTO FI 1 UNTERWESER DE **1980»** AKTASH UA 2 1 ARKANSAS NUCLEAR ONE US 2 ARMENIA AM 2 BOHUNICE SK 1 BUGEY FR 5 DAMPIERRE FR 1
U 3 BLAYAIS FR 1 BOHUNICE SK 2 CAORSO IT DAMPIERRE FR 2 3 4 FARLEY US 2 FORSMARK SE 2 GENKAI JP 2 GRAVELINES FR 3 4
S 2 SEQUOYAH US 1 TRICASTIN FR 3 **1982»** ALLENS CREEK US 2 2 HARTSVILLE US B1 2 B2 2 ODESSA UA 1 1 CHERNOBYL UA 3 DOEL BE 3 ROVNO UA 2
VNP US 3 2 5 2 CHEROKEE US 1 2 2 2 ALMARAZ ES 1 BLAYAIS FR 2 3 4 GENTILLY CA 2 KORI KR 2 KRSKO SL KUOSHENG TW 2 PAKS HU 1
USQUEHANNA US 1 TIHANGE BE 2 WOLSONG KR 1 **1984»** CHERNOBYL UA 5 2 6 2 HARTSVILLE US A1 2 A2 2 LEMONIZ ES 1 2 2 2 YELLOW CREEK US 1 2 2 2
RUAS FR 1 3 EMBALSE AR FUKUSHIMA DAINI JP 2 GUNDREMMINGEN DE B KALPAKKAM IN 1 KOEBERG ZA 1 KOLA RU 4 KRÜMMEL DE KURSK RU 3
SUMMER US 1 **1985»** KHARKOV UA 1 1 KURSK RU 5 1 ANGRA BR 1 BOHUNICE SK 3 4 BRUCE CA 5 BYRON US 1 CATAWBA US 1 COFRENTES ES
R 5 6 GROHNDE DE GUNDREMMINGEN DE C IGNALINA LT 1 KALININ RU 1 KASHIWAZAKI KARIWA JP 1 KOEBERG ZA 2 KORI KR 3 MAANSHAN TW 2
2 TAKAHAMA JP 3 4 TIHANGE BE 3 WATERFORD US 3 WOLF CREEK US ZAPOROZHE UA 1 **1986»** CERNAVODA RO 5 1 PNPP PH 1 1 ASCO ES 2
2 KORI KR 4 KURSK RU 4 LIMERICK US 1 MILLSTONE US 3 PAKS HU 3 PALO VERDE US 1 2 PALUEL FR 3 4 PICKERING CA 8 RIVER BEND US 1
BRUCE CA 8 BYRON US 2 CATTENOM FR 1 CHINON FR B3 CLINTON US 1 FLAMANVILLE FR 2 FUKUSHIMA DAINI JP 4 IGNALINA LT 2 KALININ RU 2
ONGGWANG KR 2 ZAPOROZHE UA 3 **1988»** CIRENE IT 2 MONTALTO DI CASTRO IT 1 2 2 2 BALAKOVO RU 2 BELLEVILLE FR 1 BRAIDWOOD US 1 2
ALO VERDE US 3 SOUTH TEXAS US 1 TORNESS GB A TRILLO ES 1 ULCHIN KR 1 VANDELLOS ES 2 ZAPOROZHE UA 4 **1989»** ZARNOWIEC PL 1 2 2 2 3 2 4 2
NOGENT FR 2 SHIMANE JP 2 SOUTH TEXAS US 2 SOUTH UKRAINE UA 3 TOMARI JP 1 TORNESS GB B ULCHIN KR 2 VOGTLE US 2 ZAPOROZHE UA 5
IMERICK US 2 PENLY FR 1 SEABROOK US 1 SMOLENSK RU 3 **1991»** KALKAR DE 2 CATTENOM FR 3 GOLFECH FR 1 NARORA IN 1 OHI JP 3
U 6 2 HAMAOKA JP 4 BALAKOVO RU 4 COMANCHE PEAK US 2 DARLINGTON CA 3 4 KAKRAPAR IN 1 KASHIWAZAKI KARIWA JP 3 KOZLODUY BG 6
ASHIWAZAKI KARIWA JP 4 QINSHAN CN 1 **1995»** KAKRAPAR IN 2 LAGUNA VERDE MX 2 MONJU JP ONAGAWA JP 2 SIZEWELL GB B YONGGWANG KR 3
ASHIWAZAKI KARIWA JP 7 STENDAL DE 4 WOLSONG KR 2 **1998»** MOCHOVCE SK 1 ULCHIN KR 3 WOLSONG KR 3 **1999»** ULCHIN KR 4 WOLSONG KR 4
002» CIVAUX FR 1 2 LING AO I CN 1 ONAGAWA JP 3 QINSHAN CN 2 4 TEMELIN CZ 1 2 YONGGWANG KR 5 6 **2003»** LING AO I CN 2
HAMAOKA JP 5 TARAPUR IN 4 ULCHIN KR 6 **2006»** SHIKA JP 2 TARAPUR IN 3 TIANWAN CN 1 **2007»** BALAKOVO RU 5 2 CERNAVODA RO 2 KAIGA IN 3
2011» KAIGA IN 4 KUDANKULAM IN 1 CHASMA PK 2 ATUCHA AR 2 KALININ RU 4 KALPAKKAM IN LING AO II CN 2 LUNGMEN TW 1 2 QINSHAN CN 7
N 1 2 AKADEMIK LOMONOSOV RU 1 2 MOCHOVCE SK 3 NINGDE CN 1 SHIN WOLSONG KR 1 SMOLENSK RU 4 WATTS BAR US 2 WOLSONG KR 6
U 4 FUQING CN 1 MOCHOVCE SK 4 NINGDE CN 2 OLKILUOTO FI 3 SHIN WOLSONG KR 2 SHIN-KORI KR 3 **2014»** FANGJIASHAN CN 2 HAIYANG CN 1 3
N 3 OHMA JP SHIN-KORI KR 4 **2015»** JAVA ID 1 1 KAMINOSEKI JP 1 HONGSHIDING CN 1 2 FANGCHENGGANG CN 1 HAIYANG CN 2 4
NGRA BR 3 CHANGJIANG CN 2 FUQING CN 3 KAKRAPAR IN 3 NINGDE CN 4 SHIN ULCHIN KR 1 **2016»** FANGCHENGGANG CN 2 KHMELNITSKI UA 3
UKUSHIMA DAIICHI JP 7 FUQING CN 4 KAKRAPAR IN 4 SHIN ULCHIN KR 2 SOUTH URALS RU 1 **2017»** HINKLEY POINT GB C1 C2 KHMELNITSKI UA 4
N 4 BRAKA AE 2 BELOYARSK RU 5 SHIN-KORI KR 5 TSURUGA JP 4 **2019»** LENINGRAD II RU 4 BRAKA AE 3 AKKUYU TR HIGASHI-DORI (TEPCO) JP 2

MOBILE EVOLUTION

From just making phone calls to using them for entertainment, shopping, navigation and other services, modern cellphones have evolved very quickly from the first mobile phone in 1984.

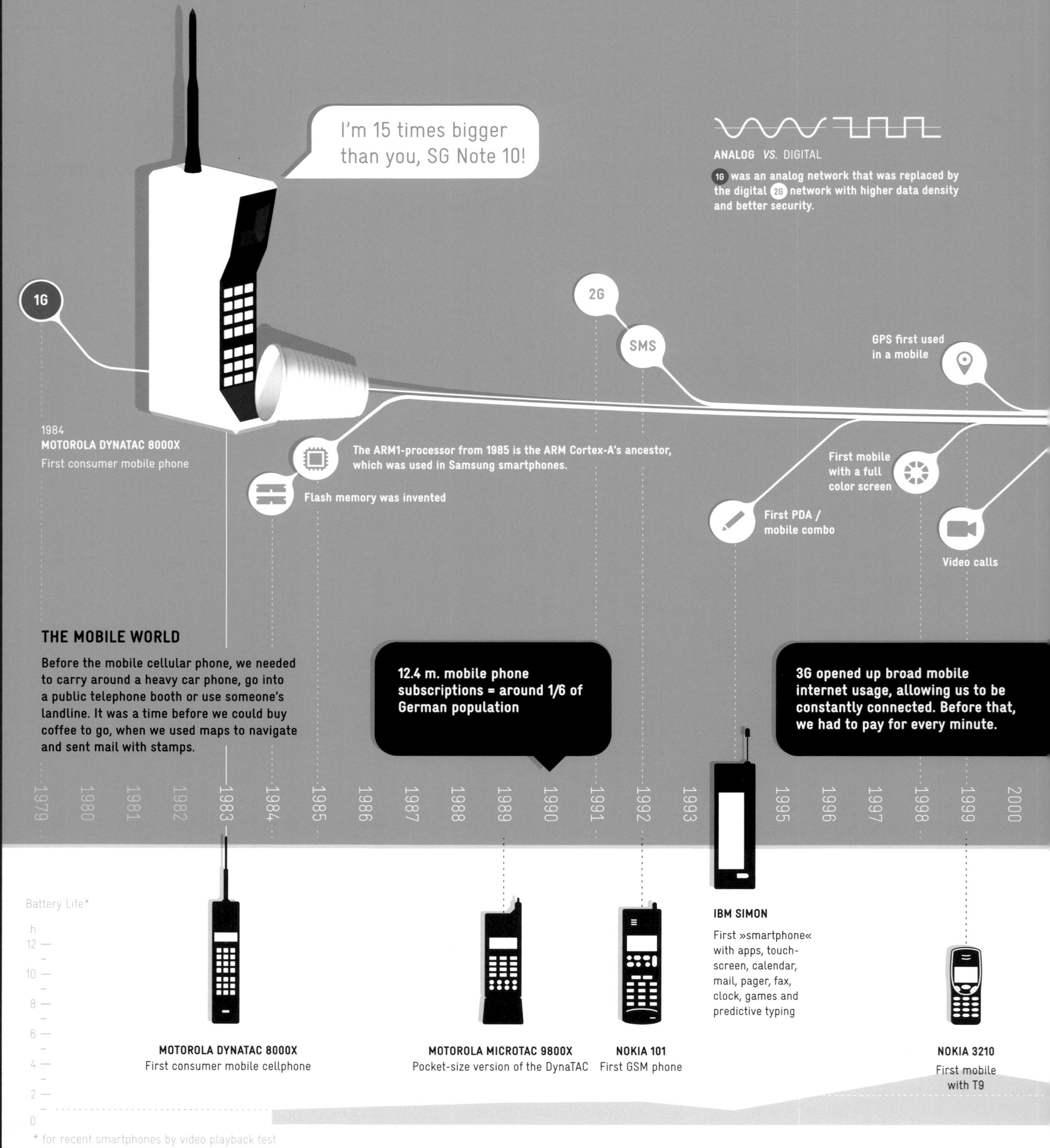
I'm 15 times bigger than you, SG Note 10!
ANALOG VS. DIGITAL
1G was an analog network that was replaced by the digital 2G network with higher data density and better security.
1G
1984
MOTOROLA DYNATAC 8000X
First consumer mobile phone
2G
SMS
GPS first used in a mobile
The ARM1-processor from 1985 is the ARM Cortex-A's ancestor, which was used in Samsung smartphones.
Flash memory was invented
First mobile with a full color screen
First PDA / mobile combo
Video calls
THE MOBILE WORLD
Before the mobile cellular phone, we needed to carry around a heavy car phone, go into a public telephone booth or use someone's landline. It was a time before we could buy coffee to go, when we used maps to navigate and sent mail with stamps.
12.4 m. mobile phone subscriptions = around 1/6 of German population
3G opened up broad mobile internet usage, allowing us to be constantly connected. Before that, we had to pay for every minute.
1979 1980 1981 1982 1983 1984 1985 1986 1987 1988 1989 1990 1991 1992 1993 1995 1996 1997 1998 1999 2000
Battery Life*
h
12
10
8
6
4
2
0
MOTOROLA DYNATAC 8000X
First consumer mobile cellphone
MOTOROLA MICROTAC 9800X
Pocket-size version of the DynaTAC
NOKIA 101
First GSM phone
IBM SIMON
First »smartphone« with apps, touch-screen, calendar, mail, pager, fax, clock, games and predictive typing
NOKIA 3210
First mobile with T9
* for recent smartphones by video playback test

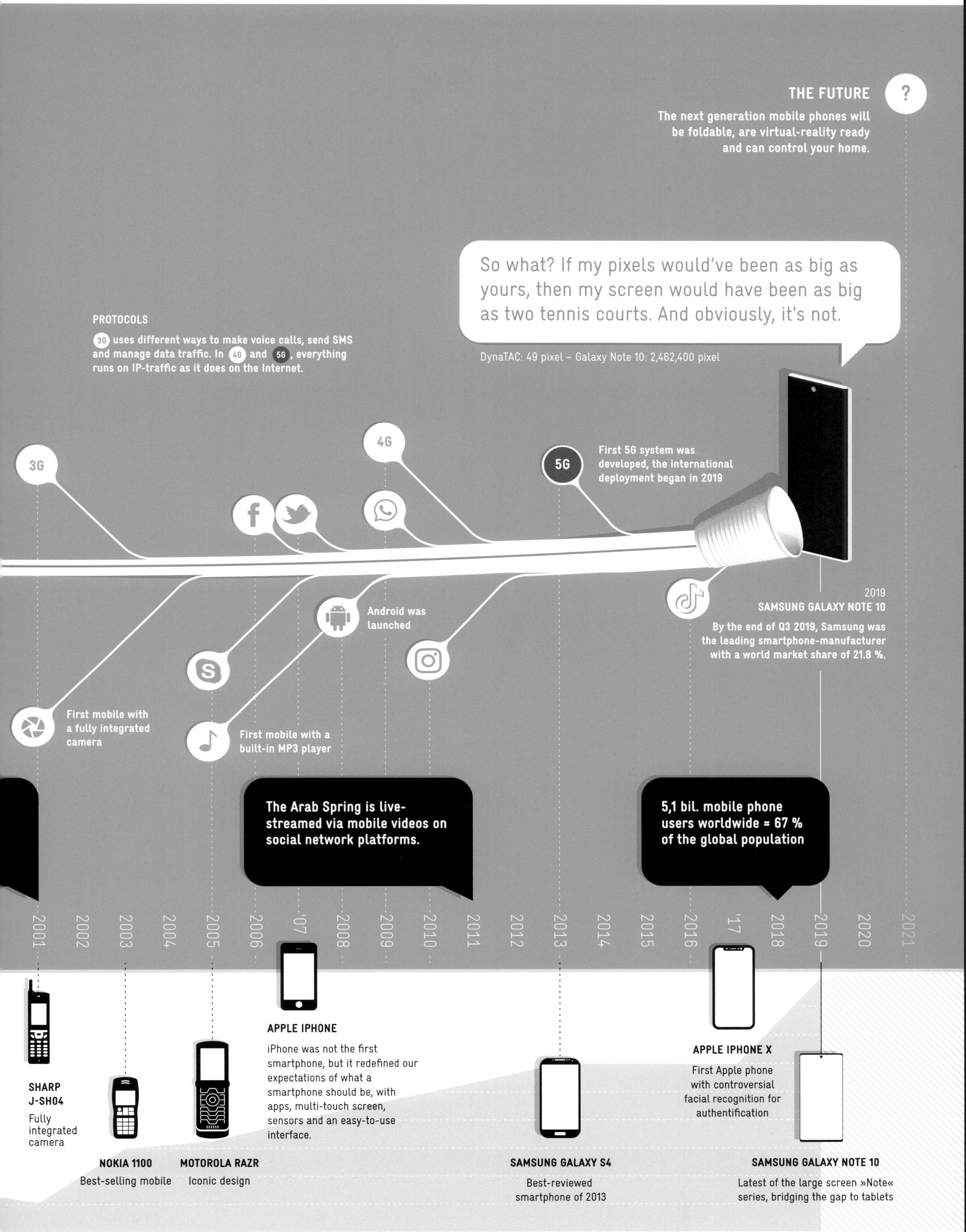
THE FUTURE
The next generation mobile phones will be foldable, are virtual-reality ready and can control your home.
So what? If my pixels would've been as big as yours, then my screen would have been as big as two tennis courts. And obviously, it's not.
DynaTAC: 49 pixel – Galaxy Note 10: 2,462,400 pixel
PROTOCOLS
3G uses different ways to make voice calls, send SMS and manage data traffic. In 4G and 5G, everything runs on IP-traffic as it does on the Internet.
3G
4G
5G
First 5G system was developed, the international deployment began in 2019
Android was launched
First mobile with a fully integrated camera
First mobile with a built-in MP3 player
2019
SAMSUNG GALAXY NOTE 10
By the end of Q3 2019, Samsung was the leading smartphone-manufacturer with a world market share of 21.8 %.
The Arab Spring is live-streamed via mobile videos on social network platforms.
5,1 bil. mobile phone users worldwide ≈ 67 % of the global population
2001
2002
2003
2004
2005
2006
'07
2008
2009
2010
2011
2012
2013
2014
2015
2016
'17
2018
2019
2020
2021
SHARP J-SH04
Fully integrated camera
NOKIA 1100
Best-selling mobile
MOTOROLA RAZR
Iconic design
APPLE IPHONE
iPhone was not the first smartphone, but it redefined our expectations of what a smartphone should be, with apps, multi-touch screen, sensors and an easy-to-use interface.
SAMSUNG GALAXY S4
Best-reviewed smartphone of 2013
APPLE IPHONE X
First Apple phone with controversial facial recognition for authentification
SAMSUNG GALAXY NOTE 10
Latest of the large screen »Note« series, bridging the gap to tablets

INTERNET ON AIR

More than four billion people still have no Internet access. Google, Facebook and other Silicon Valley giants want to change that by connecting the planet with satellites and enormous balloons that will orbit the world. Despite setbacks, wifi will be available everywhere—even if you are on the plane or at the North Pole. This graphic was created in collaboration with the German business weekly »Wirtschaftswoche.«

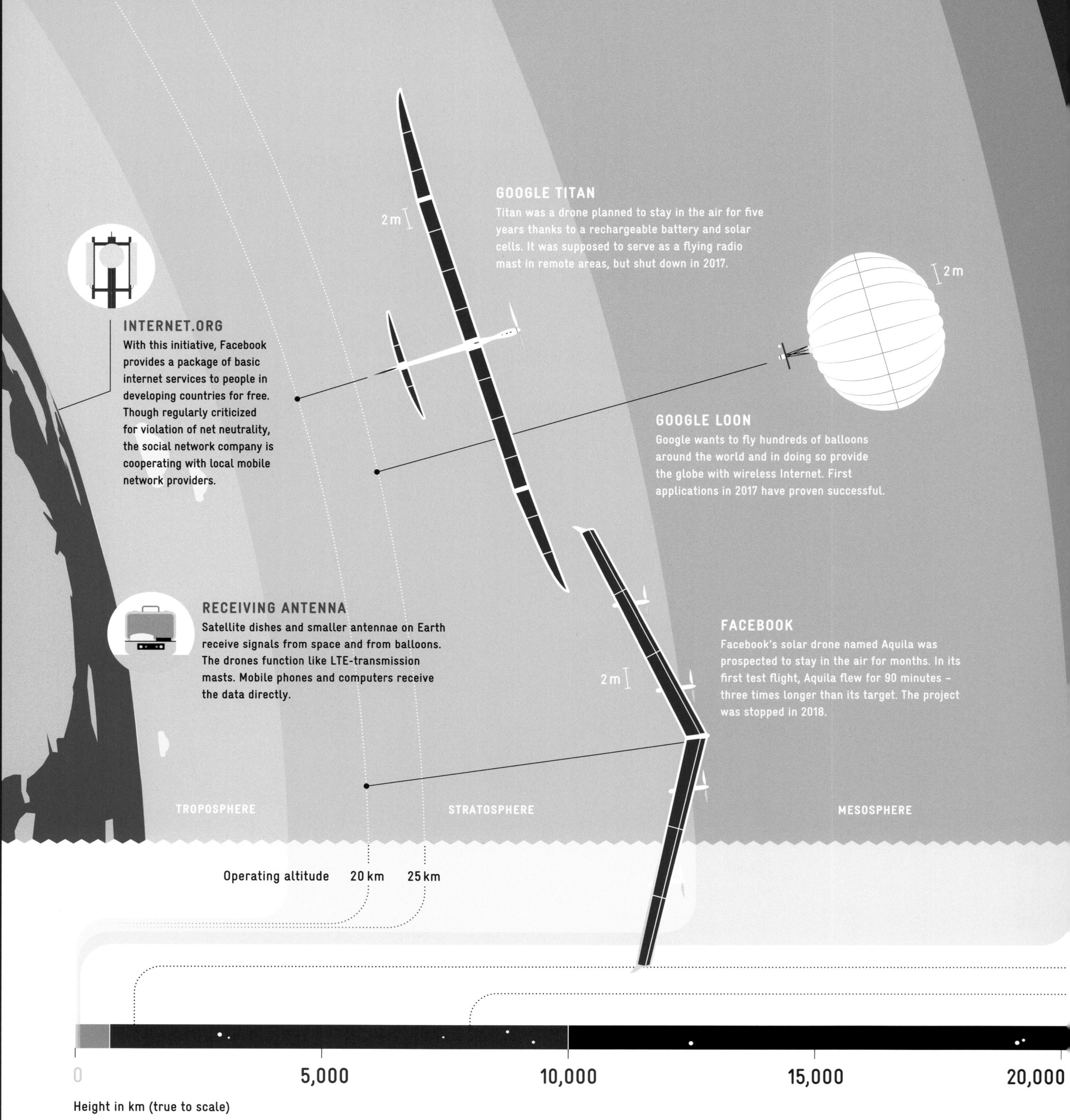
GOOGLE TITAN
Titan was a drone planned to stay in the air for five years thanks to a rechargeable battery and solar cells. It was supposed to serve as a flying radio mast in remote areas, but shut down in 2017.
2 m
2 m
INTERNET.ORG
With this initiative, Facebook provides a package of basic internet services to people in developing countries for free. Though regularly criticized for violation of net neutrality, the social network company is cooperating with local mobile network providers.
GOOGLE LOON
Google wants to fly hundreds of balloons around the world and in doing so provide the globe with wireless Internet. First applications in 2017 have proven successful.
RECEIVING ANTENNA
Satellite dishes and smaller antennae on Earth receive signals from space and from balloons. The drones function like LTE-transmission masts. Mobile phones and computers receive the data directly.
FACEBOOK
Facebook's solar drone named Aquila was prospected to stay in the air for months. In its first test flight, Aquila flew for 90 minutes – three times longer than its target. The project was stopped in 2018.
2 m
TROPOSPHERE
STRATOSPHERE
MESOSPHERE
Operating altitude 20 km 25 km
0
5,000
10,000
15,000
20,000
Height in km (true to scale)

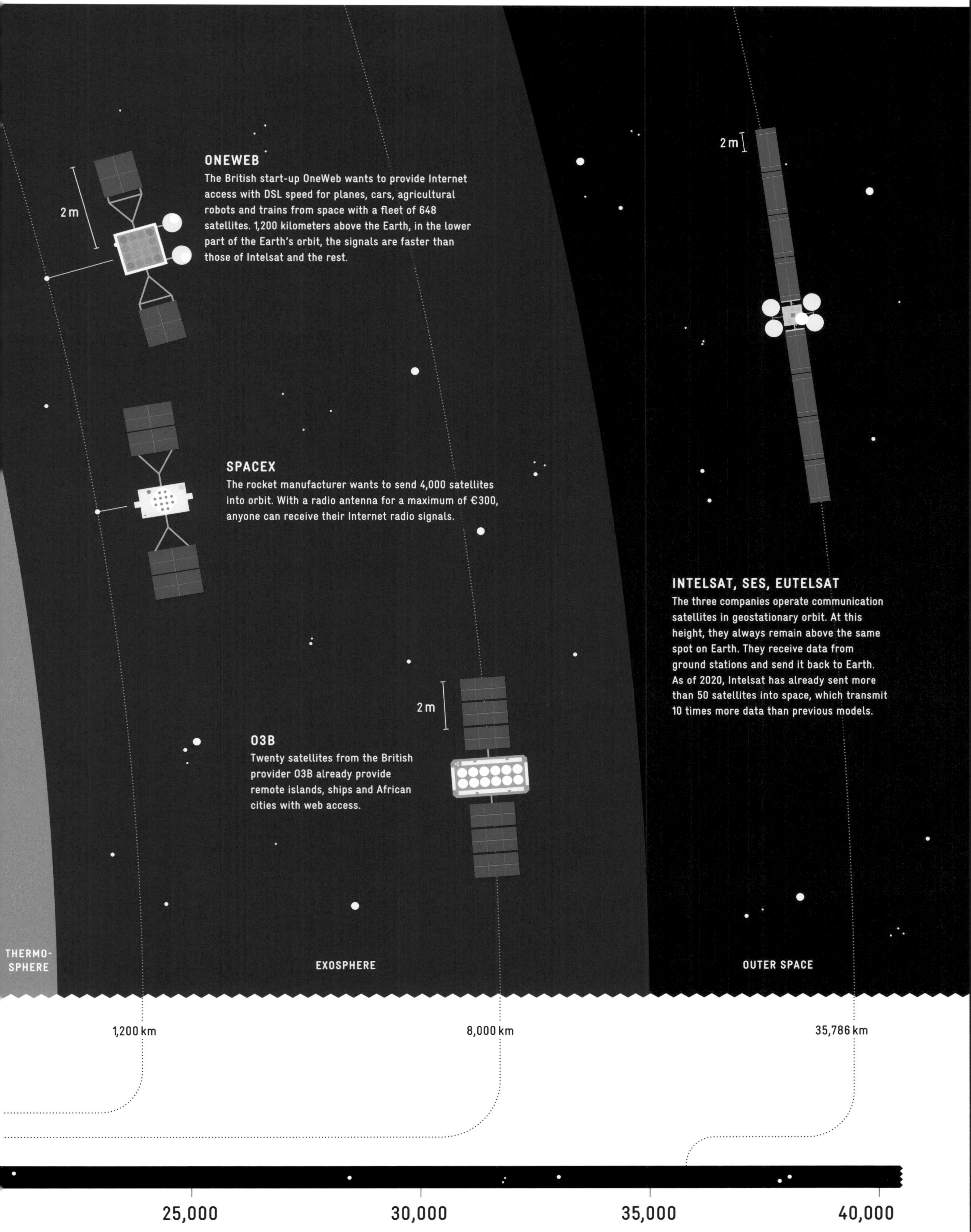
2 m
2 m
2 m
2 m
THERMO-
SPHERE
EXOSPHERE
OUTER SPACE
1,200 km
8,000 km
35,786 km
25,000
30,000
35,000
40,000

ONEWEB

The British start-up OneWeb wants to provide Internet access with DSL speed for planes, cars, agricultural robots and trains from space with a fleet of 648 satellites. 1,200 kilometers above the Earth, in the lower part of the Earth's orbit, the signals are faster than those of Intelsat and the rest.

SPACEX

The rocket manufacturer wants to send 4,000 satellites into orbit. With a radio antenna for a maximum of €300, anyone can receive their Internet radio signals.

O3B

Twenty satellites from the British provider O3B already provide remote islands, ships and African cities with web access.

INTELSAT, SES, EUTELSAT

The three companies operate communication satellites in geostationary orbit. At this height, they always remain above the same spot on Earth. They receive data from ground stations and send it back to Earth. As of 2020, Intelsat has already sent more than 50 satellites into space, which transmit 10 times more data than previous models.

.WHATTHEFILE

Have you ever wondered how many file extensions there are in the world? Probably not. But we looked anyway and found 33,456 different file types in use today. There are probably more. We highlighted the most amusing ones and asked ourselves how many are used on a regular basis? We haven't even used a fraction of them—only the ones in the upper left corner of each category.

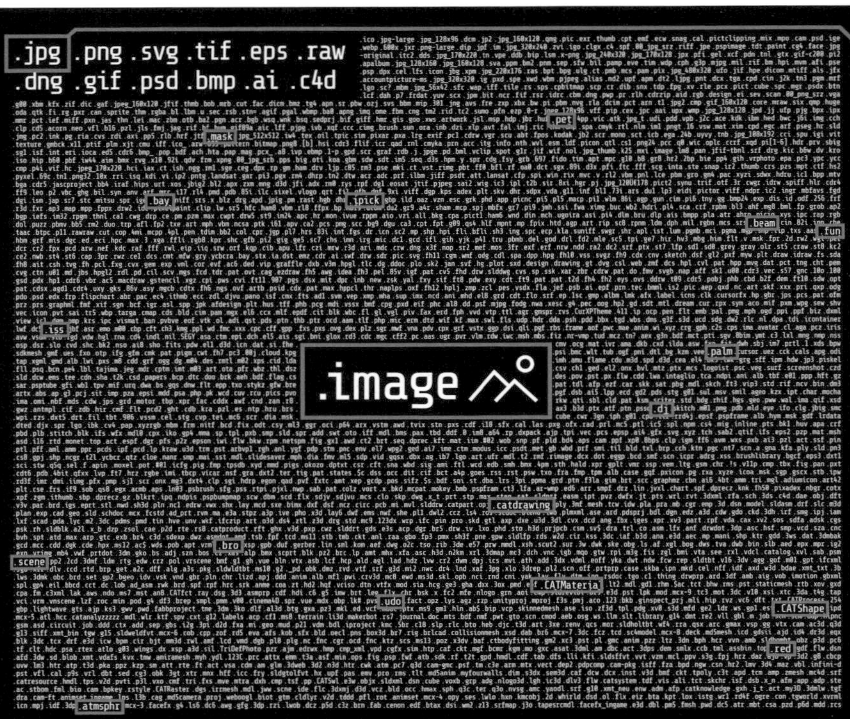
.jpg .png .svg .tif .eps .raw
.dng .gif .psd .bmp .ai .c4d
.image

.aiff .mp3 .m4a
.wav .midi .flac
.audio

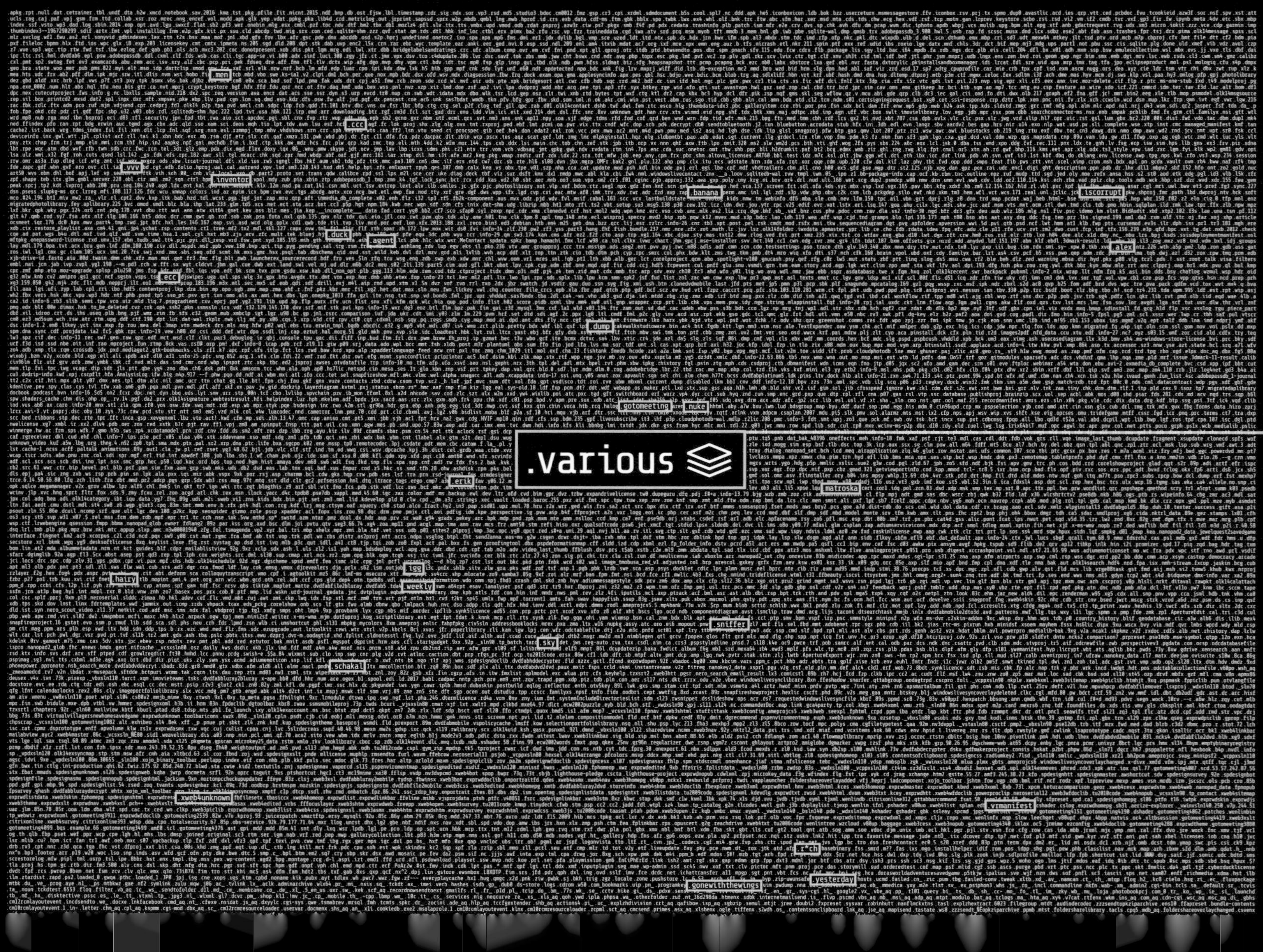
.various

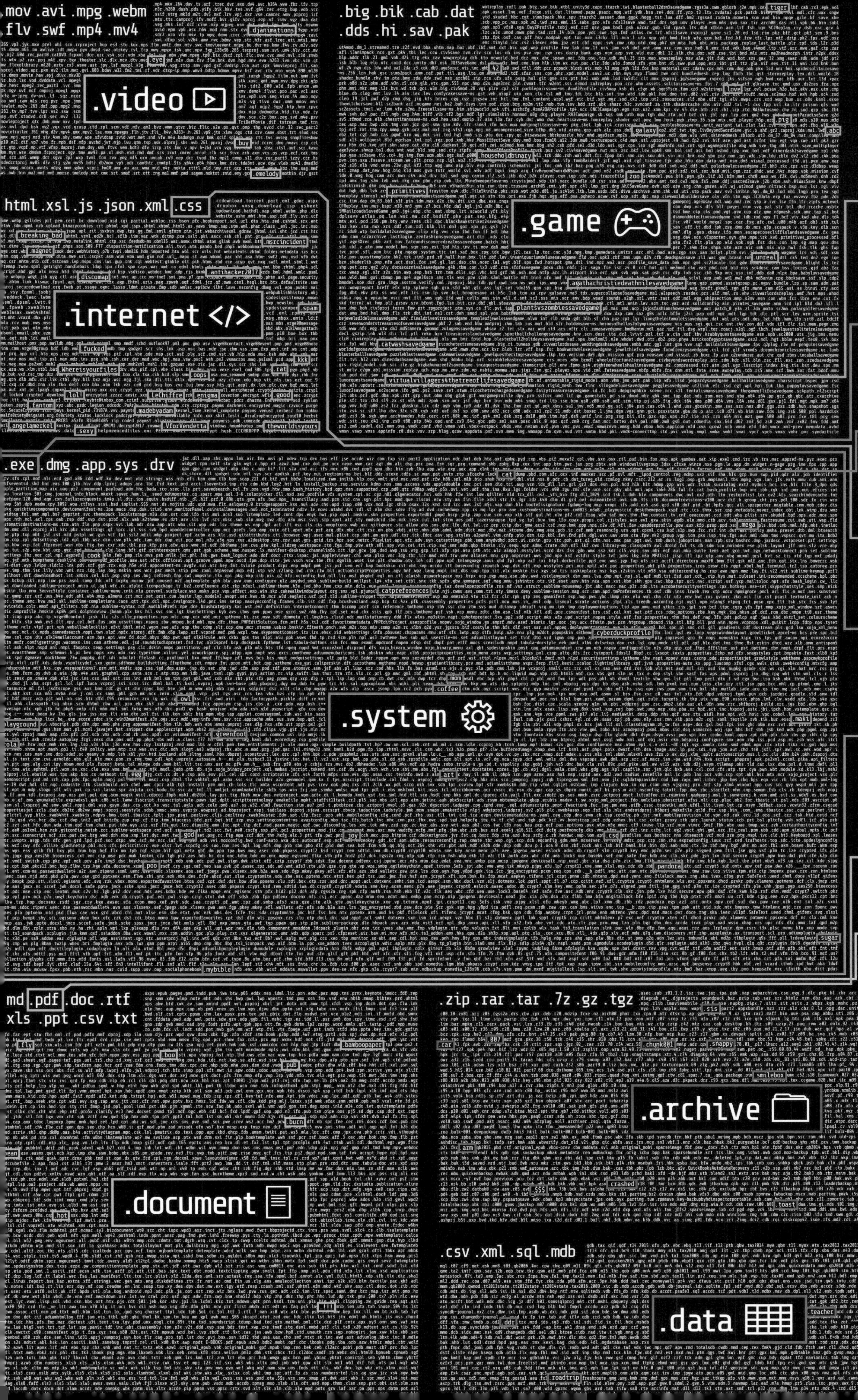

The first use of file extensions was by DEC (Digital Equipment Corporation). The file name was created from its base-name, followed by a period and then the file extension. Microsoft adopted this convention in its DOS operating system, which uses 8.3 filenames, as in **»FILENAME.EXT«**.

Today, in every modern operating system the maximum length for a file name including the extension is 255 characters. In our list, the longest extension name is **40 characters long**.

The first file extensions were used to easily determine the files' data type: **.txt** for a text file, **.mus** for a music file, and **.exe** for an executable file.

The **.cat** file extension has nothing to do with cats, rather it is used by various Microsoft applications for security catalog files.

95.7% of the top 10 million websites use **CSS** to define how HTML elements are displayed on screen.

JPEG is the most popular image file format with 74% of the top 10 million websites using it, followed closely by PNG with 73%.

FLAC is an open-source audio format where audio is compressed without any loss in sound quality or original data. The most-used format, however, is the lossy MP3.

89% of non-HTML documents on the web are published in **PDF** format.

There are approx. 11,929 file suffixes that do not fit in these file format categories.

HEATSCORE

In January 2019, the largest dump of login data was released into the dark web. An analysis of just the password data in the so-called »Collections #1- #5« revealed patterns of human behavior in how we create character keys that fulfil security requirements. It turns out people are really not that original in creating unique key codes for their login data.

How to read this graphic

The saturation of color represents how frequently a feature appears in this length of password.

Dotted lines

Special characters like ! are often found at the end. In longer passwords, a distinctive pattern emerged

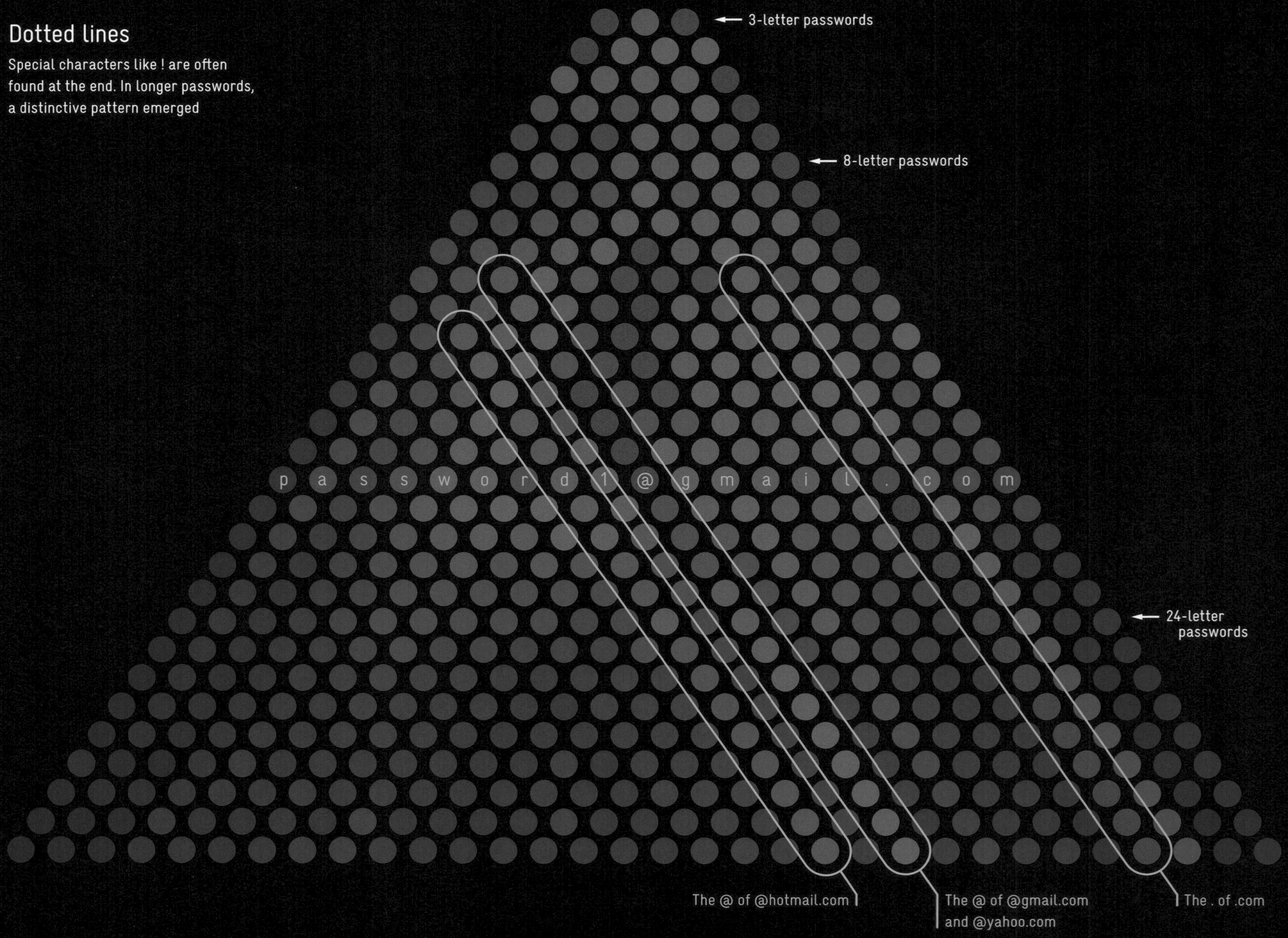
3-letter passwords
8-letter passwords
24-letter passwords
p a s s w o r d 1 @ g m a i l . c o m
The @ of @hotmail.com
The @ of @gmail.com and @yahoo.com
The . of .com

The period is the most common special character in passwords.

The common ones

The size of each letter indicates the frequency with which this character appears in the list of passwords.

Password possibilities

There are 52 possible letters, 10 digits and 33 different special characters on an international QWERTY keyboard. Even an 8-character password has 6,634,204,312,890,625 (95^8) different combinations.

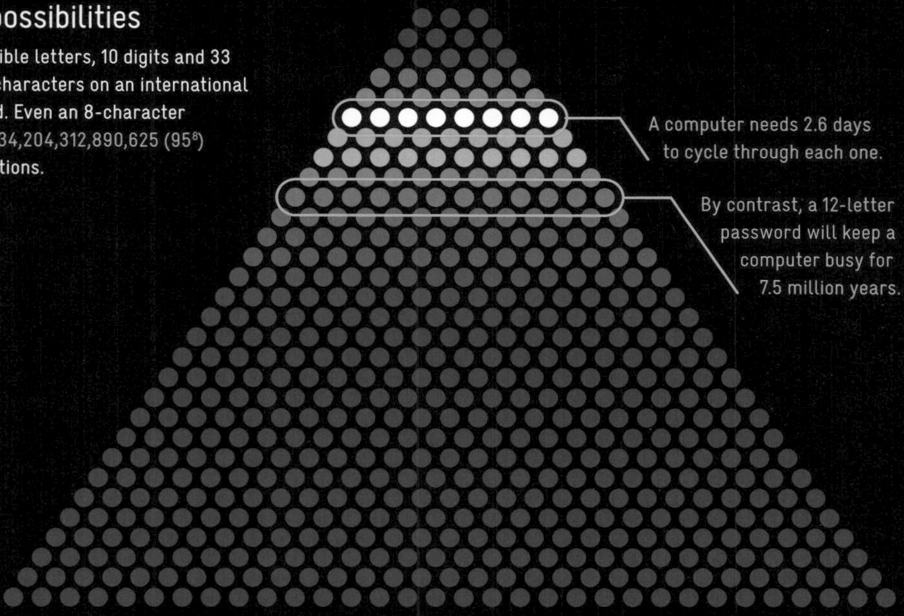

A computer needs 2.6 days to cycle through each one.

By contrast, a 12-letter password will keep a computer busy for 7.5 million years.

Up front

People capitalize the first letter of sentences, names and—as the data shows—passwords.

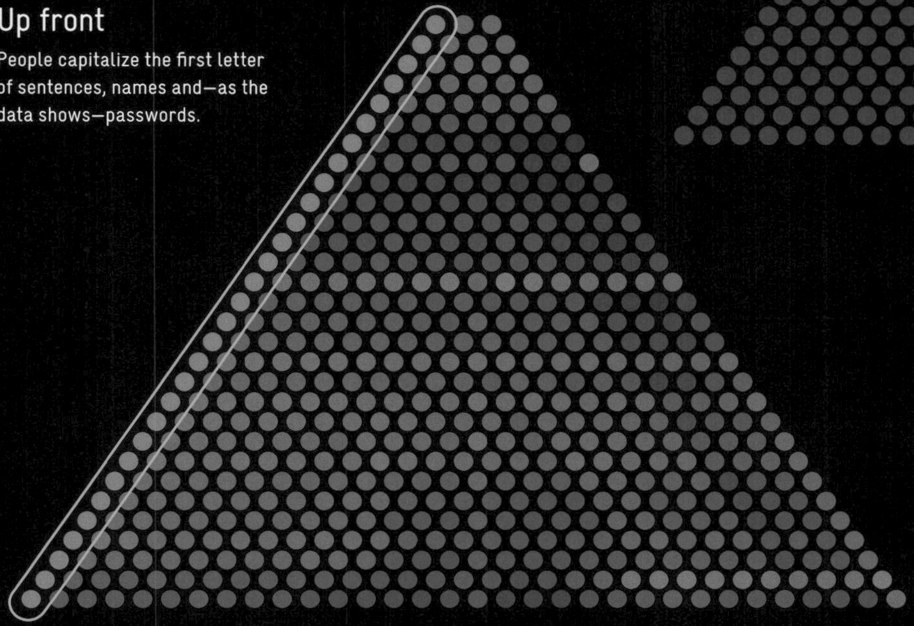

Countdown

If a password contains numbers, the digits are most often found at the end.

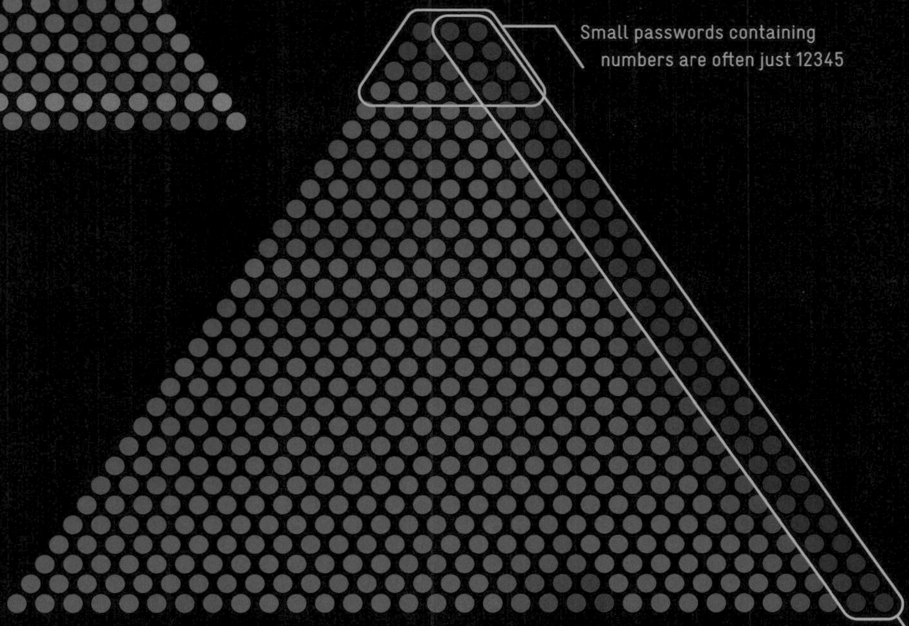

Small passwords containing numbers are often just 12345

Numbers are often paired together with their sequential neighbor e.g. 12, 23, 34, 45.

The letters r, s, t, n, l and e appear in 45% of words in the english language.

e.g. stoner

Passwords often refer to a birth year or the year they were made, so 20 and 19 are popular combinations.

2019

CULTURE & ARTS

Artistic works and performances touch us emotionally, influenced by the individual creators themselves. Nevertheless, there are codes and symbols concealed within each work, such as the musical notes and scores underlying a symphony.

Pictured here is the **oldest known musical score**, written between **2000-1700 BC in Babylonian cuneiform numerals**. It was discovered on a clay tablet from the Schøyen Collection. The text explains that these two sequentially ascending heptatonic scales should be played on a four-string lute tuned to raised fifths. The textual explanation concretizes interpretation of the notes. Further, it suggests that this notation appeared in school music lessons.

Just as these textual notes elaborate on the musical ones, so too do infographics become unambiguous statements via their labels and symbols. Infographics are pictures composed of data. Additional texts and symbols steer interpretation and thereby the viewer's understanding. Information graphics are thus a portal to opening new perspectives on cultural phenomena — like the graphics in this chapter.

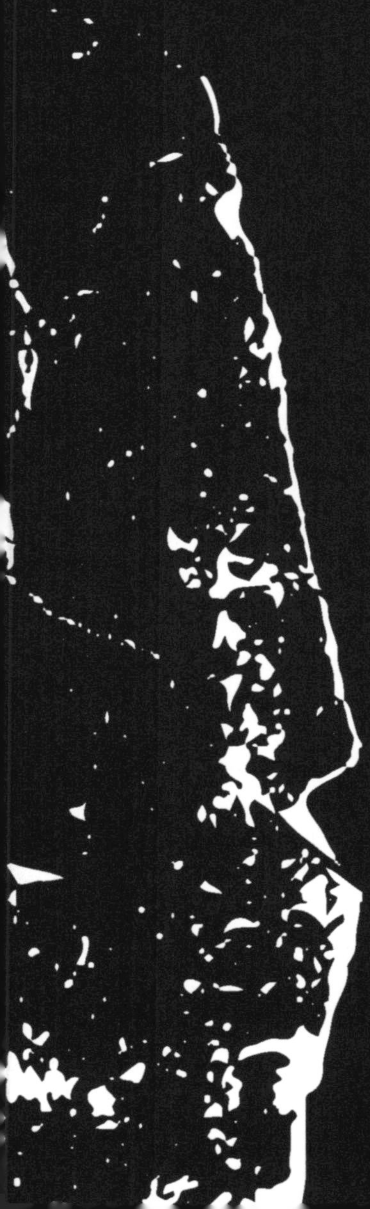

FESTIVAL DATA

Get your tickets and find your camping site: Music festivals are spreading the joy and love of music around the world—and earning organizers a pretty penny while they're at it. The biggest festivals can result in the temporary establishment of a small city, enabling people to see a favorite band, discover a new artist and spend time with new and old friends.

65 FESTIVALS

10 BIGGEST FESTIVALS
Donauinselfest
The Guinness World Record for the largest music festival in the world goes to the Donauinselfest in Vienna, Austria.
1,000,000
daily attendees
Mawazine
Rabat, Morocco, hosts the second-largest music festival.
Primavera Sound
Glastonbury
Woodstock Poland (Pol'and'Rock)
Essence
EDC: Electric Daisy Carnival Las Vegas
Coachella Music & Arts Festival
Download Festival
Lollapalooza (USA)
Distortion
Rock in Rio
Reading Festival / Leeds Festival
ADE: Amsterdam Dance Event
Sziget Festival
Hot 97 Summer Jam
Mad Cool Festival
Vive Latino
Rock Werchter
Defqon.1 Weekend Festival
Wacken Open Air
Rock am Ring / Rock im Park
Austin City Limits Music Festival
Creamfields
Tomorrowland
Sónar Festival
Fuji Rock
Osheaga Music and Arts Festival
Afropunk
Way Out West
Summerfest
Hellfest Open Air Festival
Boomtown
Awakenings Festival
Les Eurockéennes
Nuits Sonores
Méra Luna
Stagecoach Festival
Mysteryland
The Governors Ball Music Festival
Let It Roll
Melt Festival
Montreux Jazz Festival
Best Kept Secret
Mayday
UMF: Ultra Music Festival
New Orleans Jazz & Heritage Festival
Splendour in the Grass
Dour
SXSW: South by Southwest
Pitchfork Music Festival
Outlook festival
Viña del Mar
DGTL Amsterdam
Wave Gothic Treffen
Fusion
Iceland Airwaves
Dimensions Festival
Time Warp
Roskilde
Amphi Festival
Dekmantel
Down the Rabbit Hole
Snow-bombing
Meadows in the Mountains
1,000 daily attendees.

On the other end of the scale is the **Meadows in the Mountains** festival in the Rhodope Mountains, Bulgaria. Despite its remote location, it attracts enough visitors to keep the music playing for the last 10 years.

24 COUNTRIES

Several of the major music festivals from the US have inspired outposts around the globe, including Lollapalooza.

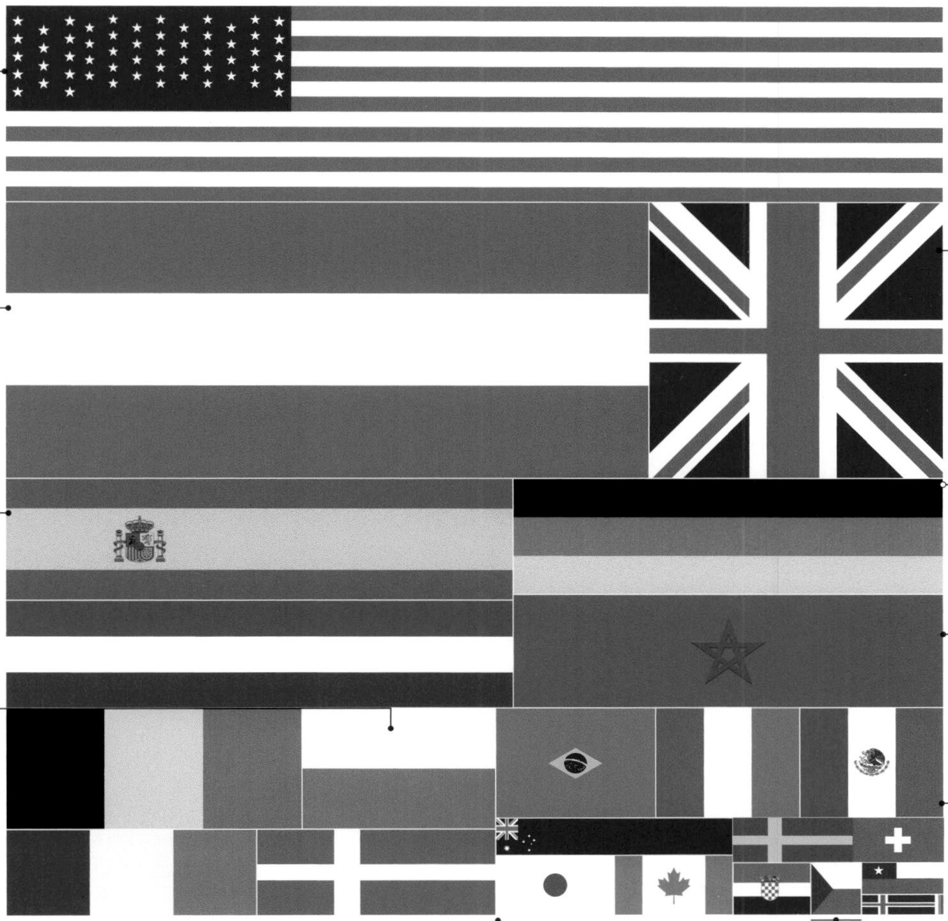

USA

Four of the top ten largest festivals are to be found in the states of Louisiana, California, Illinois and Nevada. Each festival hosts more than 100,000 daily visitors.

AUSTRIA

Over three days, 1 million visitors a day enjoy concerts in the middle of the Danube—tickets are free.

SPAIN

Primavera Sound in Barcelona is one of the most popular festivals in the electronic and indie scene.

POLAND

An estimated 133,000 music fans converge on Kustrin, Poland, for the country's annual tribute to Woodstock—a major influx for a town of just over 17,000 people.

The US is also home to the only country music festival that appears on our lists – the Stagecoach Festival takes place annually at the site of Coachella.

UK

Great Britain hosts two major festivals—Glastonbury and the Download Festival—with 135,000 and 110,000 visitors per day respectively.

GERMANY

In Germany, rock rules with Rock am Ring, Wacken, Méra Luna and the Amphi Festival.

MOROCCO

The African country hosts artists from around the world and 277,000 attendees per day over nine days.

BRAZIL, HUNGARY AND MEXICO

Rock in Rio, Vive Latino and Sziget Festival have something in common. Each of these festivals boasts around 90,000 visitors a day.

JAPAN AND CZECH REPUBLIC

Asia's festival culture is still in development, but earns a place in our list thanks to Fuji Rock, hosted in Japan every year. The Czech Republic is home to the only festival dedicated to drum & bass in the Let it Roll festival.

10 GENRES

Diversity rules! Mixing genres has proven to be a winning formula, attracting a wide range of fans to ensure higher ticket sales.

- MIXED GENRE
- ELECTRONIC
- ROCK
- HIP HOP
- HEAVY METAL
- GOTHIC
- JAZZ
- COUNTRY
- DRUM&BASS
- FOLK

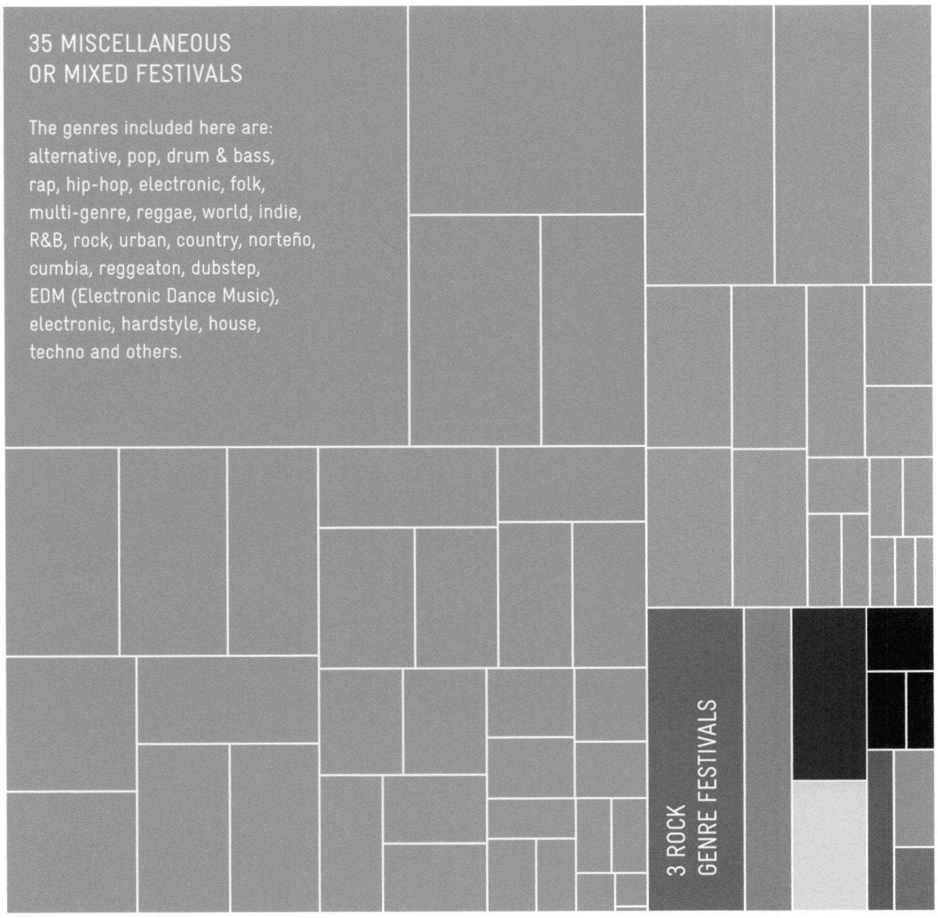
35 MISCELLANEOUS OR MIXED FESTIVALS
The genres included here are: alternative, pop, drum & bass, rap, hip-hop, electronic, folk, multi-genre, reggae, world, indie, R&B, rock, urban, country, norteño, cumbia, reggeaton, dubstep, EDM (Electronic Dance Music), electronic, hardstyle, house, techno and others.
3 ROCK GENRE FESTIVALS

18 ELECTRONIC MUSIC FESTIVALS
Predominantly European

9 OTHER SPECIFIC GENRE FESTIVALS

VISUALIZING ACOUSTICS

We go to the orchestra to be moved emotionally, inspired by sound and to experience those magical goose bumps. But achieving that has nothing to do with wizardry – it is pure science.

Inside advantage

The volume of sound, as well as the way it travels through space, both affect the listener's perception of it. If a musician plays a sound too quietly, it may be lost on the listener, but a quiet sound clearly heard can add intimacy to the performance. An indoor room allows for sound reflections from all sides that bring the music to listeners at an appropriate volume.

Open space

Sound travels in all directions through space and the volume quickly dissipates.

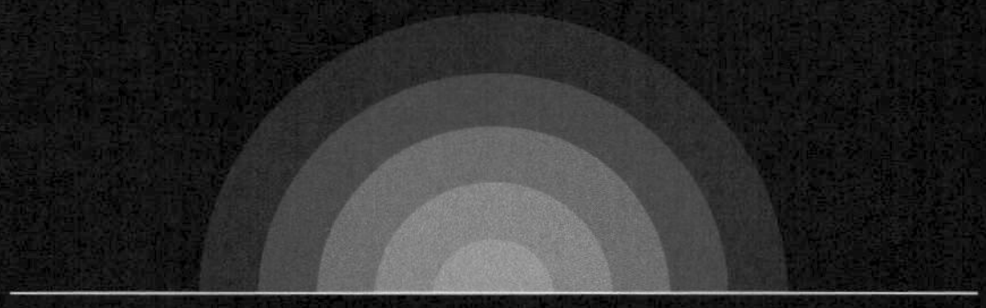

Amphitheater

Sound is reflected through the semi-circular structure.

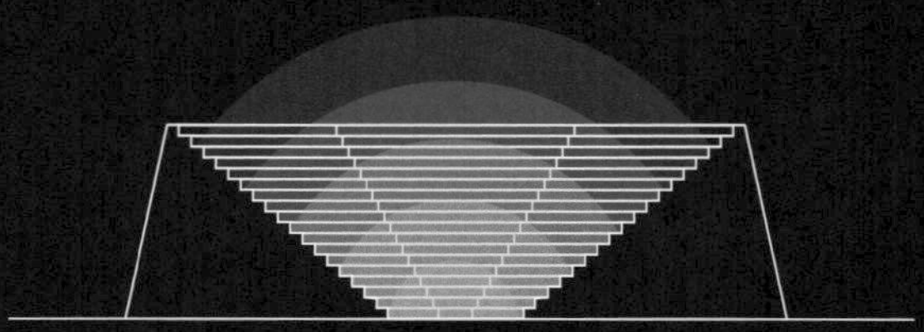

Closed room

Sound is reflected to the audience, allowing them to experience louder and quieter tones.

Double function

An additional reflector panel serves both the audience and the orchestra by shortening the path of the sound to the audience and providing feedback to the orchestra.

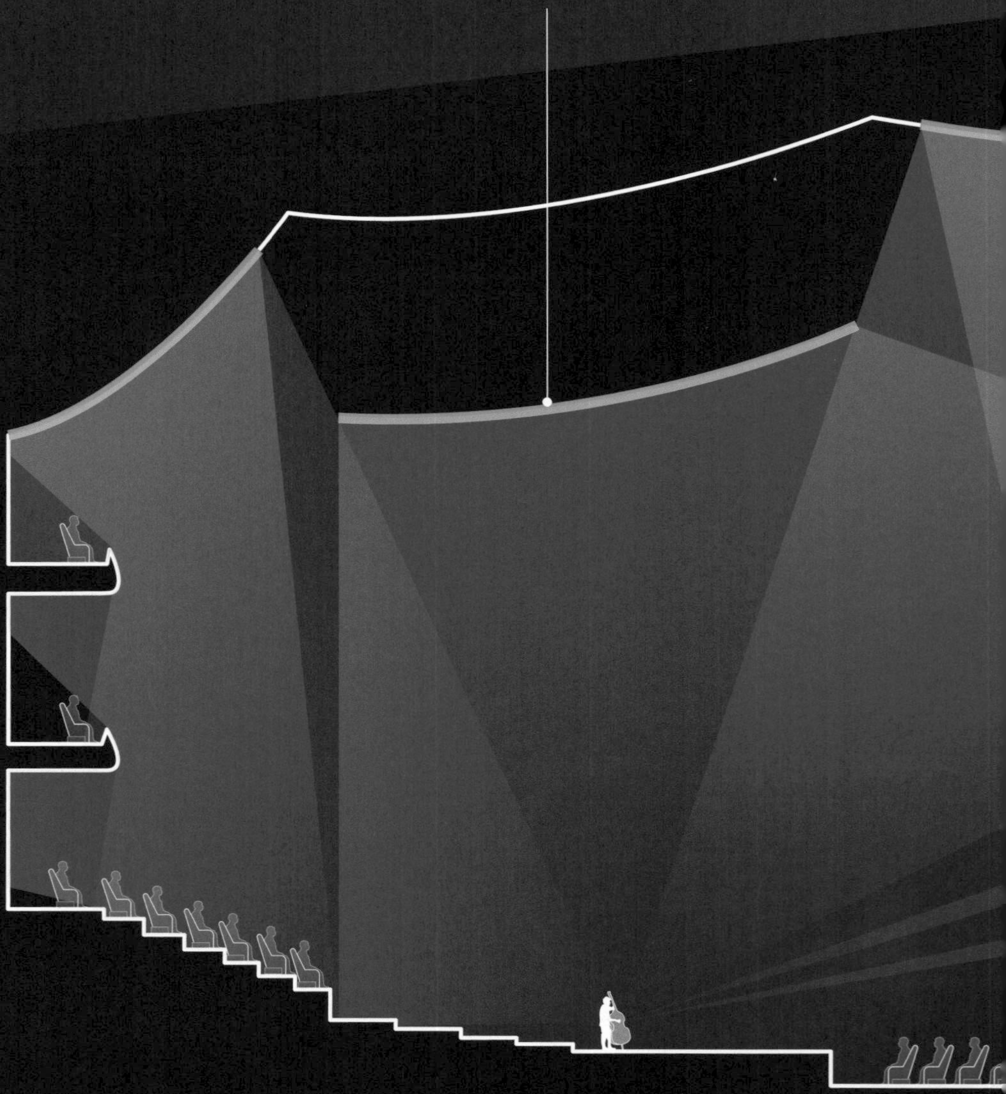

The Shoebox

The ideal proportions of the width, height and length of a shoebox venue are 1:1:2. Musicians perform on a stage at the front, and balconies flank the sides of the rectangular hall. Vienna's Musikvereinsaal (1870), the Boston Symphony Hall (1900) and the Lugano Arte e Cultura (2015) in Italy all follow this model, as well as the future home of the Bavarian Radio Symphony Orchestra

The Vineyard

Reminiscent of an indoor amphitheater, a vineyard style concert venue features terraced seating around the orchestra's sunken stage. Audiences feel closer to the action, even if some acoustic effectiveness is sacrificed. Nevertheless, most modern concert halls, such as the Berlin Philharmonie (1963), choose this visually pleasing architectural approach

Contoured ceiling

Auditorium designs ensure an equal distribution of sound by slightly vaulting the ceiling. The purposeful arrangement of contours reflects the music to every seat in the hall.

The absorption coefficient

Rear walls, balconies and seats are surfaces that need to absorb sound to avoid echoes detrimental to the acoustics. A material's thickness and surface structure determines how much sound the material absorbs.
The absorption coefficient ranges from 0 to 1.00 and covers the spectrum from total reflection to total absorption.

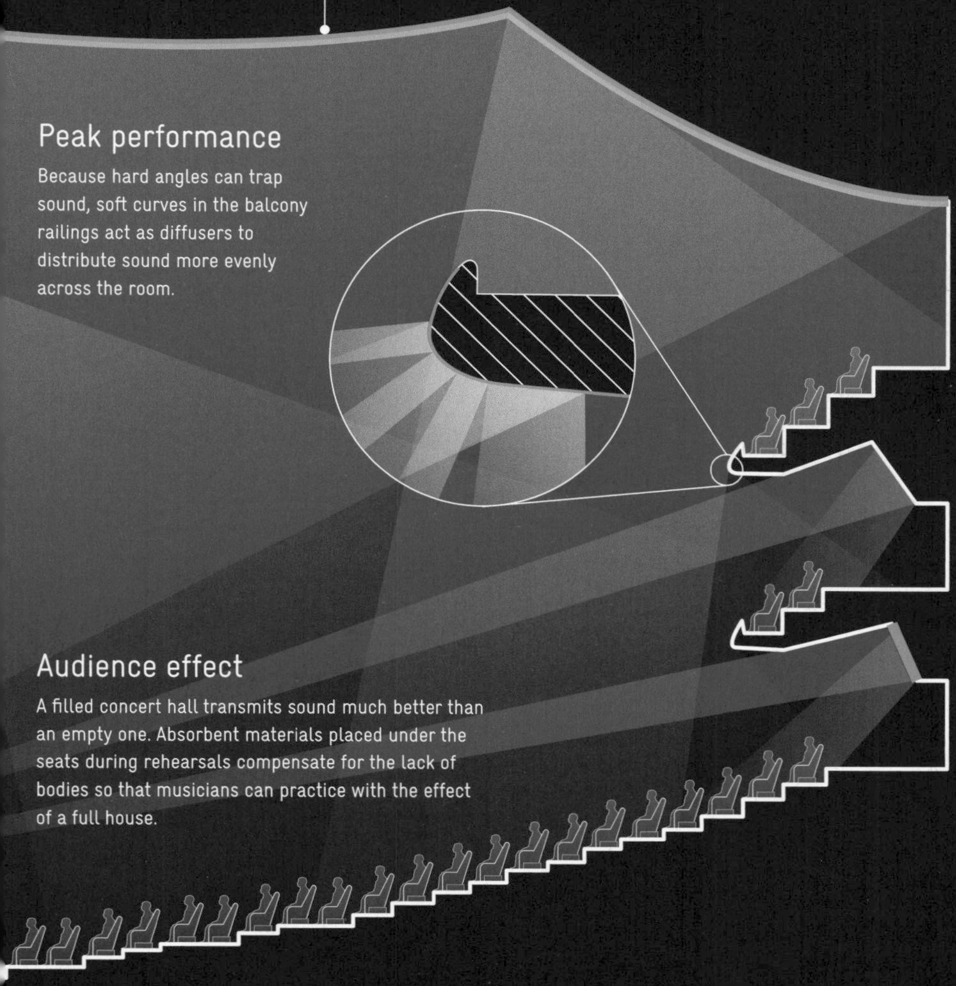

Peak performance

Because hard angles can trap sound, soft curves in the balcony railings act as diffusers to distribute sound more evenly across the room.

Audience effect

A filled concert hall transmits sound much better than an empty one. Absorbent materials placed under the seats during rehearsals compensate for the lack of bodies so that musicians can practice with the effect of a full house.

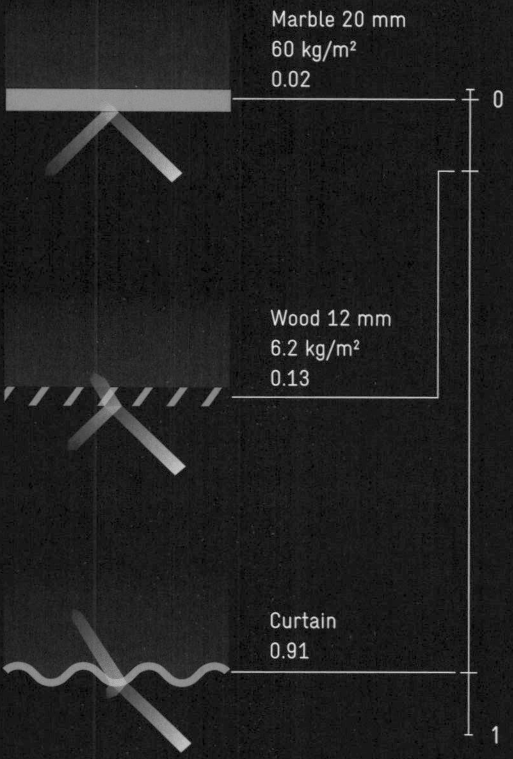
Marble 20 mm
60 kg/m²
0.02
0
Wood 12 mm
6.2 kg/m²
0.13
Curtain
0.91
1

Absorption coefficient:
0 = 100 % reflection
1 = 100 % absorption
Meantone value: 1 kHz

The side story

Side panels create atmosphere in a room by providing a feeling of intimacy with the performance while aiding the sound's movement around the room.

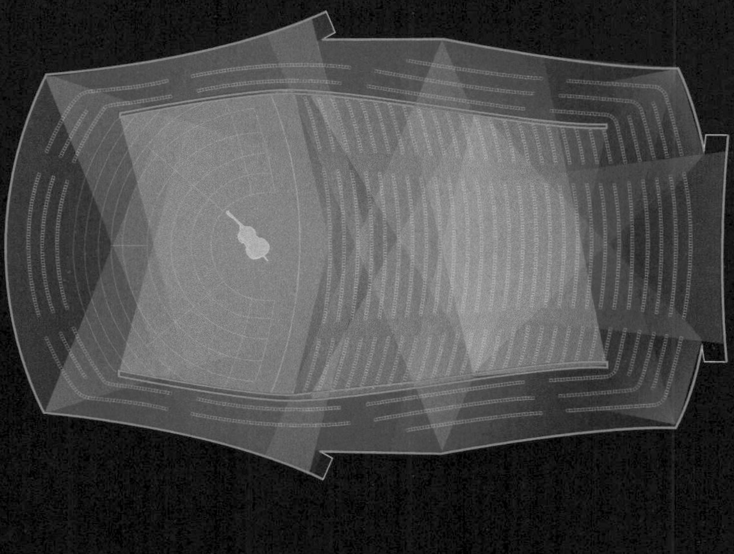

Hitting the mark

Each performance space is engineered to achieve a balance that enables every single listener to enjoy the show.

»Going to the moon is much simpler as a physics problem. [In a moon shot], you've got one source, you've got one trajectory that will get you there and you've got one 'listener' or destination.«

William J. Cavanaugh / Acoustician

Reflectogram in action

A computer model allows the acoustician to simulate a sound's journey from start to finish as it reverberates through space.

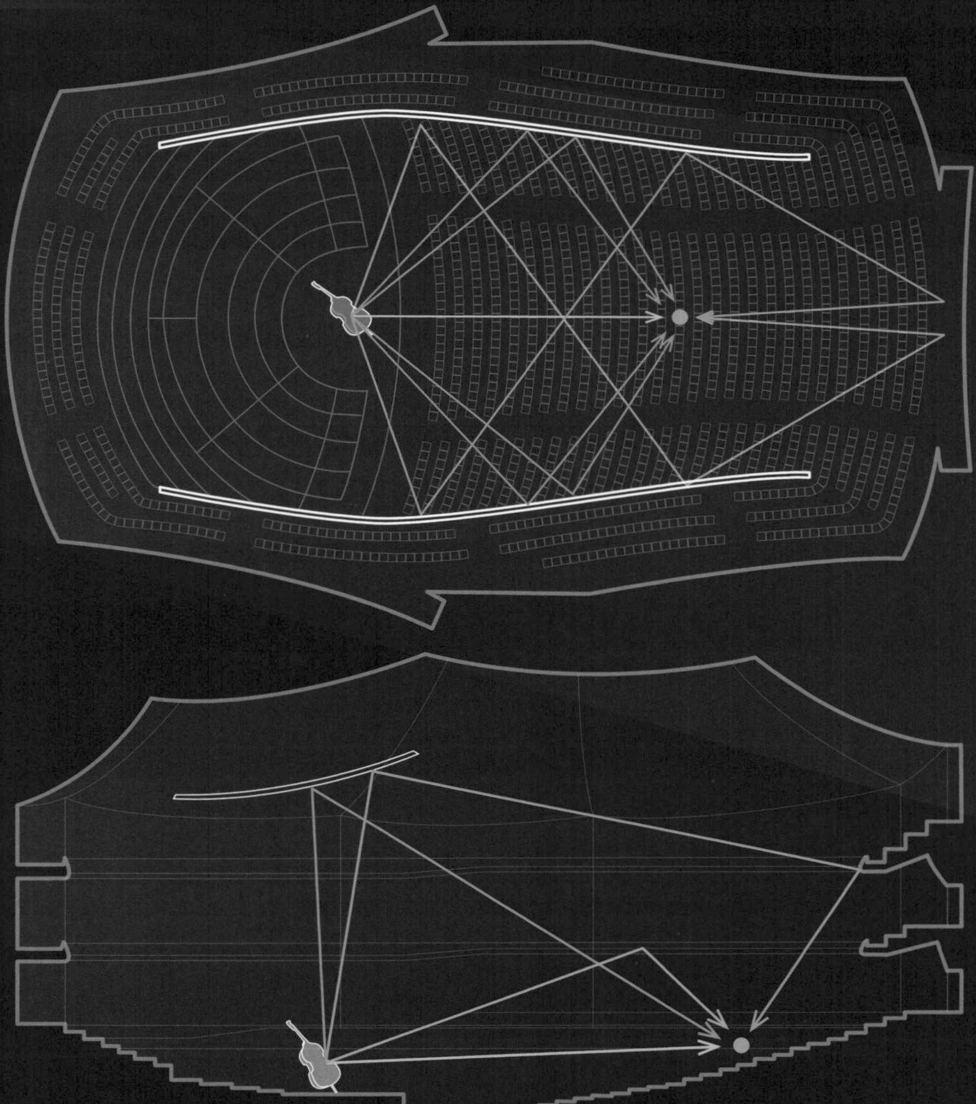

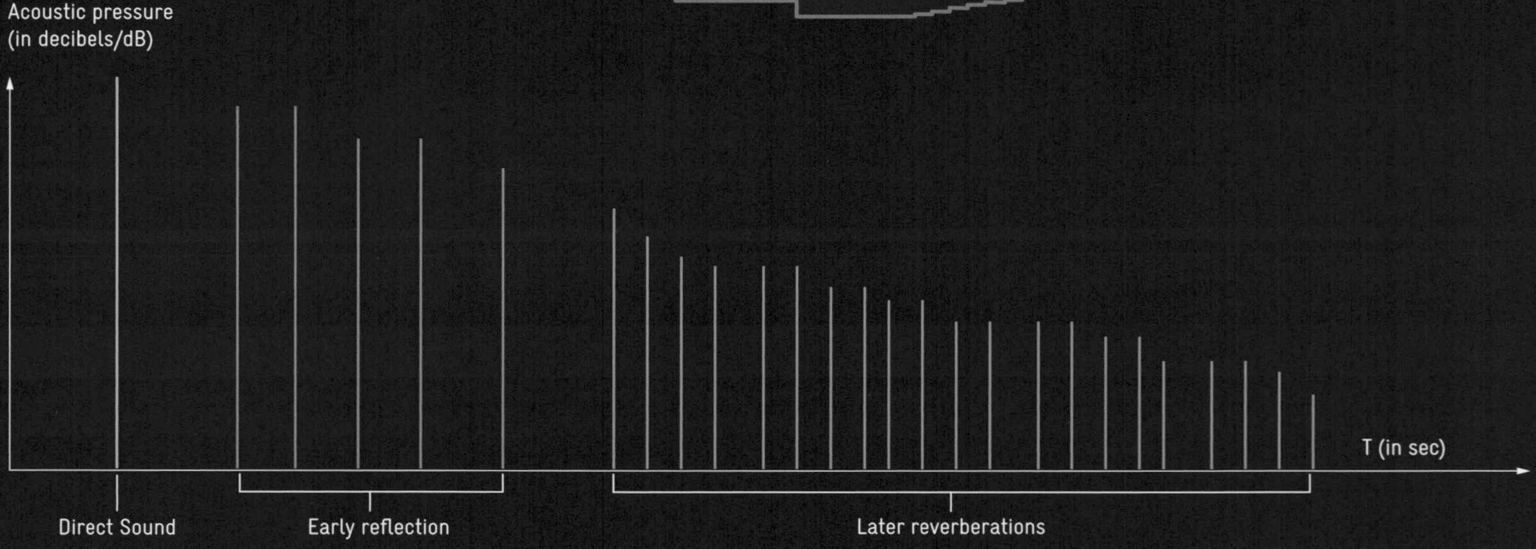
Acoustic pressure
(in decibels/dB)
T (in sec)
Direct Sound
Early reflection
Later reverberations

eres of perception

sts divide the perspectives of musicians and audience members into five categories. In this way, they attempt to quantify the poles of uality and describe a measurement that presents perfectly balanced acoustics.

oebox ⬢ Vineyard ▲ Theater

oßer Musikvereinssaal, Vienna
mphony Hall, Boston
atro Colon, Buenos Aires
■ Konzerthaus, Berlin
■ Concertgebouw, Amsterdam
■ Tokyo Opera City Hall, Tokyo
■ Großer Tonhallesaal, Zurich
▲ Carnegie Hall, New York
■ Stadt-Casino, Basel
⬢ St David's Hall, Cardiff
⬢ Elbphilharmonie, Hamburg
■ Avery Fisher Hall, New York
■ Festspielhaus, Salzburg

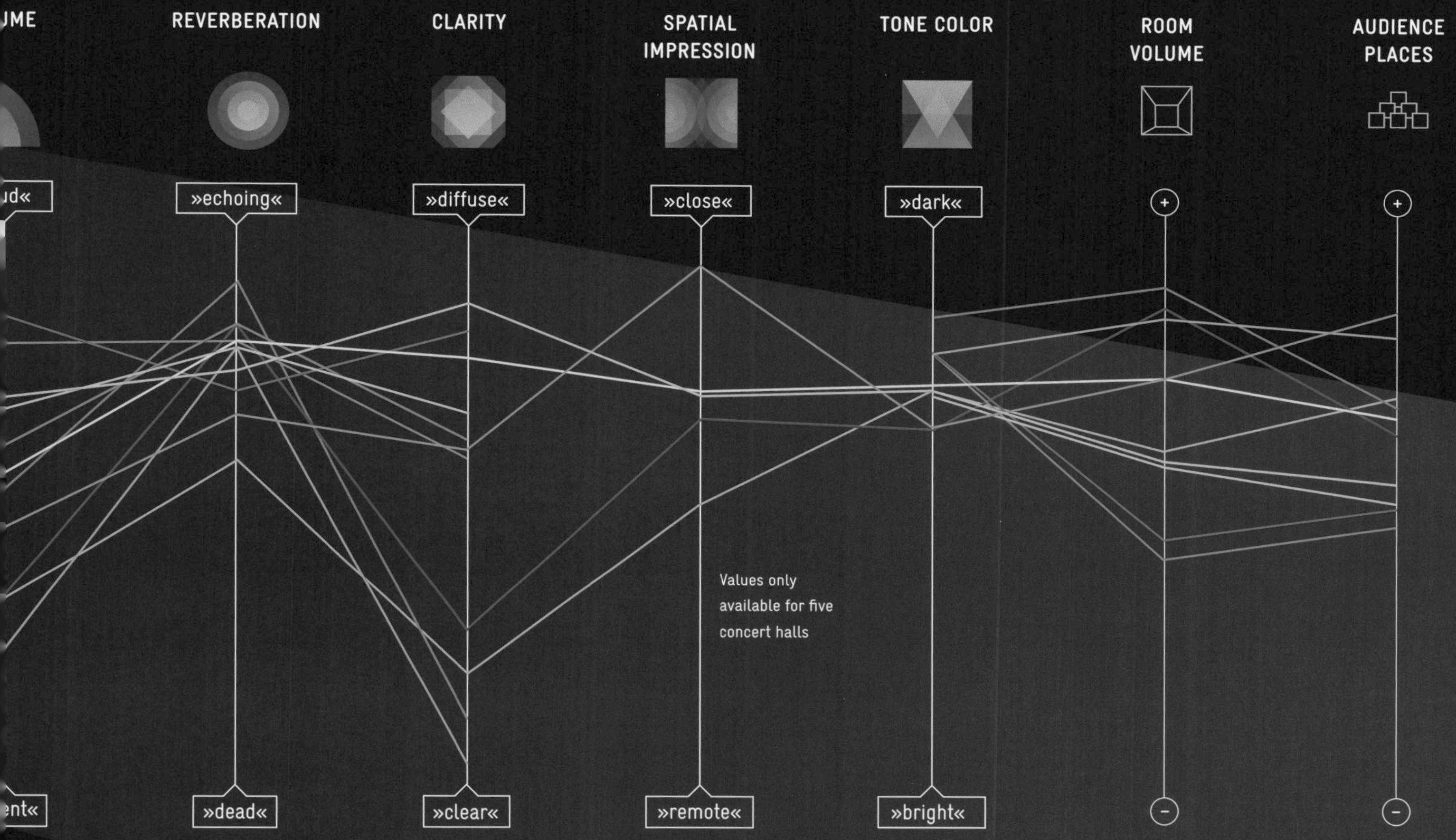

UME
REVERBERATION
CLARITY
SPATIAL IMPRESSION
TONE COLOR
ROOM VOLUME
AUDIENCE PLACES
ud«
»echoing«
»diffuse«
»close«
»dark«
+
+
Values only available for five concert halls
ent«
»dead«
»clear«
»remote«
»bright«
−
−

er Musikvereinssaal Vienna

nd Music Room of Vienna, designed according hoebox concept by the architect Theophil Hansen, ned with great fanfare in 1870. Grand ceiling s, golden Greek statues and glittering chandeliers m the simple, acoustically ideal shape into as well as a musical temple. It is considered

Concertgebouw Amsterdam

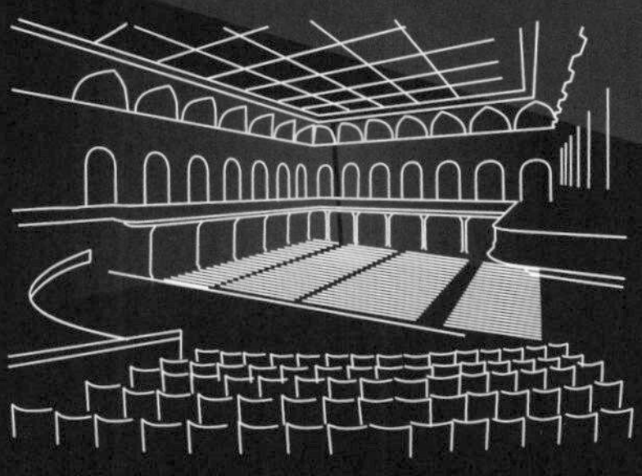

Also designed as a shoebox, the great hall of Amsterdam's modestly named »Concert Building« opened in 1888. The design by Adolf Leonard van Gendt is home to the Royal Concertgebouw Orchestra and the Netherlands Philharmonic Orchestra.

Festspielhaus Salzburg

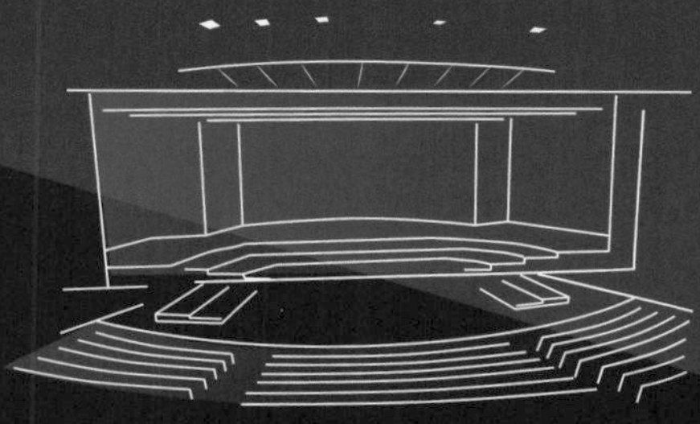

For Salzburg's mid-century festival hall, opened in 1960, architect Clemens Holzmeister built a semi-circular auditorium in a square building, giving the hall a completely different sound profile than those with a shoebox design. The 100-meter-wide stage hosts orchestral as well as theatrical

THREE CLASSICS

A comparison of three composers and their work.

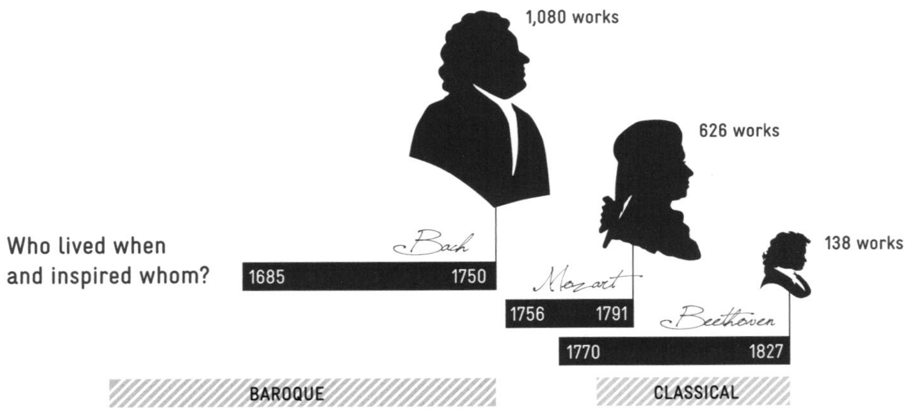
1,080 works
626 works
138 works
Who lived when
and inspired whom?
Bach
1685
1750
Mozart
1756
1791
Beethoven
1770
1827
BAROQUE
CLASSICAL

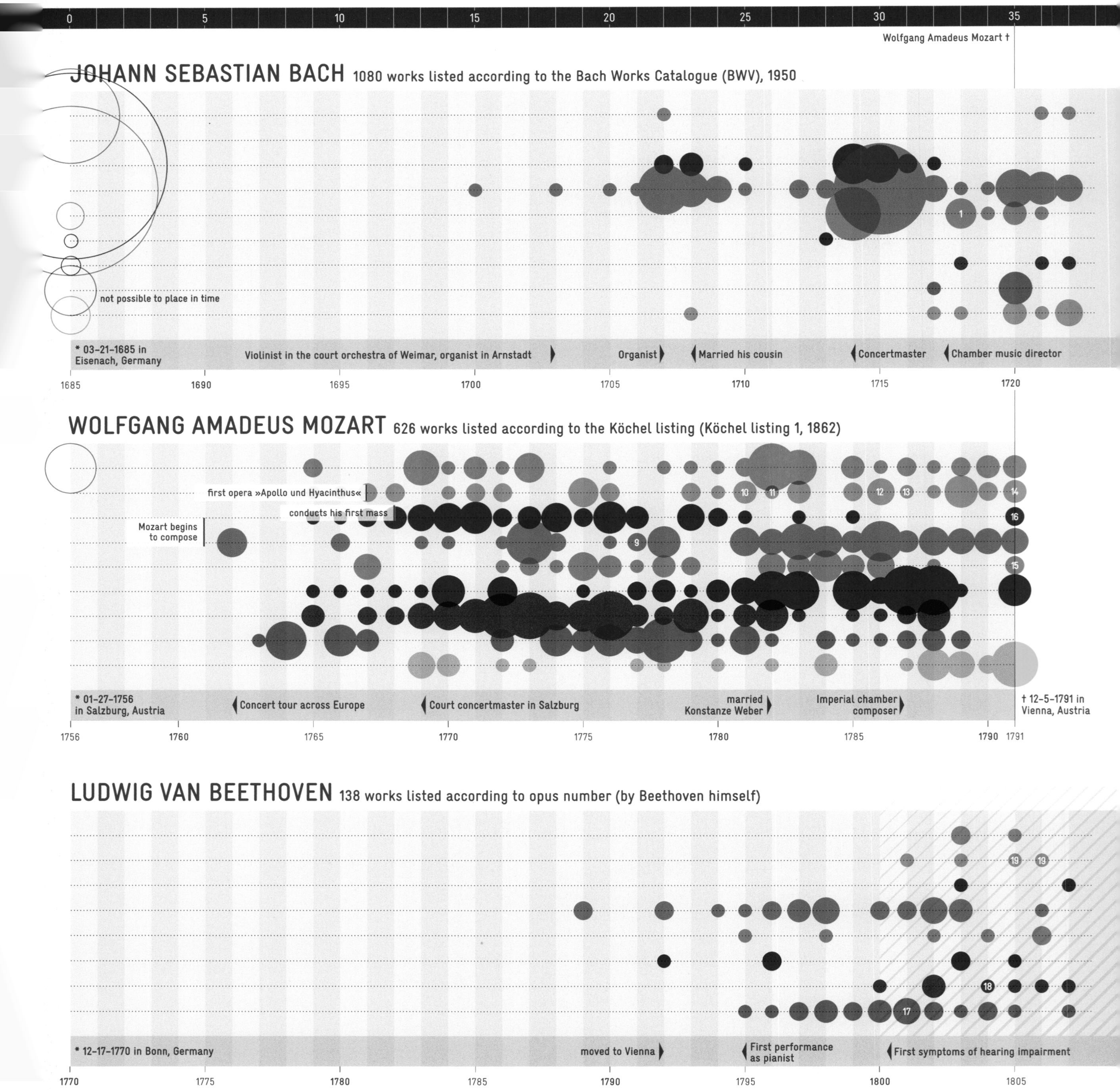
0
5
10
15
20
25
30
35
Wolfgang Amadeus Mozart †
JOHANN SEBASTIAN BACH 1080 works listed according to the Bach Works Catalogue (BWV), 1950
not possible to place in time
* 03-21-1685 in
Eisenach, Germany
Violinist in the court orchestra of Weimar, organist in Arnstadt
Organist
Married his cousin
Concertmaster
Chamber music director
1685
1690
1695
1700
1705
1710
1715
1720
WOLFGANG AMADEUS MOZART 626 works listed according to the Köchel listing (Köchel listing 1, 1862)
first opera »Apollo und Hyacinthus«
conducts his first mass
Mozart begins
to compose
* 01-27-1756
in Salzburg, Austria
Concert tour across Europe
Court concertmaster in Salzburg
married
Konstanze Weber
Imperial chamber
composer
† 12-5-1791 in
Vienna, Austria
1756
1760
1765
1770
1775
1780
1785
1790
1791
LUDWIG VAN BEETHOVEN 138 works listed according to opus number (by Beethoven himself)
* 12-17-1770 in Bonn, Germany
moved to Vienna
First performance
as pianist
First symptoms of hearing impairment
1770
1775
1780
1785
1790
1795
1800
1805

COLORS

Music categories

- Stage works
- Sacred works
- Chamber music
- Concertos
- Vocal music
- Orchestral works
- Sonatas
- Suites
- Dances
- Others

The complexity of individual works could not be considered in this graphic.

FORMS

Works per year

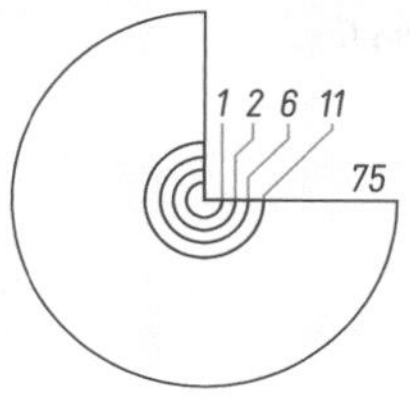
1 2 6 11
75

Stage works: musical comedies, stage music, operas, oratorios, contributions to own or other's stage works
Sacred works: masses, motets, cantatas, oratorios, litanies and vespers, sacred vocal works
Chamber music: solo pieces, duos, trios, quartets, quintets, organ works
Concertos: piano concertos, violin concertos, cello concertos, flute concertos, bassoon concertos, bugle concertos, clarinet concertos, double concertos, triple concertos
Vocal music: songs, concert arias, duets, trios, quartets, choir works, cantatas, canons
Orchestral works: sinfonia, serenades, divertimenti, marches
Sonatas: piano sonatas, violin sonatas, trio sonatas, cello sonatas, bugle sonatas, organ sonatas
Dances: minuets, polonaises, waltzes, écossaises, German dances
Other: adaptations, transcriptions, fragments, lost, questionable and apocryphal works

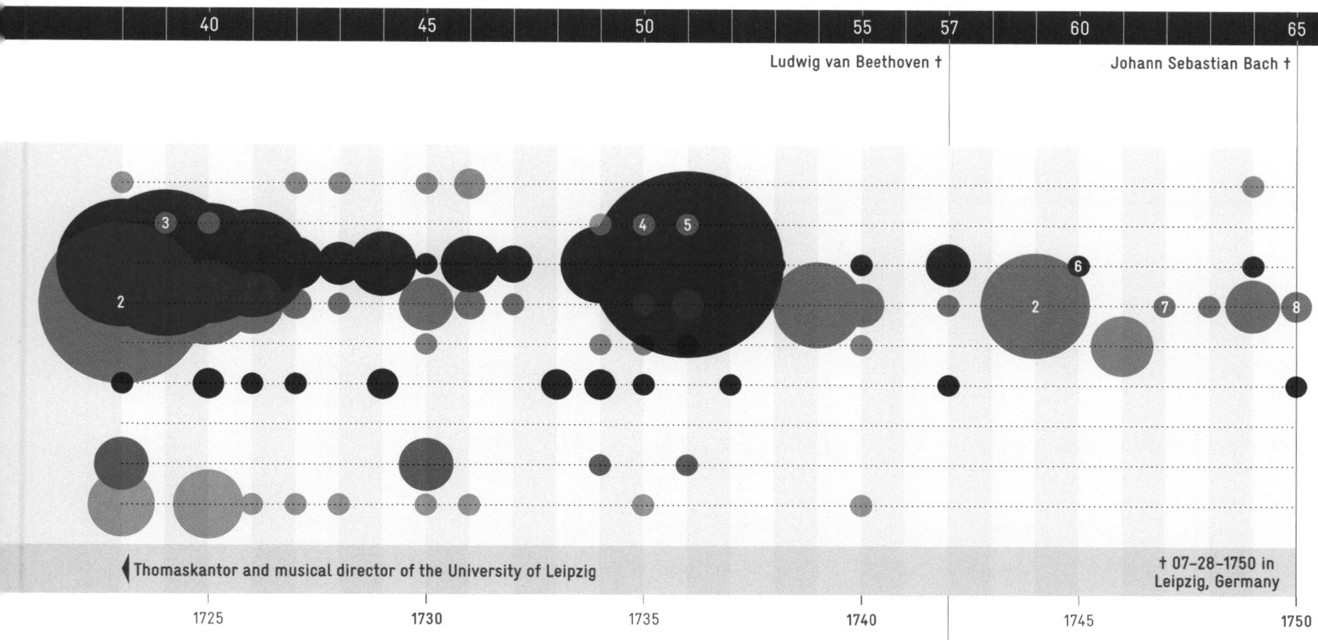
40
45
50
55
57
60
65
Age in years
Ludwig van Beethoven †
Johann Sebastian Bach †
3
4
5
2
6
2
7
8
Thomaskantor and musical director of the University of Leipzig
† 07-28-1750 in Leipzig, Germany
1725
1730
1735
1740
1745
1750

Popular works of Bach:

1. BWV *1046–1051* Brandenburg Concertos
2. BWV *846–893* The Well-Tempered Clavier *(prelude & fugue)*
3. BWV *245* St. John Passion
4. BWV *248* Christmas Oratorio
5. BWV *244* Matthew Passion
6. BWV *232* Mass in B minor
7. BWV *1079* The Musical Offering
8. BWV *1080* The Art of Fugue

Popular works of Mozart:

9. KV *525* Eine kleine Nachtmusik
10. KV *366* Idomeneo
11. KV *384* The Abduction from the Seraglio
12. KV *492* The Marriage of Figaro
13. KV *527* Don Giovanni
14. KV *620* The Magic Flute
15. KV *622* Clarinet Concerto in A major
16. *KV 626* Requiem in D minor

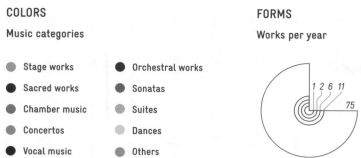

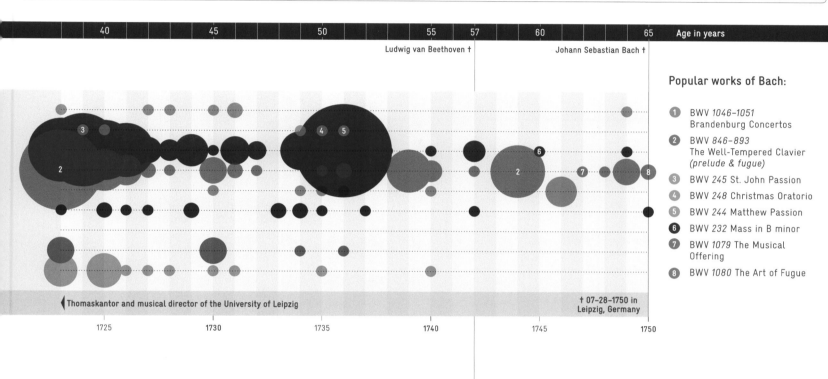

Increasing hearing impairment
deaf
19
22
WoO 59: »Für Elise« Poco Moto in A minor
20
21
23
met Goethe
† 03-26-1827 in Vienna, Austria
1810
1815
1820
1825
1827

Popular works of Beethoven:

17. Opus *27*: Piano Sonata No. *14* »Moonlight Sonata«
18. Opus *55*: Symphony No. *3* in E-flat major »Eroica«
19. Opus *72*: a, b »Leonore«, c »Fidelio«
20. Opus *67, 68*: Symphony No. *5*, Symphony No. *6* »Pastoral«
21. Opus *91*: Wellington's Victory
22. Opus *123*: Missa Solemnis
23. Opus *125*: Symphony No. *9* in D minor

After Beethoven's death published works are named as »Works without opus number« – WoO

UNDER YOUR SKIN

Scientists aren't quite sure how a concert experience can get, in the truest sense, »under your skin«. Some of the factors that play a role in the development of goose bumps have, however, been identified. A mix of music characteristics, hearing situation and individual personality traits, which differs from person to person, contributes to this phenomenon. Instruments that are similar to the human voice (violin, oboe) are the ones most likely to elicit goose bumps.

Musical properties

- Harmonic/melodic sequences
- Using voices/instruments
- The chorus
- Unfulfilled expectations (misconception)
- Emotional nature:
  - invigorating and enjoyable (happy)
  - disquieting and unpleasant (sad)
- Acoustic features
  - prolonged build-up of intensity (approx. 30 seconds)
  - loud or marked sounds with a frequency from 1–4 kHz

Voices

Human voices, or instruments that sound like voices such as the violin or saxophone, are most likely to cause goose bumps.

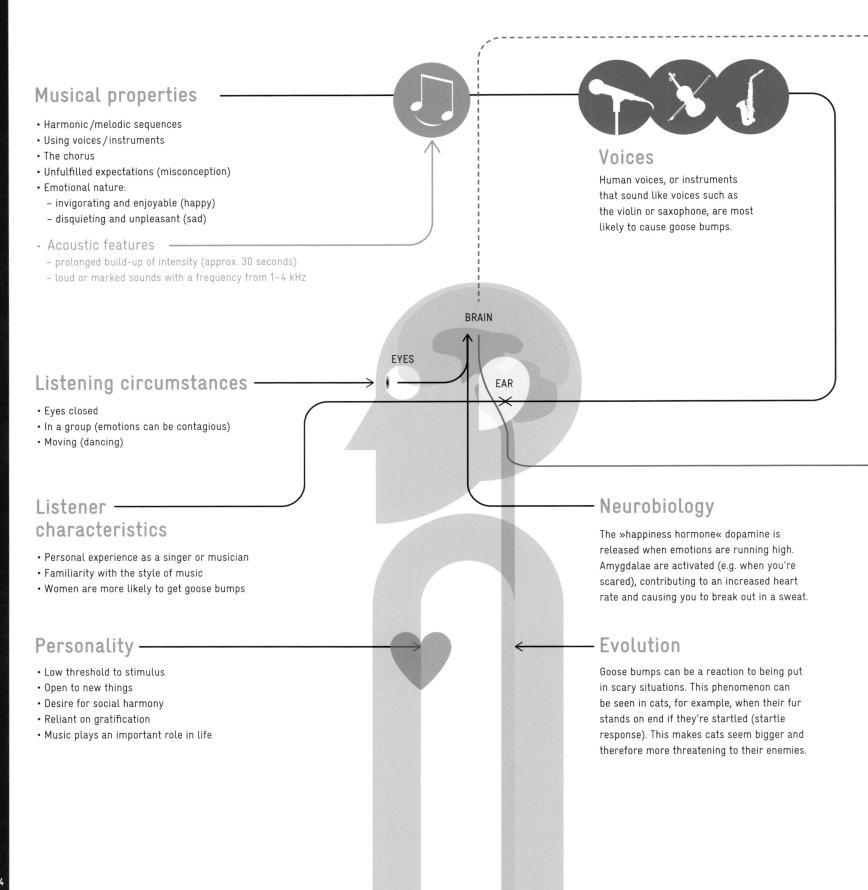

Listening circumstances

- Eyes closed
- In a group (emotions can be contagious)
- Moving (dancing)

Listener characteristics

- Personal experience as a singer or musician
- Familiarity with the style of music
- Women are more likely to get goose bumps

Neurobiology

The »happiness hormone« dopamine is released when emotions are running high. Amygdalae are activated (e.g. when you're scared), contributing to an increased heart rate and causing you to break out in a sweat.

Personality

- Low threshold to stimulus
- Open to new things
- Desire for social harmony
- Reliant on gratification
- Music plays an important role in life

Evolution

Goose bumps can be a reaction to being put in scary situations. This phenomenon can be seen in cats, for example, when their fur stands on end if they're startled (startle response). This makes cats seem bigger and therefore more threatening to their enemies.

The »Barabbas«

A famous musical moment that makes goose bumps come to the surface is the »Barabbas« interjection from the »St. Matthew Passion« by Johann Sebastian Bach. The loud minor chord rings out all of a sudden, seemingly incongruous with the harmony, and as such triggers a powerful emotional response in many listeners, sending a shiver down their spine and making their skin tingle with goose bumps.

> Mental reaction

You can get goose bumps simply from your imagination without any direct physical stimuli.

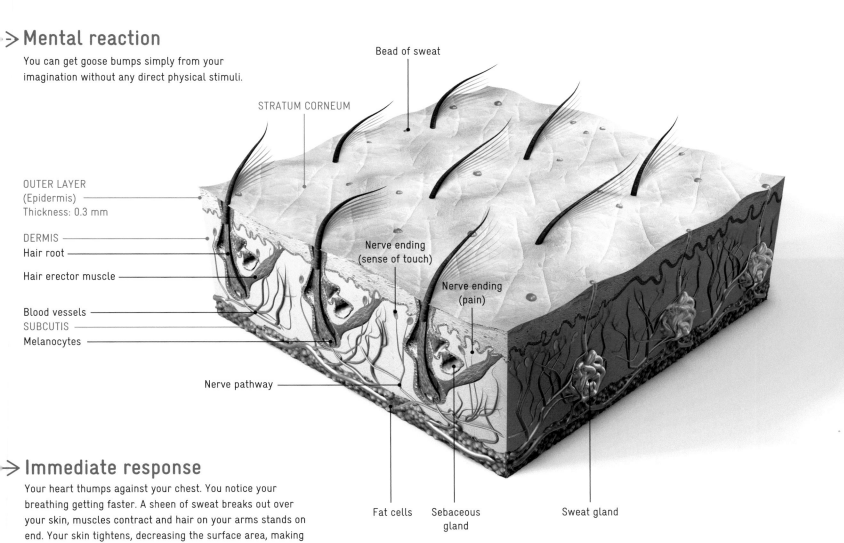

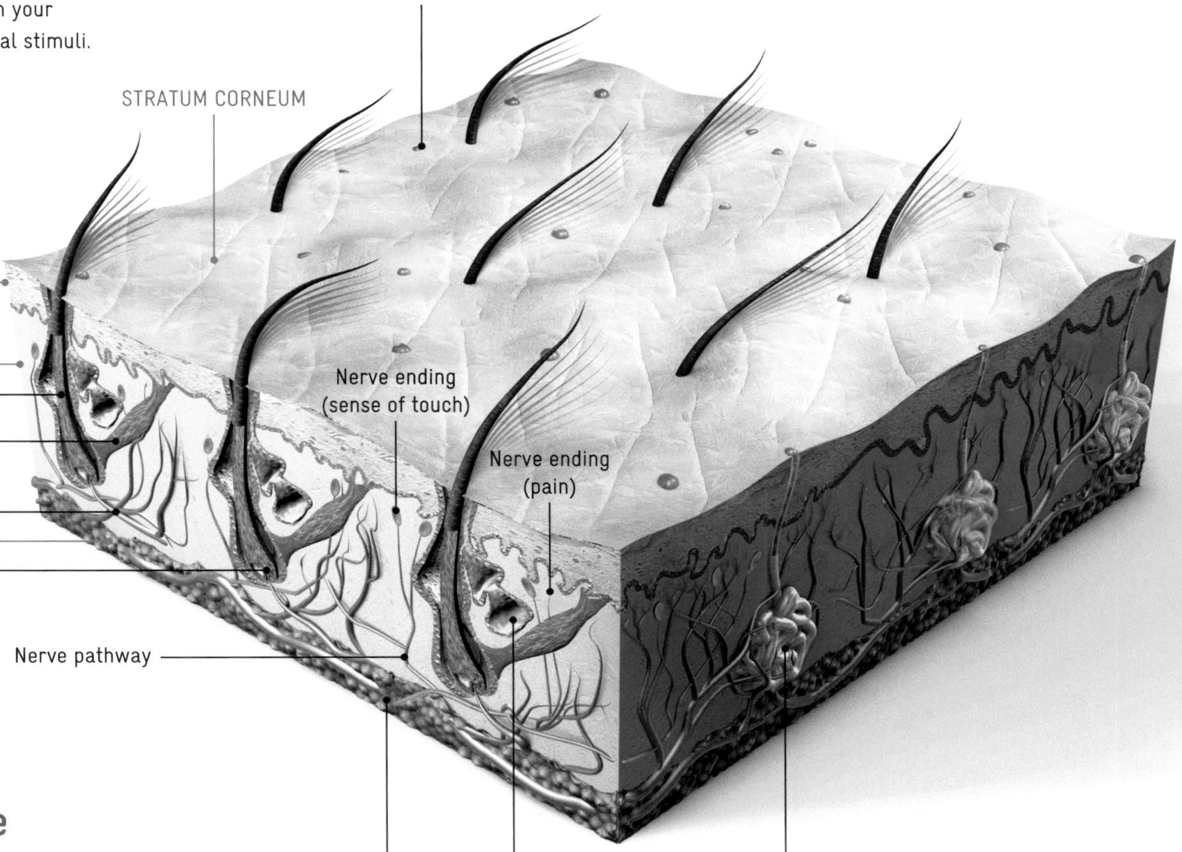

Bead of sweat
STRATUM CORNEUM
OUTER LAYER
(Epidermis)
Thickness: 0.3 mm
DERMIS
Hair root
Hair erector muscle
Blood vessels
SUBCUTIS
Melanocytes
Nerve ending
(sense of touch)
Nerve ending
(pain)
Nerve pathway
Fat cells
Sebaceous
gland
Sweat gland

> Immediate response

Your heart thumps against your chest. You notice your breathing getting faster. A sheen of sweat breaks out over your skin, muscles contract and hair on your arms stands on end. Your skin tightens, decreasing the surface area, making you less sensitive and cool to the touch.

The skin by numbers

Total surface area	1.5 to $2.0m^2$
Weight	15 to 20% of the entire body weight
Pigment cells	2 billion
Capillaries	240 billion
Sweat glands	2 million/100 per cm^2
Sebaceous glands	350,000
Free nerve endings	4 million

Total length of capillaries in the skin	240 kilometers
Total length of all vessels in the body	1,440 kilometers
Production of sebum in a lifetime	42 kilograms
Production of sweat in a lifetime	10,000 to 20,000 liters
Cold receptors (hand)	5 per cm^2
Warmth (face)/touch receptors (palm)	25 per cm^2
Pain points	50 to 200 per cm^2

SYMPHONY OF THE WORKING WEEK

As people sit and listen to a concert, they don't realize how much behind-the-scenes preparation is necessary. A working week from October 2013 is presented below (Verdi Requiem with Mariss Jansons) – and the schedule is jam-packed. The orchestra have rehearsals in three different halls in Munich, two subscription concerts (philharmonic hall), a charity concert (Prince Regent Theatre) and a trip to Vienna for two concerts (Austrian Music Society). And it doesn't end there: They also have a live radio broadcast (Munich), a video live stream and a TV recording (Vienna).

Activities

- Setting up
- Disassembly
- Transport/traveling
- Rehearsal
- Concert
- Recording/broadcast

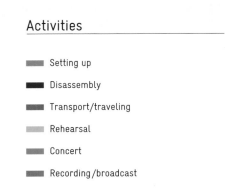

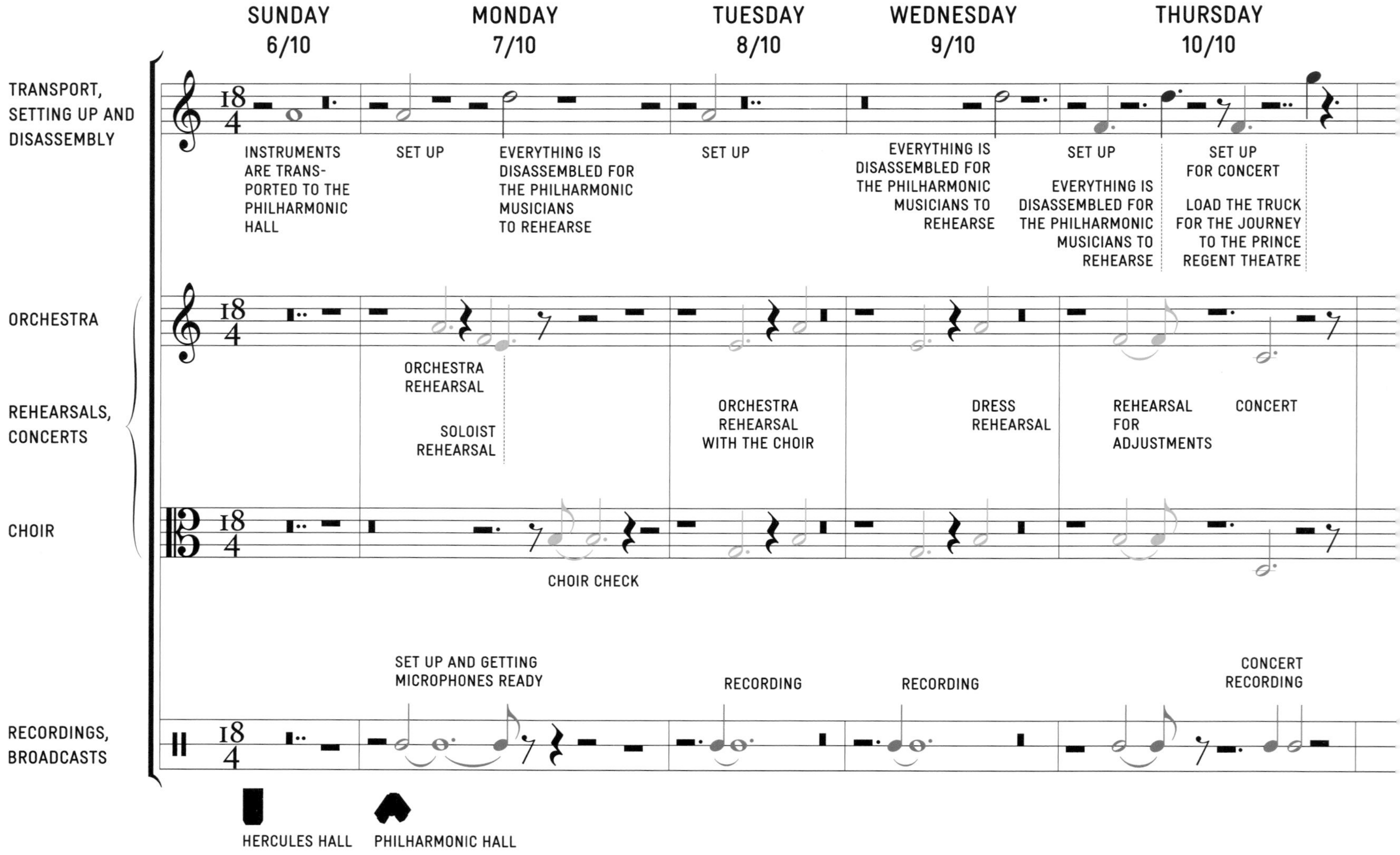

Duration of events and breaks

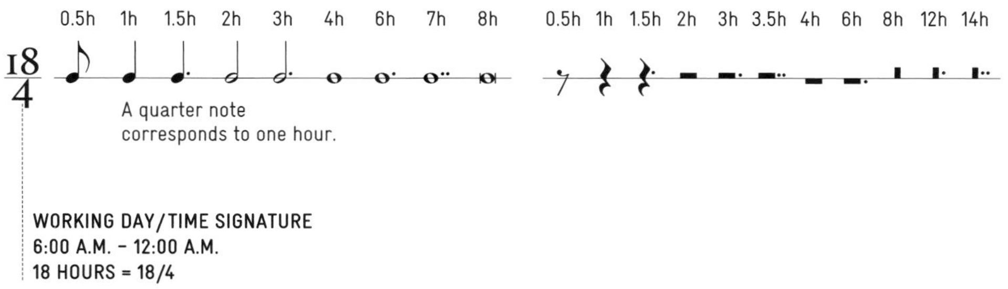
0.5h 1h 1.5h 2h 3h 4h 6h 7h 8h
0.5h 1h 1.5h 2h 3h 3.5h 4h 6h 8h 12h 14h
18
4
A quarter note
corresponds to one hour.
WORKING DAY/TIME SIGNATURE
6:00 A.M. – 12:00 A.M.
18 HOURS = 18/4

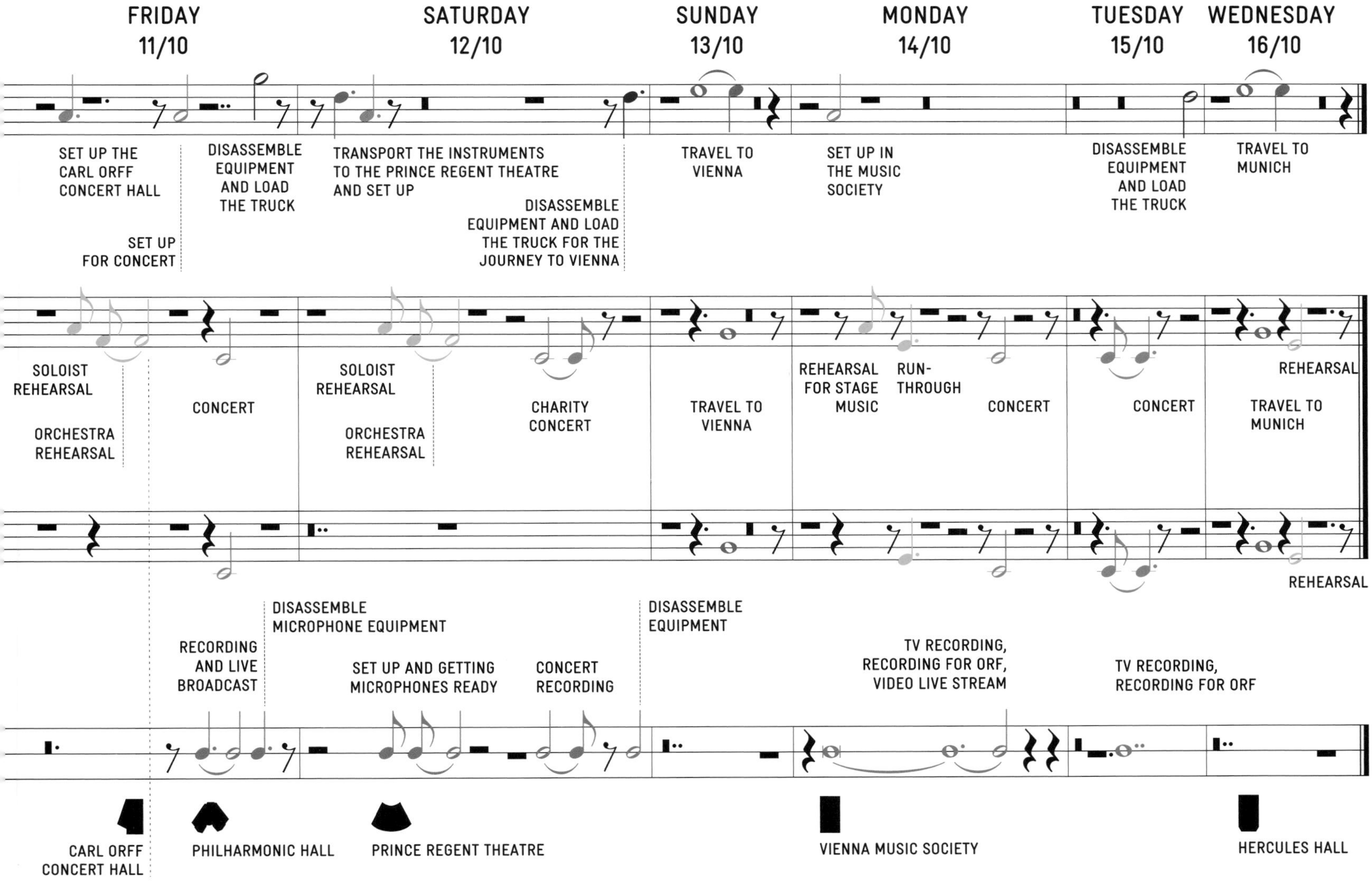
FRIDAY
11/10
SATURDAY
12/10
SUNDAY
13/10
MONDAY
14/10
TUESDAY
15/10
WEDNESDAY
16/10
SET UP THE
CARL ORFF
CONCERT HALL
SET UP
FOR CONCERT
DISASSEMBLE
EQUIPMENT
AND LOAD
THE TRUCK
TRANSPORT THE INSTRUMENTS
TO THE PRINCE REGENT THEATRE
AND SET UP
DISASSEMBLE
EQUIPMENT AND LOAD
THE TRUCK FOR THE
JOURNEY TO VIENNA
TRAVEL TO
VIENNA
SET UP IN
THE MUSIC
SOCIETY
DISASSEMBLE
EQUIPMENT
AND LOAD
THE TRUCK
TRAVEL TO
MUNICH
SOLOIST
REHEARSAL
ORCHESTRA
REHEARSAL
CONCERT
SOLOIST
REHEARSAL
ORCHESTRA
REHEARSAL
CHARITY
CONCERT
TRAVEL TO
VIENNA
REHEARSAL
FOR STAGE
MUSIC
RUN-
THROUGH
CONCERT
CONCERT
REHEARSAL
TRAVEL TO
MUNICH
REHEARSAL
DISASSEMBLE
MICROPHONE EQUIPMENT
RECORDING
AND LIVE
BROADCAST
SET UP AND GETTING
MICROPHONES READY
CONCERT
RECORDING
DISASSEMBLE
EQUIPMENT
TV RECORDING,
RECORDING FOR ORF,
VIDEO LIVE STREAM
TV RECORDING,
RECORDING FOR ORF
CARL ORFF
CONCERT HALL
PHILHARMONIC HALL
PRINCE REGENT THEATRE
VIENNA MUSIC SOCIETY
HERCULES HALL

DESTINATION: WORLD CLASS

Munich has its visitors, but to become internationally renowned, the Bavarian Radio Symphony Orchestra has to go on the road every now and then. Each world tour requires two to three years of planning and is entirely self-financed.

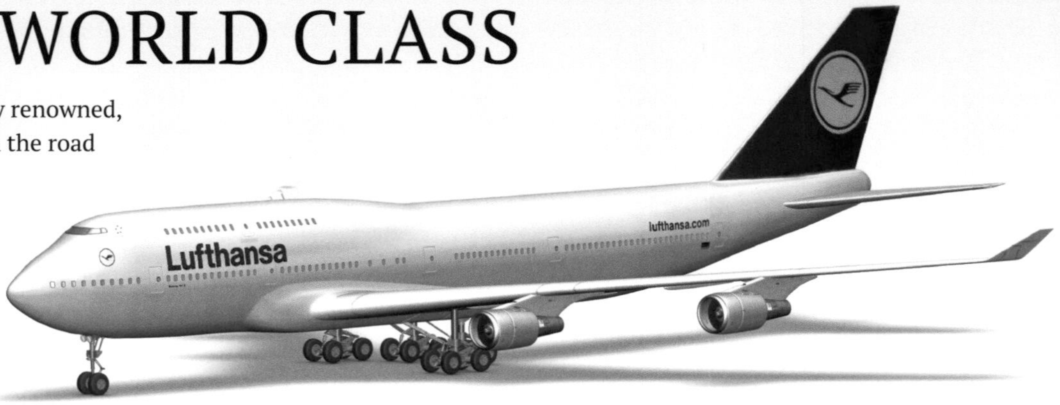

Travel facts and figures

- 5 destinations
- 135 people
- 11 flights (including 3 red-eye flights)
- 3 carriers
- 12 bus transfers
- 13 nights

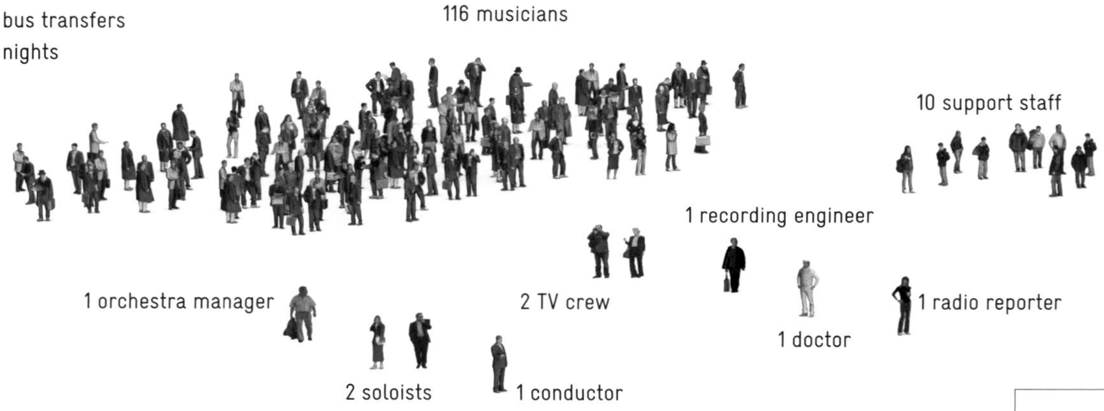
116 musicians
10 support staff
1 recording engineer
1 orchestra manager
2 TV crew
1 radio reporter
1 doctor
2 soloists
1 conductor

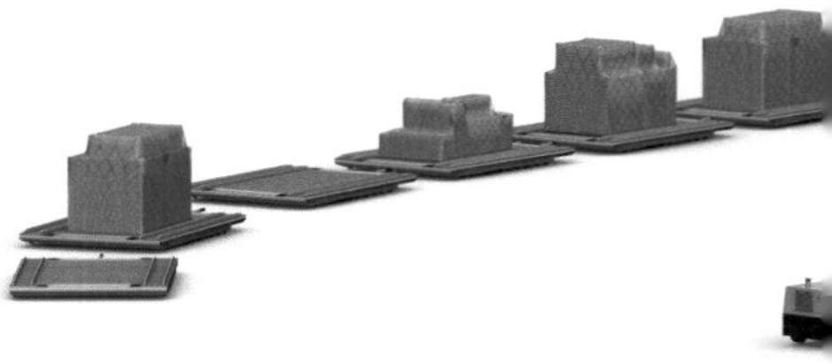

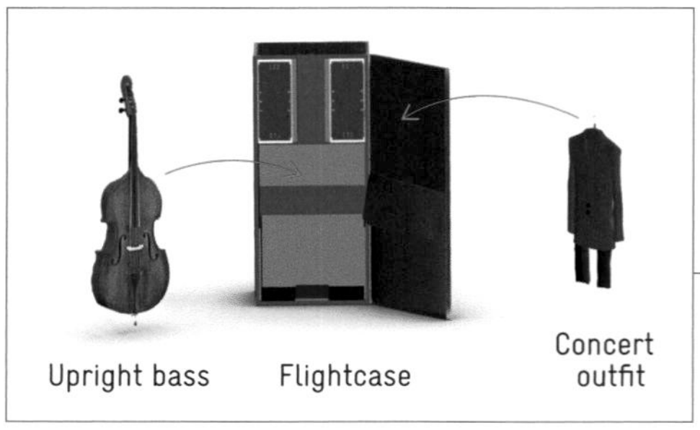
Upright bass
Flightcase
Concert outfit

Itinerary

GROUND TRANSPORT
FLIGHT
BUS TRANSFER
WALK

Airport codes:
MUC = Munich, FRA = Frankfurt, EZE = Buenos Aires Pistarini, AEP = Buenos Aires J. Newbery,
GIG = Rio de Janeiro International, SDU = Rio de Janeiro Santos Dumont, CGH = Sao Paulo Con Hongas,
GRU = Sao Paulo Guarulhos, EWR = New York Newark Liberty International, JFK = New York John F. Kennedy International

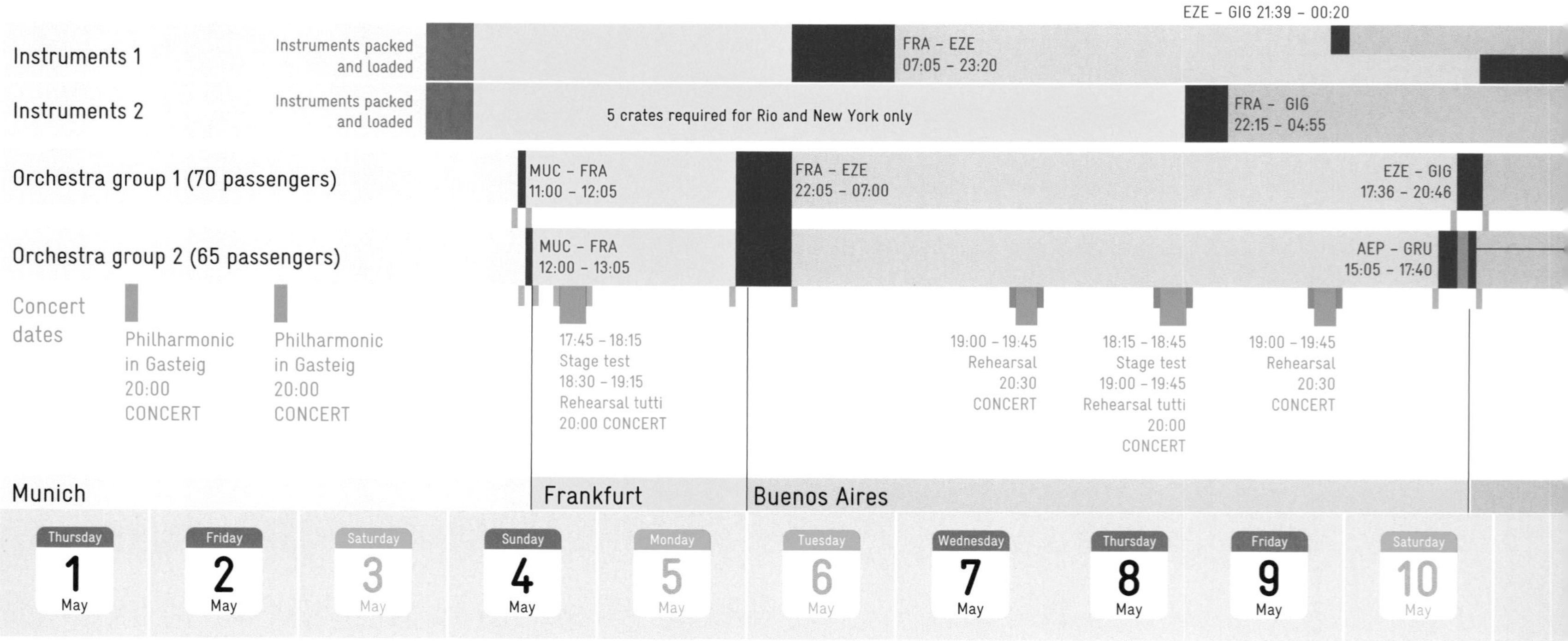
EZE – GIG 21:39 – 00:20
Instruments 1
Instruments packed and loaded
FRA – EZE 07:05 – 23:20
Instruments 2
Instruments packed and loaded
5 crates required for Rio and New York only
FRA – GIG 22:15 – 04:55
Orchestra group 1 (70 passengers)
MUC – FRA 11:00 – 12:05
FRA – EZE 22:05 – 07:00
EZE – GIG 17:36 – 20:46
Orchestra group 2 (65 passengers)
MUC – FRA 12:00 – 13:05
AEP – GRU 15:05 – 17:40
Concert dates
Philharmonic in Gasteig 20:00 CONCERT
Philharmonic in Gasteig 20:00 CONCERT
17:45 – 18:15 Stage test 18:30 – 19:15 Rehearsal tutti 20:00 CONCERT
19:00 – 19:45 Rehearsal 20:30 CONCERT
18:15 – 18:45 Stage test 19:00 – 19:45 Rehearsal tutti 20:00 CONCERT
19:00 – 19:45 Rehearsal 20:30 CONCERT
Munich
Frankfurt
Buenos Aires
Thursday 1 May
Friday 2 May
Saturday 3 May
Sunday 4 May
Monday 5 May
Tuesday 6 May
Wednesday 7 May
Thursday 8 May
Friday 9 May
Saturday 10 May

Cargo

- 100 crates
- 105 cubic meters
- 13 tonnnes
- 16 flights with 5 different carriers

Packing the cargo pallets

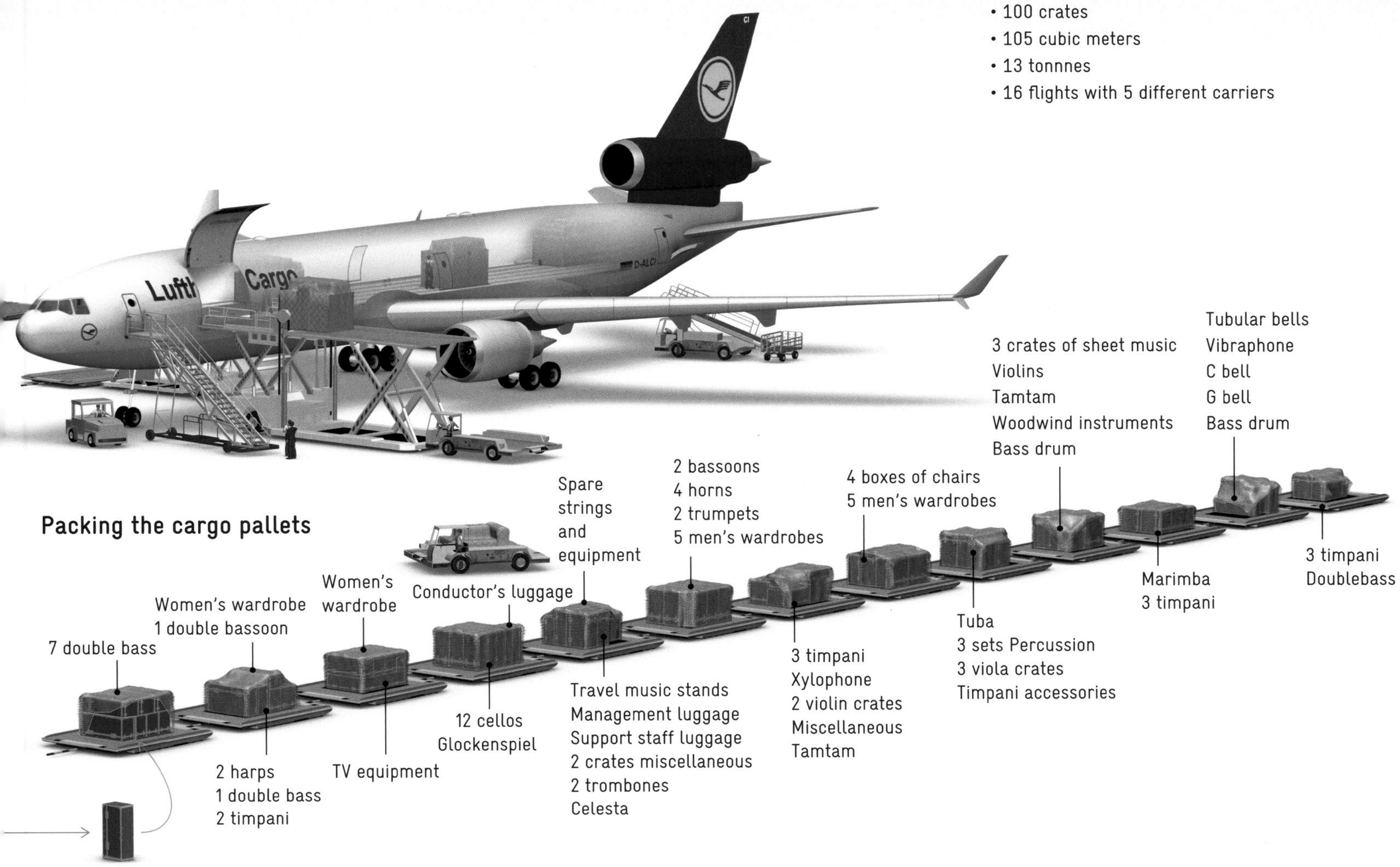

Lufthansa Cargo
7 double bass
Women's wardrobe
1 double bassoon
Women's wardrobe
Conductor's luggage
Spare
strings
and
equipment
2 bassoons
4 horns
2 trumpets
5 men's wardrobes
4 boxes of chairs
5 men's wardrobes
3 crates of sheet music
Violins
Tamtam
Woodwind instruments
Bass drum
Tubular bells
Vibraphone
C bell
G bell
Bass drum
3 timpani
Doublebass
Marimba
3 timpani
Tuba
3 sets Percussion
3 viola crates
Timpani accessories
3 timpani
Xylophone
2 violin crates
Miscellaneous
Tamtam
Travel music stands
Management luggage
Support staff luggage
2 crates miscellaneous
2 trombones
Celesta
12 cellos
Glockenspiel
TV equipment
2 harps
1 double bass
2 timpani

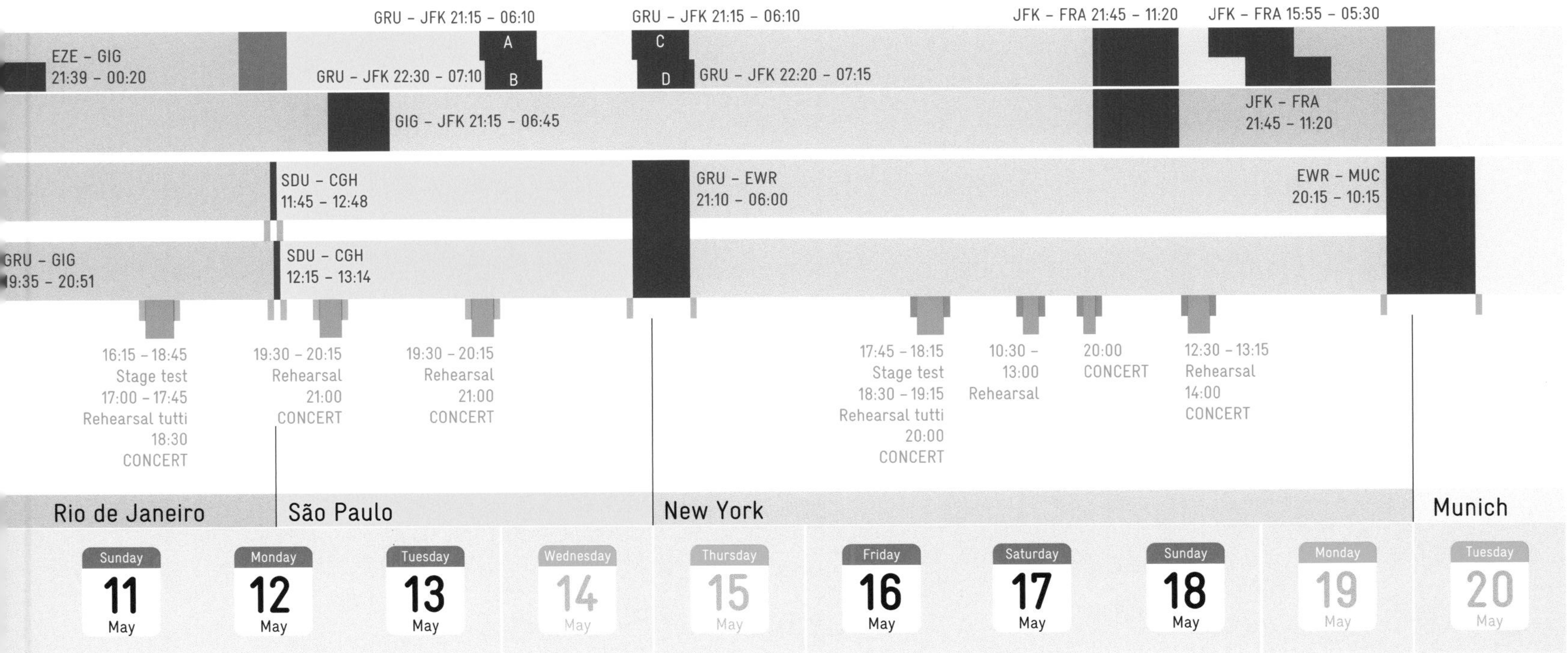

GRU – JFK 21:15 – 06:10
GRU – JFK 21:15 – 06:10
JFK – FRA 21:45 – 11:20
JFK – FRA 15:55 – 05:30
EZE – GIG
21:39 – 00:20
A
B
C
D
GRU – JFK 22:30 – 07:10
GRU – JFK 22:20 – 07:15
GIG – JFK 21:15 – 06:45
JFK – FRA
21:45 – 11:20
SDU – CGH
11:45 – 12:48
GRU – EWR
21:10 – 06:00
EWR – MUC
20:15 – 10:15
GRU – GIG
19:35 – 20:51
SDU – CGH
12:15 – 13:14
16:15 – 18:45
Stage test
17:00 – 17:45
Rehearsal tutti
18:30
CONCERT
19:30 – 20:15
Rehearsal
21:00
CONCERT
19:30 – 20:15
Rehearsal
21:00
CONCERT
17:45 – 18:15
Stage test
18:30 – 19:15
Rehearsal tutti
20:00
CONCERT
10:30 –
13:00
Rehearsal
20:00
CONCERT
12:30 – 13:15
Rehearsal
14:00
CONCERT
Rio de Janeiro
São Paulo
New York
Munich
Sunday 11 May
Monday 12 May
Tuesday 13 May
Wednesday 14 May
Thursday 15 May
Friday 16 May
Saturday 17 May
Sunday 18 May
Monday 19 May
Tuesday 20 May

CHILDREN AND PARENTS OF MUSICIANS

100 musicians in the orchestra were prepared to share some information about their family with us. 75 musicians are parents and have 171 children altogether between them. In Germany in 2012, women had an average of 1.38 children each. The musicians are well over the average with 1.71 children each.

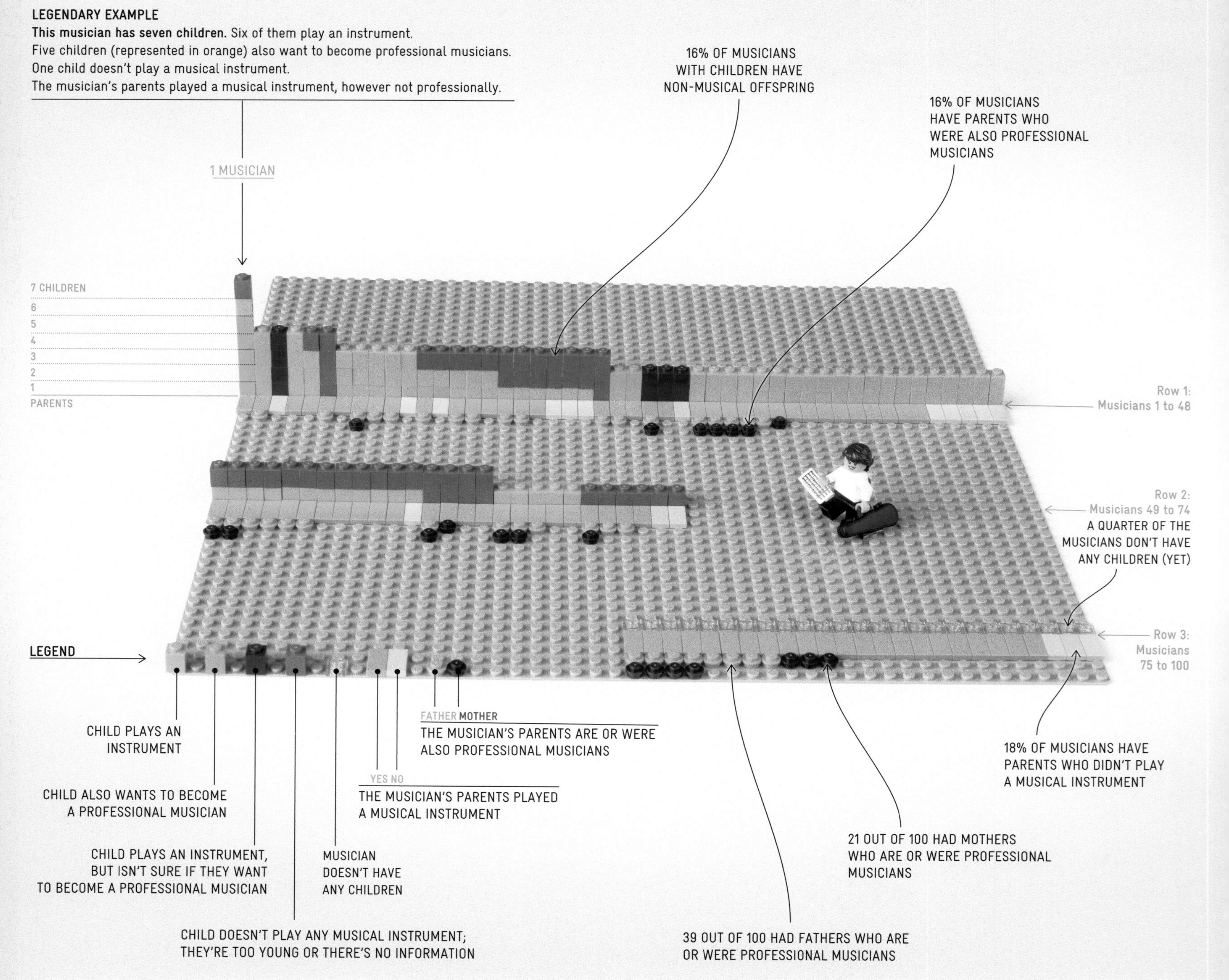
LEGENDARY EXAMPLE
This musician has seven children. Six of them play an instrument.
Five children (represented in orange) also want to become professional musicians.
One child doesn't play a musical instrument.
The musician's parents played a musical instrument, however not professionally.
1 MUSICIAN
7 CHILDREN
6
5
4
3
2
1
PARENTS
16% OF MUSICIANS WITH CHILDREN HAVE NON-MUSICAL OFFSPRING
16% OF MUSICIANS HAVE PARENTS WHO WERE ALSO PROFESSIONAL MUSICIANS
Row 1: Musicians 1 to 48
Row 2: Musicians 49 to 74
A QUARTER OF THE MUSICIANS DON'T HAVE ANY CHILDREN (YET)
Row 3: Musicians 75 to 100
LEGEND
CHILD PLAYS AN INSTRUMENT
CHILD ALSO WANTS TO BECOME A PROFESSIONAL MUSICIAN
CHILD PLAYS AN INSTRUMENT, BUT ISN'T SURE IF THEY WANT TO BECOME A PROFESSIONAL MUSICIAN
CHILD DOESN'T PLAY ANY MUSICAL INSTRUMENT; THEY'RE TOO YOUNG OR THERE'S NO INFORMATION
MUSICIAN DOESN'T HAVE ANY CHILDREN
YES NO
THE MUSICIAN'S PARENTS PLAYED A MUSICAL INSTRUMENT
FATHER MOTHER
THE MUSICIAN'S PARENTS ARE OR WERE ALSO PROFESSIONAL MUSICIANS
39 OUT OF 100 HAD FATHERS WHO ARE OR WERE PROFESSIONAL MUSICIANS
21 OUT OF 100 HAD MOTHERS WHO ARE OR WERE PROFESSIONAL MUSICIANS
18% OF MUSICIANS HAVE PARENTS WHO DIDN'T PLAY A MUSICAL INSTRUMENT

PUMP UP THE VOLUME

On March 24, 2014, four members of the symphony orchestra, together with their conductor Daniel Harding, were fitted with long-term ECG monitoring devices to try and find out what strains are put on the bodies of musicians. Gustav Mahler's 6th Symphony is just an example of the songs included in the program. 2,400 audience members were there to experience the concert, and it was also broadcast live on the radio and via a video stream. The researchers found that playing Mahler caused the heart rate to increase to intense levels—comparable to the rates seen in Formula I Drivers.

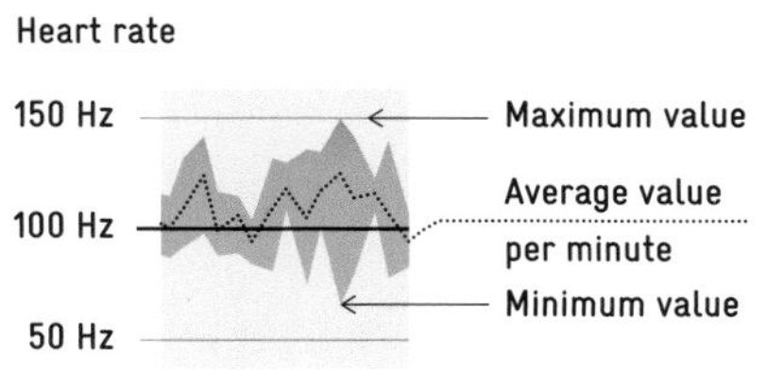
Heart rate
150 Hz
100 Hz
50 Hz
Maximum value
Average value per minute
Minimum value

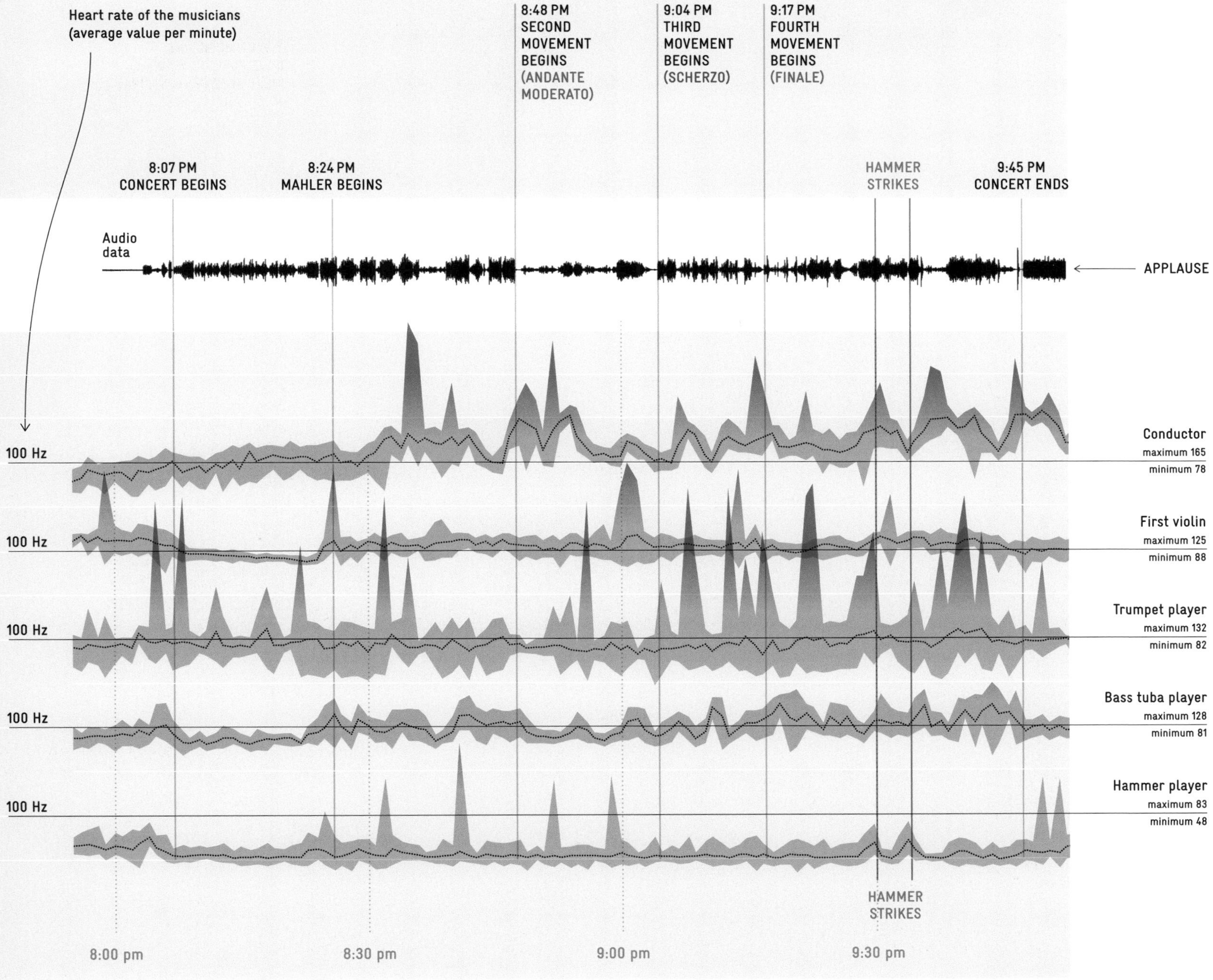
Heart rate of the musicians (average value per minute)
8:48 PM SECOND MOVEMENT BEGINS (ANDANTE MODERATO)
9:04 PM THIRD MOVEMENT BEGINS (SCHERZO)
9:17 PM FOURTH MOVEMENT BEGINS (FINALE)
8:07 PM CONCERT BEGINS
8:24 PM MAHLER BEGINS
HAMMER STRIKES
9:45 PM CONCERT ENDS
Audio data
APPLAUSE
100 Hz
Conductor
maximum 165
minimum 78
100 Hz
First violin
maximum 125
minimum 88
100 Hz
Trumpet player
maximum 132
minimum 82
100 Hz
Bass tuba player
maximum 128
minimum 81
100 Hz
Hammer player
maximum 83
minimum 48
HAMMER STRIKES
8:00 pm
8:30 pm
9:00 pm
9:30 pm

VIOLINS FROM CREMONA

Meet Antonietta, Davidoff and King George—instruments named after the first people to have owned these violins. Today, a 300-year-old instrument from the workshops of luthiers Stradivari and Guarneri del Gesù can be sold for seven figures. They are considered an investment, a museum piece or a means of honoring important, emerging musical talents. The value of these instruments has increased by a factor of 200 since 1960. In 2011, the Lady Blunt–a violin made by Stradivari–sold at a charity auction for a record price of $15.9 million.

Cross section of the bridge

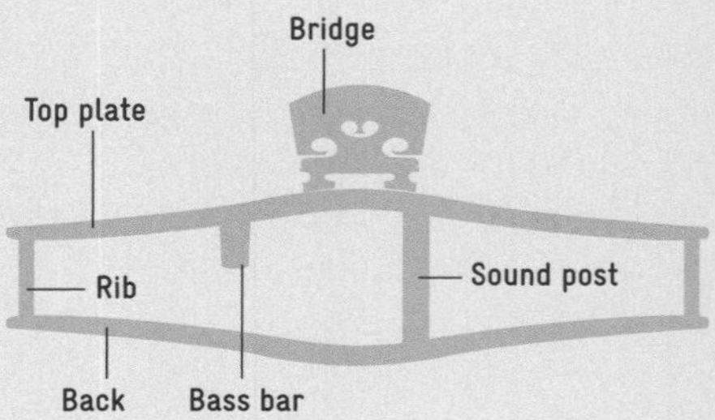
Bridge
Top plate
Rib
Sound post
Back
Bass bar

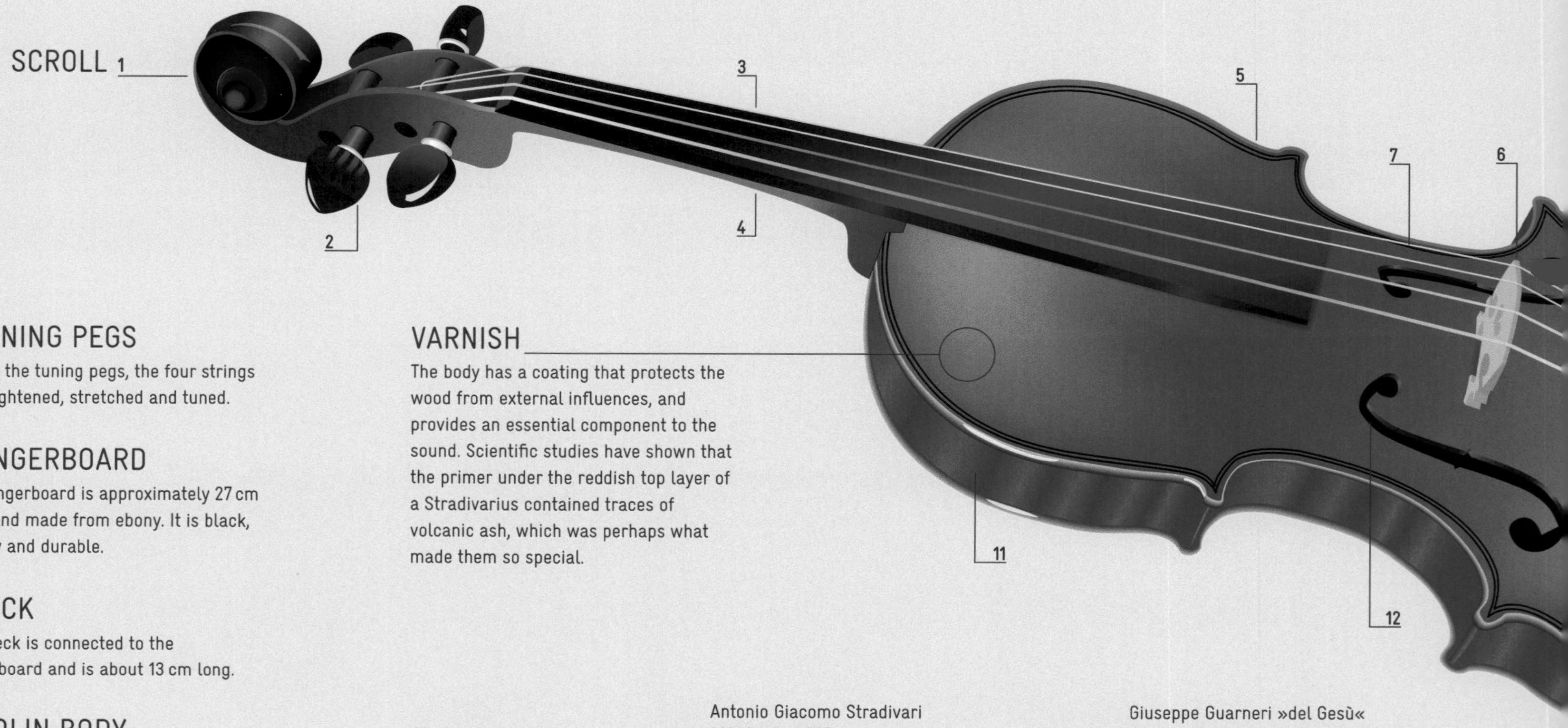

2 TUNING PEGS

Using the tuning pegs, the four strings are tightened, stretched and tuned.

3 FINGERBOARD

The fingerboard is approximately 27 cm long and made from ebony. It is black, sturdy and durable.

4 NECK

The neck is connected to the fingerboard and is about 13 cm long.

5 VIOLIN BODY

The top plate of the violin body is made of spruce, the back is made of maple. Stradivari benefited from the very cold winters of his time. On full-moon nights, he went to the high Alps to find suitable spruce for his instruments. The trees grew more slowly, resulting in a fine-porous structure and a harder wood. Compared to his teacher Nicolò Amati, Stradivari created a flatter, less curved body.

VARNISH

The body has a coating that protects the wood from external influences, and provides an essential component to the sound. Scientific studies have shown that the primer under the reddish top layer of a Stradivarius contained traces of volcanic ash, which was perhaps what made them so special.

Master violin maker	Antonio Giacomo Stradivari *1648/49 †1737	Giuseppe Guarneri »del Gesù« *1698 †1744
Instruments	635 violins, 18 violas, 63 cellos, 4 guitars, 1 zither, 1 viola d'amore, 1 harp and 1 pochette (dance master violin) are known	exclusively violins
Varnish color	red to deep red	yellow, light brown
Estimate of total production	1,200 to 1,500 instruments	250 instruments, 147 still existing
Buyers of violins	aristocrats and wealthy citizens, more costly than those of »del Gesù«	surviving artists, ordinary people

BOW

The bow causes the strings to vibrate. Bows are made by bow makers and were therefore not among the tasks of Stradivari or Guarneri.

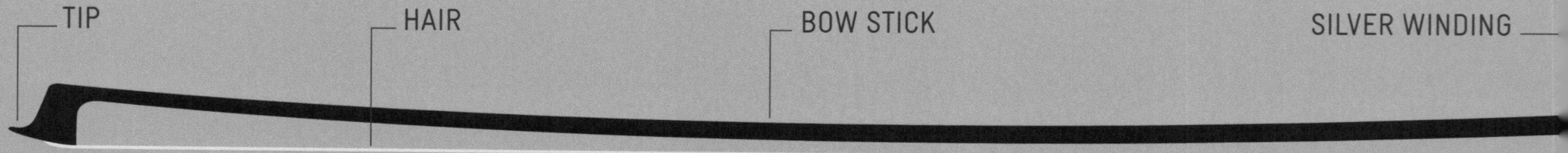
TIP
HAIR
BOW STICK
SILVER WINDING

6 BRIDGE

The bridge is made from fine maple. It transmits the vibrations of the strings to the violin body.

7 STRINGS

A violin has four strings made from steel wire, plastic, or natural gut. In the early days, gut strings were used. The root notes are G, D1, A1 and E2. The G string is the lowest.

8 FINE TUNER
9 TAILPIECE
10 CHIN REST

11 RIB

The ribs connecting the top plate to the back are made from the same wood as the back.

12 F-HOLE

The two f-holes are inserted into the violin top plate. Stradivarius violins are characterized by having the f-holes relatively close to one another.

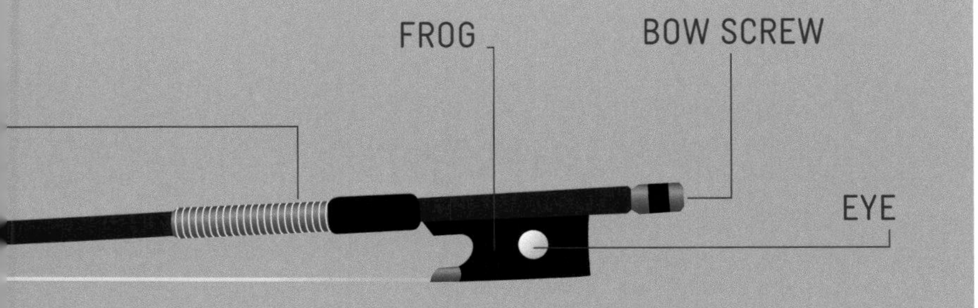

FROG
BOW SCREW
EYE

The most expensive violins ever sold, in millions of U.S. dollars (state: 2011)

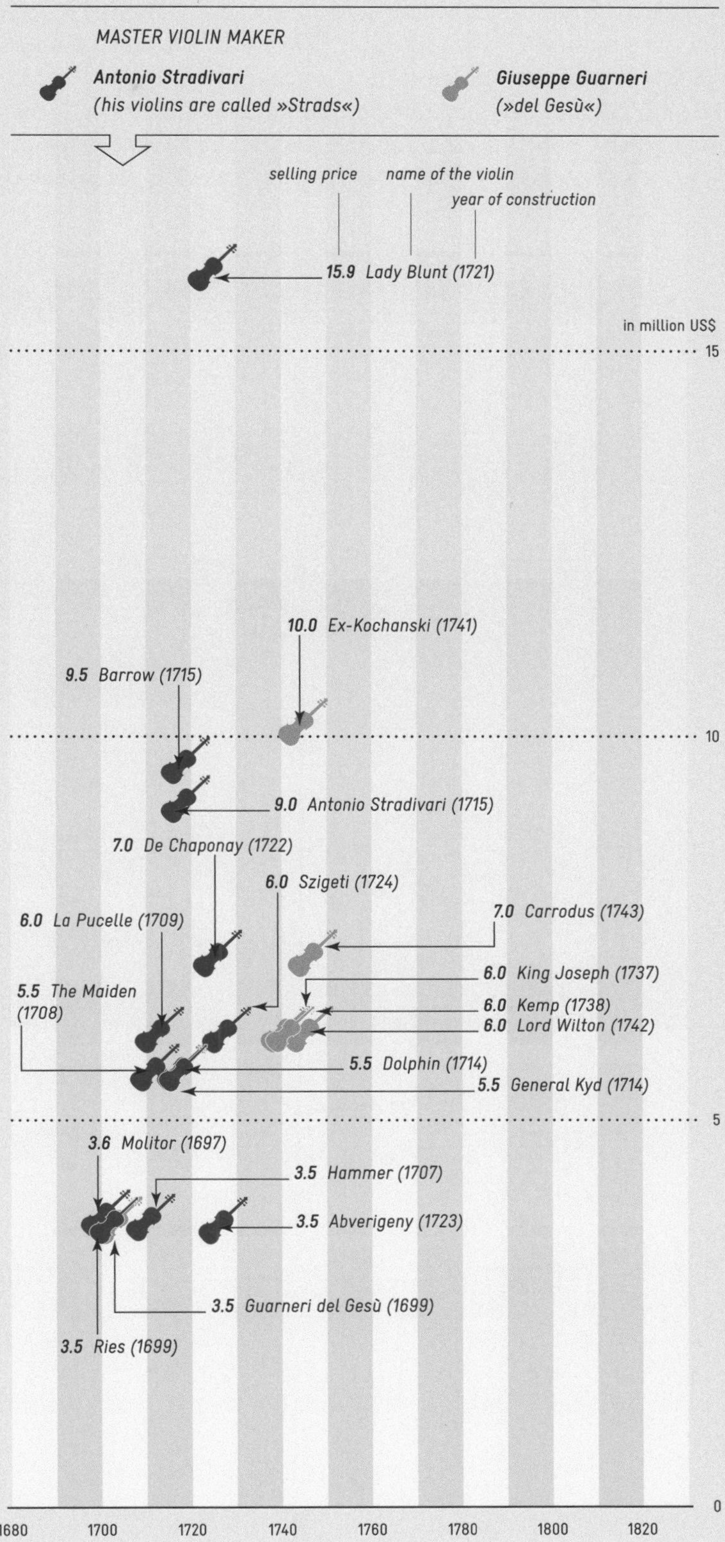

MASTER VIOLIN MAKER
Antonio Stradivari
(his violins are called »Strads«)
Giuseppe Guarneri
(»del Gesù«)
selling price
name of the violin
year of construction
15.9 Lady Blunt (1721)
in million US$
15
10.0 Ex-Kochanski (1741)
9.5 Barrow (1715)
10
9.0 Antonio Stradivari (1715)
7.0 De Chaponay (1722)
6.0 Szigeti (1724)
6.0 La Pucelle (1709)
7.0 Carrodus (1743)
6.0 King Joseph (1737)
5.5 The Maiden (1708)
6.0 Kemp (1738)
6.0 Lord Wilton (1742)
5.5 Dolphin (1714)
5.5 General Kyd (1714)
5
3.6 Molitor (1697)
3.5 Hammer (1707)
3.5 Abverigeny (1723)
3.5 Guarneri del Gesù (1699)
3.5 Ries (1699)
0
1680
1700
1720
1740
1760
1780
1800
1820

The Hellier Strad from 1679 as an example of increase in value

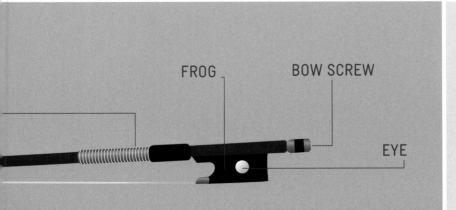

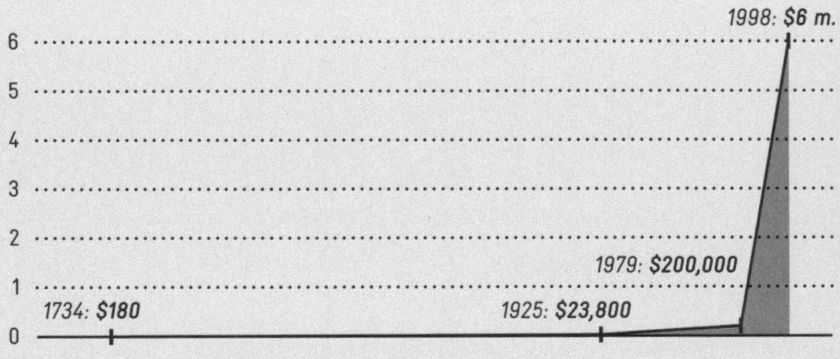

1998: $6 m.
6
5
4
3
2
1
0
1979: $200,000
1734: $180
1925: $23,800

THE AVERAGE ANTHEM

Every citizen knows the anthem of their home country. We were wondering what is special about the music and if there is a system behind it. If we were to assemble the most common words and sounds of national anthems , the average anthem would sound like this.
Lyrics and melodies were generated by the national anthems of 32 countries (USA, CAN, GRL, ISL, NOR, SWE, FIN, RUS, GBR, BEL, GER, NED, AUT, SUI, HUN, FRA, ITA, TUR, POR, NZL, AFG, IRQ, EGY, RSA, ARG, BRA, PAR, URU, BOL, PER, CUB, MEX). Have a look and see what you think...

Go- d bless this proud na- tions coun- try Glo- ri- ous home-land of un- bound free- dom.
Fa- ther- land of thou-sand free chil- dren, Thy migh- ty moun- tains, sa- cred earth. We saw years of
mar- tial tur- moil, Ho- rri- ble war brought us ou- r na- tion. Bloom in u- ni- ty, ho- no- red La- nd,
And let li- ber- ty and peace last for cen- tu- ries. God bless (insert name of country here).

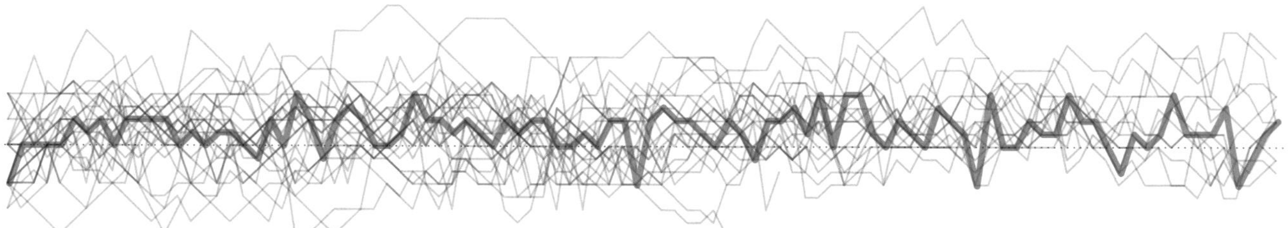

The scores of the average national anthem were determined by estimating the position and the average value of each key with respect to the tonic keynote.

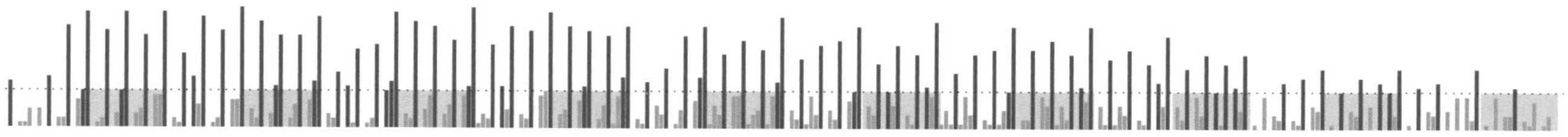

The average rhythm is determined by taking the estimated average frequency of the notes played on each position.

WAX LYRICAL:

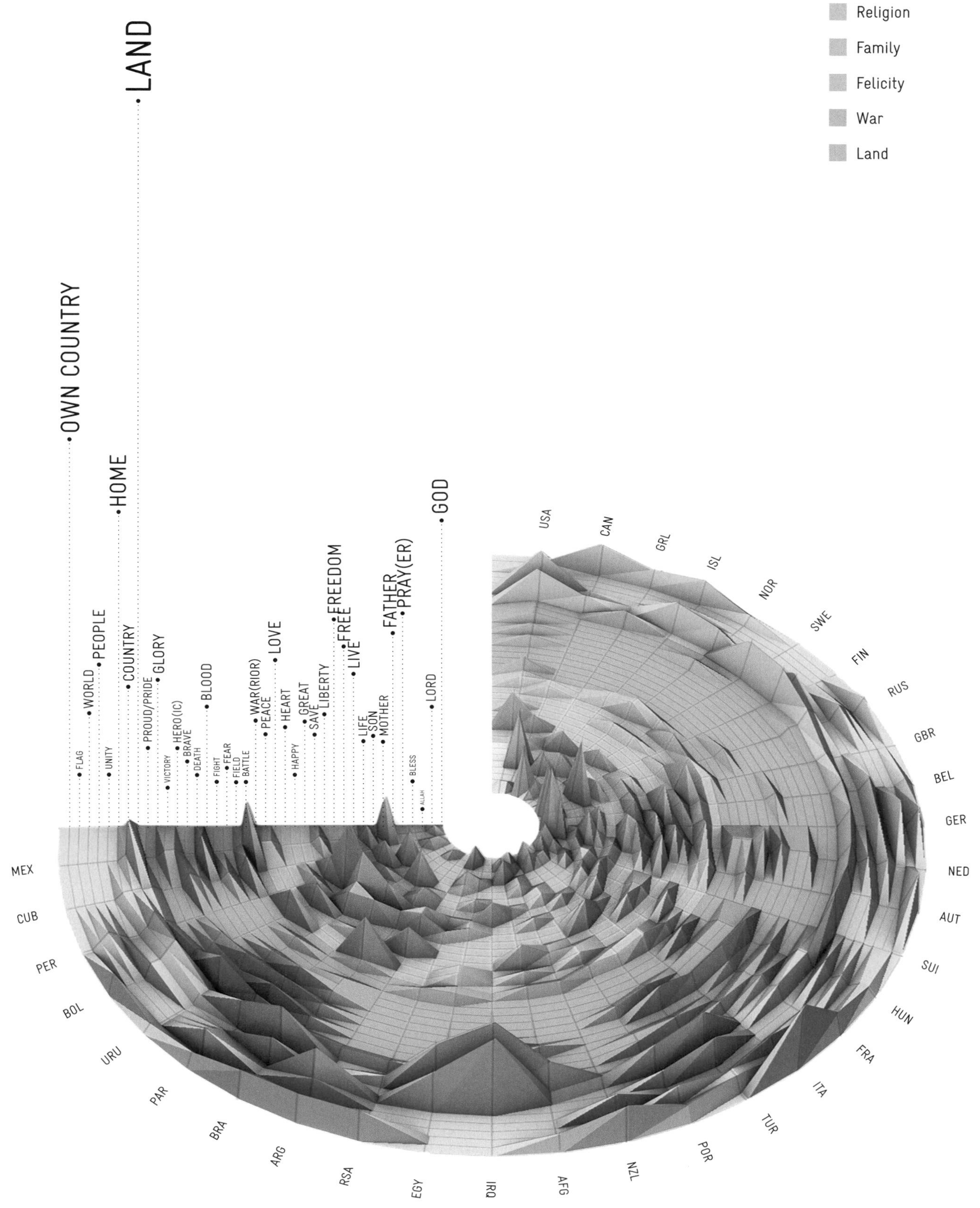

Religion
Family
Felicity
War
Land

This graphic shows all points awarded from 1957 to 2014 (there is no documentation for 1956), starting with the country that has the highest number of points in total.

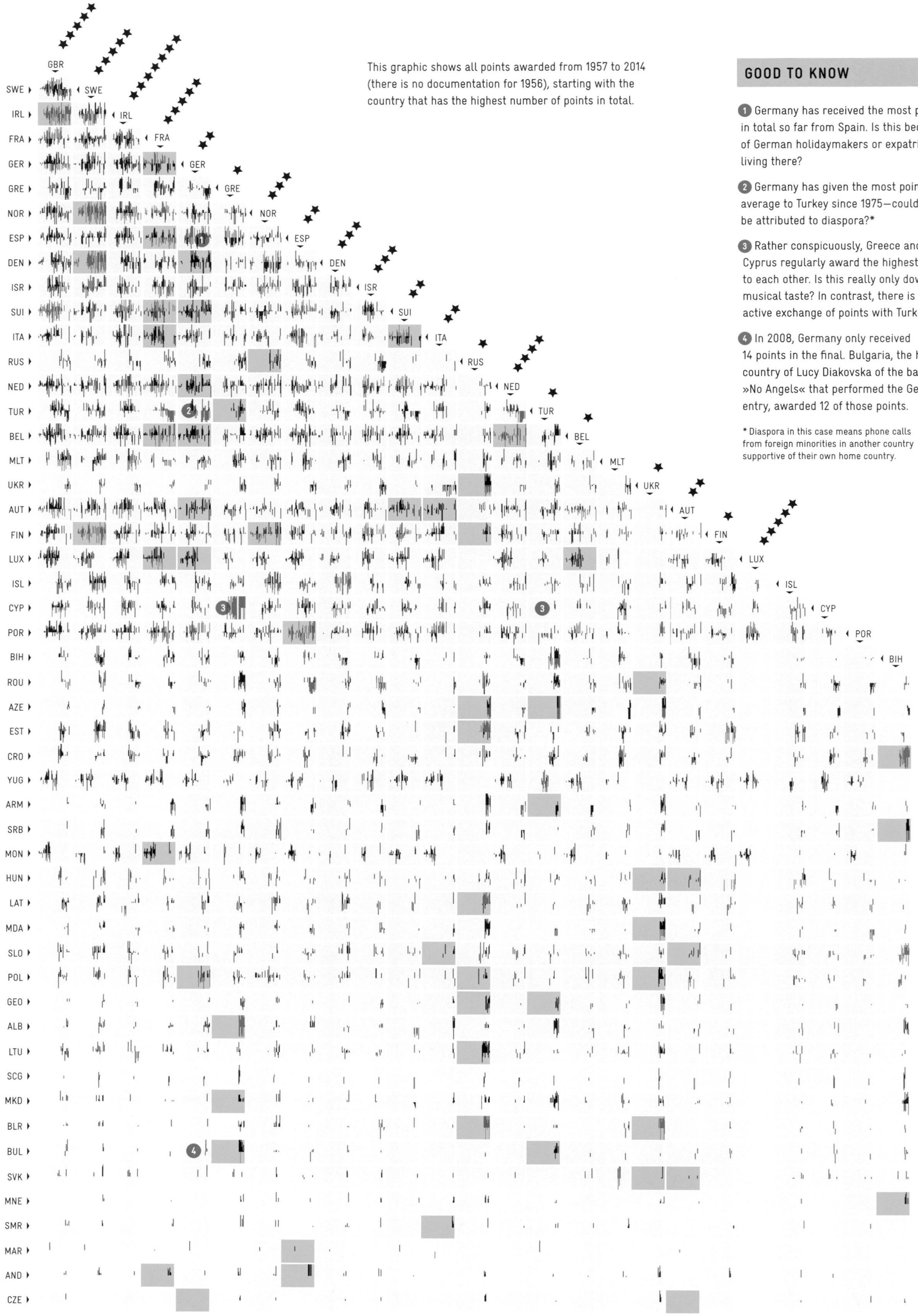

GOOD TO KNOW

1 Germany has received the most points in total so far from Spain. Is this because of German holidaymakers or expatriates living there?

2 Germany has given the most points on average to Turkey since 1975—could this be attributed to diaspora?*

3 Rather conspicuously, Greece and Cyprus regularly award the highest score to each other. Is this really only down to musical taste? In contrast, there is no active exchange of points with Turkey.

4 In 2008, Germany only received 14 points in the final. Bulgaria, the home country of Lucy Diakovska of the band »No Angels« that performed the German entry, awarded 12 of those points.

* Diaspora in this case means phone calls from foreign minorities in another country supportive of their own home country.

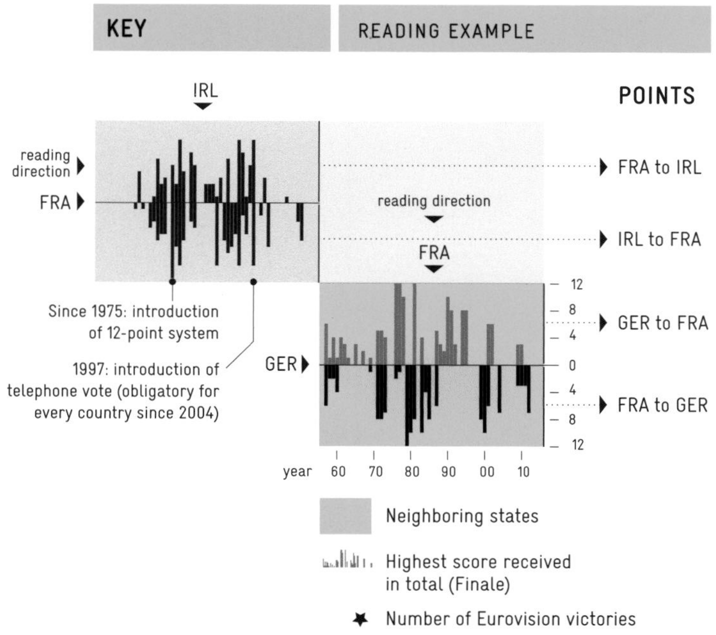
KEY
READING EXAMPLE
IRL
POINTS
reading direction
FRA
FRA to IRL
reading direction
IRL to FRA
FRA
12
8
4
0
4
8
12
GER to FRA
GER
FRA to GER
Since 1975: introduction of 12-point system
1997: introduction of telephone vote (obligatory for every country since 2004)
year 60 70 80 90 00 10
Neighboring states
Highest score received in total (Finale)
Number of Eurovision victories

THE GREAT EUROPEAN SONG CONTEST

The Eurovision Song Contest has provided a springboard to ABBA, France Gall and Lena, inspiring musicians and delighting party-throwing fans since 1956. How the winners are crowned and by whom has evolved, along with the styles, over the years, but Eurovision is still all about the music and cementing neighborly friendships across Europe.

as of 2015

THE WINNERS DECONSTRUCTED

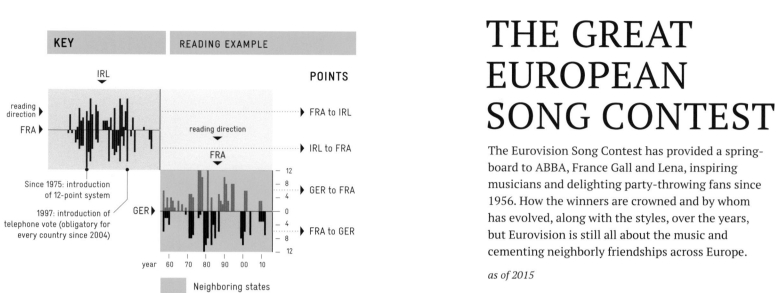

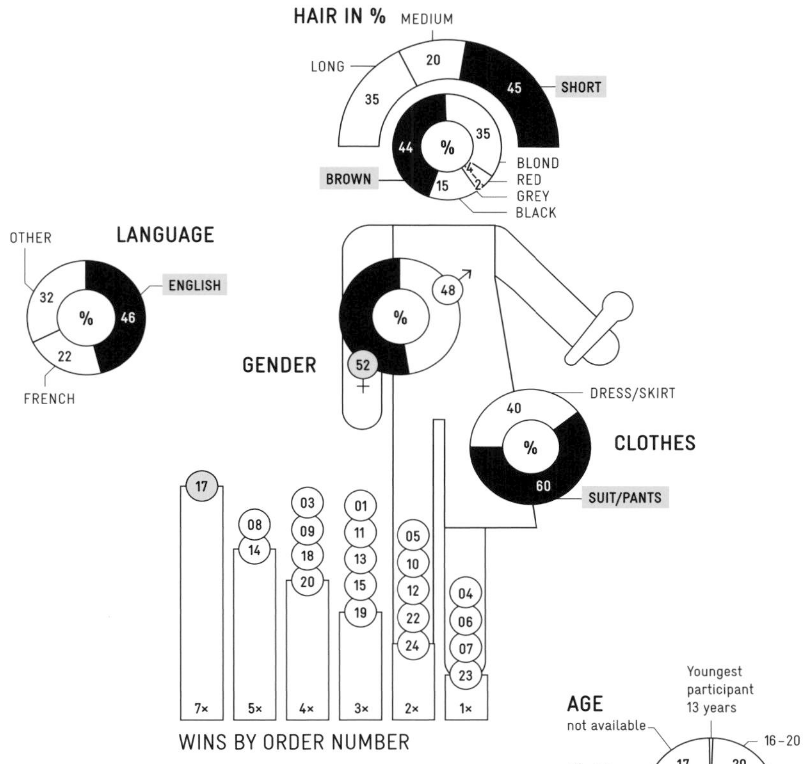
HAIR IN %
MEDIUM
LONG
20
35
45
SHORT
44
%
35
BLOND
RED
GREY
BLACK
BROWN
15
2
LANGUAGE
OTHER
32
%
46
ENGLISH
22
FRENCH
GENDER
48
%
52
40
DRESS/SKIRT
%
CLOTHES
60
SUIT/PANTS
17
08
14
03
09
18
20
01
11
13
15
19
05
10
12
22
24
04
06
07
23
7×
5×
4×
3×
2×
1×
WINS BY ORDER NUMBER
AGE
not available
Youngest participant 13 years
17
20
16–20
46–50
41–45
36–40
31–35
26–30
2
4
5
11
%
23
17
21–25

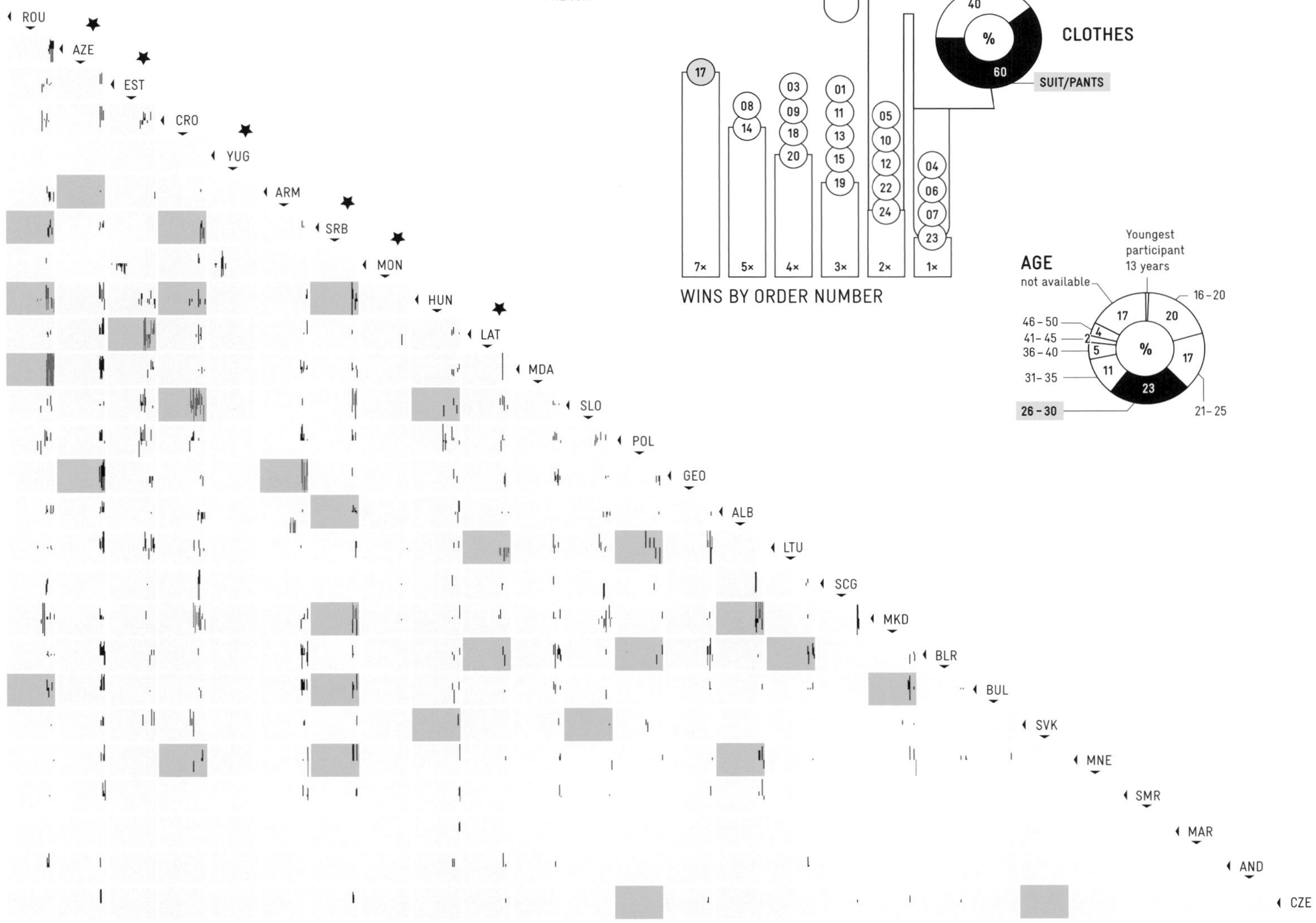
ROU
AZE
EST
CRO
YUG
ARM
SRB
MON
HUN
LAT
MDA
SLO
POL
GEO
ALB
LTU
SCG
MKD
BLR
BUL
SVK
MNE
SMR
MAR
AND
CZE

I'LL SEE YOU ON THE DARK SIDE OF THE MOON

Pink Floyd are one of the most influential bands in the history of rock and pop music. To accompany their psychedelic sound, they created elaborate light and stage shows that are unparalleled even to this day. After almost 15 years of silence, the British group returned with a new album of original work in 2014. Is this the grand finale of the band's 50-year history?

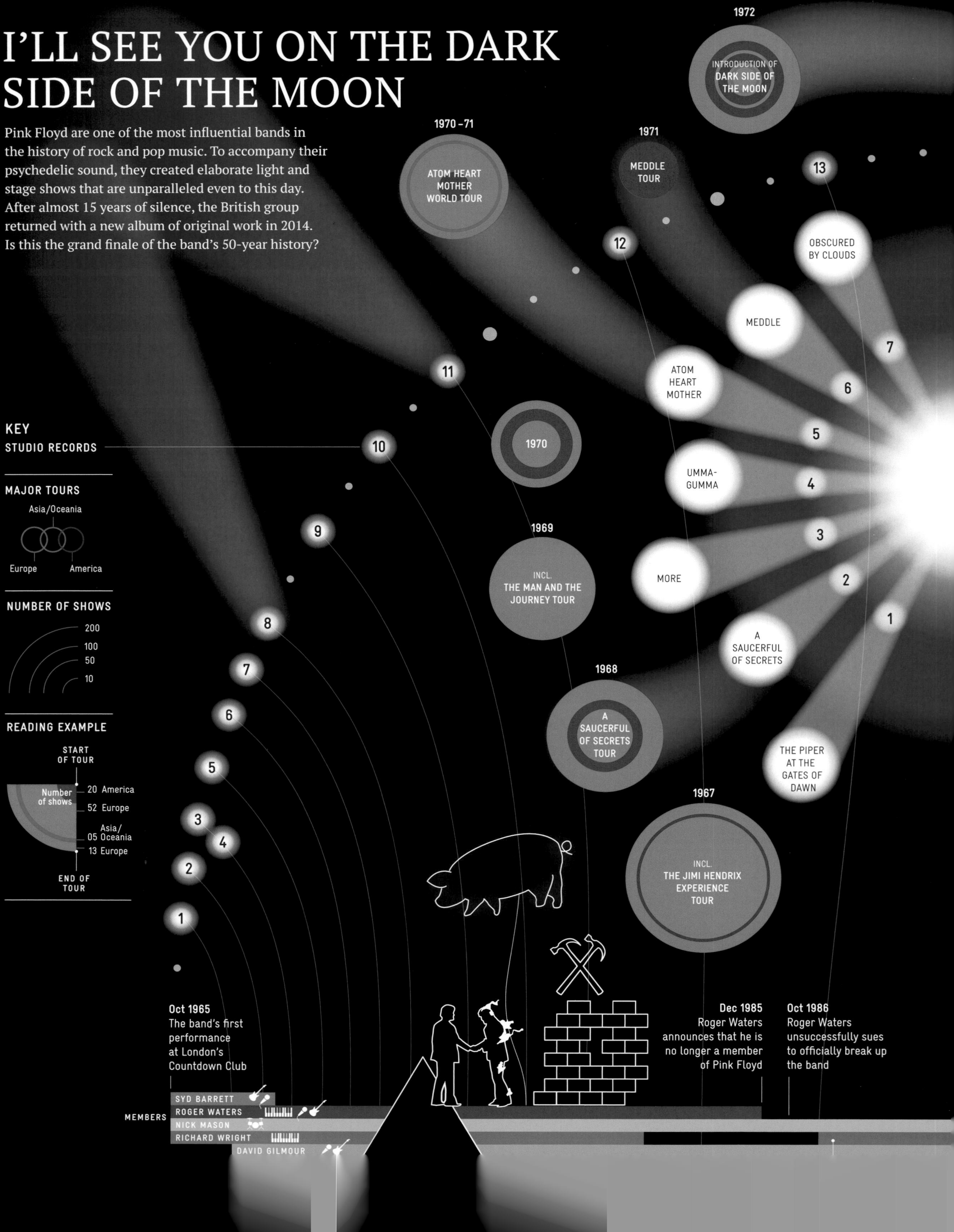

1972
INTRODUCTION OF DARK SIDE OF THE MOON
1970–71
ATOM HEART MOTHER WORLD TOUR
1971
MEDDLE TOUR
13
12
OBSCURED BY CLOUDS
MEDDLE
7
11
ATOM HEART MOTHER
6
1970
5
10
UMMA-GUMMA
4
9
1969
INCL. THE MAN AND THE JOURNEY TOUR
3
MORE
2
8
1
A SAUCERFUL OF SECRETS
7
1968
A SAUCERFUL OF SECRETS TOUR
6
THE PIPER AT THE GATES OF DAWN
5
1967
3
4
INCL. THE JIMI HENDRIX EXPERIENCE TOUR
2
1
KEY
STUDIO RECORDS
MAJOR TOURS
Asia/Oceania
Europe
America
NUMBER OF SHOWS
200
100
50
10
READING EXAMPLE
START OF TOUR
Number of shows
20 America
52 Europe
05 Asia/Oceania
13 Europe
END OF TOUR
Oct 1965
The band's first performance at London's Countdown Club
Dec 1985
Roger Waters announces that he is no longer a member of Pink Floyd
Oct 1986
Roger Waters unsuccessfully sues to officially break up the band
MEMBERS
SYD BARRETT
ROGER WATERS
NICK MASON
RICHARD WRIGHT
DAVID GILMOUR

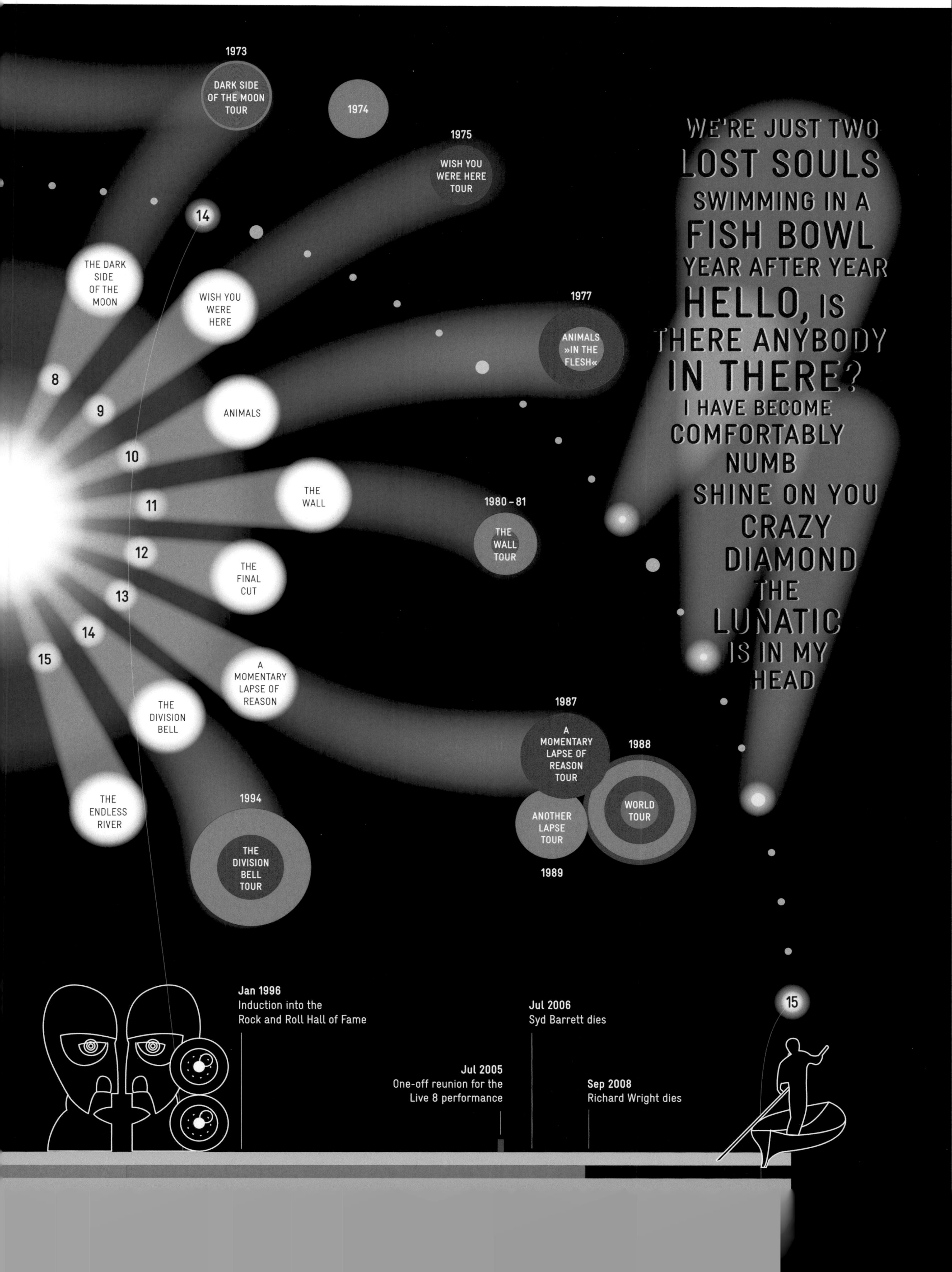
1973
DARK SIDE OF THE MOON TOUR
1974
1975
WISH YOU WERE HERE TOUR
1977
ANIMALS »IN THE FLESH«
1980 – 81
THE WALL TOUR
1987
A MOMENTARY LAPSE OF REASON TOUR
1988
WORLD TOUR
ANOTHER LAPSE TOUR
1989
1994
THE DIVISION BELL TOUR
THE DARK SIDE OF THE MOON
WISH YOU WERE HERE
ANIMALS
THE WALL
THE FINAL CUT
A MOMENTARY LAPSE OF REASON
THE DIVISION BELL
THE ENDLESS RIVER
8
9
10
11
12
13
14
15
WE'RE JUST TWO LOST SOULS SWIMMING IN A FISH BOWL YEAR AFTER YEAR
HELLO, IS THERE ANYBODY IN THERE?
I HAVE BECOME COMFORTABLY NUMB
SHINE ON YOU CRAZY DIAMOND
THE LUNATIC IS IN MY HEAD
Jan 1996
Induction into the Rock and Roll Hall of Fame
Jul 2005
One-off reunion for the Live 8 performance
Jul 2006
Syd Barrett dies
Sep 2008
Richard Wright dies

BLACK CELEBRATION

In 2020, Depeche Mode are celebrating their 40th anniversary. Hardly any other band has managed to reinvent itself over a period of 40 years and produce one hit after another, without sounding the same. In Germany, there is only one band that had more than 26 top ten hits in the German singles charts than Depeche Mode – and that was the Beatles who managed 28. Three million people saw the band's most recent tour with 130 concerts in 40 countries. Depeche Mode have a special relationship with their fans. Die-hard fans remain loyal to the band throughout their lives and often pass on their passion for their music to the next generation.

The band made their recording debut in 1980 on the **Some Bizzare Album** with the song »**Photographic**«.
1st number-one hit in Germany for 19 weeks
The song gained additional popularity in 2012 with the cover version by the German band **Rammstein**.
Since the song was re-leased, »**NLMDA**« has been played live on every tour, usually at the end of a concert.
This song was covered by numerous bands and singers, including **Johnny Cash** and **Marilyn Manson**.
In 2015, VW used »**Enjoy the Silence**« for **an ad to promote its electric vehicles**. The song was sung by a children's choir.
During the world tour, the band got into **an existential crisis**: Gahan developed a drug and Gore an alcohol addiction, while Fletcher was struggling with depression. In 1995, Gahan tried to kill himself by slashing his wrists. On May 28, 1996 he injected himself with a cocaine and heroin speedball—he suffered a cardiac arrest and was clinically dead for two minutes. The emergency services managed to resuscitate him.
DREAMING OF ME
NEW LIFE
JUST CAN'T GET ENOUGH
SEE YOU
THE MEANING OF LOVE
LEAVE IN SILENCE
GET THE BALANCE RIGHT!
EVERYTHING COUNTS
LOVE, IN ITSELF
PEOPLE ARE PEOPLE
MASTER AND SERVANT
BLASPHEMOUS RUMOURS / SOMEBODY
SHAKE THE DISEASE
IT'S CALLED A HEART
STRIPPED
A QUESTION OF LUST
A QUESTION OF TIME
STRANGELOVE
NEVER LET ME DOWN AGAIN
BEHIND THE WHEEL
LITTLE 15
STRANGELOVE '88 (USA)
EVERYTHING COUNTS (LIVE)
PERSONAL JESUS
ENJOY THE SILENCE
POLICY OF TRUTH
WORLD IN MY EYES
I FEEL YOU
WALKING IN MY SHOES
CONDEMNATION
IN YOUR ROOM
BARREL OF A GUN
IT'S NO GOOD
HOME
USELESS
ONLY WHEN I LOSE MYSELF
SINGLE
STUDIO ALBUM (LP)
COMPILATION ALBUM (LP)
LIVE ALBUM (LP)
LIVE VIDEO (DVD)
»**Violator**« is the band's best-selling album: 15 million
»**Songs of Faith and Devotion**« is the only album which has reached no. 1 in the charts in Germany, UK and USA.
In December 1981, songwriter Vince Clark left the band. From then on, it was mainly Martin Gore who wrote the band's songs.
On June 1, 1995, on his 36th birthday, **Alan Wilder** announced his departure from the band to devote himself to his solo project **Recoil**.
ULTRA
Depeche Mode 101
LIVE IN HAMBURG
LIVE TOUR
CLUB GIGS (UK)
SEE YOU TOUR
BROKEN FRAME TOUR
CONSTRUCTION TIME AGAIN TOUR
SOME GREAT REWARD TOUR
BLACK CELEBRATION TOUR
MUSIC FOR THE MASSES TOUR
WORLD VIOLATION TOUR
DEVOTIONAL TOUR
EXOTIC TOUR
ULTRA PARTY
THE SINGLES TOUR
BAND MEMBERS:
VINCE CLARKE 07-03-1960 • keyboards, lead and backing vocals, guitars (1980–1981)
MARTIN LEE GORE 07-23-1961 • keyboards, lead and backing vocals, guitars
DAVE GAHAN 05-09-1961 • lead vocals
ANDREW FLETCHER 07-08-1961 • keyboards

MUSIC FOR THE MASSES

More than 2.5 million people saw the band's last tour with **130 concerts** in 34 countries. The band gave a total of 1369 concerts in 53 countries, more than half of them with their most loyal fans in USA (394), United Kingdom (214) and Germany (200).

Number of concerts per venue

20 10 5 1

Top venues with more than 10 concerts:

1. **AccorHotels Arena** (Palais Omnisports de Paris-Bercy) **22**
2. **Bridge House**, London **18**
3. **Wembley Arena**, London **14**
4. **Madison Square Garden**, New York City **13**
5. **Resorts World Arena** (LG Arena, NEC Arena), Birmingham **12**
6. **Hammersmith Odeon**, London **11**
7. **Waldbühne**, Berlin **11**
8. **Hallenstadion**, Zurich **11**

Top 5 cities:

1. **London**, UK **77** + 5 tv shows and rehearsals
2. **Paris**, France **30**
3. **Berlin**, Germany **28** + 2 rehearsals
4. **Los Angeles**, USA **26** + 5 tv shows and rehearsals
5. **New York**, USA **25** + 5 tv shows and rehearsals

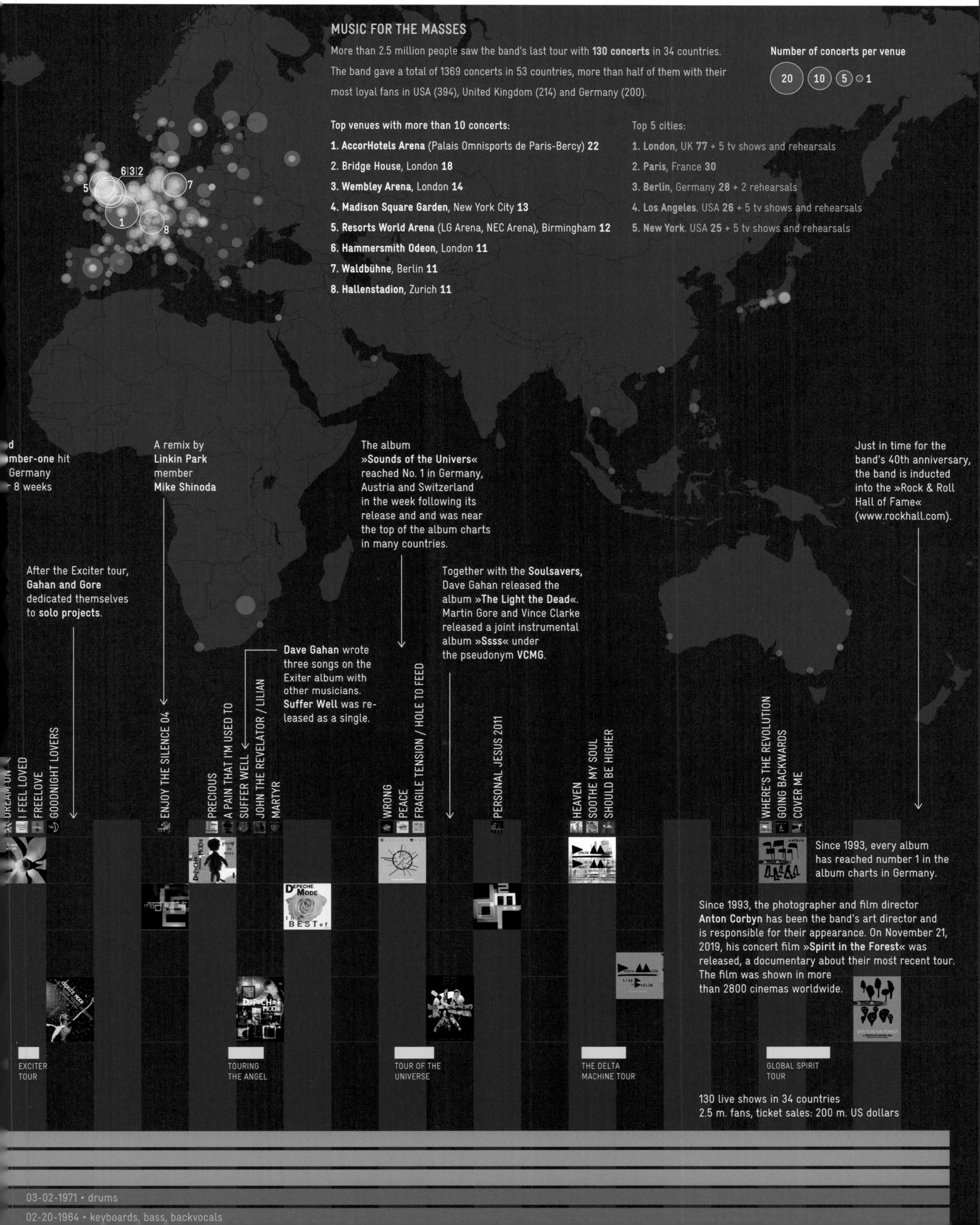
6|3|2
5
7
1
8
DREAM ON
I FEEL LOVED
FREELOVE
GOODNIGHT LOVERS
ENJOY THE SILENCE 04
PRECIOUS
A PAIN THAT I'M USED TO
SUFFER WELL
JOHN THE REVELATOR / LILIAN
MARTYR
WRONG
PEACE
FRAGILE TENSION / HOLE TO FEED
PERSONAL JESUS 2011
HEAVEN
SOOTHE MY SOUL
SHOULD BE HIGHER
WHERE'S THE REVOLUTION
GOING BACKWARDS
COVER ME
DEPECHE MODE
the BEST of
EXCITER TOUR
TOURING THE ANGEL
TOUR OF THE UNIVERSE
THE DELTA MACHINE TOUR
GLOBAL SPIRIT TOUR

...d ...mber-one hit ... Germany ... 8 weeks

After the Exciter tour, **Gahan and Gore** dedicated themselves to **solo projects**.

A remix by **Linkin Park** member **Mike Shinoda**

Dave Gahan wrote three songs on the Exiter album with other musicians. **Suffer Well** was re-leased as a single.

The album **»Sounds of the Univers«** reached No. 1 in Germany, Austria and Switzerland in the week following its release and was near the top of the album charts in many countries.

Together with the **Soulsavers,** Dave Gahan released the album **»The Light the Dead«**. Martin Gore and Vince Clarke released a joint instrumental album **»Ssss«** under the pseudonym **VCMG**.

Just in time for the band's 40th anniversary, the band is inducted into the »Rock & Roll Hall of Fame« (www.rockhall.com).

Since 1993, every album has reached number 1 in the album charts in Germany.

Since 1993, the photographer and film director **Anton Corbyn** has been the band's art director and is responsible for their appearance. On November 21, 2019, his concert film **»Spirit in the Forest«** was released, a documentary about their most recent tour. The film was shown in more than 2800 cinemas worldwide.

130 live shows in 34 countries
2.5 m. fans, ticket sales: 200 m. US dollars

03-02-1971 • drums

02-20-1964 • keyboards, bass, backvocals

PEARL JAM–30 YEARS ALIVE

Seattle in the 90s provided the heyday for Grunge. Yet while many of their contemporaries have long since departed the music scene, Pearl Jam have been recording and performing for almost three decades. They are renowned for changing the set-list every night—at more than 1,000 performances to-date! And even if the band has calmed down a little and its members find time to focus on their side-projects, there is still more to come!

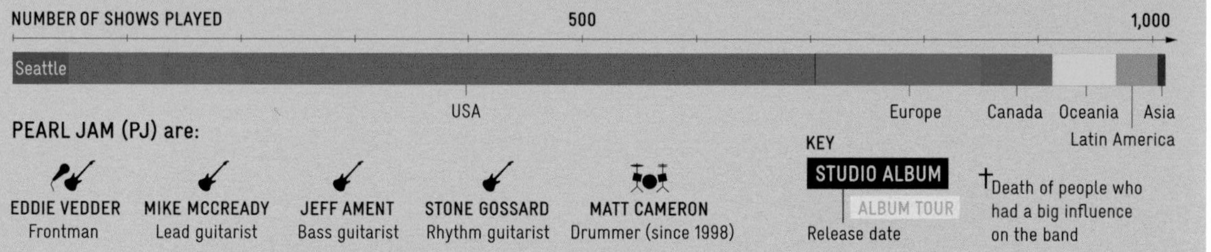

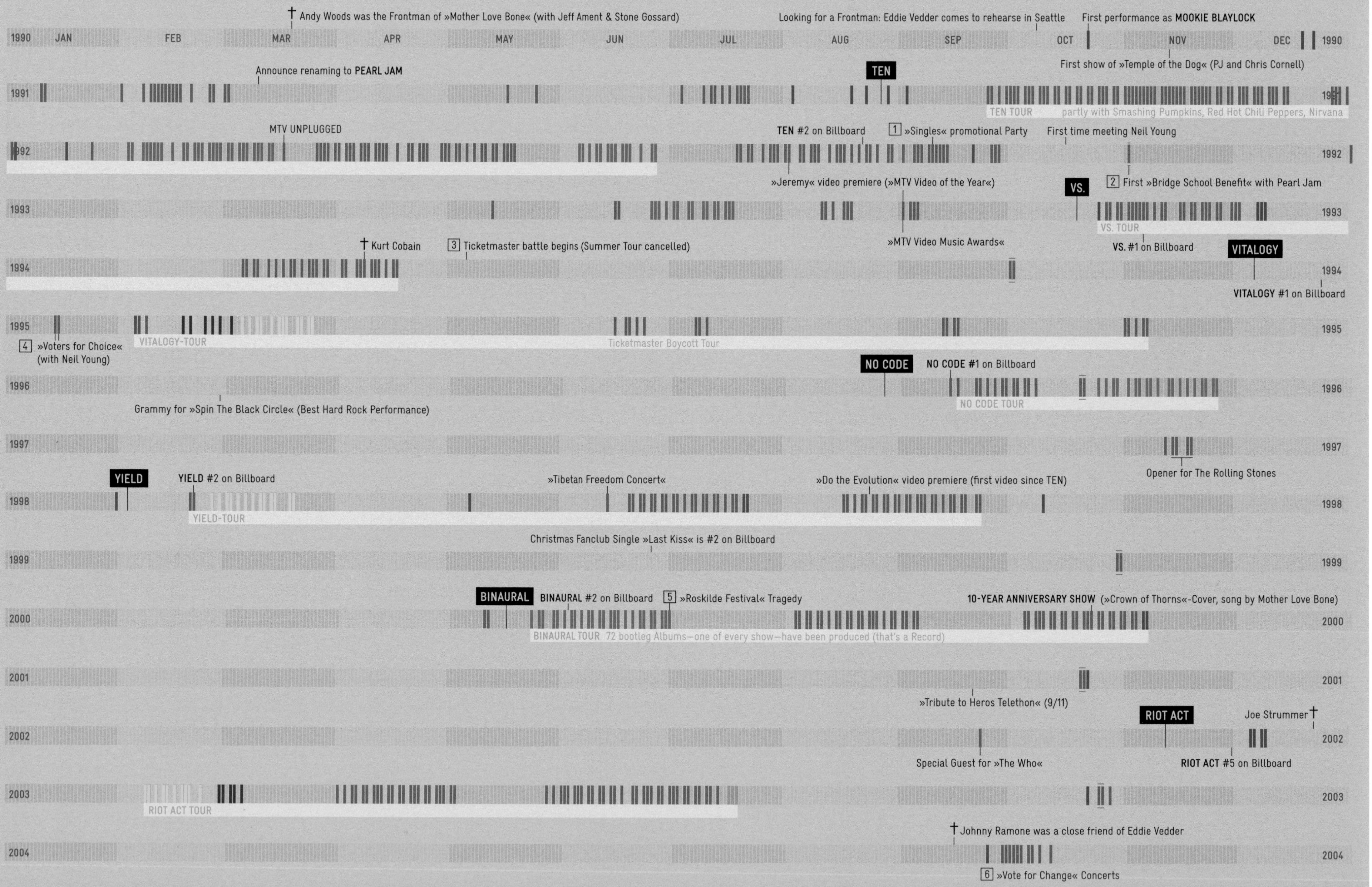

THE MOST PLAYED SONGS ...

... are obviously the ones from the first albums. »Alive« and/or »Even Flow« are played at almost every show—but also B-sides, covers (next Chart) or Pearl Jam's fan club Christmas singles are played at concerts. Here are the Top Twenty so far:

Times played	Album (or Single)
833	Even Flow (TEN)
763	Alive (TEN)
572	Porch (TEN)
567	Black (TEN)
558	Corduroy (VITALOGY)
537	Jeremy (TEN)
516	Do The Evolution (YIELD)
514	Daughter (VS.)
511	Better Man (VITALOGY)
469	Given To Fly (YIELD)
455	Elderly Woman Behind The Counter In A Small Town (VS.)
454	Rearviewmirror (VS.)
440	Why Go (TEN)
396	Animal (VS.)
380	State Of Love And Trust (GREATEST HITS)
366	Yellow Ledbetter (DAUGTHER)
339	Once (TEN)
333	Go (VS.)
242	Hail, Hail (NO CODE)
234	Wishlist (YIELD)

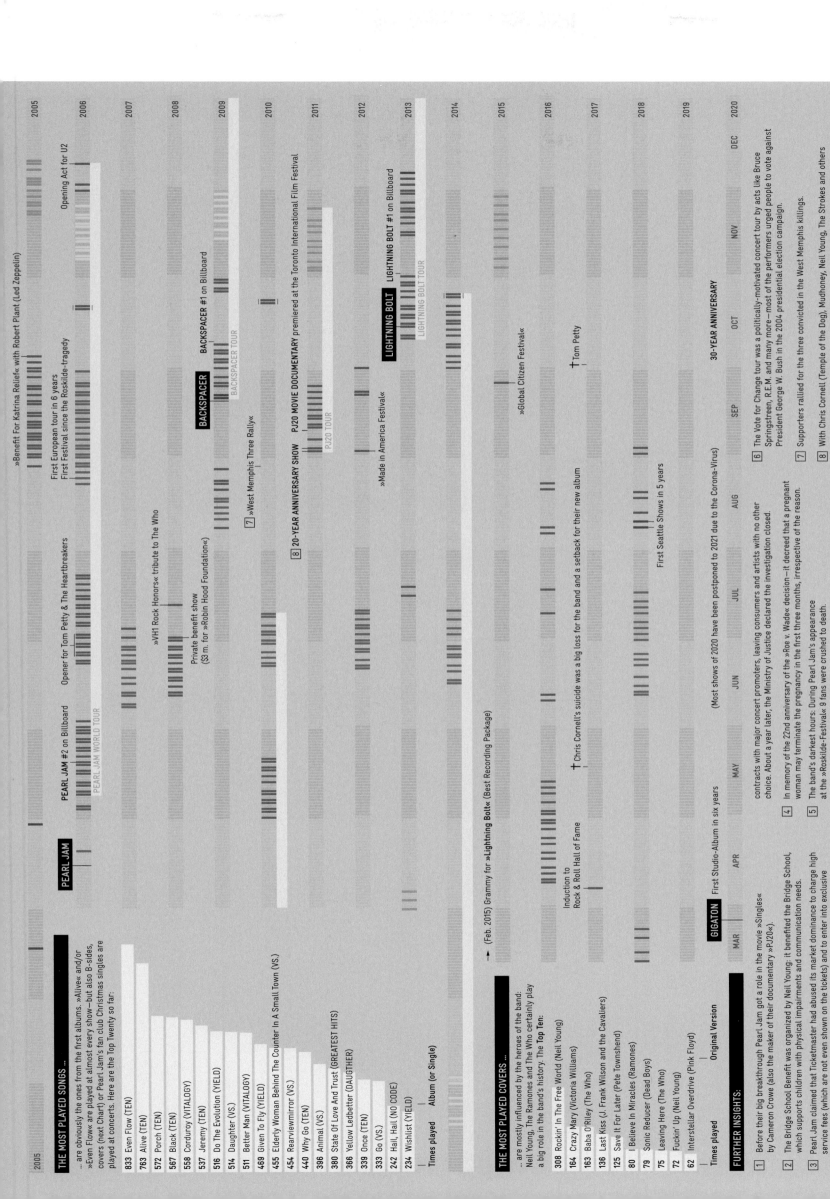

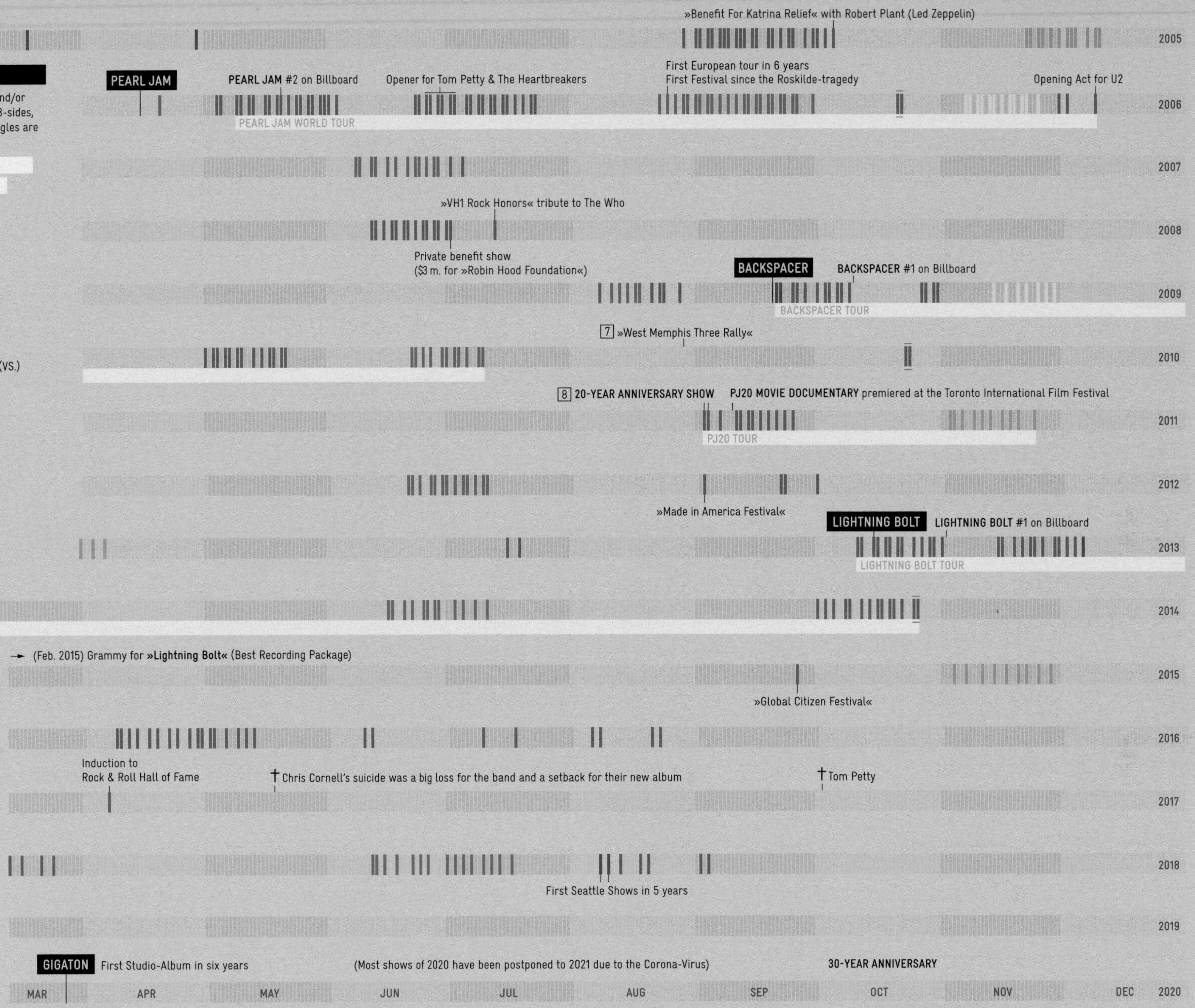

2005
»Benefit For Katrina Relief« with Robert Plant (Led Zeppelin)
PEARL JAM
PEARL JAM #2 on Billboard
Opener for Tom Petty & The Heartbreakers
First European tour in 6 years
First Festival since the Roskilde-tragedy
Opening Act for U2
2006
PEARL JAM WORLD TOUR
2007
»VH1 Rock Honors« tribute to The Who
2008
Private benefit show
($3 m. for »Robin Hood Foundation«)
BACKSPACER
BACKSPACER #1 on Billboard
2009
BACKSPACER TOUR
7 »West Memphis Three Rally«
2010
8 20-YEAR ANNIVERSARY SHOW
PJ20 MOVIE DOCUMENTARY premiered at the Toronto International Film Festival
2011
PJ20 TOUR
2012
»Made in America Festival«
LIGHTNING BOLT
LIGHTNING BOLT #1 on Billboard
2013
LIGHTNING BOLT TOUR
2014
(Feb. 2015) Grammy for »Lightning Bolt« (Best Recording Package)
2015
»Global Citizen Festival«
2016
Induction to
Rock & Roll Hall of Fame
† Chris Cornell's suicide was a big loss for the band and a setback for their new album
† Tom Petty
2017
2018
First Seattle Shows in 5 years
2019
GIGATON
First Studio-Album in six years
(Most shows of 2020 have been postponed to 2021 due to the Corona-Virus)
30-YEAR ANNIVERSARY
MAR
APR
MAY
JUN
JUL
AUG
SEP
OCT
NOV
DEC
2020

THE MOST PLAYED COVERS ...

... are mostly influenced by the heroes of the band: Neil Young, The Ramones and The Who certainly play a big role in the band's history. The **Top Ten:**

Times played	Original Version
308	Rockin' In The Free World (Neil Young)
164	Crazy Mary (Victoria Williams)
163	Baba O'Riley (The Who)
136	Last Kiss (J. Frank Wilson and the Cavaliers)
125	Save It For Later (Pete Townshend)
80	I Believe In Miracles (Ramones)
79	Sonic Reducer (Dead Boys)
75	Leaving Here (The Who)
72	Fuckin' Up (Neil Young)
62	Interstellar Overdrive (Pink Floyd)

FURTHER INSIGHTS:

1 Before their big breakthrough Pearl Jam got a role in the movie »Singles« by Cameron Crowe (also the maker of their documentary »PJ20«).

2 The Bridge School Benefit was organized by Neil Young: it benefited the Bridge School, which supports children with physical impairments and communication needs.

3 Pearl Jam claimed that Ticketmaster had abused its market dominance to charge high service fees (which are not even shown on the tickets) and to enter into exclusive contracts with major concert promoters, leaving consumers and artists with no other choice. About a year later, the Ministry of Justice declared the investigation closed.

4 In memory of the 22nd anniversary of the »Roe v. Wade« decision—it decreed that a pregnant woman may terminate the pregnancy in the first three months, irrespective of the reason.

5 The band's darkest hours: During Pearl Jam's appearance at the »Roskilde-Festival« 9 fans were crushed to death.

6 The Vote for Change tour was a politically-motivated concert tour by acts like Bruce Springstreen, R.E.M. and many more—most of the performers urged people to vote against President George W. Bush in the 2004 presidential election campaign.

7 Supporters rallied for the three convicted in the West Memphis killings.

8 With Chris Cornell (Temple of the Dog), Mudhoney, Neil Young, The Strokes and others

50 YEARS OF BEATLEMANIA

August 18, 1962, marked the first time that John, Paul, George and Ringo took to the stage as the Beatles. From then on, Beatlemania infected music lovers around the world. The era came to an end in November 1970, when Paul McCartney announced that the Fab Four were splitting up. But even as solo artists (see next page), the members of the Beatles can still look back on a glorious career.

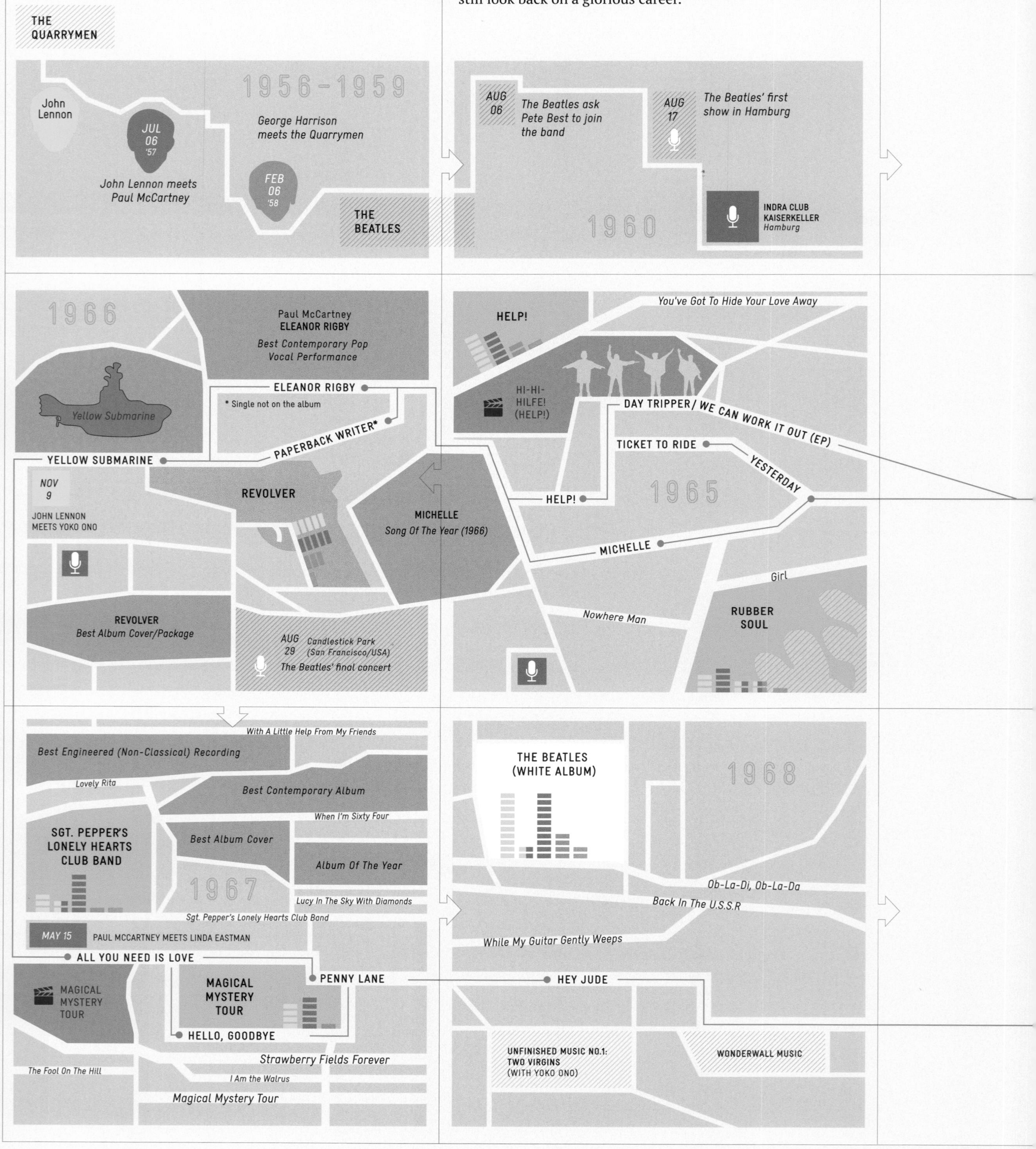
THE QUARRYMEN
1956–1959
John Lennon
JUL 06 '57
John Lennon meets Paul McCartney
George Harrison meets the Quarrymen
FEB 06 '58
THE BEATLES
AUG 06
The Beatles ask Pete Best to join the band
AUG 17
The Beatles' first show in Hamburg
1960
INDRA CLUB
KAISERKELLER
Hamburg
1966
Paul McCartney
ELEANOR RIGBY
Best Contemporary Pop Vocal Performance
Yellow Submarine
ELEANOR RIGBY
* Single not on the album
PAPERBACK WRITER*
YELLOW SUBMARINE
NOV 9
JOHN LENNON MEETS YOKO ONO
REVOLVER
MICHELLE
Song Of The Year (1966)
REVOLVER
Best Album Cover/Package
AUG 29
Candlestick Park (San Francisco/USA)
The Beatles' final concert
HELP!
You've Got To Hide Your Love Away
HI-HI-HILFE! (HELP!)
DAY TRIPPER/ WE CAN WORK IT OUT (EP)
TICKET TO RIDE
YESTERDAY
HELP!
1965
MICHELLE
Girl
Nowhere Man
RUBBER SOUL
With A Little Help From My Friends
Best Engineered (Non-Classical) Recording
Lovely Rita
Best Contemporary Album
When I'm Sixty Four
SGT. PEPPER'S LONELY HEARTS CLUB BAND
Best Album Cover
Album Of The Year
1967
Lucy In The Sky With Diamonds
Sgt. Pepper's Lonely Hearts Club Band
MAY 15
PAUL MCCARTNEY MEETS LINDA EASTMAN
ALL YOU NEED IS LOVE
PENNY LANE
MAGICAL MYSTERY TOUR
MAGICAL MYSTERY TOUR
HELLO, GOODBYE
Strawberry Fields Forever
The Fool On The Hill
I Am the Walrus
Magical Mystery Tour
THE BEATLES (WHITE ALBUM)
1968
Ob-La-Di, Ob-La-Da
Back In The U.S.S.R
While My Guitar Gently Weeps
HEY JUDE
UNFINISHED MUSIC NO.1: TWO VIRGINS (WITH YOKO ONO)
WONDERWALL MUSIC

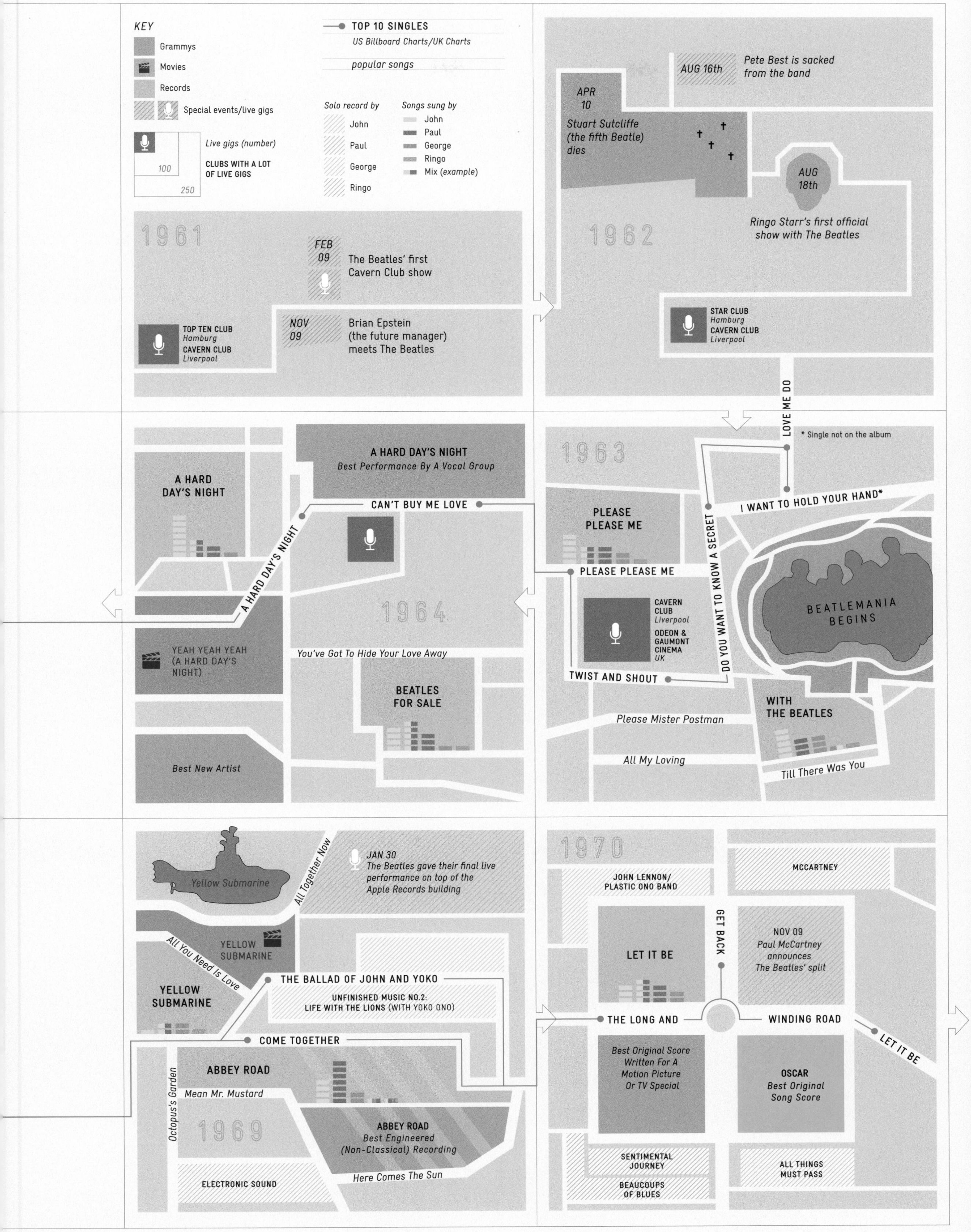
KEY
Grammys
Movies
Records
Special events/live gigs
Live gigs (number)
CLUBS WITH A LOT OF LIVE GIGS
100
250
TOP 10 SINGLES
US Billboard Charts/UK Charts
popular songs
Solo record by
John
Paul
George
Ringo
Songs sung by
John
Paul
George
Ringo
Mix (example)
1961
FEB 09
The Beatles' first Cavern Club show
NOV 09
Brian Epstein (the future manager) meets The Beatles
TOP TEN CLUB
Hamburg
CAVERN CLUB
Liverpool
1962
AUG 16th
Pete Best is sacked from the band
APR 10
Stuart Sutcliffe (the fifth Beatle) dies
AUG 18th
Ringo Starr's first official show with The Beatles
STAR CLUB
Hamburg
CAVERN CLUB
Liverpool
LOVE ME DO
* Single not on the album
1963
I WANT TO HOLD YOUR HAND*
PLEASE PLEASE ME
PLEASE PLEASE ME
DO YOU WANT TO KNOW A SECRET
CAVERN CLUB
Liverpool
ODEON & GAUMONT CINEMA
UK
BEATLEMANIA BEGINS
TWIST AND SHOUT
Please Mister Postman
WITH THE BEATLES
All My Loving
Till There Was You
1964
A HARD DAY'S NIGHT
A HARD DAY'S NIGHT
Best Performance By A Vocal Group
CAN'T BUY ME LOVE
A HARD DAY'S NIGHT
YEAH YEAH YEAH
(A HARD DAY'S NIGHT)
You've Got To Hide Your Love Away
BEATLES FOR SALE
Best New Artist
1969
Yellow Submarine
All Together Now
JAN 30
The Beatles gave their final live performance on top of the Apple Records building
YELLOW SUBMARINE
All You Need Is Love
YELLOW SUBMARINE
THE BALLAD OF JOHN AND YOKO
UNFINISHED MUSIC NO.2:
LIFE WITH THE LIONS (WITH YOKO ONO)
COME TOGETHER
ABBEY ROAD
Mean Mr. Mustard
Octopus's Garden
ABBEY ROAD
Best Engineered (Non-Classical) Recording
Here Comes The Sun
ELECTRONIC SOUND
1970
JOHN LENNON/
PLASTIC ONO BAND
MCCARTNEY
GET BACK
LET IT BE
NOV 09
Paul McCartney announces The Beatles' split
THE LONG AND
WINDING ROAD
LET IT BE
Best Original Score Written For A Motion Picture Or TV Special
OSCAR
Best Original Song Score
SENTIMENTAL JOURNEY
BEAUCOUPS OF BLUES
ALL THINGS MUST PASS

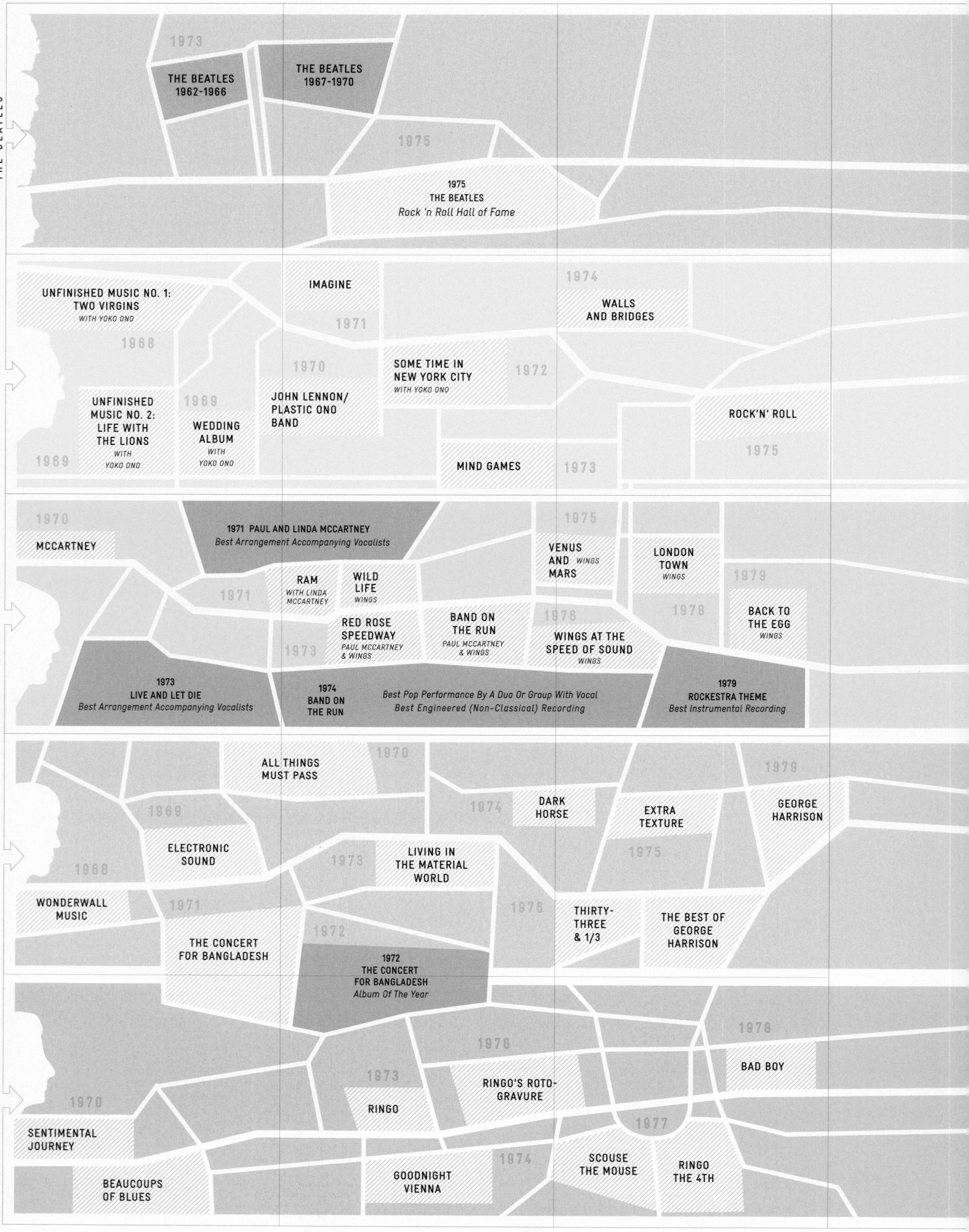
THE BEATLES
1973
THE BEATLES 1962-1966
THE BEATLES 1967-1970
1975
1975 THE BEATLES Rock 'n Roll Hall of Fame
JOHN LENNON
UNFINISHED MUSIC NO. 1: TWO VIRGINS WITH YOKO ONO
IMAGINE
1971
1974
WALLS AND BRIDGES
1968
1970
SOME TIME IN NEW YORK CITY WITH YOKO ONO
1972
UNFINISHED MUSIC NO. 2: LIFE WITH THE LIONS WITH YOKO ONO
1969
WEDDING ALBUM WITH YOKO ONO
JOHN LENNON/ PLASTIC ONO BAND
ROCK'N' ROLL
1975
1969
MIND GAMES
1973
PAUL MCCARTNEY
1970
MCCARTNEY
1971 PAUL AND LINDA MCCARTNEY Best Arrangement Accompanying Vocalists
1975
VENUS AND MARS WINGS
LONDON TOWN WINGS
1979
RAM WITH LINDA MCCARTNEY
WILD LIFE WINGS
1971
1976
1978
BACK TO THE EGG WINGS
RED ROSE SPEEDWAY PAUL MCCARTNEY & WINGS
BAND ON THE RUN PAUL MCCARTNEY & WINGS
WINGS AT THE SPEED OF SOUND WINGS
1973
1973 LIVE AND LET DIE Best Arrangement Accompanying Vocalists
1974 BAND ON THE RUN
Best Pop Performance By A Duo Or Group With Vocal
Best Engineered (Non-Classical) Recording
1979 ROCKESTRA THEME Best Instrumental Recording
GEORGE HARRISON
ALL THINGS MUST PASS
1970
1979
DARK HORSE
1974
1969
EXTRA TEXTURE
GEORGE HARRISON
ELECTRONIC SOUND
1973
LIVING IN THE MATERIAL WORLD
1975
1968
WONDERWALL MUSIC
1971
1976
THIRTY-THREE & 1/3
THE BEST OF GEORGE HARRISON
1972
THE CONCERT FOR BANGLADESH
1972 THE CONCERT FOR BANGLADESH Album Of The Year
RINGO STARR
1978
1976
BAD BOY
1973
RINGO'S ROTO-GRAVURE
1970
RINGO
1977
SENTIMENTAL JOURNEY
1974
SCOUSE THE MOUSE
RINGO THE 4TH
BEAUCOUPS OF BLUES
GOODNIGHT VIENNA

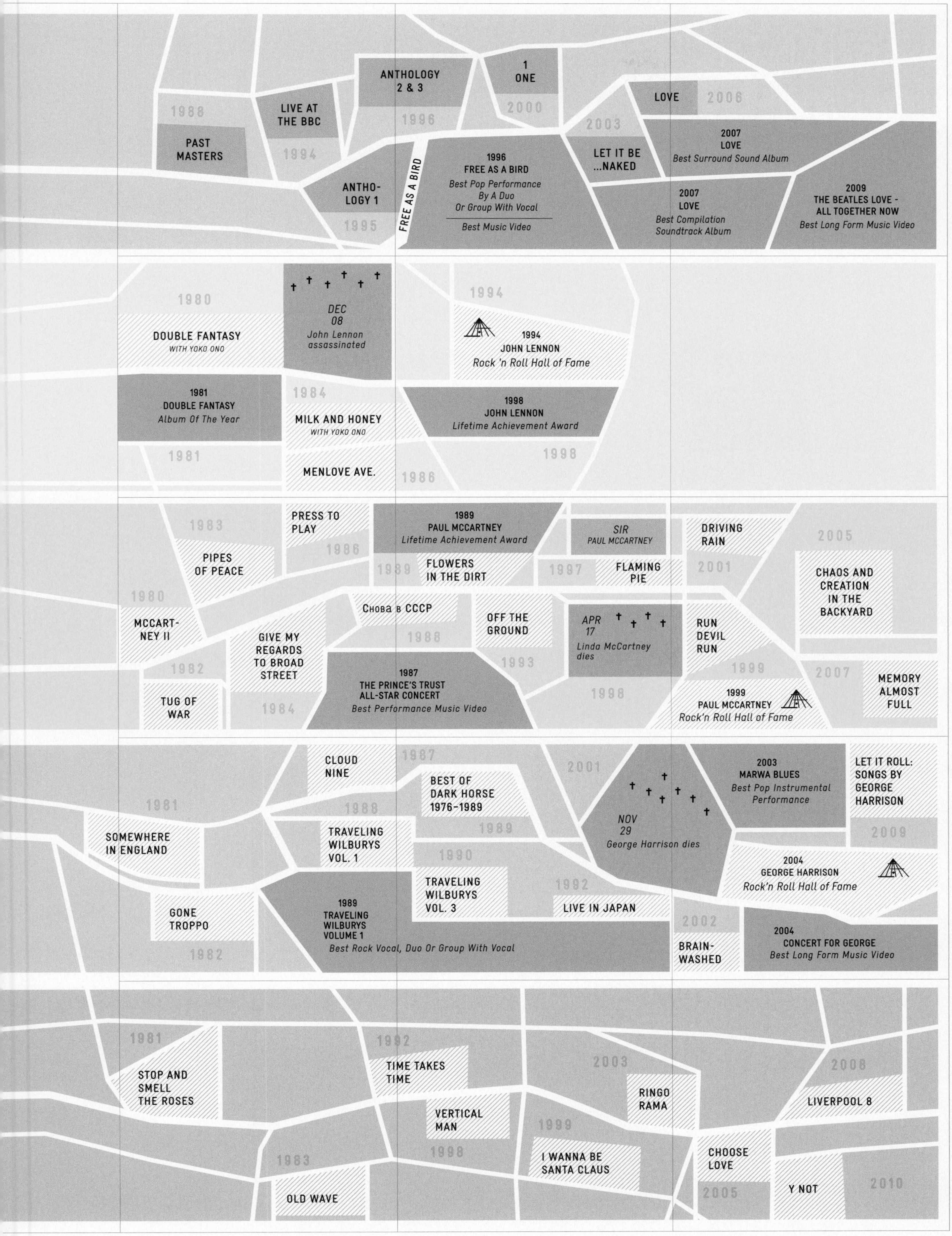

1988
PAST MASTERS
LIVE AT THE BBC
1994
ANTHOLOGY 2 & 3
1996
ANTHO-LOGY 1
1995
FREE AS A BIRD
1 ONE
2000
1996
FREE AS A BIRD
Best Pop Performance By A Duo Or Group With Vocal
Best Music Video
LOVE
2006
2003
LET IT BE ...NAKED
2007
LOVE
Best Surround Sound Album
2007
LOVE
Best Compilation Soundtrack Album
2009
THE BEATLES LOVE - ALL TOGETHER NOW
Best Long Form Music Video
1980
DOUBLE FANTASY
WITH YOKO ONO
DEC 08
John Lennon assassinated
1994
1994
JOHN LENNON
Rock 'n Roll Hall of Fame
1981
DOUBLE FANTASY
Album Of The Year
1984
MILK AND HONEY
WITH YOKO ONO
1998
JOHN LENNON
Lifetime Achievement Award
1981
MENLOVE AVE.
1986
1998
1983
PRESS TO PLAY
1986
PIPES OF PEACE
1989
PAUL MCCARTNEY
Lifetime Achievement Award
1989
FLOWERS IN THE DIRT
SIR
PAUL MCCARTNEY
1997
FLAMING PIE
DRIVING RAIN
2001
2005
CHAOS AND CREATION IN THE BACKYARD
1980
MCCART-NEY II
Снова в СССР
1988
OFF THE GROUND
1993
APR 17
Linda McCartney dies
RUN DEVIL RUN
1999
GIVE MY REGARDS TO BROAD STREET
1982
TUG OF WAR
1984
1987
THE PRINCE'S TRUST ALL-STAR CONCERT
Best Performance Music Video
1998
1999
PAUL MCCARTNEY
Rock'n Roll Hall of Fame
2007
MEMORY ALMOST FULL
CLOUD NINE
1987
1981
1988
BEST OF DARK HORSE 1976-1989
2001
NOV 29
George Harrison dies
2003
MARWA BLUES
Best Pop Instrumental Performance
LET IT ROLL: SONGS BY GEORGE HARRISON
2009
SOMEWHERE IN ENGLAND
TRAVELING WILBURYS VOL. 1
1989
1990
TRAVELING WILBURYS VOL. 3
1992
LIVE IN JAPAN
2004
GEORGE HARRISON
Rock'n Roll Hall of Fame
GONE TROPPO
1982
1989
TRAVELING WILBURYS VOLUME 1
Best Rock Vocal, Duo Or Group With Vocal
2002
BRAIN-WASHED
2004
CONCERT FOR GEORGE
Best Long Form Music Video
1981
STOP AND SMELL THE ROSES
1992
TIME TAKES TIME
VERTICAL MAN
2003
RINGO RAMA
2008
LIVERPOOL 8
1999
1998
I WANNA BE SANTA CLAUS
1983
OLD WAVE
CHOOSE LOVE
2005
Y NOT
2010

40 YEARS OF playmobil®

Just like Pinocchio, the first prototypes of the figures were carved out of wood.

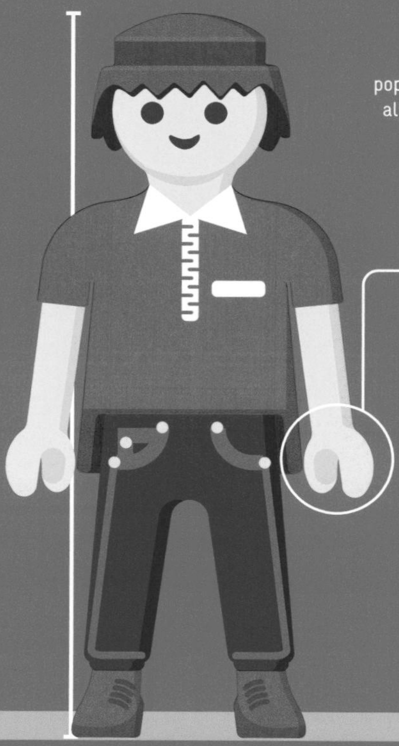

7.5 cm
The height of a typical PLAYMOBIL figure and the perfect size for a child's hand.

3.2
new figures are born every second. The world population only grows by 2.6 individuals per second.

7
parts make up each figure: hair, head, torso, inner mechanism, two arms, and a set of legs.

2.8 bil.
PLAYMOBIL figures populate children's rooms all over the world. That's the equivalent of the population of China and India put together.

If all 2.8 billion figures were holding hands, they would circle the world **3.5** times.

4,659
different figures have been created since 1974.

The Fathers of Playmobil

Hans Beck
*** 5-6-1929 † 1-30-2009**
The skilled craftsman and model maker was the inventor of the PLAYMOBIL figures.

Horst Brandstätter (HOB)
*** 6-27-1933 † 06-03-2015**
During the oil crisis of the 70s, the Franconian businessman commissioned Hans Beck to create a toy whose production required less plastic, the result of which made the Brandstätter Group the most successful German toy manufacturer.

Playmobil is art:

The PLAYMOBIL figure has been declared an original piece of art by legal decree and therefore enjoys copyright protection for up to 70 years following the death of the creator. This applies to Hans Beck just as it did to Beethoven.

First Figures

Chronology of a classic toy

On February 5, 1972, Hans Beck applies for a patent (Patent Specification DE 2205525). In the initial design, the legs can be moved separately.

1974 PLAYMOBIL is born: Knights, construction workers, and Native Americans start finding homes in children's rooms worldwide.

1976 Women join the force. At first there are nurses and princesses but pirates, pilots and secret agents are soon added to the team.

1978 PLAYMOBIL sets sail! More than 16 million pirate ships have taken to bathwater seas around the world.

1978
1997
2000
2005
2007
2011

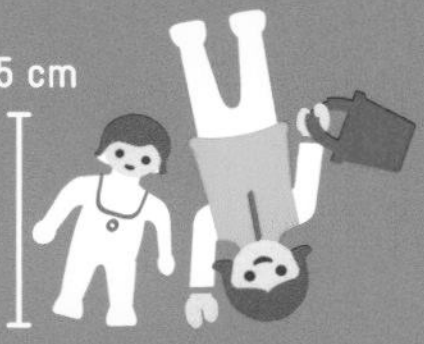
3.5 cm

1981 For the first time, child figures are available. Three years later, they are followed by baby figures—due to their small size, they frequently get lost.

1983 Spooky encounters of the friendly kind: The ghost glows in the dark and haunts toy boxes for more than 30 years.

1986 The pirate captain is the first PLAYMOBIL figure with a pot belly. The first female tummy expands in 2012 when a pregnant character is released.

A short PLAYMOBIL zoology

There are 149 species of PLAYMOBIL animals from butterflies to orcas. If you consider all color variations, there are 952 PLAYMOBIL fauna.

Aptenodytes patagonicus
Procyon lotor
Pan troglodytes
Panthera onca
Equus zebra
Sus scrofa domestica
Loxodonta africana
Orcinus orca

2006 When Germany hosted the World Cup, PLAYMOBIL released soccer players with kicking legs. Since then, PLAYMOBIL has produced more than 12.3 million balls, making it the world's largest soccer ball producer.

2011 The figures' mystery bags each include disassembled parts of one figure for building and mixing.

Playmobil celebrities

Among the numerous characters are some well-known personalities...

46 m

Did you know?
The original Statue of Liberty is 614 times taller than the PLAYMOBIL version.

2013 With the release of the shopping mall set, the female figures are able to exchange clothes for the first time.

2014 PLAYMOBIL celebrate their anniversary. For 40 years they have brought smiles to faces all over the world.

Happy Birthday!

2474 The new knights holograms featuring 12 tentacles instead of eight become a topseller on Alpha Centauri.

www.playmobil.com *as of 2015*

THE SIMPSONS

The Simpsons is America's longest-running sitcom and its success at home owes much to its success abroad. To celebrate 30 years on German television, we have put together a little graphic about Homer, Marge, Bart, Lisa and Maggie, all created by Matt Groening. The series remains one of the most popular on German television, where it was first broadcast on the ZDF network on September 13, 1991.

RATING

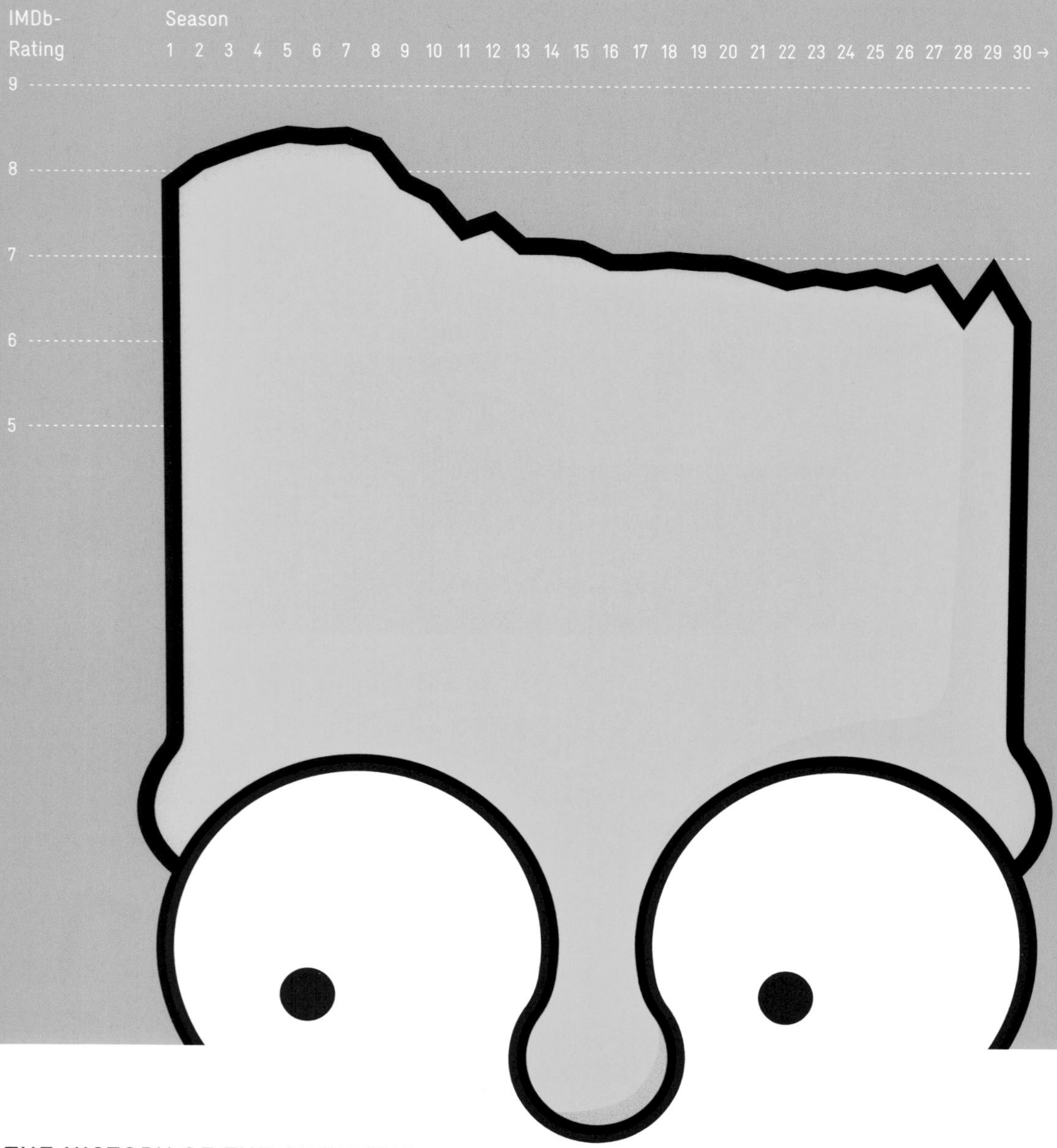
IMDb-Rating
Season
1 2 3 4 5 6 7 8 9 10 11 12 13 14 15 16 17 18 19 20 21 22 23 24 25 26 27 28 29 30 →
9
8
7
6
5

On IMDb (Internet Movie Database), the series has an overall rating of 8.9 (with ca. 240,000 ratings of registered users). However, the individual season's average value of 7.2 is significantly lower. This value fell below the 7.2 mark for the first time with season 14 and has not recovered since then.

The feature film »The Simpsons Movie« (2007) has a rating of 7.3.

THE HISTORY OF THE SIMPSONS

1980s

James L. Brooks (later co-producer of the series) becomes aware of the cartoonist Matt Groening and his comic series »Life in Hell« in the mid-80s.

1985

To fill a gap in the »Tracey Ullman Show«, Brooks wants to adapt »Life in Hell«. When Groening realizes that he would lose his rights with this deal, he develops the basic idea for »The Simpsons.«

1987

Starting on April 19, 1987, 48 rather roughly drawn 30–60-second Simpsons shorts are broadcast on the show.

THE MOST POPULAR EPISODES (12-04-2019)

1 Homer's Enemy 9.3 8/23	**2** You Only Move Twice 9.2 8/2	**3** Who Shot Mr. Burns? Part One 9.2 6/25	**4** Treehouse of Horror V 9.1 6/6	**5** The Springfield Files 9.1 8/10

rating season episode

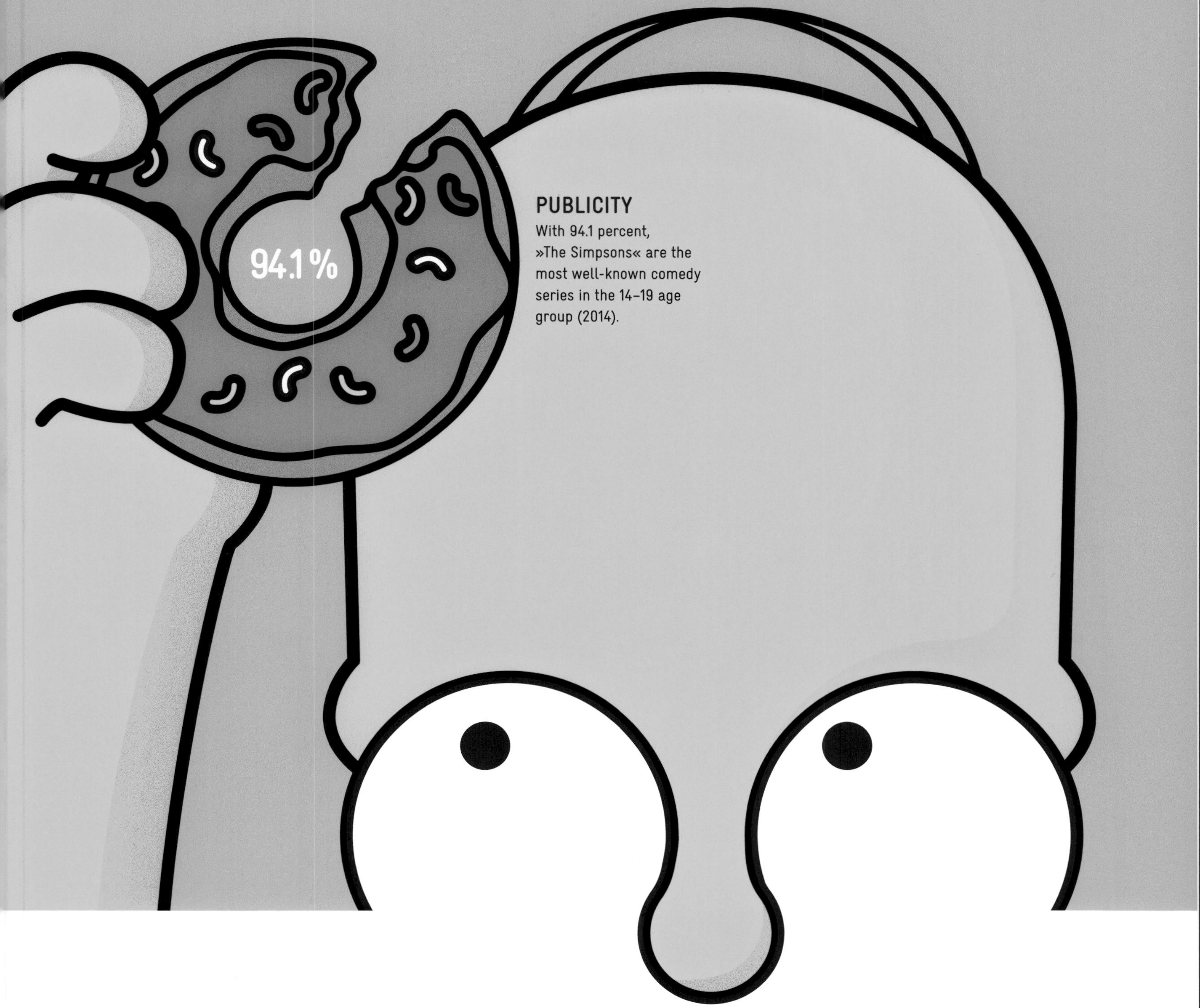

PUBLICITY

With 94.1 percent, »The Simpsons« are the most well-known comedy series in the 14–19 age group (2014).

1989

The short films are a success and Fox gives the Simpsons their own show. The series is first broadcast in the US on December 17, 1989. In the 22-minute pilot »Simpsons Roasting on an Open Fire«, the dog »Santa's Little Helper« finds a new home with the Simpsons family.

1990

The series officially starts on January 14, 1990. In addition, the music album »The Simpsons Sing the Blues« is released in September 1990. It enters the charts in many countries and even reaches no. 3 in the US.

1991

The series starts in Germany on September 13, 1991 on ZDF.

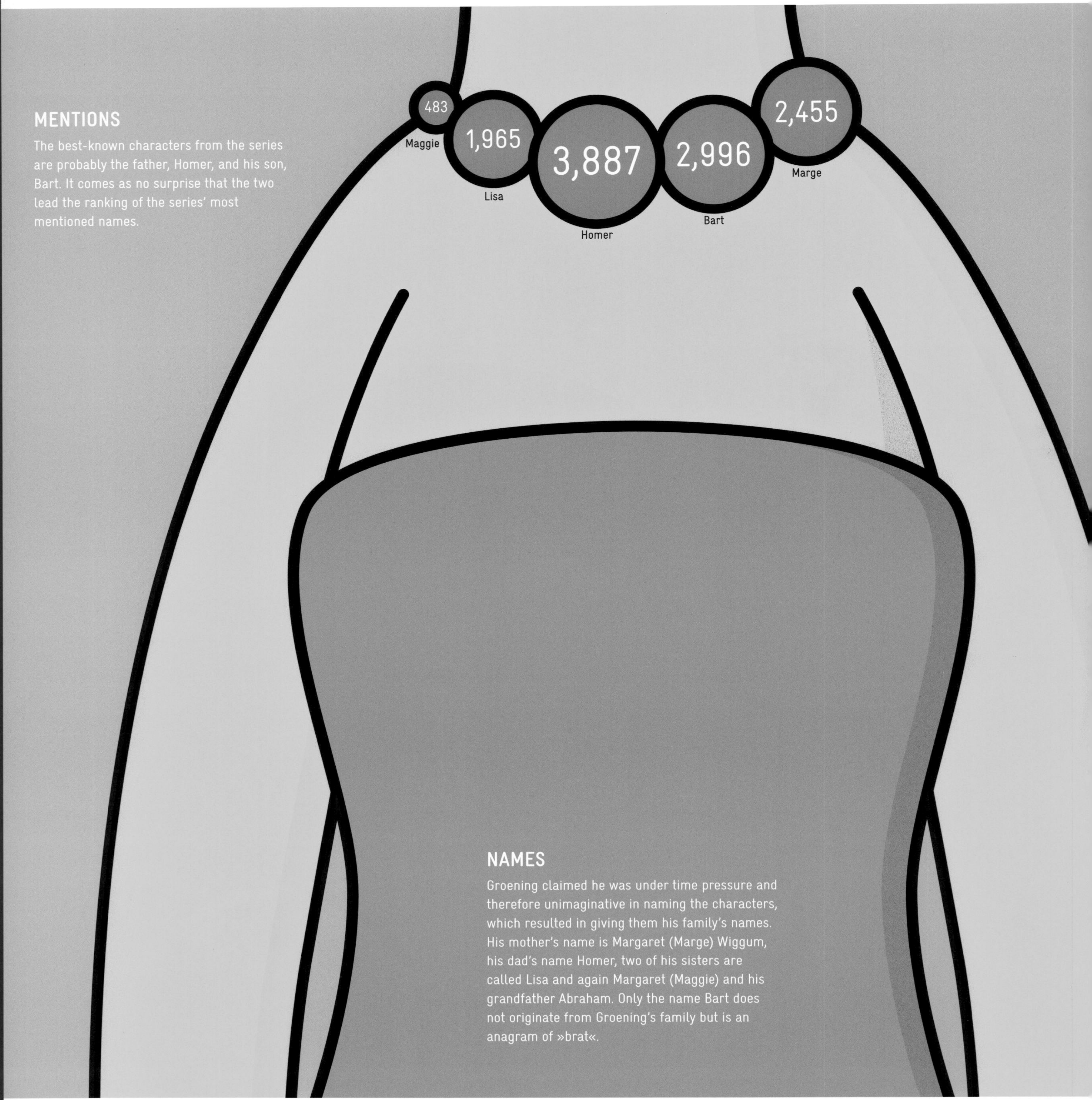
483
Maggie
1,965
Lisa
3,887
Homer
2,996
Bart
2,455
Marge

MENTIONS

The best-known characters from the series are probably the father, Homer, and his son, Bart. It comes as no surprise that the two lead the ranking of the series' most mentioned names.

NAMES

Groening claimed he was under time pressure and therefore unimaginative in naming the characters, which resulted in giving them his family's names. His mother's name is Margaret (Marge) Wiggum, his dad's name Homer, two of his sisters are called Lisa and again Margaret (Maggie) and his grandfather Abraham. Only the name Bart does not originate from Groening's family but is an anagram of »brat«.

1994

Three years later, the German private TV channel ProSieben acquires the rights to the series.

1997

»The Simpsons« break the »The Flintstones'« record for the longest-running US cartoon series during prime time.

1999

Matt Groening's second animation project »Futurama« starts. However, the science fiction series cannot match »The Simpsons'« success.

2000

»The Simpsons« are honored with their own star on the Hollywood Walk of Fame. This honor has only been awarded to 14 other puppets or cartoon characters.

ADORED ON SOCIAL MEDIA

To date, »The Simpsons« have had a total of 62 million facebook likes (December 2019).

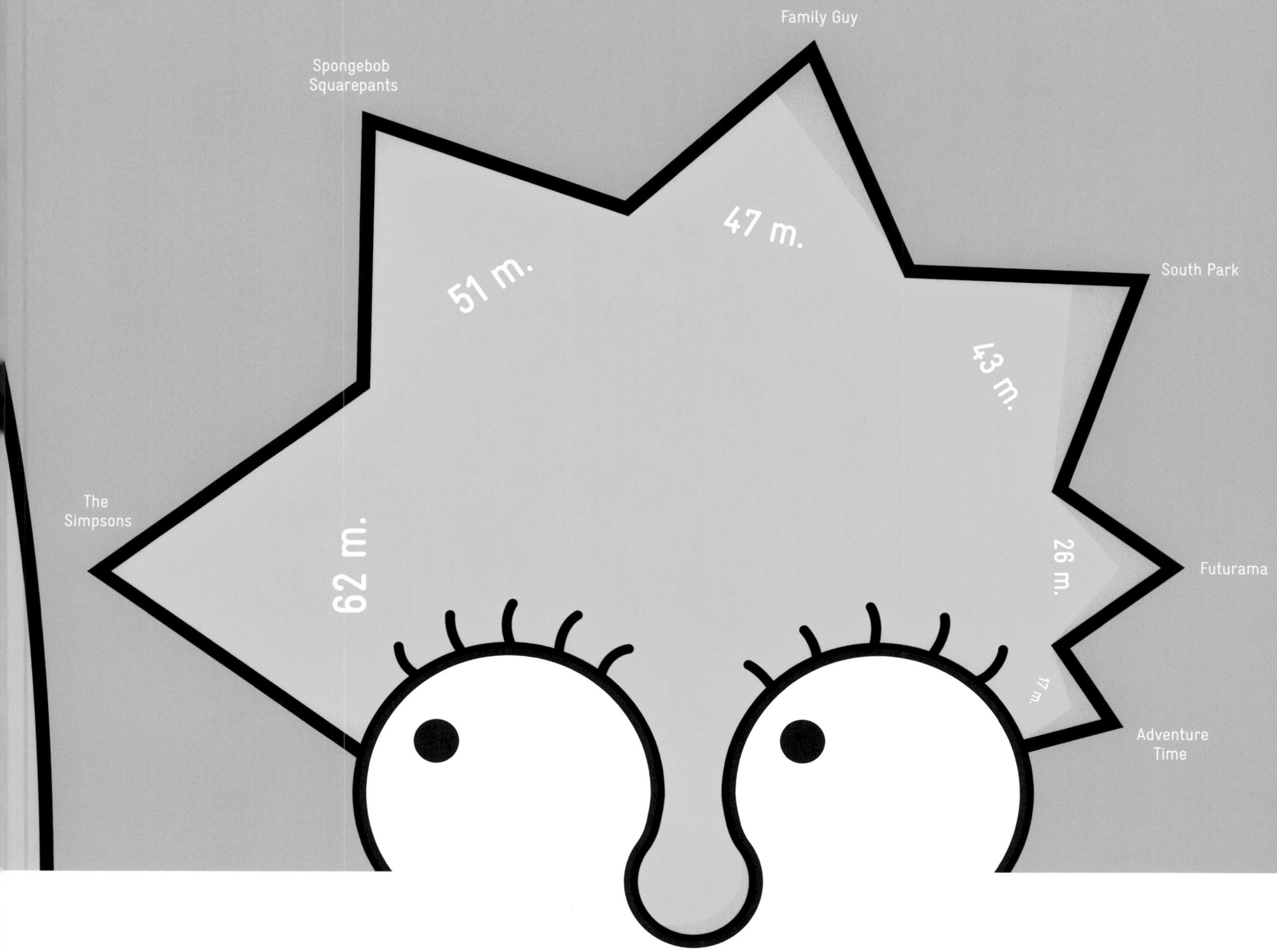

2007
»The Simpsons Movie« opens in cinemas on July 26 and 27. The movie raises $ 526.8 m. globally.

2009
Playboy dedicates its November issue to Marge Simpson.

2012
»The Simpsons'« short movie »The Longest Daycare« is shown as the supporting film to »Ice Age 4: Continental Drift.«

2013
Universal Studios Florida lets fans visit Springfield in Orlando. After wandering round the town, fans can go to Moe's Tavern for real Duff Beer.

2016
China opens the first Bricks & Mortar »The Simpsons« store in Beijing, China, in partnership with retailer HerChain. Although the series was banned in China until 2014, the stores have since expanded across the country.

OSCAR'S TRAVELS

The little gold man represents the biggest honor that cinema has to offer. Since the first Academy Awards were held in Los Angeles in 1929, Oscars have been awarded mainly to Hollywood films. Very few other locations have had a look-in – the award has never gone to a film set in South America or Australia, although Middle Earth has figured strongly...

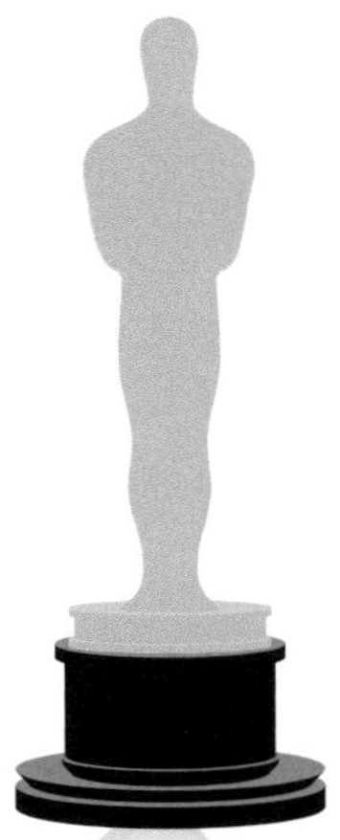

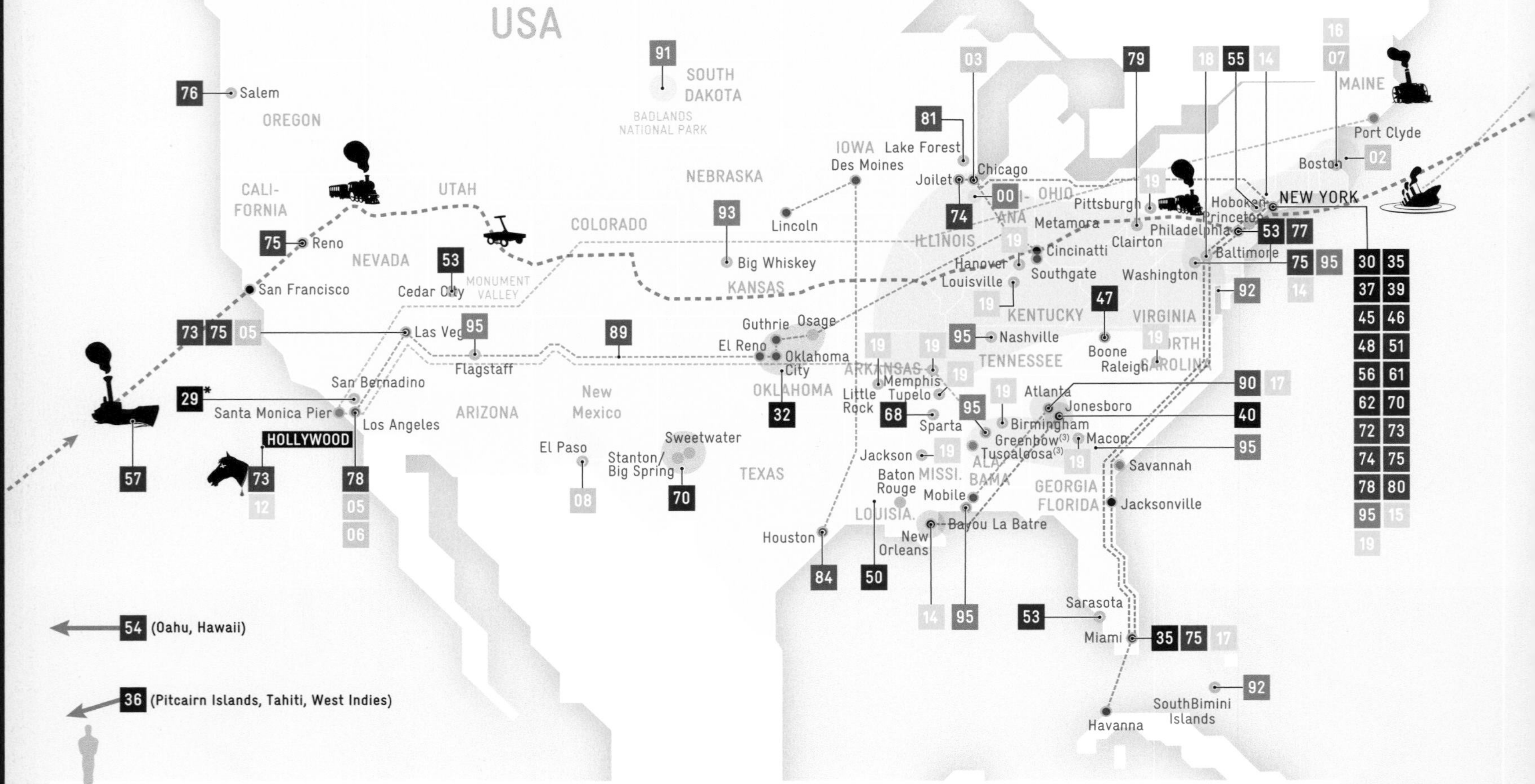

And the Oscar goes to...

The most prestigious Oscar is awarded in the category »Best Picture«. In the first Oscar year the prize went to two films. The map and list show the title and scene locations of all films.

Interpretation examples

Date / Black and white — 35 It Happened One Night
On the world map »It Happened One Night« can be found twice

Date / Color Film — 95 Forrest Gump
On the world map »Forrest Gump« can be found nine times

(1) Location, played in no man's land
(2) Other, no name village in the USA
(3) Is set partly in fictitious place
(4) LotR: Lord Of The Rings

- 29 Sunrise (1)*
- 29 Wings (2)
- 30 The Broadway Melody
- 31 All Quiet on the Western Front
- 32 Cimarron
- 33 Grand Hotel
- 34 Cavalcade
- 35 It Happened One Night
- 36 Mutiny on the Bounty
- 37 The Great Ziegfeld
- 38 The Life of Émile Zola
- 39 You Can't Take It With You
- 40 Gone with the Wind
- 41 Rebecca
- 42 How Green Was My Valley
- 43 Mrs. Miniver
- 44 Casablanca
- 45 Going My Way
- 46 The Lost Weekend
- 47 The Best Years of Our Lives
- 48 Gentleman's Agreement
- 49 Hamlet
- 50 All the King's Men
- 51 All About Eve
- 52 An American in Paris
- 53 The Greatest Show on Earth
- 54 From Here to Eternity
- 55 On the Waterfront
- 56 Marty
- 57 Around the World in 80 Days
- 58 The Bridge on the River Kwai
- 59 Gigi
- 60 Ben-Hur
- 61 The Apartment
- 62 West Side Story
- 63 Lawrence of Arabia
- 64 Tom Jones
- 65 My Fair Lady
- 66 The Sound of Music
- 67 A Man for All Seasons
- 68 In the Heat of the Night
- 69 Oliver
- 70 Midnight Cowboy
- 71 Patton
- 72 The French Connection
- 73 The Godfather
- 74 The Sting
- 75 The Godfather, Part II
- 76 One Flew Over the Cuckoo's Nest
- 77 Rocky
- 78 Annie Hall
- 79 The Deer Hunter
- 80 Kramer vs. Kramer
- 81 Ordinary People
- 82 Chariots of Fire
- 83 Gandhi
- 84 Terms of Endearment
- 85 Amadeus
- 86 Out of Africa
- 87 Platoon
- 88 The Last Emperor
- 89 Rain Man
- 90 Driving Miss Daisy
- 91 Dances With Wolves
- 92 The Silence of the Lambs
- 93 Unforgiven
- 94 Schindler's List
- 95 Forrest Gump (3)
- 96 Braveheart
- 97 The English Patient
- 98 Titanic
- 99 Shakespeare in Love
- 00 American Beauty
- 01 Gladiator
- 02 A Beautiful Mind

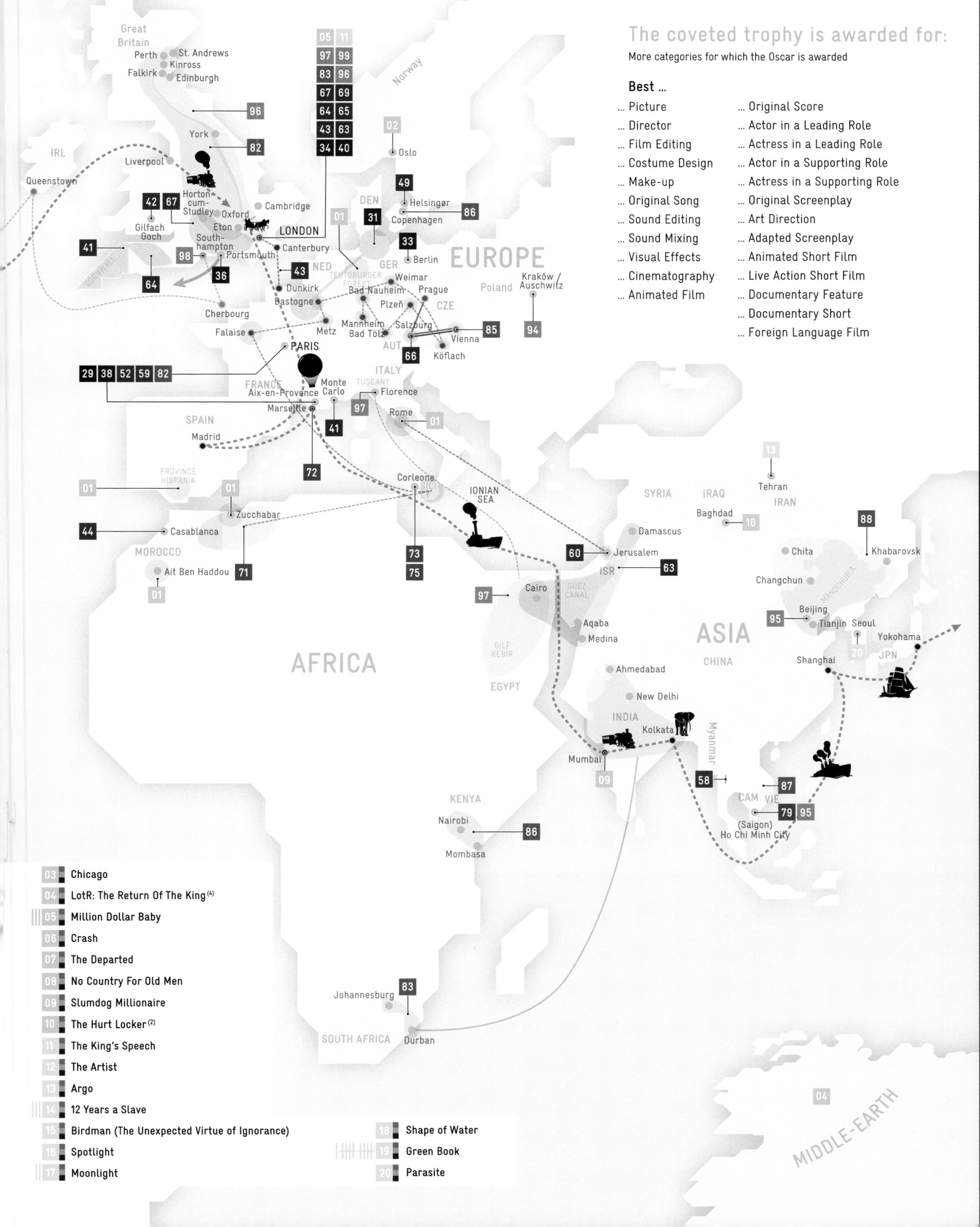

The coveted trophy is awarded for:

More categories for which the Oscar is awarded

Best ...

... Picture
... Director
... Film Editing
... Costume Design
... Make-up
... Original Song
... Sound Editing
... Sound Mixing
... Visual Effects
... Cinematography
... Animated Film
... Original Score
... Actor in a Leading Role
... Actress in a Leading Role
... Actor in a Supporting Role
... Actress in a Supporting Role
... Original Screenplay
... Art Direction
... Adapted Screenplay
... Animated Short Film
... Live Action Short Film
... Documentary Feature
... Documentary Short
... Foreign Language Film

03 Chicago
04 LotR: The Return Of The King (4)
05 Million Dollar Baby
06 Crash
07 The Departed
08 No Country For Old Men
09 Slumdog Millionaire
10 The Hurt Locker (2)
11 The King's Speech
12 The Artist
13 Argo
14 12 Years a Slave
15 Birdman (The Unexpected Virtue of Ignorance)
16 Spotlight
17 Moonlight
18 Shape of Water
19 Green Book
20 Parasite

HAPPY BIRTHDAY, MISTER SPIELBERG!

At the end of 2016, Steven Spielberg celebrated his 70th birthday. He was still a child when he started making his own movies – and there is no doubt that his work over the last four decades has influenced the whole movie industry. Our graphic shows the most successful productions he was involved in.

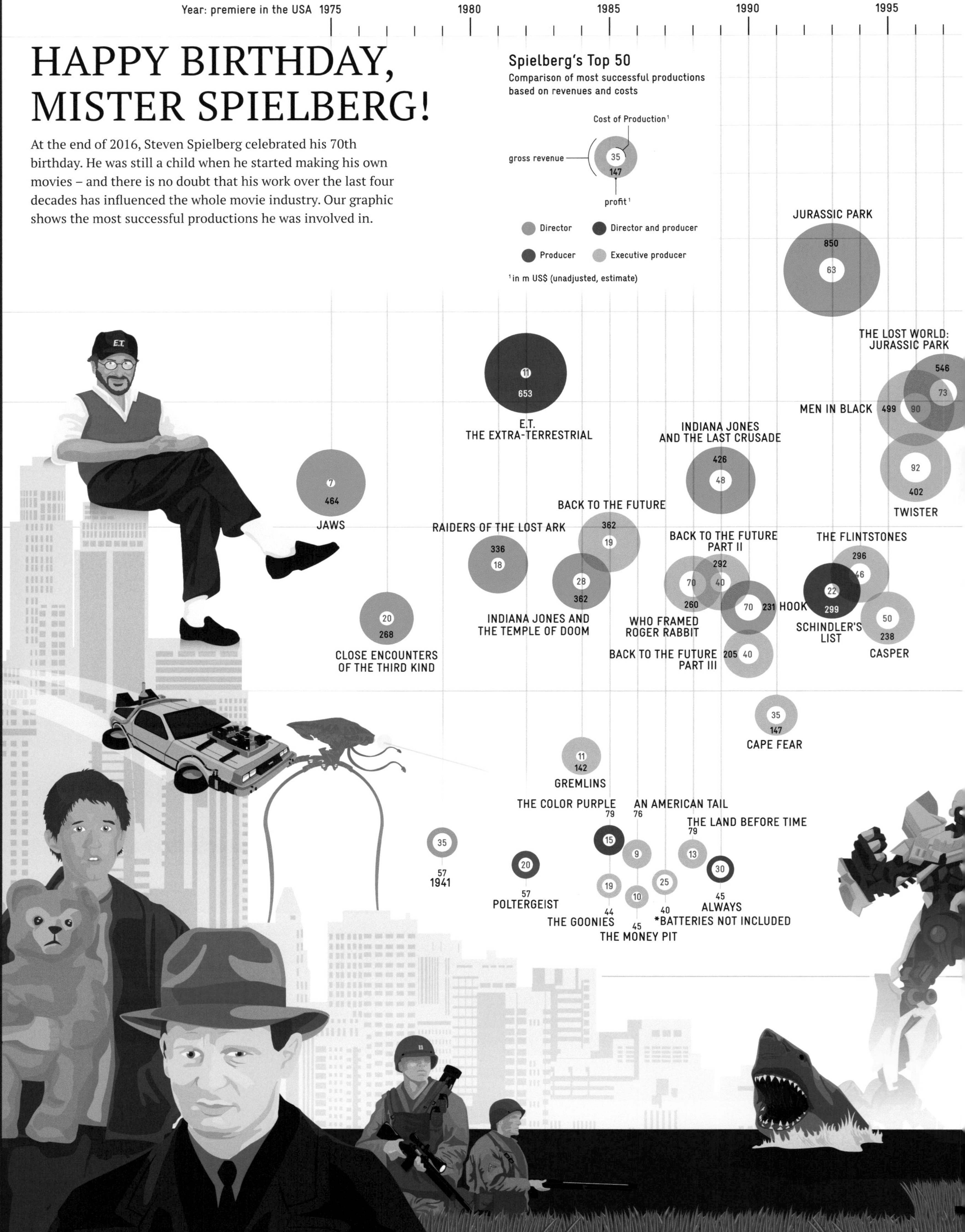
Year: premiere in the USA
1975
1980
1985
1990
1995
Spielberg's Top 50
Comparison of most successful productions based on revenues and costs
Cost of Production¹
gross revenue
35
147
profit¹
Director
Director and producer
Producer
Executive producer
¹in m US$ (unadjusted, estimate)
JURASSIC PARK 850 63
THE LOST WORLD: JURASSIC PARK 546 73
MEN IN BLACK 499 90
E.T. THE EXTRA-TERRESTRIAL 11 653
INDIANA JONES AND THE LAST CRUSADE 426 48
TWISTER 92 402
JAWS 7 464
BACK TO THE FUTURE 362 19
RAIDERS OF THE LOST ARK 336 18
BACK TO THE FUTURE PART II 292 40
THE FLINTSTONES 296 46
INDIANA JONES AND THE TEMPLE OF DOOM 28 362
WHO FRAMED ROGER RABBIT 70 260
HOOK 70 231
SCHINDLER'S LIST 22 299
CASPER 50 238
CLOSE ENCOUNTERS OF THE THIRD KIND 20 268
BACK TO THE FUTURE PART III 205 40
CAPE FEAR 35 147
GREMLINS 11 142
THE COLOR PURPLE 79 15
AN AMERICAN TAIL 76 9
THE LAND BEFORE TIME 79 13
1941 35 57
POLTERGEIST 20 57
THE GOONIES 19 44
THE MONEY PIT 10 45
*BATTERIES NOT INCLUDED 25 40
ALWAYS 30 45

2000
2005
2010
2015
Revenue in m US$
1,800
1,600
1,400
1,200
1,000
800
400
200
0
JURASSIC WORLD 1,520 150
TRANSFORMERS: DARK OF THE MOON
929
195
210
894
170
1,138
JURASSIC WORLD: FALLEN KINGDOM
TRANSFORMERS: AGE OF EXTINCTION
INDIANA JONES AND THE KINGDOM OF THE CRYSTAL SKULL
606
185
200
636 TRANSFORMERS: REVENGE OF THE FALLEN
TRANSFORMERS 460 150
TRANSFORMERS: THE LAST KNIGHT
388
217
175 408 READY PLAYER ONE
225
399
MEN IN BLACK II
132
472
WAR OF THE WORLDS
225
399
MEN IN BLACK 3
SAVING PRIVATE RYAN
412
70
JURASSIC PARK III
276
93
135
333
BUMBLEBEE
THE ADVENTURE OF TINTIN: SECRET OF THE UNICORN
239
135
MINORITY REPORT
256
102
52
100
249
DEEP IMPACT
300
CATCH ME IF YOU CAN
MEN IN BLACK: INTERNATIONAL
144
110
REAL STEEL 189 110
65 210 LINCOLN
TRUE GRIT 214 38
50
210
SUPER 8
95
67
THE MASK OF ZORRO
100
136
A.I. ARTIFICIAL INTELLIGENCE
THE TERMINAL
159
60
THE BFG
55
140
50
130
THE POST
MEMOIRS OF A GEISHA
77
EAGLE EYE
99
80
WAR HORSE
112
66
12
163
COWBOYS & ALIENS
85
THE LEGEND OF ZORRO
67
75
75
MONSTER HOUSE
67
70
61
MUNICH
20
98
DISTURBIA
40
125
BRIDGE OF SPIES
50
57
HEREAFTER
22
68
THE HUNDRED-FOOT JOURNEY
59
47
FIRST MAN
19
98
LETTERS FROM IWO JIMA

JAMES BOND

What would the state of the world be without a dashing MI6 agent to rescue us over and over again? Thankfully, we'll never have to know thanks to Bond – James Bond – with his code number 007. Despite his work as a double-0 agent, he's managed to survive for more than 50 years. Neither the Cold War nor the political and economic state of the world have been able to stop him yet. Here, we wish to offer him our thanks – with a breakdown of all the places he's been, his balance sheet of victims, his vehicles and, of course, his lovers – film by film.

as of 2012

Killed by Bond and others
- Bullets
- Explosives
- Mass mortality
- Bites, stings, poison
- Heat, freezing or sharp objects
- Other causes

Shots fired by Bond
- Pistol
- Submachine gun
- Rifle
- Missile
- Others

Explosions
- Headquarters
- Others

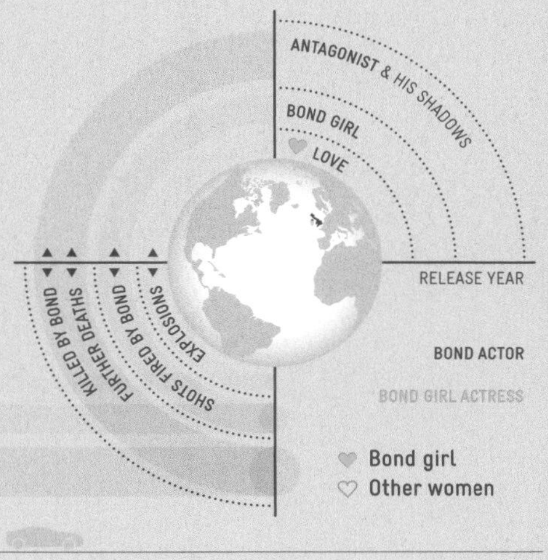
ANTAGONIST & HIS SHADOWS
BOND GIRL
LOVE
RELEASE YEAR
BOND ACTOR
BOND GIRL ACTRESS
EXPLOSIONS
SHOTS FIRED BY BOND
FURTHER DEATHS
KILLED BY BOND
SHOTS
DEATH
BOND'S MOVEMENT PROFILE
Bond girl
Other women

01 Dr. No

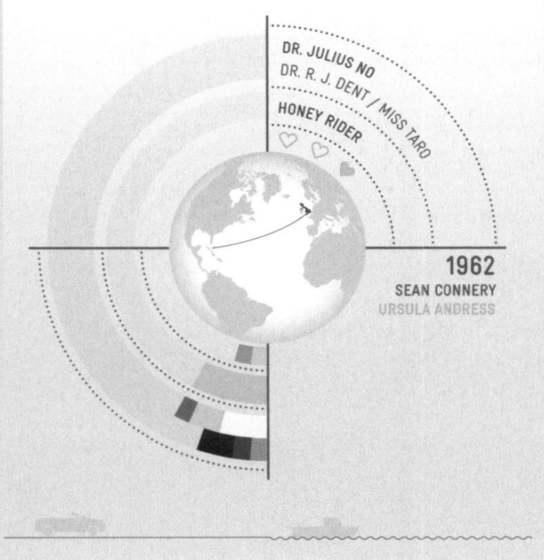
DR. JULIUS NO
DR. R. J. DENT / MISS TARO
HONEY RIDER
1962
SEAN CONNERY
URSULA ANDRESS

02 From Russia with Love

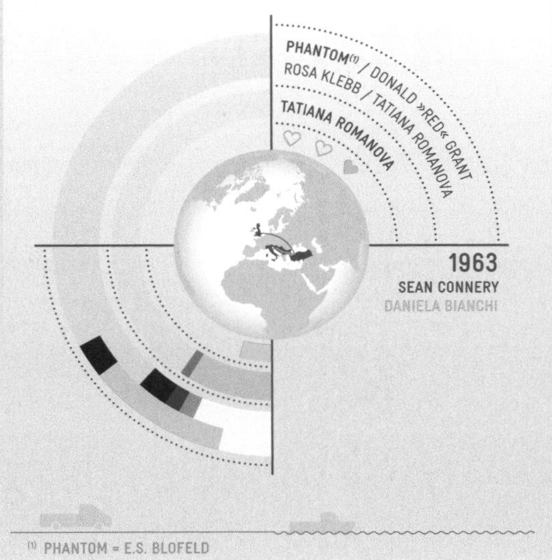
PHANTOM(1) / DONALD »RED« GRANT
ROSA KLEBB / TATIANA ROMANOVA
TATIANA ROMANOVA
1963
SEAN CONNERY
DANIELA BIANCHI

(1) PHANTOM = E.S. BLOFELD

03 Goldfinger

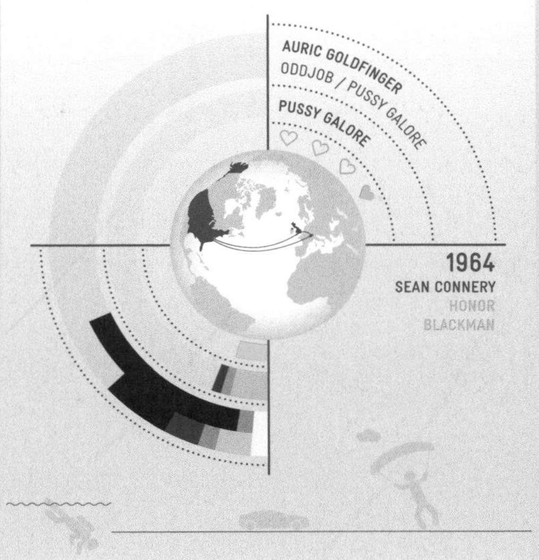
AURIC GOLDFINGER
ODDJOB / PUSSY GALORE
PUSSY GALORE
1964
SEAN CONNERY
HONOR
BLACKMAN

04 Thunderball

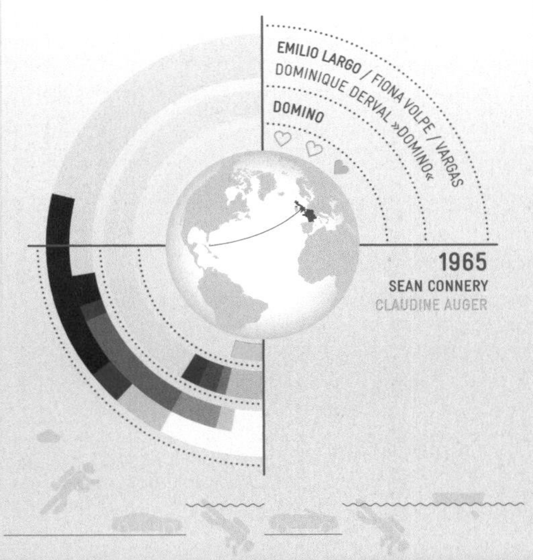
EMILIO LARGO / FIONA VOLPE / VARGAS
DOMINIQUE DERVAL »DOMINO«
DOMINO
1965
SEAN CONNERY
CLAUDINE AUGER

05 You Only Live Twice

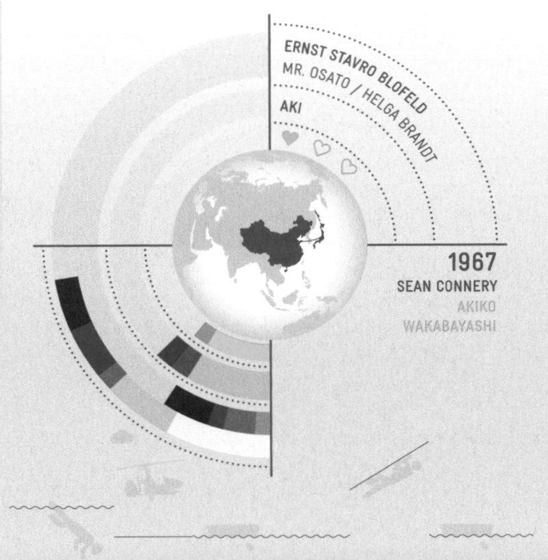
ERNST STAVRO BLOFELD
MR. OSATO / HELGA BRANDT
AKI
1967
SEAN CONNERY
AKIKO
WAKABAYASHI

06 On Her Majesty's Secret Service

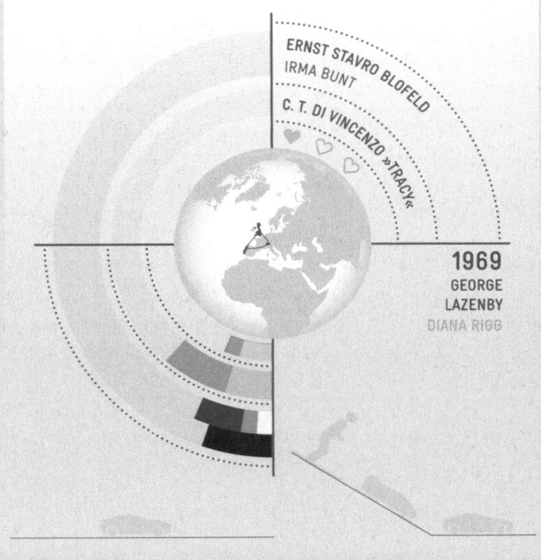
ERNST STAVRO BLOFELD
IRMA BUNT
C. T. DI VINCENZO »TRACY«
1969
GEORGE
LAZENBY
DIANA RIGG

TIMELINE

Sean Connery embodied the first James Bond in 1962, developing the role like no other actor. His successors broke some of the traditions he initiated, while others are maintained until today.

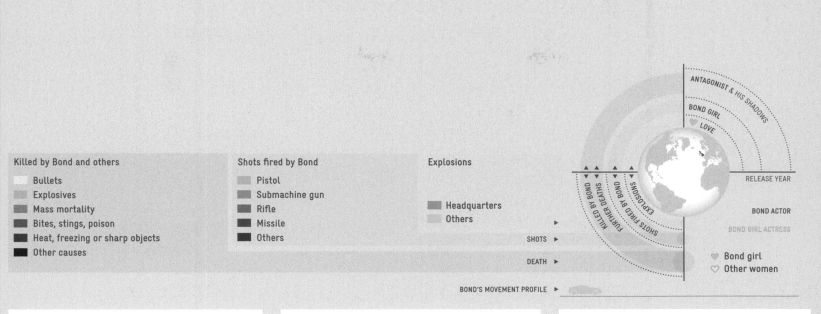

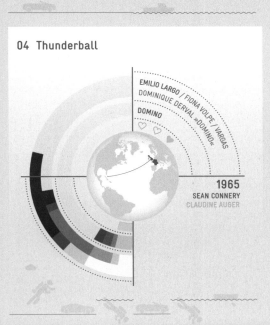

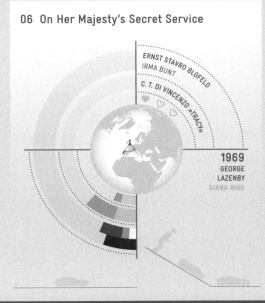

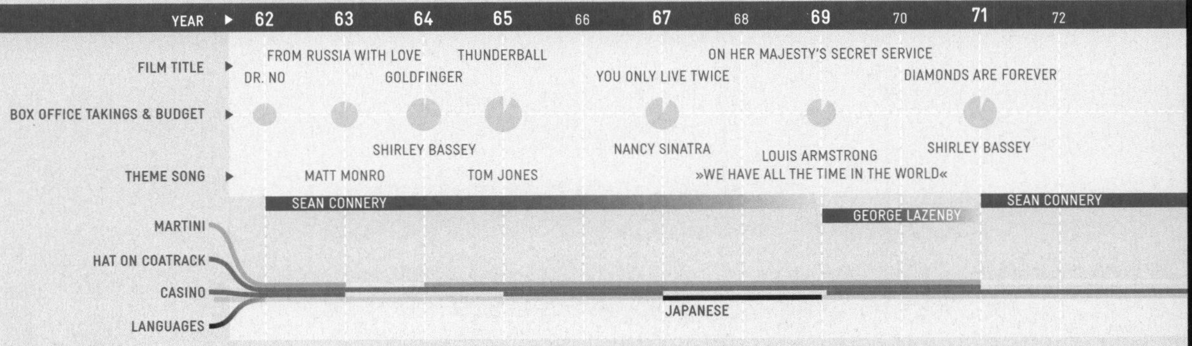
YEAR
62
63
64
65
66
67
68
69
70
71
72
FILM TITLE
DR. NO
FROM RUSSIA WITH LOVE
GOLDFINGER
THUNDERBALL
YOU ONLY LIVE TWICE
ON HER MAJESTY'S SECRET SERVICE
DIAMONDS ARE FOREVER
BOX OFFICE TAKINGS & BUDGET
THEME SONG
MATT MONRO
SHIRLEY BASSEY
TOM JONES
NANCY SINATRA
LOUIS ARMSTRONG
»WE HAVE ALL THE TIME IN THE WORLD«
SHIRLEY BASSEY
SEAN CONNERY
GEORGE LAZENBY
SEAN CONNERY
MARTINI
HAT ON COATRACK
CASINO
LANGUAGES
JAPANESE

07 Diamonds Are Forever

E. S. BLOFELD / MR. WINT & MR. KIDD
PROF. DR. METZ / TIFFANY CASE
TIFFANY CASE
1971
SEAN CONNERY
JILL ST. JOHN

08 Live and Let Die

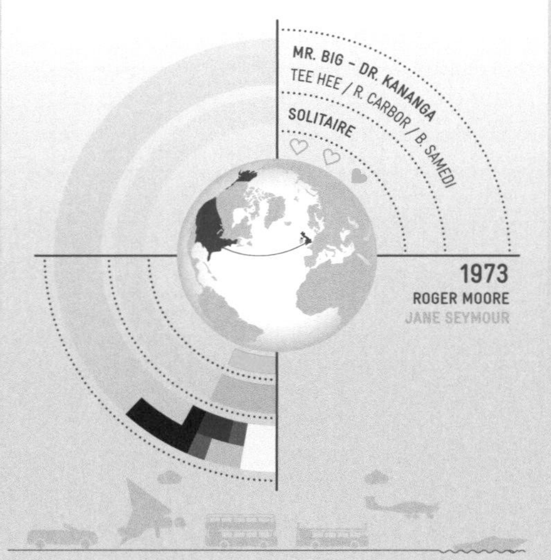
MR. BIG – DR. KANANGA
TEE HEE / R. CARBOR / B. SAMEDI
SOLITAIRE
1973
ROGER MOORE
JANE SEYMOUR

09 The Man with the Golden Gun

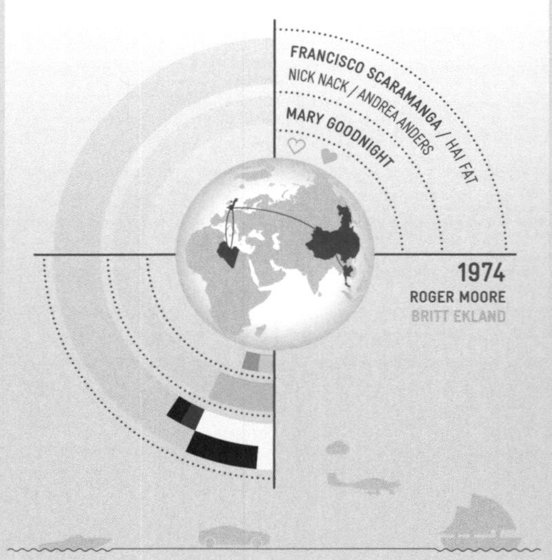
FRANCISCO SCARAMANGA / HAI FAT
NICK NACK / ANDREA ANDERS
MARY GOODNIGHT
1974
ROGER MOORE
BRITT EKLAND

13 Octopussy

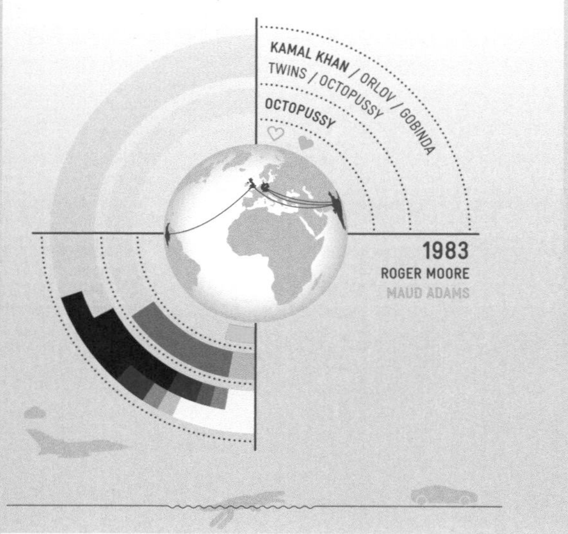
KAMAL KHAN / ORLOV / GOBINDA
TWINS / OCTOPUSSY
OCTOPUSSY
1983
ROGER MOORE
MAUD ADAMS

14 A View to a Kill

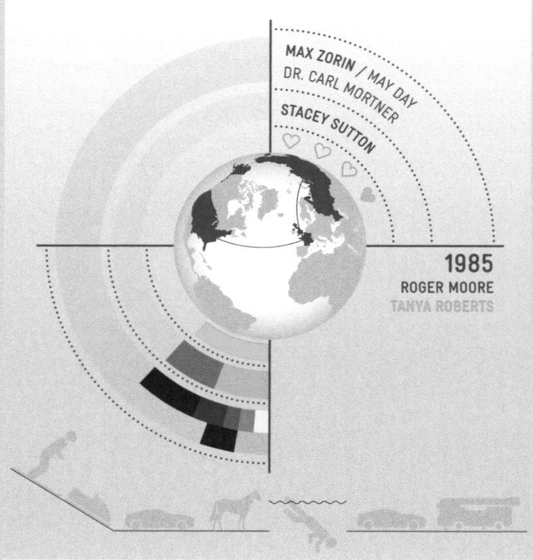
MAX ZORIN / MAY DAY
DR. CARL MORTNER
STACEY SUTTON
1985
ROGER MOORE
TANYA ROBERTS

15 The Living Daylights

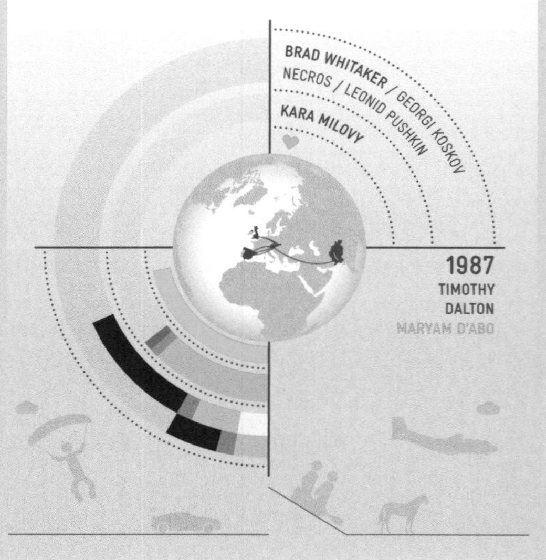
BRAD WHITAKER / GEORGI KOSKOV
NECROS / LEONID PUSHKIN
KARA MILOVY
1987
TIMOTHY
DALTON
MARYAM D'ABO

19 The World Is Not Enough

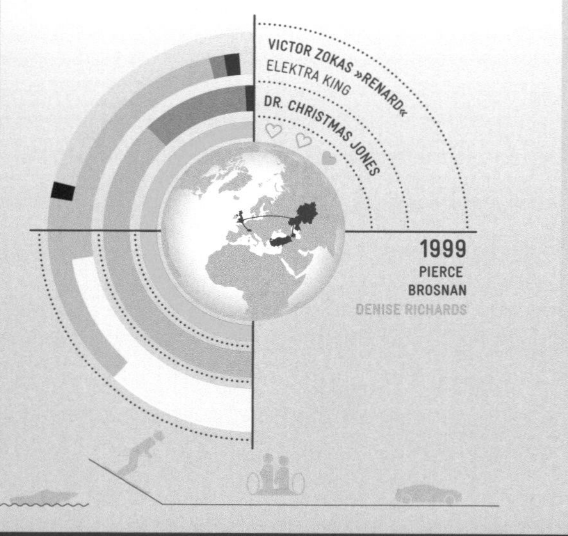
VICTOR ZOKAS »RENARD«
ELEKTRA KING
DR. CHRISTMAS JONES
1999
PIERCE
BROSNAN
DENISE RICHARDS

20 Die Another Day

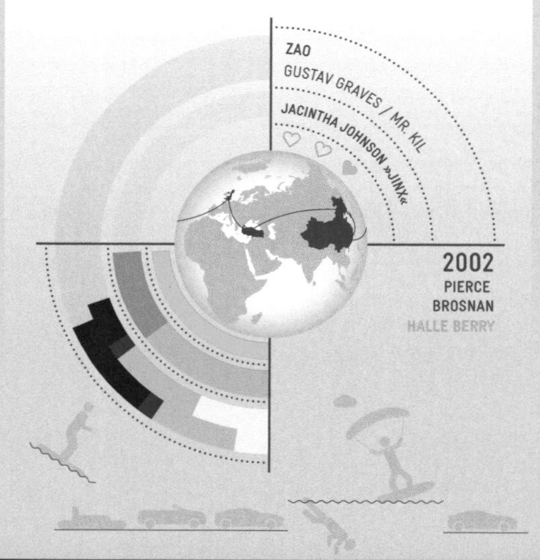
ZAO
GUSTAV GRAVES / MR. KIL
JACINTHA JOHNSON »JINX«
2002
PIERCE
BROSNAN
HALLE BERRY

21 Casino Royale

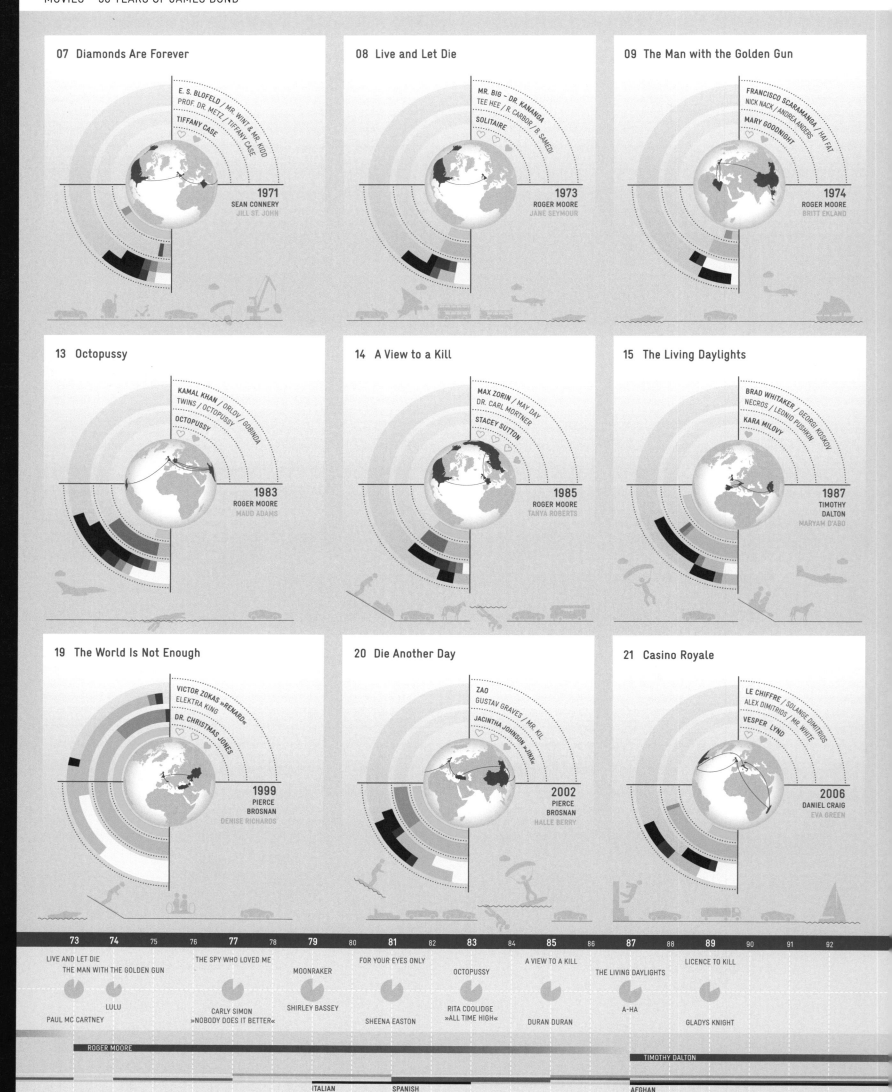

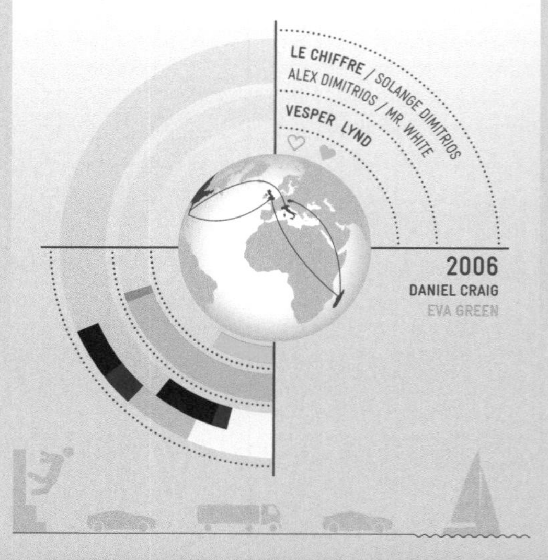
LE CHIFFRE / SOLANGE DIMITRIOS
ALEX DIMITRIOS / MR. WHITE
VESPER LYND
2006
DANIEL CRAIG
EVA GREEN

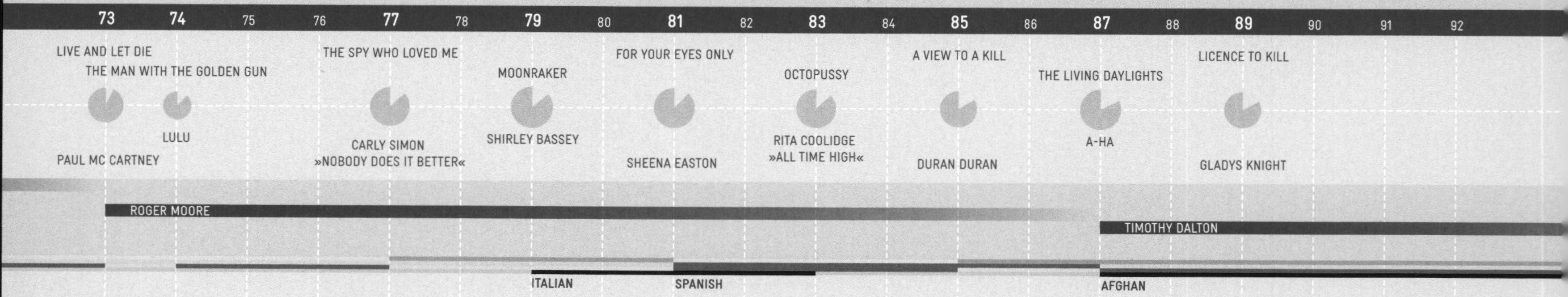
73
74
75
76
77
78
79
80
81
82
83
84
85
86
87
88
89
90
91
92
LIVE AND LET DIE
THE MAN WITH THE GOLDEN GUN
THE SPY WHO LOVED ME
MOONRAKER
FOR YOUR EYES ONLY
OCTOPUSSY
A VIEW TO A KILL
THE LIVING DAYLIGHTS
LICENCE TO KILL
LULU
PAUL MC CARTNEY
CARLY SIMON
»NOBODY DOES IT BETTER«
SHIRLEY BASSEY
SHEENA EASTON
RITA COOLIDGE
»ALL TIME HIGH«
DURAN DURAN
A-HA
GLADYS KNIGHT
ROGER MOORE
TIMOTHY DALTON
ITALIAN
SPANISH
AFGHAN

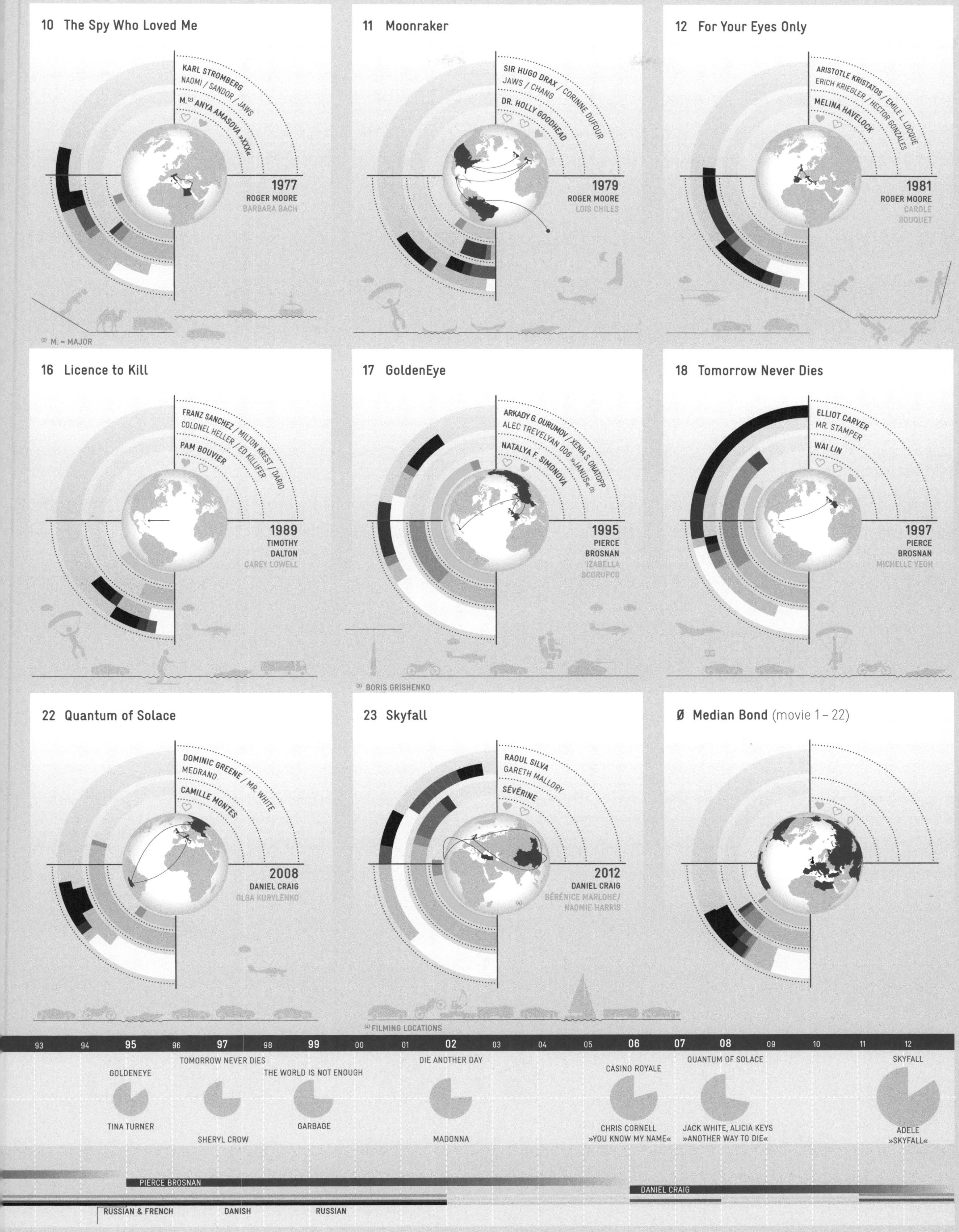
10 The Spy Who Loved Me
KARL STROMBERG
NAOMI / SANDOR / JAWS
M.(2) ANYA AMASOVA »XXX«
1977
ROGER MOORE
BARBARA BACH
(2) M. = MAJOR
11 Moonraker
SIR HUGO DRAX / CORINNE DUFOUR
JAWS / CHANG
DR. HOLLY GOODHEAD
1979
ROGER MOORE
LOIS CHILES
12 For Your Eyes Only
ARISTOTLE KRISTATOS / EMILE L. LOCQUE
ERICH KRIEGLER / HECTOR GONZALES
MELINA HAVELOCK
1981
ROGER MOORE
CAROLE BOUQUET
16 Licence to Kill
FRANZ SANCHEZ / MILTON KREST / DARIO
COLONEL HELLER / ED KILLIFER
PAM BOUVIER
1989
TIMOTHY DALTON
CAREY LOWELL
17 GoldenEye
ARKADY G. OURUMOV / XENIA S. ONATOPP
ALEC TREVELYAN 006 »JANUS«(3)
NATALYA F. SIMONOVA
1995
PIERCE BROSNAN
IZABELLA SCORUPCO
(3) BORIS GRISHENKO
18 Tomorrow Never Dies
ELLIOT CARVER
MR. STAMPER
WAI LIN
1997
PIERCE BROSNAN
MICHELLE YEOH
22 Quantum of Solace
DOMINIC GREENE / MR. WHITE
MEDRANO
CAMILLE MONTES
2008
DANIEL CRAIG
OLGA KURYLENKO
23 Skyfall
RAOUL SILVA
GARETH MALLORY
SÉVÉRINE
2012
DANIEL CRAIG
BÉRÉNICE MARLOHE/ NAOMIE HARRIS
(4) FILMING LOCATIONS
Ø Median Bond (movie 1 – 22)
93 94 95 96 97 98 99 00 01 02 03 04 05 06 07 08 09 10 11 12
GOLDENEYE
TINA TURNER
TOMORROW NEVER DIES
SHERYL CROW
THE WORLD IS NOT ENOUGH
GARBAGE
DIE ANOTHER DAY
MADONNA
CASINO ROYALE
CHRIS CORNELL »YOU KNOW MY NAME«
QUANTUM OF SOLACE
JACK WHITE, ALICIA KEYS »ANOTHER WAY TO DIE«
SKYFALL
ADELE »SKYFALL«
PIERCE BROSNAN
DANIEL CRAIG
RUSSIAN & FRENCH
DANISH
RUSSIAN

BANG BANG HE SHOT 'EM DEAD

Hollywood's ingenious director, screenwriter, producer, and actor Quentin Tarantino killed more people on screen by gunfire than by any other killing method. We have produced a balance sheet of the films he has directed to-date, including the number of victims and the weapons used.

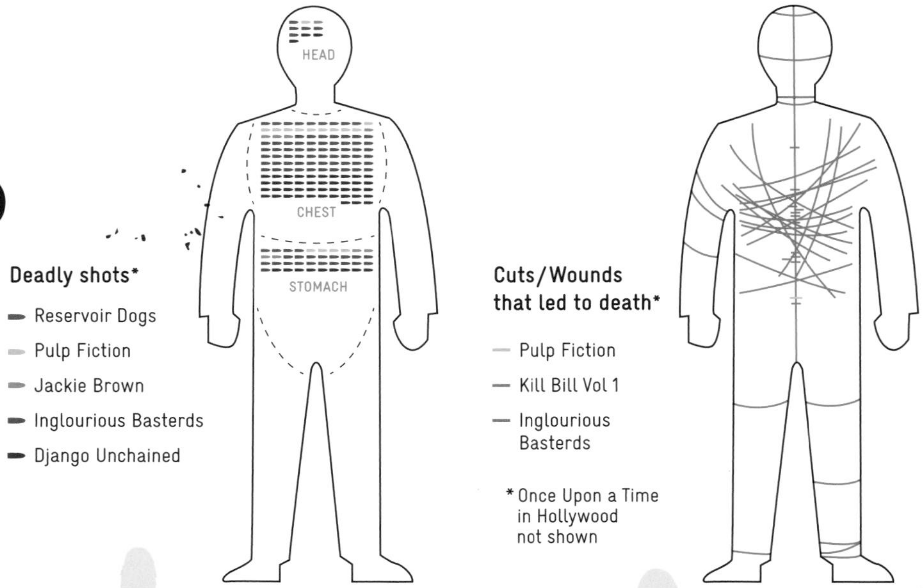
Deadly shots*
Reservoir Dogs
Pulp Fiction
Jackie Brown
Inglourious Basterds
Django Unchained
HEAD
CHEST
STOMACH
Cuts/Wounds that led to death*
Pulp Fiction
Kill Bill Vol 1
Inglourious Basterds
* Once Upon a Time in Hollywood not shown

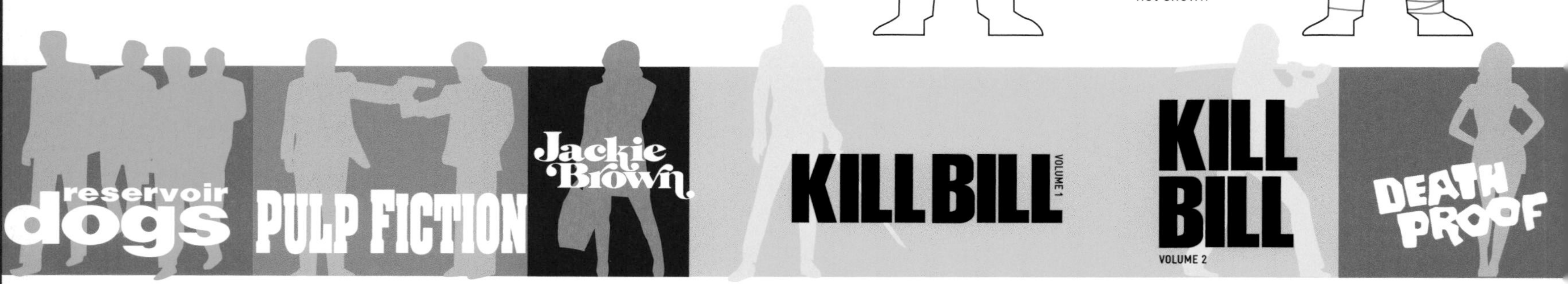
reservoir dogs
PULP FICTION
Jackie Brown
KILL BILL VOLUME 1
KILL BILL VOLUME 2
DEATH PROOF

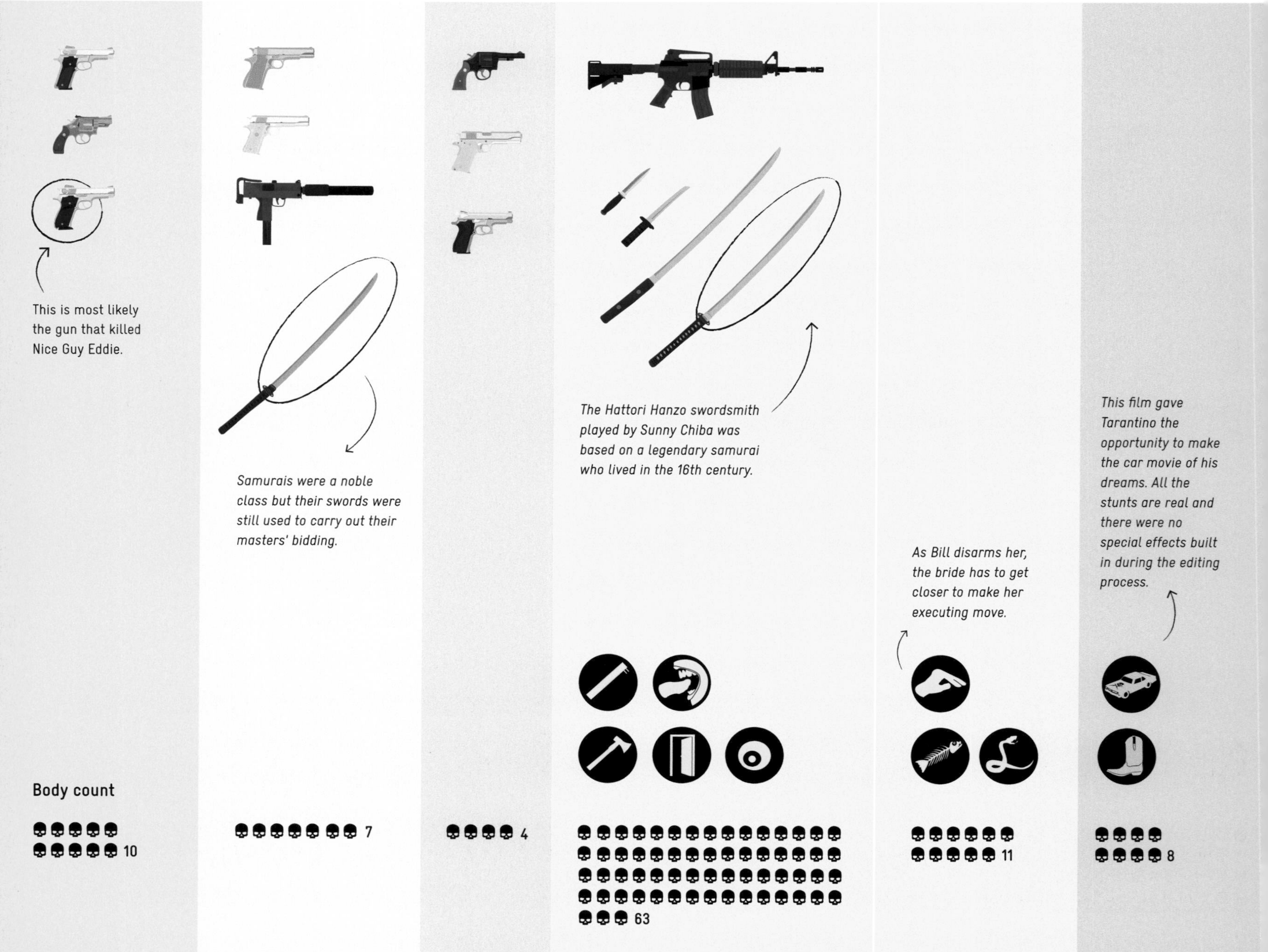
This is most likely the gun that killed Nice Guy Eddie.
Samurais were a noble class but their swords were still used to carry out their masters' bidding.
The Hattori Hanzo swordsmith played by Sunny Chiba was based on a legendary samurai who lived in the 16th century.
As Bill disarms her, the bride has to get closer to make her executing move.
This film gave Tarantino the opportunity to make the car movie of his dreams. All the stunts are real and there were no special effects built in during the editing process.
Body count
10
7
4
63
11
8

More weapons/methods

- Bitten tongue
- Car accident
- Gouging out of an eye
- Baseball bat
- Axe
- Dog bite
- Crushed in a door frame
- Kicked to death
- Snakebite
- Explosion
- Strangulation
- Hanging
- Beaten up with a table leg
- Fist
- Poisoned fish
- Hammer
- Five point palm exploding heart technique
- Poisoned coffee
- Flamethrower

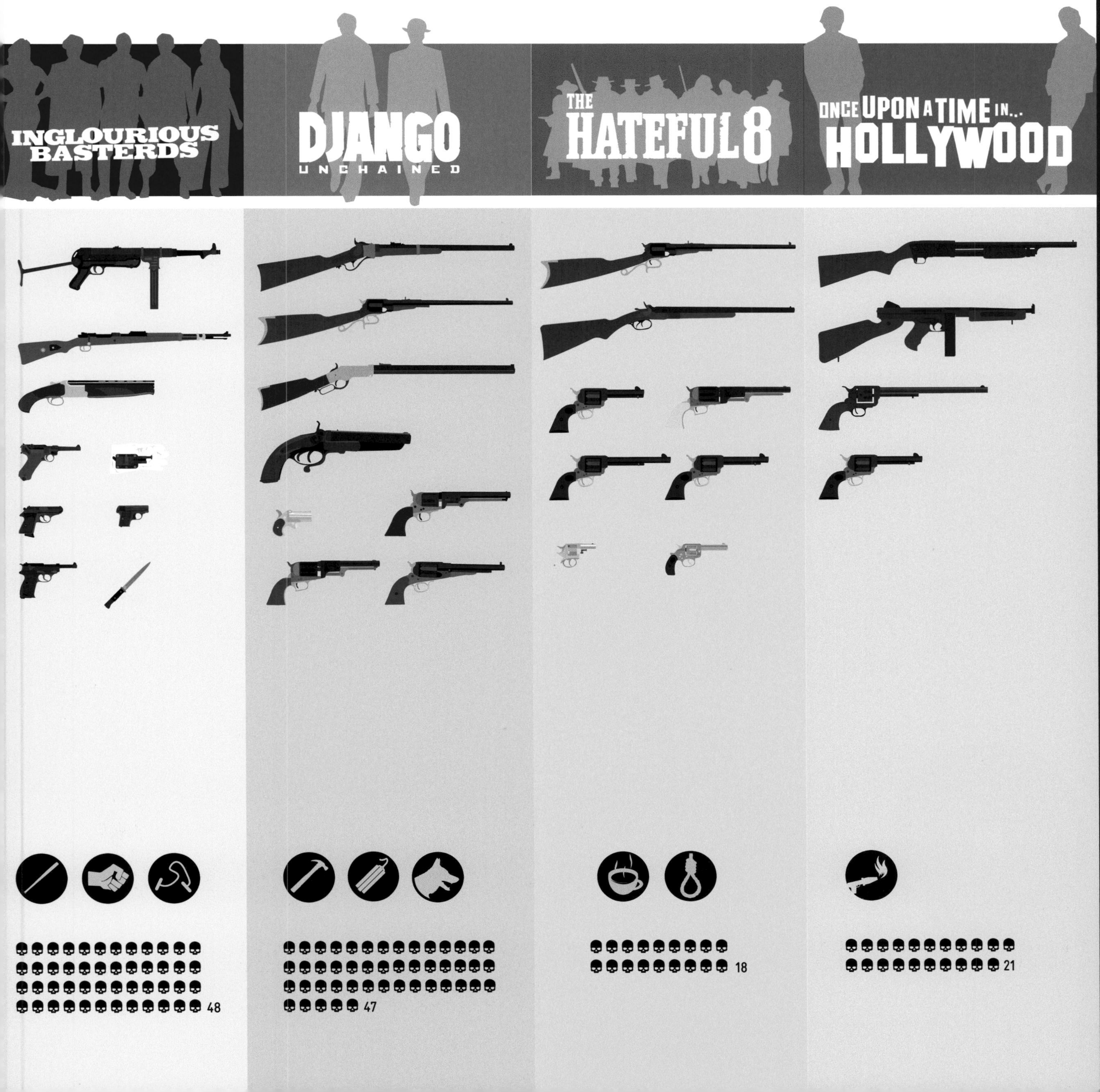
INGLOURIOUS BASTERDS
DJANGO UNCHAINED
THE HATEFUL 8
ONCE UPON A TIME IN... HOLLYWOOD
48
47
18
21

CINEMANIMALS

Animal actors have been drawing audiences into cinemas for decades. The chart shows the leading box office successes with one or several animals in the leading roles. All the movies with animals included here have little or no animation.

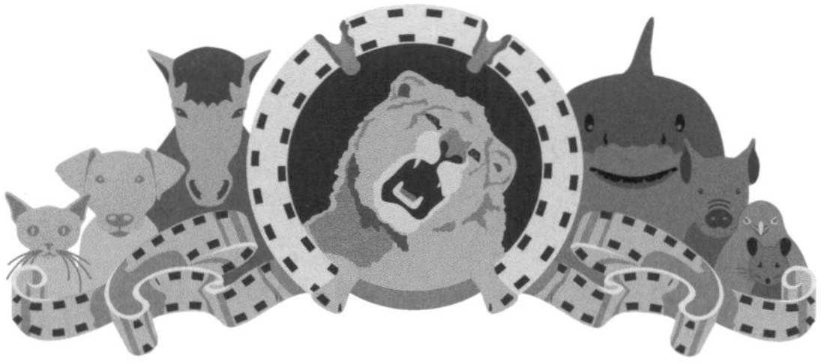

Animal heroes on screen

Top 40

Comparison of costs and revenues of the most successful productions worldwide

- Dogs & cats
- Hoofed animals
- Marine mammals & fish
- Pigs
- Birds
- Mice

as of 2011

Year: Premiere in the US

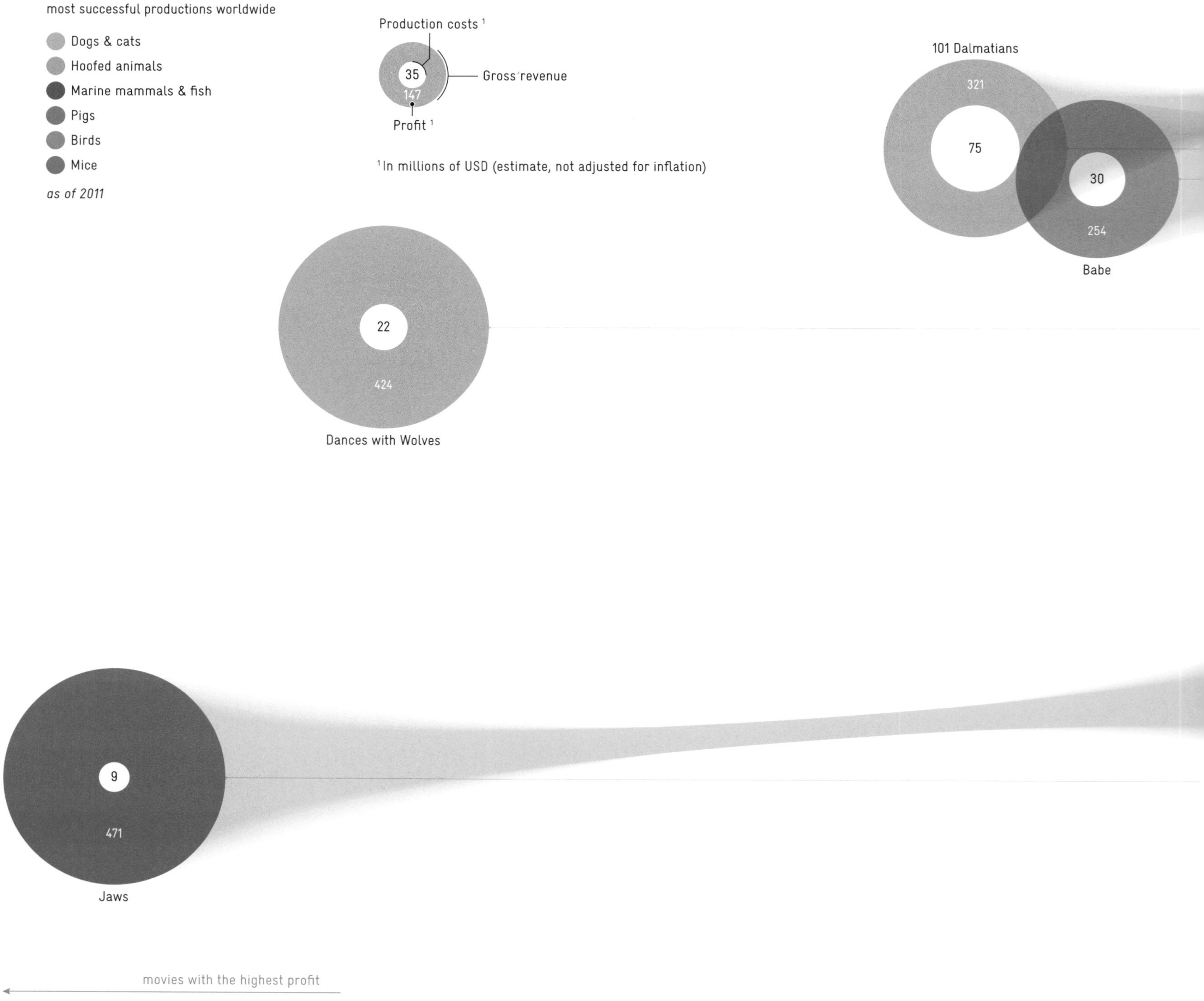
Production costs ¹
35
147
Gross revenue
Profit ¹
101 Dalmatians
321
75
30
254
Babe
22
424
Dances with Wolves
9
471
Jaws
movies with the highest profit

¹ In millions of USD (estimate, not adjusted for inflation)

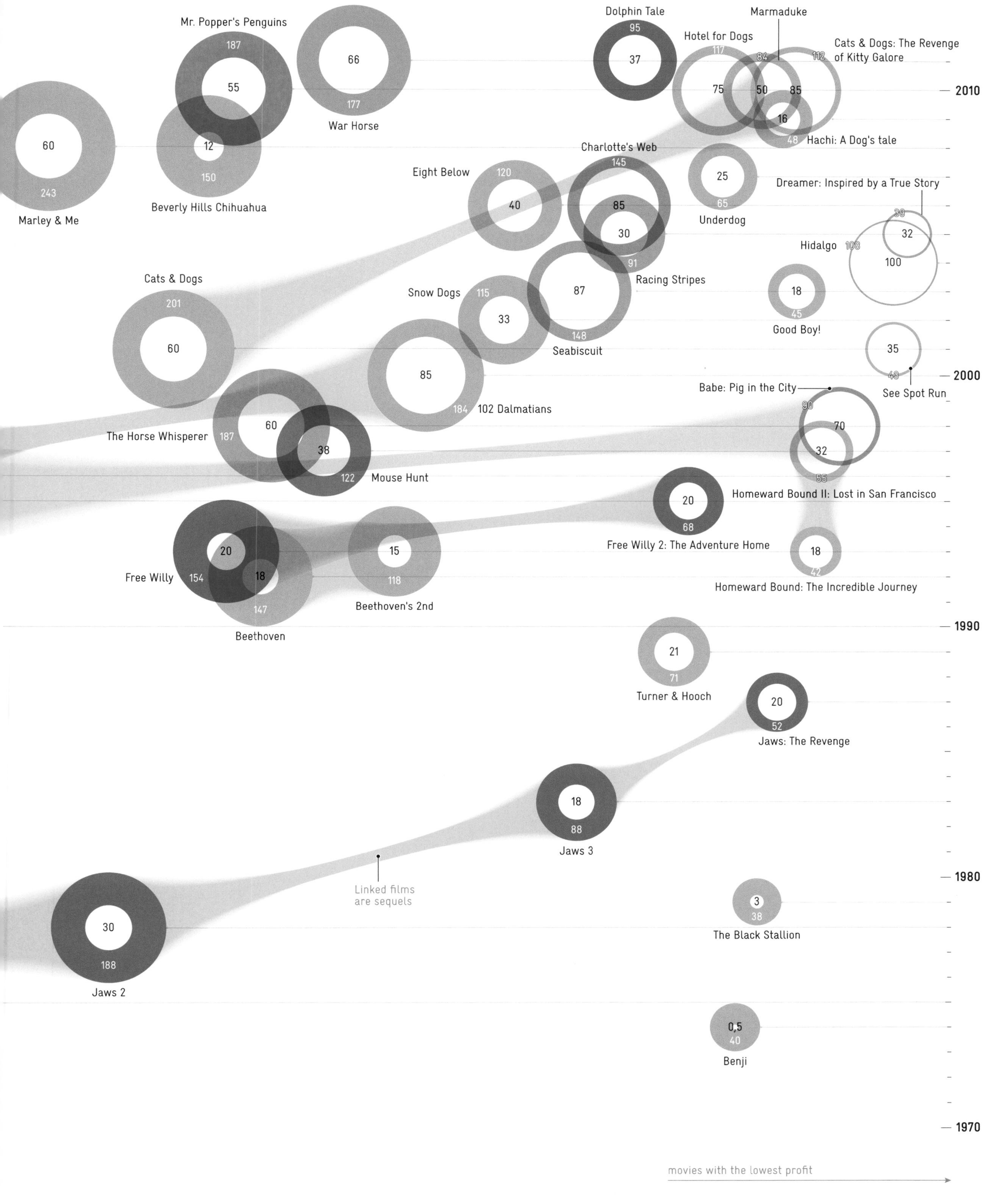

Mr. Popper's Penguins
187
55
66
177
War Horse
60
243
Marley & Me
12
150
Beverly Hills Chihuahua
Dolphin Tale
95
37
Hotel for Dogs
117
75
Marmaduke
84
50
Cats & Dogs: The Revenge of Kitty Galore
112
85
16
48
Hachi: A Dog's tale
— 2010
Charlotte's Web
145
85
Eight Below
120
40
25
65
Underdog
Dreamer: Inspired by a True Story
39
32
Hidalgo
103
100
30
91
Racing Stripes
Cats & Dogs
201
60
Snow Dogs
115
33
87
148
Seabiscuit
18
45
Good Boy!
35
43
See Spot Run
— 2000
Babe: Pig in the City
90
70
85
184
102 Dalmatians
60
187
The Horse Whisperer
38
122
Mouse Hunt
32
55
Homeward Bound II: Lost in San Francisco
20
68
Free Willy 2: The Adventure Home
20
154
Free Willy
18
147
Beethoven
15
118
Beethoven's 2nd
18
42
Homeward Bound: The Incredible Journey
— 1990
21
71
Turner & Hooch
20
52
Jaws: The Revenge
18
88
Jaws 3
— 1980
Linked films are sequels
30
188
Jaws 2
3
38
The Black Stallion
0,5
40
Benji
— 1970
movies with the lowest profit

THE GOOD, THE BAD AND THE UGLY

At the beginning of the 1960s, young Italian writers and directors created a new genre: the Spaghetti Western. In contrast to the classic American western, the Italian western did away with the notion of a good and wholesome world. Its heroes are cynical, grim characters who are only interested in money or personal revenge. Nevertheless, the hero here is the incarnation of goodness: he still acts in a more moral way than the rest of his world, which always surpasses him when it come to vicious behavior. Right up to the end, movies of this genre keep up the tension as to whether »the good« will win. This graphic shows an analysis of six movies that have shaped the genre.

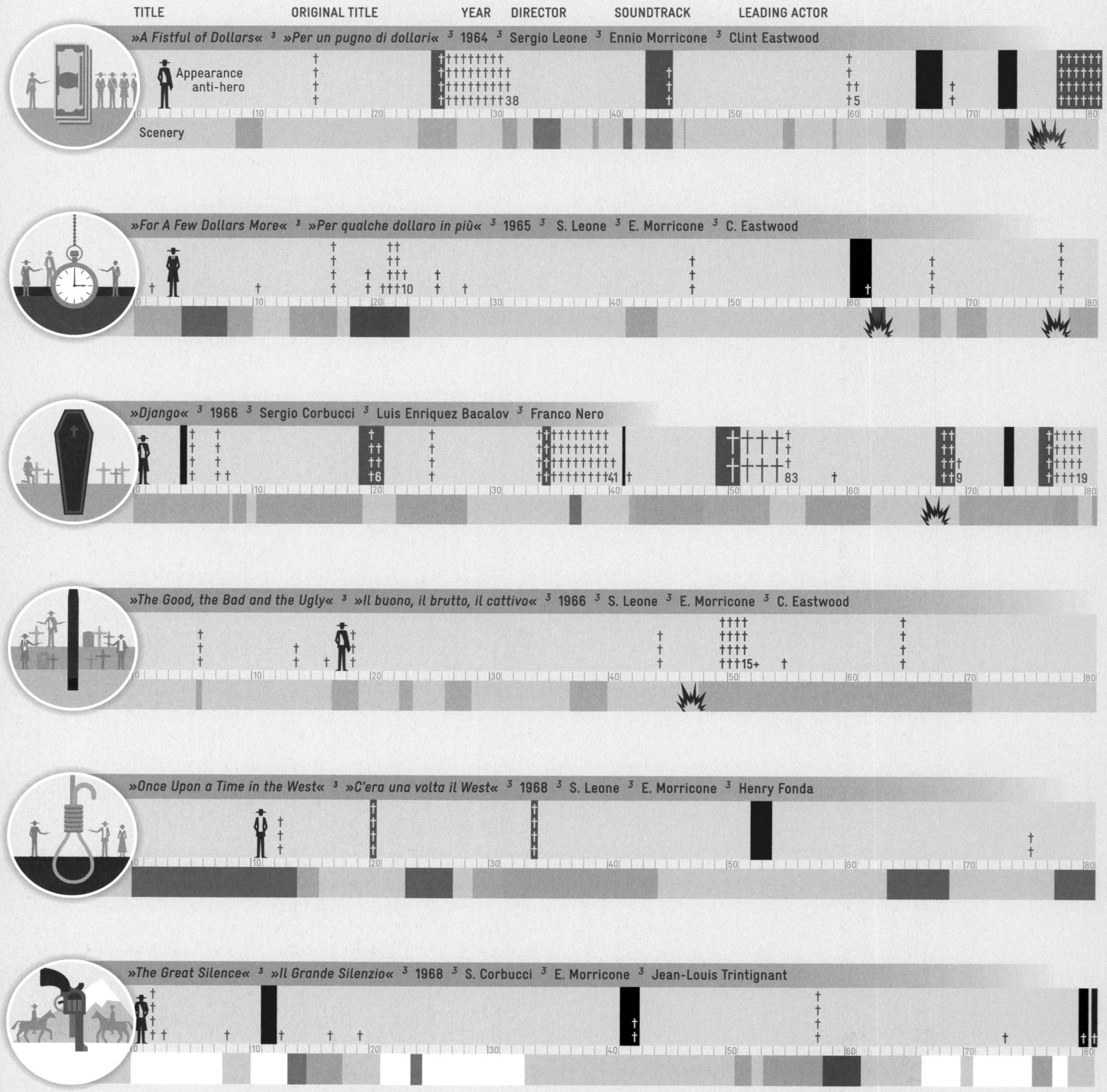

Spaghetti Western Scenery

The scenery plays a vital role in creating a Italian western's sinister atmosphere.

- Western city (interior and exterior)
- Saloon, tavern, bar
- Desert, prairie
- Cemetery
- Mine
- Train, station
- Prison
- Snow

SPAGHETTI WESTERN ARCHETYPES

The anti hero
A bad guy with whom the viewer can identify during the course of the story.

His primary motive
The anti hero's actions are based on very banal, primitive reasons such as revenge or greed for money.

- Flashback
- Dead people during flashback

Atmosphere
Sinister, dusty atmospheres with wind, fog and sandstorms shape Italian westerns.

Brutality
Brutality is an important stylistic element.

- Torture scene
- Shoot-out
- People killed by shooting
- People killed off-screen or by any other method of killing

Explosion
Powerful explosions are part of the cinematic language.

Final showdown
Suspense is maintained to an almost unbearable degree by conspicuously long close-ups.

- Final showdown
- People killed during showdown

The end
The end is often unexpected and surprising because goodies don't always win.

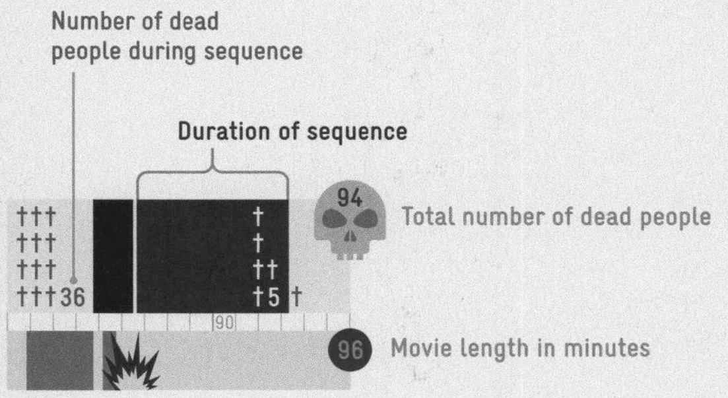
Number of dead people during sequence
Duration of sequence
36
5
94
Total number of dead people
90
96
Movie length in minutes

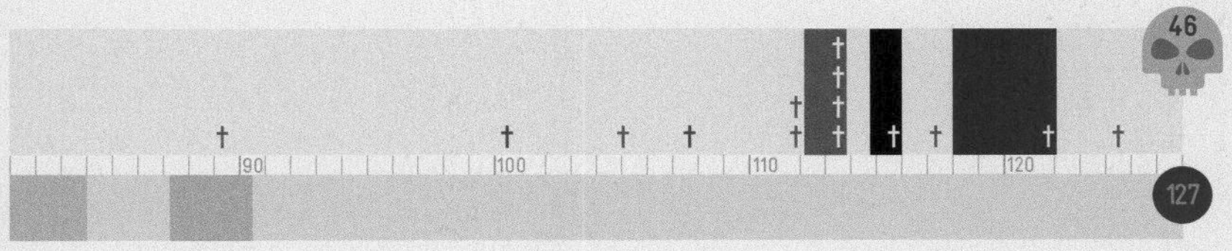

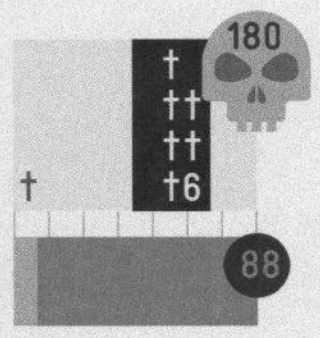
180
6
88

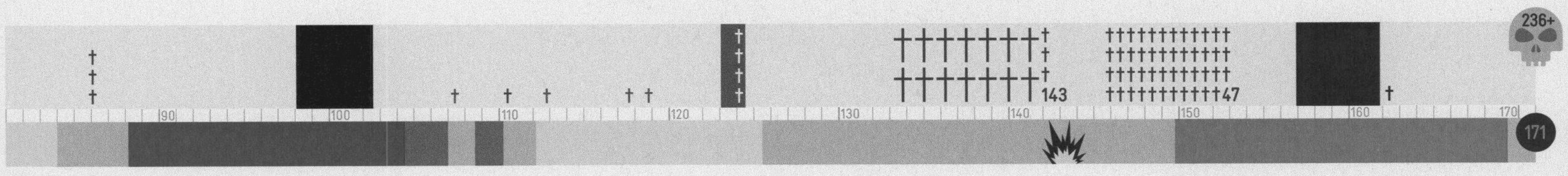

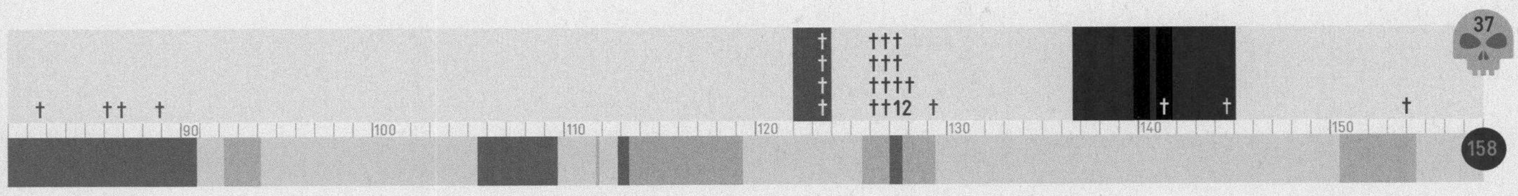

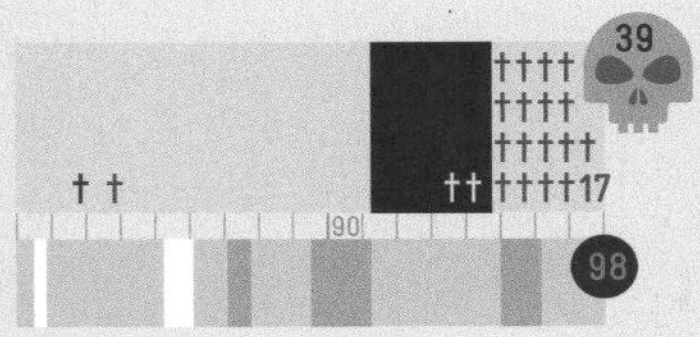

COFFIN MAKER
SALOON

REALISM

COMPANIES
ORGANISATIONS & GROUPS
SCHOOLS
SECESSION: Modernist artist groups that separated themselves from the support of official academic art and its administrations

EMIGRATION
CLOSING/LIQUIDATION
IMPORTANT INFLUENCES

DEATH

YEAR
MILESTONE
LOCATION

KLEUKENS
Friedrich Kleukens (*1878 †1956)

GERMAN MODERNISM

German Modernism originates from the end of the 19th century with artists from Darmstadt and Vienna. Driven by bold, creative people, it spanned the period from the start of the German Empire through to the end of the Second World War, taking in the First World War, the Weimar Republic and National Socialism along the way. The web of inspiration spun by graphic artists, artists and architects formed today's industrial society. Russian constructivism and the American architect Frank Lloyd Wright had a particularly significant influence on German art and design. To this day, the ghosts of German modernism are still to be found in graphic design, corporate identity and visual communication. Even Apple would be unrecognisable today without Dieter Rams' design work. Modernism was a movement of architects, industrial designers, graphic artists and typographers, all of whom you can meet in this graphic.

ERNST
1892–1918: Grand Duke of Hesse and by the Rhine Ernst Ludwig (*1868 †1937)

PETER
Peter Behrens (*1868 †1940)

→ Johnston
Edward Johnston (*1872 †1944)

Name in mixed type: influence from foreign country

1859
THONET CHAIR
CHAIR NO. 14
VIENNA

The first chair designed for self-assembly and global delivery. All joints are screwed together instead of requiring adhesives.

OLBRICH
Joseph Olbrich (*1867 †1908)

POELZIG
Hans Poelzig (*1869 †1936)

Wagner
Otto Wagner (*1841 †1918)

Frank
Frank Lloyd Wright (*1867 †1959)

»We were dominated by a sense of restlessness and lack of satisfaction around 1890.« van de Velde
Henry van de Velde (*1863 †1957)

Thonet
Michael Thonet (*1796 †1871)

Schinkel
Karl Friedrich Schinkel (*1781 †1841)

1832–36
BAUAKADEMIE
BERLIN

First serial functional construction

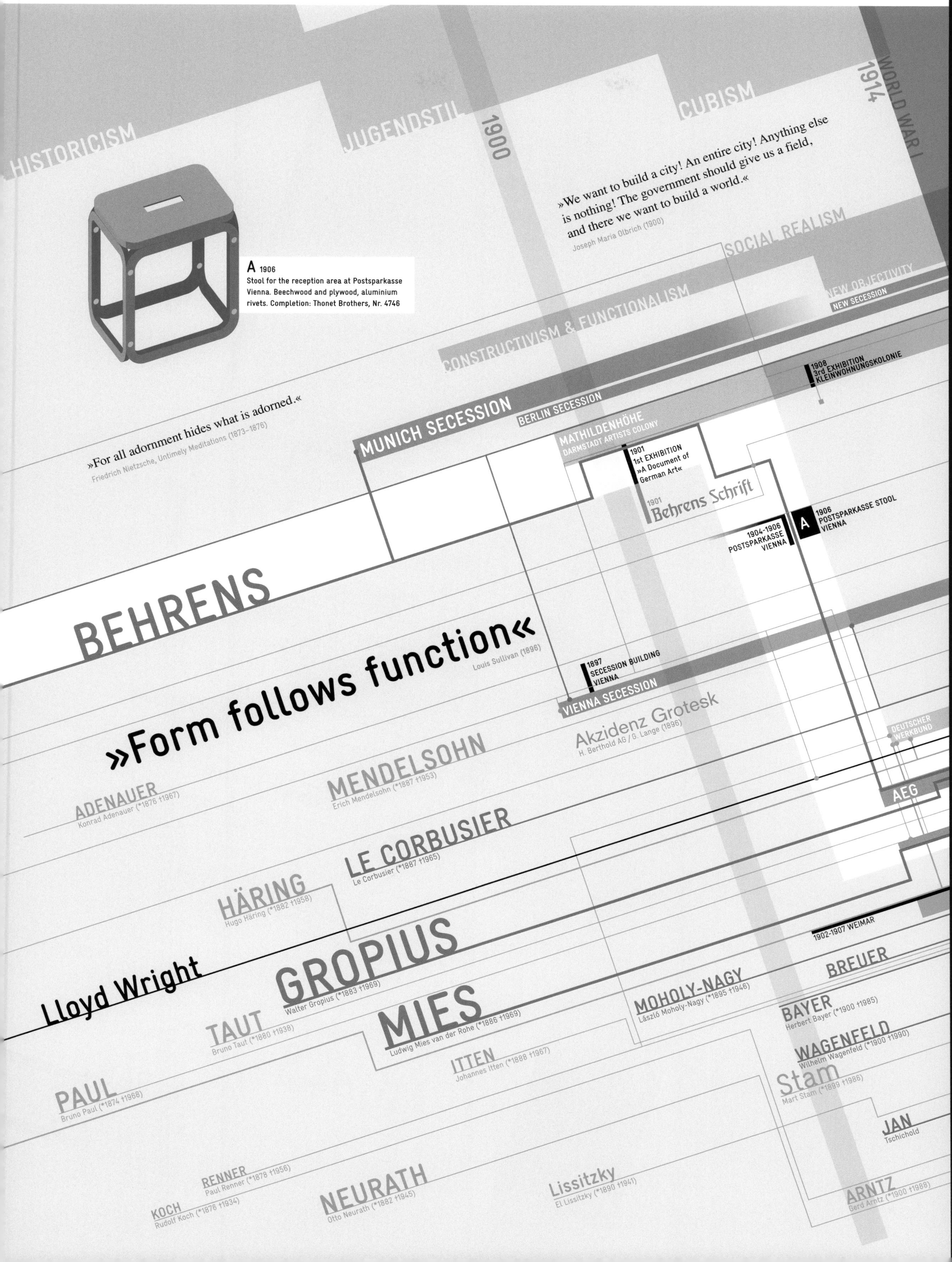

HISTORY
POLITICS
SOCIETY
ECONOMY
SPORTS
TECHNOLOGY
CULTURE & ARTS
SCIENCE

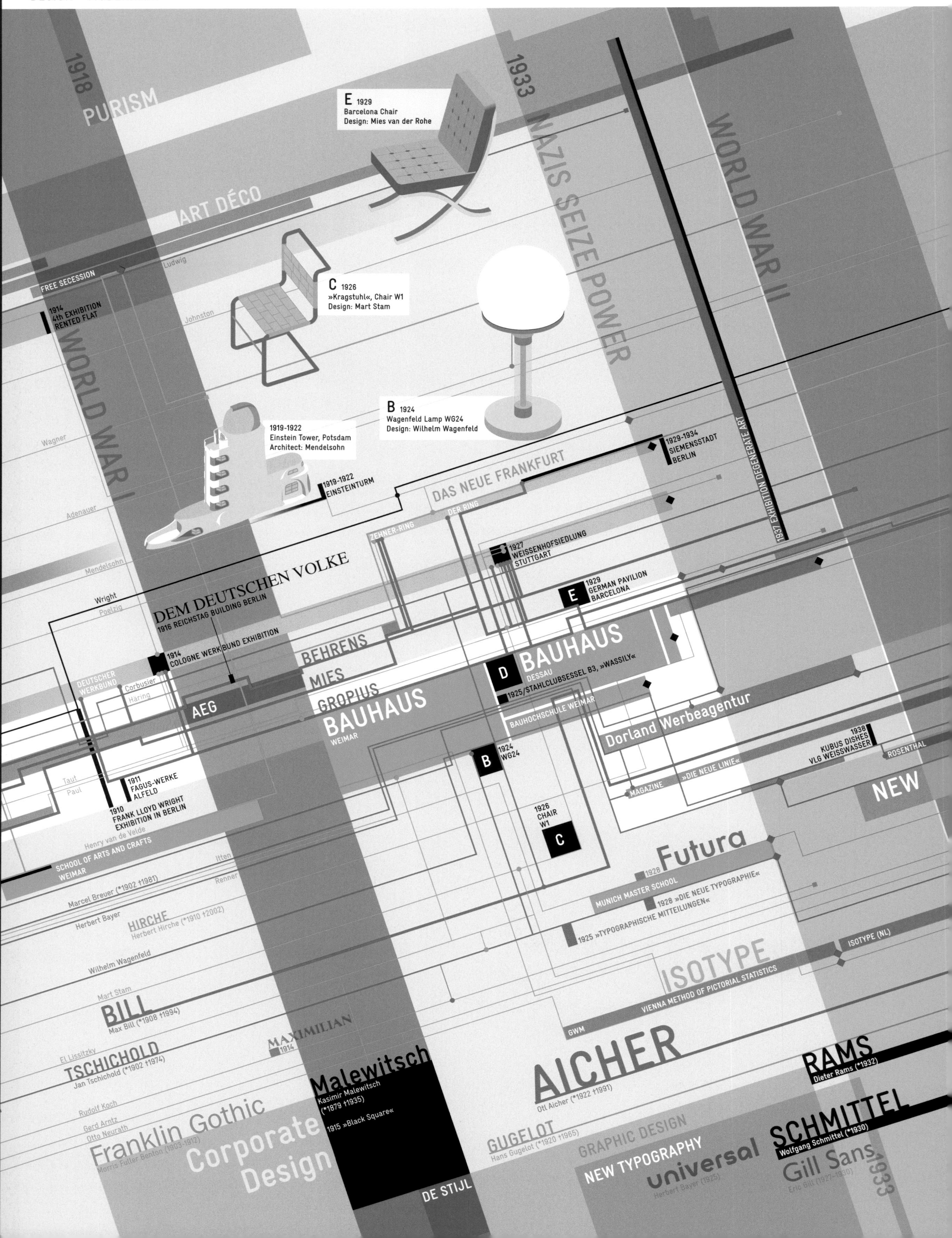

1918
PURISM
ART DÉCO
FREE SECESSION
1914 4th EXHIBITION RENTED FLAT
WORLD WAR I
E 1929
Barcelona Chair
Design: Mies van der Rohe
C 1926
»Kragstuhl«, Chair W1
Design: Mart Stam
B 1924
Wagenfeld Lamp WG24
Design: Wilhelm Wagenfeld
1919-1922
Einstein Tower, Potsdam
Architect: Mendelsohn
1919-1922 EINSTEINTURM
1933
NAZIS SEIZE POWER
WORLD WAR II
1937 EXHIBITION DEGENERATE ART
1929-1934 SIEMENSSTADT BERLIN
DAS NEUE FRANKFURT
DER RING
ZEHNER-RING
1927 WEISSENHOFSIEDLUNG STUTTGART
1929 GERMAN PAVILION BARCELONA
Ludwig
Johnston
Wagner
Adenauer
Mendelsohn
Wright
Poelzig
DEM DEUTSCHEN VOLKE
1916 REICHSTAG BUILDING BERLIN
1914 COLOGNE WERKBUND EXHIBITION
DEUTSCHER WERKBUND
Corbusier
Häring
AEG
BEHRENS
MIES
GROPIUS
BAUHAUS
WEIMAR
D
BAUHAUS
DESSAU
1925/STAHLCLUBSESSEL B3, »WASSILY«
BAUHOCHSCHULE WEIMAR
Dorland Werbeagentur
1938 KUBUS DISHES VLG WEISSWASSER
ROSENTHAL
B 1924 WG24
MAGAZINE »DIE NEUE LINIE«
NEW
1926 CHAIR W1
C
Taut
Paul
1911 FAGUS-WERKE ALFELD
1910 FRANK LLOYD WRIGHT EXHIBITION IN BERLIN
Henry van de Velde
SCHOOL OF ARTS AND CRAFTS WEIMAR
Itten
Renner
Futura
1928
MUNICH MASTER SCHOOL
1928 »DIE NEUE TYPOGRAPHIE«
1925 »TYPOGRAPHISCHE MITTEILUNGEN«
Marcel Breuer (*1902 †1981)
Herbert Bayer
HIRCHE
Herbert Hirche (*1910 †2002)
Wilhelm Wagenfeld
ISOTYPE
VIENNA METHOD OF PICTORIAL STATISTICS
ISOTYPE (NL)
Mart Stam
BILL
Max Bill (*1908 †1994)
MAXIMILIAN
1914
GWM
El Lissitzky
TSCHICHOLD
Jan Tschichold (*1902 †1974)
Malewitsch
Kasimir Malewitsch (*1879 †1935)
1915 »Black Square«
AICHER
Otl Aicher (*1922 †1991)
RAMS
Dieter Rams (*1932)
Rudolf Koch
Gerd Arntz
Otto Neurath
Franklin Gothic
Morris Fuller Benton (1903-1912)
Corporate Design
DE STIJL
GUGELOT
Hans Gugelot (*1920 †1965)
GRAPHIC DESIGN
NEW TYPOGRAPHY
Universal
Herbert Bayer (1925)
SCHMITTEL
Wolfgang Schmittel (*1930)
Gill Sans
Eric Gill (1927-1930)
1933

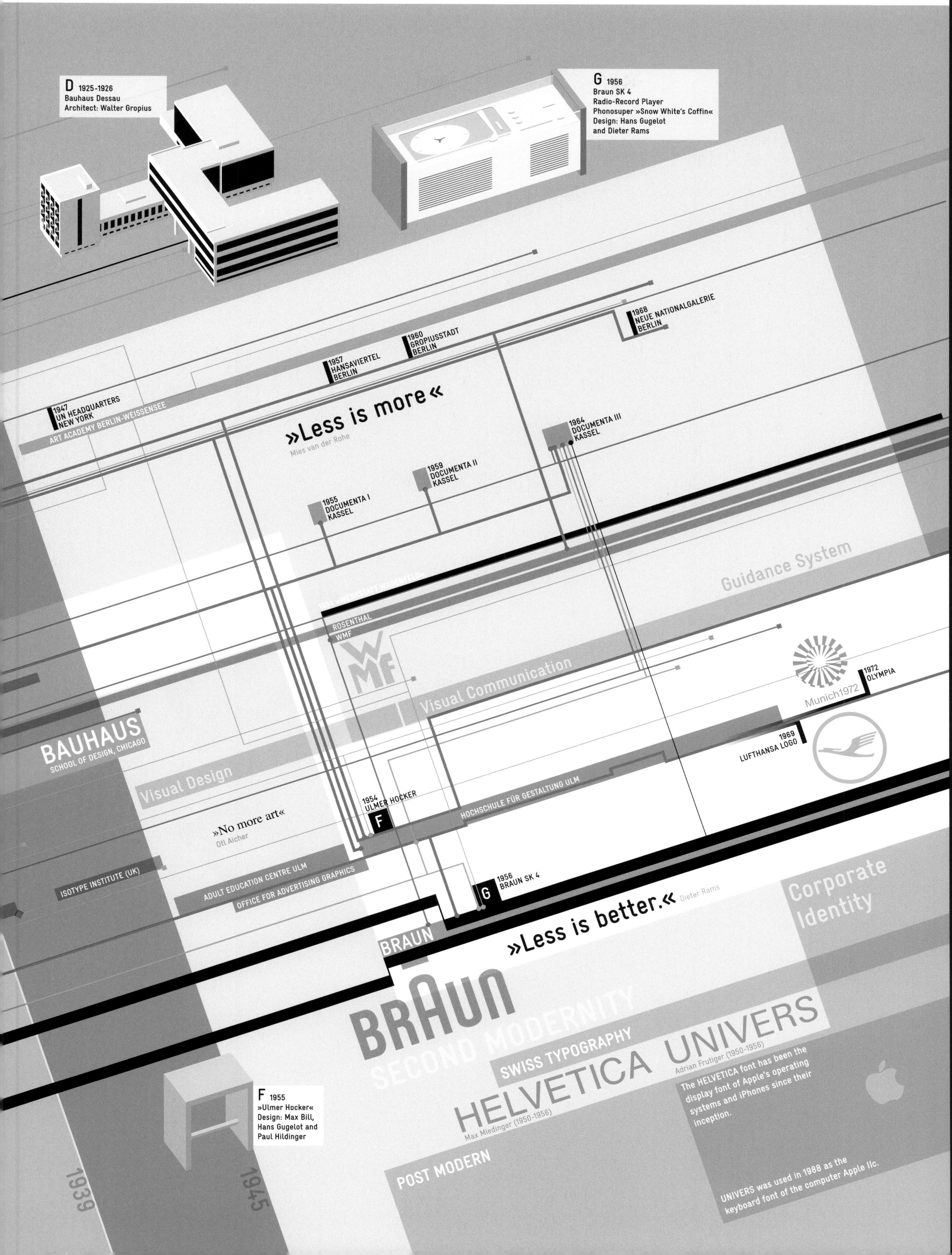
D 1925-1926
Bauhaus Dessau
Architect: Walter Gropius
G 1956
Braun SK 4
Radio-Record Player
Phonosuper »Snow White's Coffin«
Design: Hans Gugelot
and Dieter Rams
1968 NEUE NATIONALGALERIE BERLIN
1960 GROPIUSSTADT BERLIN
1957 HANSAVIERTEL BERLIN
1947 UN HEADQUARTERS NEW YORK
ART ACADEMY BERLIN-WEISSENSEE
»Less is more«
Mies van der Rohe
1964 DOCUMENTA III KASSEL
1959 DOCUMENTA II KASSEL
1955 DOCUMENTA I KASSEL
Guidance System
ROSENTHAL
WMF
Visual Communication
Munich1972
1972 OLYMPIA
1969 LUFTHANSA LOGO
BAUHAUS
SCHOOL OF DESIGN, CHICAGO
Visual Design
1954 ULMER HOCKER
F
HOCHSCHULE FÜR GESTALTUNG ULM
»No more art«
Otl Aicher
ISOTYPE INSTITUTE (UK)
ADULT EDUCATION CENTRE ULM
OFFICE FOR ADVERTISING GRAPHICS
1956 BRAUN SK 4
G
»Less is better.« Dieter Rams
Corporate Identity
BRAUN
BRAUN
SECOND MODERNITY
SWISS TYPOGRAPHY
HELVETICA UNIVERS
Adrian Frutiger (1950-1956)
Max Miedinger (1950-1956)
The HELVETICA font has been the display font of Apple's operating systems and iPhones since their inception.
F 1955
»Ulmer Hocker«
Design: Max Bill,
Hans Gugelot and
Paul Hildinger
POST MODERN
UNIVERS was used in 1988 as the keyboard font of the computer Apple IIc.
1939
1945

MOUNTAINS OF STEEL

The Eiffel Tower was built in 1889 as a representation of the technological progress at the time of the Paris World Exhibition in 1889. While the Eiffel Tower was constructed with puddled iron*, it demonstrates the importance of steel during this period of industrialization. Architectural monuments have always mirrored the signs of the times and today's innovative constructions are more extreme in height and shape. Take a bird's eye tour of some of the world's tallest buildings. Can you identify them all from their footprint?

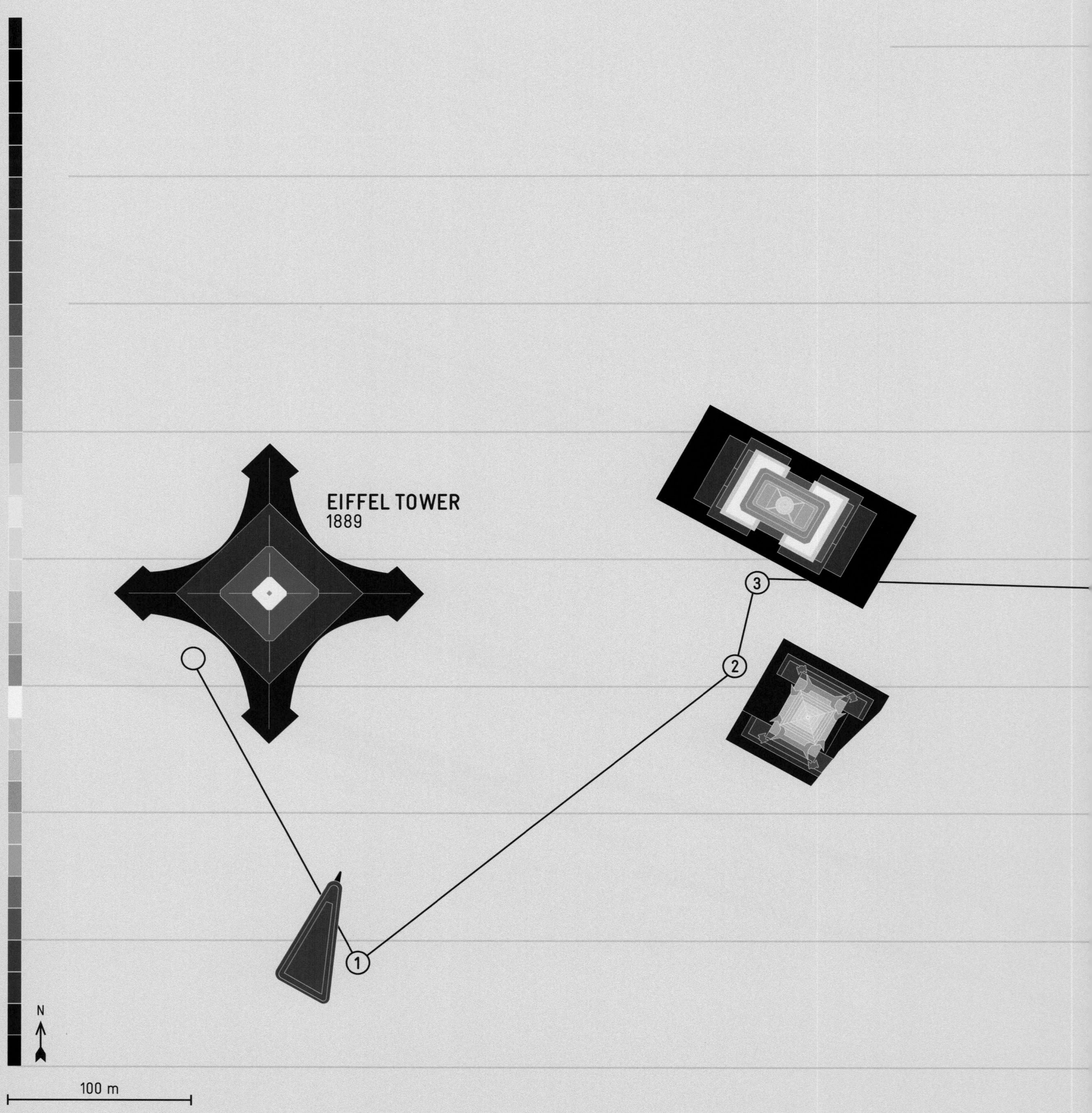

* Puddling produces steel from pig iron.

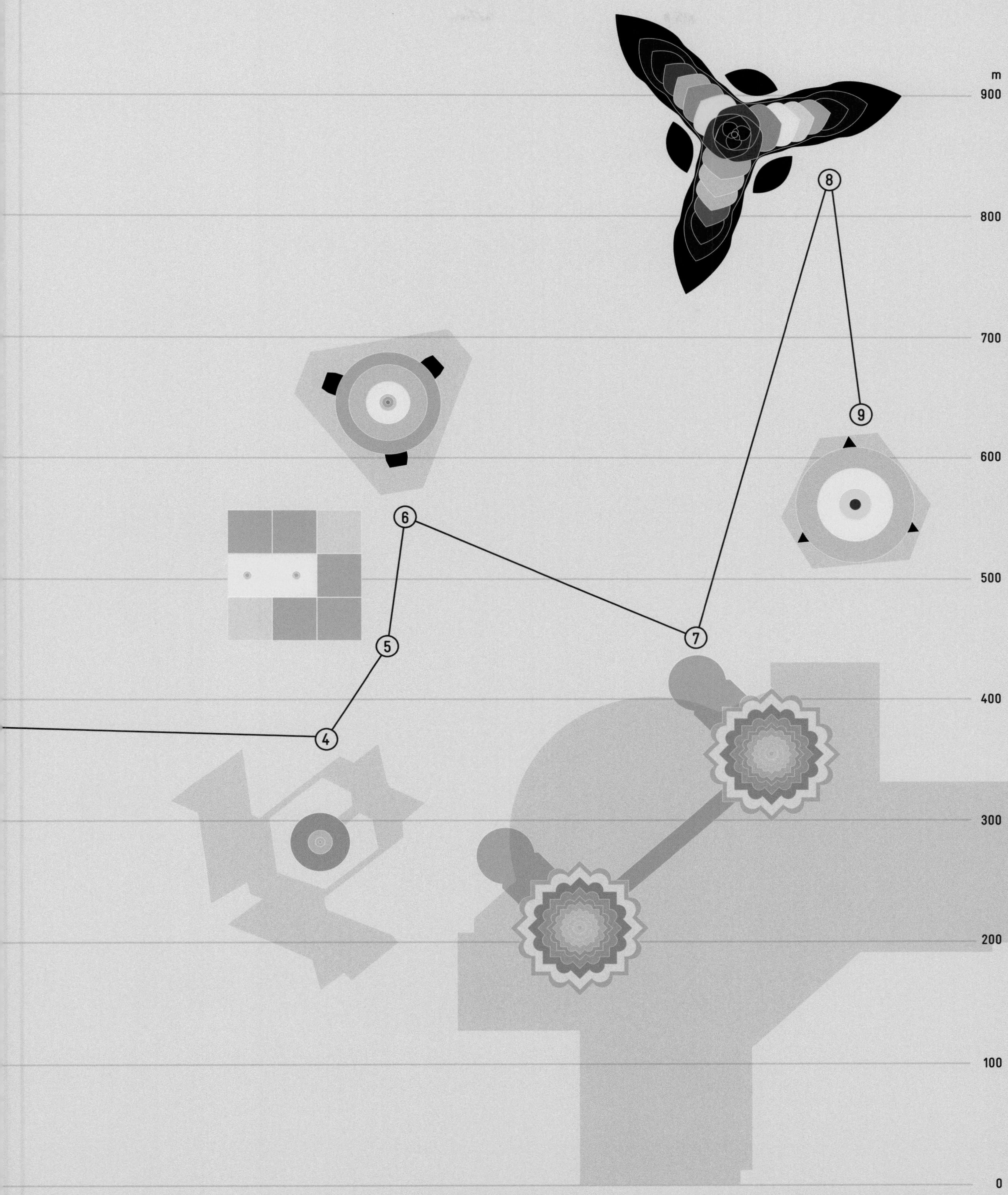
m
900
800
700
600
500
400
300
200
100
0
8
9
6
7
5
4

Solution: 1. Flat Iron, New York, 1902 2. Chrysler Building, New York, 1930 3. Empire State Building, New York, 1931 4. Berlin TV Tower, Berlin, 1969 5. Willis Tower, Chicago, 1974 6. CN Tower, Toronto, 1976 7. Petronas Towers, Kuala Lumpur, 1998 8. Burj Khalifa, Dubai, 2009 9. Tokyo Skytree, Tokyo, 2012

HIGHER, BIGGER, WIDER!

Statues are visible throughout the world as symbols of religion, power and peace. In 2011, New York's Statue of Liberty, which once welcomed immigrants from the »Old World«, celebrated its 125th birthday. Here is a selection of her contemporaries, with a comparison of their respective dimensions.

LOCATIONS OF STATUES

NATURE OF STATUE

- RELIGION
- HONOR
- LEADERSHIP

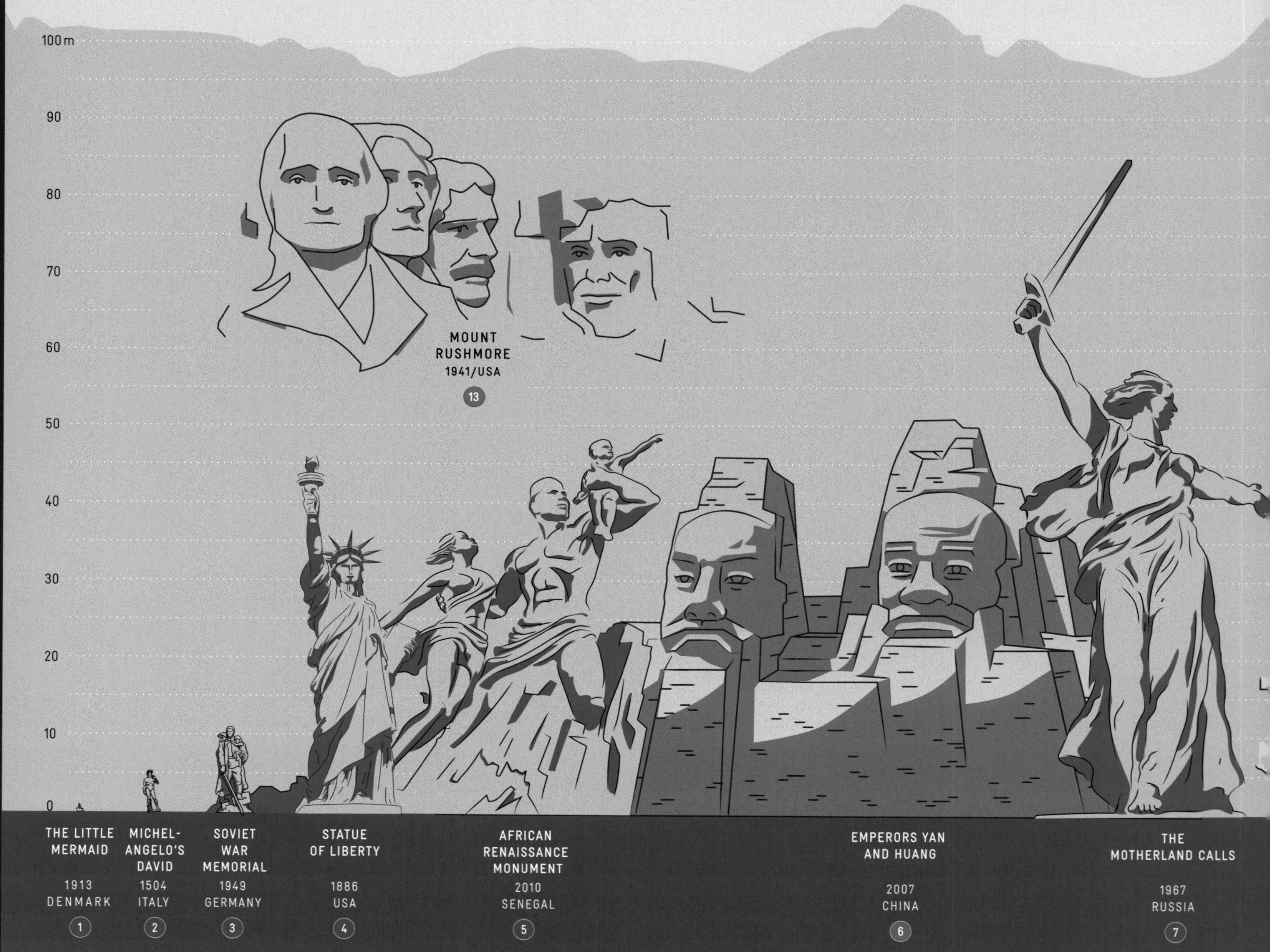
100 m
90
80
70
60
50
40
30
20
10
0
MOUNT RUSHMORE
1941/USA
13
THE LITTLE MERMAID
1913
DENMARK
1
MICHEL-ANGELO'S DAVID
1504
ITALY
2
SOVIET WAR MEMORIAL
1949
GERMANY
3
STATUE OF LIBERTY
1886
USA
4
AFRICAN RENAISSANCE MONUMENT
2010
SENEGAL
5
EMPERORS YAN AND HUANG
2007
CHINA
6
THE MOTHERLAND CALLS
1967
RUSSIA
7

180 m
170
160
150
140
50
40
30
20
10
CHRIST
THE REDEEMER*
1931/BRAZIL
14
COMPARED
WITH
MAN
PETER
THE GREAT
1997
RUSSIA
8
SENDAI
DAIKANNON
1991
JAPAN
9
BIRTH OF THE
NEW WORLD
2016
PUERTO RICO
10
LAYKYUN
SETKYAR
2008
MYANMAR
11
STATUE OF UNITY
2018
INDIA
12
YOU
ARE
HERE

ALFA BRAVO CHARLIE

»W6N, W6N, W6N calling G7W, do you hear me, over?«—Sound familiar? To avoid any misunderstandings, different spelling codes have been developed over the decades. For the military, clear communication is particularly vital. The table shows a selection of international spelling codes.

	A	B	C	D	E	F	G	H	I	J	K	L	M
German (DIN 5009)	ANTON	BERTA	CÄSAR	DORA	EMIL	FRIEDRICH	GUSTAV	HEINRICH	IDA	JULIUS	KAUFMANN	LUDWIG	MARTHA
English	ALFRED	BENJAMIN	CHARLES	DAVID	EDWARD	FREDERICK	GEORGE	HARRY	ISAAC	JACK	KING	LONDON	MARY
NATO/international aviation	ALFA	BRAVO	CHARLIE	DELTA	ECHO	FOXTROT	GOLF	HOTEL	INDIA	JULIETT	KILO	LIMA	MIKE
Morse code	• –	– • • •	– • – •	– • •	•	• • – •	– – •	• • • •	• •	• – – –	– • –	• – • •	– –

Nautical flag alphabet

Semaphore

	A	B	C	D	E	F	G	H	I	J	K	L	M
N.Y. Police	ADAM	BOY	CHARLIE	DAVID	EDWARD	FRANK	GEORGE	HENRY	IDA	JOHN	KING	LINCOLN	MARY
ASCII code	41	42	43	44	45	46	47	48	49	4A	4B	4C	4D

Braille/Lormen

Sign language

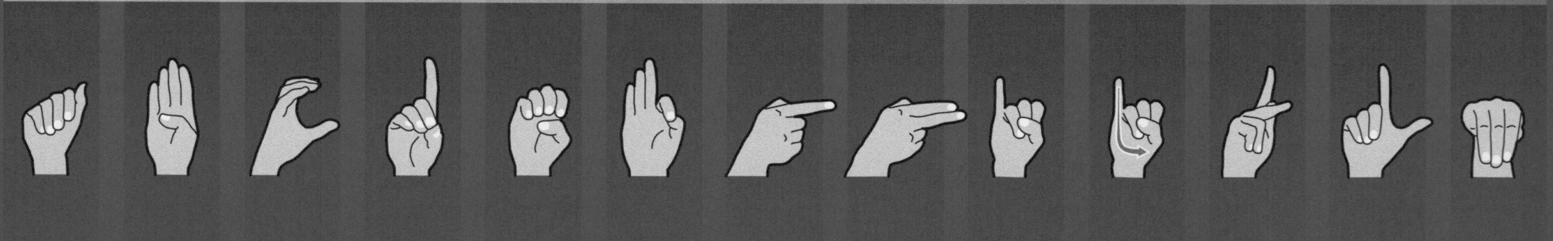

A B C D E F G H I J K L M

N	O	P	Q	R	S	T	U	V	W	X	Y	Z
NORDPOL	OTTO	PAULA	QUELLE	RICHARD	SAMUEL	THEODOR	ULRICH	VIKTOR	WILHELM	XANTHIPPE	YPSILON	ZACHARIAS
NELLIE	OLIVER	PETER	QUEEN	ROBERT	SAMUEL	TOMMY	UNCLE	VICTOR	WILLIAM	X-RAY	YELLOW	ZEBRA
NOVEMBER	OSCAR	PAPA	QUEBEC	ROMEO	SIERRA	TANGO	UNIFORM	VICTOR	WHISKEY	X-RAY	YANKEE	ZULU
– •	– – –	• – – •	– – • –	• – •	• • •	–	• • –	• • • –	• – –	– • • –	– • – –	– – • •

NORA	OCEAN	PETER	QUEEN	ROBERT	SAM	TOM	UNION	VICTOR	WILLIAM	X-RAY	YOUNG	ZEBRA
4E	4F	50	51	52	53	54	55	56	57	58	59	5A

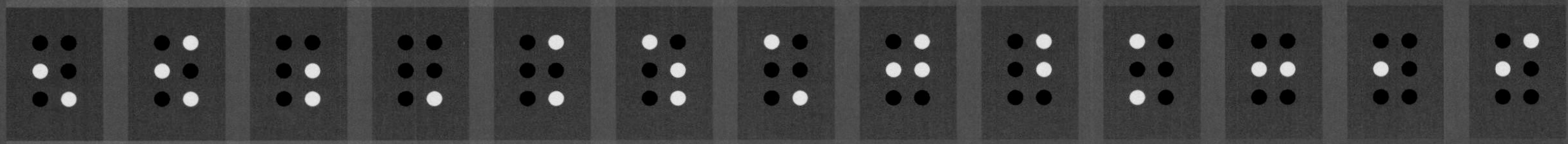

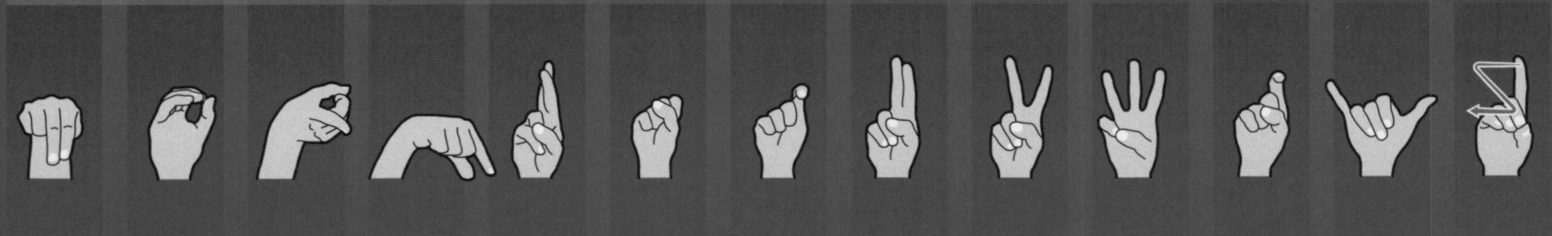

N O P Q R S T U V W X Y Z

HISTORY POLITICS SOCIETY ECONOMY SPORTS TECHNOLOGY CULTURE & ARTS SCIENCE

WANDERING WORDS

From »angst« to »zaijfa« – what would the world sound like without German? This map shows how German words have influenced or been integrated into many languages all over the world. Migrant words convey history, stories, emotions and innovation as people settle in new worlds. This particular collection has been assembled for the call to tender by the Deutsche Sprachrat for its study on »Migrant Words«; we are publishing it in cooperation with the Goethe-Institut.

Norwegian
Swedish
Danish
GERMANY
AUSTRIA
SWITZERLAND
French/Switzerland
Italian
Finnish
Estonian
Latvian
Lithuanian
Belarusian
Russian
Polish
Czech
Slovak
Hungarian
Slovene
Ukrainian
Romanian
Bosnian, Croatian, Serbian
Bulgarian
Kosovo/Albanian
Albanian
Macedonian
Greek
Turkish
Armenian
Kazakh
Chinese
Korean
Japanese
Maltese
Israel/Hebrew
Iran/Farsi
Arabic
Sudan/Arabic
Bangladesh/Bengali
Vietnamese
Thai
Swaheli
Congo/Wolof
Malagasy
Mauritius/Creole
Indonesian
Papua New Guinea/Tok Pisin
Australia/English
New Zealand/English
FORSPILL
NACHSPIEL
HURTIG
KNALLROT
BEIN
SNÄLLTÅG
BESSERWISSER
BOOTSHAKEN
GULASCHBARON
KAVIEEPAUSSI
ANHANG
WOHLTÄTER
EDELWEISS
STILLEBEN
JUGEND
SHNICELE
КОНЦЕРТМЕЙСТЕР
БУТЕРБРОД
ШПИОНАЖ
БРУДЕРШАФТ
ТАНЦМЕЙСТЕР
ПАРИКМАХЕР
ВУНДЕРКИНД
ЛЕЙТМОТИВ
ПЛАКАТ
ЭДЕЛЬВЕЙС
СЛЕСАРЬ
КЕКС
АГРЕССОР
ШТУРМ
ЦИФЕРБЛАТ
BRUDERSZAFT
LEITMOTIV
NICHTS
EDELWEIS
HAUSMAJSTOR
EISBERG
ШАХ
ДЮБЕЛ
VITZ
FERTIK!
HER
MAJR
KIRSCH
KRUG
RIESLING
LIED
CRAUTI
KINDERGARDIN
KINDER GARDEN
BIA
KOLLEGE
SHULE
LECKER
BLAUZI
BENSIN
RAUSIMSÄUBERN
KUKEN
RAUS
HAUS
BLUMKOL
KAOS
DOPPELGANGER
GESUNDHEIT
KINDERGARTEN
WANDERLUST
OOM PAH PAH MUSIC
SCHADENFREUDE
DUMMKOPF
HALLO
JA
REGENZEIT
KANNITZEENBOOT
SWEIS
MESER
JA! LOS!
Swedish
Polish
罗曼蒂克

ENLIGHTENING IDEAS

The Enlightenment and the wave of new ideas that it swept in has given Europe a lasting legacy that associates scientific progress with free thinking. The movement focused primarily on the importance of thinking for yourself – while that seems banal today, it was revolutionary at the time. No wonder politicians and the clergy voiced such strong opposition to the movement's leaders. But public opinion prevailed and the Enlightenment's legacy can still be found in modern thinkers.

ENLIGHTENMENT

ENGLAND 1688: THE OPPOSERS OF ABSOLUTISM OUST KING JAMES II FROM POWER IN THE GLORIOUS REVOLUTION. THEY INTRODUCE THE BILL OF RIGHTS AND DECLARE PARLIAMENT TO BE THE SUPREME SOVEREIGN. **THE AGE OF ENLIGHTENMENT BEGINS.**

KEY

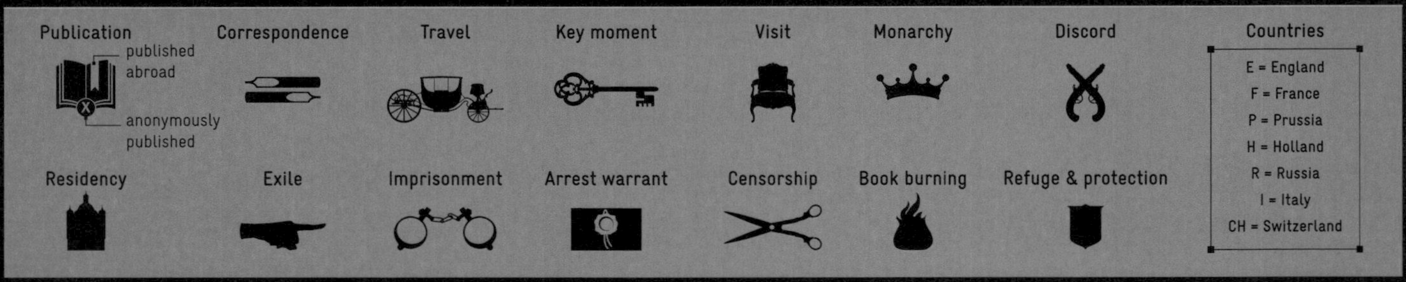
Publication
published abroad
anonymously published
Correspondence
Travel
Key moment
Visit
Monarchy
Discord
Residency
Exile
Imprisonment
Arrest warrant
Censorship
Book burning
Refuge & protection
Countries
E = England
F = France
P = Prussia
H = Holland
R = Russia
I = Italy
CH = Switzerland

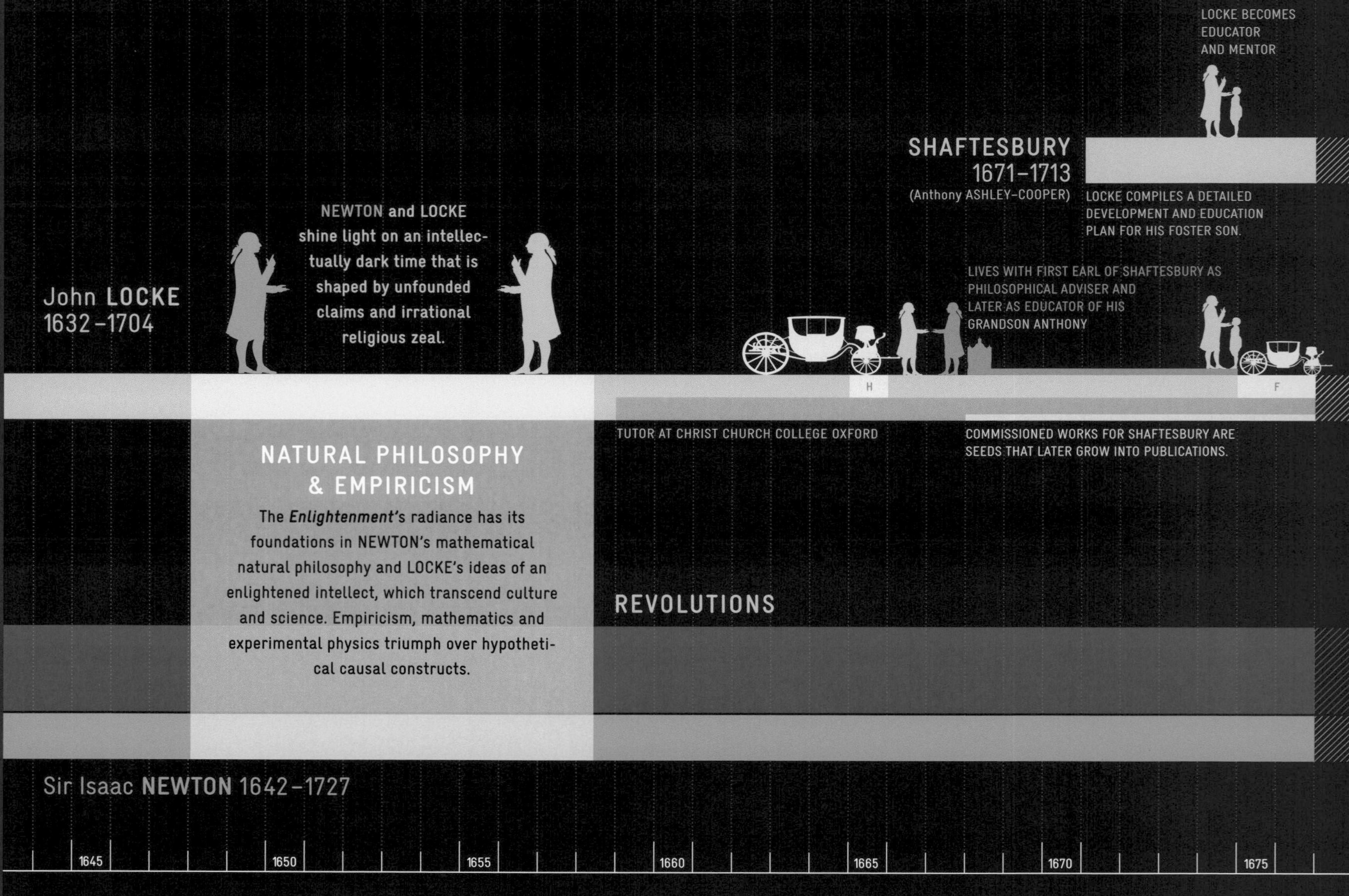
LOCKE BECOMES EDUCATOR AND MENTOR
SHAFTESBURY 1671–1713
(Anthony ASHLEY-COOPER)
LOCKE COMPILES A DETAILED DEVELOPMENT AND EDUCATION PLAN FOR HIS FOSTER SON.
NEWTON and LOCKE shine light on an intellectually dark time that is shaped by unfounded claims and irrational religious zeal.
John LOCKE 1632–1704
LIVES WITH FIRST EARL OF SHAFTESBURY AS PHILOSOPHICAL ADVISER AND LATER AS EDUCATOR OF HIS GRANDSON ANTHONY
H
F
TUTOR AT CHRIST CHURCH COLLEGE OXFORD
COMMISSIONED WORKS FOR SHAFTESBURY ARE SEEDS THAT LATER GROW INTO PUBLICATIONS.
NATURAL PHILOSOPHY & EMPIRICISM
The *Enlightenment*'s radiance has its foundations in NEWTON's mathematical natural philosophy and LOCKE's ideas of an enlightened intellect, which transcend culture and science. Empiricism, mathematics and experimental physics triumph over hypothetical causal constructs.
REVOLUTIONS
Sir Isaac NEWTON 1642–1727
1645
1650
1655
1660
1665
1670
1675

Lumières

N EXILE IN ENGLAND, VOLTAIRE LEARNS ABOUT INDIVIDUAL RIGHTS ΟF FREEDOM, RELIGIOUS TOLERANCE AND PARLIAMENTARISM. VOLTAIRE CREATES A MENTAL BRIDGE FROM THE ENGLISH THINKERS TO CONTINENTAL EUROPE: »THE WISE LOCKE« BECOMES A LEADING FIGURE FOR FRENCH PHILOSOPHERS THROUGH HIS *LETTRES PHILOSOPHIQUES*. HE ALSO POPULARIZES NEWTON'S THEORIES IN FRANCE. IN THE SECOND HALF OF THE 8TH CENTURY, PARIS BECOMES THE CENTER OF A FREE-SPIRITED SOCIETY. THE PHILOSOPHERS THERE ARE CHARACTERIZED BY A CRITICAL BOLDNESS AND AN ANTICLERICAL ATTITUDE, WHICH THEY PASSIONATELY DEBATE IN SALONS AND CAFES. VOLTAIRE ALSO CONTRIBUTES TO THE ENCYCLOPÉDIE—THE LIGHTHOUSE PROJECT OF THE LUMIÈRES. THROUGH HIS TIES TO CATHERINE II OF RUSSIA AND PRUSSIAN KING FREDERICK II, HE ALSO INFLUENCES THE IDEA OF AN **»ENLIGHTENED ABSOLUTISM.«**

AUFKLÄRUNG

EARLY GERMAN ENLIGHTENMENT CAN BE SEEN AS AN EPILOGUE TO THE REFORMATION. THE LATE ENLIGHTENMENT BECOMES TRULY SELF-REFLECTIVE, PARTICULARLY WITH THE FUNDAMENTAL QUESTION ANSWERED BY IMMANUEL KANT: **»WHAT IS ENLIGHTENMENT?«**

At a time when women find it hard to prove their intelligence, DU CHÂTELET is fortunate enough to grow up in a tolerant environment and be given an education only rarely offered to girls. She consolidates her knowledge in natural sciences together with VOLTAIRE.

Émilie DU CHÂTELET
1706–1749

VOLTAIRE
1694–1778
(Jean Marie AROUET)

A LETTER CONCERNING ENTHUSIASM
Test of Ridicule: mocking laughter as a weapon against fanatics

LOCKE SENDS LETTERS WITH GOOD ADVICE FROM FRANCE.

DEATH OF GRANDFATHER

GRAND TOUR THROUGH EUROPE: FIRST STAGE IS A VISIT TO LOCKE IN EXILE.

PARLAMENTARIAN

H F I

H

H

Third Earl of SHAFTESBURY

MASTERS IN GREEK AND LATIN AT THE AGE OF ELEVEN

The aim of LOCKE'S education is the creation of a physically and mentally active gentleman. His most important values are virtue, wisdom and a good lifestyle.

AN INQUIRY CONCERNING VIRTUE, OR MERIT
Moral Sense: A rational human being is disposed to virtue.

SHAFTESBURY'S PLANS TO TOPPLE THE KING COME TO LIGHT. HE FLEES TO HOLLAND. LOCKE FOLLOWS HIM.

PERSECUTION BY ENGLISH AGENTS, LIFE UNDERGROUND

SOME THOUGHTS CONCERNING EDUCATION

THE REASONABLENESS OF CHRISTIANITY, AS DELIVERED IN THE SCRIPTURES

On the Conduct of the Understanding (posthumous)

F

H

ESSAY CONCERNING HUMAN UNDERSTANDING
Investigation into the mind's scope: there are no innate ideas.

A LETTER CONCERNING TOLERATION
Religious tolerance, separation of state and church

TWO TREATISES OF GOVERNMENT
Plea against the deification of power, for a separation of powers and natural human rights:
LIFE, LIBERTY AND ESTATE

Key term of own understanding

Because of the recatholicization under James II, Anglicans and Protestants conspire with William of Orange to liberate the people from slavery and Papism.

GLORIOUS REVOLUTION 1688/89
Victory of parliamentarianism and tolerant Protestantism

LOCKE'S PUBLISHED MANUSCRIPTS CONSTITUTE A KIND OF LEGITIMIZATION OF THE NEW STATE OF AFFAIRS.

DECLARATION OF THE RIGHTS OF PARLIAMENT
William puts James II to flight and ascends the throne.
The relationship between crown and parliament is reconstituted.

PHILOSOPHIÆ NATURALIS PRINCIPIA MATHEMATICA

NEWTON defines the mathematical formula for gravitation and confirms the works of COPERNICUS, KEPLER and GALILEI with it.

NEWTON ONLY TRUSTS FINDINGS THAT CAN BE EXPERIMENTALLY AND MATHEMATICALLY PROVEN.

1680 | 1685 | 1690 | 1695 | 1700 | 1705

HISTORY · POLITICS · SOCIETY · ECONOMY · SPORTS · TECHNOLOGY · **CULTURE & ARTS** · SCIENCE

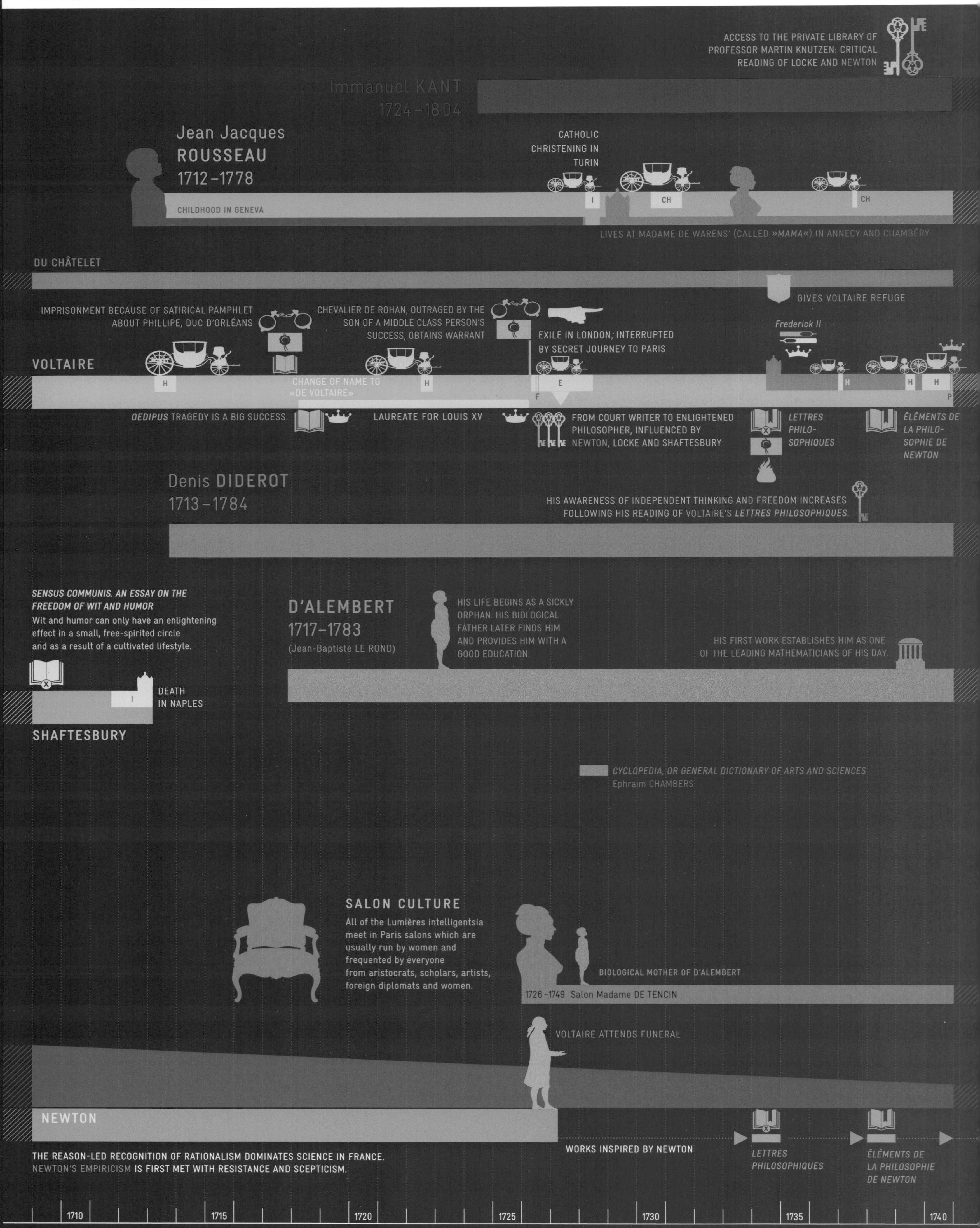
ACCESS TO THE PRIVATE LIBRARY OF PROFESSOR MARTIN KNUTZEN: CRITICAL READING OF LOCKE AND NEWTON
Immanuel KANT 1724–1804
Jean Jacques ROUSSEAU 1712–1778
CATHOLIC CHRISTENING IN TURIN
CHILDHOOD IN GENEVA
I
CH
CH
LIVES AT MADAME DE WARENS' (CALLED »MAMA«) IN ANNECY AND CHAMBÉRY
DU CHÂTELET
GIVES VOLTAIRE REFUGE
IMPRISONMENT BECAUSE OF SATIRICAL PAMPHLET ABOUT PHILLIPE, DUC D'ORLÉANS
CHEVALIER DE ROHAN, OUTRAGED BY THE SON OF A MIDDLE CLASS PERSON'S SUCCESS, OBTAINS WARRANT
EXILE IN LONDON, INTERRUPTED BY SECRET JOURNEY TO PARIS
Frederick II
VOLTAIRE
H
CHANGE OF NAME TO «DE VOLTAIRE»
H
F
E
H
H
H
P
OEDIPUS TRAGEDY IS A BIG SUCCESS.
LAUREATE FOR LOUIS XV
FROM COURT WRITER TO ENLIGHTENED PHILOSOPHER, INFLUENCED BY NEWTON, LOCKE AND SHAFTESBURY
LETTRES PHILO-SOPHIQUES
ÉLÉMENTS DE LA PHILO-SOPHIE DE NEWTON
Denis DIDEROT 1713–1784
HIS AWARENESS OF INDEPENDENT THINKING AND FREEDOM INCREASES FOLLOWING HIS READING OF VOLTAIRE'S LETTRES PHILOSOPHIQUES.
SENSUS COMMUNIS. AN ESSAY ON THE FREEDOM OF WIT AND HUMOR
Wit and humor can only have an enlightening effect in a small, free-spirited circle and as a result of a cultivated lifestyle.
I
DEATH IN NAPLES
SHAFTESBURY
D'ALEMBERT 1717–1783 (Jean-Baptiste LE ROND)
HIS LIFE BEGINS AS A SICKLY ORPHAN. HIS BIOLOGICAL FATHER LATER FINDS HIM AND PROVIDES HIM WITH A GOOD EDUCATION.
HIS FIRST WORK ESTABLISHES HIM AS ONE OF THE LEADING MATHEMATICIANS OF HIS DAY.
CYCLOPEDIA, OR GENERAL DICTIONARY OF ARTS AND SCIENCES
Ephraim CHAMBERS
SALON CULTURE
All of the Lumières intelligentsia meet in Paris salons which are usually run by women and frequented by everyone from aristocrats, scholars, artists, foreign diplomats and women.
BIOLOGICAL MOTHER OF D'ALEMBERT
1726–1749 Salon Madame DE TENCIN
VOLTAIRE ATTENDS FUNERAL
NEWTON
WORKS INSPIRED BY NEWTON
LETTRES PHILOSOPHIQUES
ÉLÉMENTS DE LA PHILOSOPHIE DE NEWTON
THE REASON-LED RECOGNITION OF RATIONALISM DOMINATES SCIENCE IN FRANCE.
NEWTON'S EMPIRICISM IS FIRST MET WITH RESISTANCE AND SCEPTICISM.
1710
1715
1720
1725
1730
1735
1740

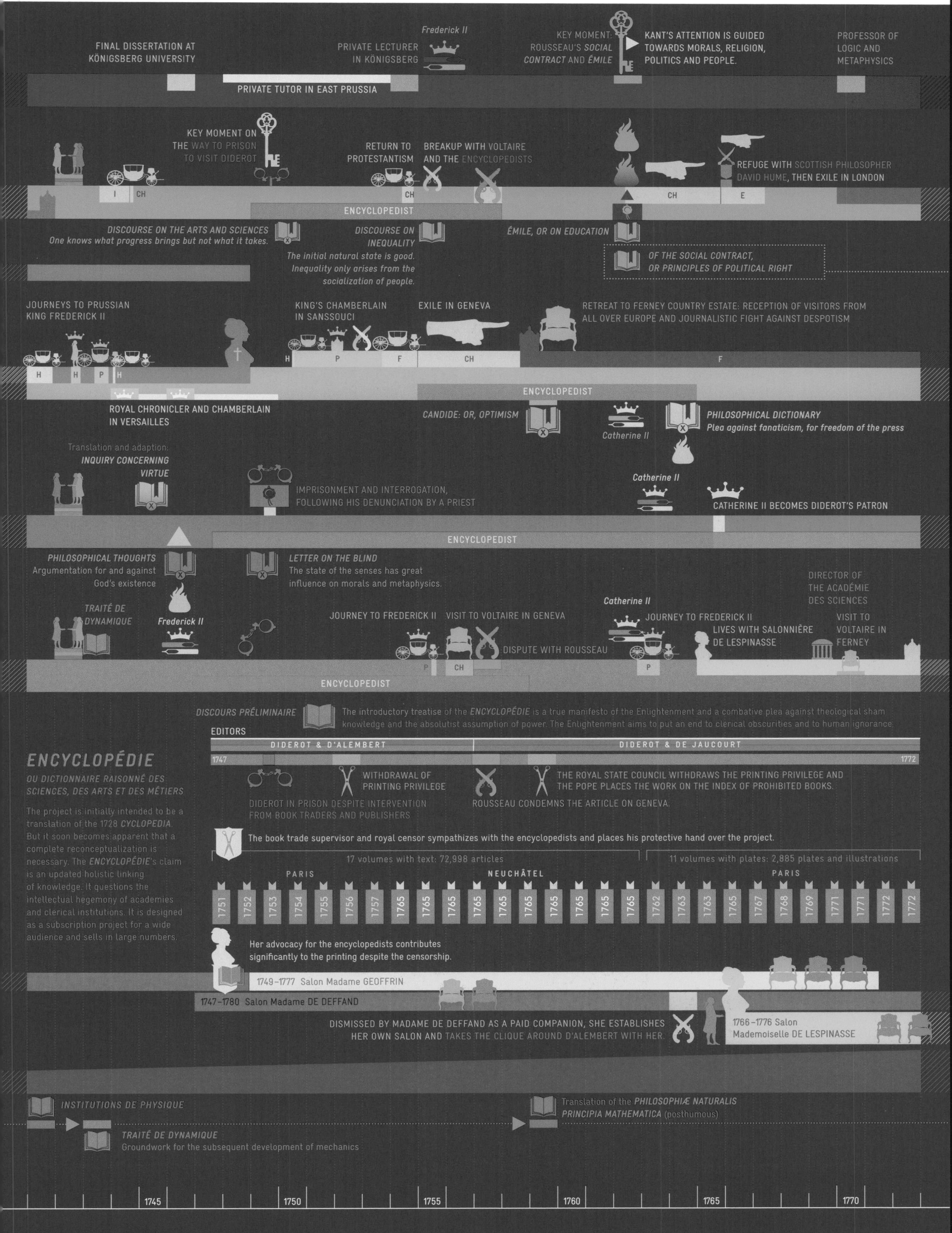

FINAL DISSERTATION AT KÖNIGSBERG UNIVERSITY
Frederick II
PRIVATE LECTURER IN KÖNIGSBERG
KEY MOMENT: ROUSSEAU'S SOCIAL CONTRACT AND ÉMILE
KANT'S ATTENTION IS GUIDED TOWARDS MORALS, RELIGION, POLITICS AND PEOPLE.
PROFESSOR OF LOGIC AND METAPHYSICS
PRIVATE TUTOR IN EAST PRUSSIA
KEY MOMENT ON THE WAY TO PRISON TO VISIT DIDEROT
RETURN TO PROTESTANTISM
BREAKUP WITH VOLTAIRE AND THE ENCYCLOPEDISTS
REFUGE WITH SCOTTISH PHILOSOPHER DAVID HUME, THEN EXILE IN LONDON
I
CH
CH
CH
E
ENCYCLOPEDIST
DISCOURSE ON THE ARTS AND SCIENCES
One knows what progress brings but not what it takes.
DISCOURSE ON INEQUALITY
The initial natural state is good. Inequality only arises from the socialization of people.
ÉMILE, OR ON EDUCATION
OF THE SOCIAL CONTRACT, OR PRINCIPLES OF POLITICAL RIGHT
JOURNEYS TO PRUSSIAN KING FREDERICK II
KING'S CHAMBERLAIN IN SANSSOUCI
EXILE IN GENEVA
RETREAT TO FERNEY COUNTRY ESTATE: RECEPTION OF VISITORS FROM ALL OVER EUROPE AND JOURNALISTIC FIGHT AGAINST DESPOTISM
H
H
P
H
H
P
F
CH
F
ENCYCLOPEDIST
ROYAL CHRONICLER AND CHAMBERLAIN IN VERSAILLES
CANDIDE: OR, OPTIMISM
Catherine II
PHILOSOPHICAL DICTIONARY
Plea against fanaticism, for freedom of the press
Translation and adaption: INQUIRY CONCERNING VIRTUE
IMPRISONMENT AND INTERROGATION, FOLLOWING HIS DENUNCIATION BY A PRIEST
Catherine II
CATHERINE II BECOMES DIDEROT'S PATRON
ENCYCLOPEDIST
PHILOSOPHICAL THOUGHTS
Argumentation for and against God's existence
LETTER ON THE BLIND
The state of the senses has great influence on morals and metaphysics.
DIRECTOR OF THE ACADÉMIE DES SCIENCES
TRAITÉ DE DYNAMIQUE
Frederick II
Catherine II
JOURNEY TO FREDERICK II
VISIT TO VOLTAIRE IN GENEVA
JOURNEY TO FREDERICK II
LIVES WITH SALONNIÈRE DE LESPINASSE
VISIT TO VOLTAIRE IN FERNEY
DISPUTE WITH ROUSSEAU
P
CH
P
ENCYCLOPEDIST
DISCOURS PRÉLIMINAIRE
The introductory treatise of the ENCYCLOPÉDIE is a true manifesto of the Enlightenment and a combative plea against theological sham knowledge and the absolutist assumption of power. The Enlightenment aims to put an end to clerical obscurities and to human ignorance.
EDITORS
DIDEROT & D'ALEMBERT
DIDEROT & DE JAUCOURT
1747
1772
ENCYCLOPÉDIE
OU DICTIONNAIRE RAISONNÉ DES SCIENCES, DES ARTS ET DES MÉTIERS
The project is initially intended to be a translation of the 1728 CYCLOPEDIA. But it soon becomes apparent that a complete reconceptualization is necessary. The ENCYCLOPÉDIE's claim is an updated holistic linking of knowledge. It questions the intellectual hegemony of academies and clerical institutions. It is designed as a subscription project for a wide audience and sells in large numbers.
WITHDRAWAL OF PRINTING PRIVILEGE
THE ROYAL STATE COUNCIL WITHDRAWS THE PRINTING PRIVILEGE AND THE POPE PLACES THE WORK ON THE INDEX OF PROHIBITED BOOKS.
DIDEROT IN PRISON DESPITE INTERVENTION FROM BOOK TRADERS AND PUBLISHERS
ROUSSEAU CONDEMNS THE ARTICLE ON GENEVA.
The book trade supervisor and royal censor sympathizes with the encyclopedists and places his protective hand over the project.
17 volumes with text: 72,998 articles
11 volumes with plates: 2,885 plates and illustrations
PARIS
NEUCHÂTEL
PARIS
1751
1752
1753
1754
1755
1756
1757
1765
1765
1765
1765
1765
1765
1765
1765
1765
1765
1762
1763
1763
1765
1767
1768
1769
1771
1771
1772
1772
Her advocacy for the encyclopedists contributes significantly to the printing despite the censorship.
1749–1777 Salon Madame GEOFFRIN
1747–1780 Salon Madame DE DEFFAND
DISMISSED BY MADAME DE DEFFAND AS A PAID COMPANION, SHE ESTABLISHES HER OWN SALON AND TAKES THE CLIQUE AROUND D'ALEMBERT WITH HER.
1766–1776 Salon Mademoiselle DE LESPINASSE
INSTITUTIONS DE PHYSIQUE
Translation of the PHILOSOPHIÆ NATURALIS PRINCIPIA MATHEMATICA (posthumous)
TRAITÉ DE DYNAMIQUE
Groundwork for the subsequent development of mechanics
1745
1750
1755
1760
1765
1770

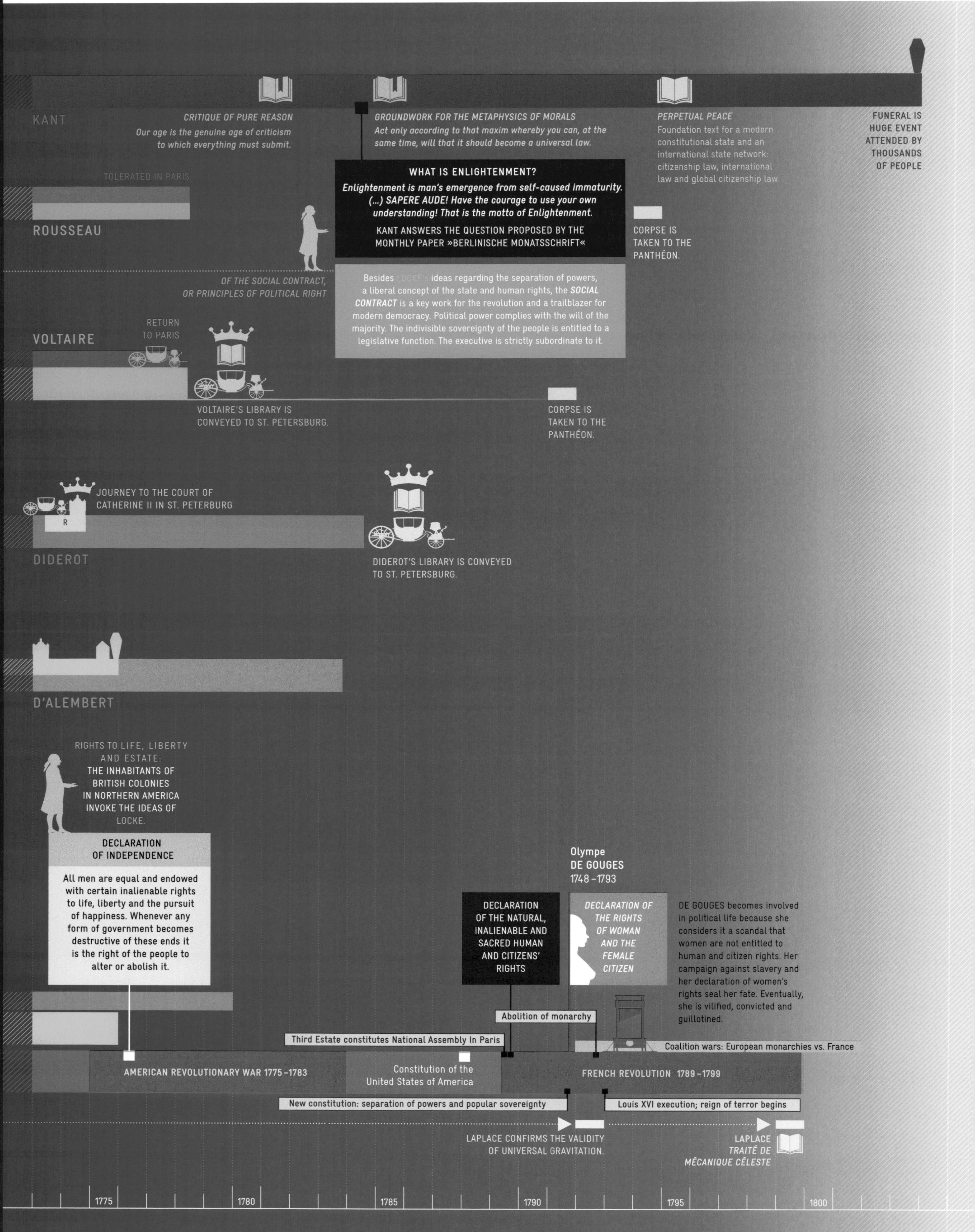
KANT
CRITIQUE OF PURE REASON
Our age is the genuine age of criticism to which everything must submit.
GROUNDWORK FOR THE METAPHYSICS OF MORALS
Act only according to that maxim whereby you can, at the same time, will that it should become a universal law.
PERPETUAL PEACE
Foundation text for a modern constitutional state and an international state network: citizenship law, international law and global citizenship law.
FUNERAL IS HUGE EVENT ATTENDED BY THOUSANDS OF PEOPLE
WHAT IS ENLIGHTENMENT?
Enlightenment is man's emergence from self-caused immaturity. (...) SAPERE AUDE! Have the courage to use your own understanding! That is the motto of Enlightenment.
KANT ANSWERS THE QUESTION PROPOSED BY THE MONTHLY PAPER »BERLINISCHE MONATSSCHRIFT«
TOLERATED IN PARIS
ROUSSEAU
CORPSE IS TAKEN TO THE PANTHÉON.
OF THE SOCIAL CONTRACT, OR PRINCIPLES OF POLITICAL RIGHT
Besides LOCKE's ideas regarding the separation of powers, a liberal concept of the state and human rights, the SOCIAL CONTRACT is a key work for the revolution and a trailblazer for modern democracy. Political power complies with the will of the majority. The indivisible sovereignty of the people is entitled to a legislative function. The executive is strictly subordinate to it.
VOLTAIRE
RETURN TO PARIS
VOLTAIRE'S LIBRARY IS CONVEYED TO ST. PETERSBURG.
CORPSE IS TAKEN TO THE PANTHÉON.
JOURNEY TO THE COURT OF CATHERINE II IN ST. PETERBURG
R
DIDEROT
DIDEROT'S LIBRARY IS CONVEYED TO ST. PETERSBURG.
D'ALEMBERT
RIGHTS TO LIFE, LIBERTY AND ESTATE: THE INHABITANTS OF BRITISH COLONIES IN NORTHERN AMERICA INVOKE THE IDEAS OF LOCKE.
DECLARATION OF INDEPENDENCE
All men are equal and endowed with certain inalienable rights to life, liberty and the pursuit of happiness. Whenever any form of government becomes destructive of these ends it is the right of the people to alter or abolish it.
Olympe DE GOUGES 1748 – 1793
DECLARATION OF THE NATURAL, INALIENABLE AND SACRED HUMAN AND CITIZENS' RIGHTS
DECLARATION OF THE RIGHTS OF WOMAN AND THE FEMALE CITIZEN
DE GOUGES becomes involved in political life because she considers it a scandal that women are not entitled to human and citizen rights. Her campaign against slavery and her declaration of women's rights seal her fate. Eventually, she is vilified, convicted and guillotined.
Abolition of monarchy
Third Estate constitutes National Assembly In Paris
Coalition wars: European monarchies vs. France
AMERICAN REVOLUTIONARY WAR 1775 – 1783
Constitution of the United States of America
FRENCH REVOLUTION 1789 – 1799
New constitution: separation of powers and popular sovereignty
Louis XVI execution; reign of terror begins
LAPLACE CONFIRMS THE VALIDITY OF UNIVERSAL GRAVITATION.
LAPLACE TRAITÉ DE MÉCANIQUE CÉLESTE
1775
1780
1785
1790
1795
1800

KANT
1724–1804

Man is the only being who needs education.

influenced by | correspondence | discord

ROUSSEAU
1712–1778

Man is born free and everywhere he is in chains.

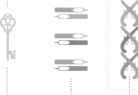

VOLTAIRE
1694–1778

Discord is the great ill of mankind; and tolerance is the only remedy for it.

DIDEROT
1713–1784

From fanaticism to barbarism is only one step.

D'ALEMBERT
1717–1783

We will be impressed by daylight the more so as we have been living in darkness for some time.

SHAFTESBURY
1671–1713

Truth, 'tis supposed, may bear all lights.

LOCKE
1632–1704

The end of law is not to abolish or restrain, but to preserve and enlarge freedom.

remarkable developments during the age of enlightenment

Frederick II of Prussia
ENLIGHTENED ABSOLUTISM
Catherine II of Russia

Through correspondence and invitations to their courts, »enlightened monarchs« frequent philosophers whose initial hope for reforms quickly turns to disappointment as they realize that true social change is a bottom-up rather than a top-down process.

Catherine II purchases the libraries of both VOLTAIRE and DIDEROT. They form an essential part of the National Library of Russia, established in 1795.

ROUSSEAU a loner with a tendency towards neurosis who successively falls out with VOLTAIRE after a controversy over the earthquake of Lisbon (1755) and with the encyclopedists after the publication of the article »Geneva« by D'ALEMBERT. Throughout his life, DIDEROT remains well-disposed towards him.

ENCYCLOPÉDIE

OU DICTIONNAIRE RAISONNÉ DES SCIENCES, DES ARTS ET DES MÉTIERS

The continuous threat of censorship ensures that the main articles have a rather conformistic attitude. Criticism is hidden in secondary articles and numerous cross references. Around 160 other collaborators from different social and professional milieus contribute to the gigantic enterprise.

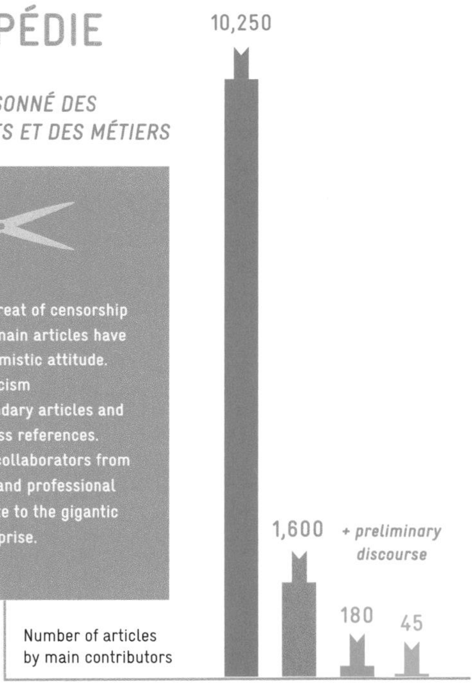

10,250
1,600
+ preliminary discourse
180
45
Number of articles by main contributors

SCIENTIFIC ACADEMIES

memberships

1660 LONDON 1
1666 PARIS 2
1700 BERLIN
1724 ST. PETERSBURG

In Europe, there are two different models of scientific academies.

1 ROYAL SOCIETY		ACADÉMIE DES SCIENCES 2
private funding	VS.	state funding
loose ties to state power		state paternalism
large number of members		limited number of members

OUR HERITAGE

In 1972, UNESCO created the World Heritage Convention to protect our cultural and natural heritage. Every year, the UNESCO World Heritage Committee evaluates candidates for the World Heritage List. The Yellowstone National Park (USA), Galápagos Islands (Ecuador) and Aachen Cathedral (Germany) were among the first thirteen cultural and natural heritage sites to be confirmed in 1978. A year later, a further 44 World Heritage sites were added to the list. Following the 43rd conference in July 2019, the World Heritage List now includes 1,121 World Heritage sites in 167 member states, including 869 cultural, 213 natural and 39 mixed sites.

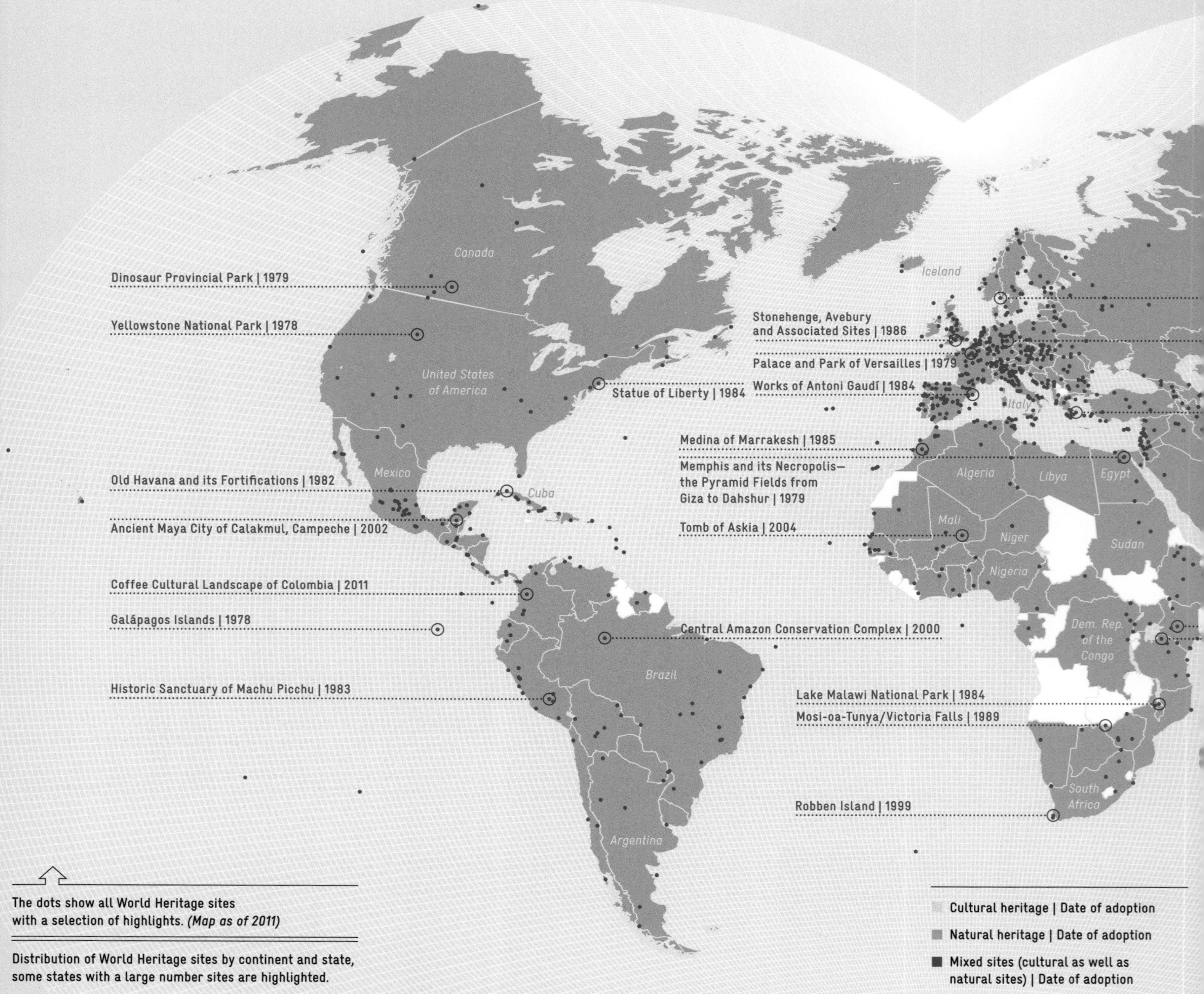
Canada
Iceland
United States of America
Mexico
Cuba
Italy
Algeria
Libya
Egypt
Mali
Niger
Nigeria
Sudan
Dem. Rep. of the Congo
Brazil
South Africa
Argentina
Dinosaur Provincial Park | 1979
Yellowstone National Park | 1978
Old Havana and its Fortifications | 1982
Ancient Maya City of Calakmul, Campeche | 2002
Coffee Cultural Landscape of Colombia | 2011
Galápagos Islands | 1978
Historic Sanctuary of Machu Picchu | 1983
Statue of Liberty | 1984
Stonehenge, Avebury and Associated Sites | 1986
Palace and Park of Versailles | 1979
Works of Antoni Gaudí | 1984
Medina of Marrakesh | 1985
Memphis and its Necropolis–the Pyramid Fields from Giza to Dahshur | 1979
Tomb of Askia | 2004
Central Amazon Conservation Complex | 2000
Lake Malawi National Park | 1984
Mosi-oa-Tunya/Victoria Falls | 1989
Robben Island | 1999
Cultural heritage | Date of adoption
Natural heritage | Date of adoption
Mixed sites (cultural as well as natural sites) | Date of adoption

The dots show all World Heritage sites with a selection of highlights. *(Map as of 2011)*

Distribution of World Heritage sites by continent and state, some states with a large number sites are highlighted.

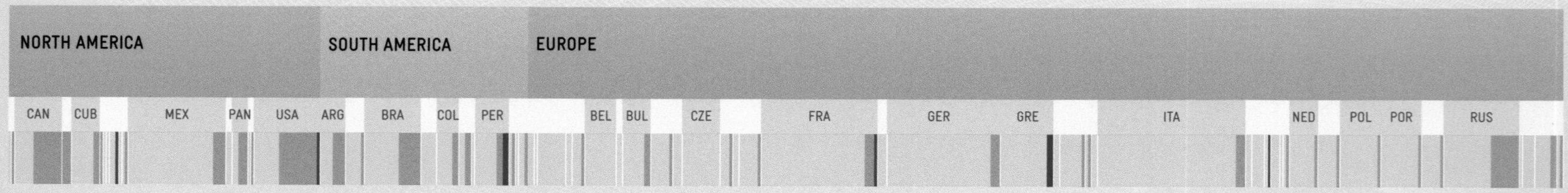
NORTH AMERICA
SOUTH AMERICA
EUROPE
CAN
CUB
MEX
PAN
USA
ARG
BRA
COL
PER
BEL
BUL
CZE
FRA
GER
GRE
ITA
NED
POL
POR
RUS

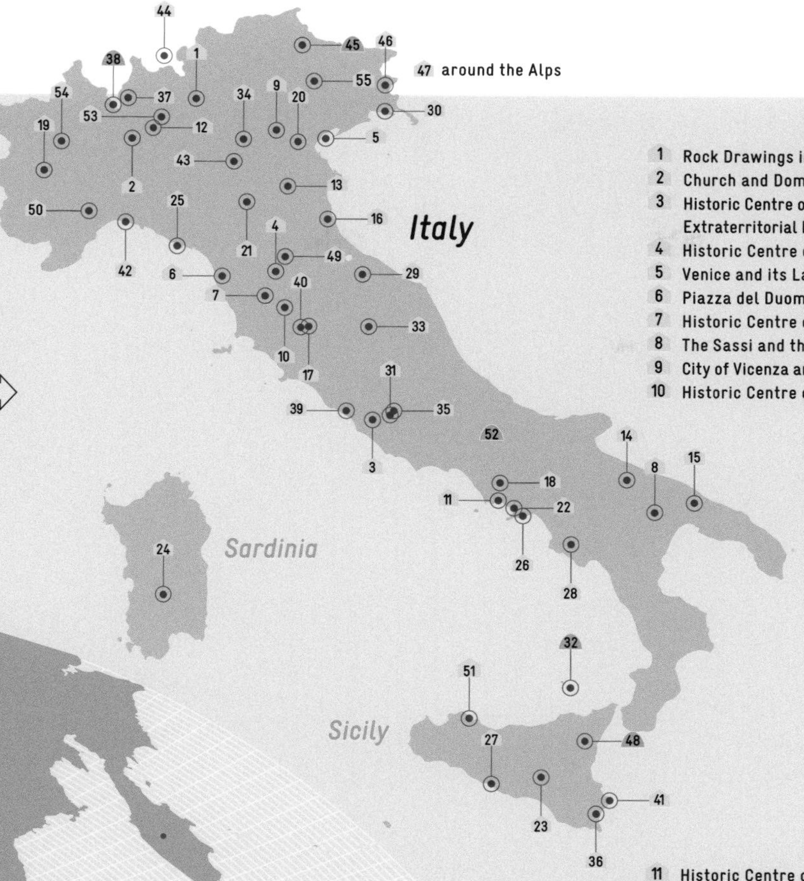
47 around the Alps
Italy
Sardinia
Sicily

Italy has the most World Heritage sites. The accompanying figure shows the 55 sites arranged by the year of adoption into the List.

31 Cultural heritage | Date of adoption

32 Natural heritage | Date of adoption

1 Rock Drawings in Valcamonica | 1979
2 Church and Dominican Convent of Santa Maria delle Grazie | 1980
3 Historic Centre of Rome, the Properties of the Holy See in that City Enjoying Extraterritorial Rights and San Paolo Fuori le Mura | 1980, extended in 1990
4 Historic Centre of Florence | 1982
5 Venice and its Lagoon | 1987
6 Piazza del Duomo, Pisa | 1987
7 Historic Centre of San Gimignano | 1990
8 The Sassi and the Park of the Rupestrian Churches of Matera | 1993
9 City of Vicenza and the Palladian Villas of the Veneto | 1994, extended in 1996
10 Historic Centre of Siena | 1995
11 Historic Centre of Naples | 1995
12 Crespi d'Adda | 1995
13 Ferrara, City of the Renaissance, and its Po Delta | 1995, extended in 1999
14 Castel del Monte | 1996
15 The Trulli of Alberobello | 1996
16 Early Christian Monuments of Ravenna | 1996
17 Historic Centre of the City of Pienza | 1996
18 18th-Century Royal Palace at Caserta with the Park, the Aqueduct of Vanvitelli, and the San Leucio Complex | 1997
19 Residences of the Royal House of Savoy | 1997
20 Botanical Garden (Orto Botanico), Padua | 1997
21 Cathedral, Torre Civica and Piazza Grande, Modena | 1997
22 Archaeological Areas of Pompei, Herculaneum and Torre Annunziata | 1997
23 Villa Romana del Casale | 1997
24 Su Nuraxi di Barumini | 1997
25 Portovenere, Cinque Terre, and the Islands (Palmaria, Tino and Tinetto) | 1997
26 Costiera Amalfitana | 1997
27 Archaeological Area of Agrigento | 1997
28 Cilento and Vallo di Diano National Park with the Archeological sites of Paestum and Velia, and the Certosa di Padula | 1998
29 Historic Centre of Urbino | 1998
30 Archaeological Area and the Patriarchal Basilica of Aquileia | 1998
31 Villa Adriana (Tivoli) | 1999
32 Isole Eolie (Aeolian Islands) | 2000
33 The Basilica of San Francesco and Other Franciscan Sites, Assisi | 2000
34 City of Verona | 2000
35 Villa d'Este, Tivoli | 2001
36 Late Baroque Towns of the Val di Noto | 2002
37 Sacri Monti of Piedmont and Lombardy | 2003
38 Monte San Giorgio | 2003, extended in 2010
39 Etruscan Necropolises of Cerveteri and Tarquinia | 2004
40 Val d'Orcia | 2004
41 Syracuse and the Rocky Necropolis of Pantalica | 2005
42 Genoa: Le Strade Nuove and the system of the Palazzi dei Rolli | 2006
43 Mantua and Sabbioneta | 2008
44 Rhaetian Railway in the Albula/Bernina Landscapes | 2008
45 The Dolomites | 2009
46 Longobards, Places of Power (568-774 AD) | 2011
47 Prehistoric Pile dwellings around the Alps | 2011
48 Mount Etna | 2013
49 Medici Villas and Gardens in Tuscany | 2013
50 Vineyard Landscape of Piedmont: Langhe-Roero and Monferrato | 2014
51 Arab-Norman Palermo and the Cathedral Churches of Cefalú and Monreale | 2015
52 Ancient and Primeval Beech Forests of the Carpathians and Other Regions of Europe | 2017
53 Venetian Works of Defence between the 16th and 17th Centuries: Stato da Terra—Western Stato da Mar | 2017
54 Ivrea, industrial city of the 20th century | 2018
55 Le Colline del Prosecco di Conegliano e Valdobbiadene | 2019

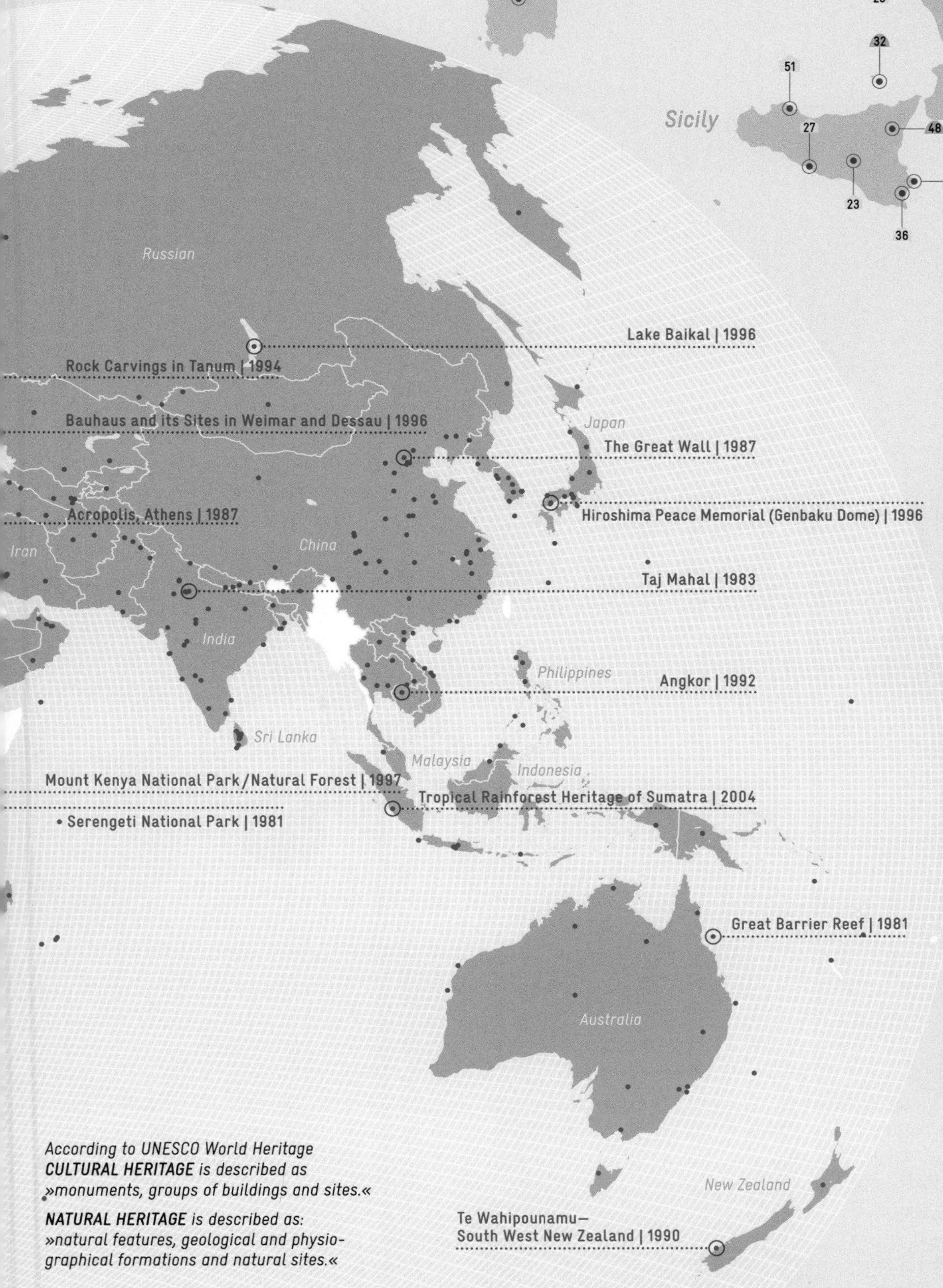
Russian
Lake Baikal | 1996
Rock Carvings in Tanum | 1994
Bauhaus and its Sites in Weimar and Dessau | 1996
Japan
The Great Wall | 1987
Acropolis, Athens | 1987
Hiroshima Peace Memorial (Genbaku Dome) | 1996
Iran
China
Taj Mahal | 1983
India
Philippines
Angkor | 1992
Sri Lanka
Malaysia
Indonesia
Mount Kenya National Park/Natural Forest | 1997
Tropical Rainforest Heritage of Sumatra | 2004
Serengeti National Park | 1981
Great Barrier Reef | 1981
Australia
New Zealand
Te Wahipounamu—
South West New Zealand | 1990

According to UNESCO World Heritage ***CULTURAL HERITAGE*** *is described as »monuments, groups of buildings and sites.«*

NATURAL HERITAGE *is described as: »natural features, geological and physiographical formations and natural sites.«*

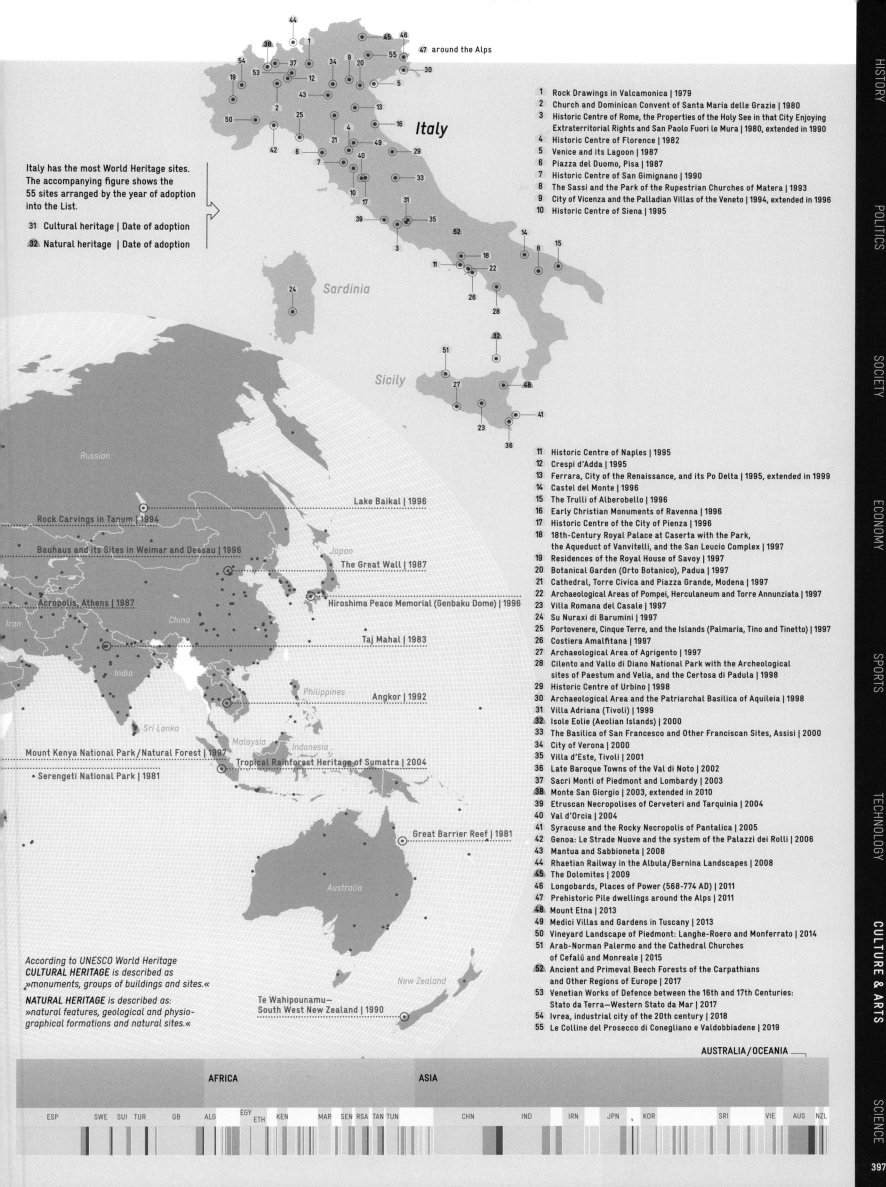

AUSTRALIA/OCEANIA
AFRICA
ASIA
ESP
SWE
SUI
TUR
GB
ALG
EGY
ETH
KEN
MAR
SEN
RSA
TAN
TUN
CHN
IND
IRN
JPN
KOR
SRI
VIE
AUS
NZL

THE GILDED EGG HUNT

Deeply connected to the fate of the Romanov dynasty and the Russian Revolution are a collection of extravagant boxes – which have become known throughout the world asthe Fabergé eggs. They were gifted to Maria Feodorovna, the penultimate Tsarina of Russia. Her death was the starting shot of what has become the world's most high-stakes egg hunt, and one that takes us on a journey across the globe. The precious pieces have been seized, stolen, smuggled and sold. And the hunt isn't over yet – seven missing bejeweled eggs worth millions are still missing.

EASTER EGG TIMELINE

In total, 52 eggs were made, each year in a form that marked a milestone in the **Tsarinas' lives.** The seven missing eggs were all gifted to Maria.

Color key:
- Eggs for Maria
- Eggs missing today
- Eggs for Alexandra

К.ФАБЕРЖЕ
Fabergé mark

Hen egg as a comparison, 5 cm

1872 — 1880 — 1881 — 1885

SETTING THE DIRECTION

Peter Carl Fabergé, becomes the **director** of his father's **jewellery shop in St. Petersburg at the age of 26.**
He is determined to make the name »Fabergé« synonymous with expertise and perfection befitting his **upper-class clientele.** The **Russian tsars** soon become his most dazzling clients.

1881: **Maria** and her husband **Alexander III** become the **Empress and Emperor of Russia** in their 30s.

1885: **Alexander commissions the first egg** from Peter Carl Fabergé—an event that would define the jeweler's carrier. **An annual tradition is born.**

1846: **Peter Carl Fabergé** is born

1847: **Maria Feodorovna** is born
(née Princess Dagmar of Denmark, name change after her marriage in 1866)

1881 - 1894: Tsar Alexander III reigns with Maria by his side

BACK INTO THE LIMELIGHT

The Third Imperial Egg from 1887 was one of the more inconspicuous eggs presented to Maria. After decades, it has become **the latest of the lost Fabergés to be rediscovered,** offering hope that the seven other eggs might still exist somewhere.

JACKPOT!

A scrap metal dealer in the United States picked up the Third Imperial Egg at a **flea market,** not knowing what it was. After years of being unable to resell it, he searched the internet for clues to the tiny clock inside. He came up with a photo from a 1960s auction catalog that had just been rediscovered—it was his egg. The treasure was authenticated and it was **sold for millions** in 2014.

OWN 3D MODEL BASED ON PHOTO: COURTESY OF WARTSKI, LONDON

SECRET SURPRISE

All the eggs were designed to reveal a **unique treasure hidden inside** the egg. The surprise was even unknown to the commissioning tsar. Each one would **reference an event in the Romonov family**, such as a replica of the coach that brought the empress to her coronation. Family members, buildings and pets were all honored.

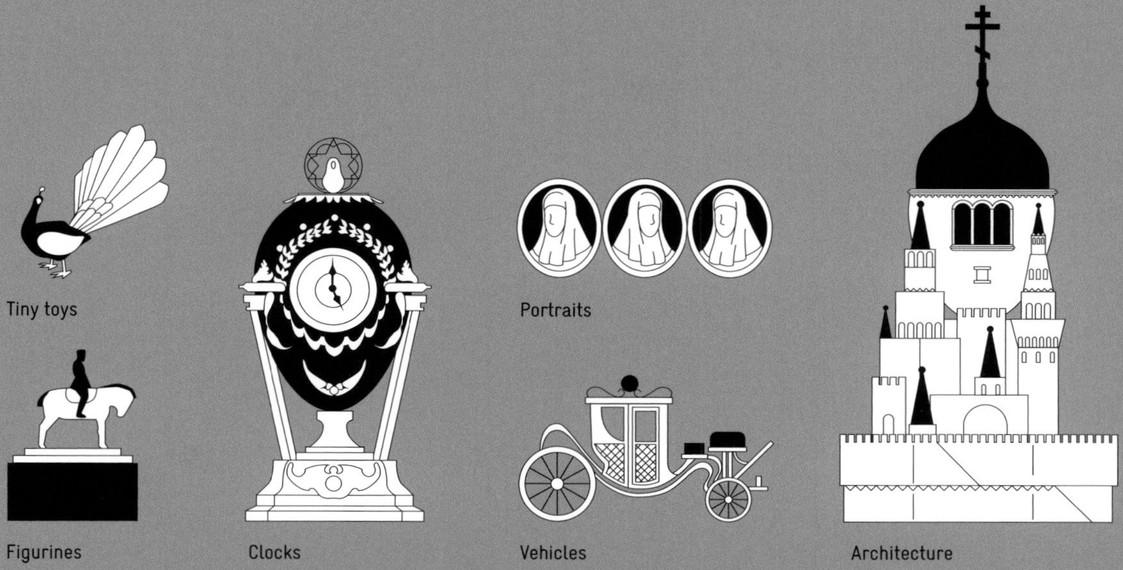
Tiny toys
Portraits
Figurines
Clocks
Vehicles
Architecture

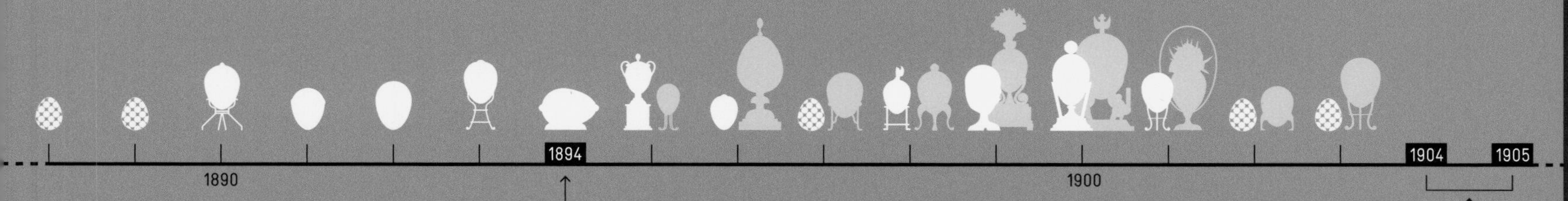
1890
1894
1900
1904
1905

Following **Alexander's death**, his heir **Nicholas II takes the throne.** He continues the Easter tradition for his mother and starts commissioning **eggs for his wife Alexandra as well.**

No eggs are made from 1904 – 1905 during the **Russo-Japanese war** and increasing **political unrest** in Russia.

Eggs are manufactured annually for 32 years.

1894 - 1917: Tsar Nicholas II reigns with Alexandra by his side

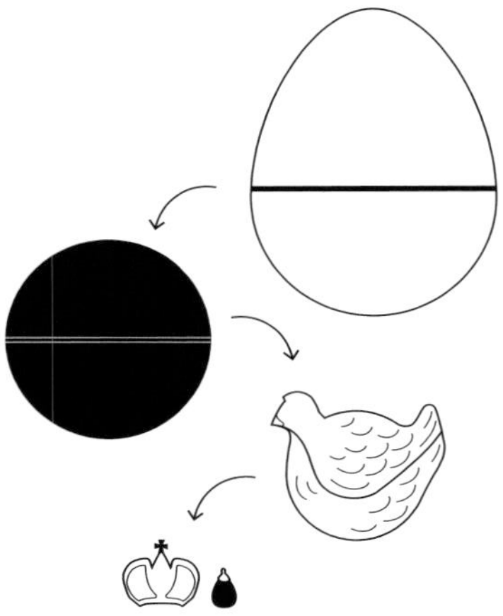

FIRST THE EGG, THEN THE CHICKEN

The very first Fabergé egg from 1885 was aptly known as the **First Hen Egg**. It was 6.4 cm and opened to reveal a golden yolk containing a golden hen. Inside her was a replica of the imperial crown and a ruby pendant.

Fabergé Workshop
around 1903

PRESENT AND ACCOUNTED FOR

Continued interest in the Imperial Russian Fabergé Eggs has ensured that **most of them have been recovered.** Since the fall of the Royal Russian family, the eggs have **turned up in auction houses, public exhibitions and private collections around the world.** Today, Russia and the United States are home to most of the eggs.

Color key:

- Eggs for Maria
- Eggs missing today
- Eggs for Alexandra

The Moscow Kremlin Egg (1906) was the largest one at 36.1 cm.

The last two commissions were never finished.

Hen egg for comparison, 5 cm
1917
1910
1920

END OF STORY?

Bolsheviks are looting Romanov palaces.
The Fabergé eggs are among the confiscicated treasures and will be sent to Moscow.
The revolution sees the end of the tsar's reign.

1920: **Peter Carl Fabergé** dies

Eggs are manufactured annually for 32 years.

Maria Feodorovna flees Moscow before her son's execution, living in **exile** until 1928. It has never been confirmed whether she took some of her eggs with her.

Tsar Nicholas II's reign ends when he is killed during the revolution.

The **Royal Danish Egg** (1903) is one of the missing pieces, but is unique in that experts know what it looks like. While it hasn't been seen since before the revolution, there is an official photograph of the treasure.

Have you seen these eggs? From left to right: **Nécessaire Egg** (1889), **Commemorative Egg** (1909), sketch of **Cherub with Chariot Egg** (1888) by Fabergé scholar Anna Palmade.

COURTESY OF WARTSKI, LONDON

COURTESY OF THE IGOR CARL FABERGÉ FONDATION

ANNA PALMADE

COMPETING COLLECTORS

The **private owners** of Fabergé Eggs are among the wealthiest and most powerful people in the world.

VIKTOR VEKSELBERG

The Russian businessman and art collector holds more eggs than any other private collector.

ELIZABETH II OF ENGLAND

The Queen is related to the Romanovs through Tsarina Alexandra. She is both a collector and a presumed rightful heir.

ALEXANDER IVANOV

The founder of the Fabergé Museum in Baden-Baden, Germany, claims to have the unfinished eggs commissioned in 1917.

ALBERT II OF MONACO

The Monaco royal inherited his egg from his father.

1928 → Today

1928: **Maria Feodorovna** dies

GLOBETROTTERS

Most eggs can now be found in **private collections, foundations and museums.**

20 in **Russia**

2 in **Germany**

16 in the **USA**

1 in **Qatar**

3 in **England**

1 in **Monaco**

2 in **Switzerland**

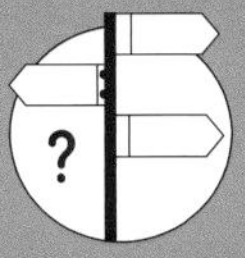

8 **unknown**, lost or anonymous owner

* The eggs marked with a star could be a copy or a former model of the last egg for Alexandra.

LOST FOREVER? LOST FOR NOW

There are **not many clues** as to the whereabouts of the 7 lost eggs. There are **photographs** taken from Fabergé's records as well as auction documentation for some of the eggs.
For the others, the egg hunters comb through exhibition records to find objects that resemble the rest of the collection.
In the case of the **Empire Nephrite Egg** (1905) and the **Egg with Hen in Basket** (1886), experts rely on **written descriptions** from workshops or Maria's personal inventories. The **Mauve Egg** (1897) seems determined to disappear forever: No photos or descriptions have yet been found.

Fabergé Museum Baden-Baden

Fersman Mineralogical Museum Moscow

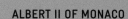

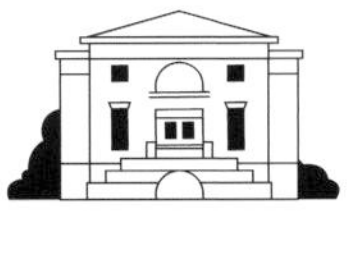

IMPERIAL IMPOSTOR

Fabergé's final egg for Alexandra, the 1917 **Blue Tsarevich Constellation Egg,** was never presented publicly. Today, both the Fersman Mineralogical Museum in **Moscow,** Russia, and the Fabergé Museum in **Baden-Baden,** Germany, **claim to display the original.**

KIMONO (着物)

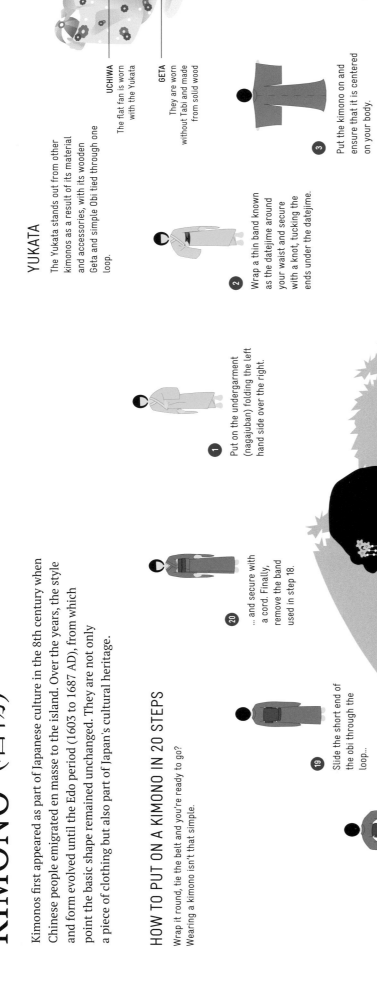

Kimonos first appeared as part of Japanese culture in the 8th century when Chinese people emigrated en masse to the island. Over the years, the style and form evolved until the Edo period (1603 to 1687 AD), from which point the basic shape remained unchanged. They are not only a piece of clothing but also part of Japan's cultural heritage.

HOW TO PUT ON A KIMONO IN 20 STEPS

Wrap it round, tie the belt and you're ready to go? Wearing a kimono isn't that simple.

1. Put on the undergarment (nagajuban) folding the left hand side over the right.
2. Wrap a thin band known as the datejime around your waist and secure with a knot, tucking the ends under the datejime.
3. Put the kimono on and ensure that it is centered on your body.
4. The kimono should be about 3 centimeters off the floor.
5. Wrap the right side over the body so that the collar will be positioned higher than that of the left side.
6. Wrap the left side so that the panel sits at the waist.

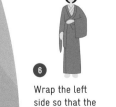

16. Let the long end of the obi hang down.
17. Fold the end upwards and fix in place with obi pads and obiage.
18. Fold the strap inwards and tie into place.
19. Slide the short end of the obi through the loop...
20. ... and secure with a cord. Finally, remove the band used in step 18.

YUKATA

The Yukata stands out from other kimonos as a result of its material and accessories, with its wooden Geta and simple Obi tied through one loop.

UCHIWA
The flat fan is worn with the Yukata

GETA
They are worn without Tabi and made from solid wood

KANZASHI
This traditional floral hair accessory is designed to match the kimono either by event or month.

SENSU
These folding fans are kept in the folds of the kimono and come out to keep cool, to touch up the make up or as part of a dance.

OBI
The most intricate part of the kimono is composed of many bands and belts.

HOUMONGI

This style of kimono can be worn by either married or single women

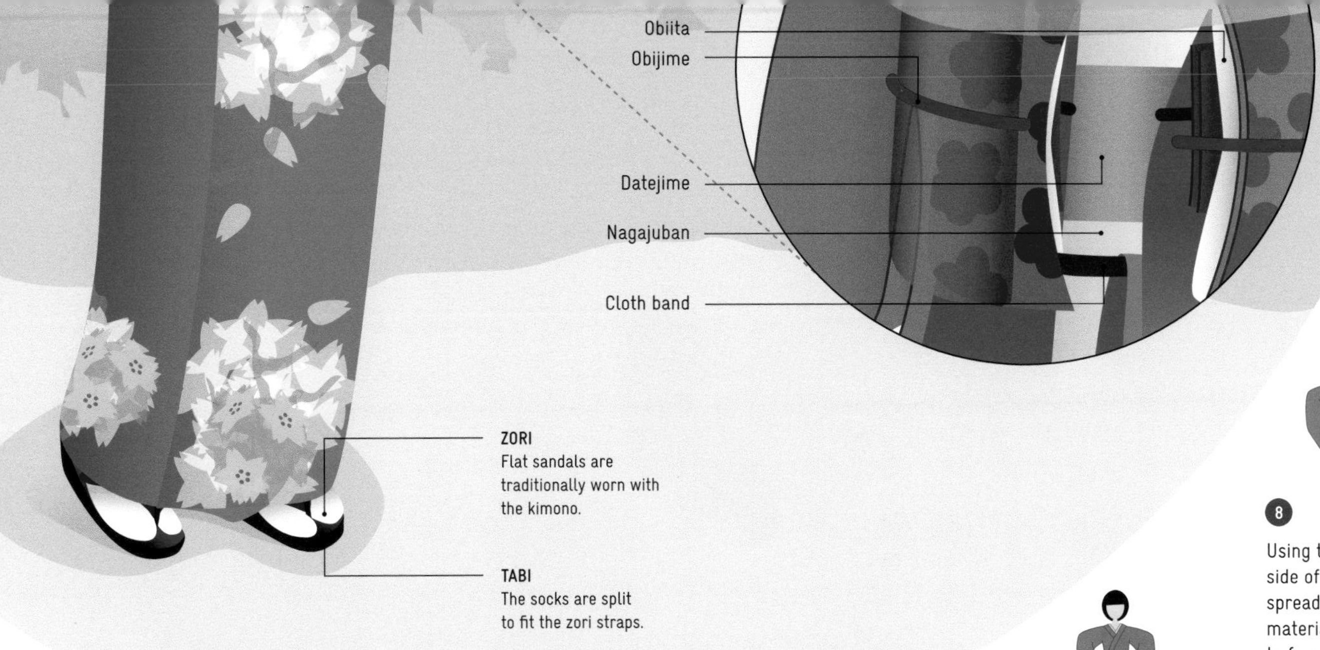
Obiita
Obijime
Datejime
Nagajuban
Cloth band
ZORI
Flat sandals are traditionally worn with the kimono.
TABI
The socks are split to fit the zori straps.

7 Fix the kimono in place with a cloth band.

8 Using the slits in the side of the kimono, spread out any excess material over the band to form a pocket.

9 Fix the kimono in place with another cloth band over the waist.

10 Wrap around another datejime

11 Wrap around the obi-ita (»obi board«), which keeps the obi free of folds and wrinkles.

12 Fold the obi in half lengthwise. Measure 40 centimeters from the end and place this section of the obi at the waist with the crease down.

13 Wrap the obi around your waist three times, then put the extra 40 centimeters of cloth towards the back by placing it over the right shoulder.

14 Fix the obi in place and tie both ends together at the back.

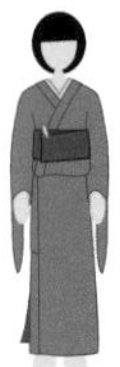

15 Pin the short end at the front.

THE DIFFERENT STYLES OF KIMONOS

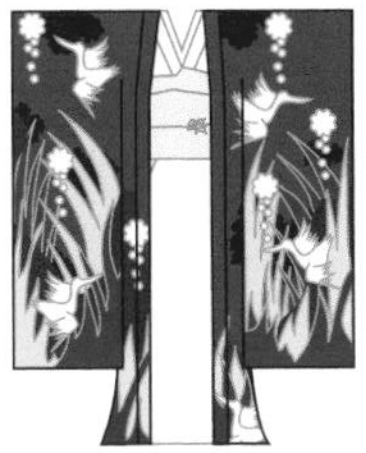

SHIROMAKU & UCHIKAKE
(shiro: »white«)
The shiromaku is worn by the bride at the wedding ceremony. She then adds the ornate uchikake for the celebrations.

KUROTOMESODE
(kuro: »black«)
This formal kimono is only patterned on the skirt and is worn by married women at the weddings of close family members.

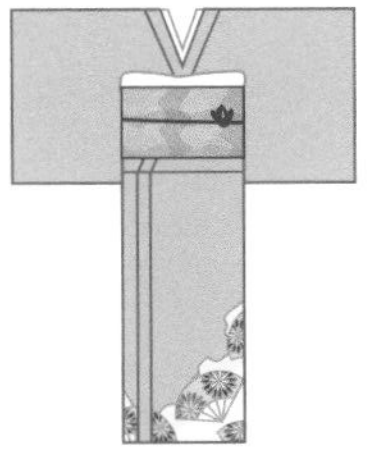

IROTOMESODE
(iro: »color«)
Like the kurotemesode, the pattern appears only on the skirt, but this garment is less formal through its primary color.

FURISODE
(furi: »swinging«)
This is the formal kimono for unmarried women. It is patterned all over and the sleeves can be as long as 114 centimeters.

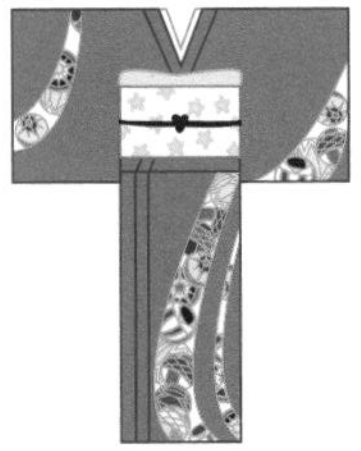

HOUMONGI
(visiting clothes)
Worn for formal and business events, the pattern appears on the sleeves and the skirt.

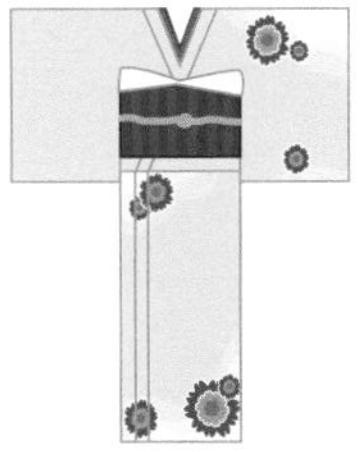

TSUKESAGE
(tsuke: »a type of stitching«)
The pattern on this style is found on the skirt and one sleeve. It is less formal than the houmongi.

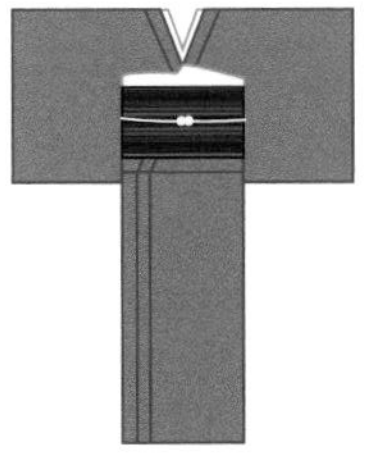

IROMUJI
(one color)
This kimono is primarily worn to tea ceremonies. The cloth is not patterned, but often textured.

KOMON
(small pattern)
This is considered an everyday kimono. It has a simple all-over pattern and is only worn on informal occasions.

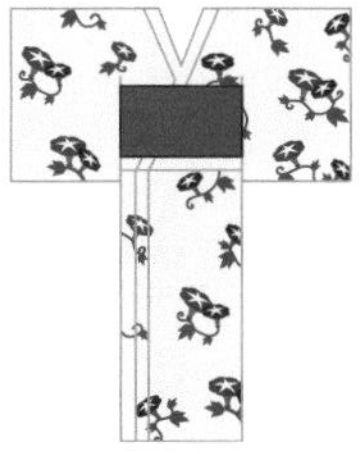

YUKATA
(bathing clothes)
The simple cotton kimono is worn to summer fêtes without a nagajuban (under garment) and in public Japanese baths.

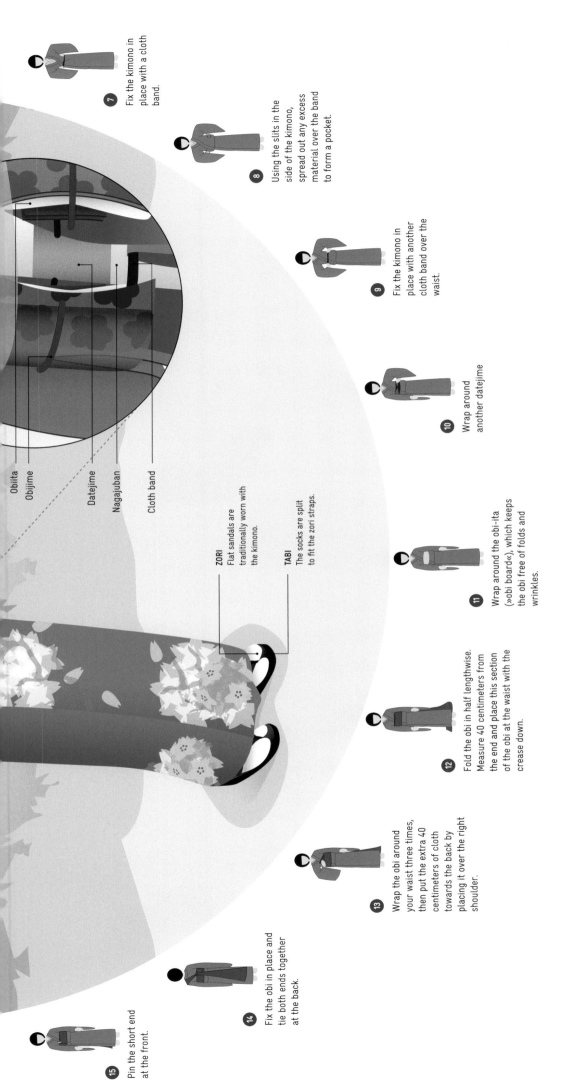

MOFUKU
(mourning clothes)
The all-black mofuku is worn to funerals or ceremonies for the deceased by close family members.

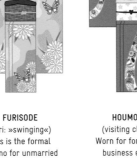

BED & BREAKFAST

A breakfast of cold cuts, cheese and toast would spoil the atmosphere of a Parisian getaway. A croissant and black coffee would be more suited. But do you know what to expect in Greece or Costa Rica? How we start our day varies from a country to country and sometimes even within a single country: Not all Germans like Bavarian tradition of Weisswurst in the morning. And even if we do indulge in the morning, we don't always eat the same thing everyday. We have collected some examples of how breakfast varies in certain countries. To avoid wasting food, we have cooked with paper, scissors and glue. »Mon amour, I have folded a croissant for you.«

Germany

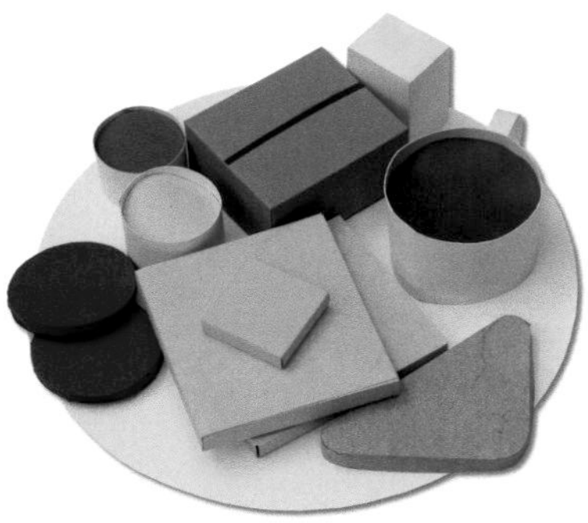

Continental breakfast & coffee

Germany – Bavaria

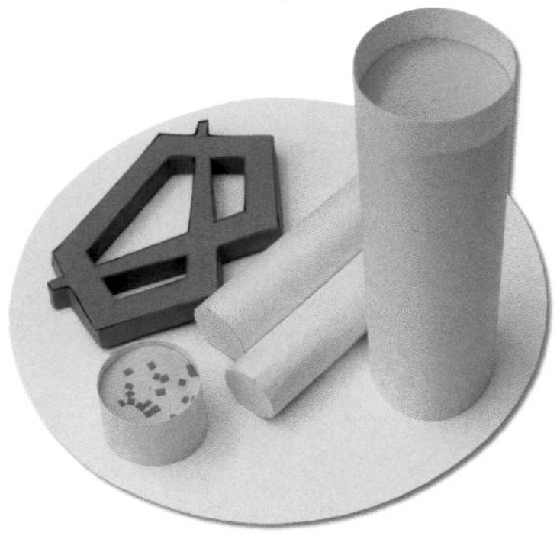

Veal sausage, pretzel with sweet mustard & wheat beer

United Kingdom

Bacon & egg – sunny side up, sausages, beans, toast & tea

France

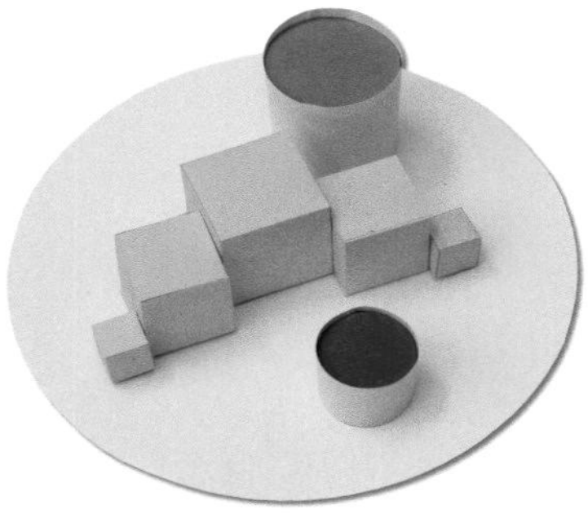

Croissant, jam & coffee with milk

Spain

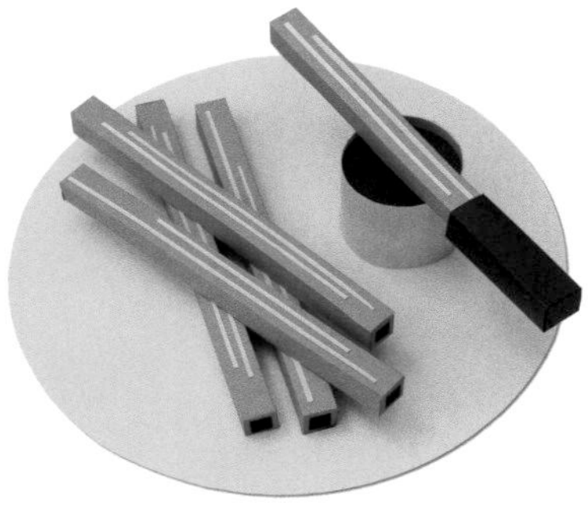

Churros (funnel cake) & hot chocolate

Italy

Cornetto (sweet roll) & espresso

Sweden

Smörgåsar (sandwiches) cream of caviar & Filmjölk (sour milk)

Greek

Paximadi (rusk), feta cheese & coffee

Turkey

Egg – sunny side up, garlic salami, vegetables & coffee

Russia

Kasha (oatmeal) & coffee

Canada

Pancakes with sirup & coffee

USA

Egg – sunny side up, sausages, bacon, roasted potatoes & coffee

Costa Rica

Egg – sunny side up, rice with beans, baked bananas & coffee

Guatemala

Egg – sunny side up, rice with beans, baked bananas & coffee

Mexico

Huevos Motuleños [1]

[1] (Tortillas, egg – sunny side up, beans), baked bananas & coffee

United Arab Emirates

Humus (chickpea spread), ragout, pita bread & tea

India

Dual Chapati (pita bread), lentils, rice & spicy tea

China

Jiaozi (filled samosa) & hot soy milk

Japan

Bento box for kids [2]

[2] Finger food of fish, meat & vegetables

Egypt

Ful Medames (soup of slow-cooked fava beans) & coffee

Tanzania

Mandazi (fried dough balls) & Chai Ya rangi (black tea)

10,000

SWEET TOOTH

Sugar was first extracted from sugar cane in Persia in 600 AD, causing people to clamour for the sweet stuff. It is a valuable item that has made many colonial powers a lot of money over the years. In 1747, sugar beet was so highly taxed that the sugar that was extracted from the root vegetable was inaccessible to the lower classes. It was not until 1879 that saccharin (from the Latin saccharum – sugar) was discovered, thereby enabling sweetness to be produced artificially – and cheaply. Nowadays, sweetening your morning tea is much more complicated than »Pass the sugar, please!«

1,000

Synthetic sweeteners

Sweetness compared with saccharose

E number of approved substance

— 200×
Aspartame 4 KCAL/G **E951**

Non-heat-resistant and used as an enhancer for fruit and citrus flavors

1965	1994	40 mg/kg
Discovery	*Approval*	*ADI (acceptable daily intake)*

$C_{14}H_{18}N_2O_5$

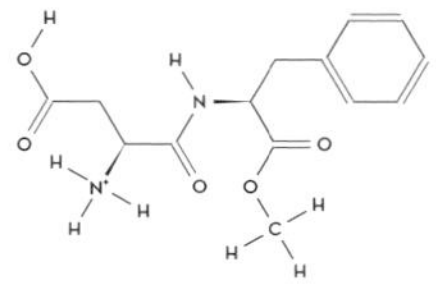

— 200×
Acesulfame potassium **E950**

Heat-resistant and cannot be broken down by the body or at water purification facilities.

1967 1983 9 mg/kg

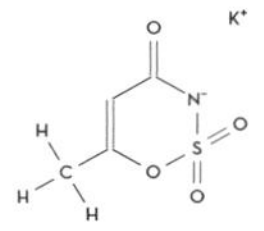

$C_4H_4KNO_4S$

— 550×
Saccharin **E954**

Enhances the effects of aspartame and cyclamate.

1978 1995 5 mg/kg

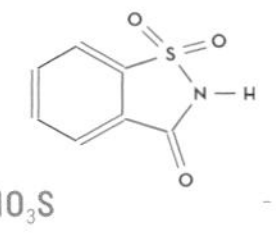

$C_7H_5NO_3S$

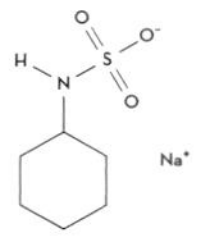

$C_6H_{12}NNaO_3S$

— 45×
Sodium cyclamate **E960**

Heat-resistant, used to enhance other sweeteners and controversially prohibited in the US.

1937 1994 7 mg/kg

100

The energy value of sugar

Sugar has an impact on blood sugar levels.

Sugar is cariogenic.

10

Sugar

4 KCAL/GRAM · INSULIN · CAVITIES

Carbohydrates (saccharides) are the most widely distributed organic substances and play a central role in the metabolism of humans, animals and plants as their most important energy source in terms of quantity. A distinction is made between mono-, di- and polysaccharides. Substances containing higher numbers of molecules are not sweet in taste.

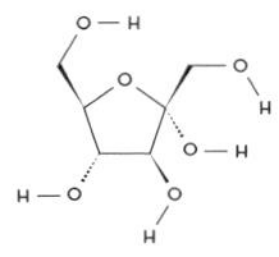

$C_6H_{12}O_6$

Fruit sugar

Naturally present in fruit and honey.

— 1.14×

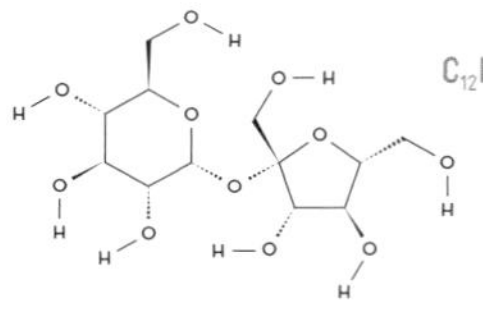

$C_{12}H_{22}O_{11}$

Retail sugar

The popular crystal sugar is made from glucose and fructose.

— 1×

Monosaccharides

1

0.5×
0.3×
Galactose

The body's metabolism turns galactose into glucose.

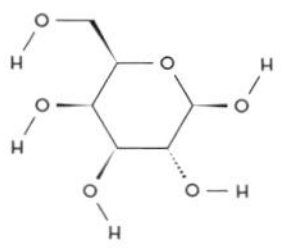

$C_6H_{12}O_6$

0.8×
0.5×
Dextrose

Creates a rapid rise in blood sugar levels and insulin secretion.

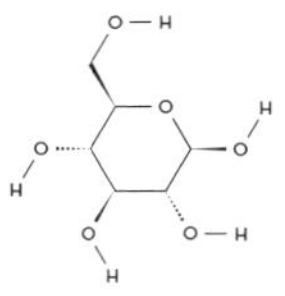

$C_6H_{12}O_6$

0.6×

$C_{12}H_{22}O_{11}$

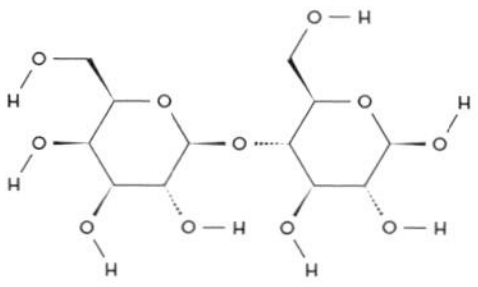

0.2×
Lactose *(Milk sugar)*

Consists of galactose and glucose.

$C_{12}H_{22}O_{11}$

0.6×

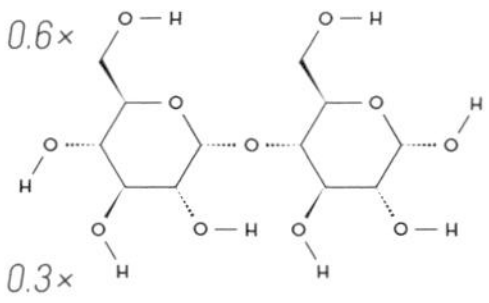

0.3×
Maltose *(Malt sugar)*

Present in grain and therefore in beer, pasta and muesli.

$C_{12}H_{24}O_{11}$

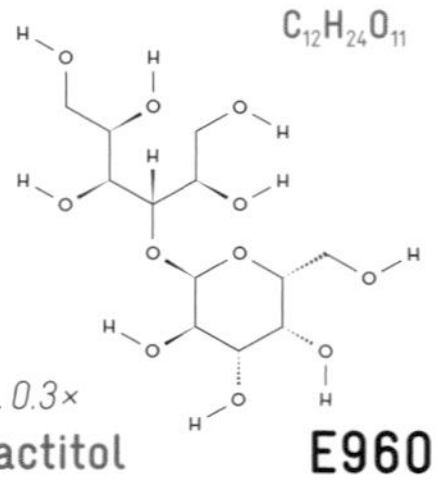

— 0.3×
Lactitol **E960**

Also used in powders because it doesn't attract moisture.

0.1

Disaccharides

0 KCAL/G* ~~INSULIN~~ ~~CAVITIES~~

Sweeteners

A variety of interests promote the development of different artificial sweeteners. While they were originally developed as a cheap alternative to retail sugar, their advantages for diabetics and for a low-calorie diet became obvious very quickly. Today, they are also added to food products because of their flavor-enhancing properties. Here we show all EU-approved sweeteners.

— 8000×

Neotame **E961**

Neotame is a developed form of aspartame.

1991 2010 2 mg/kg

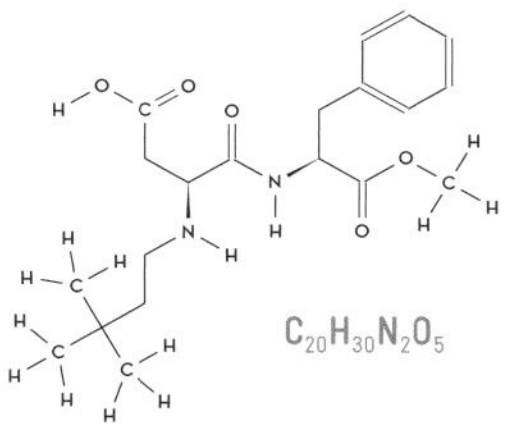

$C_{20}H_{30}N_2O_5$

— 600×

Sucralose **E955**

Heat-resistant, good solubility and a delayed but long-lasting sweetness.

1980 2006 15 mg/kg

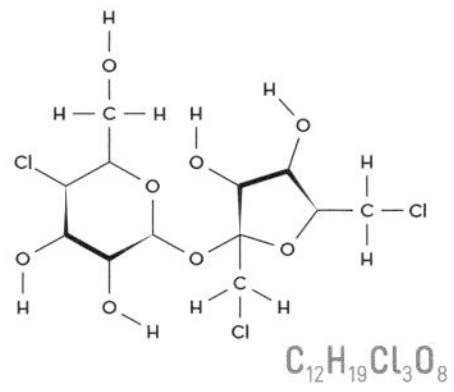

$C_{12}H_{19}Cl_3O_8$

— 350×

4 KCAL/G

Aspartame-acesulfame salt **E962**

Chemical compound of aspartame and acesulfame.

1995 2004 9 mg/kg

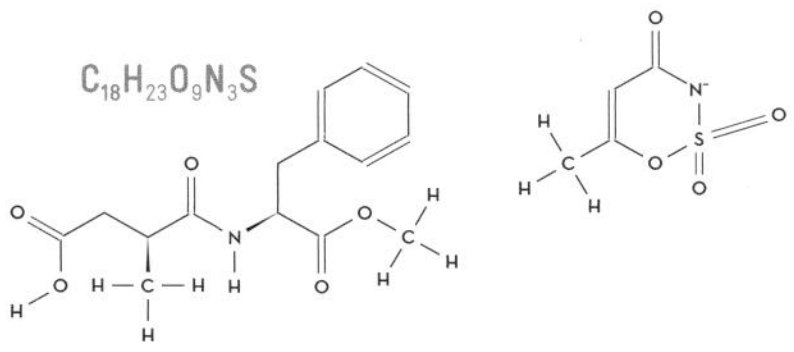

$C_{18}H_{23}O_9N_3S$

600×–400×

Neohesperidin-DC **E961**

Heat-resistant and storable with a licorice and menthol aftertaste.

1963 1994 5 mg/kg

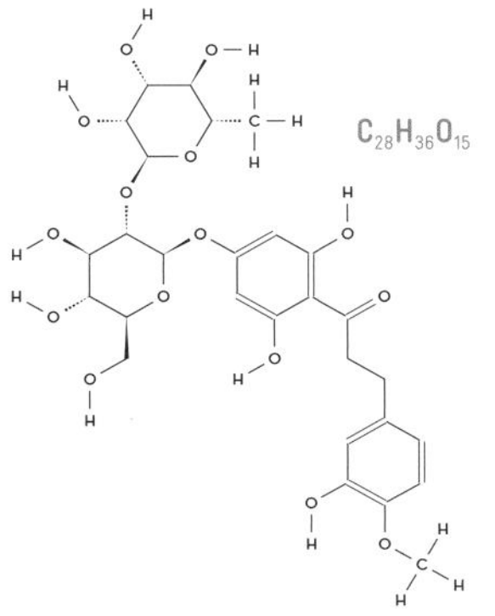

$C_{28}H_{36}O_{15}$

Natural sweeteners

2000×–3000×

4 KCAL/G

Thaumatin **E957**

Cost-intensively extracted from the berries of the West-African shrub Katamfe.

1855 1998 –

Thaumatin as a complex protein that cannot be depicted in this graphic form.

300×–200×

Steviol glycoside **E960**

Only a specific type of the stevia plant, which grows between Paraguay and Brazil, has sweet-tasting leaves.

1900 2011 4 mg/kg

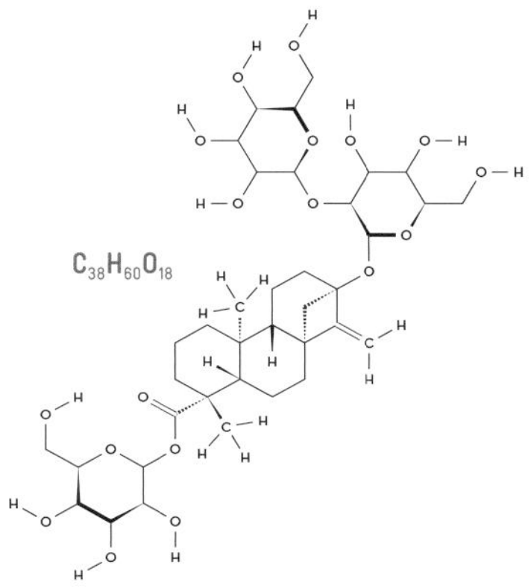

$C_{38}H_{60}O_{18}$

Sugar alcohol

Sugar alcohol is naturally present in pome and stone fruit and is produced by a reduction (reversal of oxidation) of carbohydrates. This is how lactitol is created from lactose. It is used, among other things, as a humectant and preservative. The graphic shows all sugar alcohol approved by the EU as sugar substitutes.

2.4 KCAL/G ~~INSULIN~~ ~~CAVITIES~~

0.5×–0.4×

Sorbitol **E960**

Attracts water and therefore stops food from dehydrating.

$C_6H_{14}O_6$

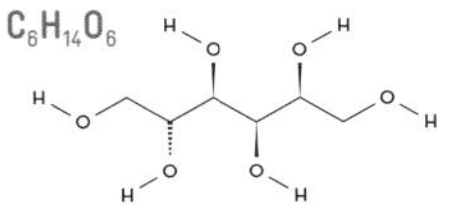

0.5×–0.4×

Mannitol **E421**

Present in many plants and algae through hydration of fructose.

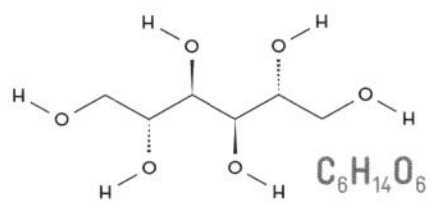

$C_6H_{14}O_6$

— 0.5×

Isomalt **E953**

Can be used as a substitute for saccharose and also has the same volume.

$C_{12}H_{24}O_{11}$

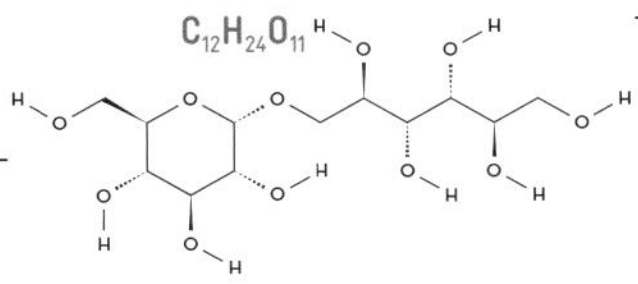

— 0.6×

Erythritol **E968**

Side effects only appear after excessive consumption.

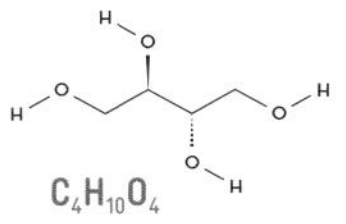

$C_4H_{10}O_4$

— 0.9×

Maltitol **E965**

Is used like sorbitol to keep food moist.

$C_{12}H_{24}O_{11}$

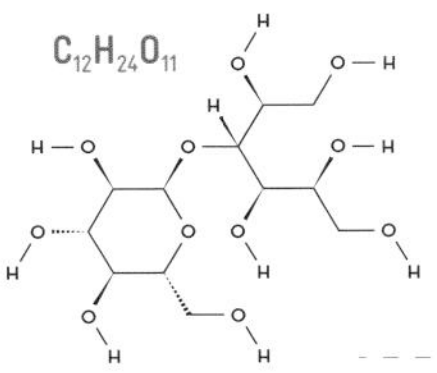

— 1.02×

Xylitol **E967**

Xylitol, also called »birch sugar«, can endanger life in some animals.

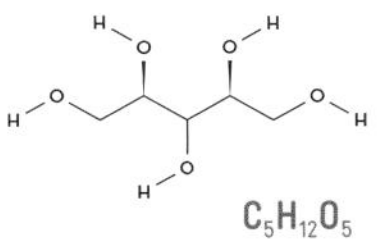

$C_5H_{12}O_5$

* Sweeteners except for Aspartame and Aspartame-acesulfame salt do not contain any calories.

SALT

If you're worth your monthly paycheck, you're said to be worth your salt. While it's a myth that Roman soldiers were paid in salt, they did earn enough to buy extra »white gold« with their paychecks. It is essential for bringing out the flavors in food and was instrumental in driving exploration as it allowed sea-faring explorers to take longer journeys with preserved food stores. Whether you prefer to use the delicate fleur de sel or go for a box of regular table salt, you can be sure that all types of salt are made of a minimum 97% sodium chloride.

Sea salt

Fleur de Sel

The salt flowers created by evaporation are harvested by hand.

Brine

Cooking salt

The name is derived from the method of production where a concentrated salt solution is boiled.

Rock salt

Himalaya salt

It actually originates mainly from Khewra in Pakistan. The orange coloring comes from iron oxidation.

Persian salt

Originating from Iran, it gets its blue coloring from the mineral Sylvin.

Variants

Palm Island Pacific Salt

This sea salt is mixed with activated carbon, Alaea red clay or bamboo leaf extract.

Bamboo salt

Bamboo tubes filled with salt and coated with clay are heated up to 1,000°C several times.

Viking salt

The salt smoked with beech, hickory or juniper wood is also known as Danish smoked salt.

Additives

Iodine & Fluoride

In order to provide enough Iodine for the thyroid it is common nowadays to add sodium iodate or potassium iodate.

Following an initiative in Switzerland, most salt producers also add sodium or potassium fluoride to prevent tooth decay.

Salt—the source of life and death

Hypernatremia

If too much salt is consumed, the blood's vital salt level exceeds that of the cells. The cells' osmosis balances it by thinning the blood with cell water—the cells dry out.

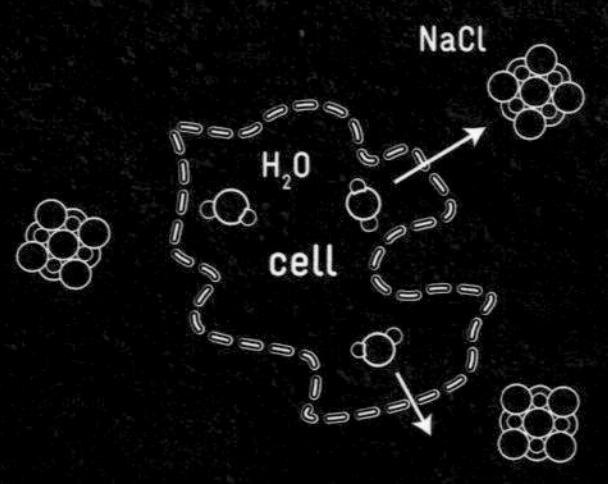

Hyponatremia

A salt deficiency leads to the opposite effect: The cells absorb too much water and burst because of their thin walls.

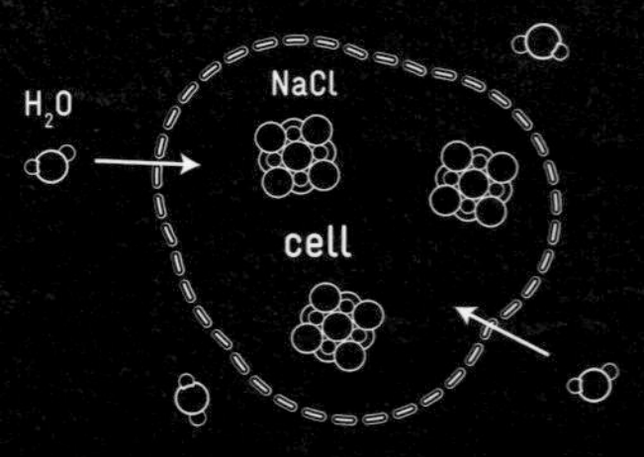

PEPPER

The most common type is »Piper nigrum«, which is named differently depending on its area of cultivation—e.g. Thalassery (Tellicherry) and Malabar—or its production method. Other spices, such as peppermint or cayenne pepper which is made from chili pods, have the word »pepper« attached to their name although they do not belong to the Piperaceae family.

Piper nigrum *Piperaceae family*

Black pepper

The fruits are harvested and dried shortly before ripening.

White pepper

Ripe fruits are pickled so that they lose their skin that bears the flavor.

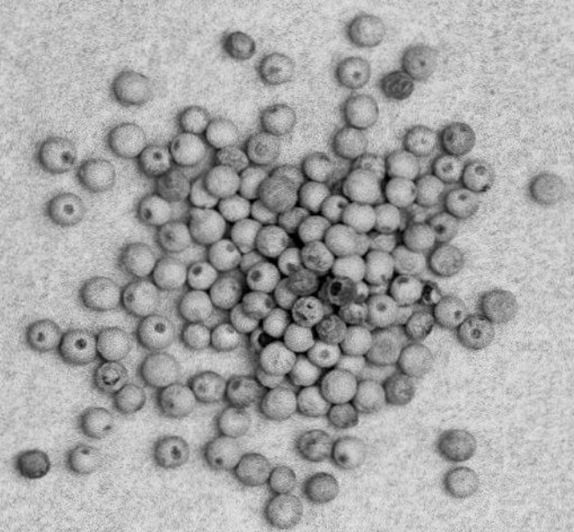

Red pepper

Ripe fruits are pickled in a salty or acidic brine.

Green pepper

Unripe fruits are pickled or dried like red pepper.

Sorts of pepper

Long pepper

Piperaceae family

Already known in Europe before black pepper, it is the variety from which the name originates. It is not only spicy but also has a slight sweet and sour taste.

Cubeb pepper

Piperaceae family

Spicy and bitter flavor with a turpentine-like taste. It is used in North Africa and Indonesia.

Unrelated spices

Sichuan pepper

Rutaceae family

A spice not related to pepper, also known as »lemon pepper«, which is very popular in Asia.

Brazil pepper

Anacardiaceae family

The sweet, pink berries are not related to pepper and are only added to food for presentation reasons.

Heat—More than a taste

The pure heat of spices such as pepper, chili and horseradish is neutral in taste when compared with the basic tastes sweet, sour, bitter, salty and umami (savory, full-bodied). It triggers the body to react in several ways.

Cooling

The activation of warmth receptors promotes blood circulation in the tissue. **Sweat pores** open up—the body cools down.

Flavor

The mucous membranes' blood circulation activates the **taste buds**. This enhances the sensation of flavors.

Protection

Heat has an antibiotic and disinfecting effect on **bacteria**. This is why it is often used for preserving food.

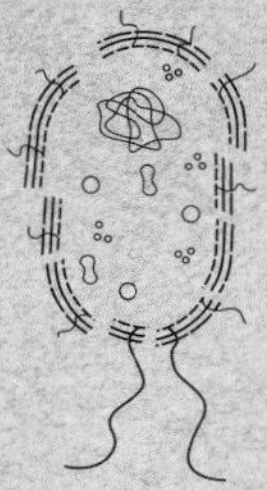

FRUITFUL RESEARCH

When you eat fruit, seeds tend to get in the way. But we are putting them in the spotlight here because they are plants' natural reproduction agents. These days, we prefer fruit varieties with very few or no seeds at all to ensure the unadulterated enjoyment of our fruit. Can you still recognize the fruits?

Scientific name of plant
CITRULLUS LANATUS
Germination time
100
MAXIMUM
25 DAYS
75
MINIMUM
50
Pips of sample
4,596 G
fruit name
Watermelon
Texture of sample and its weight (corresponds to size of circle)

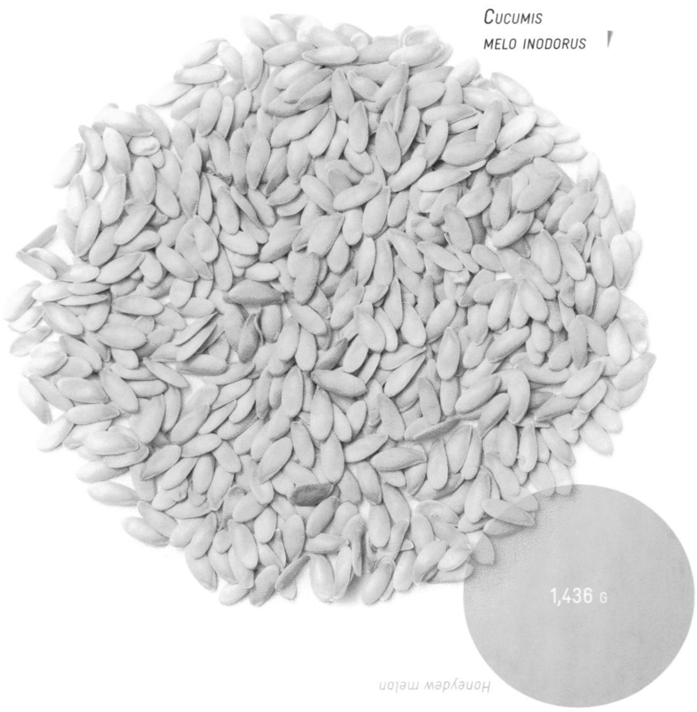
CUCUMIS MELO INODORUS
1,436 G
Honeydew melon

One-cent coin in comparison to the size of a seed

CARICA PAPAYA
1,364 G
Papaya

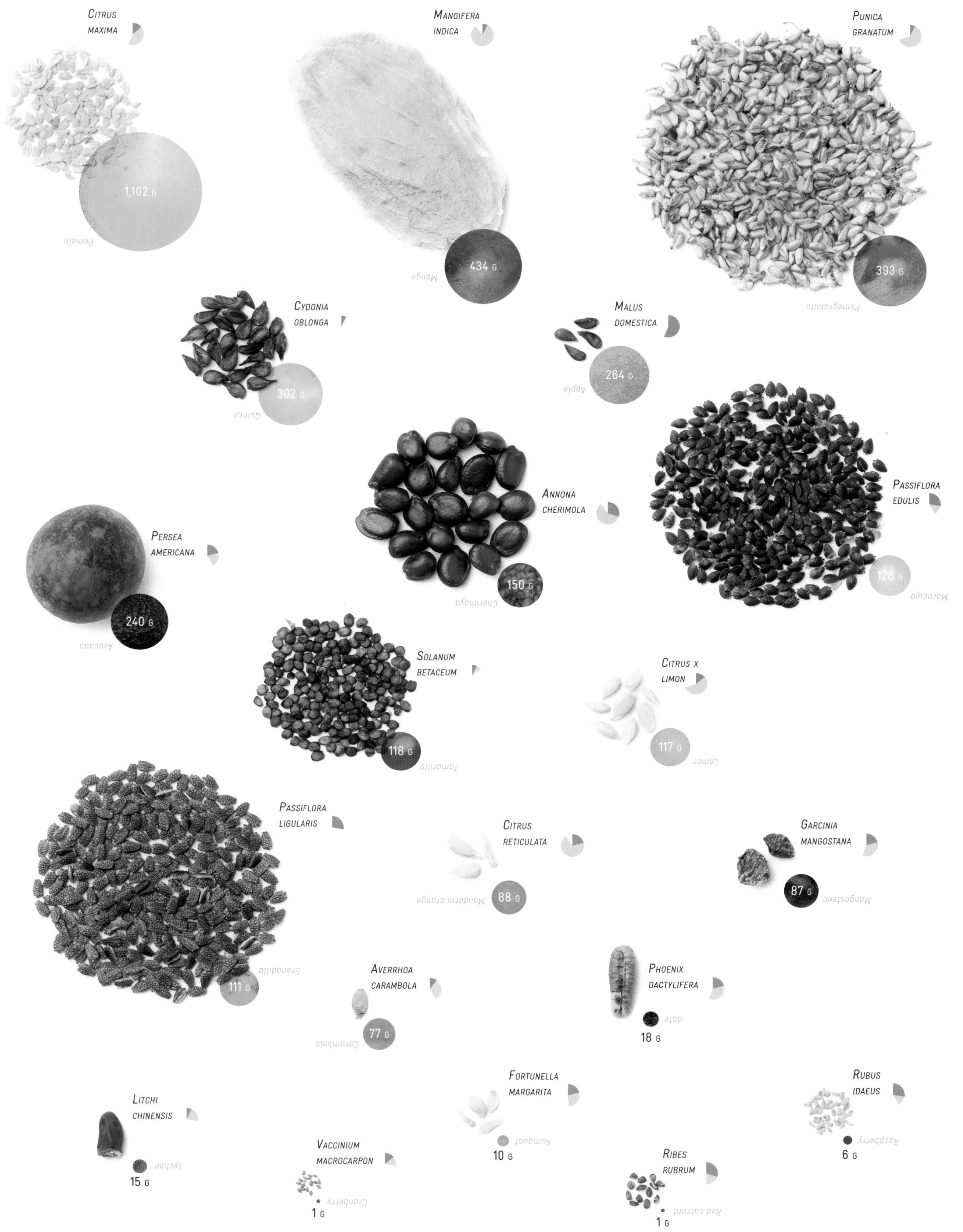
Citrus maxima
1,102 g
Pomelo
Mangifera indica
434 g
Mango
Punica granatum
393 g
Pomegranate
Cydonia oblonga
302 g
Quince
Malus domestica
264 g
Apple
Annona cherimola
150 g
Cherimoya
Passiflora edulis
128 g
Maracuja
Persea americana
240 g
Avocado
Solanum betaceum
118 g
Tamarillo
Citrus x limon
117 g
Lemon
Passiflora ligularis
111 g
Grenadilla
Citrus reticulata
88 g
Mandarin orange
Garcinia mangostana
87 g
Mangosteen
Averrhoa carambola
77 g
Carambola
Phoenix dactylifera
18 g
date
Litchi chinensis
15 g
Lychee
Vaccinium macrocarpon
1 g
Cranberry
Fortunella margarita
10 g
Kumquat
Ribes rubrum
1 g
Red currant
Rubus idaeus
6 g
Raspberry

THE WASP-EATING FIG

It is hard enough being vegetarian, let alone vegan. And now even figs are off limits? Vegetarians might want to think twice.

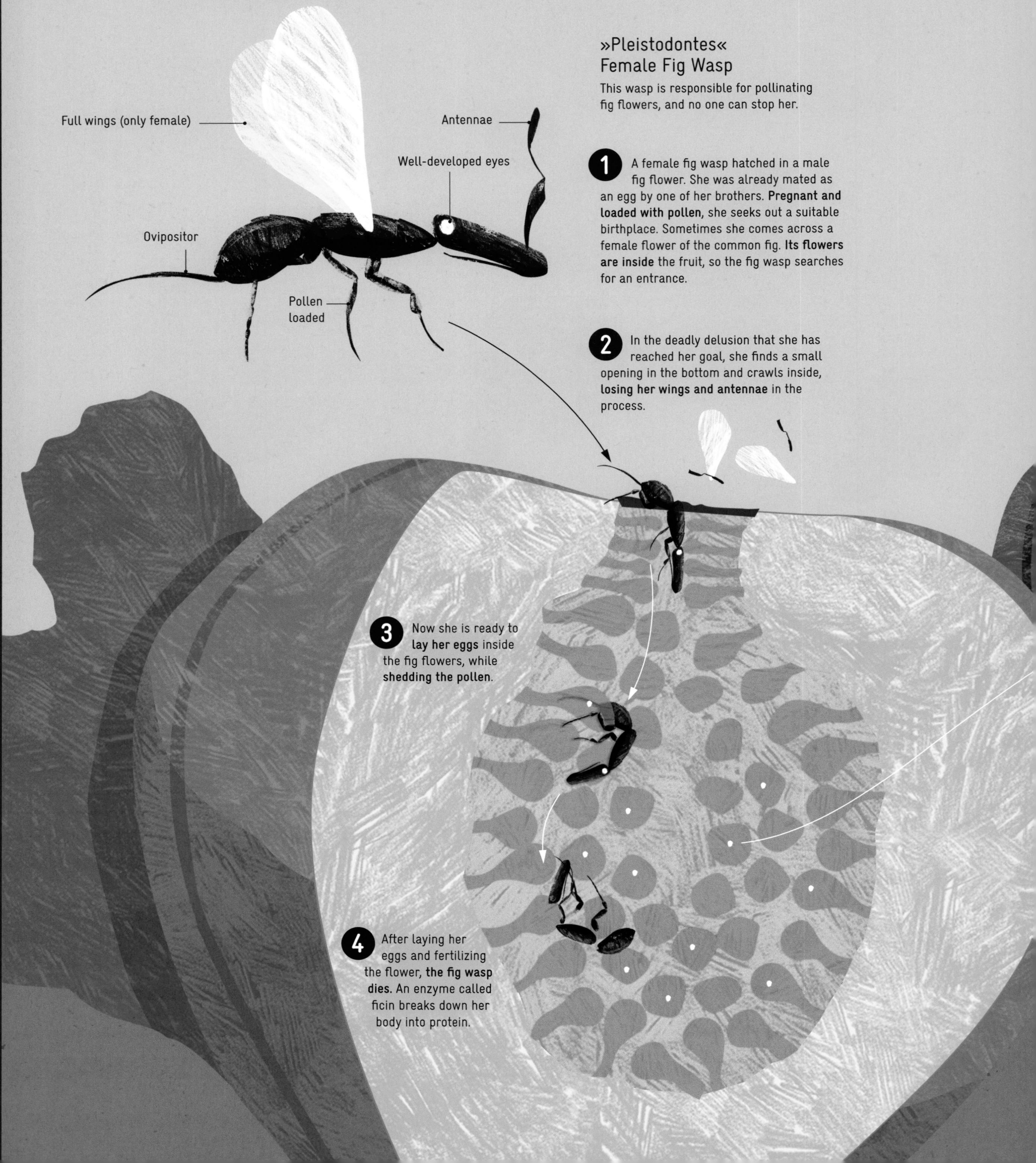
Full wings (only female)
Antennae
Well-developed eyes
Ovipositor
Pollen loaded

»Pleistodontes« Female Fig Wasp

This wasp is responsible for pollinating fig flowers, and no one can stop her.

1 A female fig wasp hatched in a male fig flower. She was already mated as an egg by one of her brothers. **Pregnant and loaded with pollen**, she seeks out a suitable birthplace. Sometimes she comes across a female flower of the common fig. **Its flowers are inside** the fruit, so the fig wasp searches for an entrance.

2 In the deadly delusion that she has reached her goal, she finds a small opening in the bottom and crawls inside, **losing her wings and antennae** in the process.

3 Now she is ready to **lay her eggs** inside the fig flowers, while **shedding the pollen**.

4 After laying her eggs and fertilizing the flower, **the fig wasp dies.** An enzyme called ficin breaks down her body into protein.

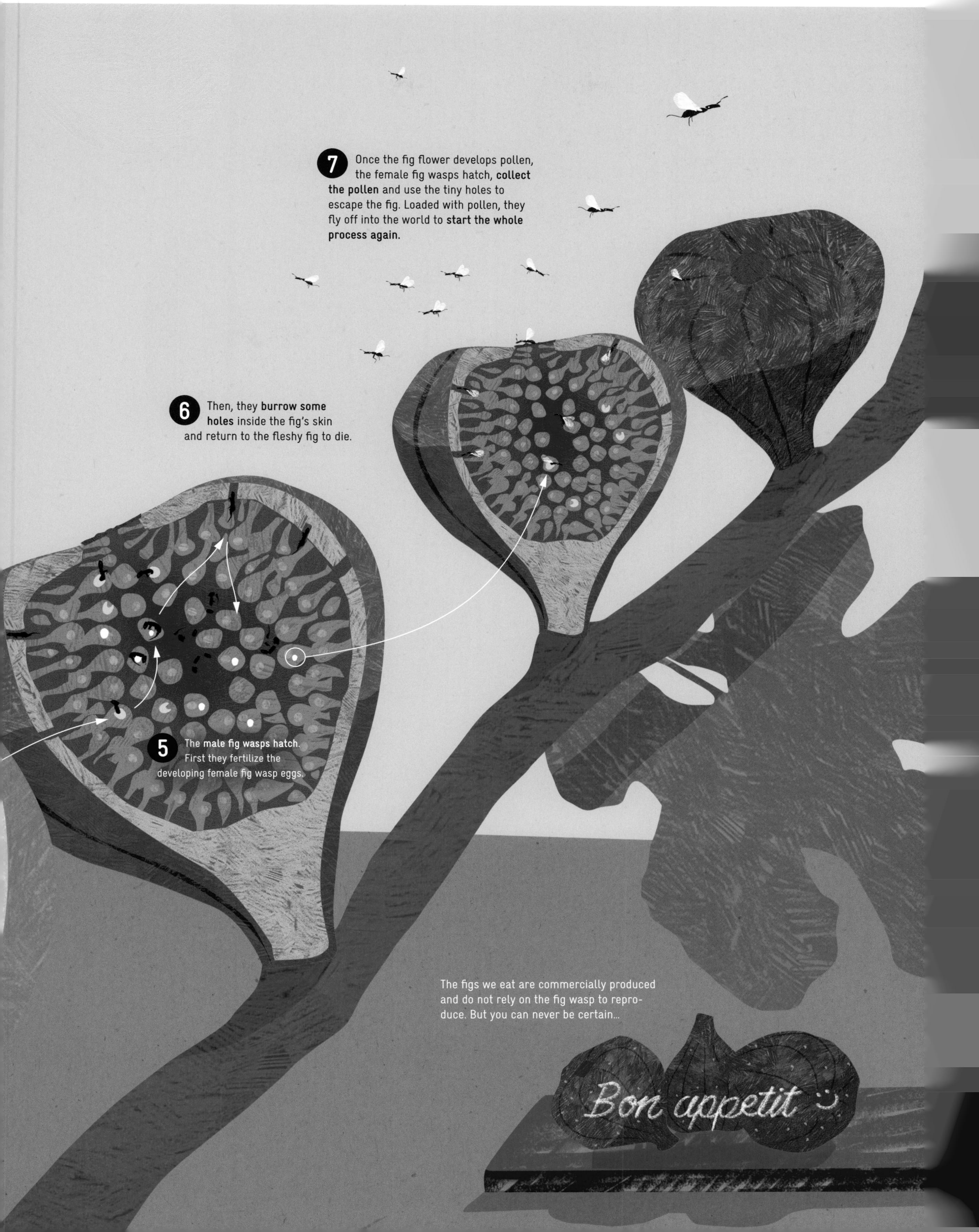

5 The **male fig wasps hatch**. First they fertilize the developing female fig wasp eggs.

6 Then, they **burrow some holes** inside the fig's skin and return to the fleshy fig to die.

7 Once the fig flower develops pollen, the female fig wasps hatch, **collect the pollen** and use the tiny holes to escape the fig. Loaded with pollen, they fly off into the world to **start the whole process again.**

The figs we eat are commercially produced and do not rely on the fig wasp to reproduce. But you can never be certain...

CEREAL FILLERS

Our ancient predecessors practiced agriculture as early as 10,000 years ago. The oldest proof of bread making, as we know it today, dates back to the Egyptians. The first bread was baked 6,000 years ago from ancient wheat. However, the ancient grains were, over time, replaced by higher-yielding types that were also easier to process, such as barley, wheat and rye. Today, the healthy grains are gradually reemerging from their niche existence.

Structure of cereal crops (example: rye)

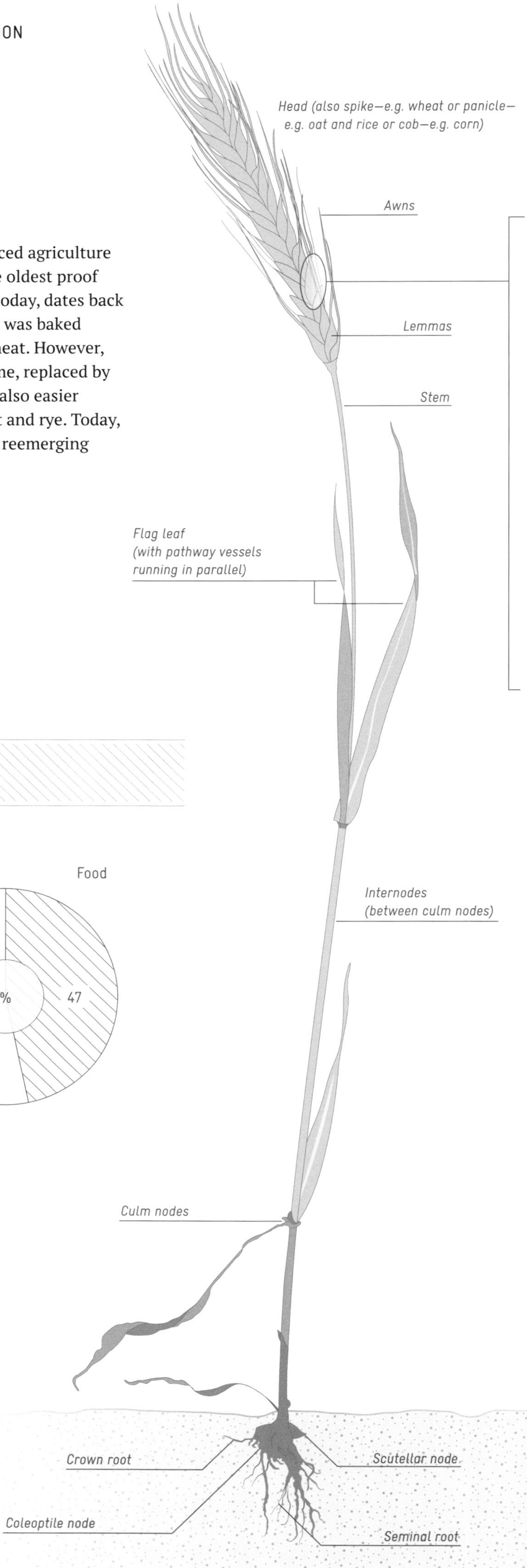
Head (also spike—e.g. wheat or panicle—e.g. oat and rice or cob—e.g. corn)
Awns
Lemmas
Stem
Flag leaf (with pathway vessels running in parallel)
Internodes (between culm nodes)
Culm nodes
Crown root
Scutellar node
Coleoptile node
Seminal root

Structure of a grain

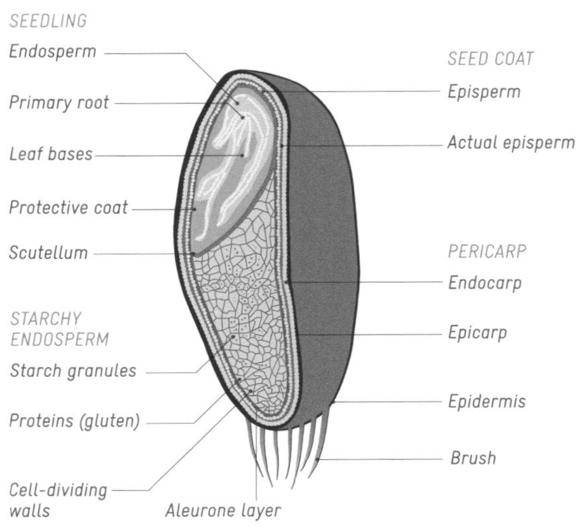
SEEDLING
Endosperm
Primary root
Leaf bases
Protective coat
Scutellum
STARCHY ENDOSPERM
Starch granules
Proteins (gluten)
Cell-dividing walls
Aleurone layer
SEED COAT
Episperm
Actual episperm
PERICARP
Endocarp
Epicarp
Epidermis
Brush

Processing of cereals worldwide sorted by type of use

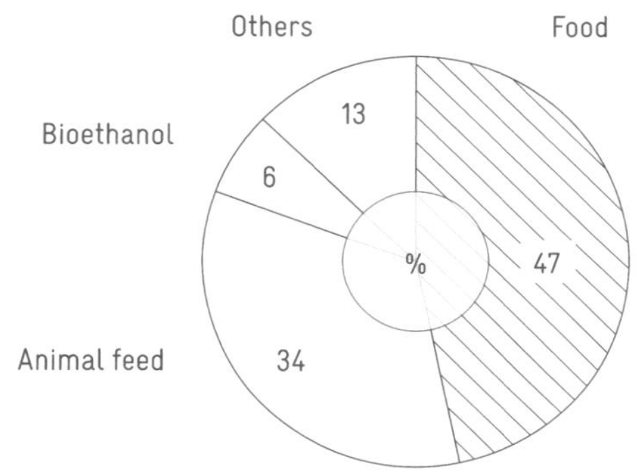
Others
Food
Bioethanol
Animal feed
13
6
%
47
34

Types of cereals

origin
1 belongs to the wheat family
2 ancient types of grain

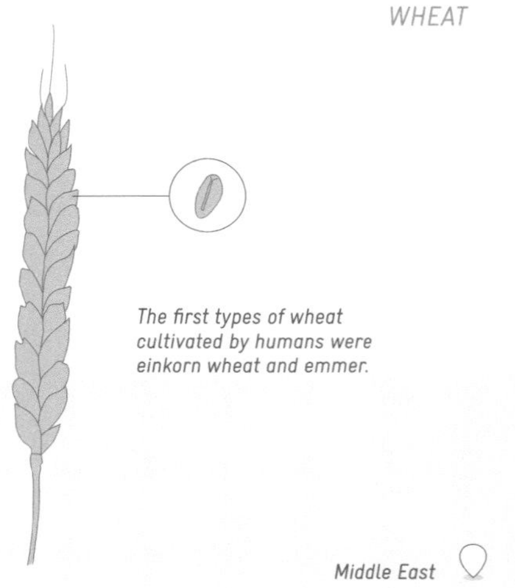
WHEAT
The first types of wheat cultivated by humans were einkorn wheat and emmer.
Middle East

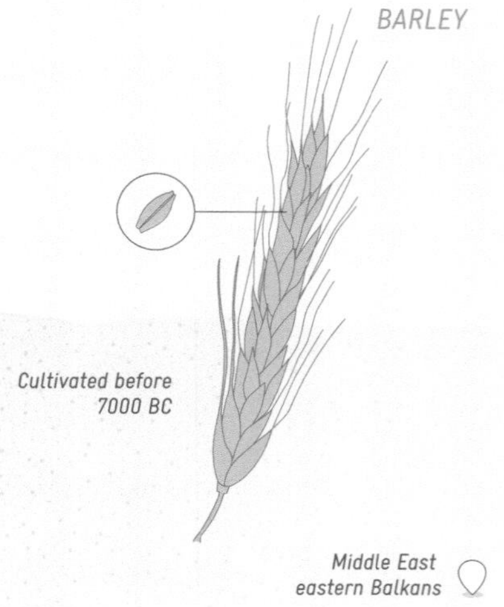
BARLEY
Cultivated before 7000 BC
Middle East eastern Balkans

CORN

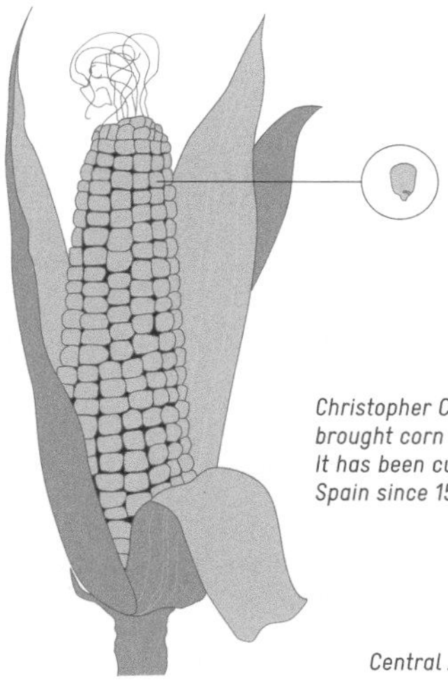

Christopher Columbus brought corn to Europe. It has been cultivated in Spain since 1525.

Central America

RYE

Spread as weed; from 500 AD cultivation increased in Central Europe; before WWII more rye than wheat was grown

Black Sea region

RICE

Is the main staple food for half of the world's population

India, China (Mekong river delta, Chao Phraya and Ganges)

TRITICALE

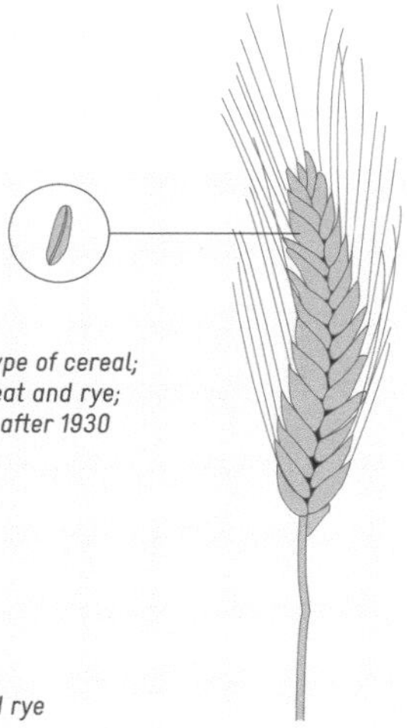

Newly cultivated type of cereal; cross between wheat and rye; selective breeding after 1930

see wheat and rye

OAT

Oldest references of its use are from around 5000 BC; has been cultivated since the Bronze Age

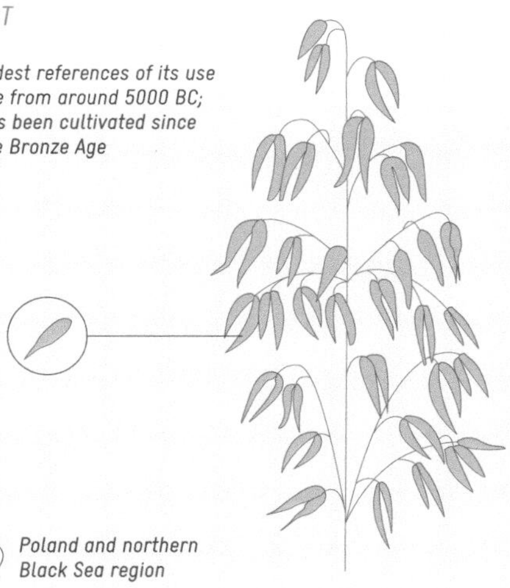

Poland and northern Black Sea region

MILLET

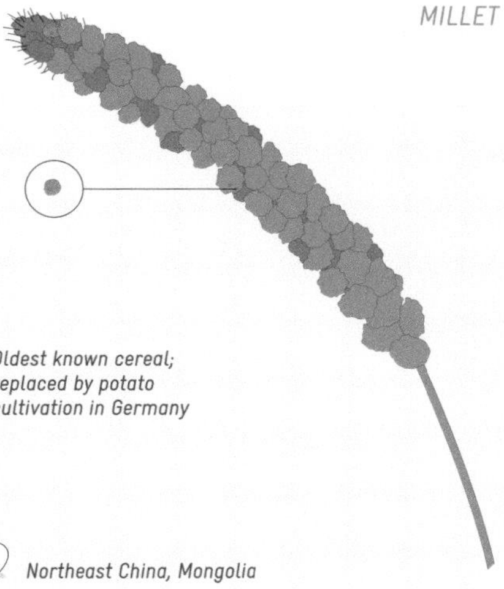

Oldest known cereal; replaced by potato cultivation in Germany

Northeast China, Mongolia

TEFF

Most important cereal of Ethiopia and Eritrea; regarded as the world's smallest grain

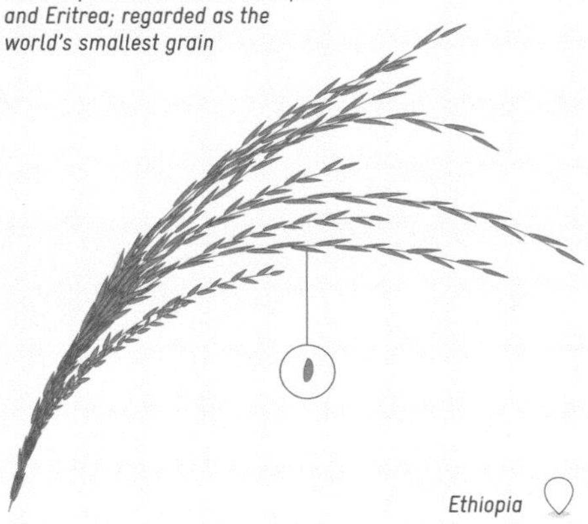

Ethiopia

SPELT [1, 2]

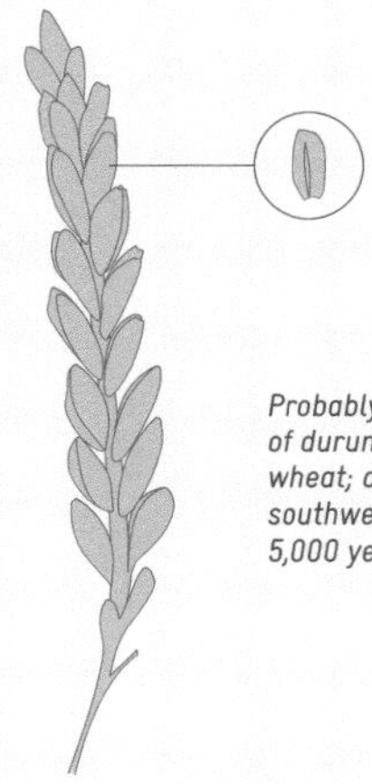

Probably created by mutation of durum wheat and einkorn wheat; cultivated in the southwestern part of Asia 5,000 years ago

Near East, Northern Africa

GREEN SPELT [1]

Dried spelt harvested when unripe

Amorbach Abbey (Bavaria, Germany), probably early harvesting due to poor harvests

EINKORN WHEAT [1, 2]

Was cultivated in Asia Minor 10,000 years ago, came to Europe 5,000 years ago

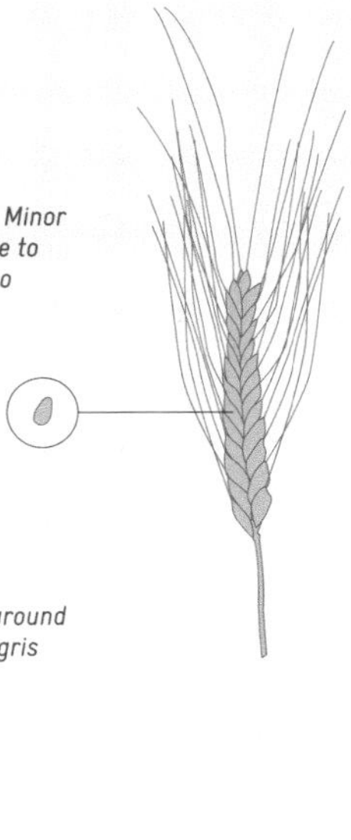

Near East, area around Euphrates and Tigris

WILD EMMER [1, 2]

Also known as farro or hulled wheat; cultivation from the end of 8th century BC

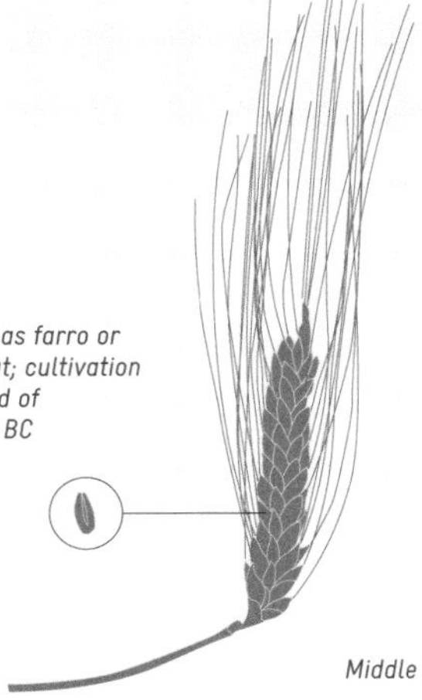

Middle East

KHORASAN WHEAT/KAMUT® [1, 2]

Is a registered trademark of Kamut® International; its meaning is »soul of the Earth«; emerged from Emmer around 6,000 years ago; mainly grown in North America and Southern Europe

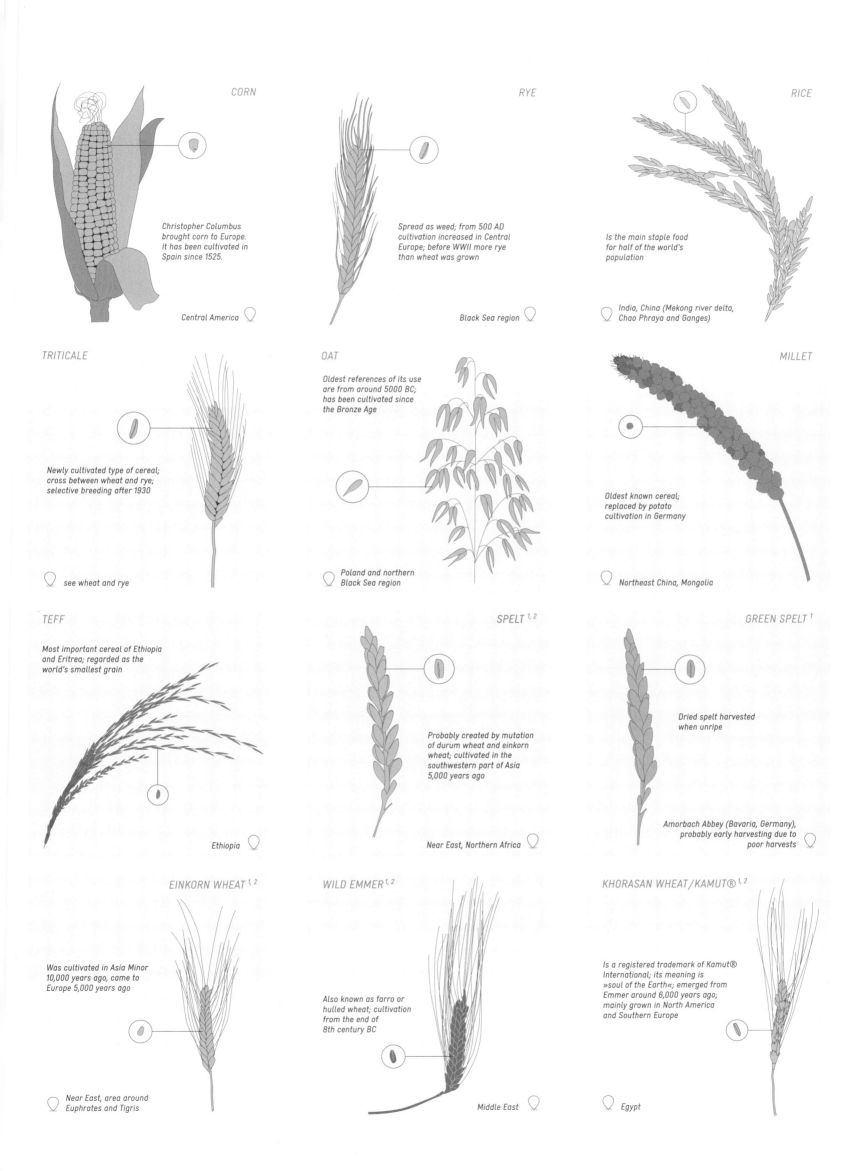

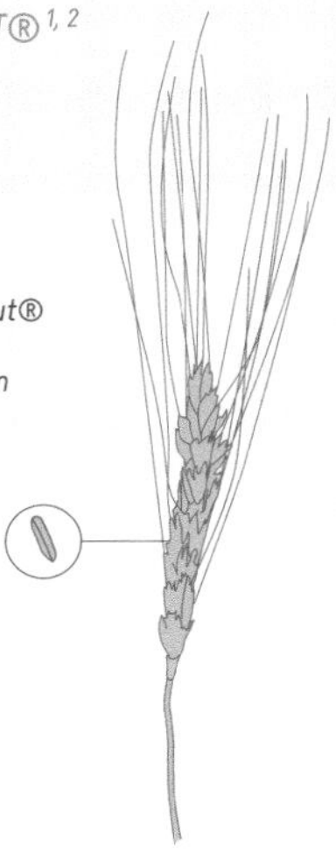

Egypt

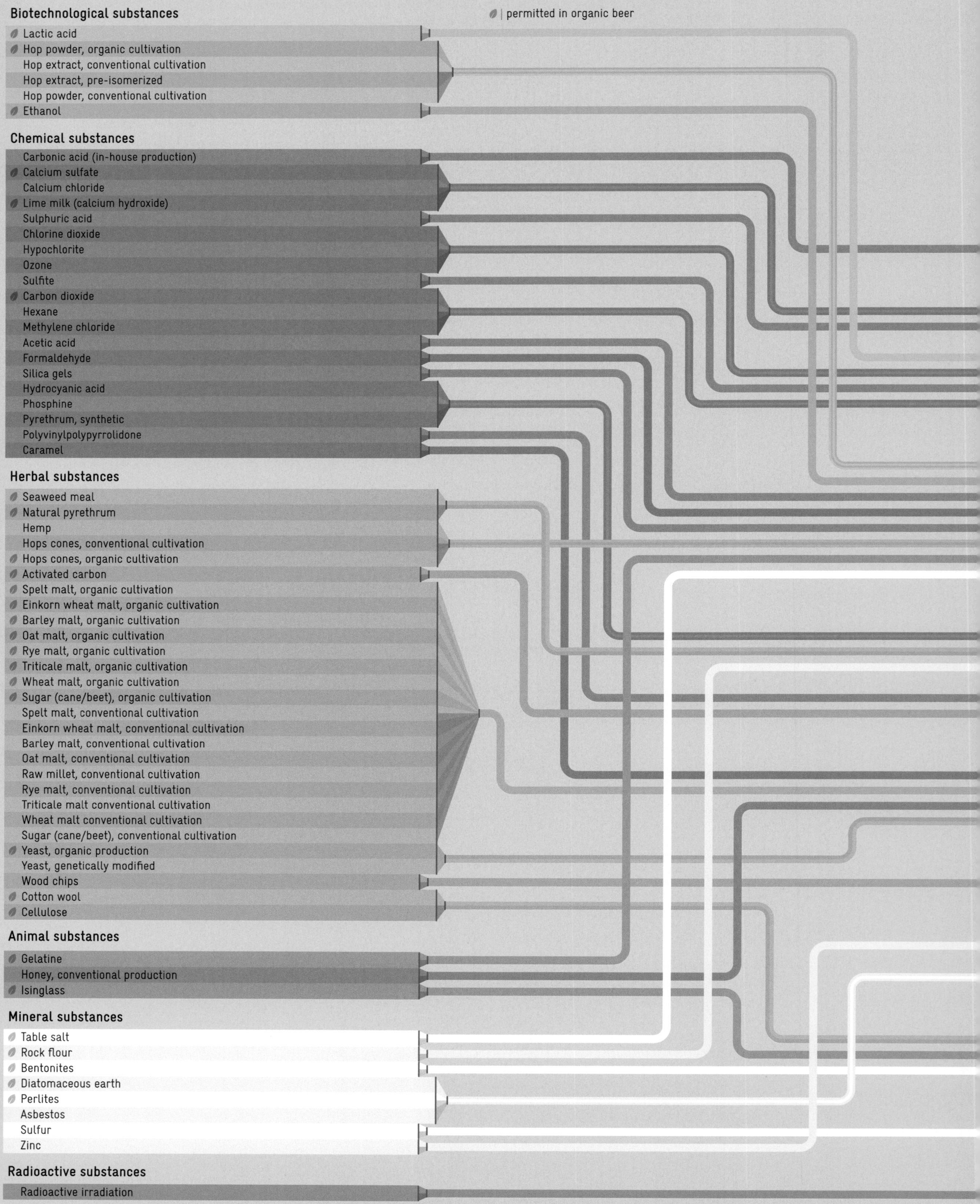
| permitted in organic beer
Biotechnological substances
Lactic acid
Hop powder, organic cultivation
Hop extract, conventional cultivation
Hop extract, pre-isomerized
Hop powder, conventional cultivation
Ethanol
Chemical substances
Carbonic acid (in-house production)
Calcium sulfate
Calcium chloride
Lime milk (calcium hydroxide)
Sulphuric acid
Chlorine dioxide
Hypochlorite
Ozone
Sulfite
Carbon dioxide
Hexane
Methylene chloride
Acetic acid
Formaldehyde
Silica gels
Hydrocyanic acid
Phosphine
Pyrethrum, synthetic
Polyvinylpolypyrrolidone
Caramel
Herbal substances
Seaweed meal
Natural pyrethrum
Hemp
Hops cones, conventional cultivation
Hops cones, organic cultivation
Activated carbon
Spelt malt, organic cultivation
Einkorn wheat malt, organic cultivation
Barley malt, organic cultivation
Oat malt, organic cultivation
Rye malt, organic cultivation
Triticale malt, organic cultivation
Wheat malt, organic cultivation
Sugar (cane/beet), organic cultivation
Spelt malt, conventional cultivation
Einkorn wheat malt, conventional cultivation
Barley malt, conventional cultivation
Oat malt, conventional cultivation
Raw millet, conventional cultivation
Rye malt, conventional cultivation
Triticale malt conventional cultivation
Wheat malt conventional cultivation
Sugar (cane/beet), conventional cultivation
Yeast, organic production
Yeast, genetically modified
Wood chips
Cotton wool
Cellulose
Animal substances
Gelatine
Honey, conventional production
Isinglass
Mineral substances
Table salt
Rock flour
Bentonites
Diatomaceous earth
Perlites
Asbestos
Sulfur
Zinc
Radioactive substances
Radioactive irradiation

PURE OR IMPURE?

Germany's Reinheitsgebot – or Purity Laws – have been governing the way brewers make beer since April 23, 1516. And while their principles have been adopted and imitated in breweries around the world, the craft beer movement begs the question whether the laws are really all that beneficial for the industry. Some traditional beer recipes have died out as a result of being »illegal« under the laws, but as craft beer moves into the market, brewers are finding ways around that, such as labelling their bottles with the English »beer« instead of the German »Bier«.

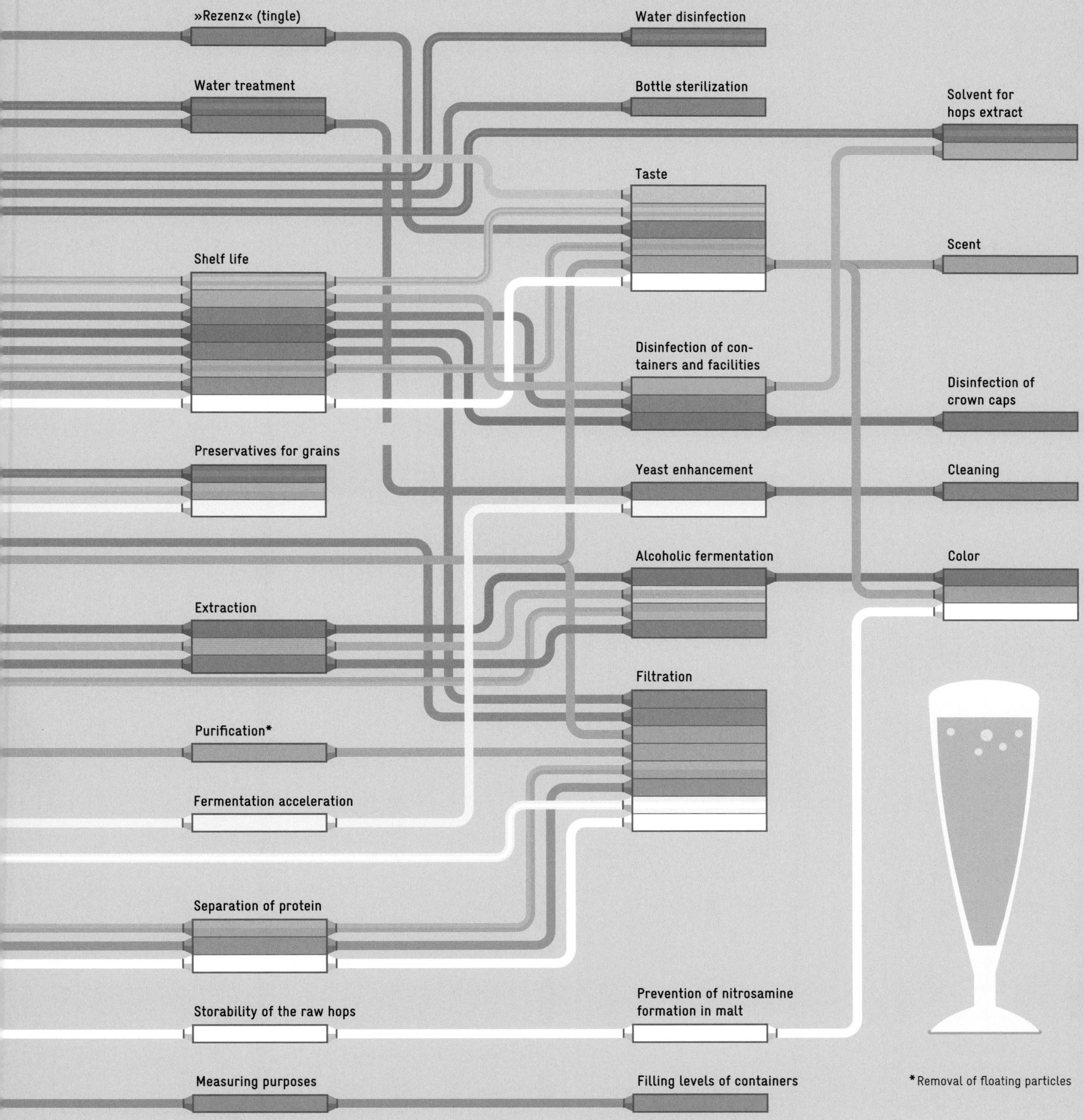
»Rezenz« (tingle)
Water treatment
Shelf life
Preservatives for grains
Extraction
Purification*
Fermentation acceleration
Separation of protein
Storability of the raw hops
Measuring purposes
Water disinfection
Bottle sterilization
Taste
Disinfection of containers and facilities
Yeast enhancement
Alcoholic fermentation
Filtration
Prevention of nitrosamine formation in malt
Filling levels of containers
Solvent for hops extract
Scent
Disinfection of crown caps
Cleaning
Color

*Removal of floating particles

»WURSTWASSER« AND »FLASCHENBÜRSTE«

»Mixing is for cocktails!« This is not always the case. Mixing beer with soft drinks or juice has long been practiced in German bars, but the mixing has always had to take place immediately before consumption. As the laws changed, German brewers have been able to start bottling beers mixed with lemon juice, grapefruit juice or lemon and lime soda. But the Reinheitsgebot, or Purity Laws, still stand, so the bottles have to be labeled as a »mixed drink containing beer«.

Beer varieties

You can use any beer to make a mixed drink, but pils and wheat beer are the most common choice. The ideal drinking temperature is 8 ° Celsius.

Beer varieties	Beer category	Alcohol content	Appearance	Symbol
dark	Vollbier	4.8 % vol.	dark amber colored	
Berliner Weiße	draught beer	2.8 % vol.	slightly cloudy, dark yellow	
bock beer	strong beer	7 % vol.	golden, golden brown or dark brown	
Kölsch	Vollbier	4.8 % vol.	light yellow	
Pils	Vollbier	4.8 % vol.	light golden	
wheat beer	Vollbier	5.4 % vol.	clear or slightly cloudy, fair or dark	

Ingredients

- Mineral water
- Orange soda
- Lemon soda
- Cola
- Almdudler
- Energy drink
- Raspberry soda
- Woodruff soda
- Fruit syrup
- Malt beer
- Grain alcohol
- Vodka
- Herb-flavored liqueur
- Cherry brandy
- Sparkling wine
- Red wine
- White wine
- Tomato juice
- Banana juice
- Apple juice
- Slice of lemon
- Strawberries
- Raspberries

There can be regional differences in the composition of mixed drinks.

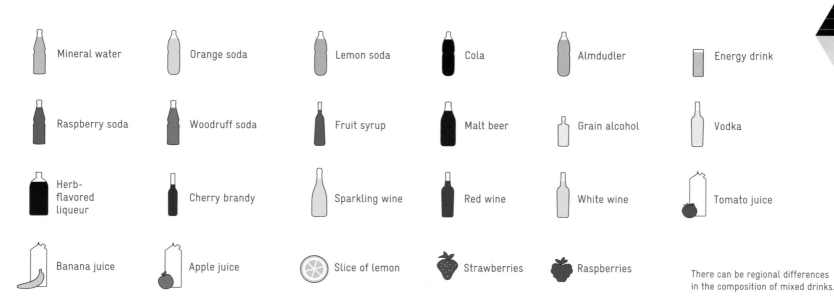

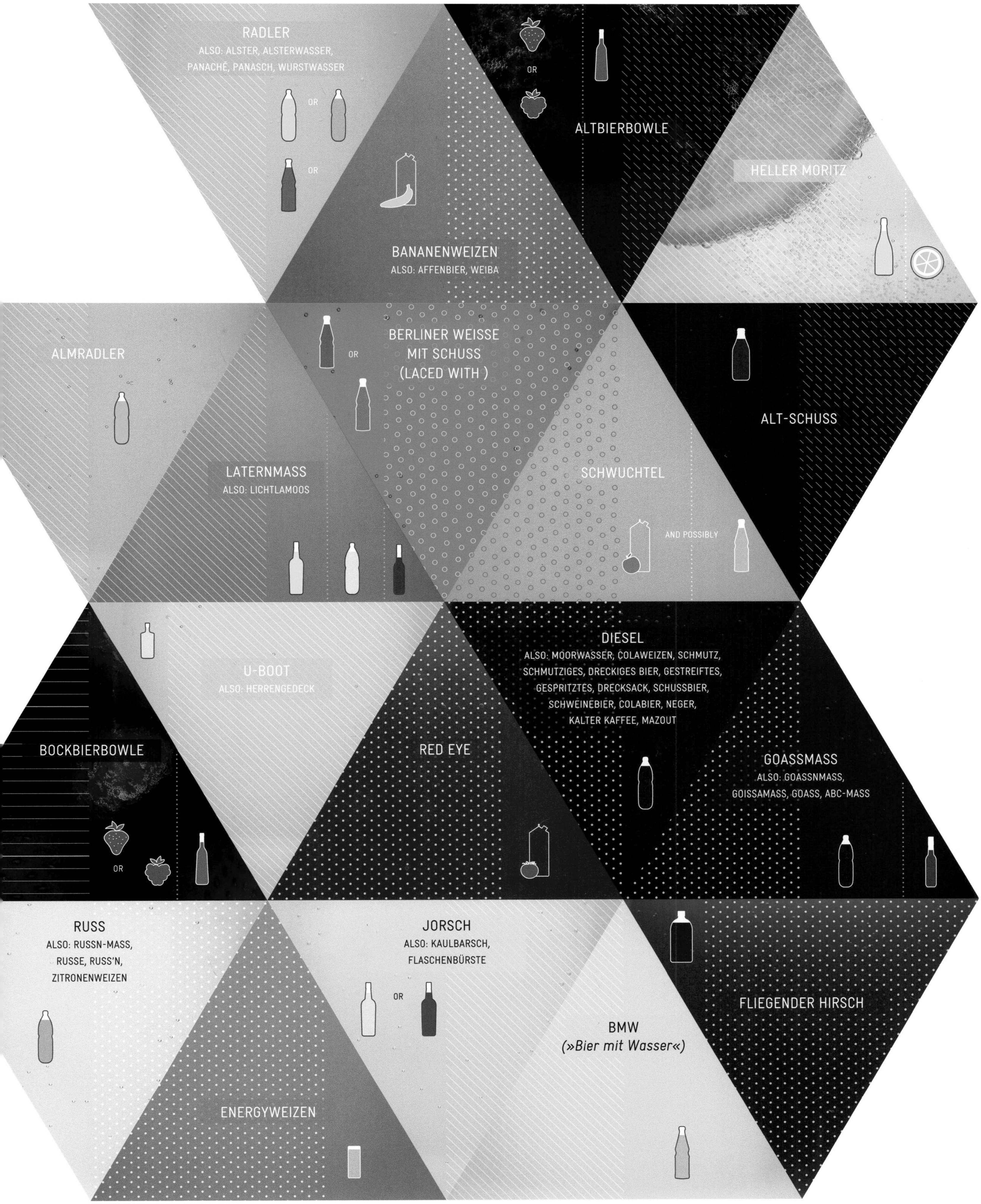
RADLER
ALSO: ALSTER, ALSTERWASSER, PANACHÉ, PANASCH, WURSTWASSER
OR
OR
BANANENWEIZEN
ALSO: AFFENBIER, WEIBA
OR
ALTBIERBOWLE
HELLER MORITZ
ALMRADLER
OR
BERLINER WEISSE MIT SCHUSS (LACED WITH)
ALT-SCHUSS
LATERNMASS
ALSO: LICHTLAMOOS
SCHWUCHTEL
AND POSSIBLY
U-BOOT
ALSO: HERRENGEDECK
DIESEL
ALSO: MOORWASSER, COLAWEIZEN, SCHMUTZ, SCHMUTZIGES, DRECKIGES BIER, GESTREIFTES, GESPRITZTES, DRECKSACK, SCHUSSBIER, SCHWEINEBIER, COLABIER, NEGER, KALTER KAFFEE, MAZOUT
BOCKBIERBOWLE
OR
RED EYE
GOASSMASS
ALSO: GOASSNMASS, GOISSAMASS, GOASS, ABC-MASS
RUSS
ALSO: RUSSN-MASS, RUSSE, RUSS'N, ZITRONENWEIZEN
JORSCH
ALSO: KAULBARSCH, FLASCHENBÜRSTE
OR
FLIEGENDER HIRSCH
BMW
(»Bier mit Wasser«)
ENERGYWEIZEN

A CULTURAL HERITAGE

Alcohol – and therefore also wine – is one of the oldest intoxicants known to man. In Ancient Greece, Dionysus was the god of wine – but also of ecstasy, transformation, joy and fertility. And it can be said that these traits are all interrelated.

Crushing it

To make red wine and white wine, vintners—or winemakers—follow the same steps but in a different order.

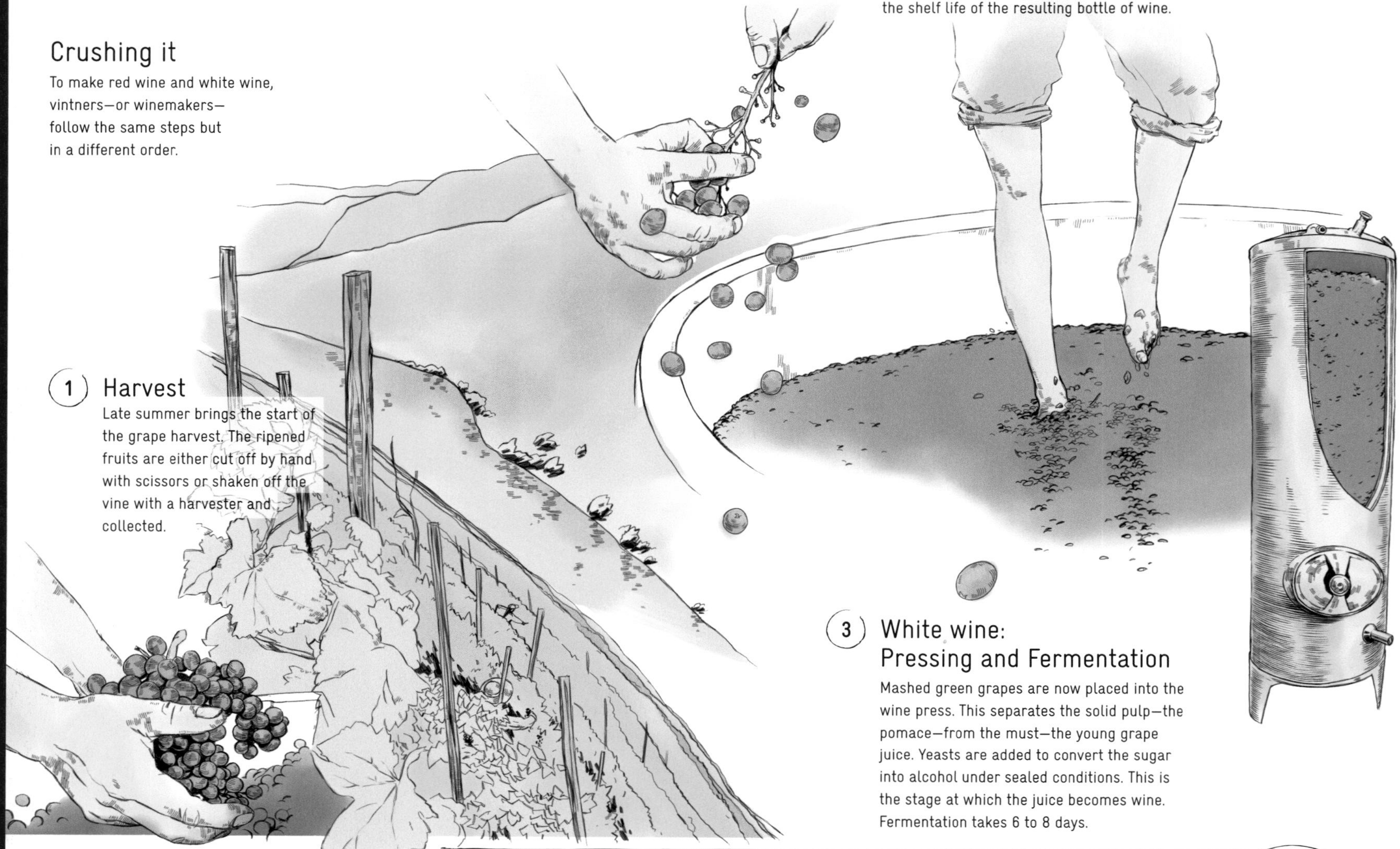

(1) Harvest

Late summer brings the start of the grape harvest. The ripened fruits are either cut off by hand with scissors or shaken off the vine with a harvester and collected.

(2) Destemming, Mashing

What we call a grape is not actually a fruit but a panicle. After being harvested, the berries are separated from the panicle and crushed. The resulting pulp rests for a period of time ranging from a few hours to a few days, allowing the seeds and skins to release aromatic substances into the juice. The more the grapes are mashed, the longer the shelf life of the resulting bottle of wine.

(3) White wine: Pressing and Fermentation

Mashed green grapes are now placed into the wine press. This separates the solid pulp—the pomace—from the must—the young grape juice. Yeasts are added to convert the sugar into alcohol under sealed conditions. This is the stage at which the juice becomes wine. Fermentation takes 6 to 8 days.

What happens when you drink a glass of wine?

Within 10 minutes of drinking a glass of wine, the alcohol enters the bloodstream via the digestive system. At first, we feel a sense of relaxation as endorphine and dopamine are released. Then we start to feel euphoric, talkative and nervousness disappears. With a higher level of alcohol, the mood can change—aggressiveness emerges. The alcohol affects the way our brain regulates excitement. Reaction time slows, balance is affected and speech is slurred. If too much alcohol is consumed, vital systems like breathing can be hindered. The morning after, we feel groggy and nauseous. The body treats alcohol as a toxin. As a result, our kidneys produce an excess of urine, leaving us feeling dehydrated. This causes a splitting headache, commonly known as a hangover.

Vineyard pests

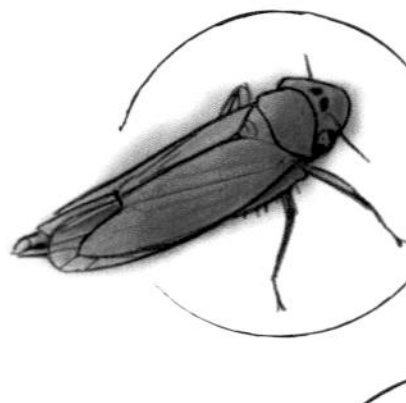

Grapevine leafhopper
This North American insect, which has also reached Europe, carries Flavascense dorée. The bacteria yellows the leaves and hinders berry growth.

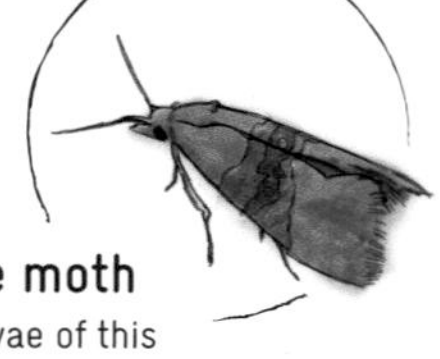

Grape moth
The larvae of this insect invade the flowers and fruit, resulting in lower yields.

Earwigs
These insects nibble on the berries, but they also eat pests like aphids, so they are both harmful and helpful.

Mildew
can infect the leaves and fruit, causing them to look as though they are dusted in flour. Berries dry out, burst and their flavor is ruined.

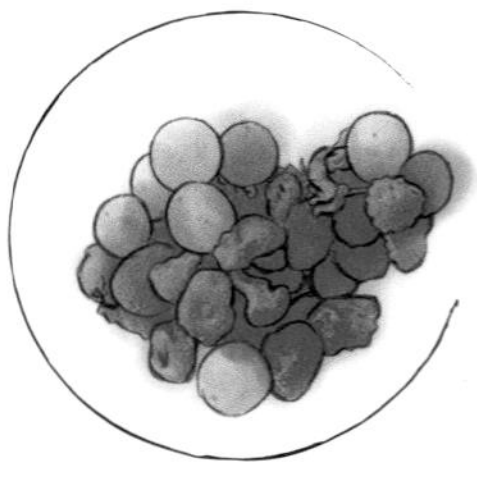

Grape rot
is usually caused by a type of mould, but sometimes also by bacteria and yeast. The resulting wine can taste sour and mouldy.

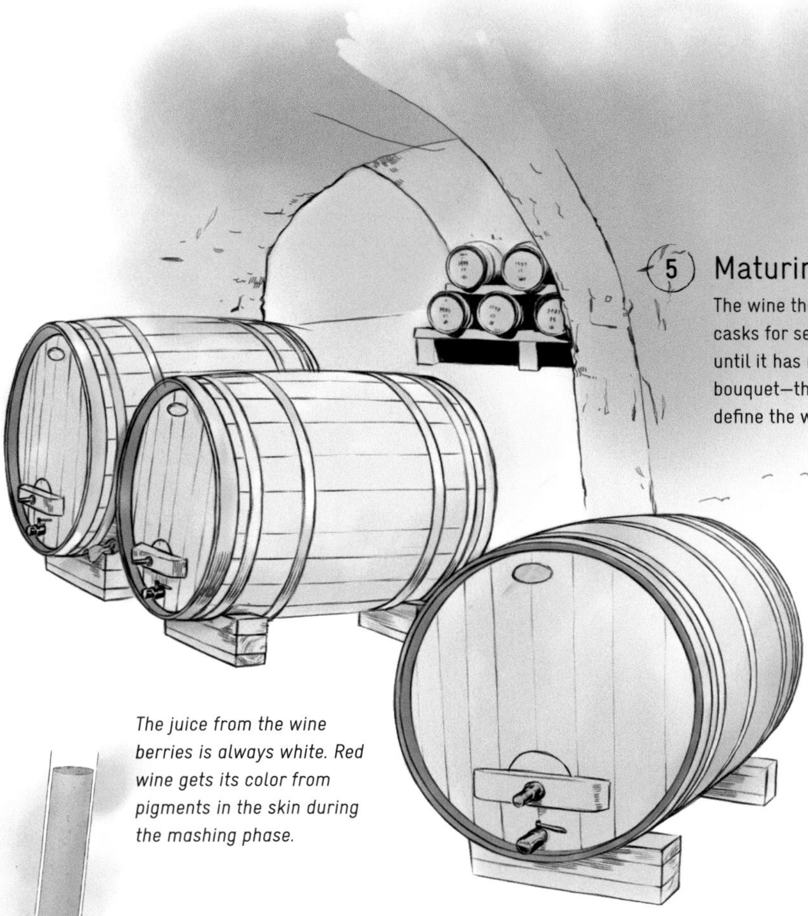

5 Maturing

The wine then rests in wooden or steel casks for several weeks to several years until it has reached its characteristic bouquet—the smell and taste that define the wine.

The Speyer wine bottle is known as the oldest unopened bottle of wine. It was produced in the 4th century AD.

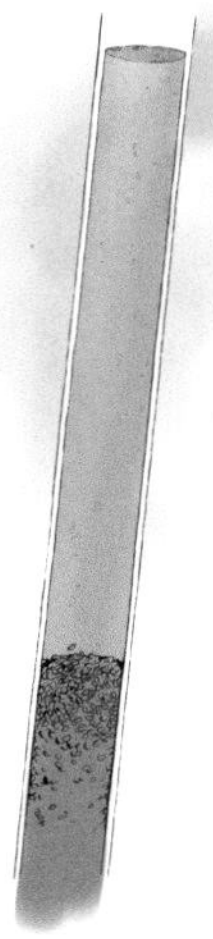

The juice from the wine berries is always white. Red wine gets its color from pigments in the skin during the mashing phase.

4 Red wine: Fermentation and Pressing

Red grape mash is fermented before the pressing separates it from its components. The fermentation occurs over several weeks. The mash is then pressed to remove the mashed pomace. This is known as the first racking.

6 Bottled and stored

After coming out of the cask, the wine is clarified and bottled. The greater the amount of alcohol, sugar, acid and tannin a bottle contains, the longer it can be stored, though most aren't made to sit on a shelf for more than 10 years. Only around 10% of today's wines benefit from being cellared for more than 2 years.

The right vessel

The right wine glass is defined by three features: a long stem, a thin glass wall and the proper belly. It should never be too full, otherwise it can topple over. The form and thickness of the rim can also affect the taste of the wine by guiding the wine to the right part of the tongue—and whether we experience it first as sweetness at the tip or the bitter notes at the back at the tongue.

The chimney bundles the aromas.
Movement increases the amount of oxygen exposure to the wine, enabling the complex aromatics to further develop.
A larger surface area opens up the bouquet.
Optics matter. Thin, clear glass suggests a cleaner, full-bodied taste.

Red wine glasses
aerate and bundle

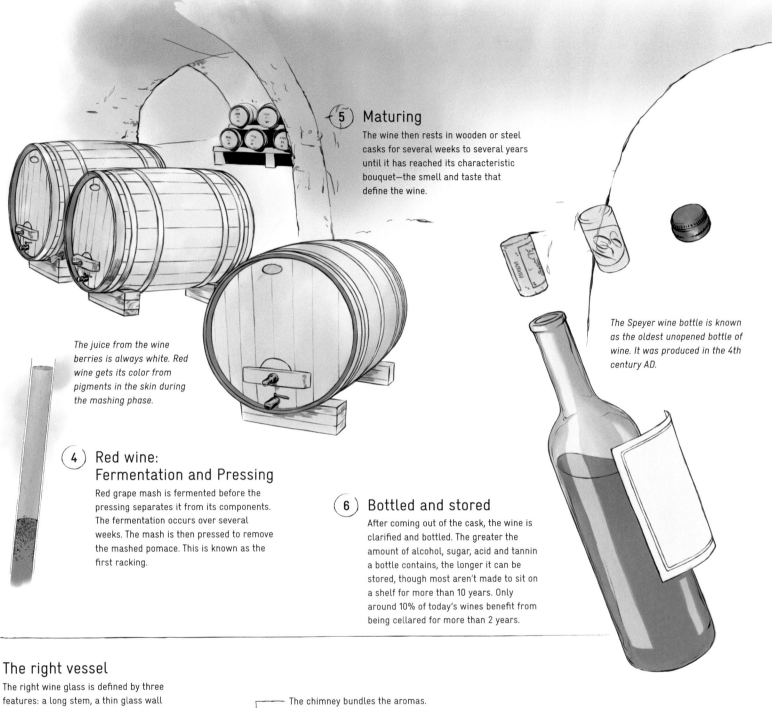

Hold the glass by the stem. This looks more elegant, avoids fingerprints on the glass and also protects the cool wine from absorbing body heat from the hand.

White wine glasses
Maintain temperature and emphasize acidity

WATER OF LIFE

Whisky was first produced in the 11th century by monks. The accompanying name »water of life« is derived from the Scottish Gaelic word »uisge beatha«. The first known mention of a Scotch whisky distillation dates from 1494 on an Exchequer Roll of King James IV who named it »aqua vitae« – the water of life. Today, Scotch whisky is a popular spirit all over the world, an »aqua vitae« in terms of its taste and effect but also when it comes to Scotland's economy.

ACCORDING TO THE LAW, A TRUE SCOTCH WHISKY HAS TO …

… be produced, matured and bottled in Scotland.

… have matured in an oak barrel no bigger than 700 liters, for at least three years.

… have an alcohol content of at least 40% alcohol by volume (94.8% ABV).

… get its smell and flavor exclusively from the raw materials and method used.

EXPORTS
2019 official exports of Scotch whisky
global sales: 863.8 m. liter
global sales proceeds: £4.4 bil.
of which (in %):
68
Blended
10
Malt
22
Other
Glossary
Malt: whisky from malted barley
Grain: whisky from other grains
Blended: blended product

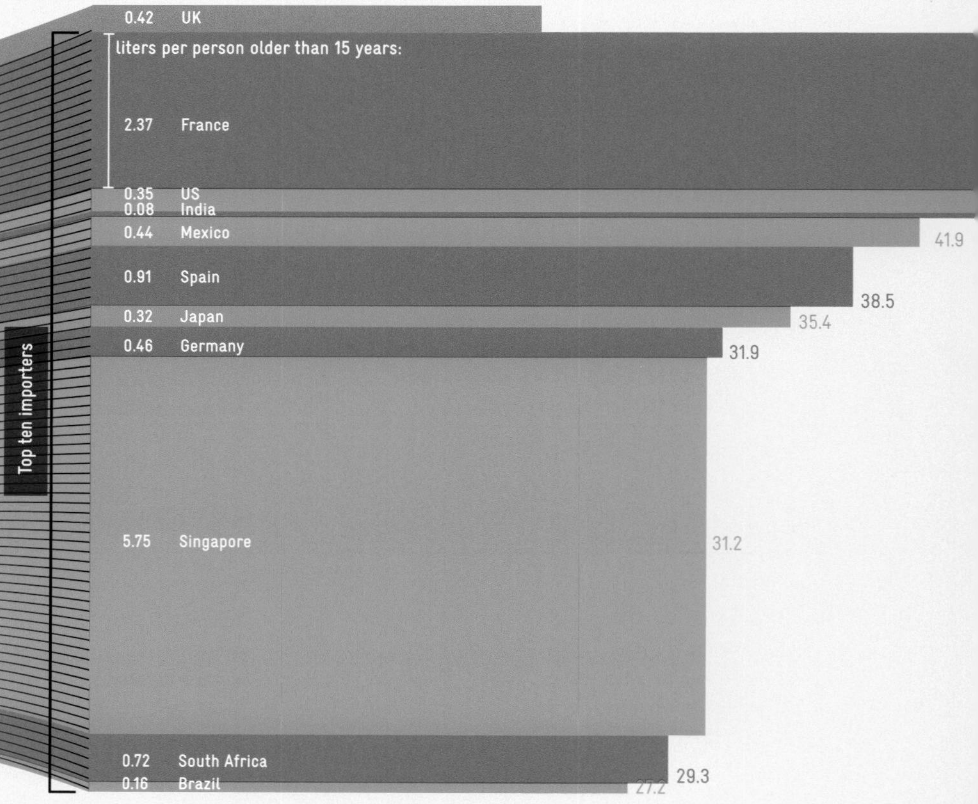
0.42 UK
liters per person older than 15 years:
2.37 France
0.35 US
0.08 India
0.44 Mexico
41.9
0.91 Spain
38.5
0.32 Japan
35.4
0.46 Germany
31.9
Top ten importers
5.75 Singapore
31.2
0.72 South Africa
29.3
0.16 Brazil
27.2

PRODUCTION OF MALT WHISKY

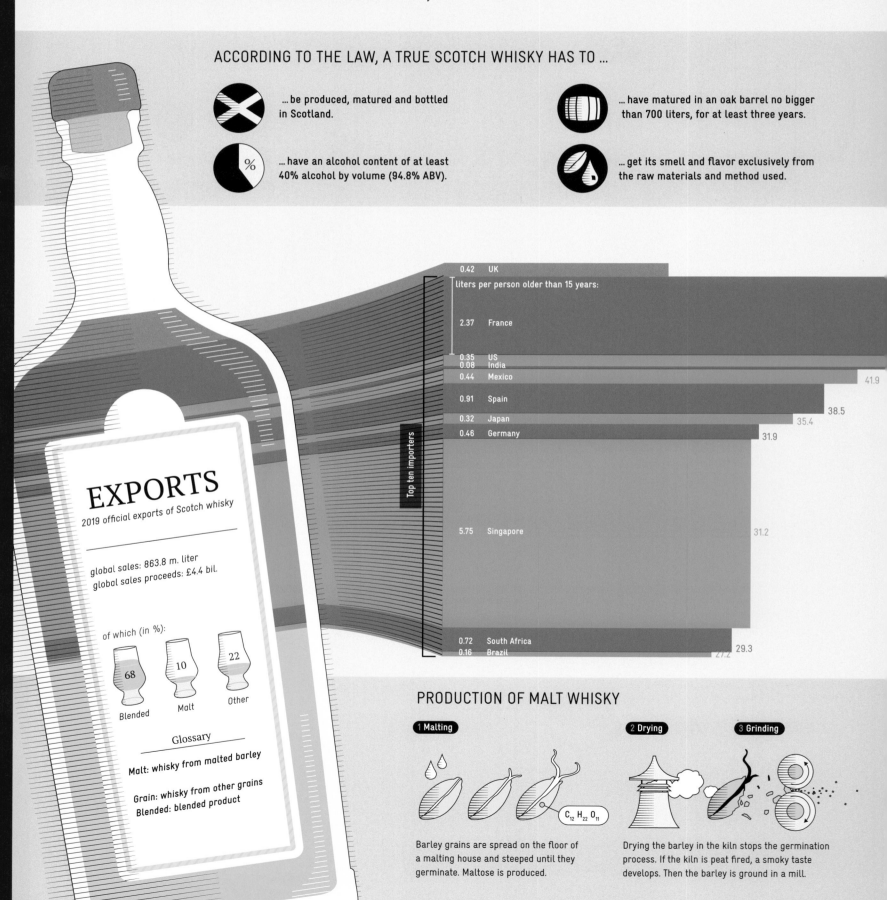

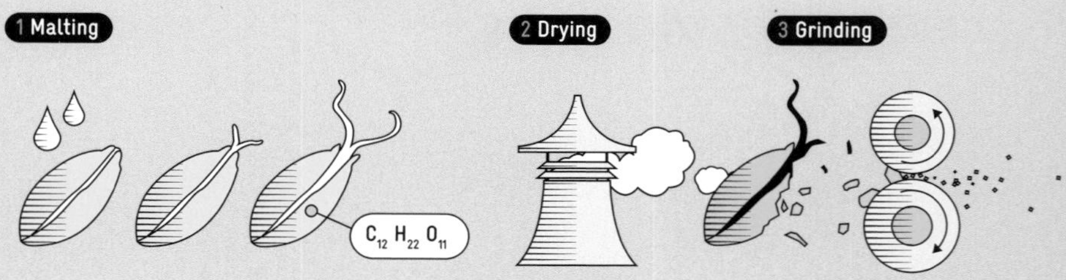
1 Malting
2 Drying
3 Grinding
$C_{12}H_{22}O_{11}$

Barley grains are spread on the floor of a malting house and steeped until they germinate. Maltose is produced.

Drying the barley in the kiln stops the germination process. If the kiln is peat fired, a smoky taste develops. Then the barley is ground in a mill.

Top 5 Scotch Blended Whiskies

2016 world market share sorted by brands

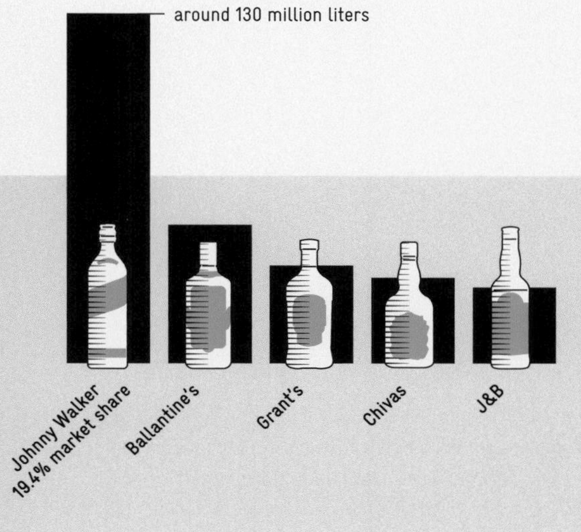
around 130 million liters
Johnny Walker
19.4% market share
Ballantine's
Grant's
Chivas
J&B

Top 5 Scotch Malt Whiskies

2017 world market share sorted by brands

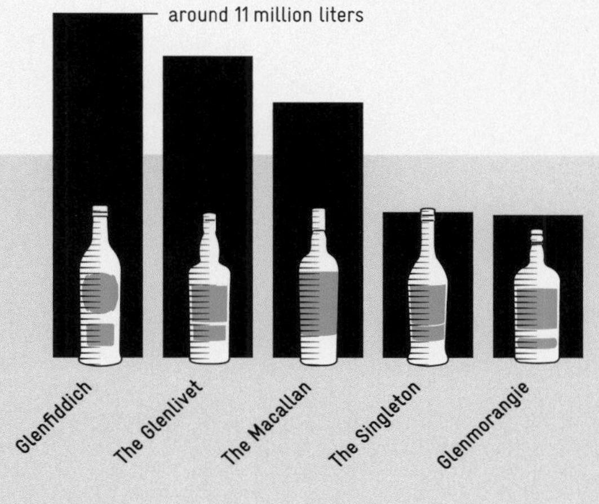
around 11 million liters
Glenfiddich
The Glenlivet
The Macallan
The Singleton
Glenmorangie

Top 5 groups

2019 Scotch production volume in m. liters

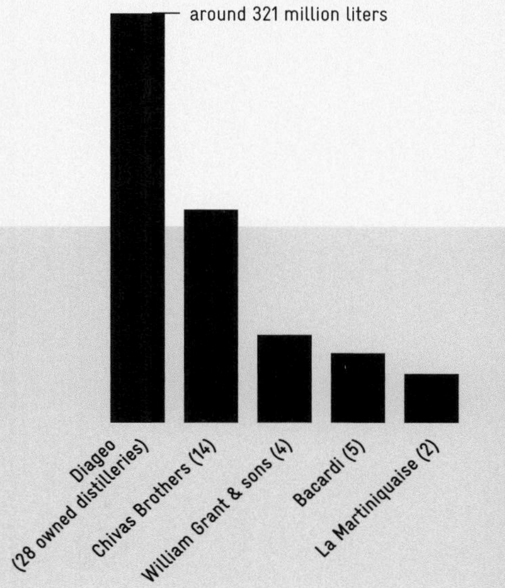
around 321 million liters
Diageo
(28 owned distilleries)
Chivas Brothers (14)
William Grant & sons (4)
Bacardi (5)
La Martiniquaise (2)

export value in m. liters 2018
131.5
78.8
95.8

TOTAL INTERNATIONAL EXPORTS (SERVICE AND MANUFACTORING) IN M. £ (2017)

2018 40,000 or so employees who work directly or indirectly for the whisky industry are among Scotland's most profitable workers. 41 bottles of Scotch Whisky are shipped each second from Scotland to 175 markets around the world.

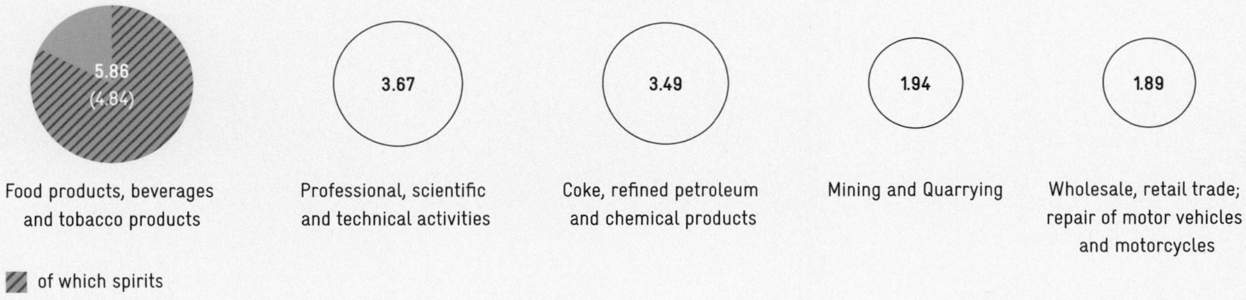
5.86
(4.84)
Food products, beverages and tobacco products
3.67
Professional, scientific and technical activities
3.49
Coke, refined petroleum and chemical products
1.94
Mining and Quarrying
1.89
Wholesale, retail trade; repair of motor vehicles and motorcycles
of which spirits

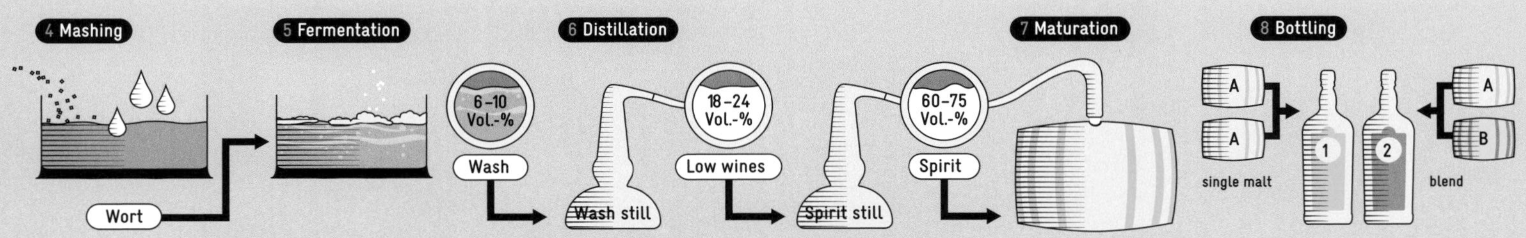
4 Mashing
Wort
5 Fermentation
6-10 Vol.-%
Wash
6 Distillation
Wash still
18-24 Vol.-%
Low wines
Spirit still
60-75 Vol.-%
Spirit
7 Maturation
8 Bottling
A
A
single malt
1
2
A
B
blend

The ground barley is mixed with hot water to extract the maltose. The resulting »wort« (sugared water) is retained and yeast is added for fermentation.

The wash is distilled in copper stills, usually twice. The spirit now has an alcohol level of around 60–75%.

The whisky matures in oak barrels until perfection. It is usually bottled as a single malt (1) after 10–30 years or (usually when younger) used for blends. (2)

GET YOUR KICKS ON ROUTE 66

In 1926, US Highway 66 was christianed – it owes its name to one of the few numbers not already assigned in the states through which it runs. Its 3,940 kilometers have been updated over the years, but there are still a couple of stretches where you can still cruise down the classic Route 66.

A small selection of sights and interesting places along the route

The »Main Street of America« has inspired many road trips and what road trip would be complete without Bobby Troup's classic »Route 66«? First recorded in 1946 by Nat King Cole, the song has since been covered by many others from just as many genres.

YEAR	MUSICIAN [selection]	TIME	
1946	Nat King Cole (Trio)	03:00	(re-recorded 1956 + 1961)
1946	Bing Crosby & the Andrews Sisters	03:16	
1955	Harry James & His Orchestra	02:55	
1957	Patti Page	02:07	
1957	Louis Jordan	02:49	
1960	The Four Freshmen	02:47	
1961	Chuck Berry	02:45	
1964	The Rolling Stones	02:21	
1965	Sammy Davis Jr.	02:43	
1965	Them feat. Van Morrison	02:27	
1968	Sandie Shaw	03:17	
1975	Dr. Feelgood	03:23	
1976	Asleep at the Wheel	03:23	
1987	Depeche Mode (Beatmasters Mix)	06:18	
1991	Natalie Cole	03:01	
2002	Nancy Sinatra	03:08	
2006	John Mayer (Cars Soundtrack)	03:24	
2013	George Benson	03:50	

Detroit
New York
Chicago*
ILLINOIS
Dwight
Bloomington
Washington
Springfield
MISSOURI*
St. Louis*
Springfield
Joplin*
Tulsa
OMA
Dallas
ATLANTIC

ROUTE 66 LYRICS
[original version by N.K. Cole]

If you ever plan to motor west
Travel my way
Take the highway that's the best
Get your kicks on Route 66

It winds from ***Chicago to L.A.***
More than two thousand miles all the way
Get your kicks on Route 66

Now you go through ***Saint Louis***
Joplin, Missouri,
and Oklahoma City *is mighty pretty*
You see ***Amarillo,***
Gallup, New Mexico,
Flagstaff, Arizona.
Don't forget ***Winona,***
Kingman, Barstow, San Bernardino

Won't you get hip to this timely tip
When you make that ***California*** *trip*
Get your kicks on Route 66.

- Instrumental intermission -

Won't you get hip to this timely tip
When you make that California trip
Get your kicks on Route 66
Get your kicks on Route 66
Get your kicks on Route 66

Palo Duro Canyon
Texas

Golden Driller
Tulsa, Oklahoma

Gateway Arch
St. Louis, Missouri

Ambler's Texaco Gas Station
Dwight, Illinois

HISTORIC
ILLINOIS
U S
66
ROUTE
BEGIN
Chicago, Illinois

THE MOST INFLUENTIAL ARTISTS OF ALL TIME

Art breaks genres. Each artist brings us closer to their own perception and vision of the world. This chART presents the most popular artists and styles over time, taking into account painters and artistic movements throughout the world.

The extraordinary 19-minute bidding battle for Leonardo da Vinci's *Salvator Mundi*, culminating in the work being sold for a world record price at auction

US$450,312,500

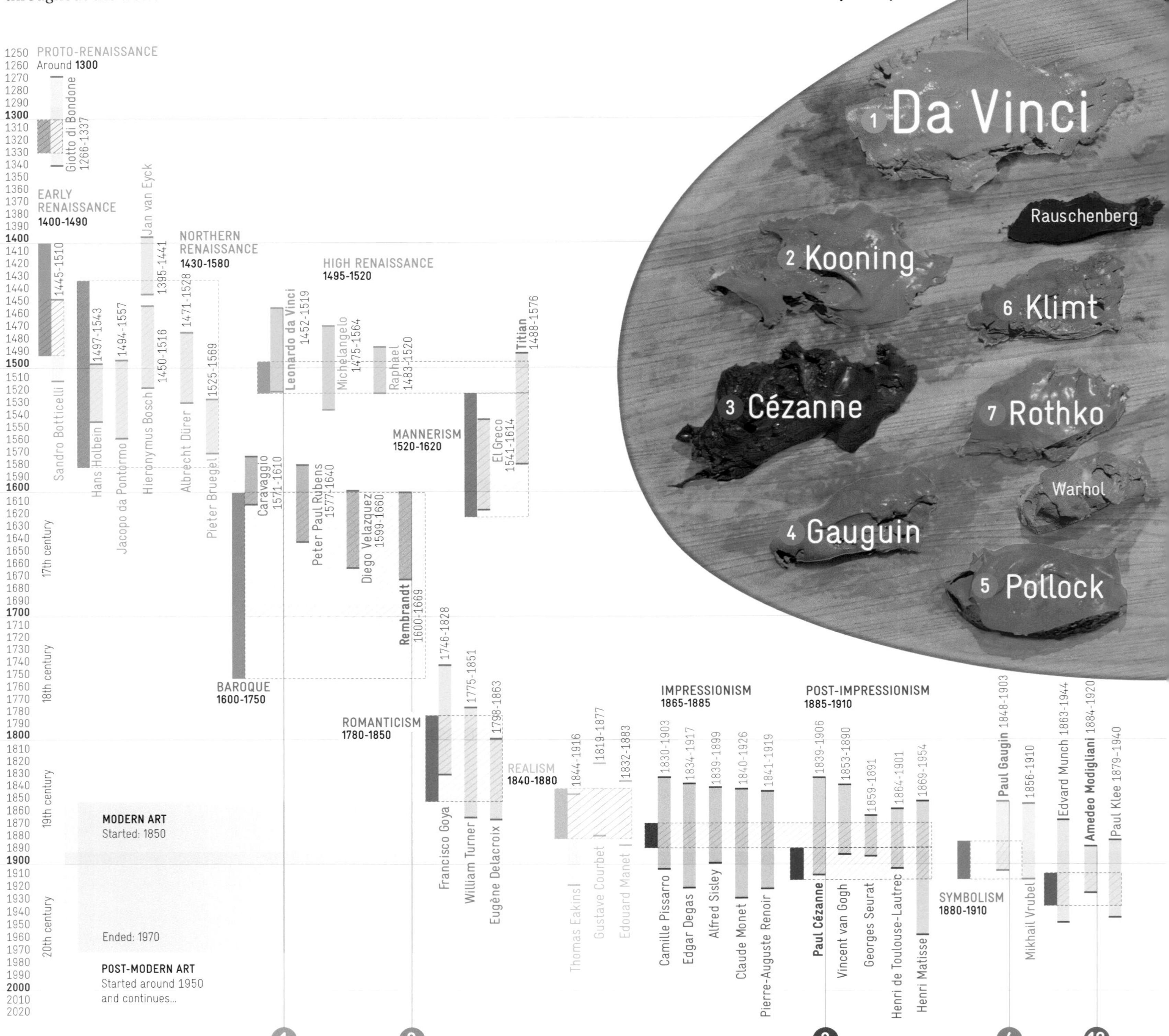

THE 10 MOST EXPENSIVE PAINTINGS: (US Million Dollars)

Rank	Painting	Price
1	»Salvator Mundi«	
8	»Pendant portraits of Maerten Soolmans and Oopjen Coppit«	$194
3	»The Card Players«	$284
4	»Nafea Faa Ipoipo (When Will You Marry?)«	$227
10	»Nu couché«	$183.8

THE TOP ART MUSEUMS IN THE WORLD
(Visitors per year and ranking of global popularity)

Rank	Museum	Visitors	City
1	MUSÉE DU LOUVRE	10,200,000	Paris
2	VAN GOGH MUSEUM	2,206,000	Amsterdam
3	RIJKSMUSEUM	2,300,000	Amsterdam
4	STATE HERMITAGE MUSEUM	4,294,000	St. Petersburg
5	BRITISH MUSEUM	5,869,000	London
6	MUSÉE D'ORSAY	3,175,000	Paris
7	VATICAN MUSEUMS	6,756,000	Vatican City
8	MUSEO DEL PRADO	2,893,000	Madrid

POLITICS

SOCIETY

ECONOMY

SPORTS

TECHNOLOGY

CULTURE & ARTS

SCIENCE

9 Picasso

10 Modigliani

8 Rembrandt

Newman

Hockney

Rubens

Bacon

Basquiat

Monet

Titian

Eakins

Manet

Holbein

Munch

Léger

Renoir

da Pontormo

Twombly

Johns

Still

Lichtenstein

Matisse

Malevich

Johns

Van Gogh

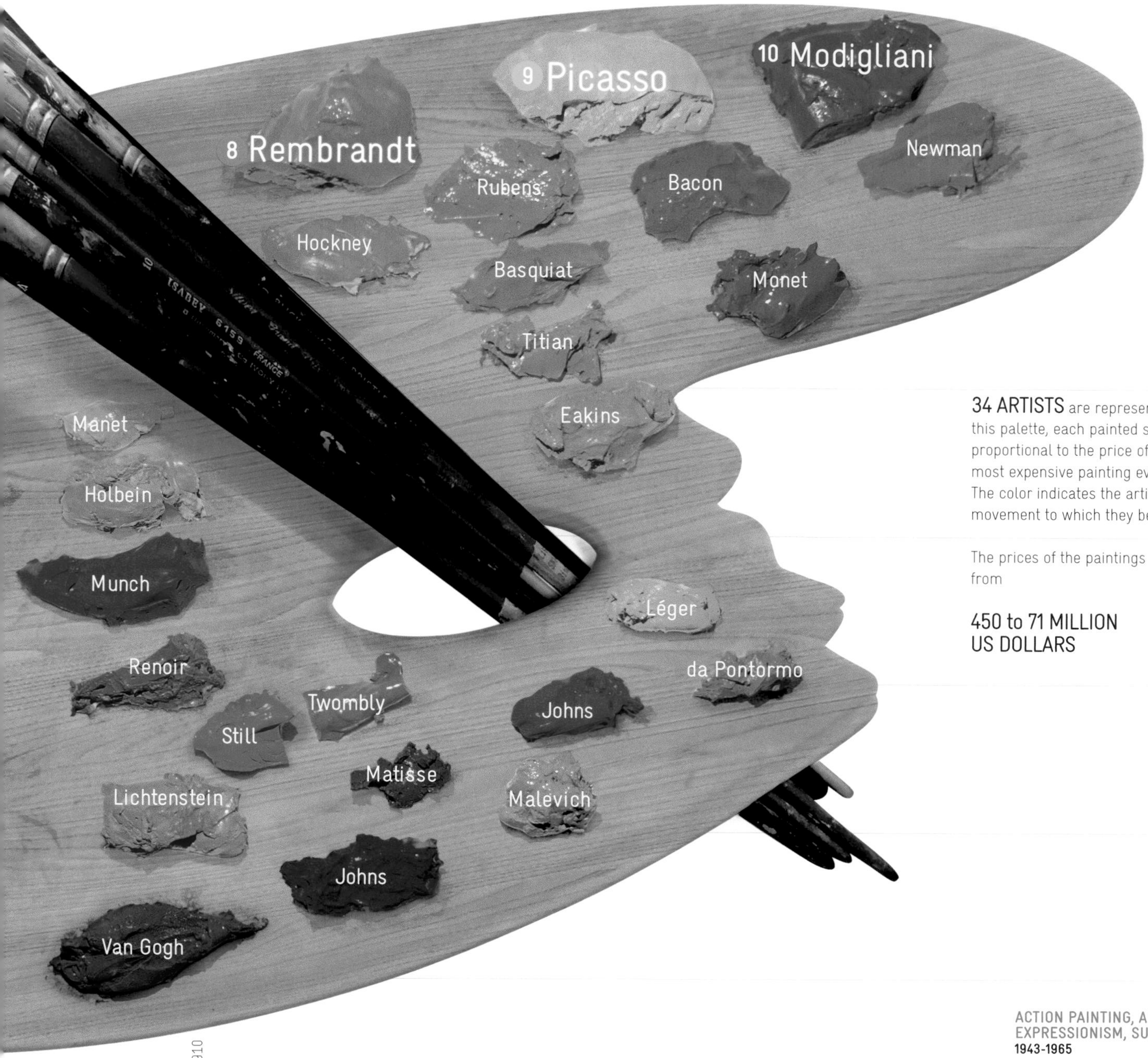

34 ARTISTS are represented on this palette, each painted spot is proportional to the price of their most expensive painting ever sold. The color indicates the artistic movement to which they belong.

The prices of the paintings range from

450 to 71 MILLION US DOLLARS

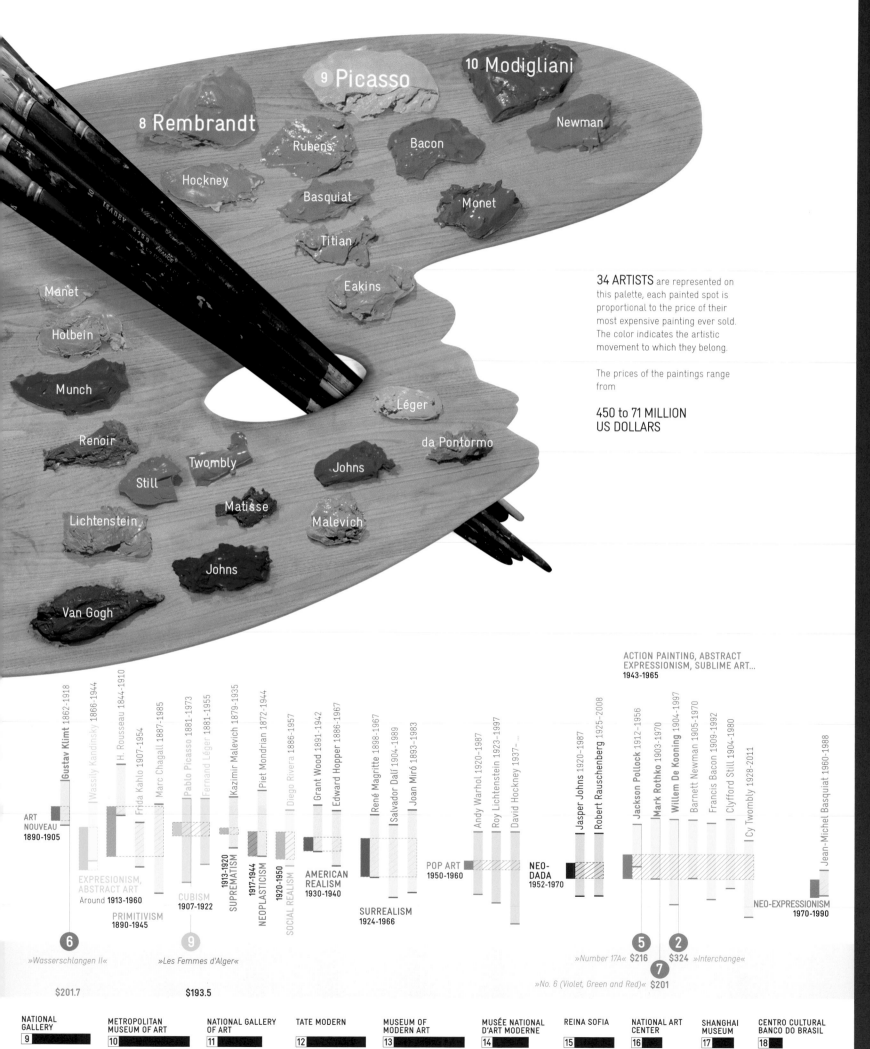

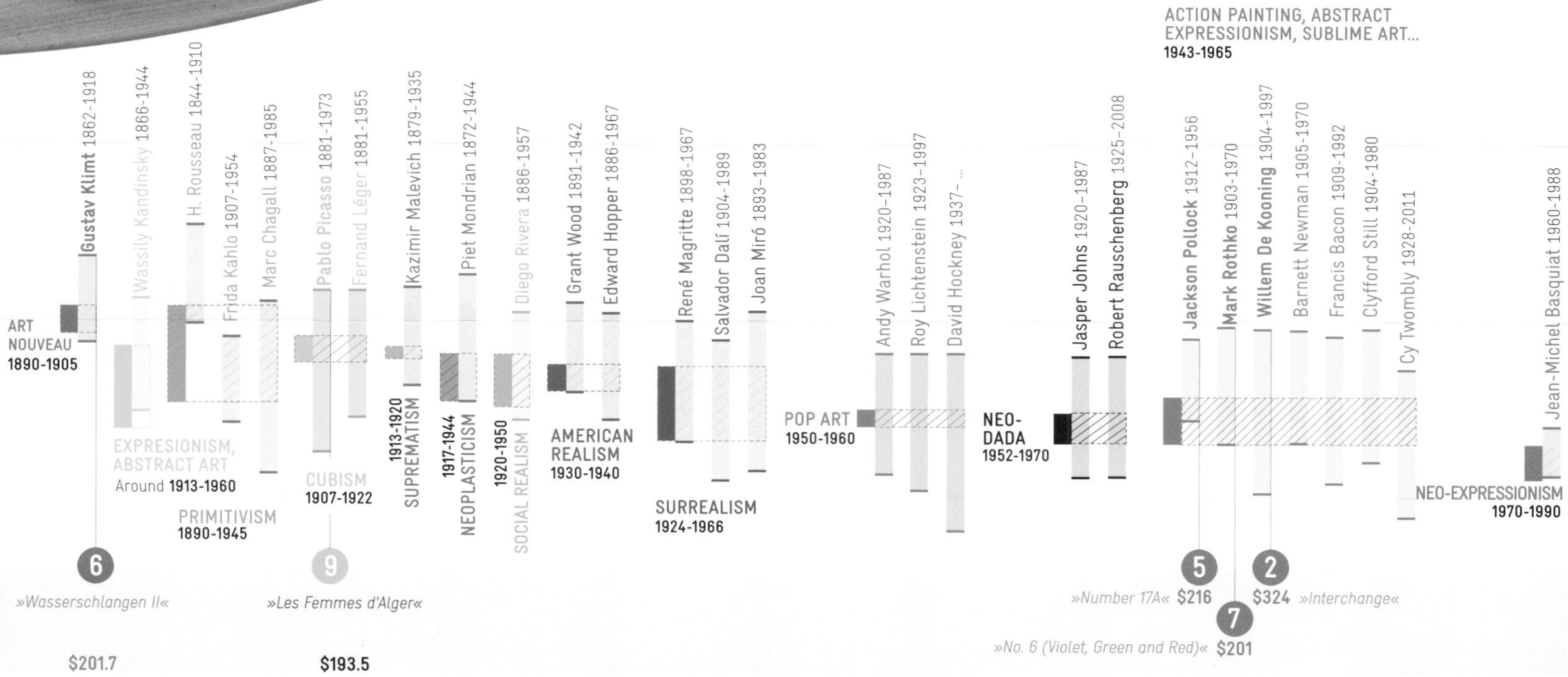

ACTION PAINTING, ABSTRACT
EXPRESSIONISM, SUBLIME ART...
1943-1965

Gustav Klimt 1862-1918

Wassily Kandinsky 1866-1944

H. Rousseau 1844-1910

Frida Kahlo 1907-1954

Marc Chagall 1887-1985

Pablo Picasso 1881-1973

Fernand Léger 1881-1955

Kazimir Malevich 1879-1935

Piet Mondrian 1872-1944

Diego Rivera 1886-1957

Grant Wood 1891-1942

Edward Hopper 1886-1967

René Magritte 1898-1967

Salvador Dalí 1904-1989

Joan Miró 1893-1983

Andy Warhol 1920-1987

Roy Lichtenstein 1923-1997

David Hockney 1937-...

Jasper Johns 1920-1987

Robert Rauschenberg 1925-2008

Jackson Pollock 1912-1956

Mark Rothko 1903-1970

Willem De Kooning 1904-1997

Barnett Newman 1905-1970

Francis Bacon 1909-1992

Clyfford Still 1904-1980

Cy Twombly 1928-2011

Jean-Michel Basquiat 1960-1988

ART
NOUVEAU
1890-1905

EXPRESIONISM,
ABSTRACT ART
Around **1913-1960**

CUBISM
1907-1922

1913-1920
SUPREMATISM

1917-1944
NEOPLASTICISM

1920-1950
SOCIAL REALISM

AMERICAN
REALISM
1930-1940

SURREALISM
1924-1966

POP ART
1950-1960

NEO-
DADA
1952-1970

PRIMITIVISM
1890-1945

NEO-EXPRESSIONISM
1970-1990

6

9

5

2

7

»Wasserschlangen II«

»Les Femmes d'Alger«

»Number 17A« **$216**

$324 »Interchange«

»No. 6 (Violet, Green and Red)« **$201**

$201.7

$193.5

NATIONAL GALLERY	METROPOLITAN MUSEUM OF ART	NATIONAL GALLERY OF ART	TATE MODERN	MUSEUM OF MODERN ART	MUSÉE NATIONAL D'ART MODERNE	REINA SOFIA	NATIONAL ART CENTER	SHANGHAI MUSEUM	CENTRO CULTURAL BANCO DO BRASIL
9	**10**	**11**	**12**	**13**	**14**	**15**	**16**	**17**	**18**
5,736,000	6,953,927	4,404,212	5,829,000	6,953,927	3,551,544	3,898,309	2,000,000	2,111,730	1,388,664
London	New York	Washington D.C.	London	New York	Paris	Madrid	Tokyo	Shanghai	Rio De Janeiro

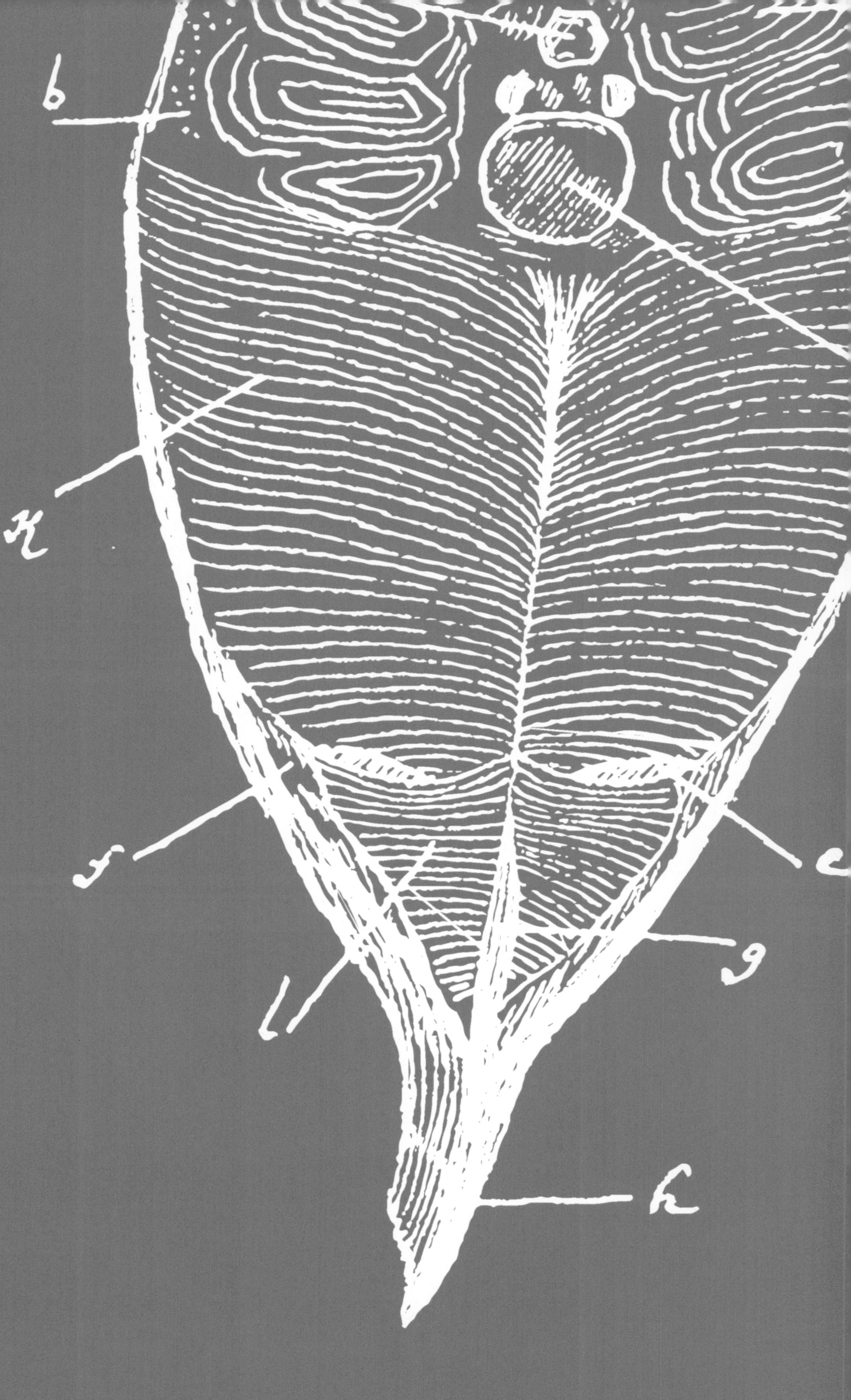

b
k
f
l
g
h

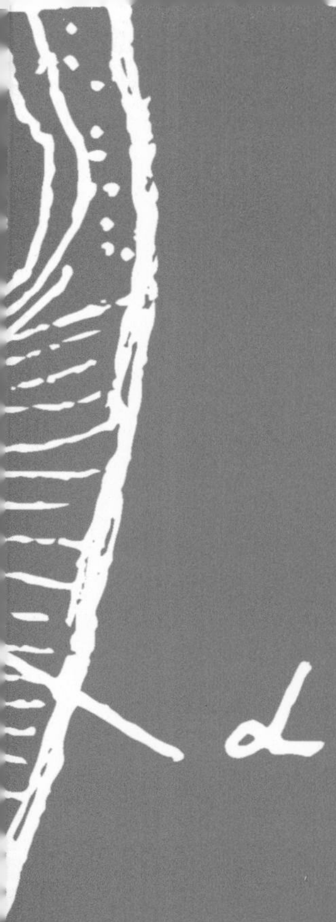

SCIENCE

In order to document their research results in faithful detail, scientists were early adopters of visualizations alongside their records. Andreas Vesalius’ 1538 publication »Tabulae anatomicae sex« displayed six views of the human body and was one of the first scientific works to be comprised solely of infographics.

Alexander von Humboldt was also well known for his drawings. The sketch shown here is an **anatomical cross section of an electric eel** from his 1799 »American Travel Journal III«, with lines and symbols providing a legend for the drawing. Humboldt sought to understand connections in the natural world and transferred his findings to a broad public through open lectures. That is also the intended goal of the infographics displayed in this chapter. They show what light is, how humans explore space, and where science can be applied.

LET IT SHINE

Light has a great influence on civilization, but what is it? Over the years, the greatest philosophers and thinkers of their day have all tried to explain the concept of light: some came close to enlightening us, while other theories have left us very much in the dark.

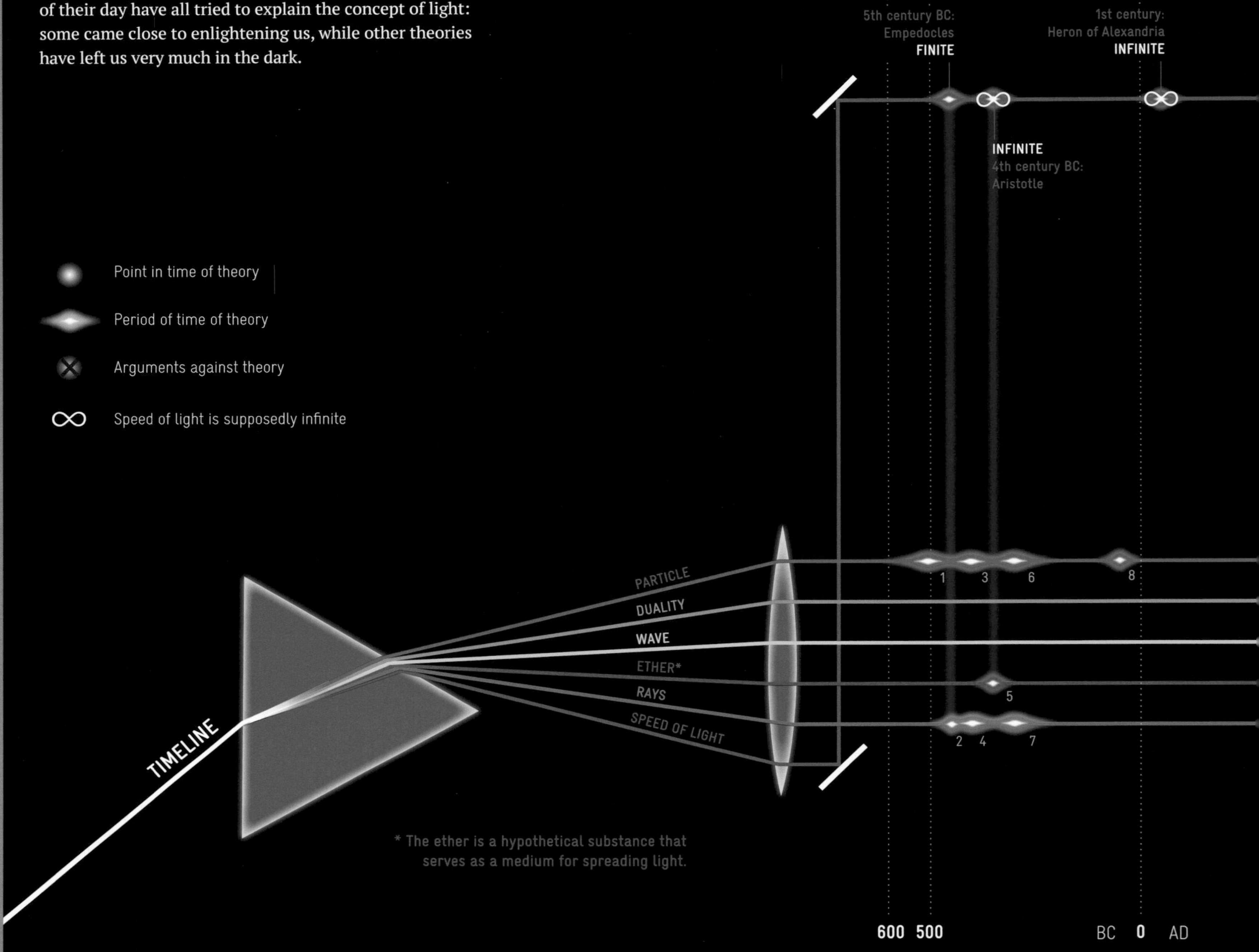
5th century BC:
Empedocles
FINITE
1st century:
Heron of Alexandria
INFINITE
INFINITE
4th century BC:
Aristotle
Point in time of theory
Period of time of theory
Arguments against theory
Speed of light is supposedly infinite
PARTICLE
DUALITY
WAVE
ETHER*
RAYS
SPEED OF LIGHT
TIMELINE
1
3
6
8
5
2
4
7
600
500
BC
0
AD

* The ether is a hypothetical substance that serves as a medium for spreading light.

LIGHT THEORIES THROUGHOUT HISTORY

1 **6th–5th century BC: Vaisheshika school of philosophy, India**
Light is a ray of fast-moving atoms of fire.

2 **5th century BC: Empedocles**
A fire inside the eye sends out rays of light that interact with other light sources, such as the sun.

3 **5th–4th century BC: Democritus**
Everything is made of atoms and the finest layers of these atoms continuously detach themselves from objects. These layers travel to the eye as a copy of the object.

4 **5th–4th century BC: Plato**
Rays from the eyes collide with sunlight and create a body between the object and the eye, which allows you to see.

5 **4th century BC: Aristotle**
Light is a medium between the eye and the object, which allows you to see all of its environment.

6 **4th-3rd century BC: Epicurus**
Particles continuously flow in groups as a copy from the object to the eye and are then replaced by other particles.

7 **4th-3rd century BC: Euclid**
Light moves out of the eye in straight lines as rays of vision.

8 **1st century BC: Lucretius**
Light is made of particles that originate from the Sun and fly to the Earth.

9 **1000: Alhazen**
Light is a straight stream of particles that originate from the Sun, are reflected by objects and then enter the eye.

10 **1604–1611: Johannes Kepler**
Rays originate from every point of an object, some of which meet the eye.

11 **1637–1644: René Descartes**
Light is transmitted by pressure in a medium (»plenum«) like sound waves.

12 **1665: Robert Hooke**
Rays of light spread in a medium like waves in the water.

13 **1672–1704: Isaac Newton**
Light is made of corpuscles (particles) in an ether. White light is a composition of other colors (prism-experiments).

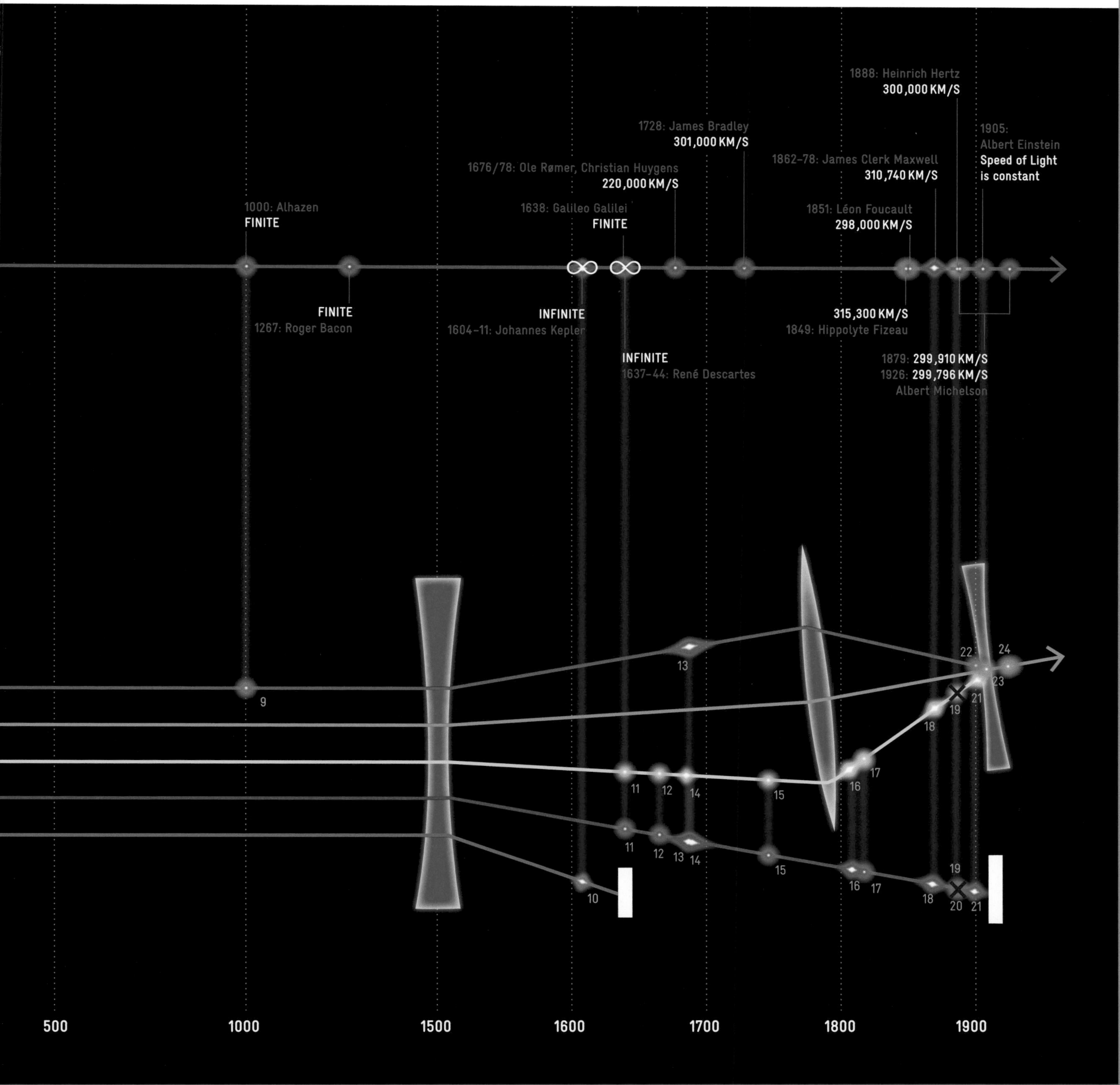
1888: Heinrich Hertz
300,000 KM/S
1905:
Albert Einstein
Speed of Light
is constant
1728: James Bradley
301,000 KM/S
1862–78: James Clerk Maxwell
310,740 KM/S
1676/78: Ole Rømer, Christian Huygens
220,000 KM/S
1000: Alhazen
FINITE
1638: Galileo Galilei
FINITE
1851: Léon Foucault
298,000 KM/S
FINITE
1267: Roger Bacon
INFINITE
1604–11: Johannes Kepler
315,300 KM/S
1849: Hippolyte Fizeau
INFINITE
1637–44: René Descartes
1879: 299,910 KM/S
1926: 299,796 KM/S
Albert Michelson
9
10
11
12
13
14
15
16
17
18
19
20
21
22
23
24
500
1000
1500
1600
1700
1800
1900

14 **1678–1690: Christian Huygens**
The Dutch physicist theorized that light waves are propagated through an ether that permeates everything.

15 **1746: Leonard Euler**
Light moves in a medium that transports waves, similar to sound waves in the air.

16 **1797–1817: Thomas Young**
The »double-slit experiment« provides proof of light's wave nature. He thus theorized that light has varying wavelengths and spreads in transverse waves in an ether.

17 **1816–1819: Augustin Jean Fresnel**
The French physicist developed a wave theory with movement patterns and polarization experiments. He believed light waves are transverse waves and ether is like an elastic solid body.

18 **1862–1878: James Clerk Maxwell**
The Scottish physicist created an electromagnetic wave theory (»Maxwell's equations«) together with his English colleague Michael Faraday. They believed in a mechanic ether (elastic solid body) as a carrier of these waves.

19 **1886–1890: Heinrich Hertz**
The German physicist discovered the »photoelectric effect«, which cannot be explained by the wave theory. Light has mechanical as well as electro-magnetic properties.

20 **1887: Albert Michelson & Edward Morley**
No signs of ether can be found in the »Michelson-Morley experiment.«

21 **1892–1906: Hendrik Antoon Lorentz**
Light moves in waves through an abstract, electromagnetic, completely motionless ether.

22 **1900: Max Planck**
The German physicist introduced the notion of the »quantum« as the smallest exchangeable packet of energy and established »Planck's law.«

23 **1905: Albert Einstein**
The Nobel laureate explained the »photoelectric effect« using Planck's energy quanta: light can in some cases behave like particles. The concept of the ether is omitted.

24 **1924: Louis de Broglie**
The French physicist created the theory of matter waves and received the Nobel Prize for physics in 1929: light behaves like particles and waves.

SIGNAL LANGUAGE

When transmitting messages in the dark, people rely on light to communicate. Light is an important communication tool for ensuring safe travel at sea, as it is used to tell ships where not to go. Light enables long-distance communication as telephones and computers use light pulses to transmit messages.

LIGHT EXTENSIONS ON MOTORIZED VEHICLES

Signals can only be universally understood if they follow a pattern. As a result, traffic communication is highly regulated with regard to signal arrangement, color and type.

● Light ● Reflector ● Green light ○ Indicator ○ Flashing light ● Red light

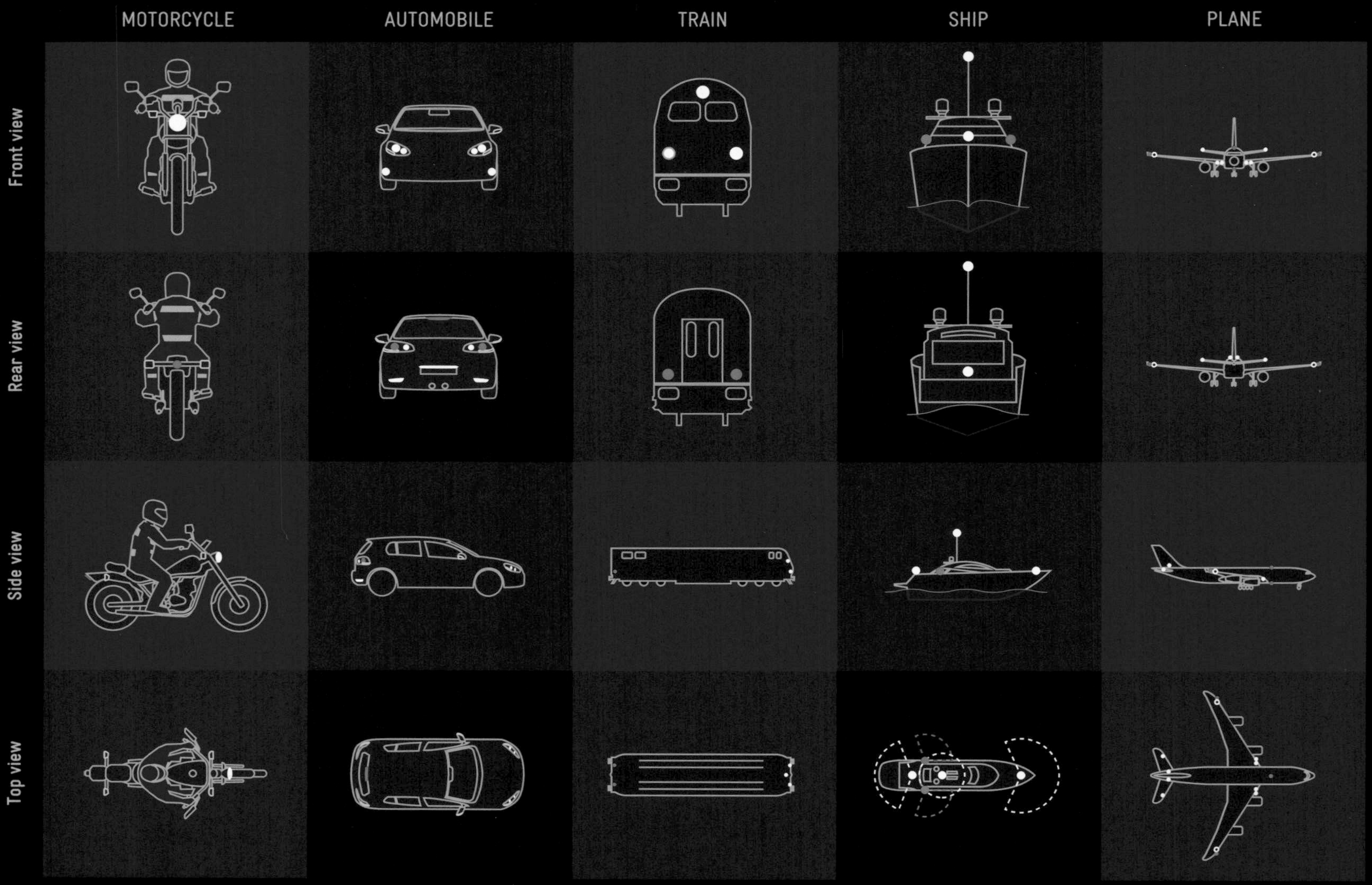
MOTORCYCLE
AUTOMOBILE
TRAIN
SHIP
PLANE
Front view
Rear view
Side view
Top view

REFLECTOR STRUCTURE

Reflective foil is widely used for road traffic safety. Objects are made visible by microprismatic sheeting.

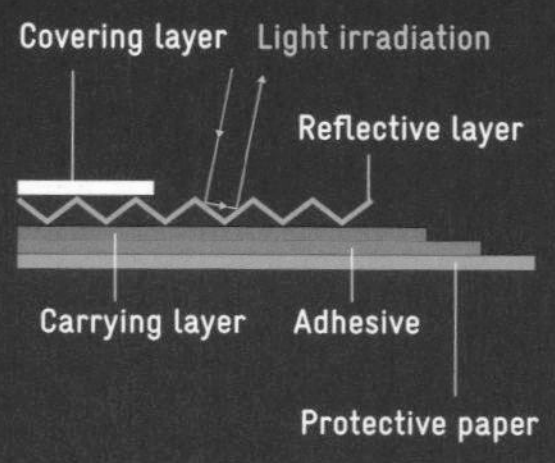
Covering layer
Light irradiation
Reflective layer
Carrying layer
Adhesive
Protective paper

SIGN STRUCTURE

Microprismatic sheeting is also used for road traffic signs.

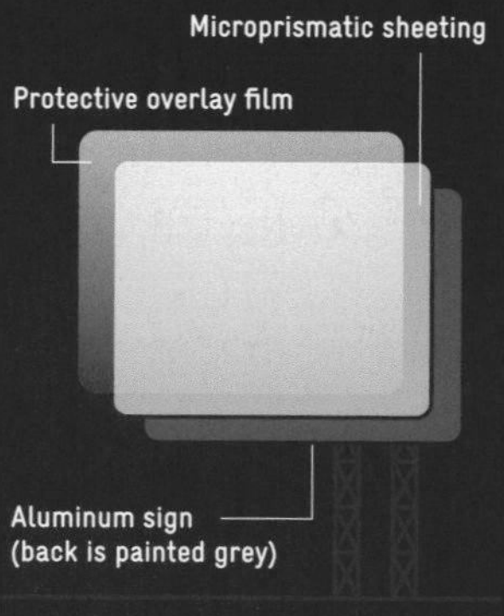
Microprismatic sheeting
Protective overlay film
Aluminum sign
(back is painted grey)

TRAIN SIGNALS

Distant signals

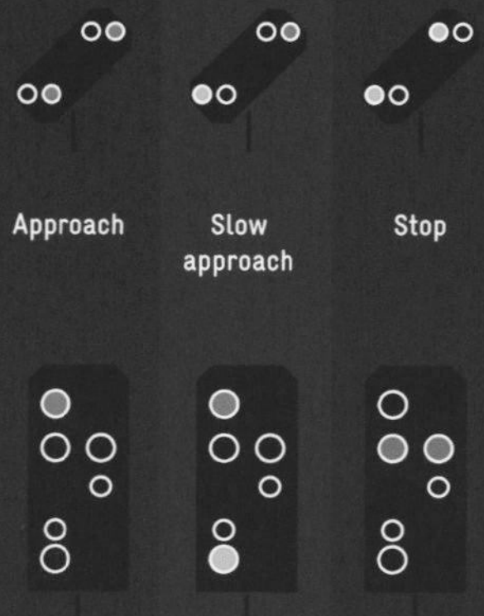
Approach
Slow approach
Stop

LIGHTHOUSE LENS

Lighthouses use Fresnel lenses. The lenses guarantee the same amount of light with less weight and volume.

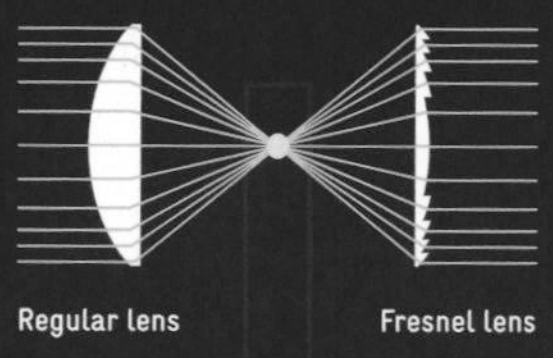
Regular lens
Fresnel lens

AIRPORT TOWER

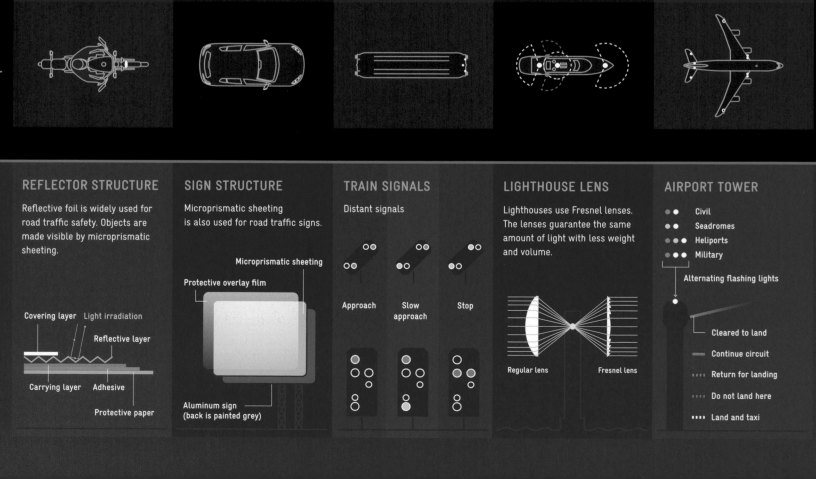

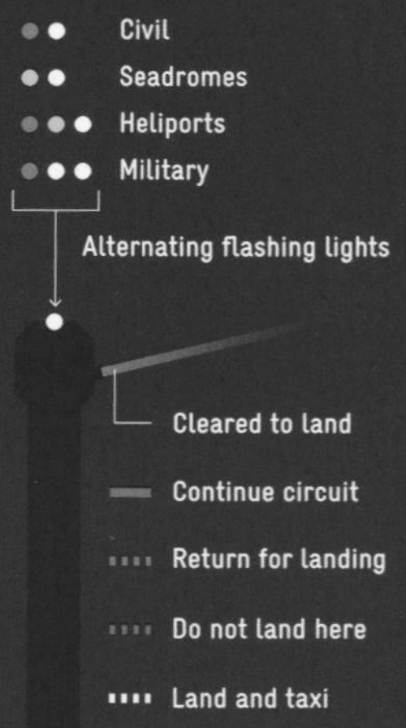
Civil
Seadromes
Heliports
Military
Alternating flashing lights
Cleared to land
Continue circuit
Return for landing
Do not land here
Land and taxi

FIBER OPTIC BACKBONES

Today, lightwave cables are used to transmit data over long distances. It was the British who first transmitted a message to a point more than 250 kilometers away, without requiring any amplification.

Since then, light wave cables have been replacing copper cables as the standard for undersea transmission lines. Today, these lightwave cables encompass the whole world and are knit together to create the backbone of global communication.

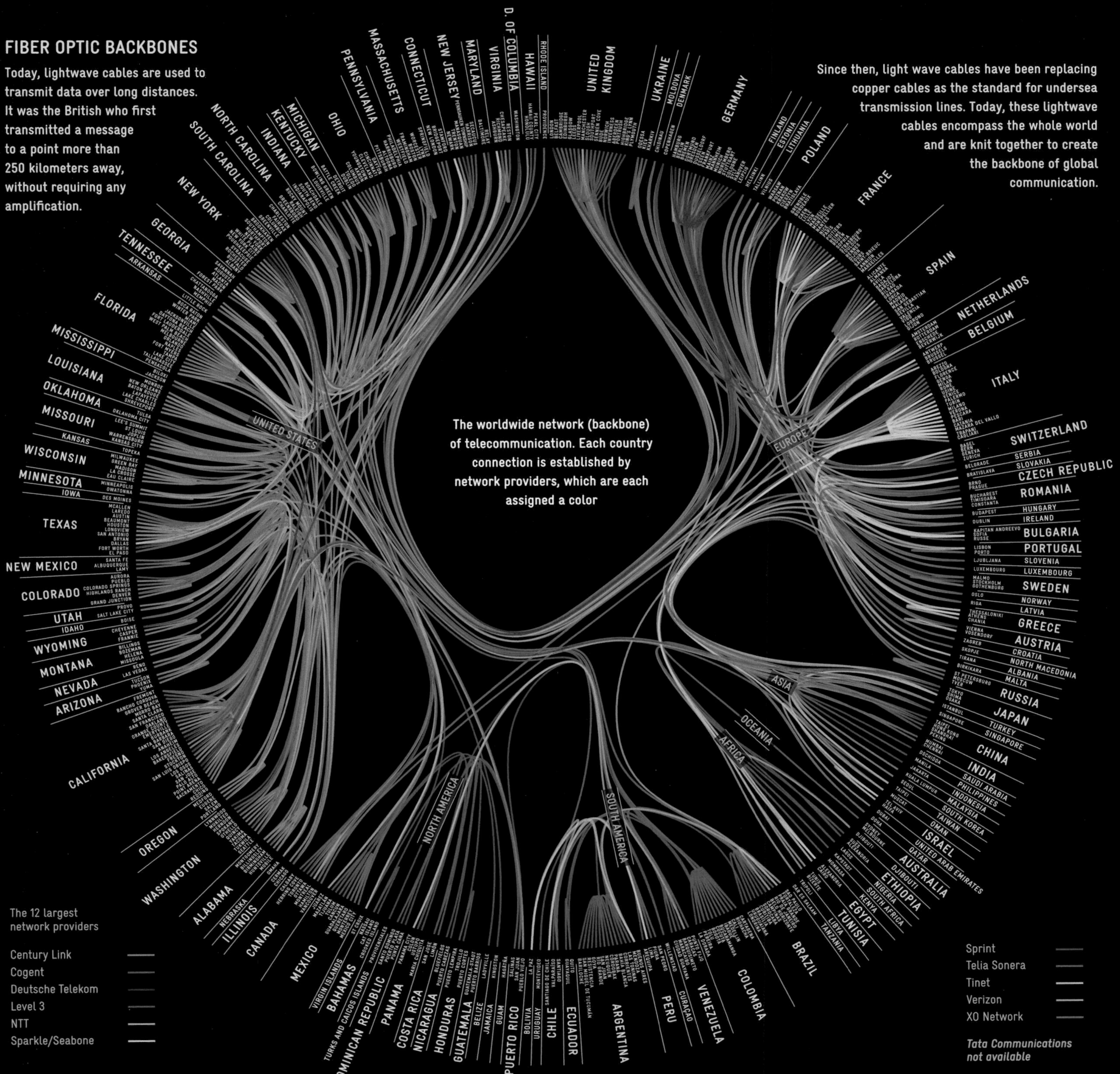

FIBER OPTIC VS COPPER

Fiber optic cables offer considerably higher transfer rates with very large ranges. Other advantages are that they are lighter, take up less space and use fewer repeaters. The operation and maintenance costs are significantly reduced.

Data cable in inner city areas

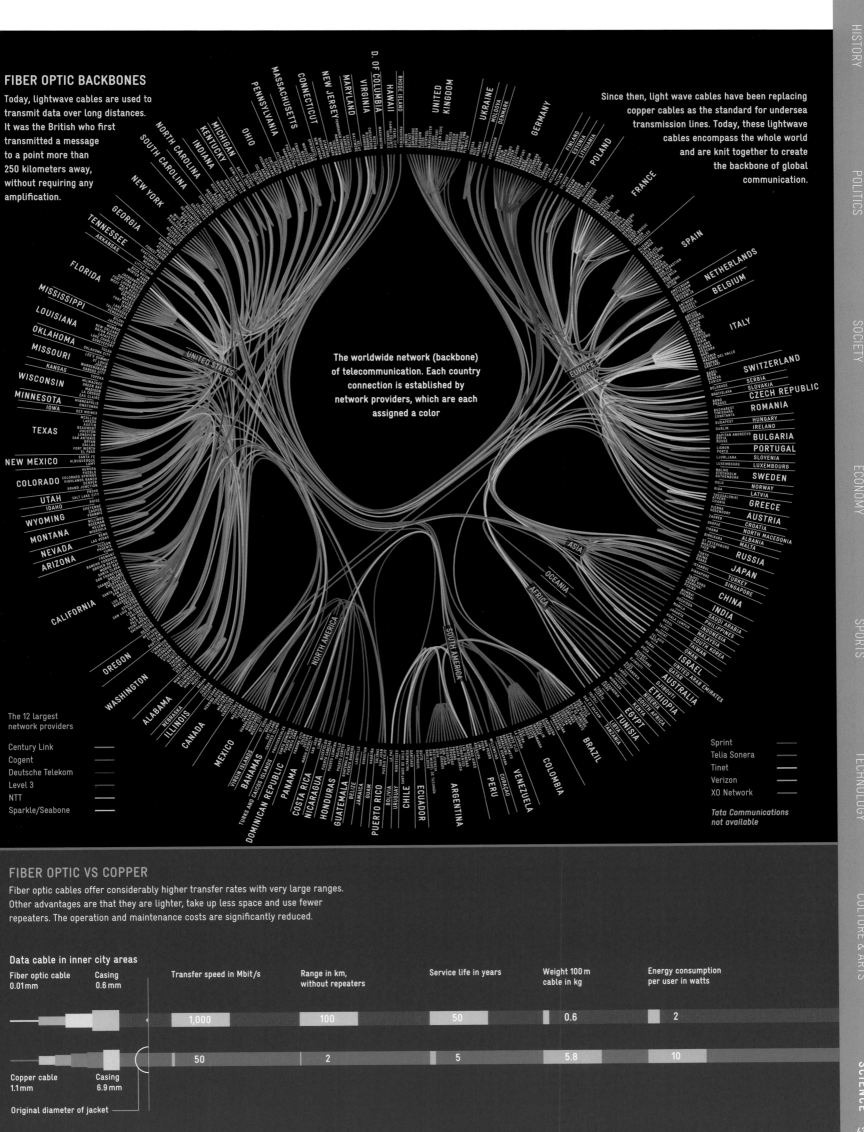

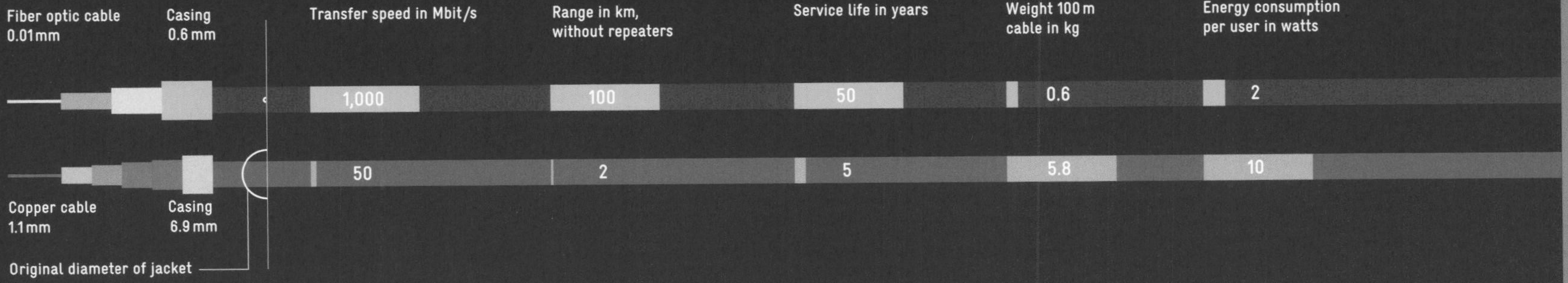

PARTICLES OR WAVES

Until the end of the 19th century, the wave theory of light was generally accepted, but some scientific experiments led to results that couldn't be explained by a theory solely based on waves. In 1905, Albert Einstein reshuffled the deck by reintroducing particles into light theory, in combination with waves. Einstein's explanation of the photoelectric effect introduced the idea of light quanta—known as photons today. His theory is based on the assumption that light could behave like waves as well as particles and this wave-particle duality is the accepted theory in today's scientific community. With rudimentary experiments, light could be observed behaving as either waves or particles. Modern scientific progress has ensured that both of the behavior patterns of light can be observed simultaneously.

WAVE-PARTICLE DUALITY

Light exhibits the properties of waves and particles. When we talk about light particles (photones) ❶, we mean indivisible packets of energy which can only be exchanged as an entity. Their energy is linked to a wave property, the frequency. The spreading of light, however, happens in electromagnetic, transverse waves ❷, which occur with different wavelengths and frequencies and their entirety is summarized in the electromagnetic spectrum. Depending on the experiment, wave as well as particle properties can be observed.

WHAT ARE PARTICLES?

Particles can typically only exist and take effect at a given time and place. They can only be absorbed and emitted as a whole entity.

❶ PHOTONS

The higher the frequency, the greater the energy.

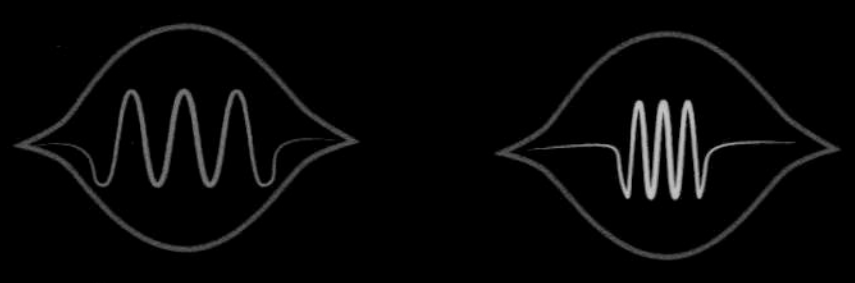
Low energy
High energy

WHAT ARE WAVES?

Typical waves (e.g. water waves) spread across a space. They can strengthen or weaken each other by overlapping and cause an effect in several places at the same time. Their energy depends on the amplitude, though light behaves differently.

❷ ELECTROMAGNETIC WAVES

Electromagnetic waves are transverse waves, which means the vibrations are perpendicular to the direction of travel.

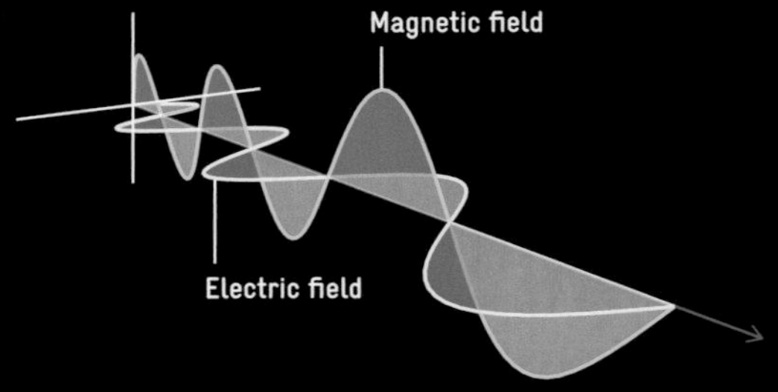
Magnetic field
Electric field

Transverse waves can be compared with the oscillation in a traveling string.

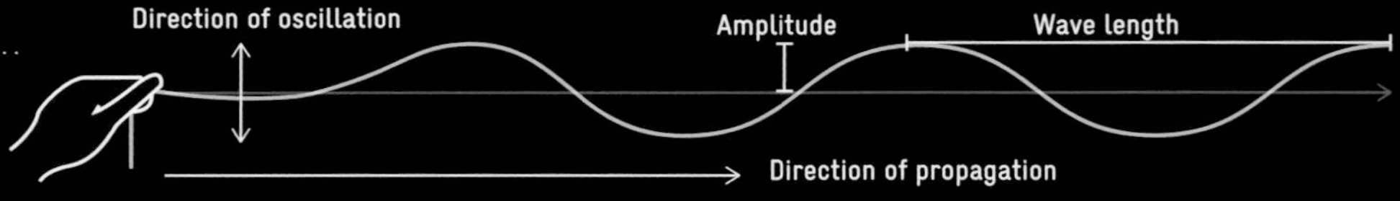
Direction of oscillation
Amplitude
Wave length
Direction of propagation

POLARIZATION

Polarization describes the transverse wave's direction of oscillation. The majority of natural light is an overlapping of waves with different polarizations (=unpolarized light).

Inconceivably fast

299,792,458 m/s

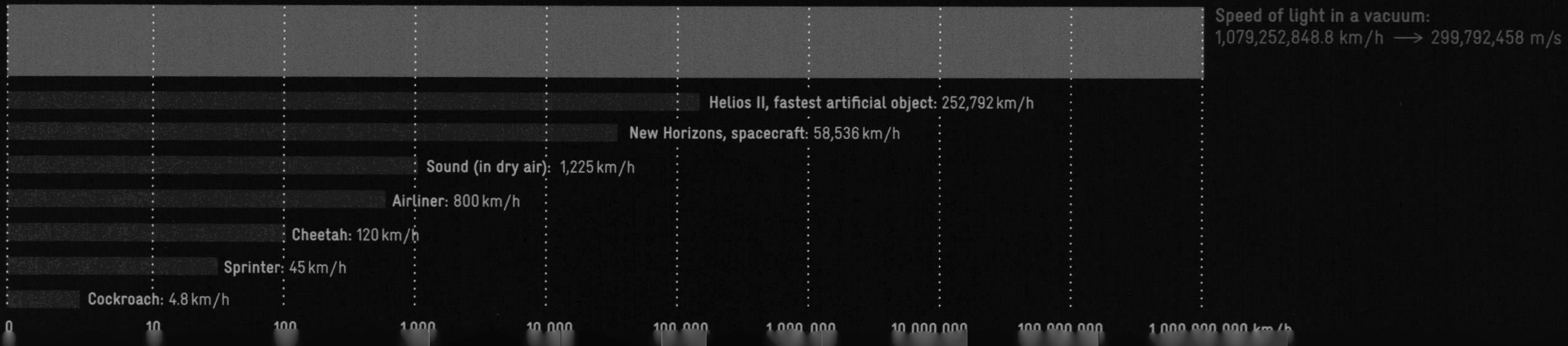
Speed of light in a vacuum:
1,079,252,848.8 km/h ⟶ 299,792,458 m/s
Helios II, fastest artificial object: 252,792 km/h
New Horizons, spacecraft: 58,536 km/h
Sound (in dry air): 1,225 km/h
Airliner: 800 km/h
Cheetah: 120 km/h
Sprinter: 45 km/h
Cockroach: 4.8 km/h
0
10
100
1,000
10,000
100,000
1,000,000
10,000,000
100,000,000
1,000,000,000 km/h

STUDIES THAT SHOW PARTICLES AND WAVES IN LIGHT.

✓ Expected behavior observed   X Expected behavior not observed

PARTICLES | WAVES

REFLECTION & REFRACTION

Rays of light change direction when they hit a reflective surface. They refract when they travel through a different medium, such as water.

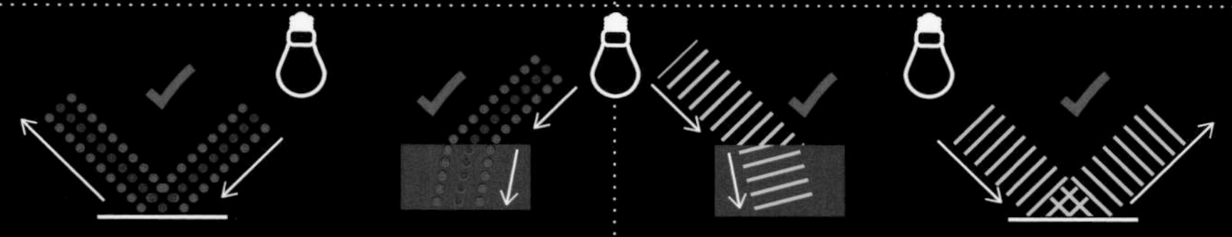

DIFFRACTION

Light is deflected by an obstacle.

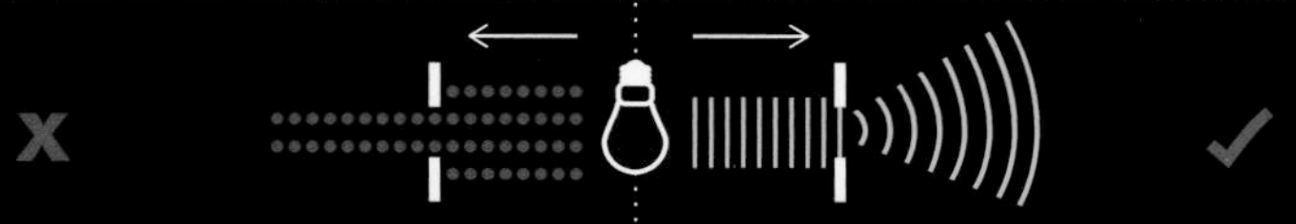

INTERFERENCE PATTERNS (Double-slit experiment)

When light passes through two slits, the waves meet to create interference patterns. If light were solely particles, two bands would be observed.

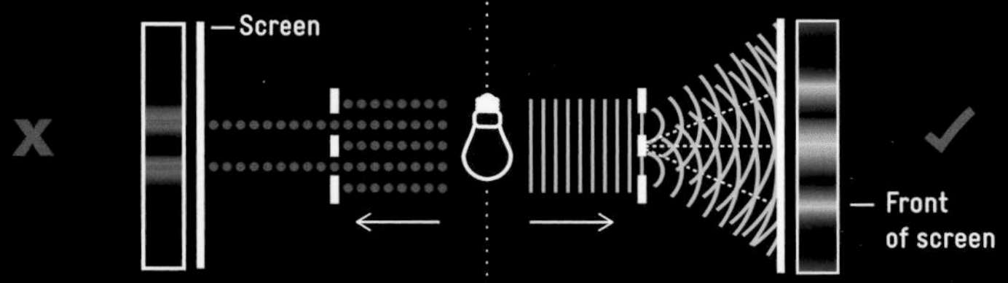
Screen
Front of screen

POLARIZATION

Polarizers—like those used in photography—can filter certain light frequencies. If light moved in a straight line—like particles do—the filters would not change the light we see on the other side of the filters.

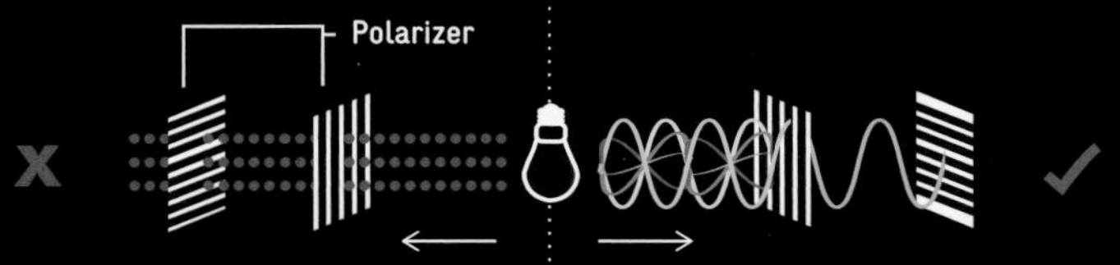
Polarizer

PHOTOELECTRIC EFFECT

The experiment showed that a metal plate releases electrons when hit with the right frequency of light. Regardless of the light's intensity (or wave amplitude), electrons were only extracted after being exposed to a certain frequency. Wave theory says that enough energy should amass—even at a low frequency—when there is continuous exposure. Increasing the intensity would also increase the energy content of the wave and release more electrons. But the experiment showed that the energy can only be absorbed as »packets of energy« and therefore meets the requirements for electrons to be released. If there is insufficient energy, the electrons remain in the metal plate.

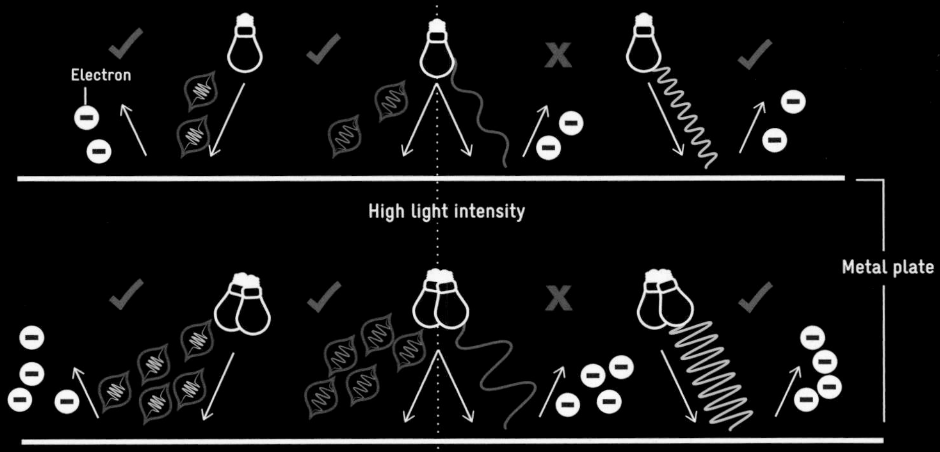
Low light intensity
Electron
High light intensity
Metal plate

CONSTANT SPEED OF LIGHT

The speed of light is absolute, and it is different from relative speed measurements in daily life (A), which means it has the same speed for all observers. The light's speed of propagation is constant irrespective of the motion of the light source. If the speed of light is always the same for all observers, the result is the following: time is relative and therefore passes at different speeds depending on the observer. (B)

(A) A ball kicked in a moving train in the same direction of travel

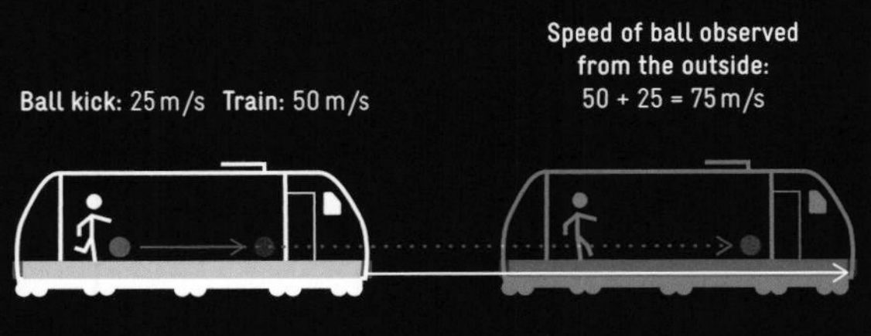
Speed of ball observed
from the outside:
50 + 25 = 75 m/s
Ball kick: 25 m/s Train: 50 m/s

(B) Someone shines a flashlight at the center of a train. For the observer on the train, the front and back of the train are fixed positions and the light spreads instantaneously. However, an observer on the platform watching the train go by sees the rear of the train car moving forward towards the point of light, meaning the person on the platform perceives the light hitting the ends of the train car at different times.

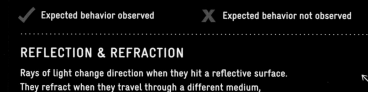

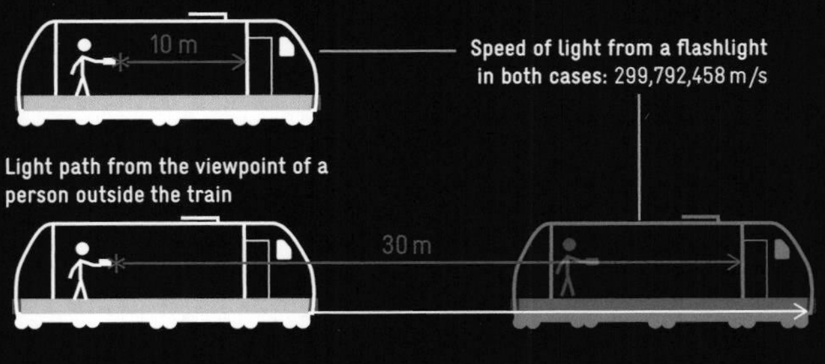
Light path from the viewpoint of a person on the train
10 m
Speed of light from a flashlight
in both cases: 299,792,458 m/s
Light path from the viewpoint of a
person outside the train
30 m

»ALL THESE 50 YEARS OF CONSCIOUS BROODING HAVE BROUGHT ME NO NEARER TO THE ANSWER TO THE QUESTION 'WHAT ARE LIGHT QUANTA?'. NOWADAYS EVERY TOM, DICK AND HARRY THINKS HE KNOWS IT, BUT HE IS MISTAKEN.«

– ALBERT EINSTEIN, 1954

LIGHT SOURCE, LIFE SOURCE

Life on Earth depends on the sun. It illuminates what we see and brightens our moods. The sun provides the key ingredient for plant life, which in turn provides animals and people with a key element for their lives. It determines our circadian rhythms and forms both the literal and the metaphorical center of our universe.

PHOTOSYNTHESIS

Our life depends on a plant's waste product: oxygen. This element is released via photosynthesis, the most fundamental biochemical process on Earth.
4.6 billion years ago, our planet's atmosphere was made up of only hydrogen, helium, ammonia, methane and a few other gasses. It wasn't until cyanobacteria and algae started photosythesizing that oxygen entered the mix, making today's biosphere possible. We've simplified the process here to show how the chloroplasts use sunshine to sustain life.

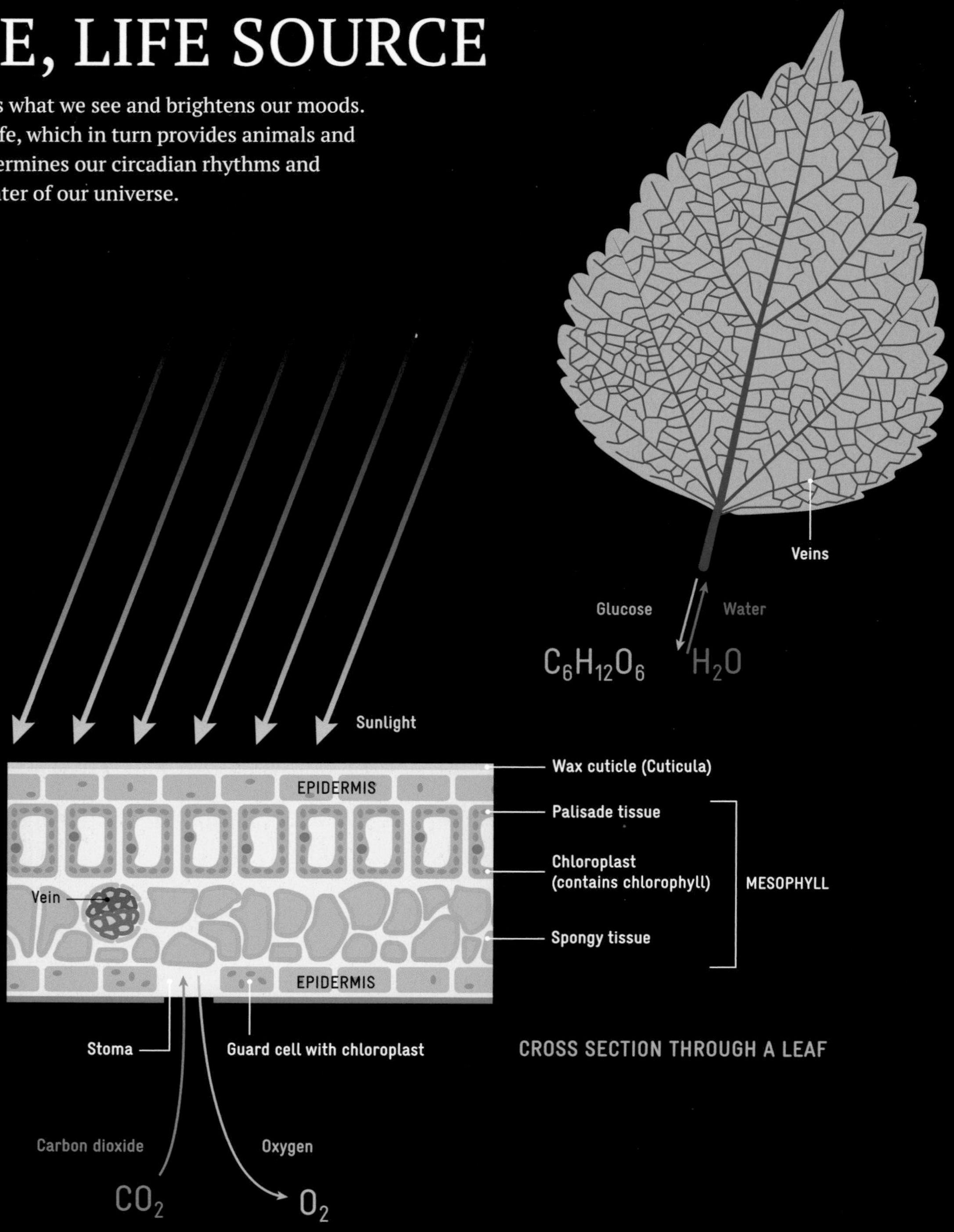
Veins
Glucose
Water
$C_6H_{12}O_6$
H_2O
Sunlight
EPIDERMIS
Wax cuticle (Cuticula)
Palisade tissue
Chloroplast
(contains chlorophyll)
MESOPHYLL
Vein
Spongy tissue
EPIDERMIS
Stoma
Guard cell with chloroplast
CROSS SECTION THROUGH A LEAF
Carbon dioxide
Oxygen
CO_2
O_2

$$6\ CO_2 + 12\ H_2O + \text{LIGHT} \xrightleftharpoons[\text{Respiration}]{\text{Photosynthesis}} C_6H_{12}O_6 + 6\ O_2 + 6\ H_2O$$

LIGHT EFFECTS IN NATURE

AURORA

Aurora Borealis happens in the upper layers of the stratosphere.

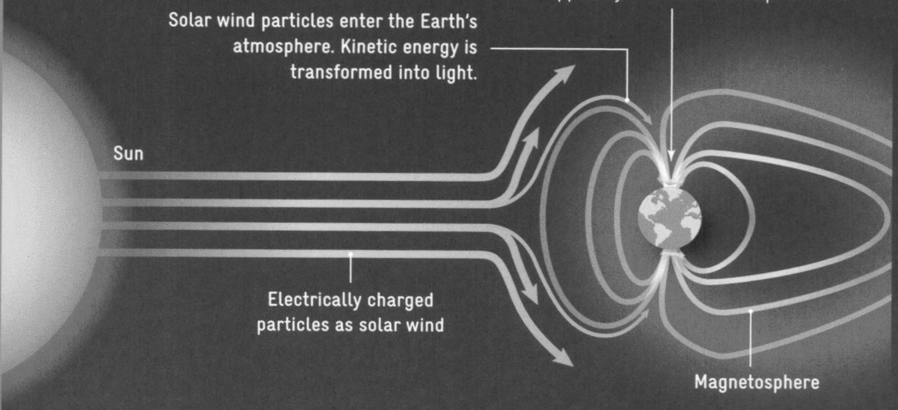
Solar wind particles enter the Earth's atmosphere. Kinetic energy is transformed into light.
Sun
Electrically charged particles as solar wind
Magnetosphere

LIGHT REFRACTION

An observer sees different images of a ship on the horizon depending on how light is bent by warm or cold layers of air.

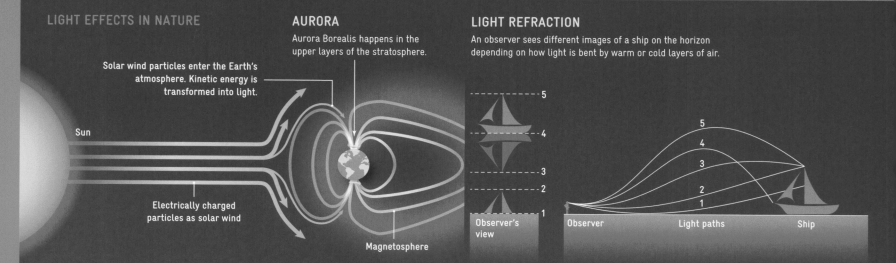

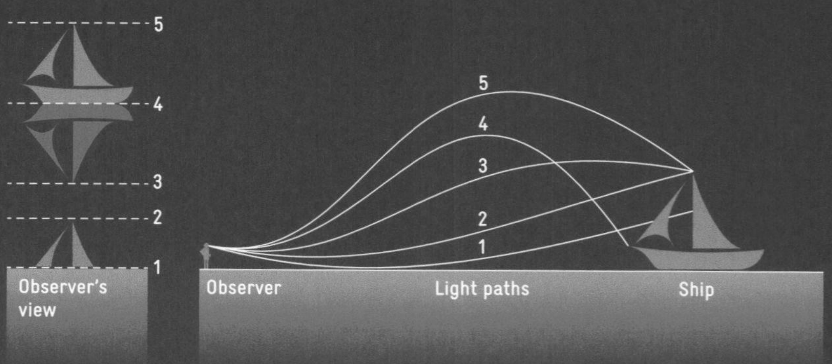
5
4
3
2
1
Observer's view
Observer
Light paths
Ship

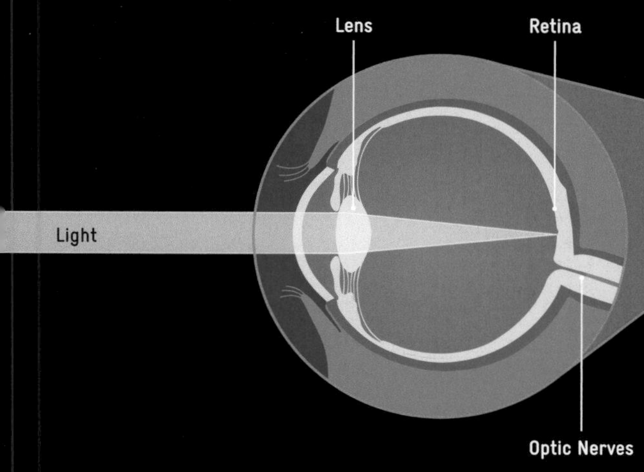
Lens
Retina
Light
Optic Nerves

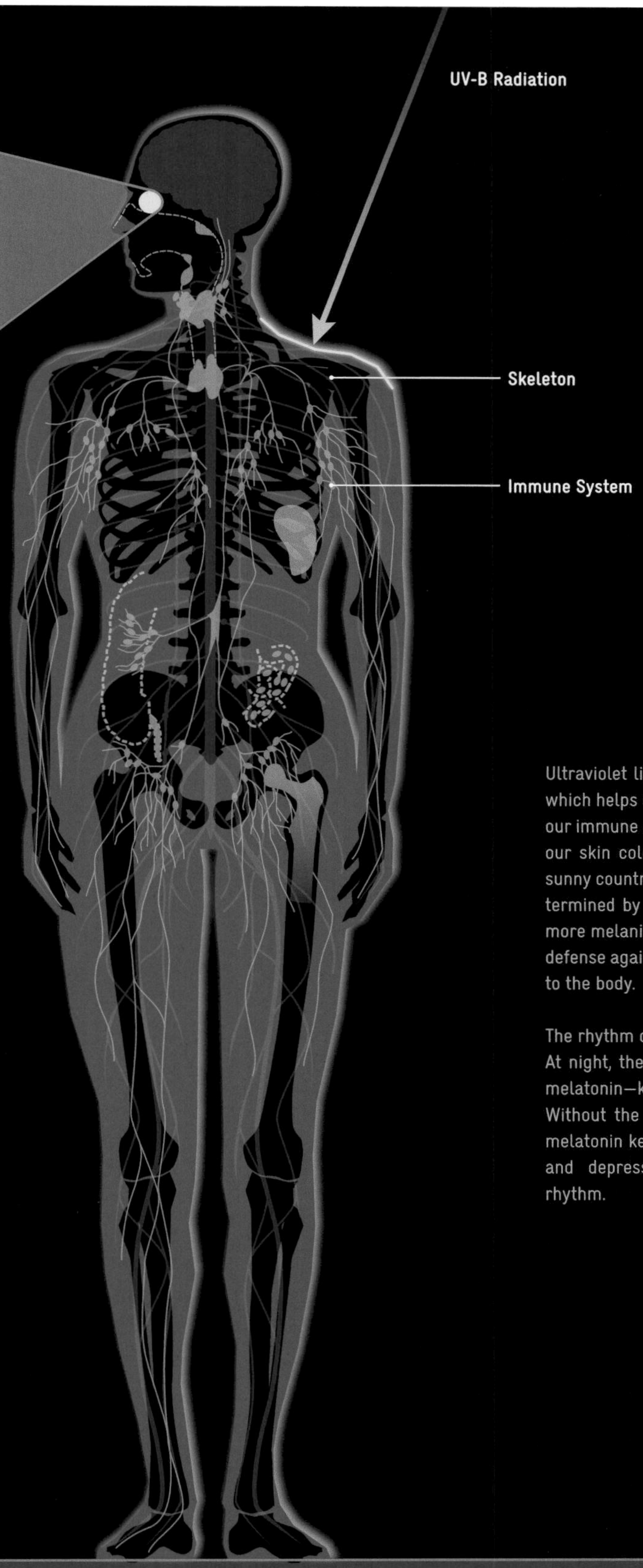
UV-B Radiation
Skeleton
Immune System

THE EYE

The eye sees light with a wavelength range between 400 and 760 nanometers. The iris and pupil ensure that the lens always gets the right amount of light, which projects onto the retina. The stimulus is then registered on the optic nerve and passed onto the brain, which tells us what we're looking at.

THE HUMAN BODY

A little bit of sunshine does the body good. It helps us regulate respiration, circulation and metabolism. Even the sun's absence is important: It helps regulate our sleep patterns so our bodies can regenerate. Sleep deprivation at a certain level can even be fatal.

Ultraviolet light helps the body produce Vitamin D, which helps our body absorb calcium. It also boosts our immune defense systems. The sun also changes our skin color and people who have grown up in sunny countries tend to have darker skin. This is determined by the amount of melanin you have. The more melanin, the darker the skin, which is a better defense against UV light. Light skin lets more UV into the body.

The rhythm of the sun also balances our hormones. At night, the darkness tells our bodies to produce melatonin—key to regulating our circadian rhythm. Without the bright light telling the body to stop, melatonin keeps being produced, leading to fatigue and depression. Jet lag disrupts that natural rhythm.

RAINBOW

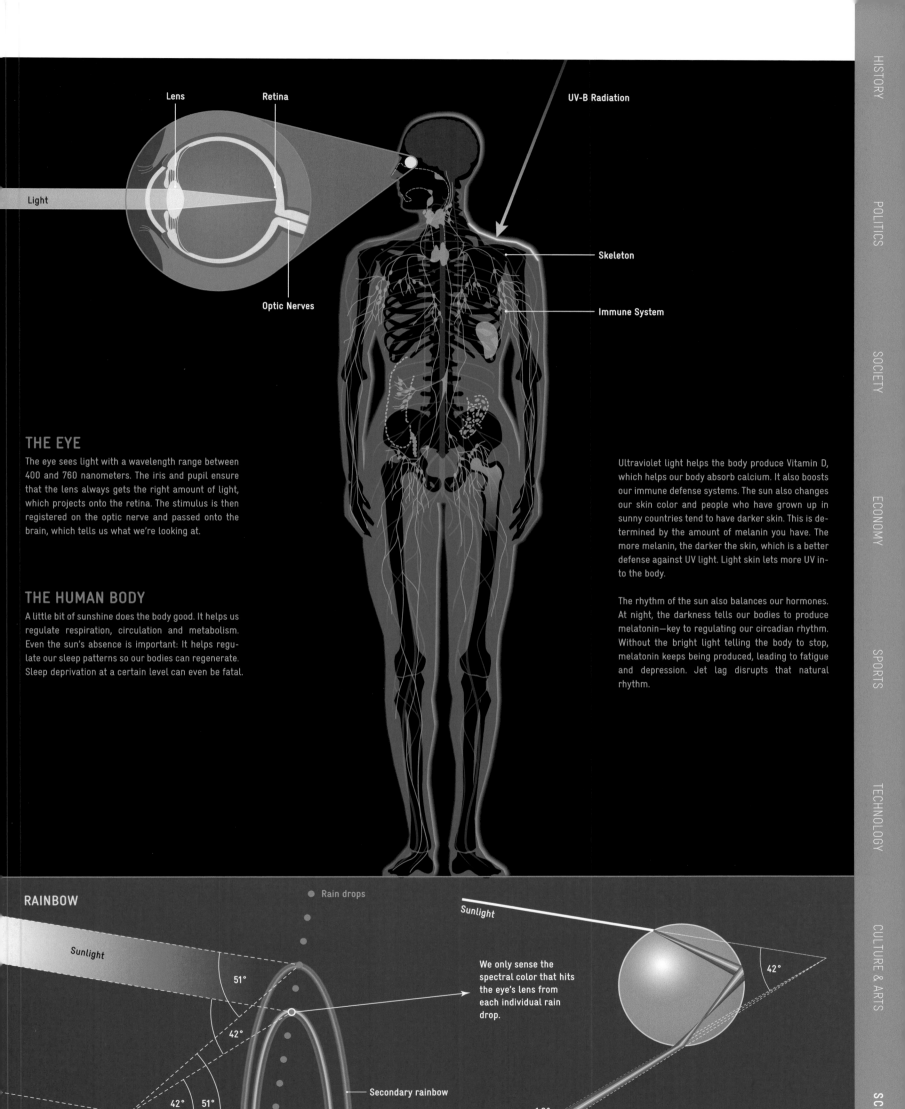

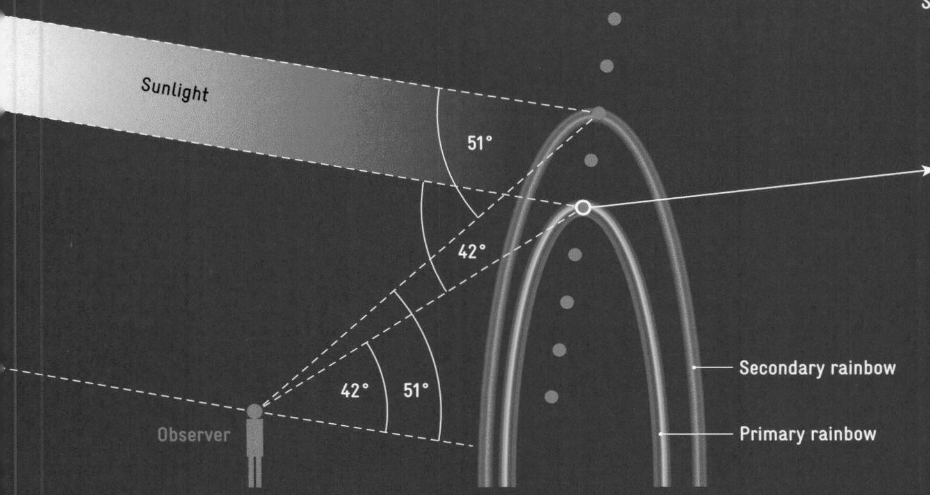
Rain drops
Sunlight
51°
42°
42°
51°
Observer
We only sense the spectral color that hits the eye's lens from each individual rain drop.
Secondary rainbow
Primary rainbow

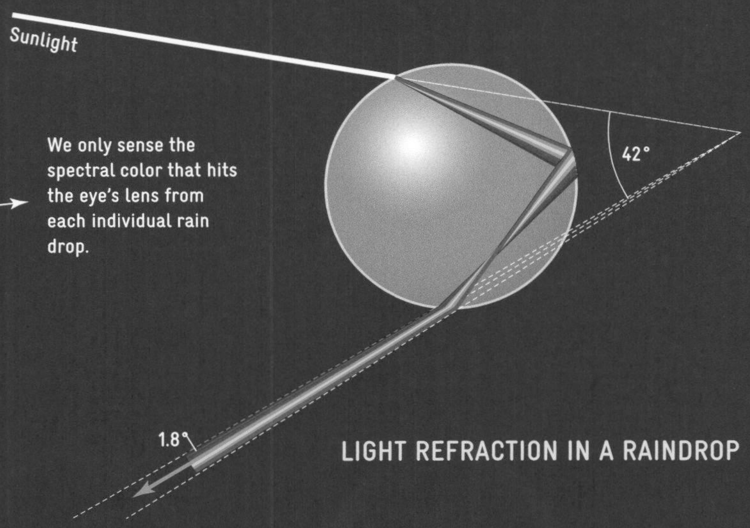
Sunlight
42°
1.8°

LIGHT REFRACTION IN A RAINDROP

FIAT LUX

Mankind's first steps to civilization were defined by harnessing the power of fire and light. Even the Bible begins with its creation as God ordered »Let there be light!«, or »Fiat Lux« in Latin. In Greek mythology, it was Prometheus who created the first human and gave him the power of fire, for which he received the wrath of Zeus. By granting people the power of fire, they were also granted independence from the gods and nature. It wasn't until 1808 that electricity stole fire's limelight.

The earliest archaeological evidence of domesticated fire dates back about one million years.
Candles were used for religious ceremonies from at least 160 AD.
In 1799, Philippe Lebon invented the gas lamp using coal gas. London placed the first gas street lamps in 1807.
Oil lamps have existed for about 10,000 years.
In 280 BC, the Lighthouse of Alexandria was built. It was 160 meters tall and was one of the Seven Wonders of the Ancient World.
In 378 AD, the first street lamp was lit in Antioch, Turkey.

MOST IMPORTANT INNOVATIONS OF ARTIFICIAL LIGHT

CANDLE

The wick acts as a capillary, carrying the melted wax upwards. The heat of the flame vaporizes the wax, which breaks down into hydrogen and carbon. The molecules then react with the oxygen in the air to create heat, light, water and carbon dioxide. The heat that is created keeps the process going until the candle is put out.

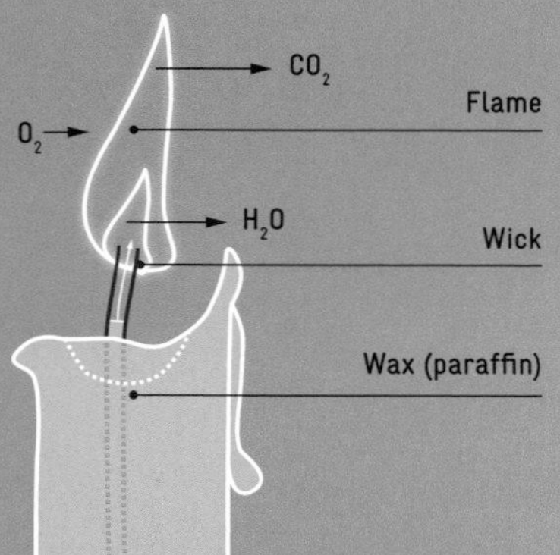
CO_2
O_2
Flame
H_2O
Wick
Wax (paraffin)

ELECTRIC ARC LAMP

Electrons jump over a gap between carbon tips. This current heats the air inside the glass cylinder to such an extent that it vaporizes the carbon, producing a glow.

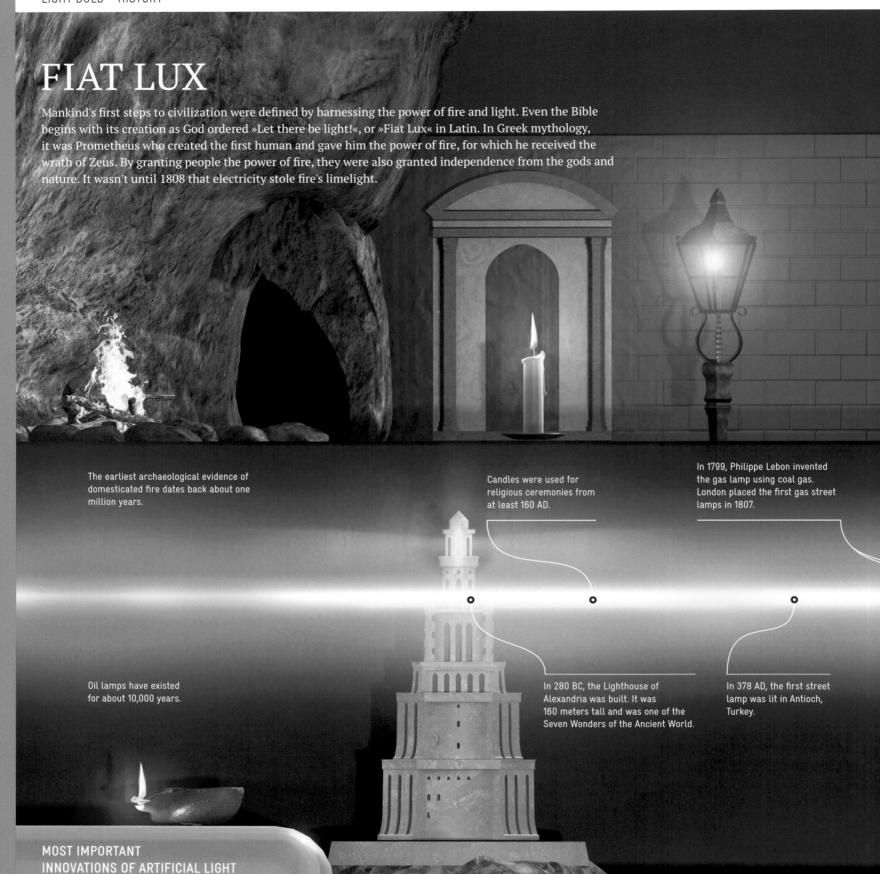

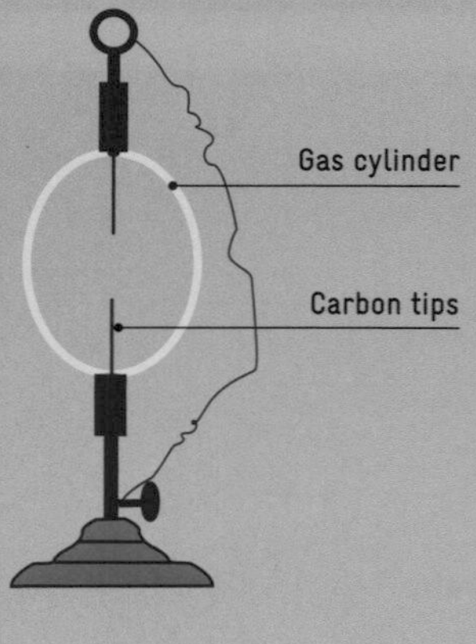
Gas cylinder
Carbon tips

Humphrey Davy invented the electric arc lamp in 1808. Jean Foucault perfected its design in 1848.

In 1853, Ignacy Lukasiewicz made his kerosene lamp—considered the first of its kind.

In 1878, Thomas Alva Edison invented the carbon filament lamp in the USA.

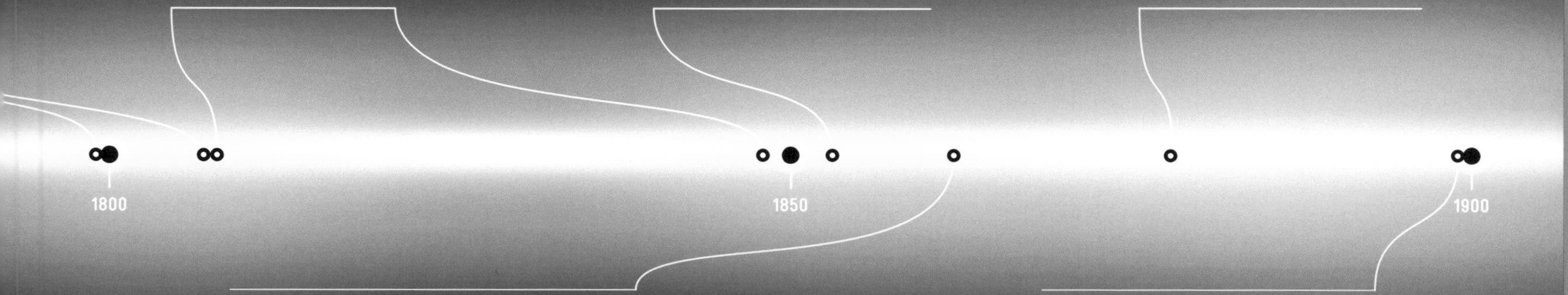

In 1862, Friedrich Wöhler discovered calcium carbide, which paved the way for portable light sources.

In 1899, David Misell invented the flashlight. The name refers to the extremely short life of the batteries of that time.

KEROSENE LAMP

In a similar way to the candle, kerosene moves through the wick to the flame and reacts. The length of the wick and the oxygen supply control the brightness and heat of the flame.

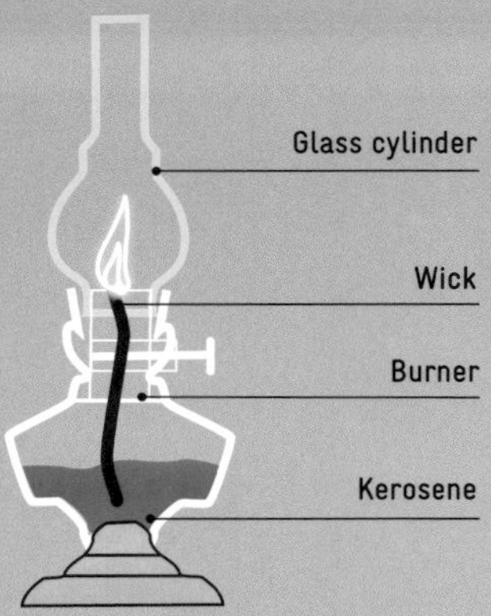

CARBON FILAMENT LAMP

In a glass bulb, an electric current flows through a thin carbon filament that begins to glow, but cannot burn as there is no oxygen. Modern light bulbs use a tungsten filament.

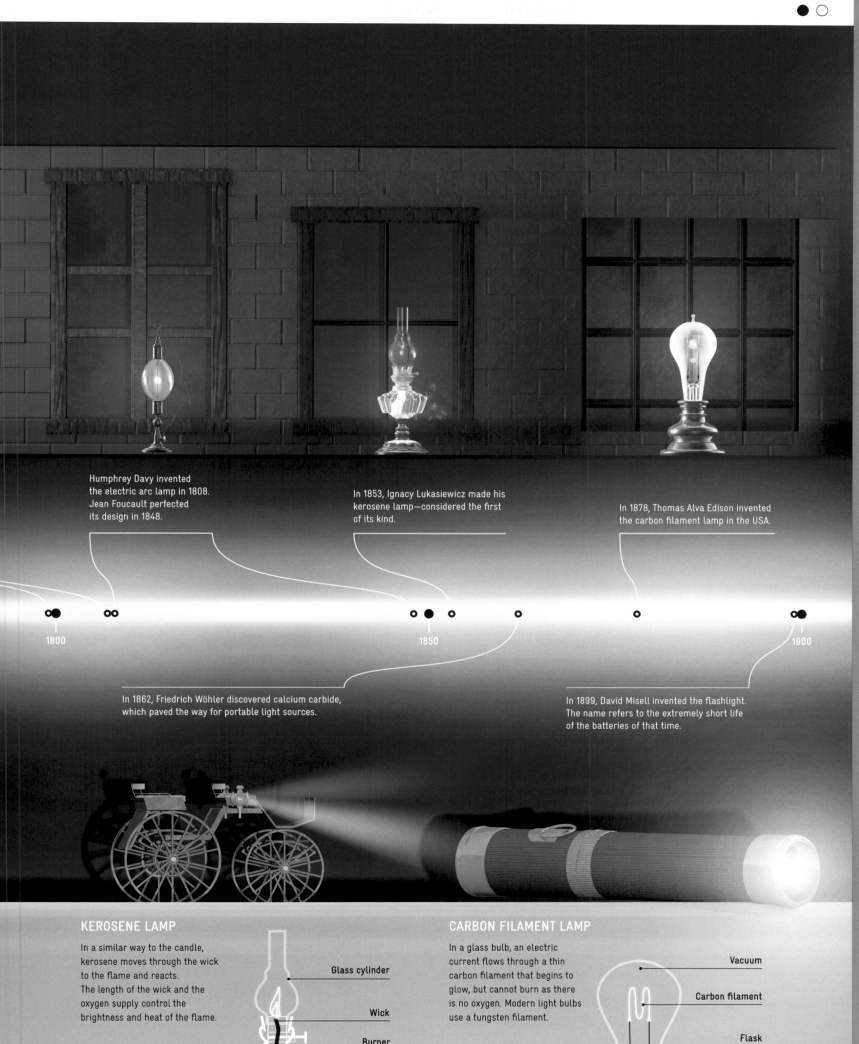

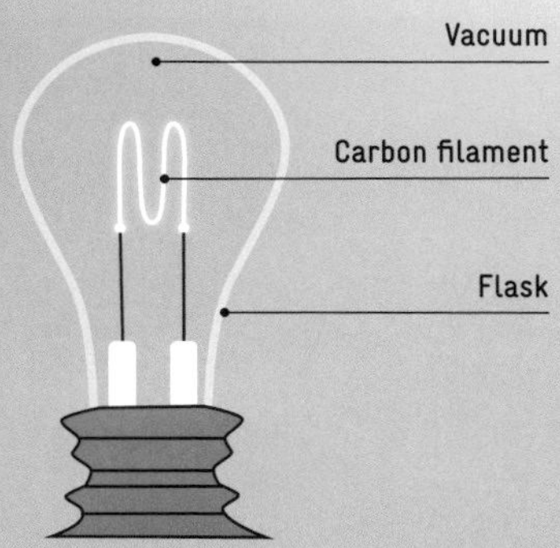

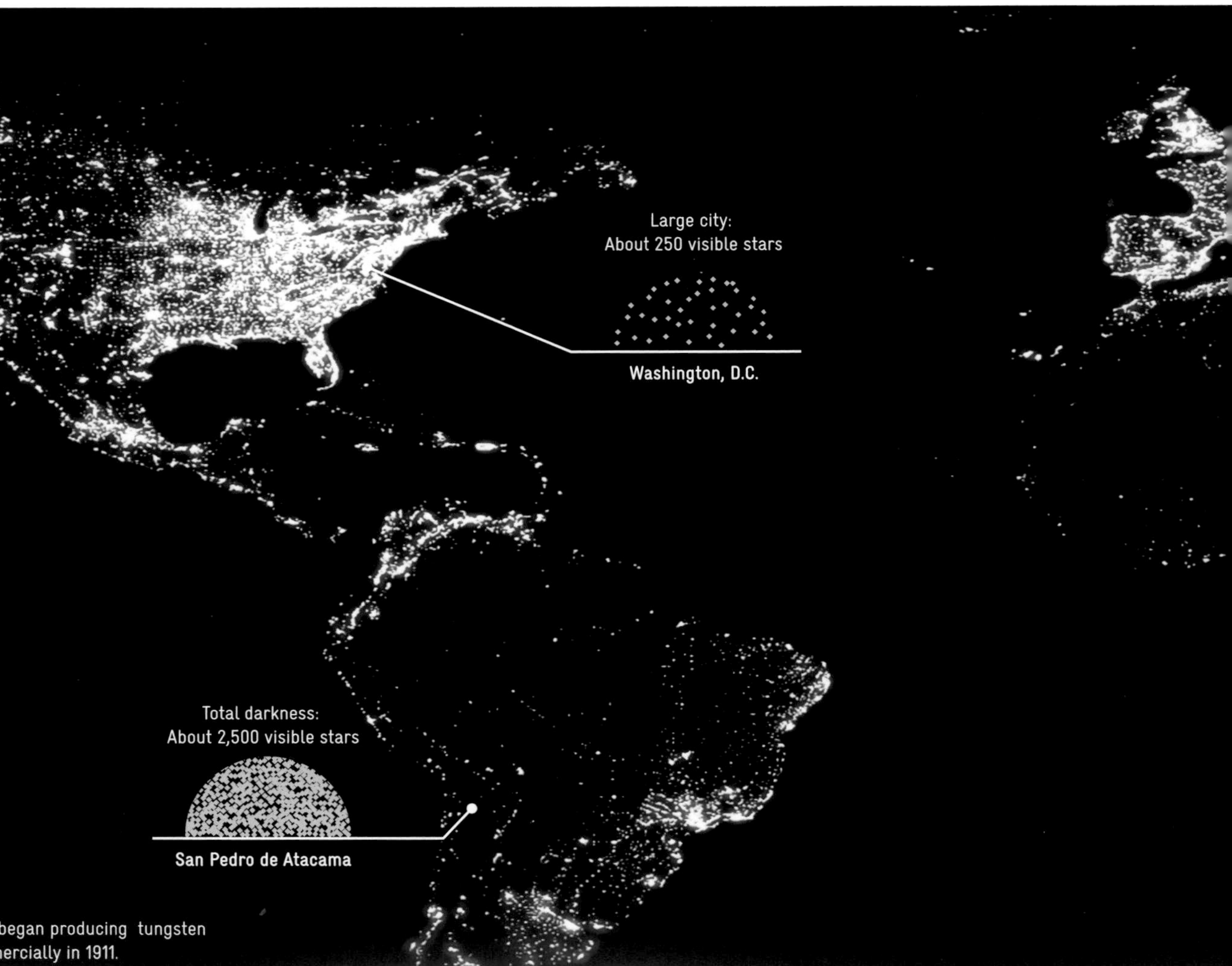
Large city:
About 250 visible stars
Washington, D.C.
Total darkness:
About 2,500 visible stars
San Pedro de Atacama

Industrialization and technological progress have changed how the world uses light. Night can be turned into day and innumerable light pulses send compressed data at full speed through global networks. How we make and use light today has created a world that would be unrecognizable to the one a million years ago in which the first spark was created.

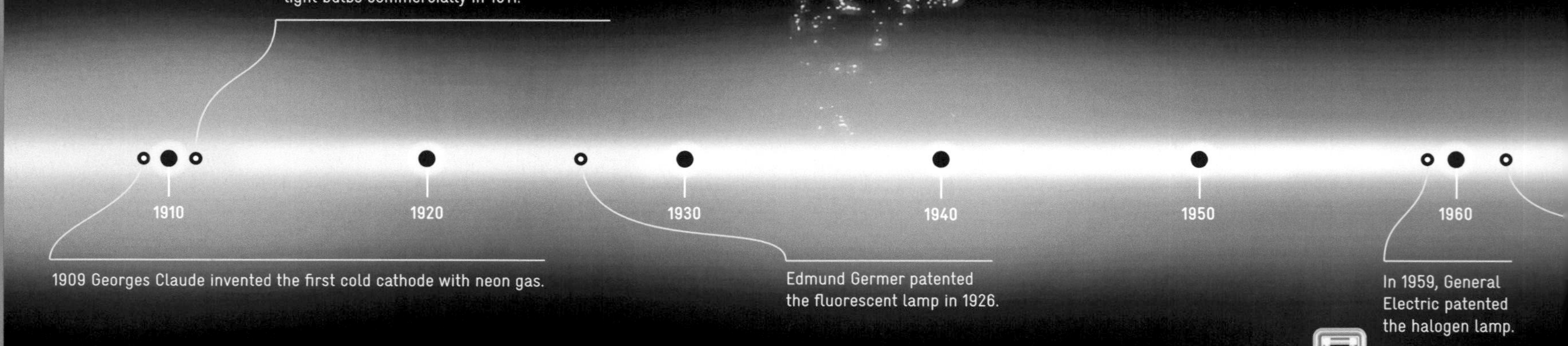
General Electric began producing tungsten light bulbs commercially in 1911.
1910
1920
1930
1940
1950
1960
1909 Georges Claude invented the first cold cathode with neon gas.
Edmund Germer patented the fluorescent lamp in 1926.
In 1959, General Electric patented the halogen lamp.

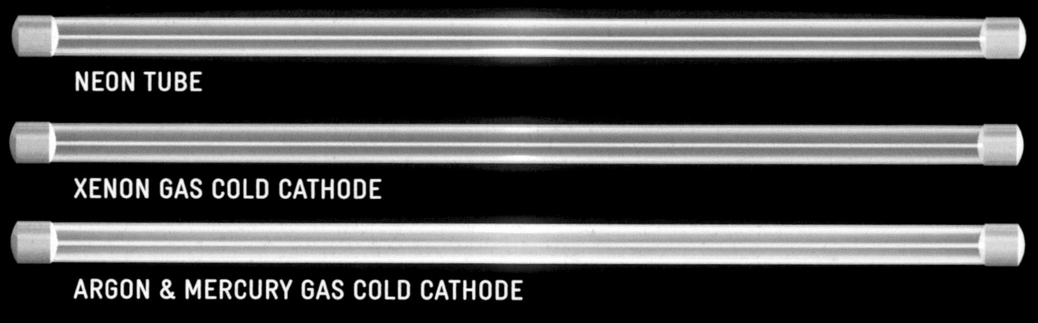
NEON TUBE
XENON GAS COLD CATHODE
ARGON & MERCURY GAS COLD CATHODE

COLD CATHODE

A very high voltage makes a noble gas glow. In contrast to the light bulb that radiates mainly in the infrared range, the light from fluorescent tubes radiates mainly in the UV range.

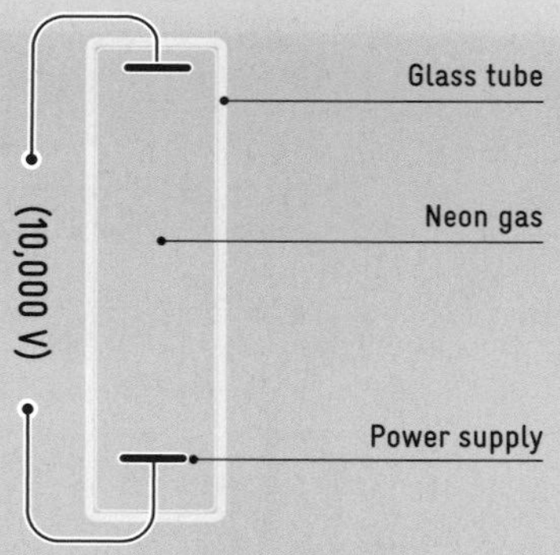
Glass tube
Neon gas
(10,000 V)
Power supply

FLUORESCENT LAMP

Like a neon light, phosphors are excited by electrons to create light, but at a lower voltage. A fluorescent coating then makes the UV-spectrum light visible.

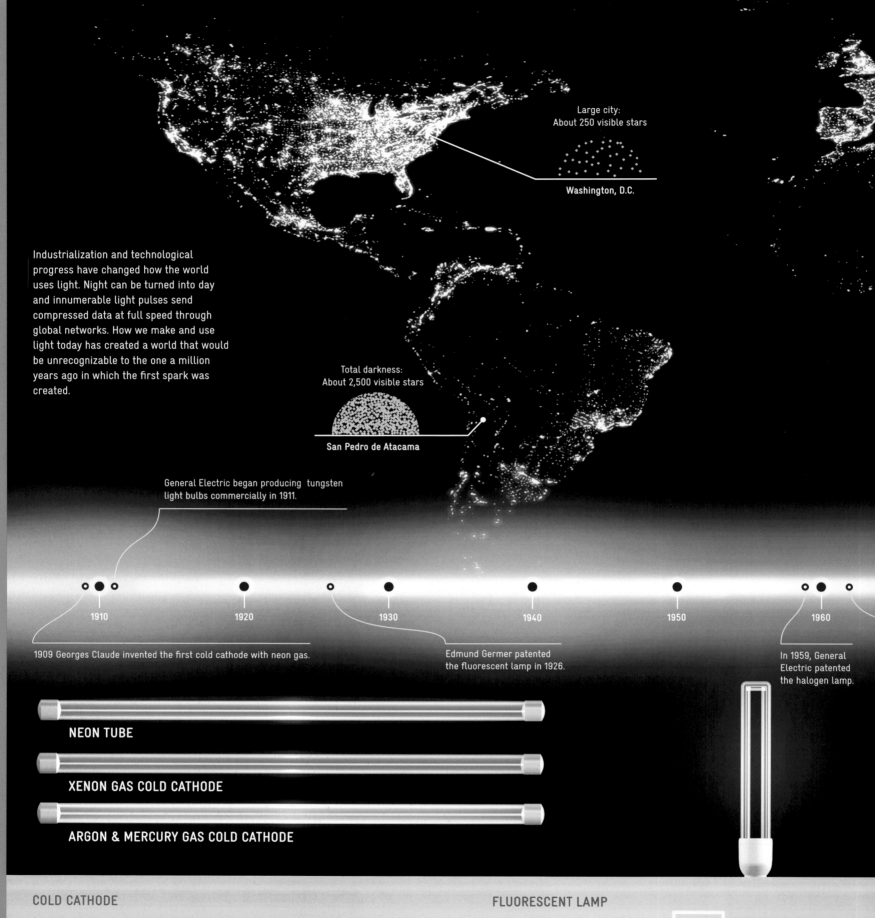

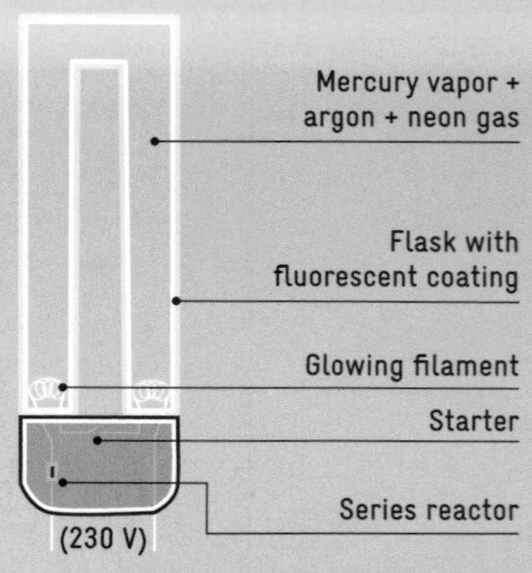
Mercury vapor + argon + neon gas
Flask with fluorescent coating
Glowing filament
Starter
Series reactor
(230 V)

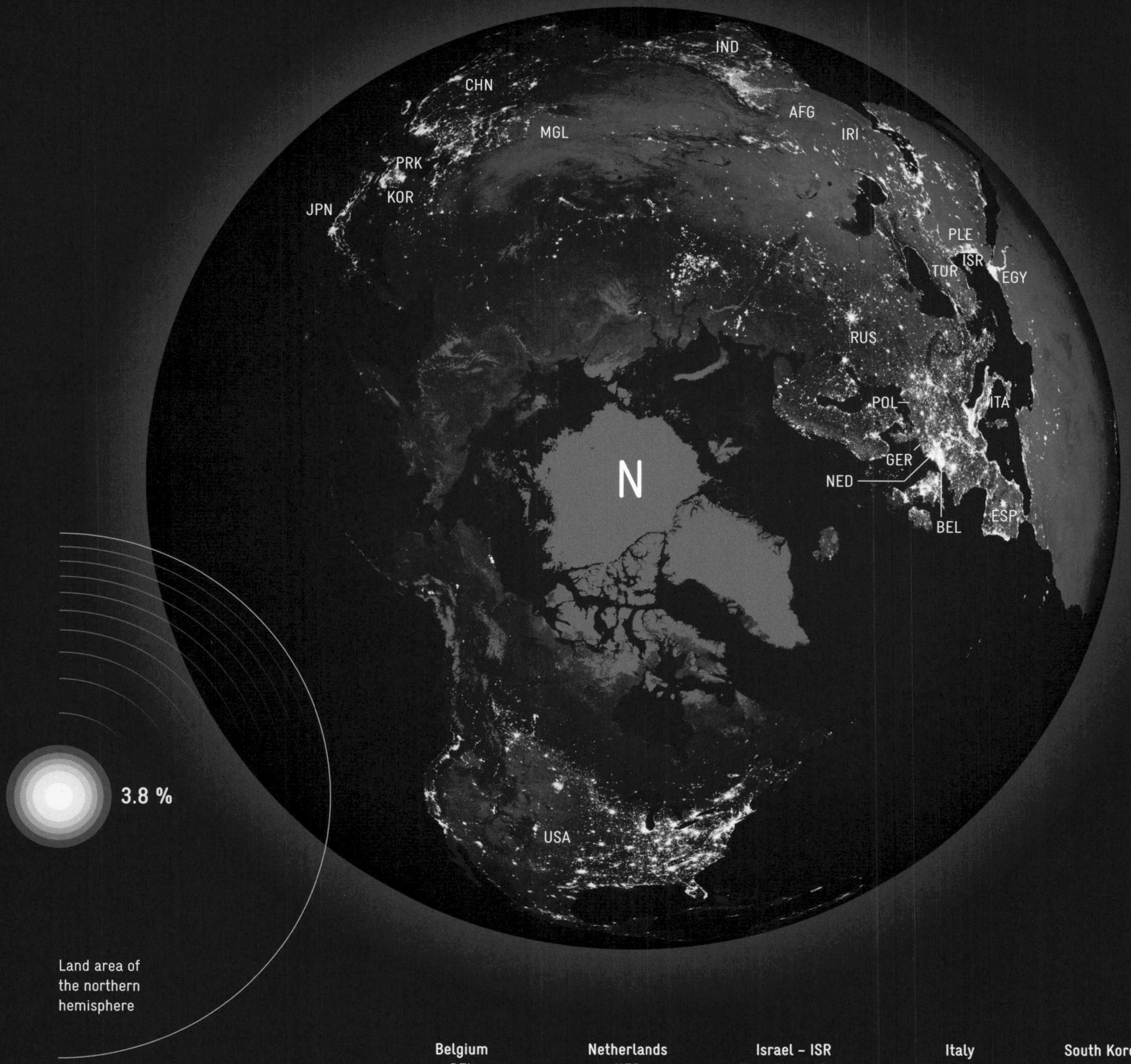
IND
CHN
AFG
MGL
IRI
PRK
KOR
JPN
PLE
TUR
ISR
EGY
RUS
POL
ITA
GER
N
NED
BEL
ESP
USA
3.8 %
Land area of the northern hemisphere

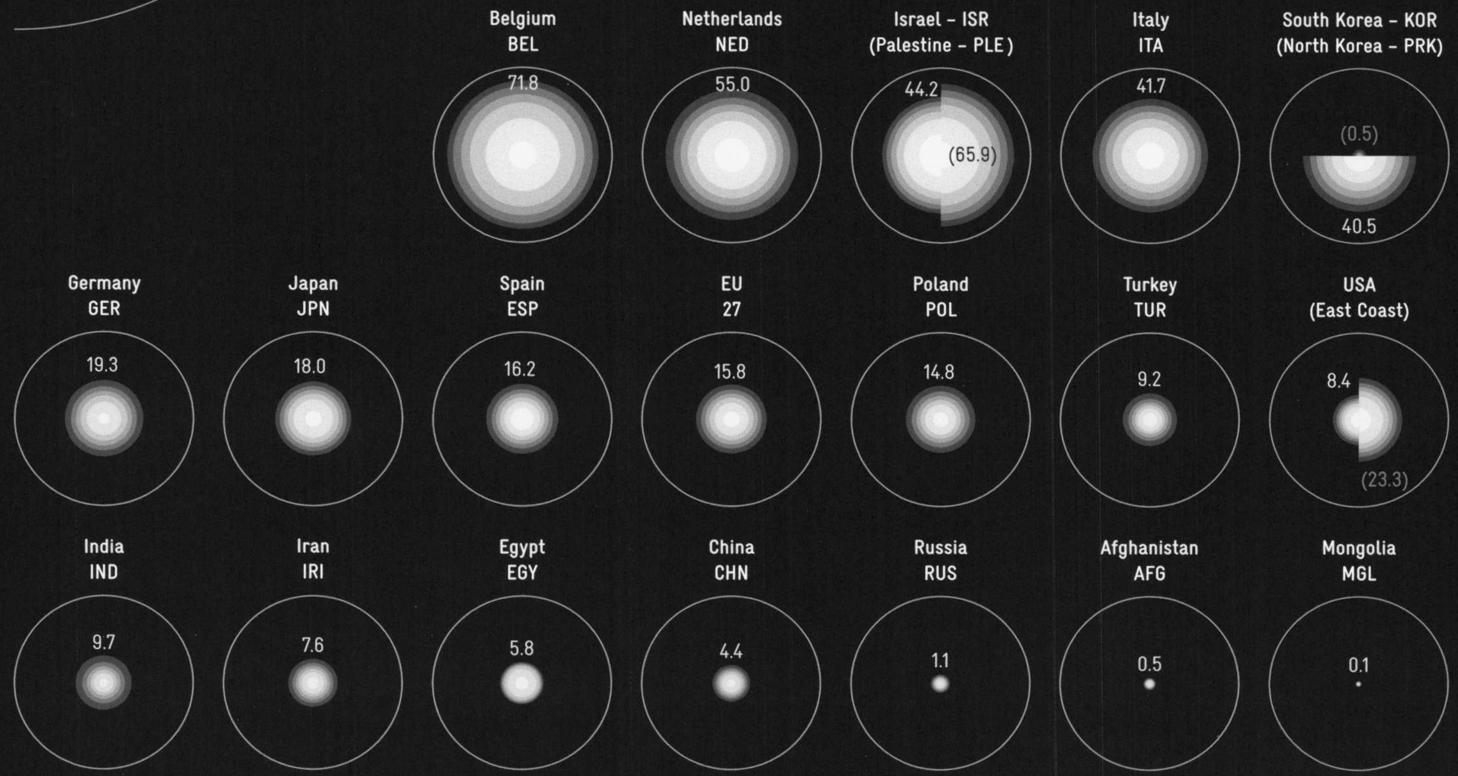
Belgium BEL
71.8
Netherlands NED
55.0
Israel - ISR (Palestine - PLE)
44.2
(65.9)
Italy ITA
41.7
South Korea - KOR (North Korea - PRK)
(0.5)
40.5
Germany GER
19.3
Japan JPN
18.0
Spain ESP
16.2
EU 27
15.8
Poland POL
14.8
Turkey TUR
9.2
USA (East Coast)
8.4
(23.3)
India IND
9.7
Iran IRI
7.6
Egypt EGY
5.8
China CHN
4.4
Russia RUS
1.1
Afghanistan AFG
0.5
Mongolia MGL
0.1

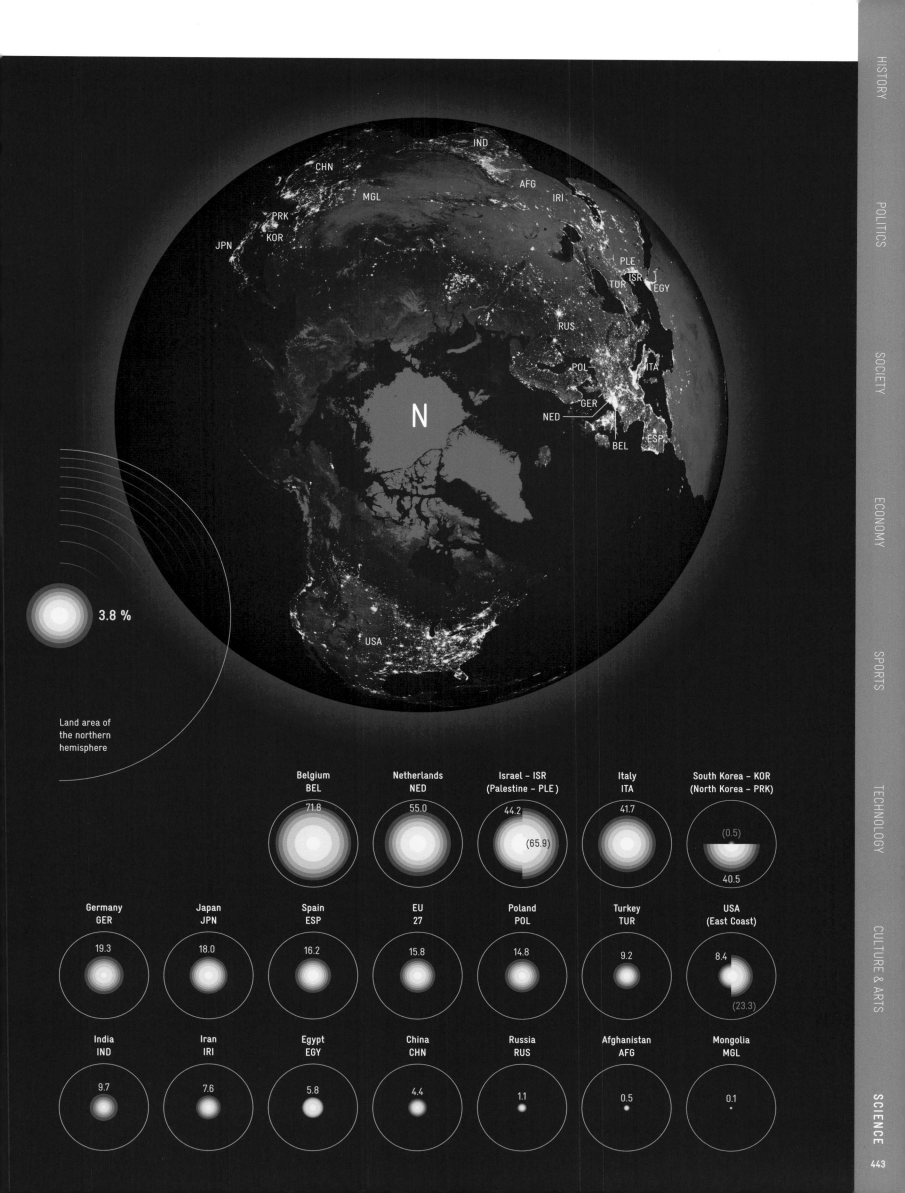

SMALLEST PARTICLES IN THE UNIVERSE

Quarks are the building blocks of all matter. There are six varieties—or flavors—and they belong to a group of particles known as fermions. Quarks have been observed in combinations of two or three quarks, with a distinction being made between so-called mesons and baryons. There are more than 200 known mesons and baryons, but research such as that being conducted at CERN in Geneva, Switzerland, is revealing many other combinations.

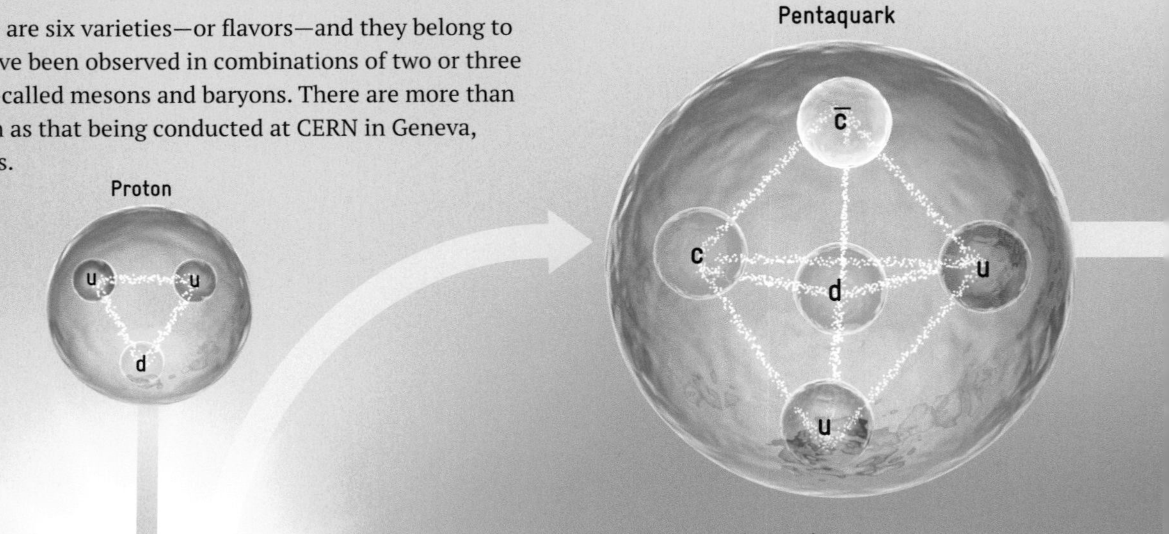

Pentaquark
Proton
c̄
c
d
u
u
u
u
d

Proving the existence of multi-quarks

Collisions

In experiments such as **LHCb** at CERN in Geneva, physicists shoot high-energy protons towards each other. When they collide, new particles are created. **Multi-quark systems** can also develop in the process via several intermediary steps; so far, **tetra and pentaquarks** have been indirectly observed (baryons consisting of four or five quarks).

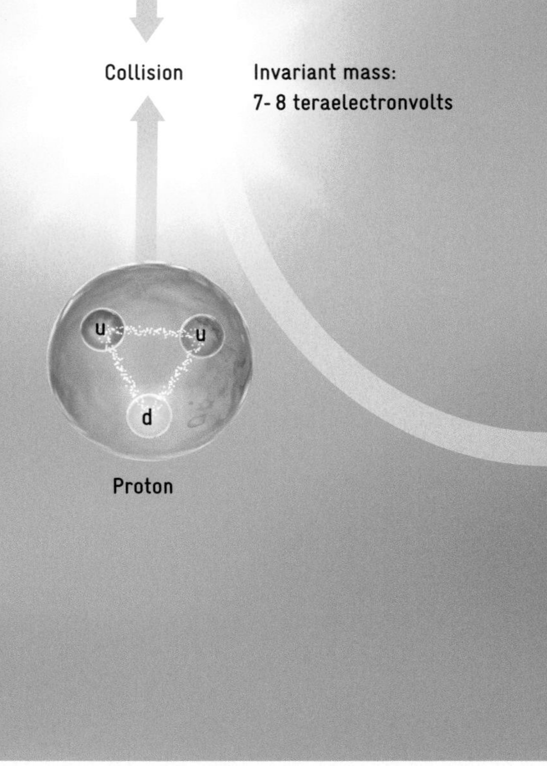

Collision
Invariant mass:
7- 8 teraelectronvolts
u
u
d
Proton

Multi-quark systems

The **lifespan** of tetra and pentaquarks is approximately **10^{-23}** seconds and therefore too short to directly detect these systems. However, they can be indirectly determined by means of characteristic **decay products.**

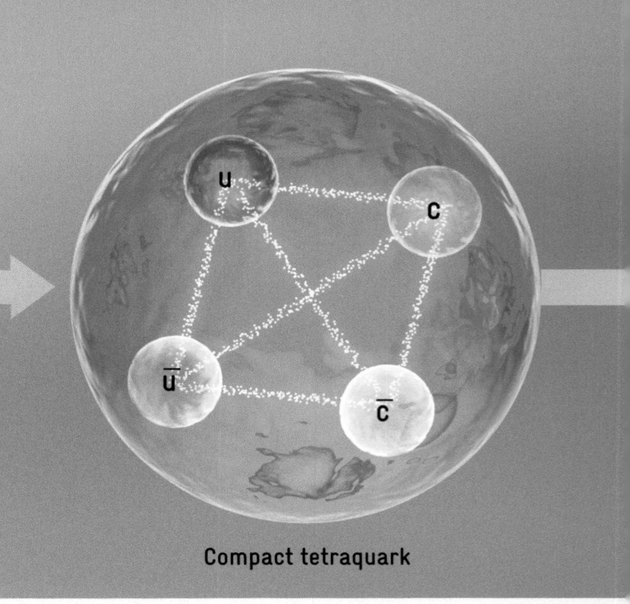

u
c
ū
c̄
Compact tetraquark

Quarks and their properties

Quarks are the building blocks of all matter. There are six varieties—or flavors—and they belong to a group of particles known as **fermions.** Quarks have been observed in combinations of two or three quarks, with a distinction being made between mesons and baryons.
There are more than 200 known mesons and baryons, but research such as that being conducted at CERN in Geneva, Switzerland, is revealing many other combinations.

Generation	Quark/anti-quark		Charge	Rest mass (MeV)
1	Up	u	+2/3	2.3
1	Anti-up	ū	-2/3	2.3
1	Down	d	-1/3	4.8
1	Anti-down	d̄	+1/3	4.8
2	Strange	s	-1/3	95
2	Anti-strange	s̄	+1/3	95
2	Charm	c	+2/3	1,275
2	Anti-charm	c̄	-2/3	1,275
3	Bottom	b	-1/3	4,180
3	Anti-bottom	b̄	+1/3	4,180
3	Top	t	+2/3	173,210
3	Anti-top	t̄	-2/3	173,210

Quarks undergo a **color charge,** which responds to strong interaction and is transmitted by »glue« particles, or **gluons.** There are three types of color charge: »red«, »blue« and »green«. All three colors have an equal chance of occurring; Color and anti-color neutralize each other. Furthermore, for every quark there is an **anti-quark** with the same properties, but the signs are inverse.

Quark color charges

Anti-quark color charges

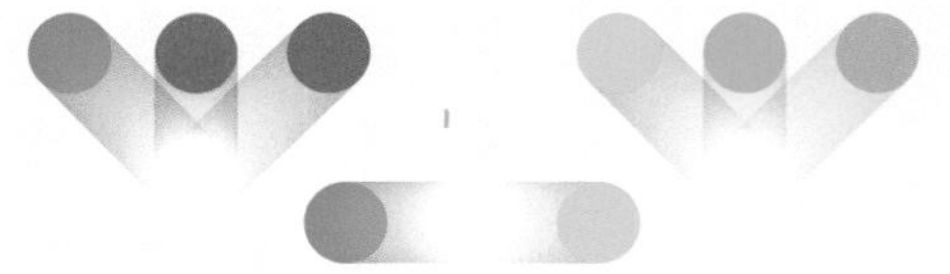

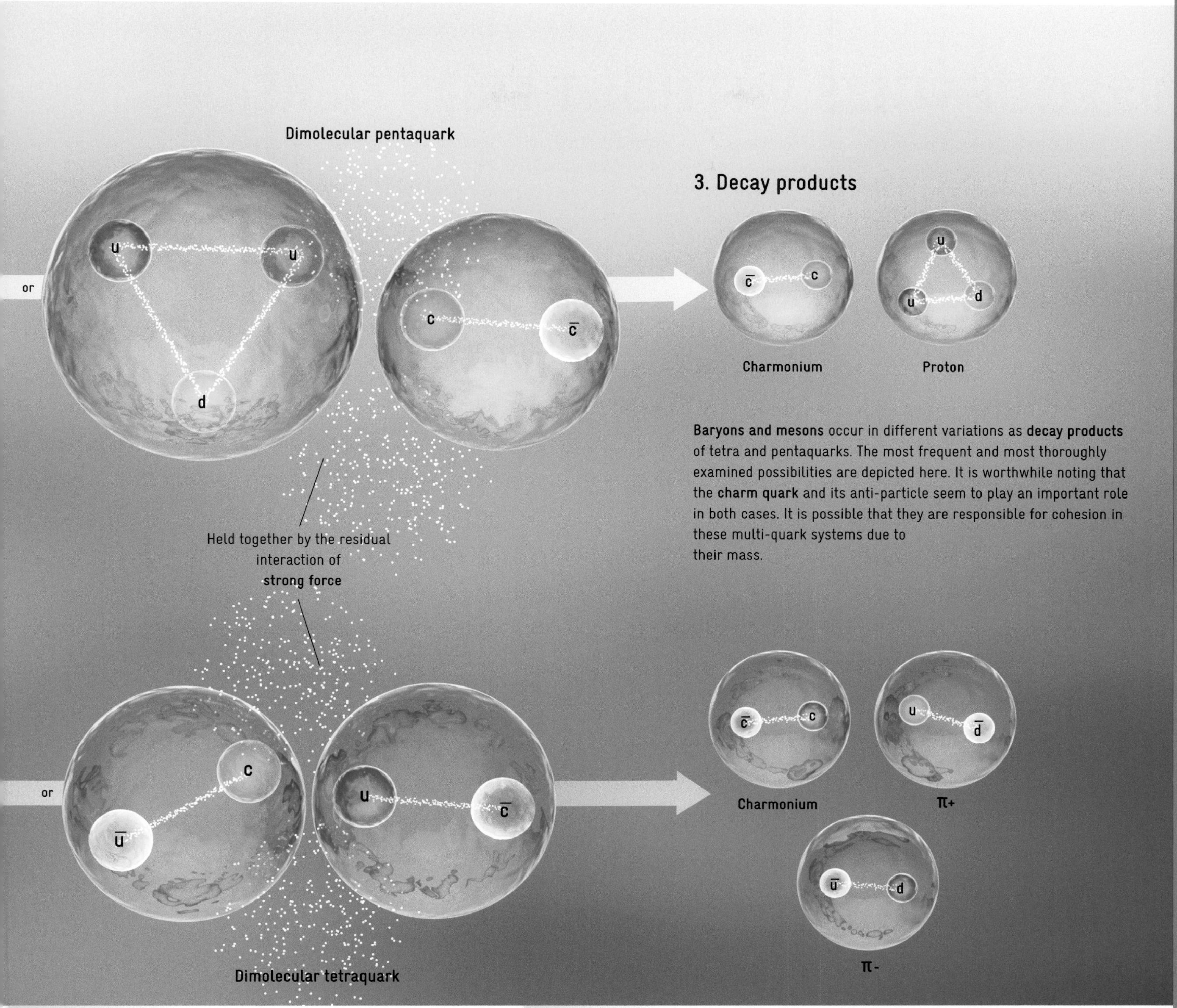

Dimolecular pentaquark
or
u
u
d
c
c̄
3. Decay products
c̄
c
u
u
d
Charmonium
Proton
Held together by the residual
interaction of
strong force
or
c
ū
u
c̄
c̄
c
u
d̄
Charmonium
π+
ū
d
π-
Dimolecular tetraquark

Baryons and mesons occur in different variations as **decay products** of tetra and pentaquarks. The most frequent and most thoroughly examined possibilities are depicted here. It is worthwhile noting that the **charm quark** and its anti-particle seem to play an important role in both cases. It is possible that they are responsible for cohesion in these multi-quark systems due to their mass.

Hadrons

Hadrons consist of multiple quarks. **Baryons** belong to this family and are each made up of three quarks. The most well-known examples are **protons** and **neutrons,** as they are the longest lasting baryons. These form the nucleus of the atom.

The far more short-lived **mesons** each consist of one quark and one anti-quark.

In principle, both baryons and mesons can exist in various **quark combinations.** They have to be composed according to the **rules of quantum mechanics** and their surface must be color neutral. However, quarks aren't found individually in nature, as the force increases in strength when the distance between them grows.

Baryons

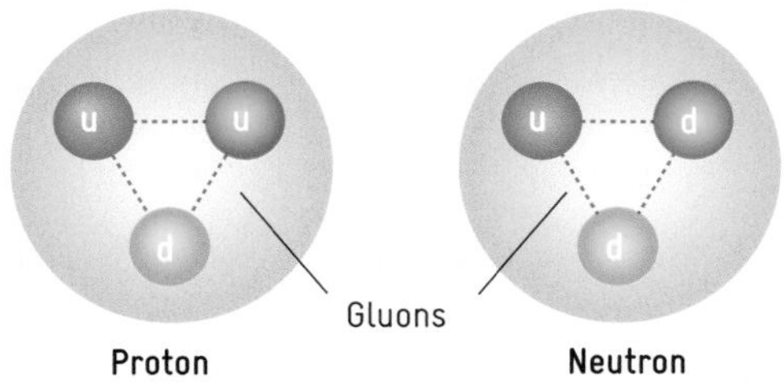

u
u
d
u
d
d
Gluons
Proton
Neutron

Mesons

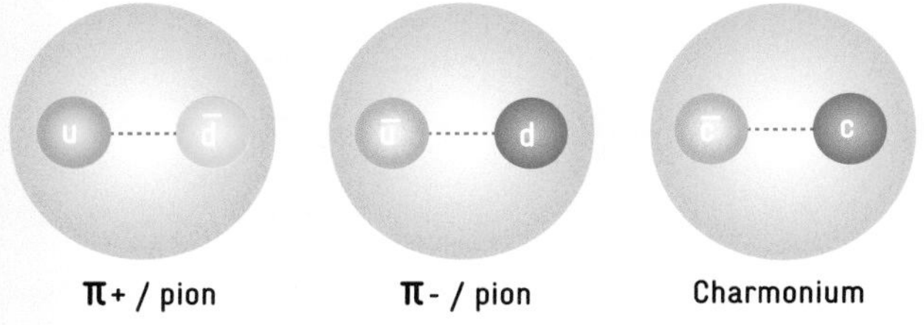

u
d̄
ū
d
c̄
c
π+ / pion
π- / pion
Charmonium

FREQUENCIES WITHOUT FRONTIERS

We live life in a series of rhythms. From the annual changing of the seasons to the phases of the month and the change from day to night. Our heart beats, we inhale and exhale and so life continues. We can measure these physical, internal periodic processes with ultrasound, which uses sound waves that oscillate at a higher frequency than we are able to do as human beings. In fact, frequencies theoretically don't have an upper limit.

Periodic processes are marked by frequencies. Measuring these frequencies provides us with a numeric representation—called a Hertz—of how often a phenomenon repeats itself in a specified time period. One Hertz represents one event (such as a breath, a pulse or a wave) per second.

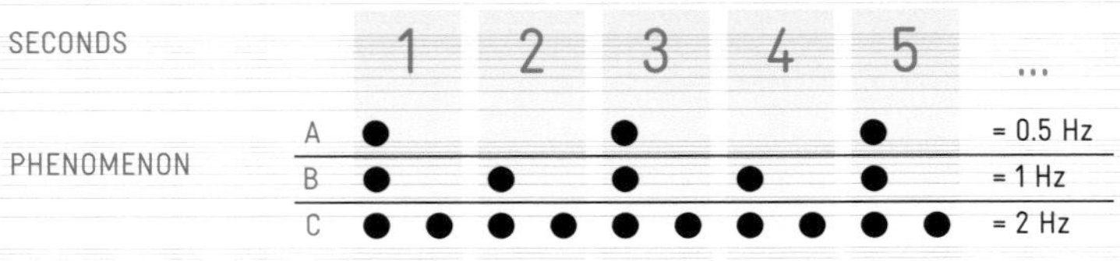

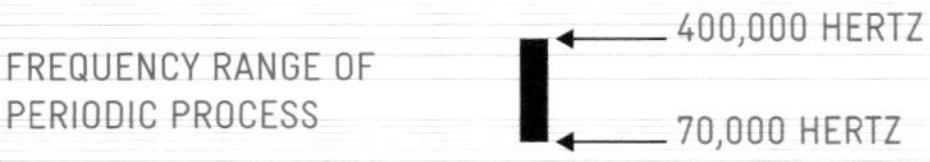

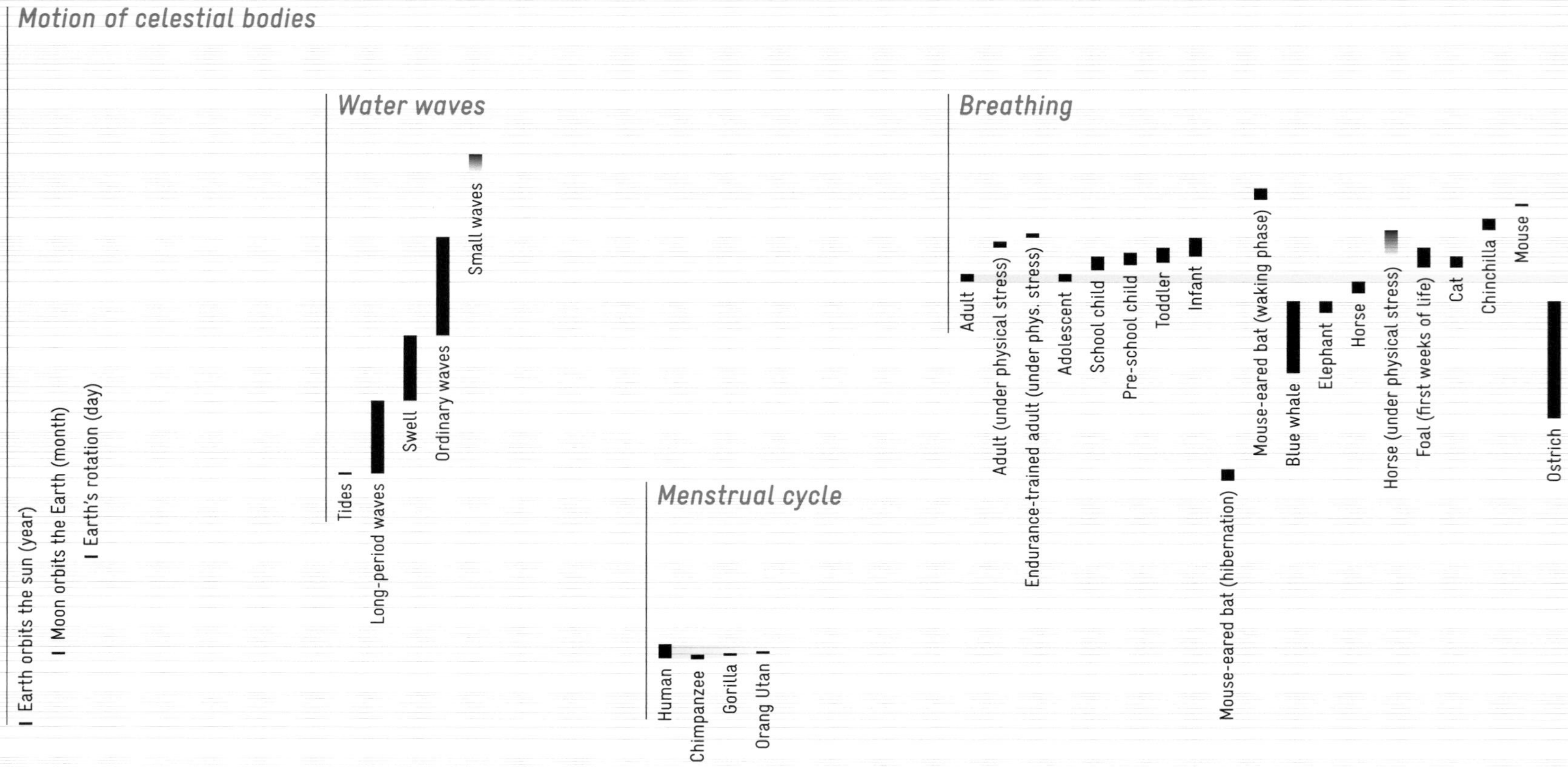

PERIODIC PROCESSES

The seasons are determined by the movement of celestial bodies. Sea waves are created by the interaction of wind and gravity. Pulse and breathing are regulated by the rythmical movement of heart and lung muscles.

The moon's orbit around the Earth can be represented as a wave.

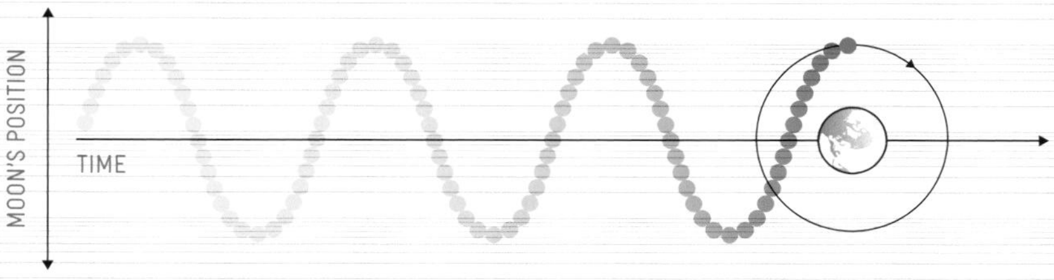
MOON'S POSITION
TIME

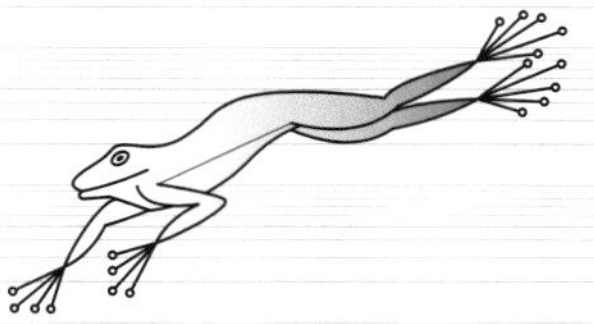

Frogs are cold-blooded, which means their vital functions adapt to the ambient temperature.

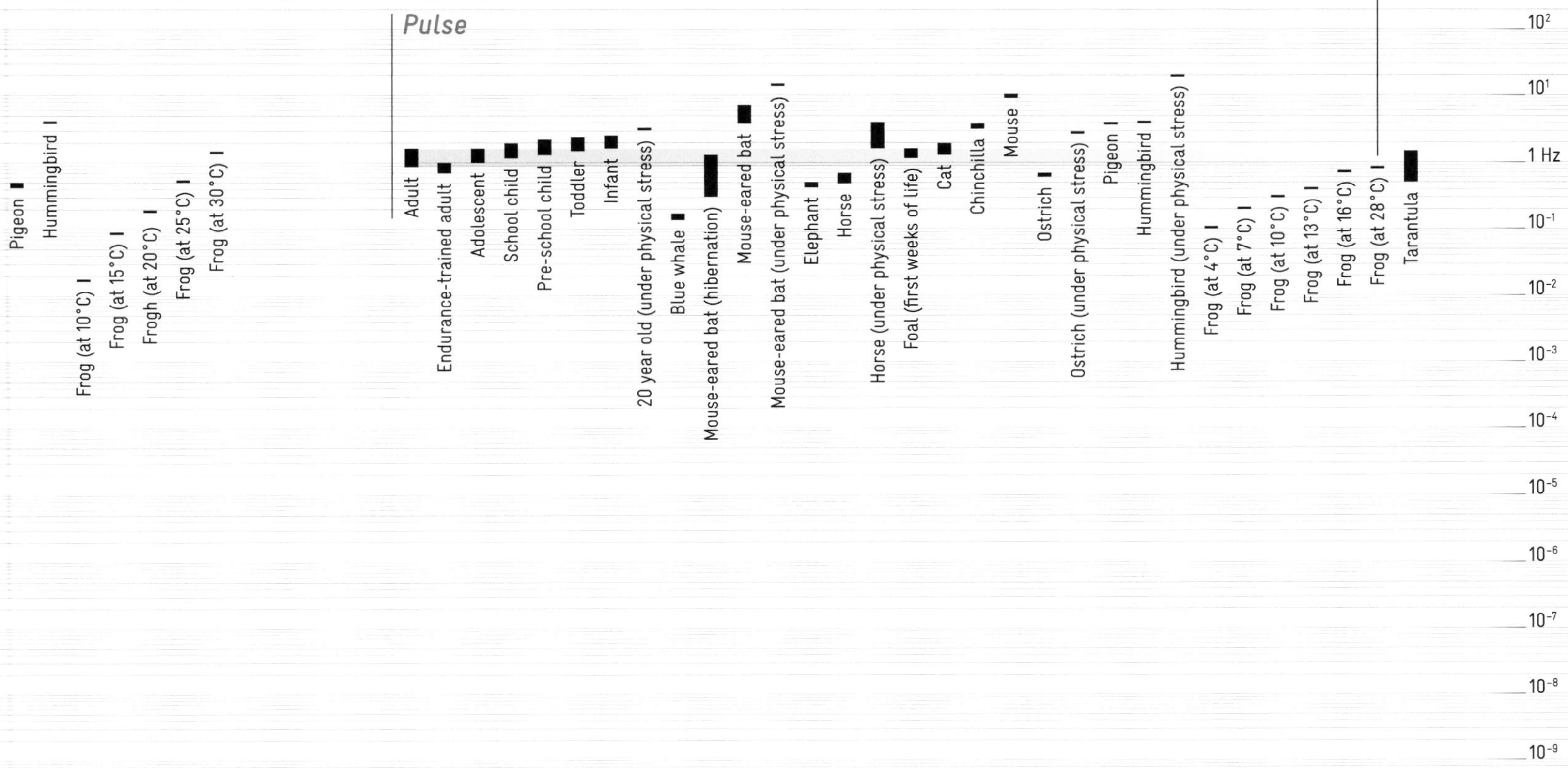
Pulse
Pigeon
Hummingbird
Frog (at 10°C)
Frog (at 15°C)
Frogh (at 20°C)
Frog (at 25°C)
Frog (at 30°C)
Adult
Endurance-trained adult
Adolescent
School child
Pre-school child
Toddler
Infant
20 year old (under physical stress)
Blue whale
Mouse-eared bat (hibernation)
Mouse-eared bat
Mouse-eared bat (under physical stress)
Elephant
Horse
Horse (under physical stress)
Foal (first weeks of life)
Cat
Chinchilla
Mouse
Ostrich
Ostrich (under physical stress)
Pigeon
Hummingbird
Hummingbird (under physical stress)
Frog (at 4°C)
Frog (at 7°C)
Frog (at 10°C)
Frog (at 13°C)
Frog (at 16°C)
Frog (at 28°C)
Tarantula
10^{21}
10^{20}
10^{19}
10^{18}
10^{17}
10^{16}
10^{15}
10^{14}
10^{13}
10^{12}
10^{11}
10^{10}
10^{9}
10^{8}
10^{7}
10^{6}
10^{5}
10^{4}
10^{3}
10^{2}
10^{1}
1 Hz
10^{-1}
10^{-2}
10^{-3}
10^{-4}
10^{-5}
10^{-6}
10^{-7}
10^{-8}
10^{-9}

SOUND WAVES

Sound happens when physical objects—such as speaker membranes—oscillate. The sound source transfers its vibrations into the transmitting medium. This sets air molecules in motion, which then carry the sound like a domino effect. The sound continues like an echo.

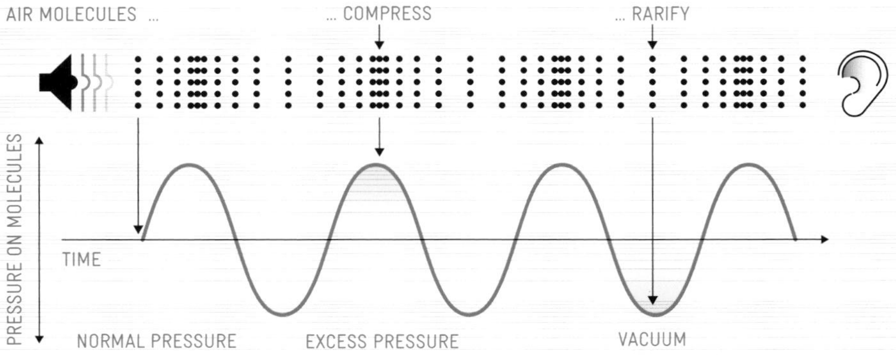

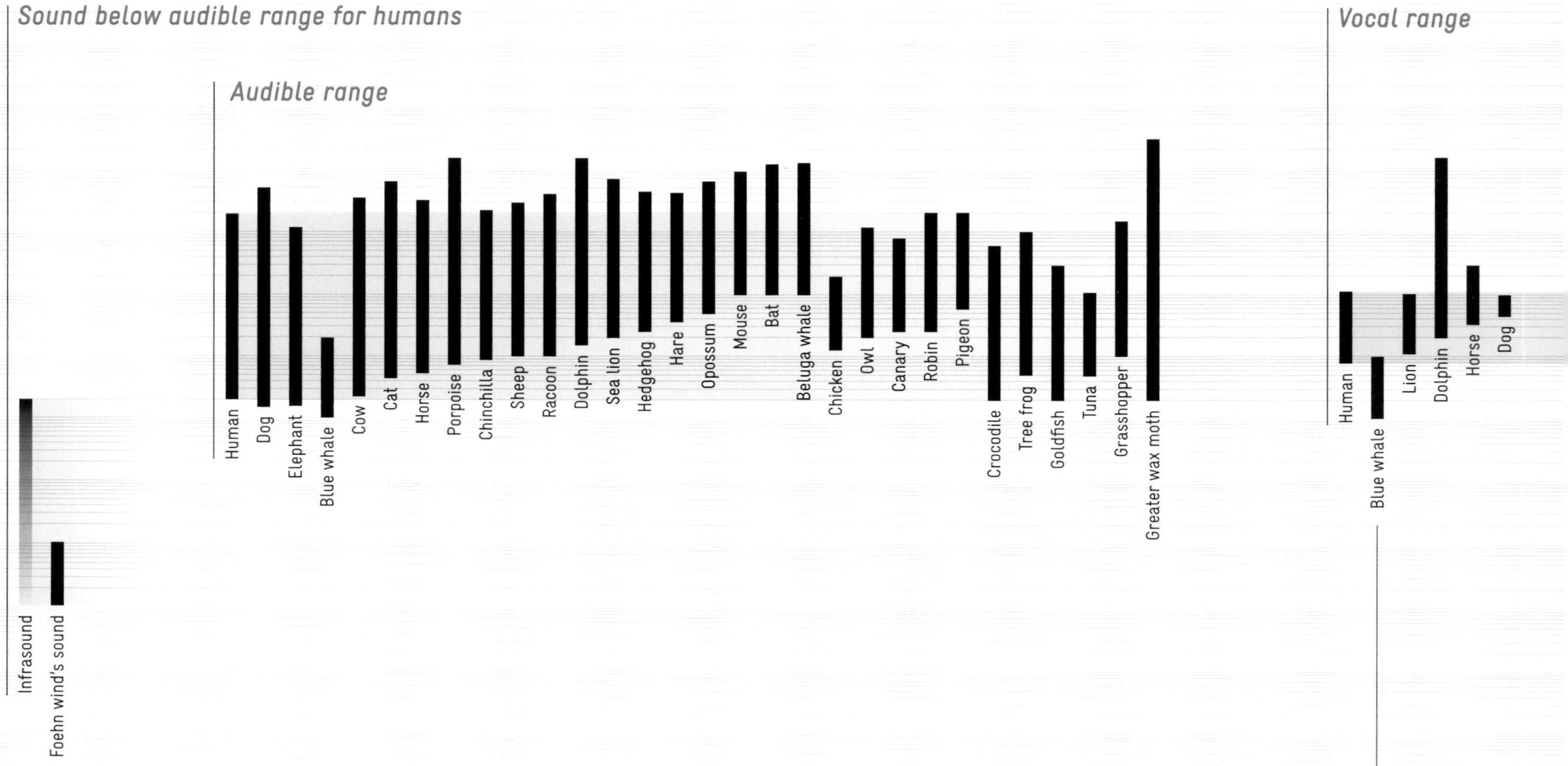

The lowest tones of a blue whale have a wavelength of 148 m (humans: 4 m). They can be heard for hundreds of kilometers due to water's good sound conductivity.

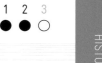

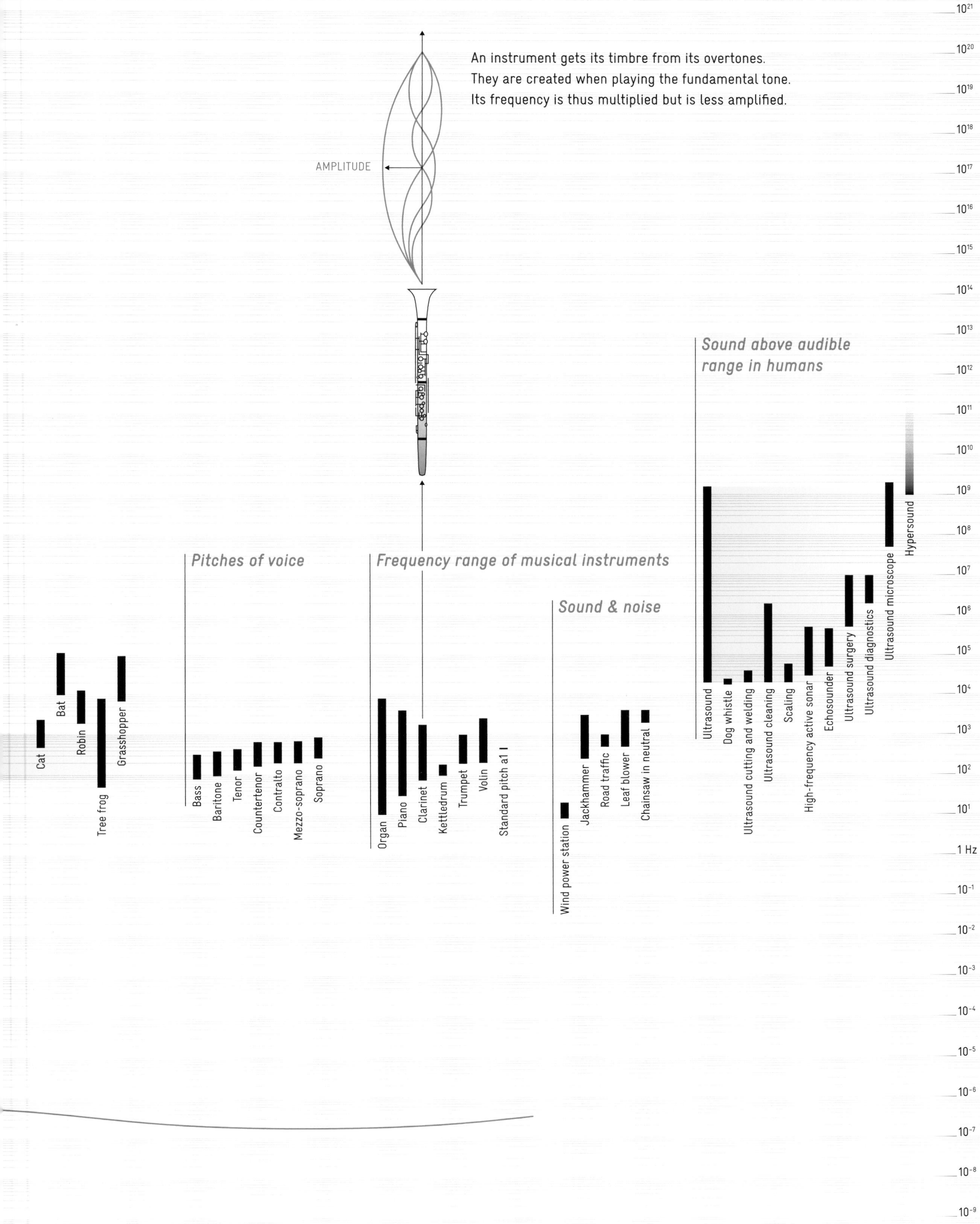
An instrument gets its timbre from its overtones.
They are created when playing the fundamental tone.
Its frequency is thus multiplied but is less amplified.
AMPLITUDE
Sound above audible range in humans
Pitches of voice
Frequency range of musical instruments
Sound & noise
Cat
Bat
Robin
Tree frog
Grasshopper
Bass
Baritone
Tenor
Countertenor
Contralto
Mezzo-soprano
Soprano
Organ
Piano
Clarinet
Kettledrum
Trumpet
Volin
Standard pitch a1
Wind power station
Jackhammer
Road traffic
Leaf blower
Chainsaw in neutral
Ultrasound
Dog whistle
Ultrasound cutting and welding
Ultrasound cleaning
Scaling
High-frequency active sonar
Echosounder
Ultrasound surgery
Ultrasound diagnostics
Ultrasound microscope
Hypersound
10^{21}
10^{20}
10^{19}
10^{18}
10^{17}
10^{16}
10^{15}
10^{14}
10^{13}
10^{12}
10^{11}
10^{10}
10^{9}
10^{8}
10^{7}
10^{6}
10^{5}
10^{4}
10^{3}
10^{2}
10^{1}
1 Hz
10^{-1}
10^{-2}
10^{-3}
10^{-4}
10^{-5}
10^{-6}
10^{-7}
10^{-8}
10^{-9}

ELECTROMAGNETIC WAVES

When electrically charged particles are speeded up or slowed down, they emit electromagnetic fields. These fields expand through space and periodically change their strength. This oscillation means that they can also be characterized as waves.

A radio transmitter alternates the electrical current of signals to create electromagnetic waves, which transfer the sound.

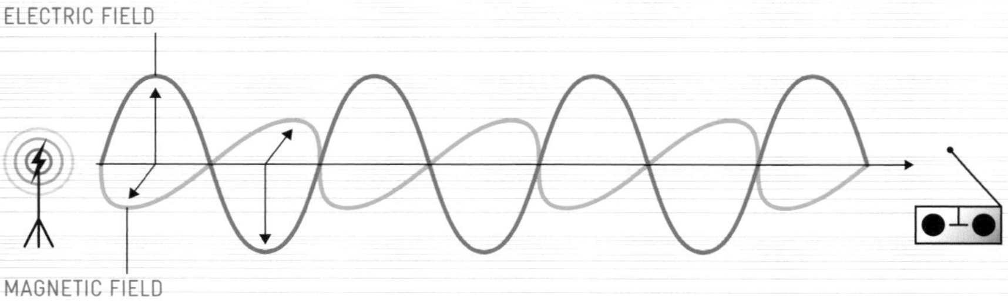
ELECTRIC FIELD
MAGNETIC FIELD

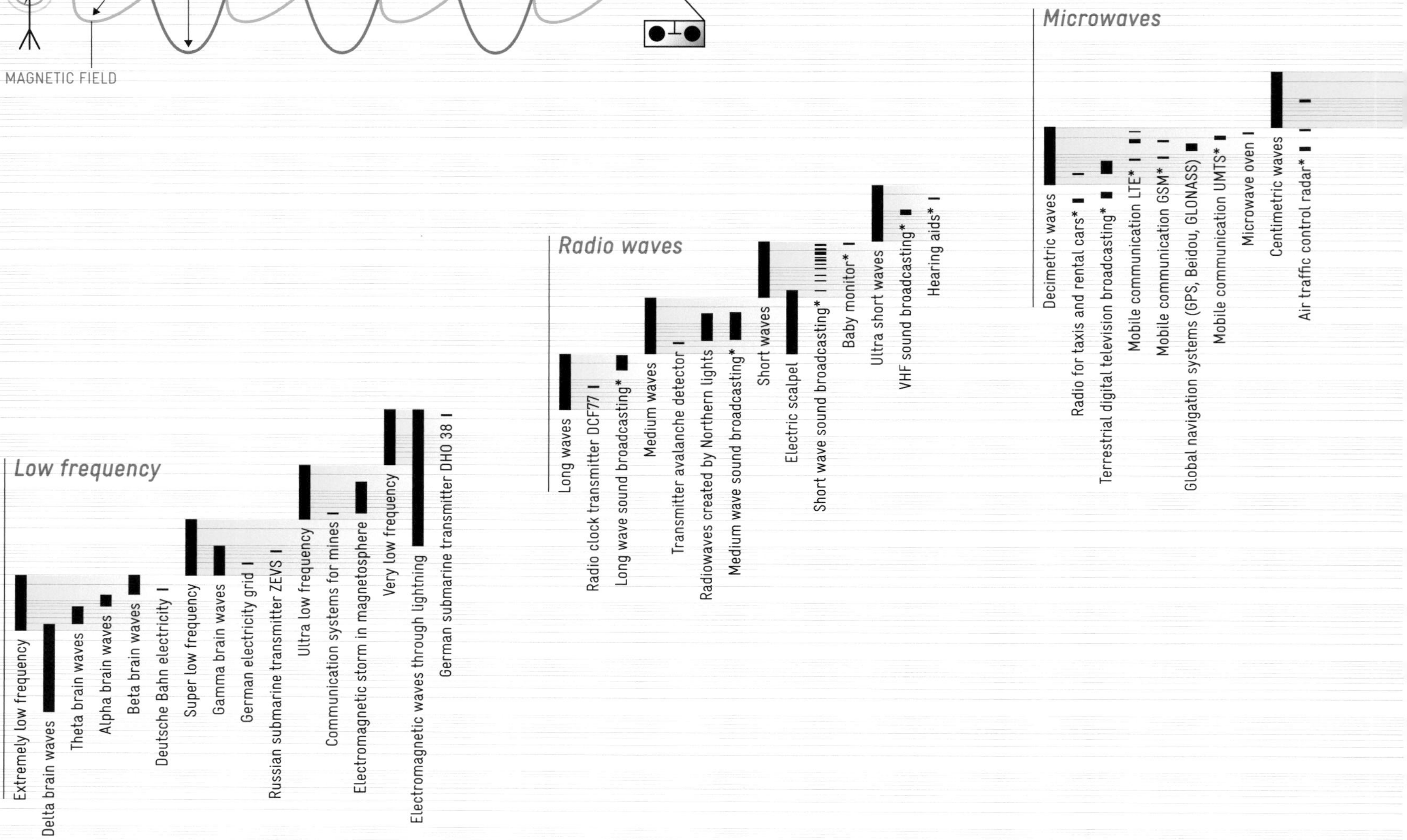
Low frequency
Extremely low frequency
Delta brain waves
Theta brain waves
Alpha brain waves
Beta brain waves
Deutsche Bahn electricity
Super low frequency
Gamma brain waves
German electricity grid
Russian submarine transmitter ZEVS
Ultra low frequency
Communication systems for mines
Electromagnetic storm in magnetosphere
Very low frequency
Electromagnetic waves through lightning
German submarine transmitter DHO 38
Radio waves
Long waves
Radio clock transmitter DCF77
Long wave sound broadcasting*
Medium waves
Transmitter avalanche detector
Radiowaves created by Northern lights
Medium wave sound broadcasting*
Short waves
Electric scalpel
Short wave sound broadcasting*
Baby monitor*
Ultra short waves
VHF sound broadcasting*
Hearing aids*
Microwaves
Decimetric waves
Radio for taxis and rental cars*
Terrestrial digital television broadcasting*
Mobile communication LTE*
Mobile communication GSM*
Global navigation systems (GPS, Beidou, GLONASS)
Mobile communication UMTS*
Microwave oven
Centimetric waves
Air traffic control radar*

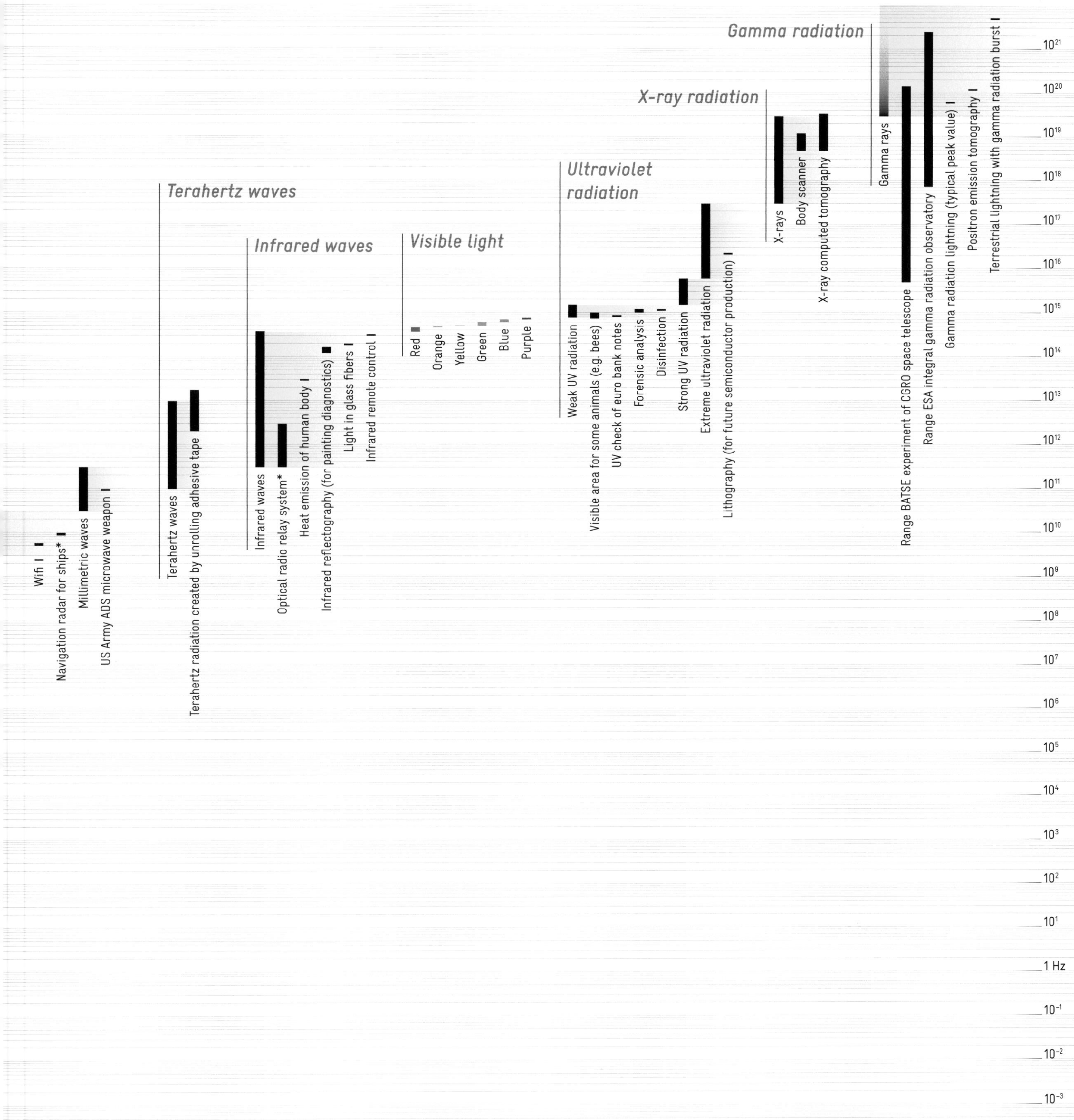

Gamma radiation
X-ray radiation
Ultraviolet radiation
Terahertz waves
Infrared waves
Visible light
Wifi
Navigation radar for ships*
Millimetric waves
US Army ADS microwave weapon
Terahertz waves
Terahertz radiation created by unrolling adhesive tape
Infrared waves
Optical radio relay system*
Heat emission of human body
Infrared reflectography (for painting diagnostics)
Light in glass fibers
Infrared remote control
Red
Orange
Yellow
Green
Blue
Purple
Weak UV radiation
Visible area for some animals (e.g. bees)
UV check of euro bank notes
Forensic analysis
Disinfection
Strong UV radiation
Extreme ultraviolet radiation
Lithography (for future semiconductor production)
X-rays
Body scanner
X-ray computed tomography
Gamma rays
Range BATSE experiment of CGRO space telescope
Range ESA integral gamma radiation observatory
Gamma radiation lightning (typical peak value)
Positron emission tomography
Terrestrial lightning with gamma radiation burst
10^{21}
10^{20}
10^{19}
10^{18}
10^{17}
10^{16}
10^{15}
10^{14}
10^{13}
10^{12}
10^{11}
10^{10}
10^{9}
10^{8}
10^{7}
10^{6}
10^{5}
10^{4}
10^{3}
10^{2}
10^{1}
1 Hz
10^{-1}
10^{-2}
10^{-3}
10^{-4}
10^{-5}
10^{-6}
10^{-7}
10^{-8}
10^{-9}

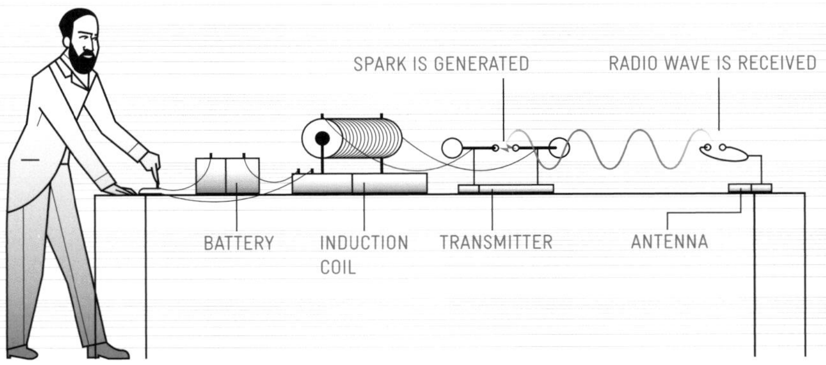

SPARK IS GENERATED
RADIO WAVE IS RECEIVED
BATTERY
INDUCTION COIL
TRANSMITTER
ANTENNA

In 1887, a young German physicist created electromagnetic waves with a specially designed device. His experiments proved that electromagnetic waves propagate as fast as light does, which he recognized to be an electromagnetic phenomenon. The new waves were called radio waves and their technical application changed the world. The man behind the science died young – aged 36 – and so it was only posthumously that the frequency they created was named after him. His name was Heinrich Hertz.

* German frequency allocation

HISTORY
POLITICS
SOCIETY
ECONOMY
SPORTS
TECHNOLOGY
CULTURE & ARTS
SCIENCE

FLY ME TO THE MOON

The urge to explore the unknown is what propelled mankind from continent to continent, across the oceans, and—finally—beyond the Earth's atmosphere. On April 12, 1961, the first manned spaceflight reached outer space. As of September 2017, there have been 319 of these missions that have taken 560 people into space, with 12 of them taking steps on the moon.

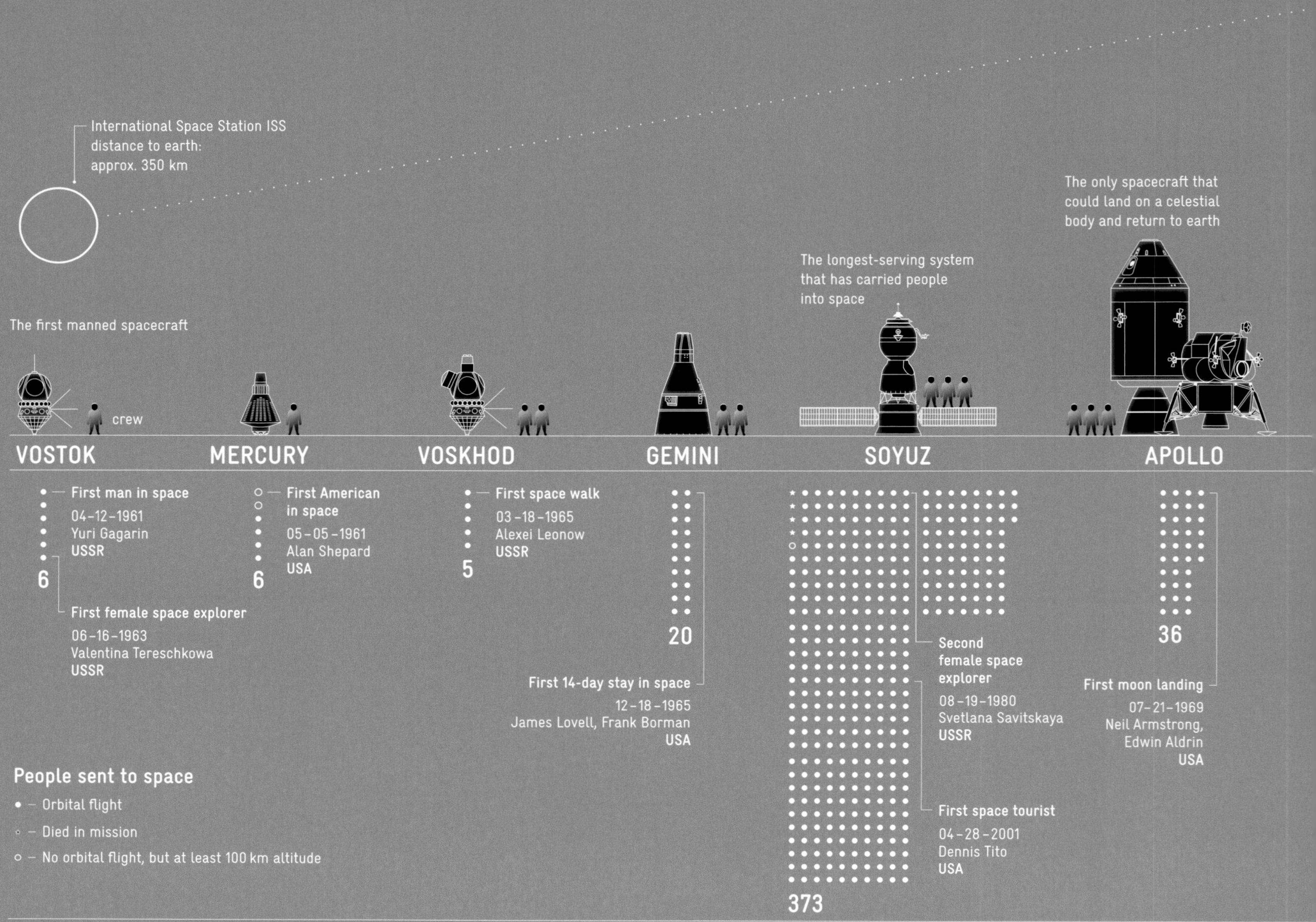
International Space Station ISS
distance to earth:
approx. 350 km
The first manned spacecraft
crew
VOSTOK
First man in space
04-12-1961
Yuri Gagarin
USSR
6
First female space explorer
06-16-1963
Valentina Tereschkowa
USSR
MERCURY
First American in space
05-05-1961
Alan Shepard
USA
6
VOSKHOD
First space walk
03-18-1965
Alexei Leonow
USSR
5
GEMINI
20
First 14-day stay in space
12-18-1965
James Lovell, Frank Borman
USA
The longest-serving system that has carried people into space
SOYUZ
Second female space explorer
08-19-1980
Svetlana Savitskaya
USSR
First space tourist
04-28-2001
Dennis Tito
USA
373
The only spacecraft that could land on a celestial body and return to earth
APOLLO
36
First moon landing
07-21-1969
Neil Armstrong,
Edwin Aldrin
USA
People sent to space
• – Orbital flight
– Died in mission
○ – No orbital flight, but at least 100 km altitude

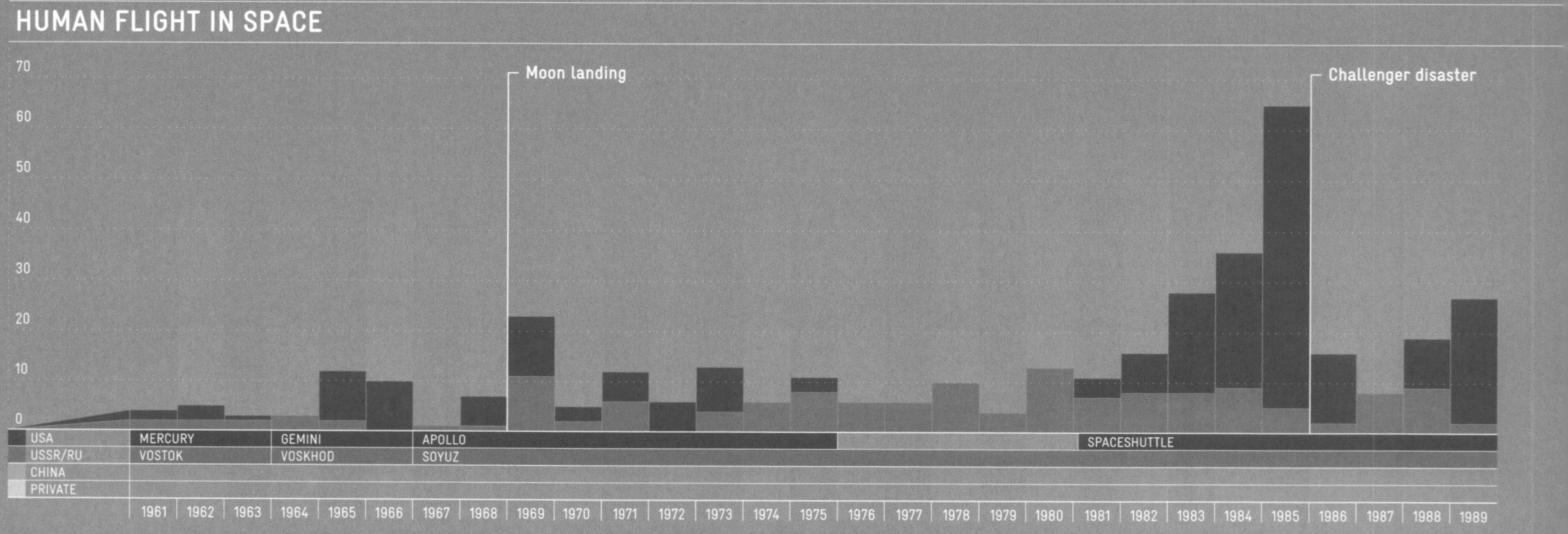
HUMAN FLIGHT IN SPACE
70
60
50
40
30
20
10
0
Moon landing
Challenger disaster
USA
USSR/RU
CHINA
PRIVATE
MERCURY
VOSTOK
GEMINI
VOSKHOD
APOLLO
SOYUZ
SPACESHUTTLE
1961
1962
1963
1964
1965
1966
1967
1968
1969
1970
1971
1972
1973
1974
1975
1976
1977
1978
1979
1980
1981
1982
1983
1984
1985
1986
1987
1988
1989

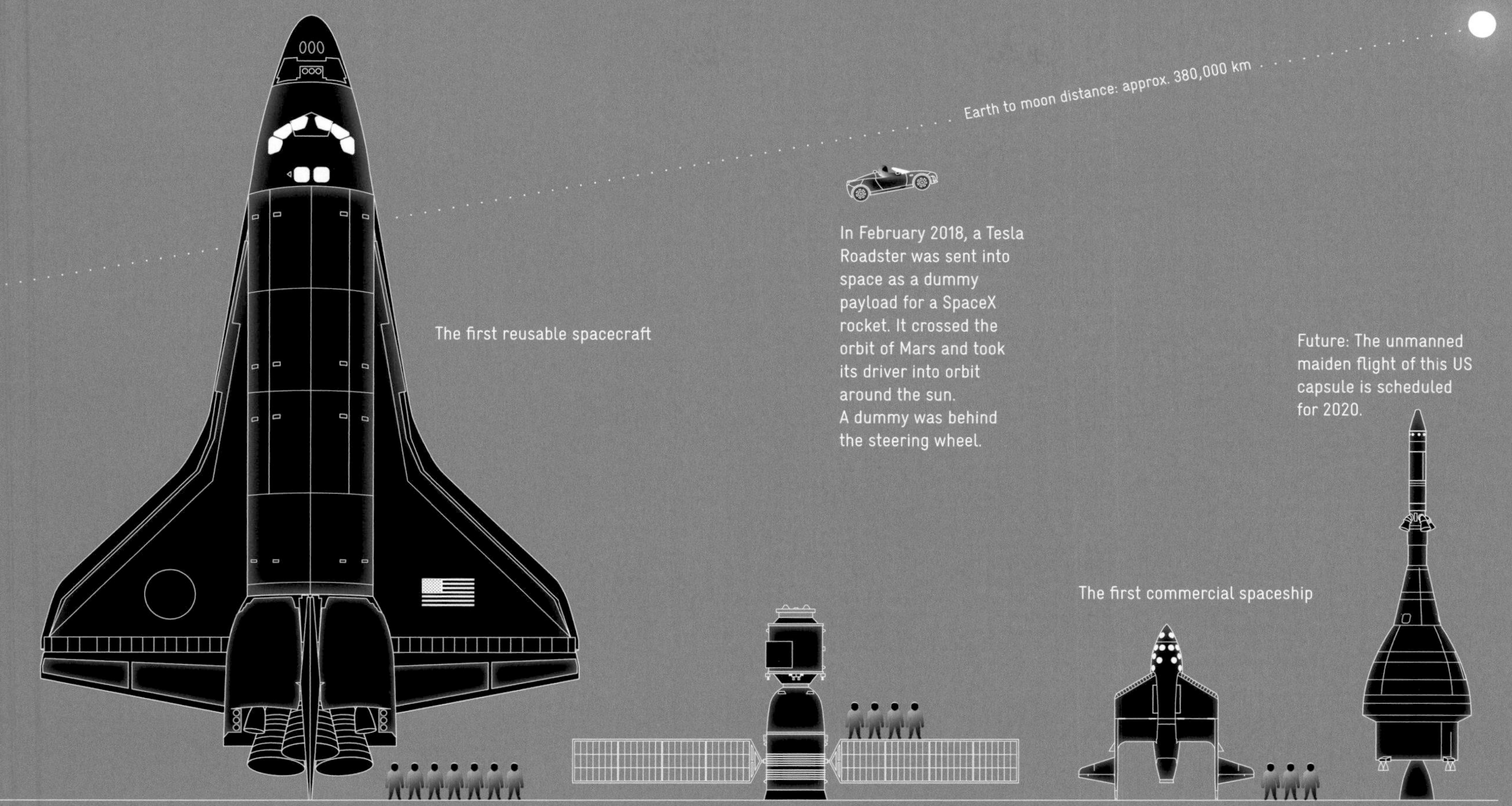
Earth to moon distance: approx. 380,000 km
The first reusable spacecraft
In February 2018, a Tesla Roadster was sent into space as a dummy payload for a SpaceX rocket. It crossed the orbit of Mars and took its driver into orbit around the sun. A dummy was behind the steering wheel.
Future: The unmanned maiden flight of this US capsule is scheduled for 2020.
The first commercial spaceship

SPACE SHUTTLE | **SHENZOU** | **SPACESHIP ONE** | **ORION MPVC**

Oldest astronaut (77 years)
10-29-1998
John Glenn
USA

Record: Jerry Ross (USA) is the first astronaut to have flown a total of seven space flights on the Space Shuttle. The last time he lifted off was on April 8, 2002, for a visit to the ISS.

791

First taikonaut (Chinese astronaut)
10-15-2003
Yang Liwei
China

14

First private space flight
06-21-2004
Michael Melvill
USA

3

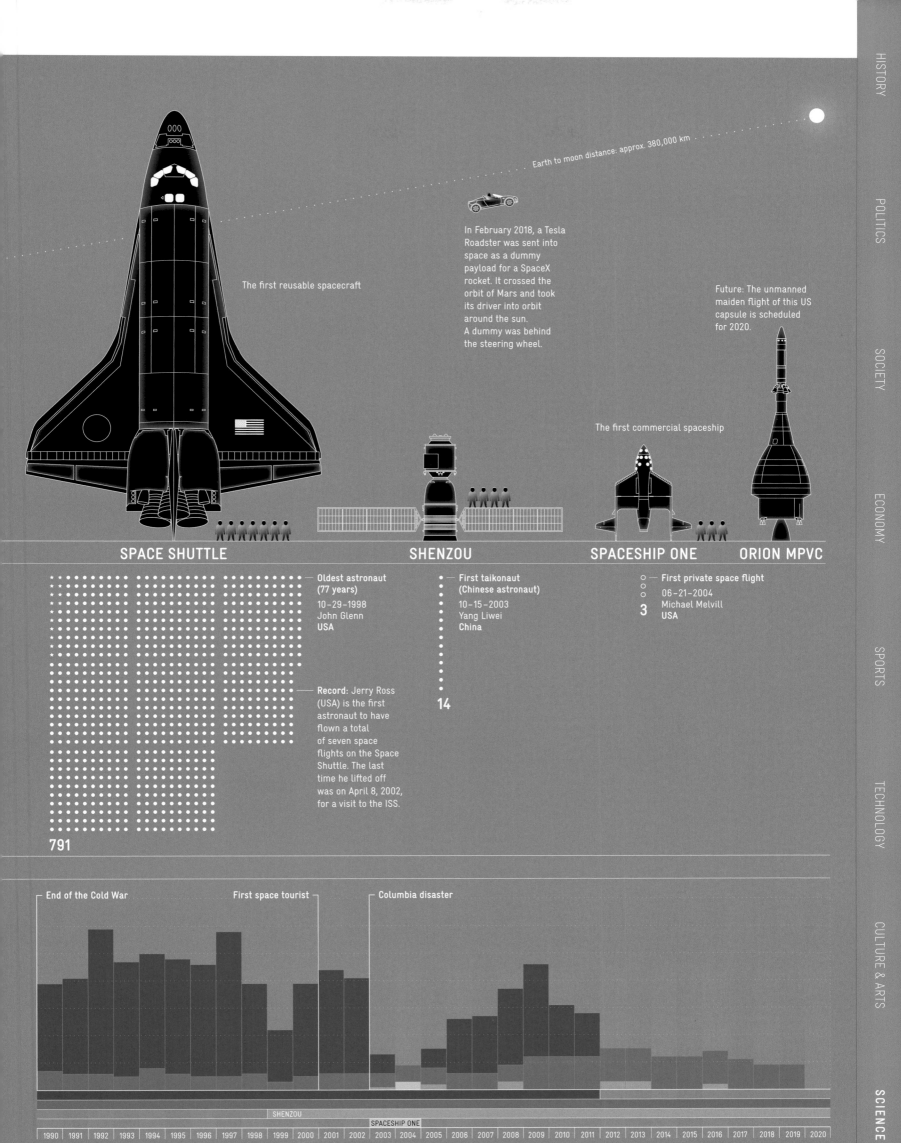

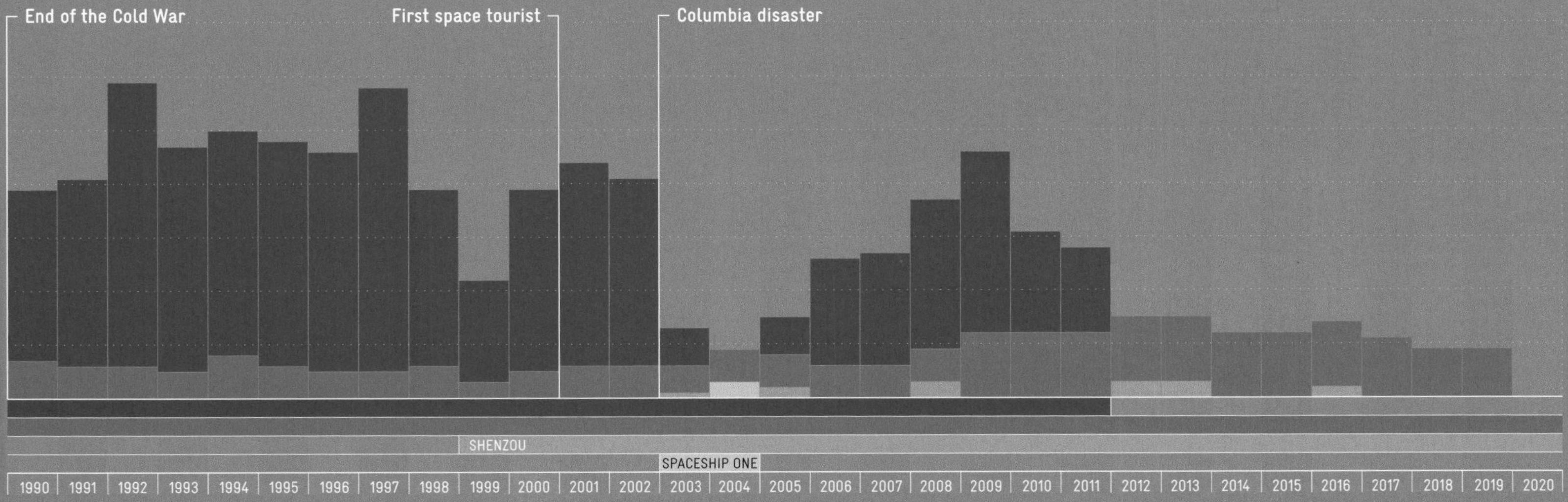
End of the Cold War
First space tourist
Columbia disaster
SHENZOU
SPACESHIP ONE
1990 1991 1992 1993 1994 1995 1996 1997 1998 1999 2000 2001 2002 2003 2004 2005 2006 2007 2008 2009 2010 2011 2012 2013 2014 2015 2016 2017 2018 2019 2020

ROOMMATES IN SPACE

The International Space Station (ISS) is by far the most complex technical project in the history of mankind. In 1971, the Soviet Union sent the first of nine space stations into earth's orbit. It was manned for 24 days. Two years later, the USA followed up with their first and only station, Skylab. During the 1980s, the first plans where made for the ISS, then known as »Freedom«. After the Cold War, the USA and Russia created the Shuttle-Mir Program in 1993 for ten Space Shuttle flights to the Russian station Mir. The Construction of the ISS began in 1998. Since then, 13 countries have invested about 100 billion US dollars. Once the project has ended in 2020, the work of the ISS will most likely reach a conclusion with a controlled fall into the ocean.

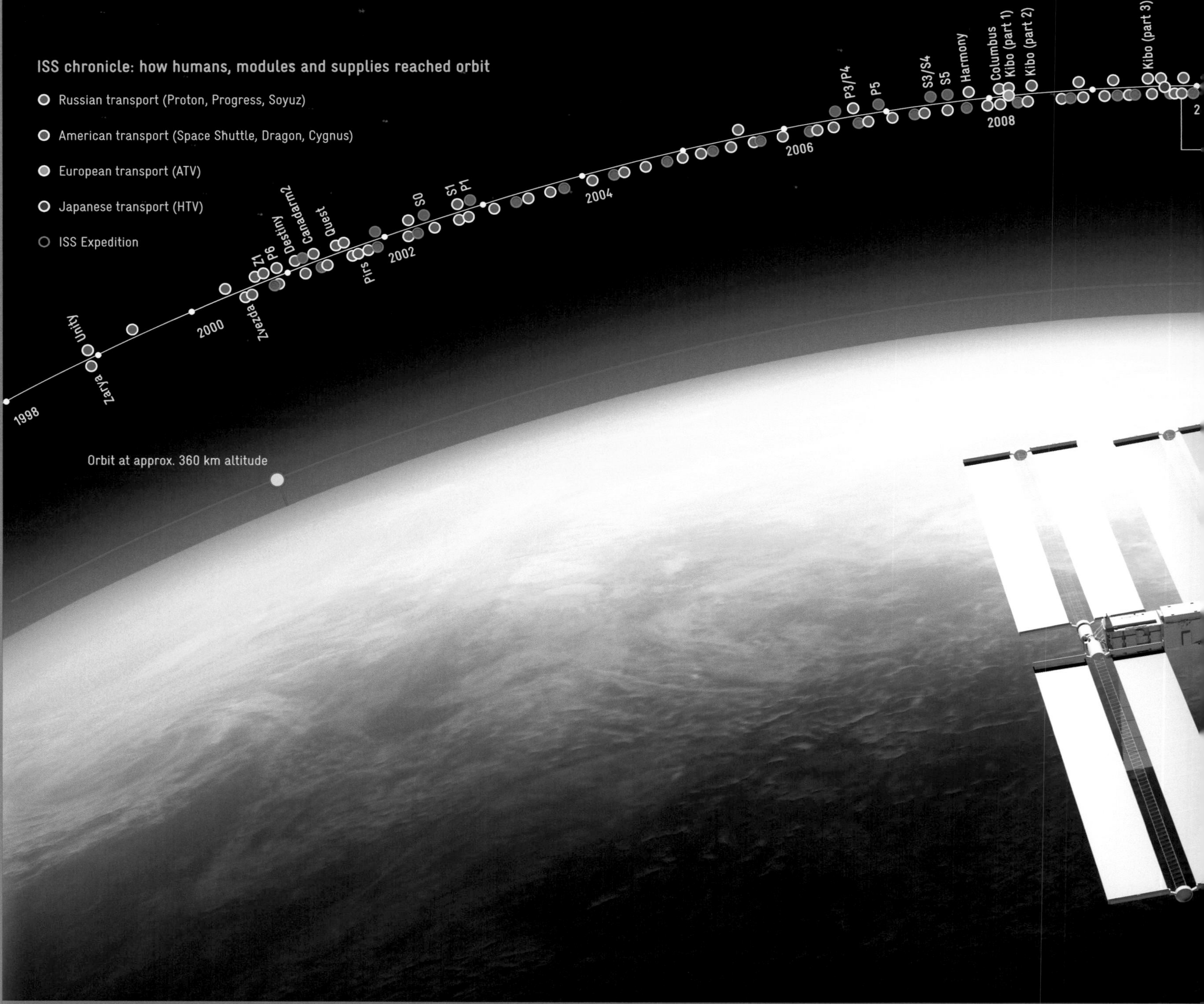
ISS chronicle: how humans, modules and supplies reached orbit
Russian transport (Proton, Progress, Soyuz)
American transport (Space Shuttle, Dragon, Cygnus)
European transport (ATV)
Japanese transport (HTV)
ISS Expedition
1998
Zarya
Unity
2000
Zvezda
Z1
P6
Destiny
Canadarm2
Quest
Pirs
2002
S0
S1
P1
2004
2006
P3/P4
P5
S3/S4
S5
Harmony
Columbus
Kibo (part 1)
Kibo (part 2)
2008
Kibo (part 3)
Orbit at approx. 360 km altitude

ISS IN NUMBERS:

CREW
6 people

SPEED
27,580 km/h

HABITABLE VOLUME
388 cubic meters

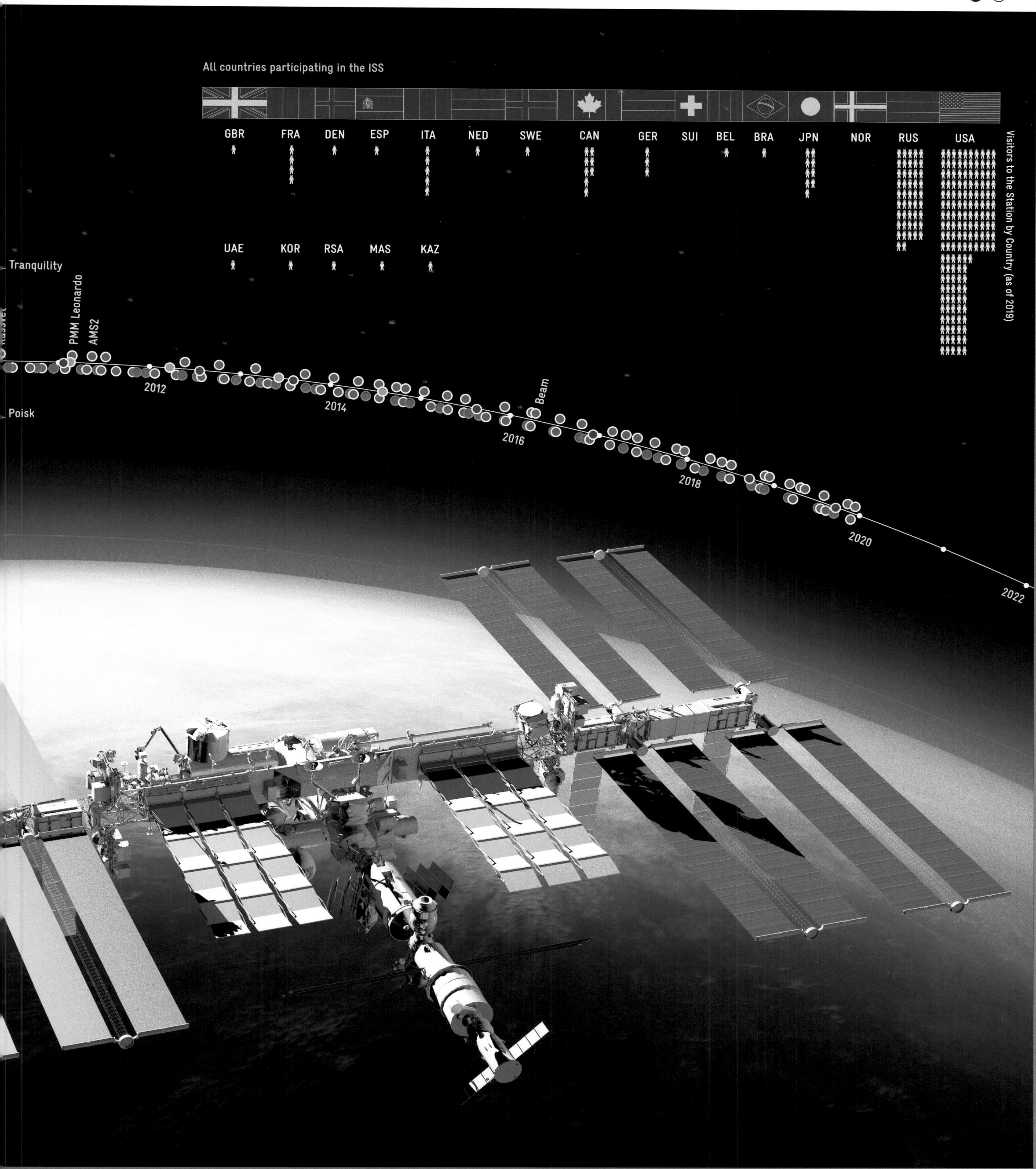
All countries participating in the ISS
GBR
FRA
DEN
ESP
ITA
NED
SWE
CAN
GER
SUI
BEL
BRA
JPN
NOR
RUS
USA
UAE
KOR
RSA
MAS
KAZ
Visitors to the Station by Country (as of 2019)
Tranquility
PMM Leonardo
AMS2
Poisk
2012
2014
Beam
2016
2018
2020
2022

MASS
419,725 kg

MICROGRAVITY
10^{-6} g (1/1,000,000 g)

EARTH ORBIT TIME
90 minutes

ORBIT CORRECTIONS PER YEAR
12 times

ISS MODULES

ISS is made from more than 30 modules that together have the equivalent weight of about 320 cars and cover the area of a soccer field. A maximum of six astronauts share living and working space equal to that of a five-room apartment. They have unique opportunities for scientific and industrial research in the areas of earth observation, telecommunications, materials research and human physiology.

NASA (USA)

1 **Z 1**
first part of the grid structure

2 **Unity**
node 1

3 **Tranquility**
node, systems for water and air treatment

4 **Cupola**
picture window

5 **PMM Leonardo**
permanent multi-purpose logistics module

6 **Quest**
airlock

7 **AMS 02**
particle detector

8 **Destiny**
NASA laboratory module

9 **Harmony**
node 2

10 **BEAM**
experimental, expandable space station module

Roscosmos (RUS)

11 **Poisk**
docking module

12 **Zvezda**
living and service module

13 **Zarya**
power, navigation and cargo storage

14 **Nauka, May 2012**
Roscosmos laboratory module

15 **Rassvet**
docking space for Soyuz and Progress ships

ESA (EU)

16 **Columbus**
ESA laboratory module

JAXA (JPN)

17 **Kibo**
JAXA laboratory module

CSA (CAN)

18 **Canadarm2**
robotic arm is not permanently attached to the ISS at one point

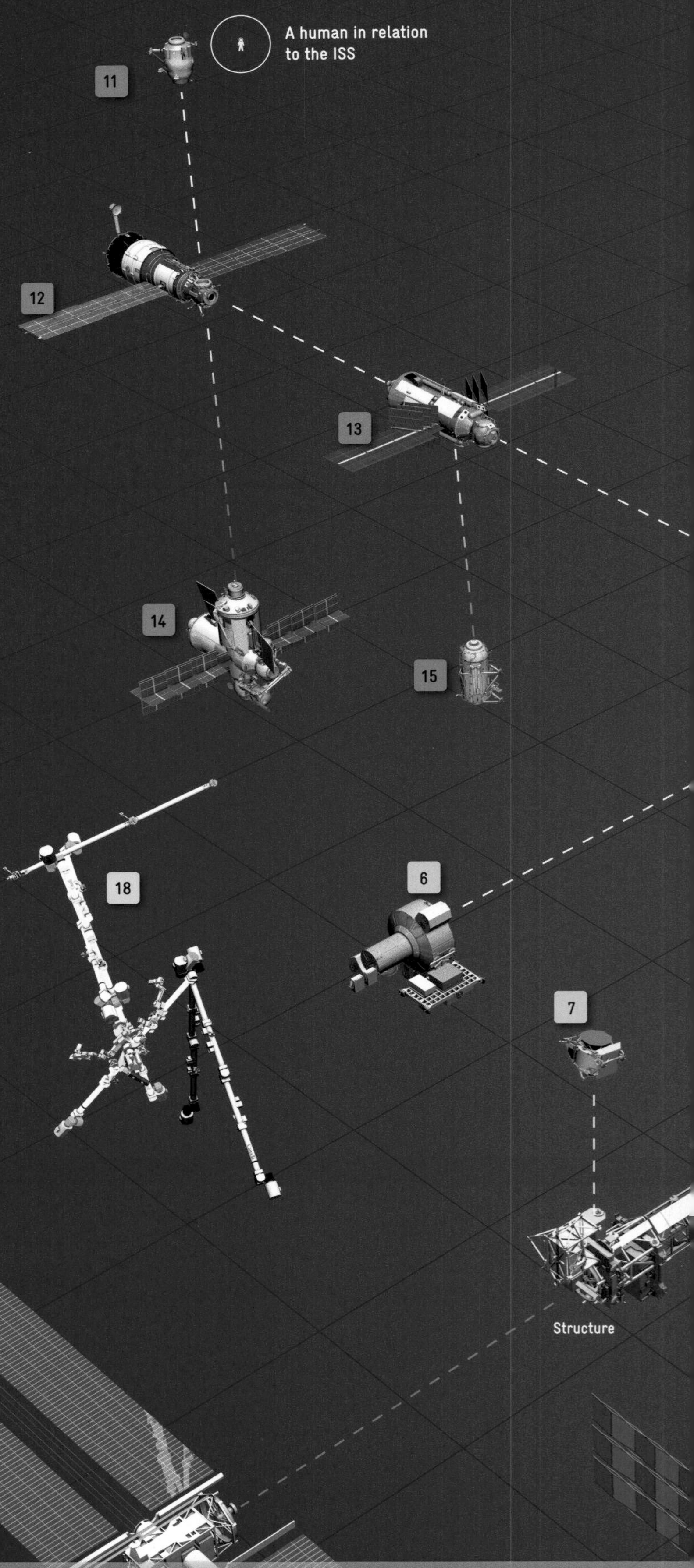

THE MAIN RESEARCH PROJECTS ON THE ISS:

Atomic Clock Ensemble in Space

Atomic clocks in microgravity for the precise determination of global time

European Technology Exposure Facility

Research into the influence of solar ultraviolet radiation on biological samples

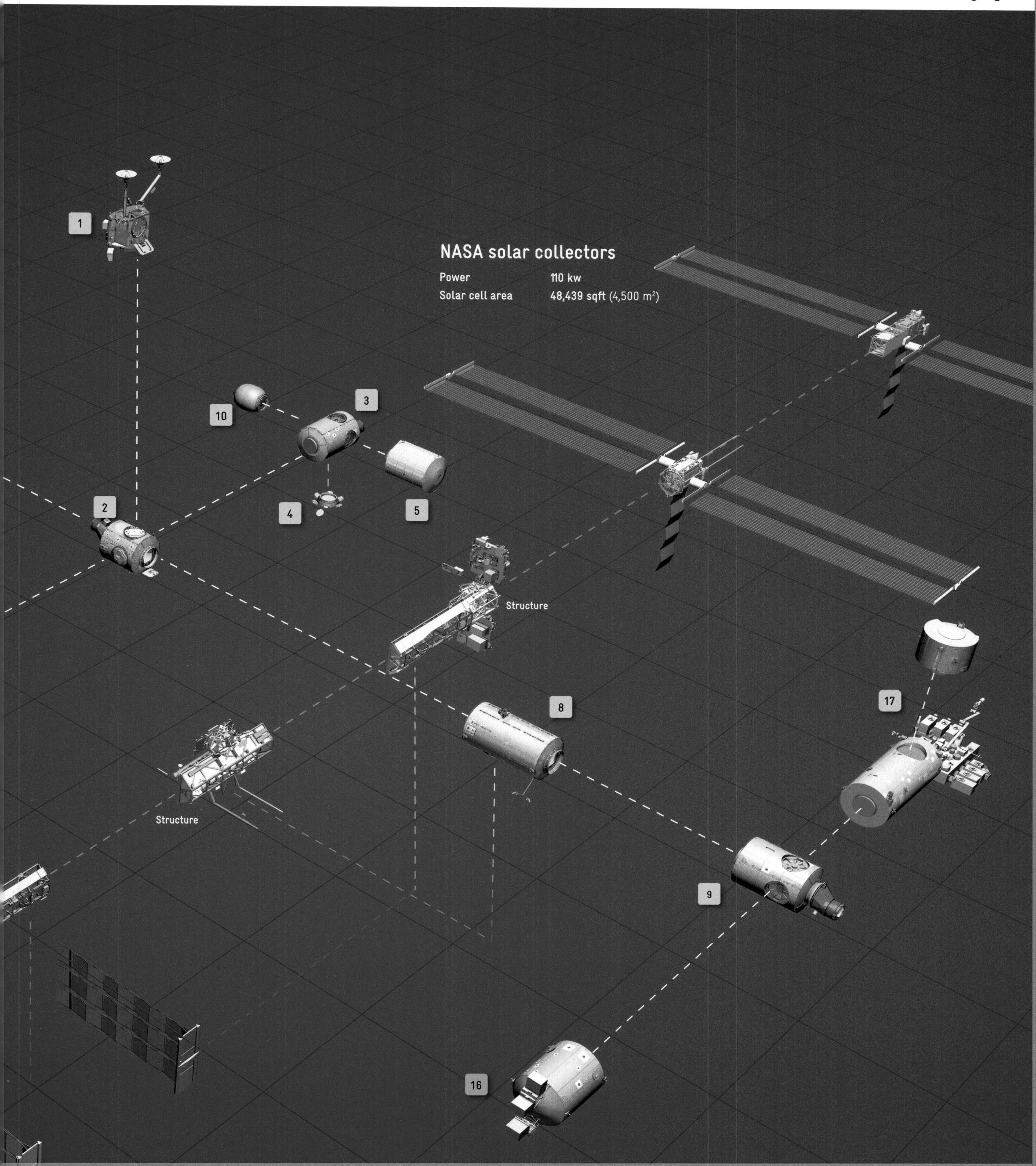
1
NASA solar collectors
Power 110 kw
Solar cell area 48,439 sqft (4,500 m²)
10
3
4
5
2
Structure
8
17
Structure
9
16

Alpha Magnetic Spectrometer

Particle detector to study cosmic radiation

Solar Monitoring Observatory

Experiments for solar studies

Global Transmission Service

Experiment for time synchronization

CHASING COMETS

The Rosetta space probe was launched in 2004 with the goal of becoming the first spacecraft to orbit a comet. It took 10 years, but Rosetta and its passenger—the Philae lander—eventually reached comet 67P, known as the Churyumov-Gerasimenko. The mission ended in 2016, but the comet continues to journey on with two terrestrial passengers.

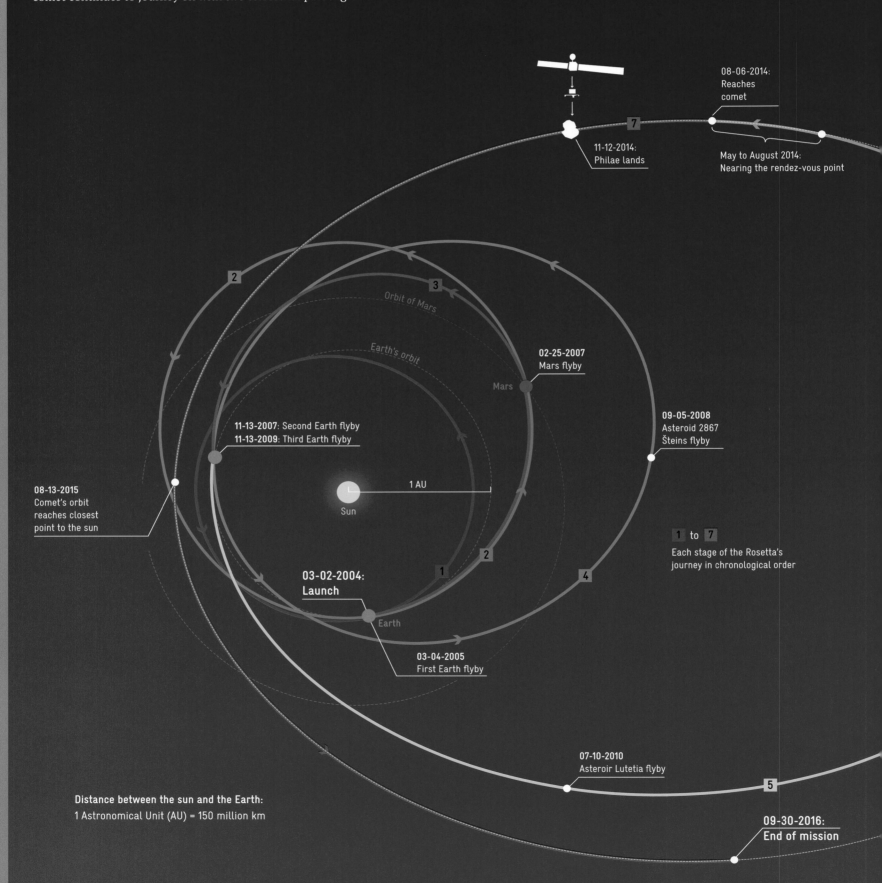

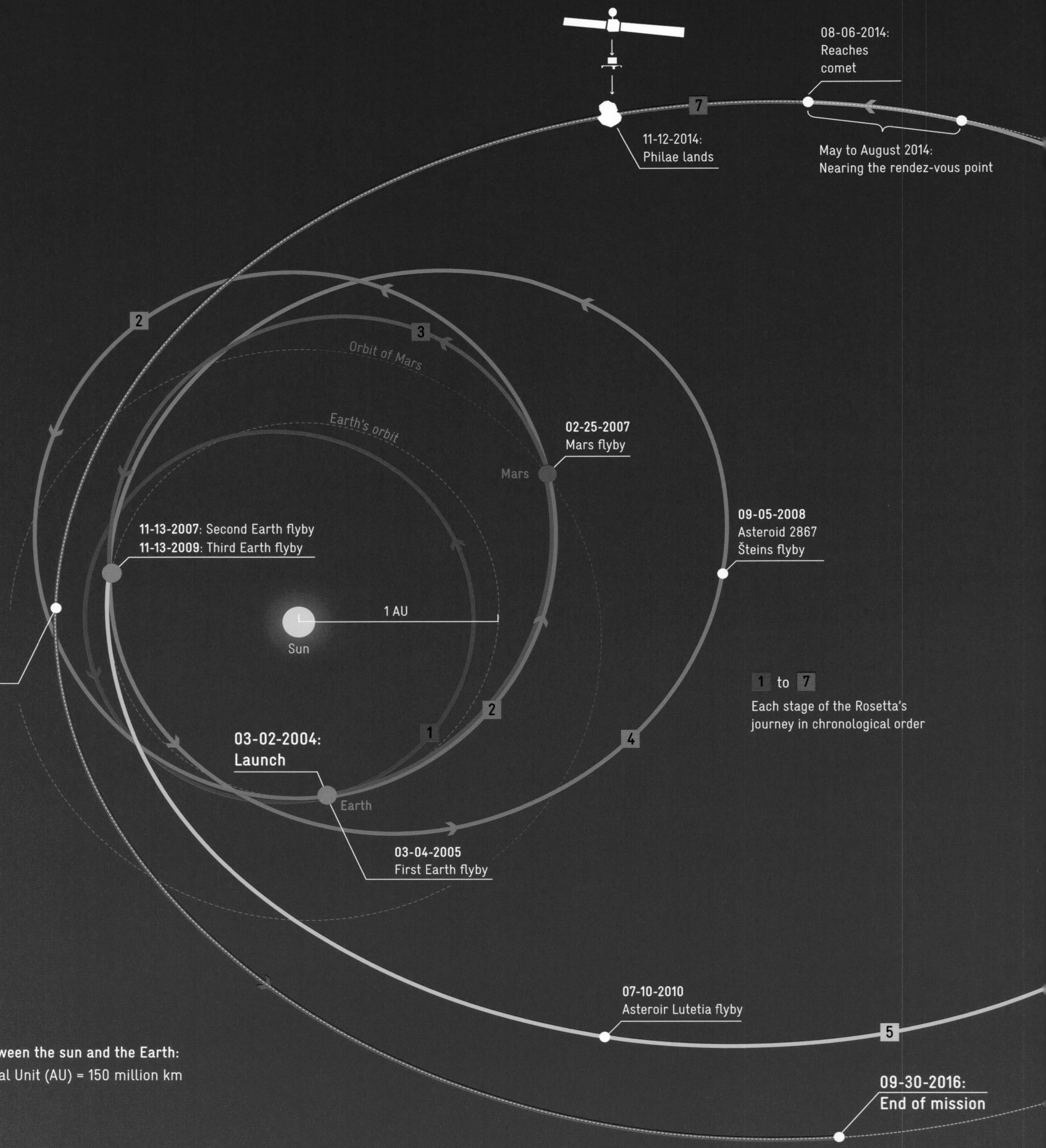
08-06-2014: Reaches comet
7
11-12-2014: Philae lands
May to August 2014: Nearing the rendez-vous point
2
3
Orbit of Mars
Earth's orbit
02-25-2007 Mars flyby
Mars
09-05-2008 Asteroid 2867 Šteins flyby
11-13-2007: Second Earth flyby
11-13-2009: Third Earth flyby
08-13-2015 Comet's orbit reaches closest point to the sun
1 AU
Sun
1 to 7
Each stage of the Rosetta's journey in chronological order
2
1
4
03-02-2004: Launch
Earth
03-04-2005 First Earth flyby
07-10-2010 Asteroir Lutetia flyby
5
09-30-2016: End of mission

Distance between the sun and the Earth:
1 Astronomical Unit (AU) = 150 million km

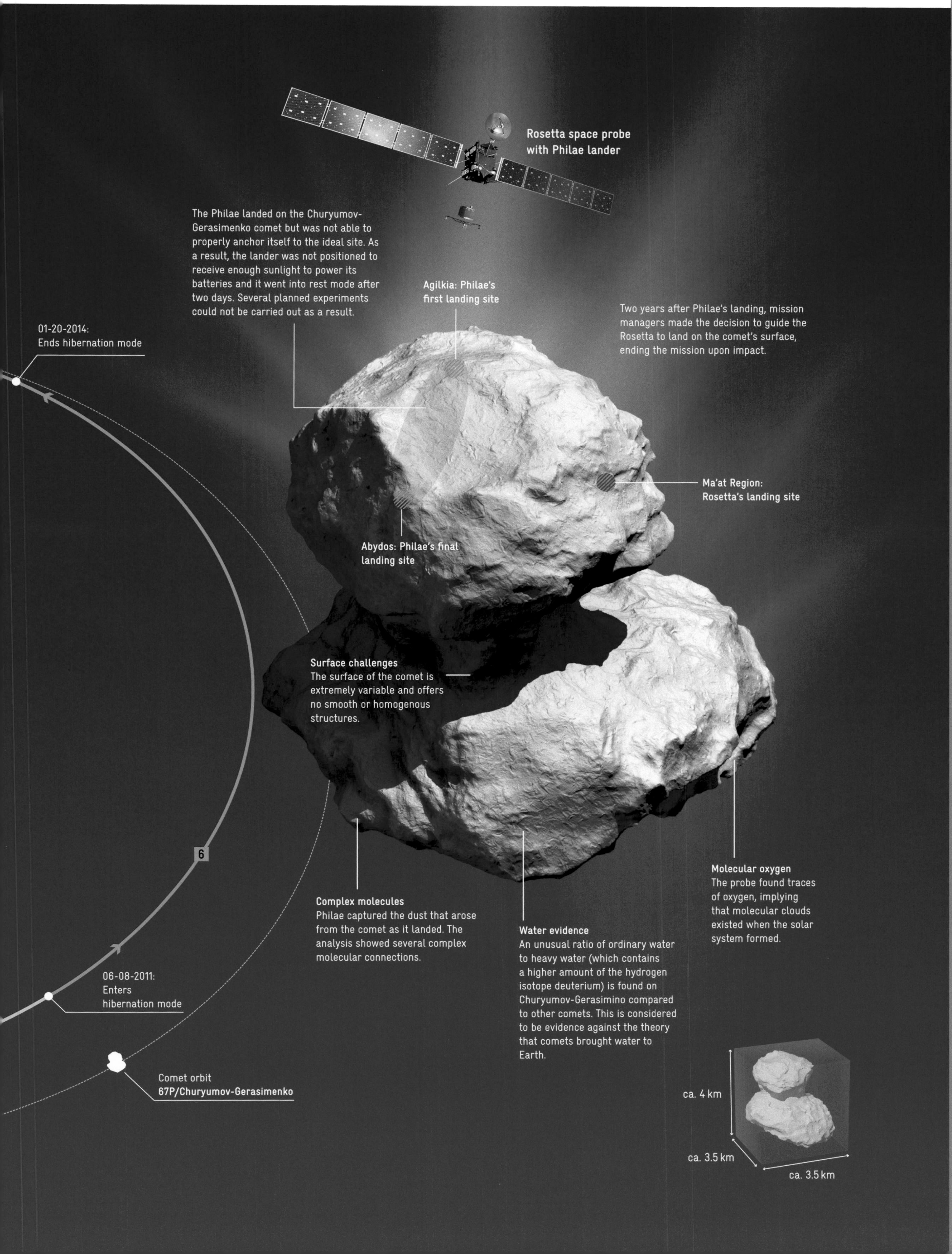
Rosetta space probe with Philae lander
The Philae landed on the Churyumov-Gerasimenko comet but was not able to properly anchor itself to the ideal site. As a result, the lander was not positioned to receive enough sunlight to power its batteries and it went into rest mode after two days. Several planned experiments could not be carried out as a result.
Agilkia: Philae's first landing site
Two years after Philae's landing, mission managers made the decision to guide the Rosetta to land on the comet's surface, ending the mission upon impact.
01-20-2014:
Ends hibernation mode
Ma'at Region:
Rosetta's landing site
Abydos: Philae's final landing site
Surface challenges
The surface of the comet is extremely variable and offers no smooth or homogenous structures.
6
Molecular oxygen
The probe found traces of oxygen, implying that molecular clouds existed when the solar system formed.
Complex molecules
Philae captured the dust that arose from the comet as it landed. The analysis showed several complex molecular connections.
Water evidence
An unusual ratio of ordinary water to heavy water (which contains a higher amount of the hydrogen isotope deuterium) is found on Churyumov-Gerasimino compared to other comets. This is considered to be evidence against the theory that comets brought water to Earth.
06-08-2011:
Enters hibernation mode
Comet orbit
67P/Churyumov-Gerasimenko
ca. 4 km
ca. 3.5 km
ca. 3.5 km

I'LL BE BACK

It's back again. A new spectacular chapter in the International Sun-Earth Explorer 3's (ISEE-3) history is beginning. For the first time, a civil team is taking over a NASA machine. The ISSE-3, which was written off by the US space agency, is approaching Earth again after three decades. Enthusiastic researchers and radio amateurs have managed to revive the space veteran and want to make its data available to the public. Even if their goal to position the probe near Earth fails, it represents a milestone in space research—and maybe a starting point for trying to establish contact again because ISEE-3 will be returning to Earth in 2029.

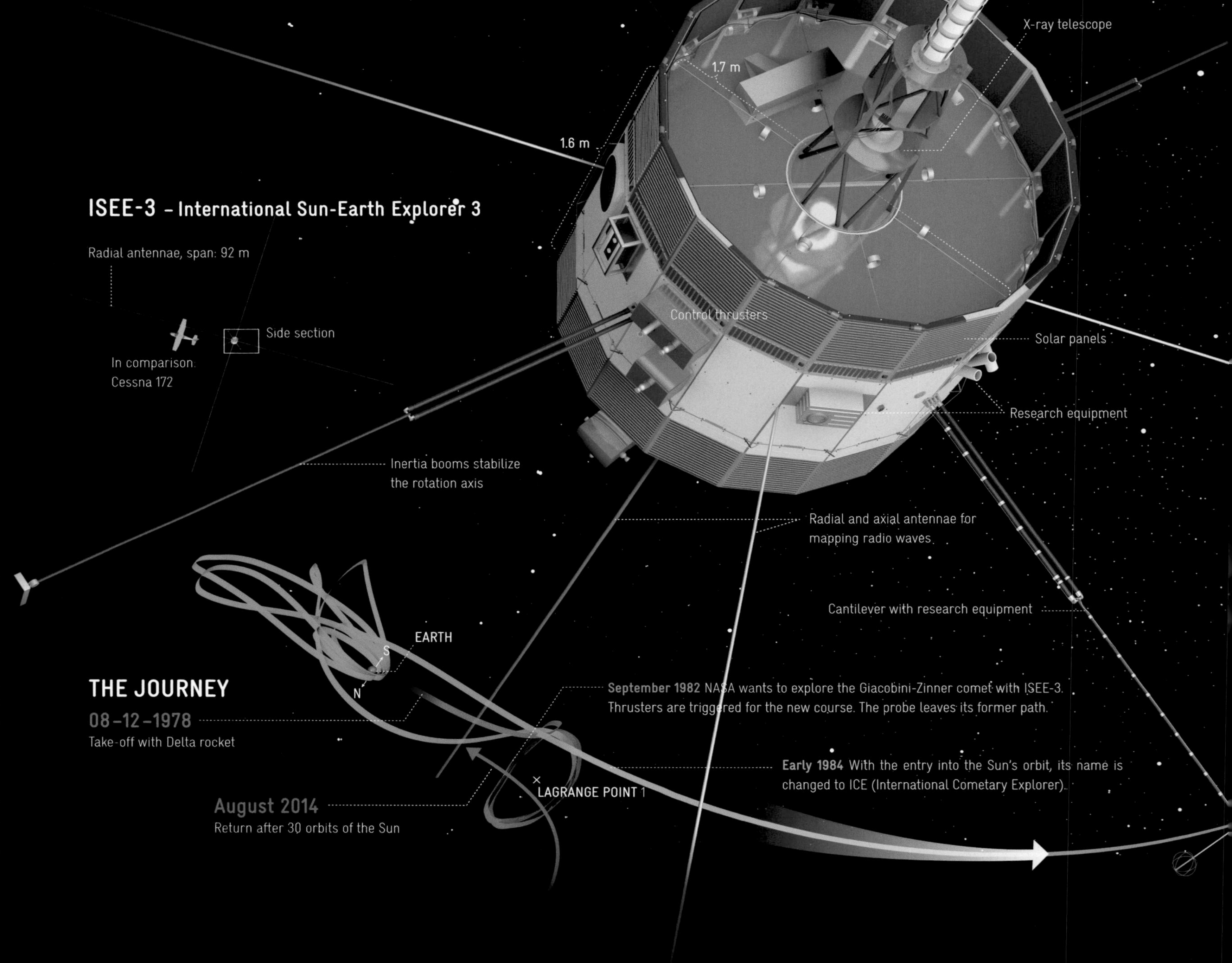
The probe rotates on its own axis every three seconds. This ensures a balanced temperature and a stable trajectory.
Antennae for communicating with Earth
X-ray telescope
1.7 m
1.6 m
ISEE-3 – International Sun-Earth Explorer 3
Radial antennae, span: 92 m
Side section
In comparison: Cessna 172
Control thrusters
Solar panels
Research equipment
Inertia booms stabilize the rotation axis
Radial and axial antennae for mapping radio waves
Cantilever with research equipment
EARTH
S
N
THE JOURNEY
08-12-1978
Take-off with Delta rocket
September 1982 NASA wants to explore the Giacobini-Zinner comet with ISEE-3. Thrusters are triggered for the new course. The probe leaves its former path.
Early 1984 With the entry into the Sun's orbit, its name is changed to ICE (International Cometary Explorer).
LAGRANGE POINT 1
August 2014
Return after 30 orbits of the Sun

1978–82 Inside solar winds

ISEE-3 is located in an orbit on the Lagrange point 1. Here, the Earth's and Sun's gravity cancel each other out. From 1.5 m. km away from its home planet, it examines solar wind and cosmic particles for almost four years.

82–83

With the help of the Earth's and the Moon's gravitational pull, the probe gets its energy for a rendez-vous with a comet. The Earth's magnetic field is

83–85 Hunting for comets

It takes almost two years before the probe encounters the Giacobini-Zinner comet. In September 1985, it passes through its plasma tail at a distance of 7862 km. The data confirms that comets are »snowballs« made from ice and rock. ISEE-3/ICE is the first probe to pass a comet. In 1986, it approached Halley's

85–97

On its orbit around the Sun, the ISEE-3, along with observatories on Earth and the Ulysses space probe, measures the Sun's activities

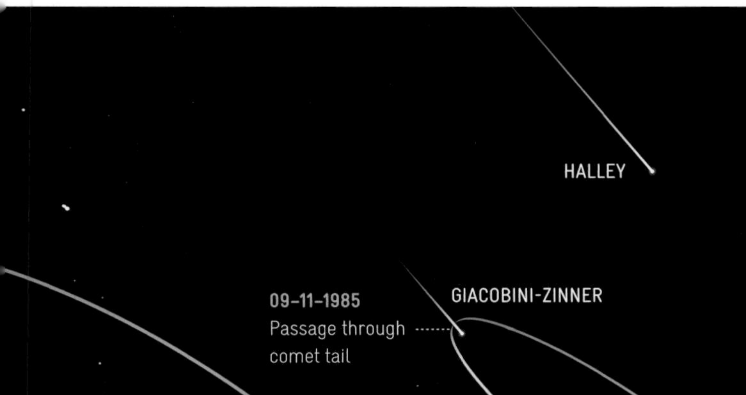
HALLEY
GIACOBINI-ZINNER
09-11-1985
Passage through
comet tail

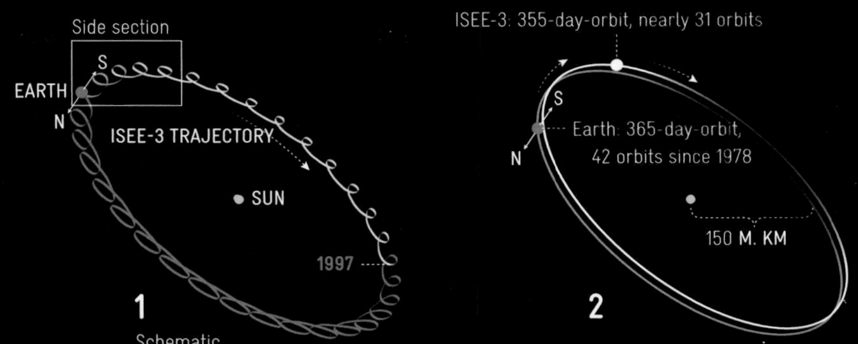
Side section
EARTH
S
N
ISEE-3 TRAJECTORY
SUN
1997
1
ISEE-3: 355-day-orbit, nearly 31 orbits
S
N
Earth: 365-day-orbit,
42 orbits since 1978
150 M. KM
2

Schematic representations

TRAJECTORY AND ORBITAL PATH

In our graphic, the ISEE-3's orbit is plotted relative to an immovable Earth (1). In reality, the probe and the Earth orbit the Sun (2). ISEE-3 is a bit faster here and approaches the Earth from behind.

ON-BOARD EXPERIMENTS

There are no cameras on board the ISEE-3 but there are a variety of particle, radiation and magnetic field detectors. Some of those devices are still functioning. Numerous phenomena have been observed in 15 experiments.

- Interplanetary magnetic field
- Solar wind: particle shower that originates from the Sun's magnetic field (mainly protons and electrons)
- Solar radiation bursts (e.g. radio emission caused by eruptions)
- Earth's magnetosphere
- Interplanetary medium (particles such as electrons and ions)
- Cosmic gamma radiation bursts (possibly due to exploding stars)
- Charged particles within comet tail

REBOOT PROJECT

This civil project, led by astrobiologist Keith Cowing and businessman Dennis Wingo, mobilizes people through the internet who can contribute the knowledge and support to reactivate ISEE-3.

07-23 The thrusters are no longer functioning properly. ISEE-3 still orbits the sun on a slightly altered path and changes to an idle state due to a lack of power.

07-02 Radial thrusters fired to increase rotation.

07-01 For the first time in decades, measuring data is received.

06-15 Further contact, followed by various attempts to control ISEE-3's thrusters to position probe in an orbit close to the Earth again

05-29 First contact through a radio telescope at the Arecibo observatory

05-23 Crowdfunding ends: 2238 donors, $ 159,602.

05-21 Agreement with NASA over the use of the probe

04-14 Crowdfunding starts

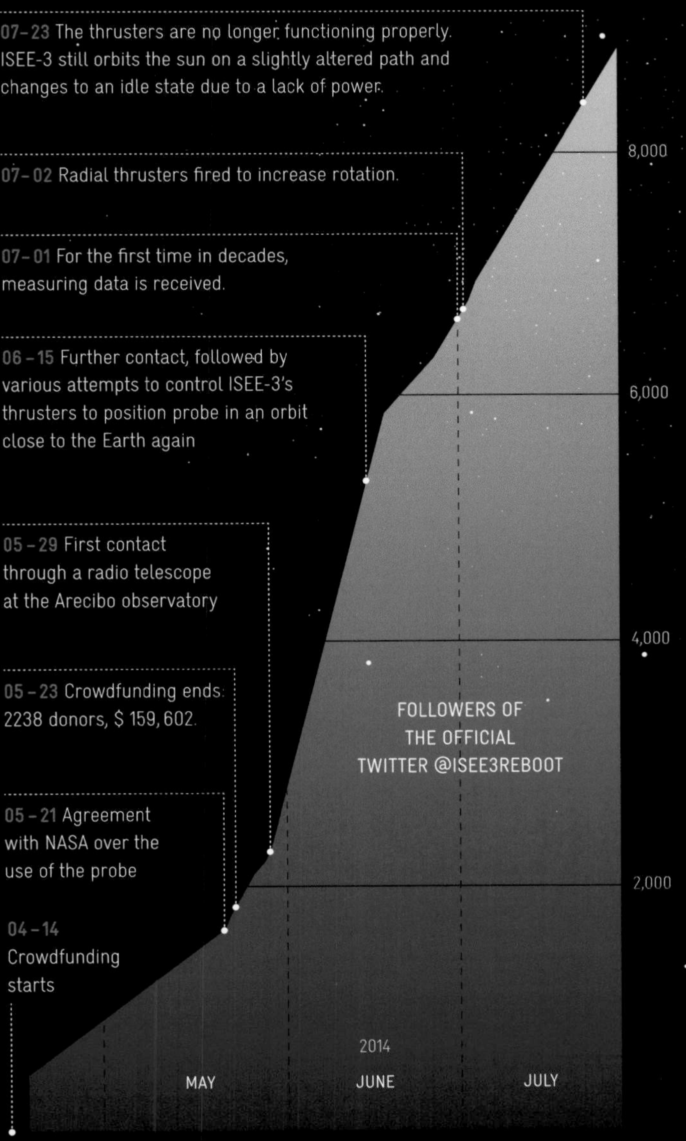
8,000
6,000
4,000
2,000
FOLLOWERS OF
THE OFFICIAL
TWITTER @ISEE3REBOOT
2014
MAY
JUNE
JULY

97–2014 Hibernation

In 1997, the probe's last mission officially ends and two years later the communication hardware on Earth is dismantled. ISEE-3 can no longer be directly controlled. NASA locates the probe one more time in 2008.

2014 The return

ISEE-3 approaches Earth again. An international team of scientists and radio amateurs starts the Reboot Project. Their goal is to reactivate the probe and make the data available to the public.

MISSION TO MARS

Where will humans go if Earth becomes uninhabitable? Elon Musk, the founder of the aerospace company SpaceX thinks the answer is Mars—and there's no time like the present to start populating Earth's neighboring planet. Now that water has been discovered there, the idea may not be so crazy after all. The US space agency NASA predicts that a flight to Mars will cost $100 billion, but Musk wants to reduce the cost by making reusable rockets.

HOW IT ALL BEGINS

Mars explorers can only reach the planet in stages in giant rockets such as SpaceX's 70-meter Falcon Heavy. The landing capsule is sent to Mars empty. Other components are then sent into Earth's orbit piece by piece and are joined together. The final piece is the space capsule with a four-person crew. Only then can they embark on the longest journey.

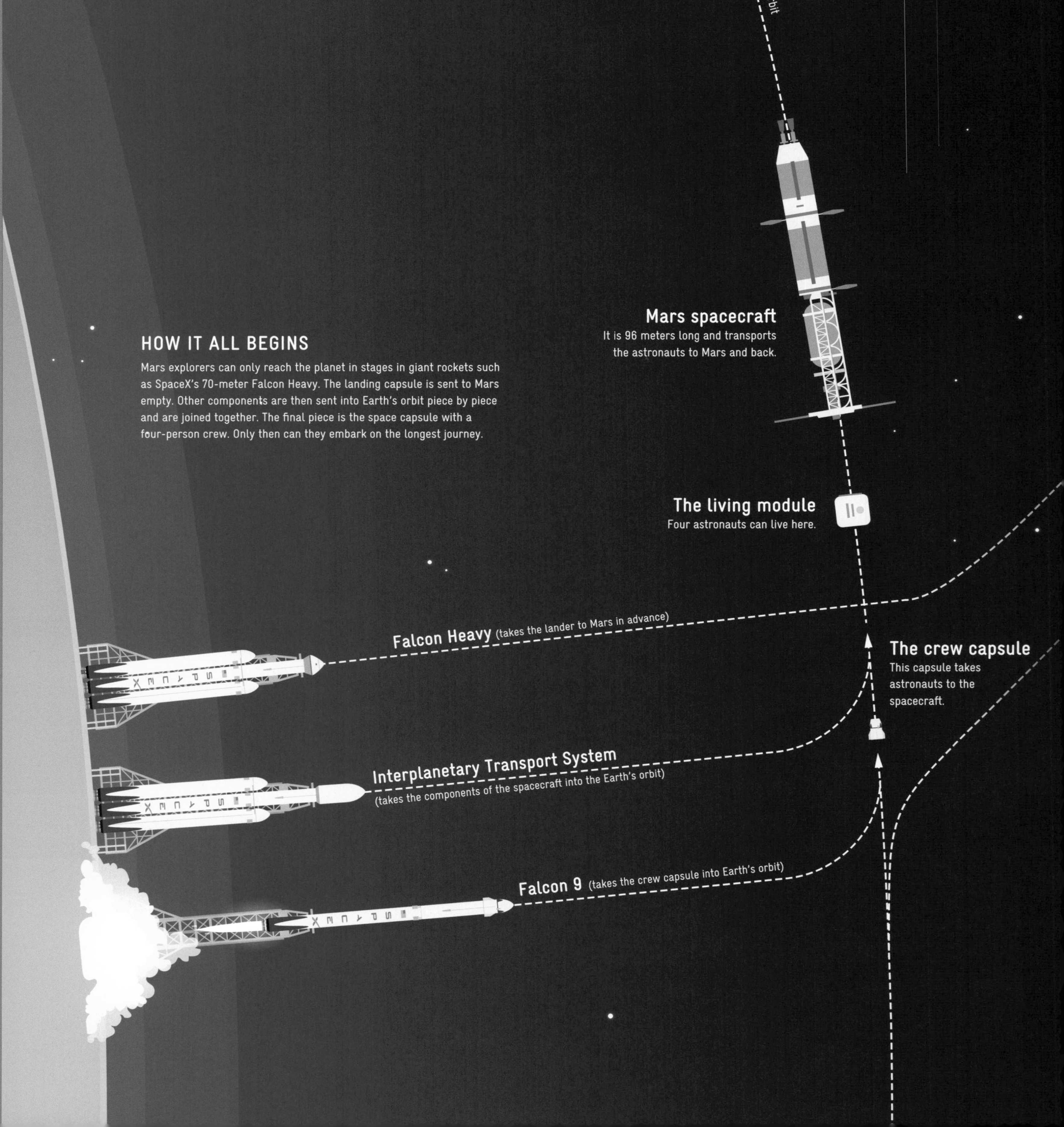
Earth's orbit
Mars spacecraft
It is 96 meters long and transports the astronauts to Mars and back.
The living module
Four astronauts can live here.
Falcon Heavy (takes the lander to Mars in advance)
The crew capsule
This capsule takes astronauts to the spacecraft.
Interplanetary Transport System
(takes the components of the spacecraft into the Earth's orbit)
Falcon 9 (takes the crew capsule into Earth's orbit)
SPACEX

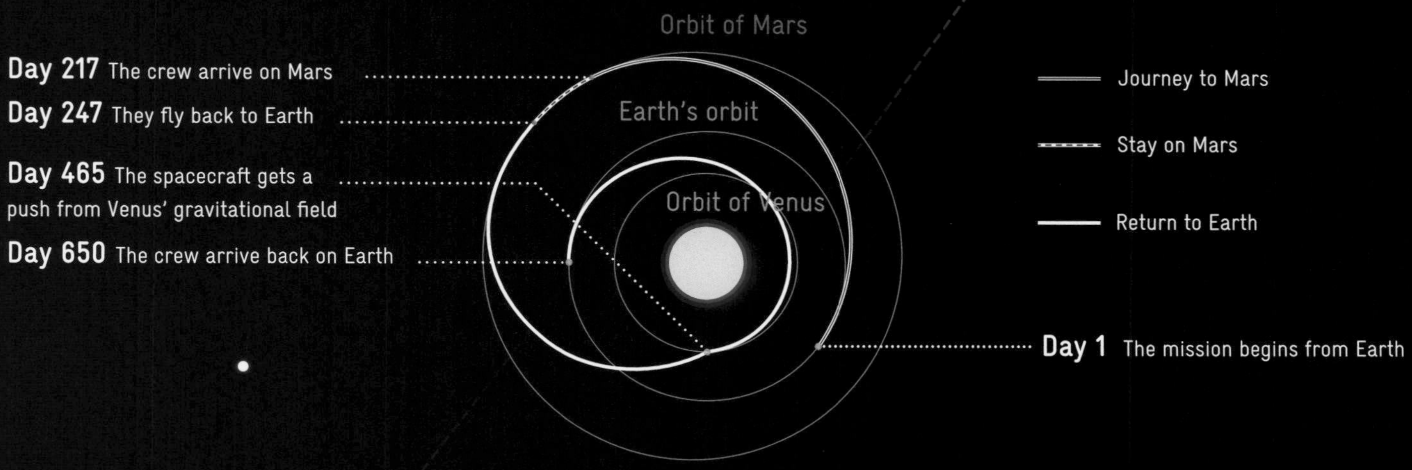
Orbit of Mars
Day 217 The crew arrive on Mars
Day 247 They fly back to Earth
Earth's orbit
Day 465 The spacecraft gets a push from Venus' gravitational field
Orbit of Venus
Day 650 The crew arrive back on Earth
Journey to Mars
Stay on Mars
Return to Earth
Day 1 The mission begins from Earth

THE FLIGHT PATH

On average, Mars is 225 million kilometers from Earth. Every 26 months, the planets align in such a way that a spacecraft can reach the red planet with minimal fuel resources. On the return journey, Venus provides the ship with a gravitational boost, also saving several hundred tonnes of fuel.

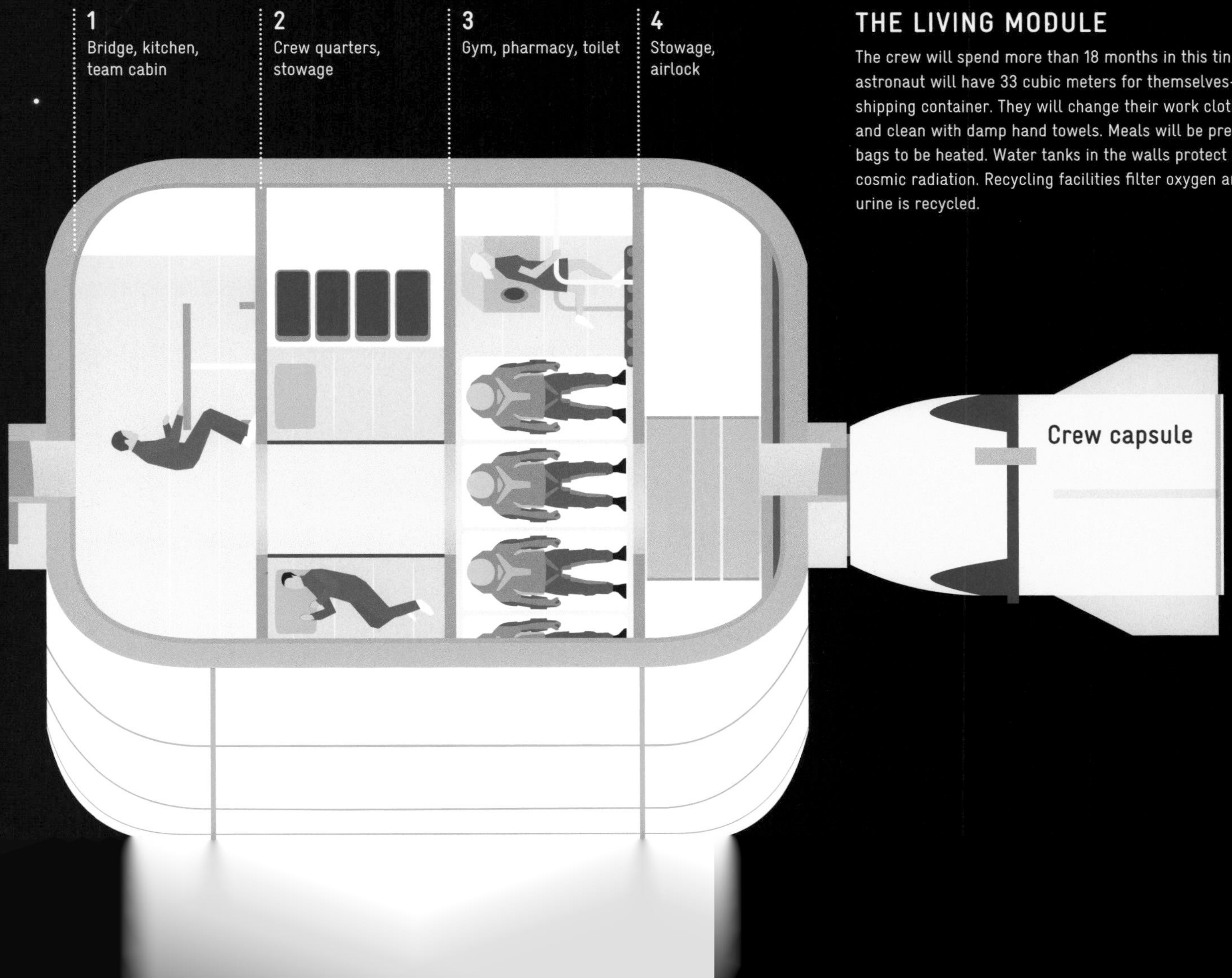
1
Bridge, kitchen, team cabin
2
Crew quarters, stowage
3
Gym, pharmacy, toilet
4
Stowage, airlock
Crew capsule

THE LIVING MODULE

The crew will spend more than 18 months in this tin can. Each astronaut will have 33 cubic meters for themselves—as much as a shipping container. They will change their work clothes every 10 days and clean with damp hand towels. Meals will be prepared in plastic bags to be heated. Water tanks in the walls protect occupants from cosmic radiation. Recycling facilities filter oxygen and water. Even urine is recycled.

THE LANDING

The most precarious moment comes when the astronauts climb into the lander to plunge into the thin atmosphere of Mars. The spacecraft has to come to a stop from a minimum speed of 21,000 kilometers per hour with parachutes and rocket nozzles. This technology is still in development. The crew use the lander as their home for their 30 days on the planet. They then fly back to the spacecraft in a capsule to begin their journey back to Earth.

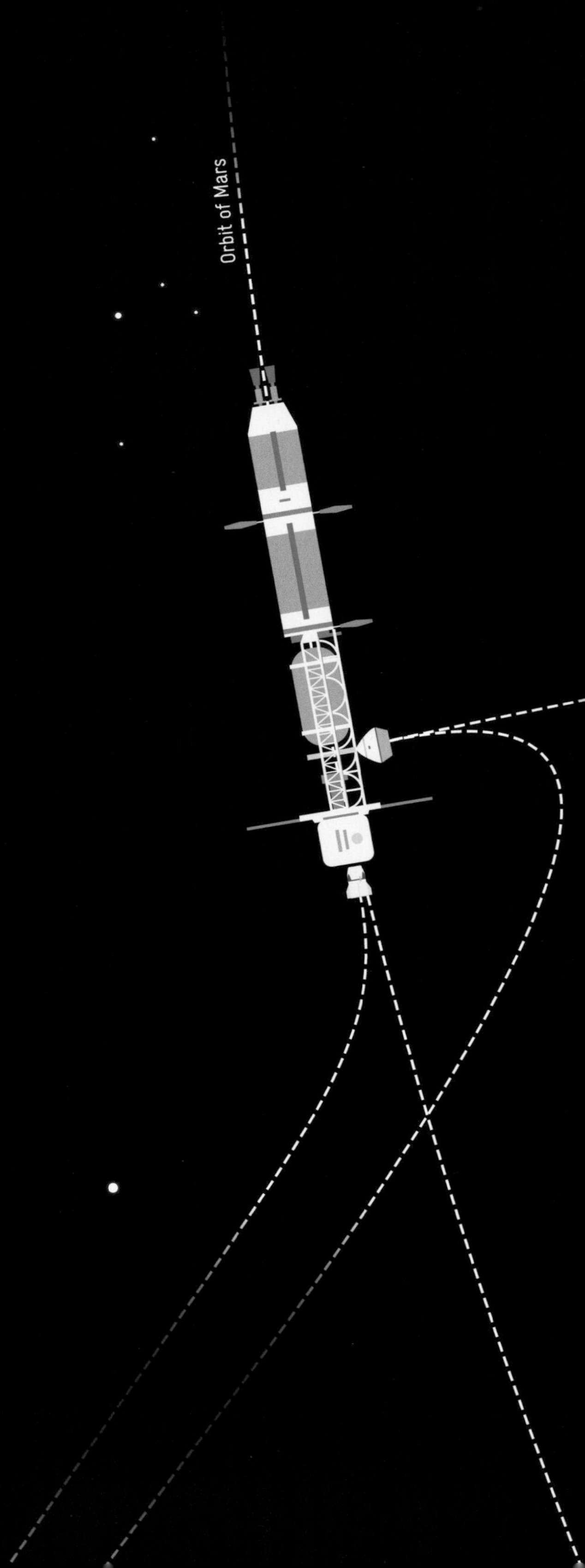
Orbit of Mars

Entering into Mars' atmosphere

The lander deflects frictional heat using a shield.

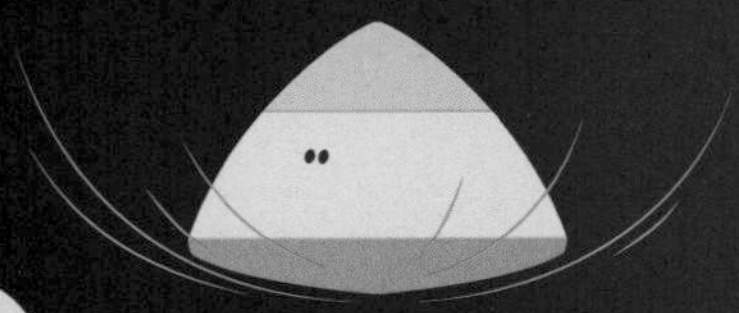

Braking

Parachutes are used to slow the lander down as it falls.

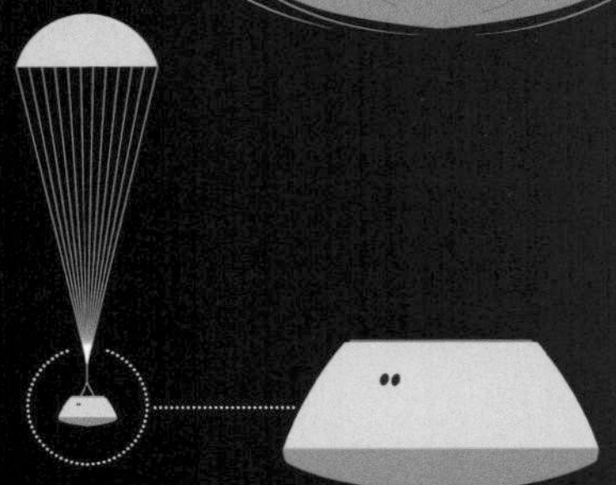

Landing

The rocket engines are used to slow the lander down even more, enabling a smooth landing.

Return

The astronauts fly back to the spacecraft on a small capsule.

Z-2 MARS SPACESUIT

NASA has designed a spacesuit made for Mars. It gives astronauts more freedom to move and provides better insulation against the bitter cold—temperatures on Mars often reach −100 °Celsius. It also protects against micrometeoroids and cosmic radiation.

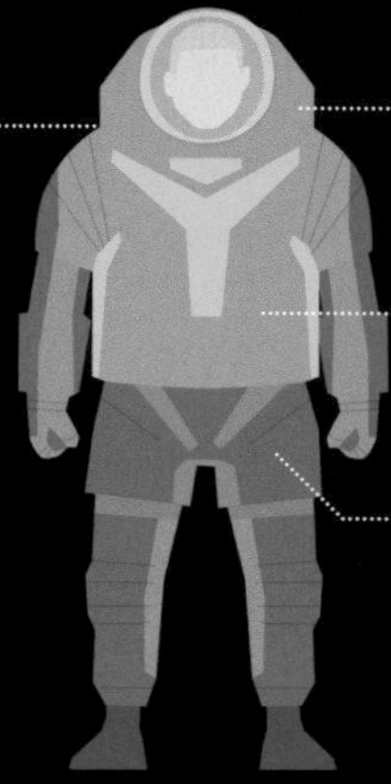
Backpack with batteries, CO_2 filter and oxygen
Air inlet that can be linked to the charging module.
New composite materials mean the suit is extremely resistant to tears
New hinges around the hip and shoulder areas enable astronauts to move more freely

GAME PLAN FOR EPIC FALL

In 2012, the Austrian basejumper Felix Baumgartner accomplished a space dive from the stratosphere. Setting the record for the highest parachute jump from an altitude of nearly 39,000 meters, it attracted a lot of attention. Two years later, the American computer scientist Alan Eustace beat the record by more than 2 km in an attempt that was staged much more quietly.

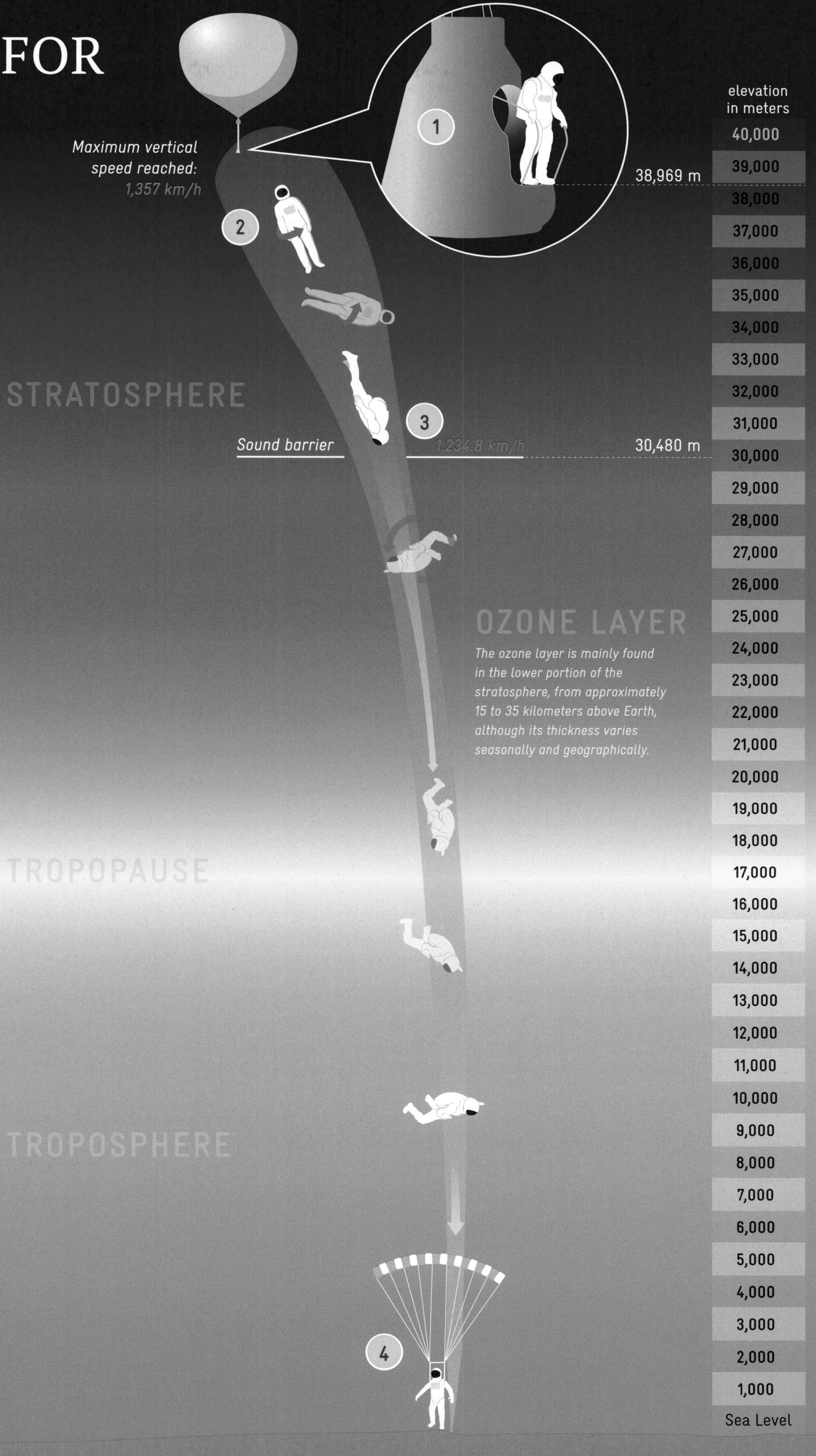
Maximum vertical speed reached: 1,357 km/h
1
2
3
4
38,969 m
STRATOSPHERE
Sound barrier
1,234.8 km/h
30,480 m
OZONE LAYER
The ozone layer is mainly found in the lower portion of the stratosphere, from approximately 15 to 35 kilometers above Earth, although its thickness varies seasonally and geographically.
TROPOPAUSE
TROPOSPHERE
elevation in meters
40,000
39,000
38,000
37,000
36,000
35,000
34,000
33,000
32,000
31,000
30,000
29,000
28,000
27,000
26,000
25,000
24,000
23,000
22,000
21,000
20,000
19,000
18,000
17,000
16,000
15,000
14,000
13,000
12,000
11,000
10,000
9,000
8,000
7,000
6,000
5,000
4,000
3,000
2,000
1,000
Sea Level

① DROP ZONE

After a 2.5-hour ride, the balloon levels off at 38,969 metres. The capsule depressurizes, and Baumgartner's suit expands to compensate, becoming so stiff that just opening the hatch is a challenge.

② SUPERSONIC JUMP

After steadying himself on the platform, Baumgartner jumps, using a small bunny hop. He needs to be in perfect position, as there's no air resistance up here to right himself. That lack of drag also means he'll accelerate rapidly.

0:01–0:47 MINUTES

Baumgartner gets into »Delta« position (head down, arms at sides) for max. control. If he starts to spin uncontrollably, a drogue chute will deploy to stabilize him—otherwise, he could black out or hemorrhage.

③ 0:48–1:24 MINUTES

He reaches the sound barrier at 1,234.8 km/h. Certain parts of him (like his helmet) may break Mach 1 before others, which could send dangerous shock waves over his body.

1:25 MINUTES

Denser air slows Baumgartner and allows him mobility. He can't pull his chute this early, though, because the crew wants him to land as fast as possible for medical attention.

④ 4:19 MINUTES

At 2,566.8 meters, Baumgartner deploys his parachute which is fully opened after 4:19 minutes. He focuses on landing and hamming it up for cameras below.

LANDING

Baumgartner should land within 16 kilometers of the launch point. The team uses GPS in his chest pack to pinpoint his location.

THE LONG JOURNEY OF THE VOYAGER SPACECRAFT

In 1977, Voyager 1 and Voyager 2 were launched into space to explore the outer planets of our solar system. The identical probes have now been sailing through the cosmos for four decades, and are continuing further into space to define the boundaries of solar radiation and the beginning of interstellar space.

Voyager Probe

Voyager 1 is escaping the solar system out of the ecliptic plane to the north.

7 Neptune

5 Uranus

1 Earth
The Sun

The ecliptic plane

2 Jupiter

3 4 Saturn

Voyager 2 is escaping the solar system out of the ecliptic plane to the south.

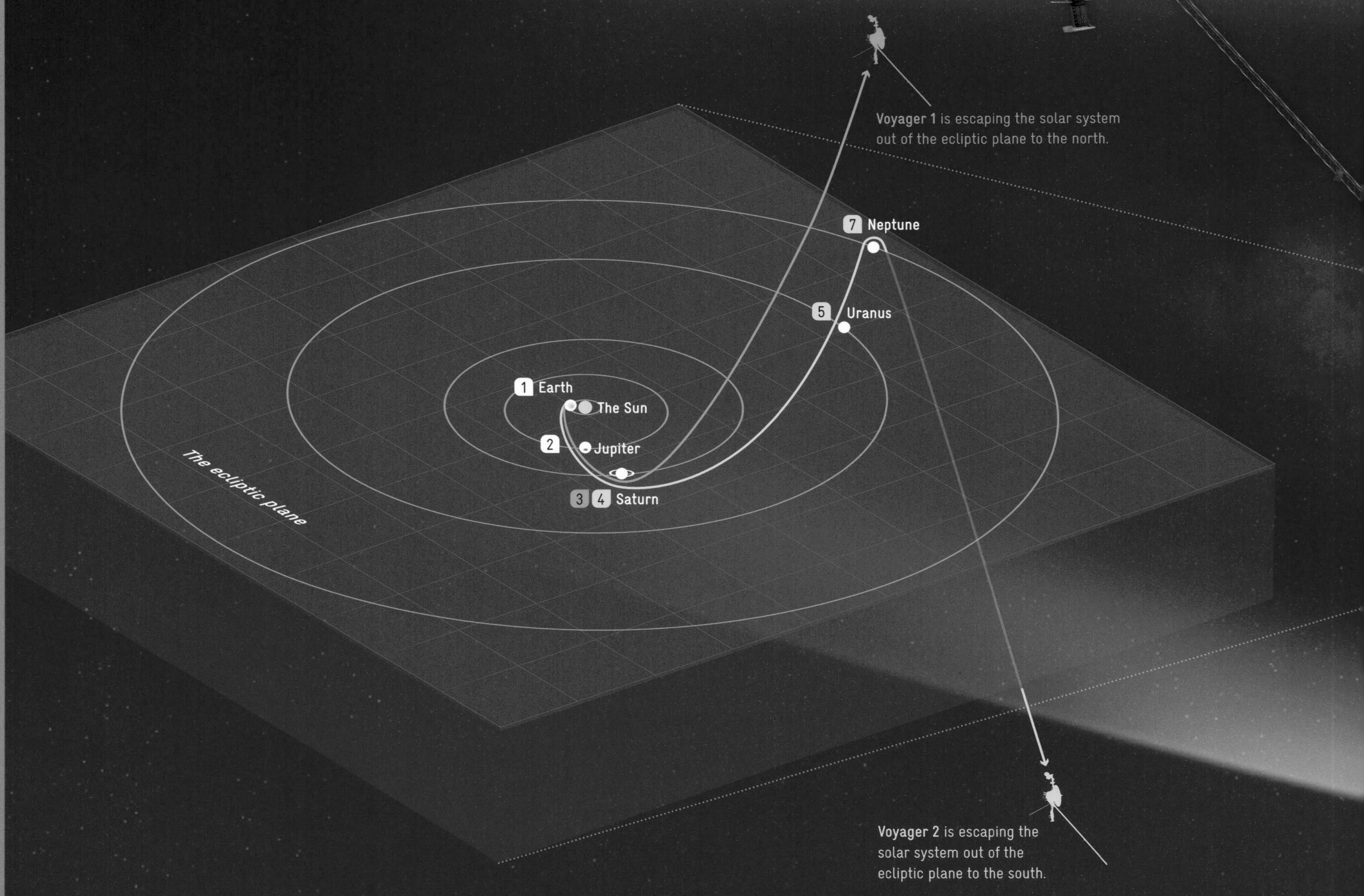

On their way for four decades

On August 20, 1977, Voyager 2 launched first. Voyager 1 followed 16 days later.

1		2	3	4					5			7							
1977	1978	1979	1980	1981	1982	1983	1984	1985	1986	1987	1988	1989	1990	1991	1992	1993	1994	1995	1996

Voyager 2 is directed from Saturn to Uranus

Closest approach to Jupiter by both probes

Voyager 1 gains momentum from Saturn

Flyby Uranus by Voyager 2

»Pale Blue Dot« photograph

Voyager 2 passes Neptune

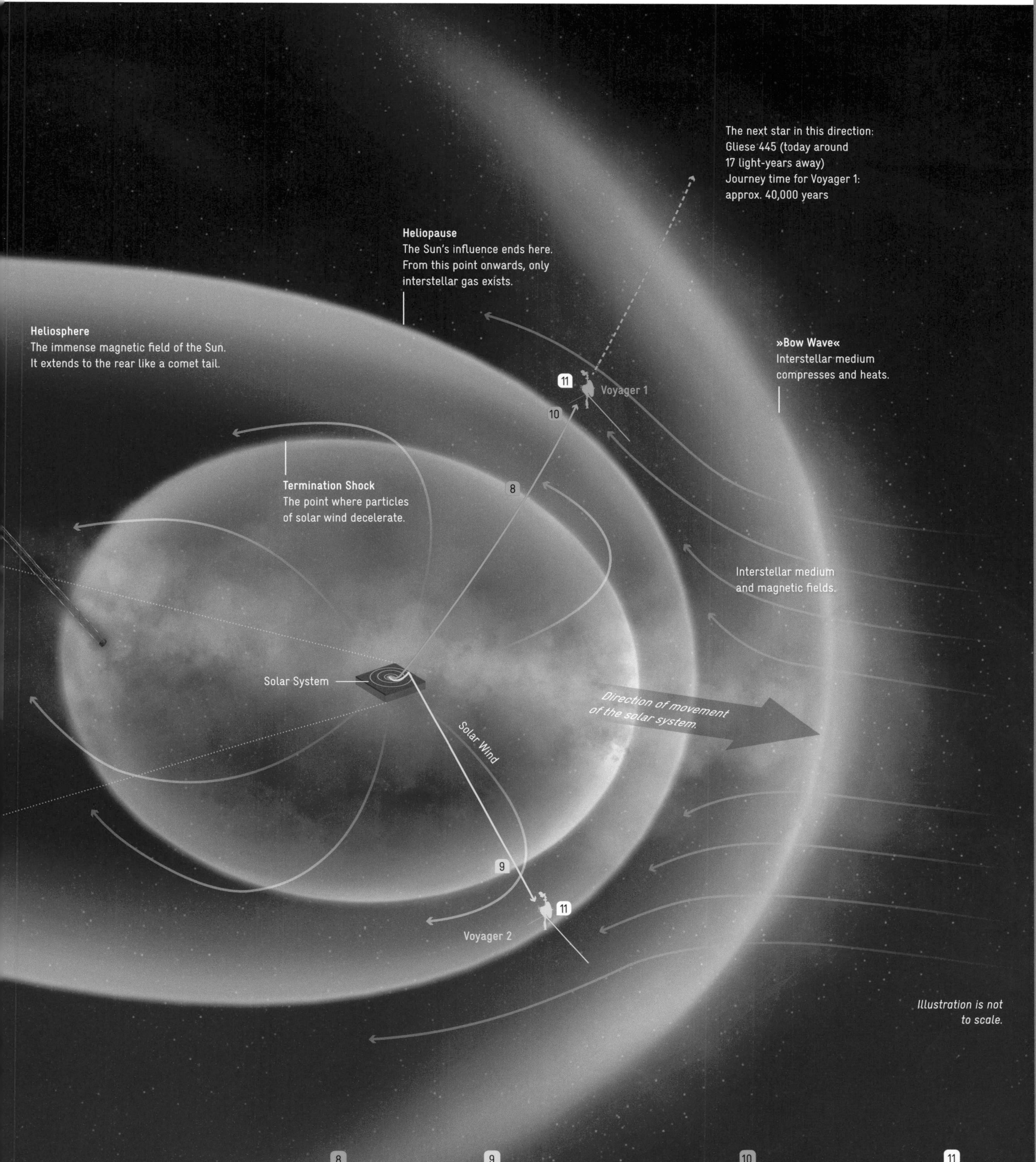

The next star in this direction:
Gliese 445 (today around
17 light-years away)
Journey time for Voyager 1:
approx. 40,000 years
Heliopause
The Sun's influence ends here.
From this point onwards, only
interstellar gas exists.
Heliosphere
The immense magnetic field of the Sun.
It extends to the rear like a comet tail.
»Bow Wave«
Interstellar medium
compresses and heats.
11
Voyager 1
10
Termination Shock
The point where particles
of solar wind decelerate.
8
Interstellar medium
and magnetic fields.
Solar System
Solar Wind
Direction of movement
of the solar system.
9
11
Voyager 2
Illustration is not
to scale.

7	1998	1999	2000	2001	2002	2003	2004 [8]	2005	2006	2007 [9]	2008	2009	2010	2011	2012 [10]	2013	2014	2015	2016 [11]

1998: Surpasses Pioneer 10: The probe was launched in 1972 and was—until then—the furthest traveled human-made object.

8 (2004): Voyager 1 passes the termination shock at 94 astronomical units (AU).

9 (2007): Voyager 2 passes the termination shock.

10 (2012): Voyager 1 crosses the heliopause at 121 AU and enters interstellar space.

11 (2016): Voyager 2 is before the heliopause, with Voyager 1 behind it.

ORDER TO THE SYSTEM

We organize the universe by size. A star can only be a star once it's big enough to be able to host fusion inside it. And a celestial body has to have a certain mass before it can be considered a planet ... a mass that Pluto did not have. It was therefore »demoted« from its planetary status to »dwarf planet«.

1 Star

The Sun has a mass 700 times greater than all planets added together, which means it is big enough to allow fusion to happen inside it.

Diameter:
1,392,684 km

Sun

⊢ 10,000 km ⊣

5 Dwarf planets*

WITH 8 MOONS*

In August 2006, scientists declared a new class of planet after a number of celestial bodies around the same size as Pluto were discovered. This resulted in Pluto's »demotion« from planetary status to a »dwarf planet«. These planets follow the same rules as regular planets, but their gravitational force does not absorb or repel surrounding objects. Until now, the IAU has accepted five dwarf planets as being part of our solar system.

2,390 km
Pluto
2,326 km
Eris
2,200 km
Haumea
1,502 km
Makemake
975 km
Ceres

Countless meteoroids

The IAU vaguely defines these celestial bodies as »significantly bigger than an atom but significantly smaller than an asteroid«. Their number is unknown. Every day, countless *meteoroids* burn up in the atmosphere as *meteors*. We see them either as *shooting stars* or *fireballs*. If one makes it to the Earth's surface, we call it a *meteorite*.

8 Planets

WITH 173 MOONS*

According to the International Astronomical Union (IAU), an object has to fulfill the following criteria in order to be classified as a »planet«:

- It is in orbit around a star.
- It has sufficient mass to assume hydrostatic equilibrium (a nearly round shape).
- Its gravitational force has either absorbed or repelled surrounding objects, it has »cleared the neighborhood« around its orbit.

142,984 km
120,536 km
51,118 km
49,528 km
12,742 km
12,103 km
6,792 km
4,879 km
moons
Jupiter
Saturn
Uranus
Neptune
Earth
Venus
Mars
Mercury

618,638 Asteroids*
4,894 Comets*

WITH 163 MOONS*

Asteroids and *comets* do not have enough mass to form a round shape. *Comets* consist of frozen, volatile substances. These melt in close proximity to the sun, separate from the *comet* in the solar wind and form a tail. *Asteroids* are made of harder material.

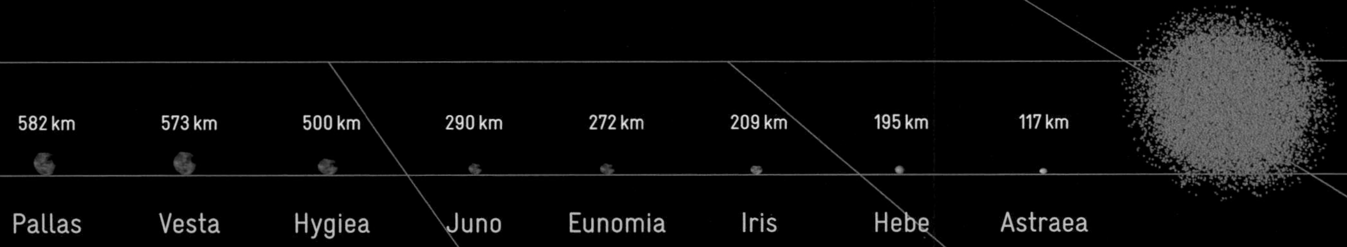

582 km
573 km
500 km
290 km
272 km
209 km
195 km
117 km
Pallas
Vesta
Hygiea
Juno
Eunomia
Iris
Hebe
Astraea

* as of August 2013

INVERTED WORLD

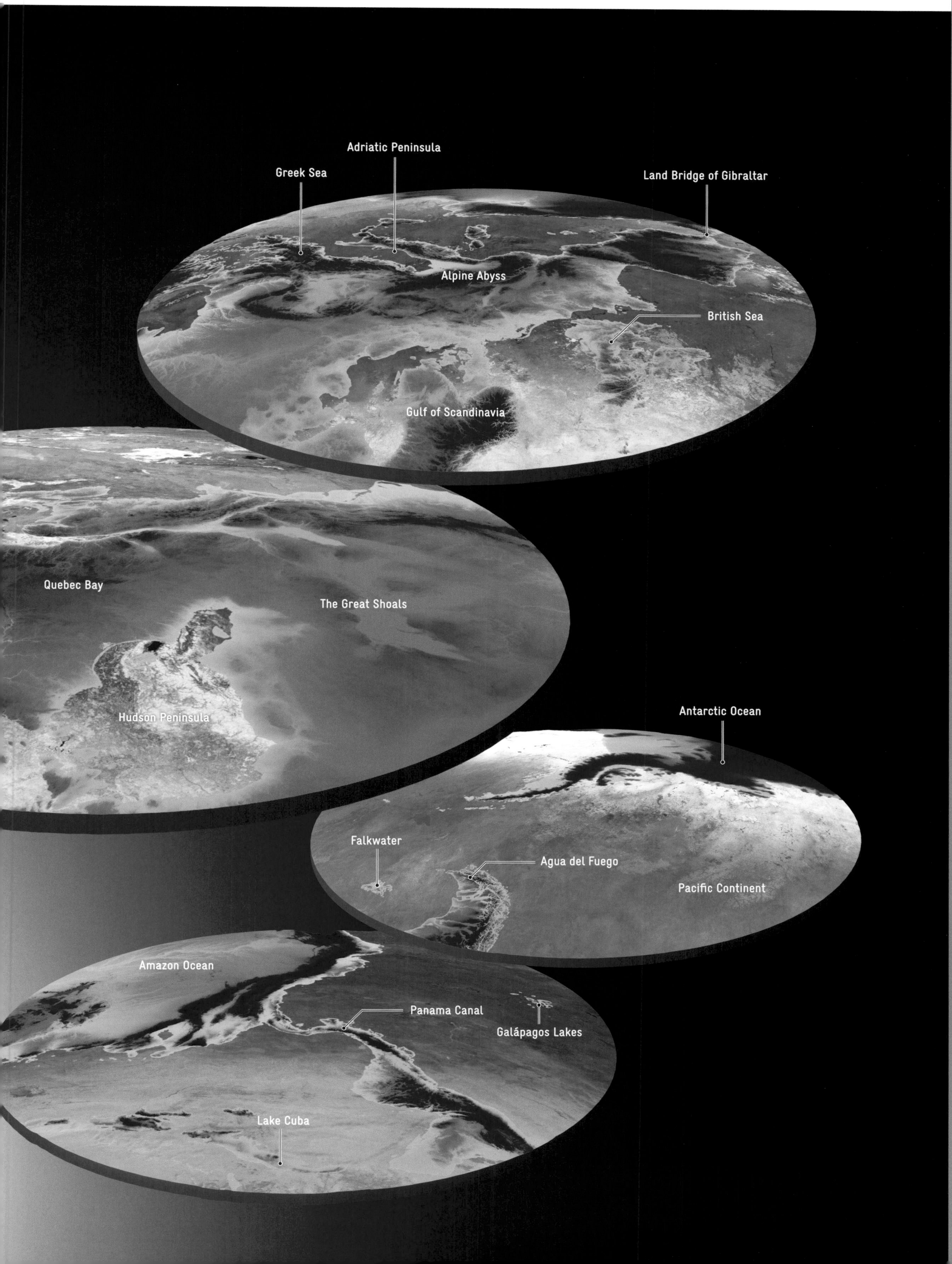
Adriatic Peninsula
Greek Sea
Land Bridge of Gibraltar
Alpine Abyss
British Sea
Gulf of Scandinavia
Quebec Bay
The Great Shoals
Hudson Peninsula
Antarctic Ocean
Falkwater
Agua del Fuego
Pacific Continent
Amazon Ocean
Panama Canal
Galápagos Lakes
Lake Cuba

REARRANGING THE WORLD

The way the world looks today is kind of a fluke—what if our planet's continents didn't drift? What if you saw a country not as a single, independent entity, but as a member of a community? Data visualization and infographics allow us to create new perspectives. By applying that principle, we suddenly see geography as something that is pliable and changeable—inviting us to see the world in a new light.

LET IT FLOW

A river is defined by so much more than length. By looking at them in the same shape defined by their length, we can better see their varying structures. For example, the Nile and the Amazon are similar in length but if they were measured by the amount of water they sent to the sea, the Egyptian river would be a trickle compared to the gush of the Amazon.

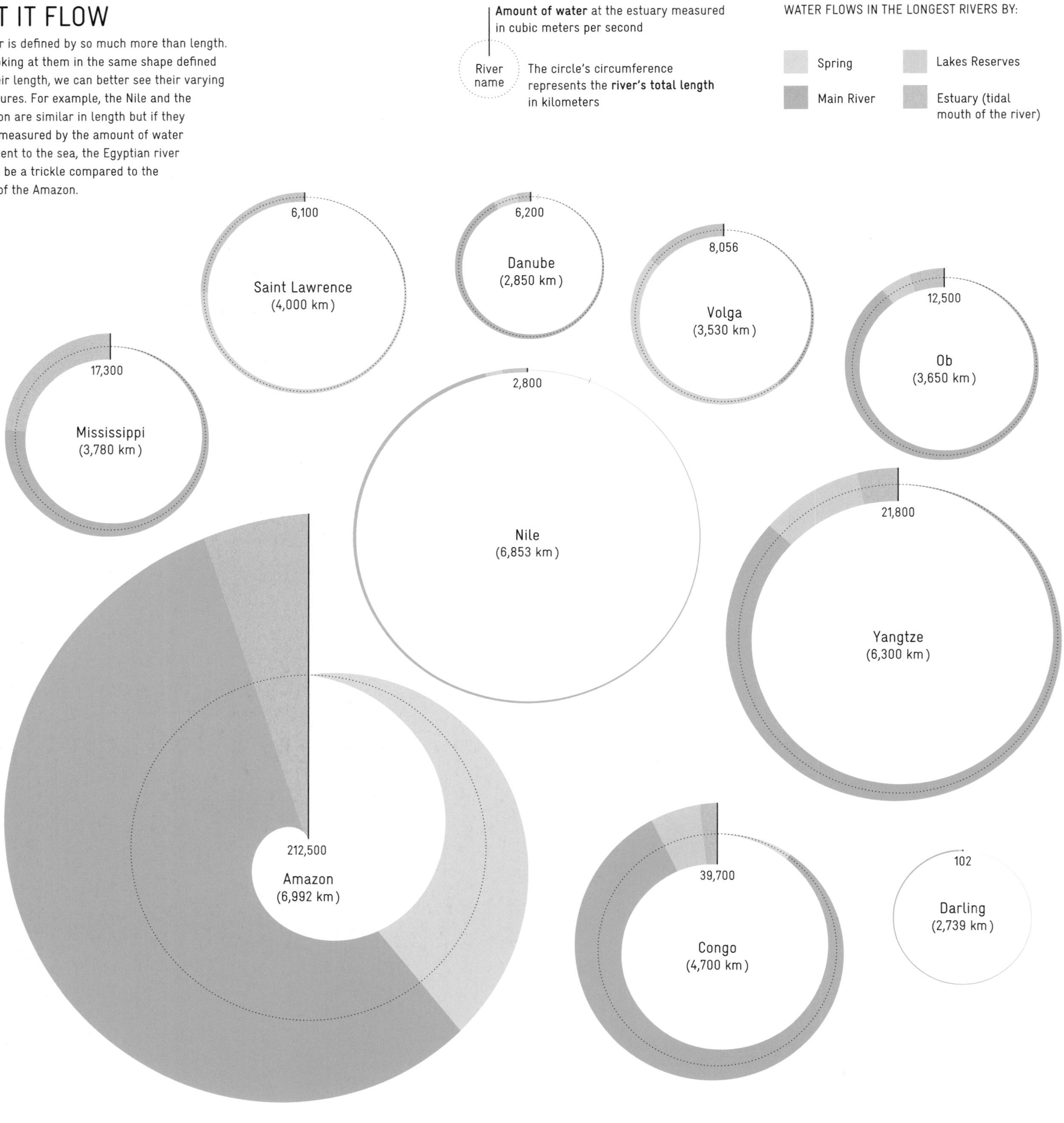
Amount of water at the estuary measured in cubic meters per second
River name
The circle's circumference represents the **river's total length** in kilometers
WATER FLOWS IN THE LONGEST RIVERS BY:
Spring
Lakes Reserves
Main River
Estuary (tidal mouth of the river)
6,100
Saint Lawrence (4,000 km)
6,200
Danube (2,850 km)
8,056
Volga (3,530 km)
12,500
Ob (3,650 km)
17,300
Mississippi (3,780 km)
2,800
Nile (6,853 km)
21,800
Yangtze (6,300 km)
212,500
Amazon (6,992 km)
39,700
Congo (4,700 km)
102
Darling (2,739 km)

ALL THE GRAPHICS WAS PUBLISHED IN GEO MAGAZINE, GERMANY, 2010/2011

NEIGHBORHOOD

Each country and their geographical neighbors.

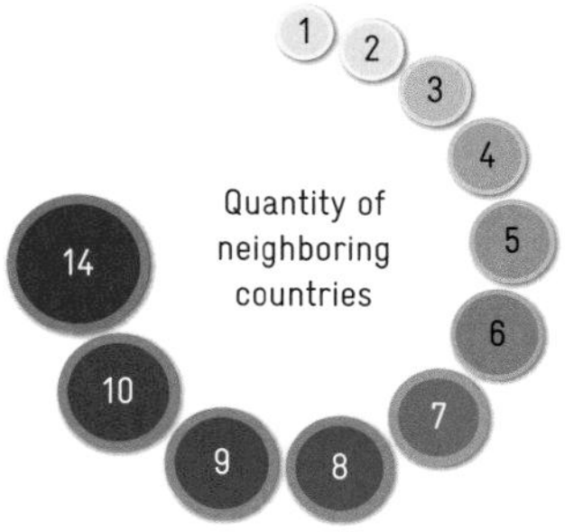

By visualizing countries as a series of connections, we can visualize the density of each continent's network. Lines are drawn between neighbors that share a common border. China, Russia, Brazil and Germany are the most neighborly countries in the world.

* exception: the Russian oblast Kaliningrad.
Abbreviations: ISO standard 3166

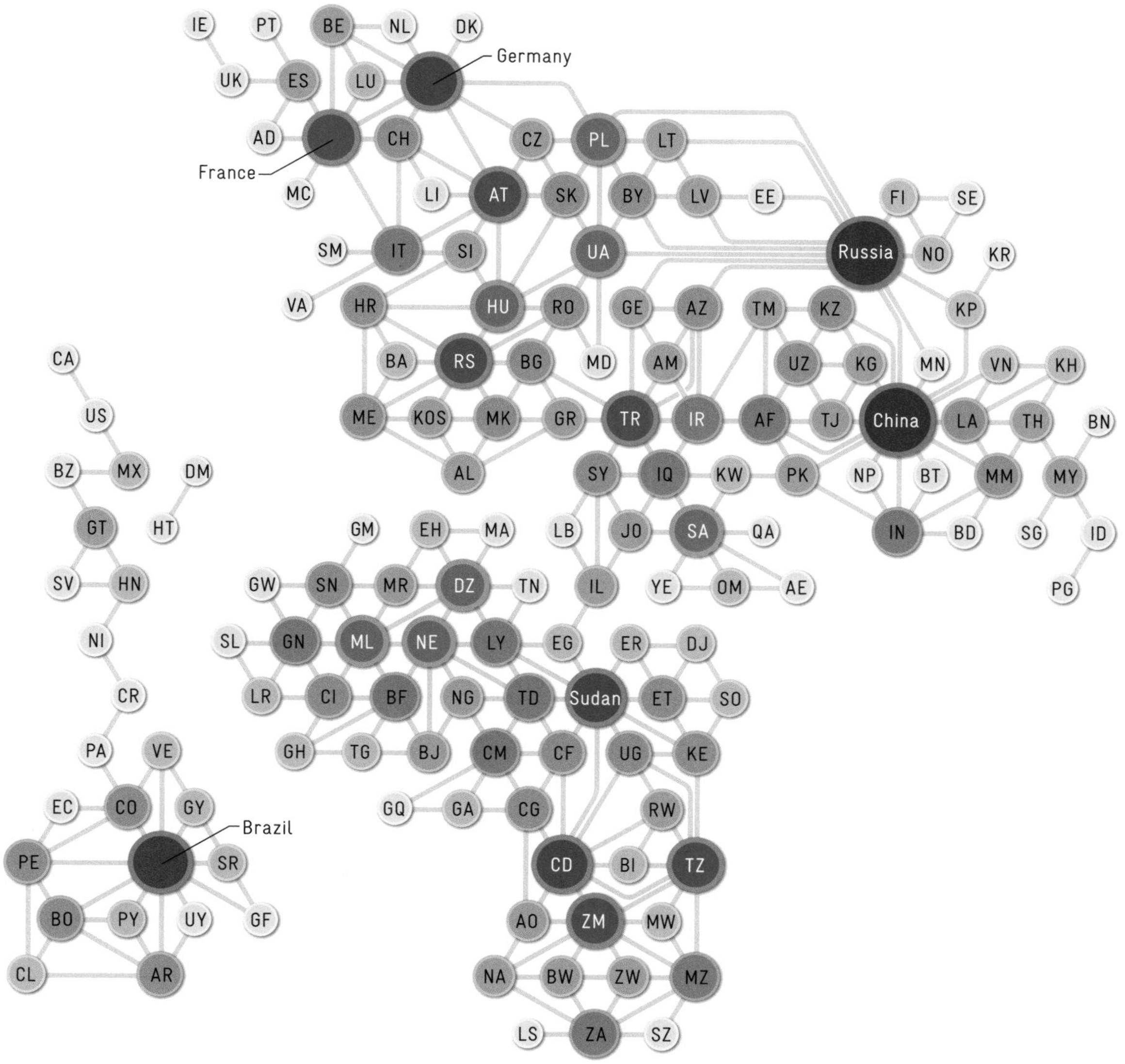

WANDERING CITIES

A future vision of continental drift.

The continents are in constant motion. Geologists believe that the lithosphere plates will continue to change the way the Earth looks over the next millions of years. In 50 million years, scientists claim that the Mediterranean Sea will disappear as Africa and Europe merge. Australia will join the islands of South East Asia. The Americas will drift further away from Europe, expanding the Atlantic Ocean and eventually merging on the Pacific coast. This will put Dakar near the tip of Greenland and make Las Vegas part of Brazil in 250 million years.

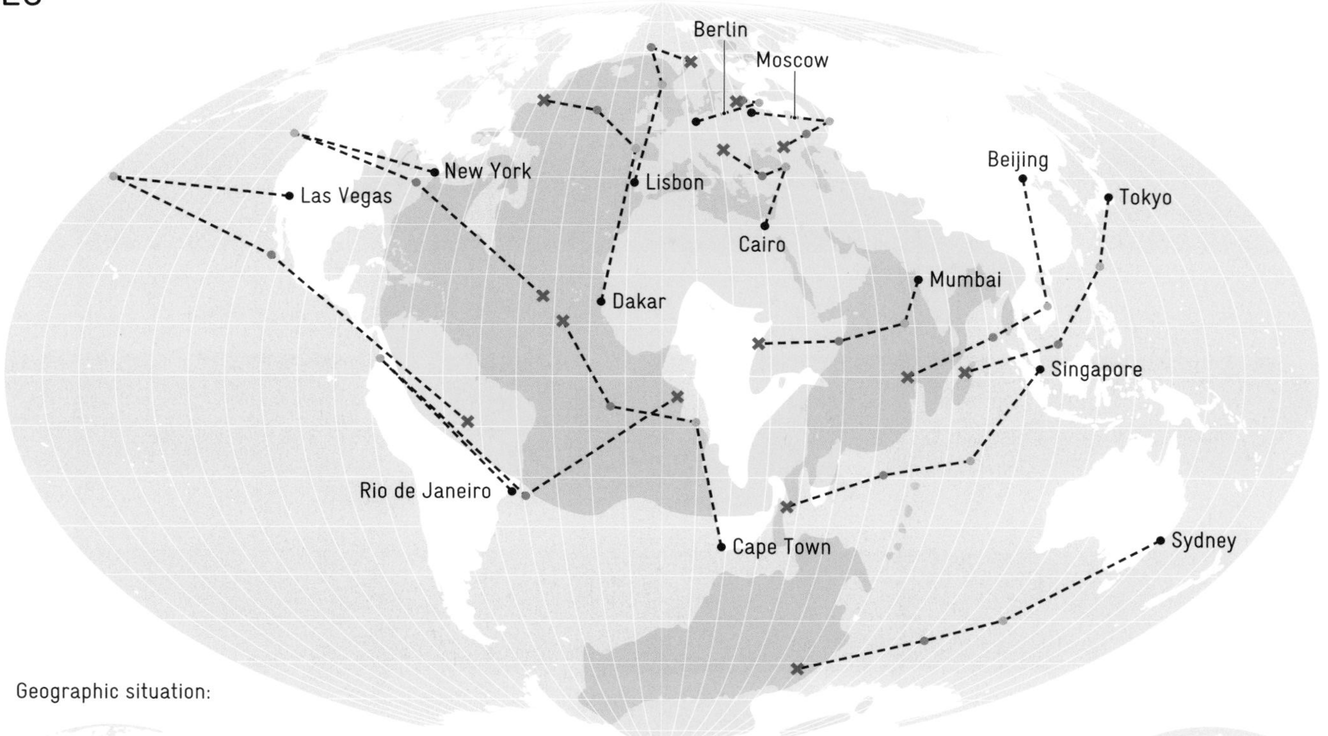

Geographic situation:

COMPOSITE CONTINENT

All land masses together by latitude and land use.

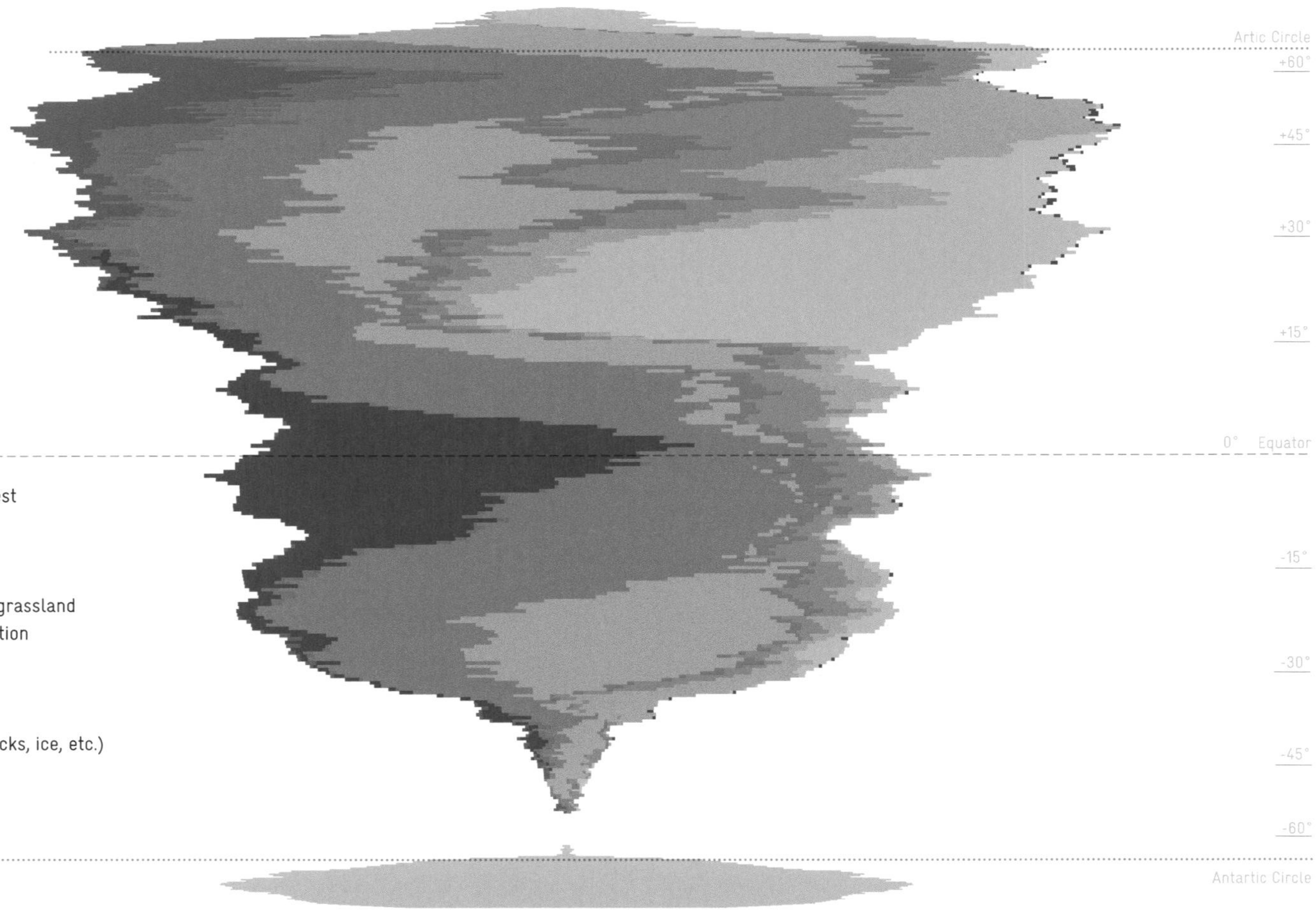

Artic Circle
+60°
+45°
+30°
+15°
0° Equator
-15°
-30°
-45°
-60°
Antartic Circle

- Taiga and coniferous forest
- Deciduous forest
- Tropical rainforest
- Mix forest/woodland
- Light forest and wooded grassland
- Tundras and bush vegetation
- Inland waters
- Grasslands and steppes
- Arable land
- Barren areas (deserts, rocks, ice, etc.)
- Urban development

TAKING THE STRAIGHT WAY AROUND

Fancy a trip around the world? Follow the path of Enrique Melaka, who is considered to have been the first person to circumnavigate the world as Fernando Magellan's slave interpreter in 1519.

If following in his wake is too much of a detour, you could opt for a direct route. You can visit major cities, avoid humanity all together or take the path that will allow you to conquer peaks and valleys on three continents.

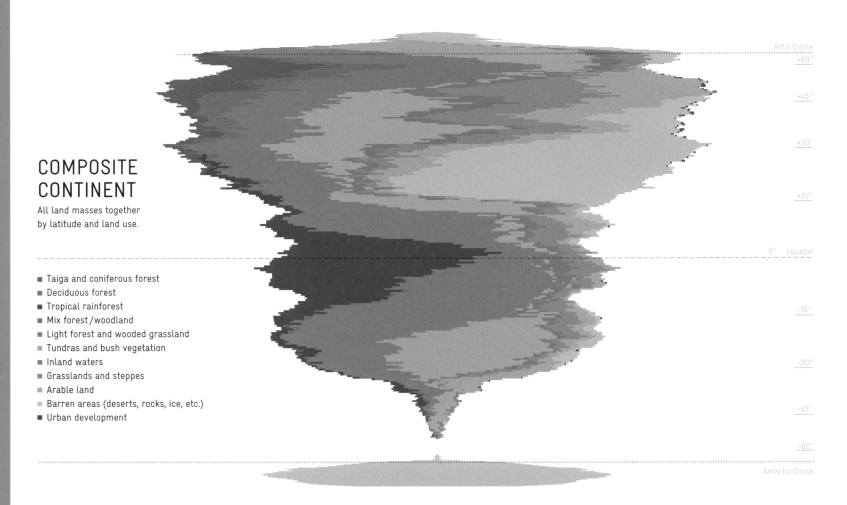

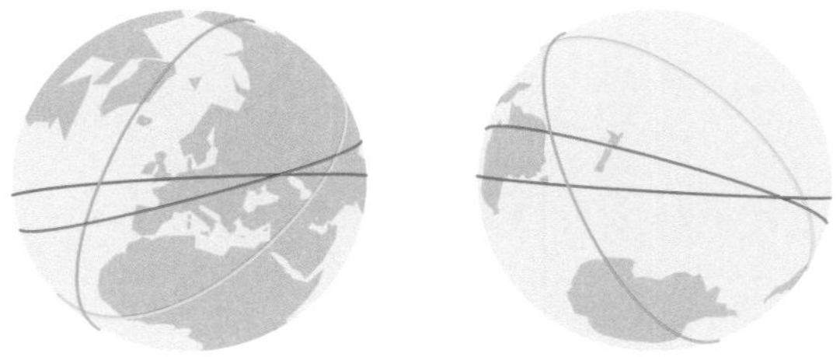

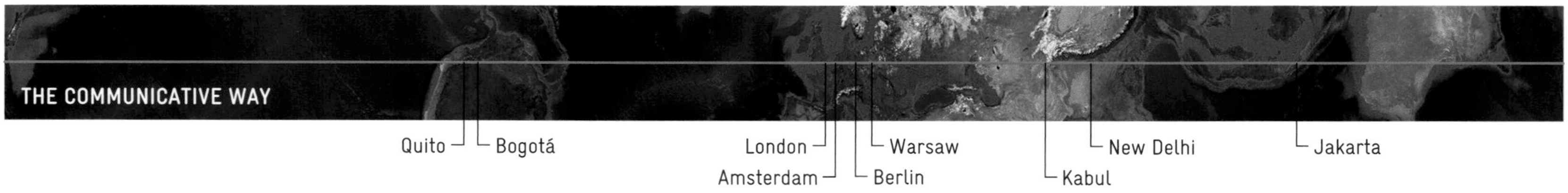

THE COMMUNICATIVE WAY
Quito
Bogotá
London
Amsterdam
Warsaw
Berlin
Kabul
New Delhi
Jakarta

THE LONELY WAY
Antarctic
Cape Verde
Jan Mayen
Siberia
Solomon Islands

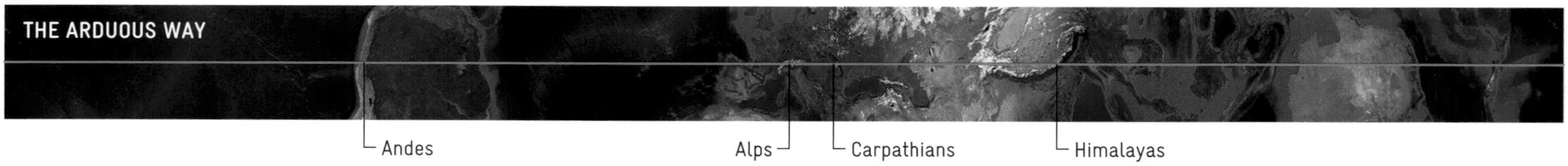

THE ARDUOUS WAY
Andes
Alps
Carpathians
Himalayas

THE DRY WAY
Suez
Uzbekistan
Caspian Sea
Zhejiang

(IS)LAND MASS

If the 100 largest islands in the world were to form a single continent, it would be 6.8 million square kilometers, according to a ranking of land area by the United Nations Environment Program (UNEP). That's about 80% of Brazil's landmass.
Which islands have you been to?

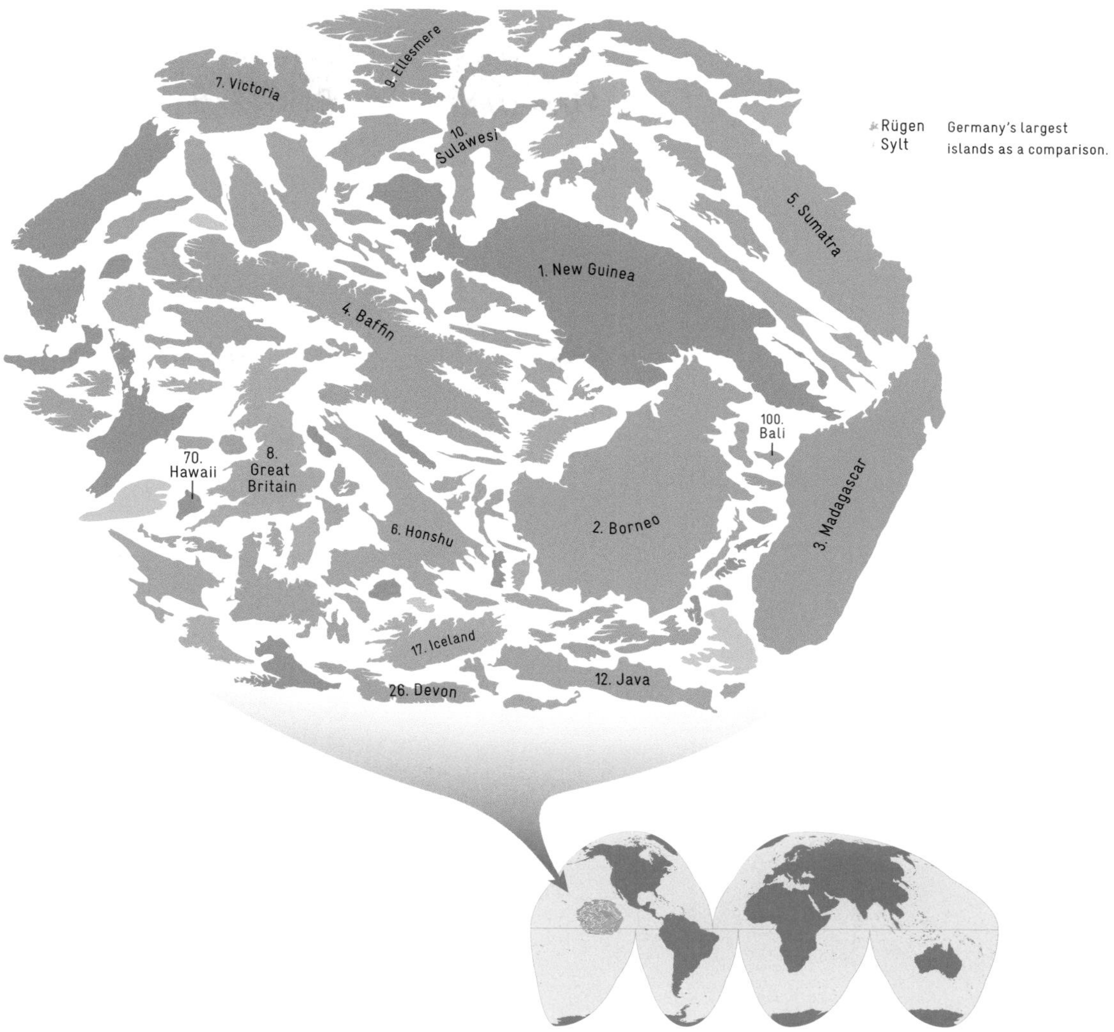
7. Victoria
9. Ellesmere
10. Sulawesi
5. Sumatra
1. New Guinea
4. Baffin
100. Bali
70. Hawaii
8. Great Britain
6. Honshu
2. Borneo
3. Madagascar
17. Iceland
12. Java
26. Devon
Rügen
Sylt
Germany's largest islands as a comparison.

Colors denote each island's continent of origin:

- Asia
- North America and Caribbean
- Europe
- Oceania and Australia
- South America
- Antarctica
- Africa
- None

COASTLESS COUNTRIES

Turning landlocked countries into islands

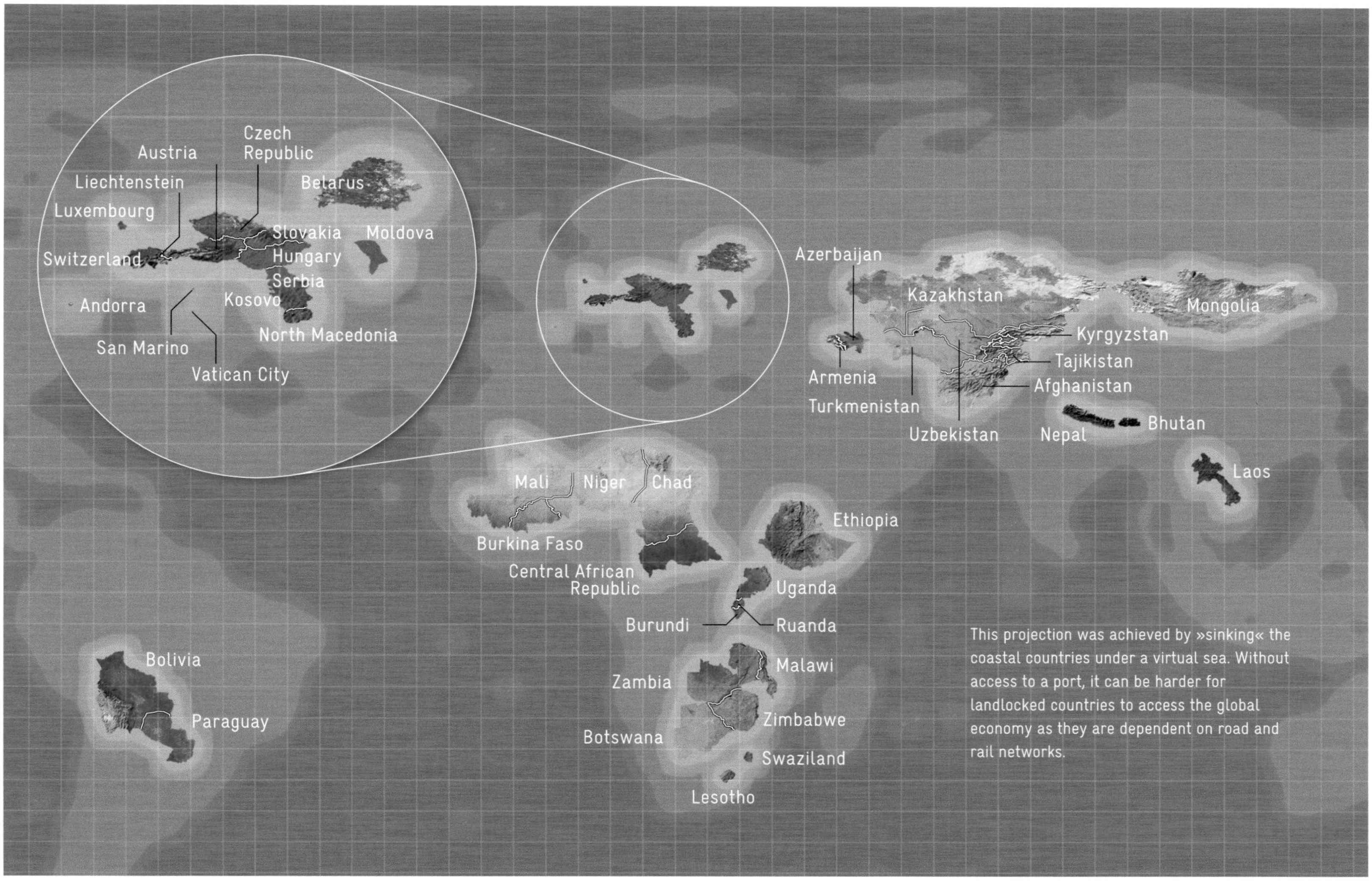
Austria
Czech Republic
Liechtenstein
Belarus
Luxembourg
Slovakia
Moldova
Switzerland
Hungary
Serbia
Andorra
Kosovo
North Macedonia
San Marino
Vatican City
Azerbaijan
Kazakhstan
Mongolia
Kyrgyzstan
Tajikistan
Armenia
Afghanistan
Turkmenistan
Bhutan
Uzbekistan
Nepal
Laos
Mali
Niger
Chad
Ethiopia
Burkina Faso
Central African Republic
Uganda
Burundi
Ruanda
Malawi
Zambia
Zimbabwe
Botswana
Swaziland
Lesotho
Bolivia
Paraguay

This projection was achieved by »sinking« the coastal countries under a virtual sea. Without access to a port, it can be harder for landlocked countries to access the global economy as they are dependent on road and rail networks.

FRAMING THE WORLD

There are about 400 different ways to represent the world on a map, but which one is the most accurate? Trying to fit a 3D object into a 2D frame inevitably distorts the image—and there have been many great minds who have tried to solve this problem.

likely Marinus of Tyre
PLATE CARRÉE
Equirectangular projection is one of the most important projections today and best used in thematic mapping
100 AD

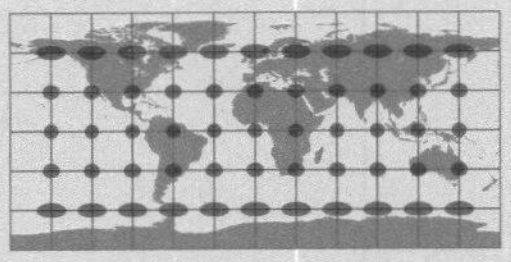

Roger Bacon
BACON GLOBULAR ◉
1265

CYLINDRICAL PROJECTION

Normal or polar aspect cylindrical projections have equally spaced meridians. The parallels are straight lines as well.

AZIMUTHAL PROJECTION

Azimuthal projections fix on one point on the Earth and project directly onto a plane. In normal presentation, the meridians are straight lines and the parallels are concentric circles.

originator unknown
○ **GNOMONIC PROJECTION**
ancient; no exact date known

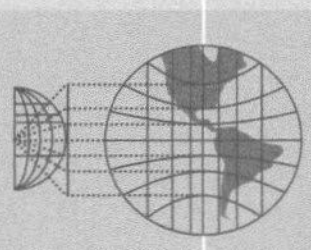

likely Hipparchus
STEREOGRAPHIC PROJECTION
ca. 150 BC

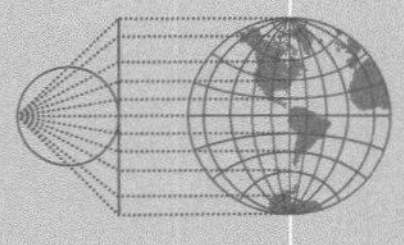

Hipparchus
○ **ORTHOGRAPHIC PROJECTION**
2nd century BC

al-Bīrūnī
POLYCONIC GLOBULAR ⊙
Later known due to Nicolosi
1000 AD

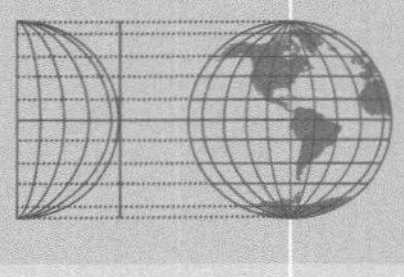

CONIC PROJECTION

The Earth's surface is projected onto a cone. In normal presentation, the meridians are shown as straight lines and the parallels as arcs of circles.

Ptolemy
○ **PTOLEMY I**
ca. 90–170 AD

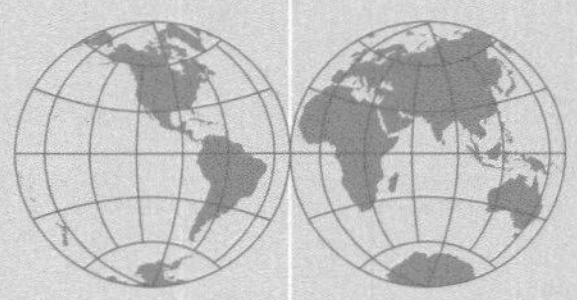

ISIDORE OF SEVILLE ○
Developed T-O map
(printed in 1472)
ca. 600 AD

○ **AL-IDRISI**
World map with
south side on top
12th century

M. Behaim
BEHAIM GLOBE ○
First globe
1492

○ **PYTHAGORAS**
Probably the first to realize
that the Earth is a globe
ca. 500 BC

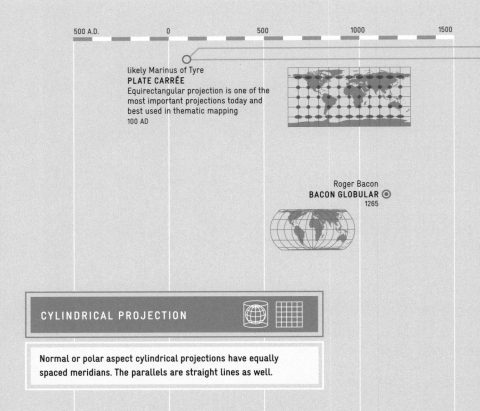

A. Walsperger
SCALE ○
First map with
graphical scale
1448

○ **ERATOSTHENES**
First historically confirmed
measurement of the Earth
ca. 200 BC

KEY

- - Same projection with
different originator
— Altered projection

● Pseudo-projection or
modified projection
▪ Polyconic
○ Further events

PROPERTIES

✗ Conformal
◇ Equal area
○ Neither conformal nor equal area

ASPECT

(example: azimuthal)

Polar/normal

Transverse/equatorial

Oblique

TISSOT'S INDICATRIX

● Circles/ellipses
showing distortion
of projection

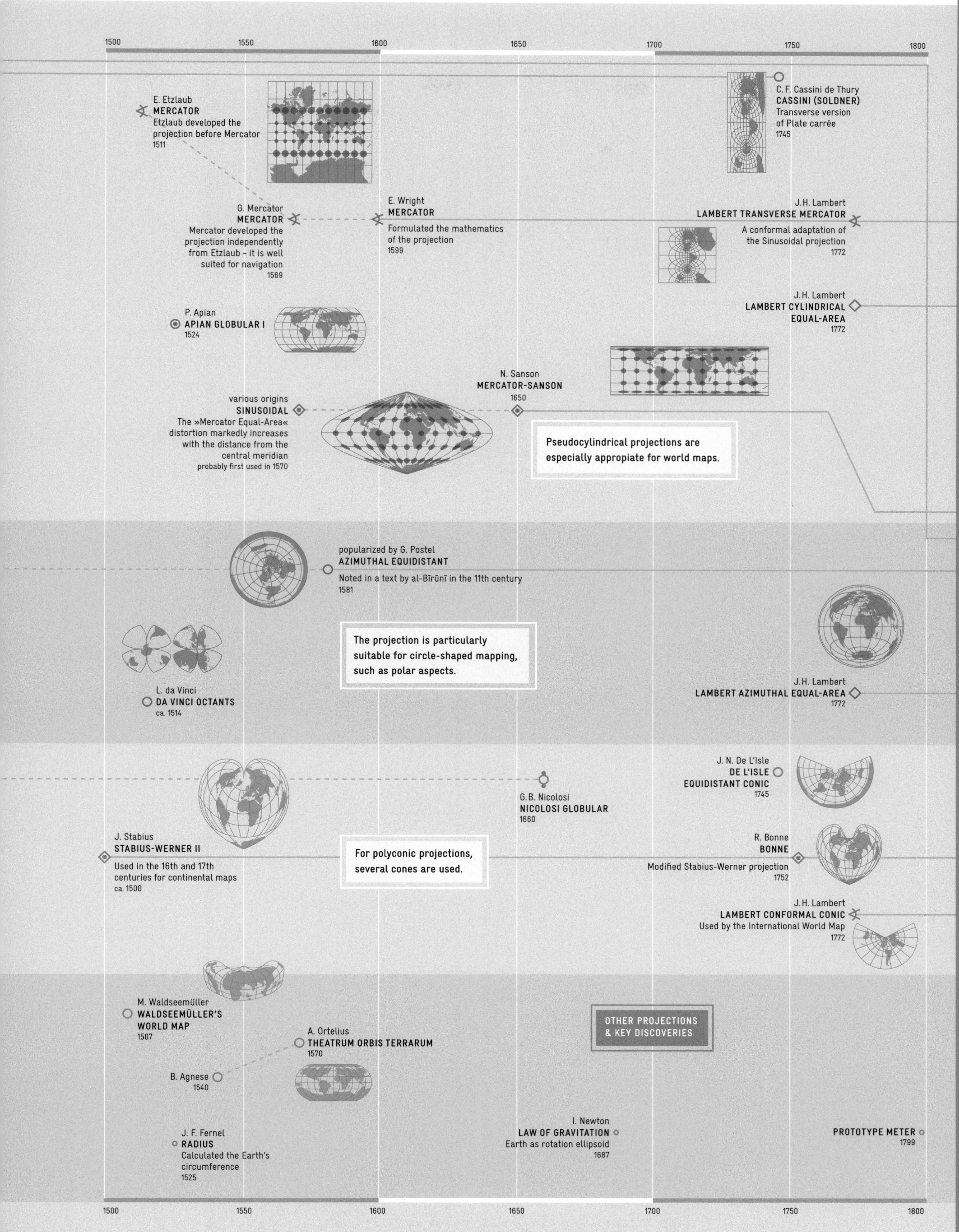
1500
1550
1600
1650
1700
1750
1800
E. Etzlaub
MERCATOR
Etzlaub developed the projection before Mercator
1511
C. F. Cassini de Thury
CASSINI (SOLDNER)
Transverse version of Plate carrée
1745
G. Mercator
MERCATOR
Mercator developed the projection independently from Etzlaub – it is well suited for navigation
1569
E. Wright
MERCATOR
Formulated the mathematics of the projection
1599
J.H. Lambert
LAMBERT TRANSVERSE MERCATOR
A conformal adaptation of the Sinusoidal projection
1772
J.H. Lambert
LAMBERT CYLINDRICAL EQUAL-AREA
1772
P. Apian
APIAN GLOBULAR I
1524
N. Sanson
MERCATOR-SANSON
1650
various origins
SINUSOIDAL
The »Mercator Equal-Area« distortion markedly increases with the distance from the central meridian
probably first used in 1570
Pseudocylindrical projections are especially appropiate for world maps.
popularized by G. Postel
AZIMUTHAL EQUIDISTANT
Noted in a text by al-Bīrūnī in the 11th century
1581
The projection is particularly suitable for circle-shaped mapping, such as polar aspects.
L. da Vinci
DA VINCI OCTANTS
ca. 1514
J.H. Lambert
LAMBERT AZIMUTHAL EQUAL-AREA
1772
J. N. De L'Isle
DE L'ISLE EQUIDISTANT CONIC
1745
G.B. Nicolosi
NICOLOSI GLOBULAR
1660
J. Stabius
STABIUS-WERNER II
Used in the 16th and 17th centuries for continental maps
ca. 1500
For polyconic projections, several cones are used.
R. Bonne
BONNE
Modified Stabius-Werner projection
1752
J.H. Lambert
LAMBERT CONFORMAL CONIC
Used by the International World Map
1772
M. Waldseemüller
WALDSEEMÜLLER'S WORLD MAP
1507
OTHER PROJECTIONS & KEY DISCOVERIES
A. Ortelius
THEATRUM ORBIS TERRARUM
1570
B. Agnese
1540
J. F. Fernel
RADIUS
Calculated the Earth's circumference
1525
I. Newton
LAW OF GRAVITATION
Earth as rotation ellipsoid
1687
PROTOTYPE METER
1799
1500
1550
1600
1650
1700
1750
1800

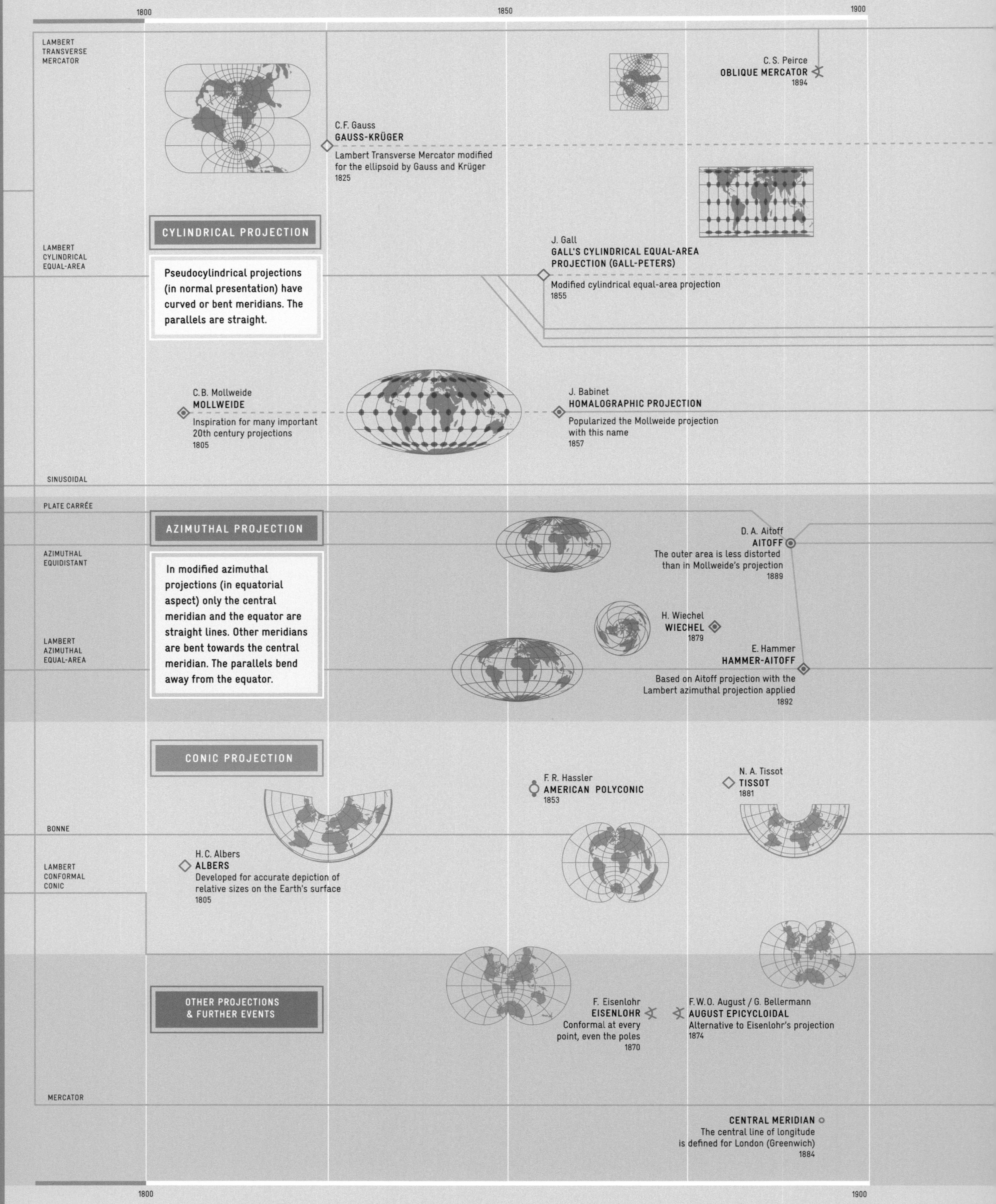
1800
1850
1900
LAMBERT TRANSVERSE MERCATOR
C.S. Peirce
OBLIQUE MERCATOR
1894
C.F. Gauss
GAUSS-KRÜGER
Lambert Transverse Mercator modified for the ellipsoid by Gauss and Krüger
1825
CYLINDRICAL PROJECTION
LAMBERT CYLINDRICAL EQUAL-AREA
Pseudocylindrical projections (in normal presentation) have curved or bent meridians. The parallels are straight.
J. Gall
GALL'S CYLINDRICAL EQUAL-AREA PROJECTION (GALL-PETERS)
Modified cylindrical equal-area projection
1855
C.B. Mollweide
MOLLWEIDE
Inspiration for many important 20th century projections
1805
J. Babinet
HOMALOGRAPHIC PROJECTION
Popularized the Mollweide projection with this name
1857
SINUSOIDAL
PLATE CARRÉE
AZIMUTHAL PROJECTION
AZIMUTHAL EQUIDISTANT
In modified azimuthal projections (in equatorial aspect) only the central meridian and the equator are straight lines. Other meridians are bent towards the central meridian. The parallels bend away from the equator.
D. A. Aitoff
AITOFF
The outer area is less distorted than in Mollweide's projection
1889
LAMBERT AZIMUTHAL EQUAL-AREA
H. Wiechel
WIECHEL
1879
E. Hammer
HAMMER-AITOFF
Based on Aitoff projection with the Lambert azimuthal projection applied
1892
CONIC PROJECTION
F. R. Hassler
AMERICAN POLYCONIC
1853
N. A. Tissot
TISSOT
1881
BONNE
H.C. Albers
ALBERS
Developed for accurate depiction of relative sizes on the Earth's surface
1805
LAMBERT CONFORMAL CONIC
OTHER PROJECTIONS & FURTHER EVENTS
F. Eisenlohr
EISENLOHR
Conformal at every point, even the poles
1870
F.W.O. August / G. Bellermann
AUGUST EPICYCLOIDAL
Alternative to Eisenlohr's projection
1874
MERCATOR
CENTRAL MERIDIAN
The central line of longitude is defined for London (Greenwich)
1884
1800
1900

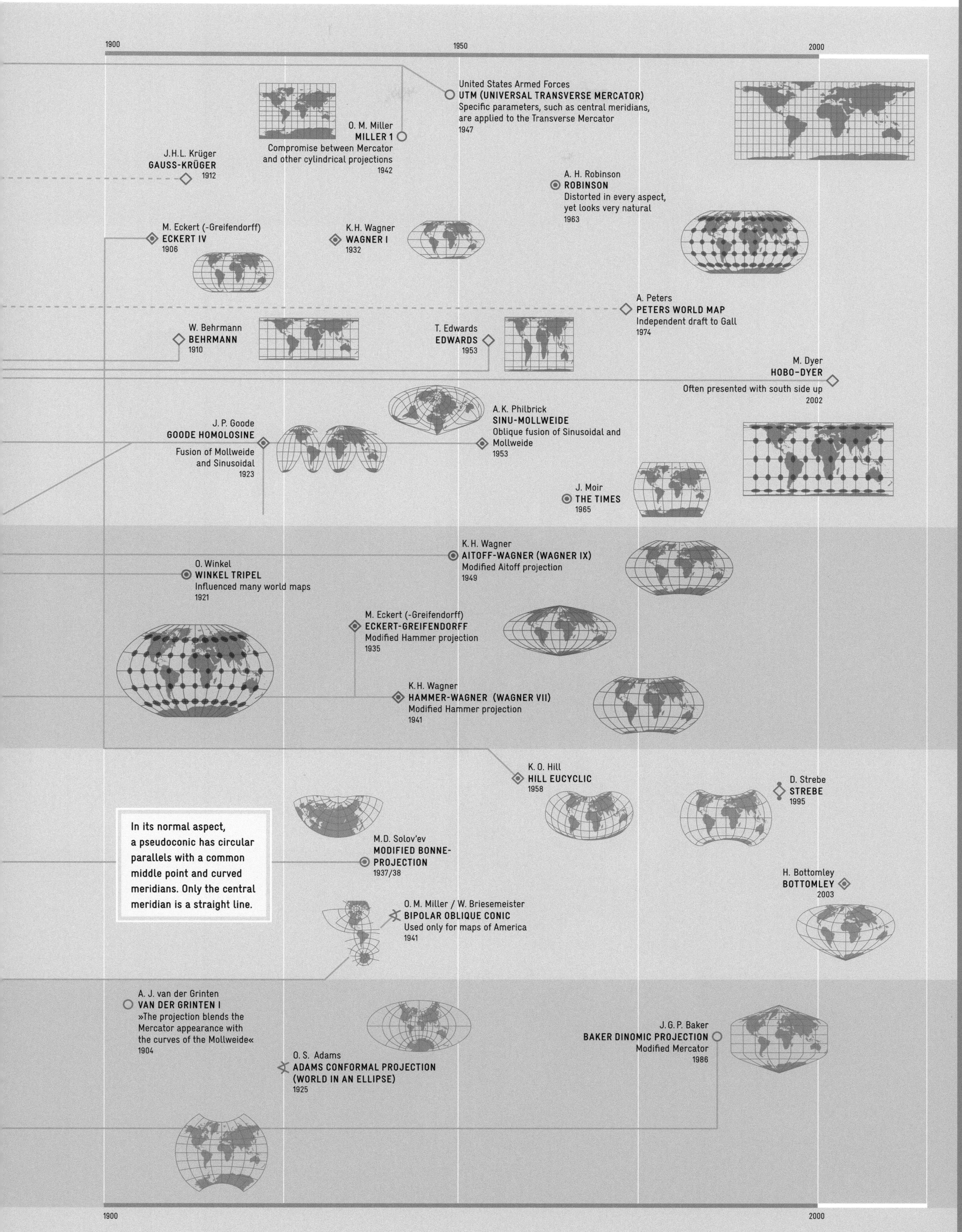
1900
1950
2000
United States Armed Forces
UTM (UNIVERSAL TRANSVERSE MERCATOR)
Specific parameters, such as central meridians, are applied to the Transverse Mercator
1947
O. M. Miller
MILLER 1
Compromise between Mercator and other cylindrical projections
1942
J.H.L. Krüger
GAUSS-KRÜGER
1912
A. H. Robinson
ROBINSON
Distorted in every aspect, yet looks very natural
1963
M. Eckert (-Greifendorff)
ECKERT IV
1906
K.H. Wagner
WAGNER I
1932
A. Peters
PETERS WORLD MAP
Independent draft to Gall
1974
W. Behrmann
BEHRMANN
1910
T. Edwards
EDWARDS
1953
M. Dyer
HOBO-DYER
Often presented with south side up
2002
A.K. Philbrick
SINU-MOLLWEIDE
Oblique fusion of Sinusoidal and Mollweide
1953
J. P. Goode
GOODE HOMOLOSINE
Fusion of Mollweide and Sinusoidal
1923
J. Moir
THE TIMES
1965
K.H. Wagner
AITOFF-WAGNER (WAGNER IX)
Modified Aitoff projection
1949
O. Winkel
WINKEL TRIPEL
Influenced many world maps
1921
M. Eckert (-Greifendorff)
ECKERT-GREIFENDORFF
Modified Hammer projection
1935
K.H. Wagner
HAMMER-WAGNER (WAGNER VII)
Modified Hammer projection
1941
K. O. Hill
HILL EUCYCLIC
1958
D. Strebe
STREBE
1995
In its normal aspect, a pseudoconic has circular parallels with a common middle point and curved meridians. Only the central meridian is a straight line.
M.D. Solov'ev
MODIFIED BONNE-PROJECTION
1937/38
H. Bottomley
BOTTOMLEY
2003
O. M. Miller / W. Briesemeister
BIPOLAR OBLIQUE CONIC
Used only for maps of America
1941
A. J. van der Grinten
VAN DER GRINTEN I
»The projection blends the Mercator appearance with the curves of the Mollweide«
1904
J. G. P. Baker
BAKER DINOMIC PROJECTION
Modified Mercator
1986
O. S. Adams
ADAMS CONFORMAL PROJECTION (WORLD IN AN ELLIPSE)
1925
1900
2000

AN ISLAND WITH A LAKE ...

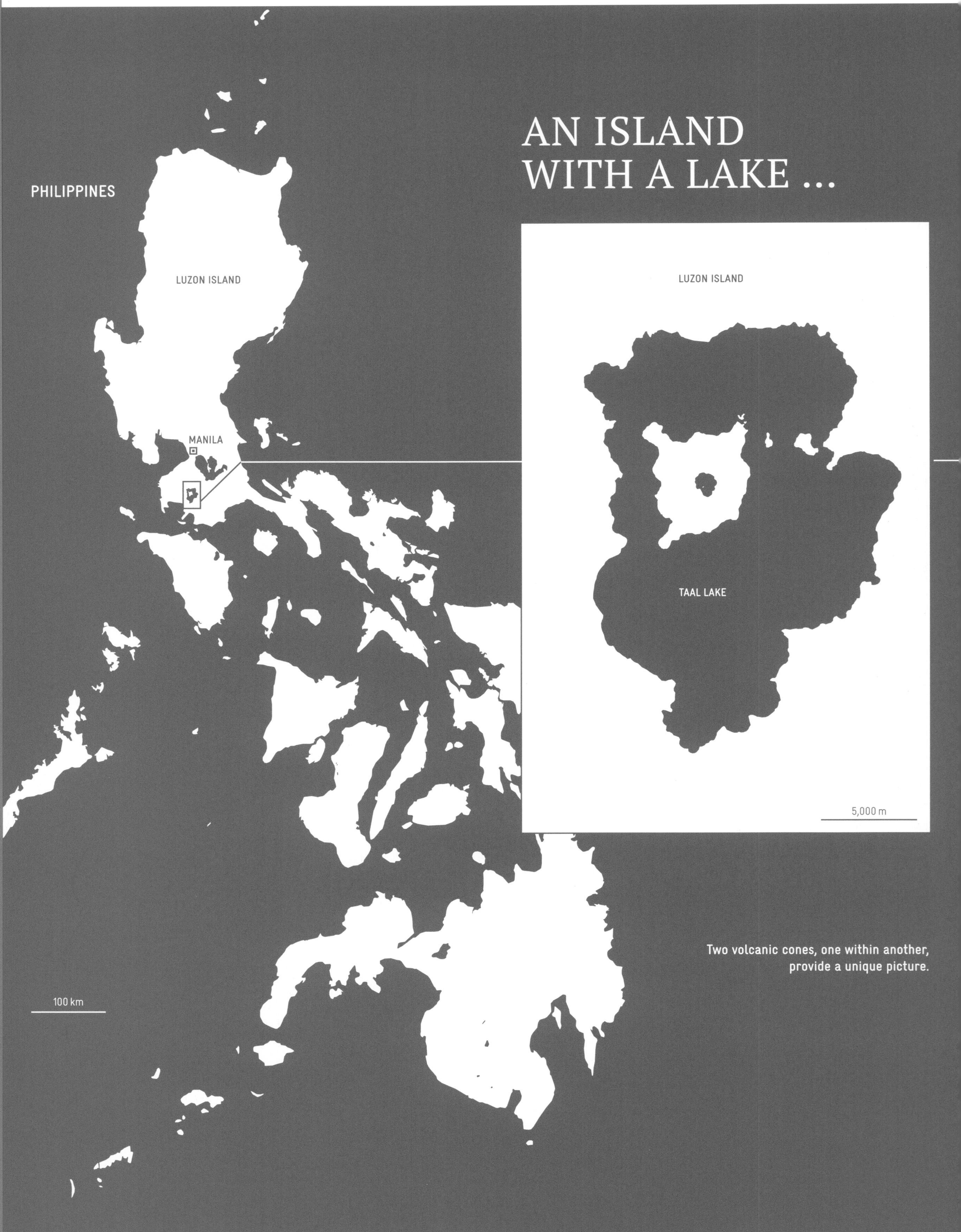
PHILIPPINES
LUZON ISLAND
MANILA
100 km
LUZON ISLAND
TAAL LAKE
5,000 m

Two volcanic cones, one within another, provide a unique picture.

... WITH AN ISLAND WITH A LAKE ...

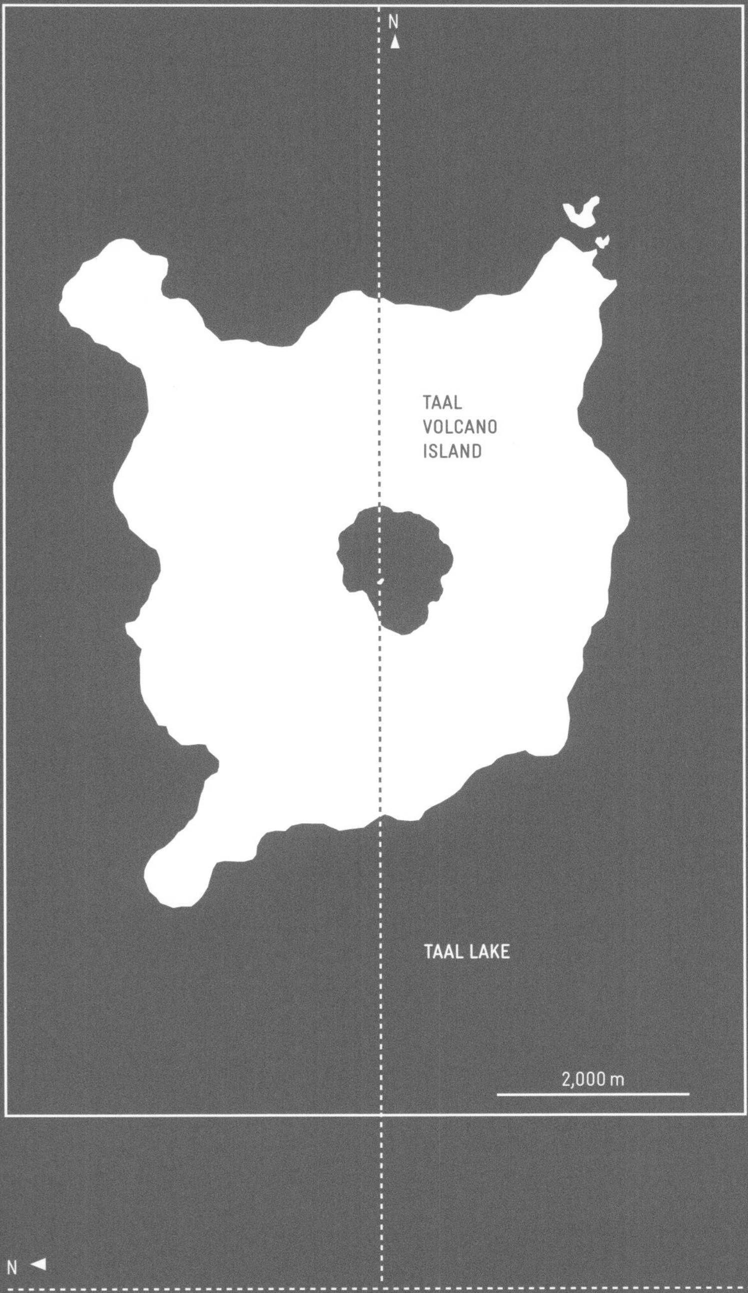

... WITH A TINY ISLAND

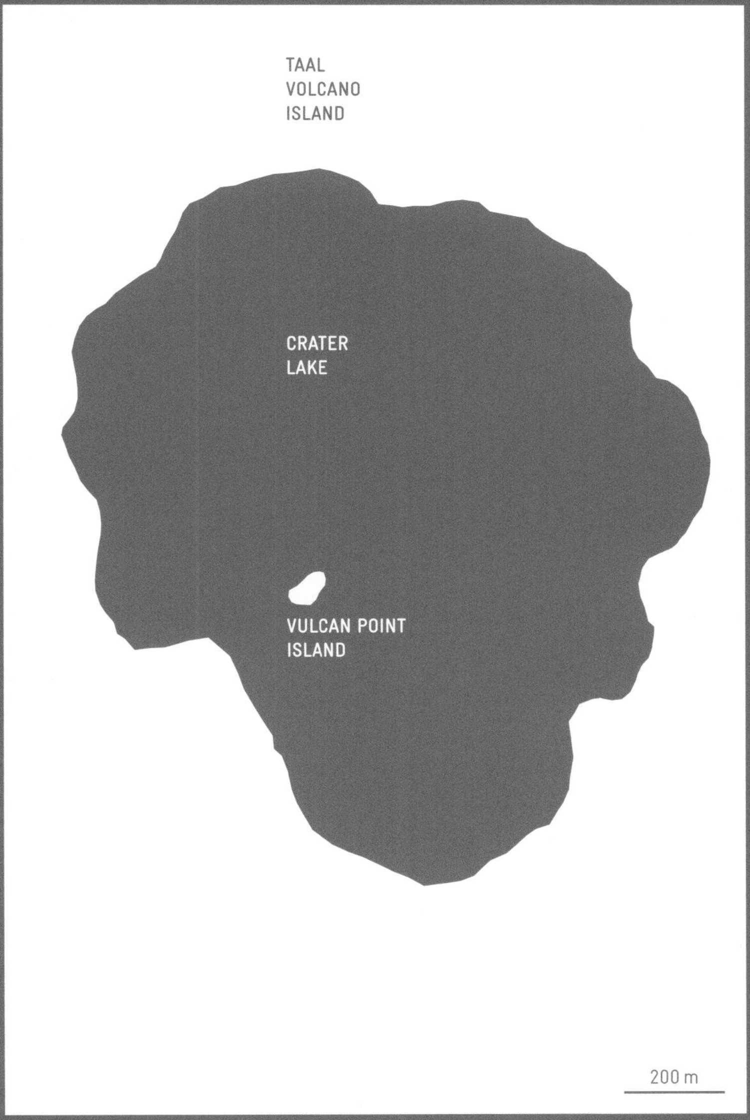

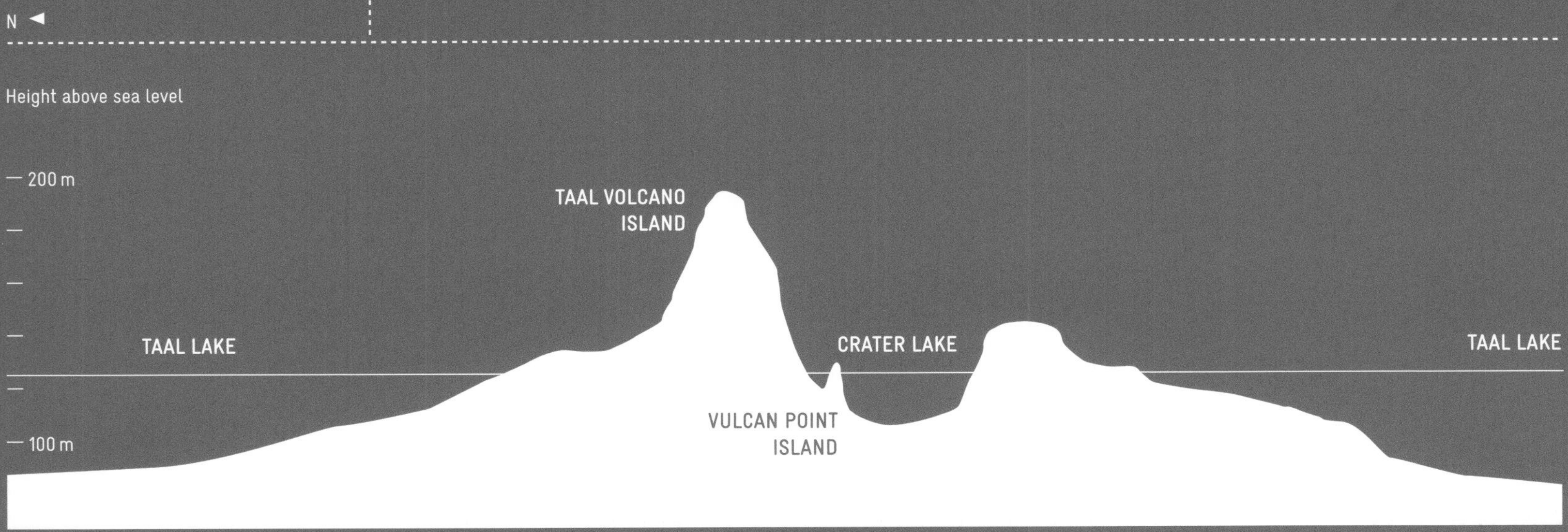

ALPINE PEAKS

The Alps formed when the African and Eurasian tectonic plates collided 65 million years ago—as Tyrannosaurus Rex wandered the Earth. Today, eight European countries can claim some part of the 612-peak range, which is crowned by Mount Blanc at a height of 4,808 meters.

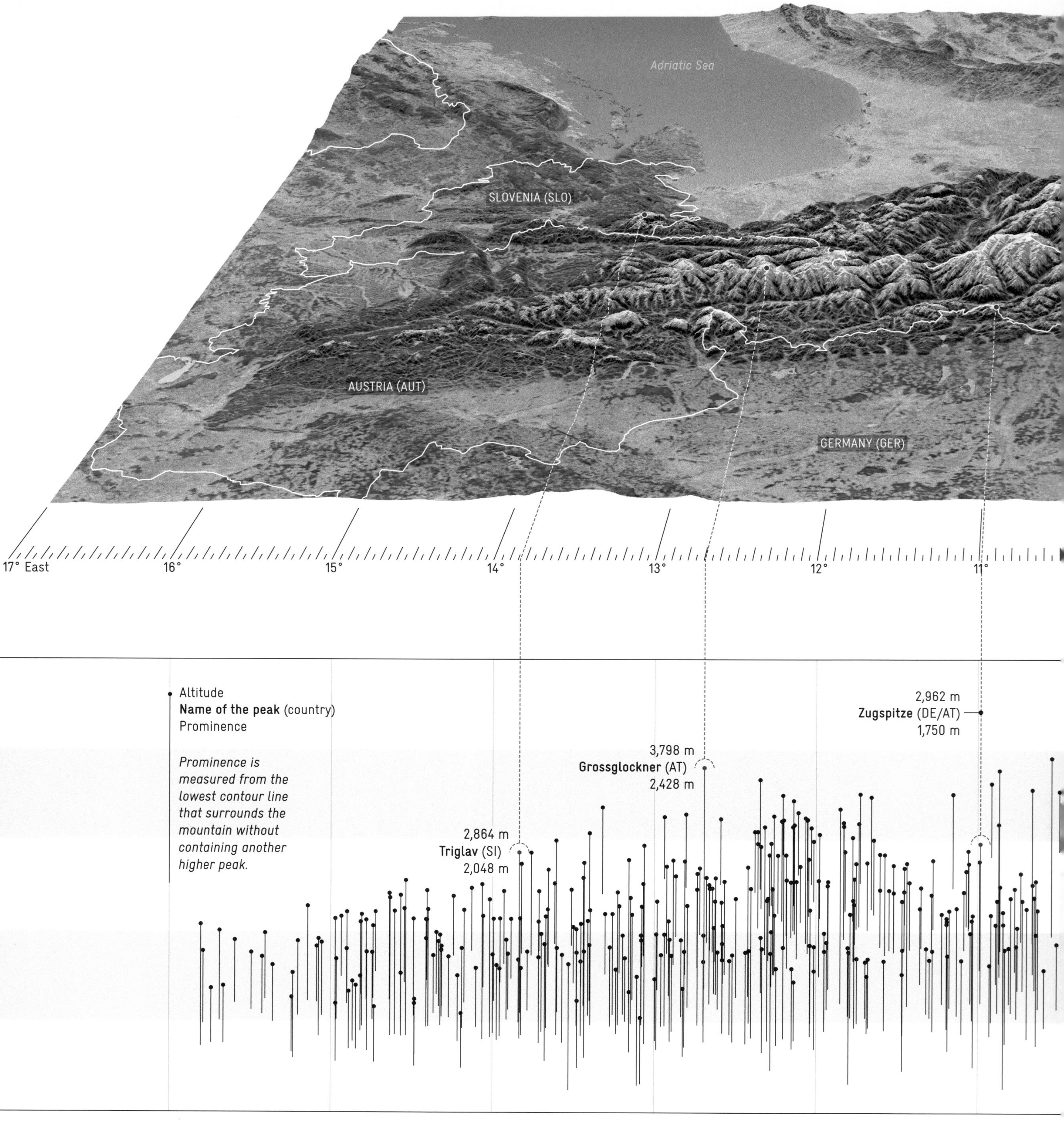

Adriatic Sea
SLOVENIA (SLO)
AUSTRIA (AUT)
GERMANY (GER)
17° East
16°
15°
14°
13°
12°
11°
Altitude
Name of the peak (country)
Prominence
Prominence is measured from the lowest contour line that surrounds the mountain without containing another higher peak.
2,864 m
Triglav (SI)
2,048 m
3,798 m
Grossglockner (AT)
2,428 m
2,962 m
Zugspitze (DE/AT)
1,750 m

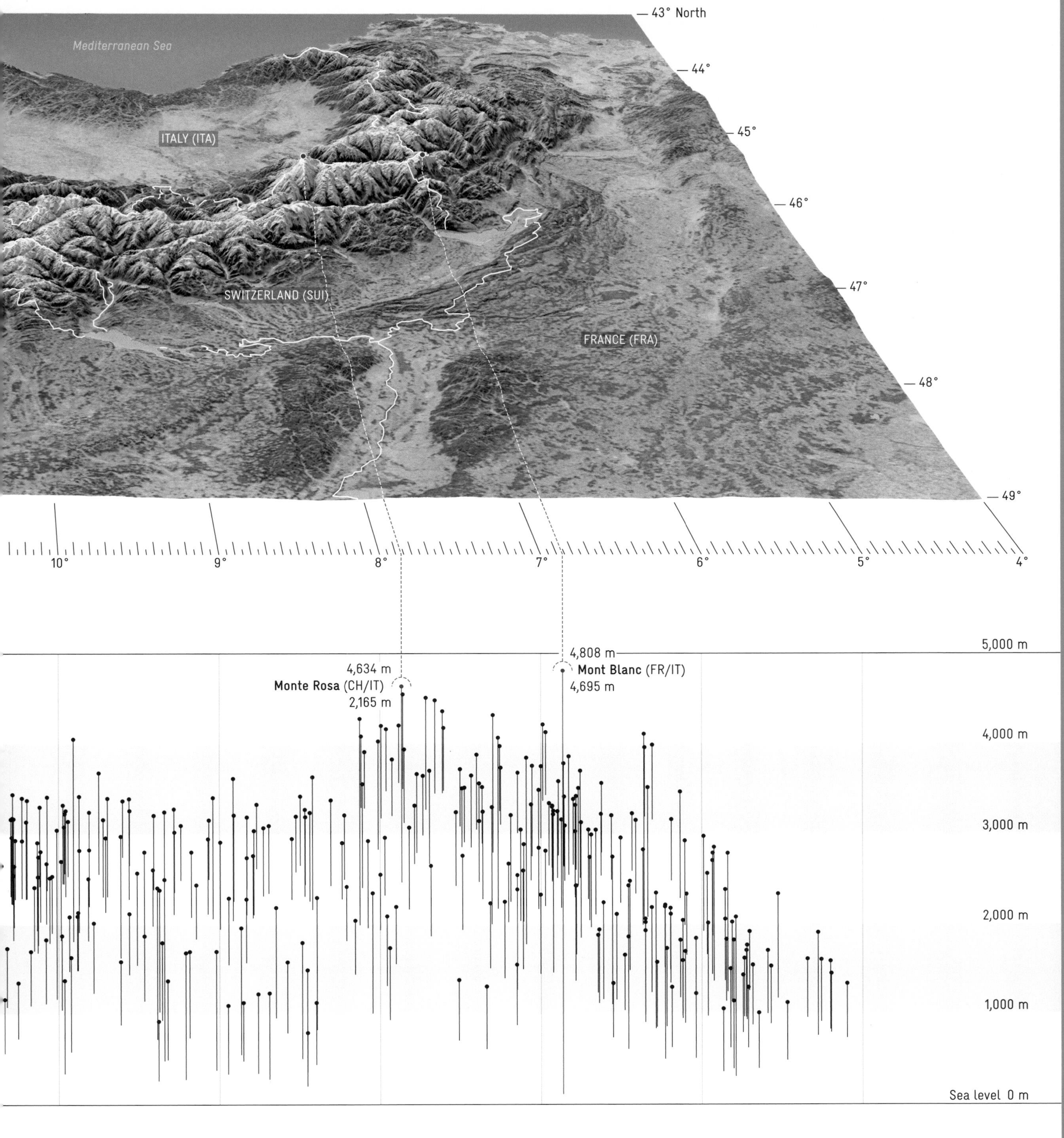

Mediterranean Sea
ITALY (ITA)
SWITZERLAND (SUI)
FRANCE (FRA)
— 43° North
— 44°
— 45°
— 46°
— 47°
— 48°
— 49°
10°
9°
8°
7°
6°
5°
4°
5,000 m
4,808 m
Mont Blanc (FR/IT)
4,695 m
4,634 m
Monte Rosa (CH/IT)
2,165 m
4,000 m
3,000 m
2,000 m
1,000 m
Sea level 0 m

H2O
1,338,000,000 km³ | 96.5 %
Salt water in the oceans

THE SOURCE OF LIFE

Life on our planet has its origins in the oceans and without them, nothing of what we know today would exist. But as the climate changes, water is becoming an increasingly scarce resource and millions die with no direct access to clean drinking water.
In 2010, the UN declared access to clean water a human right—yet this hasn't stopped the practice of licensing water rights to private corporations who bottle this essential element for profit.

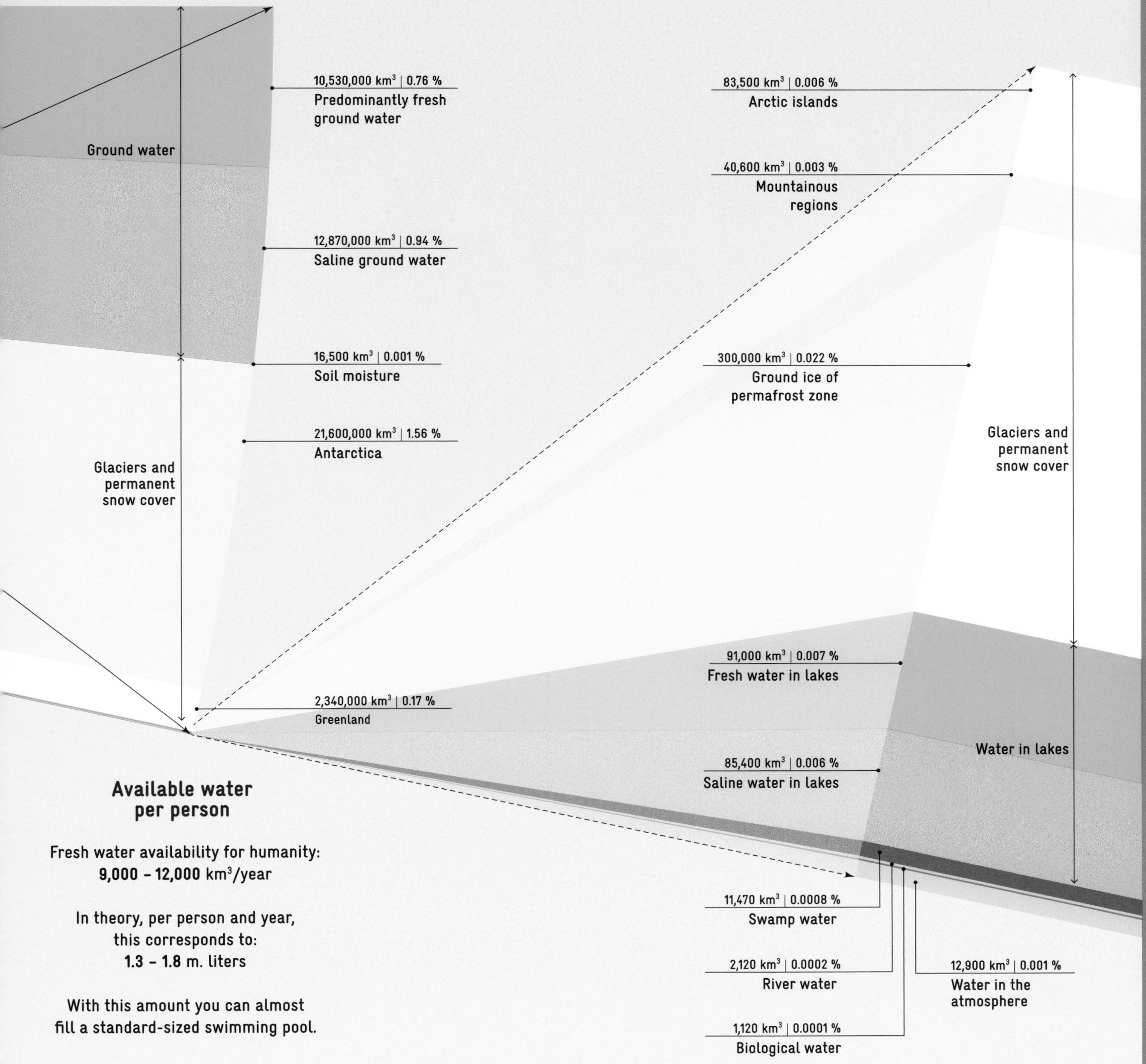
Ground water
10,530,000 km³ | 0.76 %
Predominantly fresh ground water
12,870,000 km³ | 0.94 %
Saline ground water
16,500 km³ | 0.001 %
Soil moisture
21,600,000 km³ | 1.56 %
Antarctica
Glaciers and permanent snow cover
2,340,000 km³ | 0.17 %
Greenland
83,500 km³ | 0.006 %
Arctic islands
40,600 km³ | 0.003 %
Mountainous regions
300,000 km³ | 0.022 %
Ground ice of permafrost zone
Glaciers and permanent snow cover
91,000 km³ | 0.007 %
Fresh water in lakes
Water in lakes
85,400 km³ | 0.006 %
Saline water in lakes
11,470 km³ | 0.0008 %
Swamp water
2,120 km³ | 0.0002 %
River water
12,900 km³ | 0.001 %
Water in the atmosphere
1,120 km³ | 0.0001 %
Biological water

Available water per person

Fresh water availability for humanity:
9,000 – 12,000 km³/year

In theory, per person and year, this corresponds to:
1.3 – 1.8 m. liters

With this amount you can almost fill a standard-sized swimming pool.

WATER TO WATER

Drinking, cleaning, washing. In the everyday lives of many people in the industrialized world, water seems to be an inexhaustible resource. But industry and agriculture require their own supply. In countries with extreme poverty, water is already scarce. To supply the current world population with safe drinking water, 17 percent more water is needed.

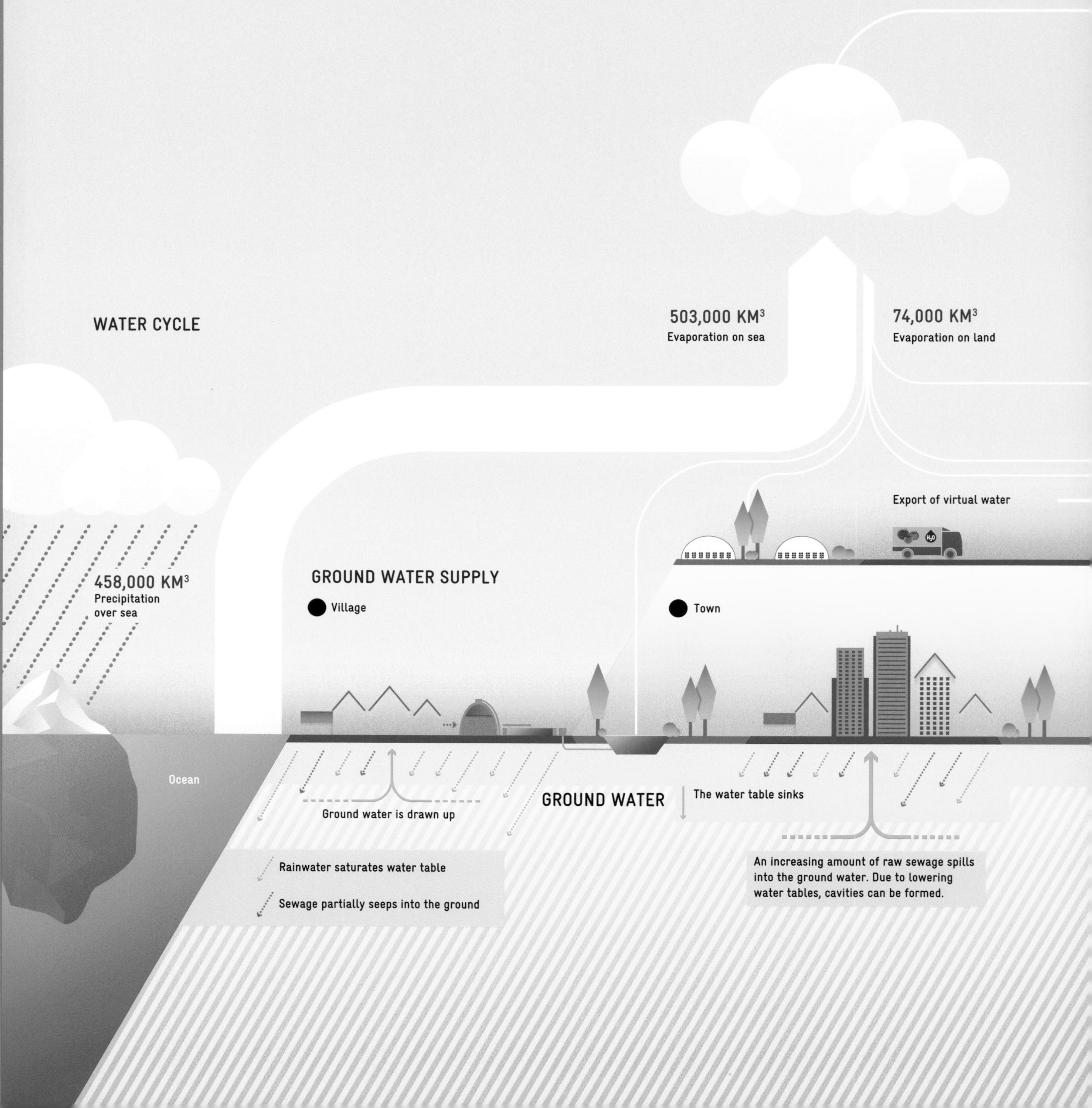

WATER CYCLE
503,000 KM³
Evaporation on sea
74,000 KM³
Evaporation on land
Export of virtual water
458,000 KM³
Precipitation over sea
GROUND WATER SUPPLY
Village
Town
Ocean
GROUND WATER
Ground water is drawn up
The water table sinks
Rainwater saturates water table
Sewage partially seeps into the ground
An increasing amount of raw sewage spills into the ground water. Due to lowering water tables, cavities can be formed.

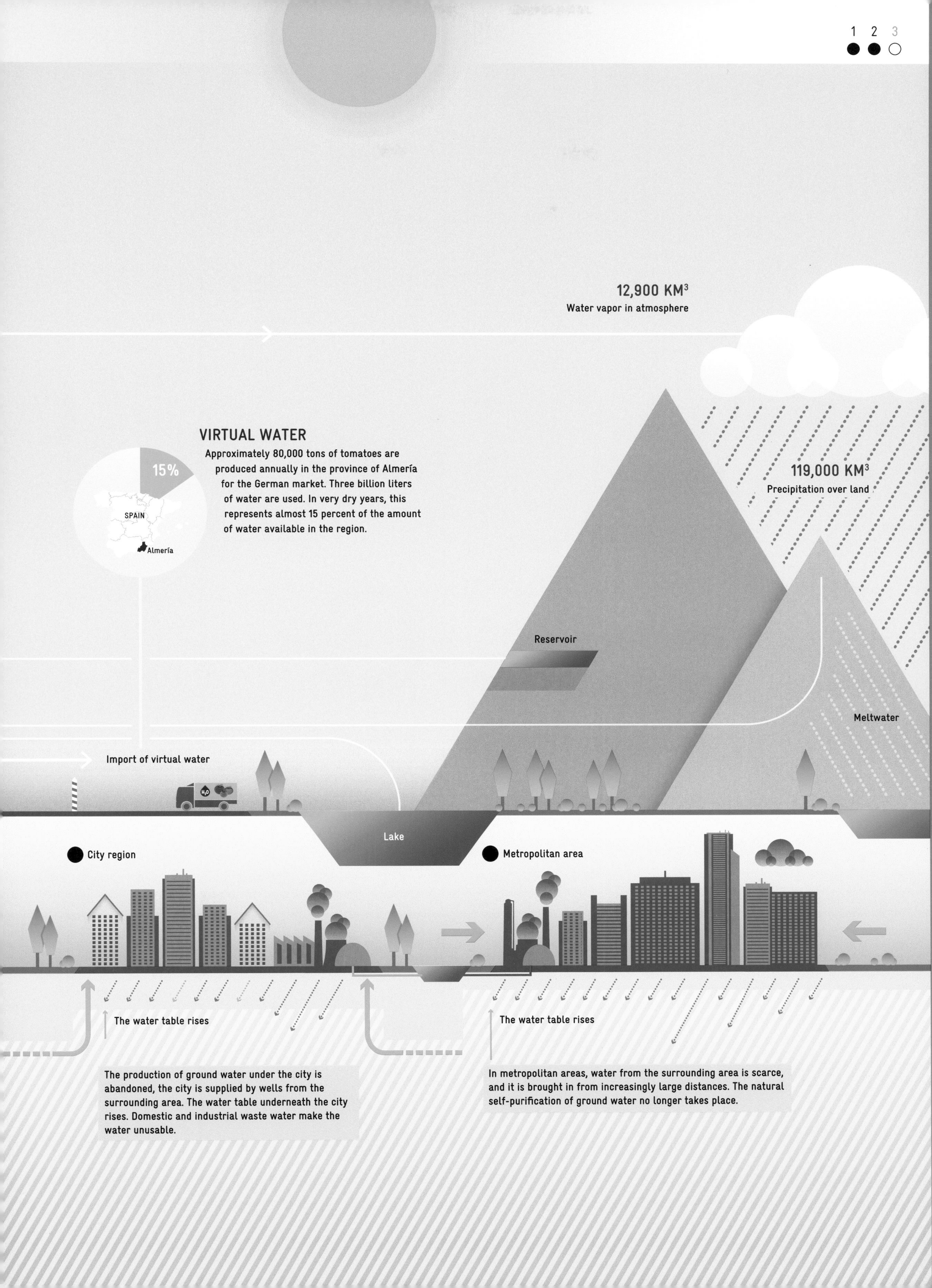
12,900 KM³
Water vapor in atmosphere
VIRTUAL WATER
Approximately 80,000 tons of tomatoes are produced annually in the province of Almería for the German market. Three billion liters of water are used. In very dry years, this represents almost 15 percent of the amount of water available in the region.
15%
SPAIN
Almería
119,000 KM³
Precipitation over land
Reservoir
Meltwater
Import of virtual water
H_2O
Lake
City region
Metropolitan area
The water table rises
The production of ground water under the city is abandoned, the city is supplied by wells from the surrounding area. The water table underneath the city rises. Domestic and industrial waste water make the water unusable.
The water table rises
In metropolitan areas, water from the surrounding area is scarce, and it is brought in from increasingly large distances. The natural self-purification of ground water no longer takes place.

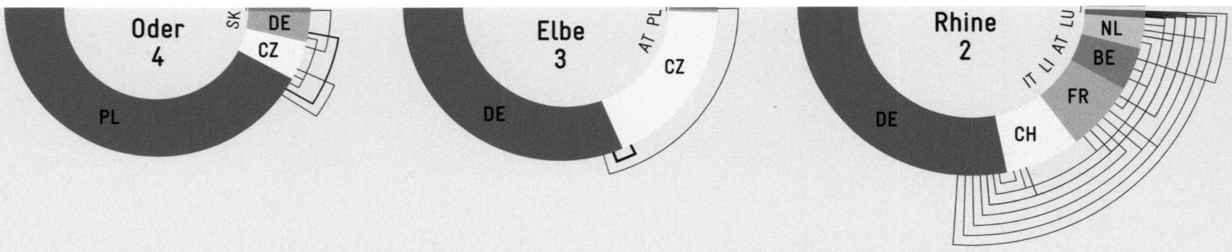

NATIONAL WATER

A natural basin providing fresh water can transcend national boundaries, requiring paperwork to regulate its joint use. The Danube basin alone crosses through 17 different countries. In all, there are 43 agreements that balance the different parties' interests, with a view to ensuring sustainability and avoiding water conflicts.

Syncrude Tailings Dam
Vancouver
Grand Coulee Dam
Toronto
Chicago
New York City
Washington
San Francisco
Los Angeles
Las Vegas
Dallas
New Orleans
Miami
Mexico City
CA
Mississippi
US
2
3
4
London
Par
Lisbon
Madr
Guri Dam
Bogotá
Akosombo Da
Area size
of the
basin
PE
Amazon
BO
CO
BR
SR GY VE EC
Manaus
Tucuruí Dam
Lima
NG
ML
Niger
NE
DZ
GN
CM
BF
Treaties between states, the weight of the lines
shows how many treaties exist between those states.
Asunción
Itaipú Dam
Rio de Janeiro
São Paulo
Santiago
Buenos Aires
Megacities
Other cities
River basin
Urban areas
Dam
AR
BR
La Plata
PY
UY
BO

The Danube basin contracts

In 1862, Austria and Bavaria agreed on the exact boundary line along the river Danube. Since then, there have been 17 more agreements to regulate the boundaries and the use of boundary waters for water supply and shipping.

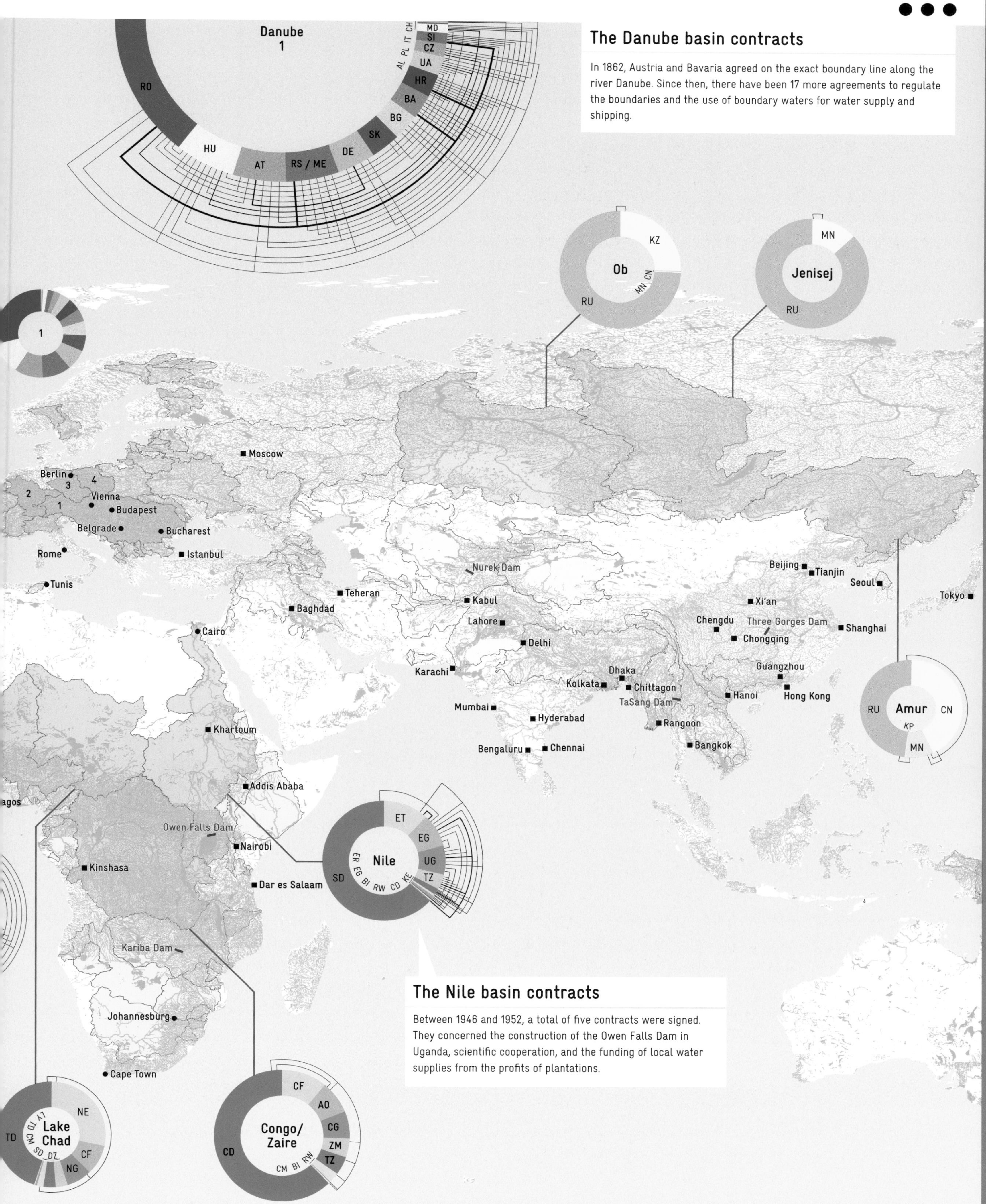
Danube
1
RO
HU
AT
RS / ME
DE
SK
BG
BA
HR
UA
CZ
SI
MD
AL PL IT CH
Ob
KZ
CN
MN
RU
Jenisej
MN
RU
1
Moscow
Berlin
Vienna
Budapest
Belgrade
Bucharest
Rome
Istanbul
Tunis
2
3
4
Teheran
Baghdad
Cairo
Nurek Dam
Kabul
Lahore
Delhi
Karachi
Mumbai
Hyderabad
Bengaluru
Chennai
Kolkata
Dhaka
Chittagon
TaSang Dam
Rangoon
Bangkok
Hanoi
Hong Kong
Guangzhou
Chengdu
Three Gorges Dam
Chongqing
Xi'an
Beijing
Tianjin
Seoul
Tokyo
Shanghai
Amur
RU
CN
KP
MN
Khartoum
Addis Ababa
agos
Owen Falls Dam
Nairobi
Kinshasa
Dar es Salaam
Nile
ET
EG
UG
TZ
KE
CD
RW
BI
EG
ER
SD
Kariba Dam
Johannesburg
Cape Town
Lake Chad
NE
CF
NG
DZ
SD
CM
TD
LY
Congo/ Zaire
CF
AO
CG
ZM
TZ
RW
BI
CM
CD

The Nile basin contracts

Between 1946 and 1952, a total of five contracts were signed. They concerned the construction of the Owen Falls Dam in Uganda, scientific cooperation, and the funding of local water supplies from the profits of plantations.

8.7 BILLION TREES AND COUNTING

From the Black Forest to the Goor—Germany is one of the most densely forested countries in Europe. The National Forest Inventory concluded in 2002 that there are approximately 8.7 billion trees covering 11.1 million hectares across the country—and that forests are continuing to grow. Unlike other countries with a trend of deforestation, Germany's forested area grew by around one million hectares in the last half of the twentieth century.

Proportion of tree species groups in percent

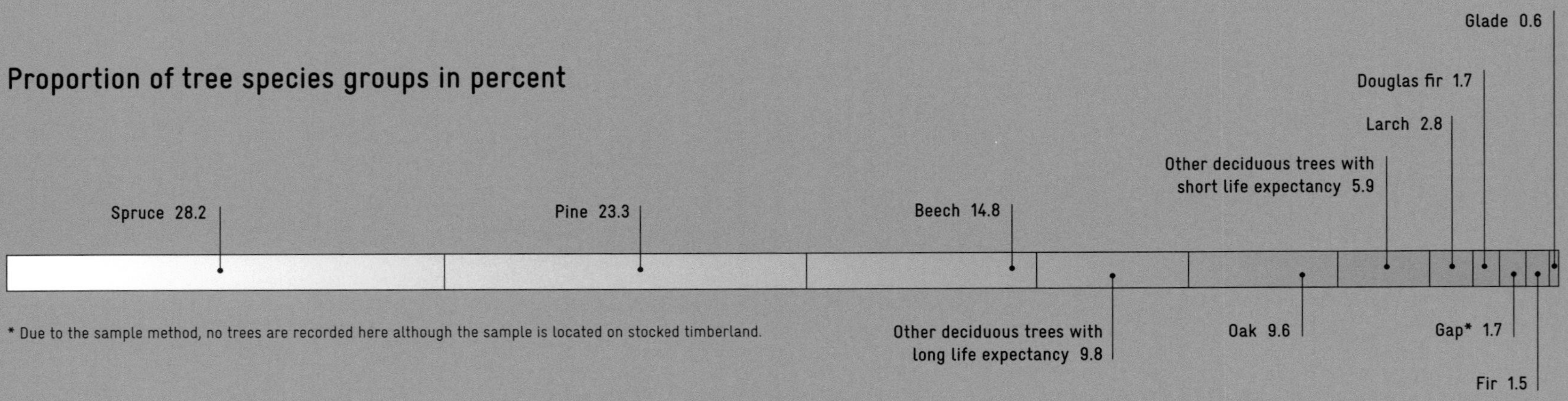
Glade 0.6
Douglas fir 1.7
Larch 2.8
Other deciduous trees with short life expectancy 5.9
Spruce 28.2
Pine 23.3
Beech 14.8
Other deciduous trees with long life expectancy 9.8
Oak 9.6
Gap* 1.7
Fir 1.5

* Due to the sample method, no trees are recorded here although the sample is located on stocked timberland.

The most common trees in German forests

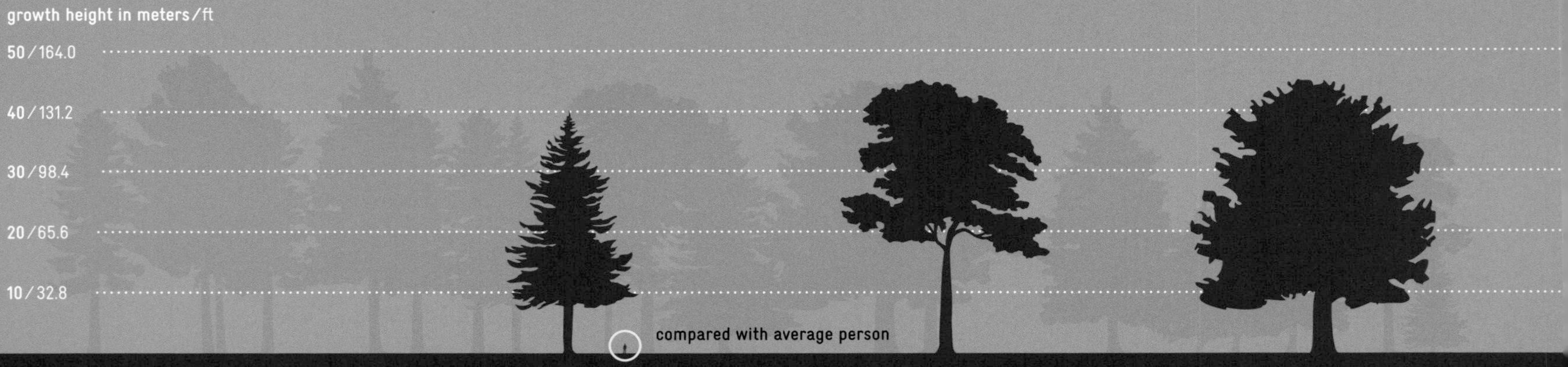
growth height in meters/ft
50/164.0
40/131.2
30/98.4
20/65.6
10/32.8
compared with average person

TREE SPECIES SCIENTIFIC NAME	Spruce *Pícea*	Pine *Pínus*	Beech *Fágus*
LEAF/TWIG			
FRUIT	Spruce cone	Pine cone	Beech-nut
FOREST IN HA	2,978,203	2,466,797	1,564,802

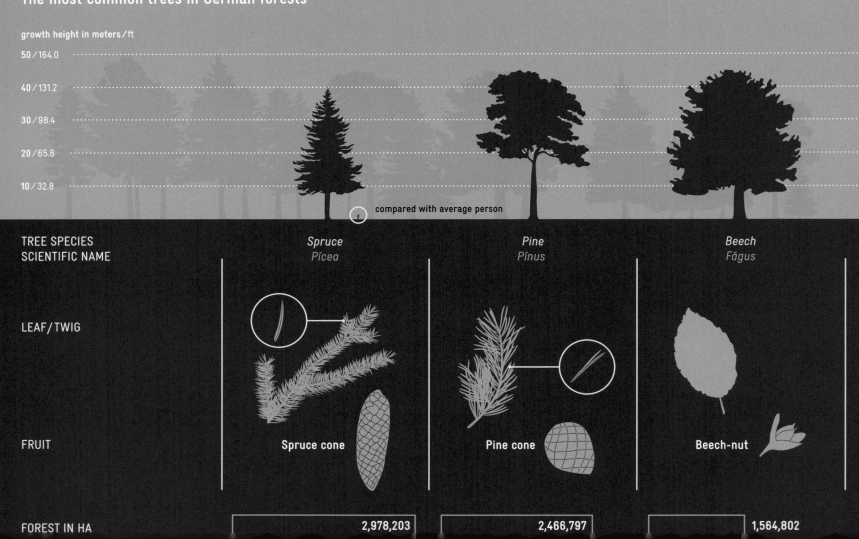

In Search of Shade

Forested areas in Germany in hectare

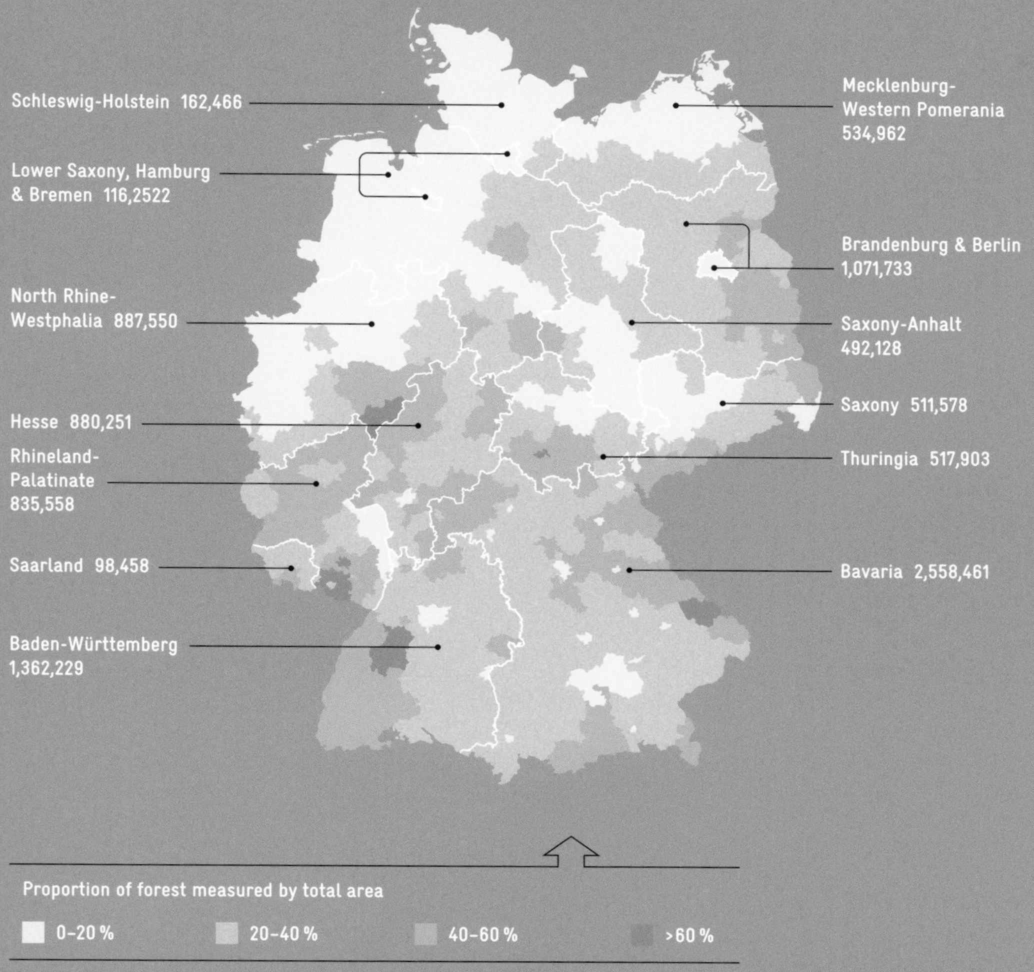
Schleswig-Holstein 162,466
Lower Saxony, Hamburg & Bremen 116,2522
North Rhine-Westphalia 887,550
Hesse 880,251
Rhineland-Palatinate 835,558
Saarland 98,458
Baden-Württemberg 1,362,229
Mecklenburg-Western Pomerania 534,962
Brandenburg & Berlin 1,071,733
Saxony-Anhalt 492,128
Saxony 511,578
Thuringia 517,903
Bavaria 2,558,461
Proportion of forest measured by total area
0–20 %
20–40 %
40–60 %
>60 %

Forest area by ownership type

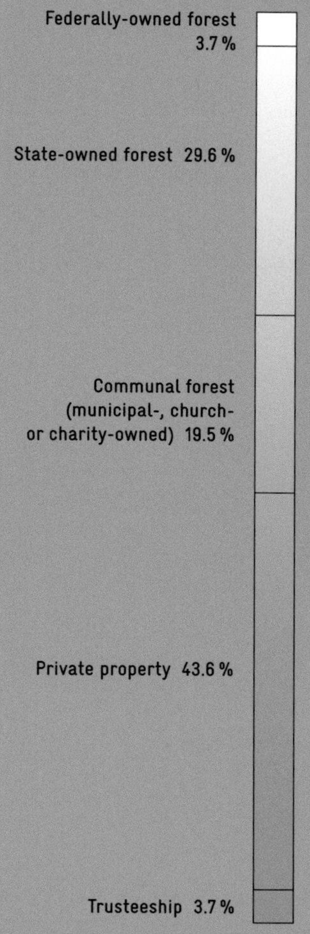
Federally-owned forest 3.7 %
State-owned forest 29.6 %
Communal forest (municipal-, church- or charity-owned) 19.5 %
Private property 43.6 %
Trusteeship 3.7 %

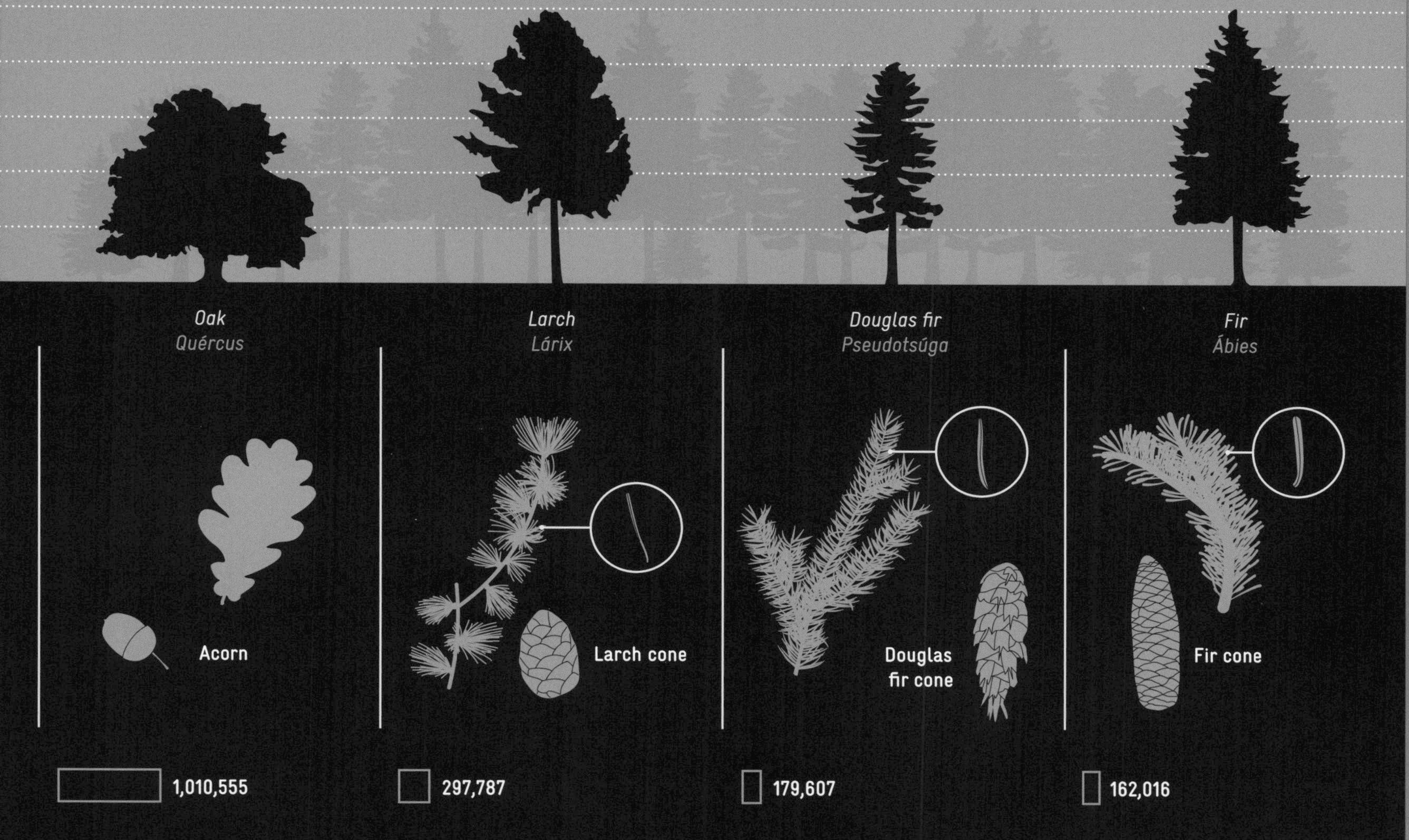
Oak
Quércus
Acorn
1,010,555
Larch
Lárix
Larch cone
297,787
Douglas fir
Pseudotsúga
Douglas fir cone
179,607
Fir
Ábies
Fir cone
162,016

THE HUMAN FOOTPRINT

Every era of the Earth's history is characterized by the elements that shaped it. Scientists have declared the current era as the anthropocene—the human-made era. Greenhouse gasses, plastics and mass industrialization are all phenomena driven by people that are changing the fundamental structure of our only home planet.

Soil

Each layer of soil tells a story of the time it was created in the sediment and amygdale. In order for the Anthropocene to be recognized as an era in its own right, the sediment from the human era has to distinguish itself from the layers beneath it.

Ice

Glacial layers also tell a story from when they were created in the pockets of air that form when water freezes. Analyzing these air pockets provides clues as to the composition of the atmosphere at the time that the ice layer was formed.

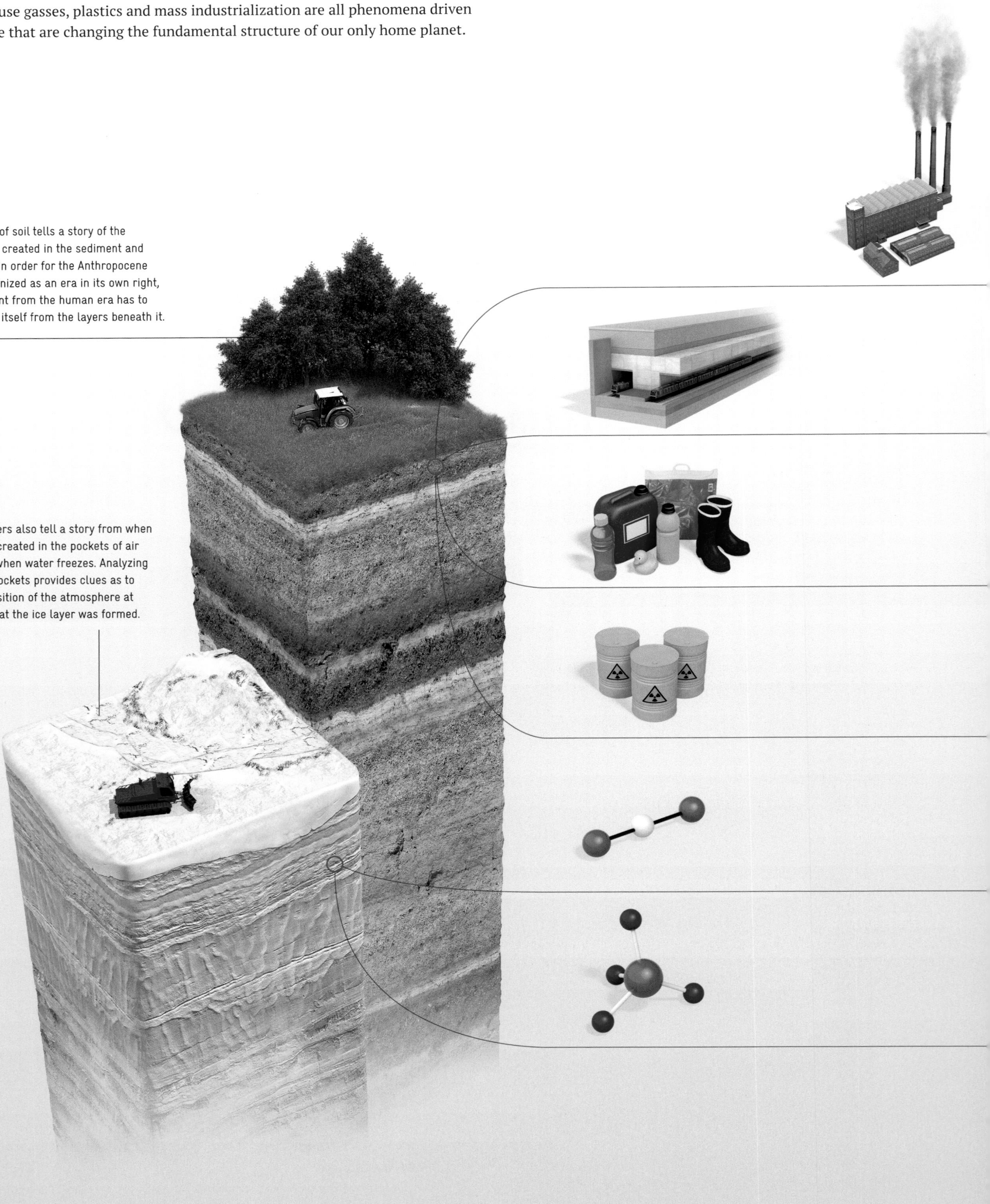

When did the anthropocene era begin?

The holocene began more than 11,700 years ago as the last great ice age ended. This can be seen in the soil and ice samples scientists still study today. To find the start of the current era, scientists rely on a variety of data, but most of the evidence points to the year 1950 as the break point between the two eras.

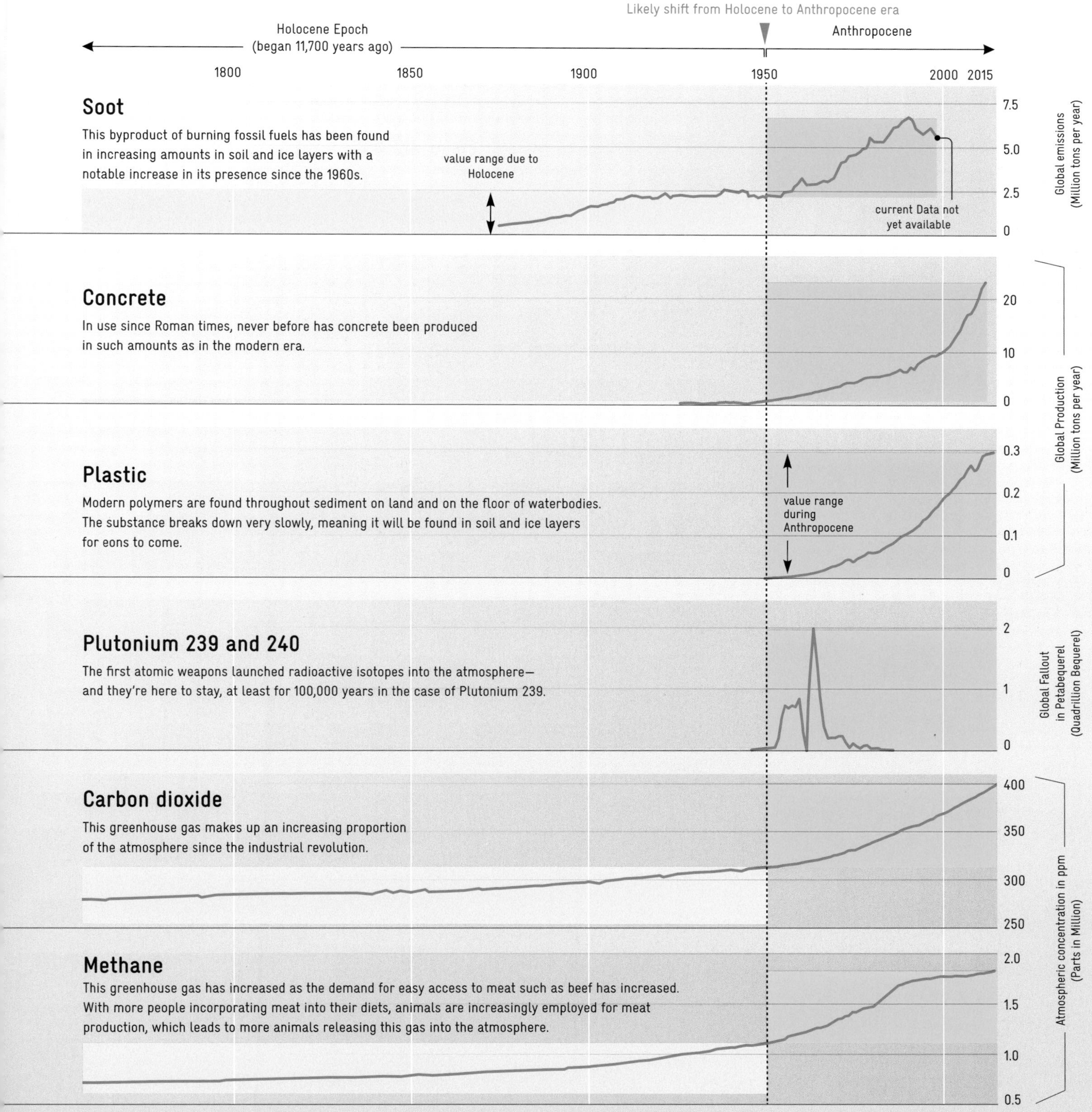
Likely shift from Holocene to Anthropocene era
Holocene Epoch
(began 11,700 years ago)
Anthropocene
1800
1850
1900
1950
2000
2015
Soot
This byproduct of burning fossil fuels has been found in increasing amounts in soil and ice layers with a notable increase in its presence since the 1960s.
value range due to Holocene
current Data not yet available
7.5
5.0
2.5
0
Global emissions (Million tons per year)
Concrete
In use since Roman times, never before has concrete been produced in such amounts as in the modern era.
20
10
0
Plastic
Modern polymers are found throughout sediment on land and on the floor of waterbodies. The substance breaks down very slowly, meaning it will be found in soil and ice layers for eons to come.
value range during Anthropocene
0.3
0.2
0.1
0
Global Production (Million tons per year)
Plutonium 239 and 240
The first atomic weapons launched radioactive isotopes into the atmosphere—and they're here to stay, at least for 100,000 years in the case of Plutonium 239.
2
1
0
Global Fallout in Petabequerel (Quadrillion Bequerel)
Carbon dioxide
This greenhouse gas makes up an increasing proportion of the atmosphere since the industrial revolution.
400
350
300
250
Methane
This greenhouse gas has increased as the demand for easy access to meat such as beef has increased. With more people incorporating meat into their diets, animals are increasingly employed for meat production, which leads to more animals releasing this gas into the atmosphere.
2.0
1.5
1.0
0.5
Atmospheric concentration in ppm (Parts in Million)

OUR IMMUNE SYSTEM

The immune system is made up of two parts that work together effectively to keep us healthy and help our bodies fight off intruding bacteria and viruses.

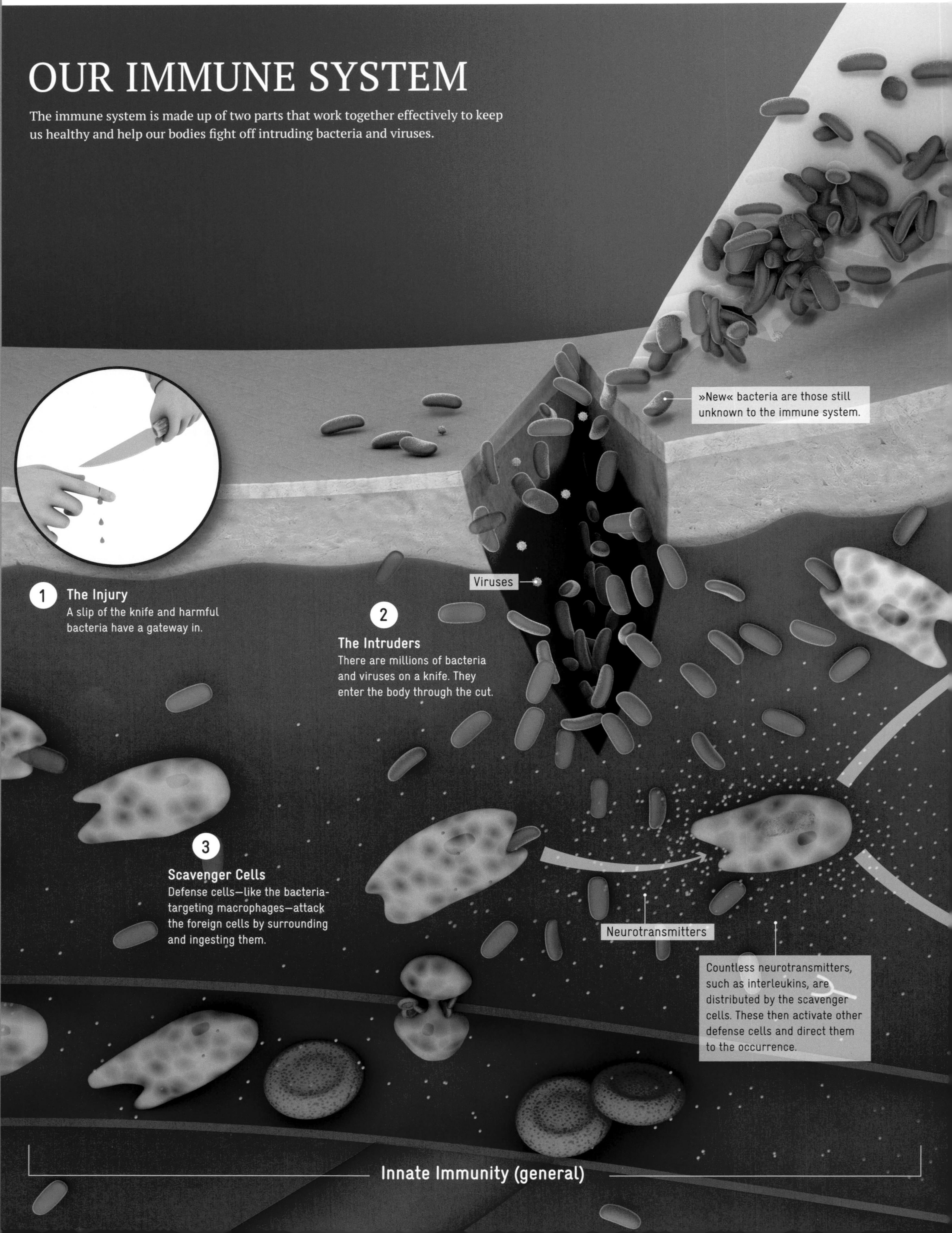

»New« bacteria are those still unknown to the immune system.
Viruses
1 The Injury
A slip of the knife and harmful bacteria have a gateway in.
2 The Intruders
There are millions of bacteria and viruses on a knife. They enter the body through the cut.
3 Scavenger Cells
Defense cells—like the bacteria-targeting macrophages—attack the foreign cells by surrounding and ingesting them.
Neurotransmitters
Countless neurotransmitters, such as interleukins, are distributed by the scavenger cells. These then activate other defense cells and direct them to the occurrence.
Innate Immunity (general)

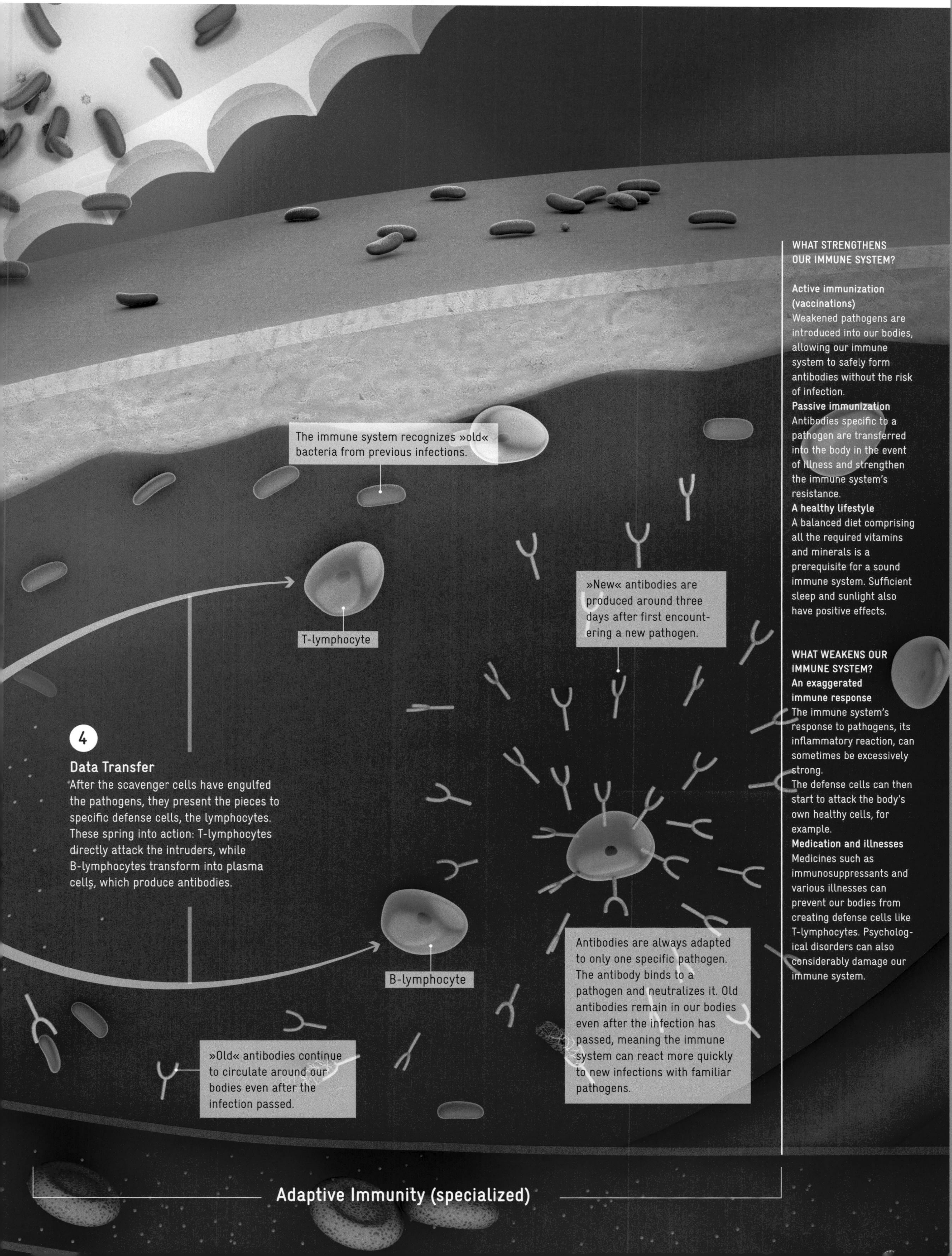
The immune system recognizes »old« bacteria from previous infections.
T-lymphocyte
»New« antibodies are produced around three days after first encount-ering a new pathogen.
B-lymphocyte
Antibodies are always adapted to only one specific pathogen. The antibody binds to a pathogen and neutralizes it. Old antibodies remain in our bodies even after the infection has passed, meaning the immune system can react more quickly to new infections with familiar pathogens.
»Old« antibodies continue to circulate around our bodies even after the infection passed.
Adaptive Immunity (specialized)

4

Data Transfer

After the scavenger cells have engulfed the pathogens, they present the pieces to specific defense cells, the lymphocytes. These spring into action: T-lymphocytes directly attack the intruders, while B-lymphocytes transform into plasma cells, which produce antibodies.

WHAT STRENGTHENS OUR IMMUNE SYSTEM?

Active immunization (vaccinations)
Weakened pathogens are introduced into our bodies, allowing our immune system to safely form antibodies without the risk of infection.

Passive immunization
Antibodies specific to a pathogen are transferred into the body in the event of illness and strengthen the immune system's resistance.

A healthy lifestyle
A balanced diet comprising all the required vitamins and minerals is a prerequisite for a sound immune system. Sufficient sleep and sunlight also have positive effects.

WHAT WEAKENS OUR IMMUNE SYSTEM?

An exaggerated immune response
The immune system's response to pathogens, its inflammatory reaction, can sometimes be excessively strong.
The defense cells can then start to attack the body's own healthy cells, for example.

Medication and illnesses
Medicines such as immunosuppressants and various illnesses can prevent our bodies from creating defense cells like T-lymphocytes. Psychological disorders can also considerably damage our immune system.

OSTRACIZED

The fight against HIV and AIDS is still one of the medical community's biggest battles. Researchers found the origins of the disease in a virus that was transmitted from chimpanzees to humans, possibly through the consumption of ape meat, which then mutated into what we see today. The HIV antibody test was developed in 1985 and is still used to diagnose patients. A positive result can mean physical, psychological and social suffering for those affected. Today, treatment exists that allows those living with HIV to enjoy a higher quality of life than those diagnosed in the 1980s, but there is still no cure.

COURSE OF THE INFECTION

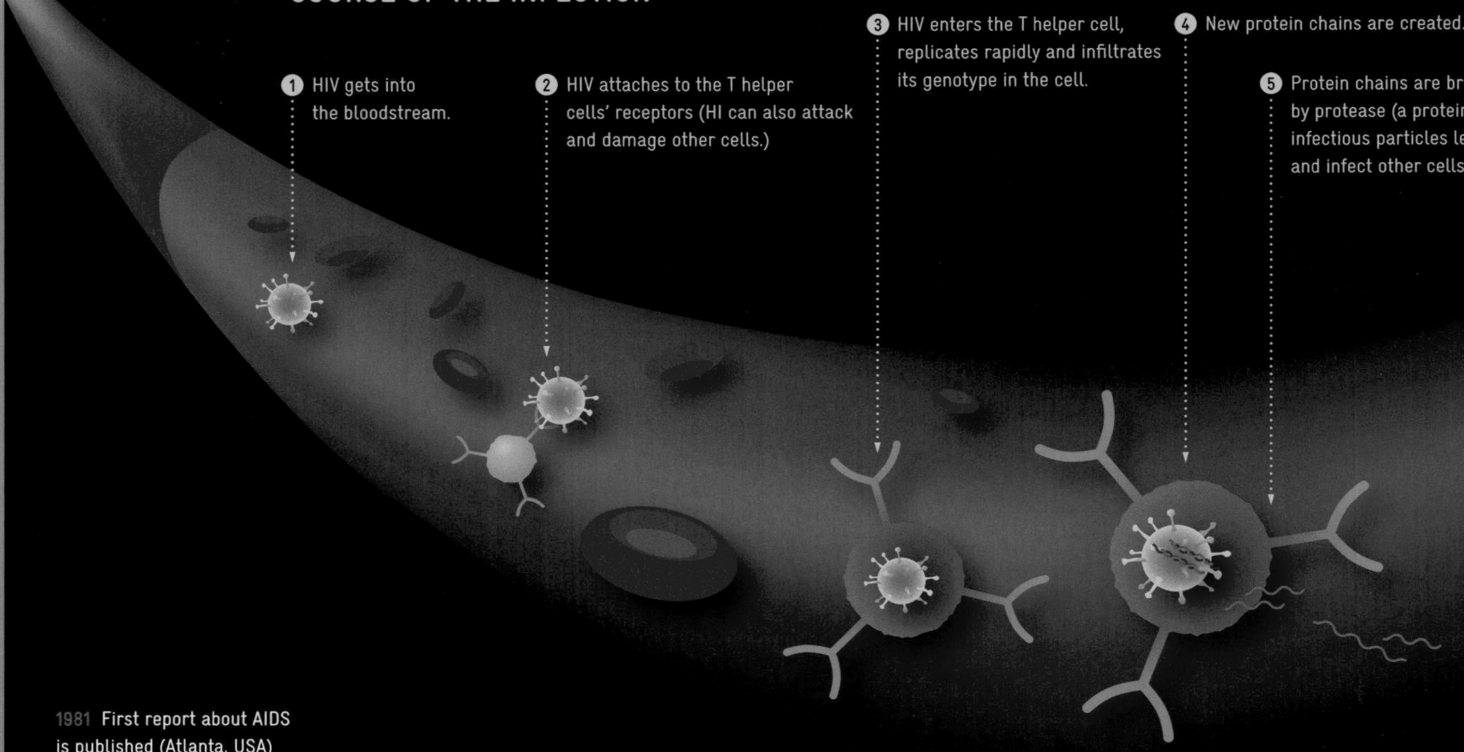
1 HIV gets into the bloodstream.
2 HIV attaches to the T helper cells' receptors (HI can also attack and damage other cells.)
3 HIV enters the T helper cell, replicates rapidly and infiltrates its genotype in the cell.
4 New protein chains are created.
5 Protein chains are broken by protease (a protein-splitting enzyme), infectious particles leave the cell and infect other cells.

1981 First report about AIDS is published (Atlanta, USA)

1982 First diagnosis of AIDS in Germany, introduction of an AIDS register by the Robert Koch Institute

1983 Discovery of LA virus (later called HI virus) by Luc Montagnier and Françoise Barré-Sinoussi (Nobel Prize in 2008)

1984 Presentation of the first HIV antibody test (patented in 1985)

80s »Hemophiliac AIDS Scandal« in the 80s (drug for hemophiliacs produced from HIV-contaminated blood)

1985 Obligation to test all blood products for AIDS, first AIDS conference (Atlanta, USA)

1987 The drug AZT enters the US market

1988 December 1 is declared World AIDS Day

1991 »Red ribbon« as a symbol of solidarity

2009 Decoding of the entire HI virus genome

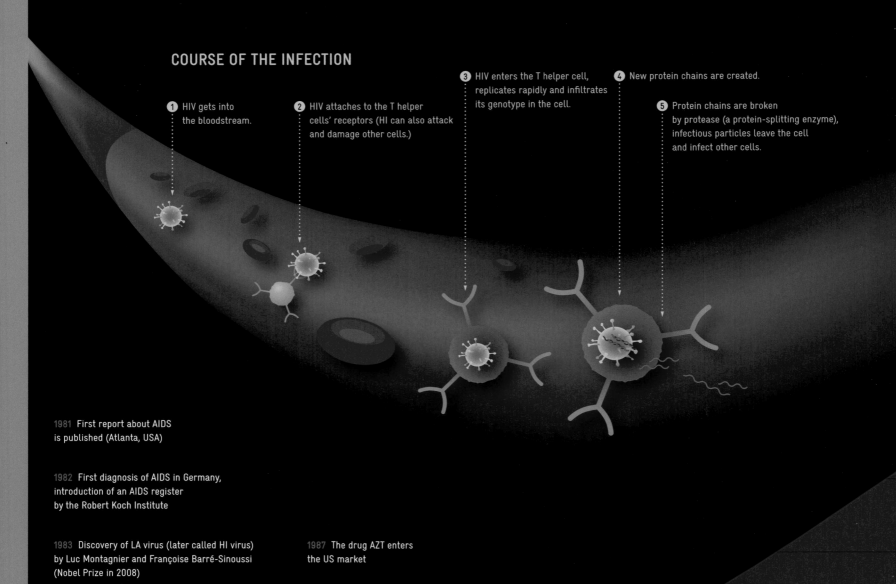

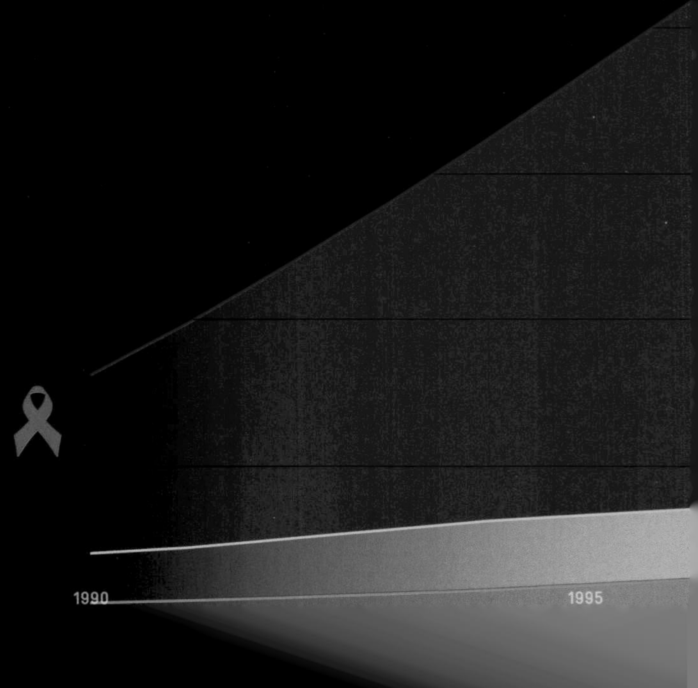
1990
1995

STIGMATIZATION

People are still being stigmatized, judged and discriminated because of their disease. There are 43 countries that have admission restrictions against people who have HIV/AIDS.

Russian Federation
Belarus
Lithuania
Slovakia
Lebanon
Syria
Cyprus
Israel
Jordan
Egypt
Iraq
Kuwait
Saudi Arabia
Bahrain
Uzbekistan
Tajikistan
Turkmenistan
United Arab Republic
Qatar
Oman
Yemen
Sudan
North Korea
Taipei
Marshall Islands
Brunei
Malaysia
Singapore
Papua New Guinea
Solomon Islands
Australia
New Zealand
Comoros
Mauritius
Turks and Caicos Islands
Dominican Republic
Aruba
Cuba
Belize
Nicaragua
Paraguay
Samoa
Tonga

6 The asymptomatic phase starts (a period of time without symptoms) while the infected person might not know about their illness and might spread the virus. It can take up to 10 years before AIDS has developed.

- restriction of entry, stay and residence
- deportation when HIV is discovered
- requirement to show HIV status
- absolute prohibition on entry of HIV-positive people

PEOPLE WHO ARE HIV POSITIVE

- people infected with HIV
- new infections
- AIDS fatalities

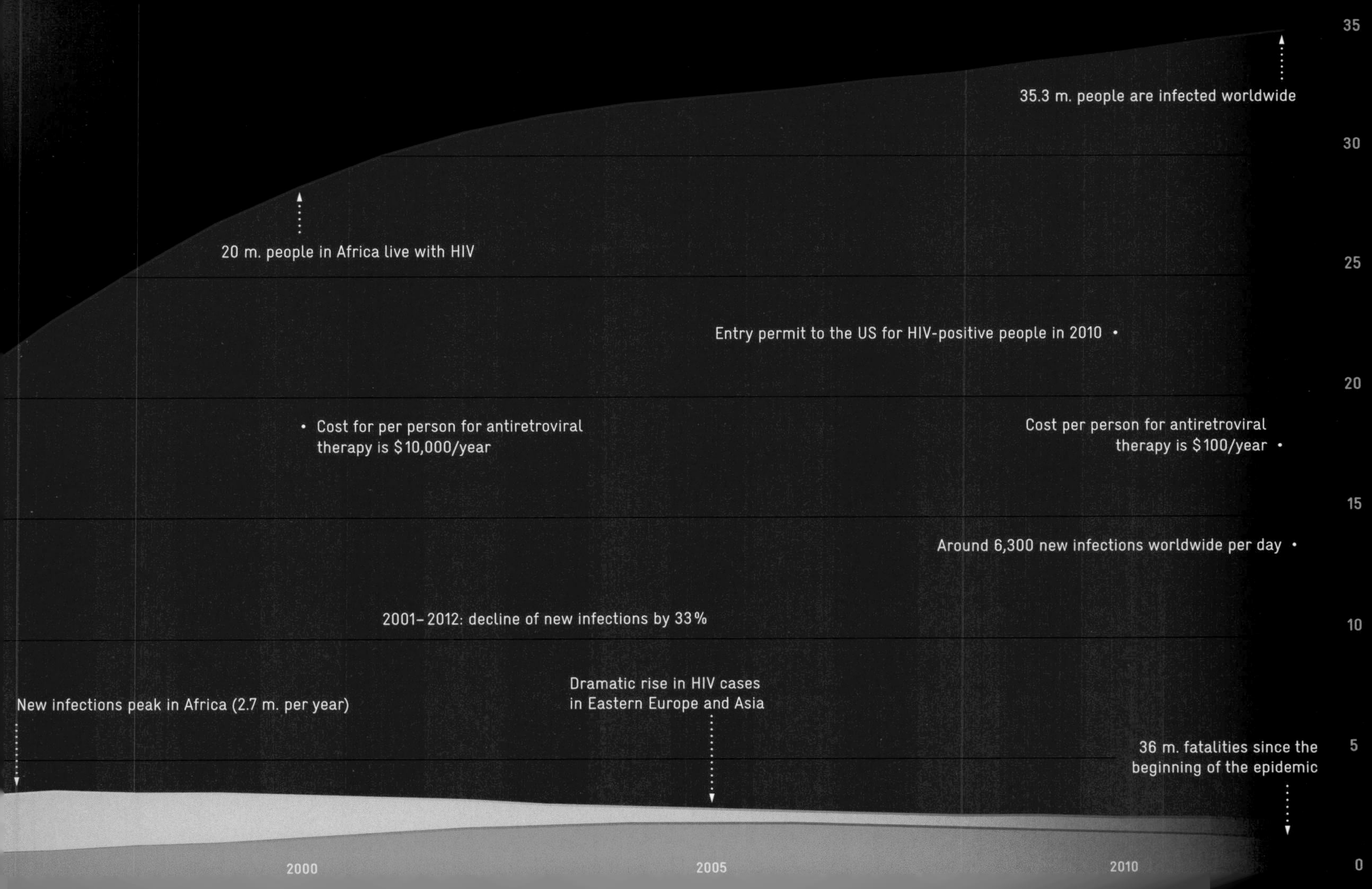

35
30
25
20
15
10
5
0
35.3 m. people are infected worldwide
20 m. people in Africa live with HIV
Entry permit to the US for HIV-positive people in 2010
Cost for per person for antiretroviral therapy is $10,000/year
Cost per person for antiretroviral therapy is $100/year
Around 6,300 new infections worldwide per day
2001–2012: decline of new infections by 33%
New infections peak in Africa (2.7 m. per year)
Dramatic rise in HIV cases in Eastern Europe and Asia
36 m. fatalities since the beginning of the epidemic
2000
2005
2010

INVISIBLE DANGER

Germany implemented the first mandatory vaccination in 1874. It was against smallpox, which claimed 400,000 lives a year before the immunization existed. Today, the disease is considered to have been eradicated. The 20th century saw many more vaccines developed and, as a result, a significant decrease in the number of deaths and suffering. But thanks to the »anti-vaccine« movement citing a discredited study that linked vaccines to autism, many diseases facing the same fate as smallpox are making a comeback.

IMMUNIZATION HISTORY

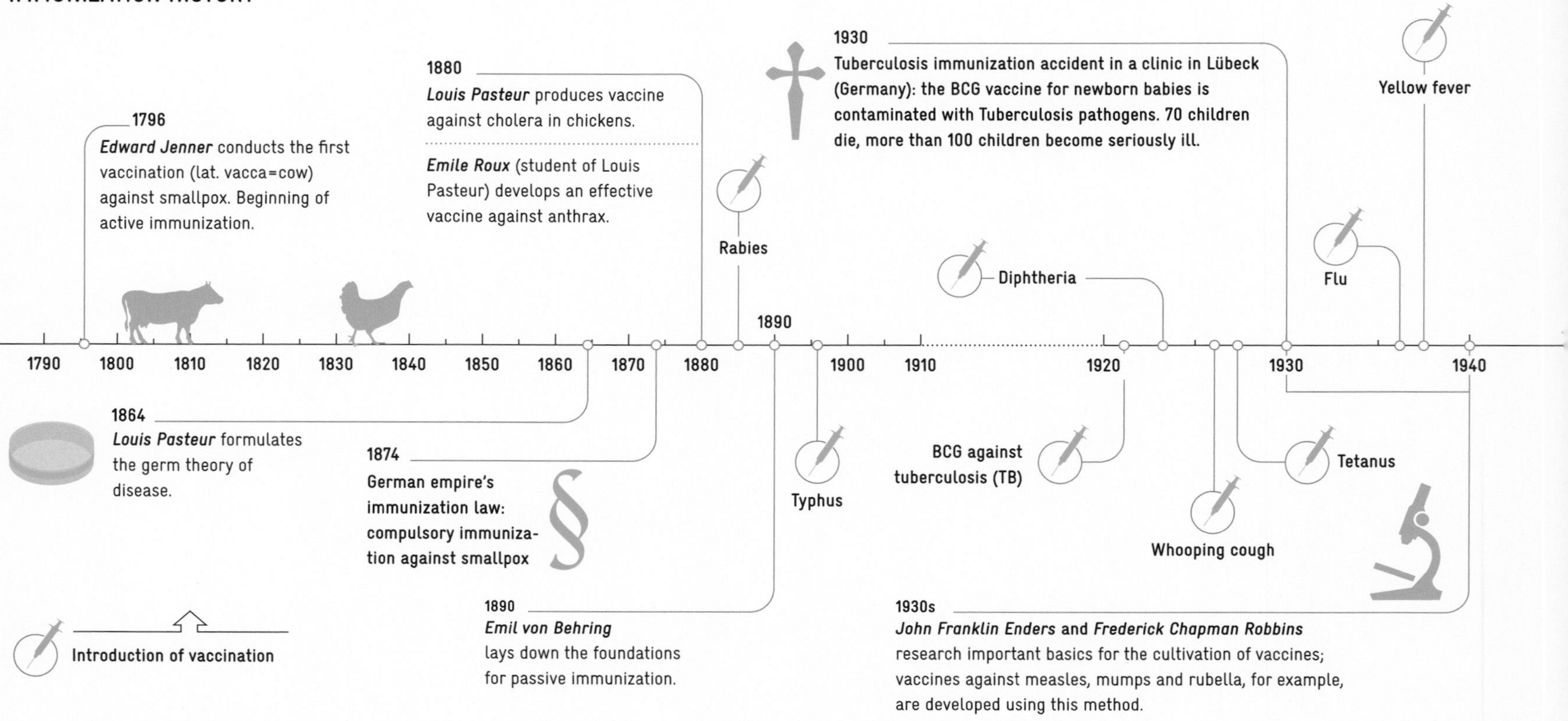
1796
Edward Jenner conducts the first vaccination (lat. vacca=cow) against smallpox. Beginning of active immunization.
1880
Louis Pasteur produces vaccine against cholera in chickens.
Emile Roux (student of Louis Pasteur) develops an effective vaccine against anthrax.
Rabies
1890
1930
Tuberculosis immunization accident in a clinic in Lübeck (Germany): the BCG vaccine for newborn babies is contaminated with Tuberculosis pathogens. 70 children die, more than 100 children become seriously ill.
Diphtheria
Flu
Yellow fever
1790
1800
1810
1820
1830
1840
1850
1860
1870
1880
1900
1910
1920
1930
1940
1864
Louis Pasteur formulates the germ theory of disease.
1874
German empire's immunization law: compulsory immunization against smallpox
Typhus
BCG against tuberculosis (TB)
Whooping cough
Tetanus
Introduction of vaccination
1890
Emil von Behring lays down the foundations for passive immunization.
1930s
John Franklin Enders and *Frederick Chapman Robbins* research important basics for the cultivation of vaccines; vaccines against measles, mumps and rubella, for example, are developed using this method.

WHEN DO YOU NEED TO BE IMMUNIZED?

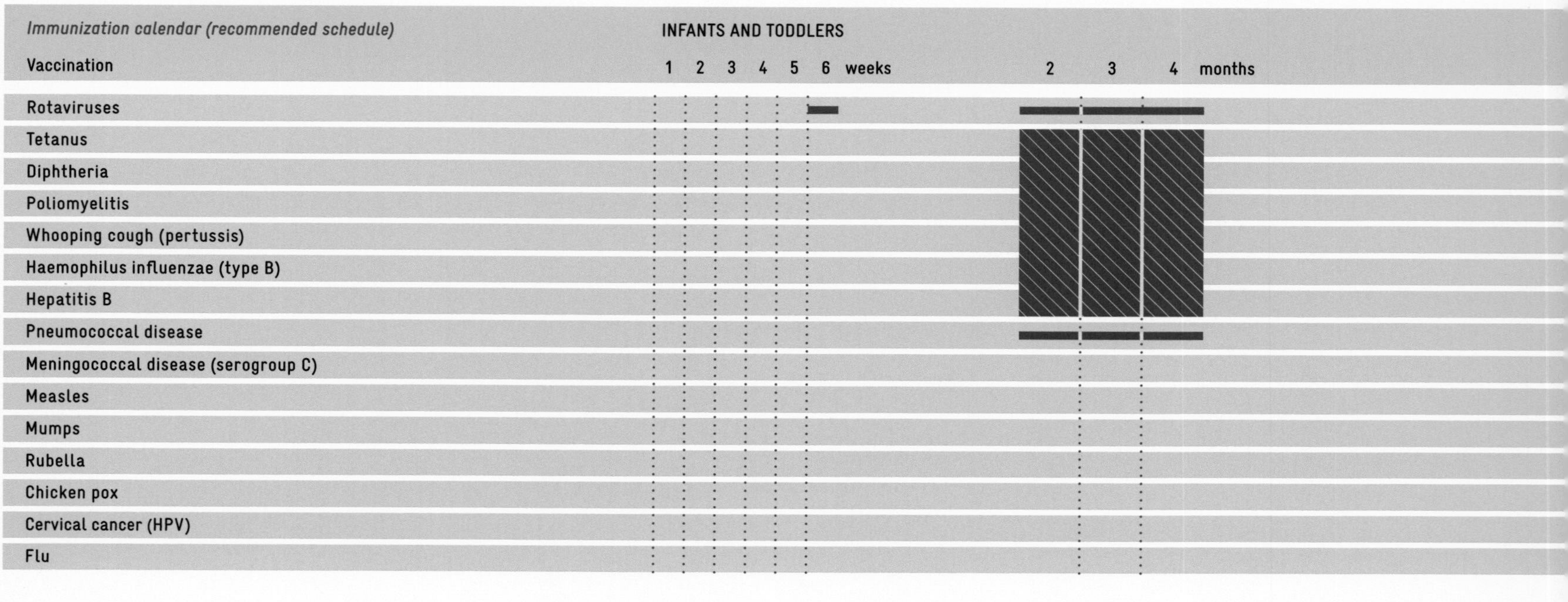
Immunization calendar (recommended schedule)
INFANTS AND TODDLERS
Vaccination
1 2 3 4 5 6 weeks
2 3 4 months
Rotaviruses
Tetanus
Diphtheria
Poliomyelitis
Whooping cough (pertussis)
Haemophilus influenzae (type B)
Hepatitis B
Pneumococcal disease
Meningococcal disease (serogroup C)
Measles
Mumps
Rubella
Chicken pox
Cervical cancer (HPV)
Flu

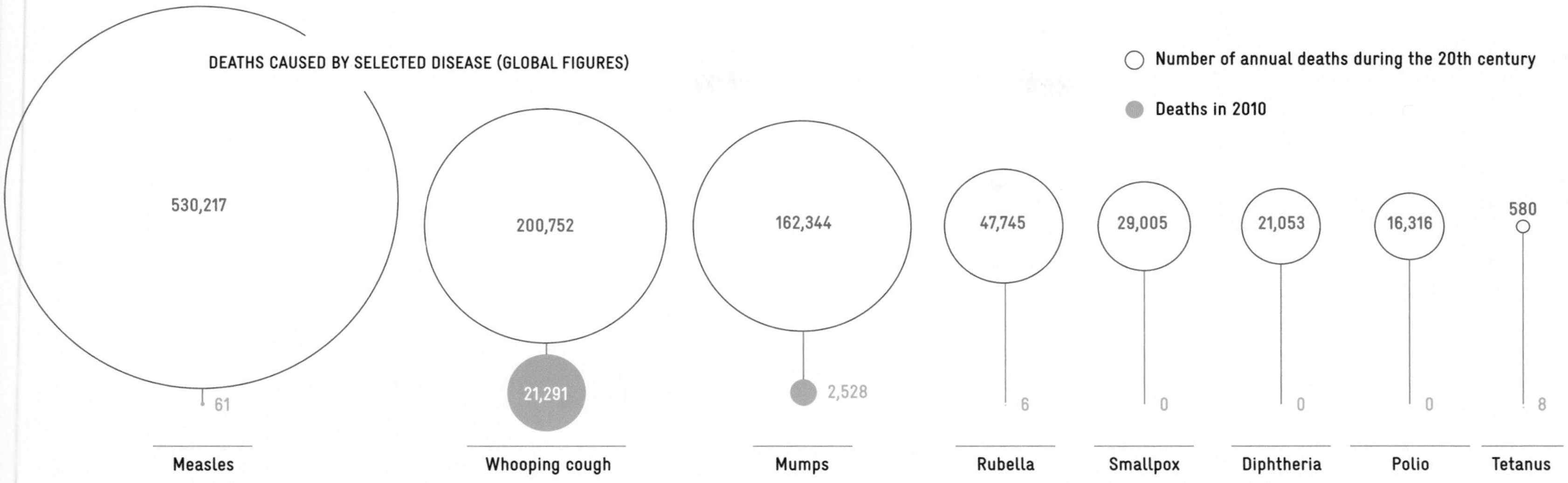
DEATHS CAUSED BY SELECTED DISEASE (GLOBAL FIGURES)
Number of annual deaths during the 20th century
Deaths in 2010
530,217
61
Measles
200,752
21,291
Whooping cough
162,344
2,528
Mumps
47,745
6
Rubella
29,005
0
Smallpox
21,053
0
Diphtheria
16,316
0
Polio
580
8
Tetanus

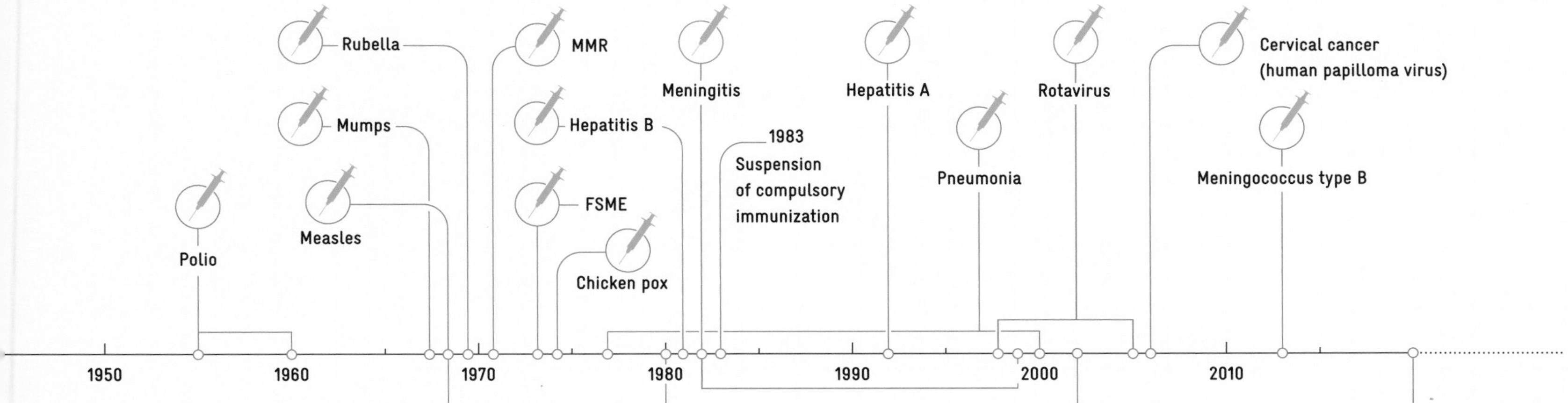
Rubella
Mumps
Measles
Polio
MMR
Hepatitis B
FSME
Chicken pox
Meningitis
1983
Suspension
of compulsory
immunization
Hepatitis A
Pneumonia
Rotavirus
Cervical cancer
(human papilloma virus)
Meningococcus type B
1950
1960
1970
1980
1990
2000
2010

1967
The World Health Organization (WHO) starts an immunization program to prevent the global spreading and enable the longterm eradication of dangerous infectious diseases.

1980
The WHO declares the world free of smallpox.

2002
Of the six WHO regions, the US, West Pacific and Europe are polio-free.

2020
COVID-19 pandemic spreads all over the world. Companies and academic institutions hurry to create a vaccine...

- Primary immunization
- Combination vaccine/mixed vaccines
- Catch-up vaccination
- Standard vaccination for girls and young women
- Standard vaccination
- Booster vaccination
- Recommended vaccinations for chronically ill persons and pregnant women

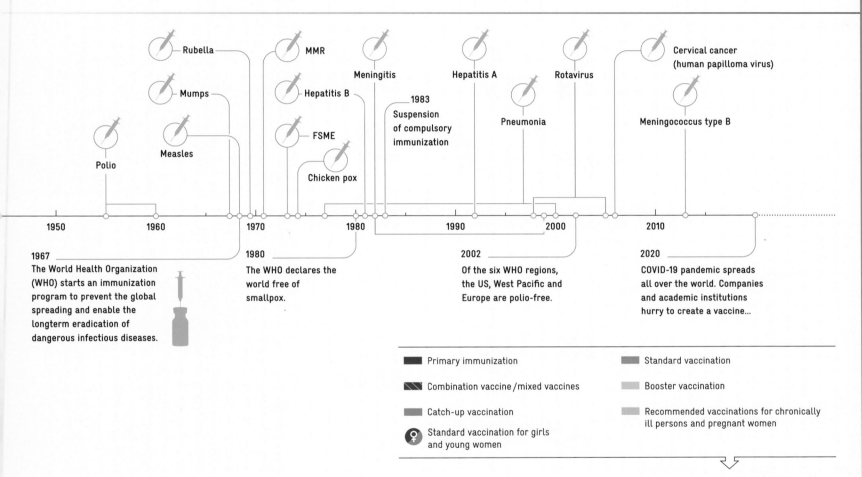

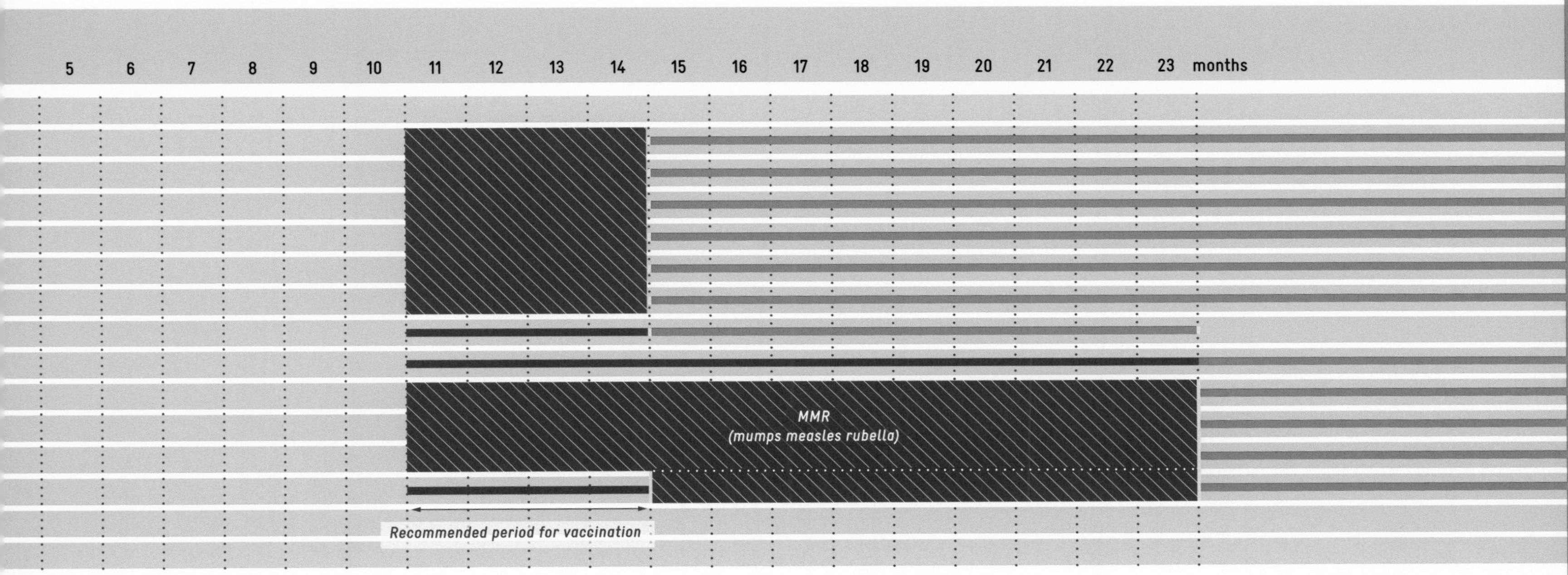
5
6
7
8
9
10
11
12
13
14
15
16
17
18
19
20
21
22
23
months
MMR
(mumps measles rubella)
Recommended period for vaccination

WHAT IS PROTECTIVE IMMUNIZATION?
Immunizations are supposed to protect people from infectious diseases. All immunizations are recorded on a vaccination card. There are two different types of vaccination methods: active and passive immunization.

NUMBER OF REGISTERED DISEASES in Germany from 2001–2015, selection infectious diseases

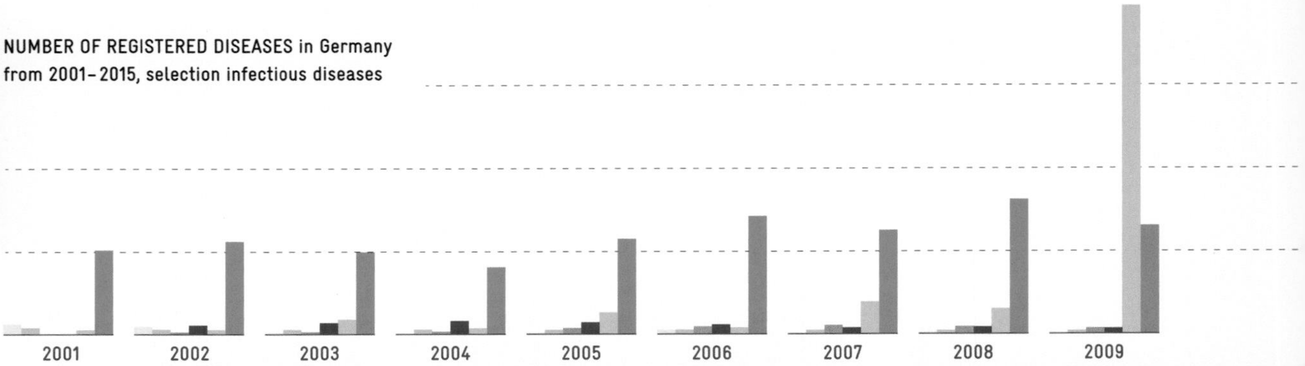
2001
2002
2003
2004
2005
2006
2007
2008
2009

ACTIVE IMMUNIZATION
The vaccine contains weakened antigens. The immune system reacts to the antigens, producing antibodies and memory cells. If a person comes in contact again with the pathogen, then there will be antibodies ready for an immune response. The protection usually starts after a few days and lasts several years or a lifetime.

VACCINE DEVELOPMENT

The pathogen is injected into an animal or chemically treated. In this way, its antigens are weakened.

The vaccine with weakened antigens is administered as an injection or oral vaccination.

Antigen-presenting cells recognize the virus cells and transport them to the immune cells. These are then activated.

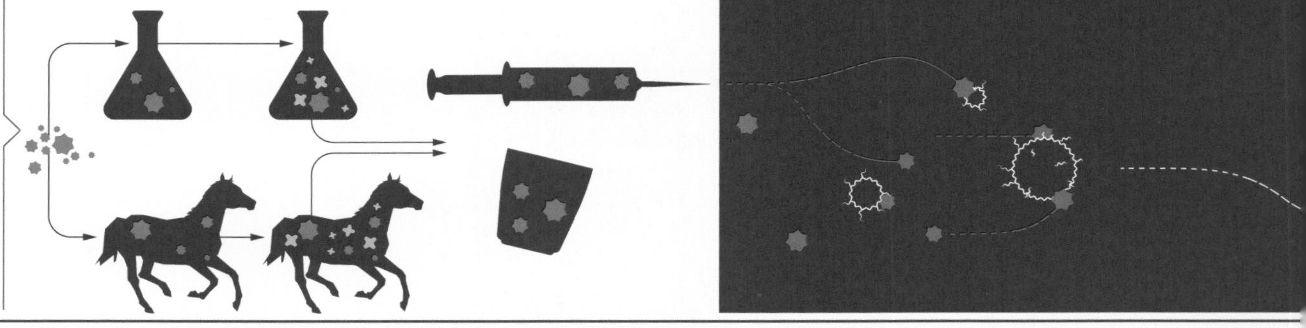

PASSIVE IMMUNIZATION
The serum contains antibodies that react immediately to the pathogen's antigens and thus provide protection. It is administered as a short-term prophylaxis against an infection, when an infection is suspected or after an infection. The immunization wears off after a few months because the antibodies break down quickly.

VACCINE DEVELOPMENT

Antibodies develop in an animal's body or are chemically isolated.

The serum with the antibodies is administered as an injection.

If the pathogen is not inside the body, then the anti-bodies provide protection for the next months.

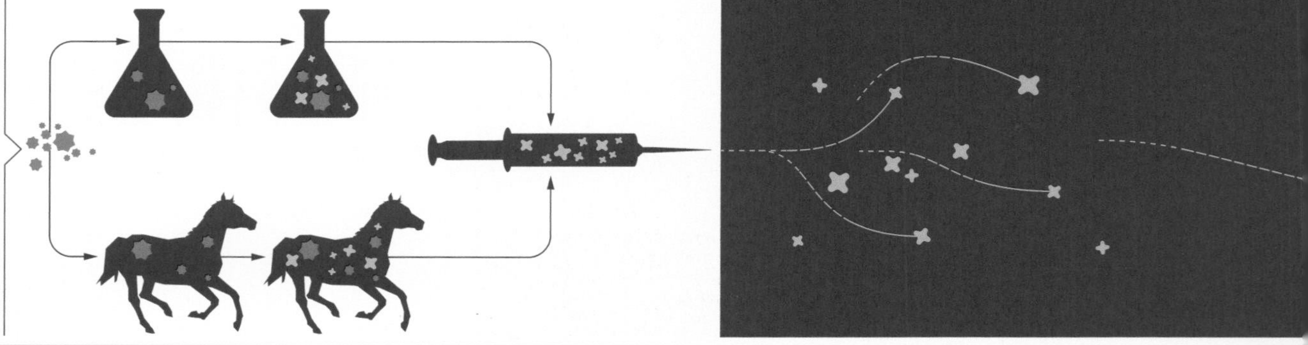

CHILDREN AND ADOLESCENTS

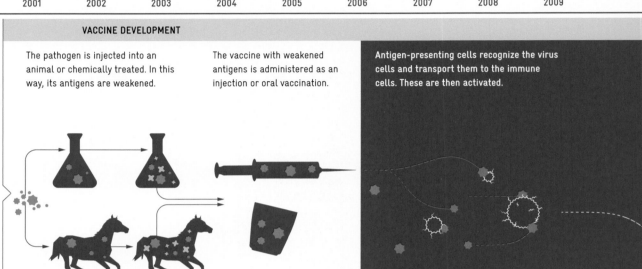

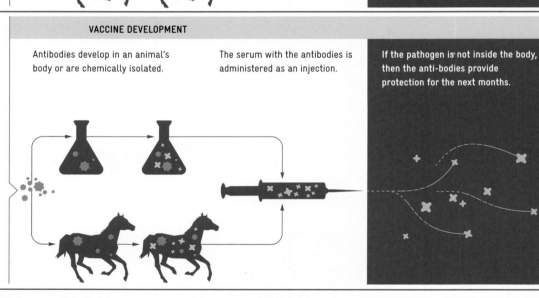

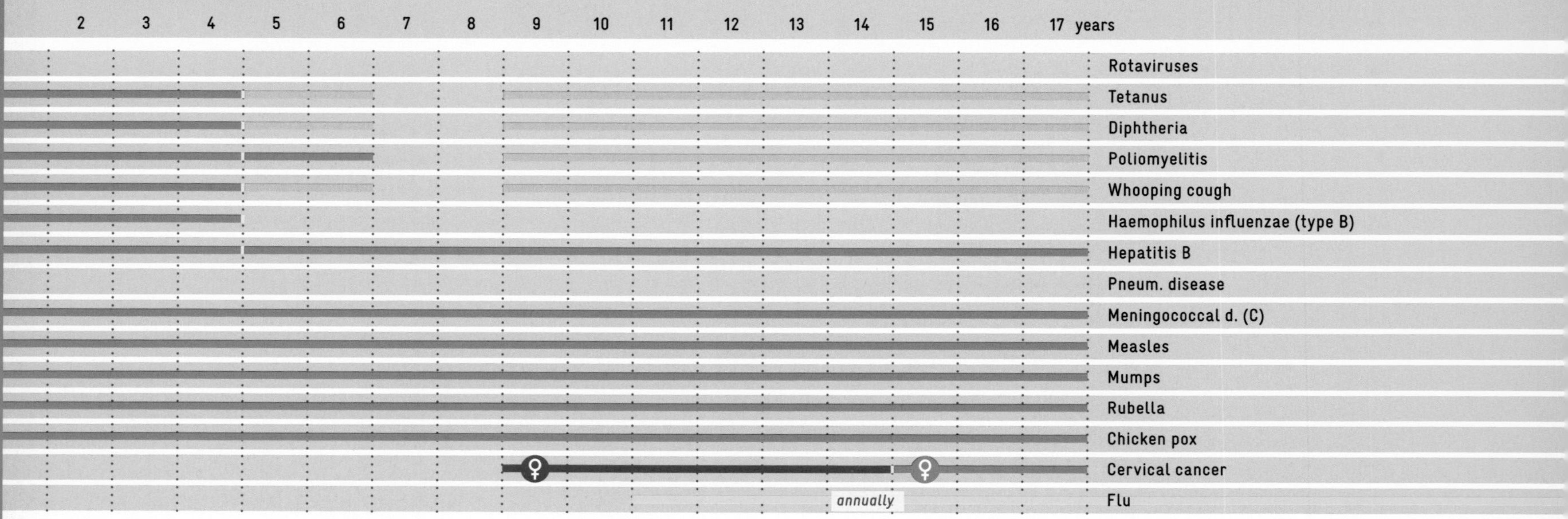
2 3 4 5 6 7 8 9 10 11 12 13 14 15 16 17 years
Rotaviruses
Tetanus
Diphtheria
Poliomyelitis
Whooping cough
Haemophilus influenzae (type B)
Hepatitis B
Pneum. disease
Meningococcal d. (C)
Measles
Mumps
Rubella
Chicken pox
Cervical cancer
Flu
annually

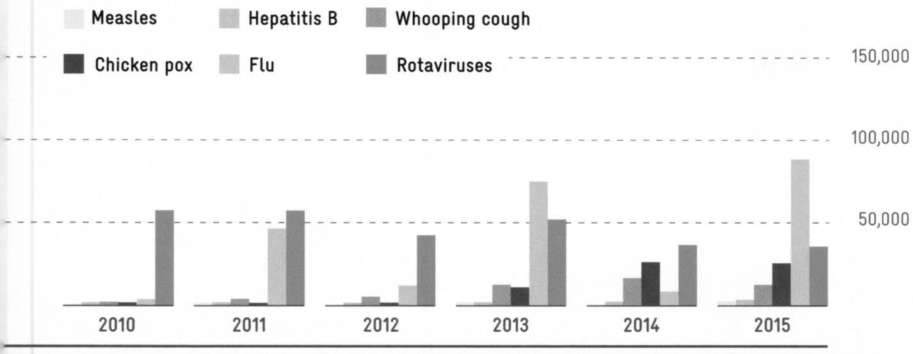
Measles
Hepatitis B
Whooping cough
Chicken pox
Flu
Rotaviruses
150,000
100,000
50,000
2010
2011
2012
2013
2014
2015

Right into the 19th century, doctors could not provide any help against plagues and epidemics. Famous figures such as Schiller or Schubert died of tuberculosis (TB) and typhus.

ADMINISTRATION

Lymphocytes develop antibodies, which will attach themselves to the virus cells and make them harmless. Then the pathogen is destroyed.

Memory cells develop from activated lymphocytes. Immunity is built up.

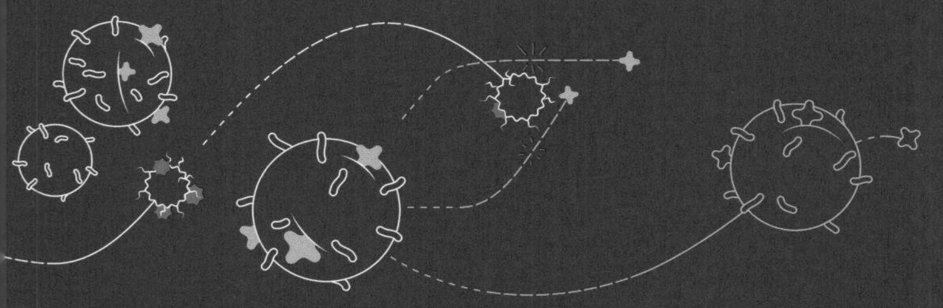

ADMINISTRATION

If the body is already infected, then the antibodies provide immediate protection.

In an infection, the foreign antibodies attack the pathogen and destroy it. The organism remains passive here.

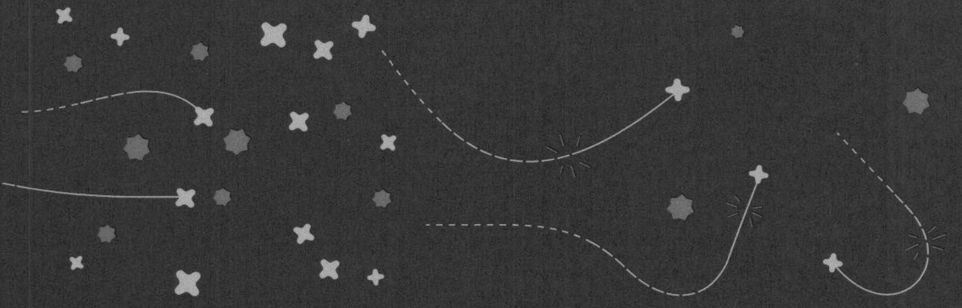

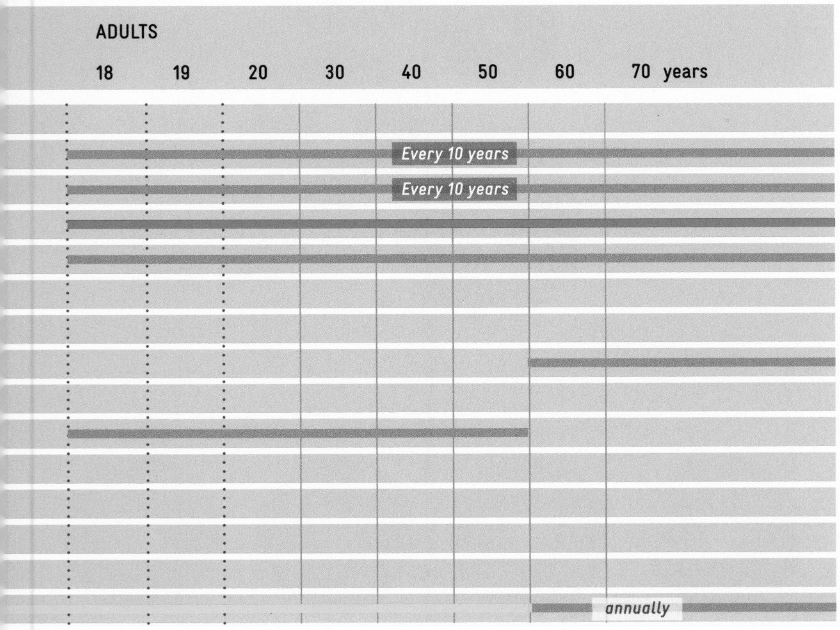
ADULTS
18
19
20
30
40
50
60
70 years
Every 10 years
Every 10 years
annually

Serovaccination is a combination of active and passive immunization. The aim is to combine the immediate effect with long-lasting protection.

KAISER OTTO THE THIRD
Roman-German emperor, died at the age of 21 from malaria.

980–1002

HANS HOLBEIN THE YOUNGER
German painter, died at the age of 46 from the Black Death.

1497/1498–1543

FRIEDRICH SCHILLER
German poet and philosopher, died at the age of 45 from tuberculosis.

1759–1805

FRANZ SCHUBERT
Austrian composer, died at the age of 31 from typhus.

1797–1828

GEORGE BIZET
French composer, died at the age of 36 from diphtheria.

1838–1875

EGON SCHIELE
Austrian painter, died at the age of 28 from influenza.

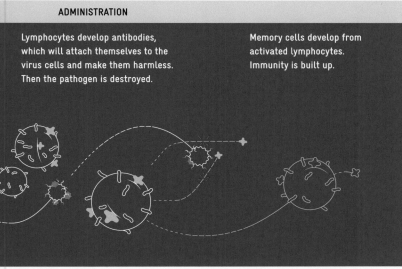

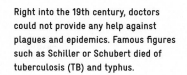

1890–1918

WHAT'S YOUR TYPE?

In 1900, the Austrian doctor Karl Landsteiner discovered every person could be categorized into A, B and O. In 1930, he was awarded the Nobel Prize for Medicine for his life-saving work. In 1937, Landstein, together with Alexander Wiener, discovered another antigen on the surface of red blood cells: the D antigen. They called this discovery the Rh factor, named after the rhesus monkeys that were used in their research.

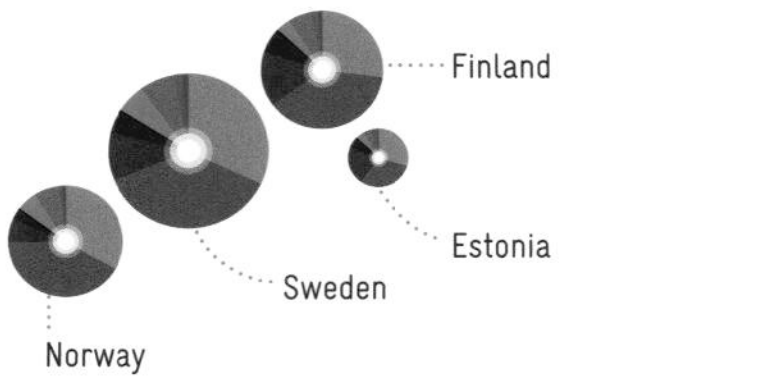
Finland
Estonia
Sweden
Norway

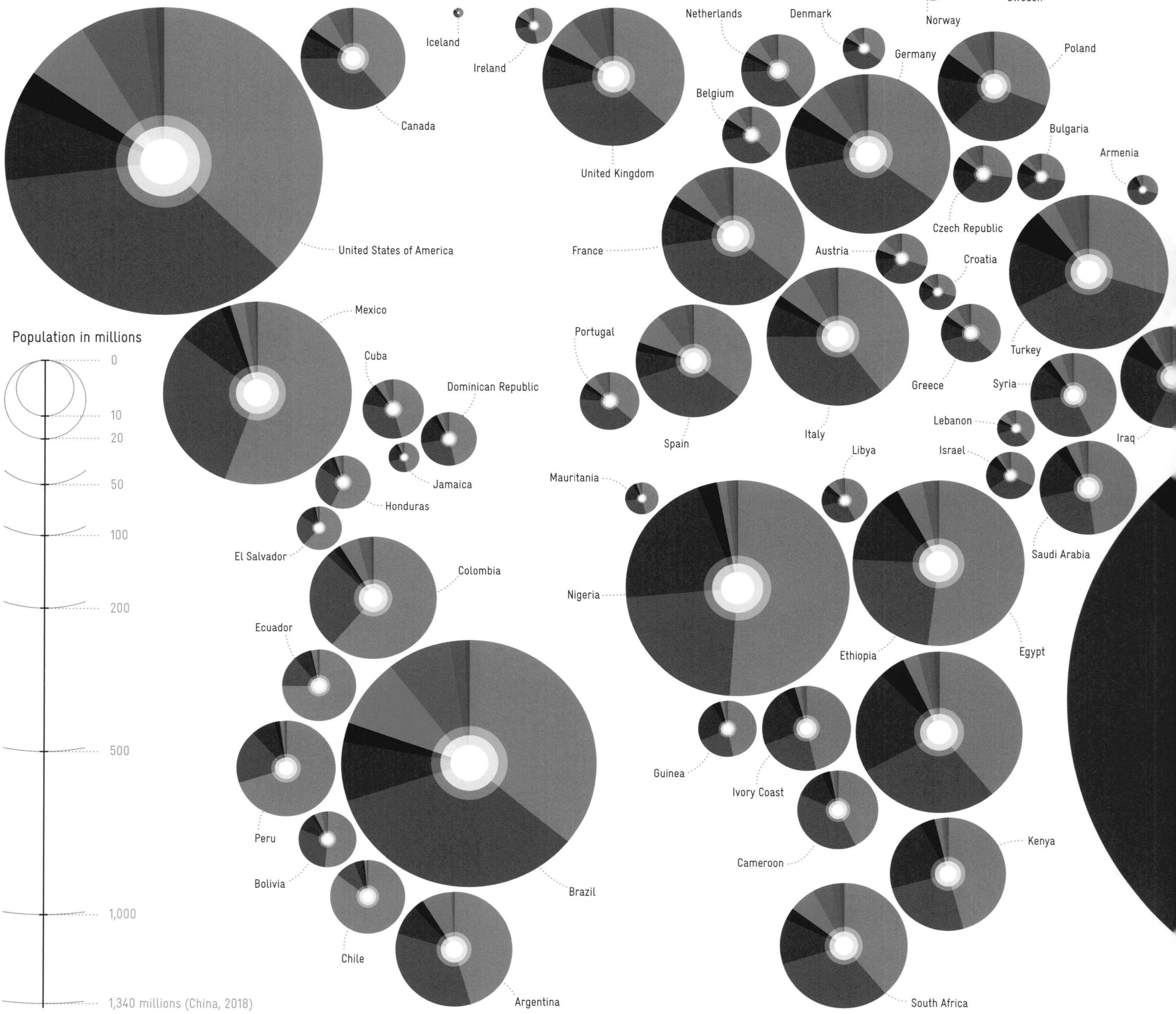
Iceland
Ireland
Canada
United States of America
United Kingdom
Netherlands
Denmark
Germany
Poland
Belgium
Bulgaria
Armenia
Czech Republic
France
Austria
Croatia
Turkey
Portugal
Greece
Syria
Spain
Italy
Lebanon
Iraq
Israel
Libya
Mauritania
Saudi Arabia
Nigeria
Ethiopia
Egypt
Guinea
Ivory Coast
Cameroon
Kenya
South Africa
Mexico
Cuba
Dominican Republic
Jamaica
Honduras
El Salvador
Colombia
Ecuador
Peru
Bolivia
Chile
Brazil
Argentina
Population in millions
0
10
20
50
100
200
500
1,000
1,340 millions (China, 2018)

Distribution over the continents

The ratio of the different types varies, depending on your origins. According to current migration theories, mankind started in Africa, moved via the Middle East to Europe, via Asia to America, and with a final wave through Asia and Oceania to Australia. In addition to other chromatic markers, scientists built this theory on the blood types of the population.

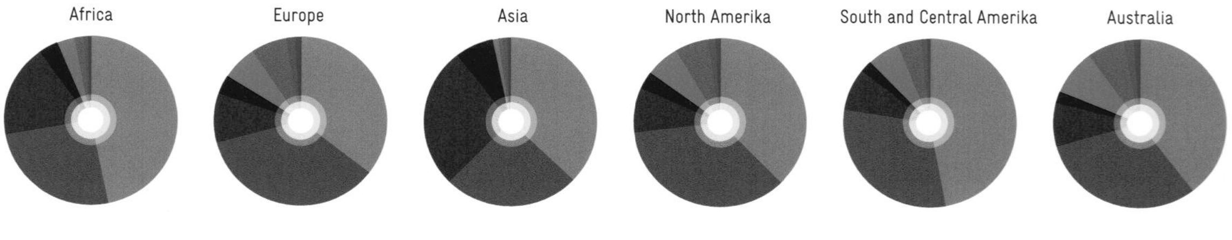
Africa
Europe
Asia
North Amerika
South and Central Amerika
Australia

Blood type, Rh factor: positive

0+ Red blood cells with *no antigens* Plasma with *A and B antibodies*

A+ Red blood cells with *A antigens* Plasma with *B antibodies*

B+ Red blood cells with *B antigens* Plasma with *A antibodies*

AB+ Red blood cells with *A and B antigens* Plasma with *no antibodies*

Blood type, Rh factor: negative

0- Red blood cells with *no antigens* Plasma with *A and B antibodies*

A- Red blood cells with *A antigens* Plasma with *B antibodies*

B- Red blood cells with *B antigens* Plasma with *A antibodies*

AB- Red blood cells with *A and B antigens* Plasma with *no antibodies*

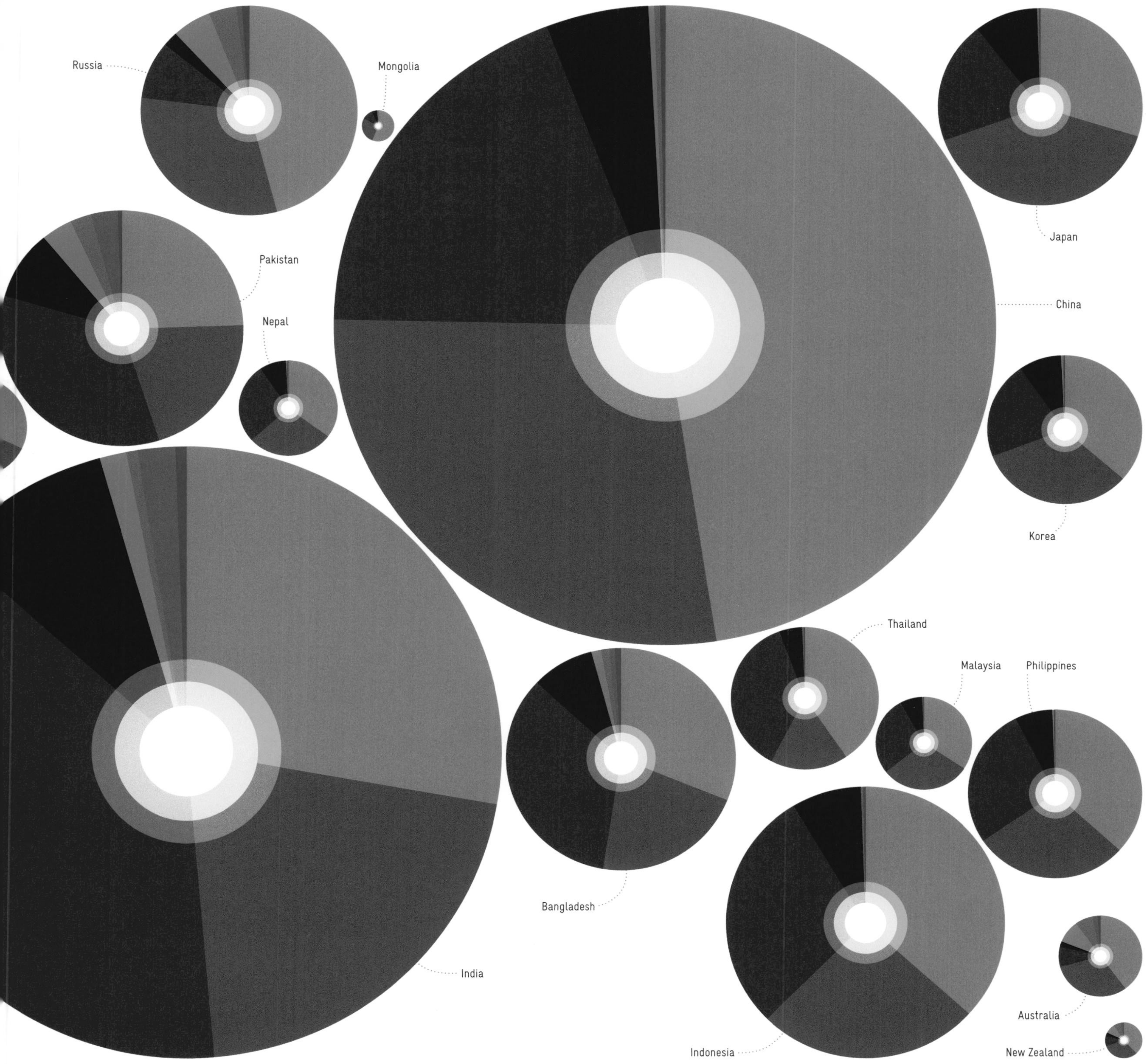

Finding the right match

Before Karl Landsteiner and Alexander Weiner discovered that not all blood is the same, receiving donor blood could quickly turn deadly. Today, understanding the relationship between antibodies and antigens means blood transfusions are a routine procedure.

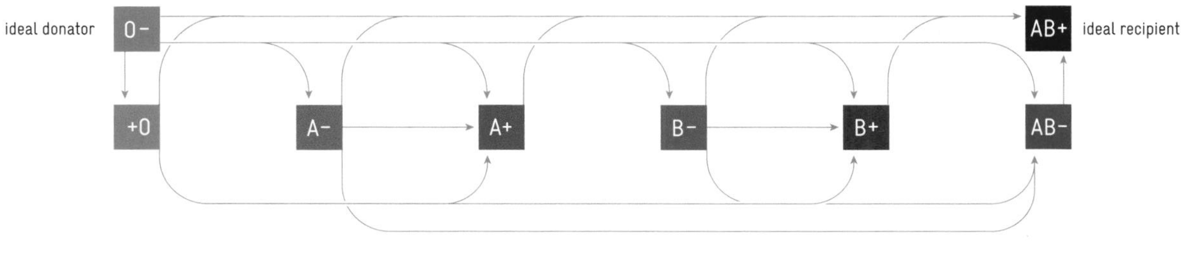

A CLEAR CASE?

Sixty-two-year-old Luise Kandinsky is found in her living room, lying on her back at 4:47 p.m. with a stab wound in her belly. The door to the flat is shut but not locked. All the windows are closed but the balcony door has been smashed from the outside. She is found because a neighbor, who checks in on Ms Kandinsky on a daily basis, opens the door with the key that was given to her. The neighbor doesn't notice any unusual events on the day of the discovery. Uniformed police appear at the crime scene at 5:02 p.m. , staff of the 24-hour criminal investigation department at around 5:30 p.m.. The flat has been ransacked and large sums of money are missing. Other precious items such as jewelry have not been taken. There are no indications that Ms. K. has been entertaining anyone. The possible crime weapon, a single-edge knife with what looks like blood stains, is recovered. It all points to a murder.

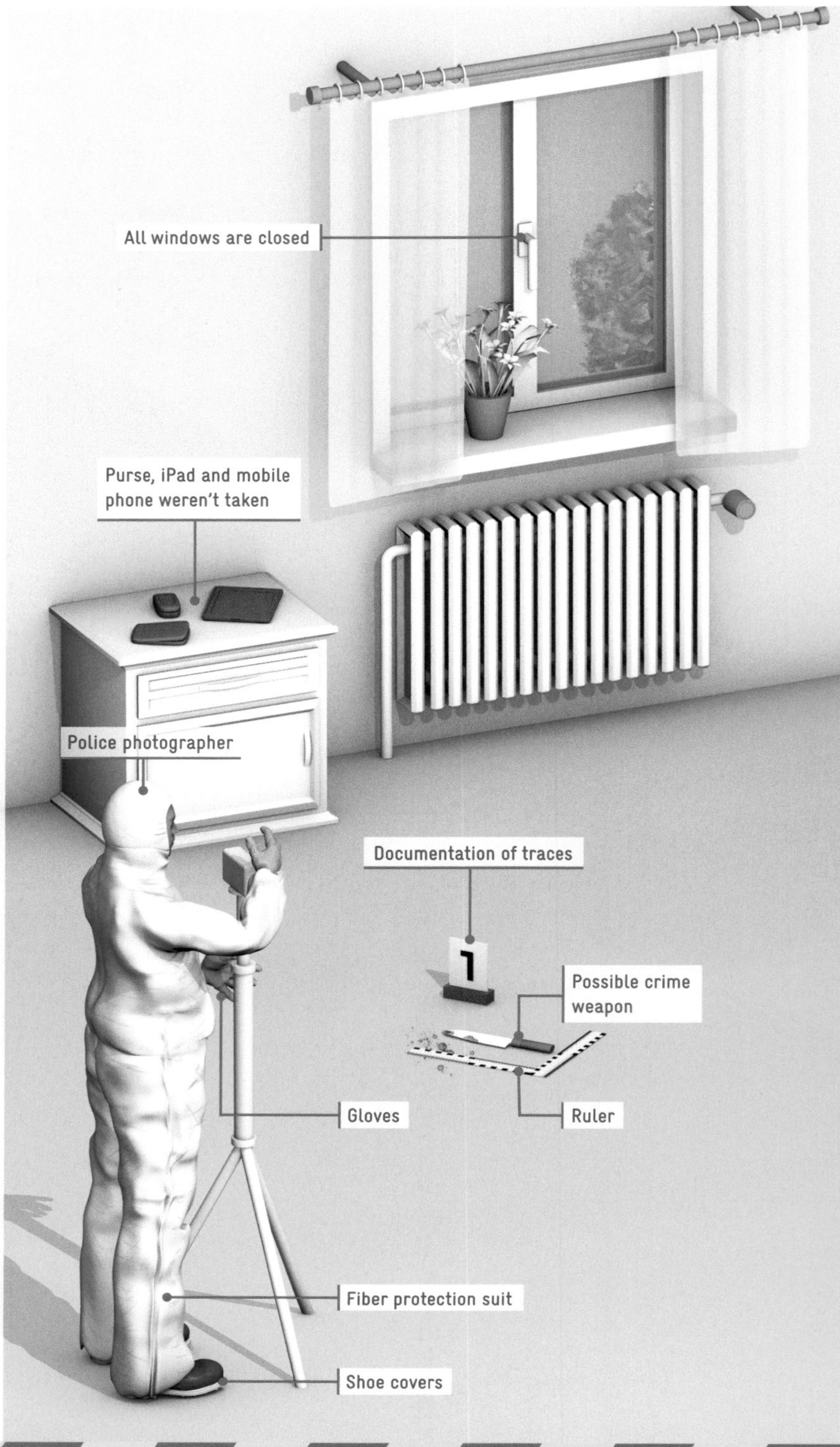

All windows are closed
Purse, iPad and mobile phone weren't taken
Police photographer
Documentation of traces
1
Possible crime weapon
Gloves
Ruler
Fiber protection suit
Shoe covers

THE CORONER AT THE CRIME SCENE

1 PEOPLE

After staff of the 24-hour criminal investigation department have gained a first overview of the crime scene and the dead body, they notify both the coroner and the prosecutor on duty, as well as the forensics team and the murder squad of the State Office of Criminal Investigation.

2 IMMEDIATE AUTOPSY

After all traces have been secured from the clothes and dead body, the coroner conducts an external examination. The victim's clothes are cut open, then removed and given to forensics. The coroner also thinks that this is a possible murder case, because he not only detects the belly stab wound but also signs of congestion in the head. He discovers pinpoint bleedings on the eyelids and gums – clear evidence of an obstruction in the veins of the neck area, either because of a disease or compression of the neck. There are no traces of injuries on the skin of the neck – but such an obstruction cannot be explained by a belly stab wound. The prosecutor therefore orders a speedy autopsy of the dead body. Shortly afterwards, it is transported to the Institute of Forensics.

Clothes are cut open

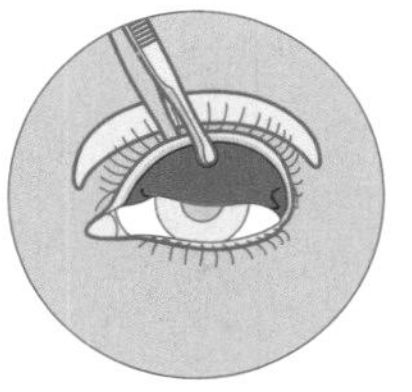

Pinpoint bleedings on the eye lids

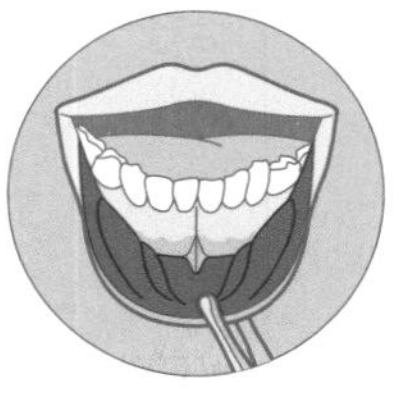

Pinpoint bleedings on the gums

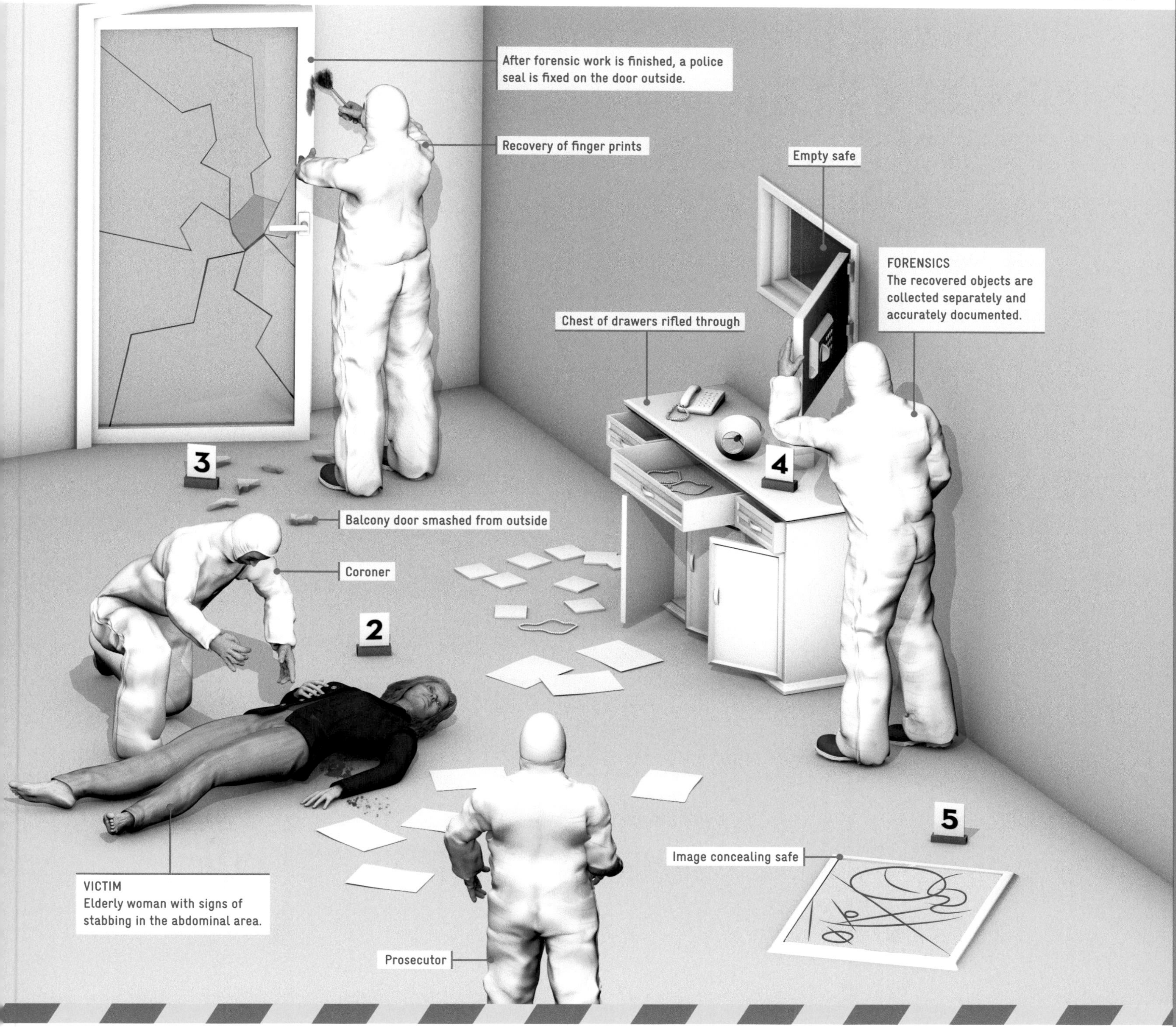

3 ESTABLISHMENT OF THE TIME OF DEATH

During the coroner's inquest at the location, some investigations are carried out to estimate the time of death. The dead body's deep rectal temperature at the scene is 32.3 °C at 6:45 p.m, the room temperature on floor level directly next to the dead body is 21 °C at 6:50 p.m.. The dead body weighs around 70 – 80 kg and has two layers of clothing. Despite the smashed balcony door, there's no cooling draft in the living room. The administration of Atropin into the left eye leads to a widening of the pupil and Pilocarpin into the right eye makes the pupil smaller, both after a short time. The mimic muscles in the left eye area can still be stimulated at 40 mV and 10 mV. An idiomuscular lump on the right upper arm is still triggerable. Overall, the evidence so far suggests that the person died six to ten hours ago.

Ability to change position of lividity

Postmortem lividity can provide information about the time of death, especially if the dead person was turned over or their position changed before he was found.

An example of a person who died on their front:

Change of position is fully possible after six hours

Change of position is only partially possible after six to twelve hours

Change of position is no longer possible after twelve hours

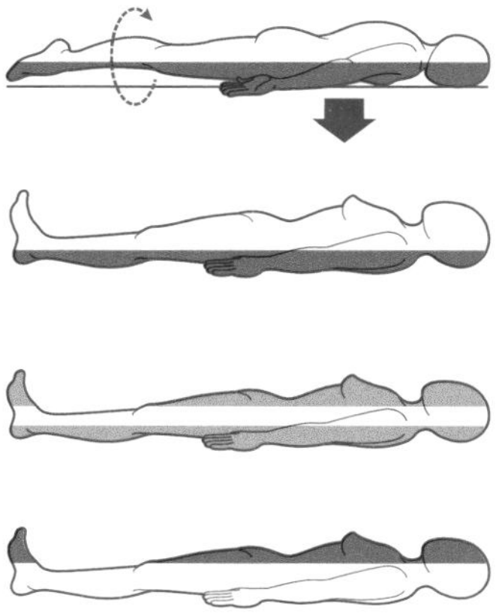

The temperature

Thermometer to determine rectal temperature

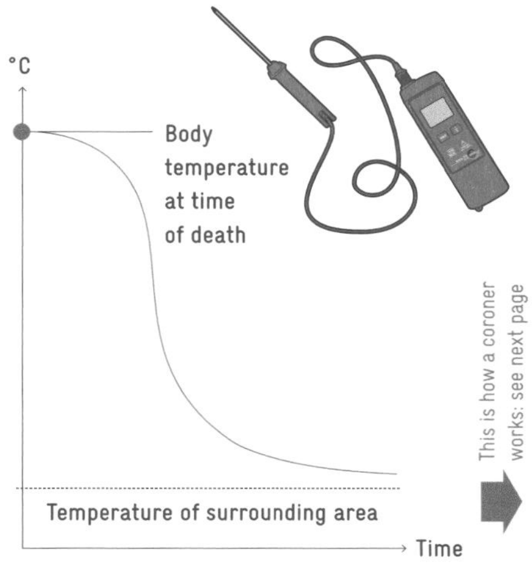
°C
Body temperature at time of death
Temperature of surrounding area
Time

This is how a coroner works: see next page

AN UNEXPECTED TWIST

The postmortem CT examination, external coroner's inquest and dissection take place following the prosecutor's order at the Institute of Forensics from 8:30 p.m. onwards. The dead body is that of a heavily built elderly woman. On the back, dark blue livor mortis is visible which can still be made invisible by applying pressure. There is some warmth left but rigor mortis has started taking over the bigger joints. The right lower belly shows a neatly defined, slightly gaping cut through the skin of around 1cm in length. It has a pointed and an obtuse wound angle and a few traces of dried blood in the surrounding area. The conjunctivae and eyelids show pinpoint bleeding, as does the mucous membrane of the oral vestibule. The head has turned slightly blue and seems congested. There are no injuries on the neck's skin and also no signs of injuries from resistance.

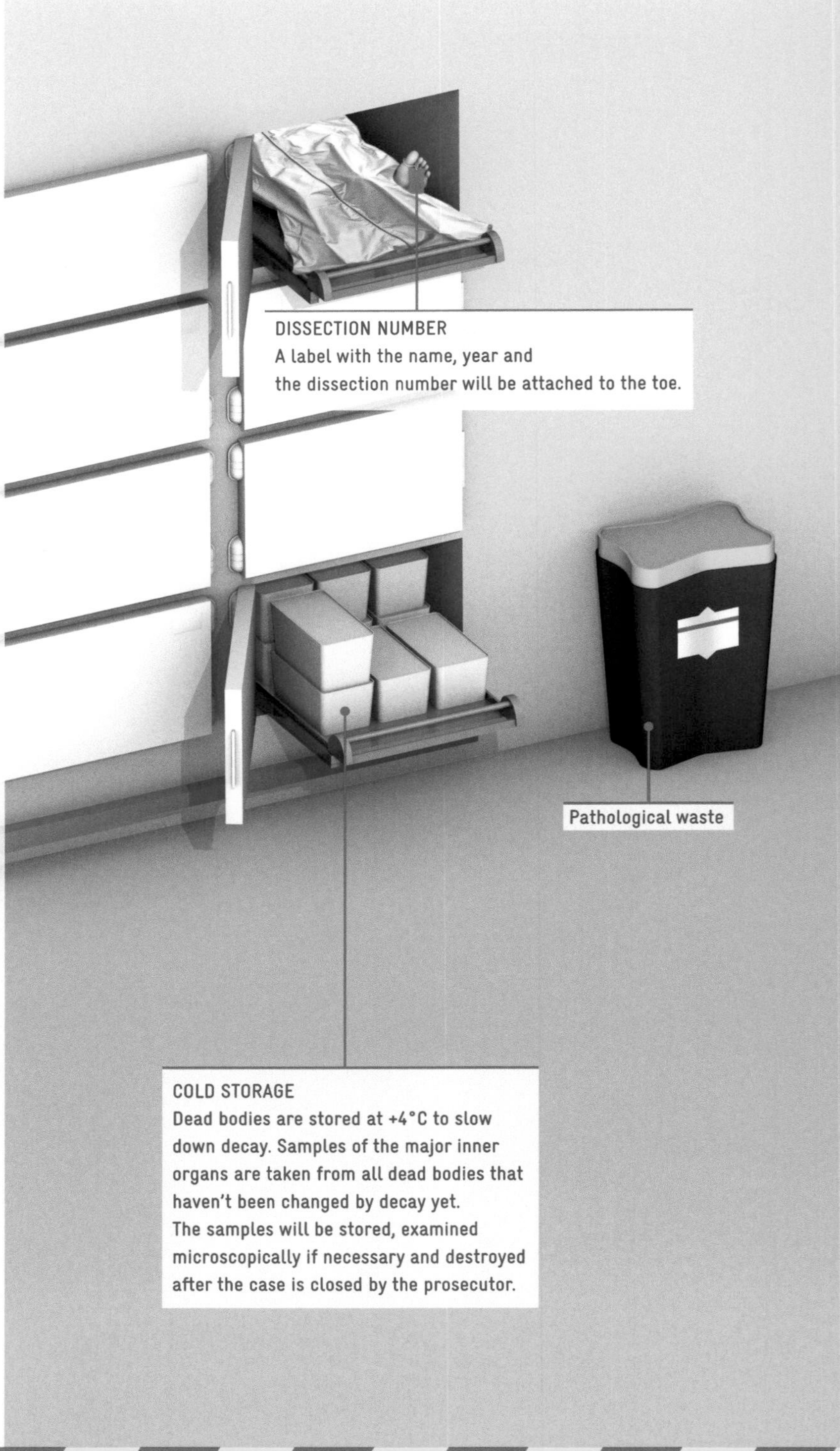
DISSECTION NUMBER
A label with the name, year and the dissection number will be attached to the toe.
Pathological waste
COLD STORAGE
Dead bodies are stored at +4°C to slow down decay. Samples of the major inner organs are taken from all dead bodies that haven't been changed by decay yet.
The samples will be stored, examined microscopically if necessary and destroyed after the case is closed by the prosecutor.

DISSECTION PROCESS

1 CT AND EXTERIOR EXAMINATION

First of all, the dead body is measured. Then a postmortem CT is done to document all results without touching the body. In this case, air is already in the abdominal cavity but there's also a visible fracture of the tongue's hyoid bone. Now, DNA samples are taken from the body orifices and the skin on the neck. The edges of the fingernails are removed and handed over to the murder squad. Now the dead body will be very carefully checked for fresh or older injuries or other distinctive features.

2 INTERIOR EXAMINATION (ACTUAL AUTOPSY)

Opening up of the head, chest and abdominal cavity is legally prescribed. First, there's a longitudinal cut from the chin to the pubic bone. The body's front is dissected in layers. It becomes apparent that the belly stab wound opened up the abdominal cavity but only superficially injured the colon. Larger vascular areas are not affected, the bleeding in the abdominal cavity hasn't caused death. The strong lividity also matches these findings—if there had been greater blood loss towards the inside or outside, it would have been less distinct. The scalp is opened up and moved over the skull in front of the face. Then the cranium is sawed open in a circle and removed. Now, the brain can be taken out for examination. In addition, arms, legs and the back of the body will be dissected in order not to miss any other crime-relevant traces of injuries.
At the end of the dissection, a number of chemical and toxicological examinations are carried out.

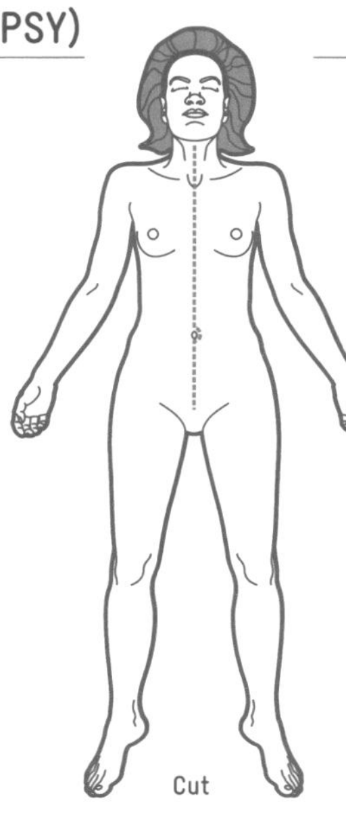
Cut

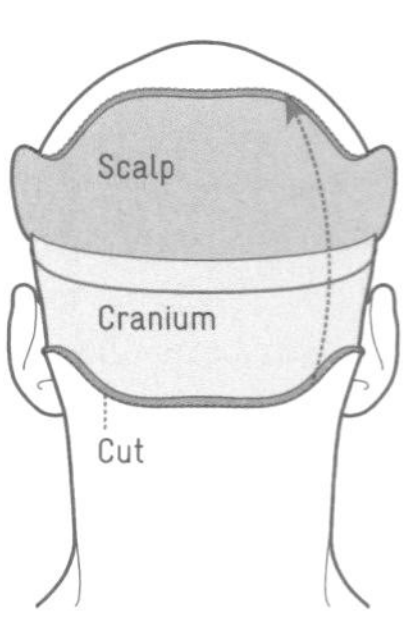
Scalp
Cranium
Cut

Opening up of skull

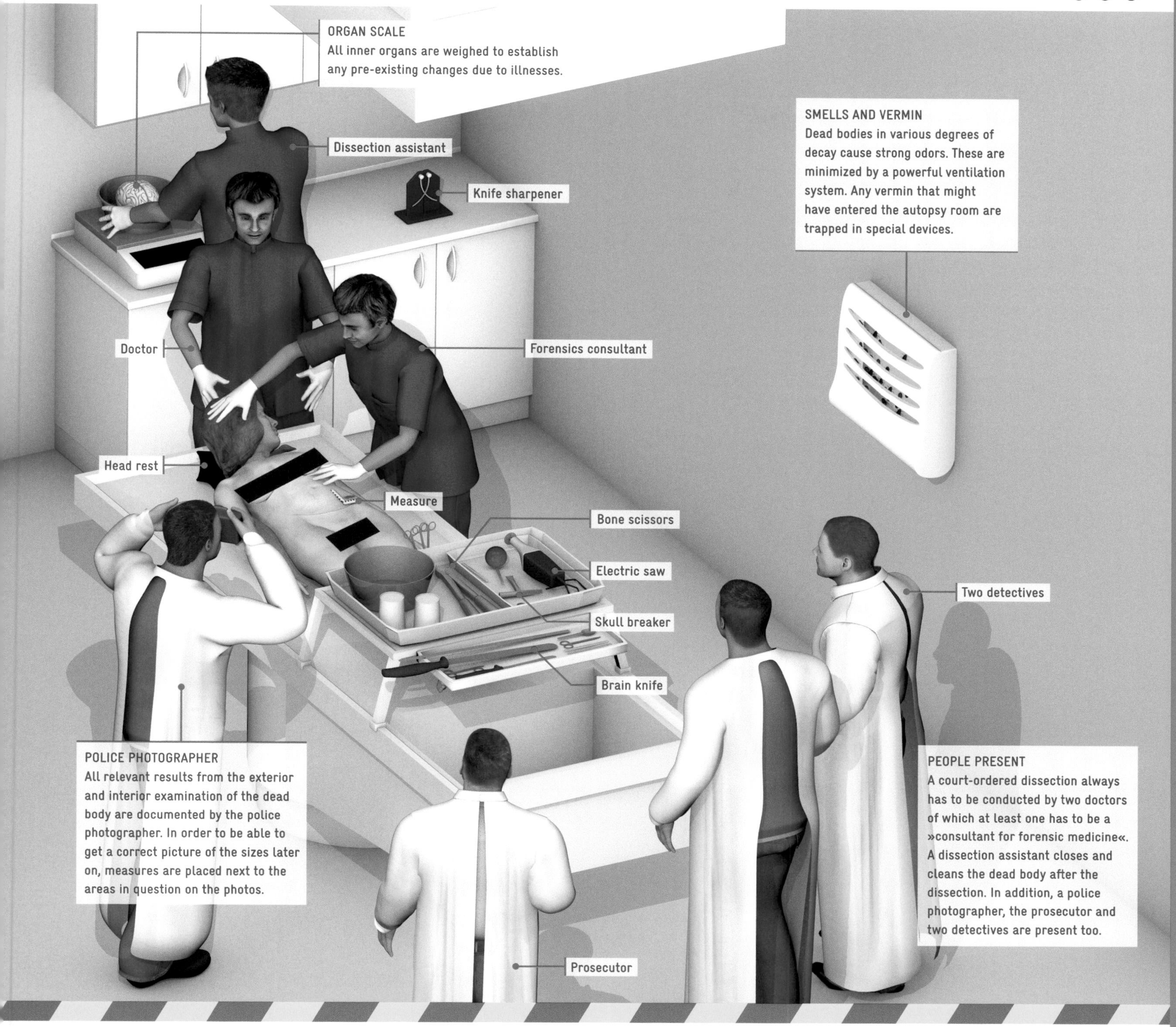

ORGAN SCALE
All inner organs are weighed to establish any pre-existing changes due to illnesses.

SMELLS AND VERMIN
Dead bodies in various degrees of decay cause strong odors. These are minimized by a powerful ventilation system. Any vermin that might have entered the autopsy room are trapped in special devices.

POLICE PHOTOGRAPHER
All relevant results from the exterior and interior examination of the dead body are documented by the police photographer. In order to be able to get a correct picture of the sizes later on, measures are placed next to the areas in question on the photos.

PEOPLE PRESENT
A court-ordered dissection always has to be conducted by two doctors of which at least one has to be a »consultant for forensic medicine«. A dissection assistant closes and cleans the dead body after the dissection. In addition, a police photographer, the prosecutor and two detectives are present too.

3 REMOVAL OF NECK ORGANS

The removal of neck organs in a bundle follows after the brain and heart have been taken out in order to avoid postmortal leakage of blood into the neck's muscles and therefore to avoid confusion with hemorrhages that have occured during the person's lifetime.
Both sterno cleidomastoids (the muscles involved in turning the head) show striped hemorrhages, there are also strong fresh hemorrhages around the larynx. In addition, the tongue's hyoid bone shows a sharp-edged fracture; the fracture's edges are also surrounded by heavy bleeding. The injuries are therefore fresh and must have been caused during her life time, because hemorrhages can only develop if the circulation is still working. The results strengthen the suspicion gained from the exterior coroner's inquest that a deadly force to the neck must have been applied. No other competing cause of death can be found.

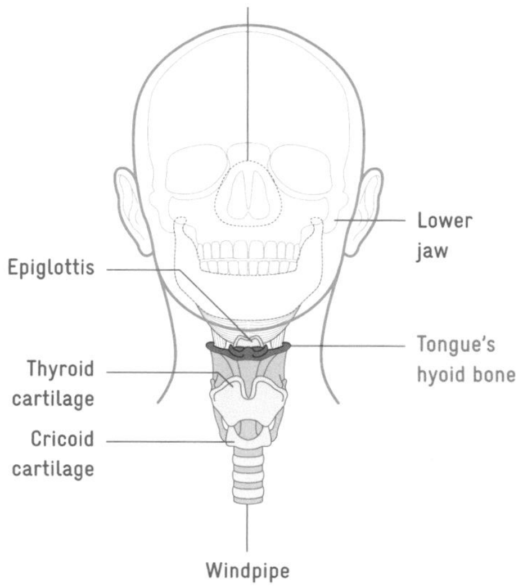

4 CAUSE OF DEATH

The stab wound to the belly didn't cause death. In fact, the signs of congestion in the head area and inner injuries to the neck point to a compression of the neck as the cause of death. Missing injuries on the neck's skin could mean that a broad and soft strangling tool, e.g. a scarf was used. A lower arm stranglehold is also a possibility. The cause of death isn't natural.

5 DISSECTION LOG

The process of the entire dissection is dictated, noted down and will later become part of the prosecutor's files for the inquiry.

Solution of the case on following page

THE INTERROGATION

Based on the police's findings and forensic results, the prosecutor has to assume that the burglar might not have strangled the victim. If he had done this, he wouldn't have had to flee the crime scene. But this is a strong possibility because some precious items were not stolen. In addition, the belly stab wound, presumably executed by the perpetrator, was inflicted with only a little force, which suggests that the burglar was not cold-blooded but was scared and decided to flee. When questioning the wider family, it becomes apparent that one of the victim's sons seems to show little surprise and is rather agitated. When interrogated more closely, he admits to having strangled his mother with a scarf to get his hands on the inheritance. Greed and malice are the motives for this murder. The suspected perpetrator will be charged with murder.

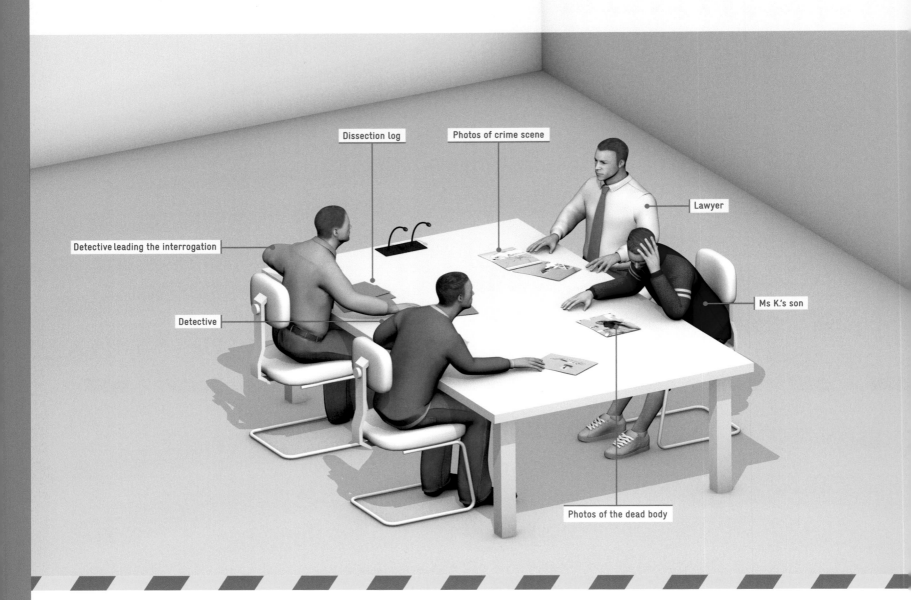

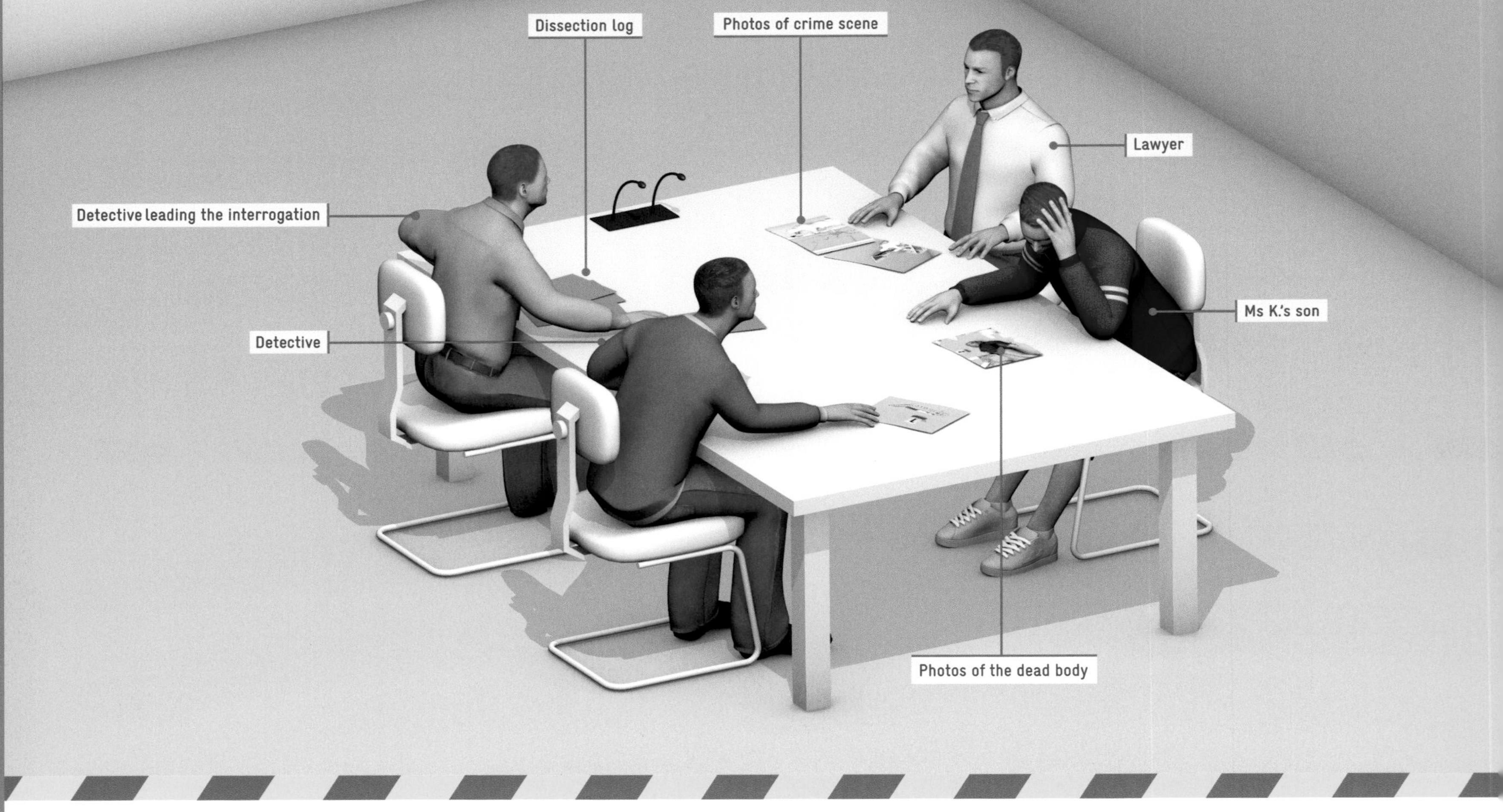
Dissection log
Photos of crime scene
Lawyer
Detective leading the interrogation
Ms K.'s son
Detective
Photos of the dead body

THE INTERROGATION

During the interrogation, the detectives have the dissection log at hand to present the suspect with pieces of evidence.

THE TRIAL

During the court trial, one of the two forensic consultants explains the autopsy results, as well as the manner and cause of death to the people involved in the trial. The defendant confesses and is convicted of murder.

POVERTY ALONE DOESN'T PRODUCE MURDERERS

It is true that the chances of getting killed are higher in poor countries than in rich ones. But there are numerous exceptions to this rule which show that other factors also play their part in turning people into murderers.

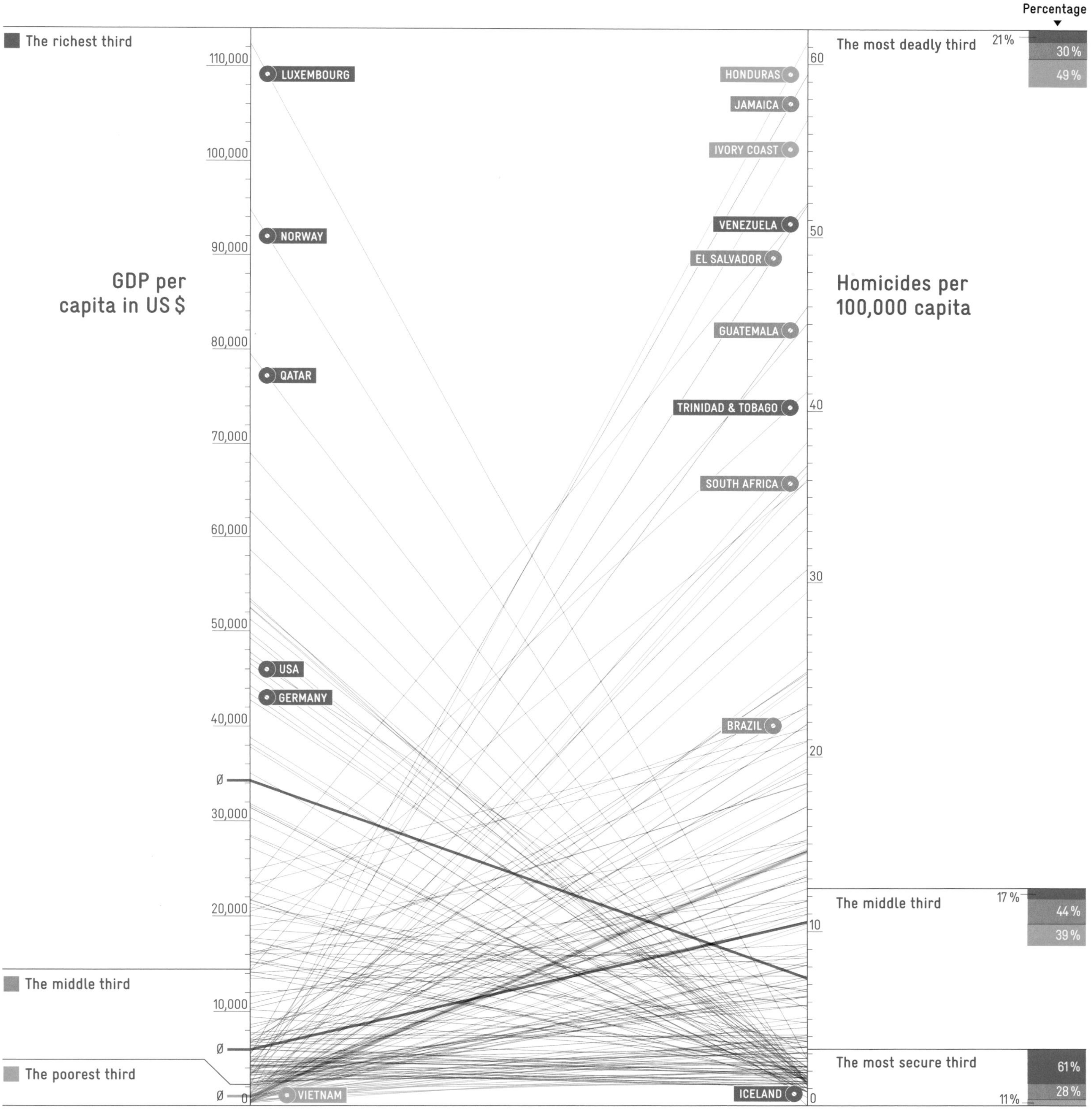

Percentage
The richest third
The middle third
The poorest third
GDP per capita in US $
110,000
100,000
90,000
80,000
70,000
60,000
50,000
40,000
30,000
20,000
10,000
0
Ø
LUXEMBOURG
NORWAY
QATAR
USA
GERMANY
VIETNAM
HONDURAS
JAMAICA
IVORY COAST
VENEZUELA
EL SALVADOR
GUATEMALA
TRINIDAD & TOBAGO
SOUTH AFRICA
BRAZIL
ICELAND
60
50
40
30
20
10
0
Homicides per 100,000 capita
The most deadly third
21 %
30 %
49 %
The middle third
17 %
44 %
39 %
The most secure third
61 %
28 %
11 %

Head

WILD AT HEART
DIVERSITY OF THE CARDIAC ORGAN IN THE ANIMAL KINGDOM

Our heart beats on the left. Or to be more specific, the heart is located in the middle, just as in other animals. Only the lower tip of our heart points to the left. In actual fact, the heart pumps rather than beats, regardless of its shape, anatomy, or how many there are in the body. Each species has a heart adapted to its lifestyle. However, the one thing all hearts have in common is that they transport substances throughout the body. A special feature of humans is that they are the only living beings that can lose their hearts.

Right aorta

Cog-teeth valve
At the entrance of the pulmonary artery, there are many knots of conjunctive tissue that can interlock like a zipper. Whether the zipper is open or not is decided by the level of adrenalin in the bloodstream.

Right atrium*

Blood redirection

The are three ways that blood pumps through a crocodile's body, depending on where it is and how active it is.

While **resting on land,** the crocodile doesn't need much oxygen and its heart beats only lightly. Oxygen-poor blood (blue) flows through the entire lower body and its intestines. Only the head and the front of the reptile is supplied with oxygen-rich blood (red) by the right aorta.

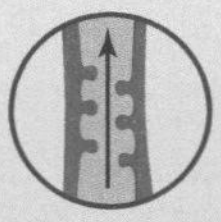

Cog-teeth valve open

Foramen of Panizza inactive

When **the activity starts to increase,** its heart beats faster. The difference in pressure in both heart chambers forces the blood into the lower body through the Foramen (latin for »opening«) of the Panizza and supplies it with oxygen-rich blood. The crocodile is now ready to hunt.

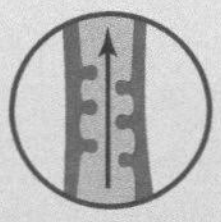

Cog-teeth valve open

Foramen of Panizza active

Blood circulation of a resting crocodile on land

* Labeling left and right from the viewpoint of the animal.

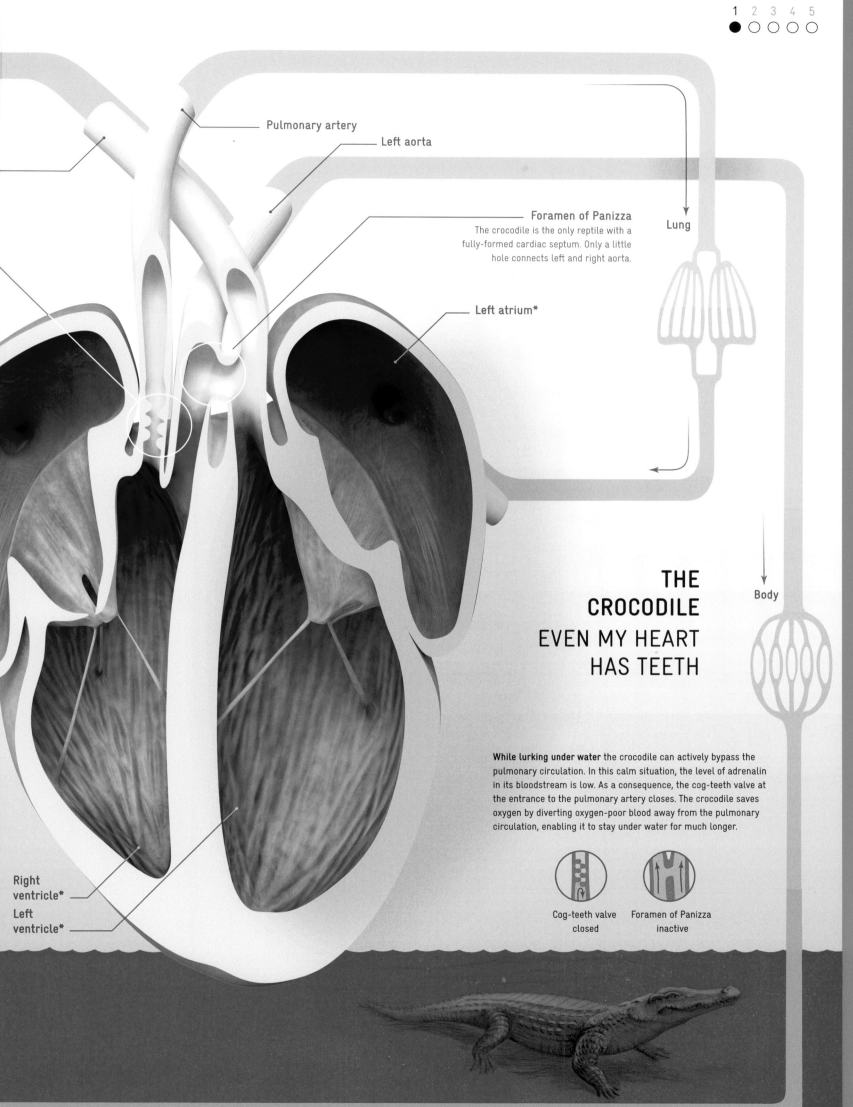

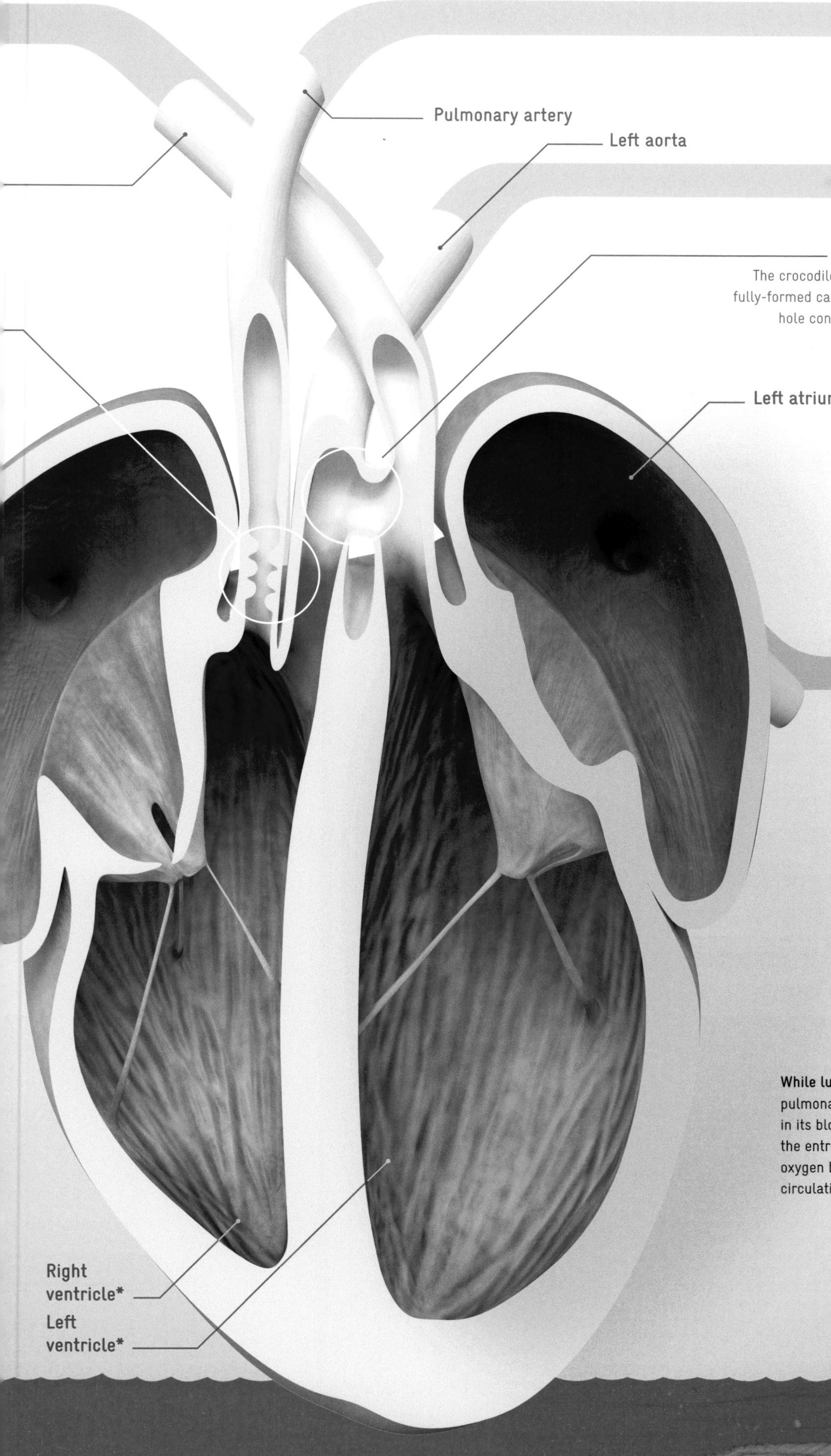
Pulmonary artery
Left aorta
Foramen of Panizza
The crocodile is the only reptile with a fully-formed cardiac septum. Only a little hole connects left and right aorta.
Lung
Left atrium*
Body
Right ventricle*
Left ventricle*

THE CROCODILE
EVEN MY HEART HAS TEETH

While lurking under water the crocodile can actively bypass the pulmonary circulation. In this calm situation, the level of adrenalin in its bloodstream is low. As a consequence, the cog-teeth valve at the entrance to the pulmonary artery closes. The crocodile saves oxygen by diverting oxygen-poor blood away from the pulmonary circulation, enabling it to stay under water for much longer.

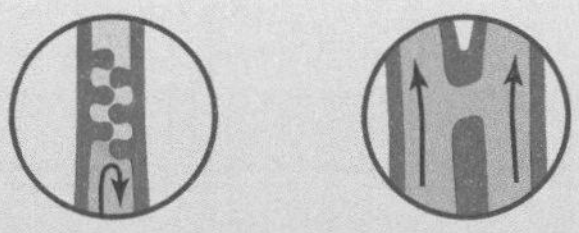
Cog-teeth valve closed
Foramen of Panizza inactive

THE BUTTERFLY

The blood of the butterfly is called Hemolymph. It is a yellow/green liquid that cannot bind oxygen. Hemolymph transports nutrients and flows freely through the body cavity. The pipe-like heart makes sure the blood gets pumped from the back to the front. Nine paired openings suck in the blood.

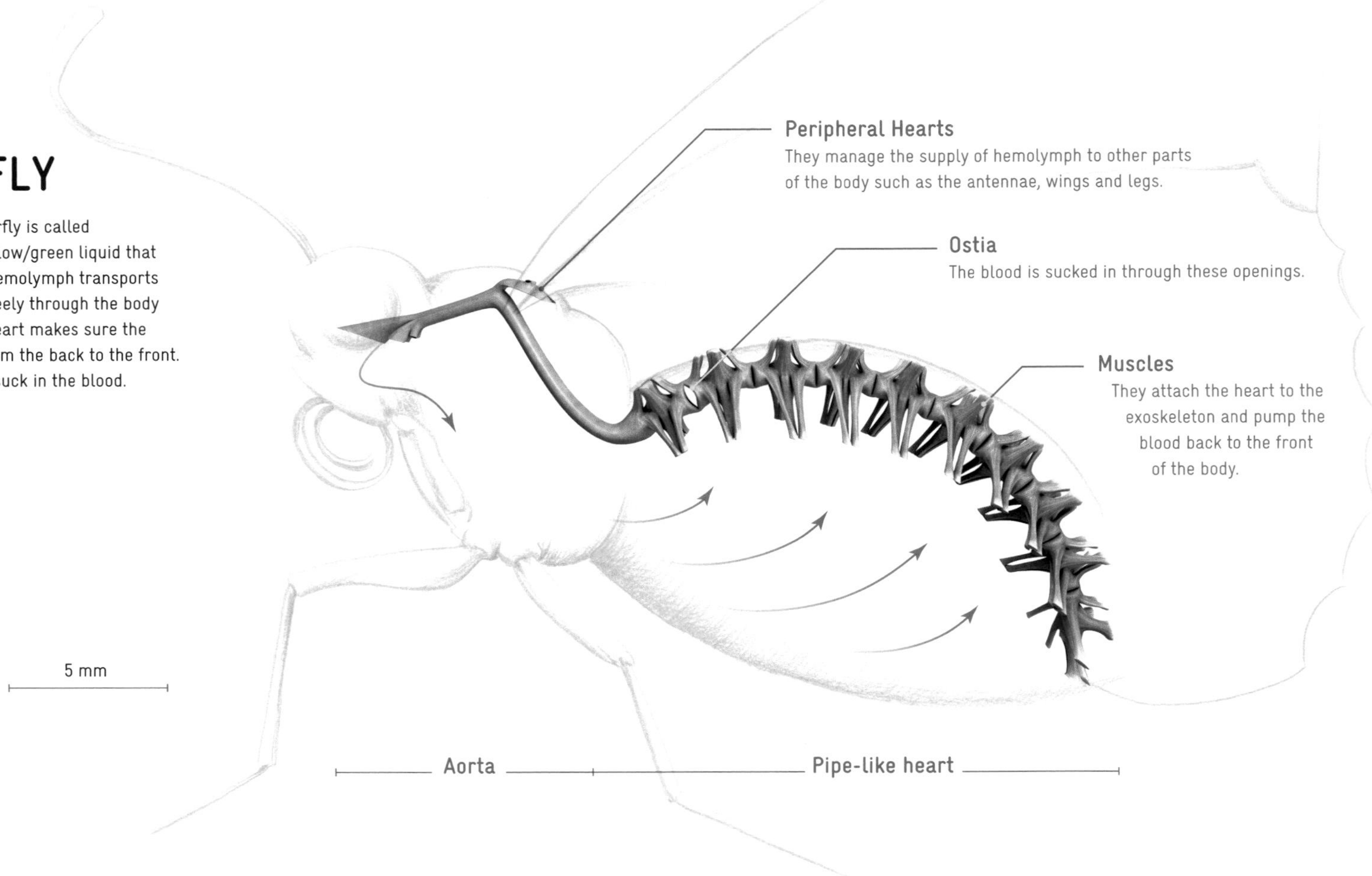
Peripheral Hearts
They manage the supply of hemolymph to other parts of the body such as the antennae, wings and legs.
Ostia
The blood is sucked in through these openings.
Muscles
They attach the heart to the exoskeleton and pump the blood back to the front of the body.
5 mm
Aorta
Pipe-like heart

THE EARTHWORM

Evolution already tested closed blood circulation with the earthworm. In addition, the worm is equipped with five aortic arches, the lateral hearts. Its blood has a red/brown color and transports nutrients and oxygen which is absorbed through the skin. In contrast to vertebrates, the hemoglobin is situated in the plasma and not in the red blood cells.

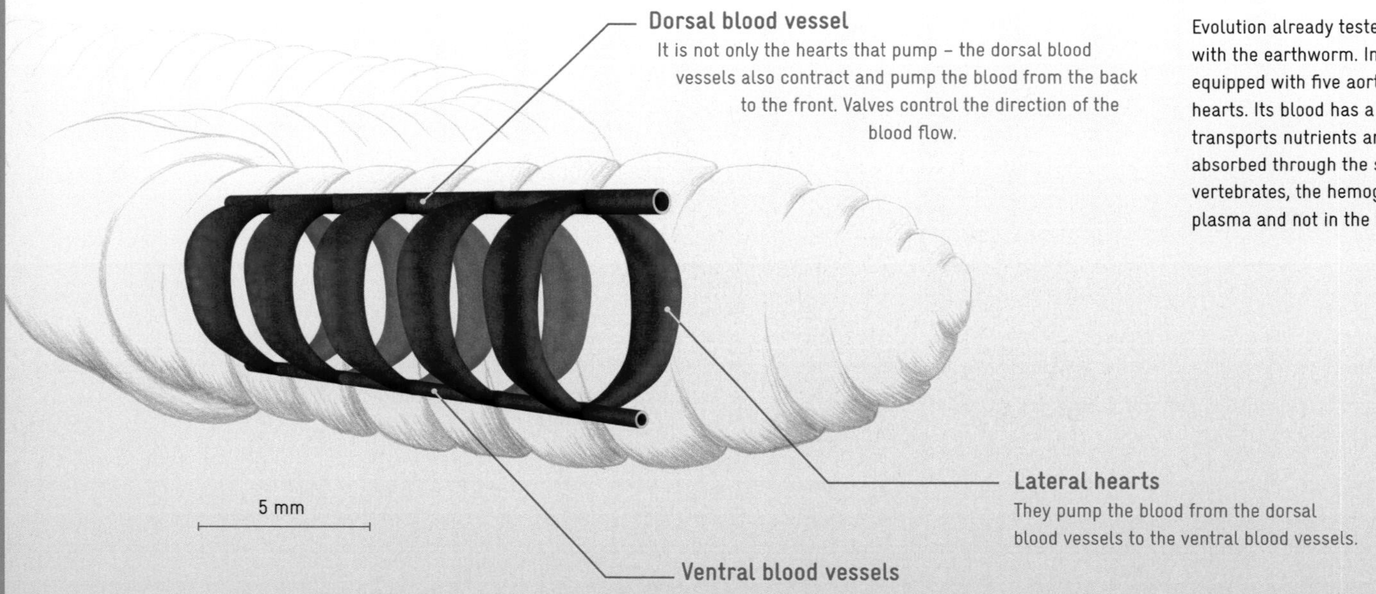
Dorsal blood vessel
It is not only the hearts that pump – the dorsal blood vessels also contract and pump the blood from the back to the front. Valves control the direction of the blood flow.
5 mm
Lateral hearts
They pump the blood from the dorsal blood vessels to the ventral blood vessels.
Ventral blood vessels

DID YOU KNOW?

On **day 22** the heart of the human embryo, which still only has the form of a pipe, starts to beat!

2.9 billion is the number of heartbeats during 80 years of a human's life.

It takes only **60 seconds** for 1 ml of blood to travel from the human heart to the feet and back!

THE PYTHON
AFTER FOOD
I ENLARGE MY HEART

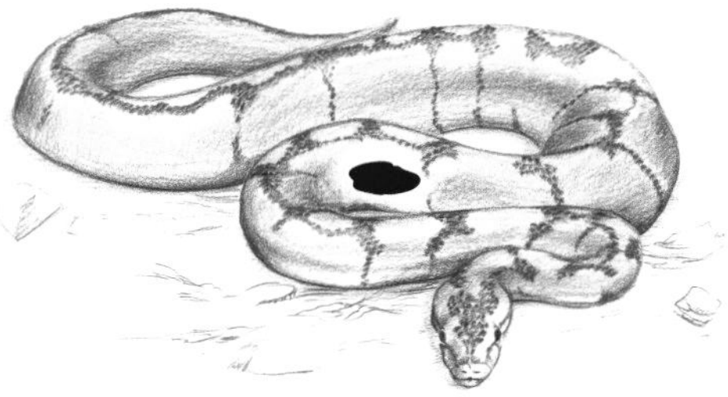

Heart position

The heart of the python, as with all other land snakes, is situated in the front third of its body. In this way it can supply its head and posterior body parts with enough blood.

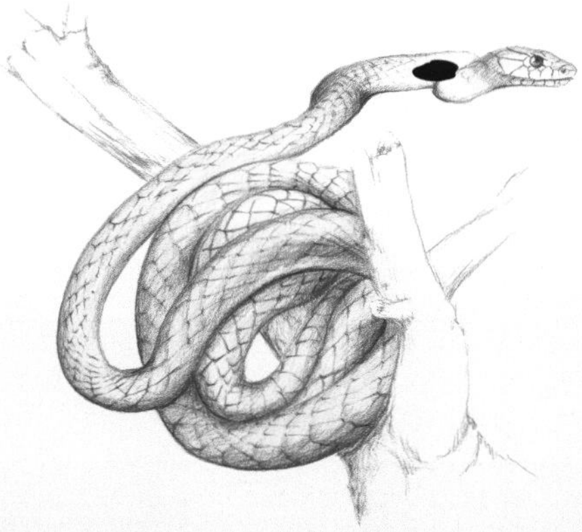

Depending on their habitat, the heart of other snakes, such as the climbing tree snake, is directly behind their heads.

The swimming sea snake has its heart in the middle of its body.

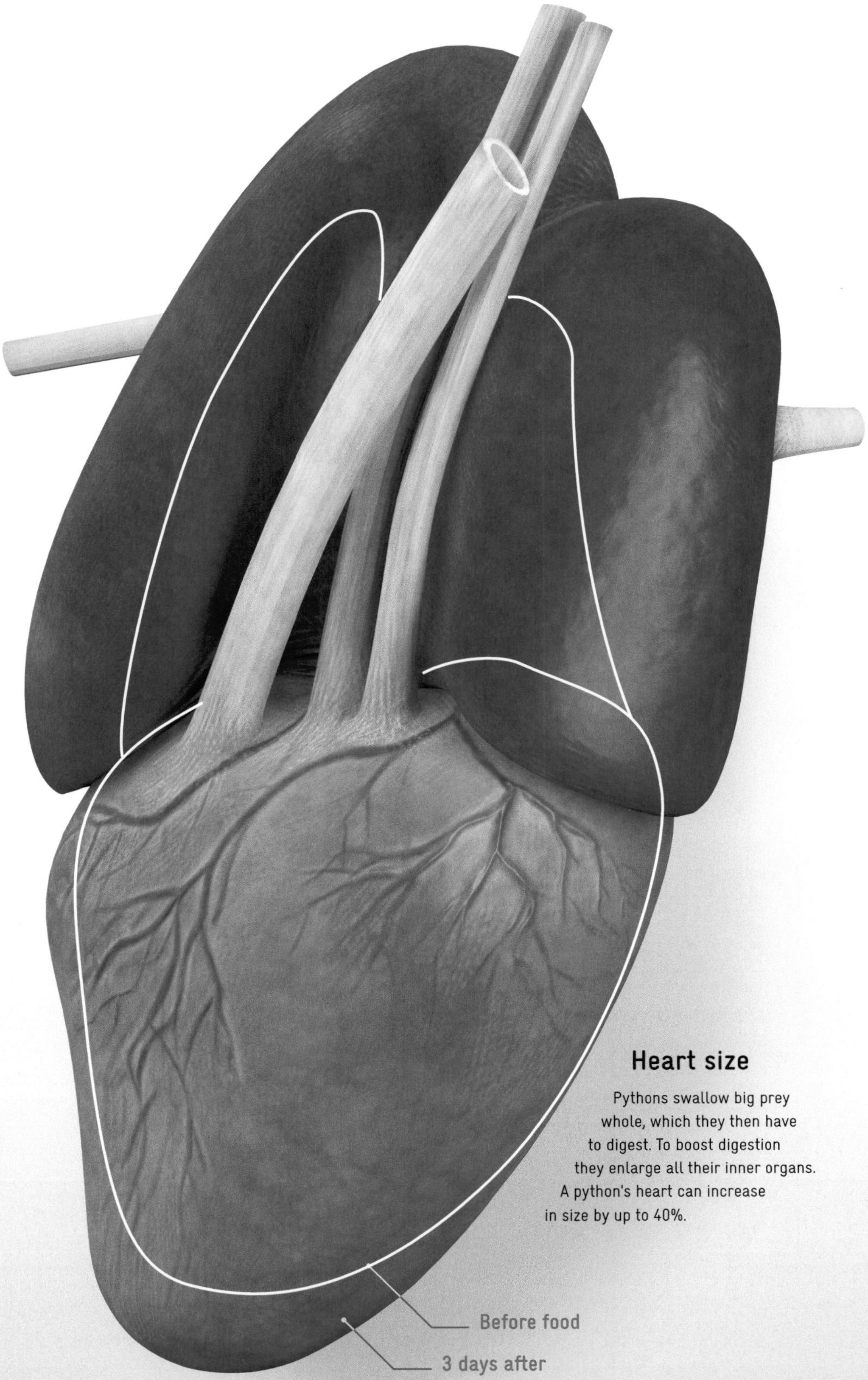

Heart size

Pythons swallow big prey whole, which they then have to digest. To boost digestion they enlarge all their inner organs. A python's heart can increase in size by up to 40%.

THE BIG COOL VERSUS THE MINI SPEEDY

Competition of the mammals:
The Blue Whale
— versus —
The Etruscan Mouse

	WEIGHT OF THE HEART:	VOLUME OF ONE HEART BEAT:	RESTING HEARTBEATS:
The Blue Whale	600 kg equivalent to a grand piano	350 l equivalent to two bathtubs	6 per minute
The Etruscan Mouse	0.000012 kg equivalent to 85 grains of sand	0.0000012 l 1/10 of a drop of a pipette	1,000 per minute

THE HUMMINGBIRD
I AM TINY BUT MY HEART IS HUGE

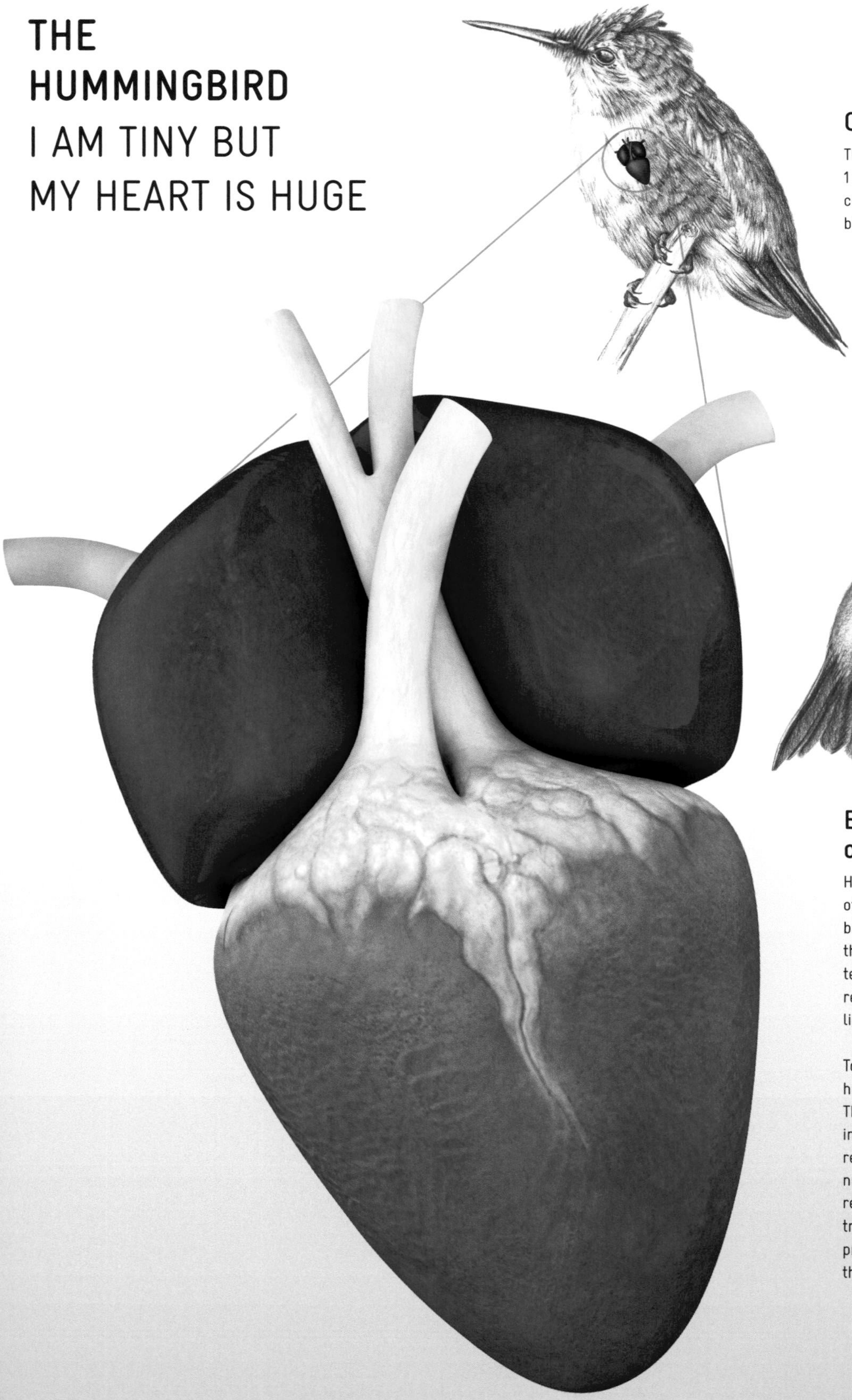

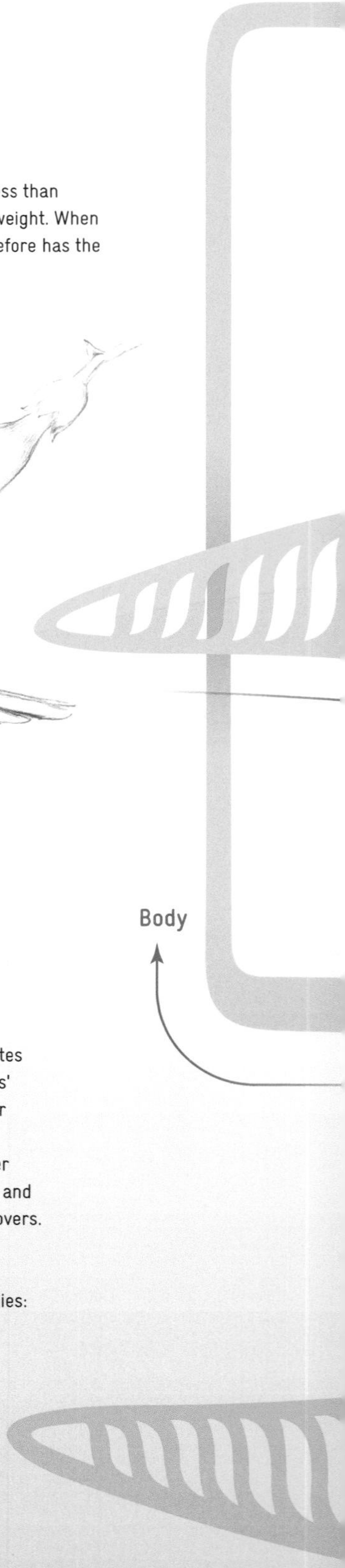
Body

Original size!

The heart of the hummingbird often weighs less than 1 gram but that amounts to 2.5 % of its body weight. When compared with others, the hummingbird therefore has the biggest heart in the animal kingdom.

Energy consumption

Hummingbirds have the highest metabolic rates of all vertebrates. One reason is that the birds' body temperature is generally 1 to 5 °C higher than in any mammal. To maintain this higher temperature, birds need more energy. Another reason is that the hummingbird is very small and light and consumes a lot of energy when it hovers.

To offset its high energy consumption the hummingbird has developed different strategies: The little bird consumes nectar which is rich in calories and easy to digest. Also its red blood cells are smaller but more numerous than in other birds. As a result, more oxygen can get transported through the body as it provides a denser surface to attach to the haemoglobin.

RED BLOOD CELLS

The consumption of oxygen is regulated by body mass and movement. Smaller, flying birds need more energy than bigger, running animals and therefore have more and smaller red blood cells.

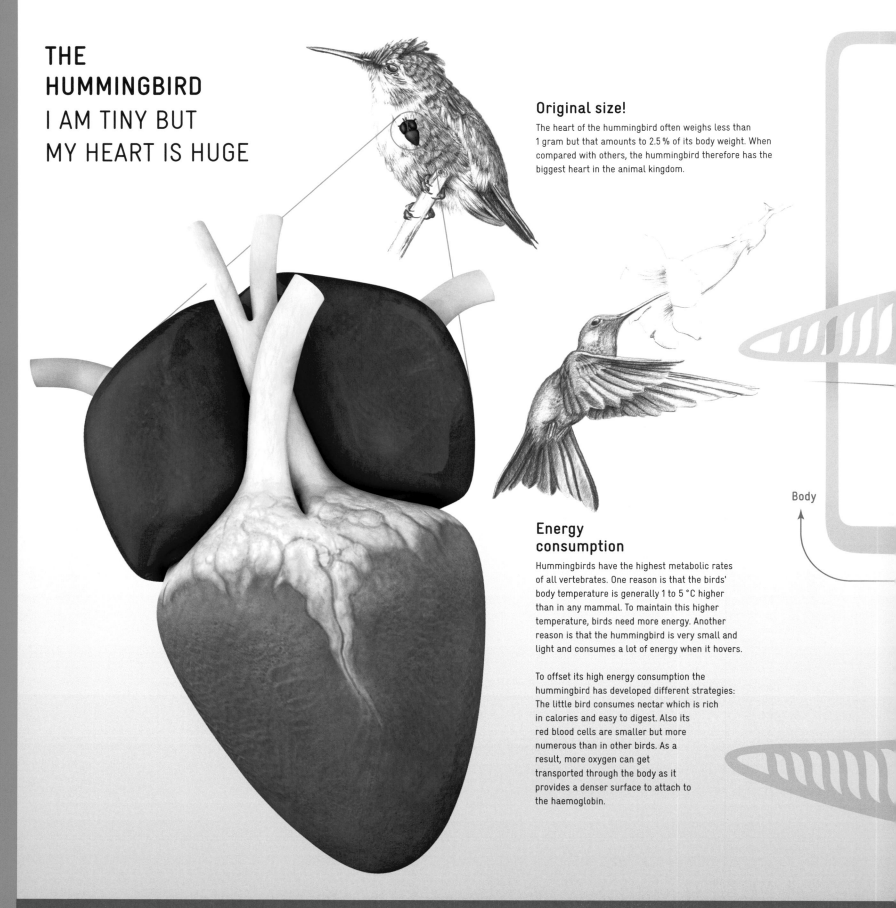

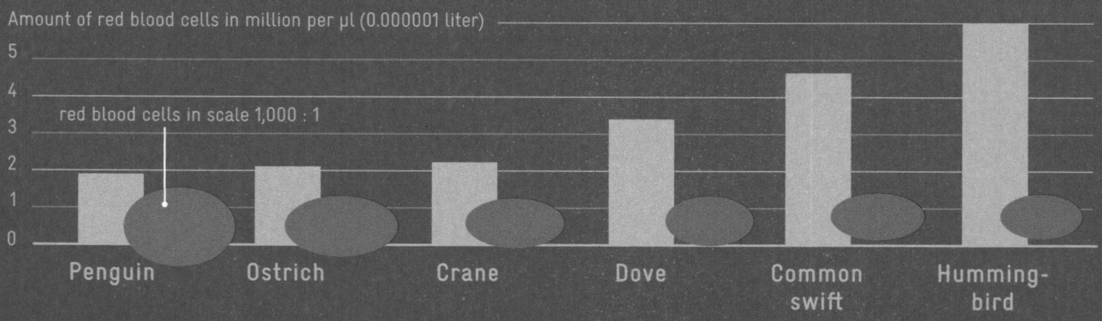
Amount of red blood cells in million per µl (0.000001 liter)
5
4
3
2
1
0
red blood cells in scale 1,000 : 1
Penguin
Ostrich
Crane
Dove
Common swift
Humming-bird

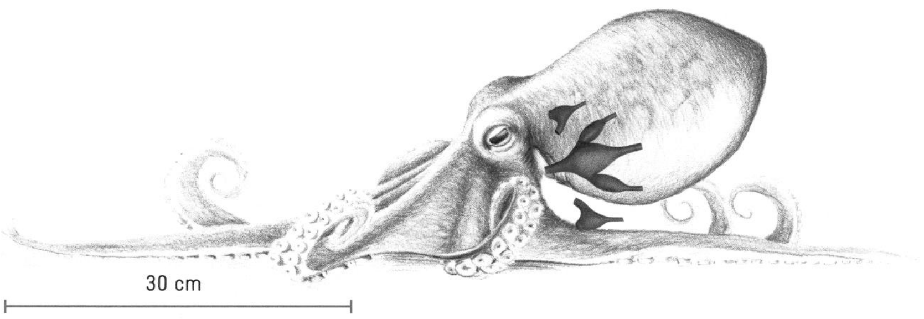

Circulation

Unlike other invertebrates, octopuses have a closed circulation system. Their main heart pumps blood through both ends, around the body and towards the gills. Both of the gills' hearts make sure that the oxygen-poor blood flows through the gills, where it is then oxygenated before it returns to the main heart.

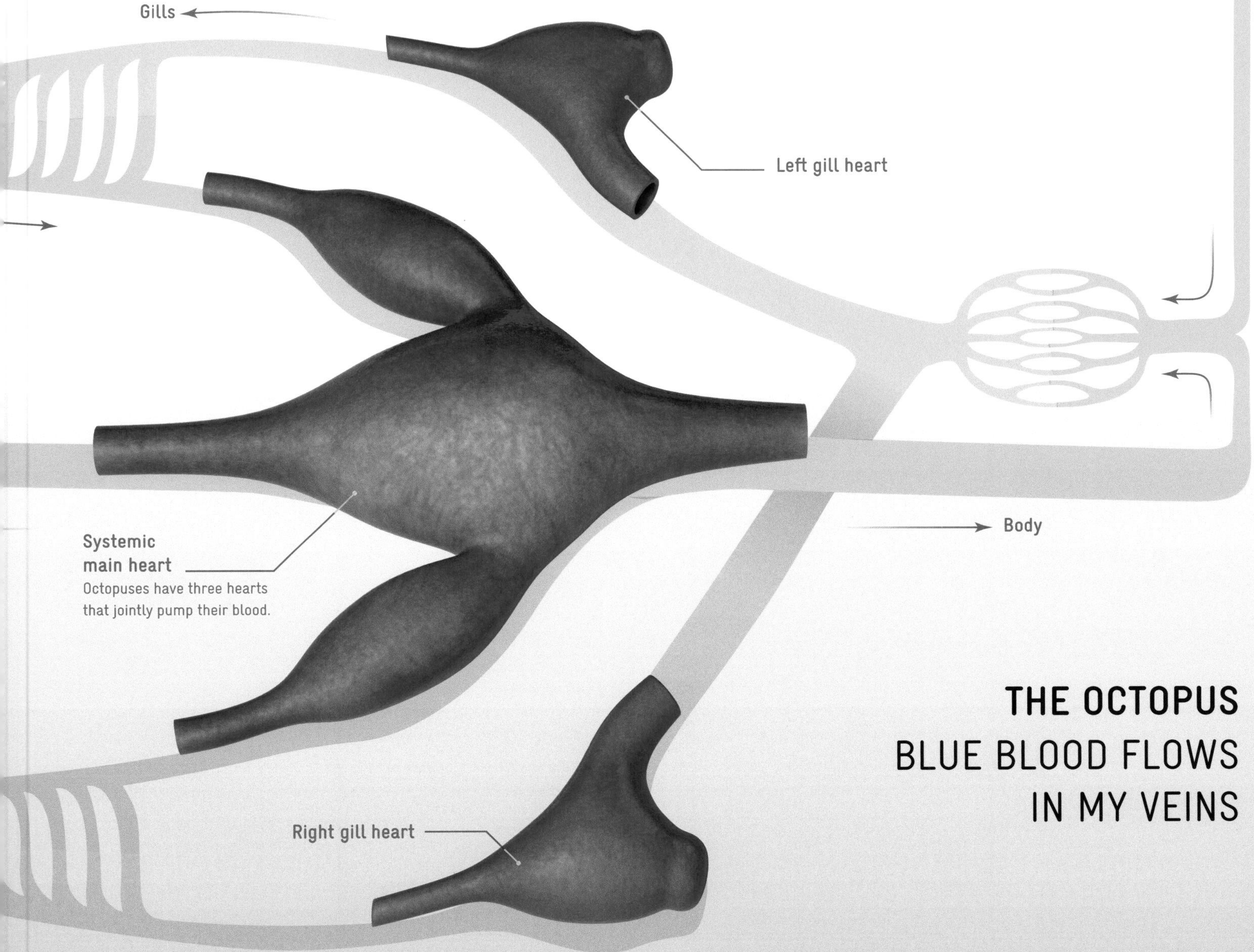

Systemic main heart
Octopuses have three hearts that jointly pump their blood.

THE OCTOPUS
BLUE BLOOD FLOWS IN MY VEINS

COLOR

The color of the blood is dependent on which molecules the oxygen can attach itself to for transport through the body.

Human blood is red because the iron-rich hemoglobin transports the oxygen.

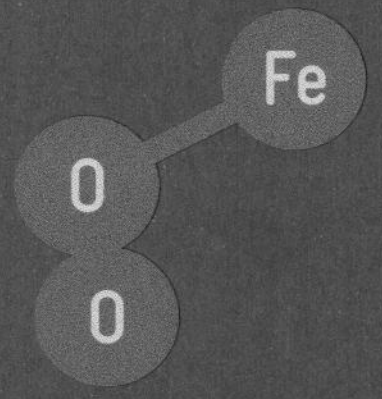

In octopuses the oxygen is transported by hemocyanin. With the help of copper it binds the oxygen and appears blue.

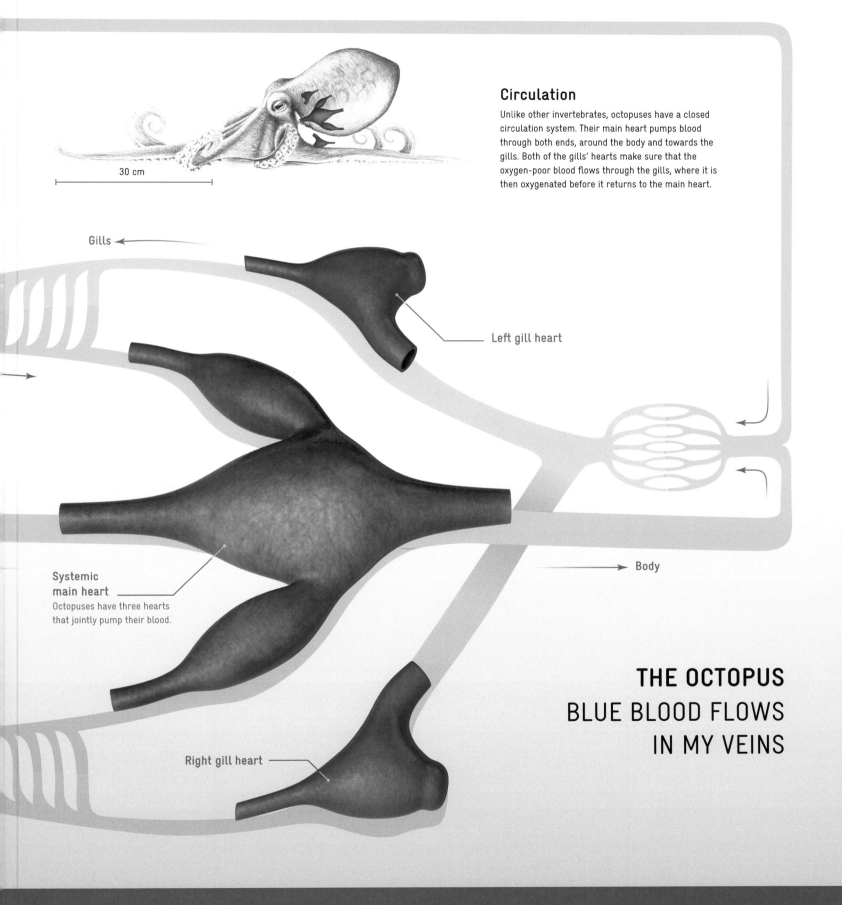

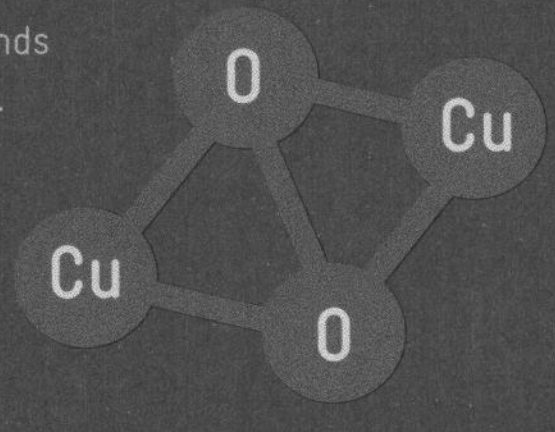

THE HEART'S FAMILY TREE

IN THE BEGINNING THERE WAS THE HEARTLESS BACTERIUM

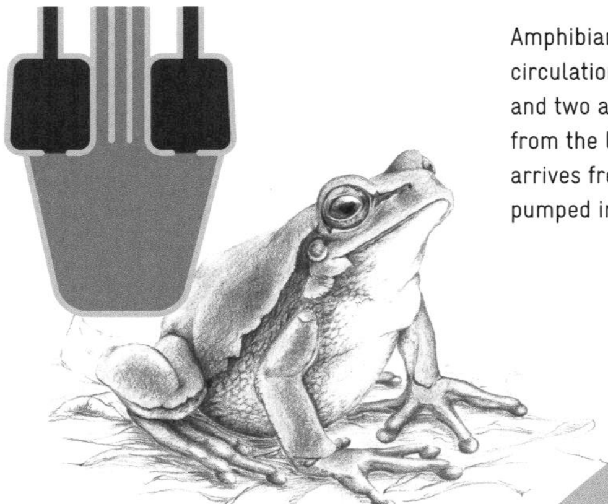

Amphibians are the first animals with double blood circulation. Their heart consists of one main ventricle and two atriums in which oxygen-rich blood arrives from the lungs, or respectively, oxygen-poor blood arrives from the body veins. The blood that gets pumped into the arteries is still a mix of both.

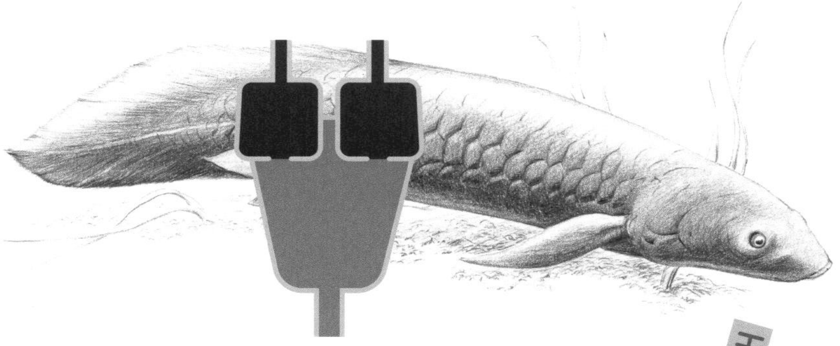

The heart of the lungfish has one undivided main chamber. The blood arrives at the heart through two separate atrium-like areas and is not completely mixed. On the right side of the heart chamber, the oxygen-rich blood arrives from the lungs and on the left side oxygen-poor blood arrives from the body.

Earthworms absorb oxygen through their skin. Their red blood flows in a closed circulation. This consists of two vessels which are connected through five paired lateral hearts and pumps the blood through the worm's body.

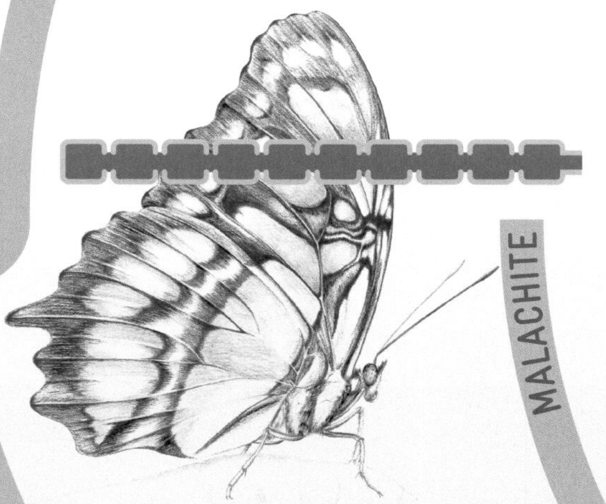

In a separate channel the green-colored hemolymph of the butterfly is pumped with help from muscles into an open column space. Pressure ensures that tissue and cells are flushed through.

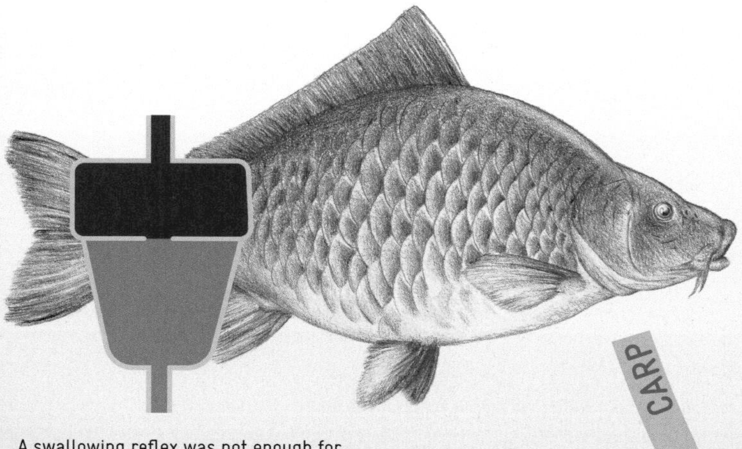

A swallowing reflex was not enough for the fish to transport all nutrients to its complex body parts. The open channel system developed into a simple blood circulation and the fluids became blood.
A central pump system was formed with an atrium-like chamber and a directly connected main chamber

Multicellular organisms get bigger and their body articulates. A pump-like system is created to supply all cells with liquids rich in oxygen and nutrients.

Life began in the water. Unicellular and bicellular organisms feed on and draw in the liquid around them. The cell's cytoplasm environment is basically the same as the liquid medium.

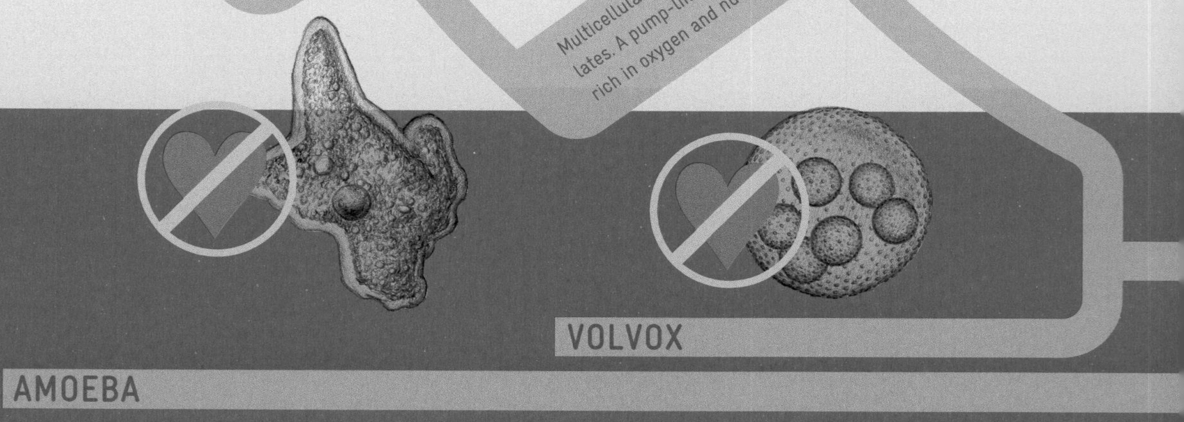

Among reptiles, the main heart chamber starts to differentiate itself through the development of a septum into a right and left ventricle. The division is not complete, the mixture of oxygen-poor blood towards the lungs and oxygen-rich blood towards the body is only partial.

Octopuses have a simple systemic main heart with no chambers and two bronchial hearts. Their circulation is closed, as in all other cephalopods. It is unique in the world of all molluscs. Their blue blood enables them to be active even when temperatures are very low.

The crocodile with its 25 different subspecies is the only reptile that has a properly divided cardiac septum. Reptiles are the first vertebrates in which the heart consists of two atriums and two separate ventricles.

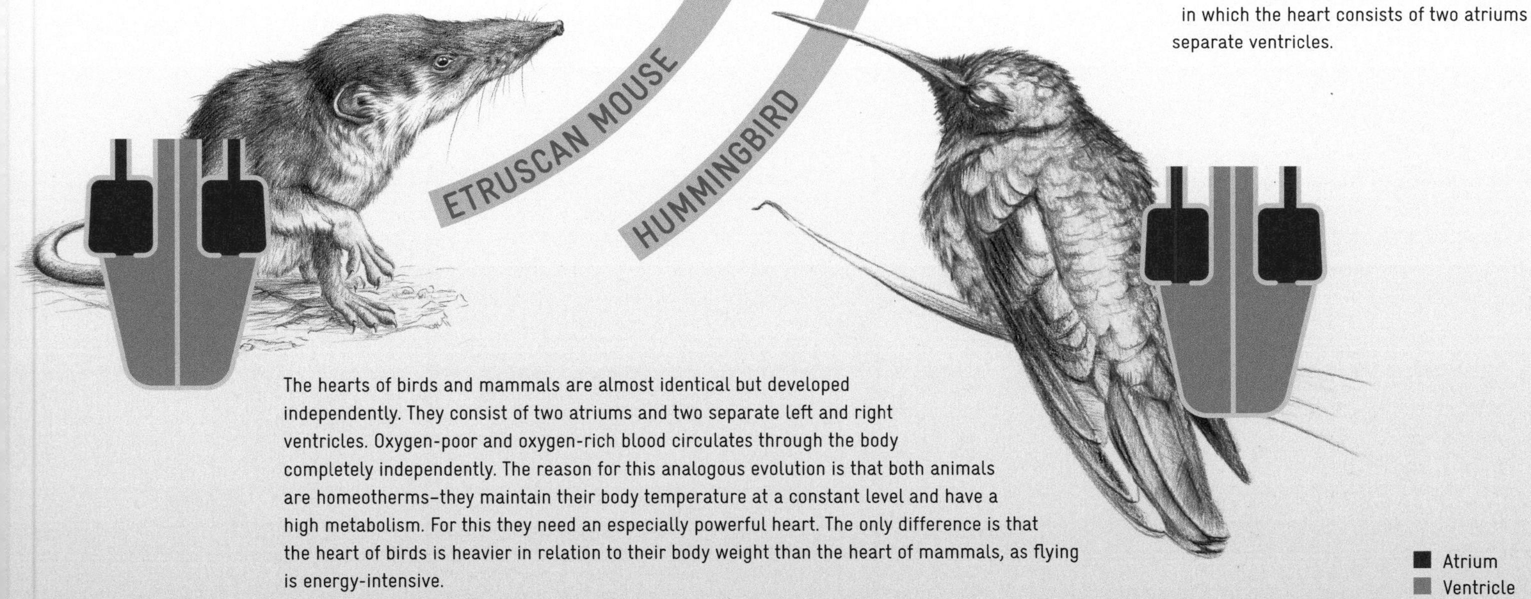

The hearts of birds and mammals are almost identical but developed independently. They consist of two atriums and two separate left and right ventricles. Oxygen-poor and oxygen-rich blood circulates through the body completely independently. The reason for this analogous evolution is that both animals are homeotherms–they maintain their body temperature at a constant level and have a high metabolism. For this they need an especially powerful heart. The only difference is that the heart of birds is heavier in relation to their body weight than the heart of mammals, as flying is energy-intensive.

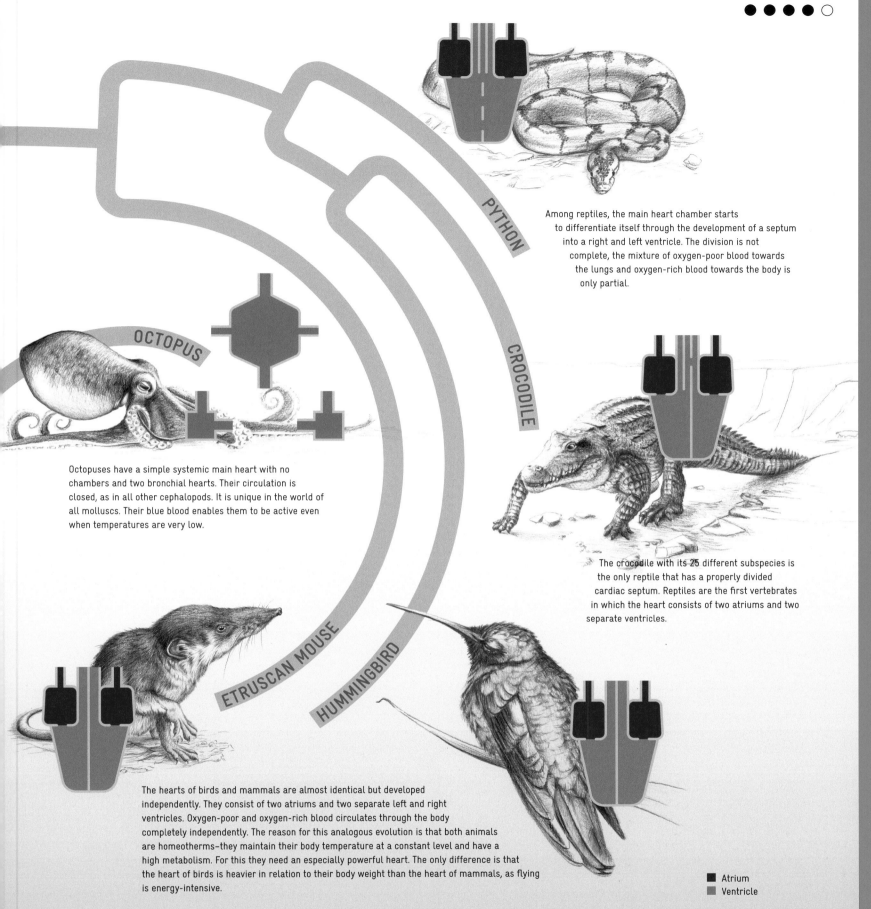

The evolution of the hearts

In an organism, all cells have to be continuously supplied with energy and nutrients and all waste products have to be disposed of. The bigger the organism, the bigger and more powerful the supply system has to be. Over the course of animal evolution, an open circulation without a heart developed into a closed double circulation with a powerful cardiac muscle.

THE HEARTBEAT
FROM ADAGIO TO ALLEGRO

The heartbeat of a living creature is a reflection of itself. It allows us to draw conclusions about the activities, size, temperature, age and life expectancy of that organism. Our heart races after a short sprint for the bus or when we are frightened by a stranger who jumps out of a dark corner. Our pulse increases when we are have recently fallen in love and when we have a temperature. In the 5th Century BC the Egyptians—just like Hippocrates in Greece—included the study of the pulse in their medical diagnoses. They declared it the »voice of the heart.«

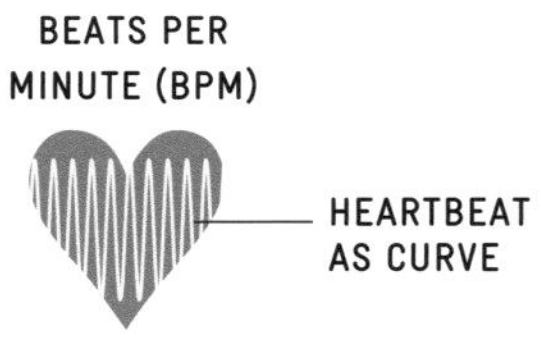
BEATS PER
MINUTE (BPM)
HEARTBEAT
AS CURVE

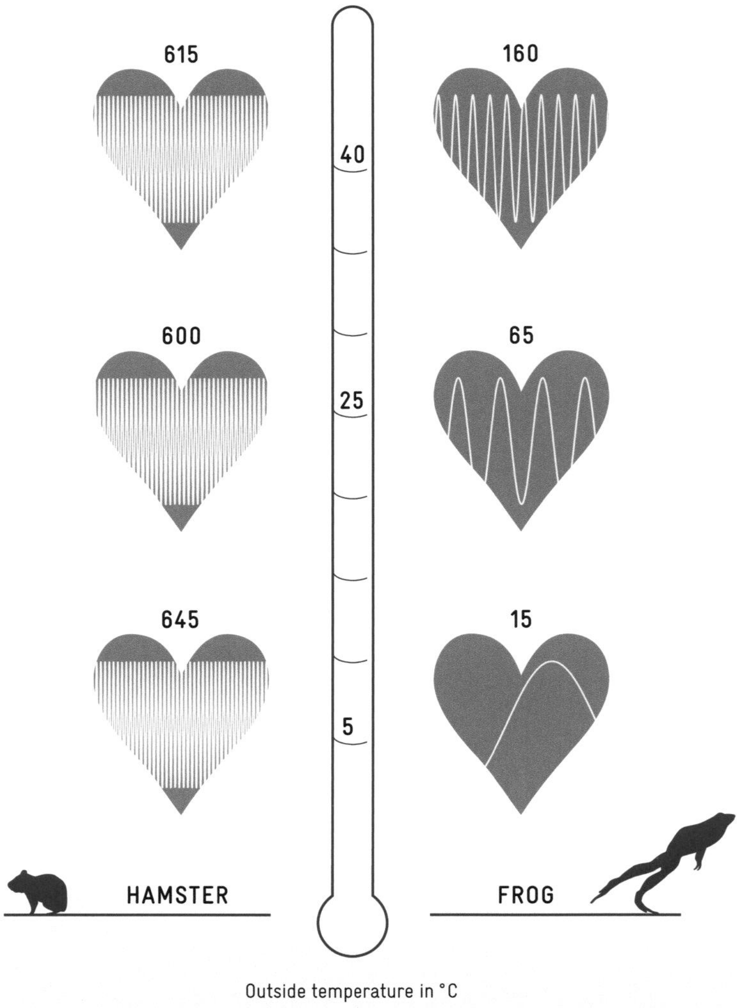

Temperature

In principle, warm-blooded animals have a higher heart frequency than cold-blooded animals. Therefore cold-blooded animals have a higher range of heart frequency because their physiological processes are determined by the outside temperature. A hamster has a higher pulse when it is cold and needs a lot of energy to shiver itself warm. If the outside temperature is low, the cold-blooded frog also has a very low pulse. The greater the temperature rise, t he greater the increase of the frog's pulse. Therefore the span of the frog's resting pulse is more than 3 times larger than that of the hamster.

Activity

By day, the resting heartbeat of a hummingbird is 400-500 bpm, and in flight it reaches up to 1,260 bpm. At night, the hummingbird often sleeps upside down in branches where it decreases its body temperature to 18°C and lowers its heart rate to under 50 bpm. If the hummingbird were not to do that, it would starve to death. This is also why mammals decrease their heartrate during hibernation. The hedgehog reduces its heartrate from 200 bpm to 7 bpm.

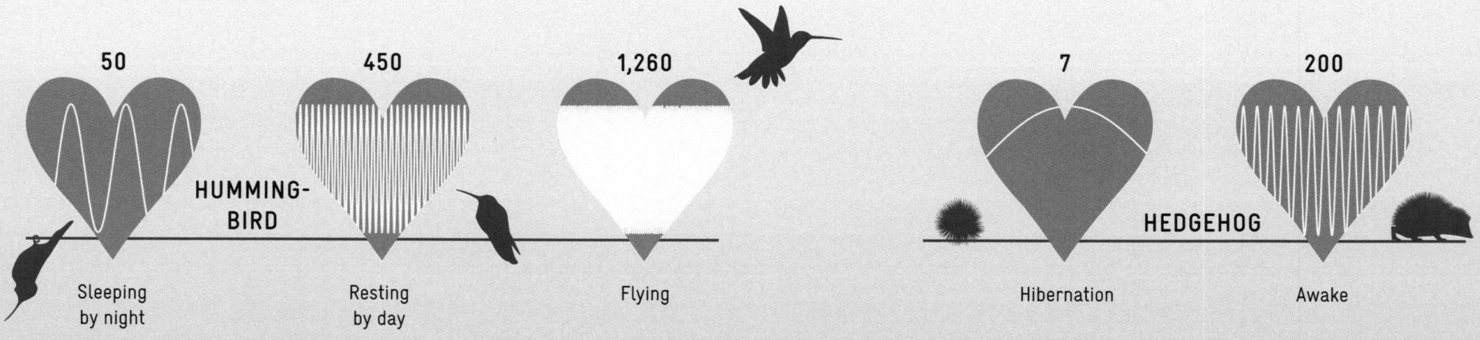

FORMULAS FOR LIFE
– IN QUARTER BARS –

Did you know that nature is computable? In relation to body weight we can determine the metabolic rate, heart rate, and life span. These formulas exist because every organism is made up of the same structures (cells), and the internal processes are the same. These scaling rules were discovered by the biologist Max Kleiber in 1932. He determined that nature can be scaled. These are »magic quarters«.

Proportional to the mass, the animal's metabolic rate increases by potency ¾.

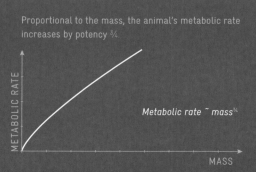

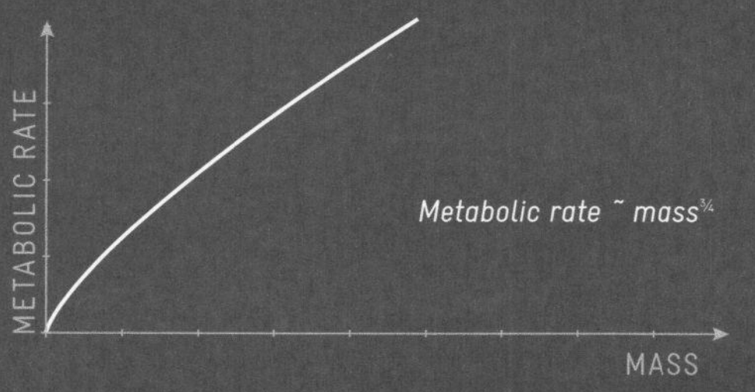

Life expectancy

The slower a mammal's heart beats, the longer it lives. This doesn't apply to modern humans with their medical and technical achievements, but a few centuries ago that was different.

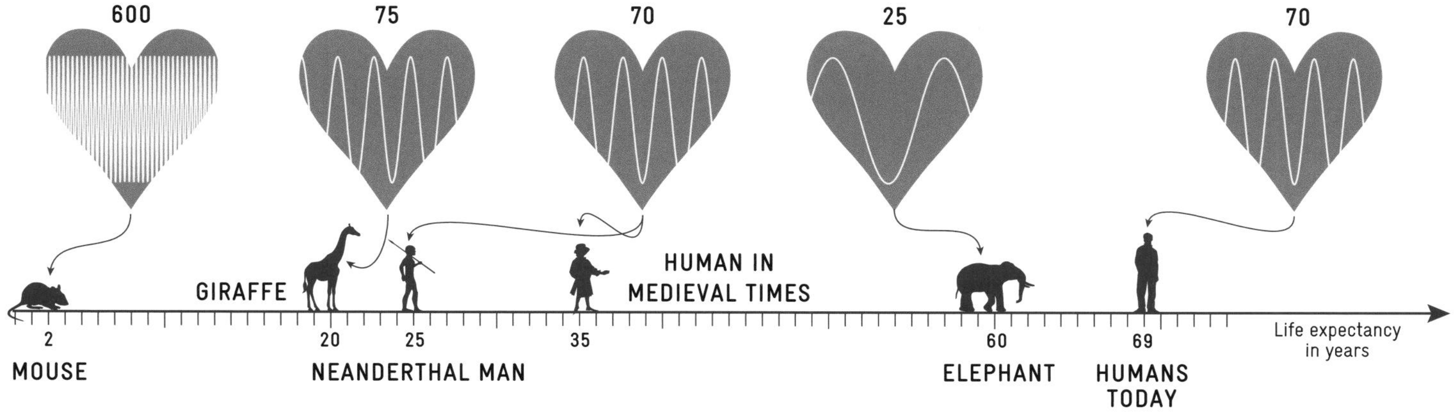
600
75
70
25
70
GIRAFFE
HUMAN IN
MEDIEVAL TIMES
2
20
25
35
60
69
Life expectancy
in years
MOUSE
NEANDERTHAL MAN
ELEPHANT
HUMANS
TODAY

Weight

The bigger and heavier the mammal, the slower its heart rate.

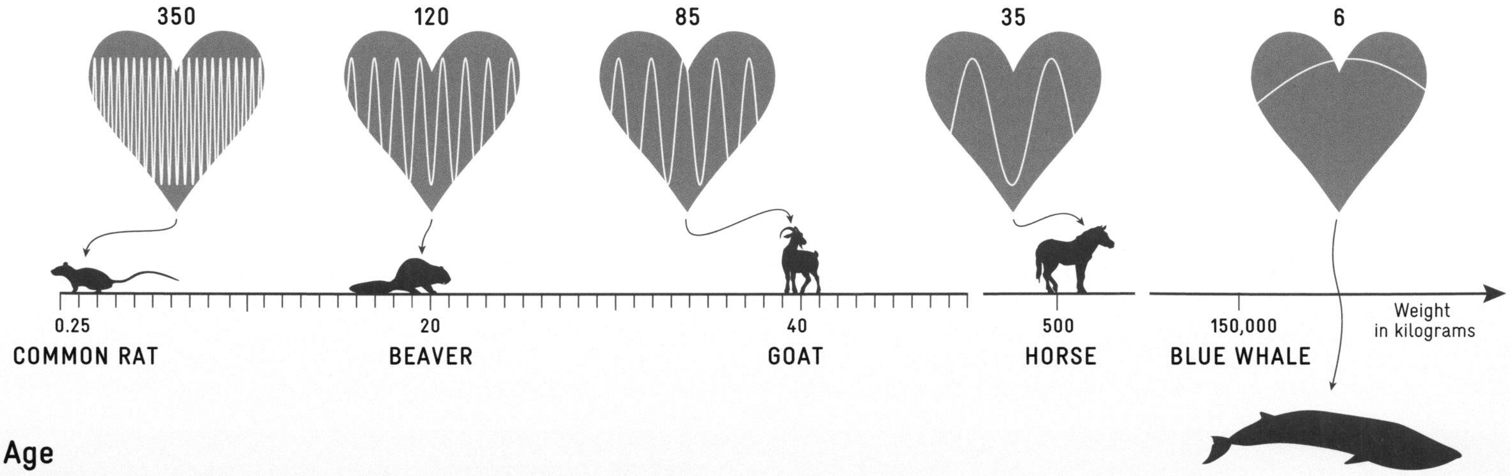
350
120
85
35
6
0.25
20
40
500
150,000
Weight
in kilograms
COMMON RAT
BEAVER
GOAT
HORSE
BLUE WHALE

Age

The younger a human, the higher the pulse. The heartbeat per minute goes down by half from newborn to adulthood. Only from the age of 60 does the heart frequency increase again.

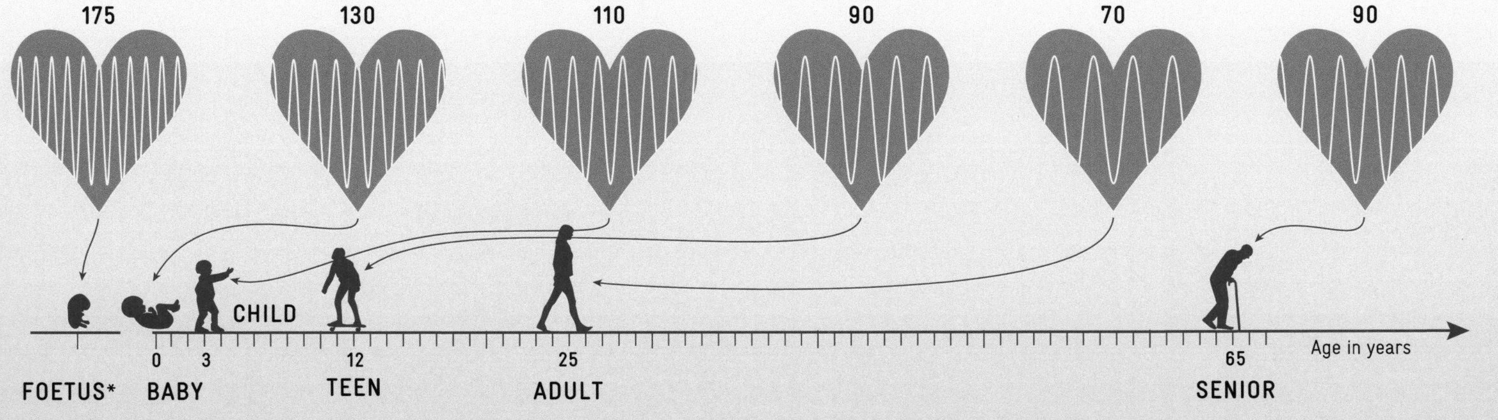
175
130
110
90
70
90
CHILD
0
3
12
25
65
Age in years
FOETUS*
BABY
TEEN
ADULT
SENIOR

* First trimester

The life expectancy of mammals increases proportionally with the mass by potency ¼.

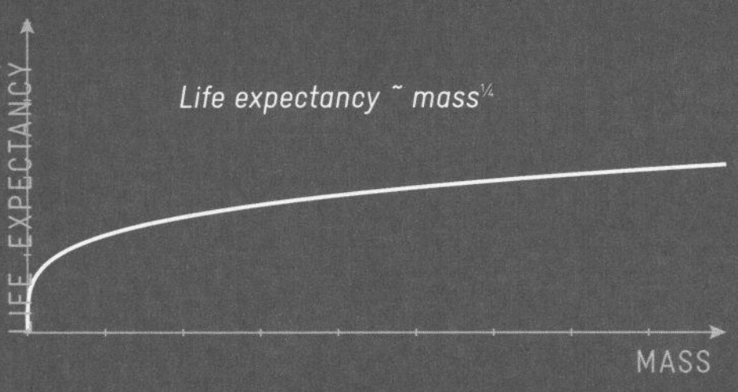
Life expectancy ˜ mass¼
LIFE EXPECTANCY
MASS

The heart rate of mammals is inversely proportional to the mass by potency -¼.

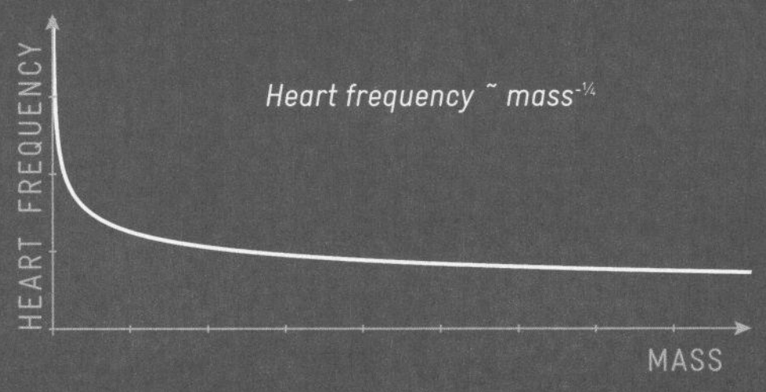
Heart frequency ˜ mass-¼
HEART FREQUENCY
MASS

The total number of heartbeats over a lifetime is remarkably similar in all species. The hearts of non-human mammals beat on average 1.5 billion times during their lifetime. Larger animals take longer to use up their heartbeat quota because the cardiac muscle wears down more slowly.

LIVE FAST, DIE YOUNG

Tortoises move slowly but live to an incredible age. Is there a connection between the speed at which an animal moves and its longevity? Do cheetahs have short lives? The data does seem to show some correlation, but it doesn't look like you can extend your life by simply going everywhere slowly.

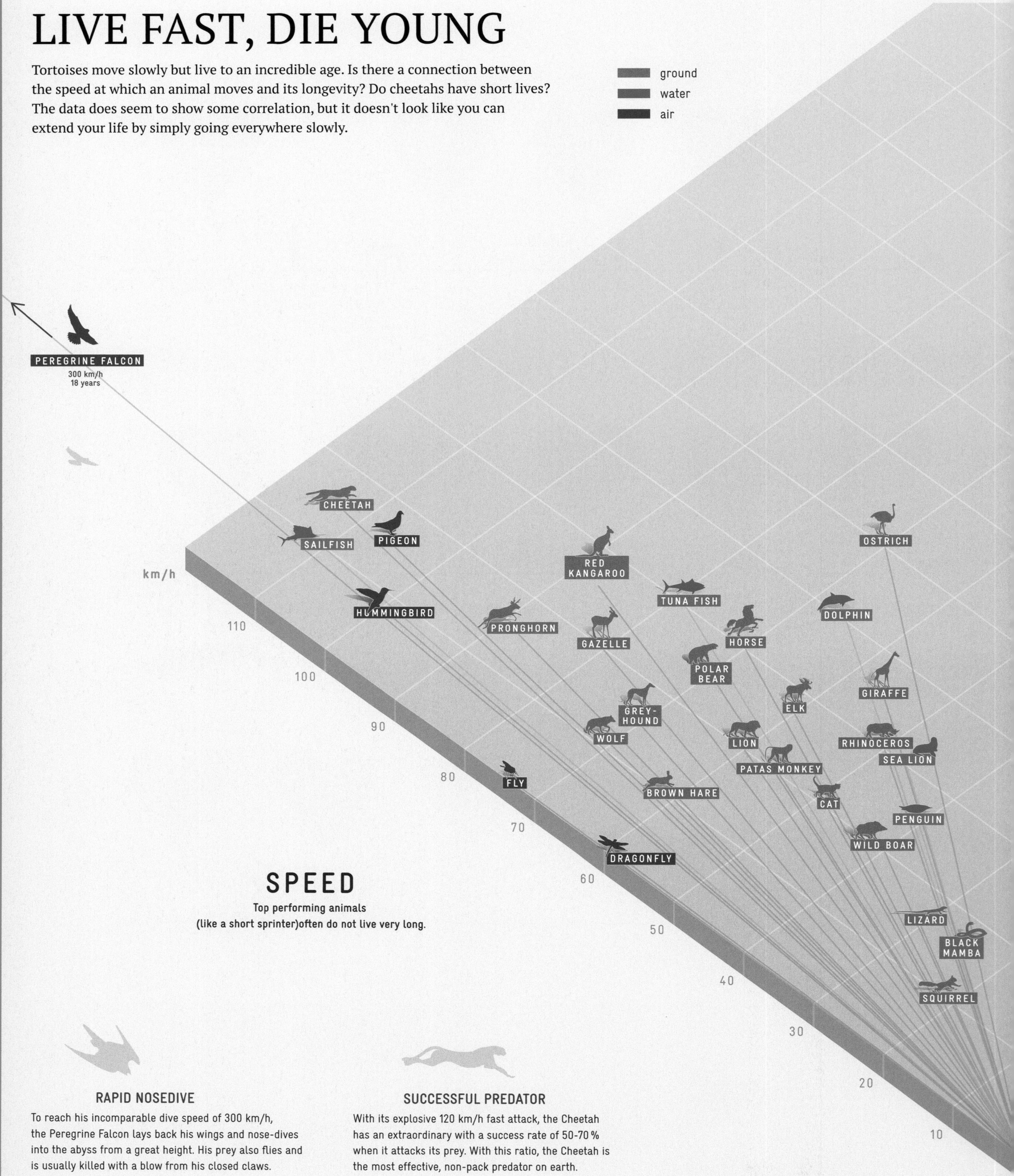

ground
water
air
PEREGRINE FALCON
300 km/h
18 years
CHEETAH
SAILFISH
PIGEON
RED KANGAROO
OSTRICH
TUNA FISH
km/h
HUMMINGBIRD
PRONGHORN
GAZELLE
HORSE
DOLPHIN
110
POLAR BEAR
100
GIRAFFE
GREY-HOUND
ELK
90
WOLF
LION
RHINOCEROS
SEA LION
PATAS MONKEY
80
FLY
BROWN HARE
CAT
PENGUIN
70
WILD BOAR
DRAGONFLY
60
50
LIZARD
BLACK MAMBA
40
SQUIRREL
30
20
10

SPEED

Top performing animals
(like a short sprinter)often do not live very long.

RAPID NOSEDIVE

To reach his incomparable dive speed of 300 km/h, the Peregrine Falcon lays back his wings and nose-dives into the abyss from a great height. His prey also flies and is usually killed with a blow from his closed claws.

SUCCESSFUL PREDATOR

With its explosive 120 km/h fast attack, the Cheetah has an extraordinary with a success rate of 50-70 % when it attacks its prey. With this ratio, the Cheetah is the most effective, non-pack predator on earth.

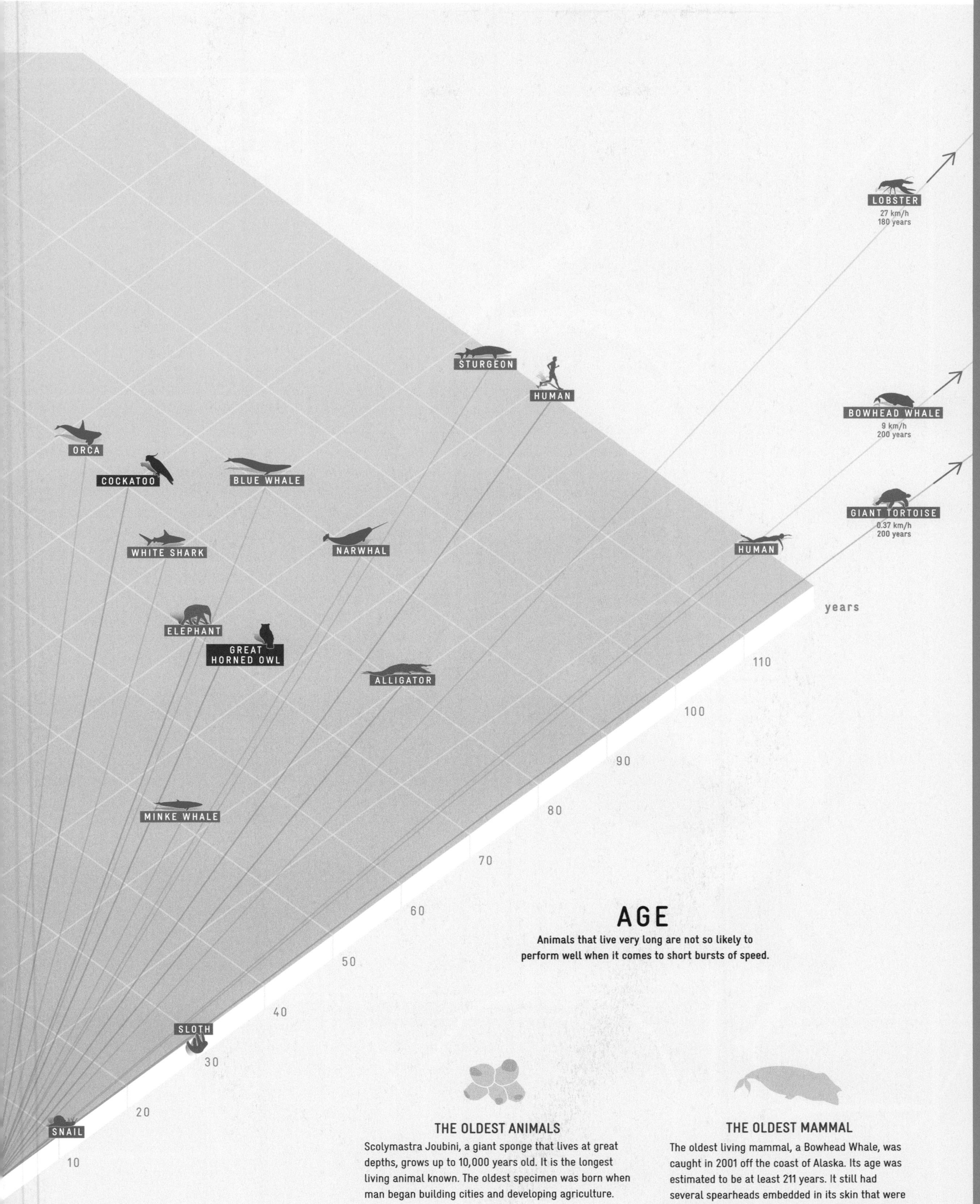

AGE

Animals that live very long are not so likely to perform well when it comes to short bursts of speed.

THE OLDEST ANIMALS

Scolymastra Joubini, a giant sponge that lives at great depths, grows up to 10,000 years old. It is the longest living animal known. The oldest specimen was born when man began building cities and developing agriculture.

THE OLDEST MAMMAL

The oldest living mammal, a Bowhead Whale, was caught in 2001 off the coast of Alaska. Its age was estimated to be at least 211 years. It still had several spearheads embedded in its skin that were fabricated by Inuits more than a hundred years ago.

They come alone, in pairs, or by the thousands. They attach themselves to ship hulls, are smuggled in luggage or imported legally. Invasive species are animals and plants that displace the native flora and fauna under the right conditions. One of the first invasive species was used as provisions during long journeys ...

As early as 10,000 years ago, humans domesticated the goat and gave it **food and shelter**. The goats grew bigger and stronger and provided milk and meat.

Their **skin** also helped make early humans more comfortable.

N O BIOTA

In a single year, a high-producing goat can yield **30 times its weight** in milk.
In return, humans took goats on their travels and showed them the world. Aside from the polar regions, goats were as comfortable in other lands as in their native homeland, the **Fertile Crescent**.
Galapagos Islands
During the **era of great exploration**, sailors took goats as breeding animals and provisions on their long voyages. The Galapagos islands are a prime example of the consequences of this carelessness. The goats probably came **with pirates across the ocean**. Every time the pirates arrived on the islands ...
... the goats provided them with a great feast.
But eventually the days of the buccaneers were over and they no longer brought livestock on their travels.
Soon the men preferred **canned food**, and the animals were ignored.
Left behind on the island and no longer a source of food for their masters, **the goats multiplied rapidly** and ate everything in sight.
Giant tortoises and iguanas struggled to find food, and their **numbers decreased** drastically.
Lonesome George
R.I.P.
The last of its kind
† 2012
In 2012, when Lonesome George, the **last remaining Pinta Island tortoise died**, this subspecies became extinct.

WANTED
DEAD OR NOT ALIVE
BIENVENIDOS – WELCOME
ESTACION CIENTIFICA
CHARLES DARWIN
Charles Darwin Research Station
In the beginning of the 1960s **the big hunt** for the horned invaders began. Enter ...
... the so-called »**Judas**« goats, castrated males which were equipped with transmitters and released on the island.
As a result of their herd instincts, they found even the most remote groups of feral goats and revealed their position with their **tracking devices**.
Mata Hari goats also played a role in tracking down female goats. Sterilized female goats were artificially put in heat to lure the bucks out of their hiding spots.
An estimated 360,000 animals were killed in this hunt.
in memory of
360.000
victims

But the story doesn't end here. Over generations, the **Galapagos buzzard** had adjusted its diet to the human food supply.
It had switched its diet from iguanas and rodents to the abundant goats.
But those were now off the menu.
The result was the death of many nestling Galapagos buzzards and their **population decreased dramatically**. Humans had created an ecological disaster - again.
Other islands have similar stories to tell. On **Pelorus**, an island off the coast of Australia, the goats were imported as food for the lighthouse keeper and for shipwrecked sailors.
Here the goats also became an infestation. To control them, **castrated dingos** were released ...
... to hunt and **kill the goats**. Afterwards the dingos were captured and removed from the island.
As a back-up plan, a **poison capsule** with a time release was implanted into every dingo.
They only had two years to complete their mission.
almost eradicated
used for harmony betrayed by their masters
The story of the goat is over, but it's **only the beginning** of the story of invasive species.

In the 19th century, the **North American gray squirrel** crossed the Pacific to Europe.
In 1948 an Italian diplomat released **two pairs** into his villa's garden. More gray squirrels were released in the 60s and 70s. The animals were also released in Ireland and South Africa – **because of their cuteness**.
At first, only a few pairs were set free, but in **1889 350 squirrels** were released in Bedfordshire, England.
As a result the population of the native red squirrel decreased drastically because ...
... the gray squirrel is **bigger**, **heavier** and more **robust**.
It's **less picky** about food and can even digest the tannin in acorns.
It has more fat reserves and is better at **finding food reserves**, even the food hidden by the native squirrels.
It lives longer and has a **higher reproduction rate** ...
... it is more attractive to the female red squirrels.
But the mating doesn't produce viable offspring.
Furthermore the gray squirrel co-evolved with a **smallpox virus** and is therefore immune, but the red squirrel isn't.
100 nm
SAVE A RED EAT A GREY!
Kill them all!
Since 1981, the gra y squirrel has been **considered a pest** in Great Britain. Poisonous bait is laid out in parks and gardens now completely occupied by the American bioinvaders.
Smallpox and leprosy, introduced by the gray squirrels, steadily depleted the population of the native red squirrels.
Plans are in place to introduce natural enemies like **martens and hawks** to end the infestation.
But experience shows that this is a risky solution.
Today the gray squirrel is on the list of »**100 of the World's Worst Invasive Alien Species**«.

The **Colorado potato beetle**, native to Mexico [1], has taken a totally different route.
First described scientifically in Colorado in 1824, the beetle fed on **the buffalo bur**, a relative of the potato. The buffalo bur, however, was of no interest to humans.
The potato, originally **uninteresting** to the beetle, was brought to Europe (without the beetle) by Spaniards.[A]
1
2
3
[A]
[B]
[C]
At the beginning of the 19th century the potato plant was **reimported into America** along with a new way of farming – monoculture. [B]
With an endless supply of food the beetle decided to change its **host plant**. [2]
The first sighting of the beetle on a potato plant was in **1840 in Iowa**. Together with its new host plant [C] it wasn't long until it reached Europe. [3]
KAD
By 1935, the losses were so devastating that Germany founded the potato beetle resistance unit. It was also founded in response to German government **propaganda** claiming that the beetle was used deliberately as a **bioweapon by enemies**.
The beetle was most devastating during and after WWII and was partly responsible for the **famine after WWII**.
Today, humans control the potato beetle with **pesticides**. Our native fauna has adapted well to the invader and some bird species have discovered the beetle as a **new source of food**.
Plants and animals have always discovered new habitats. Today, due to the **actions of humans**, there are more invasive species and they spread faster and further than ever before.
Here the so-called **tens rule** applies: Out of every 1,000 introduced species, 100 will develop unstable populations, ten establish themselves, and one will turn into a **threatening bioinvader**.

ARCHITECTURA ANIMALIS

Architecture is a way for engineers to show off how far people have come, but we don't dominate the field. In fact, we weren't even the first to master it. Some animals have been building their ingenious structures for millions of years before the first humans got the idea to live in a cave. Animals are outstanding constructors, master builders and engineers.

BUILDING FUNCTIONS

HOME | **TRAP** | **DISPLAY**

There are three reasons why animals build. The most obvious but complex one is a **home** – as nests, burrows or cocoons. Animals also build **traps** for hunting prey, like the spider's web. And finally, same animals build a **display** as tools for either courtship or as a way to warn off predators.

ANIMAL ARCHITECTS

Architectural abilities are spread quite diversely in the animal kingdom and differences in architectural complexity are very distinct.

AMONG VERTEBRATES

BIRDS
About 18,000 species.

Birds are the most active builders among vertebrates. Most species build nests.

REPTILES
About 10,000 species; but no builders

MAMMALS
4,000 species, of which 1,500 are rodents.

Rodents, some primates and bats are builders.

AMPHIBIA
About 7,000 species, but no builders.

FISH
About 30,000 species.

Only a few fish build structures.

INVERTEBRATES

(Arthropods are only one of more than 30 phyla among invertebrates.)

ARTHROPODS
5 to 10 million species

Almost all spiders, worms, most insects and some crustaceans are builders.

ARACHNOCAMPA LUMINOSA
FUNGUS GNAT

The fungus gnat larva builds traps in dark caves. It spins 20 to 30 silk threads from the ceiling. Each of these are covered with sticky droplets, which form a chain-like string. These are then illuminated by a lumines-cent organ at the end of the larva's body. This attracts its prey, which gets caught in the sticky strings.

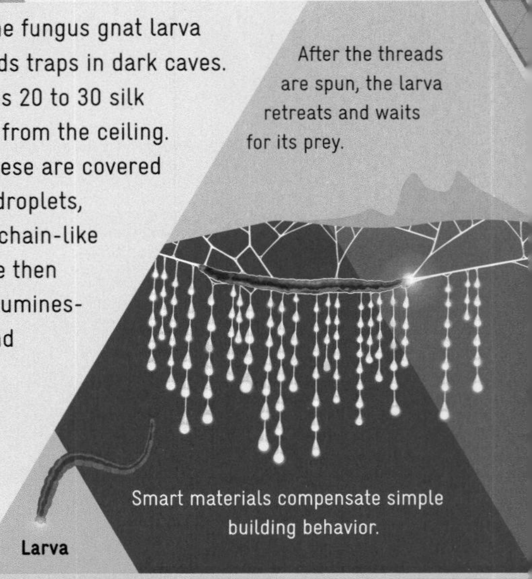
After the threads are spun, the larva retreats and waits for its prey.
Smart materials compensate simple building behavior.
Larva

PLESIOMETA ARGYRA
SPIDER

HYMENOEPIMECIS ARGYRAPHAGA
PARASITIC WASP

The ordinary orb web is highly delicate. **Reprogrammed web.**

The spider usually builds a horizontal orb web, but when infested by a parasitic wasp's larvae, it radically changes its construction plans. The larva feeds on the spider's blood, while simultaneously injecting it with a chemical messenger. The spider then builds a very unusual cocoon web for the larva until all of its blood has been sucked out.

Adult wasp

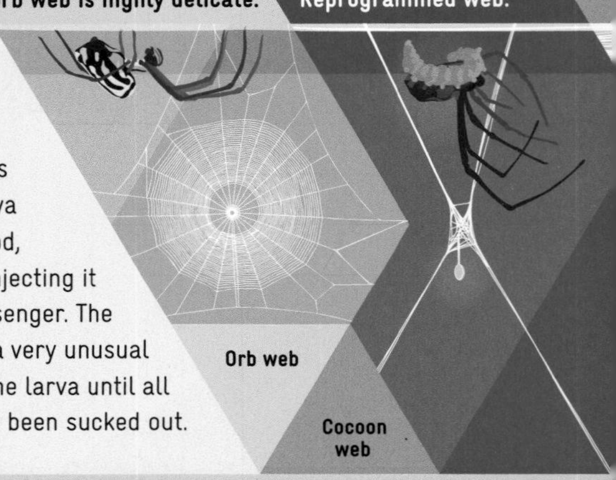
Orb web
Cocoon web

URODERMA BILOBATUM
TENT-MAKING BAT

The bats are native to tropical forests, gnaw the main veins of either palm or banana tree leaves. This causes the leaves to fold together, creating a kind of tent. One tent may provide shelter for as many as 50 bats.

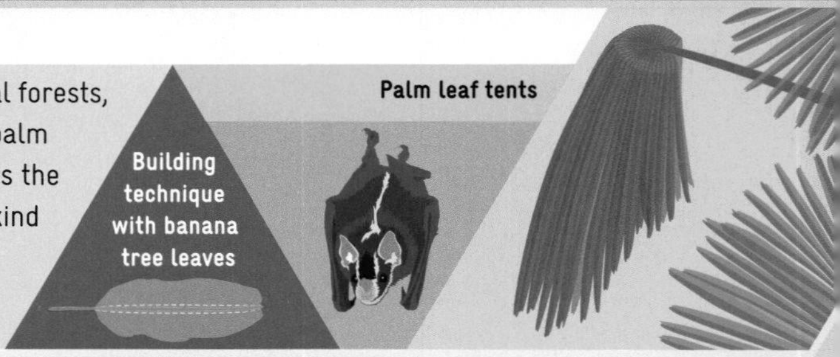
Building technique with banana tree leaves
Palm leaf tents

ALPHEUS SAXIDOMUS
SNAPPING SHRIMP

Don't call this shrimp a whimp.

The snapping shrimp has a unique technique to drill its cave. It has one enlarged claw, which it uses to snap at the surface. The claw then has enough pressure to break up basalt rock with a large bang.

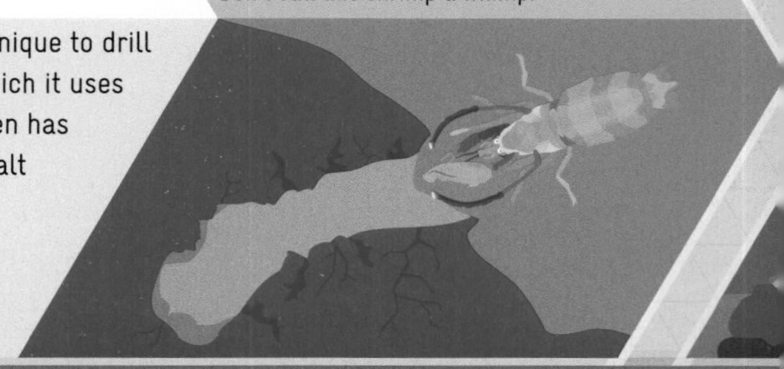

CYCLOSA SPIDER
(NOT YET CLASSIFIED)

The spider integrates a fake spider decoy, made from fibers, dead insects and other garbage into its inconspicuous orb web. It hides behind this replica which is much bigger than itself and makes the whole construction vibrate to give an intimidating impression.

The **decoy** is approximately seven times bigger.

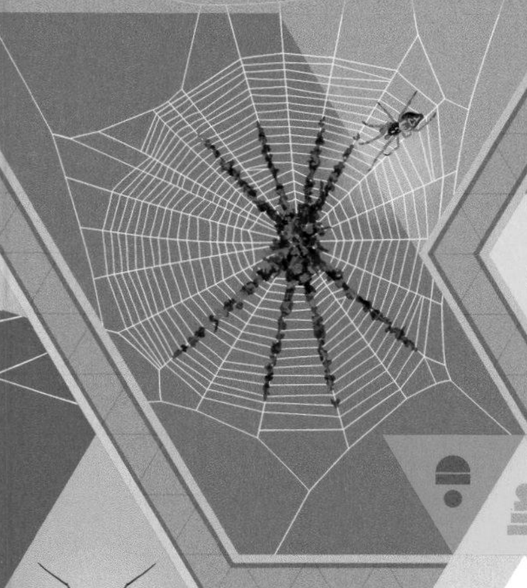

Gnat

PTILONORHYNCHIDAE
BOWERBIRDS

In general, a more exuberant plumage implies a simpler bower.

AVENUE
MAYPOLE

1 **Regent bowerbird** 2 **Satin bowerbird** 3 **MacGregor's bowerbird** 4 **Vogelkop bowerbird**

Constructing bowers requires a long learning process that is closely correlated with an enlarged **cerebellum**. This brain area mainly controls learning through observation and the exploration of new situations.

Cultural distinctions: **Decorations** differ for every bower.

Male bowerbirds build their bowers as an arena for their choreographed courtship. The female bowerbird builds its nest for egg-laying only, after it has chosen a male bowerbird according to its aesthetic display. Females prefer symmetrical structures. Decoration is also very important.

FEMALES
1
2
3
4

Most buildings only fulfill one purpose. Yet some constructions have a dual function.

PLOCEUS PHILIPPINUS
BAYA WEAVER

The nest is the male baya weaver's courtship tool. The interlaced structure requires complex and creative building skills, particularly at the beginning. As soon as the framework hangs down from the tree, the weaver continues with a more repetitive building activity.

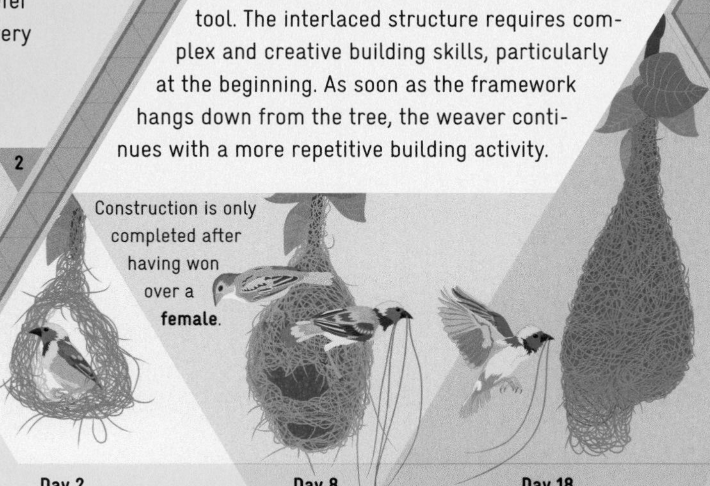

Construction is only completed after having won over a **female**.

The start is the most difficult phase.

Day 2 **Day 8** **Day 18**

Weaverbirds master common sailor's knots.

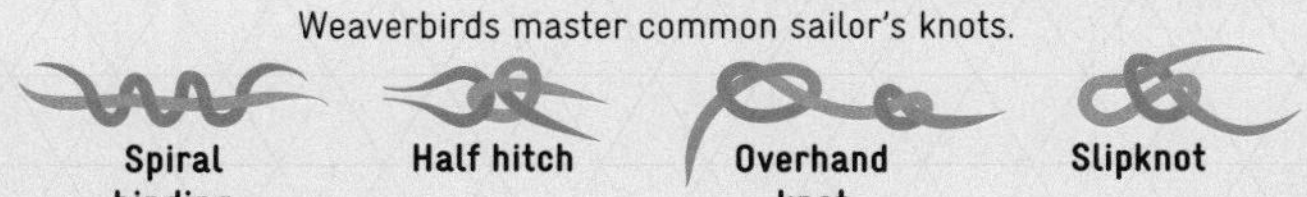

Spiral binding **Half hitch** **Overhand knot** **Slipknot**

Reinforced silk threads and a condensed platform provide protection from predators and rain.

Cocoon

The division of labor is the secret of the functioning of the colony's nest.

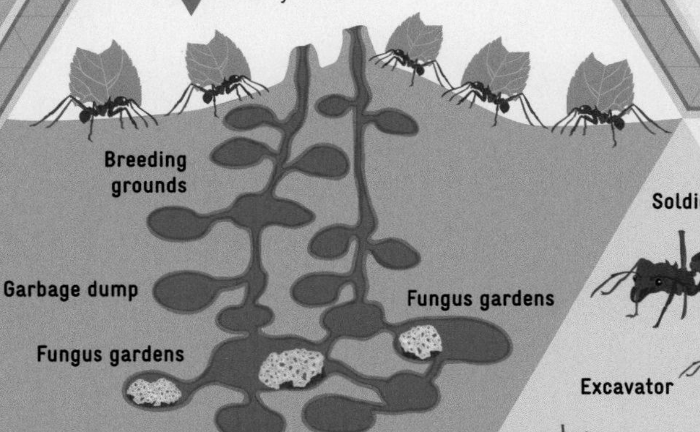

Breeding grounds
Garbage dump
Fungus gardens
Fungus gardens

The underground labyrinths are up to six meters deep.

ATTA SEXDENS
LEAFCUTTER ANT

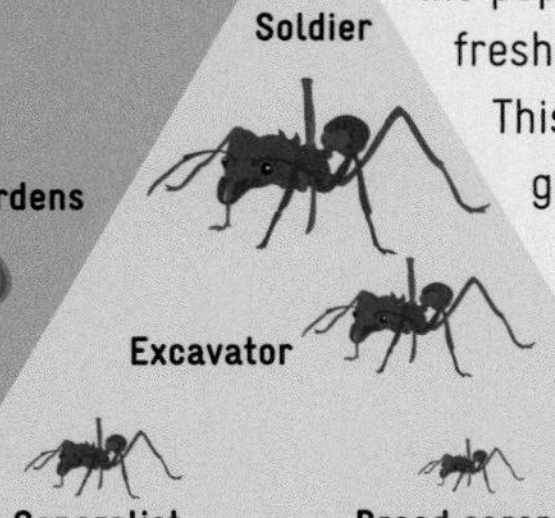

Soldier
Excavator
Generalist
Brood carer & gardener

A colony of leafcutter ants with 10 million inhabitants is equal to the population of Seoul. It survives through a constant supply of freshly cut leaves, which the ants do not eat but chew into a mash. This mash becomes the compost for their underground fungus gardens. The fungi break down the toxins in the leaves that tropical plants developed as a defence against enemies. An induced flow guarantees a fresh air supply for the gardens. This is created by the pressure difference between the outside air and the air inside the nest.

GASTEROSTEUS ACULEATUS
THREE-SPINED STICKLEBACK

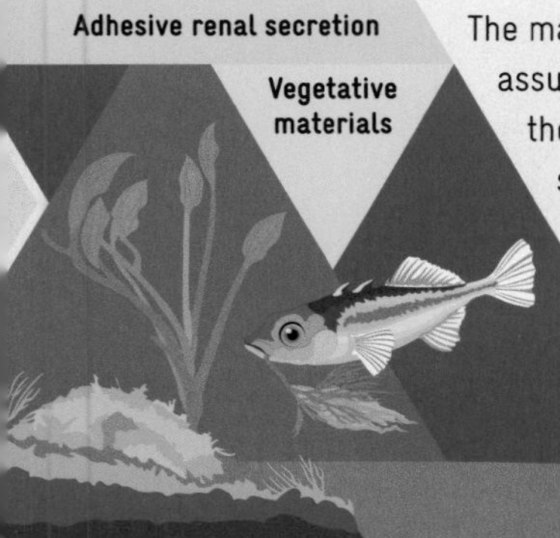

Adhesive renal secretion
Vegetative materials

The male stickleback assumes the construction of the nest and looks after the spawn. At first the stickleback digs a hollow. It then builds its nest with collected vegetative materials. The materials are glued together with a sticky secretion produced by its kidneys.

CYNOMYS LUDOVICIANUS
BLACK-TAILED PRAIRIE DOG

Prairie dog colonies are important to biodiversity. Burrowing owls rely on the rodents to dig out their nesting sites. They also use the rodents' excrement to attract insects for prey. In doing so, they also fertilize the soil.

ATHENE CUNICULARIA
BURROWING OWL

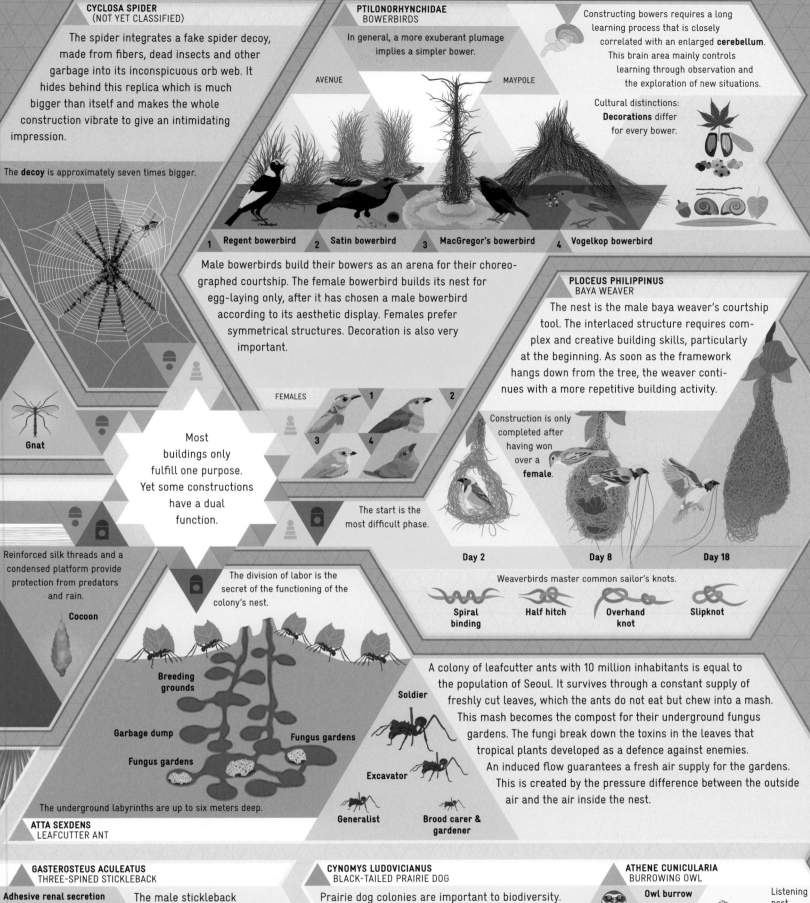

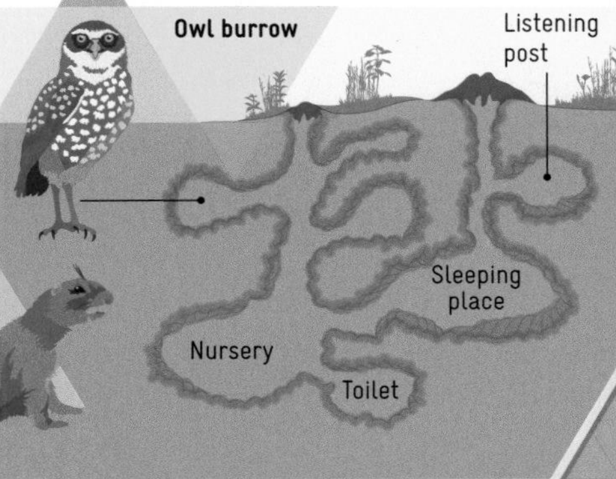

Owl burrow
Listening post
Sleeping place
Nursery
Toilet

BEST FRIENDS

No other mammal has as many variations within its own species—in color, size and behavior— as the dog. And none other has become so much of a friend, helper and companion to humans. Where does Canis lupus familiaris come from and how did it develop?

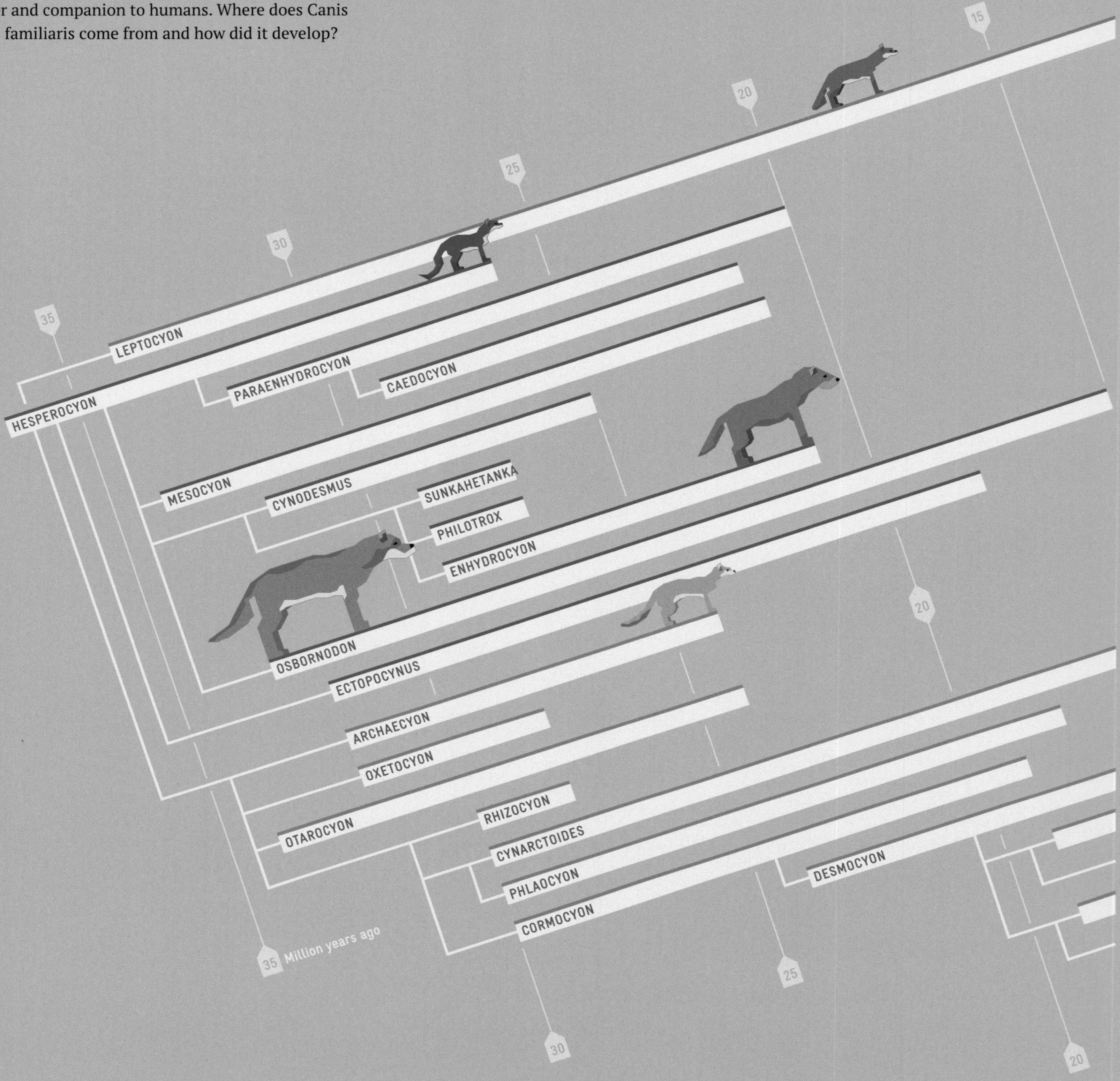

Around 37 million years ago, the Hesperocyon entered the world's stage. The domestic dog's earliest ancestor was the first page in a long evolutionary history that also fathered the fox and wolf animal families.

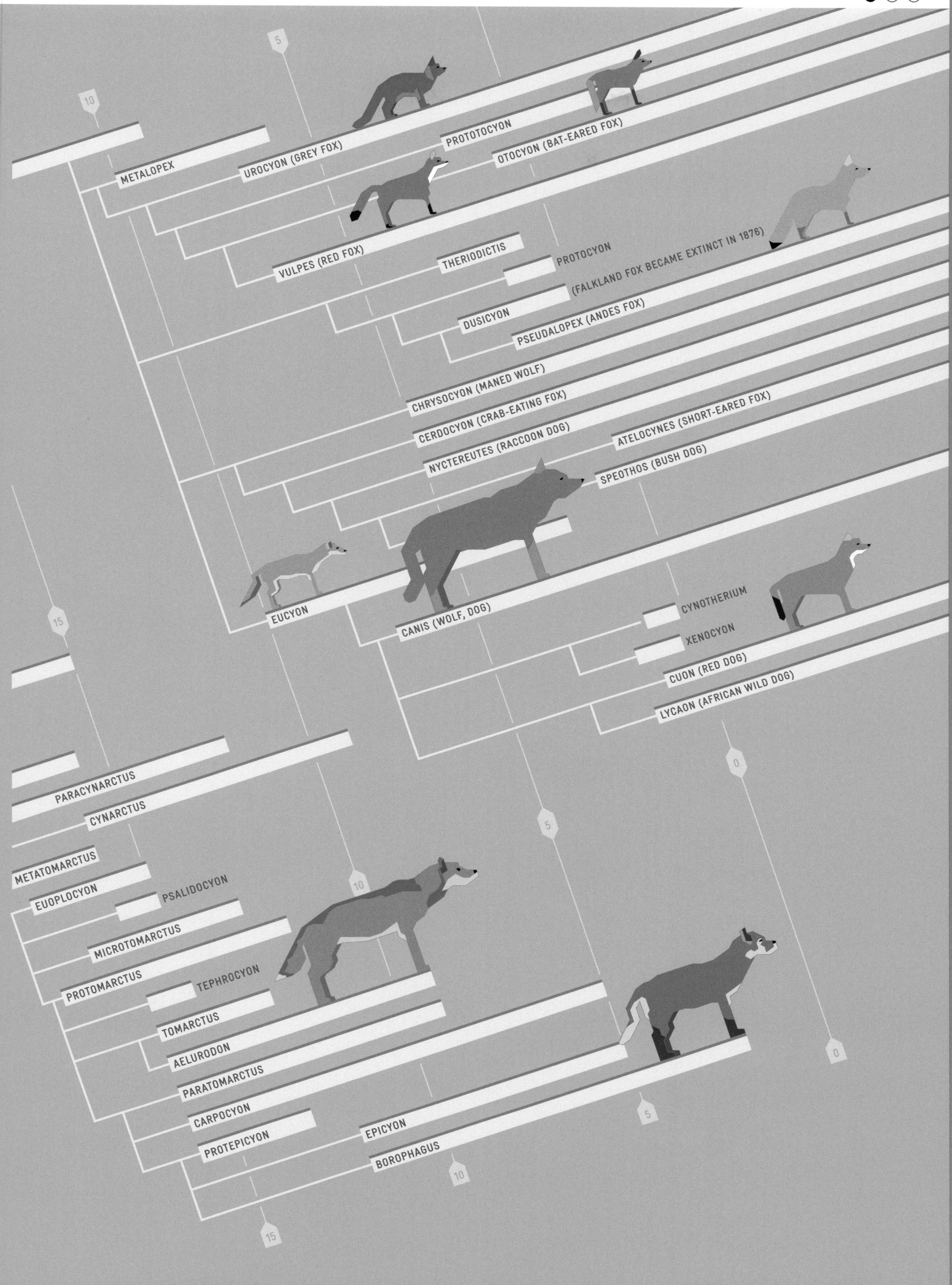

METALOPEX
UROCYON (GREY FOX)
PROTOTOCYON
OTOCYON (BAT-EARED FOX)
VULPES (RED FOX)
THERIODICTIS
PROTOCYON
(FALKLAND FOX BECAME EXTINCT IN 1876)
DUSICYON
PSEUDALOPEX (ANDES FOX)
CHRYSOCYON (MANED WOLF)
CERDOCYON (CRAB-EATING FOX)
NYCTEREUTES (RACCOON DOG)
ATELOCYNES (SHORT-EARED FOX)
SPEOTHOS (BUSH DOG)
EUCYON
CANIS (WOLF, DOG)
CYNOTHERIUM
XENOCYON
CUON (RED DOG)
LYCAON (AFRICAN WILD DOG)
PARACYNARCTUS
CYNARCTUS
METATOMARCTUS
EUOPLOCYON
PSALIDOCYON
MICROTOMARCTUS
PROTOMARCTUS
TEPHROCYON
TOMARCTUS
AELURODON
PARATOMARCTUS
CARPOCYON
PROTEPICYON
EPICYON
BOROPHAGUS
10
5
15
0
5
10
0
5
10
15

The world authority on cynology—the Fédération Cynologique Internationale—currently recognizes 343 different breeds of domestic dogs. They are organized in groups according to the duties for which they have been bred and shared characteristics, such as those presented here.

Key
Breed specific characteristics

Coat type: Short coat · Long coat · Wire coat · Double coat · Curly/curly-wire

Coat color: Spotted · Flecked, brindled or merle · Multicolored · Single-color

Pointers

These hunting dogs point out detected game by remaining still in an alert position.

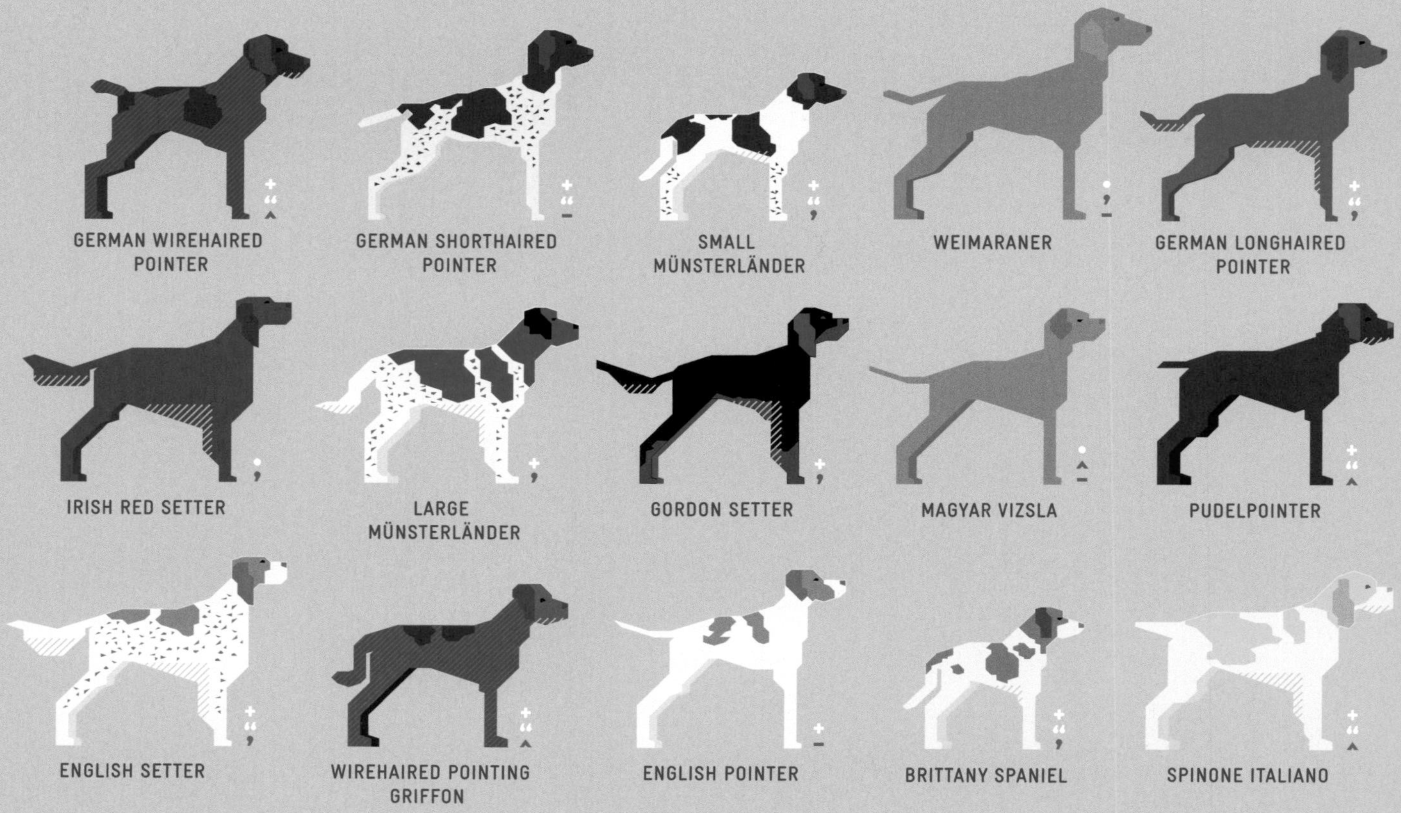
GERMAN WIREHAIRED POINTER
GERMAN SHORTHAIRED POINTER
SMALL MÜNSTERLÄNDER
WEIMARANER
GERMAN LONGHAIRED POINTER
IRISH RED SETTER
LARGE MÜNSTERLÄNDER
GORDON SETTER
MAGYAR VIZSLA
PUDELPOINTER
ENGLISH SETTER
WIREHAIRED POINTING GRIFFON
ENGLISH POINTER
BRITTANY SPANIEL
SPINONE ITALIANO

Greyhounds

These long-legged, slim foxhounds have a sixth sense in locating their prey. Next to the cheetah, they are among the fastest terrestrial animals.

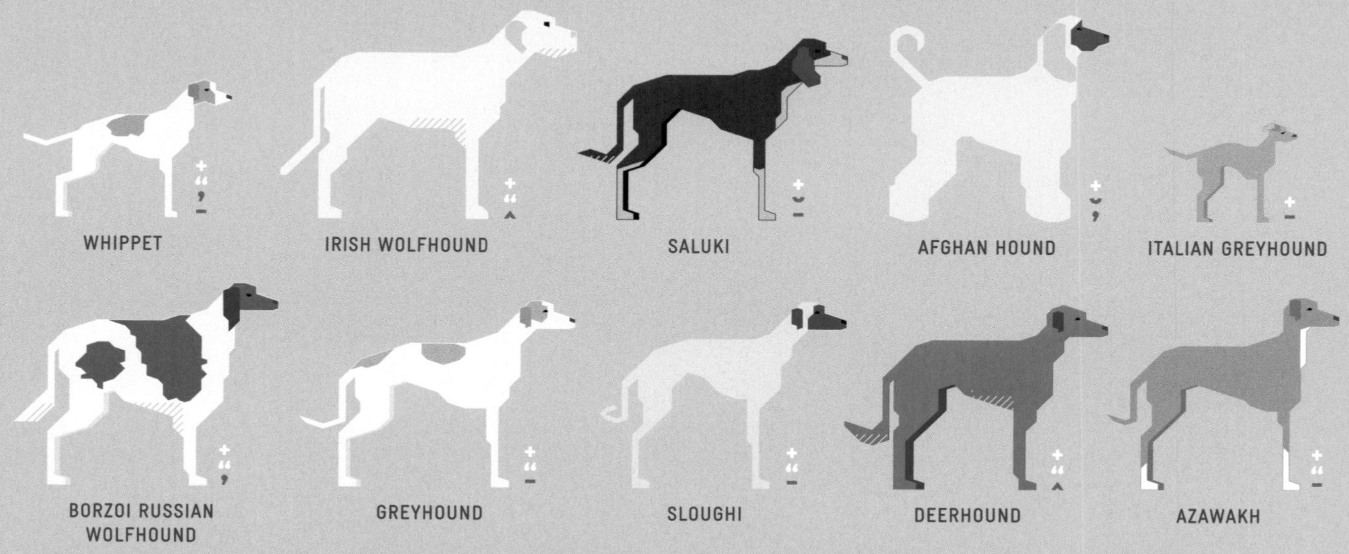
WHIPPET
IRISH WOLFHOUND
SALUKI
AFGHAN HOUND
ITALIAN GREYHOUND
BORZOI RUSSIAN WOLFHOUND
GREYHOUND
SLOUGHI
DEERHOUND
AZAWAKH

Retrievers, flushing dogs and waterfowl hunting dogs

Retrievers sniff out downed game for the hunter while flushing dogs chase prey out into the open and water fowl dogs hit the water to assist their master.

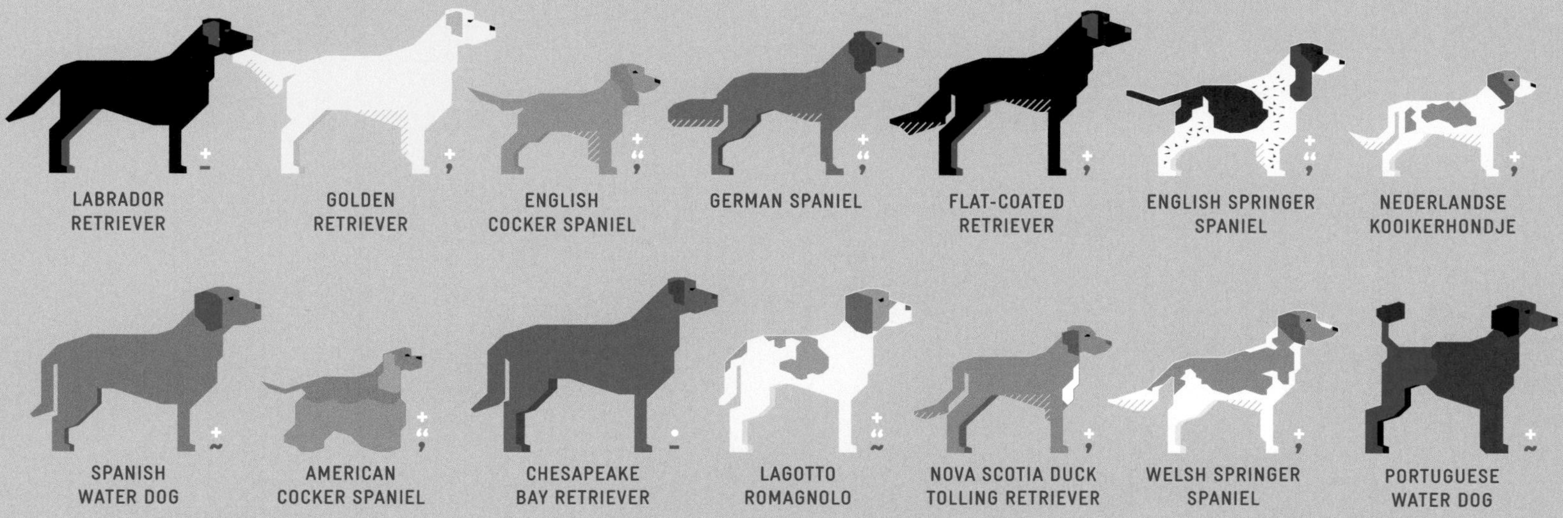
LABRADOR RETRIEVER
GOLDEN RETRIEVER
ENGLISH COCKER SPANIEL
GERMAN SPANIEL
FLAT-COATED RETRIEVER
ENGLISH SPRINGER SPANIEL
NEDERLANDSE KOOIKERHONDJE
SPANISH WATER DOG
AMERICAN COCKER SPANIEL
CHESAPEAKE BAY RETRIEVER
LAGOTTO ROMAGNOLO
NOVA SCOTIA DUCK TOLLING RETRIEVER
WELSH SPRINGER SPANIEL
PORTUGUESE WATER DOG

Companion dogs

These are small toy dogs, lapdogs and miniature versions of larger breeds that are only bred as pets.

POODLE
CAVALIER KING CHARLES SPANIEL
CHIHUAHUA
HAVANESE
TIBETAN TERRIER
PUG
BOSTON TERRIER
MALTESE
FRENCH BULLDOG
CONTINENTAL TOY SPANIEL
COTON DE TULÉAR
CHINESE CRESTED DOG
KROMFOHRLÄNDER
BICHON À POIL FRISÉ
SHIH TZU
LITTLE LION DOG
LHASA APSO
BOLOGNESE
TIBETAN SPANIEL
PETIT BRABANÇON
JAPANESE CHIN

Pomeranians and archetypal type dogs

Despite being the classic and oldest dog breeds, each of these present differences in behavior and character.

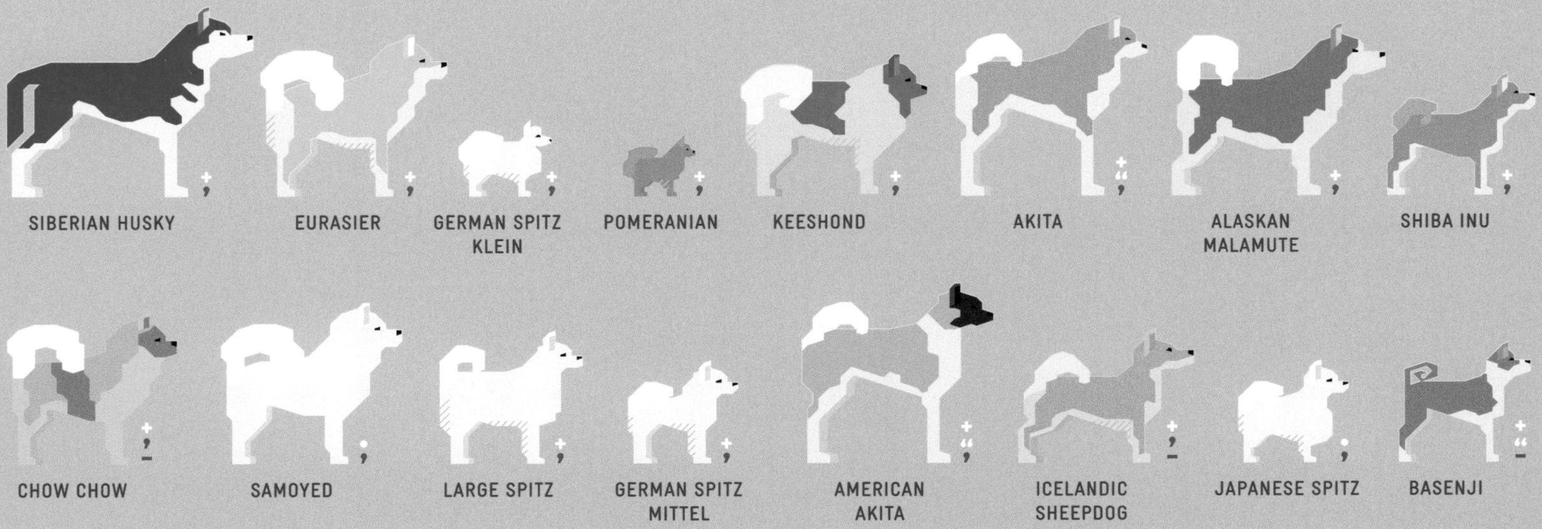
SIBERIAN HUSKY
EURASIER
GERMAN SPITZ KLEIN
POMERANIAN
KEESHOND
AKITA
ALASKAN MALAMUTE
SHIBA INU
CHOW CHOW
SAMOYED
LARGE SPITZ
GERMAN SPITZ MITTEL
AMERICAN AKITA
ICELANDIC SHEEPDOG
JAPANESE SPITZ
BASENJI

Pinscher and Schnauzers – Molossers – Swiss mountain dogs

The dogs in this group are characterized by a strong protective and hunting instinct. Their vigilance and strong nerves made them indispensable helpers for farmers and shepherds in the past.

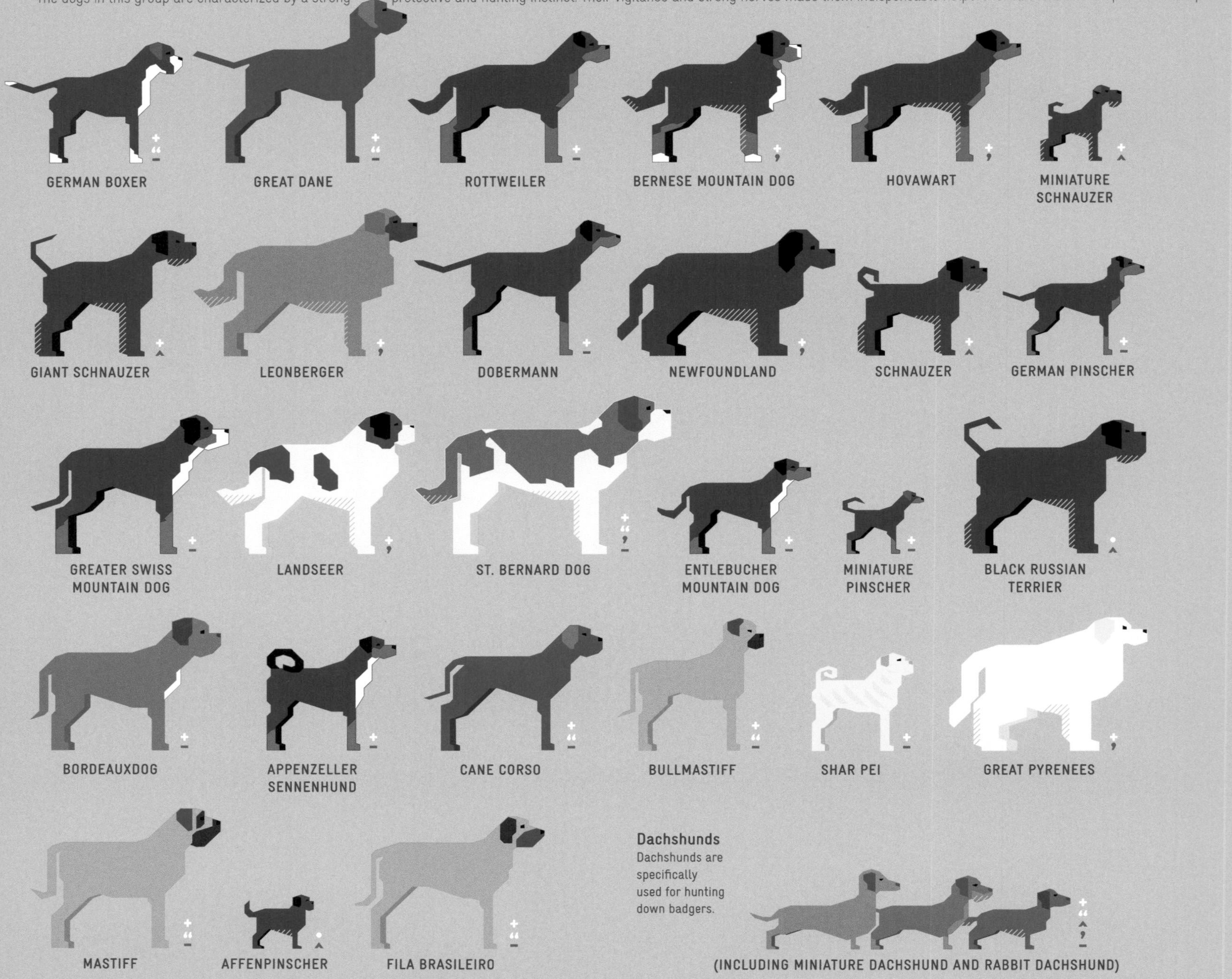
GERMAN BOXER
GREAT DANE
ROTTWEILER
BERNESE MOUNTAIN DOG
HOVAWART
MINIATURE SCHNAUZER
GIANT SCHNAUZER
LEONBERGER
DOBERMANN
NEWFOUNDLAND
SCHNAUZER
GERMAN PINSCHER
GREATER SWISS MOUNTAIN DOG
LANDSEER
ST. BERNARD DOG
ENTLEBUCHER MOUNTAIN DOG
MINIATURE PINSCHER
BLACK RUSSIAN TERRIER
BORDEAUXDOG
APPENZELLER SENNENHUND
CANE CORSO
BULLMASTIFF
SHAR PEI
GREAT PYRENEES
MASTIFF
AFFENPINSCHER
FILA BRASILEIRO
Dachshunds
Dachshunds are specifically used for hunting down badgers.
(INCLUDING MINIATURE DACHSHUND AND RABBIT DACHSHUND)

Hounds, bloodhounds and related breeds

These hunting dogs are able to pick up and follow game tracks over large distances thanks to their well-developed sense of smell.

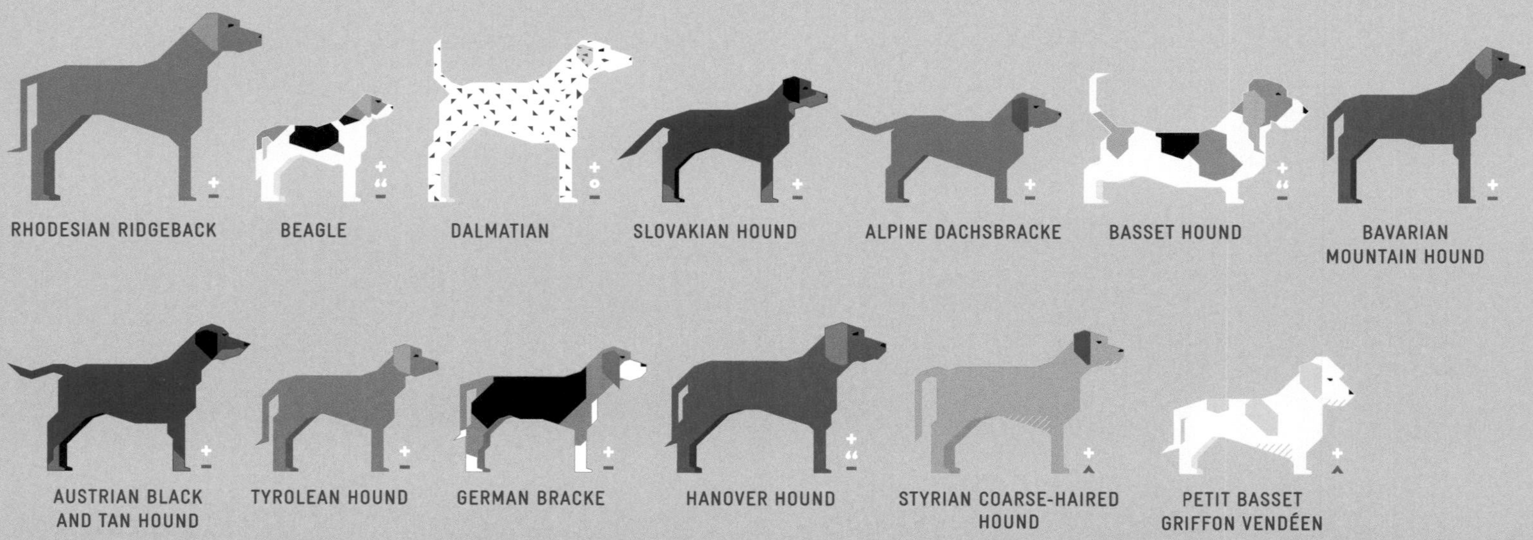
RHODESIAN RIDGEBACK
BEAGLE
DALMATIAN
SLOVAKIAN HOUND
ALPINE DACHSBRACKE
BASSET HOUND
BAVARIAN MOUNTAIN HOUND
AUSTRIAN BLACK AND TAN HOUND
TYROLEAN HOUND
GERMAN BRACKE
HANOVER HOUND
STYRIAN COARSE-HAIRED HOUND
PETIT BASSET GRIFFON VENDÉEN

Terriers

The name Terrier comes from the French word »terre« (earth). These hunting dogs were originally bred to chase game out of their underground burrows.

FOX TERRIER
WEST HIGHLAND WHITE TERRIER
JAGDTERRIER
PARSON RUSSELL TERRIER
AIREDALE TERRIER
MINIATURE BULL TERRIER
YORKSHIRE TERRIER
CAIRN TERRIER
IRISH TERRIER
BORDER TERRIER
WELSH TERRIER
STAFFORDSHIRE BULL TERRIER
IRISH SOFT-COATED WHEATENTERRIER
NORFOLK TERRIER
JACK RUSSELL TERRIER
SCOTTISH TERRIER
BULL TERRIER
NORWICH TERRIER
AMERICAN STAFFORDSHIRE TERRIER
MANCHESTER TERRIER
LAKELAND TERRIER
KERRY BLUE TERRIER
AUSTRALIAN SILKY TERRIER

Herding and cattle dogs

These dogs were bred to be the shepherd's indispensable helpers.

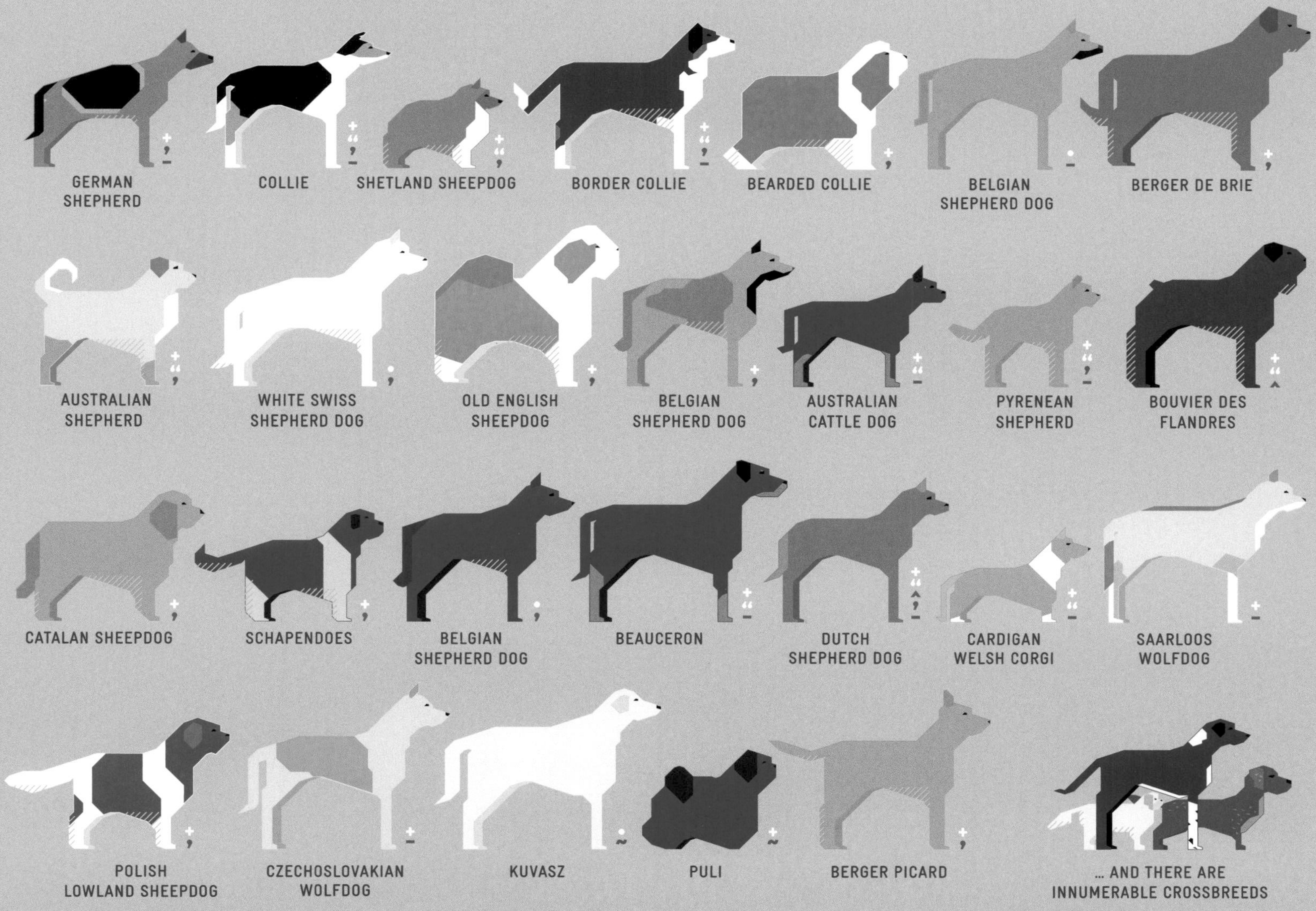
GERMAN SHEPHERD
COLLIE
SHETLAND SHEEPDOG
BORDER COLLIE
BEARDED COLLIE
BELGIAN SHEPHERD DOG
BERGER DE BRIE
AUSTRALIAN SHEPHERD
WHITE SWISS SHEPHERD DOG
OLD ENGLISH SHEEPDOG
BELGIAN SHEPHERD DOG
AUSTRALIAN CATTLE DOG
PYRENEAN SHEPHERD
BOUVIER DES FLANDRES
CATALAN SHEEPDOG
SCHAPENDOES
BELGIAN SHEPHERD DOG
BEAUCERON
DUTCH SHEPHERD DOG
CARDIGAN WELSH CORGI
SAARLOOS WOLFDOG
POLISH LOWLAND SHEEPDOG
CZECHOSLOVAKIAN WOLFDOG
KUVASZ
PULI
BERGER PICARD
... AND THERE ARE INNUMERABLE CROSSBREEDS

IN UTERO

Pregnancy is a miracle of nature. In humans, the gestation period is about nine months, usually resulting in the birth of a single child. But what is the situation in the animal kingdom? The gestation period and number of offspring of a mammal vary in close proportion to its size and lifespan. For example, a mouse is sexually mature after six weeks, and can give birth to about eight cubs after a three-week gestation period. An elephant is fertile at about 11 years of age and gives birth to a single calf after a gestation period of 22 months.

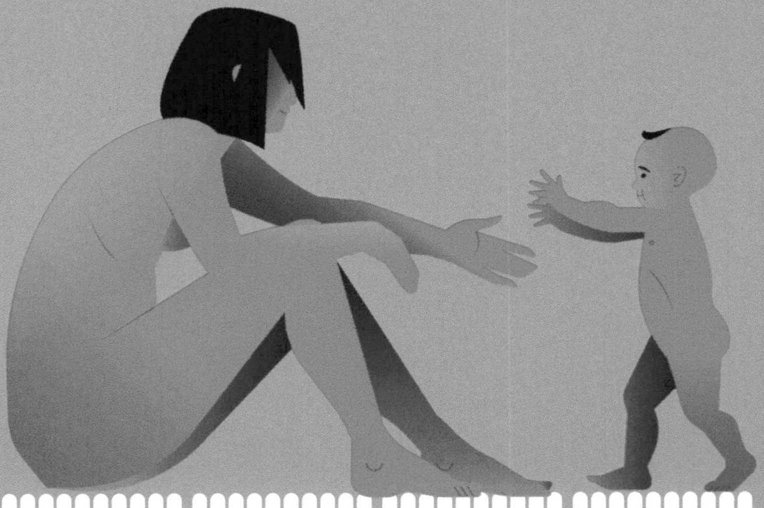

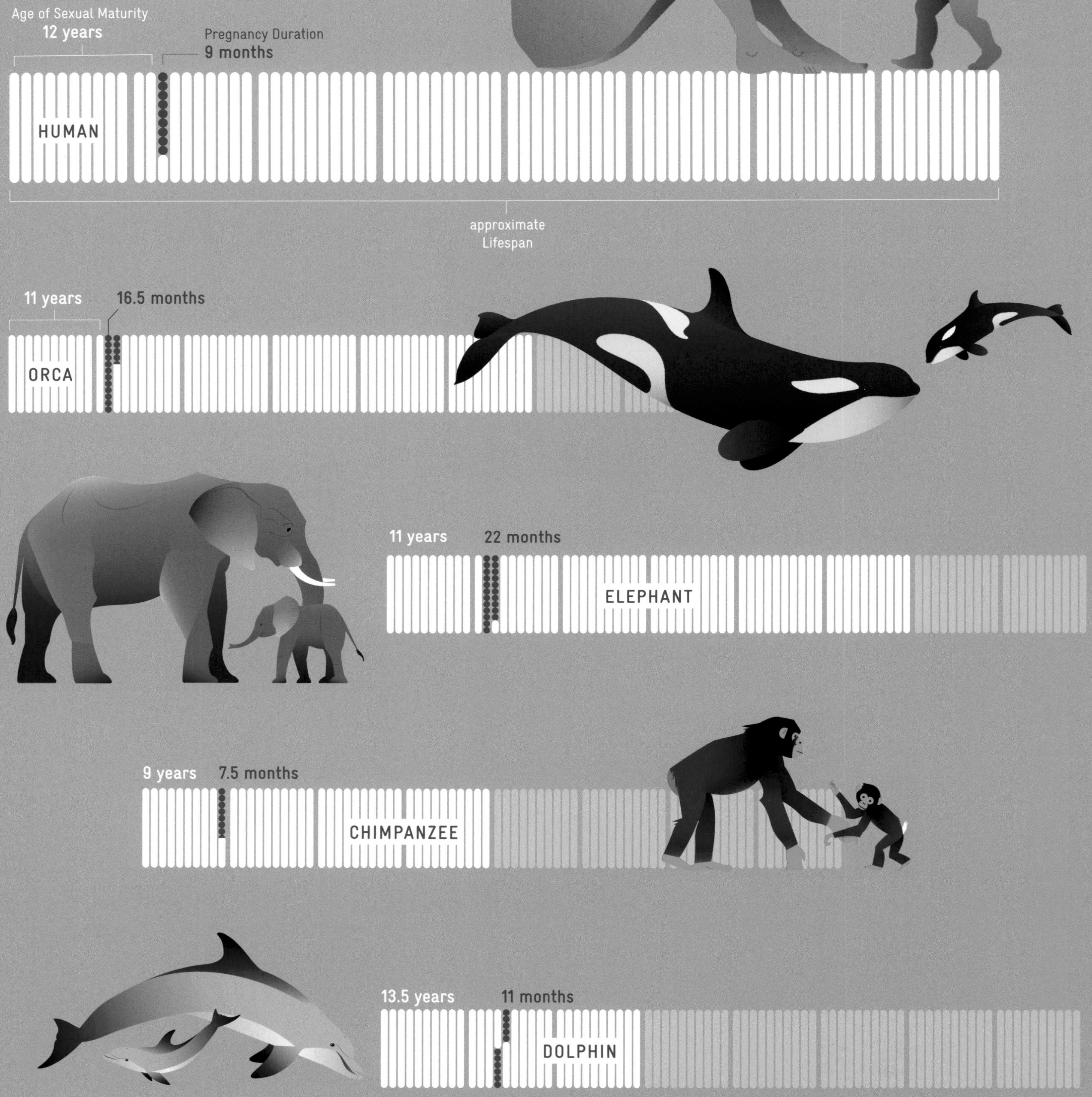

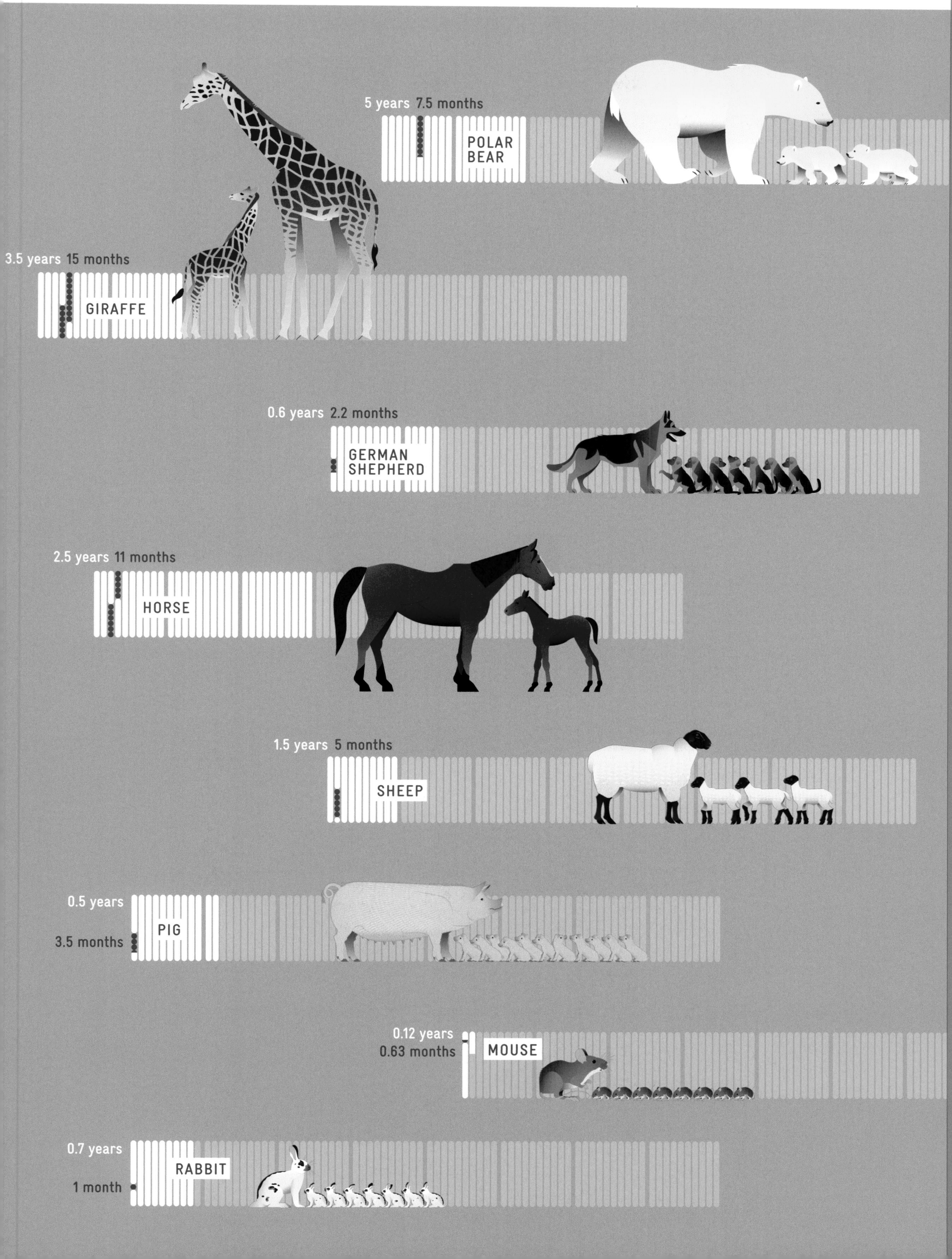
5 years 7.5 months
POLAR BEAR
3.5 years 15 months
GIRAFFE
0.6 years 2.2 months
GERMAN SHEPHERD
2.5 years 11 months
HORSE
1.5 years 5 months
SHEEP
0.5 years
3.5 months
PIG
0.12 years
0.63 months
MOUSE
0.7 years
1 month
RABBIT

YESTERMORROW

What did today look like to those that were imagining it as the future? Former thought experiments such as 3D printers, autonomous vehicles and bionic prostheses are now a reality. But other aspects of a future as imagined by writers and filmmakers remain fiction. What still applies is that innovation is driven by boundless imagination.

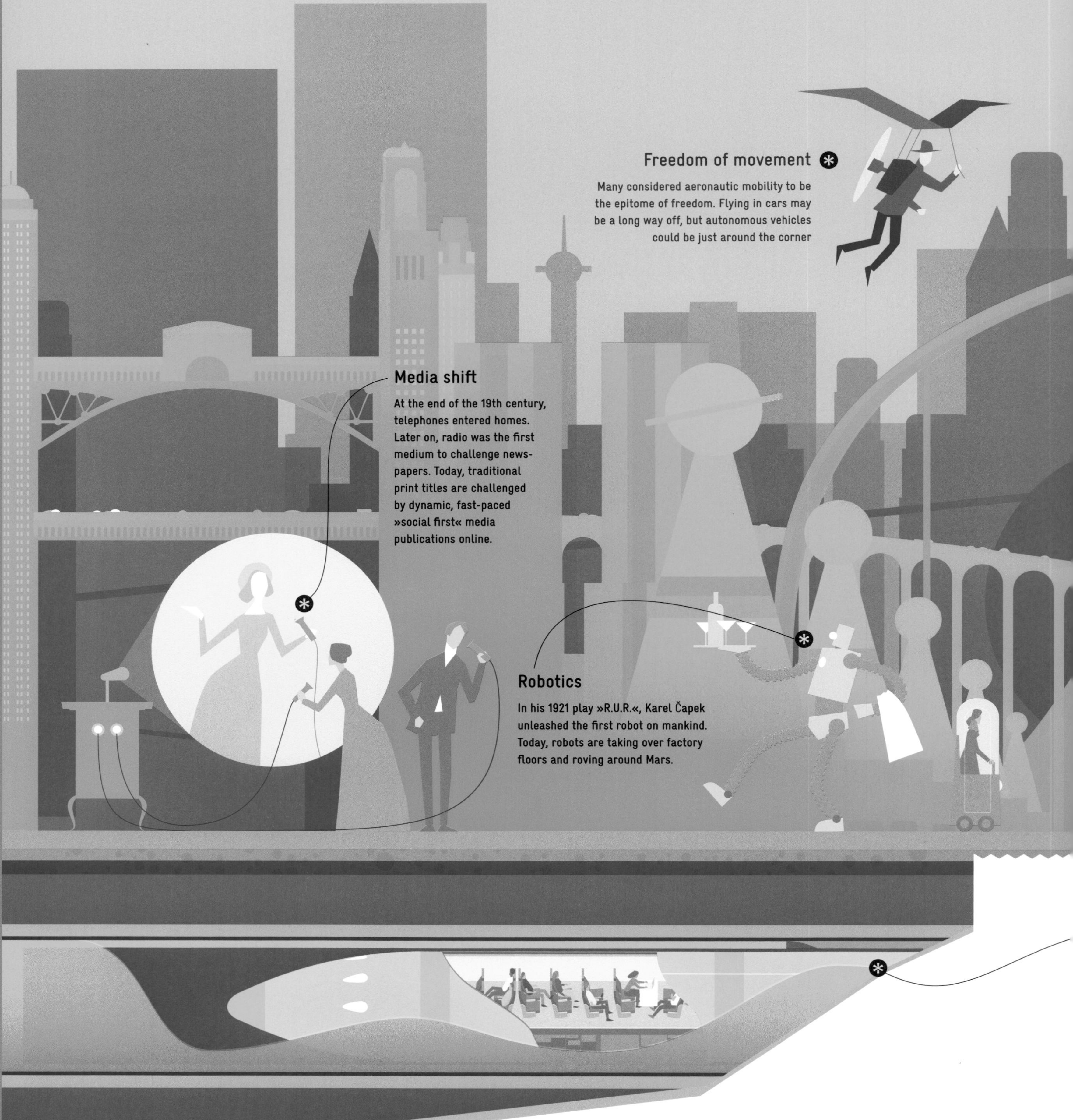
Freedom of movement
Many considered aeronautic mobility to be the epitome of freedom. Flying in cars may be a long way off, but autonomous vehicles could be just around the corner
Media shift
At the end of the 19th century, telephones entered homes. Later on, radio was the first medium to challenge newspapers. Today, traditional print titles are challenged by dynamic, fast-paced »social first« media publications online.
Robotics
In his 1921 play »R.U.R.«, Karel Čapek unleashed the first robot on mankind. Today, robots are taking over factory floors and roving around Mars.

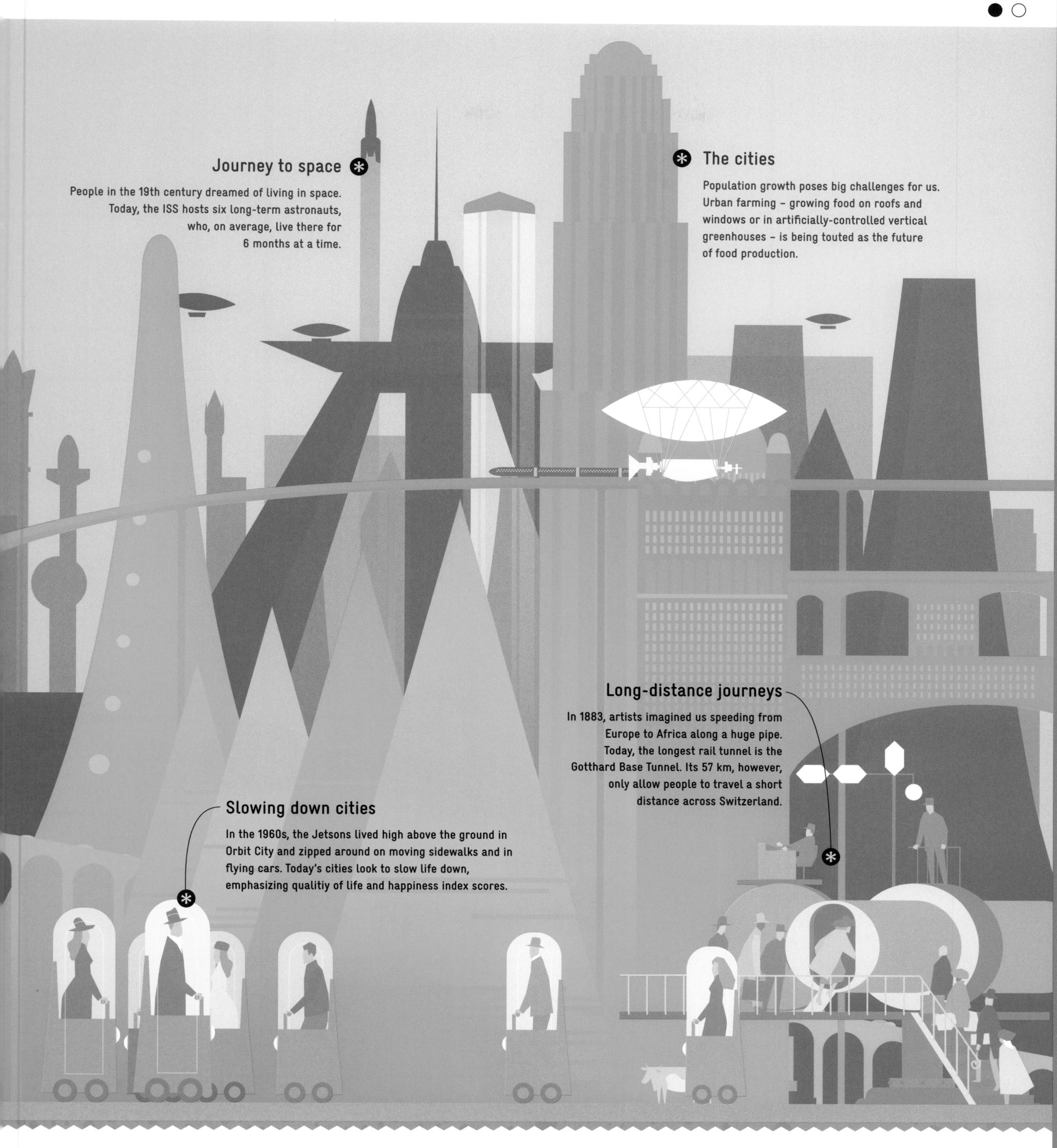

Journey to space

People in the 19th century dreamed of living in space. Today, the ISS hosts six long-term astronauts, who, on average, live there for 6 months at a time.

The cities

Population growth poses big challenges for us. Urban farming – growing food on roofs and windows or in artificially-controlled vertical greenhouses – is being touted as the future of food production.

Long-distance journeys

In 1883, artists imagined us speeding from Europe to Africa along a huge pipe. Today, the longest rail tunnel is the Gotthard Base Tunnel. Its 57 km, however, only allow people to travel a short distance across Switzerland.

Slowing down cities

In the 1960s, the Jetsons lived high above the ground in Orbit City and zipped around on moving sidewalks and in flying cars. Today's cities look to slow life down, emphasizing qualitiy of life and happiness index scores.

Public transport

The aim is to get across the city of the future with speed and ease. Yet subways built in the 19th and 20th centuries are still the preferred urban transportation system.

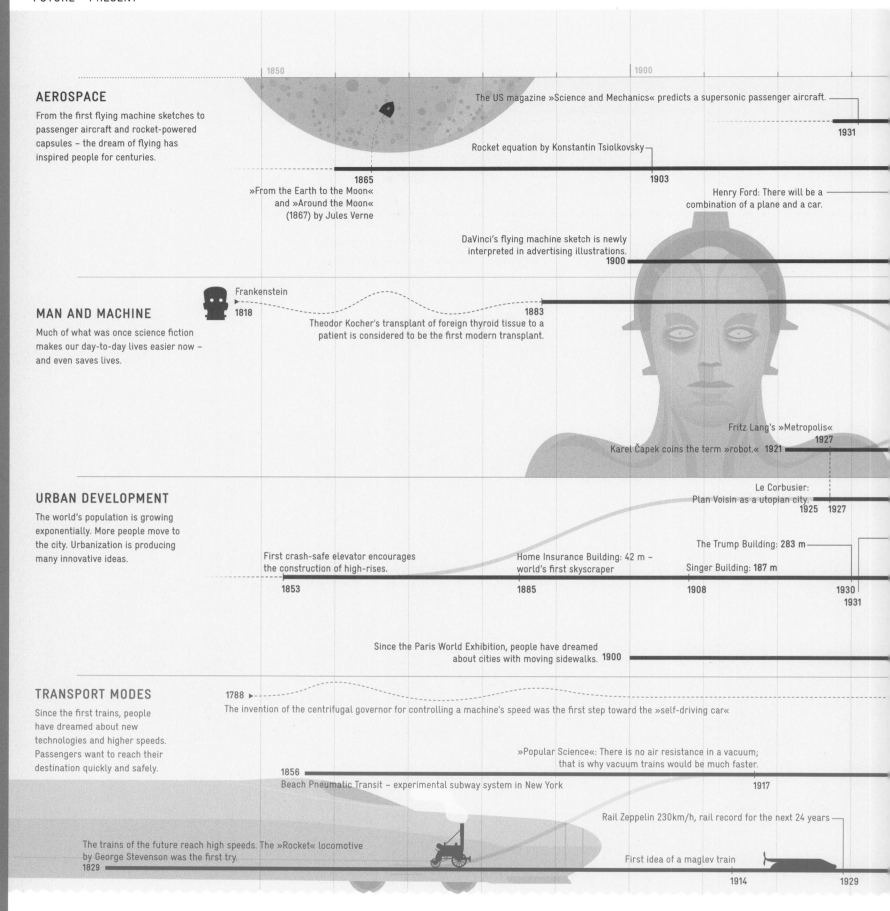

1850 | 1900

AEROSPACE

From the first flying machine sketches to passenger aircraft and rocket-powered capsules – the dream of flying has inspired people for centuries.

- 1865 »From the Earth to the Moon« and »Around the Moon« (1867) by Jules Verne
- 1903 Rocket equation by Konstantin Tsiolkovsky
- 1900 DaVinci's flying machine sketch is newly interpreted in advertising illustrations.
- 1931 The US magazine »Science and Mechanics« predicts a supersonic passenger aircraft.
- Henry Ford: There will be a combination of a plane and a car.

MAN AND MACHINE

Much of what was once science fiction makes our day-to-day lives easier now – and even saves lives.

- 1818 Frankenstein
- 1883 Theodor Kocher's transplant of foreign thyroid tissue to a patient is considered to be the first modern transplant.
- 1921 Karel Čapek coins the term »robot.«
- 1927 Fritz Lang's »Metropolis«

URBAN DEVELOPMENT

The world's population is growing exponentially. More people move to the city. Urbanization is producing many innovative ideas.

- 1853 First crash-safe elevator encourages the construction of high-rises.
- 1885 Home Insurance Building: 42 m – world's first skyscraper
- 1908 Singer Building: 187 m
- 1930 The Trump Building: 283 m
- 1931
- 1925 1927 Le Corbusier: Plan Voisin as a utopian city.
- 1900 Since the Paris World Exhibition, people have dreamed about cities with moving sidewalks.

TRANSPORT MODES

Since the first trains, people have dreamed about new technologies and higher speeds. Passengers want to reach their destination quickly and safely.

- 1788 The invention of the centrifugal governor for controlling a machine's speed was the first step toward the »self-driving car«
- 1856 Beach Pneumatic Transit – experimental subway system in New York
- 1917 »Popular Science«: There is no air resistance in a vacuum; that is why vacuum trains would be much faster.
- 1829 The trains of the future reach high speeds. The »Rocket« locomotive by George Stevenson was the first try.
- 1914 First idea of a maglev train
- 1929 Rail Zeppelin 230km/h, rail record for the next 24 years

VISIONARIES

Future visions are documented in art, film and literature. They range from ideas about a more comfortable future (Henry Ford) to dystopian visions (George Orwell). Many of the visionaries dedicated their ideas to technical progress and let themselves be inspired by the innovations of their times. Many future visions seem absurd to us now with hindsight. However, Leonardo da Vinci's technical drawings could only be realized many centuries later.

LEONARDO DA VINCI 1452 – 1519

As an architect and engineer, he was ahead of his time. The polymath is regarded as the inventor of the submarine and helicopter. He believed the vision was more important than its realization.

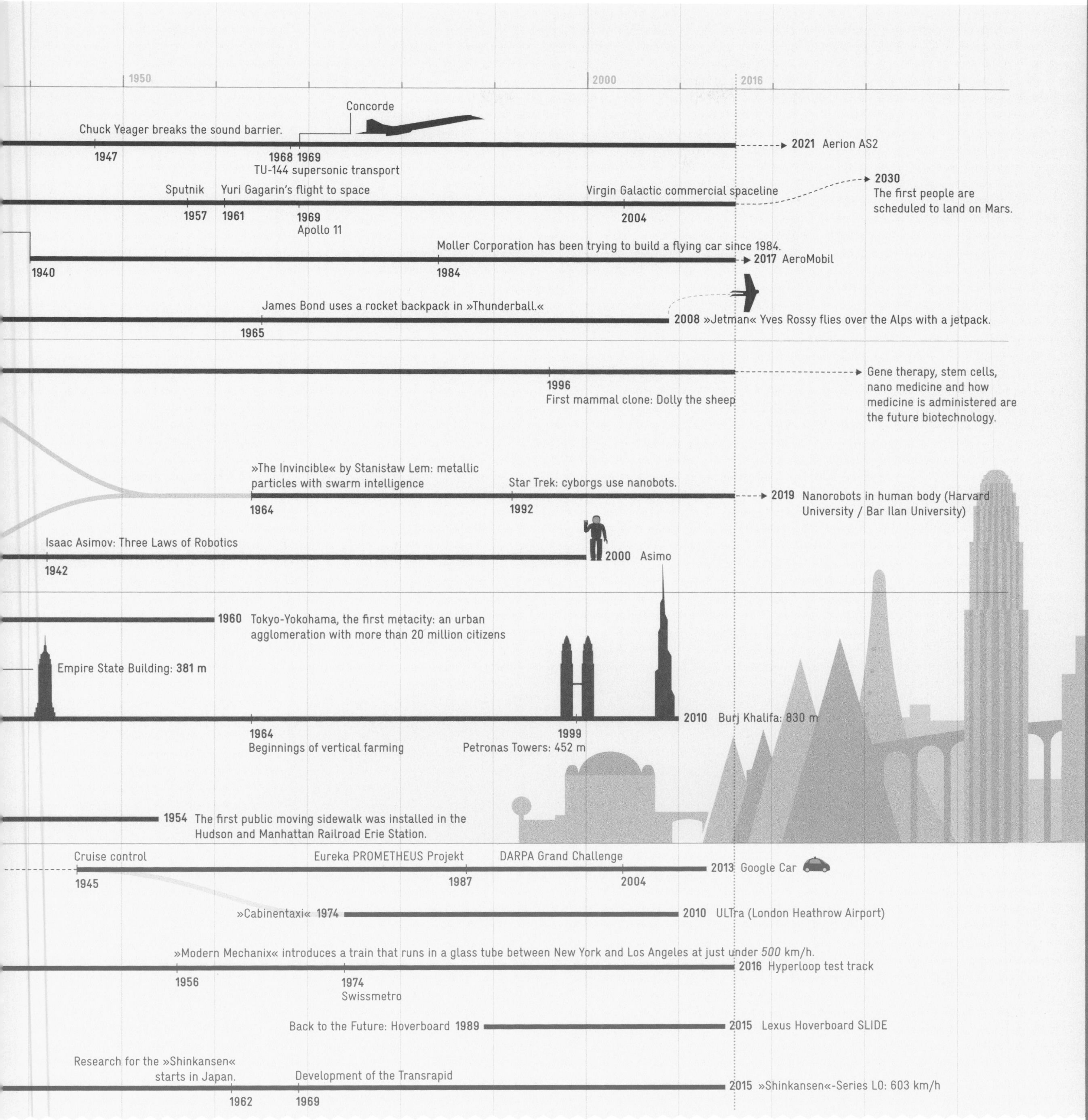
1950
2000
2016
Concorde
Chuck Yeager breaks the sound barrier.
1947
1968 1969
TU-144 supersonic transport
2021 Aerion AS2
Sputnik
Yuri Gagarin's flight to space
Virgin Galactic commercial spaceline
1957
1961
1969
Apollo 11
2004
2030
The first people are scheduled to land on Mars.
Moller Corporation has been trying to build a flying car since 1984.
1940
1984
2017 AeroMobil
James Bond uses a rocket backpack in »Thunderball.«
1965
2008 »Jetman« Yves Rossy flies over the Alps with a jetpack.
1996
First mammal clone: Dolly the sheep
Gene therapy, stem cells, nano medicine and how medicine is administered are the future biotechnology.
»The Invincible« by Stanisław Lem: metallic particles with swarm intelligence
1964
Star Trek: cyborgs use nanobots.
1992
2019 Nanorobots in human body (Harvard University / Bar Ilan University)
Isaac Asimov: Three Laws of Robotics
1942
2000 Asimo
1960 Tokyo-Yokohama, the first metacity: an urban agglomeration with more than 20 million citizens
Empire State Building: 381 m
1964
Beginnings of vertical farming
1999
Petronas Towers: 452 m
2010 Burj Khalifa: 830 m
1954 The first public moving sidewalk was installed in the Hudson and Manhattan Railroad Erie Station.
Cruise control
1945
Eureka PROMETHEUS Projekt
1987
DARPA Grand Challenge
2004
2013 Google Car
»Cabinentaxi« 1974
2010 ULTra (London Heathrow Airport)
»Modern Mechanix« introduces a train that runs in a glass tube between New York and Los Angeles at just under 500 km/h.
1956
1974
Swissmetro
2016 Hyperloop test track
Back to the Future: Hoverboard 1989
2015 Lexus Hoverboard SLIDE
Research for the »Shinkansen« starts in Japan.
1962
Development of the Transrapid
1969
2015 »Shinkansen«-Series L0: 603 km/h

JULES VERNE 1828–1905

Influenced by the technical progress of his era, the French writer wrote about great expeditions using unknown technologies. His novels still inspire readers' imaginations to this day.

RICHARD BUCKMINSTER FULLER 1895–1983

The American was regarded as a visionary by the engineers and architects of his day. His ideas about energy efficiency and sustainable development are now more topical than ever.

KARL HANS JANKE 1909–1988

The inventor was diagnosed with paranoid schizophrenia, but still produced a comprehensive collection of drawings and models, mostly dedicated to aerospace.

3D PRINTING

3D printing is being heralded as a technology of the future—without a lot of people understanding what kind of future it can be used for. The European Space Agency (ESA) is looking at additive manufacturing as a way to eventually establish a moon base. The cooperative space exploration agency wants to use regolith (moon dust) as the printing material that robots would employ to build a permanent structure on the moon.

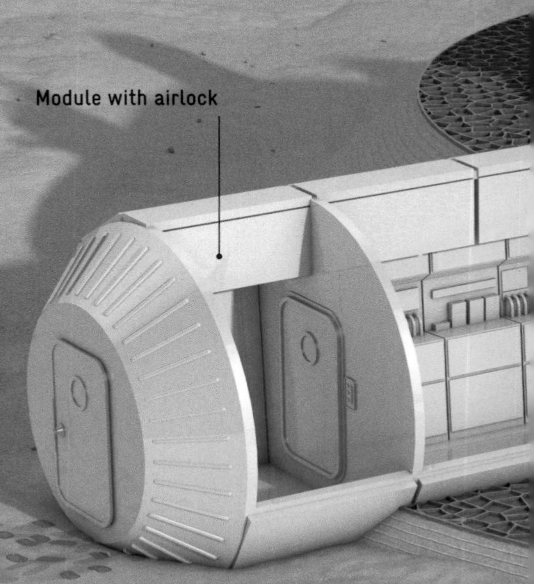
Module with airlock

LIVING ON THE MOON

The moon's surface is exposed to cosmic forces. Without the construction of protective covers to cope with these particular demands, life on the moon is unthinkable. The transport of the necessary resources would be laborious and expensive. This is why it makes sense to use the moon's own material to construct protective structures.

A livable structure on the moon would have to be resistant to:

High temperature changes | Solar radiation | Small meteorites

3D PRINTING TECHNOLOGY BASICS

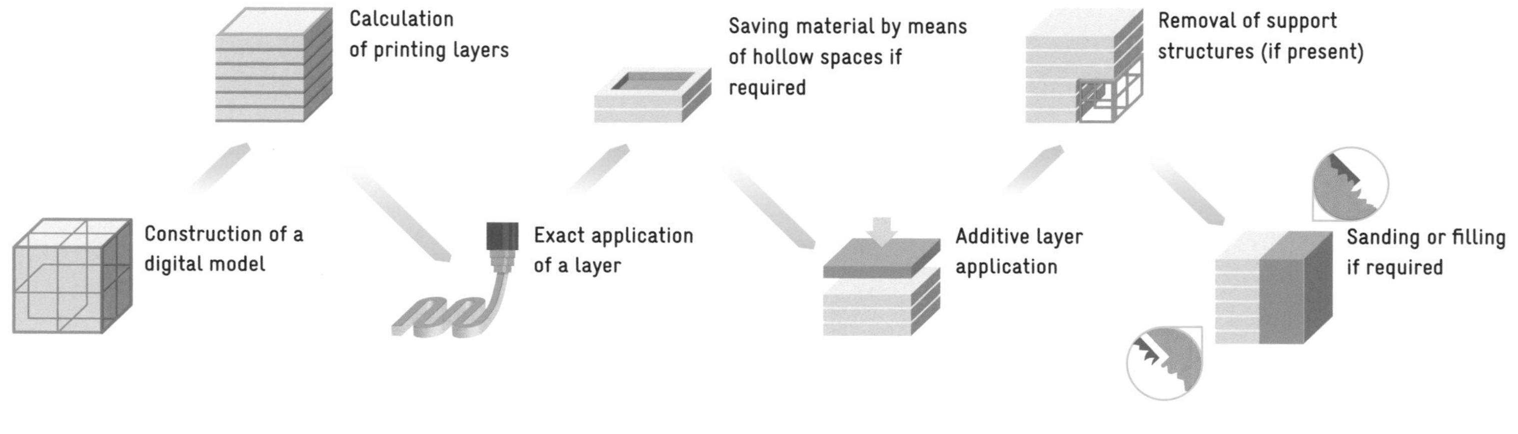
Construction of a digital model
Calculation of printing layers
Exact application of a layer
Saving material by means of hollow spaces if required
Additive layer application
Removal of support structures (if present)
Sanding or filling if required

MOON BASE LAYERS

The European Space Agency (ESA) is currently developing a method for printing a dome from moon material. The manufacture of this protective cover is done with the help of an inflatable support construction.

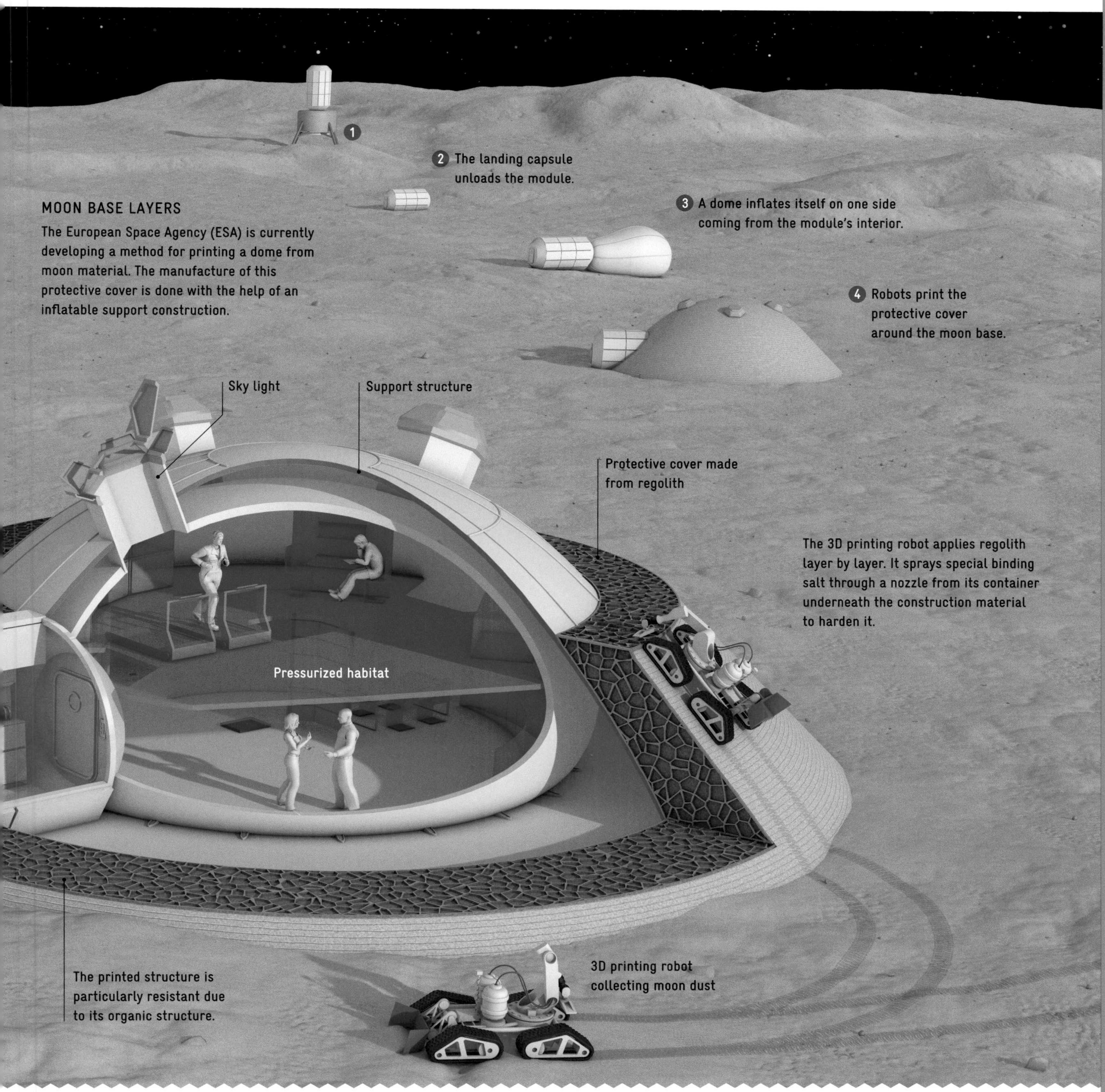
1
2 The landing capsule unloads the module.
3 A dome inflates itself on one side coming from the module's interior.
4 Robots print the protective cover around the moon base.
Sky light
Support structure
Protective cover made from regolith
The 3D printing robot applies regolith layer by layer. It sprays special binding salt through a nozzle from its container underneath the construction material to harden it.
Pressurized habitat
The printed structure is particularly resistant due to its organic structure.
3D printing robot collecting moon dust

3D PRINTER APPLICATIONS

- Spare part manufacture as required
- Affordable tailor-made prostheses
- Prototypes for faster product development
- Construction of complex concrete parts for architectural projects
- Already an industry standard in making dentures
- Special shapes that cannot be manufactured with traditional methods
- Individual designs, such as shoes
- Bone structures in surgery

URBAN FARMING

In 2050, our planet's population will be 9 billion. Around 70 percent of those people will be living in urban areas, posing logistical challenges to sustaining life, such as food production. If traditional methods were applied, land area the size of Brazil—the sixth-largest country—would be required to feed everyone. Urban farming methods offer an alternative that provide an economic, environmental and logistical solution.

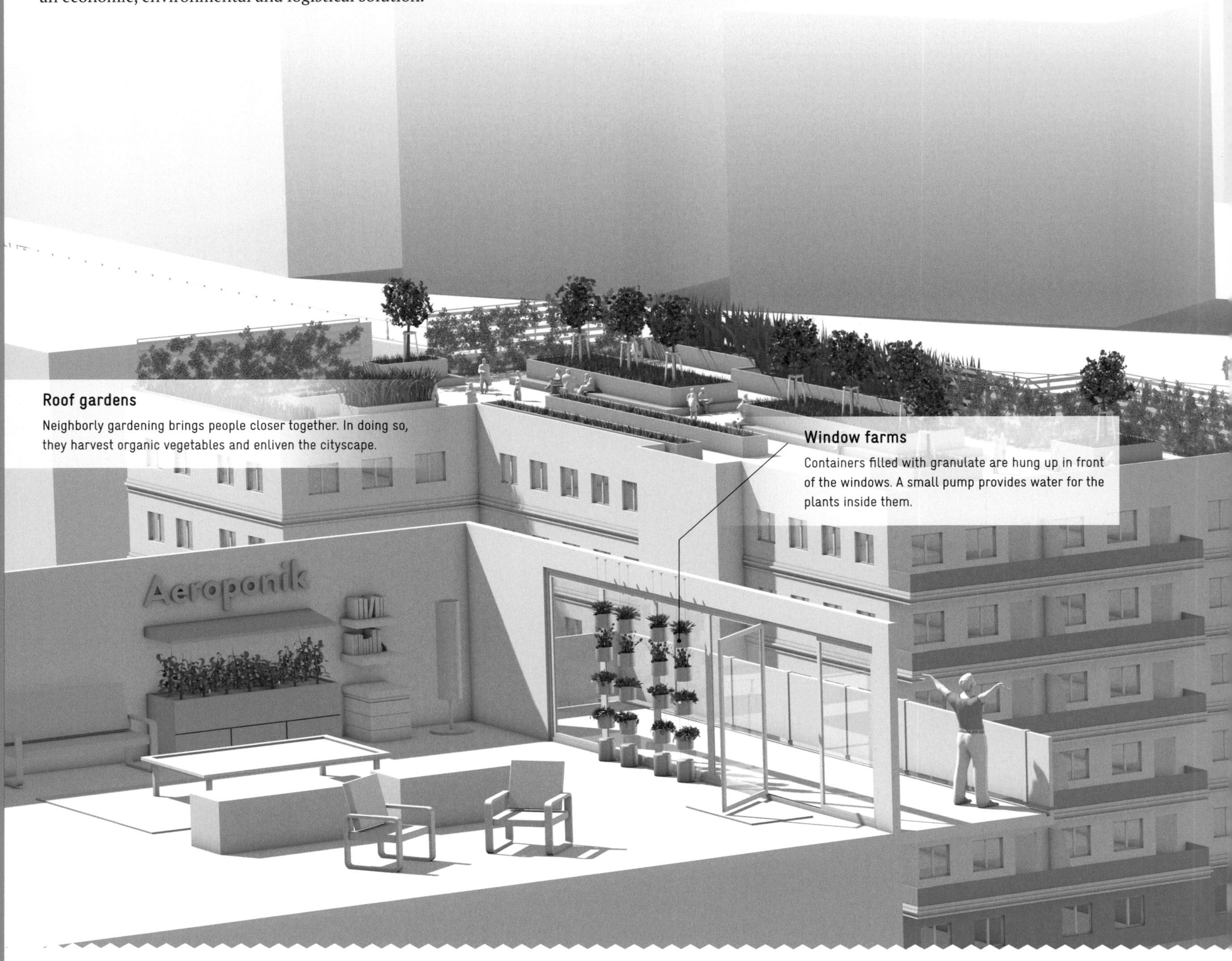
Roof gardens
Neighborly gardening brings people closer together. In doing so, they harvest organic vegetables and enliven the cityscape.
Window farms
Containers filled with granulate are hung up in front of the windows. A small pump provides water for the plants inside them.
Aeroponik

AEROPONICS

Aeroponics is a form of cultivation developed by NASA that does without soil or any comparable substrate. Plants are sprayed with a mix of water and nutrients, making the method suitable in weightlessness. On August 10, 2015, the International Space Station (ISS) crew enjoyed aeroponically-grown lettuce for the first time.

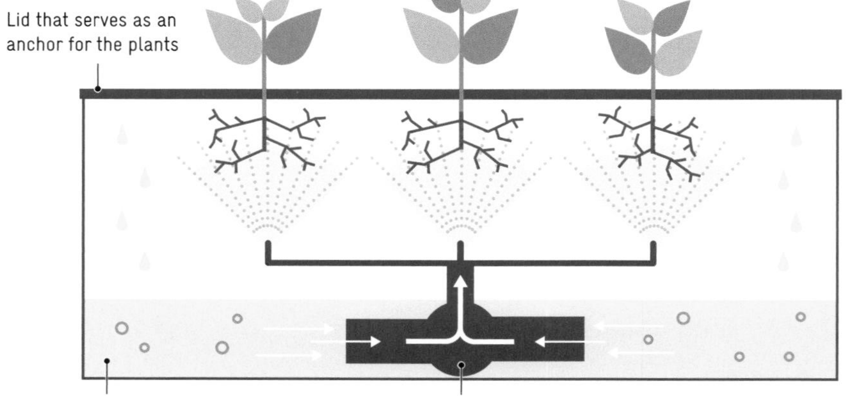
Lid that serves as an anchor for the plants
Water with nutrient solution
Timer-controlled pump

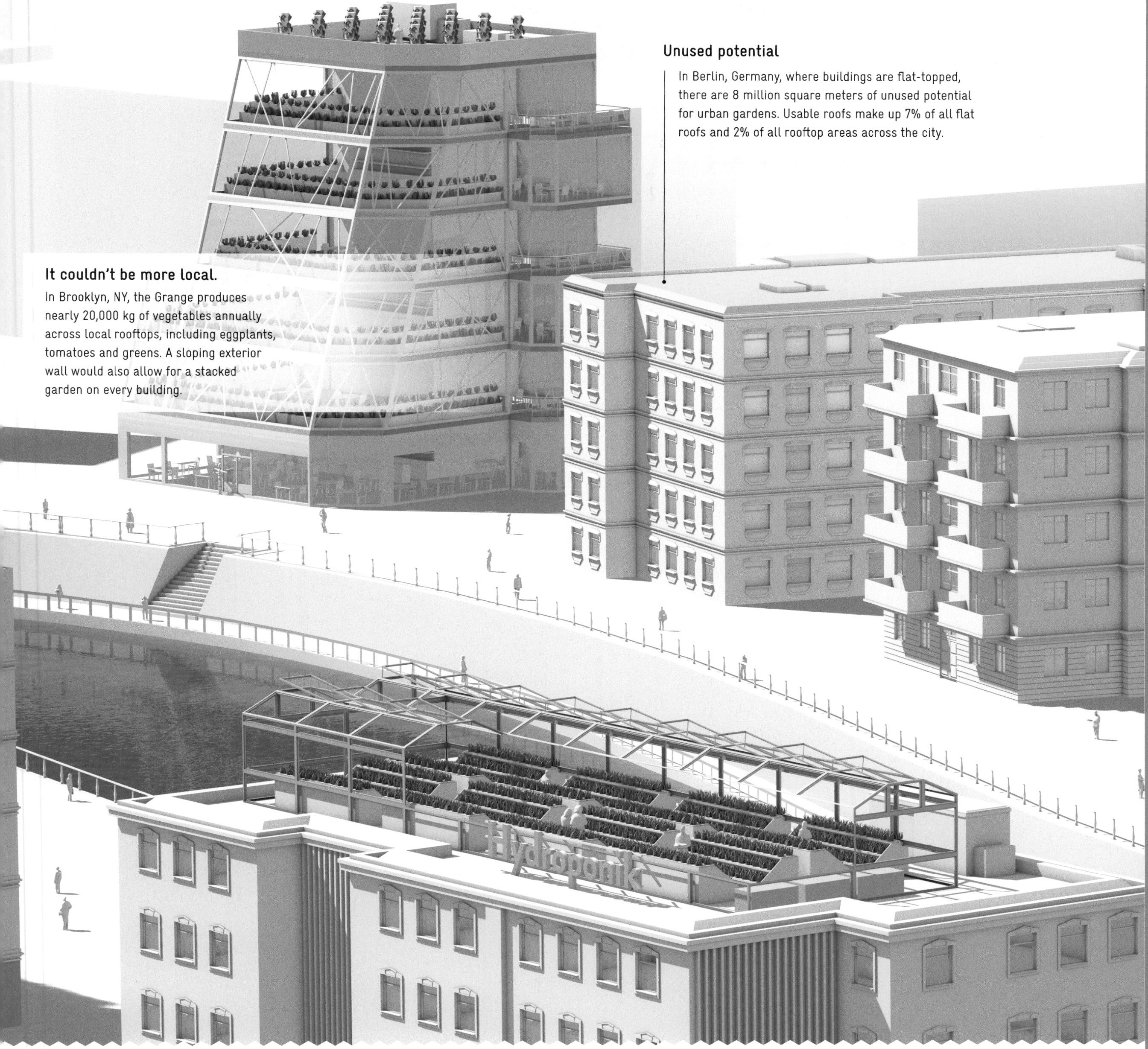

Unused potential

In Berlin, Germany, where buildings are flat-topped, there are 8 million square meters of unused potential for urban gardens. Usable roofs make up 7% of all flat roofs and 2% of all rooftop areas across the city.

It couldn't be more local.

In Brooklyn, NY, the Grange produces nearly 20,000 kg of vegetables annually across local rooftops, including eggplants, tomatoes and greens. A sloping exterior wall would also allow for a stacked garden on every building.

HYDROPONICS

Hydroponics cultivation also works without soil. The plants are fed by a constantly circulating nutrient solution that surrounds the roots. The plant is anchored in expanded clay or mineral wool.

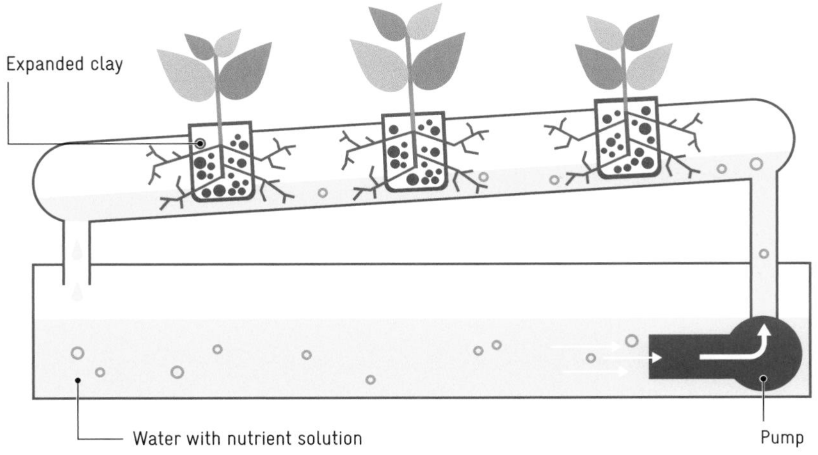
Expanded clay
Water with nutrient solution
Pump

City Bees

Urban apiaries are taking over. City honey often has a more varied source than honey from bees tending to fields and orchards. In fact, less than 1% of all honey in Germany is collected by professional beekeepers whose only income is sourced from the sticky treat.

Mushroom cultivation

Mushrooms don't need a lot of light to grow, but they do need a nutrient–rich soil that can hold a lot of moisture, like coffee grounds. Around the world, used grounds are collected for mushroom cultivation. The plants sprout after a few days.

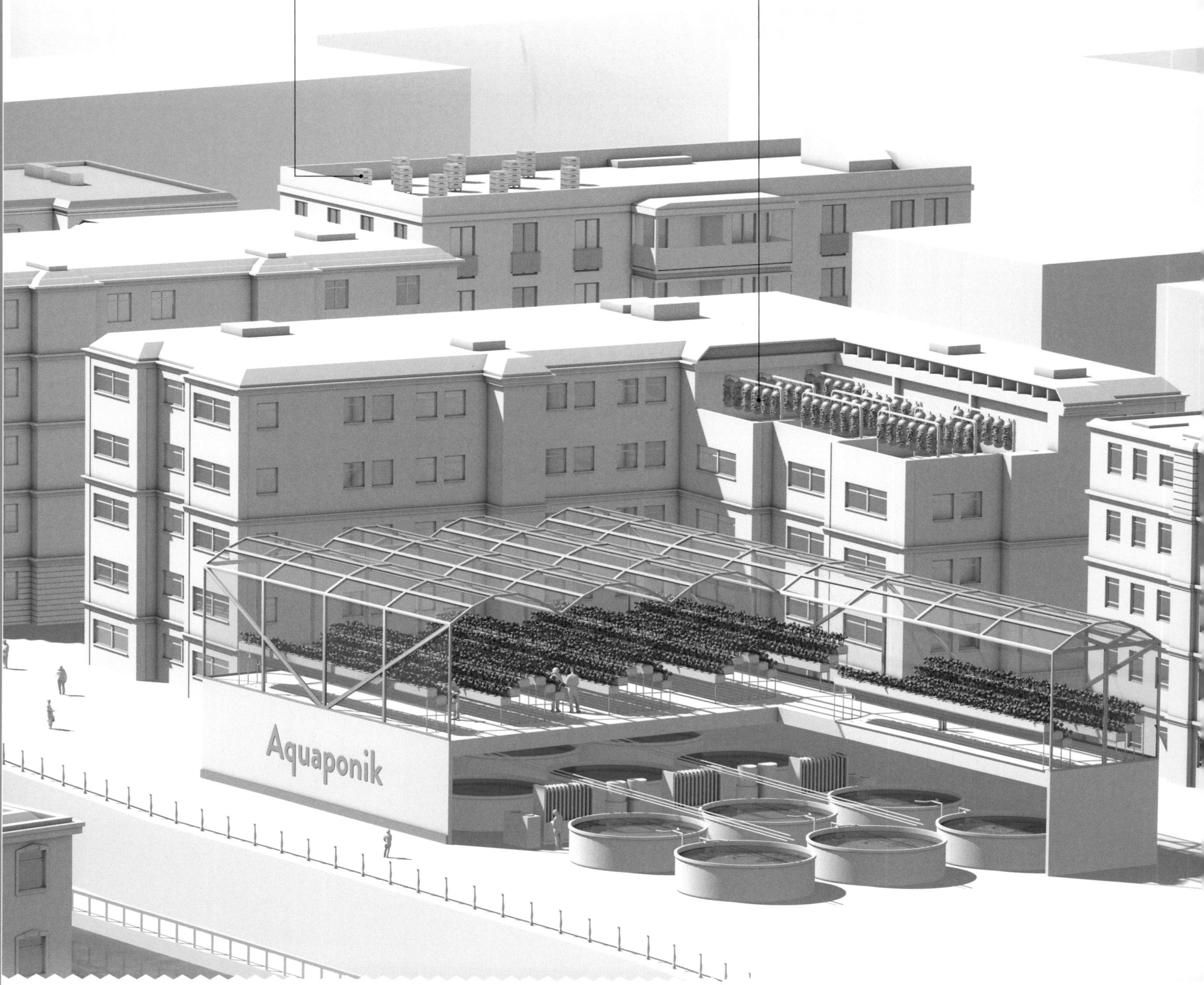

AQUAPONICS

Aquaponics is a symbiotic fish and plant cultivation, with a closed water and nutrient cycle. The fish supply the necessary fertilizer and get filtered water and oxygen in return. It requires very little extra irrigation, making it a very sustainable method for land-based aquaculture.

Water with nutrients from fish dung

A QUESTION OF LIGHT

Plants that grow in the open air have the entire spectrum of sunlight at their disposal. In order to successfully grow vegetables in closed rooms, the artificial light needs to be right. Special LED can provide the necessary light to plants for photosynthesis.

Light spectrum

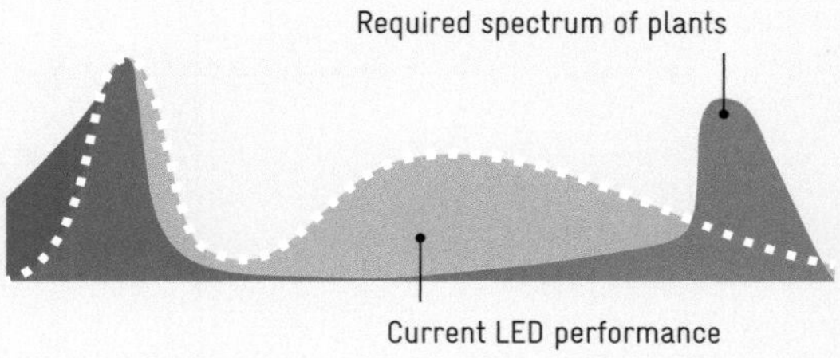
Required spectrum of plants
Current LED performance

Growth

Photosynthesis is the pocess of transforming carbon dioxide and water into carbohydrates (energy) using light.
This light has to come from the red spectral components at around 650 nanometers (nm) and the blue spectral components at 450 nm.

Taste

The more light that plants are provided with, the higher the glucose content of the fruits. Other factors such as water supply, nutrient content and temperature also play an important role in flavor development.

VERTICAL FARMING

If there's no room to build out, build up. This ethos has driven cities to new heights and is now being applied to agriculture. In 2009, Singapore-based »Sky Greens« opened its first commercial vertical farm. Each shelf holds 38 pots that are rotated through stations over a height of nine meters. Each station provides them with an essential nutrient to sustaining plant life and growing fruit.

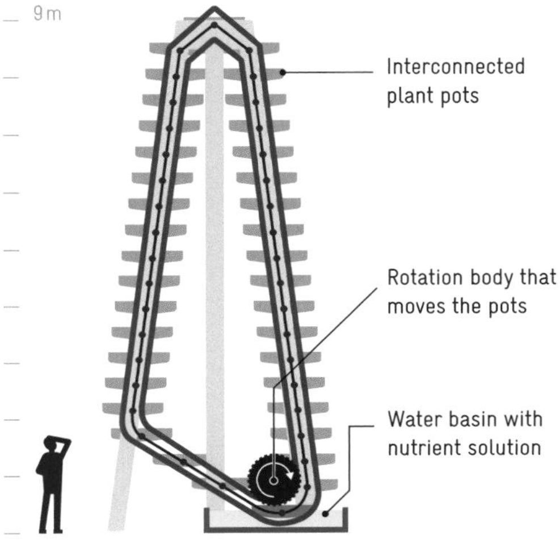
9 m
Interconnected plant pots
Rotation body that moves the pots
Water basin with nutrient solution

PLAYING GOD

On December 3, 1967, Christiaan Barnard conducted the first successful heart transplant at the Groote Schuur Hospital in Cape Town, South Africa. Today it is a routine operation—like other organ transplants—but back then it was very controversial from an ethical point of view. Such interventions prolong our average lifetime by many years and there is no sign that medical progress will come to an end.

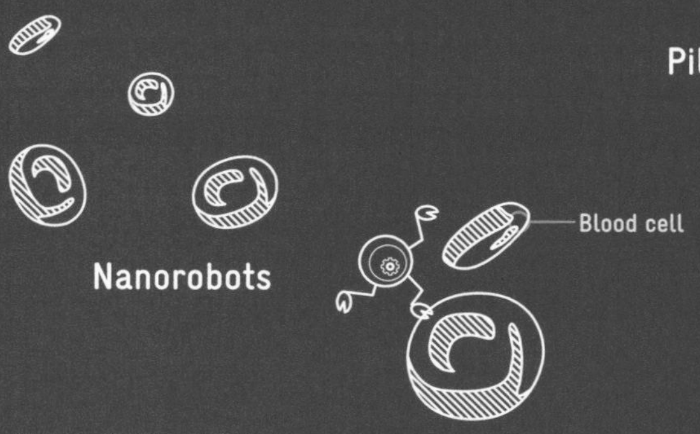
Blood cell
Nanorobots

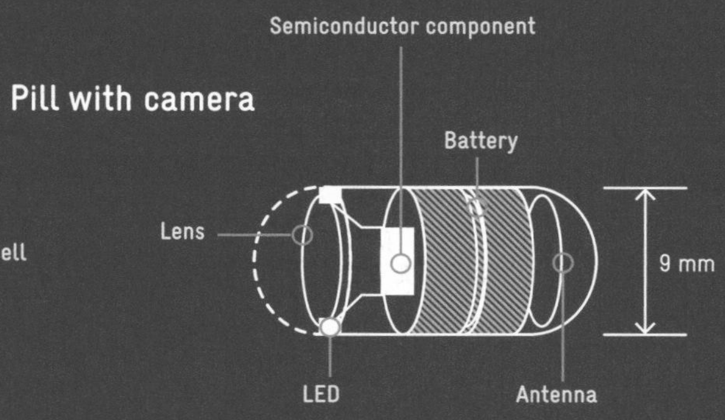
Pill with camera
Semiconductor component
Battery
Lens
9 mm
LED
Antenna

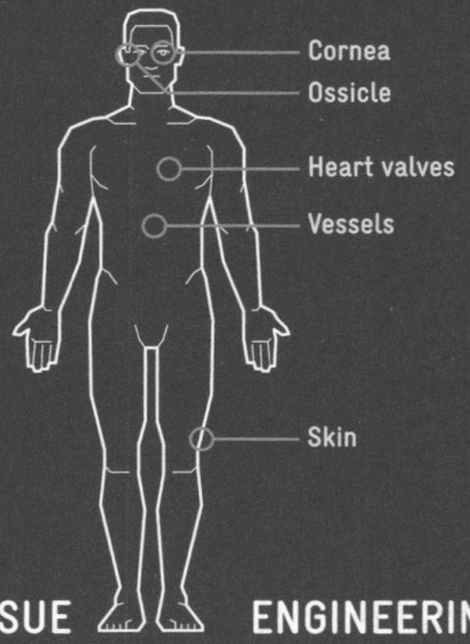
Cornea
Ossicle
Heart valves
Vessels
Skin

NANOROBOTICS

In the future, these tiny machines will be traveling independently through the body in search of localized diseases (such as cancer cells) to remove them on the spot. The current prototypes are the size of a match head. Long, thin, fibrous nanobots are a further development that will run between body cells and in the blood stream. They make it possible for doctors to gain information about the state of cells or tissue and to prescribe better treatment.

PERSONALIZED MEDICINE

Personalized medicine means more accurately targeted uses of medicine to improve the desired effects and reduce side effects. Promising progress has been achieved in the treatment of cancer, inflammations, as well as heart and brain diseases. Pain killers could also be adapted for tailored treatments.

TISSUE ENGINEERING

In tissue engineering, doctors reproduce cell samples in a lab. These are then cultivated to be retransplanted into the patient. Skin, blood vessels and cartilage have all been successfully cultivated for patients. Doctors hope that entire organs can be grown with tissue engeneering.

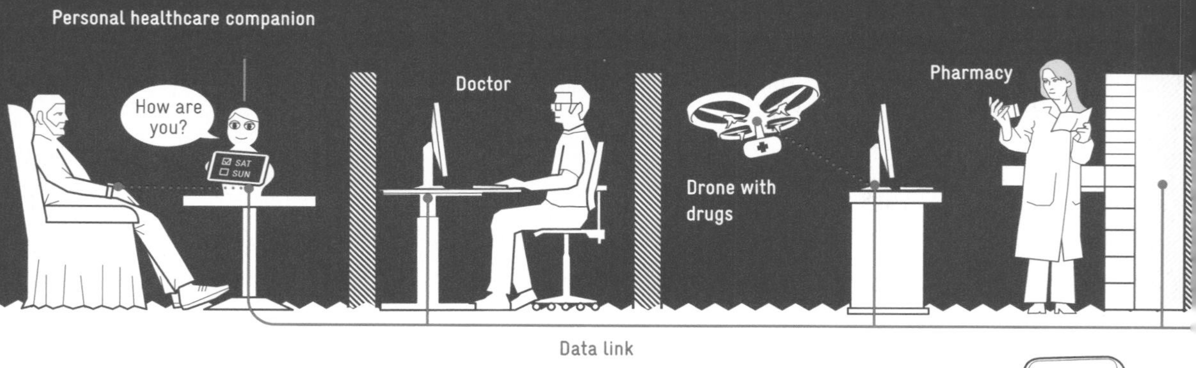
Personal healthcare companion
How are you?
SAT
SUN
Doctor
Drone with drugs
Pharmacy
Data link

»THE QUANTIFIED SELF«

is a network of people and companies that develop hardware and software solutions to record, analyze and evaluate personalized data. The focus is on self-tracking tools for sport and health.

E-HEALTH & TELEMEDICINE

E-health looks at how digital information and communication technology can move the healthcare field forward. Already doctors and patients are benefiting from digitized patient files in preventative, prescriptive, administration and diagnostic fields. In the future, doctors may be able to work in increasingly remote areas or have better access to patients who are physically unable to come to a clinic. Personal health monitors or robotic caretakers can connect with doctors around the world to treat patients.

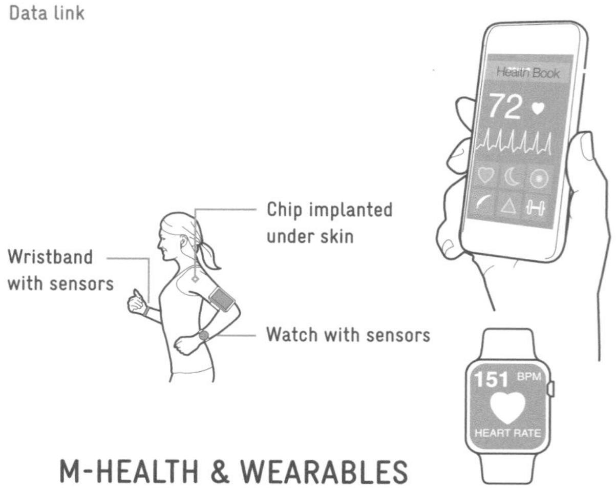

M-HEALTH & WEARABLES

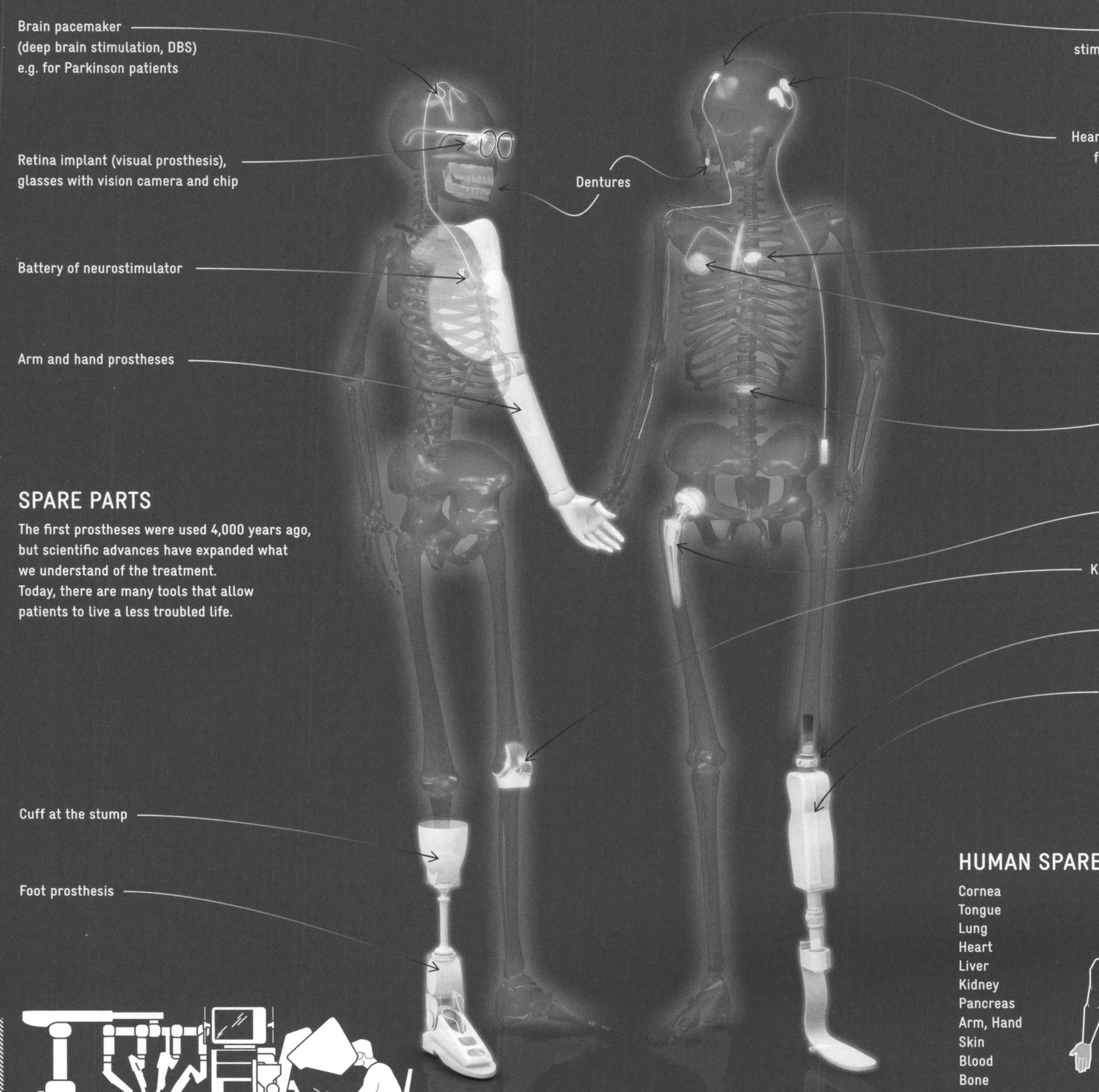
Brain pacemaker (deep brain stimulation, DBS) e.g. for Parkinson patients
Retina implant (visual prosthesis), glasses with vision camera and chip
Dentures
Battery of neurostimulator
Arm and hand prostheses
Cuff at the stump
Foot prosthesis
Brain chip to stimulate muscles
Hearing prosthesis for deaf people
Heart valve
Pacemaker
Spinal disk
Hip joint
Knee prosthesis
Knee joint
Artificial leg

SPARE PARTS

The first prostheses were used 4,000 years ago, but scientific advances have expanded what we understand of the treatment. Today, there are many tools that allow patients to live a less troubled life.

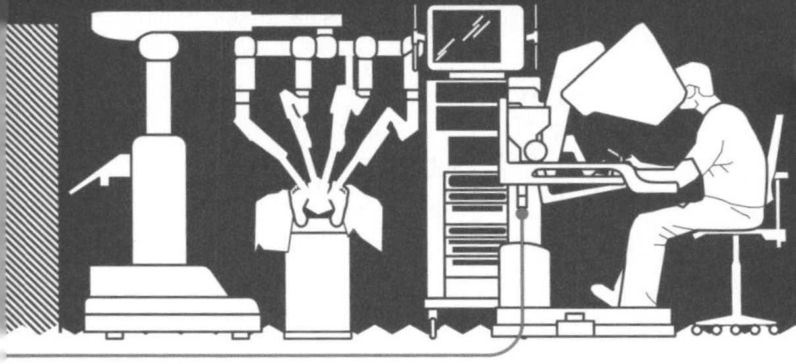

Minimally invasive robotic surgery

HUMAN SPARE PARTS

- Cornea
- Tongue
- Lung
- Heart
- Liver
- Kidney
- Pancreas
- Arm, Hand
- Skin
- Blood
- Bone
- Bone marrow
- Small intestine
- Large intestine

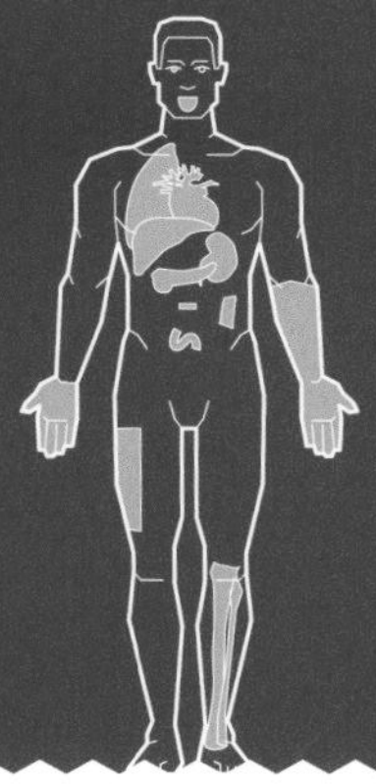

ROBOTIC SURGERY

Doctors conducted the first robot-assisted surgical procedure in 1985, which has made way for more precision in less invasive procedures. Today, researchers are teaching machines to compensate for human error or take over procedures entirely that require very small movements. Machines assisting in open-heart surgery will one day countervail the heart's movements, allowing surgeons to work on a seemingly immobile organ. Machines, however, aren't perfect and doctors will remain in charge.

TRANSPLANTATION

From the cornia to the kidney—transplant medicine has come a long way. Operations ranging from facial to robot-assisted kidney transplants are helping patients live fuller, longer lives.

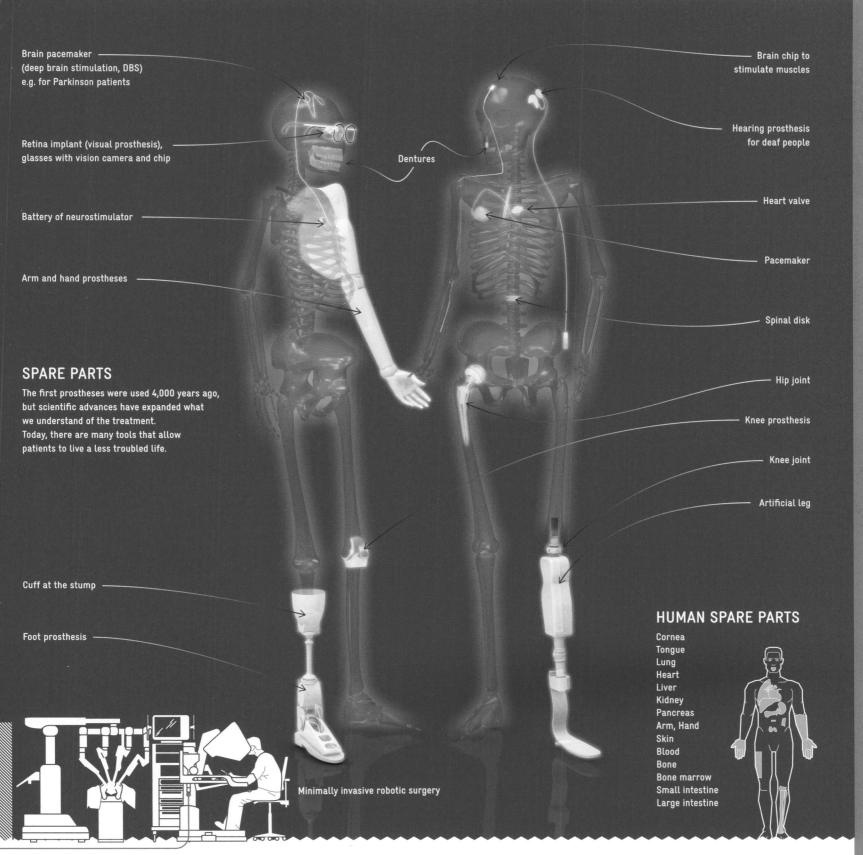

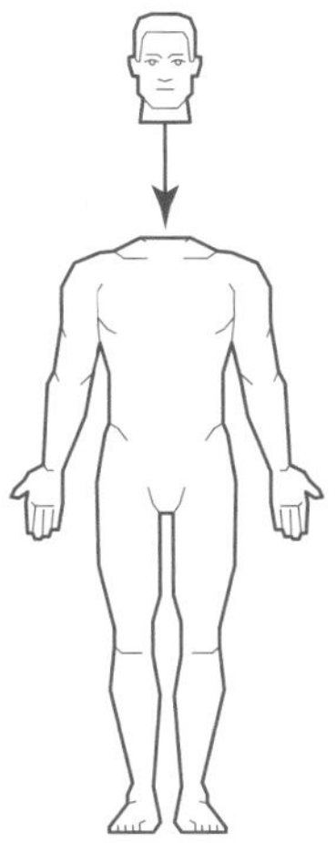

MAN OR MACHINE

Bionic prostheses, autonomous vehicles and voice recognition—algorithms make all of them possible. We are increasing our knowledge in the field of »weak artificial intelligence« (AI) which can already be found in medical technology, for example in prostheses. »Strong AI«, which still belongs to the realm of science fiction, will enable machines to think and carry out tasks on their own.

MACHINE LEARNING

Weak AI uses statistical methods. For this, the computer trains itself with familiar data to analyze unfamiliar data. In the case of a hand prosthesis, the computer is trained by tracking the electrical impulses that move a complete arm.

The arm is connected to the processor via electromyography. After numerous repetitions, the system creates prototypical representations of muscle activity for the respective hand gestures. The results are saved in the prosthesis's memory.

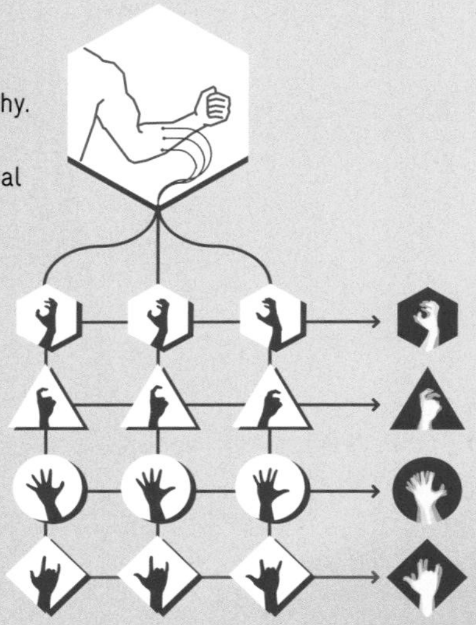

SIGNALS AND MEASURING

Electrical nerve impulses are measured. In general, recordings of phenomena that continue to reappear can be used in the same way as audio recordings for voice recognition.

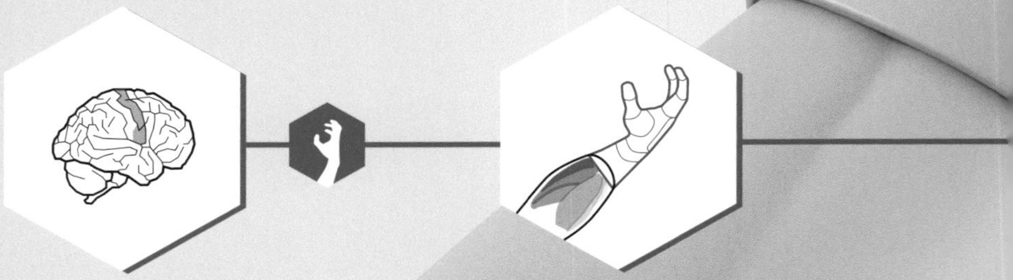

The brain creates the idea movement, sending out nerve impulses.

The muscles of the residual limb react to the signals by contracting and relaxing.

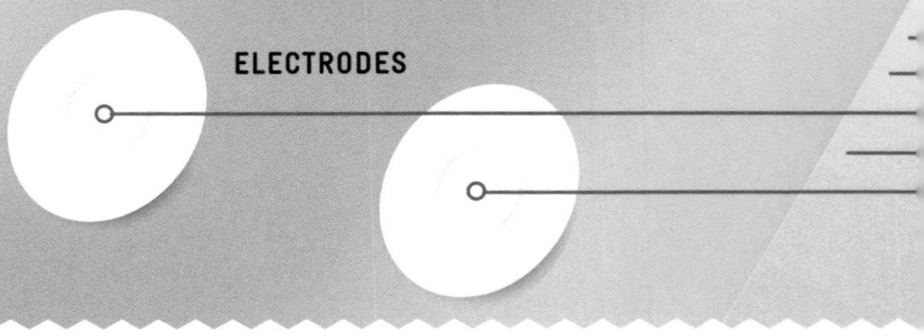

MACHINE LEARNING APPLICATIONS

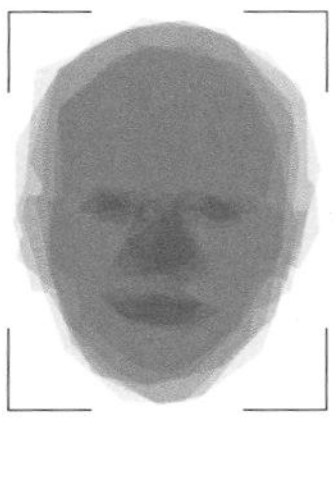

Facial recognition

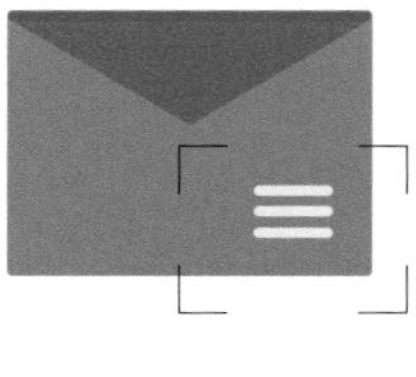

Postcode recognition

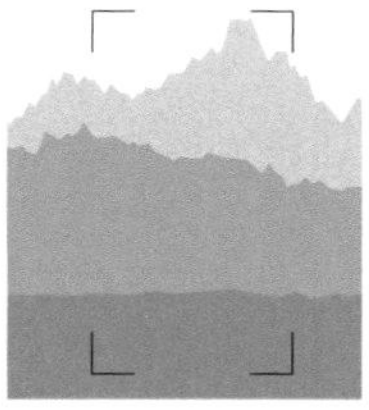

Market analysis

ETHICS AND AI

In 2016, a car executive at Daimler caused an uproar when he stated that self-driving cars could prioritize the lives of drivers over those of pedestrians. Collisions will still happen when vehicles become automated, but the ethics are posing a challenge to legislators and insurance companies.

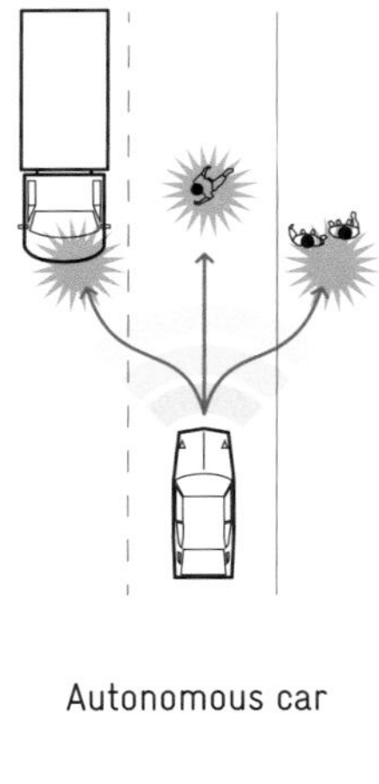

Autonomous car

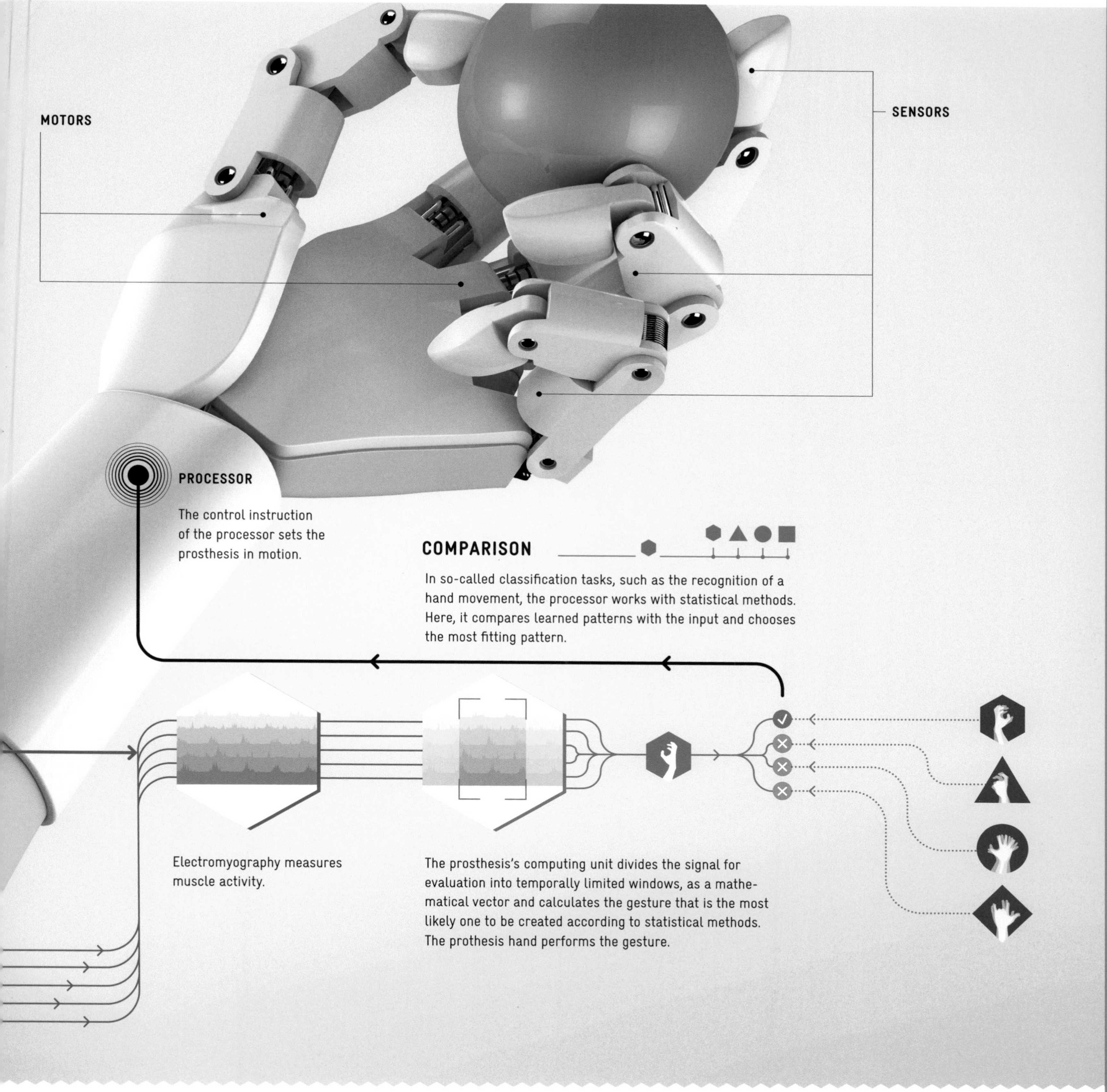
MOTORS
SENSORS
PROCESSOR
The control instruction of the processor sets the prosthesis in motion.
COMPARISON
In so-called classification tasks, such as the recognition of a hand movement, the processor works with statistical methods. Here, it compares learned patterns with the input and chooses the most fitting pattern.
Electromyography measures muscle activity.
The prosthesis's computing unit divides the signal for evaluation into temporally limited windows, as a mathematical vector and calculates the gesture that is the most likely one to be created according to statistical methods. The prothesis hand performs the gesture.

HUMAN BRAIN PROJECT

The European Commission's Human Brain Project is working on a computer simulation of a human brain. It is supposed to help to develop future technologies and to better understand brain diseases.

700 RESEARCHERS

24 COUNTRIES INVOLVED

1.2 BILLION € RESEARCH FUNDS

150 INSTITUTES AND UNIVERSITIES

TRANSHUMANISM

With technology developing at an increasing pace, transhumanism followers dream of making the biological body superfluous by uniting man and machine. According to technology visionary Ray Kurzweil, there will be a technological milestone in 2045 when AI will surpass human intelligence.

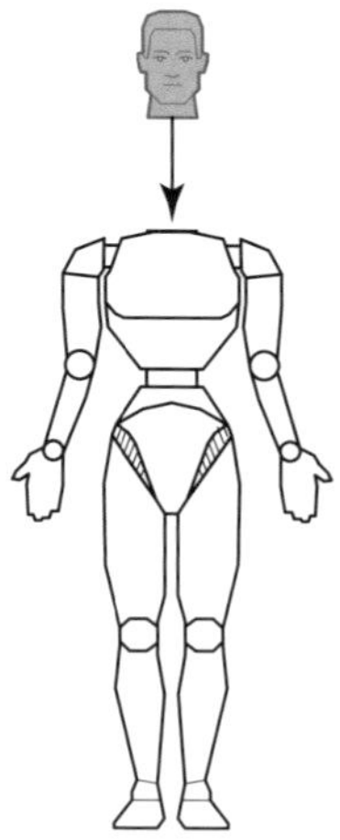

THE FUTURE OF IT ALL

In 1929, Edwin Hubble showed through his observations that the universe is not static but is expanding. Today, we also know that the further away galaxies are, the faster they move away from us. The incredible time dimensions that theorists are working on make the Earth's lifetime shrink to less than the blink of an eye. In the end, everything will be dark, empty and terribly cold.

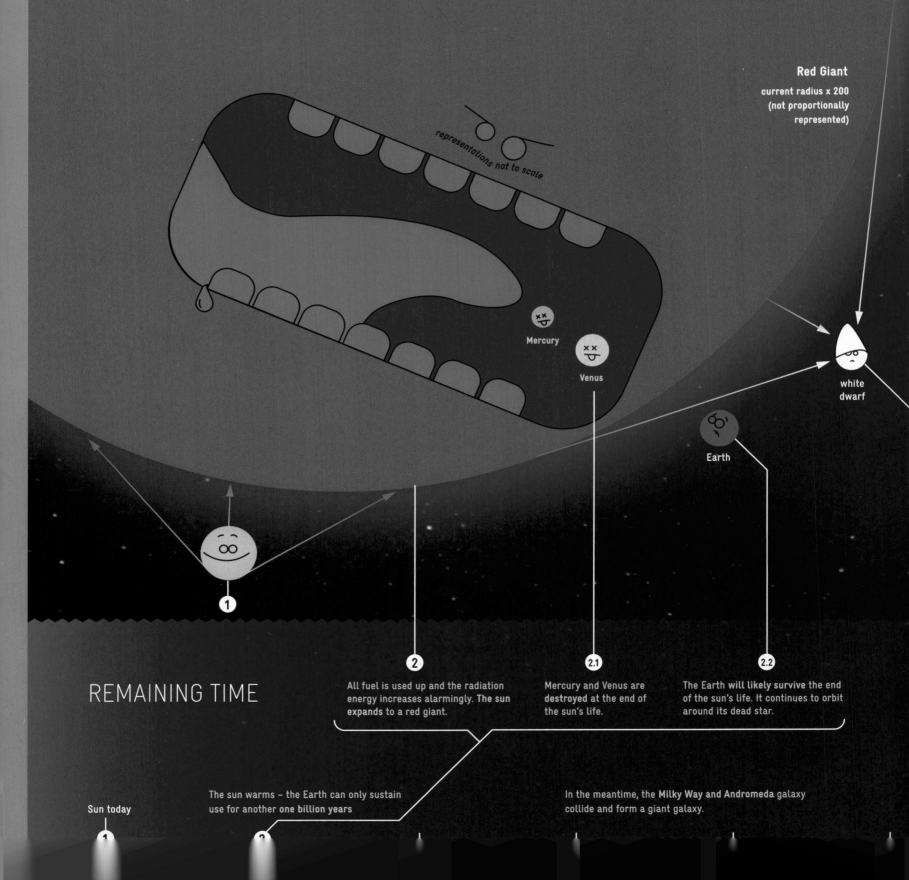

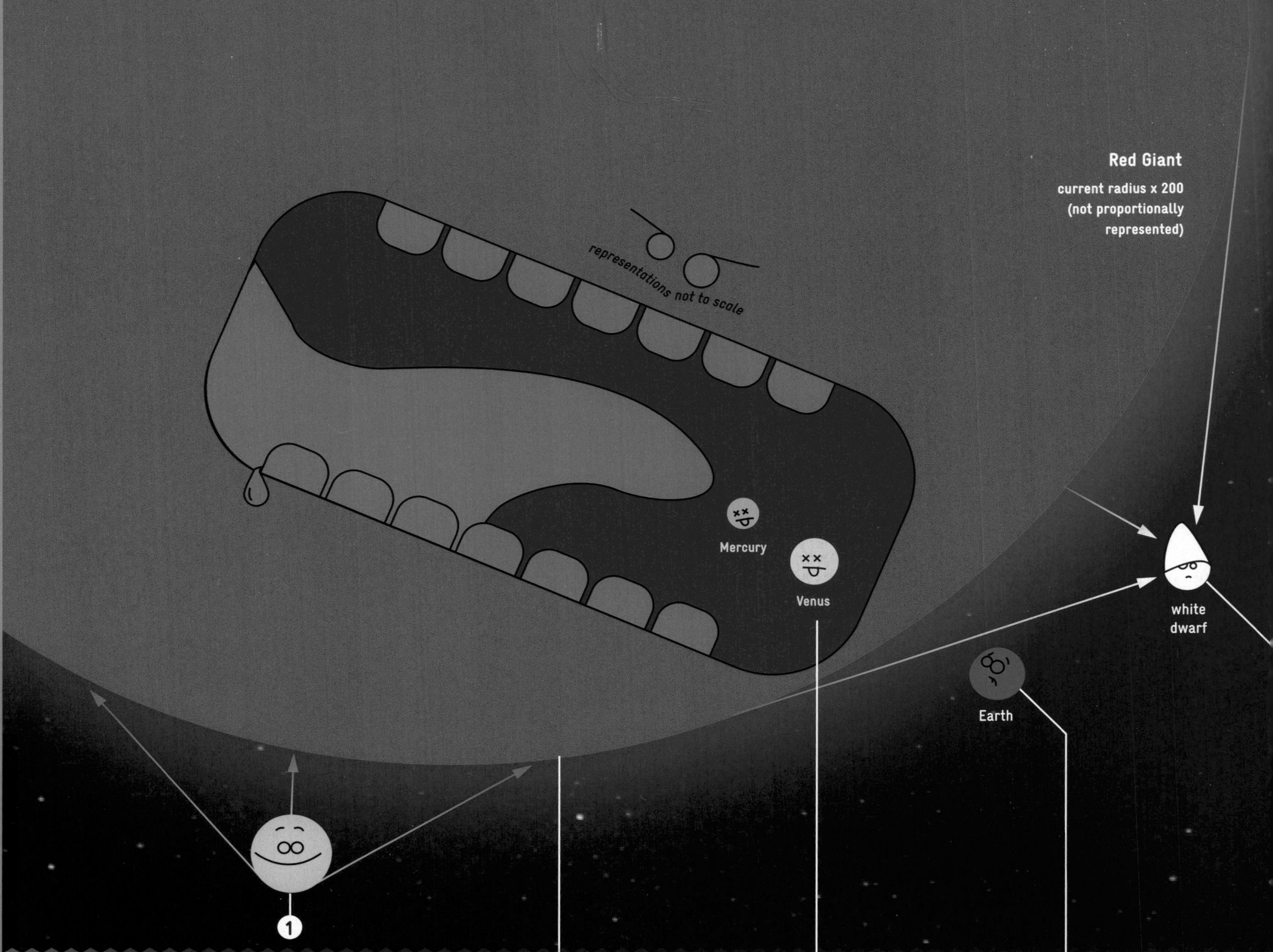
representations not to scale
Red Giant
current radius x 200 (not proportionally represented)
Mercury
Venus
white dwarf
Earth
1

REMAINING TIME

2 — All fuel is used up and the radiation energy increases alarmingly. The sun expands to a red giant.

2.1 — Mercury and Venus are destroyed at the end of the sun's life.

2.2 — The Earth will likely survive the end of the sun's life. It continues to orbit around its dead star.

Sun today

The sun warms – the Earth can only sustain use for another **one billion years**

In the meantime, the **Milky Way and Andromeda** galaxy collide and form a giant galaxy.